Evidence

Text & Materials

Gregory Durston

OXFORD
UNIVERSITY PRESS

Great Clarendon Street, Oxford OX2 6DP

Oxford University Press is a department of the University of Oxford.
It furthers the University's objective of excellence in research, scholarship,
and education by publishing worldwide in

Oxford New York

Auckland Cape Town Dar es Salaam Hong Kong Karachi
Kuala Lumpur Madrid Melbourne Mexico City Nairobi
New Delhi Shanghai Taipei Toronto

With offices in

Argentina Austria Brazil Chile Czech Republic France Greece
Guatemala Hungary Italy Japan Poland Portugal Singapore
South Korea Switzerland Thailand Turkey Ukraine Vietnam

Oxford is a registered trade mark of Oxford University Press
in the UK and in certain other countries

Published in the United States
by Oxford University Press Inc., New York

British Library Cataloguing in Publication Data

Data available

Library of Congress Cataloging in Publication Data

Data available

Typeset by Newgen Imaging Systems (P) Ltd., Chennai, India
Printed in Great Britain
on acid-free paper by
L.E.G.O S.p.A

ISBN 978–0–19–921548–5

10 9 8 7 6 5 4 3 2 1

To my students, past and present

PREFACE

The law of evidence has undergone enormous changes in recent years as a result of important and far-reaching new statutes, such as the Criminal Justice Act 2003, and the ongoing effects of the Human Rights Act 1998. Together, these have transformed many areas of the subject. New statutes have, in turn, spawned numerous appellate-level decisions seeking to interpret or apply their frequently novel (and sometimes confusing) provisions. However, despite such innovation, several other areas of the discipline have witnessed little or no parliamentary intervention over the past few decades and, in a few topics, authorities drawn from the nineteenth century are still highly relevant. This book reproduces extracts from important judgments in some of the more significant cases on the law of evidence, both old and new, along with a modest amount of important statutory material (to reduce the need for constant cross-referencing to a statute book). As a result, it allows students ready access to the 'raw material' on which this area of English adjectival law is built.

Although the 'law' is, of course, contained in statutes and cases it is also the subject of (sometimes heated) academic, political and professional debate, reflected in numerous journal articles, books and proposals for reform. In England and Wales the law of evidence was relatively late in becoming established as a major field for academic study. However, as the excerpts from legal journals, books and reports that are reproduced in this volume suggest, this has been remedied over the past 40 years, as an ever growing number of outstanding scholars have followed in the pioneering footsteps of Sir Rupert Cross and analysed the subject from a variety of very different perspectives. I trust that this book will provide an effective introduction to their work and ideas as well as to some of the debates that they have initiated and pursued.

Additionally, while it might be said that, like the French essayist Michel de Montaigne, I have drawn together a posie of other men's (and women's) flowers and only the thread that binds them together is my own, I also hope that, in this case at least, the linking text offers a straightforward and lucid, but also thorough and up-to-date, introduction to the relevant law in this complex and fast changing subject.

I would like to thank the libraries of Kingston University and Lincoln's Inn for their help with the collection of materials. Thanks are also due to Philippa Russell, Edward Meers, and the staff at Oxford University Press for their assistance with the preparation of the manuscript. Having taught the law of evidence for over 20 years I have, inevitably, accrued a considerable debt to the generations of students who have taken my course on the subject and it is to them that this book is dedicated.

Gregory Durston
London
Christmas 2007

GUIDE TO THE BOOK

Evidence: Text & Materials is enhanced with a number of different features that are designed to enrich your learning and provide additional support as you progress through your law of evidence module. This guide highlights these features and will help you get the most out of your textbook.

Definitions

Legal burden The obligation placed on a party to litigation to e
that s/he will fail on that issue if s/he does not prove them to the

Evidential burden The obligation to make an issue 'live' by calli
that the tribunal of fact is obliged to decide whether one of the
on that issue.

Reverse onus burden A legal burden that is placed on a defer
the normal position which places such burdens on the Crown.

'Golden thread of English justice' The general principle that

Definitions

Each chapter opens with a short list of definitions of the key terms and concepts relevant to that chapter. These will help to highlight the key topics discussed, and clearly explain any jargon or terminology that you will encounter. These terms are collected in a glossary which can be found on the Online Resource Centre that accompanies this book.

 Cross-reference Box

Matters asserted and admitted in such documents cease t
facts can be determined without the formal adduction of e
more on this, go to chapter 1, at pp. 18–24.

Cross-reference boxes

It can be challenging to keep track of how the many elements of the law of evidence relate to each other. This feature does the hard work of cross-referencing from chapter to chapter for you, by directing you straight to the relevant page elsewhere in the text.

 Pause for reflection

Do you feel that, in the modern era, it is appropriate that sp
allowed not to testify for the prosecution against their partn

Pause for reflection boxes

These boxes are ideally placed to help you stop, reflect on and assess the law that you have been considering. Most encourage you to place the law in context, and consider its social or moral implications.

 Exam tip

Competence and compellability are only rarely set as proble
of course, a lecturer/exam setter has a particular interest in
appended to a question on other aspects of the law of evide

Exam tips

These tips highlight areas of the law that are frequently raised in exam questions, and offer invaluable advice on how you should approach them.

Summary

- As a general rule, under English common law (and unlike t
  evidence does not need to be supported to found a convic
- However, at common law, a small number of situations d
  was necessary in criminal matters, while in others, there v
  be warned about the dangers of convicting in its absence. T
  highly technical in its legal requirements.
- In the modern era, both of these two general categories
  a need to give a corroboration warning, nor is there an

Summaries

At the end of each chapter is a short summary that reiterates the key points that have been covered. You should use these to check your understanding and return to any areas that aren't now completely clear.

Further reading

Mike Redmayne, 'The Structure of Evidence Law' (2006) O
4, 805–822

Alex Stein, *Foundations of Evidence Law* (2005, Oxford Uni

Laird C Kirkpatrick, 'Evidence Law in the Next Millennium
363–368, at 363

David Ormerod and Diane Birch, 'The Evolution of the Dis
Crim LR 38–159

Further reading

These suggestions for additional reading have been carefully selected to highlight key areas and to help you deepen your knowledge of the subject.

Questions for Discussion

1. Rachel, a cocaine addict, is arrested for taking part in ar
   in a very cold and unheated cell, in January, for 12 hours, t
   Detective Sergeant. Shaun, who is unaware of Rachel's add
   cooperative can influence bail decisions'. Rachel, who is d
   sions to the crime, implicates Delia in the offence, and gives
   proceeds of the robbery (packets of money) can be discove
   The police search the location she has described, and dis
   which are found to have Rachel's fingerprints on them.

Questions for discussion

The questions that close each chapter provide the ideal opportunity for you to test your understanding of a topic. They challenge you to apply your knowledge in a practical situation – either by preparing a full answer to a question, or by debating the issues it raises with your fellow students. Guidelines on how to approach each of these questions are available on the Online Resource Centre.

GUIDE TO THE ONLINE RESOURCE CENTRE

This book is accompanied by an Online Resource Centre that complements the text and is designed to enhance your learning experience.

www.oxfordtextbooks.co.uk/orc/durston/

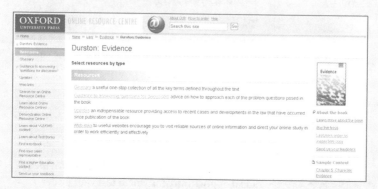

Regular updates

An indispensable resource providing access to recent cases and developments in the law that have occurred since publication of the book. These updates are accompanied by page references to the textbook, so you can see how the new developments relate to the existing case law.

The recent case of *R v Beedall (Lee James)* [2007] EWCA Crim 23 has reaffirmed that s.41 of the Youth Justice and Criminal Evidence Act 1999, which prevents the cross-examination of a complainant in a sexual offence case (such as rape) on his/her own sexual history, except in the special circumstances set out in s.41(3) and s.41(5), can lead to the exclusion of potentially relevant evidence. Additionally, it indicates a determination on the part of the courts that, notwithstanding the decision in *R v A (No.2)* [2002] 1 AC 45, the impact of s.41 will not lightly be watered down, as occurred, it has been argued by some observers, with its predecessor (s.2 of the (now repealed) Sexual Offences (Amendment) Act 1976).

R v Beedall (Lee James) [2007] EWCA Crim 23 involved an allegation of homosexual rape. The complainant, a youth of 17, and the defendant had met (for the first time) at a taxi rank, after both had been out drinking. The defendant then led the alleged victim to a secluded location nearby on the premise that he knew that a taxi could be found there. Once there, he produced a knife, threatened the youth and had non-consensual oral and anal intercourse with him. After the defendant was arrested, some five weeks later, he initially denied any involvement but, when presented with DNA evidence, admitted rape. However, at trial he claimed that all sexual activity had been consensual.

Glossary

A useful one-stop collection of all the key terms defined throughout the text.

Web links

Links to useful websites encourage you to visit reliable sources of online information and direct your online study in order to work efficiently and effectively.

Guidance to answering 'questions for discussion'

Advice on how to approach each of the problem questions posed in the book is provided on the ORC, to aid your exam preparation and help refine your analytical skills.

SOURCE ACKNOWLEDGEMENTS

Grateful acknowledgement is made to all the authors and publishers of copyright material which appears in this book, and in particular to the following for permission to reprint material from the sources indicated.

Parliamentary copyright material is reproduced with the permission of the Controller of Her Majesty's Stationery Office on behalf of Parliament. Other Crown copyright material is reproduced under Class Licence Number C2006010631 with the permission of the Controller of HMSO and the Queen's Printer for Scotland.

ICLR:
McQuaker v Goddar, CA, [1940] 1 KB 687
A v Secretary of State for the Home Department, HL, (No 2) [2006] 2 A.C. 221
Jones v University of Warwick, CA, [2003] 1 WLR 954
Regina (Saifi) v Governor of Brixton Prison and another, DC, [2001] 1 WLR 1134
R v Looseley, HL, [2001] 1 WLR 2060
Woolmington v DPP, HL, [1935] AC 462
R v Edwards, CA, [1975] QB 27
R v Lambert HL, [2002] 2 AC 545
R v Johnstone, HL, [2003] 1 WLR 1736
Sheldrake v DPP, HL, [2005] 1 AC 264
Levison and another v Patent Steam Carpet Cleaning Co. Ltd (CA), [1978] QB 69
R v Gill CCA, [1963] 1 WLR, 841
R v Lobell, CCA [1957] 1 QB 547
R v Vye, CA, [1993] 1 WLR 471
R v Hanson, Gilmore and Pickering, CA, [2005] 1 WLR 3169
O'Brien v Chief Constable of the South Wales Police, HL, [2005] 2 WLR 1038
R v Andrews, HL, [1987] AC 281
R v Al-Khawaja, CA, [2006] 1 WLR 1078
R v Gunewardene, CCA, [1951] 2 KB 600
R v Hayter, HL, [2005] 1 WLR 605
R v Brophy, HL, [1982] AC 477
David Mitchell v The Queen, PC, [1998] AC 695
R v Mushtaq, HL, [2005] 1 WLR 1513
R v Condron, CA, [1997] 1 WLR 827
R v Momodou, CA, [2005] 1 WLR 3442
Polanski v Conde Nast Publications Ltd, HL, [2005] 1 WLR 637
R v A, HL, [2002] 1 AC 45
R v Turner, CA, [1975] QB 834
English Exporters (London) Ltd, v Eldonwall Ltd, HC, [1973] Ch 415
Armstrong and anor v First York Ltd, CA, [2005] 1 WLR 275
R v Makanjuola, CA, [1995] 1 WLR 1348
Benedetto and Labrador v The Queen, PC, [2003] 1 WLR 1545
R v Turnbull, CA, [1977] QB 224
D v NSPCC, HL, [1978] AC 171

Rogers v Home Secretary, HL, [1973] AC 388

R v Keane, CA, [1994] 1 WLR 746

Savage v Chief Constable of Hampshire, CA, (1997) 1 WLR 1061

R v Johnson (Kenneth), CA, [1988] 1 WLR 1377

R v H, R v C, HL, (2004) 2 AC 134

BSC v Granada TV, HL, [1981] AC 1096

R v Manchester Crown Court, ex parte Rogers, QBD, [1999] 1 WLR 832

Kuwait Airways Corporation v Iraqi Airways Co. (No. 6) CA, [2005] 1 WLR 2734. Reprinted with kind permission of ICLR

JSB publications:

Specimen Directions, fifth edition, para. 23. Defendant's Character—good. Judicial Studies Board, Crown Court Bench, Book. 1. www.jsboard.co.uk/criminal law/cbb/index.htm

LexisNexis:

Campbell v Hamlet PC, [2005] 3 All ER 1116. Reprinted with the permission of LexisNexis

Oxford University Press and the author:

Mike Redmayne, 'The Structure of Evidence Law'. *Oxford Journal of Legal Studies* (2006), vol. 26, no. 4 pp. 805–822 (extract)

Sweet and Maxwell Ltd, extracts from:

R v Doheny, CA, [1997] 1 Cr App R 369

R v Derek William Bentley (Deceased), CA, [2001] 1 Cr App R 21

R v Acott, HL, [1997] 2 Cr App R 94

R v Gray, CA, (1974) 58 Cr App R 177

R v Stephens, CA, [2002] EWCA Crim 1529

R v Redgrave, CA, (1981) 74 Cr App Rep 10

R v Gray, CA, [2004] 2 Cr App R 30

R v Tirnameanue, CA, [2007] 2 Cr App R 23

R v Anthony Sawonuik, CA, [2000] 2 Cr App R 220

R v Chopra, CA, [2007] 1 Cr App R 16

R (on the application of Robinson) v Sutton Coldfield Magistrates' Court, DC, [2006] 2 Cr App R 13

R v Edwards (Karl) and others, CA, [2006] 1 Cr App R 3

R v Edwards (Stewart) and others, CA, [2006] 2 Cr App R 4

R v Nelson, CA, [2006] EWCA Crim 3412

R v Singh (James Paul), CA, [2007] EWCA Crim 2140

R v Antony Weir and others, CA, [2006] 1 Cr App R 19

R v S (Andrew), CA, [2006] 2 Cr App R 31

R v Taylor, CA, [2006] 2 Cr App R 14

R v Finch (David Barry), CA, (2007) WL 2843

Welsh v Stokes, CA, [2007] PIQR p. 27

R v Elleray, CA, [2003] 2 Cr App R 11

R v Newsome, CA, (1980) 71 Cr App R 325

R v Blackburn, CA, [2005] 2 Cr App R 30

R v Wahab, CA, [2003] 1 Cr App R 15

R v El-Hannachi (Samir) and others, CA, [1998] 2 Cr App R 226

R v McAfee (John James), (2006) WL 3880356

R v O, CA, [2006] 2 Cr App R 27

R v Thompson, CA, (1976) 64 Cr App Rep 96

R v David and Ellis, CA, [2006] 2 Cr App R 32

R v Martin, CA, [2004] 2 Cr App R 22

R v White (Andre Barrington), CA, [2004] EWCA Crim 946

R v Peter John Chard, CA, (1972) 56 Cr App R 268

R v Pinfold and Mackenny, CA, [2004] 2 Cr App R 32

R v Blackburn, CA, [2005] 2 Cr App R 30

R v Harris (Lorraine), CA, [2005] 1 Cr App R 55

R v Trevor Alan Oakley, CA, (1980) 70 Cr App R 7

R v Clare and Peach, CA, [1995] 2 Cr App Rep 333

R v Stockwell, CA, (1993) 97 Cr App R 260

R v Steven Abadom, CA, (1983) 76 Cr App R 48

R v O'Doherty, CA, (NI), [2003] 1 Cr App R 77

R v Fergus (Ivan), CA, (1994) 98 Cr App R 313

Paul Roberts, 'Taking the Burden of Proof Seriously'. [1995] Crim LR p. 783

Ian Dennis, 'Reverse Onuses and the Presumption of Innocence: In search of principle'. [2005] Crim LR pp. 901–936

L. Hoyano, 'Striking a balance between the rights of defendants and vulnerable witnesses; will special measures directions contravene guarantees of a fair trial?' [2005] 1 WLR 637

N. Kibble, 'Judicial discretion and the admissibility of prior sexual history evidence under section 41 of the Youth Justice and Criminal Evidence Act 1999: sometimes sticking to your guns means shooting yourself in the foot: Part 2' [2005] Crim LR 263–274 (extract)

Ian Dennis, 'Sexual history evidence: Evaluating section 41' [2006] Crim LR 869–870

Vathek Publishing:

Deirdre Dwyer, 'Can a marriage be delayed in the public interest so as to maintain the compellability of a prosecution witness? R (on the application of the Crown Prosecution Service) v Registrar General of Births, Marriages and Deaths' (2003) E & P 7(3): 191–196 (extract)

Andy Roberts, 'The problem of mistaken identification: Some observations on process' (2004) 8 E & P 100 (extract)

SUMMARY CONTENTS

DETAILED CONTENTS

2   Judicial Discretion

⑤ Character Evidence

6 Hearsay Evidence

7 Confession Evidence and Related Matters

8 Competence and Compellability

9 The Course of the Evidence: Examination in Chief

10 The Course of the Evidence: Cross-examination and Re-examination

12 Corroboration and Identification Evidence

TABLE OF CASES

TABLE OF LEGISLATION

TABLE OF STATUTORY INSTRUMENTS

1 INTRODUCTION TO THE LAW OF EVIDENCE

Definitions

Admissibility Whether potential evidence can be adduced at trial or is caught by an exclusionary rule.

Cogency The degree of weight or importance ascribed to relevant and admissible evidence.

Evidence Material adduced at trial to establish disputed facts.

Prejudice Unjustified significance that might be placed on some (often emotive) forms of evidence, by a tribunal of fact.

Relevance Whether potential evidence makes disputed facts more or less likely, using common-sensical notions of logic.

Voir dire The special hearing conducted during a criminal trial in which the admissibility of some types of evidence is determined.

Exclusionary rule Evidential rule that prevents parties from adducing certain forms of relevant evidence.

Free proof The system of determining admissibility under which the only test is relevance, and which characterizes the civil law tradition.

---

1. What is 'Evidence' and Why is it Important?

Introduction

In the modern Western tradition, the aim of litigation, whether criminal or civil, is usually to recreate events, in a forensic environment, that have occurred at some point in the past, and then to apply the substantive law to them. For example, a court might have to decide whether: the widgets supplied pursuant to a contract made on 12 July last year were of satisfactory quality under s. 14(2) of the Sale of Goods Act 1979; a criminal defendant was the man who robbed a bank in the High Street on 5 January a year ago; a particular husband committed adultery in Brighton some two years earlier; or a fairground amusement ride was operated negligently the previous summer.

Of course, this is not invariably the case; occasionally, facts are not disputed, merely the interpretation to be placed on the law governing them, and a trial will consequently consist largely of legal argument. Nevertheless, the vast majority of cases involve a factual dispute, at least to some degree, and constitute an attempt at determining what happened at an earlier time. As the eminent eighteenth-century jurist William Blackstone observed, in his celebrated *Commentaries*: '...experience will abundantly show, that above a hundred of our lawsuits arise from disputed facts, for one where the law is doubted of'.

Although to modern observers the adduction of information about such earlier events—an expert's analysis of the widgets, an eyewitness description of the man who carried out the robbery, a receptionist's account of the couple who checked into a seafront hotel, a passenger's description of how a big dipper crashed—appears to be the 'obvious' way to resolve such a dispute, this has not always, or invariably, been the case.

In the West, prior to the Fourth Lateran Council of 1215, trial by ordeal was sometimes employed to decide a dispute as to facts. For example, occasionally, an accused person's guilt might be determined by whether their hand festered or healed within a certain period after they had carried a red-hot iron for several paces. As a result, guilt might be resolved by a party's medical powers of recovery, though it was believed that this would be directly influenced by divine intervention (it was also normally necessary for there to be a clear prima facie case against the accused before the procedure could be employed). A similar approach to the adjudication of disputed facts is still occasionally found amongst some tribal societies, in remote parts of the Third World.

 Pause for reflection

Is there any merit in such 'non-rational' approaches to adjudication?

However, given that modern trials *are* normally premised on attempts at recreating past events, it is obvious that contested cases will only ever be as strong as the information that is adduced to support them. Having the substantive law on their side will not be of any benefit to litigants if they cannot also persuade a tribunal of fact—whether judge, jury or magistrates—to believe their 'version' of events, or, as it is sometimes described by advocates, their 'theory of a case'. This is done by adducing 'evidence', which may be described as information, whether correct or not, supplied to establish the truth of any given issue in a forensic environment.

The 'law of evidence' is the body of legal rules that determines whether (and how) such evidence can be adduced. It regulates what material is legally admissible for the purpose of establishing facts in dispute, the manner in which it may be placed before the court, and even, on occasion, how the tribunal should consider it.[1] In theory, it should ensure a fair and efficient trial process.

---

[1] J Buzzard et al (eds), *Phipson on Evidence* (13th edn, 1982, Sweet & Maxwell) at 1.

This makes the law of evidence of vital practical significance to lawyers. It may not create substantive legal rights, duties or liabilities in the way that, for example, the law pertaining to contract, crime and tort does, but it defines the means by which such substantive law is applied in practice. This also means that it often shapes the 'investigative' stage of proceedings, prior to a matter coming to trial or litigation even being initiated. If a party cannot identify any admissible evidence to support their case, however strong it might at first appear, they are likely to be firmly advised by their legal advisers not to start proceedings.

As this suggests, a firm grasp of the law of evidence is particularly useful for those engaged in litigation, and especially advocacy, as objections to questionable pieces of evidence often have to be raised or opposed in court with little prior notice, before being immediately ruled upon by a judge or magistrates. In some serious cases this position has been slightly modified by the existence of interlocutory evidential decisions made before trial, under, for example, s. 35 of the Criminal Procedure and Investigations Act 1996, and determined by judges at preparatory hearings, combined with the possibility of appealing such decisions prior to the substantive hearing. Nevertheless, there will often be little opportunity to research an evidential topic in depth, prior to its being considered and ruled on by the relevant tribunal.

Evidence and Procedure

The 'sister' subject to evidence in adjectival law is that pertaining to civil and criminal procedure. However, the two are also often inextricably interlinked; procedural rules govern how questions of evidential admissibility will be determined in court. For a common law example of this, consider the operation of the *voir dire* or, as it is colloquially known, the 'trial within a trial' (see below).

This interlinked relationship between procedure and evidence is, perhaps, most clearly seen in the influence of the Civil Procedure Rules of 1998 (CPR 1998) and the Criminal Procedure Rules of 2005 (CPR 2005). These statutory instruments regulate (amongst other things) the procedures for adducing a huge range of evidence in civil and criminal forums respectively. For example, paras 27–36 of the CPR 2005 govern the adduction of hearsay, bad character and expert opinion in criminal trials, though it should be observed that, unlike their civil counterparts, the impact of the CPR 2005 in practice has been relatively modest so far. It may be that these rules will become more significant as lawyers and the judiciary become better acquainted with them.

Additionally, procedural tactics can, sometimes, be used out of court to secure or safeguard evidence at an early stage in proceedings. Thus, in the past, victims of fraud would often be advised to apply for an 'Anton Piller' order, enabling a claimant to search the defendant's home or office for documents, and requiring the defendant to allow immediate inspection, so as to prevent their destruction. Such orders have been replaced by 'search orders', which are now made *ex parte* to a High Court judge, pursuant to s. 7(1) of the Civil Procedure Act 1997 and r. 25 of the CPR 1998. They are more rarely granted in the modern era than formerly, being subject to strict prerequisites. Because such orders are granted in secret, the person whose premises are to be searched first knows of the procedure when they are served with the relevant order by the solicitor who is supervising a 'search party'. Such an order requires the recipient to allow the search party to search listed premises for relevant documents and to copy computer files. They do not permit forced entry, but a failure on the part of the recipient to comply with a search order can be punished as a contempt of court. Any discussion of evidence will necessarily touch on aspects of procedure, if only briefly.

This book is primarily concerned with the law regulating the adduction of evidence. It should, however, also be noted that, in the common law tradition at least, there has been a tendency to equate evidence as a subject purely with its legal aspects, and to neglect other important dimensions, such as witness psychology, the philosophy and logic of proof, and the evidentiary significance of forensic science in the trial process.[2] As Jeremy Bentham observed (although he focused his own energy on judicial evidence), the '...field of evidence is no other than the field of knowledge'.

The subject stretches across disciplines and excites popular interest in many of its non-legal aspects via television programmes, such as 'CSI Miami', which focus on innovative scientific techniques in forensic detection. In recent decades, the use of genetic profiling based on DNA has been of great practical importance in many trials, especially, but not solely, criminal ones. Techniques for recovering genetic profiles have also improved enormously since their advent in the 1980s, so that those employed today are very much more sensitive, and require much smaller traces, than those available even a decade ago (though this also increases the risk of accidental contamination). As a result, many 'cold cases' involving serious crimes (especially rape and murder) have been reviewed, and even solved, in recent years. Similarly, there has been much modern research on how witness psychology affects the giving of evidence in a forensic environment. However, although these are all very important areas, some are largely outside the remit of a work of this nature, and will merely be alluded to in passing, while others will be touched on only briefly.

William Twining, 'Evidence as a multi-disciplinary subject' (2003) Law, Probability and Risk, vol 2, 91–107 (Extract)

The label 'evidence' has a number of different associations depending on context. . . . For example, a historian might think that it is artificially narrow to separate inferential reasoning from broader concerns about narrative and truth; for some the main interest lies in particular kinds of data, such as archaeological remains, DNA or psychological findings about memory or bias. Some are interested in particular problems of collecting evidence, or preserving it, or assessing its credibility.

When Do the Rules Of Evidence Apply?

It should be noted that the strict rules of evidence do not apply, in their entirety, to all legal forums with an adjudicative function. Thus, and most importantly, they do not operate (or operate fully) in many tribunals. For example, in *Re A Solicitor* [1992] 2 WLR 552, the Divisional Court accepted, without question, that the normal rules of evidence did not apply to a disciplinary hearing conducted by the Law Society over a very serious allegation against a solicitor. Similarly, employment tribunals are not required to apply formal rules of evidence, by dint of the following statutory instrument.

---

[2] T Anderson, W Twining and D Schum, *Analysis of Evidence* (2nd edn, 2005, Cambridge University Press) at 78.

The Employment Tribunals (Constitution and Rules of Procedure) Regulations 2004 (SI/1861)

Rule 14(2): So far as it appears appropriate to do so, the chairman or tribunal shall seek to avoid formality in his or its proceedings and shall not be bound by any enactment or rule of law relating to the admissibility of evidence in proceedings before the courts.

Pause for reflection

Why should some legal tribunals not be subject to the full law of evidence?

2. What is Evidence Adduced to Establish?

All matters determined by litigation (whether criminal or civil) can be broken down into discrete issues; these are sometimes called the 'facts in issue', these being matters of substantive law that one of the parties must establish to succeed. Thus, in criminal matters, these are usually the 'essential elements' of the offence charged, plus any special defences that have been raised by the defendant. For example, the elements that the prosecution must establish in a theft case are: (1) dishonest, (2) appropriation of (3) property, (4) belonging to another, (5) with the intention of permanently depriving that other of it. If the defendant alleges that he has a defence of insanity to such a charge, this will add another issue to the case. Similarly, if he were to claim that he stole as result of duress (threats of violence from a third party), and adduced some evidence to support this, yet another issue would be added to the trial (which the prosecution would then have the duty of disproving).

Cross-reference Box

Since the defence of duress places an 'evidential burden' on the defendant in a criminal case, he is required to adduce some evidence that he was acting under such duress before the prosecution are obliged to prove that this was not so. For more information on evidential burdens, go to pp. 118–126.

In civil matters, such as an action for breach of contract, the facts in issue might be: the establishment of the existence of a contract and its contents; breach of a term of that contract; and resulting and foreseeable loss. Similarly, in a case of tortious negligence, they might be: the establishment of a duty of care towards the claimant, breach of that duty and resultant (and non-remote) damage.

However, it should also be noted that lawyers sometimes speak of an *ultimate probabandum*, that is the very matter that the prosecution or claimant ultimately has to establish. For example, did the defendant murder the man named on the indictment or were the widgets not of a satisfactory quality as alleged in a claimant's statement of case?

All disputed facts in issue, as well as collateral matters going to the credit of witnesses (where they are permitted), must normally be proved by the adduction of admissible evidence. Counsel, in their personal capacity, cannot furnish the court with information that the tribunal of fact can then use to reach a decision; for example, via an unsubstantiated submission to the judge, magistrates or jury. Thus, in recent years, the Court of Appeal has stressed that formal evidence must be adduced to support any explanation for a failure to testify that is advanced by the defence in a criminal trial, so as to avoid an adverse inference direction under s. 35 of the Criminal Justice and Public Order Act 1994 (CJPOA 1994) being given to a jury; the same court has also warned against advocates giving evidence dressed up as a legal submission.

Cross-reference Box

Until the advent of the 1994 Act a trial judge had to direct a jury that no significance could be placed on a defendant's failure to testify at trial. In particular, an adverse inference could not be drawn from such a failure. This has now changed as a result of the CJPOA 1994, at least in some situations. For more on this, go to pp. 387–392.

Pause for reflection.

Why should counsel not normally be allowed to furnish the court with information on which it can act?

What will be acceptable in establishing disputed facts will depend, to some extent, on the nature of the case and the type of tribunal concerned. The following extract, which also gives a valuably succinct overview of the operation of the entire Law of Evidence, and recent trends in its development, makes this clear:

Mike Redmayne, 'The Structure of Evidence Law' (2006) Oxford Journal of Legal Studies, vol 26, no 4, 805–822

Here is a fairly straightforward sketch of the theoretical structure of evidence law. Fact-finding involves decision-making under uncertainty, that is, in situations where we cannot be absolutely sure of where the truth lies. The best that fact-finders can do, then, is assess the probability of liability. Fact-finding should be conducted rationally, therefore we can think of it as governed by the rules of probability theory. These rules provide a framework within which fact-finders should draw on their general experience to assess the probability of the evidence presented and, ultimately, of the facts in issue. Because fact-finders make decisions under uncertainty, evidence law needs to provide rules specifying the degree of certainty required for a verdict. Such rules are termed standards of proof. Standards of proof can only be set by considering what is at stake in a finding of liability, so at this point accounts of the rules governing civil and criminal trials diverge. In civil trials, the basic presumption is one of equality between claimant and defendant: a mistake affecting one side is as serious as a mistake affecting the other. Decision theory can then be used to show that the civil standard of proof should be set at a probability of 0.5, the 'balance of probabilities', a rule which has the additional merit of minimizing the number of expected fact-finding errors. The presumption of equality does not apply to criminal trials, where the censure involved in a finding of liability, as well as the 'hard treatment' that frequently follows such a finding, point to a higher standard of proof.

Overlying this basic decisional structure are rules excluding evidence and instructing fact-finders on how to reason about evidence. Evidence may be excluded for one of a number of policy reasons: for example, to preserve confidentiality between lawyers and their clients, or to preserve the integrity of a trial (as when, in a criminal case, illegally or unfairly obtained evidence is excluded). Evidence may also be excluded in order to promote accurate fact-finding. Thus evidence of D's criminal record may be excluded on the grounds that its probative value is outweighed by its prejudicial effect (we will refer to this concern as 'PV/PE'). Evidence might also be excluded because it is not the 'best evidence'; in this way second hand evidence may be excluded in order to encourage the parties to seek out and present first hand evidence (this might provide a justification for the hearsay rule). Where the concern is with the confusion of fact-finders, a less drastic means of promoting verdict accuracy is to instruct them to be cautious about a particular type of evidence. In recent times, exclusionary rules of the second-accuracy promoting-type have not been favoured. The trend is to trust fact-finders not to fall into error, especially when the less drastic 'caution' type rule can be used instead.

3. The Role of Judge, Magistrates and Jury

Introduction

What might be termed 'classical' evidence theory was premised on a bifurcation between the tribunal of fact and law, and, at the start of the nineteenth century, this was still very much the norm in reality. Both civil and criminal matters were largely determined by juries and presided over by professional judges. As a result, the latter could determine questions of evidential admissibility in the absence of the former, who would not be exposed to evidence that was ultimately deemed to be inadmissible in the process.

However, this has changed greatly in the modern era. The advent of the County Courts in 1846, and the loss of juries from nearly all High Court trials in the early twentieth century, combined with the steady growth of summary jurisdiction in criminal matters (magistrates determine most criminal cases today), means that the classic 'judge and jury' environment, against which backdrop most evidential rules emerged, no longer applies in the vast majority of situations. It has largely retreated to relatively serious criminal matters and defamation actions.

This has had enormous practical significance for the law of evidence, albeit that much of the theory has altered little. For example, the general (and now considerably diluted) rule that the tribunal of fact should not normally be aware of a defendant's previous convictions is often unrealistic where an habitual criminal is being tried by his local magistrates, who may well have seen him on numerous earlier occasions.[3] Even if they have not done so, if the prosecution make an application to adduce his convictions under s. 101(1)(d) of the Criminal Justice Act 2003, perhaps because they feel that they show a propensity to offend in a certain manner, the magistrates decide that the statutory prerequisites for this provision have not been met, and the convictions are consequently deemed to be inadmissible, they will still have been exposed to them. Although the justices of the peace (JPs) are then supposed to put the convictions out of

---

[3] See on this, generally, P Darbyshire, 'Previous Misconduct and Magistrates' Courts—Some tales from the real world' [1997] Crim LR 105.

their minds when determining the defendant's guilt or innocence, essentially speculating as to what verdict another hypothetical bench, uncontaminated by such information, would reach, this will not necessarily be easy.

Cross-reference Box

The prosecution can only adduce a defendant's previous convictions, or other aspects of his bad character, if they can introduce it under one of the gateways set out in s. 101 of the Criminal Justice Act 2003. For more on this important provision, go to pp. 184–220.

Of course, such problems raise the obvious question as to whether, as is currently the case, exactly the same evidential rules should apply whether a jury is present or not. It is probably neither practicable nor desirable to distinguish between criminal matters being tried summarily, and those being heard on indictment, especially as this would produce separate regimes for either-way cases depending on the forum in which they were heard, something to which the courts have traditionally (and rightly) been very averse.

Even so, the absence, in most cases, of civil juries has undoubtedly contributed to the great relaxation in evidential rules in non-criminal matters that has occurred over the last 50 years. Arguably, if juries did not exist, it would be possible to dispense with significant areas of the law of evidence in criminal cases. Against this, however, it might be asserted that judges are not quite as immune to cognitive or reasoning errors as is sometimes claimed. Judicial expertise in evaluating evidence may occasionally be exaggerated.

Pause for reflection

Do you feel that a judge is better equipped than you are to make judgments of fact (rather than law)?

When it comes to determining the admissibility of evidence, applications will often involve questions of law that can be determined by a judge simply by hearing legal argument from counsel, albeit that, in the Crown Court, this will usually be in the absence of the jury. Nevertheless, sometimes, the very decision will necessitate the adduction and examination of evidence. This will require the first instance judge to hold a *voir dire*, or, as it is sometimes termed, a 'trial within a trial', in which he hears evidence to determine whether other evidence should be admitted. This procedure, conducted in the absence of the jury, is most commonly used to determine the admissibility of a contested confession and so will be considered in detail in chapter 7. Even so, it should be noted that its use is certainly not confined to confession evidence, and can also be used, for example, to decide whether a witness is competent to testify and in a variety of other situations.

It is often (and correctly) said that judges determine questions of law, and juries matters of fact, so that questions of evidential admissibility are decided by the judiciary, while how much importance to place on that evidence (if it is admitted), is determined by jurors. However, as the *voir dire* procedure suggests, there is not a hermetic seal between the two. Thus, when determining the admissibility of certain types of evidence a first instance judge will often have to make an assessment of its cogency. For example, where there is a disputed identification in a criminal case, the trial judge will have to decide whether the identification is of sufficient quality to justify going before the jury at all, under the principles set out in *R v Turnbull* [1977] QB

224. As a result, he will have to consider the effects on the identification of various factors, such as light, distance, the presence of obstructions, etc.

Cross-reference Box

Experience over the years has demonstrated that identification evidence is much less reliable than is popularly appreciated, and, in the past, has been a major cause of mistaken convictions. For this reason, in *R v Turnbull* [1977] QB 224, the Court of Appeal set out firm guidelines as to when cases that turned on identification could be left to a jury, and the warnings that a trial judge had to give juries on identification evidence if they were. For more on this topic see pp. 539–552.

Additionally, when directing the jury at the end of a criminal trial, one of a judge's functions is to reiterate and summarize the evidence that has been heard, as well as to identify the accused person's defence, during which process he is also allowed to comment on the evidence, albeit in very circumspect terms, *provided* he also makes it clear that the jurors are fully entitled to disagree with his views, and should disregard his comments if they do: *R v Jackson* [1992] Crim LR 214. Thus, in the case of *R v Cohen and Bateman* (1909) 2 Cr App R 197, still approved and cited today, the Criminal Court of Appeal observed that: 'Of course, questions of fact are for the jury and not for the judge, yet the judge has experience on the bearing of evidence, and in dealing with the relevancy of questions of fact, and it is therefore right that the jury should have the assistance of the judge.' This is unlike the situation found in many American states, which have a 'no judicial-comment' on evidence rule for judicial summing up, with the trial judge merely directing jurors on the law. Even in England, the past 50 years have seen a marked decline in the extent to which a trial judge can make negative comments about a defendant's case.[4]

Pause for reflection

Do you think that judges should be allowed to give their views on evidence, even in the most anodyne terms, to English and Welsh juries?

Submissions of No Case to Answer

Another aspect of judicial control of the trial, and the admissibility of evidence, is that a first instance judge will have to determine submissions of 'no case to answer'. These can be made by the defendants in both criminal and civil cases, at the end of the prosecution or claimant's evidence. If they are successful, the case will be 'thrown out' and, in the Crown Court, a jury will be directed to acquit. In these situations, the defendant is, essentially, saying that the evidence being brought against him is so poor that he should not be required to answer the allegations being made by calling his own evidence in reply or to risk a 'perverse' verdict, against the evidence, being returned by a jury. For example, there might not be any evidence on an essential element of a criminal offence, and thus no prima facie case.

Submissions of 'no case' are made much more rarely in civil matters than during criminal trials. This is because, normally, a judge will only entertain such a submission after putting a defendant

---

[4] N Madge, 'Summing Up-a Judge's Perspective' [2006] Crim LR 817–827, at 824–825.

to his election as to whether to give evidence: *Graham v Chorley Borough Council* [2006] EWCA Civ 92. If he proposes to give evidence, he cannot usually make such a submission. Thus, unless a civil defendant is supremely confident, or has no evidence at all to give in reply to a claimant's case (rarely the situation), a submission of no case to answer will not normally be made.

In criminal hearings, where they are far more common, there are two, subtly different tests, for such a submission, depending on whether it is being made in the Crown Court or the Magistrates Court. In the former, it is governed by the principles set out in the case of *R v Galbraith* [1981] 1 WLR 1039, in the latter, it is regulated by a practice direction issued by Lord Parker CJ over 45 years ago: *Practice Direction (Submission of no case)* [1962] 1 WLR 227. The main difference between the two is that the Practice Direction appears to give magistrates slightly greater scope to make a qualitative assessment as to whether they would convict on the evidence adduced. Although it may appear strange that the test for such submissions is not exactly the same in the two forums, one rationale given for this difference is that as magistrates (unlike judges) are the tribunal of both fact and law it is right that they should be allowed a little more leeway to make an assessment as to the quality of the prosecution evidence.

Pause for reflection

What are the dangers of allowing a trial judge in the Crown Court excessive latitude in accepting submissions of no case to answer?

R v Galbraith [1981] 1 WLR 1039, CA

Lord Lane CJ

How then should the judge approach a submission of 'no case'? (1) If there is no evidence that the crime alleged has been committed by the defendant, there is no difficulty. The judge will of course stop the case. (2) The difficulty arises where there is some evidence but it is of a tenuous character, for example because of inherent weakness or vagueness or because it is inconsistent with other evidence. (a) Where the judge comes to the conclusion that the prosecution evidence, taken at its highest, is such that a jury properly directed could not properly convict upon it, it is his duty, upon a submission being made, to stop the case. (b) Where however the prosecution evidence is such that its strength or weakness depends on the view to be taken of a witness's reliability, or other matters which are generally speaking within the province of the jury and where on one possible view of the facts there is evidence upon which a jury could properly come to the conclusion that the defendant is guilty, then the judge should allow the matter to be tried by the jury. . . . There will of course, as always in this branch of the law, be borderline cases. They can safely be left to the discretion of the judge.

4. Who Adduces Evidence?

Introduction

The common law fact-finding process is an adversarial system, founded on a belief that the 'truth' can best be established by a neutral and (largely) passive adjudicator, whether jury, judge or magistrates, presiding over a clash between forensic opponents. Each party seeks its own evidentiary material, selects and prepares it, and uses it in a manner that best advances its tactical interests. In common law theory, if two competent lawyers argue the evidence for and against the defendant in a case, to the best of their ability, its real significance will be tested and become clear to the tribunal of fact. Of course, this assumes that there is an 'equality of arms' between litigants. If financial constraints limit access to competent lawyers, unfairness might result. This is one argument for the judge-dominated inquisitorial system (see below) that is often advanced by continental lawyers and those who are sympathetic towards such systems.

Inevitably, there are also some constraints (both professional and legal) on this general position. For example, it is the professional duty of the prosecutor in a criminal trial to present the evidence for the Crown as fairly as possible, and not to strive for a conviction by every means in his power. A prosecuting barrister should: '... not regard himself as appearing for a party'.[5] Similarly, although the prosecution has an unfettered discretion as to what witnesses to call to prove their case prior to the service of witness statements on the defence, once these have been issued they ought to call any witness whose statement has been served who is also capable of belief: *R v Haringey Justices ex parte DPP* [1996] 2 Cr App R 119. Nevertheless, these constraints are relatively modest, especially with regard to defendants (generally) and claimants in civil matters.

R v Russell-Jones [1995] 1 Cr App R 538, CA

Kennedy LJ

The principles which emerge from the authorities and from rules of practice appear to be: (1) Generally speaking the prosecution must have at court all the witnesses named on the back of the indictment (nowadays those whose statements have been served as witnesses on whom the prosecution intend to rely), if the defence want those witnesses to attend. ... (2) The prosecution enjoy a discretion whether to call, or tender, any witness it requires to attend, but the discretion is not unfettered. (3) The first principle which limits this discretion is that it must be exercised in the interests of justice, so as to promote a fair trial. ... (4) The next principle is that the prosecution ought normally to call or offer to call all the witnesses who give direct evidence of the primary facts of the case, unless for good reason, in any instance, the prosecutor regards the witness's evidence as unworthy of belief. ... The defence cannot always be expected to call for themselves witnesses of the primary facts whom the prosecution has discarded. For example, the evidence they may give, albeit at variance with other evidence called by the Crown, may well be detrimental to the defence case. ... (5) It is for the prosecution to decide which witnesses give direct evidence of the primary facts of the case. ... (6) The prosecutor is also, as we have said, the primary judge of whether or not a witness to the material events is incredible, or unworthy of belief. ... (7) A prosecutor properly exercising his discretion will not therefore be obliged to proffer a witness merely in order to give the defence material with which to attack the credit of other witnesses on whom the Crown relies.

The alternative to the common law adversarial approach to evidence is that found in the civil law 'inquisitorial' system, in which the court, or its officers, take[s] an active role in gathering and adducing evidence, and which also do not make a rigid separation between the investigative process prior to trial and the hearing itself.[6]

---

[5] See, for example, the Code of Conduct of the Bar of England and Wales (8th edn), Section 3, at para. 10.1.

[6] J Cooper, 'Criminal Investigations in France' (1991) New Law Journal, issue 141, 381–382 at 381.

Thus, and typically of such systems, in Holland, much pre-trial evidence gathering in criminal cases is done under the supervision of an investigating judge or magistrate. The ensuing criminal trial focuses heavily on the resulting dossier, which contains statements made to both the police and judge. The court also conducts the primary examination of witnesses, and may adjourn from time to time to call extra witnesses or for the further compilation of evidence for the dossier. As a result, the proceedings and the taking of evidence are, to a considerable extent, court rather than party-driven,[7] though lawyers in such systems sometimes suggest improvements in the wording of the judicial summaries of witness evidence in the dossier (witness testimony is seldom recorded verbatim).[8] More widely, and as a very crude generalization, it can be noted that most civil law systems are culturally attuned to placing less significance on oral evidence (and more on that found in documents) than their common law counterparts.

John Langbein, *The Origins of Adversary Trial* (2003, Oxford University Press), at 1–2

The lawyer-conducted criminal trial, our so-called adversary system, is the defining feature of criminal justice in England and in countries like the United States that are founded on the English common law. What distinguishes criminal adjudication in the Anglo-American world from the European and European derived systems is not simply that our system allows lawyers for prosecution and defense. The European procedure does too. The striking peculiarity of the Anglo-American trial is that we remit to the lawyer-partisans the responsibility for gathering, selecting, presenting, and probing the evidence. Our trial court, traditionally a jury sitting under the supervision of the judge, conducts no investigation of its own. The court renders a verdict of guilt or innocence by picking between or among the evidence that the contesting lawyers have presented to it. In the European systems, by contrast, evidence is gathered by judges or judge-like investigators, public officers who operate under a duty to seek the truth. Criminal investigation is understood to be a public rather than a private function. At trial, the presiding judge examines the witnesses. The lawyers for the prosecution and defense play subordinate roles, mostly recommending lines of inquiry, sometime supplementing the court's questioning of witnesses.

Limited Judicial Role in Adducing Evidence

In the English system, judges are heavily constrained in their input to the development of a case, and have little active involvement in the process. As far back as the seventeenth century, Sir Francis Bacon suggested that in civil matters, where there were advocates available to conduct the hearing, it was not a judge's role to find material that he might have heard: '…in due time from the bar; or to show quickness of conceit, in cutting off evidence or counsel too short; or to prevent information by questions—though pertinent'.[9] (As will be seen, the absence of lawyers from many serious criminal trials meant that activist judges were much more common in such hearings, prior to the 1780s.)

---

[7] JF Nijboer et al (eds), 'The Requirement of a Fair Process and the Law of Evidence in Dutch Criminal Proceedings' in *Forensic Expertise and the Law of Evidence* (1993, Royal Netherlands Academy) at 161.

[8] JH Langbein, 'The German Advantage in Civil Procedure' (1985) University of Chicago Law Review, vol 52, no 4, 823–866, at 835.

[9] Sir Francis Bacon, 'On Judicature' in the Everyman series, *The Essays* (1906, JM Dent) at 162–165.

In the modern era, appellate courts have taken an even more robust approach towards interventionist judges. Thus, in *Jones v National Coal Board* [1957] 2 QB 55, Lord Denning famously argued that: 'In the system of trial which we have evolved in this country, the judge sits to hear and determine the issues raised by the parties, not to conduct an investigation or examination on behalf of society at large.' Indeed, so firmly was this established that a judge was not normally allowed to call a witness in a civil case whom he thought might throw some light on the facts: 'He must rest content with the witnesses called by the parties.' Similarly, in *Laker Airways Ltd v Department of Trade* [1977] 2 All ER 182 Lawton LJ gave his own, rather 'sporting', view of the judicial role: 'I regard myself as a referee. I can blow my judicial whistle when the ball goes out of play; but when the game restarts I must neither take part in it nor tell the players how to play.' This approach has been reiterated on several occasions in the more recent past.

Pause for Reflection

Do you think that such judicial passivity in the trial process is a good thing?

The judicial power to question witnesses called by the parties is also very limited, at least in theory. In *R v Webb and Simpson* [2000] WL 1544617, where the appellants were convicted after a lengthy trial for tax evasion and false accounting, one of the grounds of appeal was the manner in which the trial judge had personally questioned the defendants. The Court of Appeal noted that a trial judge was entitled to ask questions to clear up ambiguities, and even to deal with matters not covered by counsel, but observed that when doing so he must be careful not to 'enter the arena'. Where there was competent legal representation on both sides it would normally be inappropriate for a large number of questions to come from the bench.

In *Webb and Simpson*, the judge had asked 175 questions and, the Court of Appeal concluded, was, at times, assuming the role of a prosecutor and was not displaying appropriate judicial impartiality. Illustrative of this, the judge had asked 25 questions of his own during the cross-examination of a single witness by experienced leading counsel. The Court of Appeal opined that there was no justification for the appellant having been questioned in this manner (though the convictions were held to be safe on the evidence).

However, it is not simply the number, but also the nature of judicial questions or observations that will be significant. More recently, in *R v H* [2006] EWCA 853, where a 14-year-old boy was accused of raping a younger child by oral penetration, an interjection by the trial judge, in circumstances that many lay observers might consider reasonable, was criticized by the Court of Appeal.

R v H [2006] EWCA 853, CA

Rix LJ

The third ground of appeal arises from an intervention by the Judge in the course of the cross-examination of T on the third day of the trial. Mr Jeary was asking him about his account of how the assaults took place, and invited him to confirm that both the appellant and E were standing, a point on which his evidence was inconsistent with that of his brother. At this point Mr Jeary asked T, 'why are you putting your head down when you are telling us about these things?' The Judge intervened: 'Maybe because he is twelve years old and he witnessed his brother, according to him, having oral sex against his will, Mr Jeary'. Mr Jeary submitted that the Judge

> should not have intervened in this way, and that the jury might have understood that the Judge was indicating his own thoughts about the facts of the case. We can understand the Judge wishing to reassure a young witness, but in our judgment free from the immediate pressures that the Judge faced, the intervention was unfortunate. It is true that, as Ms Rowley observed, it included the words 'according to him', but we do not consider that this justified it. Nor do we consider that the criticism is answered by the observation that in his summing up the Judge told the jury not to adopt views about the facts that he might appear to express unless they agreed with him. That said, however, we are unable to accept that this intervention on the third day of a six day trial can realistically be supposed to have influenced the jury's verdicts or gives rise to a risk that they are unsafe.

Nevertheless, this is not to say that judges have *no* role at all in the adduction or examination of evidence. As *Webb and Simpson* also makes clear, they can ask questions of witnesses to clear up ambiguities. Furthermore, *in practice* if not in theory, in recent years some members of the judiciary have taken a slightly more assertive role with regard to witnesses, and there is even some limited appellate support for such a position.

For example, in the little-reported case of *R v Saville* (1993) Archbold Cr App Office Index 1, 98, the Court of Appeal described a Recorder's fairly active conduct of a theft trial as 'impeccable'. The part-time judge had, inter alia, asked a prosecution witness whether she had embezzled the missing money, so denying defence counsel the opportunity of subsequently suggesting this possibility to the jury. The appellant's contention that the judge had 'descended into the arena' and assumed the role of an advocate was rejected, the court noting that if a trial judge perceived a risk that a case might go off on a wholly wrong basis because of some lacuna in the evidence, it was not incumbent on him to remain silent and watch justice miscarry. In any event, the Court of Appeal appears to be reluctant to quash convictions because of excessive judicial interventions, unless they are extreme.

Additionally, although in civil cases a judge can only call a witness with the permission of the parties, in criminal cases he can do so on his own initiative in exceptional circumstances. The exercise of such a power is tightly circumscribed and very rarely used, though it is sometimes suggested that judges should be more willing to employ it. Even so, in *R v Haringey Justices ex parte DPP* [1996] 2 Cr App R 119 it was held to have been wrong for magistrates not to have exercised this discretion to call a policeman, one of two officers who were the alleged victims in an assault case, who was not called by the prosecution because he had subsequently been suspended from duty.

R v Haringey Justices ex parte DPP [1996] 2 Cr App R 119, DC

Stuart-Smith LJ

Where in the exercise of their unfettered discretion the prosecution choose not to call a witness, such witnesses will fall into one of two categories. First, there are those whose evidence is helpful to the defence and tends to contradict the Crown's case. On being notified of the existence of such a witness, the defence can make arrangements to call him. Secondly, there are those whose evidence supports the Crown's case but, for whatever reason, it is decided not to call him or her. In the ordinary way the defence will obviously not wish such a witness to be called. But there may be exceptional cases where the defence do wish such a witness to be called. The instant case was such a one. Rightly or wrongly the defence considered that they would have a better prospect of establishing their case, which was that the two police officers were out to harass and assault two young black men, if they could cross-examine both officers and no doubt try to exploit discrepancies between them to show that the evidence was fabricated. Where the witness is a police officer it is in my view unrealistic to require the defence to call him and I do not think it is in the interests of justice that they should be required to do so. The situation with other witnesses may well be different and each case will have to be considered in the light of its own facts. . . . If the court is satisfied that the interests of justice require that he should give evidence and that it would be unfair to the defence that he should not do so, they should so rule, though I would emphasise that in my view this will be an exceptional case and the justices should not lightly reach this conclusion.

In extreme cases, a presiding judge also has the power to impose time limits for questioning during either examination in chief or cross-examination as part of his case management role, even in criminal trials. Thus, where counsel cross-examining a rape complainant had spent large amounts of time on irrelevant matters, having already put her case properly, and had become prolix and repetitious, a first instance judge's decision to prevent her from continuing her questioning, after several warnings, and where it did not occasion any unfairness to the defendant, was upheld by the Court of Appeal in *R v B* [2006] Crim LR 54.

Criticism of Party Adduction of Evidence

The traditional common law emphasis on party adduction and examination of evidence has been criticized for creating a 'bipolar tension' in which there is little middle ground. Because witnesses are usually specifically associated with one or other of the litigants, there is a risk that they are not viewed as 'neutral' and independent sources of information. Additionally, witnesses themselves may come to feel associated with the side that is calling them, and subconsciously shape their evidence to support that party. Where they are paid for their testimony, as with experts, this risk becomes even more acute.

The parties are also given an incentive to adopt what have been termed 'truth defeating stratagems' when questioning witnesses, to prevent them producing unhelpful material; for example, counsel might ask that a witness, who wishes to give a qualified answer to a question posed in cross-examination, 'Answer this question, yes or no.' Some have argued that this partisanship, the so-called 'combat effect', when combined with the 'wealth effect', which disadvantages those who cannot afford to hire skilled counsel at trial or pay for the thorough investigation of available evidence, means that the adversarial system is fundamentally flawed.[10]

Such observers tend to support the inquisitorial, civil (or 'Roman') law tradition found on the continent, where there is much greater judicial involvement in fact gathering, and where the lawyers' role in eliciting evidence is more restricted. It is argued that although adversaries might sometimes bring into court evidence that would otherwise be overlooked, this is an argument for *including* them in the fact-gathering process rather than letting them *dominate* it. To this end, and for example, German civil procedure allows lawyers to nominate witnesses, attend and supplement court questioning, and develop adversary positions on the significance of the evidence adduced. However, in Germany the court ultimately decides which witnesses, including expert witnesses, it wishes to hear from (whether nominated or not), and the judge

---

[10] See, for an example, JH Langbein, *The Origins of Adversary Trial* (2003, Oxford University Press) at 1–2.

serves as the examiner-in-chief. Only at the conclusion of his interrogation of each witness does counsel for either party pose additional questions, if they wish to do so.[11]

It might also be noted that in criminal matters at least, the modern common law form of lawyer-dominated trial is less than 250 years old. An absence of counsel from felony hearings until well into the eighteenth century (they were legally forbidden to defendants until the 1730s), meant that judges necessarily had to dominate proceedings and conduct much of the questioning of witnesses. Thus, in 1680 the barrister, Sir John Hawles noted that because of their experience, judges were presumed to be best qualified to ask pertinent questions: '…they therefore commonly examine the witnesses in the Court'.[12] As a result, the judicial contribution was substantially inquisitorial, with such proofs as were adduced being as likely to be the fruits of the judge's questioning as of the parties' efforts.[13]

However, against such criticism, supporters of the modern common law approach to the gathering and adduction of evidence argue that it has, in its turn, many strengths; it is also claimed that these are often absent from continental systems. For example, it ensures that all evidence is normally tested thoroughly by an opponent, who will also seek out any potential material available to support his own case, and to discredit that of his opponent, and will consider all realistic options open to his client on the evidence. Additionally, it does not assume that fact finders are completely impartial components of the justice system, free of normal human limitations, beliefs or prejudices, and so incapable of jumping to conclusions or adopting a theory in any given case and then 'running' with it, while ignoring conflicting indications in the process. Arguably, the adversarial system is also less susceptible to corruption and the effects of extrinsic pressure, because it reduces judicial (and so state) involvement in the process, although this consideration will be far more relevant in some parts of the world than in others.

 Pause for reflection

Do you think it should be the parties who largely decide what evidence should be adduced at trial in England and Wales?

There has also been some academic criticism of judicial involvement in fact-finding. Thus, it has been argued by the American judge and legal academic, Richard Posner that it is both expensive and potentially ineffectual. Posner also asserts that inherent balances within the adversarial system mean that the amount of evidence secured, and the resources devoted to this process, are more likely to be proportionate to the gravity of a case, at least in serious commercial matters.

Richard A Posner, 'An Economic Approach to the Law of Evidence' (1999) Stanford Law Review, vol 51, no 6, 1477–1490, at 1488 (Extract)

It might seem that our searcher-judge would be an extremely efficient searcher, because of selection, training, and experience. But maybe not. Since it is difficult to evaluate legal fact finding and

---

[11] JH Langbein, 'The German Advantage in Civil Procedure' (1985) University of Chicago Law Review, vol 52, no 4, 823–866, at 835.

[12] Sir J Hawles, *The Englishmans Right* (1680, printed for Richard Janesway) at 4.

[13] S Landsman, 'The rise of the contentious spirit: Adversary procedure in Eighteenth Century England' (1990) Cornell Law Review, vol 75, 505–506.

thus to criticize a judge for having made erroneous findings or praise him for good ones, the judge's incentive to exert himself to do a good job will be limited. In addition, if he is highly paid, the cost of search may be substantial. The amount of search conducted, moreover, will depend on the number of judges and auxiliary judicial personnel, and that number may be determined without much regard to the socially optimal amount of search. In addition, the public may lack confidence in the judge's search and in the conclusions he draws from it because the process of judicial inquiry in an inquisitorial system, like grand jury proceedings in the United States, is carried on mainly behind closed doors. And there is a danger that the judge will render the 'popular' result in a case, irrespective of justice.

In the adversarial process exemplified by the modern American civil jury trial, the evidence search is conducted separately by the lawyers for the opposing sides and presented to a non-expert, ad hoc, multi-headed tribunal for decision. Because trial lawyers are compensated directly or indirectly on the basis of success at trial, their incentive to develop evidence favourable to their client and to find the flaws in the opponent's evidence is very great and, if it is a big money case, their resources for obtaining and contesting evidence will be ample. If the size of the stakes in a case is at least a rough proxy for the social costs of an inaccurate decision, there will be at least a rough alignment between the amount of search that is actually conducted and the amount that is socially optimal.

It should, perhaps, also be stressed that no legal system in the world is purely inquisitorial or adversarial, as reality never conforms to 'ideal typical' models, however helpful they might be for lecturing purposes. There are inquisitorial elements in the current English law of evidence and adversarial elements in continental practice. Thus, and very obviously, under the Criminal Appeal Act 1995, when dealing with suspected miscarriages of criminal justice, the Court of Appeal can direct the Criminal Cases Review Commission to investigate and report to the Court on any matter that appears relevant to the determination of an appeal. Also very importantly, and again by way of example, in civil cases the reforms to procedure effected by the Civil Procedure Rules 1998 have introduced an inquisitorial element to many hearings, not least via judicial case-management. This is unsurprising; Lord Woolf, whose work and reports during the 1990s led to the introduction of the Civil Procedure Rules, specifically identified excessive adversarialism as contributing to the high cost and delay commonly associated with civil litigation in the late twentieth century.

Conversely, there is a considerable degree of adversarialism in nearly all civil law systems, some of which have actively taken steps to imitate some aspects of the common law trial, especially in criminal matters. Thus, and for example, although the Japanese legal system is essentially based on the nineteenth-century German form of Roman law, its criminal procedure and rules of evidence contain many elements adopted from the American version of common law. The trial is adversarial in character; the parties, rather than the judge, take the initiative in adducing and examining evidence, and even hearsay can be excluded in certain circumstances.[14] Similarly, and if only for practical reasons, the judicial input in adducing evidence in Roman law countries in less serious non-criminal matters, and in trivial criminal cases, is usually very much more modest than that found with regard to serious crimes such as murder.

[14] H Oda, *Japanese Law* (1992, Butterworths) at 401–402.

5. What Matters can be Established Without Adducing Evidence?

Introduction

Facts in issue, and relevant collateral facts (where allowed), must normally be proved by the adduction of admissible evidence. However, it is not always necessary to call evidence to prove matters that are before the court. They can, sometimes, be established by other mechanisms. Amongst these are legal presumptions (specifically dealt with in chapter 4). Others include: statements of case, formal admissions and the doctrine of judicial notice; to these might be added earlier findings, in other (and separate) criminal proceedings, when those findings are adduced at a subsequent trial to establish their truth. These will be dealt with in turn.

Cross-reference Box

With a true presumption, on proof of fact A, fact B will necessarily follow, even though no evidence has been called on it, unless the opposing side does something. For more on this, go to pp. 151–159.

Statements of Case in Civil Matters

In a civil matter, many issues are determined before trial via the exchange of 'statements of case' (formerly known as 'pleadings'). These are the formal documents that set out the claimant's and defendant's respective cases. Thus, the various parts of r. 16 of the CPR 1998 require that the parties to litigation set out their allegations in their Particulars of Claim (if claimants) and identify those allegations that they take issue with in their Defence (if defendants). For example, in a breach of contract case the claimant will often begin by averring in his statement of claim that there was a contract with certain terms, and these facts will frequently be admitted by the defendant in his defence; however, the claimant will also allege that one of the terms was broken, and this allegation will be denied by the defendant. It is the breach that is the issue in the case, not the existence of a contract. After the admissions made by the defendant in his defence, the existence of the contract and its contents cease to be an issue, or to require proof, at trial.

One of the principal aims of the exchange of such documents is to define disputed facts as narrowly as possible prior to the hearing, reducing the length (and cost) of contested civil hearings and so focusing the court's mind on the real crux of a case. Less commonly, facts in issue and related matters in a civil matter can also be admitted by an exchange of letters between the parties prior to trial.

Formal Admissions in Criminal Cases

The situation in criminal cases is rather different; a plea of 'not guilty' puts every element of an offence in issue: *R v Sims* [1946] KB 531. This remains the case, even if the defendant does not intend to take issue with some of them. Thus, and for example, the defendant in a theft case may not dispute that he appropriated property belonging to another, and may merely wish to take issue with the fact that he did so dishonestly. Even so, the prosecution must still prove *all* the elements of the offence, including appropriation and ownership (beyond reasonable doubt). The main way round this is for the defendant to make a 'formal' admission pursuant to s. 10 of the Criminal Justice Act 1967. This has to be made in writing, unless done in open court (though it is still usually made in writing, even in court, to avoid the risk of ambiguity).

Section 10(1) of the Criminal Justice Act 1967

Subject to the provisions of this section, any fact of which oral evidence may be given in any criminal proceedings may be admitted for the purpose of those proceedings by or on behalf of the prosecutor or defendant, and the admission by any party of any such fact under this section shall as against that party be conclusive evidence in those proceedings of the fact admitted.

In the past, such admissions were not made very frequently. They are much more common in the modern era. Nevertheless, the dangers of lightly making s. 10 admissions were emphasized in *R v Kolton* [2000] Crim LR 761, where it transpired that the defence had admitted crucial movements by the accused which significantly strengthened the prosecution case, yet which could not otherwise be proved by the Crown. The court will not allow such admissions to be withdrawn unless there is cogent evidence that the admission had been made by mistake or under a misunderstanding.

Pause for reflection

Would it be possible, or desirable, to introduce the equivalent of 'statements of case' or 'pleadings' in criminal matters?

However, such admissions are often made because they are helpful for expediting proceedings, focusing the tribunal's minds and, in some situations, might also be useful for avoiding prejudice to an accused person. Thus, in a case of driving whilst disqualified, where there is no dispute that the defendant was disqualified at a certain period, and he wishes to avoid the prejudice of having the details of the conviction for which he was banned from driving adduced (perhaps because they reflect very badly upon him), he might make a formal admission to having been disqualified at the relevant time, in which case the prosecution would merely have to establish that he drove on a public road at that time.

Of course, if a defendant does not intend to dispute one of the elements of an offence, he is unlikely to take issue with it in cross-examination, so implicitly accepting it. Traditionally, when summing up to a jury, a trial judge was (and is) likely to make this obvious (though still leaving the matter to their determination), perhaps using a phrase such as 'this was not challenged by the defence and it may be that it will not trouble you excessively' when directing them on that issue. This was likely to be taken as a sign by the jurors that they should find the matter to be proved. Furthermore, in the modern era, it is not uncommon for a trial judge to discuss his proposed directions to a jury with counsel, at the close of the trial, and in the former's absence.

If defence counsel assents, the judge can simply direct jurors that a matter is agreed. The issue is then, effectively, withdrawn from the jury.

> ### Cross-reference Box
>
> At trial, a party must 'put his case' in cross-examination, that is he must ask a witness who can speak to the facts in issue whether he agrees with his (the party's) version of events, and if he does not, make this clear to the witness and the court. For more on this topic, go to pp. 430–431.

Judicial Notice

Another way in which a fact can be established, without evidence for it having to be adduced at trial, is for a first instance judge to take 'judicial notice' of it, that is to formally recognize its existence without requiring evidence to be adduced to establish it. In *R v Simpson (Calvin)* (1984) 78 Cr App R 115, the Court of Appeal noted that there are at least two reasons as to why a doctrine of judicial notice should exist. In the first place, it expedites the hearing of many cases. Much time would be wasted if every conceivable fact that was not expressly admitted by the opposing side had to be the subject of specific evidence that would, in many instances, also be very costly and difficult to obtain. Secondly, the doctrine tends to produce uniformity of decision-making on certain recurring matters of fact, in situations where a diversity of findings might be distinctly embarrassing; for example, on whether a certain type of bladed implement should be considered to be an offensive weapon per se.

Thus, in *DPP v Hynde* [1998] 1 WLR 1222, the defendant was charged with unlawful possession of a butterfly knife in Heathrow Airport, contrary to s. 4 of the Aviation Security Act 1982. On hearing the information the stipendiary magistrate held, on a submission of no case to answer, that the prosecution had failed to prove an essential element of the charge, namely that a butterfly knife was 'made or adapted for causing injury', and consequently dismissed the information. The prosecutor's appeal by way of case stated to the Divisional Court was allowed, on the basis that the magistrate should have taken judicial notice of the fact that a butterfly knife was necessarily made for use for causing injury to a person. As a result, no further evidence was required to establish this point.

Frequently of course, matters are tacitly recognized by the courts without even being the subject of formal judicial notice, as they are taken to 'go without saying'; for example, that Monday follows Sunday, that winter days are shorter than summer ones, etc. Thus, if a suspect is caught running from where a nearby bank has been held up, the courts will not normally bother to formally 'notice' that fleeing a crime scene might be circumstantial evidence that the accused was involved in the crime; it is 'taken as read'. It is, after all, impossible to assess evidence without assuming something that has not been formally proved in court or having recourse to generalizations based on personal experience of the world.

DPP v Hynde [1998] 1 WLR 1222, DC

Henry LJ

While my impression is that the courts have not had to deal with nearly as many butterfly knives as flick knives, the fact remains that Parliament was sufficiently concerned as to them to outlaw them to the extent that section 141 of the Act of 1988 and the Order made under it did. And there has not, so far as I am aware, been any complaint that they are objects of ordinary, everyday utility manufactured for peaceful purposes which should not have been so proscribed. Just as the courts have taken judicial notice of the fact that flick knives are offensive weapons, so I believe that butterfly knives should also be so treated, because it is in my judgment clear that they are essentially the same weapon involving the same features of concealment, speed and surprise as the flick knife. Both have been outlawed by Parliament, and in all the circumstances justice would be affronted if either in every such case there had to be oral evidence of the manufacturer's intention, or that the same butterfly knife might be found to be an offensive weapon by one fact finding tribunal and not by another. The mischief goes further than that, if in this case the manufacturer or importer or person who sold the butterfly knife to the defendant had been accused with her, then they would have had to be convicted under the provisions of the Order on the basis that the butterfly knife was an offensive weapon covered by section 141 of the Act of 1988, but the defendant could be acquitted because the fact finding tribunal did not consider the matter proved, despite the fact that the same statutory test was involved. Such a result would bring the law into disrepute.

I would answer the question in this case as follows. The stipendiary magistrate was not correct in holding that further evidence was required to establish that a butterfly knife was an article 'made . . . for use for causing injury to . . . a person.' . . . In my judgment the stipendiary magistrate could and should have taken judicial notice of that fact.

The Two Forms of Judicial Notice

There are two forms of judicial notice: that made following inquiry, and that made without such inquiry. The latter refers to matters that are deemed to be so notorious or of such common knowledge amongst ordinary people that they could not be open to serious question or dispute. For example, that Christmas Day (in the Latin tradition) falls on 25 December, or that in human beings pregnancy normally lasts about nine months: *Preston-Jones v Preston-Jones* [1951] AC 391. In these situations, the trial judge or magistrates would simply state in open court that they are 'noticing' the matter in question. This is, effectively, just 'one step up' from the situation in which something is 'taken as read'.

Notice after inquiry occurs where the trial judge consults a source of information, such as a treatise or reference work of almost undisputed accuracy, before formally taking notice of the relevant material, even if it is not necessarily 'generally' known. For example, he might consult a reliable almanac to establish the state of the moon on a certain night. Alternatively, in some situations, he might take notice after being advised by an appropriate government official. Thus, in *The Fagernes* [1927] P 311, Atkin LJ observed that whether a foreign land was a Crown territory was a matter of which a: ' . . . court takes judicial notice. The court has, therefore, to inform itself from the best material available; and on such a matter it may be its duty to obtain its information from the appropriate department of Government. Any definite statement from the proper representative of the Crown as to the territory of the Crown must be treated as conclusive'. Although this might appear similar to receiving 'evidence' on a topic, this is definitely not the case. It is the judge, not the parties, who seeks out the source of information. Once a higher court has formally 'noticed' something after inquiry it can also be legally binding on inferior tribunals, in appropriate circumstances, in subsequent cases.

Arguably, a loose hierarchy exists when it comes to forensic hearings. At its base lies information or assumptions that are implicitly accepted when considering evidence without recourse to the notice procedure at all. It is assumed, for example, that umbrellas are used to keep off the rain in winter. Above this level is information where such an unmentioned assumption does not occur, but which is still (nevertheless) deemed to be so notorious that it can be accepted by taking express judicial notice without any further inquiry, such as that there are 30 days in September. In these situations, the trial judge will merely state in court that he is 'noticing' the fact. Above this again, is information of which judicial notice can be taken, but only following inquiry from an authoritative source; for example, whether 1999 was a leap year or not (after viewing a reliable calendar). Finally, at its apex, are situations where formal evidence, in the normal matter, must be adduced to satisfy the tribunal of fact on an issue.

A very long list of subjects has been expressly 'noticed' by the courts, with or without inquiry, and setting them all out would serve little useful purpose in a work of this nature. They include matters as diverse as the fact that many members of the general public watch trial reconstructions on television, via Oxford University being an institution for the advancement of learning, to Jamaica and Amsterdam being locations that are frequently involved in drug dealing and supply. Obviously, some of the things that can be noticed will change over time. For example, most well-educated and intelligent men in the early years of the twentieth century would have been expected to understand what was meant by commonplace allusions to the Classics or Scripture, in a way that is not necessarily the case a hundred years later. Conversely, it is probably no longer necessary to adduce evidence to persuade a court that CDs can be used to store information; it would have been very different when they were first invented.

Although easy to state in outline, the dividing line between these various categories can be very hard to identify in borderline cases. For example, judicial notice without further inquiry has sometimes been taken of things that might be viewed as at least open to question, and certainly not 'notorious'. Thus, in the celebrated case of *Home Office v Dorset Yacht Co Ltd* [1970] AC 1004, Lord Diplock stated that it was: '…common knowledge, of which judicial notice may be taken, that Borstal training often fails to achieve its purpose of reformation, and that trainees when they have ceased to be detained in custody revert to crime'. Although it is probable that most observers in his era would have shared his lack of confidence in the reformatory power of borstal training, as has been observed by Roderick Munday, this might not quite have been 'common knowledge'. Similarly, not everyone might think that the life of a criminal is necessarily an unhappy one, even if it is an immoral existence, although the former proposition has been expressly 'noticed' by the courts: *Burns v Edman* [1970] 2 QB 541.

Assessing how far the doctrine can be taken can also pose acute problems. For example, in *Morris v KLM Royal Dutch Airlines* [2001] 3 WLR 351, the claimant alleged that she had been physically molested on a long haul flight by another passenger. Lord Phillips MR stated in the Court of Appeal that judges could take judicial notice of the fact that passengers travelling in economy flew in relatively cramped conditions, something that brought them into close proximity to their neighbours. However, should judicial notice be taken of the fact that charter flights are usually even more cramped than the economy class found in scheduled flights, or that economy seats in Air New Zealand (apparently) have more space than is customarily found in most other airlines?

In like manner, there is sometimes difficulty in determining what matters allow notice to be taken only after inquiry has been made from an authoritative source, and what things can be noticed without further ado. Even when inquiry is made, the results can be inconclusive. By way of illustration, in *McQuaker v Goddard* [1940] 1 KB 687, the plaintiff had been bitten by a camel while at the defendant's zoo and liability turned on whether the camel was deemed to be a wild or domestic animal. Ultimately, the issue was resolved by the judge taking judicial notice of its status, after making his own inquiries, although this is something that some zoologists would, at least, view as open to debate. (Nevertheless, and irrespective of the actual decision, the case provides a useful analysis of the doctrine.) Finally, the dividing line between situations that allow notice after inquiry and those that require formal evidence can also pose problems.

 Pause for reflection

Is it possible to hold a trial without taking notice, whether expressly or impliedly, of many matters of fact?

As these problems suggest, the doctrine of judicial notice is not without its dangers. Although inadequate use of the doctrine might entail considerable (and tedious) delay to forensic hearings and produce inconsistency in decision making, excessive recourse to the procedure can usurp the role of the tribunal of fact and sometimes risk adjudicative error. For this reason alone, a degree of caution is warranted in the use of the doctrine, in both its forms.

McQuaker v Goddard [1940] 1 KB 687, CA

Clauson LJ

I should like, however, to add a word as to the part taken in the matter by the evidence given as to the facts of nature in regard to camels. That evidence is not, it must be understood, in the ordinary sense evidence bearing upon an issue of fact. In my view the exact position is this. The judge takes judicial notice of the ordinary course of nature, and in this particular case of the ordinary course of nature in regard to the position of camels among other animals. The reason why the evidence was given was for the assistance of the judge in forming his view as to what the ordinary course of nature in this regard in fact is, a matter of which he is supposed to have complete knowledge. The point is best explained by reading a few lines from that great work, the late Mr. Justice Stephen's, 'Digest of the Law of Evidence'. In the 12th edition, Article 62 is as follows: 'No evidence of any fact of which the Court will take judicial notice need be given by the party alleging its existence; but the judge, upon being called upon to take judicial notice thereof, may, if he is unacquainted with such fact, refer to any person or to any document or book of reference for his satisfaction in relation thereto, or may refuse to take judicial notice thereof unless and until the party calling upon him to take such notice produces any such document or book of reference.' From that statement it appears that the document or book of reference only enshrines the knowledge of those who are acquainted with the particular branch of natural phenomena; and in the present case, owing to some extent to the fact that there appears to be a serious flaw in a statement in a well-known book of reference on the matter here in question, the learned judge permitted, and properly permitted, oral evidence to be given before him by persons who had, or professed to have, special knowledge with regard to this particular branch of natural history. When that evidence was given and weighed up with the statements in the books of reference which were referred to, the facts became perfectly plain; and the learned judge was able without any difficulty whatever to give a correct statement of the natural phenomena material to the matter in question, of which he was bound to take judicial notice.

6. The Findings of Earlier Proceedings

Introduction

At common law, verdicts reached in earlier trials could not be adduced as evidence of the facts on which such findings had been based in subsequent and separate hearings (whether between the same, or different, parties). This was for a variety of reasons, amongst the most important of them being that a verdict is, essentially, only a statement of opinion (on the part of the tribunal of fact in the earlier case) and so caught by the general exclusionary rule against opinion evidence (see chapter 11). This principle is sometimes known as the 'rule in *Hollington v Hewthorn* (1943) KB 587', after the case which clarified the common law situation in this regard. The facts of this case are illustrative of its operation. In it the plaintiff in a negligence action was not allowed to adduce the defendant's (criminal) conviction for careless driving, arising out of the very same incident as his cause of action, as evidence that the defendant had been negligent, for the purposes of the subsequent civil matter.

In some situations, and especially with regard to a matter proved on the balance of probabilities in a civil court at an earlier hearing, this might be a sensible rule. In a 'close' civil trial, a slight change in the evidence, or the way in which it was given or viewed, might have led to a very different verdict. However, its application to verdicts reached in earlier criminal cases, that have necessarily been proved 'beyond reasonable doubt' (in either the Crown Court or a Magistrates Court) and which, under the rule, could not be adduced in later civil or criminal trials, was a matter of general concern. It was felt that the rule could occasion considerable vexation, expense and delay. As a result, the common law principle has been qualified in both areas (civil and criminal) by major statutory reform, this being effected by the Civil Evidence Act 1968 and the Police and Criminal Evidence Act 1984 respectively.

 Cross-reference Box

The 'balance of probabilities' is the standard of proof employed in civil cases (unlike 'beyond reasonable doubt' in criminal matters). It means 'more probable than not', and, unlike beyond reasonable doubt can be reduced to a mathematical formula: a 51% probability. For more on this go to pp. 134–138.

Civil Cases

As the facts of *Hollington v Hewthorn* suggest, this lacuna in the law was felt to be most glaring in civil matters, especially where the civil action arose from exactly the same facts as an earlier criminal case, and even though the matter in question only had to be established on a 'balance of probabilities' at the civil trial. Thus, and for example, might be considered the situation in which Adam assaults Brenda on 1 January, giving her two blacks eyes, and is subsequently convicted of inflicting actual bodily harm (for that assault) in the Crown Court, on 1 June. At common law, this jury verdict could not be adduced at a later civil trial, heard on 1 December of the same year, and brought against Adam by Brenda in the County Court, with a view to obtaining damages for her personal injuries. The same evidence that had been adduced in the Crown Court on 1 June would have to be received all over again by the County Court on 1 December, so that it could determine whether such an assault had actually occurred on 1 January.

This situation changed as a result of the statutory reform effected by s. 11(1) of the Civil Evidence Act 1968 (CEA 1968), which allowed the adduction of a domestic criminal conviction in civil proceedings as 'evidence' (where relevant) that the convicted party committed the offence for which they were found guilty. Under s. 11(2) of the same statute, such a conviction, when adduced into evidence, creates a (rebuttable) legal presumption that the relevant party committed the offence for which they were convicted. Particulars of the indictment or charge sheet can also be adduced in such cases, pursuant to s. 11(2)(b) of the CEA 1968, to assist the civil court in determining the relevance of the earlier criminal conviction to its own proceedings.

Section 11 of the Civil Evidence Act 1968

Convictions as evidence in civil proceedings.

(1) In any civil proceedings the fact that a person has been convicted of an offence by or before any court in the United Kingdom or by a court-martial there or elsewhere shall (subject to subsection (3) below) be admissible in evidence for the purpose of proving, where to do so is relevant to any issue in those proceedings, that he committed that offence, whether he was so convicted upon a plea of guilty or otherwise and whether or not he is a party to the civil proceedings; but no conviction other than a subsisting one shall be admissible in evidence by virtue of this section.

(2) In any civil proceedings in which by virtue of this section a person is proved to have been convicted of an offence by or before any court in the United Kingdom or by a court-martial there or elsewhere—

(a) he shall be taken to have committed that offence unless the contrary is proved; and

(b) without prejudice to the reception of any other admissible evidence for the purpose of identifying the facts on which the conviction was based, the contents of any document which is admissible as evidence of the conviction, and the contents of the information, complaint, indictment or charge-sheet on which the person in question was convicted, shall be admissible in evidence for that purpose.

As a result, and purely by way of illustration, in *McCauley v Hope* (1999) 1 WLR 1977 the claimant was injured in a car crash while being driven as a passenger in a friend's vehicle. Under s. 11(1), the defendant's subsequent conviction by magistrates for driving without due care and attention was admissible as part of the plaintiff's case against him in a negligence action, although as this case also suggests, there is nothing to prevent the defendant trying to prove that his earlier criminal conviction was mistaken. (In this instance, by adducing a new traffic accident investigator's report suggesting that the accident was not his fault.)

McCauley v Hope (1999) 1 WLR 1977, CA

Sir Patrick Russell

The closing words of that section [11(2)(a)] 'unless the contrary is proved' provide, in my judgment, the clearest possible mandate to a defendant in a road traffic accident case to attack his earlier conviction provided he has some good cause for so doing and can discharge the burden of proof to a civil standard that the section imposes upon him. . . . Miss Gumbel for the plaintiff acknowledged that under the provisions of section 11 the defendant was at liberty to prove if she could that her conviction was erroneous but she submitted that the abuse of process arose out of the attempt to overturn the conviction simply on the evidence of the expert's report to which I have referred. I do not think that this argument is sustainable...

This provision only covers subsisting convictions (those not overturned on appeal) arising from a United Kingdom (not just an English or Welsh) court, albeit that it also extends to those from a British Court Martial conducted abroad. It does not apply to foreign convictions, which remain inadmissible under the rule in *Hollington v Hewthorn*. Thus, in *Union Carbide Corporation v Naturin Ltd.* [1987] FSR 538, five employees of one of the defendants had been convicted by a French court of stealing confidential information belonging to a subsidiary of the plaintiff. The plaintiff pleaded this in their statement of case, as relevant to their civil action, but on appeal this was struck out.

There has been (and still is) some dispute as to whether a conviction adduced under s. 11(1) merely creates a presumption (which must then be rebutted by the opposing side), or whether it is also, itself, of evidential weight; something that can go into the balance when deciding whether sufficient evidence has been adduced for the presumption to be rebutted (and which would then require much more evidence from the defendant to displace).[15] The latter analysis was favoured by Lord Denning in *Stupple v Royal Insurance Co Ltd.* [1970] 3 All ER 230, who felt that the earlier conviction was a weighty, albeit not conclusive, piece of evidence in its own right. In this case, the conviction of the plaintiff for bank robbery was adduced to suggest that money found in his flat was part of the proceeds of that robbery, and so could be recovered by the insurance company that had reimbursed the bank. Lord Denning's analysis (in this, if not other respects) was reiterated in *Hunter v Chief Constable of West Midlands* [1982] AC 549.

Hunter v Chief Constable of West Midlands [1982] AC 549, HL

Lord Diplock

Section 11 makes the conviction prima facie evidence that the person convicted did commit the offence of which he was found guilty; but does not make it conclusive evidence; the defendant is permitted by the statute to prove the contrary if he can. The section covers a wide variety of circumstances; the relevant conviction may be of someone who has not been made a defendant to the civil action and the actual defendant may have had no opportunity of determining what evidence should be called on the occasion of the criminal trial; the conviction, particularly of a traffic offence, may have been entered upon a plea of guilty accompanied by a written explanation in

---

[15] For a detailed discussion of presumptions, see chapter 3.

mitigation; fresh evidence, not called on the occasion of his conviction, may have been obtained by the defendant's insurers who were not responsible for the conduct of his defence in the criminal trial, or may only have become available to the defendant himself since the criminal trial. This wide variety of circumstances in which section 11 may be applicable includes some in which justice would require that no fetters should be imposed upon the means by which a defendant may rebut the statutory presumption that a person committed the offence of which he has been convicted by a court of competent jurisdiction. In particular I respectfully find myself unable to agree with Lord Denning M.R. that the only way in which a defendant can do so is by showing that the conviction was obtained by fraud or collusion, or by adducing fresh evidence (which he could not have obtained by reasonable diligence before) which is conclusive of his innocence. The burden of proof of 'the contrary' that lies upon a defendant under section 11 is the ordinary burden in a civil action: proof on a balance of probabilities; although in the face of a conviction after a full hearing this is likely to be an uphill task.

Criminal Cases

In the modern era, earlier criminal convictions in a UK court of someone 'other than the accused' can, sometimes, also be adduced in subsequent criminal proceedings, where to do so is relevant to those proceedings. This is by dint of s. 74(1) of the Police and Criminal Evidence Act 1984 (PCEA 1984) which is, very broadly, the criminal equivalent of s. 11 of the CEA 1968, and which was introduced after an earlier recommendation from the Criminal Law Revision Committee. Under s. 75(1) of the PCEA 1984, the details of the charge sheet or indictment on which the earlier conviction was secured can also be adduced (again, to assist the court in determining its relevance to the case in hand).

Section 74(1) might be particularly significant in those situations where an offence presupposes the commission of an earlier crime (though, as will be seen, it is not confined to such cases). Where the provision applies, it reverses the application of the rule in *Hollington v Hewthorn* in criminal trials, as seen in *R v Spinks* [1982] 78 Cr App R 263. In this case, it was noted in obiter comments that at the trial of a defendant for attempting to impede the apprehension of a person who had committed an arrestable offence, contrary to s. 4 of the Criminal Law Act 1967 (by hiding a knife used in an earlier affray and wounding), any conviction of the person accused of the arrestable offence could not have been adduced to show that such a crime had actually been committed, although proving this was an essential element of the s. 4 offence. The matter would have had to have been proved afresh at the s. 4 trial.

However, in part because the standard of proof is so much higher, and the consequences of a mistake usually so much greater in criminal cases than it is in civil matters, the application of s. 74 of the PCEA 1984 is rather less straightforward than that of s. 11 of the CEA 1968. In particular, the adduction of such convictions by the prosecution might be prevented by an exercise of the judicial discretion contained in s. 78 of the PCEA 1984 (see below). It should also be noted that the wording of s. 74 was amended by the Criminal Justice Act 2003 (CJA 2003), which, inter alia, added the phrase 'where evidence of his [the third party] having done so is admissible'. This allows for compliance with s. 100 of the CJA 2003, which puts limitations on the adduction of third party 'bad character' evidence (including convictions) generally, limiting it to the situations set out in s. 100(1)(a)–(c). A conviction adduced under s. 74 of the PCEA 1984 must now necessarily also comply with s. 100 of the CJA 2003.

Cross-reference Box

Section 100 of the CJA 2003 places firm limits on when the bad character of non-defendants, whether witnesses or not, can be adduced at trial. Such evidence now has to satisfy a quality threshold, so that third party bad character evidence of little value is not adduced. Nevertheless, this is unlikely to have affected most of the pre-2003 cases on s. 74 of the PCEA 1984, as they would probably have met the requisite threshold. For more information on s. 100 of the CJA 2003, go to pp. 221–230.

There is a potential overlap between many of the factors that will influence a court in deciding whether the requirements of s. 100(1) of the CJA 2003 have been met, and those that might affect a decision to exclude evidence of a conviction under s. 78, and it is likely that the issues of admissibility will, to an extent, be dealt with holistically by the courts.

Section 74 of the PCEA 1984

(1) In any proceedings the fact that a person other than the accused has been convicted of an offence by or before any court in the United Kingdom or by a Service court outside the United Kingdom shall be admissible in evidence for the purpose of proving that that person committed that offence, where evidence of his having done so is admissible, whether or not any other evidence of his having committed that offence is given.

(2) In any proceedings in which by virtue of this section a person other than the accused is proved to have been convicted of an offence by or before any court in the United Kingdom or by a Service court outside the United Kingdom, he shall be taken to have committed that offence unless the contrary is proved.

For an example of the operation of s. 74 in practice, the situation in which a defendant is prosecuted for receiving stolen goods might be considered. The prosecution wish to prove that someone else has already been convicted of stealing the very same goods, with a view to establishing that the relevant goods were, in fact, stolen (an essential element of any handling charge). In this situation, the third party's conviction for theft might be adduced under s. 74. Similarly, in *R v Pigram* [1995] Crim LR 808, the Court of Appeal held that a co-defendant's earlier guilty plea to handling stolen video recorders could be adduced at trial against a defendant for the purposes of proving that the same videos were stolen.

The interpretation placed on the wording of s. 74 of the PCEA 1984 by the courts is relatively broad, allowing convictions to be adduced not simply to help establish essential elements of an offence, as in *Pigram*, but also, in some cases, important evidential matters that support the prosecution case in other ways: *R v Robertson and Golder* [1987] QB 920. In this case, a defendant was tried on a count of conspiring with two other named men to commit burglaries in commercial premises. The two other men pleaded not guilty to conspiracy, but guilty to 16 relevant counts of burglary with which the defendant was not charged. At the defendant's trial for conspiracy, the prosecution sought and received leave under s. 74 to adduce evidence of the two men's convictions on the 16 counts, even though this did not go directly to an essential issue in the case against him (as the two men had not pleaded guilty to entering any conspiracy). The defendant was convicted and appealed. However, in dismissing his appeal, the Court of Appeal concluded that s. 74(1) extended to evidential issues arising during the course of proceedings.

Nevertheless, simply because the conviction that it is proposed to adduce under s. 74 has some relevance to the instant proceedings, does not mean that it will necessarily be admitted. The Court of Appeal has expressly discouraged excessive recourse to s. 74, urging that prosecutors use the provision selectively and only where it is necessary to do so.

R v Robertson and Golder [1987] QB 920, CA

Lord Lane CJ

It only remains to add this. Section 74 is a provision which should be sparingly used. There will be occasions where, although the evidence may be technically admissible, its effect is likely to be so slight that it will be wiser not to adduce it. This is particularly so where there is any danger of a contravention of section 78. There is nothing to be gained by adducing evidence of doubtful value at the risk of having the conviction quashed because the admission of that evidence rendered the conviction unsafe or unsatisfactory. Secondly, where the evidence is admitted, the judge should be careful, as Judge Owen Stable was here, to explain to the jury the effect of the evidence and its limitations.

Very importantly, and even ignoring the strict prerequisites set out in s. 100 of the CJA 2003, if the prosecution seeks to adduce a conviction under s. 74, it may be prevented by an exercise of the judicial discretion contained in s. 78 of the Police and Criminal Evidence Act 1984. This was demonstrated early on in the provision's existence in *R v O'Connor* (1987) 85 Cr App R 298. In this case, a defendant was accused of conspiracy to obtain property by deception, by agreeing with another man (one Beck) to make a false insurance claim after pretending that a Vauxhall van had been stolen. Beck had subsequently pleaded guilty to this charge and, at the defendant's trial, this was adduced under s. 74(1) as part of the case against him, with the details of the charge to which he had pleaded guilty being revealed under s. 75 of the same Act. Having been exposed to these, which indicated that Beck had pleaded guilty to conspiring with the defendant, the Court of Appeal concluded that it was inevitable that a jury would have concluded that not only had Beck conspired with the defendant (as the indictment to which he had pleaded guilty made clear), but that the converse must also have taken place (otherwise Beck would not have admitted it). Beck, of course, would not have been present to be challenged by the defence at the defendant's trial, making the accused's position even more difficult.

In the circumstances, the Court of Appeal concluded that the evidence should have been excluded under s. 78 of the PCEA 1984. Inevitably, even this is a matter of degree; if the circumstances were changed slightly, it may be that the evidence would have been admissible under s. 74, even in *R v O'Connor*. For example, suppose that Beck had pleaded guilty to conspiring with a large number of other people, including the defendant. In this situation, he may have been able to effectively challenge his participation in the conspiracy without questioning its existence.

R v O'Connor (1987) 85 Cr App R 298, CA

Taylor J

Once the conviction was put in evidence, all those details went in as being admitted by Beck. It would be very difficult to contend realistically that a jury would not be entitled to draw the inference from that admission and those details that not only had Beck conspired with O'Connor, but also the converse had taken place. We find this a difficult point, and, without deciding the full scope of section 74, for the purposes of this case, it is sufficient to say that if it was appropriate within the section to admit the conviction of Beck in the proceedings, we take the view that it would have resulted in a very unfair state of affairs. For the reasons already given, it was not open to the defence to challenge what had been said by Beck. The result was that not only was what he had said in the appellant's absence admitted, but it was not exposed to any kind of challenge or test. In those circumstances we take the view that section 78 ought to have been brought into play by the learned judge. This was a case in which the admission of the evidence would have such an adverse effect on the fairness of the proceedings that the court ought not to have admitted it.

7. Three Key Concepts: Relevance, Cogency, Admissibility

Relevance

In all common law systems (indeed, in all 'rational' legal systems), admissible evidence must be 'relevant'. As r. 402 of the American Federal Rules of Evidence succinctly notes: 'Evidence which is not relevant is not admissible.' Relevance means that the proposed evidence makes the facts in issue more or less likely. A number of broadly similar definitions of the concept have been advanced, by both judiciary and legislatures, around the common law world, and can be considered for purposes of comparison. Thus, Lord Simon gave a valuably concise definition in *Director of Public Prosecutions v Kilbourne* [1973] AC 729, when he observed that: '…relevant evidence is logically probative or disprobative of the facts in issue'. Similarly, Lord Steyn noted in *R v A* (No 2) [2002] 1 AC 45 that: '…to be relevant the evidence need merely have some tendency in logic and common sense to advance the proposition in issue'.

Going abroad, in America, r. 401 of the Federal Rules of Evidence, provides that it is material having: '…any tendency to make the existence of any fact that is of consequence to the determination of the action more probable or less probable than it would be without the evidence'. In like manner, in New South Wales, s. 55 of the Australian State's Evidence Act of 1995 declares that: 'Evidence is relevant if it is evidence which, if accepted, could rationally affect the assessment of the probability of a fact in issue in the proceedings.'

What do these definitions mean in practice? To give a rather fanciful illustration, if a man is accused of murder, committed by stabbing another to death, but denies involvement, the fact that shortly after the alleged killing he was seen with a bloodied dagger in his hand is potentially relevant as to whether he was guilty of the killing. However, the same could not, prima facie, be said of the fact that he was a former All England Come Dancing Champion. If the prosecution sought to take up court time to establish this fact, it would swiftly be interrupted, by both trial judge and defence counsel asking to know why such evidence was being adduced. Of course, in other given situations such a fact *might* become relevant. If, again, identity was in issue, the deceased man had been killed at a *Thé Dansant*, and a professional ballroom dancing instructor, who was an eye-witness to the crime, said that his assailant had, minutes earlier, danced the Rumba with brilliance, it *could* be relevant in helping to establish the identity of the defendant as the killer, by showing that he had such dancing abilities.

English common law normally approaches the notion of relevance with an intuitive approach rather than by adopting a mathematical or scientific one. Thus, in *Corke v Corke & Cook* [1958] 2 WLR 110, Morris LJ was of the view that: '...relevance is to be judged by applying a fair-minded common-sense approach'. For the same reason, in *R v Adams* [1996] 2 Cr App R 467 the Court of Appeal discouraged jury use of, and reliance on, Bayes Theorem, a calculation employed by statisticians to assess mathematical probability, when dealing with DNA evidence. The court noted that jurors evaluated evidence not by means of a scientific formula, but by the joint application of their common sense and knowledge of the world to the evidence before them. More recently, in *R v Randall* [2004] 1 WLR 56, Lord Steyn noted that relevance was, 'determined, for the most part, by common sense and experience'.

Not everyone has approved of such a pragmatic approach. One critic complained, after approaching several lawyers' magazines with a view to writing about Bayes Theorem, that the legal profession knew little and cared less about the 'rational' use of evidence.[16] However many other observers have expressed concern that adopting such 'scientific' approaches to the treatment of evidence would simply engender confusion, especially amongst lay jurors and JPs. Additionally, as Rose LJ noted in *Adams*, concealed within Bayes Theorem and other similar formulae there are often still a large number of subjective assessments as to the weight to be given to component parts of the evidence, so that, in reality, it is much less 'scientific' than might at first appear.

R v Adams [1996] 2 Cr App R 467, CA

Rose LJ

More fundamentally, however, the attempt to determine guilt or innocence on the basis of a mathematical formula, applied to each separate piece of evidence, is simply inappropriate to the jury's task. Jurors evaluate evidence and reach a conclusion not by means of a formula, mathematical or otherwise, but by the joint application of their individual common sense and knowledge of the world to the evidence before them. It is common for them to have to evaluate scientific evidence, both as to its quality and as to its relationship with other evidence. Scientific evidence tendered as proof of a particular fact may establish that fact to an extent which, in any particular case, may vary between slight possibility and virtual certainty. For example, different blood spots on an accused's clothing may, on testing, reveal a range of conclusions from 'human blood' via 'possibly the victim's blood' to 'highly likely to be the victim's blood'. Such evidence is susceptible to challenge as to methodology and otherwise, which may weaken or even, in some cases, strengthen the impact of the evidence. But we have never heard it suggested that a jury should consider the relationship between such scientific evidence and other evidence by reference to probability formulas. That such a course would in any event be impossible of sensible achievement by a jury, at least so far as the use of the Bayes Theorem is concerned, is demonstrated by the practical application of the stage of that theorem's methodology that involves numerical assessment of the various items of evidence. Individual jurors might differ greatly not only according to how cogent they found a particular piece of evidence (which would be a matter for discussion and debate between the jury as a whole), but also on the question of what percentage figure for probability should be placed

---

[16] R Mathews, 'Why new evidence doesn't always carry conviction' *Sunday Telegraph*, London, 8 July 2001, at 33.

on that evidence. ...Quite apart from these general objections, as the present case graphically demonstrates, to introduce Bayes Theorem, or any similar method, into a criminal trial plunges the jury into inappropriate and unnecessary realms of theory and complexity deflecting them from their proper task.

It should, perhaps, also be observed that mathematical models of proof have often occasioned considerable problems for lawyers, as well as laymen. Thus, can be considered the so-called 'prosecutors' fallacy' that bedevilled the early days of DNA evidence. It was sometimes suggested that if a DNA sample suggested that only one in 500,000 people could have left the trace (whether via blood, semen or hair, etc.) this necessarily indicated that there was only a 500,000 to one chance of the identification being wrong.

Of course, what it really means is that the defendant is one of 120 people in the United Kingdom who could have left the trace. If the trace were the only evidence against the accused, this would be woefully inadequate to prove guilt. However, if it can be combined with other evidence, the DNA becomes much more valuable. For example, suppose the trace was taken from a crime scene in a very small village where the suspect resides, and there is some other circumstantial evidence linking him to the crime. The DNA evidence then becomes a compelling piece of circumstantial evidence in its own right. Such problems are much less pressing today, as modern DNA matches are often almost unique to an individual, identical twins apart, as Phillips LJ (as he then was) anticipated in the following case.

R v Doheny [1997] 1 Cr App R 369, CA

Phillips LJ

It is easy, if one eschews rigorous analysis, to draw the following conclusion:

1. Only one person in a million will have a DNA profile which matches that of the crime stain. 2. The defendant has a DNA profile which matches the crime stain. 3. Ergo there is a million to one probability that the defendant left the crime stain and is guilty of the crime. Such reasoning has been commended to juries in a number of cases by prosecuting counsel, by judges and sometimes by expert witnesses. It is fallacious and it has earned the title of 'The Prosecutor's Fallacy'. The propounding of the prosecutor's fallacy in the course of the summing-up was the reason, or at least one of the reasons, why the appeal against conviction was allowed in Deen. ... Taking our example, the prosecutor's fallacy can be simply demonstrated. If one person in a million has a DNA profile which matches that obtained from the crime stain, then the suspect will be 1 of perhaps 26 men in the United Kingdom who share that characteristic. If no fact is known about the Defendant, other than that he was in the United Kingdom at the time of the crime the DNA evidence tells us no more than that there is a statistical probability that he was the criminal of 1 in 26. The significance of the DNA evidence will depend critically upon what else is known about the suspect. If he has a convincing alibi at the other end of England at the time of the crime, it will appear highly improbable that he can have been responsible for the crime, despite his matching DNA profile. If, however, he was near the scene of the crime when it was committed, or has been identified as a suspect because of other evidence which suggests that he may have been responsible for the crime, the DNA evidence becomes very significant. The possibility that two of the only 26 men in the United Kingdom with the matching DNA should have been in the vicinity of the crime will seem almost incredible

and a comparatively slight nexus between the defendant and the crime, independent of the DNA, is likely to suffice to present an overall picture to the jury that satisfies them of the defendant's guilt. The reality is that, provided there is no reason to doubt either the matching data or the statistical conclusion based upon it, the random occurrence ratio deduced from the DNA evidence, when combined with sufficient additional evidence to give it significance, is highly probative. As the art of analysis progresses, it is likely to become more so, and the stage may be reached when a match will be so comprehensive that it will be possible to construct a DNA profile that is unique and which proves the guilt of the defendant without any other evidence. So far as we are aware that stage has not yet been reached.

Sometimes, it is not immediately apparent that evidence being tendered by a party to litigation is relevant, because it will require other, yet to be admitted, evidential material to be adduced for it to become clearly probative in the case (obviously, different types of evidence cannot be admitted simultaneously). In these situations, the tendered evidence might be adduced on the basis of 'conditional relevance' or, as it is sometimes termed, *de bene esse*. This means that it is admitted on the understanding, and often following an express undertaking, that it will subsequently be shown to be relevant by later admissible evidence. If it is not, the trial judge will have to direct the jury (or himself) to disregard the evidence. If the material that was admitted on a conditional basis was very prejudicial, he might even have to discharge the jury in a criminal case.

Cogency

This is sometimes referred to as 'weight' and signifies the probative value of the evidence adduced. Not all relevant evidence is of equal worth; some is of only marginal importance, some of vital significance. Let us consider again the defendant accused of murder and found in possession of a bloodied knife. If the blood is proved to have belonged to the same blood group as the victim that would make it even more cogent evidence of the defendant's involvement in the murder. If it is proved to have the same DNA series as that of the victim this will enormously increase its probative value once again. In all three situations, blood on the knife with no further information, blood on the knife of the same blood group as the victim, blood of the same DNA as the victim, the evidence is relevant and probative. However, the evidence provided by the third situation is more cogent than that of the first two and that provided by the second situation, more cogent than that of the first.

Admissibility

Under the common law system it has been noted that: 'All admissible evidence is relevant, but not all relevant evidence is admissible.' This is because much relevant evidence is kept from the tribunal of fact, especially in criminal cases, because it is caught by exclusionary rules of admissibility. As the popular writer, John Mortimer QC has observed (albeit slightly cynically), lawyers are trained in 'no-go' areas: 'They are accustomed to find truth concealed behind barriers marked "inadmissible evidence".[17] Similarly, an old, possibly apocryphal, and certainly hackneyed anecdote, often related to law students, describes a judge who has become increasingly irritated by the technical evidential objections being taken by defence counsel, eventually asking in exasperation: 'Am I to hear the truth in this case or not?' At which, counsel for the defendant immediately replies: 'No, my Lord, you are to hear the evidence!' At a judicial level, Sellers LJ noted in *Corke v Corke & Cook* [1958] P 93 that: 'Evidence is not a matter of mere logic. Evidence which is hearsay might well be relevant to the issues and of probative value but it is excluded and made inadmissible for practical consideration.' The body of exclusionary rules, together with numerous exceptions to the rules (whether statutory or common law), provide much of the *corpus* of the English law of evidence.

The exclusionary rules generally operate to prevent the admission of evidence that is—or was at some time in the past—considered to be inherently unreliable, difficult to assess, 'improper' for reasons of public policy or hard to challenge effectively. The existence of such exclusionary rules has numerous practical consequences. For example, the proof of evidence of a witness drawn up by a solicitor prior to trial, will exclude anything to which the witness could speak but which would be legally inadmissible in oral testimony. Similarly, the Code for Crown Prosecutors working for the CPS requires that an 'Evidential Test' be satisfied when making the decision on whether to prosecute. There must be a 'realistic prospect of conviction' against each defendant on each charge (para. 5.1 of the code) and, in deciding this, a Crown Prosecutor must consider whether the evidence available can be used in court (that is, is admissible). Additionally, as will be seen (in chapter 2), even relevant evidence that is not caught by a specific exclusionary rule may still be excluded, in some situations, by an exercise of judicial discretion if, for example, its probative value is deemed to be substantially outweighed by the dangers of unfair prejudice or confusion of the issues.

Pause for reflection

Is it right that relevant evidence should ever be withheld from a court or tribunal?

Sometimes, material will be admissible for one purpose, but not for another. In these cases of 'conditional' admissibility, the judge will give the jurors (or, in theory, himself) a direction as to the permissible use that can be made of it, and a warning that they must disregard it for other purposes. Thus, if an out of court statement is admitted for a purpose other than its testimonial effect he will warn the jury that it only goes to the fact that it was made, not to the truth of its contents. How effective such directions are is a matter of fierce dispute. The government's white paper, *Delivering Justice*, published in July 2002, called following these directions an 'almost impossible task' (para. 4.54).

Pause for reflection

Would you be able to exclude from your mind evidence that you had already heard when reaching a decision, if you were a judge or magistrate?

Some social scientists have argued that juries are unable to comprehend many judicial instructions, and are less than confident about the ability of jurors to follow highly technical and subtle directions on evidential matters in particular. Thus, an American study, conducted in 1991,

---

[17] J Mortimer QC, *Clinging to the Wreckage* (1982, Weidenfeld and Nicolson) at 234.

concluded that: '…real jurors understand…fewer than half of the instructions they receive at trial'. Several other (but not all) American studies suggest that even when jurors do understand judicial directions, they sometimes decide to ignore them.[18] Against this, research conducted with mock juries at the London School of Economics over 30 years ago suggested that such directions are often fairly effective. Thus, and for example, in many situations a judicial direction to disregard a defendant's previous convictions, where they were adduced purely to undermine credit (rather than going directly to the issue of guilt), as was often then the practice, successfully averted prejudicial effect.[19]

Mistakes on the Admissibility of Evidence

It should also be noted that if a trial judge makes a mistake about the admissibility of an item of evidence it will not automatically render the ensuing trial unfair, and so liable to be quashed on appeal, unless it is considered to be of a sufficiently serious nature. As Lord Bingham observed in the Privy Council decision of *Randall v R* [2002] 1 WLR 2237, not every departure from good practice will have this effect: 'Inevitably, in the course of a long trial, things are done or said which should not be done or said. Most occurrences of that kind do not undermine the integrity of the trial, particularly if they are isolated and particularly if, where appropriate, they are the subject of a clear judicial direction.' However, some mistakes as to the admissibility of evidence are deemed to be so grave that any ensuing conviction will nearly always be quashed.

Similarly, and perhaps equally inevitably, sometimes evidence that is inadmissible will be inadvertently revealed to the tribunal, whether by a witness, counsel or the judge himself. In these circumstances, the trial judge in, for example, a Crown Court hearing has a choice as to whether to discharge the jury and order a retrial, or simply to let the case proceed, perhaps after giving the jury a curative direction in which he tells them to ignore the evidence that they have improperly heard. If a conviction ensues in such circumstances, it will not necessarily be deemed to be unsafe if appealed. Everything will turn on the facts of the individual case, and whether a fair-minded and informed observer would feel that the jury would be prejudiced against the defendant by the inadmissible information, so that a conviction became unsafe. In making such an assessment, the court will have regard to a multiplicity of factors; for example, how the information came to be revealed, whether the trial judge gave a curative direction (though sometimes this might make the situation worse by putting undue stress on the evidence), etc.

However, in such cases, the Court of Appeal will not lightly substitute its own judgment for that of the first instance judge: *R v Lawson and others* [2007] 1 Cr App R 20. In this case, the defendants were accused of importing a large quantity of cannabis resin. Their defence was that they thought that they were illicitly importing tobacco, not drugs. The trial judge decided that the jurors should not be aware that a third party, who was also known to the defendants, had been arrested for drug dealing. However, the same judge inadvertently later revealed in court that this had, in fact, occurred. He concluded that a curative direction would be sufficient, without the need to discharge the jury. On appeal, his decision was upheld. Similarly, in *R v Noden* [2007] EWCA Crim 2050, and on the particular facts of that case, a conviction was upheld even though prosecuting counsel had 'opened' his case to the jury by referring to a confession that was subsequently deemed to be inadmissible.

---

[18] F J Macchiarola, 'Finding the truth in an American Criminal Trial: some observations' (1997) Cardozo Journal of International and Comparative Law, Yeshiva University, issue 97, 104.

[19] WR Cornish and AP Sealy, 'Juries and the Rules of Evidence' [1973] Crim LR 208; and AP Sealy and WR Cornish, 'Jurors and their Verdicts' (1973) Modern Law Review 496.

R v Lawson and others [2007] 1 Cr App R 20, CA

Auld LJ

Whether or not to discharge the jury is a matter for evaluation by the trial judge on the particular facts and circumstances of the case, and this court will not lightly interfere with his decision. It follows that every case depends on its own facts and circumstances, including: 1) the important issue or issues in the case; 2) the nature and impact of improperly admitted material on that issue or issues, having regard, inter alia to the respective strengths of the prosecution and defence cases; 3) the manner and circumstances of its admission and whether and to what extent it is potentially unfairly prejudicial to a defendant; 4) the extent to and manner in which it is remediable by judicial direction or otherwise, so as to permit the trial to proceed. We repeat, all these matters and their combined effect are very much an evaluative exercise for the trial judge in all the circumstances of the case. The starting point is not that the jury should be discharged whenever something of this nature is put in evidence through inadvertence. Equally, there is no sliding scale so as to increase the persuasive onus on a defendant seeking a discharge of a jury on this account according to the weight or length of the case or the stage it has reached when the point arises for determination. The test is always the same, whether to continue with the trial would or could, by reason of the admission of the unfairly prejudicial material, result in an unsafe conviction.

8. Confusion in Terminology

Introduction

Although the three concepts of relevance, cogency and admissibility are distinct, the conceptual waters are often 'muddied' by the courts using such terminology rather loosely. Thus, and for example, evidence which is theoretically (or 'logically') relevant, but of such little cogency that the court does not feel that it is justifiable to take up forensic time, or risk jury/tribunal confusion by creating a multiplicity of side issues in adducing it, is often referred to as 'irrelevant' and so not admitted. It would, in such situations, be better conceptually to state clearly that the court is excluding the evidence for the reasons set out in r. 403 of the American Federal Rules of Evidence, which provides that: '[R]elevant, evidence may be excluded if its probative value is substantially outweighed by the danger of...confusion of the issues, or misleading the jury, or by considerations of undue delay, waste of time, or needless presentation of cumulative evidence.'

However, this approach was expressly recognized by a domestic forum in *R v Funderburk* (1990) 90 Cr App R 466, in which the Court of Appeal observed that relevance is a: '...matter of degree in each case, the question in reality is whether or not the evidence is or is not sufficiently relevant'. This was because it was both necessary and in the interests of justice to keep criminal trials within bounds, and so to assist the jury in concentrating on what really matters, without them being distracted by doubts as to 'marginal' events or a multiplicity of side issues.

The court in *Funderburk* went on to note that determining this is always a matter for the first instance judge, having regard to the evidence and the way the case is presented at trial. This is also tacitly recognized by r. 1.1(2)(e) of the CPR 2005, which requires cases to be dealt with 'efficiently and expeditiously', having regard to the gravity of the allegation in question. In practice, however, evidence that is theoretically relevant, but of minimal cogency, is regularly described and excluded as 'irrelevant', accepting Lord Steyn's analysis that 'Relevance is typically a question of degree': *R v Randall* [2004] 1 WLR 56.

Periodically, the courts also occasion confusion by misusing the concept of relevance to exclude evidence that they think is actually 'unfair' and so should not be admitted. Thus, in the case of *R v Blastland* [1986] AC 46, some members of the House of Lords suggested that evidence that an individual with a paedophile tendency ('Mark') was aware of a child murder, before it became public knowledge, was not 'relevant' to an accused's defence that he was not the killer, because there were a variety of ways in which Mark could have come by the knowledge. As a result, according to Lord Bridge, Mark's knowledge that the child had been murdered was irrelevant to the issue, even though the appellant was seeking to establish Mark as a possible, if not probable, murderer of the child. The judge concluded that what was relevant was not the fact of Mark's knowledge, but how he had come by that knowledge. He might have done so in a number of ways, but the two most obvious possibilities were either that he had witnessed the commission of the murder by the appellant or that he had committed it himself. Lord Bridge felt that the statements indicating Mark's knowledge of the murder provided no rational basis on which the jury could be invited to draw an inference as to the source of that knowledge, which would, consequently, have been 'mere speculation' and so 'irrelevant'.

With respect to the distinguished judge, this analysis must be mistaken, as almost all circumstantial evidence can be the subject of a variety of alternative explanations. These may reduce its weight, but they do not prevent its admissibility. As Lord Steyn later noted in *R v A (No 2)* [2002] 1 AC 45: 'Relevance and sufficiency of proof are different things. The fact that the accused a week before an alleged murder threatened to kill the deceased does not prove an intent to kill on the day in question. But it is logically relevant to that issue.' Perhaps fortunately, as the law then stood, the evidence in *Blastland* was clearly inadmissible (at the time), even if relevant, as it was caught by the hearsay exclusionary rule. Nevertheless, it is, arguably, not helpful for the judiciary to separate what, in the popular mind, might be termed 'logical' relevance from 'legal' relevance.

The concept of relevance has continued to occasion difficulties for the courts in recent years. For example, in cases of dangerous driving, the prosecution is normally allowed to adduce the fact that the defendant has been drinking excessively (that is, is over the legal limit), on the basis that this would make it more likely that he had driven dangerously, but not normally permitted to adduce evidence that he has drunk alcohol but is still within the legal limit.

Thus, that a normal sized man has drunk two pints of (normal strength) beer, cannot usually go before the tribunal in such cases, but that he has consumed four pints can. The mere fact that he has consumed alcohol is not deemed to be 'relevant', even though most scientists would argue that two pints is enough to have *some* effect on driving ability: *R v Woodward* [1995] 2 Cr App R 388. By contrast, it seems that any amount of cocaine in the bloodstream, however minimal, is deemed relevant per se to such an allegation: *R v Pleydell* [2006] Crim LR 425. It might be argued that there is a clear inconsistency in these decisions.

Evidence of Lifestyle

An area that has occasioned particular difficulties for the courts in respect to both relevance and admissibility, and which, as a consequence, is highly illustrative of the attendant problems, involves evidence of defendant 'lifestyle' adduced by the prosecution in drugs cases. For example, that a defendant has been found in possession of large amounts of cash in used bills. This is something that is commonly associated with drug dealers, who are obviously unlikely to receive payment by cheque or credit card. Essentially, the argument is that, just as finger scales, a supply of small plastic bags, disposable mobile phones and the presence of a weapon might be circumstantial evidence that someone is a drug dealer, so might large amounts of cash. However, possession of a substantial quantity of cash is, of course, also associated with some forms of legitimate business, a distrust of the banking system and other, less serious, forms of nefarious activity, such as working in the 'black' economy. As a result, there is a danger that a tribunal might give it more significance than it properly deserves.

In the case of *R v Grant* [1996] 1 Cr App R 73, Lord Taylor CJ held that, in a case involving simple possession of drugs (without intent to supply), the presence of cash was not relevant to the charge; someone purchasing a personal 'fix' of a banned substance (usually a small quantity) does not need large amounts of cash to do so. However, the judge went on to observe that, in trials for the possession of drugs with intent to supply, a jury could consider the presence of large sums of money (in this case over £900) as indicative of the charge. Nevertheless, he also concluded that, in such a situation, it was necessary for a trial judge to warn the jury that if they concluded that there was any possibility of the cash being held for any other reason, it was not to be viewed as probative. The jury could only use such evidence to determine intent if it was also satisfied that the presence of the money indicated ongoing dealing in drugs. Unfortunately, a criticism of this approach is that it involves a 'circular' argument. The suggestion appears to be that the possession of the money can, in some way, be compartmentalized from that of the possession of the drugs.

Despite this, the separate approach to the two types of drugs charge (simple possession and intent to supply) was approved in *R v Guney* [1998] 2 Cr App R 242, where the defendant was accused of possessing five kilos of heroin with intent to supply. The drugs had been discovered in a wardrobe, along with a gun and almost £25,000 in cash. In this case, the accused man's defence was that the items had been planted on him. Because of this, the presence of the cash would not normally have been deemed to be admissible, as the issue would be a simple question of fact for the jury; that is, was the accused knowingly in possession of the drugs or not, as there was no suggestion that such a huge quantity of heroin could possibly have been for personal use. (However, on the special facts of the case it was deemed admissible for other reasons.)

Drawing more general threads together from these cases, it seems that if someone is charged with laundering tens of millions of pounds of drugs money the Crown will wish to include evidence of his lavish and luxurious lifestyle, such as the consumption of vintage champagne. But if the prosecution sought to adduce such evidence in a murder trial, even where lifestyle might be technically relevant but of very small cogency (perhaps because it involved a contract killing made against the backdrop of organized crime), a trial judge would be likely to exclude it from the jury if, for example, the crucial issue at trial was whether the accused person's defence of alibi to the killing in question was correct.

R v Guney [1998] 2 Cr App R 242, CA

Judge LJ

Relevance and admissibility are distinct questions. Provided evidence is sufficiently relevant to the issues in any particular case it is normally admissible provided 'the evidence tendered does not infringe any of the exclusionary rules that may be applicable to it' (Cross & Tapper on Evidence, (8th ed., 1995), p. 66). The question whether evidence is relevant depends not on abstract legal theory but on the individual circumstances of each particular case.... In our judgment evidence of possession of cash will often lack any probative value. The defendant's possession of a large sum of cash, or enjoyment of a wealthy lifestyle, does not, on its own, prove anything very much, and certainly not possession of drugs. If there is a little additional but highly tenuous evidence which links the defendant with drugs, cash or lifestyle evidence may remain valueless, or do no more than provide an occasion for 'the inadmissible chain of reasoning' identified by Lord Hailsham. Nevertheless in our judgment the relevance of any particular piece of evidence should be decided on a case by case basis. Accordingly although evidence of cash and lifestyle may only rarely be relevant where the charge is simple possession, we are unable to accept that as a matter of law such evidence must, automatically, be excluded as irrelevant. In any event when the accused is charged with possession with intent the Crown is seeking to prove a distinct aggravated offence, and, contrary to the assumption made earlier, the evidential considerations are not identical. Even if evidence of cash and lifestyle were automatically excluded in cases where simple possession is alleged, it would not follow from the sensible forensic tactic of conceding the intent to supply that cash and lifestyle evidence in cases alleging possession with intent should be excluded. The different ingredients of this offence should not be artificially compartmentalised. Ultimately the jury has to decide whether the particular charge has been proved, and for this purpose is entitled to consider all the relevant evidence. In our judgment where possession with intent is charged, there are numerous sets of circumstances in which cash and lifestyle evidence may be relevant and admissible to the issue of possession itself, not least to the issue of knowledge as an ingredient of possession.

9. The History of Exclusionary Rules and their Reform

Introduction

This book is largely about the various exclusionary rules found in the modern law of evidence, and the numerous exceptions, both statutory and common law, to those rules. However, it is worth (very briefly) considering their origins, if only to see what light this might throw on their current status. This is not easy; it has often been observed that attempts at making a scientific categorization of evidence have largely failed because the discipline was not developed in a scientific way. It is a pragmatic subject, shaped by the necessities and realities of practice at various points in the past.[20]

Evidential rules, though sometimes already present in proto-form, were still very flexible at the end of the seventeenth century. The first major text on the Law of Evidence, by William Nelson, only appeared in 1717. Indeed, the rules of criminal evidence were still fairly rudimentary in

---

[20] P Murphy, *Murphy on Evidence* (9th edn, 2005, Oxford University Press) at 7–12.

the middle decades of the eighteenth century.[21] As Lord Sankey later observed, during the 1760s the: '…law of evidence was in a very fluid condition. Indeed in some civil cases it differed on different circuits'.[22]

However, and at the risk of oversimplifying a complex historical process, during the latter decades of the eighteenth century, English lawyers and members of the judiciary developed an acute concern about the quality of the evidence that was received in criminal trials. It is likely that this development was partly linked to the advent, and growth in the use of, lawyers in felony (serious criminal) trials, combined with public anxiety about 'entrepreneurial' policing, as seen, for example, in the substantial rewards offered for prosecuting felons to conviction and the extensive use of accomplice evidence (given in exchange for immunity from prosecution).

This concern was manifest in the growing rigidity with which a number of major exclusionary rules were applied. These prevented certain types of 'suspect' evidence, such as hearsay, from being received at trial, or only allowed such evidence to be received if certain prerequisites were satisfied (as with admissible confessions). The presence of laymen on the tribunal of fact may have encouraged this process, even if it was not directly its cause, as fears grew that jurors were unable to properly assess certain types of evidence.[23] There was also a more generally perceived need, at a time when there were few, if any, ways of appealing a jury's decision, and many potentially capital crimes, to provide extra procedural safeguards for a defendant.

The process reached a peak during the 1780s, when an influx of able criminal barristers, working in the Old Bailey and at provincial Assizes, was accompanied by a sharp increase in their willingness to aggressively pursue their clients' interests, accelerating the acceptance into criminal law of firmer rules of evidence, as counsel took issue with proposed evidence that they felt to be flawed in some way.[24] It is, perhaps, not surprising that so much of the English law of evidence can attribute its provenance to the later eighteenth century. Indeed, Langbein suggests that the modern law of evidence, far from tracing its ancestry *back* to civil cases, as some older authorities suggested, was in reality heavily influenced by the aggressive adversary procedure developed by counsel in the criminal courts towards the end of the eighteenth century. These trials may then have set the tone for civil cases, as normal criminal 'practice' was transferred to civil courts.[25]

This process seems to have rapidly developed a dynamic of its own. As the rules became universal to both criminal and civil cases they were driven to extremes. Few could have foreseen that the early cases firmly excluding direct hearsay evidence (rather than merely reducing its weight), within little more than half a century, would have led to the interpretation of the hearsay rule manifest in *Wright v Doe d. Tatham* (1837) 7 A & E 313, which held that the rule against hearsay applied to *implied* assertions of fact (assertions not intended by their maker) as well as to express ones. Even Baron Parke, in his judgment in that case, accepted that the inference to be drawn from the excluded evidence was logical in the 'ordinary affairs of life', albeit

---

[21] JH Langbein, 'Historical Foundations of the Law of Evidence: A View From the Ryder Sources' (June 1996) Columbia Law Review 1172.

[22] *Woolmington v DPP* [1935] AC 462.

[23] JM Beattie, *Crime and the Courts in England 1660–1800* (1986, Oxford University Press) at 147.

[24] JM Beattie, 'Scales of Justice: Defence Counsel and the English Criminal Trial in the Eighteenth and Nineteenth Centuries' (1991) Law and History Review 9, 221–267.

[25] Langbein, (n 21 above) at 1202.

not permissible. From providing safeguards against injustice, evidential rules were on the way to acquiring a degree of technicality that would have significant ramifications.

> **Pause for reflection**
>
> Can you think of other areas of the law where activism on the part of lawyers has had a major effect? What are the disadvantages of such 'unplanned' legal developments?

By the early nineteenth century virtually all of the common law evidential rules were formed, often in a fairly rigid manner. To soften some of their implications, a series of common law exceptions to the general rules had also developed in tandem with them, usually where the tendered evidence considered to be inherently reliable or was otherwise unobtainable. Some of these, such as the now abolished 'dying declaration' in homicide cases, built on much older roots. This development was largely complete by the 1840s. Nevertheless, as late as the case of *Myers v DPP* [1965] AC 1001, and in response to arguments by counsel, the House of Lords was forced to state that the era of new, judicially created, common law exceptions to the rules of evidence was long over. Any future changes were for Parliament (though arguably, there have been some small judge-created exceptions since this date).

John Langbein, *The Origins of Adversary Trial* (2003, Oxford University Press) at 178–179

The other response to the dangers that emerged from prosecutorial practice in this period was to devise rules of evidence that excluded certain problematic types of proof. These rules ultimately coalesced into a body of law that for a time was thought of as a distinct field, the law of criminal evidence, but which has since been largely subsumed in the general law of evidence. Although the creation of the law of criminal evidence was the work of the bench, it played into the hands of the lawyers, who would find in the exclusionary principle one of the levers that would help them wrest control of the criminal trial.

Are the Evolved Rules of Evidence Satisfactory?

Are the English rules of evidence satisfactory? Different individuals have held very different perspectives on the subject over the last 200 years. Thus, the first edition of John Pitt Taylor's *Treatise on the Law of Evidence*, published in 1848, was laudatory:

> The student will not fail to observe the symmetry and beauty of this branch of the law, under whatever disadvantages it may labour from the manner of treatment, and will rise from the study of its principles convinced, with Lord Erskine, that, with some few exceptions, 'they are founded in the charities of religion—in the philosophy of nature—in the truths of history—and in the experience of common life'!

By contrast, Jeremy Bentham, the English utilitarian philosopher, was scathing. He believed that they were almost purpose made to prevent the establishment of the truth in any given case and were designed to provide work for lawyers.

A similar dichotomy can be found in the twentieth century. According to Cyril Pearce Harvey, in his much quoted *The Advocate's Devil* of 1958, there has never been a:

> ...more slapdash, disjointed and inconsequent body of rules than that which we call the Law of Evidence. Founded apparently on the propositions that all jury-men are deaf to reason, that all witnesses are presumptively liars and that all documents are presumptively forgeries, it has been added to, subtracted from and tinkered with for two centuries until it has become less of a structure than a pile of builder's debris.

However, only six years later, in the Privy Council case of *Sparks v R* (1964) AC 964, Lord Morris was persuaded that, whatever their short-term deficiencies, taken overall, they greatly served the interests of justice, especially as: 'The cause of justice is...best served by adherence to rules which have long been recognised and settled.'

More recently, some senior policemen have expressed fears that the rules of evidence obstruct justice and correctness of adjudication. Thus, Sir David Phillips, when president of the Association of Chief Police Officers, claimed that: 'A huge amount of hard evidence is simply inadmissible in Britain, whereas in other countries such as France it can be considered.' In particular, and for example, he wished to see evidence of wealth for which defendants could not account being routinely admissible in court (unlike the present situation).[26] It has also been claimed that the English law of evidence is incomprehensible to most lawyers and nearly all laymen. It is sometimes suggested that this is partly because, until recently, Parliament left much of the relevant law-making to the higher courts and partly because, until the pioneering work of the late Professor Sir Rupert Cross (whose major work on the subject was first published as recently as 1958), academic lawyers often ignored this branch of the law.

Reform

As the above accounts suggest, the emergence of common law evidential rules was not an entirely 'rational' or coherent process. It was a piecemeal development that reflected the concerns of the time, some of which are no longer viewed as being very important. Nor has there ever been a time when the subject did not attract critics. Unsurprisingly, some traditional evidential rules did not appear to make a great deal of 'sense' to many twentieth-century observers. As a result, in 1974, Sir Rupert Cross could note that he profoundly regretted Parliament's failure to implement most of the radical recommendations contained in the Criminal Law Revision Committee's (CLRC) 11th Report on Evidence of 1972, as he felt that the drastic changes proposed would have given England and Wales the best criminal rules of evidence of any common law country, and would have gone far towards: '...eliminating the illogicality in which the law of evidence has come to be rooted'.[27]

As a consequence of such perceptions, in the post-war era, many academic and judicial observers called for a full reassessment of the principles underlying the law of evidence and the extent to which evidential rules detracted from, or supported, wider objectives in the justice system. Reflecting this, when, in the 1990s, the then Lord Chancellor appointed Lord Justice Auld to report on the working of the criminal courts, his terms of reference included

---

[26] D Bamber (Home Affairs Correspondent), 'Justice system cannot handle criminal gangs', *Daily Telegraph*, 9 December 2001.

[27] R Cross, *An Attempt to Update the Law of Evidence* (1947, The Magnes Press) at 27.

an examination of the rules of evidence applied at every level, with a view to ensuring that the courts delivered justice fairly.

However, numerous specific proposals for reform have been made, and some acted on, in the past 30 years. The CLRC's approach has already been noted, but there have been many others. For example, the Royal Commission on Criminal Justice, which reported in 1993, proposed that hearsay evidence should be admitted to a greater degree in criminal trials, and also that the admissibility of evidence relating to a defendant's previous convictions should not be restricted to cases covered by the then 'similar fact' exception (now abolished in criminal cases).[28]

Subsequently, the Law Commission produced similar recommendations, as did Lord Justice Auld, who felt that particular consideration should be given to the reform of the rules governing the refreshing of memory, the use of witness statements, hearsay, unfair evidence, previous misconduct of the defendant, the evidence of children and expert evidence. Auld wished to see reform go considerably further than had previously been the case, and also to identify and establish coherent principles that would make the law of evidence an efficient and 'simple' agent for securing justice. Similarly, the government's white paper, *Delivering Justice*, published in July 2002, and which presaged major changes in the law pertaining to criminal evidence, asserted that the existing rules of evidence were 'difficult to understand', hard to apply and likely to exclude relevant material. Like (and influenced by) Auld LJ, it argued for a coherent rewriting of the rules of evidence, so that tribunals could give evidence the weight it properly 'deserved' (at para. 4.52 of the report).

Pause for reflection

Do you feel that the law of evidence can ever be a 'simple' agent, if it is also to secure justice?

As a result of such proposals, a variety of statutes, and, to a lesser extent, appellate level judicial decisions, over the past 40 years, have had a major impact on both civil and criminal evidence. Most recently, many (but not all) proposals for reform have seen fruition in the radical evidential provisions of the Criminal Justice Act 2003. As a result, some of the subject's more recondite technicalities, and its more obscure or apparently unjustified evidential rules, have been abolished or reformed since the Second World War.

Auld LJ, Review of the Criminal Courts of England and Wales, 2001, paras 76–77

76 My terms of reference require me to examine the fairness and efficiency of the rules of evidence in the criminal justice process. That is an enormous subject in its own right, suffering, as Professor Colin Tapper has put it, from a 'blight' in the law of evidence as a whole. It is a blight that he and many distinguished academics have long attributed to incoherence, confusion and conflict in the aims and policy of the law of evidence. This is in large part due to our tradition of sporadic and piecemeal statutory reform and constantly evolving overlay of judge-made law softening its edges. It also suffers from a neglect of the needs of summary trial. Rules devised in the main for, or which have their origin in, jury trial are often far too complex or artificial for application in the fast

---

[28] Recommendations 189, 191, 192, 193, 194.

moving list of magistrates' courts. Magistrates, who undertake the bulk of summary work, or their advisers, cannot be expected to grapple with the minutiae and refinements devised principally for the more leisurely proceedings in the Crown Court. Indeed, I suspect that District Judges, with their equally long and arduous lists, have little time or patience for fine evidential points.

77 For these reasons there is an urgent need for a comprehensive review of the whole law of criminal evidence to make it a simple and an efficient agent for ensuring that all criminal courts are told all and only what they need to know. I believe that an important part of this exercise should be an examination of the justice and feasibility of a general move away from rules of inadmissibility to trusting fact finders to give relevant evidence the weight it deserves. It is no part of this Review to attempt a comprehensive study or to make detailed recommendations for reform in this field. As I have indicated in Chapter 1, that should be part of a principled and comprehensive exercise in the reform and codification of the criminal law, to be undertaken by a standing body working under the oversight of the Criminal Justice Council.

Nevertheless, although large areas of the law of evidence have been the subject of such statutory reform, England does not, as yet, have a unified code of evidence, though its desirability has been a matter of keen debate since the nineteenth century. It remains a judge-created structure with later, albeit very substantial, statutory accretions. This is, perhaps, ironic, as English legislators and jurists, such as James Fitzjames Stephen, the author of the Indian Evidence Act of 1879, introduced a degree of codification to many countries around the Empire.

It should, perhaps, also be noted that reform in this area can be a 'two edged' sword. The near torrent of recent legislation affecting the law of evidence has often been heavily criticized, both as to the quality of its content and as to the speed with which it has been introduced (sometimes without adequate training of court personnel). Some observers have claimed that, far from reforming and improving an already complicated situation, it has merely engendered further confusion. Despite this, it must be remembered that the debate about reform is not over. Further changes might be expected, if not at the rate of recent years.

10. The Rationale Behind Evidential Rules

Introduction

Whatever the reasons for their original emergence, various arguments are traditionally advanced for preserving existing evidential rules and even for introducing new ones. Amongst them are the need: to avoid expense, confusion and delay in the trial process; to enhance procedural fairness or personal rights; to preserve confidence in the justice system; to apportion litigation risk and, perhaps the single most commonly cited justification, to avoid adjudicative error, especially that occasioned by 'prejudice' (see below).

This last consideration is one of the subject's oldest rationales. For example, in the historic case of *R v Warwickshall* (1783) 1 Leach 263, correctness of decision making was apparently paramount in deciding that confessions that may have been coerced should be excluded; this was because of a: '…consideration whether they are or are not intitled [sic] to credit'.

Sometimes, the importance of rectitude in adjudication has also been considered as a paramount consideration amongst modern observers. Thus, the 1972 Criminal Law Revision
Committee's 11th report on evidence recommended the abolition of all cautioning requirements for questioned suspects, arguing that it often: '…interrupts the natural course of interrogation and unduly hampers the police, as there may be a good deal more information which
they wish to get'.

However, correctness of decision making has never been the only justification for having
rules of evidence. Otherwise, the prosecution in a criminal case would not have to prove their
case 'beyond reasonable doubt', so allowing many guilty defendants to walk free wherever a
tribunal harbours a small doubt about their lack of innocence. That the CLRC's proposal with
regard to cautioning has not been followed is itself indicative of a perceived need for the law of
evidence to serve several functions other than merely ensuring correctness of, and efficiency
in, adjudication. In particular, it demonstrates a belief that it should help preserve individual
'rights' and the integrity of, and public respect for, the wider justice system.

Pause for reflection

What do you consider to be the most important reasons, if any, for preserving exclusionary rules
of evidence?

This has been of particular topicality, in recent years, with regard to statements made by witnesses in foreign countries, who do not attend to give evidence in person in a domestic forum,
yet whose statements may have been obtained by torture, but are, prima facie, admissible in
England and Wales against criminal defendants, or those facing other types of proceedings.
This might be either under a statutory exception to the hearsay rule provided for by the Criminal
Justice Act 2003, or because the statement is being tendered in a forum, such as a tribunal, that
does not apply the full rules of evidence.

Cross-reference Box

Hearsay was the common law rule that prevented out of court statements (such as those made
by people who were abroad) from being adduced as truth of their contents. It is now subject to
numerous exceptions and has been abolished in civil matters as a rule of exclusion. For more on
this go to chapter 6, at p. 241.

This issue was considered by the House of Lords in *A v Secretary of State for the Home
Department (No 2)* [2006] 2 AC 221, which, in the light of Article 15 of the European
Convention on Human Rights (ECHR) and the traditional attitude taken by English common
law towards torture, concluded that evidence from a witness which had been obtained by
torture could not be admitted against a party to proceedings in a British court. In this case,
it was held that such evidence, allegedly obtained from a third party by torture conducted in
a foreign state, could not be received by a Special Immigration Appeal Commission hearing.
The hearing had been held to determine whether suspected international terrorists, who could
not be deported because of fears for their own safety, or for other practical considerations,
might be detained in the United Kingdom under ss. 21 and 23 of the Anti-terrorism, Crime
and Security Act 2001.

A v Secretary of State for the Home Department (No 2)
[2006] 2 AC 221, HL

Lord Carswell

My Lords, the abhorrence felt by civilised nations for the use of torture is amply demonstrated by the material comprehensively set out in the opinion of my noble and learned friend, Lord Bingham of Cornhill. While it is regrettably still practised by some states, the condemnation expressed in all of the international instruments to which he has referred is universal. Some of these adjure states to do their utmost to ensure that torture does not take place, while others urge them not to admit in evidence in any proceedings statements obtained by the use of torture. The objections to the admission of evidence obtained by the use of torture are twofold, based, first, on its inherent unre-liability and, secondly, on the morality of giving any countenance to the practice . . . the duty not to countenance the use of torture by admission of evidence so obtained in judicial proceedings must be regarded as paramount and that to allow its admission would shock the conscience, abuse or degrade the proceedings and involve the state in moral defilement . . .

Lord Brown

In question here is not the power of the executive but rather the integrity of the judicial process. SIAC is a court of law (indeed a superior court of record). And as was pointed out in M v Secretary of State for the Home Department [2004] 2 All ER 863, SIAC's function on an appeal under section 25 is not to review the exercise by the Secretary of State of his power of certification under section 21, but rather to decide for itself whether, at the time of the hearing, there are 'reasonable grounds' for the suspicion and belief required under section 21. True it is that the statements in question are sought to be relied upon not to convict the appellant of any offence but rather to found such suspicion and belief as would justify his continued detention under section 23. It is difficult to see, however, why this consideration should strengthen rather than weaken the Crown's argument: no court will readily lend itself to indefinite detention without charge, let alone trial. . . . At all events, for the detention to continue under the 2001 Act, Parliament required that SIAC must independently sanction this deprivation of liberty. In short, I would hold that SIAC could never properly uphold a section 23 detention order where the sole or decisive evidence supporting it is a statement estab-lished to have been coerced by the use of torture. To hold otherwise would be, as several of your Lordships have observed, to bring British justice into disrepute. And this is so notwithstanding that the appellant was properly certified and detained by the Secretary of State in the interests of national security, notwithstanding that the legislation (now, of course, repealed) allowed the appel-lant's continuing detention solely on the ground of suspicion and belief, notwithstanding that the incriminating coerced statement was made not by the appellant himself but by some third party, and notwithstanding that it was made abroad and without the complicity of any British official.

Pause for reflection

Can you envisage any type of proceedings or circumstances in which evidence obtained by torture should be admissible?

Attempts at producing a more general and coherent underlying theory that can (or should) encompass most, if not all, evidential rules have been made periodically over the past 250 years, with mixed success, as the following extract suggests.

Terence Anderson, William Twining and David Schum, *Analysis of Evidence* (2nd edn, 2005, Cambridge University Press) at 290

In the Anglo-American tradition there have been four principal attempts to develop an explicit general theory of the law of evidence. Gilbert tried to subsume all the rules of evidence under a single general principle, the 'best evidence rule'; Bentham saw the existing technical rules as an illogical and indefensible morass, and he argued that there should be no binding rules at all within the framework of the Natural System of Procedure; Stephen tried to find a coherent rational for the whole of the law of evidence in the principle of relevancy. Thayer admired Stephen's enterprise but agreed with Sir Frederick Pollock's judgment that it represented 'a splendid mistake'. Relevance was a matter of logic, not law and 'The law has no mandamus on the logical faculty'. Thayer treated the rules of evidence as a mixed group of exceptions to a principle of freedom of proof. Nearly all modern writers on evidence in the common law world have accepted some version of Thayer's thesis, and it has more or less explicitly provided the basis for most subsequent attempts to codify this branch of the law, including the Federal Rules of Evidence.

It is, perhaps, significant that it is the more pragmatic, less over-arching analysis of James Thayer, rather than the more ambitious theorizing of Jeffrey Gilbert and James Stephen that dominates in the modern era. Nevertheless, recently, in an enormously ambitious, and innovative, attempt at examining the underlying theory of evidence law in common law legal systems, the American academic, Professor Alex Stein, has combined probability theory with epistemology, economic analysis, and moral philosophy to argue that the fundamental purpose of the law of evidence is to apportion the risk of error in the face of uncertainty, rather than simply to facilitate the establishment of the truth in any given situation; that is, it serves many vital functions other than rectitude of decision making.

Alex Stein, *Foundations of Evidence Law* (2005, Oxford University Press) 133

Allocation of the risk of error in fact-finding ought to be the principal objective of evidence law. As much as it matters how adjudicators decide cases, it matters how they allocate this risk. While some adjudicators may favour equality in apportioning the risk of fact-finding error, others may opt for economic efficiency. An altogether different group of adjudicators may take a pragmatic approach and let this risk fall upon whom it happens to fall. Adjudicators should not be able to choose between these (or other) approaches as they deem fit. To be legitimate, their risk allocating decisions ought to be justified by moral and political principles.... These principles ought to reflect societal preferences in the area or risk-allocation. These general preferences need to be both adopted and adapted by the Law of Evidence. They should translate into a series of specific rules and principles that allocate the risk of fact-finding error.

Civil/Roman Law Systems and Evidence

The other great Western legal system, Roman (or 'civil') law, traditionally takes a very different approach to evidence. In 1898, Professor James Bradley Thayer, an early scholar of the subject, and the author of *A Preliminary Treatise on Evidence at the Common Law*, observed that: 'When a man raises his eyes from the common-law system of evidence, he is struck with the fact that our system is radically peculiar.' As Thayer remarked, a large amount of logically probative evidence was excluded by legal rules in the late nineteenth century, although the same matters were not excluded anywhere else. This was because: 'English-speaking countries have what we call a "Law of Evidence"; but no other country has it; we alone have generated and evolved this large, elaborate, and difficult doctrine.' As his comment suggests, such exclusionary rules of evidence are found, with national variations, in all common law countries. However, their focus on determining what is *not* evidence often appears strange to lawyers trained in the Roman Law tradition.[29]

In the civil law systems of Continental Europe (and elsewhere) the law governing evidence is of much smaller significance, often being largely procedural, with far fewer exclusionary rules preventing the admissibility of otherwise relevant evidence. These systems broadly operate on a system of 'free proof', where the test of admissibility is often limited to one of relevance, rather than relevance combined with not being caught by an exclusionary rule (as with common law countries).[30]

John Langbein, 'The German Advantage in Civil Procedure' (1985) University of Chicago Law Review, vol 52, no 4, at 823–866 (extract)

A related source of dispatch in German procedure is the virtual absence of any counterpart to the Anglo-American law of evidence. German law exhibits expansive notions of testimonial privilege, especially for potential witnesses drawn from the family. But German procedure functions without the main chapters of our law of evidence, those rules (such as hearsay) that exclude probative evidence for fear of the inability of the trier of fact to evaluate the evidence purposively. In civil litigation German judges sit without juries (a point to which this essay recurs); evidentiary shortcomings that would affect admissibility in our law affect weight or credit in German law.

Arguably, civil law systems use evidentiary rules that accord more with everyday modes of inquiry (such as a teacher resolving allegations and counter-allegations made by children), while common law evidentiary rules were, historically, designed to structure the thinking and ultimately the decision-making of jurors. (However, it should be noted that, in serious crimes, decision-makers in civil law jurisdictions, although freer in their evaluation of the material presented, must ultimately justify their decisions in writing, while a jury's verdict is presented without explanation.)[31] Thus, and for example, in France, far from there being a presumption against adducing the defendant's previous bad character in a criminal trial, it is normally an automatic part of the prosecution case and is read out at the start of the hearing. This is customary in most (though not all) continental countries.

Of course, such differences should not be exaggerated. Even today, although continental justice is still more conducive to (for example) the admission of hearsay evidence than its English counterpart, European courts recognize the weaknesses of derivative proof and often generate

---

[29] TP Gallanis, 'The Rise of Modern Evidence Law' (1999) Iowa Law Review, vol 84, 499–560, at 500.

[30] NV Demleitner, 'More Than "Just" Evidence: Reviewing Mirjan Damaska's Evidence Law Adrift' (1999) American Journal of Comparative Law, issue 47, 515–534, at 516.

[31] Demleitner, ibid.

restrictions on its free use. Additionally, in recent years, the ECHR, especially Article 6, which guarantees the right to a fair trial, has had some impact on Roman law systems (as well as that of England and Wales), and encouraged the emergence of what are, effectively, evidentiary rules. For example, the (qualified) right to question witnesses under Article 6(3)(d), places some limits on the adduction of hearsay evidence, even on the continent.

Furthermore, although some of the most important common law rules are absent in civil systems, such as those regulating the adduction of defendant bad character, there are a significant number of rules governing modes of proof taking, privileges, and even rules excluding certain forms of illegally obtained evidence. It is mistaken to imagine that the free evaluation of evidence found in continental jurisdictions is the same as freedom from all legal regulation of fact-finding activities. This unfounded perception is assisted by the absence of the 'law of evidence' as an academic subject in its own right in civil jurisdictions. Instead, it is usually appended to the law governing civil and criminal procedure.

Mirjan Damska, 'The jury and the law of evidence: real and imagined interconnections' (2006) Law, Probability and Risk, vol 5, 255–256 (extract)

In short, although it regulates fact finding in juryless trials, continental evidence law is far from negligible. It can be regarded as such only if one searches for counterparts of our rules on propensity evidence, hearsay, or a few other intrinsic exclusionary rules. And to the extent that a lingering malaise about exclusionary rules can be diagnosed on the continent, it can easily be explained on grounds we have previously examined. As in our bench trials, so in continental mixed courts: the same adjudicators decide the admissibility issue and render the final decision. The enforcement of admissibility rules in this context easily leads to interference with the decision makers' reasoning from evidence—an interference that has been *prima facie* suspect to continental lawyers since the eighteenth century rejection of the Roman-canon system of legal proof.

It must also be remembered that the Roman law approach to evidence is heavily shaped by the structural differences between civil systems and those found in common law countries. For example, the frequent presence of judicial involvement in the fact-finding process (already noted) and the fact that civil systems do not make a rigid separation between the investigation that gathers evidence of a matter and the presentation of that evidence at trial. This is unlike the common law system, with its emphasis on judicial passivity and 'day in court' justice, when all available and admissible evidence is presented to the tribunal of fact for a 'one-off' consideration.

Nevertheless, an obvious question is to ask why a system of 'free proof' should not be adopted in England, within the existing adversarial system? Even strong supporters of the exclusionary rules accept that it would be possible to dispense with them, conceding that: 'It would be quite practicable, in fact, to conduct trials without any rules of evidence at all, by the jurors simply applying their native wit and powers of reasoning to miscellaneous information that was furnished to them. There would, no doubt, be miscarriages of justice, as we have come to view them, but the system would work after a fashion.'[32] Others view such an objective as strongly desirable and question whether miscarriages of justice would ensue.

---

[32] Wells J in *Pfitzner* (1976) 15 SASR 171, 190.

Pause for reflection

Do you favour the adoption of a system of 'free proof' in England and Wales?

Over the last two centuries, many of the scholars who have specialized in the common law of evidence have taken an 'abolitionist' view towards their own subject. Thus, Jeremy Bentham attacked almost the entire body of evidence law as it existed in early nineteenth-century England. Subsequently, the American expert Dean Wigmore also called for the rejection of many exclusionary rules. More recently, Sir Rupert Cross, the leading English evidence scholar of the twentieth century, reportedly declared: 'I am working for the day when my subject is abolished.'[33]

The major reforms of recent years, in both criminal and civil matters, mean that it is possible, to a degree, to identify a general modern trend under which, in Lord Justice Auld's words, there has been a: '…move away from the technical rules of admissibility of evidence, to a system under which tribunals of fact gave evidence the weight they felt it deserved'. Although identifiable in criminal matters, this has been particularly marked in civil cases, where jurors are usually absent, and where there have been definite moves towards a system of free proof. As Balcombe LJ noted in *Ventouris v Mountain (No 2)* (1992) I WLR 887: 'The modern tendency in civil proceedings is to admit all relevant evidence and the judge should be trusted to give proper weight to evidence which is not the best evidence.'

The 1995 Civil Evidence Act is an obvious illustration of this change. Few now argue with the view expressed by the Law Commission that abolition of the exclusionary hearsay rule in civil cases, as occurred under the Civil Evidence Act 1995, would enable: '…parties to concentrate on substantive issues as opposed to technical evidential points'. To an extent, this, when viewed in conjunction with the High Court Practice Directions and Civil Procedure Rules limiting the length of oral submissions, cross-examination of witnesses and the reading aloud from documents and authorities, whilst at the same time allowing written witness statements to stand as evidence in chief and prescribing the use of skeleton arguments, means that there has also been a significant erosion of the traditional common law emphasis on orality (in civil matters).

Nevertheless, there are several reasons why a system of entirely free proof is unlikely to be accepted in England and Wales. Correctness of decision-making is, and should be, a vital principle underlying the law of evidence (even if it is not the only one). Linked to this, and perhaps the most important reason for retaining such rules, is a fear of 'prejudice', especially moral prejudice (personal animosity towards a defendant), clouding the judgement of jurors and magistrates. Significantly, perhaps, in Western Europe, laymen never retire unaided to consider a verdict on the evidence. Even under the French Assizes system the lay assessors in serious cases retire with professional judges.

The role of the jury and JPs in the common law system probably means that a system of free proof will never be felt to be appropriate in England, at least in criminal matters. In a famous comment in the *Berkeley Peerage Case* (1816) 4 Camp 401, Lord Mansfield claimed that the reason that civil law countries could employ a system of free proof (he did not use the term), and, for example, listen to hearsay evidence, was that they did not use juries, and their professional judges could be relied upon to give evidence its appropriate weight. By contrast: '…in England,

---

[33] LC Kirkpatrick, 'Evidence Law in the Next Millennium' (1998) Hastings Law Journal, issue 49, 363–368, at 363.

where the jury are the sole judges of the fact, hearsay evidence is properly excluded, because no man can tell what effect it might have upon their minds'.

Moreover, there has been significant academic criticism of a system of free proof, as well as support. Thus, Alex Stein has deprecated such a system, and especially the steps taken towards attaining it in England and Wales (where, he feels, 'this abolitionist trend is especially noticeable'), for allowing trial judges to apportion the risk of adjudicative error as they see fit. Stein also argues that the 'family adjudication' model which proponents of such a system, such as Jeremy Bentham, have traditionally advanced as an ideal, is completely inappropriate for the complexities of the wider (and much larger) society, with its competing interest groups, and expressed the fear that freedom from legal constraints in fact-finding may actually lead to judicial or other forms of tyranny.[34]

11. The Impact of ECHR/HRA 1998

Introduction

A very significant development in recent years has been the impact of the European Convention for the Protection of Human Rights and Fundamental Freedoms of 1950, with its various amending protocols (hereinafter ECHR) on the law of evidence, along with the jurisprudence on its interpretation emanating from the European Court of Human Rights (ECtHR) in Strasbourg. The Convention's significance has been greatly reinforced by the advent of the Human Rights Act of 1998 (HRA 1998), which came into force in October 2000, and which has directly incorporated European law into domestic law. The operation of the HRA 1998 will be considered in detail later in this book with regard to specific evidential provisions where it has had a major impact, such as 'reverse burdens of proof' in criminal trials, or the adduction of complainant sexual history in rape cases (see chapters 3 and 10 respectively), but can be considered here in general terms. From the perspective of the law of evidence, by far the most important provision is Article 6, which in its first part, Article 6(1) provides what is primarily a general statement of principle, followed by the more specific requirements set out at Article 6(2) and (3).

Article 6 of the ECHR

1. In the determination of his civil rights and obligations or of any criminal charge against him, everyone is entitled to a fair and public hearing within a reasonable time by an independent and impartial tribunal established by law. Judgement shall be pronounced publicly by the press and public may be excluded from all or part of the trial in the interest of morals, public order or national security in a democratic society, where the interests of juveniles or the protection of the private life of the parties so require, or the extent strictly necessary in the opinion of the court in special circumstances where publicity would prejudice the interests of justice.

---

[34] A Stein, *Foundations of Evidence Law*, (2005, Oxford University Press) at 107 and 109.

2. Everyone charged with a criminal offence shall be presumed innocent until proved guilty according to law.

3. Everyone charged with a criminal offence has the following minimum rights:

(a) to be informed promptly, in a language which he understands and in detail, of the nature and cause of the accusation against him;

(b) to have adequate time and the facilities for the preparation of his defence;

(c) to defend himself in person or through legal assistance of his own choosing or, if he has not sufficient means to pay for legal assistance, to be given it free when the interests of justice so require;

(d) to examine or have examined witnesses against him and to obtain the attendance and examination of witnesses on his behalf under the same conditions as witnesses against him;

(e) to have the free assistance of an interpreter if he cannot understand or speak the language used in court.

Article 6 has a potentially major impact on many areas of the law of evidence. Although couched in broad terms, much has been 'read in' to it. Thus, there is nothing in the wording of Article 6 about the right to silence or the right not to incriminate oneself; nevertheless, the ECtHR has concluded that (in certain circumstances) these are 'generally recognised international standards which lie at the heart of the notion of a fair procedure under Article 6': *Saunders v United Kingdom* (1996) 23 EHRR 313. Similarly, and for example, it also has the potential to affect the adduction of hearsay, as it might be argued that adducing such evidence violates a defendant's Article 6(3)(d) right to examine witnesses who give evidence against him (see chapter 5).

Several of the other Articles set out in s. 1 of the ECHR also have the potential to influence the law of evidence, even if it is only in specific circumstances, as will become apparent during the course of this book. For example, the wording of Article 3, which provides that no one should be subjected to torture or inhuman or degrading treatment, has been expressly incorporated into s. 76(2) of the PCEA 1984, which regulates the adduction of confessions (see chapter 7). Additionally, it can, at least, be argued that requiring journalists to reveal their sources is a breach of the right to receive information set out in Article 10 (see chapter 14). In like manner, it might be claimed that any attempt to prevent a man and woman from marrying, so that the latter could not take advantage of the spousal exemption from being compelled to give evidence against her husband, would be a breach of the right to marry set out under Article 12 (see chapter 8). Furthermore, it might be argued that a breach of the Article 8 right to privacy must be considered if evidence of private conversations is secretly recorded. Some of these arguments have been accepted by the ECtHR, others dismissed, at least in certain circumstances.

However, and as will also become apparent in later chapters, the ECtHR allows signatory states a significant margin of discretion when applying the Convention to evidential questions, viewing such matters as issues to be determined by national jurisdictions: *Teixeira de Castro v Portugal* (1998) 28 EHRR 101. The Court will only intervene if an evidential provision falls outside these margins. Additionally, the decided cases emanating from the ECtHR have an unfortunate tendency to be couched in general, if not positively vague, terms. Instead of saying 'yes' or 'no' to a given situation, the Court is more likely to 'sometimes yes' and 'sometimes no'; it often depends on the circumstances of the individual case and whether the evidential provision that is being challenged is 'proportionate'. This can make making predictions as to the Convention's interpretation quite difficult.

Teixeira de Castro v Portugal (1998) 28 EHRR 101, ECtHR

The judgment

The Court reiterates that the admissibility of evidence is primarily a matter for regulation by national law and as a general rule it is for the national courts to asses the evidence before them. The Court's task under the Convention is not to give a ruling as to whether statements of witnesses were properly admitted as evidence, but rather to ascertain whether the proceedings as a whole, including the way in which evidence was taken, were fair.

The Working of the Human Rights Act 1998

If incompatibility does arise between a statute and convention, the mechanisms of the HRA 1998 come into play. Most importantly, s. 3(1) of the Act provides that: 'So far as it is possible to do so, primary legislation and subordinate legislation must be read and given effect in a way which is compatible with the Convention rights.' This applies as much to evidential rules as to any other area of the law. It may mean placing a somewhat strained interpretation on the relevant provision, one that would not normally be reached using traditional canons of statutory interpretation (such as the 'golden rule' or the 'literal rule'), if that is necessary to ensure convention compliance. Thus, and for example, as Lord Cooke observed in *R v Director of Public Prosecutions, ex parte Kebilene* [2000] 2 AC 326, a legal burden of proof can be read down to become an evidential burden, so that a phrase such as 'unless the contrary is proved' can be interpreted by the courts as meaning 'unless sufficient evidence is given to the contrary', though this is clearly not the normal interpretation of such a phrase.

Cross-reference Box

Legal burdens, where they fall on the defendant, must be proved by that party on the balance of probabilities; evidential burdens merely require that he produce some tangible evidence. For more on this topic go to p. 134.

Perhaps ironically, if this sort of interpretation is not possible, because the breach manifests what Lord Hobhouse described in *Kebilene* as 'irremediable incompatibility' with the Convention, a declaration of incompatibility with Convention rights, as then required by s. 4 of the HRA 1998, will not be of benefit to a criminal defendant. This is because s. 4(6) of the 1998 Act preserves in being the provision in relation to which such a declaration is made, pending legislative change, and declares that such a declaration is not binding on the parties to the proceedings in which it is made. Perhaps for this reason, Lord Steyn in *R v A (No. 2)* [2002] 1 AC 45 viewed such a declaration of incompatibility as being very much a 'last resort' for the courts, with quite strained interpretations and implications being justified under s. 3 to avoid it.

Nevertheless, some other senior members of the judiciary have been much more cautious about this process, warning of the dangers that excessive linguistic elasticity in construction could produce, and pointing out that the judicial task is essentially to interpret legislation, not to produce what is often, effectively, judge-created law. Excessive use of s. 3 frequently involves the judiciary in making what are essentially political decisions, and risks undermining the role within the constitution of a sovereign Parliament. A declaration of incompatibility has the benefit of putting the onus back on Parliament. Nevertheless, there is, of course, no guarantee that a declaration of incompatibility under s. 4 of the HRA 1998 will lead to subsequent statutory intervention, as the following extract, discussing the controversial decision of the House of Lords in *A*, makes clear.

Aileen Kavanagh, 'Unlocking the Human Rights Act: The "Radical" Approach to Section 3(1) Revisited' (2005) EHRLR, 259–275 (Extract)

But what about the option of issuing a declaration of incompatibility under s. 4 HRA? In light of the widely acknowledged shortcomings of s.41 and the controversy surrounding it, might this not have been the ideal solution in A, so that Parliament could review the section as a whole and replace it with a more coherent provision which did not violate defendants' right to a fair trial? Whilst this might indeed have been ideal, given the legislative history of s. 41 and the role which distrust of the judiciary played in generating the Government's narrow gateways approach to this issue, it seems highly unlikely that a declaration of incompatibility would have led to a comprehensive reform of this area of the law. Declaring s. 41 to be incompatible with the Convention under s. 4 would have been a contentious step in the early days of the operation of the HRA and would, in any case, probably have failed to secure any legislative reform of the provision. More importantly, it would have also failed to protect the right to a fair trial of the defendant in A. As Lord Steyn pointed out in Ghaidan, s. 3(1) is the primary remedial provision of the HRA. A declaration of incompatibility would not have aided the defendant in the case before them. Given the importance of the right to a fair trial, and the way in which it minimises the risk of convicting the innocent, the best remedial solution in A was to opt for a strained interpretation of s. 41 under s. 3(1). This route may have disadvantages compared with a considered and comprehensive legislative reform of this area, but the latter would have come too late for the defendant in A and was, in any case, an unlikely eventuality.

Figure 1.1 Flow Chart on Compliance

Is it prima facie convention compliant using traditional canons of statutory interpretation? No. >>> Can it be interpreted under s.3 HRA 1998 to make it convention compliant? No. >>> Declaration of Incompatibility under s.4 HRA must be made. >>> Parliament must decide whether to amend the law.

12. Disclosure of Evidence Prior to Trial

In civil cases, both the claimant's cause of action and the defendant's defence is apparent from the exchange of 'statements of case' (formerly termed 'pleadings'), and the modern trend in civil litigation has been for advance disclosure of nearly all evidence, what is sometimes called a 'cards on the table' approach, via the pre-trial exchange of documents and witness statements. As a result, the parties have a very clear idea of the nature of the allegations, and the evidence that will be used to support them, prior to trial. In criminal cases, the Crown has always provided disclosure of evidence for trials on indictment via the service of committal statements, although disclosure of unused material, on which the prosecution does not propose to rely, has been considerably enhanced in recent years. In the summary trial of 'either way' cases, some disclosure has been provided for by way of advance information under the Magistrates' Courts Advance Information Rules 1985 (SI 1985/601). However, there is no duty on the Crown to provide any advance disclosure of evidence in summary only offences (such as minor cases of criminal damage) to the defence, though this can be done as a matter of discretion.

Prior to 1996, there was no general requirement for a defendant in a criminal trial to disclose his case in advance of trial. Nevertheless, there were a limited number of exceptions to this general rule, the most important of which was the requirement to serve notice of intention to adduce an alibi or to adduce expert opinion evidence. There is *still* no general requirement on a defendant to disclose evidence in summary trials, although he can do so voluntarily. In trials on indictment, however, the situation has changed as a result of the advent of the Criminal Procedure and Investigations Act 1996 (CPIA 1996), which created a statutory scheme for both prosecution and (in some situations) defence disclosure of evidence, and under which both parties must set out their allegations and responses to those allegations. The disclosure regime created by this statute is complicated, and detailed examination of the topic is more appropriate to a specialist work on criminal procedure. What follows is merely an outline of the relevant provisions.

Under s. 3 of the CPIA 1996, the prosecution must make 'primary' disclosure of their evidence, also supplying the defence with all evidence that might undermine the Crown's case that has not been previously supplied or, if in the prosecutor's opinion there is none, providing a written statement to that effect to the defendant. Where this has been done, the accused must then usually give a defence statement to the court and the prosecutor. A defence statement is, in theory, a written statement setting out in general terms the nature of the accused's defence, indicating the matters on which he takes issue with the prosecution, and setting out, in the case of each such matter, the reason why he takes issue with the Crown. If this is done, the prosecution is then required to make a second disclosure of any information that might assist the defendant in the light of his defence. The defence also has the right to apply for a court order requiring the disclosure of prosecution evidence if the accused has reasonable cause to believe there exists prosecution material that may aid their defence.

As before 1996, if the defence statement discloses an alibi, the accused must give particulars of the alibi (in the statement), including the name and address of any witness the accused person believes is able to give evidence in support of the alibi, if these are known to the accused when the statement is given, and any information in the accused's possession which might be of material assistance in finding such a witness, if his name or address is not known when the statement is given. If, at trial, a defence is put forward that is different to that contained in the pre-trial defence statement the court may draw adverse inferences against the defendant under s. 11 of the CPIA 1996. For example, if a rape defendant initially states that he intends to allege mistaken identity, and subsequently changes his defence to one of consent, prosecution counsel and the trial judge will comment on this change. However, in practice, in many cases, defence disclosure is still often couched in fairly vague and general terms.

 Pause for reflection

Can you think of any reason why evidence should not be disclosed ahead of trial?

The effectiveness of the 1996 Act has been considerably enhanced by the amendments to its wording contained in the Criminal Justice Act 2003, and by the relevant provisions contained in the Criminal Procedure Rules 2005.

13. Evidential Categories/Terminology

Introduction

It is necessary to discuss briefly some of the terminology employed in the law of evidence, and to identify the various categories of evidence, as this will facilitate comprehension of the rest of the book. It should be observed that many of these categories are not mutually exclusive. Thus, and for example, if, after a stabbing, a defendant is found in possession of a knife, it is *both* real and circumstantial evidence.

Direct Evidence

Direct evidence is evidence of the facts in issue that requires no inferential process, the only matter needing to be assessed being the credibility and reliability of the witness. For example, if an eyewitness to a homicide states at a trial for murder that he saw the defendant kill the victim with a knife, this would be direct evidence of the murder. No inference is necessary, though the tribunal must still decide whether he is an honest witness and if his observation is reliable.

Circumstantial Evidence

Circumstantial evidence, unlike 'direct evidence', requires inferences to be drawn before it can establish the facts in issue in regard to which it is adduced; ie one step more than is necessary with direct evidence. It is evidence of a fact from which the facts in issue (or their absence) *might* be inferred. Circumstantial evidence usually works on an inductive rather than a deductive basis; 'given A it is more likely that B will follow' instead of 'given A, B must follow'. The latter example is characteristic of deductive reasoning (seen most clearly in the Aristotelian syllogism).

Simply because circumstantial evidence works on an inductive basis does not necessarily mean that it is inferior, as is sometimes popularly supposed. Very strong cases can be, and frequently are, founded purely on such evidence. Often, as Pollock CB expressly noted in *R v Exall* (1886) 4 F & F 922, although a single item of circumstantial evidence might not be enough to convict in a criminal case (though this is not always so), when taken together with other pieces of circumstantial evidence, there might be ample material to justify a finding of guilt (or that a civil case has been proved).

Thus, in the notorious 1961 murder trial of James Hanratty, defence counsel was forced to open his defence by saying that the case was 'sagging with coincidences'. In light of the DNA evidence adduced at the final (and rejected) posthumous appeal of the matter in 2001, if James Hanratty was not guilty, and ignoring the fact that he had been identified at an identification parade by one of his surviving victims (which was obviously direct evidence): he had the same identifying manner of speech as the killer; he had stayed in a room the night before the crime from which the same type of bullets that had been fired from the murder weapon were subsequently recovered; the murder weapon was found concealed in a place on a bus which the defendant regarded as his personal hiding place, and the vehicle followed a route he could well have used; his DNA was found on a piece of material from the knickers of the surviving victim, where it would be expected to be if the appellant was guilty; it was also found on the handkerchief found next to the gun. In reality, as was observed in *R v Hanratty (Dec'd)* [2002] 2 Cr App R. 30: 'The number of alleged coincidences means that they are not coincidences but overwhelming proof of the safety of the conviction from an evidential perspective.'

However, because circumstantial evidence, even if it is believed, does not resolve an issue unless additional reasoning is used, and because inductive reasoning is inherently less certain in its conclusions, the possibility of alternative and innocent explanations for its existence must be considered. Thus, and for example, if a blood-stained suspect is seen running from the place where a murder victim's body was found, and forensic evidence subsequently establishes that this was at about the time the killing occurred, this would be circumstantial evidence as to whether he was the perpetrator of the killing.

Nevertheless, an alternative, and innocent, scenario can easily be envisaged. For example, that the accused man came across the body, attempted to assist or revive the victim, becoming contaminated with blood in the process, and then fled the scene in a state of shock and horror. It is rare that such an alternative scenario (albeit often a highly unlikely one) cannot be envisaged to explain circumstantial facts. Additionally, as Lord Normand observed in *Teper v R* [1952] AC 480, circumstantial evidence must sometimes be treated with caution, if only because 'evidence of this kind may be fabricated'. Furthermore, such evidence often rests on a set of assumptions and generalizations about the way in which human existence operates. Sometimes, these might turn out to be completely erroneous or, perhaps more commonly, out of date.

Common examples of circumstantial evidence are matters such as: motive, opportunity, capacity, possession of a weapon consistent with that used in the crime, a defendant's fingerprints being found at the crime scene, etc. For example, that a defendant in a murder trial had a reason to hate the dead person is obviously not conclusive as to whether or not they killed the victim (otherwise the planet would be depopulated), but is certainly relevant. Homicidal psychopaths (possibly) apart, people usually murder for a reason. Having such a reason makes it more likely that someone would commit murder. Similarly, that the modus operandi of a particular crime required a considerable degree of physical strength means that it will be relevant that an accused person was of powerful build and physique, but again certainly not conclusive (there are many sturdy people in the general population).

In some types of crime, circumstantial evidence is the only type of evidence that is likely to be available. For example, direct evidence of insider trading is exceptionally rare. There are no 'smoking guns' or physical evidence that can be scientifically linked to a perpetrator. Unless the insider trader confesses to an offence in an admissible form, the evidence against him is almost always circumstantial. It requires examining apparently innocuous events—meetings in restaurants, telephone calls from certain numbers, relationships between people, trading patterns—and drawing reasonable inferences based on their timing and surrounding circumstances. These can lead to the conclusion that the defendant bought or sold stock with the benefit of wrongfully obtained, price sensitive, inside information. The judicial studies board has provided some guidance as to how jurors might be directed on circumstantial evidence.

Crown Court Bench Book 1, Specimen Directions, fifth edition, para 19, Circumstantial Evidence in Complicated Cases

Sometimes a jury is asked to find some fact proved by direct evidence. For example, if there is reliable evidence from a witness who actually saw a defendant commit a crime; if there is a video recording of the incident which plainly demonstrates his guilt; or if there is reliable evidence of the defendant himself having admitted it, these would all be good examples of direct evidence against him. On the other hand it is often the case that direct evidence of a crime is not available, and the prosecution relies upon circumstantial evidence to prove guilt. That simply means that the prosecution is relying upon evidence of various circumstances relating to the crime and the defendant which they say when taken together will lead to the sure conclusion that it was the defendant who committed the crime. Circumstantial evidence can be powerful evidence, but it is important that you examine it with care, and consider whether the evidence upon which the prosecution relies in proof of its case is reliable and whether it does prove guilt. Furthermore, before convicting on circumstantial evidence you should consider whether it reveals any other circumstances which are or may be of sufficient reliability and strength to weaken or destroy the prosecution case.

 Pause for reflection

Can you think of any other crimes where circumstantial evidence is likely to be the only evidence available?

Real Evidence

This is tangible evidence that can be produced to the court for inspection. An example might be a knife or weapon found at the scene of a crime. This can be produced at trial as a prosecution or defence exhibit. An amusing illustration of such real evidence can be seen in the case of *R v Pieterson* [1995] 1 WLR 293, where Lord Taylor CJ held that the indication provided by a tracker dog as to the presence of someone's scent (and thus that person) at a particular place was admissible as real evidence, provided that an evidential foundation was laid for it by establishing the dog's training and reliability (usually via evidence provided by its handler). Additionally, the tribunal of fact should be warned that they must treat such evidence with caution, especially as the dog could not be called and cross-examined! Real evidence includes the demeanour of a witness when testifying in court (does he look nervous or evasive, etc?). A 'view' by a tribunal of fact, for example, a jury visit to a crime scene or a visit by a judge to the scene of an accident in a personal injury case, is also treated as a species of real evidence. In such cases, the judge and representatives of both parties should be present when the view is carried out. If a jury is determining the case, all 12 of its members must take part in the view. It is wrong for one member to participate and then report back to the other 11: *R v Gurney* [1976] Crim LR 567.

Documentary Evidence

This is written evidence produced for the inspection of the court, for example, ledgers and other records. If they are adduced to establish the truth of their contents, they will also have to be admitted via an exception to the hearsay rule (under the Criminal Justice Act 2003 or the

Civil Evidence Act 1995, say). If they are adduced merely to show their existence, for example, a signed cheque with the defendant's fingerprints on it, they are also a species of 'real' evidence. Under modern statutes, such as s. 13 of the Civil Evidence Act 1995, documents include items such as films, video recordings and tapes that record information.

Testimony

Testimony is oral evidence, given by a witness, in person, from the witness box. It might be of what they themselves perceived with one of their senses (and so direct evidence), or, in some situations, what they were told by others (and so hearsay evidence).

Hearsay Evidence

Hearsay evidence is an out of court statement tendered for the truth of its contents. It can be in a document, or related orally. Thus, an attendance record that notes, and is adduced in court to establish, that person X visited building Y, on a certain date, would come within the former. A statement from witness A that person B told him that he had seen defendant C visit the same building would be oral hearsay.

Evidence to Credit

This is evidence that goes to the question as to whether a witness is worthy of belief, ie a collateral matter (see below), rather than directly to the facts in issue. For example, does a witness have previous convictions for offences involving deception or other forms of dishonesty?

Collateral Evidence

This is evidence adduced (where permitted) on a 'collateral' matter, rather than going directly to the facts in issue. In practice, this will usually mean a matter going to the credit of a witness, and adduced so that their evidence on the facts in issue might be given appropriate weight. For example, that an important witness in the prosecution of another person has previous convictions for perjury is a collateral matter, because the trial at which they testify is not about their criminal record, it is about whether the other person is guilty of the crime with which they are charged. Nevertheless, evidence of those perjury convictions might, in some circumstances, affect the weight placed on the witness's testimony. Similarly, that a witness who claims to have overheard a whispered conversation, in which a party admitted killing someone, is himself profoundly deaf, would also be collateral to any murder trial at which they testified, but again might affect the weight ascribed to their evidence.

Cross-reference Box

The law of evidence places firm limits on the collateral matters that can be adduced or explored in the trial process. This is for fear of excessively prolonging the trial process and occasioning confusion by raising a multiplicity of side issues. For more information on what collateral matters can be the subject of evidence go to pp. 441–444.

Judicial Discretion

This is the power that a judge has to exclude (or admit) evidence that is otherwise admissible (or inadmissible) under the rules of evidence. It is an important subject that requires detailed consideration in its own right, and will be the subject of chapter 2.

14. The 'Best Evidence' Rule

The early years of the law of evidence were heavily influenced by the 'best evidence' rule. This should be considered briefly, as it survived into the modern era, in an attenuated form, and has never been formally abolished, though it has long been recognized, if sometimes only in obiter comments, as having fallen into abeyance: *Garton v Hunter* (1969) 2 QB 37.

In the early 1700s, Chief Baron Gilbert, who wrote one of the earliest treatises on evidence and who was a strong proponent of 'best evidence', felt that, generally, the rule: '. . . demands the best Evidence that the nature of the thing admits'. Thus, secondary evidence of, for example, a lease, contained in a book or other medium, was often excluded because it was 'not such good evidence' as the litigant might have adduced, the best evidence available being the original lease itself.[35]

However, even in its heyday, it was not an absolute rule. In *Saltern v Melhuish* (1754) Amb 246, Lord Hardwicke observed that there were several grounds on which inferior evidence, even oral testimony, could be received as to the contents of a deed or other document, without the adduction of the original being required. For example, if the document was in the possession of the opposing party and they refused to produce it, or, alternatively, if it had been lost or destroyed. As the same judge noted in *Whitfield v Fausset* (1750) 1 Ves Sen 387: 'The rule is that the best evidence must be used that can be had, first the original; if that cannot be had, you may be let in to prove it any way, and by any circumstances the nature of the case will admit.' However, before this could be done it was necessary to prove that the deed or document had become unobtainable.

Thus, in *Brewster v Sewell* (1830) 3 B & Ald 296, the plaintiff in a libel action sought to give secondary evidence of the contents of an insurance policy. He testified that he had searched for the original policy but was unable to find it. The court held that this was sufficient to explain his inability to produce it, and admitted his secondary evidence of its contents. Holroyd J observed that the rationale behind the best evidence rule was that if a litigant did not produce an available document, or take the necessary steps to obtain its production, but resorted to other evidence of its contents, a: '. . . fair presumption is, that the original document would not answer his purpose, and that it would differ from the secondary evidence which he gives with respect to the instrument itself.' In the same case, Best J noted that the degree of diligence that should be employed in searching for an original document, before a party was entitled to give secondary evidence of its contents, depended on the circumstances of each case. For example, is the document of a type that would have been carefully preserved or one that might more readily have been thrown away, etc?

As a result of such interpretations, by the nineteenth century, the rule was recognized by the courts as no more than a rule of practice to the effect that a court will attach little or no weight

---

[35] J Gilbert, *The Law of Evidence* (2nd edn, 1760, printed by Catherine Lintot) at 2 and 9.

to secondary evidence of the contents of a document unless the party seeking to adduce such evidence has first adequately explained the non-production of the original. This makes it little more than a common sense inference. Even the one possible exception to this general position, recognized by Lord Denning in *Garton v Hunter*, which was that if an original document is in a party's hands it must normally be produced (see below), was expressly rejected by the Court of Appeal in *Springsteen v Masquerade Music Ltd* [2001] EMLR 654. Nevertheless, as all advocates know, producing inferior evidence when better is readily available to you is likely to excite the suspicions of any tribunal of fact to a very marked degree.

Garton v Hunter (1969) 2 QB 37, CA

Lord Denning MR

It is plain that Scott L.J. had in mind the old rule that a party must produce the best evidence that the nature of the case will allow, and that any less good evidence is to be excluded. That old rule has gone by the board long ago. The only remaining instance of it that I know is that if an original document is available in your hands, you must produce it. You cannot give secondary evidence by producing a copy. Nowadays we do not confine ourselves to the best evidence. We admit all relevant evidence. The goodness or badness of it goes only to weight, and not to admissibility. So I fear that Scott L.J. was in error.

Pause for reflection

Why should this be so? Can you think of any arguments for reviving the 'Best Evidence' rule?

Summary

- The law of evidence regulates the material that can be adduced at trial to prove the various facts in issue in litigation. The aim of this material is usually to recreate events that occurred at some point in the past, so allowing the tribunal of fact to apply the substantive law to those events.

- All admissible evidence must be relevant. This is determined using a 'common sense' approach to see whether it makes the facts in issue, or relevant collateral matters, more or less likely.

- Not all relevant evidence is admissible. Some relevant evidence is caught by an exclusionary rule, and is thus deemed to be inadmissible. These rules, and their exceptions, form the bulk of the English law of evidence.

- The various exclusionary rules have a provenance reaching back several centuries, and prevent the adduction of evidence that is, or was at some time, considered to be flawed in some manner. These rules became very much more rigid in the 40 years after *c*.1780, which can be considered as a crucial formative period in the law of evidence.

- A number of justifications are advanced for preserving the exclusionary rules of evidence. Amongst them are: the need to avoid prejudice, to preserve public confidence in the judicial process and to uphold individual rights.

- In the Roman law tradition, there are comparatively few exclusionary evidentiary rules, these codes traditionally adopting what is known as a system of 'free proof', whereby all relevant evidence is admissible (with limited exceptions).

- Very occasionally, in both criminal and civil cases, but especially in the former, admissible and relevant evidence can be excluded by an exercise of judicial discretion, whether under common law or (more commonly) statutory powers.

- There has been considerable reform in the law of evidence over recent decades, with some of the more arcane exclusionary rules being abolished or modified, as a result of parliamentary or (less commonly) judicial action. This is an ongoing process and more change can be expected in the coming years.

- The advent of the HRA 1998, combined with the ECHR, has had a significant impact on the law of evidence, modifying some established principles as the courts have sought to ensure convention compliance.

- Evidence is traditionally divided into different descriptive categories: circumstantial, direct, real, etc., but these often overlap, so that an item of evidence falls within two or more categories simultaneously.

- Historically, the 'best evidence rule' required that the best potential evidence available on a matter, such as the original copy of a disputed lease, be placed before the court. Although once an important rule of evidence, there are now so many exceptions, that it amounts to nothing more than a common-sense inference.

 ## Further reading

Terence Anderson, William Twining and David Schum, *Analysis of Evidence* (2nd edn, 2005, Cambridge University Press)

WR Cornish and AP Sealy, 'Juries and the Rules of Evidence' [1973] Crim LR 208

Penny Darbyshire, 'Previous Misconduct and Magistrates' Courts—Some tales from the real world' [1997] Crim LR 105

Thomas P Gallanis, 'The Rise of Modern Evidence Law' (1999) Iowa Law Review, vol 84, 499–560

Rosemary Pattenden, 'Admissibility in criminal proceedings of third party and real evidence obtained by methods prohibited by UNCAT' (2006) International Journal of Evidence and Proof, vol 10, no 1, 1–41

Mike Redmayne, 'The Structure of Evidence Law' (2006) Oxford Journal of Legal Studies, vol 26, no 4, 805–822

Alex Stein, *Foundations of Evidence Law* (2005, Oxford University Press)

Laird C Kirkpatrick, 'Evidence Law in the Next Millennium' (1998) Hastings Law Journal, issue 49, 363

John H Langbein, 'The German Advantage in Civil Procedure' (1985) University of Chicago Law Review, vol 52, no 4, 823–866

William Twining, 'Evidence as a multi-disciplinary subject' (2003) Law, Probability and Risk, vol 2, 91–107

 ## Questions for Discussion

For suggested approaches, please visit the Online Resource Centre

1. Does the law of evidence serve any useful function in the modern era? Could it be entirely abolished?

2. What is meant by a system of 'free proof'?

3. What are the key differences between an inquisitorial and an adversarial legal system when it comes to adducing evidence?

4. What is meant by 'relevant' evidence?

5. Distinguish between relevance and cogency/weight.

6. What rationales have been advanced for the common law system of exclusionary rules?

7. Why did the common law rules of evidence develop?

8. What areas of the law of evidence have seen major reform in recent years?

9. Why should evidential rules differ between civil and criminal cases?

2 JUDICIAL DISCRETION

Definitions

Codes of Practice Binding guidance issued to investigating authorities under s. 66 of the PCEA 1984, as to the scope of police powers and duties.

Inclusionary discretion A judicial power to admit evidence that is otherwise caught by an exclusionary rule of evidence.

Exclusionary discretion A judicial power to exclude evidence that is otherwise both relevant and admissible.

Entrapment Situation in which a person is enticed (to some degree) into committing a crime by a third party (for example a police officer or journalist).

---

1. Introduction

Evidential rules are, by definition, inflexible, whatever the merits of an individual case. As a result, it is sometimes suggested—most recently, to a modest degree at least, by Lord Justice Auld in his *Review of the Criminal Court of England and Wales* of 2001—that guided judicial discretion, rather than fixed 'bright line' rules, should be the way forward in this area of adjectival law. Thus, a trial judge would not be bound by rigid exclusionary rules (or their absence), but would have a general discretion to admit or exclude evidence as he saw fit, having regard to what he perceived to be the interests of justice, albeit in the light of designated statutory criteria and the facts of the case before him.

 Pause for reflection

Can you think of any *causes célèbres* in recent years where evidential rules have meant that criminal prosecutions could not proceed?

This is certainly not a new idea. The distinguished American legal academic, James Bradley Thayer (1831–1902), who also called for a 'radical simplification of the law of evidence', and many major twentieth-century law reformers, advocated increasing the discretion given to trial judges when deciding whether to admit evidence. They proposed that the law be changed so that appellate courts would no longer craft specific and detailed evidential rules, but, instead, provide a regime of broad principles, designed to ensure substantial flexibility in trial court decision-making, and considerable immunity from subsequent appellate court review of those decisions.

Thus, John Henry Wigmore (1863–1943), a leading authority on the Anglo-American law of evidence in the first half of the twentieth century, favoured both the expansion of judicial discretion and a considerable freeing up of a trial court's evidentiary decisions from being challenged, though he differed from Thayer in believing that detailed guidelines, rather than broad principles, should direct judicial decision-making. Both men appreciated that increased judicial discretion necessarily required a 'deferential' standard of appeal court review, and a tolerance for trial court decisions that the appellate judges would not, themselves, have made, provided the requisite guidelines were applied and that a decision was not plainly perverse.[1]

Pause for reflection

Do you think that an entirely discretionary approach to evidence is viable?

As will be seen, to a small but not insignificant degree, the English law of evidence has moved in this direction, allowing more discretion to trial judges in several situations. This is manifest, for example, in the novel inclusionary power to admit otherwise inadmissible hearsay evidence in criminal cases, established by s. 114(1)(d) of the Criminal Justice Act 2003 (see chapter 6), the advent of an unprecedented general exclusionary power in civil matters, and the development of a broader exclusionary power in criminal cases (see below).

In the modern era, the Court of Appeal is also often reluctant to overturn a trial judge's decision on evidential matters, unless it manifests 'unreasonableness' in the form identified in *Associated Provincial Picture Houses Ltd v Wednesbury Corporation* [1948] 1 KB 223, ie no reasonable tribunal (rather than the individual judges sitting in the Court of Appeal), could have reached such a decision or relevant factors have not been considered at first instance. Nevertheless, when it comes to evidential matters, the growth of discretion in England and Wales remains limited, largely because of its perceived risks.

Dangers in Discretion

There are dangers as well as benefits in ignoring 'bright-line' evidential rules in favour of judicial discretion, especially if its exercise is not easily reviewable on appeal. There are, inevitably, fears that discretionary powers will be exercised arbitrarily and unfairly; that broad and ambiguous principles make evidentiary rulings unpredictable to parties preparing for trial or attempting to negotiate a settlement to a dispute, and will also result in inconsistent outcomes. Additionally, the uncertainty created by excessive discretion might have the potential to reduce public confidence in the judicial system.[2]

Significantly, perhaps, the Law Commission Report, *Hearsay And Related Topics* (No 245) of 1997, claimed (at para. 1.29 of the Report's Summary) that the discretionary provisions in the (now repealed) Criminal Justice Act 1988, relating to the adduction of hearsay evidence,

---

[1] E Swift, 'One Hundred Years of Evidence Law Reform: Thayer's Triumph' California Law Review, issue 88, 2000, at 2443–2445.

[2] Swift, ibid., at 2439 and 2476.

had not worked satisfactorily, with some judges consistently refusing to exercise their power to admit such evidence under the statute, while others were usually more liberal. In turn, the uncertainty that this created meant that the Crown often could not confidently assess the prospects of a conviction when making an initial decision as to whether to prosecute or not, while those acting for a defendant frequently found it difficult to advise on the appropriate plea or on the conduct of the defence.

From a more theoretical perspective, Professor Alex Stein has argued strongly against the growth of discretion in adjudicative fact-finding within common law systems, and deprecated, in particular, its expansion in England (manifest, for example, in statutes such as the Criminal Justice Act 2003). Instead, Stein argues that evidence law should be moving in the opposite direction, so that legal regulation of fact-finding is increased rather than being reduced. Stein identifies two fundamental precepts in the common law rules of evidence: the 'equality principle' that controls the apportionment of the risk of error in civil litigation; and the 'equal-best' standard that needs to be satisfied in every criminal case in order to convict the accused. He uses these to justify most of the major common law evidential rules that developed in Anglo-American legal systems.[3] For a combination of these reasons, both practical and conceptual, it seems unlikely that fixed evidential rules will be entirely replaced in the future by guided judicial discretion.

2. Judicial Discretion in Modern England

Introduction

Ignoring the theoretical debate about discretion, to what extent does an English or Welsh trial judge in the present era have a discretion to 'override' the strict rules of evidence? That is, can he admit evidence that is technically inadmissible or, alternatively, exclude evidence which is technically admissible? To answer this question, the subject must be broken down into inclusionary and exclusionary discretions. The former would allow a judge to admit evidence that was otherwise inadmissible, the latter to exclude evidence that was both relevant and not otherwise caught by an exclusionary rule. Additionally, the existence (or lack) of such a discretion must be considered for both civil and criminal matters. This produces four separate situations, which will be considered in turn, albeit that the exclusionary discretion in criminal cases, the most important of them, warrants specially detailed examination.

Exclusionary Discretion in Civil Cases

Traditionally, it was thought that a trial judge in a civil case had no discretion to exclude evidence, however it was obtained, provided it was both relevant and legally admissible. It was accepted that a judge could exercise considerable 'moral' pressure on counsel on this point, using his authority to discourage the adduction of evidence that he felt to have been obtained

---

[3] See generally, A Stein, *Foundations of Evidence Law* (2005, Oxford University Press).

improperly, something that his status as tribunal of both fact and law greatly facilitated (in most civil cases). However, as Potter LJ expressly observed in *Grobbelaar v Sun Newspapers Ltd* (1999) *The Times* 12 August, when giving the judgment of the Court of Appeal, the preponderance of academic opinion took the view that in civil cases there was no discretion at common law for a civil judge to exclude otherwise admissible evidence because, for example, its prejudicial effect outweighed its probative value or for some other reason. If one of the parties insisted on adducing the disputed evidence it would be adduced.

Nevertheless, and as Potter LJ also noted in *Grobbelaar*, this has changed as a result of the advent of r. 32.1 of the CPR 1998 (SI 1998/3132), which provided civil courts with a discretion to exclude otherwise relevant and admissible evidence. This was because Sch. 1, para. 4 of the Civil Procedure Act 1997, the enabling Act under which the statutory instrument was issued, made it apparent that the CPR 1998 could effect evidential changes, and this power was clearly exercised by r. 32.

Rule 32 of the CPR 1998

(1) The court may control the evidence by giving directions as to—

    (a) the issues on which it requires evidence;

    (b) the nature of the evidence which it requires to decide those issues; and

    (c) the way in which the evidence is to be placed before the court.

(2) The court may use its power under this rule to exclude evidence that would otherwise be admissible.

(3) The court may limit cross-examination.

As a result of this provision, a civil trial judge does now have the power to exclude otherwise admissible evidence. There were no express limitations set out in the CPR 1998 as to the manner and extent to which this power should be applied, although clearly it must be exercised so as to deal justly with any given case. For example, Lord Woolf has observed that while, under the new rules, a party could not be prevented from putting forward an allegation that was central to his or her defence, the court could control the manner in which this was done, and so limit the costs involved.

As this judicial comment suggests, the draftsmen behind the provision envisaged that it would be used, primarily, to exclude technically admissible evidence that was of limited weight, or which would otherwise be duplicated, with a view to keeping hearings to a length, and costs to a size, that was commensurate with the gravity of the case in hand, ie its primary purpose was 'case management', and it is for this that it is most commonly employed. However, there was nothing in the provision that *required* it to be limited to such uses, or that necessarily prevented it from being employed to exclude evidence that was deemed to be, in some way, 'unfair'.

It is now clear that the provision can be exercised to exclude evidence for reasons of fairness. However, it is also equally apparent that it will be exercised very circumspectly indeed, and utilized only rarely for such purposes, as can be seen from the Court of Appeal decision in *Jones v University of Warwick* [2003] 1 WLR 954, the leading case in this area of the law. In this case, the claimant had suffered injury to her right hand and wrist in an accident at work for which her employers, the defendants, admitted liability. However, they were sceptical about her claim for continuing disability as a result of the accident and instructed enquiry agents ('private eyes') to investigate exactly how seriously she had been injured.

At trial, the first instance judge refused to exclude video evidence, under r. 32.1(2) of the CPR 1998, that had been secretly video-recorded in the claimant's home, on two occasions, by an enquiry agent acting for the defendant's insurers. The agent had obtained access to the claimant's home by posing as a market researcher. On the basis of the video evidence, the defendant's medical expert was of the opinion that the claimant had a normal function in her injured hand, and that damages awarded for the accident should be commensurately small. It was not in dispute that the enquiry agent was guilty of trespass and that she would not have been given permission to enter had she not misled the claimant as to her identity.

On appeal, the trial judge's decision was upheld on the facts of the case. Nevertheless, the Court of Appeal did not preclude such an application being successful in other, more extreme, or less evidentially reliable, circumstances. Lord Woolf CJ, giving the judgment of the court, said that the appeal required the court to consider two competing and opposing public interests: (i) that in litigation the truth should be revealed and (ii) that the courts should not acquiesce in, let alone encourage the use of, unlawful means to obtain evidence. However, as the judge noted, it was not possible to reconcile perfectly the conflicting public interests that arose from these two considerations.

In the instant case, the court felt that the defendant's conduct was not so grave that the video evidence should be excluded. This was especially the case as fresh medical experts would have to be instructed, from whom the enquiry agent's video would have to be concealed. Additionally, it would not be possible to cross-examine the claimant properly at trial, as no mention could be made of what she had been filmed doing in her house. As a result, the Court of Appeal concluded that it would not be right to interfere with the trial judge's decision to admit the video evidence.

Even so, the Court of Appeal appreciated that under the CPR 1998, a judge, when exercising his discretion to manage litigation, also had to consider the effect of his decisions upon litigation generally and should seek to deter improper conduct by litigants. As a consequence, it suggested that a trial court could reflect its disapproval of the insurers' improper conduct, and discourage it in others, by the costs orders that it made after the conclusion of a trial. Accordingly, since, in the instant case, it was the insurers' conduct that gave rise to the litigation over the admissibility of the video evidence, it was right that the defendant should pay all the legal costs of resolving that issue (even if he won the case).

 Pause for reflection

In a major case, in which very large sums of money are being claimed, would this provide much of a disincentive?

A number of factors clearly influenced the court's decision in this case. For example, that the evidence was extremely reliable; it was not oral testimony from an eye witness but a video that the court could consider for itself. Additionally, the enquiry agent had been invited into the defendant's living room, albeit on false pretences. The Court of Appeal did not preclude other, more extreme situations, or inherently less reliable evidence, leading to the evidence being excluded. Thus, suppose for example that the enquiry agent had broken into the claimant's house and hidden under her bed to record her video or, alternatively, had asserted in evidence that she had seen the claimant freely moving her wrist but could not produce any photographic record of this, other than her oral testimony (or even that both factors were present)? Such a scenario might have produced a different result. Additionally, it should be remembered that such cases will often involve a potential breach of the other party's Article 8 right to privacy, which must also be considered, though this, too, can be breached in varying degrees of severity and with different consequences.

Jones v University of Warwick [2003] 1 WLR 954, CA

Lord Woolf CJ

The court must try to give effect to what are here the two conflicting public interests. The weight to be attached to each will vary according to the circumstances. The significance of the evidence will differ as will the gravity of the breach of article 8, according to the facts of the particular case. The decision will depend on all the circumstances. Here, the court cannot ignore the reality of the situation. This is not a case where the conduct of the defendant's insurers is so outrageous that the defence should be struck out. The case, therefore, has to be tried. It would be artificial and undesirable for the actual evidence, which is relevant and admissible, not to be placed before the judge who has the task of trying the case. We accept Mr Owen's submission that to exclude the use of the evidence would create a wholly undesirable situation. Fresh medical experts would have to be instructed on both sides. Evidence which is relevant would have to be concealed from them, perhaps resulting in a misdiagnosis; and it would not be possible to cross-examine the claimant appropriately. For these reasons we do not consider it would be right to interfere with the judge's decision not to exclude the evidence... Excluding the evidence is not, moreover, the only weapon in the court's armoury. The court has other steps it can take to discourage conduct of the type of which complaint is made. In particular it can reflect its disapproval in the orders for costs which it makes. In this appeal, we therefore propose, because the conduct of the insurers gave rise to the litigation over admissibility of the evidence which has followed upon their conduct, to order the defendant to pay the costs of these proceedings to resolve this issue before the district judge, Judge Harris and this court even though we otherwise dismiss the appeal.... In addition, we would indicate to the trial judge that when he comes to deal with the question of costs he should take into account the defendant's conduct which is the subject of this appeal when deciding the appropriate order for costs. He may consider the costs of the inquiry agent should not be recovered.... In giving effect to the overriding objective, and taking into account the wider interests of the administration of justice, the court must, while doing justice between the parties, also deter improper conduct of a party while conducting litigation. We do not pretend that this is a perfect reconciliation of the conflicting public interests. It is not; but at least the solution does not ignore the insurers' conduct.

Pause for reflection

Do you feel that the evidence of the enquiry agent should have been admitted in this case?

Inclusionary Discretion in Civil Cases

There is no general discretion to admit evidence in civil cases that is otherwise inadmissible, however cogent it might appear to be, though there are a small number of specific, statutory, inclusionary discretions, such as that to admit previous consistent statements (see chapter 7).

Nevertheless, because, in the modern era, evidential rules are usually very much less strict in civil cases, this is much less likely to be a problem than it is in criminal matters.

Inclusionary Discretion in Criminal Cases

In criminal cases, there is no general discretion to admit evidence that is otherwise excluded by one of the rules of evidence. A classic illustration of this general rule is provided by the Privy Council case of *Sparks v R* (1964) AC 964. In this case, a white American serviceman was accused of assaulting a small girl in Bermuda. The girl was deemed to be too young to give evidence (she was only four) and thus a statement that she had made to her mother about her attacker, in which she had said, 'Mummy it was a coloured boy', though obviously cogent, was held to be inadmissible (it was excluded by the rule against hearsay). On appeal, the Privy Council upheld the trial judge's decision not to admit this evidence and expressly rejected the suggestion that there was a general judicial discretion to admit highly probative evidence where it was in the interests of justice. (Interestingly, it found other grounds for allowing the appeal.) Nevertheless, and mindful of such cases, the Law Commission proposed that there should be a judicial discretion to admit hearsay evidence that would otherwise be inadmissible under any other provision, where this was in the interests of justice.[4] This was effected by s. 114(1)(d) of the Criminal Justice Act 2003 (see chapter 6).

 Pause for reflection

Would it be sensible for a trial judge to have the power, in all situations, to admit evidence that was otherwise caught by an exclusionary rule, if it was in the interests of justice?

3. Exclusionary Discretion in Criminal Cases

Introduction

Historically, rather than adopting a rigid exclusionary rule for improperly obtained evidence, England followed an inclusionary practice, whereby relevant evidence was legally admissible, regardless of its source. There was no rule of law *requiring* its exclusion. The most frequently cited authority in this regard is the decision in the case of *R v Leatham* [1861] 8 Cox CC 498, in which Crompton J famously held that: '... it matters not how you get it, if you steal it even, it would be admissible in evidence'. Subsequent cases have periodically confirmed this analysis. However, it is very important to appreciate that this refers to a rule of law *requiring* exclusion, not to the existence of a judicial *discretion* allowing the exclusion of evidence for such impropriety.

The absence of such a rule, and the significance of such a discretion, has been particularly important where evidence has been obtained by nefarious means, and especially by entrapment.

---

[4] Law Commission Report No 245, *Hearsay And Related Topics*, published 19 June 1997, Summary Of Principal Recommendations at 1.3.

This either involves inducing a person to commit a crime (pre-offence entrapment) or inducing a person to confess to, or reveal, a crime that has already been committed (post-offence entrapment). Pre-offence entrapment generally involves the use of an *agent provocateur,* who entices another person to a breach of the law that would not otherwise have occurred, and then provides evidence against that person. Nevertheless, there are numerous other forms of investigative impropriety, apart from entrapment. There are also situations where the adduction of relevant and otherwise admissible evidence might be considered 'unfair', even though there has been no impropriety. The exclusion of evidence in criminal cases, via an exercise of discretion has become particularly significant in recent years.

David Ormerod and Diane Birch, 'The Evolution of the Discretionary Exclusion of Evidence' [2004] Crim LR 767–788 (Extract)

No one would dispute the frequency of applications for the exercise of judicial discretion to exclude an item of evidence, whether in the magistrates' court or the Crown Court. The principal basis for the exercise of such a discretion is under s. 78 of PCEA, but a well-established body of other discretions are also frequently called upon including the common law power to exclude evidence where its prejudicial effect outweighs its probative value. Distinct from, but closely allied to the power of exclusion, is the ability to stay proceedings as an abuse of process. Not only is it increasingly common for the courts to be called upon to exercise these powers, but their increased significance in the trial is also generally acknowledged. At a micro-level, the exercise of exclusionary discretion may have the effect of terminating the proceedings, as when a ruling excludes a crucial confession. At a macro-level, the existence and exercise of judicial discretion to exclude evidence affects the development of the investigative, pre-trial and trial processes of the criminal justice system.

At Common Law

Despite the decision reached in *Leatham*, the existence of a general *discretion* (rather than a legal *obligation*) to exclude evidence at common law, having regard to its provenance, was periodically hinted at in several appellate level cases, though very rarely, if ever, employed. These included (although in neither case was such a discretion applied) cases such as *Kuruma, Son of Kaniu v R* [1953] AC 197 and *Jeffrey v Black* [1978] QB 490. In the latter case, in which police officers had arrested a man for stealing a sandwich in a public house and then conducted an illegal search of his flat during which drugs had been found, the court noted that if a case was 'exceptional', for example, if the police had not just entered without authority, but had also been guilty of trickery, or they had been oppressive, unfair, or: '... in other respects they have behaved in a manner which is morally reprehensible, then it is open to the justices to apply their discretion and decline to allow the particular evidence to be let in as part of the trial'. Nevertheless, in this case, such a discretion was not exercised, and the evidence of the drugs was admitted.

Arguably, an extremely rare case of this occurring, and the discretion to exclude evidence actually being exercised, can be seen in the case of *R v Payne* [1963] 1 WLR 637, where the defendant, charged with drunk driving, was induced to undergo a medical examination to see if he was 'ill', on the understanding that the doctor would not try to establish if he was fit to drive. Subsequently, it was held that evidence from the doctor of his unfitness to drive should have been excluded at trial (police practice on the use of such evidence having changed in the meantime). Nevertheless, and unlike the American experience, in post-war England, the courts took a progressively more restrictive view of the existence of such a common law discretion. Ultimately, in the important case of *R v Sang* [1980] AC 402, it was very narrowly limited to two specific situations.

More Prejudicial than Probative

First, in what was regrettably a rather confused judgment, Lord Diplock and a majority of the House of Lords in *Sang* held that a judge in a criminal trial always had a: '... discretion to refuse to admit evidence if in his opinion its prejudicial effect outweighs its probative value'. This is found, in varying forms, in all common law jurisdictions and is a key evidential concept. Thus, in America, FRE 402 provides that even relevant evidence may be excluded if its probative value is: '... substantially outweighed by the dangers of unfair prejudice'. It is particularly important in jury trials, where laymen hear the evidence.

Essentially, 'prejudice' is the difference between legitimate weight ascribed to prosecution evidence and the significance that would actually be attributed to it by the tribunal of fact. For example, if its true cogency was worth a score of 10 (on a purely hypothetical scale!) and a jury would treat it as having a value of 15, the extra five points would be 'prejudice'. This is particularly relevant in cases where the tendered evidence, by its nature, is likely to excite strong passions on the part of the tribunal of fact. Of course, if the 'true' value of evidence is particularly damning, it will be very difficult for it to produce prejudice, as jurors are unlikely to give it more importance than it deserves.

Obviously, such an exercise of discretion will require trial judges to make difficult assessments, weighing up facts on a case by case basis. Nevertheless, in England its existence was periodically reiterated throughout the twentieth century, in cases such as *R v Christie* [1914] AC 545. More recently, it was noted in *Scott v R* [1989] AC 1242 that a trial judge always has a discretion to: '... exclude evidence if it is necessary in order to secure a fair trial for the accused'. Thus, if tendered evidence is technically relevant in helping the prosecution to establish their case, but is of very low cogency and, at the same time, greatly damages the standing of the defendant, or excites acute hostility against him, it might be excluded.

For example, in child murder cases, it is quite common not to show photographs of the dead infant's body to the jury, unless it is important to do so, the prosecution often confining itself to oral evidence of the lethal injuries, because of the prejudice that seeing such photographs might occasion (a phenomenon that appears to be supported by some recent academic research in Australia). Similarly, in *R v Khan et al* (2007) *The Times* 1 May, during the trial of five men convicted of conspiracy to cause explosions as part of an Islamist bomb plot, the jury were kept unaware of the fact that two of the defendants had earlier met two of the men involved in the 7 July 2005 London suicide bomb attacks, on the basis that this would be disproportionately prejudicial (though obviously their association with other terrorists was of *some* relevance).

R v Christie [1914] AC 545, HL

Lord Moulton

The law is so much on its guard against the accused being prejudiced by evidence which, though admissible, would probably have a prejudicial influence on the minds of the jury which would be out of proportion to its true evidential value, that there has grown up a practice of a very salutary nature, under which the judge intimates to the counsel for the prosecution that he should not press for the admission of evidence which would be open to this objection, and such an intimation from the tribunal trying the case is usually sufficient to prevent the evidence being pressed in all cases where the scruples of the tribunal in this respect are reasonable. Under the influence of this practice, which is based on an anxiety to secure for every one a fair trial, there has grown up a custom of not admitting certain kinds of evidence which is so constantly followed that it almost amounts to a rule of procedure.

Pause for reflection

Do you feel that it is ever proper to withhold relevant evidence from a tribunal, simply because of a concern that they will be excessively affected by it?

Confessions and Analogous Evidence

Secondly, *Sang* also held that there was a discretion to exclude improperly obtained: '… admissions and confessions and generally with regard to evidence obtained from the accused after the commission of the offence'. These were *sui generis* and would encompass, for example, a confession that was obtained by trickery. An illustration of this would be the post-PCEA 1984 case of *R v Mason* [1988] 1 WLR 139, where the confession was obtained by deliberate deceit. Although actually excluded under s. 78 of the PCEA 1984 (see below), the Court of Appeal indicated that it could also have been excluded under the common law discretion. In *Sang*, Lord Diplock suggested that the situation in *Payne* was analogous to unfairly obtaining a confession; it was evidence obtained from a defendant after an offence, and so could be legitimately explained as a manifestation of this discretion, by applying the maxim *nemo debet prodere se ipsum*. However, this situation apart, *Sang* concluded that there was no general discretion to refuse to admit relevant and admissible evidence on the ground that it was obtained by 'improper or unfair means'. Dicta to the contrary, in cases such as *Black*, were rejected.

The limited common law discretion to exclude evidence set out in *Sang* still survives, by dint of s. 82(3) of the PCEA 1984, which expressly preserved any existing power of the court to exclude evidence at its discretion. As a result, in *R v Nadir* [1993] 4 All ER 513, Lord Taylor CJ could state that although a trial judge might exclude evidence under s. 78 of the PCEA 1984 (see below): 'He also has a general discretion to exclude evidence which was preserved by s. 82(3) of the 1984 Act which would allow the judge to exclude evidence he considers more prejudicial than probative.'

Nevertheless, in *R v Khan* [1994] 4 All ER 426, Lord Taylor also considered that the continuing significance of the common law power would be relatively small, because, as the discretion conferred on a trial judge by the advent of s. 78 was: '… at least as wide as that identified in *R v Sang* [usually] it is only necessary to consider the question of the exercise of discretion under s. 78'. Even so, it has been suggested that there might be a residual role for the common law power, because of the 'prospective' wording of s. 78, 'proposes to rely', something that might mean it could not be applied retrospectively, to 'exclude' evidence that had already been admitted (by directing a jury to disregard it): *R v Sat-Bhambra* [1988] 88 Cr App R 55.[5] Obviously, such situations would be exceptionally rare as, normally, if a judge decided that he should have exercised his discretion to exclude evidence, he would offer the defence the chance to abort the trial in favour of a fresh hearing.

4. The Advent of Section 78 of the PCEA 1984

Introduction

Section 78(1) of the PCEA 1984 was introduced by the government in response to a broader proposal made by Lord Scarman, in the House of Lords, during the passage of the Act through Parliament.

Section 78(1) of the PCEA 1984

In any proceedings the court may refuse to allow evidence on which the prosecution proposes to rely to be given if it appears to the court that, having regard to all the circumstances, including the circumstances in which the evidence was obtained, the admission of the evidence would have such an adverse effect on the fairness of the proceedings that the court ought not to admit it.

Perhaps because of the rather ad hoc manner in which s. 78 had been introduced to the Act, there was, initially, considerable confusion as to its effect. Even so, several things could be noted straightaway. First, s. 78 only applies to prosecution evidence. It cannot, for example, be used to exclude evidence being adduced by a co-defendant that implicates a fellow accused. However, *R v Mason* [1988] 86 Cr App R 349 swiftly made it apparent that s. 78 applies to *all* prosecution evidence, even if such evidence is also regulated by another specialist provision (as with confession evidence). Thus, s. 78 can be used to exclude matters as diverse as confessions, identification evidence, hearsay and the adduction of defendant bad character evidence. It will be encountered regularly during the course of this book. Section 78(2) also makes clear that the provision is without prejudice to any other rule of law *requiring* a court to exclude evidence; it does not affect the operation of any exclusionary rule of evidence.

Although, and unlike s. 76(3) of the PCEA 1984 (which deals specifically with confession evidence), there is no express statutory power for a first instance judge to raise s. 78 on his own initiative, the Divisional Court decision in *Regina (Saifi) v Governor of Brixton Prison and another* [2001] 1 WLR 1134 suggests that s. 78 is broad enough for it to be raised by the court, without an application first being made by defence counsel. However, it is also apparent that there is normally no obligation on a trial judge to consider the exercise of the discretion, if it is

---

[5] An extract from this case can be found in chapter 7, at pp. 347–348.

not raised by defence counsel, and a failure to do this will sometimes preclude the matter being considered for the first time on appeal. Additionally, and unlike the exclusion of confessions under s. 76, once the defendant has raised the exclusion of evidence under s. 78, there is no onus on the prosecution to prove (beyond reasonable doubt) that the provision should not be applied. It is entirely a matter for the judge's *discretion* and so not amenable to burdens or standards of proof, as the following extract demonstrates.

Regina (Saifi) v Governor of Brixton Prison and another
[2001] 1 WLR 1134, DC

Rose LJ

The enactment in section 76(2) of PCEA of a burden on the prosecution to prove beyond reasonable doubt that a confession was not obtained by oppression or other circumstances affecting its reliability, is a clear pointer against the validity of the argument [that such a burden exists on the Crown under s. 78, which has no such provision] . . . Section 78 confers a power in terms wide enough for its exercise on the court's own motion. The power is to be exercised whenever an issue appears as to whether the court could conclude that the evidence should not be admitted. The concept of a burden of proof has no part to play in such circumstances. No doubt it is for that reason that there is no express provision as to the burden of proof, and we see no basis for implying such a burden. The prosecution desiring to adduce and the defence seeking to exclude evidence will each seek to persuade the court about impact on fairness. We regard the position as neutral and see no reason why section 78 should be understood as requiring the court to consider upon whom the burden of proof rests. In this case it is said that the magistrate should have made findings of fact. If the section places a burden of proof upon the prosecution this would advance the applicant's fundamental attack on the magistrate's refusal to make specific findings and his failure to apply the criminal standard of proof to the prosecution's rebuttal of issues raised by the defence. In our judgment these submissions are inconsistent with the breadth of purpose of section 78. Unlike the words of section 76(2), where the burden and standard of proof is directed towards a specific issue, namely whether or not the prosecution has proved that the confession was not obtained by oppression, or in circumstances rendering it unreliable, the reach of the protection provided by section 78 is broader, namely the prevention of unfairness from the admission of any evidence, not just a confession. The objective being broader, so also is the range of circumstances having a bearing on it. The ambit is not confined to what emanates from the defence. Circumstances may appear to the court other than those raised by the defendant. . . . The absence from section 78 of words suggesting that facts are to be established or proved to any particular standard is, in our judgment, deliberate.

It should be noted that s. 78 requires the court to make an assessment of the degree of unfairness involved in any given case. It is not *any* level of unfairness that will lead to the exclusion of evidence. It must be a sufficiently severe example ('such unfairness'), that the evidence ought not to be admitted. Minor examples of unfairness may well not be enough to lead to exclusion, especially as case law has indicated that the notion of 'fairness of the proceedings' involves a consideration not only of fairness to the accused but also of fairness to the public and prosecution. Ultimately, every case will turn on its individual facts, and must be considered in its 'totality', ie in the light of all the surrounding circumstances, as the following excerpt from *Saifi* also suggests.

Regina (Saifi) v Governor of Brixton Prison and another
[2001] 1 WLR 1134, DC

Rose LJ

The purpose of the section is to enable the court to achieve fairness in the conduct of its proceedings, not by reference to the particular character or type of evidence but by having 'regard to all the circumstances'. The exercise of the power is unlikely to achieve its aim if encased in a rigid framework. That said, the outcome of the argument depends upon the proper interpretation of the section. It is obvious that, since the court cannot infer there would be unfairness without having regard to all the circumstances, there are in our judgment two aspects, rather than two stages, to the exercise of the power, namely consideration of the circumstances and assessment of their impact on fairness....Under section 78 any circumstance which can reasonably have a bearing on fairness should be considered. The weight to be attached to an individual circumstance may increase or decrease because of the presence of other related or unrelated circumstances. The preponderance of all the circumstances may show that the admission of the evidence would have such an adverse effect on fairness as to require its exclusion.

This is, inevitably, still a rather vague, if broad ranging, formula. However, case law in the past 20 years has given considerable guidance as to what factors appear to exercise the courts when they consider whether or not the discretion should be applied. Nevertheless, to determine unfairness, it is obviously helpful to have some notion of what is considered to be 'fair'.

Clearly, breaches of domestic and (in some cases) foreign law will often be highly relevant when making a decision on s. 78, as will any breach of Article 6 of the ECHR. Additionally, in *R v Khan* [1996] 3 All ER 289, the Court of Appeal observed that breaches of convention rights under the ECHR *other* than that to a fair trial set out under Article 6, such as the right to privacy set out under Article 8, would also be matters that could be considered when exercising the discretion under s. 78, though they would not be conclusive, any more than an apparent breach of domestic law would automatically be decisive on such a matter. However, much more detail as to what is deemed to be 'fair' is provided by the Codes of Practice issued (and regularly updated) pursuant to s. 66 of the PCEA 1984. In reality, specific breaches of these provisions will often provide much of the 'meat' to applications to exclude prosecution evidence under s. 78 of the PCEA 1984.

The Codes of Practice and Section 78 of the PCEA 1984

Prior to the advent of the Police and Criminal Evidence Act 1984 (PCEA 1984), police powers and responsibilities, whether when patrolling the streets, on arresting and detaining suspects, or when questioning them at police stations, were, as the Royal Commission on Criminal Procedure expressly observed in its 1981 Report, rather confused and unclear. They were governed by a mixture of common law rules and the recommendations contained in the non-binding 'Judges' Rules'. These were judicial guidelines on 'good' police practice; they were periodically issued from 1911 onwards, with the last set coming out in 1964. One of the aims of the Royal Commission was to codify and clarify the law pertaining to policing in many relevant areas and to regulate more precisely what officers should, and should not, do in most given situations. Additionally, the Commission wished to enhance safeguards for those detained and/or questioned by the police. In this regard, the impact of the 1984 Act has been very significant in the more than 20 years that have passed since it came into force on 1 January 1986.

To meet this perceived need, Codes of Practice, which provide relatively clear guidance for police conduct in a variety of areas, such as the detention, questioning, and identification of detained suspects, the searching of premises and persons, etc. are issued pursuant to s. 66 of the Act (it also extends to bodies such as the Customs and Excise). The Codes are updated periodically to take account of changing conditions. Breaches of the Codes are themselves specifically admissible in evidence under s. 67(11) of the Act, and can be considered by the courts when determining questions of evidential admissibility or exclusion, whether under the general discretion contained in s. 78, or a more specific provision like s. 76 (which deals with the admissibility of confessions; see chapter 6).

Amongst other things, the seven Codes cover the treatment of those arrested by the police. Thus, and inter alia, their accommodation and nutrition, provision of rest, refreshment and the right of access to free legal advice are all regulated by Code C. The acoustic recording and (increasingly) the video-taping of their police interviews are governed by Code E and Code F (respectively). The identification of suspects, including the correct way for holding identification procedures, is regulated by Code D. So extensive are these provisions that some judicial (and much police) comment has suggested that the balance of the investigative process may have tipped too far towards the suspect, though this has been challenged by many academic observers and defence lawyers.[6] Some of the detail of the codes of practice can be seen in the following very short extract, taken from Code C, regulating aspects of police detention and interviews.

Police and Criminal Evidence Act 1984—Code of Practice C, July 2006

12 INTERVIEWS IN POLICE STATIONS

(a) Action

12.1 If a police officer wants to interview or conduct enquiries which require the presence of a detainee, the custody officer is responsible for deciding whether to deliver the detainee into the officer's custody.

12.2 Except as below, in any period of 24 hours a detainee must be allowed a continuous period of at least 8 hours for rest, free from questioning, travel or any interruption in connection with the investigation concerned. This period should normally be at night or other appropriate time which takes account of when the detainee last slept or rested. If a detainee is arrested at a police station after going there voluntarily, the period of 24 hours runs from the time of their arrest and not the time of arrival at the police station. The period may not be interrupted or delayed, except [a number of exceptions follow] . . .

12.3 Before a detainee is interviewed the custody officer, in consultation with the officer in charge of the investigation and appropriate health care professionals as necessary, shall assess whether the detainee is fit enough to be interviewed. This means determining and considering the risks to the detainee's physical and mental state if the interview took place and determining what safeguards are needed to allow the interview to take place. See Annex G. The custody officer shall not allow a detainee to be interviewed if the custody officer considers it would cause significant

---

[6] See, for example, speech on the 'Balance of Fairness' by the then Lord Chief Justice, Lord Lane, in *R v Alladice* [1988] 87 Cr App R 380.

harm to the detainee's physical or mental state. Vulnerable suspects listed at paragraph 11.18 shall be treated as always being at some risk during an interview and these persons may not be interviewed except in accordance with paragraphs 11.18 to 11.20.

12.4 As far as practicable interviews shall take place in interview rooms which are adequately heated, lit and ventilated.

Interpretation of Section 78

At first, there was considerable confusion as to whether s. 78 went any further than the discretion to exclude evidence at common law (preserved by s. 82(3) of the PCEA 1984). Indeed, in *Mason,* Watkins LJ opined that the new statutory provision did 'no more than to restate the power which judges had at common law before the 1984 Act was passed'.

However, this interpretation was swiftly abandoned. The Act is a codifying statute, and so can be interpreted in its own terms, independent of previous common law decisions: *R v Samuel* [1988] 2 All ER 135. It is quite clear that s. 78 goes considerably beyond the restrictive position reached in *Sang.* Thus, in *R v Smurthwaite* [1994] 1 All ER 898 undercover police officers posing as contract killers were solicited to carry out a murder. Dismissing an appeal against conviction, it was held that s. 78 had not altered the substantive rule of law that entrapment or the use of an *agent provocateur* does not *per se* afford a defence in law to a criminal charge. However, the court went on to note: '. . . that is not to say that entrapment, agent provocateur or the use of a trick are irrelevant to the application of s. 78'. This was obviously a departure from the post-*Sang* common law position, in most situations.

An analysis of decided cases leads to the identification of certain factors as being important in the application of s. 78, although balancing them is sometimes like the children's game of 'Scissors, Paper, Stone'; each factor trumping another in certain circumstances. Additionally, their relative significance appears to have waxed and waned over the past 20 years. In essence, however, they seem to include: the presence or absence of 'bad faith', ie deliberate misconduct or trickery on the part of the investigating authorities; the degree of impropriety shown by the authorities, whether deliberate or not, which will often, but not invariably, be in the form of breaches of PCEA 1984 and its attendant Codes of Practice, some other area of the substantive criminal or civil law, or of the ECHR; and the effect of the impropriety on the outcome of the case, that is, did it make a practical difference?

When exercising the discretion, the courts also appear to have a variety of aims, even if they are sometimes undeclared. Frequently, s. 78 is exercised to prevent the adduction of potentially unreliable or 'prejudicial' evidence. At other times, it is utilized to ensure fairness to the defendant, to uphold his rights or to preserve the integrity and public reputation of the criminal justice system. Very occasionally, it appears that the section is being tacitly employed to serve a disciplinary function with regard to the police, preventing them from benefiting from their misconduct, even though such a use for s. 78 has also been clearly and expressly rejected by the Court of Appeal on several occasions: *R v Keenan* [1990] 2 QB 54.

Thus, and for example, where the police are deliberately deceitful, or are well aware of their wrongdoing, manifest, for example, in a conscious and deliberate violation of the PCEA 1984, their 'bad faith' might result in, or contribute to, the exclusion of evidence under s. 78. A clear example of this occurred in *R v Mason* [1987] 3 All ER 481, where the police pretended that the defendant's fingerprints had been found on the glass fragments of a petrol bomb, after he was arrested on suspicion of committing the offence of arson, thus inducing a confession. This was subsequently held not to be admissible. By contrast, in the case of *R v Alladice* [1988] Crim LR 608, where a confession was (quite exceptionally) admitted, despite the wrongful refusal of access to a solicitor (contrary to s. 58 and Code C of the PCEA 1984), the Court of Appeal, when approving the first instance judge's decision to allow the evidence to be adduced, noted that there was no indication of bad faith in the case, and commented that: '… if the police had acted in bad faith, the Court would have had little difficulty in ruling any confession inadmissible under s 78'.

Nevertheless, it appears to be necessary to distinguish malpractice outside the criminal justice system from that perpetrated by a law enforcement agency, at least to some degree. For example, journalists behaving as *agents provocateurs* in encouraging drugs offences by dressing up as Arab sheiks seeking cocaine from minor celebrities, for subsequent exposure in a popular newspaper, are not necessarily considered to be in quite the same situation as policemen, whose misbehaviour could undermine public confidence in the criminal justice system. A higher standard of conduct is expected of officers: *R v Hardwick and Thwaites* (2000) WL 1629663.

R v Hardwick and Thwaites (2000) WL 1629663, CA

Kennedy LJ

Before we leave the decision in Latif it is of some importance to note that what the court seeks not to condone is 'malpractice by law enforcement agencies' which 'would undermine public confidence in the criminal justice system and bring it into disrepute'. Obviously that is not a consideration which applies with anything like the same force when the investigator allegedly guilty of malpractice is outside the criminal justice system altogether.

Additionally, the fact that the police, although not acting in bad faith, have obtained evidence as a result of some 'impropriety', albeit inadvertently committed, will be a highly relevant factor in the exercise of s. 78 (often by far the most important factor). As already noted, this impropriety may take the form of a breach of substantive law, convention rights under the ECHR, or a failure to follow the procedures laid down by the PCEA 1984 and its Codes. The more serious the impropriety, the more likely it is that exclusion will follow.

By way of illustration, one of the most important examples of impropriety entails a failure to allow a suspect access to legal advice. Thus, in *R v Samuel* [1988] 2 All ER 135, the defendant was denied access to a solicitor after being charged with burglary. He was then re-interviewed and confessed to a separate robbery. The Court of Appeal held that refusal of access to a solicitor in breach of s. 58 of the PCEA 1984 and Code C was a breach of one of the most important rights of the citizen. Consequently, the judge should have considered whether to exclude the confession under s. 78. His failure to do this meant that the conviction was quashed.

As this case suggests, and as the Court of Appeal expressly noted in *R v Walsh* [1989] 91 Cr App R 161, if there are 'significant and substantial breaches' of s. 58 of the PCEA 1984 (dealing with the right to legal advice) or other provisions of the Codes, then: '… prima facie at least the standards of fairness set by Parliament have not been met'. This might then merit exclusion. Similarly, a failure to caution prior to questioning is always considered to be an exceptionally serious breach of the Codes and will almost always render any ensuing confession inadmissible.

By contrast, minor breaches of the Code are unlikely to lead to evidence being excluded, unless there are aggravating circumstances (such as deliberate police misconduct) or, taken cumulatively, they amount to a grave breach. For example, an inadvertent failure to offer a sus-pect a light refreshment break while he is being questioned by the police is unlikely to lead to the exclusion of any ensuing confession. Such an analysis was also expressly recognized by the Court of Appeal in *R v Keenan* [1990] 2 QB 54, where it was noted that it was clear that: '. . . not every breach or combination of breaches of the code will justify the exclusion of interview evi-dence under s. 76 or s. 78'. The same approach will apply to non-confessional evidence where there has been a breach of the Codes.

In exceptional cases, the courts will look at the practical consequences of any breach, espe-cially where there is no 'bad faith' on the part of the investigating authorities. Very occasion-ally, albeit rarely, the apparent unfairness occasioned by major breaches of the Codes might be rebutted on the facts of a given case. For example, in *R v Alladice* [1988] Crim LR 608, the defendant, who had been convicted of robbery, appealed on the basis that he had made a con-fession after wrongly being refused access to a solicitor. The Court of Appeal accepted that there had been a breach of s. 58 of the PCEA 1984, but nevertheless held that the confession was admissible. This was largely because the defendant's own evidence made it clear that he was well aware of his (then) right to remain silent, and what a solicitor's advice to him would have been (had he been present), and that the absence of a lawyer had made no difference to his actions. The case should certainly not be taken to suggest that defendants with a considerable number of previous convictions can be safely denied access to legal advice.

Pause for reflection

Which of these factors do you consider to be the most important?

Unsurprisingly, given the apparent vagueness as to its interpretation, some observers have called for a 'structured overhaul' of s. 78, one that would identify more clearly the significant factors to which magistrates and judges should attach importance when exercising the discre-tion, and their aims in doing so. Against this, such a change might inhibit judicial freedom to apply the provision in a flexible manner, although its versatility has been extremely important over the last two decades in dealing with changing conditions and novel situations.[7]

Section 78 and Entrapment

Until recently, entrapment cases were a crucial field for the exercise of the s. 78 discretion. A mass of cases, over the years, had indicated a range of matters that the courts would con-sider as relevant when determining the degree of unfairness involved in such situations, and whether it warranted exclusion under s. 78. These included: how active or passive the police officers' role in obtaining the evidence had been; whether they were acting in such a way as to entice the defendant into committing an offence that he would otherwise not have carried out or merely giving him the opportunity to offend; how well supported was their evidence by other material?

---

[7] D Ormerod and D Birch, 'The Evolution of the Discretionary Exclusion of Evidence' [2004] Crim LR 138–159, at 157–158.

However, all cases ultimately turned on their own facts, making generalizations difficult. Thus, in *R v Christou* [1992] 1 QB 979, it was stressed by the Court of Appeal, in a case involving a bogus jeweller's shop, established by the police to attract those selling stolen items, that in this situation, the: '... trick was not applied to the appellants; they voluntarily applied themselves to the trick. It is not every trick producing evidence against an accused which results in unfairness.'

As this suggests, many police 'tricks' or ruses are deemed to be acceptable. For example, in *Nottingham City Council v Amin* [2000] 1 WLR 1071, plainclothes officers had invited a taxi driver to take them to a destination, outside the terms of his licence, without disclosing their identity. He did so willingly, without any cajoling, and it was held that the officers' evidence was not to be excluded as that of *agents provocateurs*. In like manner, in *Williams* v *DPP* [1993] 3 All ER 365, the police left a van unattended and open with dummy cartons of cigarettes on view. Anyone who attempted to steal the cartons was arrested and prosecuted. The Court of Appeal accepted that although there was an element of trickery involved in this ruse, the evidence was admissible, as those convicted were: '... tempted but not persuaded by any words or pressure on the part of the police'. The appellants stole the cigarettes because of 'their own criminal instincts'.

Other cases, such as *R v Shannon* (2001) 1 WLR 51, confirmed that the fact that an offence had been committed at the behest of an *agent provocateur*, would not be sufficient, *per se*, to justify exclusion under s. 78. As these cases suggest, a key question was whether the conduct of the undercover police officer did more than provide an opportunity to offend. In *Shannon*, the defendant had appealed against his conviction for supplying cocaine and cannabis to a journalist posing as an Arab sheikh, as had occurred in *R v Hardwick and Thwaites* (2000) WL 1629663. At a *voir dire* held prior to trial the first instance judge ruled against a defence application to exclude all the prosecution evidence on the ground that it was unfairly obtained contrary to s. 78 and Article 6(1) of the ECHR. This was upheld on appeal, partly on the basis that although the defendants may have been enticed into committing offences, they were certainly not pressured to do so. (Like *Hardwick and Thwaites* the case also indicates that the standards expected of police officers do not necessarily apply where members of the public have instigated the entrapment.)

By contrast, if a youth of low intelligence and previous good character, who urgently needed money to fund his family, had been approached by undercover officers, posing as his friends, who, over a period of time, and despite his initial reluctance, had gradually enticed and cajoled him into seeking to obtain drugs for them from other residents on the rough council estate in which he lived, perhaps providing money up front, promising much more, and suggesting where he might look for a dealer, the evidence would very likely be excluded under s. 78.

Entrapment and Abuse of Process

It should be noted that the recent trend on entrapment cases has been to consider them under abuse of process principles, rather than to focus on s. 78 and the exclusion of evidence. If the courts do decide that, as a result of the action of an *agent provocateur*, allowing a case to proceed would constitute an abuse of process, because it would constitute an affront to the public conscience or offend ordinary notions of fairness, the entire proceedings will be stayed, on the basis that the accused person should not be tried at all, rather than the courts merely excluding aspects of the evidence under s. 78 at trial: *R v Looseley* [2001] 1 WLR 2060.

However, if an application to stay proceedings is refused, or not made at all, it will not preclude an application at trial to exclude individual pieces of evidence under s. 78. Nevertheless, it appears that the courts will treat the two in a similar fashion, if their effect is the same; ie if police misconduct is bad enough to warrant exclusion under s. 78, it will usually warrant staying proceedings as an abuse of process (assuming the evidence is central to the case), and vice versa, making applications under s. 78 unlikely to be successful if one has already failed under abuse of process principles. However, if the contested evidence is more peripheral, there might still be a role for exclusion under s. 78. Additionally, some observers have concluded that, as a mechanism that is primarily used to address misuse of state power, the abuse of process doctrine is inapplicable in cases of private entrapment. It is argued that this leaves exclusion of evidence under s. 78 as the only possible remedy (even if not one that the courts will necessarily employ).[8]

Looseley, and the conjoined referral for consideration by the House of Lords of the *Attorney-General's Reference (No 3 of 2000)*, also suggest that the current interpretation placed on the application of s. 78 is thought, by domestic courts, to be convention compliant under Article 6 of the ECHR. This means that if the challenged evidence could survive an application to exclude it under s. 78 its adduction would normally not violate Article 6 either. Many of the factors enunciated in earlier cases on s. 78 (some of which have already been discussed) still appear relevant to abuse of process applications, especially the crucial question as to whether a law enforcement officer has done no more than provide the defendant with an unexceptional opportunity to offend, of which he has freely taken advantage.

R v Looseley [2001] 1 WLR 2060, HL

Lord Nicholls

Accordingly, one has to look elsewhere for assistance in identifying the limits to the types of police conduct which, in any set of circumstances, are acceptable. On this a useful guide is to consider whether the police did no more than present the defendant with an unexceptional opportunity to commit a crime. I emphasise the word 'unexceptional'. The yardstick for the purpose of this test is, in general, whether the police conduct preceding the commission of the offence was no more than might have been expected from others in the circumstances. Police conduct of this nature is not to be regarded as inciting or instigating crime, or luring a person into committing a crime. The police did no more than others could be expected to do. The police did not create crime artificially. McHugh J had this approach in mind in Ridgeway v The Queen 184 CLR 19, 92, when he said:

> 'The state can justify the use of entrapment techniques to induce the commission of an offence only when the inducement is consistent with the ordinary temptations and stratagems that are likely to be encountered in the course of criminal activity. That may mean that some degree of deception, importunity and even threats on the part of the authorities may be acceptable. But once the state goes beyond the ordinary, it is likely to increase the incidence of crime by artificial means.'

24 This is by no means the only factor to be taken into account when assessing the propriety of police conduct. The investigatory technique of providing an opportunity to commit a crime touches upon other sensitive areas. Of its nature this technique is intrusive, to a greater or lesser degree, depending on the facts. It should not be applied in a random fashion, and used

---

[8] K Hofmeyr, 'The Problem of Private Entrapment' [2006] Crim LR 319–336, at 335–336.

for wholesale 'virtue-testing', without good reason. The greater the degree of intrusiveness, the closer will the court scrutinise the reason for using it. On this, proportionality has a role to play.

25 Ultimately the overall consideration is always whether the conduct of the police or other law enforcement agency was so seriously improper as to bring the administration of justice into disrepute. Lord Steyn's formulation of a prosecution which would affront the public conscience is substantially to the same effect: see R v Latif [1996] 1 WLR 104, 112. So is Lord Bingham of Cornhill CJ's reference to conviction and punishment which would be deeply offensive to ordinary notions of fairness: see Nottingham City Council v Amin [2000] 1 WLR 1071, 1076. In applying these formulations the court has regard to all the circumstances of the case. The following comments may be made on some circumstances which are of particular relevance.

26 The nature of the offence. The use of pro-active techniques is more needed and, hence, more appropriate, in some circumstances than others. The secrecy and difficulty of detection, and the manner in which the particular criminal activity is carried on, are relevant considerations.

27 The reason for the particular police operation. It goes without saying that the police must act in good faith and not, for example, as part of a malicious vendetta against an individual or group of individuals. Having reasonable grounds for suspicion is one way good faith may be established, but having grounds for suspicion of a particular individual is not always essential. Sometimes suspicion may be centred on a particular place, such as a particular public house. Sometimes random testing may be the only practicable way of policing a particular trading activity.

28 The nature and extent of police participation in the crime. The greater the inducement held out by the police, and the more forceful or persistent the police overtures, the more readily may a court conclude that the police overstepped the boundary: their conduct might well have brought about commission of a crime by a person who would normally avoid crime of that kind. In assessing the weight to be attached to the police inducement, regard is to be had to the defendant's circumstances, including his vulnerability. This is not because the standards of acceptable behaviour are variable. Rather, this is a recognition that what may be a significant inducement to one person may not be so to another. For the police to behave as would an ordinary customer of a trade, whether lawful or unlawful, being carried on by the defendant will not normally be regarded as objectionable.

29 The defendant's criminal record. The defendant's criminal record is unlikely to be relevant unless it can be linked to other factors grounding reasonable suspicion that the defendant is currently engaged in criminal activity. As Frankfurter J said, past crimes do not forever outlaw the criminal and open him to police practices, aimed at securing repeated convictions, from which the ordinary citizen is protected: see Sherman v United States 356 US 369, 383.

THE HUMAN RIGHTS CONVENTION

30 The question raised by Attorney General's Reference (No 3 of 2000) is whether, in a case involving the commission of an offence by an accused at the instigation of undercover police officers, the judicial discretion conferred by section 78 of the Police and Criminal Evidence Act 1984 or the court's power to stay proceedings as an abuse of the court has been modified by article 6 of the European Convention for the Protection of Human Rights and Fundamental Freedoms and the jurisprudence of the European Court of Human Rights. I would answer that question in the negative. I do not discern any appreciable difference between the requirements of article 6, or the Strasbourg jurisprudence on article 6, and English law as it has developed in recent years and as I have sought to describe it.

As the above criteria suggest, both staying proceedings for abuse of process and excluding evidence under s. 78 is always a matter of degree, dependent on the facts of the individual case. This can also be seen from the circumstances of *R v Lewis* [2005] Crim LR 796, in which the defendant was accused of possessing counterfeit currency. His defence was that he had been entrapped into doing so by undercover police officers requesting that he obtain fake cash. The trial judge refused to either exclude the evidence under s. 78 or stay the proceedings as an abuse of process, after which the defendant pleaded guilty. He appealed to the ECtHR, which found that there had been a breach of Article 6, in the failure to provide sufficient identification of the police officers involved at trial, but which also concluded that this did not necessarily make the conviction unsafe and refused to award compensation. Subsequently, the Court of Appeal dismissed the defendant's appeal, reiterating that entrapment did not necessarily give rise to an abuse of process, and noting that, in the instant case, the defendant had not suggested that any undue pressure had been brought to bear on him by the undercover officers, whether when interviewed by the police or at court.

Section 78 in Other Situations

Of course, the exclusion of evidence under s. 78 goes very much further than entrapment cases, as it applies to all prosecution evidence. For example, it was considered, in another context, in *R v Khan (Sultan)* [1996] 3 All ER 289. In this case, two men (who were cousins) had arrived from Pakistan, on the same flight, one of them carrying heroin. The one who was not carrying the drug was released, the other detained at the airport. However, the police subsequently attached a listening device (by a civil trespass) to a house in which the freed man was staying. A conversation was then recorded, in which he incriminated himself in the heroin importation. When the trial judge, after argument on the *voir dire*, decided to admit this evidence, the appellant changed his plea to guilty, but appealed on the basis that the evidence of the recording should not have been admitted, and that without it there was no prosecution case against him. The appeal raised two issues. First, was the evidence legally admissible at all, and secondly, if admissible, should it have been excluded by the judge in the exercise of his discretion, whether under common law or s. 78 of the PCEA 1984?

Unsurprisingly, the first point was swiftly dismissed, as it would have required a major change to the position reached in *R v Sang* [1980] AC 402 to do otherwise. Evidence obtained improperly or even unlawfully remains legally admissible. The second issue, should the judge have exercised his discretion to exclude it, was rather less straightforward. In the House of Lords, it was argued for the Crown that the trespass (it was not the defendant's house), any damage occasioned by it, and any potential breach of Article 8 of the ECHR (this issue not being entirely clear) were not sufficient to outweigh the factors militating for admitting the evidence. In particular, no crime was incited, no deliberate deceit was practised on the defendant and no oppression, misleading information or pressure was applied to him to make him speak. There was also a clear taped record of what had occurred, which was highly cogent evidence. The House of Lords agreed with these submissions, and noted that the appropriate Home Office guidelines had also been followed. Additionally, the offences being investigated were of 'great gravity', a factor that the courts also appear to put into the balance in s. 78 applications. As a result, the court had no hesitation in agreeing with the trial judge that the evidence was rightly admitted.

   Pause for reflection

To what extent, if at all, do you consider that the gravity of an allegation should be a factor influencing a decision to exercise the judicial discretion to exclude evidence?

However, the House of Lords did accept that if evidence had been obtained in circumstances that involved an apparent breach of Article 8 (respect for private life), or, for that matter, a breach of the law of a foreign country, such breaches would be potentially relevant to the exercise of the s. 78 discretion. However, the significance of such matters would normally be determined not so much by their apparent irregularity, but by their effect upon the overall fairness of the proceedings. In the instant case, the judge was fully entitled to hold that the circumstances in which the relevant evidence was obtained, even if they constituted a breach of Article 8, were not such as to require the exclusion of the evidence. Interestingly, Khan made no complaint that his right under Article 6 (1) of the ECHR to a fair trial had been infringed. This may have been because the ECtHR had, several years earlier, rejected a complaint brought under that provision by a defendant against whom an unlawfully obtained recording of a telephone conversation had been used in evidence: *Schenk v Switzerland* [1988] 13 EHRR 242.

In *R v Loveridge* [2001] 2 Cr App R 29, the applicants were convicted of robbing a post office. They had been recorded on CCTV film in a Fiesta motor vehicle, at a petrol station about an hour and a half before the robbery took place. The prosecution alleged that, having committed the robbery, the two male applicants abandoned another vehicle and met up with the female applicant, who was waiting for them in the same Fiesta. When the applicants were in custody at a Magistrates' Court, the police, without their knowledge, allowed them to be filmed by video camera, with a view to enabling comparison to be made with the pictures taken earlier by the CCTV cameras, and so to connect them with the robbery. At trial, the film was admitted in evidence and used for comparison.

The applicants appealed against conviction on the ground that the video evidence contravened s. 41 of the Criminal Justice Act 1925, which prohibits the taking of photographs in court, and so should have been excluded under s. 78 of the PCEA 1984, because it was obtained unfairly. Additionally, it was argued that filming them constituted a breach of the men's right to privacy as laid down in Article 8 of the ECHR. Nevertheless, their appeal was dismissed. Although filming the applicants in the Magistrates' Court was unlawful, the videotape evidence was held to be admissible because it did not have such an adverse effect on the fairness of the proceedings that it should have been excluded under s. 78. Article 8 of the ECHR had been contravened, because of the breach of the right to privacy, but, although such behaviour was undesirable, the contravention was only relevant to the appeal if it interfered with applicants' right to a fair trial, which, the Court of Appeal concluded, had not occurred in the instant case.

R v Loveridge [2001] 2 Cr App R 29, CA

Lord Woolf CJ

As we have already pointed out, the filming was contrary to law. We therefore have no hesitation in coming to the conclusion that in the circumstances of this case there has been a breach of Article 8. However, so far as the outcome of this appeal is concerned, the breach of Article 8 is only relevant if it interferes with the right of the applicants to a fair hearing. Giving full weight to the breach of the Convention, we are satisfied that the contravention of Article 8 did not interfere with the fairness of the hearing. The judge was entitled to rule as he did. The position is the same so far as section 78 of the Police and Criminal Evidence Act 1984 is concerned. We would here refer to the judgment of Swinton Thomas L.J. in the case of Perry, The Times April 28, 2000.

As this case suggests, where the courts have considered breaches of Article 8 of the ECHR, when deciding whether to admit evidence, it has usually been on the basis that such a breach might also result in a violation of the right to a fair trial under Article 6(1). In many cases, it seems that an award of damages, rather than the exclusion of evidence, would be considered the appropriate remedy for such a convention breach. The courts appear reluctant, if not positively unwilling, to exclude evidence for breach of Article 8 *per se*. Thus, in *R v Button* [2005] Crim LR 571, (accidentally) unauthorized video-surveillance of potential witnesses to a murder, conducted at a police-station, was subsequently admitted at their trial for the same crime, and the decision upheld on appeal, even though it was accepted that their right to privacy had been breached.

Similarly, in *R v Rosenberg* [2006] Crim LR 540, covert filmed surveillance of a neighbour by a member of the public, revealing that the neighbour was a drug dealer, but which may have infringed his right to privacy under Article 8 of the ECHR, was held admissible for the Crown in a prosecution for dealing in proscribed drugs. The degree of police involvement, or its absence, was considered a legitimate factor in deciding whether to exclude evidence under s. 78 of the PCEA 1984 and, in the instant case, the police had neither encouraged nor initiated the video-taped surveillance.

As some of these cases might also suggest, the Court of Appeal adopts a relatively high threshold before interfering with a trial judge's decision as to the exercise of his discretion under s. 78. It is not enough that the appeal judges might have exercised the discretion in a different manner. Normally, they will only substitute their own judgment if that of the trial judge comes within the realm of '*Wednesbury* unreasonableness', namely that the purported exercise of the discretionary power was so unreasonable that no reasonable court could have exercised it in that way or, alternatively, the trial judge took account of irrelevant considerations (such as an earlier, and out of date, version of the Codes of Practice), or ignored relevant ones. In these situations the Court of Appeal will substitute its own discretion for that of the first instance judge.[9]

It should be noted that there are several, very specific exclusionary discretions, contained in various statutes, allowing a trial judge to exclude certain types of specialist evidence in criminal cases. For example, s. 101(3) of the Criminal Justice Act 2003 allows a trial judge to refuse to admit evidence of defendant bad character that would otherwise be admissible under s. 101(1)(d) and (g). Its wording is very similar to that of s. 78 of the PCEA 1984. However, these provisions will be dealt with in subsequent chapters, in the context of the type of evidence to which they relate.

 Summary

- Occasionally, in both criminal and civil cases, admissible and relevant evidence can be excluded by an exercise of judicial discretion. This is exceptionally unusual in civil matters, but more commonly encountered in criminal cases.

- In civil cases this discretion is a consequence of the interpretation of the wording of r. 32.1 of the CPR 1998.

- In criminal cases, a narrow discretion to exclude evidence that was more prejudicial than probative and confession evidence obtained by underhand methods, developed at common law, and is

[9] The term comes from the leading case on this area of the law, *Associated Provincial Picture Houses Ltd v Wednesbury Corporation* [1948] 1 KB 223.

preserved in the modern era by dint of s. 82(3) of the PCEA 1984. There is no general discretion at common law to exclude improperly obtained evidence.

- More importantly, in criminal matters, is the discretion contained in s. 78 of the PCEA 1984, which allows a judge to exclude prosecution evidence if adducing it would have such an adverse effect on the fairness of the proceedings that it ought not to be admitted.

- Such a discretion might be exercised because, for example, the evidence is considered more prejudicial than probative (this discretion also existing at common law) or because it has been obtained in a seriously 'improper' manner, even if the latter was inadvertent.

- Substantive law, Articles of the ECHR, and, very importantly, breaches of the Codes of Practice issued pursuant to s. 66 of the PCEA 1984, provide indications as to what behaviour (especially by the police or other investigating authorities) might be considered 'improper'.

- At one point, the exercise of s. 78 was frequently considered with regard to entrapment cases. However, in recent years, it is more common for such cases to be dealt with under abuse of process principles, the whole prosecution sometimes being stayed, rather than for individual pieces of evidence being excluded for entrapment.

 ## Further reading

Mike Redmayne, 'The Structure of Evidence Law' (2006) Oxford Journal of Legal Studies, vol 26, no 4, 805–822

Alex Stein, *Foundations of Evidence Law* (2005, Oxford University Press)

Laird C Kirkpatrick, 'Evidence Law in the Next Millennium' (1998) Hastings Law Journal, issue 49, 363–368, at 363

David Ormerod and Diane Birch, 'The Evolution of the Discretionary Exclusion of Evidence' [2004] Crim LR 38–159

Eleanor Swift, 'One Hundred Years of Evidence Law Reform: Thayer's Triumph' (2000) California Law Review, issue 88, 2000, at 2443–2445

 ## Questions for Discussion

1. What principles, if any, govern the situations in which s. 78 of the Police and Criminal Evidence Act of 1984 (PCEA 1984) will be employed to exclude evidence? How have these been affected, if at all, by the Human Rights Act 1998?

2. Whilst answering a claimant's correspondence in relation to a civil action against their company, for breach of contract, Adam and Barbara, directors of Hammersmith Financial Management Ltd. ('the company'), accidentally reveal information that suggests the possibility of their having perpetrated a serious fraud. Caroline, the claimant's solicitor, quickly passes on a copy of the letter to the police. Afraid that Adam and Barbara might destroy evidence of the alleged fraud, PC Dennis and PC Edmund decide not to delay taking action by obtaining a search warrant, and immediately visit the company's offices, which they find to be locked. Dennis and Edmund then (unlawfully) break down a door to enter the premises, where, after an extensive search, they find no evidence of fraud, but do discover several new laser printers, which they think might have been stolen. As a result, Dennis takes one of them to the police station to check its serial number, while Edmund immediately goes to the homes of Adam and Barbara

For suggested approaches, please visit the Online Resource Centre

and arrests them. The printers do turn out to be stolen, but Adam and Barbara claim they knew nothing about them (they were discovered in a loft space in the office), until Dennis untruthfully says that Barbara's fingerprints have been found on them, and repeats this claim to their solicitors, whereupon Adam confesses. Adam has several previous convictions for theft. Meanwhile, a friend of the claimant has obtained important information relating to the civil action by posing as a chimney sweep and browsing around the premises after being let into the company's office to clean a flue.

Advise Adam and Barbara as to any evidential issues raised in the civil proceedings and also with respect to the criminal trial, for handling stolen goods, which they also subsequently face, and to which charge both plead 'not guilty'.

3. Fiona is suing George, a physiotherapist, for negligently injuring her while giving her a back massage. She says that her injuries mean that she can no longer bend down. However, George disputes the extent of her injuries and his solicitors employ Helen, an enquiry agent, to carry out an investigation. Helen gains entry to Fiona's garden by claiming to be from the Water Board and saying that she needs to survey underground pipes. She hides behind a bush, and stays in the garden for an hour; while there, she watches Fiona dig an entire potato bed. George wants to call Helen to give oral evidence, as to what she saw, at trial. Fiona argues that this is unfair and asks the judge to exclude the evidence.

Advise the parties as to any evidential issues raised on the above facts.

4. What are the advantages and disadvantages of having rigid exclusionary rules for certain types of evidence, when compared to granting a general exclusionary discretion to a trial judge?

5. DC Hard, while operating undercover, becomes familiar with Idris, an unemployed labourer with a back problem, whose wife is pestering him to take the family on a holiday to Spain. After a short acquaintanceship, Hard asks Idris if he can obtain for him some crack cocaine. Idris, who has no previous convictions, initially refuses to do this, but Hard cajoles him for several weeks, promising him a substantial financial reward if he does so, until he yields. When Idris next meets Hard with a quantity of the drug, he is arrested and prosecuted for possession with intent to supply.

Advise Idris.

3 THE BURDEN AND STANDARD OF PROOF

Definitions

Legal burden The obligation placed on a party to litigation to establish certain facts in issue, such that s/he will fail on that issue if s/he does not prove them to the relevant standard.

Evidential burden The obligation to make an issue 'live' by calling some tangible evidence on it, so that the tribunal of fact is obliged to decide whether one of the parties has satisfied a legal burden on that issue.

Reverse onus burden A legal burden that is placed on a defendant in a criminal trial, contrary to the normal position which places such burdens on the Crown.

'Golden thread of English justice' The general principle that legal burdens in criminal cases are on the Crown, not on the defendant, subject to a number of specific exceptions.

'Satisfied so that you are sure' The most common definition of the standard of proof on the prosecution in criminal cases.

'Satisfied beyond reasonable doubt' Alternative and traditional definition of the standard placed on the prosecution.

'Balance of probabilities' The standard of proof in civil cases, and also on criminal defendants (in those situations where they carry a legal burden).

---

1. Introduction

This area of the law is fraught with terminological difficulties, which require some early explanation to facilitate comprehension. As the word suggests, a 'burden' puts an obligation of some kind on the party on which it rests. There are three separate uses of the word in the law of evidence, namely: the legal, evidential and tactical burdens. Only the first two have 'academic' and formal legal significance. As will be seen, the tactical burden is purely a practitioner's concept and largely a matter of common sense. Because these concepts are so intertwined, and to facilitate comprehension, it may be advisable to first read through this chapter in outline, before going through it in more detail.

Legal (but not evidential) burdens have to be satisfied to a certain standard, ie evidence of sufficient cogency or weight must be called to persuade the tribunal of fact to a designated level. This is the realm of 'standard of proof'. Standards of proof can differ, depending on the forum in which a case is heard, the party to proceedings and even, in practice, the nature of the allegation.

However, before a tribunal of fact even has to consider whether a legal burden has been satisfied, there must be some tangible evidence that requires it to address its (collective) mind to that issue, just as the judges in a championship boxing match will only have to consider whether the challenger has wrested the title on points if he gets off his stool and is still on his feet when the final bell goes (though achieving this feat certainly does not mean that they will necessarily declare him the winner). This is the province of evidential burdens.

As was noted in chapter 1, all litigation can be broken down into discrete issues (the essential elements of an offence/cause of action, etc.). The party that bears a legal burden on such an issue is the party that will fail on that matter if they do not establish it to the appropriate standard of proof. Thus, the allocation of the burden of proof will decide who bears the risk of losing on an issue (and the case overall). It is for this reason that the legal burden is sometimes termed the 'risk of non-persuasion'.

Strictly speaking, it is a mistake to talk about the burden of proof in a case as a whole, as it can differ between separate issues decided at the same trial. Nevertheless, some generalizations are possible. For example, in a criminal trial, the Crown has the legal burden of proving all the essential elements of the prosecuted offence's *mens rea* and *actus reus*. If it fails to achieve this, it will lose on those issues, and thus also lose on the prosecution overall. In a civil case, such as an action for negligence, the claimant normally has the burden of proof on the essential matters (duty, breach and non-remote damage); if he fails to satisfy this burden, he will lose in his action. The legal burden has acquired a number of other, more rarely used names; amongst them are the 'ultimate burden' and the 'persuasive burden'.

The easiest way to decide where a legal burden lies is to ask which party in the given case will lose on an issue if no evidence at all, from either side, is called on it. Thus, if the prosecution in a theft case does not call any evidence to show that the property that forms the subject of the charge 'belong[ed] to another' it will lose on that issue (and the case overall). By contrast, if the defendant fails to call any evidence at all on this issue he will not necessarily be convicted, as he does not have a legal burden with regard to it. Similarly, in an action for breach of contract, if no evidence is called that a contract ever existed, the claimant will lose on that matter (and, again, the case overall).

2. Legal Burdens in Criminal Matters

Introduction

Generally speaking, and as already indicated, the legal burden in a criminal case is on the prosecution. This is an essential part of the presumption of innocence, and has been a much cherished maxim of English law for several centuries.

Bruce P Smith, 'The Presumption of Innocence and the English Law of Theft: 1750–1850' (2005) Law and History Review, vol 23, no 1, 133–173, at 133

No principle in Anglo-American criminal law is more vaunted than the so-called 'presumption of innocence': the doctrine that the prosecution must both *produce* evidence of guilt and *persuade* the fact-finder 'beyond a reasonable doubt'. The claim that 'every man is presumed to be innocent until he is proved guilty' has been described as 'dear to the hearts of Englishmen' and as an omnipresent feature of English criminal law. In 1895, the United States Supreme Court declared the 'presumption of innocence in favor of the accused' to be 'the undoubted law, axiomatic and elementary'—a protection that 'lies at the foundation of the administration of our criminal law'. Befitting its lofty stature in Anglo-American legal culture, the presumption has become associated, over time, with that most famous of Blackstonean maxims: '[I]t is better that ten guilty persons escape, than that one innocent suffer.'

The 'Golden Thread'

In a celebrated passage in *Woolmington v DPP* [1935] AC 462, Lord Sankey identified this maxim as the 'Golden Thread' of English justice. In this case, the defendant, a young farm labourer, had shot and killed his estranged wife. In his defence, he claimed that the weapon had gone off accidentally, while he was threatening to kill himself with it if she did not return to him. At trial, Swift J directed the jury that once the fact of the shooting and ensuing death had been proved, it was for the accused man to persuade the court that it was an accident. On final appeal to the House of Lords, however, the conviction was quashed. Lord Sankey concluded that in English criminal law: '…one golden thread is always to be seen, that it is the duty of the prosecution to prove the prisoner's guilt subject to what I have already said as to the defence of insanity and subject also to any statutory exception'.

This decision put an end to earlier, ambiguous, and conflicting decisions about the legal burden in criminal cases where a defence of accident was run. It was not, as is sometimes thought, an appellate response to a manifestly incompetent trial judge. The first instance judge had merely followed a line of authority premised on the work of the distinguished eighteenth-century jurist, Sir Michael Foster, who had suggested that in murder cases, once the killing had been proved: '…all the circumstances of accident, necessity, or infirmity are to be satisfactorily proved by the prisoner'. However, in *Woolmington*, Lord Sankey pointed out that Foster did not lay down the doctrine in a decided case, but rather in a textbook article. It was, he held, a mistaken view of the law (although it had, by then, been embodied in several colonial evidence codes).

Pause for reflection

Can you think of any arguments for following Sir Michael Foster's approach?

Woolmington v DPP [1935] AC 462, HL

Viscount Sankey LC

If at any period of a trial it was permissible for the judge to rule that the prosecution had established its case and that the onus was shifted on the prisoner to prove that he was not guilty and that unless he discharged that onus the prosecution was entitled to succeed, it would be enabling the judge in such a case to say that the jury must in law find the prisoner guilty and so make the judge decide the case and not the jury, which is not the common law. It would be an entirely different case from those exceptional instances of special verdicts where a judge asks the jury to find certain facts and directs them that on such facts the prosecution is entitled to succeed. Indeed, a consideration of such special verdicts shows that it is not till the end of the evidence that a verdict can properly be found and that at the end of the evidence it is not for the prisoner to establish his innocence, but for the prosecution to establish his guilt. Just as there is evidence on behalf of the prosecution so there may be evidence on behalf of the prisoner which may cause a doubt as to his guilt. In either case, he is entitled to the benefit of the doubt. But while the prosecution must prove the guilt of the prisoner, there is no such burden laid on the prisoner to prove his innocence and it is sufficient for him to raise a doubt as to his guilt; he is not bound to satisfy the jury of his innocence.

This is the real result of the perplexing case of Rex v. Abramovitch, which lays down the same proposition, although perhaps in somewhat involved language. Juries are always told that, if conviction there is to be, the prosecution must prove the case beyond reasonable doubt. This statement cannot mean that in order to be acquitted the prisoner must 'satisfy' the jury. This is the law as laid down in the Court of Criminal Appeal in Rex v. Davies, the head note of which correctly states that where intent is an ingredient of a crime there is no onus on the defendant to prove that the act alleged was accidental. Throughout the web of the English Criminal Law one golden thread is always to be seen, that it is the duty of the prosecution to prove the prisoner's guilt subject to what I have already said as to the defence of insanity and subject also to any statutory exception. If, at the end of and on the whole of the case, there is a reasonable doubt, created by the evidence given by either the prosecution or the prisoner, as to whether the prisoner killed the deceased with a malicious intention, the prosecution has not made out the case and the prisoner is entitled to an acquittal. No matter what the charge or where the trial, the principle that the prosecution must prove the guilt of the prisoner is part of the common law of England and no attempt to whittle it down can be entertained. When dealing with a murder case the Crown must prove (a) death as the result of a voluntary act of the accused and (b) malice of the accused. It may prove malice either expressly or by implication. For malice may be implied where death occurs as the result of a voluntary act of the accused which is (i.) intentional and (ii.) unprovoked. When evidence of death and malice has been given (this is a question for the jury) the accused is entitled to show, by evidence or by examination of the circumstances adduced by the Crown that the act on his part which caused death was either unintentional or provoked. If the jury are either satisfied with his explanation or, upon a review of all the evidence, are left in reasonable doubt whether, even if his explanation be not accepted, the act was unintentional or provoked, the prisoner is entitled to be acquitted. It is not the law of England to say, as was said in the summing-up in the present case: 'if the Crown satisfy you that this woman died at the prisoner's hands then he has to show that there are circumstances to be found in the evidence which has been given from the witness-box in this case which alleviate the crime so that it is only manslaughter or which excuse the homicide altogether by showing it was a pure accident.'

The 'Golden Thread' in the Modern Era

Lord Sankey's enunciation of the 'Golden Thread' is the starting point for considering legal burdens in criminal cases and has been reiterated on several occasions since. Thus, in the belated appeal in the *cause célèbre* involving the 1955 murder trial of Derek Bentley, who was executed for murder, it was held that the presiding judge, the then Lord Chief Justice, Lord Goddard, had failed to ensure that the jury were clearly and unambiguously instructed that the burden of proving the guilt of the accused normally lies only on the Crown, and that (subject to exceptions that were not relevant to the instant case) there was no burden on the accused to prove anything.

R v Derek William Bentley (Deceased) [2001] 1 Cr App R 21, CA

Lord Bingham CJ

Mr Fitzgerald submitted that the trial judge had failed to give the jury a clear direction on the burden of proof, and had indeed reversed the burden by suggesting that there was an onus lying on the appellant and his co-defendant.

In support of this submission Mr Fitzgerald relied first on the passage in the summing-up, already quoted, at page 132C of the transcript. In this passage the trial judge said that it was for the prosecution to prove their case and that it was not for the prisoners to prove their innocence. This was of course a correct and orthodox direction. Mr Fitzgerald, however, submitted that the effect of that direction was undermined by the passage immediately following in which the trial judge suggested that the prosecution had given abundant evidence for a case calling for an answer, and that a case had been established against the defendants, then continuing in effect to consider whether the evidence of the appellant and his co-defendant was such as to rebut that case. Mr Fitzgerald argued that that misdirection was not cured by the later direction, in the passage already quoted at page 138F of the transcript of the summing-up, that it was the duty of the jury to convict if they were satisfied with the evidence for the prosecution. Mr Fitzgerald further argued that the confusion which these directions were bound to leave in the minds of the jury was compounded by additional misdirections given to the jury in relation to the case against Craig. At page 132G of the transcript of the summing-up the trial judge said: 'Now let us take first of all the case of Craig: it is not disputed, and could not be disputed, that he fired the shot which killed that Police Constable. You are asked to say that the killing was accidental, and that therefore the offence is reduced to manslaughter. Gentlemen of the jury, it is the prerogative of the jury in any case where the charge is of murder to find a verdict of manslaughter, but they can only do it if the evidence satisfies them that the case is properly reducible to one of manslaughter—that is, not with regard to any consequence that may happen, but simply whether the facts show that the case ought to be regarded as one of manslaughter and not of murder . . .' Then, at page 133H of the summing-up, the trial judge added: 'In that case the only possible way of reducing the crime to manslaughter is to show that the act was accidental, and not wilful—the act.' These passages, Mr Fitzgerald argued, gave the jury the clear impression that there was a burden on Craig to show that the killing was accidental and that therefore the proper verdict was one of manslaughter and not murder. Mr Sweeney did not accept any of these criticisms. He relied on the opening passage at page 132C of the transcript and the closing passage at page 138F of the transcript to submit that the direction, viewed as a whole, was defensible; and pointed out that the other directions related to Craig, not the appellant. The jury must be clearly and unambiguously instructed that the burden of proving the guilt

> of the accused lies and lies only on the Crown, that (subject to exceptions not here relevant) there is no burden on the accused to prove anything and that if, on reviewing all the evidence, the jury are unsure of or are left in any reasonable doubt as to the guilt of the accused that doubt must be resolved in favour of the accused. Such an instruction has for very many years been regarded as a cardinal requirement of a properly conducted trial. The courts have not been willing to countenance departures from it. We cannot regard the direction in this case as satisfactory. By stressing the abundant evidence calling for an answer in support of the prosecution case, and by suggesting that that case had been 'established', and by suggesting that there was a burden on Craig to satisfy the jury that the killing had been accidental (however little, on the facts of this case, the injustice caused to Craig thereby), the jury in our view could well have been left with the impression that the case against the appellant was proved and that they should convict him unless he had satisfied them of his innocence. We do not regard the earlier direction as cured by the passage at page 138F of the transcript.

This fundamental principle has been neatly embodied in the current Judicial Studies Board specimen direction on burden of proof. These are usually, though not invariably, followed by first instance judges when summing a case up at the end of a trial.

JSB Crown Court Bench Book: Specimen Directions, August 2005: 2.A Burden of proof

In this case the prosecution must prove the defendant is guilty. He does not have to prove his innocence. In a criminal trial the burden of proving the defendant's guilt is on the prosecution.

Exceptions

However, although *Woolmington* decided that, as a *general* rule, the legal burden was always on the Crown, Lord Sankey himself recognized that this was qualified, and that there were two clear exceptions where legal burdens were placed on a defendant (sometimes these are termed 'reverse burdens of proof'); these are: insanity and statutory exceptions. The latter category can be further sub-divided into express and implied statutory exceptions.

Insanity

This is the only common law exception to the 'golden thread', by which a legal burden is placed on a defendant. Although it has been a principle of English law since at least the eighteenth century that an accused person must persuade a tribunal that he is insane, in the modern era it is taken to have been most clearly enunciated by the decision in *Daniel M'Naghten's Case* (1843) 10 Cl & F 200, the trial ensuing from the attempted murder of Sir Robert Peel. In this case, Tindal CJ concluded that all defendants must be presumed sane: '...until the contrary be proved to their [a jury's] satisfaction'. Thus, if a defendant is accused of murder, and wishes to secure a verdict of not guilty by reason of insanity, he must prove to the jury at his trial that he was (legally) insane.

Pause for reflection

Why do you think the legal burden of proving insanity should be placed on a defendant?

Assuming that the prosecution satisfies all of its inherent legal burdens in the case, by proving (beyond reasonable doubt) that the defendant killed the victim with malice aforethought, it will not be enough for the accused to leave the jury with the belief that there is a 'distinct possibility' that he was insane, or even a precisely 50/50 likelihood that this was the case, to secure the sought-after verdict. He must persuade them that it is true (albeit, as will be seen, only on the balance of probabilities and not beyond reasonable doubt).

It should be noted that a defence of automatism, though sometimes exhibiting similarities to that of insanity, normally merely places an evidential burden on the defendant to raise the issue, rather than a legal one to prove it: *Bratty v Attorney-General for Northern Ireland* [1963] AC 386. However, as Devlin J noted in *Hill v Baxter* [1958] 1 QB 277, if the particular nature of the automatism 'amounted to insanity in the legal sense, it is well established that the burden of proof would start with and remain throughout upon the defence'. Because of its drastic consequences, a verdict of not guilty by reason of insanity has only rarely been sought since the abolition of the death penalty for murder. Much more important in practice are statutory derogations from the 'golden thread'. These can be divided into two sorts, express and implied.

Express Statutory Exceptions

Lord Sankey clearly excluded express statutory exceptions from the golden thread. These have been in existence for several centuries, and reflect the sovereignty of the Queen in Parliament. Thus, a plethora of statutes were passed in the latter decades of the 1700s, creating relatively minor offences, that reversed the burden of proof and which allowed the prosecution to secure convictions in circumstances where traditional common law offences, such as larceny, would be difficult to prove. For example, statutes allowed magistrates to convict summarily those who failed to 'account' to an appropriate standard for goods that were in their possession in apparently suspicious circumstances.[1] Express statutory exceptions are identifiable by the language used in the enactment, being revealed by tell-tale phrases such as 'the burden whereof shall be on the defendant', 'it shall be for the defendant to prove', 'it will be assumed...unless the contrary be proved'.

For an obvious example in the modern era, consider the defence of diminished responsibility under s. 2(2) of the Homicide Act 1957, which provides that: 'On a charge of murder, it shall be for the defence to prove that the person charged is by virtue of this section not liable to be convicted of murder.' Another, more frequently encountered, express statutory exception can be found in s. 1 of the Prevention of Crime Act 1953, whereby it is an offence to carry an offensive weapon in a public place: '...without lawful authority or reasonable excuse, the proof whereof shall lie on him'.

Similarly, under s. 139 of the Criminal Justice Act 1988, if a defendant is charged with carrying a knife of certain dimensions in a public place, he commits an offence. It is for the prosecution to prove that he had the knife, that its size and shape were proscribed under the Act, and that the defendant was in a public place. However, s. 139(4) provides that: 'It shall be a defence

---

[1] BP Smith, 'The Presumption of Innocence and the English Law of Theft: 1750–1850' (2005) Law and History Review, vol 23, no 1, 133–173, at 152.

for a person charged with an offence under this section to prove that he had good reason or lawful authority for having the article with him in a public place'. As a result of the wording of this provision, the defences of 'lawful authority' and 'good reason' place a legal burden on the accused, who has the onus of proving that they apply to his case.

There are many other reverse statutory burdens under English law, albeit that some are only rarely encountered. For a more recently enacted example, consider the wording of s. 31 of the Immigration and Asylum Act 1999, 'It is a defence for a refugee...to show', which is deemed to put an express burden on the accused with regard to the defences raised: *R v Makuwa* [2006] Crim LR 911. However, as will be seen, although clearly excluded from the 'golden thread' by Lord Sankey, express statutory exceptions are now subject to the operation of the Human Rights Act 1998 and must be compatible with the European Convention of Human Rights (hereinafter ECHR).

Implied Statutory Exceptions

Somewhat more problematic, when it comes to compatibility with the 'golden thread', is the position with regard to 'implied' statutory exceptions. These have been in existence for at least two hundred years, as can be seen in cases such as *R v Turner* (1816) 5 M & S 206. Indeed, their existence appears to stem back to the petitionary nature of early modern parliamentary legislation, in which those who feared adverse consequences from the principal clause of a new statute would insert saving clauses, and the manner in which these saving clauses were then treated by seventeenth-century courts: *Jones v Axen* (1696) I Lord Raym 119.

Although Lord Sankey did not distinguish between implied and express statutory exceptions to the golden thread in his famous judgment, arguments that implied burdens should not have survived *Woolmington* were firmly rejected in both *R v Edwards* [1975] QB 27 and *R v Hunt* [1987] AC 352. In the latter case, Lord Griffiths observed: 'I cannot accept that either Viscount Sankey LC or Lord Simon LC intended to cast doubt on these long-standing decisions.'

Generally speaking, implied statutory exceptions cover situations in which a statute exempts defendants from criminal liability in certain highly specific situations, without making it expressly clear that the accused must show that he falls within those circumstances (or that the prosecution must prove their absence). Thus in *Turner* the defendant was accused of selling game (pheasants, partridges, hares, etc.) without the appropriate authority or licence. There were at least 10 situations in which selling game would have been quite legal; for example, if he had had a dealer's licence or was a major landowner. The court held that in such cases it was for the accused to show that he fell within one of the exempt categories, rather than for the prosecution to show that he did not. Similarly, in *R v Oliver* [1944] KB 68 the defendant was accused of selling sugar contrary to wartime regulations and authorization. It was held that it was for the defendant to prove that he had been granted a licence to sell sugar.

R v Turner (1816) 5 M & S 206, King's Bench

Lord Ellenborough CJ

The question is, upon whom the onus probandi lies; whether it lies upon the person who affirms a qualification, to prove the affirmative, or upon the informer, who denies any qualification to prove the negative. There are, I think, about ten different heads of qualification enumerated in the statute to which the proof may be applied; and, according to the argument of to-day, every person who lays an information of this sort is bound to give satisfactory evidence before the magistrates to negative the defendant's qualification upon each of those several heads. The argument really comes to this, that there would be a moral impossibility of ever convicting upon such an information. If the informer should establish the negative of any part of these different qualifications, that would be insufficient, because it would be said, non liquet, but that the defendant may be qualified under the other. And does not, then, common sense shew, that the burden of proof ought to be cast on the person, who, by establishing any one of the qualifications, will be well defended? Is not the Statute of Anne in effect a prohibition on every person to kill game, unless he brings himself within some one of the qualifications allowed by law; the proof of which is easy on the one side, but almost impossible on the other?

Pause for reflection

Is the notion of implied reverse burdens of proof compatible with the 'Golden Thread' of English justice?

Scope of Implied Burdens

There are often sound policy reasons for placing such burdens on the accused. To take an obvious (and very common) modern example, if a driver is accused of the summary offence of driving without insurance, it would be extremely difficult for the prosecution to prove that he was not covered by an appropriate policy. It would have to call evidence from every insurance provider in the country to show that the defendant was not 'on their books'. Additionally, it would be confronted by the difficulty of proving a negative. As a result, once the prosecution has established that the accused was driving on a public road, its case will be made out unless the defendant persuades the court that he was insured (by adducing the appropriate policy in court, etc.).

However, and more controversially, the doctrine of implied legal burdens is not confined to minor regulatory offences, or even to those where the prosecution would have enormous difficulty in establishing an absence of the relevant circumstances. Serious criminal matters, with potentially heavy penalties, can place implied legal burdens on the defendant.

Additionally, as the case of *Edwards* makes clear, and contrary to earlier suggestions by Bayley J in *Turner*, the matter on which an accused person carries an implied burden does not have to be 'peculiarly within the knowledge' of the defendant (as is the case with vehicle insurance). In *Edwards*, the defendant was accused of selling liquor without a justices' licence, contrary to the Licensing Act 1964. The lack of such a licence was something that the prosecution could quite readily have called evidence on, as the magistrates' clerk was required to keep a register of everyone in the area who was authorized to sell alcohol; nevertheless, it was still held to be a matter for the defence to establish.

When will such an implied burden fall on a defendant? In the summary courts the common law principle has been reduced to a statutory provision, currently contained in s. 101 of the Magistrates' Courts Act 1980 (though it has numerous predecessors under earlier statutes reaching far back into the nineteenth century). This section provides that where a defendant relies for his defence on, 'Any exception, exemption, proviso, excuse or qualification', the burden of proving the defence shall be on him. Thus, in the case of *Gatland v Metropolitan Police Commissioner* [1968] 2 QB 279, under s. 81 of the Magistrates' Courts Act 1952 (the immediate predecessor to s. 101), it was held that on a charge of obstructing a public road without lawful authority, the prosecution merely had to show that the defendant had obstructed such a road; the defendant then had to show that he had lawful authority to do so.

Section 101 of the Magistrates' Courts Act 1980

Onus of proving exceptions, etc. Where the defendant to an information or complaint relies for his defence on any exception, exemption, proviso, excuse or qualification, whether or not it accompanies the description of the offence or matter of complaint in the enactment creating the offence or on which the complaint is founded, the burden of proving the exception, exemption, proviso, excuse or qualification shall be on him; and this notwithstanding that the information or complaint contains an allegation negativing the exception, exemption, proviso, excuse or qualification.

However, although the position in the summary courts is now governed by statute, it is clear that there is no difference between cases determined by magistrates and those heard on indictment in the Crown Court, albeit that the latter situation is still regulated by case law. Section 101 is a statutory restatement of a common law principle. Otherwise, the invidious situation would exist in which burdens for 'either way' offences might differ depending on the forum in which they were heard: *R v Edwards* [1975] QB 27.

In *Edwards*, Lawton LJ observed that implied burdens were limited to offences arising under enactments that prohibit the doing of an act, 'save in specified circumstances or by persons of specified classes or with specified qualifications or with the licence or permission of specified authorities'. Most, but not all, cases involving implied burdens will fall into one of these categories.

R v Edwards [1975] QB 27, CA

Lawton LJ

In our judgment this line of authority establishes that over the centuries the common law, as a result of experience and the need to ensure that justice is done both to the community and to defendants, has evolved an exception to the fundamental rule of our criminal law that the prosecution must prove every element of the offence charged. This exception, like so much else in the common law, was hammered out on the anvil of pleading. It is limited to offences arising under enactments which prohibit the doing of an act save in specified circumstances or by persons of specified classes or with specified qualifications or with the licence or permission of specified authorities. Whenever the prosecution seeks to rely on this exception, the court must construe the enactment under which the charge is laid. If the true construction is that the enactment prohibits the doing of acts, subject to provisoes, exemptions and the like, then the prosecution can rely upon the exception.

In our judgment its application does not depend upon either the fact, or the presumption, that the defendant has peculiar knowledge enabling him to prove the positive of any negative aver-ment. As Wigmore pointed out in his great Treatise on Evidence (1905), vol. 4, p. 3525, this concept of peculiar knowledge furnishes no working rule. If it did, defendants would have to prove lack of intent. What does provide a working rule is what the common law evolved from a rule of pleading. We have striven to identify it in this judgment. Like nearly all rules it could be applied oppressively; but the courts have ample powers to curb and discourage oppressive prosecutors and do not hesi-tate to use them. Two consequences follow from the view we have taken as to the evolution and nature of this exception. First, as it comes into operation upon an enactment being construed in a particular way, there is no need for the prosecution to prove a prima facie case of lack of excuse, qualification or the like; and secondly, what shifts is the onus: it is for the defendant to prove that he was entitled to do the prohibited act. What rests on him is the legal or, as it is sometimes called, the persuasive burden of proof. It is not the evidential burden. When the exception as we have adjudged it to be is applied to this case it was for the defendant to prove that he was the holder of a justices' licence, not the prosecution.

Cases in which an implied burden is placed on an accused will not invariably fall into the cat-egories identified in *Edwards*; an implied burden can still be placed on a defendant in situations that are outside the examples cited by Lawton LJ, as was accepted in *R v Hunt* [1987] AC 352. In this case, a small quantity of white powder was found in the defendant's possession. Analysis revealed that it consisted of morphine (a controlled drug) mixed with caffeine and atropine (neither being controlled drugs). The defendant was charged with unlawful possession of a controlled drug under s. 5(2) of the Misuse of Drugs Act 1971.

However, Reg. 4(1) and para. 3 of Sch. 1 of the Misuse of Drugs Regulations 1973 provided that it was not unlawful to possess a compound that contained morphine, *provided* that it was less than 0.2 per cent of the total by volume, and not easily separable from the bulk. At trial, the prosecution established possession of the powder and the presence of morphine within it, but tendered no evidence as to the proportion of morphine in the compound. The defence then moved that there was no case to answer, arguing that the Crown had failed to establish that it was not readily separable or exceeded 0.2 per cent by volume, and that they bore the legal burden of proving these facts. Their submission was dismissed by the trial judge, on the basis that it was for the accused to show that the proportion was less than that amount and not easily separable. The defendant then entered a plea of guilty.

The matter went to the Court of Appeal, where the trial judge's decision was upheld. However, on further appeal to the House of Lords the defendant was acquitted. Their Lordships con-cluded that on its true construction, the Act and its attendant regulations dealt with the def-inition of an essential ingredient in the offence, not with exceptions to what would otherwise be unlawful. In reaching this conclusion, they made a number of important observations and relied heavily on the Scottish civil case of *Nimmo v Alexander Cowan & Sons Ltd* [1968] AC 107. Essentially, the court decided that, very occasionally, the wording of a statute would not make it clear whether a ground of exoneration must be established by the defendant or negated by the prosecution. In these (fairly rare) situations, policy factors could be considered when deciding where the burden of proof should fall. For example: how easy or difficult it would be for the defendant to discharge a legal burden (in drugs cases, the police will normally be in physical possession of the confiscated narcotics); that such a burden should not lightly be placed on an accused in a serious criminal matter, etc.

Pause for reflection

Do you feel that the decision reached by the House of Lords in this case was correct?

More recently, and following this approach, the Court of Appeal has concluded that the wording of s. 31 of the Immigration and Asylum Act 1999, which covered 'refugees' without making it clear who had the burden of proving that they were, or were not, entitled to that status, put a legal burden on the prosecution to prove the negative. This was largely due to policy factors such as the defendant's difficulty in securing the wider information that would confirm or deny his or her claim: *R v Makuwa* [2006] Crim LR 911.

It should be noted that this assessment of policy matters has been further complicated since the Human Rights Act 1998 came into force. Implied burdens, as much as express ones, must be convention compliant: *R (Grundy) v Halton Division Magistrates Court* (2003) 167 JP 387. Some of the factors that should be considered when deciding whether a reverse onus burden falls on a defendant by implication are also relevant when deciding whether such a provision is compliant with the 1998 Act. Amongst them, for example, is the ease or difficulty of proving the matter on which it is claimed the defendant should carry a burden of proof. In theory, when determining such cases, a two-stage process should be followed. First, is an implied legal burden placed on the defendant using the normal canons of interpretation and, if necessary, having regard to policy factors (as in *Hunt*)? Secondly, and if is, is it convention compliant? In practice, because of the overlap of policy factors, such precision on the part of the judiciary, when considering newly created (or previously unlitigated) implied burdens, may not always occur.

R v Hunt [1987] AC 352, HL

Lord Griffiths

In Reg. v. Edwards [1975] Q.B. 27, 39–40 the Court of Appeal expressed their conclusion in the form of an exception to what they said was the fundamental rule of our criminal law that the prosecution must prove every element of the offence charged. They said that the exception 'is limited to offences arising under enactments which prohibit the doing of an act save in specified circumstances or by persons of specified classes or with specified qualifications or with the licence or permission of specified authorities'.

I have little doubt that the occasions upon which a statute will be construed as imposing a burden of proof upon a defendant which do not fall within this formulation are likely to be exceedingly rare. But I find it difficult to fit Nimmo v. Alexander Cowan & Sons Ltd. [1968] A.C. 107 into this formula, and I would prefer to adopt the formula as an excellent guide to construction rather than as an exception to a rule. In the final analysis each case must turn upon the construction of the particular legislation to determine whether the defence is an exception within the meaning of section 101 of the Act of 1980 which the Court of Appeal rightly decided reflects the rule for trials on indictment. With this one qualification I regard Reg. v. Edwards as rightly decided.

My Lords, I am, of course, well aware of the body of distinguished academic opinion that urges that wherever a burden of proof is placed upon a defendant by statute the burden should be an evidential burden and not a persuasive burden, and that it has the support of the distinguished signatories to the 11th Report of the Criminal Law Revision Committee, Evidence (General) (1972) (Cmnd. 4991). My Lords, such a fundamental change is, in my view, a matter for Parliament and not a decision of your Lordships' House.

Criticism of Reverse Onus Legal Burdens

The practice of placing legal burdens, whether express or implied, on defendants in criminal trials has been heavily criticized from different quarters for many years. It amounts to a far more drastic interference with the presumption of innocence than does putting a merely evidential burden on the accused. The former necessarily involves the risk that, if a jury is faithful to the judge's direction, or magistrates follow the law, they will convict where the accused has not discharged the legal burden resting on him, but has left the tribunal of fact unsure on the point, ie a finding of guilt will be returned even though the tribunal is not sure of the accused's guilt. This risk is not present if only an evidential burden is placed on the defendant (see below).

 Pause for reflection

What do you think are the problems occasioned by placing burdens of proof on a defendant?

Despite this, the process of enacting both express and implied legal reverse burdens of proof has proceeded apace since the Second World War. As a result, Professors Andrew Ashworth and Meredith Blake were able to find 219 examples of legal burdens or presumptions operating against the defendant in 540 offences that were triable in the Crown Court (ie ignoring summary only matters where reverse burdens are even more common). At least 40 per cent of all such offences had provisions that were contrary to the 'golden thread' presumption in some way.[2] The enacting of such statutes has still not ceased, despite the advent of the Human Rights Act 1998. Parliament continues to pass Acts which place express legal burdens on a defendant, such as s. 5 of the Private Security Act 2001.

As far back as 1972 the Criminal Law Revision Committee's controversial 11th report on evidence was, 'strongly of the opinion that, both on principle and for the sake of clarity and convenience in practice, burdens on the defence should be evidential only'.[3] A number of distinguished legal academics, including the late Glanville Williams, have also been vigorous critics of statutes that placed legal burdens on defendants.

In reply, however, exponents of such reverse burdens point to strong policy factors justifying such an approach, in appropriate cases. Thus, in *Sweet v Parsley* [1970] AC 132, Lord Reid expressed surprise that, 'More use has not been made of this method'. Indeed, it was Lord Denning, speaking during a debate in the House of Lords, who suggested that the burden of proving good reason or lawful authority for possessing a proscribed blade in public, by way of defence under s. 139(4) of the Criminal Justice Act 1988, should be expressly placed on the defendant. His suggestion was subsequently accepted by Parliament.

Paul Roberts, 'Taking the Burden of Proof Seriously' [1995] Crim LR 783

The principles relating to the burden of proof are an important aspect of criminal procedure which, in turn, is a key component of political democracy. The burden of proof checks and constrains the

---

[2] A Ashworth and Meredith Blake, 'The Presumption of Innocence in English Criminal Law' (1996) Crim LR, 306–317, at 309.

[3] CLRC Eleventh Report, Evidence (General), Cmnd 4991 of 1972, para. 140.

power of the state to intervene in the lives of individuals and their families in the far-reaching and sometimes catastrophic ways sanctioned by the machinery of criminal justice. This section outlines three practical reasons which, taken together, explain why individual liberty is buttressed by placing the burden of proof on the prosecution and, conversely, that freedom is threatened when the onus of proof is reversed.

The first argument is straightforward and easily stated. Whenever the burden of proof on any particular issue rests with the defendant it follows that the jury or magistrates must convict in cases in which they remain undecided about facts material to that issue. A presumption of guilt is employed to fill the void of doubt, in place of the presumption of innocence which usually awards the benefit of any reasonable doubt to the defendant. The Criminal Law Revision Committee thought that placing probative burdens on the defendant was 'repugnant to principle'. It is manifestly illiberal inasmuch as it makes people presumptive criminals, and puts the onus on them to prove otherwise.

The structure of criminal proceedings and, in consequence, the relative ease with which a burden of proof can be discharged, points to a second reason for placing the onus on the prosecution. The prosecution has the dual advantage of dictating the nature of the proceedings and of being well prepared to participate in them. The state employs professional investigators to detect crime and to gather evidence, utilising offence definitions to structure the shape and direction of their inquiries. As proceedings develop, the facts to be proved by the prosecution are specified by the charges, which the prosecutor selects after reviewing the evidence. On the other hand, in contrast to the prosecutor who is both forewarned and forearmed, the defendant must respond to a procedural agenda that is already more or less fixed by the time that he is called on to explain himself. A moment's introspection reveals, at least to most of us, that we could not guarantee to be able to account for our past movements and motives in order to answer any charge that might, without warning, be brought against us. Guilty people may well invest time and effort in covering their tracks or in setting up false alibis, but innocent people are not generally concerned with being able to prove their innocence, unless and until they are called upon to do so; and then it might be too late. . . .

The second argument amounts to this: for as long as criminal proceedings are initiated and structured by the prosecutor's presentation of a prima facie case to answer on specified charges—as opposed, say, to requiring each of us to undergo monthly confessionals before an inquisitor—placing the burden of proof on a defendant will often deprive him of a fair opportunity to answer the allegations against him. Now it is sometimes said, to the contrary, that the mental elements of crimes are easier for a defendant to prove, because nobody knows the defendant's own mind as well as the defendant himself. Thus, in Edwards Lawton L.J. opines that 'if there ever was a matter which could be said to be peculiarly within a person's knowledge, it is the state of his own mind'. There are important philosophical objections to this superficially attractive assumption, but an excursus into the philosophy of mind is unnecessary here. It is enough to point out that the present argument is addressed to the logic and practicalities of proof, not to the grounds of knowledge. The fact that a defendant knows he is innocent will not avail him under a burden-reversing regime unless he can prove it and, as we have seen, the structure of criminal proceedings puts him at a considerable disadvantage in attempting to do so. It may be that these structural and practical considerations are at the bottom of the familiar but conceptually puzzling claim that it is harder to prove 'a negative' than it is to substantiate a positive proposition.

The third reason for placing the onus of proof on the prosecution also focuses on the practicalities of proof, specifically on the fact that the prosecution has access to investigative resources which are vastly superior to those available to most defendants in criminal cases. From the high-tech world of DNA profiling to labour-intensive house to house inquiries, the prosecution is considerably better placed to amass evidence of guilt than is a defendant trying to establish her innocence. And as Lord Griffiths noted in Hunt, the defendant's difficulties are compounded by her restricted access to physical evidence. The prosecution sometimes destroys all the available samples during testing; or fails to collect them in the first place.

The three arguments advanced in this section are mutually reinforcing. Together they amount to a compelling case for thinking that placing the burden of proof on defendants is (to quote the words of Di Birch with a little contextual latitude) 'about as far from a good thing as it is possible to get'. A policy of reversing the burden of proof in criminal proceedings might commend itself to a totalitarian regime which, for reasons of domestic order or foreign diplomacy, wished to retain the bare window dressing of legality, but it is not the badge of an administration which values and respects its citizens' freedom.

...Now, there may be sound reasons of principle or policy for placing the onus of proof on defendants in exceptional circumstances, and it is not part of the present argument to assert otherwise. But if they exist, these weighty principles or policies should be articulated clearly and the ambit of any exception should be carefully drawn so that the specific principle or policy is served without weakening the general presumption of innocence any more than is absolutely necessary. Yet statutory provisions which reverse the burden of proof are frequently unsupported by any reasoned justification. Nor has there ever been an adequate response to the argument, advanced by Glanville Williams and others, that in any case where placing a burden of proof on the defendant would be justifiable, the evidential burden would suffice. In the absence of argument to the contrary, one can only conclude that the current legislative practice is unjustifiable.

3. Reverse Burdens of Proof and Human Rights

Since October 2000, when the Human Rights Act 1998 (HRA 1998) came into force, reverse burdens, whether express or implied, must be seen against the light of their compliance with the provisions of the ECHR. It can be argued that placing a legal burden on a defendant violates important convention rights, such as the right to a 'fair' trial enshrined in Article 6(1) and, perhaps most importantly, the presumption of innocence in Article 6(2). This provides that: 'Everyone charged with a criminal offence shall be presumed innocent until proved guilty according to law.' Forcing someone to prove their innocence, even on the balance of probabilities, might be viewed as derogating from that presumption of innocence, at least in some situations.

As was noted in chapter 1, since 2000, if a court concludes that this is the case, and there is a violation of Article 6, it has a choice; it can either make a declaration of incompatibility under s. 4 of the Act (leaving it to Parliament to effect change in the law) or, alternatively, 'read down' the provision in accordance with the courts' interpretative power under s. 3 of the statute, so that it becomes convention compliant. In practice, the latter is nearly always the preferred course for appellate courts. This means treating the words as imposing an evidential and not a legal burden on the defendant, even if, conventionally interpreted, the latter is clearly what was intended by Parliament. Thus, and for example, 'to prove' in a statute becomes 'to adduce some evidence on' the matter. Placing evidential burdens on defendants has always been deemed to be compatible with the Convention, as it amounts to a far less drastic interference with the presumption of innocence than placing a legal burden on the accused: *R v Bianco* [2001] EWCA Crim 2516.

This issue was first considered at the highest level in the case of *R v Lambert* [2001] 3 WLR 206, where the appellant was convicted of possessing a controlled drug (cocaine) with intent to supply, contrary to s. 5 of the Misuse of Drugs Act 1971; he was sentenced to seven years' imprisonment. In his defence, he relied on s. 28(3)(b)(i) of that Act to assert that he did not believe or suspect, or have reason to suspect, that the duffel bag which he carried contained a proscribed drug. The judge directed the jury that the prosecution had to prove only that the defendant had, and knew that he had, the bag in his possession and that it contained a controlled drug (of any type). To establish a defence under s. 28(3)(b)(i) the defendant then had to prove that he did not know that the bag contained such a narcotic; ie he carried a legal burden on that issue. This direction was well established and unsurprising, given that s. 28(3)(b)(i) states clearly that it only applies 'if he [the defendant] proves' that he did not know, suspect or have reason to believe that the substance was a controlled drug. This is the classic language of express statutory exceptions to the 'golden thread'.

On appeal, however, it was argued that the trial judge was wrong to conclude that the statute imposed a legal, rather than an evidential, burden on the defendant. It was claimed that putting such a burden of proof on the accused to establish the defence (rather than merely to raise it) violated Article 6 of the ECHR. Despite this, the Court of Appeal upheld the trial judge's decision. Nevertheless, on further appeal to the House of Lords, the decision was reversed by a majority decision, which held that, in the light of the HRA 1998, the statute should be interpreted as imposing merely an evidential, rather than a legal, burden on defendants. The court employed s. 3 of the statute to 'read down' the provision so that 'prove' was interpreted as to 'adduce evidence on.' Once this had been done, it would be for the prosecution to prove (beyond reasonable doubt) that the defendant did know that the bag contained drugs.

Despite this decision, the House of Lords also made it clear that not all legal burdens, whether express or implied, that were placed on a defendant in a criminal trial violated the Convention generally or Article 6(2) in particular, which, the court held, was not an absolute right in all circumstances. This is, perhaps, unsurprising, as the European Court of Human Rights (ECtHR) itself expressly recognized in *Salabiaku v France* (1988) 13 EHRR 379 that: 'Presumptions of fact or of law operate in every legal system. Clearly the Convention does not prohibit such presumptions in principle.' Some reverse burdens of proof are 'convention compliant'.

Indeed, in the right circumstances, even apparently draconian reverse burdens have been held to be acceptable by the ECtHR or Commission, as is illustrated by *Bates v United Kingdom* (App No 2628) (unreported), 16 January 1996. In this case, the Commission declined to admit a complaint that s. 5(5) of the Dangerous Dogs Act 1991 infringed the Convention even though statute provided that: 'If in any proceedings it is alleged by the prosecution that a dog is one to which [the Act] applies, it shall be presumed that it is such a dog unless the contrary is shown by the accused by such evidence as the court considers sufficient.' Theoretically, if the prosecution alleged that a Chihuahua was a 'dangerous dog', it would be for its owner to prove that it was not such an animal.

Pause for reflection

Is this merely a reflection of the belief that the life of an animal is of much less significance than something that will directly affect human beings?

This raises the difficult question as to how 'acceptable' reverse legal burdens can be distinguished from those that violate the Convention. In *Lambert*, the House of Lords emphasized that the primary obligation to prove the main ingredients of an offence (for example, the physical possession of illicit drugs) must always fall upon the Crown, but thereafter the 'legality' of any reverse burden would be tested in the light of all the circumstances of the case. These included the purpose of the legislation, the fact that Parliament had deemed it fit to pass such a statute, and the ease with which the Crown could discharge the burden were it to be placed upon the prosecution. The approach to this balancing process was, essentially, that adopted by the ECtHR in *Salabiaku v France*, where it was held that Article 6 required the contracting states to remain within reasonable limits when it came to reverse burdens. Any legislative interference with the presumption of innocence requires justification and must not be greater than is necessary; ie it must be 'proportionate'.

In *Lambert*, the majority of their Lordships felt that placing a burden on the defendant on the issue of knowledge was not proportionate. Indeed, some of the judges involved in the case appeared to be eager to see the Act used to facilitate future judicial interventionism, Lord Slynn openly warning that legal 'sacred cows' might have to be 'culled' under its provisions. Others, however, were slightly more cautious.

R v Lambert [2002] 2 AC 545, HL

Lord Steyn

The principle of proportionality requires the House to consider whether there was a pressing necessity to impose a legal rather than evidential burden on the accused. The effect of section 28 is that in a prosecution for possession of controlled drugs with intent to supply, although the prosecution must establish that prohibited drugs were in the possession of the defendant, and that he or she knew that the package contained something, the accused must prove on a balance of probabilities that he did not know that the package contained controlled drugs. If the jury is in doubt on this issue, they must convict him. This may occur when an accused adduces sufficient evidence to raise a doubt about his guilt but the jury is not convinced on a balance or probabilities that his account is true. Indeed it obliges the court to convict if the version of the accused is as likely to be true as not. This is a far-reaching consequence: a guilty verdict may be returned in respect of an offence punishable by life imprisonment even though the jury may consider that it is reasonably possible that the accused had been duped. It would be unprincipled to brush aside such possibilities as unlikely to happen in practice. Moreover, as Justice has pointed out in its valuable intervention, there may be real difficulties in determining the real facts upon which the sentencer must act in such cases. In any event, the burden of showing that only a reverse legal burden can overcome the difficulties of the prosecution in drugs cases is a heavy one.

A new realism in regard to the problems faced by the prosecution in drugs cases have significantly reduced their scope. First, the relevant facts are usually peculiarly within the knowledge of the possessor of the container and that possession presumptively suggests, in the absence of exculpatory evidence, that the person in possession of it in fact knew what was in the container. This is simply a species of circumstantial evidence. It will usually be a complete answer to a no case submission. It is also a factor which a judge may squarely place before the jury. After all, it is simple common sense that possession of a package containing drugs will generally as a matter of simple common sense demand a full and adequate explanation. Secondly, the statutory provisions enabling a judge to comment on an accused's failure to mention facts when questioned or charged has strengthened the position of the prosecution: section 34 of the Criminal Justice Act 1994. Thirdly, I turn to the fears centred on the ability of an accused in a drugs case to manipulate the system by providing a mixed statement containing a self-serving explanation that he did not know what was in the package. The perceived difficulty is that the whole statement may be introduced as evidence and he may not testify. In the leading case of R v Duncan(1981) 73 Cr App R 359, 365, Lord Lane CJ observed: 'where appropriate, as it usually will be, the judge may, and should, point out that the incriminating parts are likely to be true (otherwise why say them?), whereas the excuses do not have the same weight. Nor is there any reason why, again where appropriate, the judge should not comment in relation to the exculpatory remarks upon the election of the accused not to give evidence.' This guidance has twice been approved by the House: R v Sharp (Colin) [1988] 1 WLR 7; R v Aziz [1996] AC 41. Cumulatively, these considerations significantly reduce the difficulties of the prosecution in drugs cases. Specifically, it should not be possible for an accused, in a case where his conduct calls for an explanation, to advance a submission at the end of the prosecution case that the prosecution have not eliminated a possible innocent explanation. Such submissions should generally in practice receive short shrift.

Returning to the relative merits of the transfer of a legal burden on an important element or issue to the accused, as opposed to the creation of a mere evidential burden, there have been note-worthy developments in England and in cognate legal systems. In R v Director of Public Prosecutions, Ex p Kebilene [2000] 2 AC 326 in the Divisional Court Lord Bingham of Cornhill CJ had no doubt that, in the context of a serious offence (terrorism), a reverse legal burden of proof provision on a matter central to the wrongdoing alleged against the defendant would breach Article 6(2) of the Convention. On the appeal to the House a majority suggested that, once the 1998 Act was in force, reverse legal burden provisions may have to be interpreted as imposing merely an evidential burden on the defendant. Responding to Ex p Kebilene Parliament enacted the Terrorism Act 2000 which in section 118(1) and (2) provides that the reverse onus of proof is satisfied if the person adduces evidence which is sufficient to raise an issue with respect to the matter unless the prosecution can prove the contrary beyond reasonable doubt. Comparative experience in constitutional democracies underlines the vice inherent in transfer of legal burden provisions, and the utility, in appropriate contexts, of evidential presumptions. . . .

In these circumstances I am satisfied that the transfer of the legal burden in section 28 does not satisfy the criterion of proportionality. Viewed in its place in the current legal system section 28 of the 1971 Act is a disproportionate reaction to perceived difficulties facing the prosecution in drugs cases. It would be sufficient to impose an evidential burden on the accused. It follows that section 28 is incompatible with Convention rights.

Despite such views, it should also be noted that, in the same case, Lord Hutton gave a strong (and influential) dissenting judgment, arguing that, on its facts, the transfer of the burden of proof did not infringe the presumption of innocence set out in Article 6(2); he felt that the Crown had justified the imposition of a legal burden on the defendant. It is apparent that what ultimately persuaded the judge of this was the danger posed by drugs to the wider society and the fact that the Crown still had to establish possession of the bag and its contents, which required proof that the defendant knew that he had control over the bag, and whatever object or substance was inside it. It was only then that the statutory defence became relevant, ie it was on a very narrow issue.

R v Lambert [2002] 2 AC 545, HL

Lord Hutton (dissenting judgment)

Therefore in considering whether a rebuttable presumption of knowledge created by section 28(2) and (3) is compatible with article 6(2) a number of factors (which to some extent overlap) have to be considered. (1) Is the presumption created by section 28(2) and (3) directed towards a clear and proper public objective? In my opinion it clearly is. The taking of controlled drugs is a great social evil which causes widespread suffering and the possession of controlled drugs with intent to supply is a grave and frequently committed offence which ensures the continuation of this social evil. (2) Is the creation of the presumption a reasonable measure for Parliament to take and is there a reasonable relationship of proportionality between the means employed and the aim sought to be realised? In considering this matter it is necessary, as Lord Hope of Craighead stated in Brown v Stott, to assess whether a fair balance has been struck between the general interest of the community and the personal rights of the individual. In my opinion the threat posed by drugs to the welfare of society is so grave and the difficulty in some cases of rebutting a defence that the defendant believed that he was carrying something other than drugs is so great that it was reasonable for Parliament to impose a persuasive burden as to lack of knowledge on a defendant. The question whether a fair balance has been struck depends in large measure on whether the creation of an evidential burden as opposed to a persuasive burden on a defendant would be adequate to remedy the problem with which section 28(2) and (3) were intended to deal. That problem can arise in the type of case where the Crown proves that a man was carrying a container such as a bag and that the bag contained a controlled drug, or where the Crown proves that tablets, which were a controlled drug, were on a table in the bedroom of the defendant's house and the defendant raises the defence that he believed that the object in the bag was a video film or that the tablets on the bedroom table were painkillers. In such cases it will often be very difficult to prove guilt if the prosecution has to prove beyond a reasonable doubt that the defendant knew that the bag contained a controlled drug or that the tablets were a controlled drug. It is clear from the decisions of the European Commission in X v United Kingdom and A G v Malta that the difficulty of proving knowledge on the part of the defendant is one of the factors which can justify the creation of a presumption against a defendant, where the presumption is neither irrebuttable nor unreasonable.

I am, with respect, unable to agree with the view that the problem of obtaining a conviction against a guilty person can be surmounted by imposing an evidential burden on the defendant. All that a defendant would have to do to discharge such a burden would be to adduce some evidence to raise the issue that he did not know that the article in the bag or the tablets on the table were a controlled drug, and the prosecution would then have to destroy that defence in such a manner as to leave in the jury's mind no reasonable doubt that the defendant knew that it was a controlled drug in the bag or on the table....

In my opinion it would be easy for a guilty defendant to raise the defence of lack of knowledge by an assertion in his police statement or by adducing evidence (which could be from a third person), and the Crown would then have to prove beyond a reasonable doubt that the defendant did have knowledge. Therefore I think that in a drugs case, in practice, there is little difference between the burden of proving knowledge resting throughout on the prosecution and requiring the defendant to raise the issue of knowledge before the burden of proof on that matter reverts to the prosecution.

... in my opinion the threat of drugs to the wellbeing of the community and the peculiar difficulty of proving knowledge in such cases justifies an exception to the general principle advocated by the Criminal Law Revision Committee, and this was clearly the view taken by Parliament in enacting sections 5 and 28 of the 1991 Act. Moreover the transfer of the burden of proof as to knowledge in drugs cases has the powerful support of Lord Reid and Lord Pearce in R v Warner [1969] 2 AC 256 to which I later refer.

The argument advanced against the imposition of a persuasive burden is that it creates the position that where a defendant fails to satisfy the jury on the balance of probabilities that he did not know he was carrying drugs, the jury will or may convict him notwithstanding that they have a reasonable doubt as to whether or not he had that knowledge. In theory there is force in this argument, but in my respectful opinion there is greater force in the common sense view of Lord Pearce in Sweet v Parsley [1970] AC 132 where the defendant was charged under section 5(b) of the Dangerous Drugs Act 1965 with being concerned in the management of premises used for the purpose of smoking cannabis resin. Lord Pearce said, at p 157: 'Parliament might, of course, have taken what was conceded in argument to be a fair and sensible course. It could have said, in appropriate words, that a person is to be liable unless he proves that he had no knowledge or guilty mind. Admittedly, if the prosecution have to prove a defendant's knowledge beyond reasonable doubt, it may be easy for the guilty to escape. But it would be very much harder for the guilty to escape if the burden of disproving mens rea or knowledge is thrown on the defendant. And if that were done, innocent people could satisfy a jury of their innocence on a balance of probabilities....' In my opinion it is not unprincipled to have regard to practical realities where the issue relates to knowledge in a drugs case....

My Lords, when judges of such eminence considered that transferring the burden of proof in relation to knowledge in drugs cases would not result in an unfair trial to the defendant, I consider that 30 years later when the problem has not changed there is no reason for this House to take a different view. Section 2 of the 1998 Act now requires the House in determining a question which has arisen in connection with a Convention right to take into account judgments of the European Court and decisions of the European Commission, but in my opinion the judgments and decisions to which I have referred provide no basis for the view that under the jurisprudence of the European Court the transfer of the onus of proof as to knowledge in drugs cases would constitute a violation of article 6(2).

The practical consequences of the approach taken by their Lordships in *Lambert* are that every reverse onus clause in English law must be measured for convention compliance on an individual, case-by-case, basis at an appellate level. Although it is apparent that the onus on those seeking to persuade the court that a reverse burden is necessary is a heavy one, the courts continue to uphold such provisions, if the circumstances are deemed to be right.

However, as the case of *Lambert* indicates, in these situations it is almost impossible to avoid both a strong degree of judicial subjectivity and also to prevent judges from straying into what is, essentially, a political arena. In the case of *Hunt*, Lord Ackner had observed that it was not for the courts to overturn parliamentary provisions. Nevertheless, that is exactly what use of the 1998 Act can effect. As Lord Bingham noted in *Sheldrake v DPP* [2005] 1 AC 264, the statutory provisions being considered in that case were not 'obscure and ambiguous'; prior to the advent of the 1998 Act they would have to have been interpreted as placing a legal burden on the accused and these were clearly what Parliament had intended.

It must also be remembered that, in *Lambert,* a majority of the judges who considered the reverse onus at first instance and on appeal agreed with Lord Hutton's analysis. Doubtless, Lord Hutton could easily have found himself in the majority in a differently constituted court, whose members might have sympathized with his view that the change endangered society while the provision was not unfair to the accused. His dissenting judgment may have influenced other senior members of the judiciary, as, shortly after *Lambert,* there appears to have been a subtle change in emphasis in appellate-level decisions.

In the light of *Lambert,* some observers had hoped (or feared) that the courts would interpret most reverse burdens of proof as imposing merely evidential burdens on the accused, especially if they occurred in statutes creating serious offences carrying heavy punishments. However, the subsequent decision of the House of Lords in *R v Johnstone* [2003] 1 WLR 1736 appeared to qualify this expectation. The case involved a trade-mark offence carrying a potentially long term of imprisonment. Despite this, their Lordships stressed the need for due respect to be paid to the will of Parliament and cautioned against any ready finding that the imposition of a reverse burden was a disproportionate response. It also reiterated that Article 6(2) did not stand alone; it was part of the guarantee of a fair trial provided by Article 6 as a whole, not what Lord Carswell later referred to in *Sheldrake* as a 'free-standing obligation', any departure from which would be a violation of the Convention. A reverse burden did not necessarily preclude a fair trial. It could be a proportionate response to a serious and current social or commercial mischief.

R v Johnstone [2003] 1 WLR 1736, HL

Lord Nicholls

The relevant factors to be take into account when considering whether such a reason exists have been considered in several recent authorities . . . A sound starting point is to remember that if an accused is required to prove a fact on the balance of probability to avoid conviction, this permits a conviction in spite of the fact-finding tribunal having a reasonable doubt as to the guilt of the accused: see Dickson CJ in R. v Whyte (1988) 51 DLR (4th) 481, 493. This consequence of a reverse burden of proof should colour one's approach when evaluating the reasons why it is said that, in the absence of a persuasive burden on the accused, the public interest will be prejudiced to an extent which justifies placing a persuasive burden on the accused. The more serious the punishment which may flow from conviction, the more compelling must be the reasons. The extent and nature of the factual matters required to be proved by the accused, and their importance relative to the matters required to be proved by the prosecution, have to be taken into account. So also does the extent to which the burden on the accused relates to facts which, if they exist, are readily provable by him as matters within his own knowledge or to which he has ready access.

 In evaluating these factors the court's role is one of review. Parliament, not the court, is charged with the primary responsibility for deciding, as a matter of policy, what should be the constituent elements of a criminal offence. I echo the words of Lord Woolf in Attorney-General of Hong Kong v Lee Kwong-kut [1993] AC 951, 975: 'In order to maintain the balance between the individual and the society as a whole, rigid and inflexible standards should not be imposed on the legislature's attempts to resolve the difficult and intransigent problems with which society is faced when seeking to deal with serious crime.' The court will reach a different conclusion from the legislature only when it is apparent the legislature has attached insufficient importance to the fundamental right of an individual to be presumed innocent until proved guilty.

 I turn to s. 92. (1) Counterfeiting is fraudulent trading. It is a serious contemporary problem. . . . Protection of consumers and honest manufacturers and traders from counterfeiting is an important policy consideration. (2) The offences created by s.92 have rightly been described as offences of 'near absolute liability'. The prosecution is not required to prove intent to infringe a registered trade mark. (3) The offences attract a serious level of punishment: a maximum penalty on indictment of an unlimited fine or imprisonment for up to ten years or both, together with the possibility of confiscation and deprivation orders. (4) Those who trade in brand products are aware of the need to be on guard against counterfeit goods. They are aware of the need to deal with reputable suppliers and keep records and of the risks they take if they do not. (5) The s. 92(5) defence relates to facts within the accused person's own knowledge: his state of mind, and the reasons why he held the belief in question. His sources of supply are known to him. (6) Conversely, by and large it is to be expected that those who supply traders with counterfeit products, if traceable at all by outside investigators, are unlikely to be co-operative. So, in practice, if the prosecution must prove that a trader acted dishonestly, fewer investigations will be undertaken and fewer prosecutions will take place.

> In my view factors (4) and (6) constitute compelling reasons why the s. 92(5) defence should place a persuasive burden on the accused person. Taking all the factors mentioned above into account, these reasons justify the loss of protection which will be suffered by the individual. Given the importance and difficulty of combating counterfeiting, and given the comparative ease with which an accused can raise an issue about his honesty, overall it is fair and reasonable to require a trader, should need arise, to prove on the balance of probability that he honestly and reasonably believed the goods were genuine. . . .
>
> I consider the persuasive burden placed on an accused person by the s. 92(5) defence is compatible with Article 6(2). This being so, it becomes unnecessary to consider whether, if this interpretation of s. 92(5) were incompatible with Article 6(2), s. 92(5) might be open to a different interpretation pursuant to s. 3(1) of the Human Rights Act 1998.

Subsequently, the Court of Appeal appeared to favour the less interventionist approach taken in *Johnstone* to that adopted in *Lambert* when considering appeals on reverse burdens; thus, in *Attorney-General's Reference (No 1 of 2004)* [2004] 1 WLR 2111 the court held that the former case was the latest word on the subject and that citation of other authorities should normally be discouraged. This approach was aided by the fact that the comments in *Lambert* were, strictly speaking, obiter, as the court also concluded in that case that the 1998 Act did not operate retrospectively. As a result, the next decision of the House of Lords in this area, in the conjoined appeals in *Sheldrake v DPP; A-G's Reference (No 4 of 2002)* [2005] 1 AC 264, provided an opportunity for fresh consideration of the issues and an attempt to reconcile the earlier cases emanating from that forum.

In *Sheldrake* the court concluded that Lambert should not be disregarded. It also held that it was compatible with Johnstone, *as the two decisions dealt with different types of case. Both remained valid authorities.* The primary question was always to ask whether the reverse burden was compatible with a fair trial; if not, it should be read down as merely imposing an evidential burden. However, *Sheldrake* reiterated that reverse burdens did not necessarily preclude a fair trial under Article 6. Indeed, their Lordships rejected the earlier decision of the Divisional Court in the same case.

 Pause for reflection

Do you feel that *Lambert* and *Johnstone* are easily reconcilable?

By a two-to-one majority, the lower court had decided that a defendant accused of the summary offence of being in charge of a motor vehicle while over the proscribed alcohol limit, contrary to s. 5 of the Road Traffic Act 1988, merely had an evidential burden to raise the defence set out under s. 5(2) of the Act, whereby he would not be guilty if there was no likelihood that he would drive whilst still over the limit. This was despite the prima facie wording of the provision making it clear that an express legal burden was being placed on the accused. Thus, the Divisional Court (Henriques J dissenting) had decided that once the issue was raised by the defendant it was for the prosecution to establish that this was not the case, i.e. that he was likely to drive the vehicle while still intoxicated (reported as *Sheldrake v DPP* [2003] All ER 335). The House of

Lords decided that this was wrong, and that it was for the defendant to prove that there was no likelihood of his driving,

In *Sheldrake* their Lordships also concluded that, when conducting an assessment of proportionality, it was necessary to balance society's interest in the effective suppression of a social mischief against the defendant's right to a fair trial. When weighing up these two competing interests, several factors could be considered. Amongst them were: the severity of the offence in terms of potential sentence; the ease of proof for one party or the other in relation to establishing the reverse burden (someone in charge of a motor vehicle was uniquely placed to know whether or not he would have driven it); and the danger of convicting the innocent.

Critics of *Sheldrake* have argued that, in practice, it still provides the courts with little clear guidance on how to interpret statutes that impose reverse burdens of proof. Certainly, the considerations that have been judicially identified as relevant to decision-making in such cases, such as the maximum potential penalty, are merely indicative, not conclusive. Thus, a 10-year maximum sentence of imprisonment in *Johnstone* did not preclude a legal burden being placed on the accused, although it may explain the different approach taken by their Lordships between the appeal in *Sheldrake* and that in *Attorney-General's Reference (No 4 of 2002)* where there was a six months' maximum sentence (in the former case) compared to one of 10 years (in the latter). Of course, frequently, crimes with severe maximum penalties will, by definition, often be aimed at combating serious social evils, so that the same case might produce opposing criteria

Pause for reflection

What are the potential dangers of uncertainty in this area of the law?

Sometimes, the identified considerations are also difficult to reconcile with existing cases on reverse burdens, all of which, apart from *R v Carass* [2002] 2 Cr App R 77, their Lordships approved in *Sheldrake*. In *Carass*, the Court of Appeal had decided that s. 206(4) of the Insolvency Act 1986, despite its apparently 'express' wording, only imposed an evidential burden on the accused to 'prove' (ie to raise as an issue) that he had no intention to defraud by concealing property in a liquidated company. However, and indicative of the difficulties created when applying the HRA 1998, in *Sheldrake*, the House of Lords concluded that *Carass* was 'wrongly decided'. Arguably, many of the judicially recognized factors could be interpreted either way, militating for or against a reverse onus being deemed to be convention compliant, in any given case.[4]

Academic commentators have identified a number of other criteria that sometimes appear to be considered by the courts when reaching such decisions. Amongst them is the question as to whether the offence in question is viewed as a 'mainstream' crime, one that is 'truly criminal', or a 'regulatory' matter. The latter have less social stigma and (often) lighter potential sentences and so, it appears, are less likely to produce a violation of Article 6. This distinction was expressly identified by Lord Clyde in *Lambert* and has since been referred to in several other decisions. It, too, might help explain the difference in outcome between the two appeals in *Sheldrake* and *Attorney-General's Reference (No 4 of 2002)*.

However, separating 'regulatory' from 'mainstream' offences can, itself, be very difficult. At the Divisional Court-level hearing of *Sheldrake*, two of the judges thought that an offence based

---

[4] A Ashworth, 'Case Comment' (2005) Crim LR, 215–219.

around the likelihood of an intoxicated driver driving a vehicle of which he was in charge was not a regulatory matter, while Henriques J concluded that it was such an offence. Additionally, it should be noted that the courts appear to be less likely to read down a reverse burden that was consciously and expressly passed by Parliament, than one that was imposed by implication (the former apparently requiring more 'due respect' than the latter, as more clearly deliberate).

Sheldrake v DPP [2005] 1 AC 264, HL

Lord Bingham

From this body of authority certain principles may be derived. The overriding concern is that a trial should be fair, and the presumption of innocence is a fundamental right directed to that end. The Convention does not outlaw presumptions of fact or law but requires that these should be kept within reasonable limits and should not be arbitrary. It is open to states to define the constituent elements of a criminal offence, excluding the requirement of mens rea. But the substance and effect of any presumption adverse to a defendant must be examined, and must be reasonable. Relevant to any judgment on reasonableness or proportionality will be the opportunity given to the defendant to rebut the presumption, maintenance of the rights of the defence, flexibility in application of the presumption, retention by the court of a power to assess the evidence, the importance of what is at stake and the difficulty which a prosecutor may face in the absence of a presumption. Security concerns do not absolve member states from their duty to observe basic standards of fairness. The justifiability of any infringement of the presumption of innocence cannot be resolved by any rule of thumb, but on examination of all the facts and circumstances of the particular provision as applied in the particular case.

The interpretative obligation of the courts under section 3 of the 1998 Act was the subject of illuminating discussion in Ghaidan v Godin-Mendoza [2004] 2 AC 557. The majority opinions of Lord Nicholls, Lord Steyn and Lord Rodger of Earlsferry in that case (with which Baroness Hale of Richmond agreed) do not lend themselves easily to a brief summary. But they leave no room for doubt on four important points. First, the interpretative obligation under section 3 is a very strong and far reaching one, and may require the court to depart from the legislative intention of Parliament. Secondly, a Convention-compliant interpretation under section 3 is the primary remedial measure and a declaration of incompatibility under section 4 an exceptional course. Thirdly, it is to be noted that during the passage of the Bill through Parliament the promoters of the Bill told both Houses that it was envisaged that the need for a declaration of incompatibility would rarely arise. Fourthly, there is a limit beyond which a Convention-compliant interpretation is not possible, such limit being illustrated by R (Anderson) v Secretary of State for the Home Department [2003] 1 AC 837 and Bellinger v Bellinger (Lord Chancellor intervening) [2003] 2 AC 467. In explaining why a Convention-compliant interpretation may not be possible, members of the committee used differing expressions: such an interpretation would be incompatible with the underlying thrust of the legislation, or would not go with the grain of it, or would call for legislative deliberation, or would change the substance of a provision completely, or would remove its pith and substance, or would violate a cardinal principle of the legislation (paras 33, 49, 110–113, 116). All of these expressions, as I respectfully think, yield valuable insights, but none of them should be allowed to supplant the simple test enacted in the Act: 'So far as it is possible to do so . . .' While the House declined to try to formulate precise rules (para 50), it was thought that cases in which section 3 could not be used would in practice be fairly easy to identify.

I intend no disrespect to the Court of Appeal by failing to discuss a number of cases in which that court has considered, in relation to various statutes, the presumption of innocence. But I cannot overlook the decision of an enlarged Court of Appeal (Lord Woolf CJ, Judge LJ, Gage, Elias and Stanley Burnton JJ) in Attorney General's Reference (No 1 of 2004) [2004] 1 WLR 2111 and four appeals heard at the same time. In its judgment the court considered much of the authority to which I have referred (although not Ghaidan v Godin-Mendoza, which had not been decided) and detected (para 38) a 'significant difference in emphasis' between the approach of Lord Steyn in R v Lambert [2002] 2 AC 545 and that of Lord Nicholls in R v Johnstone [2003] 1 WLR 1736. Making plain its preference for the latter, the court prefaced its guidance to the courts of England and Wales by ruling, at para 52a, that: 'Courts should strongly discourage the citation of authority to them other than the decision of the House of Lords in Johnstone and this guidance. Johnstone is at present the latest word on the subject.' Relying on this judgment, Mr Perry, for the Director of Public Prosecutions and the Attorney General, submitted in his printed case and (more tentatively) in argument that there was clearly a difference of emphasis between the approach of Lord Steyn in R v Lambert and that of Lord Nicholls in R v Johnstone, and that the latter was to be preferred. Mr Turner, for Mr Sheldrake, made a submission to the opposite effect, that the reasoning of the House in R v Johnstone should not be followed.

Both R v Lambert [2002] 2 AC 545 and R v Johnstone [2003] 1 WLR 1736 are recent decisions of the House, binding on all lower courts for what they decide. Nothing said in R v Johnstone suggests an intention to depart from or modify the earlier decision, which should not be treated as superseded or implicitly overruled. Differences of emphasis (and Lord Steyn was not a lone voice in R v Lambert) are explicable by the difference in the subject matter of the two cases. Section 5 of the Misuse of Drugs Act 1971 and section 92 of the Trade Marks Act 1994 were directed to serious social and economic problems. But the justifiability and fairness of the respective exoneration provisions had to be judged in the particular context of each case. I have already identified the potential consequence to a section 5 defendant who failed, perhaps narrowly, to make good his section 28 defence. He might be, but fail to prove that he was, entirely ignorant of what he was carrying. By contrast, the offences under section 92 are committed only if the act in question is done by a person 'with a view to gain for himself or another, or with intent to cause loss to another'. Thus these are offences committed (if committed) by dealers, traders, market operators, who could reasonably be expected (as Lord Nicholls pointed out) to exercise some care about the provenance of goods in which they deal. The penalty imposed for breaches of section 92 may be severe (see, for example, R v Gleeson [2002] 1 Cr App R (S) 485), but that is because the potential profits of fraudulent trading are often great.

31 The task of the court is never to decide whether a reverse burden should be imposed on a defendant, but always to assess whether a burden enacted by Parliament unjustifiably infringes the presumption of innocence. It may none the less be questioned whether (as the Court of Appeal ruled in para 52d) 'the assumption should be that Parliament would not have made an exception without good reason'. Such an approach may lead the court to give too much weight to the enactment under review and too little to the presumption of innocence and the obligation imposed on it by section 3.

At the extremes, it is possible to predict with some confidence as to whether a reverse burden is likely to be convention compliant. Thus, and for hypothetical example, a statute that places a burden on an accused person, where the offence is aimed at combating a very serious social evil, is generally viewed as regulatory, carries a very lenient maximum punishment, is something that the defendant is in a much better position to establish than the prosecution and is confined as narrowly as possible, will probably be convention compliant. A statute that imposes a legal burden where these factors operate in the opposite direction (serious punishment, mainstream crime, hard for a defendant to establish, etc.) will probably not be compliant.

However, there is a very large and much less clear-cut, grey area between these extremes where much might depend on the individual judge or judges involved in determining the matter. Fortunately, because the HRA 1998 has now been in force for some years, fresh decisions on compatibility will increasingly be confined to newly enacted statutes. Many longstanding reverse burdens have now been the subject of appellate review. It is also apparent that if a reverse onus provision is deemed incompatible with the 1998 Act it will almost invariably be 'read down' under s. 3 of the Act, rather than the courts having recourse to the s. 4 'declaration of incompatibility' procedure.

Ian Dennis, 'Reverse Onuses and the Presumption of Innocence: In Search of Principle' [2005] Crim LR 901–936

The main conclusions of this inquiry can now be summarised. The imposition by statute of an onus on the defendant in relation to a criminal charge raises a potential issue of compatibility of the onus with the presumption of innocence in Article 6(2) of the ECHR. The issue is resolved by a three-stage process of decision-making.

The first stage of the decision-making process deals with the question whether a statute imposes a burden of any kind on the defendant, and, if so, whether it is a legal or an evidential burden. This question is settled by ordinary principles of statutory construction. These include the effect of s. 101 of the Magistrates' Courts Act 1980, as explained and expanded by Edwards and Hunt. If the burden is an evidential one no problem of compatibility with Article 6 arises. If the burden is a legal one, the issue of compatibility must be considered.

The second stage of decision-making requires a court to decide the issue of compatibility according to whether the reverse onus (legal burden) is justified as a proportionate measure in pursuance of a legitimate aim. It is at this stage that the main problems and uncertainties arise. The debate is almost entirely about proportionality, but analysis of the case law shows considerable disagreement and inconsistency about the use of one or more of six relevant factors [deference to the judgment of parliament, ease of proof, maximum penalty that can be imposed, is it a 'truly criminal' or a 'regulatory' offence, is it an essential element or a special defence to the crime, importance of the presumption of innocence] in determining this question. If no broader principles for applying the relevant factors can be identified, the decisions as to the justifiability of particular reverse onuses will continue to resemble a forensic lottery. A search for principle suggests that issues of moral blameworthiness should be proved by the prosecution. These issues will include, in addition to the relevant prohibited acts, any requisite culpable mental states, any objective fault such as negligence, and the unavailability of any common law defences raised by the defendant. Exceptionally, legal burdens can be placed on defendants to prove formal qualifications to do certain regulated acts, and in cases where the defendant accepts the burden of proof of exculpation by virtue of voluntarily participating in a regulated activity from which he intends to derive benefit. Lord Bingham in Sheldrake adopted a further principle that where the scope of an offence is so wide as to include defendants who are not blameworthy a reverse onus on the defendant to prove lack of culpability is disproportionate. Conversely, an onus to prove facts taking the defendant outside the rationale of the offence, meaning the danger with which the prohibited, morally blameworthy, conduct is intended to deal, may be upheld. There are advantages to Lord Bingham's principle, but also significant problems.

If the reverse onus is justified as proportionate to a legitimate aim no further decision is necessary. If it is not justified according to these criteria the third stage of decision-making requires the court to read down the legal burden to an evidential burden if it is possible to do this using s. 3 of the HRA. On the basis of Sheldrake it seems that it will almost always be possible to do this; it is hard to envisage a case that would not come within the scope of Lord Bingham's reasoning. Accordingly a declaration of incompatibility of a reverse onus will almost never be necessary.

4. Legal Burdens in Civil Matters

The general proposition in civil cases (and very loosely their equivalent of the 'golden thread' in criminal matters) is that: 'He who asserts must prove.' A litigant who desires the court to take action against another party must persuade it of the need to do so: *Dickinson v Minister of Pensions* [1953] 1 QB 228. As a result, it is normally the claimant who must establish (to the appropriate standard) the main elements of his cause of action, as he is the party who brings the matter to court. In the tort of negligence, for example, these will be duty, breach and non-remote damage. In an action for breach of contract, they will be the existence of a contract, subsequent breach and consequent loss.

Of course, many of these issues are decided on the exchange of statements of case (formerly termed pleadings), narrowing down the issues to be determined at trial; the pleadings can also be employed to determine who is 'asserting': *Wilsher v Essex Area Health Authority* [1988] AC 1074. However, it is the effect, not the wording, of an allegation that decides where the burden lies. Otherwise, clever drafting could suggest that it was always the defendant who was asserting: *Soward v Legatt* (1836) 7 C & P 613.

Cross-reference Box

Matters asserted and admitted in such documents cease to be in issue. This is one way in which facts can be determined without the formal adduction of evidence (there are several others). For more on this, go to chapter 1, at pp. 18–24.

Nevertheless, although it is usually the claimant who is asserting, this is not always the case; as a result, sometimes it will be the defendant who carries a legal burden. For example, in a case involving the defence of contributory negligence, it is the defendant who has the onus of establishing 'contrib', though the claimant must still prove all the other inherent elements of his/her case. Occasionally, however, it is not immediately clear who is asserting what, and a perusal of the case law is helpful in deciding where a legal burden lies. For example, it would appear that if the defendant is seeking to show that a contract has been brought to an end by a frustrating event, such as a thunderbolt destroying its subject matter, he will have the onus of showing that such an event occurred and rendered further performance impossible. The claimant will, of course, still bear the burden of establishing that there was a contract and prima facie breach.

What if the claimant asserts that, even if an apparently frustrating event did occur, it came about because of the defendant's default or negligence? (The doctrine of frustration only applies if it was not the result of either party's fault, whether deliberate or negligent, ie it was not 'self-induced'.) The case law on this issue suggests that in such a situation the burden will return to the claimant to establish fault. Thus, in *Joseph Constantine Steamship Line Ltd v Imperial Smelting Corpn Ltd* [1942] AC 154 (HL) Lord Russell of Killowen noted that in a breach of contract action for failure to load and ship cargo, where the defence was a frustrating act (the explosion of the ship), once the explosion had been proved by the party arguing that the contract was frustrated, any attempt to defeat such a defence by asserting that the prima facie frustrating event was self-induced had to be proved by the party who asserted that it should not apply (ie the claimant). This was especially the case as, it was argued, proving a negative in such a situation would be a very difficult, if not impossible, burden to impose on a litigant.

Joseph Constantine Steamship Line v Imperial Smelting Corporation
[1942] AC 154, HL

Viscount Simon LC

It is true that he [the arbitrator] also stated that he was not satisfied that negligence on the part of the servants of the appellants did not cause or contribute to the disaster. That, in my view, amounts to a finding that, notwithstanding the evidence, there was a possibility that there had been negligence or default on the part of the servants of the appellants. If, however, I am right in the opinion above expressed that the onus of establishing absence of default did not rest on the appellants, the mere possibility of default on their part is not sufficient to disentitle them to rely on the principle of frustration. For these reasons I am of opinion that the appeal should be allowed and that the order of Atkinson J. should be restored with costs here and below.

Similarly, where a defendant argues that he should be exempt from the consequences of an alleged breach of contract, because the breach falls within an exclusion clause, he will have the onus of proving that he is covered by the terms of that clause: *The Glendarroch* [1894] P 226.

The Glendarroch [1894] P 226, CA

Lopes LJ

The question raised on this appeal is as to the onus of proof; as a general rule, it may be said that the burden of proof lies on the person who affirms a particular thing 'ei incumbit probatio qui dicit, non qui negat'. It appears to me in this case that the burden of proving that the loss which has happened is attributable to an excepted cause lies on the person who is setting it up. That in this case would be the defendants, the shipowners. If, however, the excepted cause by itself is sufficient to account for the loss, it appears to me that the burden of shewing that there is something else which deprives the party of the power of relying on the excepted cause lies on the person who sets up that contention. That in this case would be the plaintiffs, who are the shippers.

I think that is not only the result of the authorities, but of all pleadings before the Judicature Acts. The cases which have been referred to are Grill v. General Iron Screw Collier Co., Czech v. General Steam Navigation Co., Taylor v. Liverpool and Great Western Steam Co., Peninsular and Oriental Steamship Co. v. Shand, and Wyld v. Pickford.

These cases shew what I have stated with regard to the onus of proof, namely, that where a peril of the sea is set up it is sufficient for the defendant to prove the peril relied on, and he need not go on to shew that that was really not caused by him; but if the plaintiff says that it was, then he must set it up in his replication and must prove it.

However, there are a few cases where this general analysis ('he who asserts must prove') does not appear to apply. For example, in some contracts involving bailment it seems that a bailor merely has to show the bailment and a subsequent failure to restore the goods. The legal burden may then be on the bailee to prove that he was not at fault in their loss. There are policy reasons for such an approach; most importantly, the bailor has no way of establishing what happened to his goods after he handed them over: *Levison and another v Patent Steam Carpet Cleaning Co. Ltd.* [1978] QB 69, CA.

Levison and another v Patent Steam Carpet Cleaning Co. Ltd.
[1978] QB 69, CA

Lord Denning MR

On whom is the burden of proof? Take the present case. Assuming that clause 2 (a) or clause 5, or either of them, limits or exempts the cleaners from liability for negligence: but not for a fundamental breach. On whom is the burden to prove that there was fundamental breach? Upon principle, I should have thought that the burden was on the cleaners to prove that they were not Guilty of a fundamental breach. After all, Mrs. Levison does not know what happened to it. The cleaners are the ones who know, or should know, what happened to the carpet, and the burden should be on them to say what it was. It was so held by McNair J. in Woolmer v. Delmer Price Ltd. [1955] 1 Q.B. 291; and by me in J. Spurling Ltd. v. Bradshaw [1956] 1 W.L.R. 461, 466, and by the East African Court of Appeal in United Manufacturers Ltd. v. WAFCO Ltd. [1974] E.A. 233. A contrary view was expressed by this court in Hunt & Winterbotham (West of England) Ltd. v. B.R.S. (Parcels) Ltd. [1962] 1 Q.B. 617, 635. and there is a long line of shipping cases in which it has been held that, if a shipowner makes a prima facie case that the cause of the loss was one of the excepted perils, the burden is on the shipper to prove that it was not covered by the exceptions: see The Glendarroch [1894] P. 226 and Munro, Brice & Co. v. War Risks Association Ltd. [1918] 2 K.B. 78. To which there may be added Joseph Constantine Steamship Line Ltd. v. Imperial Smelting Corporation Ltd. [1942] A.C. 154 on frustration.

It is, therefore, a moot point for decision. On it I am clearly of opinion that, in a contract of bailment, when a bailee seeks to escape liability on the ground that he was not negligent or that he was excused by an exception or limitation clause, then he must show what happened to the goods. He must prove all the circumstances known to him in which the loss or damage occurred. If it appears that the goods were lost or damaged without any negligence on his part, then, of course, he is not liable. If it appears that they were lost or damaged by a slight breach—not going to the root of the contract—he may be protected by the exemption or limitation clause. But, if he leaves the cause of loss or damage undiscovered and unexplained—then I think he is liable: because it is then quite likely that the goods were stolen by one of his servants; or delivered by a servant to the wrong address; or damaged by reckless or wilful misconduct; all of which the offending servant will conceal and not make known to his employer. Such conduct would be a fundamental breach against which the exemption or limitation clause will not protect him.

It should be noted that it is always open to the parties to a contract expressly to determine who will have the legal burden on certain issues, should a dispute result in litigation, even if this is at variance to the normal position: *Levy v Assicurazioni Generali* [1940] AC 791. Additionally, a specific statutory provision will sometimes determine where a legal burden lies in a civil case. Thus, s. 98(1) of the Employment Rights Act 1996 provides that, in an unfair dismissal claim, once the dismissal has been proved, it is for the employer to establish that it was fair, although he is the respondent in the action.

5. Evidential Burdens

Introduction

A legal burden always also carries an evidential burden. This is the obligation to adduce some evidence on a matter, so that it becomes a 'live' issue and warrants consideration by the tribunal of fact (whether judge, jury or magistrates). If a party with a legal burden does not call any evidence at all on the matter that they have to prove, it will usually be thrown out following a submission of 'no case to answer' by the opposing side. In practice, these are most commonly made in criminal matters. In civil cases, such an application, if unsuccessful, usually precludes the subsequent calling of defence evidence (see chapter 1). As a result, unless a case is extremely clear-cut, the defendant has no evidence to call in rebuttal, or he receives an obvious invitation from a trial judge to make an application, such submissions are rare.

However in, for example, a theft case, if, prior to closing its case, the Crown fails to call any evidence on one (or more) of the essential elements of the offence, such as whether the property in question 'belonged to another', defence counsel will almost always ask that the matter be withdrawn from the jury, who will not then be required to decide whether the Crown has satisfied its legal burden on the issue. The defendant will be formally acquitted. In the criminal courts, submissions of no case to answer are governed by the principles set out in *R v Galbraith* [1981] 73 Cr App R 124.

 Cross-reference Box

In essence, *Galbraith* provides that such a submission must be allowed if there is no evidence on an essential matter that the prosecution has to establish, or if the trial judge concludes that, taking the prosecution's evidence at its highest, no reasonable or properly directed jury could convict. However, the judge should not normally attempt a qualitative assessment of the evidence ('do I personally believe this witness?'). For more on submissions of no case to answer go to chapter 1 at p. 9.

A jury never needs to consider whether an evidential burden has been satisfied, as it is always a matter for the tribunal of law (ie the presiding judge or magistrates), which is why it is also known colloquially as 'passing the judge'. If an issue becomes live, it goes to the tribunal of fact. If it does not, and it is a trial on indictment, the jury do not consider the defence. Magistrates, of course, should decide not to direct their minds to any issue on which an evidential burden has not been satisfied. That an evidential burden has been met does not, of course, necessarily mean that the party's legal burden on the same matter will be satisfied. A party can adduce some tangible evidence on an issue without coming close to proving it beyond reasonable doubt or even on the balance of probabilities.

 Exam tip

It is normally a cardinal mistake, in a problem question on the burden and standard of proof, to discuss jurors considering evidential burdens.

Evidential Without Legal Burdens

More rarely, a party to litigation might carry an evidential burden without also having a legal burden. This is most commonly found in the raising of certain defences in criminal trials, though it occasionally occurs in civil cases as well. Thus, in the case of the defence of duress, some evidence must be adduced to suggest that the accused was coerced to behave as he did: *R v Gill* [1963] 1 WLR 841.

R v Gill [1963] 1 WLR 841, CCA

Edmund Davies J

The issue of duress was, nevertheless, left to the jury in the present case, and that may well have been the prudent course. Having been left, did the burden rest upon the Crown conclusively to destroy this defence, in the same way as it is required to destroy such other defences as provocation or self-defence? Or was the accused required to establish it, on the balance of probabilities? For the latter view, reliance was placed on the judgment of Lord Goddard C.J. in Rex v. Steane, in the course of which he said: '...before any question of duress arises, a jury must be satisfied that the prisoner had the intention which is laid in the indictment. Duress is a matter of defence and the onus of proving it is on the accused. As we have already said, where an intent is charged on the indictment, it is for the prosecution to prove it, so the onus is the other way.'

On the other hand, in Rex v. Purdy, where a British prisoner of war was charged with treason, Oliver J., directing the jury on the defence of duress, said: 'If you believe, or if you think that it might be true, that he only did that because he had the fear of death upon him, then you will acquit him on that charge, because to act in matters of this sort under threat of death is excusable.'

Similarly, in Reg. v. Shiartos, where duress was relied upon by an accused charged with arson, Lawton J. directed the jury that: 'If, in all the circumstances of this case, you are satisfied that what he did he did at pistol point and in fear of his life, he is entitled to be acquitted. If, although you are not satisfied, you think it might well be that he was forced at pistol point to do what he had to do, then again you should acquit him, because the prosecution would not have made you feel sure that what he did he did maliciously.'

In our judgment, the law on this matter is to be found correctly stated in Dr. Glanville Williams' Criminal Law, 2nd ed. (1961), p. 762, in this way: '...although it is convenient to call duress a "defence", this does not mean that the ultimate (persuasive) burden of proving it is on the accused....But the accused must raise the defence by sufficient evidence to go to the jury; in other words, the evidential burden is on him.'

The Crown are not called upon to anticipate such a defence and destroy it in advance. The defendant, either by the cross-examination of the prosecution witnesses or by evidence called on his behalf, or by a combination of the two, must place before the court such material as makes duress a live issue fit and proper to be left to the jury. But, once he has succeeded in doing this, it is then for the Crown to destroy that defence in such a manner as to leave in the jury's minds no reasonable doubt that the accused cannot be absolved on the grounds of the alleged compulsion. It is true that this approach appears to conflict with the literal reading of the passage from Lord Goddard C.J.'s judgment in Rex v. Steane. It is to be observed, however, that that passage was obiter in that the real decision there was that it was for the Crown to prove the specific intent laid and that in the particular circumstances of that case an inference could not be drawn that the prisoner intended the natural consequences of his act. We agree with Dr. Glanville Williams that the dictum must be read as relating only to what the author calls the 'evidential' burden cast upon the accused, and not to the ultimate (or 'persuasive') burden placed upon the Crown of destroying the defence of duress where it has been substantially raised.

Similarly, non-insane automatism places an evidential burden on the accused: *Hill v Baxter* [1958] 1 QB 277. Much more commonly, where a defence of self-defence is advanced at trial, some evidence of this must be adduced before the jury are required to consider it: *R v Lobell* [1957] 1 QB 547.

R v Lobell [1957] 1 QB 547, CCA

Lord Goddard CJ

If an issue relating to self-defence is to be left to the jury there must be some evidence from which a jury would be entitled to find that issue in favour of the accused, and ordinarily no doubt such evidence would be given by the defence. But there is a difference between leading evidence which would enable a jury to find an issue in favour of a defendant and in putting the onus upon him. The truth is that the jury must come to a verdict on the whole of the evidence that has been laid before them. If on a consideration of all the evidence the jury are left in doubt whether the killing or wounding may not have been in self-defence the proper verdict would be not guilty. A convenient way of directing the jury is to tell them that the burden of establishing guilt is on the prosecution, but that they must also consider the evidence for the defence which may have one of three results: it may convince them of the innocence of the accused, or it may cause them to doubt, in which case the defendant is entitled to an acquittal, or it may and sometimes does strengthen the case for the prosecution. It is perhaps a fine distinction to say that before a jury can find a particular issue in favour of an accused person he must give some evidence on which it can be found but none the less the onus remains on the prosecution; what it really amounts to is that if in the result the jury are left in doubt where the truth lies the verdict should be not guilty, and this is as true of an issue as to self-defence as it is to one of provocation, though of course the latter plea goes only to a mitigation of the offence. Had the judge in the present case gone on to say that it was not for the accused to establish his plea with the same degree of certainty as is necessary to establish a case for the prosecution it might have been that we should have had to consider whether this was a case for the application of the proviso. There was certainly here material on which a jury might have found self-defence. But that it was the duty of the accused to satisfy them on this point was on several occasions stressed in the summing-up and we do not feel by any means satisfied that if what we now hold was the correct direction had been given the jury would be sure to have convicted. For these reasons we quashed the conviction at the close of the argument.

Perhaps more puzzlingly, it has been held that an alibi defence places an evidential burden on the defendant who advances it. Nevertheless, it could be argued that an alibi is, effectively, simply a denial that the accused was at the crime scene, something that the prosecution must prove as an inherent part of its case, in the same way that it had to prove that the killing in *Woolmington* was deliberate. Less controversially, drunkenness will place an evidential burden on a defendant who raises it to (for example) claim that he could not have formed a specific intent because of his degree of intoxication: *R v Groark* [1999] Crim LR 669.

There are a considerable number of others, less commonly encountered in practice than the examples already considered. For example, in *R v Makuwa* [2006] Crim LR 911 it was held that a defendant merely had an evidential burden to raise the fact that he was a refugee pursuant to s. 31 of the Immigration and Asylum Act 1999, the prosecution then bore the burden of proving that he was not.

In these situations, if the defendant does satisfy his evidential burden on an issue, the Crown will acquire a fresh legal burden, on top of the inherent elements of the offence; that is to prove (beyond reasonable doubt) that the accused was not acting as a result of duress, in self-defence, etc. However, the prosecution does not have such an obligation at the very outset of the trial, simply because a 'not guilty' plea is entered by the defendant. It will acquire it only if the defence is made 'live' by some tangible evidence being adduced during the hearing, though, frequently, it will be able to anticipate the defence as a result of police interviews, etc.

This situation can be contrasted to that in which an issue is an innate part of the 'affirmative' prosecution case, where there is no such burden on the defendant, and where a plea of not guilty always puts the prosecution to strict proof of all the essential elements of the offence. Thus, if a defendant accused of theft simply denies that he appropriated the property that forms the subject matter of the charge he will not have to adduce any evidence on that matter (though it might well be tactically prudent to do so).

By contrast, if he feels he should be acquitted of theft because he was compelled to steal by threats of violence from a third party, he (or someone else) will have to provide evidence of such duress before the tribunal of fact needs to consider whether the prosecution has discharged its legal burden of proving (beyond reasonable doubt) that the accused was not acting under duress. In *Sheldrake v DPP* [2005] 1 AC 264 Lord Bingham succinctly summarized the distinction: 'An evidential burden is not a burden of proof. It is a burden of raising, on the evidence in the case, an issue as to the matter in question fit for consideration by the tribunal of fact. If an issue is properly raised, it is for the prosecutor to prove, beyond reasonable doubt, that that ground of exoneration does not avail the defendant.'

As Lord Bingham's comment in *Sheldrake* makes clear, it is wrong to speak of an 'evidential burden of proof'. The party with such a burden does not have to *prove* anything; he does not have to meet any *standard* of persuasion. All that the phrase signifies is that *some* tangible evidence must be adduced on the relevant issue by the party that carries such a burden. This then raises the obvious question, how tangible should such evidence be? Clearly, for example, an unsubstantiated and rejected suggestion by counsel during the examination of witnesses is not 'evidence'.

Exam tip

It is best always to avoid the phrase 'evidential burden of proof', as this is likely to lead to confusion with the legal burden, whether in problem or essay questions.

Generally, the courts appear to approach the matter in a fairly liberal manner, especially where an evidential burden is placed on a defendant in a criminal matter. This was expressly recognized by the Privy Council in *Xavier v The State* (unreported), 17 December 1998; Appeal No 59 of 1997, which held that the threshold of credibility to satisfy such a burden was a low one. If there is *any* evidence, whether from the defendant, another witness (including those called by the prosecution) or any other source, trial judges usually allow the defence to go to the jury, if only to preclude the risk of a subsequent successful appeal.

Nevertheless, there does appear to be a qualitative threshold, albeit a low one, and the courts are not obliged to take such an indulgent attitude. In the Privy Council case of *Jayasena v The Queen* [1970] AC 618, a murder trial from Ceylon, Lord Devlin considered what would be necessary to discharge an evidential burden placed on a defendant by a defence of self-defence. He concluded that it required a defendant to collect enough evidence 'to make it possible for a reasonable jury to acquit'.

Jayasena v The Queen PC [1970] AC 618, PC

Lord Devlin

Their Lordships do not understand what is meant by the phrase 'evidential burden of proof'. They understand, of course, that in trial by jury a party may be required to adduce some evidence in support of his case, whether on the general issue or on a particular issue, before that issue is left to the jury. How much evidence has to be adduced depends upon the nature of the requirement. It may be such evidence as, if believed and if left uncontradicted and unexplained, could be accepted by the jury as proof. Or it may be, as in English law when on a charge of murder the issue of provocation arises, enough evidence to suggest a reasonable possibility. It is doubtless permissible to describe the requirement as a burden, and it may be convenient to call it an evidential burden. But it is confusing to call it a burden of proof. Further, it is misleading to call it a burden of proof, whether described as legal or evidential or by any other adjective, when it can be discharged by the production of evidence that falls short of proof. The essence of the appellant's case is that he has not got to provide any sort of proof that he was acting in private defence. So it is a misnomer to call whatever it is that he has to provide a burden of proof.

As *Jayasena* suggests, absolutely minimal evidence on an issue will not necessarily satisfy an evidential burden, though it might require a 'courageous' judge to withhold an associated defence from a defendant. Nevertheless, this is what occurred in *R v Miao* [2003] EWCA Crim 3486, and the trial judge's decision was subsequently approved by the Court of Appeal. When an evidential burden is on the prosecution, the test appears to be slightly stricter; in *Jayasena* Lord Devlin suggested that it would be satisfied by evidence that: '...if believed, and if left uncontradicted and unexplained, could be accepted by the jury as proof'. There are some sound policy reasons for such a distinction. The prosecution has to adduce evidence that can preclude a successful submission of no case to answer, and which ultimately might persuade a jury beyond reasonable doubt. The defence merely has to find enough evidence to allow a jury to be directed to consider the relevant issue, and which might be capable of raising a reasonable doubt.

If no (or no acceptable) evidential foundation is laid for a defence that carries such a burden, counsel will not be allowed to broach the subject when addressing a bench or jury. Thus, in *R v Pommell* [1995] 2 Cr App R 607, in which a defence of necessity for the possession of a firearm was advanced by counsel late in the trial, the Court of Appeal reiterated that a first instance judge was entitled to withdraw such an issue from the jury if there was no evidence to support it.

It should also be stressed that, although an evidential burden is normally satisfied by evidence called by the accused (often the testimony of the defendant himself), this is not invariably the case. Evidence adduced by a witness for the Crown, even if the 'victim', can also make such a defence 'live'. As Lord Steyn observed in *R v Acott* [1997] 2 Crim App R 94: '...it does not matter from what source that evidence emerges'.

The Trial Judge's 'Invisible Burden'

A potentially difficult situation occurs when evidence of a possible defence emerges during a criminal trial, which would be enough to satisfy the evidential burden on that defence, but where the accused chooses, for tactical reasons, not to advance or even mention it. This is particularly likely where the relevant evidence comes from a source other than the defendant; for example, a prosecution witness. Such a situation is especially common where the 'main' line of defence effectively precludes counsel from addressing the jury on any alternative possibility, for fear of undermining the primary defence.

For example, suppose that an eyewitness to an alleged murder gives testimony suggesting that the defendant, although responsible for the killing, may have struck the fatal blow to protect himself from an assault by the dead man. Nevertheless, despite this, the accused's defence is one of alibi, denying that he was anywhere near the crime scene at the relevant time. In these circumstances, it will be almost impossible for defence counsel to raise self-defence as well as alibi without seriously undermining the alibi defence. As a result, it is likely that he will make no mention of it at all when addressing the jury, rather than saying something bizarre such as: '…the defendant was nowhere near the killing, and if he was, he was acting in self defence'. However, in these situations the trial judge comes under an obligation to put any defence raised on the evidence to the jury on his own initiative, even if the issue is not expressly raised by defence counsel, *provided* that the evidential foundation for such a defence is established during the trial: *Palmer v R* (1971) 55 Cr App R 223. This is sometimes called the judge's 'invisible burden'.

A selection of cases illustrates the working of the invisible burden. Thus, in *R v Cambridge* [1994] 1 WLR 971, the Court of Appeal held that provocation should have been left to the jury, even though it was entirely inconsistent with the defence of mistaken identity being advanced by the accused, because it was raised on the evidence. The judge's failure to do so meant that the murder conviction was quashed and one of manslaughter returned.

Similarly, in the case of *R v Owino* [1996] 2 Cr App R 128, the trial judge did not put self-defence to the jury in the trial of a man for assaulting his wife (having deliberately decided not to do so as it was not referred to by either counsel during the trial), until a note from the jury raised the issue. The Court of Appeal was firmly of the opinion that if, as was clearly the situation in the instant case, the: '…issue of self-defence had been raised on the evidence, he [the judge] had a duty to put it to the jury and to direct the jury upon it. The fact, if it be a fact, that counsel had not specifically referred to self-defence in the course of their speeches was no reason for the learned judge not to deal with it in his summing up.' In this case, the police interview of the appellant had made it clear that his version of events was that any violence that he had used towards his wife was employed only when restraining her after she had attacked him.

Finally, in *R v Calvert* [2000] WL 1841611 the defendant was convicted of raping an inebriated student that he met in the street late at night. At trial, his defence was that she had consented to intercourse and this was the only issue that defence counsel or the judge put to the jury. However, his conviction was quashed because the trial judge had failed to direct the jury on a possible secondary defence that was available to the accused, namely, that he did not know that the complainant was not consenting nor was he reckless as to whether or not there was consent. The evidence, much of which came from the complainant, indicated that there had been a conversation, that she accompanied him without pressure to a secluded alley, gave no verbal or other indication to the appellant that she was unwilling to have intercourse and there was no evidence of a struggle.

The Invisible Burden and Provocation

As *Cambridge* suggests, one of the most common situations in which a judge must let a defence go to the jury that was not canvassed by the defendant, but which is potentially available on the evidence, occurs with regard to the partial defence of provocation under s. 3 of the Homicide Act 1957. This is usually because it is inconsistent with an accused person's main defence, and would undermine his chance of a complete acquittal (producing, instead, a verdict of guilty of manslaughter).

Nevertheless, in *R v Campbell* (1986) 84 Cr App R 255 Lord Lane CJ was adamant that if there was evidence of provocation a judge must leave that defence to the jury 'even if it is not relied upon by those appearing for the defendant at trial'. More detailed guidance was provided by the Privy Council in *Von Starck v The Queen* [2000] 1 WLR 1270, which concluded that there would be few, if any, circumstances in which a trial judge did not have a duty to put such a possibility before the jury.

> ### *Von Starck v The Queen* [2000] 1 WLR 1270, PC
>
> #### Lord Clyde
>
> For tactical reasons counsel for a defendant may not wish to enlarge upon, or even to mention, a possible conclusion which the jury would be entitled on the evidence to reach, in the fear that what he might see as a compromise conclusion would detract from a more stark choice between a conviction on a serious charge and an acquittal. But if there is evidence to support such a compromise verdict it is the duty of the judge to explain it to the jury and leave the choice to them.

Over forty years ago, Lord Devlin in *Lee-Chun-Chuen v R* [1963] 1 All ER 73 stressed that where provocation was raised: 'All the defence need do is to point to material which could induce a reasonable doubt.' What constitutes such 'material'? The House of Lords decision in *R v Acott* [1997] 1 All ER 706 examined in detail how the evidential burden relating to provocation might be discharged. Section 3 of the Homicide Act 1957 provides that the partial defence will only apply where there is 'evidence on which the jury find that the person charged was provoked (whether by things done or by things said or by both together) to lose his self-control'. It appears that the wording of this provision puts particular constraints on how its evidential burden can be satisfied, unlike some other defence evidential burdens.

In *Acott,* the defendant, a 48-year-old man, lived with, and was financially dependent on, his elderly mother who could be quite 'difficult,' sometimes treating him as if he was a child and frequently stressing his monetary dependence on her. On the day of his mother's death, he called an ambulance saying that she had fallen down some stairs and hurt herself. The ambulance men found her dead on the floor. She had suffered serious multiple injuries to the head and neck. Acott denied any responsibility for his mother's death, claiming that her injuries were caused by her fall, perhaps compounded by his clumsy efforts at first aid.

At trial, medical evidence was adduced to suggest that the woman had died from a sustained physical attack and that her injuries were inexplicable by the defendant's version of events. However, it was accepted by the doctor concerned that the injuries she sustained were indicative of a sudden loss of self-control by her attacker, and prosecuting counsel even put this to the defendant in cross-examination. Had Acott, who was a man of previous good character, conceded that this is what had occurred, and given evidence of what had provoked him, the partial defence would certainly have gone to the jury and, in the circumstances, might well have been successful. Instead, he resolutely maintained his version of events throughout the hearing, seeking a complete acquittal.

The trial judge directed the jury that, in light of the defence offered (a simple denial), the only issue for them to decide was whether or not the defendant murdered his mother. The jury convicted by a majority verdict. Acott's appeal to the Court of Appeal was dismissed. On a final appeal, the House of Lords held that there must be some evidence as to what was done or said to provoke the alleged loss of self-control. In the absence of evidence of a specific act or words of provocation, the trial judge should not direct the jury to speculate about possible provocation even if the circumstances might suggest that it was likely. As a result, the appeal was dismissed.

However, when counsel for the appellant in *Acott* invited the House of Lords to state exactly what would be sufficient evidence of provocation to justify it being left to the jury, his invitation was firmly rejected. This was because it was not a question of law: 'Where the line is to be drawn depends on a judgment involving logic and common sense, the assessment of matters of degree and an intense focus on the circumstances of a particular case. It is unwise to generalise on such matters: it is a subject best left to the good sense of trial judges.'

Such an approach was subsequently followed by the Court of Appeal in *R v Nicholas Paul Arnold* [1998] EWCA Crim 1617, where the appellant had killed the deceased woman during a sustained attack at his flat. He claimed he was suffering from amnesia and thus had no recollection of the killing. Obviously, in this situation, he could give no evidence of 'anything said or done' by the deceased which might conceivably have provoked him to behave as he did. The trial judge ruled that he was not prepared to leave provocation to the jury. From the nature of the victim's injuries and the inferences to be drawn from the sites of violence in the appellant's flat it was possible to infer that he lost his self-control and attacked the deceased in something of a frenzy. However, other explanations for these injuries could also be advanced. The Court of Appeal rejected the appellant's argument that, in the circumstances, there was a proper evidential basis for leaving provocation to the jury. There had to be a reasonable possibility arising on the evidence that something specific was said or done which provoked the appellant to lose his self-control. Mere speculation was not enough to found such a defence.

The approach taken in *Acott* was also followed by the Court of Appeal, in slightly less clear-cut circumstances, in *R v Miao* [2003] EWCA Crim 3486, in which the defendant allegedly killed a woman with whom he had had a stormy relationship. At trial, his defence was to deny the presence of any intent to kill or cause grievous bodily harm during the lethal assault. The trial judge refused to leave provocation to thc jury, as an alternative defence, despite being invited to do so by both prosecution and defence counsel, and although he accepted there was some 'minimal' evidence of words and deeds that could have been provocative. On appeal, his decision was upheld.

R v Acott [1997] 2 Cr App R 94, HL

Lord Steyn

It follows that there can only be an issue of provocation to be considered by the jury if the judge considers that there is some evidence of a specific act or words of provocation resulting in a loss of self-control. It does not matter from what source that evidence emerges or whether it is relied on at trial by the defendant or not. If there is such evidence, the judge must leave the issue to the jury. If there is no such evidence, but merely the speculative possibility that there had been an act of provocation, it is wrong for the judge to direct the jury to consider provocation. In such a case there is simply no triable issue of provocation. I would hold that in such circumstances our law of provocation knows no principle that 'the jury must not be deprived of their opportunity to return a perverse verdict': see the commentary by Sir John Smith on Stewart [1995] Crim.L.R. 67 but compare his later commentary on Acott [1996] Crim.L.R. 665. Counsel for the appellant invited your Lordships to go further and state what would be sufficient evidence of provocation to justify a trial judge in leaving the issue of provocation for the jury to consider. The invitation was attractively put. But it must be rejected. What is sufficient evidence in this particular context is not a question of law. Where the line is to be drawn depends on a judgment involving logic and common sense, the assessment of matters of degree and an intense focus on the circumstances of a particular case. It is unwise to generalise on such matters: it is a subject best left to the good sense of trial judges. For the same reason it is not useful to compare the facts of decided cases on provocation with one another.

For my part the certified question can be answered in the general way in which I have indicated. But the reasoning in this judgment is subject to the overriding principle that the legal burden rests on the Crown to disprove provocation on a charge of murder to the required standard of proof. In Lee Chun-Chuen v. R. [1963] A.C. 220, 229, Lord Devlin summed up the legal position as follows: '. . . It is not, of course, for the defence to make out a prima facie case of provocation. It is for the prosecution to prove that the killing was unprovoked. All that the defence need do is to point to material which could induce a reasonable doubt.'

It should be noted that provocation is not unique as a defence that has fairly specific, if not technical, requirements, before its evidential burden is satisfied. Another example occurs with regard to the defence of automatism, which, it appears, requires some medical evidence (from a qualified doctor) to make it 'live', rather than being based purely on defendant testimony: *Bratty v Attorney-General for Northern Ireland* [1963] AC 386.

Bratty v Attorney-General for Northern Ireland [1963] AC 386, HL

Lord Denning

What, then, is a proper foundation? The presumption of mental capacity of which I have spoken is a provisional presumption only. It does not put the legal burden on the defence in the same way as the presumption of sanity does. It leaves the legal burden on the prosecution, but nevertheless, until it is displaced, it enables the prosecution to discharge the ultimate burden of proving that the act was voluntary. Not because the presumption is evidence itself, but because it takes the place of evidence. In order to displace the presumption of mental capacity, the defence must give sufficient evidence from which it may reasonably be inferred that the act was involuntary. The evidence of the man himself will rarely be sufficient unless it is supported by medical evidence which points to the cause of the mental incapacity. It is not sufficient for a man to say 'I had a black-out': for 'black-out' as Stable J. said in Cooper v. McKenna, *ex parte* Cooper 'is one of the first refuges of a guilty conscience and a popular excuse'. The words of Devlin J. in Hill v. Baxter should be remembered: I do not doubt that there are genuine cases of automatism and the like, but I do not see how the layman can safely attempt without the help of some medical or scientific evidence to distinguish the genuine from the fraudulent.

6. The Standard of Proof in Criminal and Civil Matters

Introduction

Whether the evidence adduced is quantitatively enough to satisfy a proponent's burden of proof will depend on its weight or 'cogency'. As has regularly been noted, no conclusions reached in legal disputes are ever made with absolute certainty. Even apparently overwhelming evidence could, in theory, turn out to be flawed. For example, if a College of Cardinals claimed to have been eyewitnesses, at close quarters, to a crime, giving identical evidence on the matter, it is, theoretically, always possible that they had secretly been administered a hallucinatory drug and then hypnotized to believe they had seen something that had not actually occurred! As a result, the use of probabilistic concepts is necessary. These are usually expressed verbally, although one of them (the balance of probabilities) also allows for a mathematical calculation.[5]

The Standard of Proof in Criminal Cases

Perhaps because at first sight it appears intellectually less challenging than the problems occasioned by interpreting the ramifications of *Lambert* and other more arcane aspects of the burden of proof, questions as to the *degree* of cogency that evidence must reach to satisfy the various burdens in a criminal or civil trial tend to be glossed over in undergraduate and professional evidence courses, as well as in legal periodicals and textbooks. However, it is a subject that is at least as important to the outcome of the litigation process as the onus of proving an issue, usually being the key question that the tribunal of fact addresses its collective mind to. Given that by the time the issue of guilt is decided by the tribunal of fact it will have survived a potential submission of 'no case to answer' it is probably safe to assume that in many (if not most) criminal cases the key issue to be decided is whether the Crown's case leaves a doubt in the minds of JPs or jurors.

   Another reason for the lack of analysis is the conceptually almost indefinable nature of many of the questions raised, something that led the Court of Appeal in *R v Ching* (1976) 63 Cr App R 7 to conclude that: 'If judges stopped trying to define that which is almost impossible to define there would be fewer appeals.' However, encouraging judicial silence on this issue can also be unhelpful. Anecdotal evidence would appear to suggest that it is an area that creates considerable problems for juries when reaching decisions. Thus, some years ago, in a letter to a national newspaper, a former member of the jury in a complicated drug dealing case expressed concern about his colleagues' understanding of the appropriate standard. The jury had acquitted the defendant on a majority verdict, despite finding his defence 'unbelievable', having been told on numerous occasions by the defence, prosecution and trial judge that they had to be 'sure beyond reasonable doubt'. The juryman noted that: 'All my fellow jurymen and jurywomen took this

---

[5] T Anderson, W Twining and D Schum, *Analysis of Evidence* (2nd edn, 2005, Cambridge University Press) at 246.

to mean that if any of the defendants could offer any explanation—however ludicrous—we should accept it.' The trial judge clearly felt their decision perverse as he asked them to remain behind afterwards to witness the sentencing of the defendant on other drugs offences to which he had pleaded guilty.[6] (Interestingly, in this context, research over the past decade, suggests that 'sure', especially when it is unaccompanied by any mention of 'beyond reasonable doubt', is interpreted by over half of all jurors to mean 100 per cent certain.)[7]

The Prosecution Standard of Proof

In the early eighteenth century, the burden of proof in a criminal trial was not clearly fixed on the Crown, and thus the standard of proof was also not firmly established. A standard of proof that was 'beyond reasonable doubt' was not formally enunciated until the final quarter of the eighteenth century, when, in 1777, Lord Mansfield directed a jury that the evidence should irresistibly prove the crime, and that if 'not perfectly convinced you must find the accused not guilty'. However, a belief that doubts should be resolved in favour of the accused was much older, though a lack of precise formulation may have reduced its impact.[8] There are numerous intimations from the late medieval period onwards that any uncertainty should normally work in a defendant's favour.[9] Thus, although the standard of proof was often still vague in the 1460s, in serious conventional felonies at least, it was generally accepted that it was much better that: '…twenty guilty persons should escape the punishment of death, than that one innocent person should be condemned and suffer capitally'.[10]

In the past 250 years, case law has produced two widely accepted definitions of the criminal standard as well as an approved combination. Nevertheless, as the appellate courts periodically restate, there is no 'magic' in these customary phrases (although they are almost invariably used, such that any departures from them would be automatically fatal to a conviction). It is the overall tenor of the words that is significant. In *R v Kritz* [1950] 1 KB 82, Lord Goddard declared that: 'It would be a great misfortune, in criminal cases especially, if the accuracy or inaccuracy of a summing up were to depend upon whether or not the Judge or the Chairman had used a particular formula of words. It is not the particular formula of words that matters; it is the effect of the summing up.' This was reiterated by Lord Diplock in *Walters v The Queen* [1969] 1 All ER 877, PC, when he stressed that: 'It is the effect of the summing-up as a whole that matters.'

Nevertheless, as Lord Scarman noted in *Ferguson v The Queen* [1979] 1 All ER 877, although the law does not require a particular formula 'judges are wise, as a general rule, to adopt one.' The approved directions are well known, as the judge also observed in that case: 'The time honoured formula is that the jury must be satisfied beyond reasonable doubt.' Although he felt that other expressions had 'never prospered', he recognized that another well accepted direction was that encouraged by Lord Goddard (who personally disliked 'beyond reasonable doubt') in the 1950s, namely 'satisfied so that you are sure'. In *Ferguson*, Lord Scarman also approved a

---

[6] *The Independent*, 4 October 1996, at 17.

[7] W Young, 'Summing-Up to Juries in Criminal Cases—What Jury Says about Current Rules and Practice' [2003] Crim LR 665–689, at 674–675.

[8] BJ Shapiro, 'To A Moral Certainty: Theories of Knowledge and Anglo-American Juries 1600–1850' (1986) Hastings Law Journal, vol 38, 156.

[9] JH Langbein, 'The historical origins of the privilege against self-incrimination at Common Law' (1994) Michigan Law Review, vol 92, 1047–1085, at 1057.

[10] F Grigor (ed), *Sir John Fortescue's Commendation of the Laws of England* (1917, Sweet & Maxwell) at 45.

'combined' direction to the jury, incorporating both of these, so that they were warned that they must: '…be satisfied beyond reasonable doubt so that they feel sure of the defendant's guilt'.

More recently, Lord Goddard's preferred direction has found considerable favour with the Judicial Studies Board, forming the basis of its own specimen direction (normally adopted as a template by first instance judges). One reason for this is that it does not invite juries to ask for judicial clarification as to what is a 'reasonable doubt'. As a result, the board advises judges that, when directing a jury on the standard of proof, it is not necessary to use that phrase. However, where it has been used during the trial, for example, by counsel in their closing speeches, it is suggested that it is desirable to give the following explanation: 'The prosecution must make you sure of guilt, which is the same as proving the case beyond reasonable doubt.'

JSB Crown Court Bench Book: Specimen Directions, August 2005: 2.B. Standard of proof, B. Standard of proof

How does the prosecution succeed in proving the defendant's guilt? The answer is—by making you sure of it. Nothing less than that will do. If after considering all the evidence you are sure that the defendant is guilty, you must return a verdict of 'Guilty'. If you are not sure, your verdict must be 'Not Guilty'.

NOTE

Normally, when directing a jury on the standard of proof, it is not necessary to use the phrase 'beyond reasonable doubt'. But where it has been used in the trial, e.g. by counsel in their speeches, it is desirable to give the following direction: 'The prosecution must make you sure of guilt, which is the same as proving the case beyond reasonable doubt': see R v Adey, unreported (97/5306/W2), where the Court of Appeal cautioned against any attempt at a more elaborate definition of 'being sure' or 'beyond reasonable doubt'.

Pause for reflection

Which of 'beyond reasonable doubt' and 'satisfied so that you are sure' do you feel suggest the higher standard of proof?

How cogent must evidence be to satisfy the criminal standard? In the case of *Miller v Minister of Pensions* [1947] 2 All ER 372 Denning J (as he then was), in obiter comments (it was a civil case), tried to define the degree of persuasion required for criminal cases. He felt that: 'It need not reach certainty, but it must carry a high degree of probability. Proof beyond reasonable doubt does not mean proof beyond a shadow of a doubt… If the evidence is so strong against a man as to leave only a remote possibility in his favour which can be dismissed with the sentence "of course it is possible, but not in the least probable", the case is proved beyond reasonable doubt, but nothing short of that will suffice.' In this passage, Denning was trying to show that absolute certainty was not possible in human affairs, even when determining guilt in a criminal trial. Nevertheless, some commentators have argued that this direction might, by inference, be placing the standard too low. In *R v Stephens* [2002] WL 1039755, the Court of Appeal stated that it was unhelpful for a trial judge to attempt to distinguish between being 'sure' and 'certain'.

A number of phrases, when employed on their own, have been expressly disapproved by the appellate courts as being insufficient to convey the appropriate standard. Thus, 'satisfied', without being accompanied by a reference to being sure, or being satisfied beyond reasonable doubt (or some other equally high standard), is plainly inadequate: *R v Hepworth and Fearnley* [1955] 2 QB 600. Similarly, 'reasonably sure' was held to be inadequate in *R v Head* (1961) 45 Cr App R 225. However, given the growing reliance on specimen directions contained in the 'bench books' formulated for the judiciary by the Judicial Studies Board (though they are not, in theory, legally authoritative unless endorsed by an appellate court), departures from established directions are increasingly rare in domestic courts, although they still regularly appear in Privy Council cases.[11]

R v Hepworth and Fearnley [1955] 3 WLR 331, HL

Lord Goddard CJ

. . . one would be on safe ground if one said in a criminal case to a jury: 'You must be satisfied beyond reasonable doubt' and one could also say: 'You, the jury, must be completely satisfied', or better still: 'You must feel sure of the prisoner's guilt.' But I desire to repeat what I said in Rex v. Kritz: 'It is not the particular formula that matters: it is the effect of the summing-up. If the jury are made to understand that they have to be satisfied and must not return a verdict against a defendant unless they feel sure, and that the onus is all the time on the prosecution and not on the defence,' that is enough. I should be very sorry if it were thought that these cases should depend on the use of a particular formula or particular word or words. The point is that the jury should be directed first, that the onus is always on the prosecution; secondly, that before they convict they must feel sure of the accused's guilt. If that is done, that will be enough.

Comment has been made on the use by the recorder of the word 'satisfied' only, and we have come to the conclusion that the summing-up was not satisfactory; but again I emphasize that this is a case of receiving and in such a case it is always important that the onus of proof should be emphasized and explained. The jury should be told that the possession of goods recently stolen calls for an explanation, and if none is given, or one is given which the jury are convinced is untrue, that entitles them to convict. But if the explanation given leaves them in doubt as to whether the accused received the goods honestly or dishonestly the prosecution have not proved the case and they should acquit.

For the reasons I have endeavoured to give—I hope it will not be thought that we are laying down any particular form of words, but we are saying it is desirable that something more should be said than merely 'satisfied'—we think that the conviction should be quashed.

As already noted, although discouraged, periodic requests from juries for an explanation of what is a 'reasonable doubt' have also led to a variety of (reluctant) judicial attempts to define what is essentially indefinable. If a jury asks for specific guidance on this matter, judicial reticence will not always be possible. Some resulting directions have subsequently been approved at appellate level, while others have been held to place the level too low: *R v Bradbury* (1969) 53 Cr App R 217.

A direction that clearly set the standard too low (and also an indication that such a direction can be rectified if accompanied by sufficient appropriate directions) can be seen in the Privy Council case of *Codrington v R* [1996] CLY 1646, an appeal from a murder conviction in Belize. The appellant's counsel advanced as a basis of his appeal, inter alia, that the trial judge had

---

[11] For a discussion of the importance of these directions, see generally, R Munday, 'The Bench Books: Can the Judiciary Keep a Secret' (1996) Crim LR, 296–305, at 297.

placed the standard of proof at too low a level, when he directed the jury, in his summing-up, in the following terms: 'If you are left in doubt as to whether he is innocent or guilty, then again your verdict would have to be one of not guilty. If you have doubts, serious doubts, substantial doubts, as to whether he is guilty then you must return a verdict of not guilty.' He had later repeated the tenor of this direction by saying that they could not convict if: '... you find evidence which leaves a substantial or serious doubt as to whether Alfred Codrington was the person.'

The Privy Council accepted that this would have been too low had it been the only direction on standard of proof. It is not necessary for a juror to entertain a 'serious or substantial' doubt before he concludes that he is not sure. However, in the context of the summing-up as a whole, in which the judge gave a proper direction, telling the jury they must be sure and that the prosecution must prove the case beyond reasonable doubt on numerous occasions (eight and five times respectively), the Privy Council felt able to dismiss the appeal.

R v Gray (1974) 58 Cr App R 177, CA

Megaw LJ

The complaint is with reference to a short passage in the summing-up: short, but dealing with what always is a vital matter in a criminal trial: the direction by the learned judge on the standard of proof. His direction on that matter was this: 'The burden of proof here, of course, lies upon the prosecution and it remains upon the prosecution from the very start to the very end of the case. It is never any part of the accused's duty to prove his innocence and the standard of proof is a high one. It must be proved, it is sometimes said, beyond reasonable doubt, and that means simply a doubt based upon good reason and not a fanciful doubt. It is the sort of doubt which might affect you in the conduct of your everyday affairs. That is the standard of proof which is required.' There are no references anywhere else in the course of the summing-up from beginning to end of the directions to the jury as to the burden and standard of proof.

Now, so far as concerns the first three sentences, there is no complaint. In particular it should be noted that the learned judge stressed that the standard of proof is a high one. The complaint which is made is that having told the jury that it was for the prosecution to prove the offence beyond reasonable doubt, he went on to define what was meant by 'reasonable doubt', not merely by the formula 'a doubt based upon good reason and not a fanciful doubt', but by a further exposition in the sentence 'It is the sort of doubt which might affect you in the conduct of your everyday affairs.' This Court would not wish to say anything which might be treated as being relevant in relation to a direction to the jury using different words from the precise words that are here used. If the learned judge had referred, for example, to the sort of doubt which may affect the mind of a person in the conduct of important affairs, there could be, in the view of this Court, no proper criticism. Indeed that was the very sort of direction which was approved by the Judicial Committee of the Privy Council in Walters v. R. [1969] 2 A.C. 26. But in this case the direction is open to legitimate criticism. The reference to 'the conduct of your everyday affairs' might in this context suggest to a jury too low a standard of proof; because a doubt which would influence a decision on an important matter might sensibly be disregarded in a decision on some 'everyday affair'. Once again if this complaint as to direction to the jury had stood by itself with nothing more in the case, this Court would at any rate have hesitated long before deciding that that complaint about the summing-up was sufficient to require that this conviction should be quashed. But when that error, as this Court regards it as being, is taken together with the possible effect upon the jury of the fresh evidence, this Court has come to the conclusion that this is a case where the verdict is in all the circumstances unsafe or unsatisfactory. Accordingly, leave to appeal having been given, the appeal is allowed and the conviction is quashed.

One direction in a judge's summing-up on standard of proof is often sufficient. In *Mancini v Director of Public Prosecutions* [1942] AC 1 at 13 Viscount Simon LC said: 'There is no reason to repeat to the jury the warning as to reasonable doubt again and again, provided that the direction is plainly given.' However, in long summing-ups, trial judges should normally reiterate both the burden and standard of proof (this is often done at the beginning and towards the end of the judge's directions).

A failure to give any direction at all will usually, though not quite invariably, lead to any ensuing conviction being quashed. In *R v Edwards* (1983) 77 Cr App R 5, the trial judge had omitted to give a rape jury any direction at all on the standard of proof. The Court of Appeal regarded that as a serious defect, not cured by references in the speeches of counsel, but applied the then proviso to s. 2(1) of the 1968 Act (as the subsection stood before amendment in 1995). Thus, a conviction may, in exceptional circumstances, be regarded as safe despite the absence of an adequate direction even on a matter as fundamental as the standard of proof. Nevertheless, this could only be an appropriate conclusion where the case against the defendant was properly held to be overwhelming, as the court found it to be in *Edwards*. Because of the inherently intangible nature of directions on the criminal standard, juries continue to find them troubling, and, periodically, will still ask for clarification, which can sometimes lead to further confusion and provide arguable grounds for appeal, as occurred in *R v Stephens* [2002] EWCA Crim 1529.

R v Stephens [2002] EWCA Crim 1529, CA

Keene LJ

In his summing-up the judge dealt at the outset with the burden and standard of proof which the jury should apply. He said this at page 5: 'And the standard of proof is this: before you can convict the defendant you must be satisfied so that you feel sure of his guilt. That's the same thing as being satisfied beyond reasonable doubt of his guilt. Nothing less will do.' However, the jury, after retiring, sent out a number of notes. One of them read: 'What constitutes reasonable doubt? How certain do you have to be?'

Before seeking to direct the jury in answer to these questions, the judge discussed the matter with counsel. There was no issue as to what the judge proposed to say in answer to the first of those questions, but after some hesitation both prosecution and defence counsel suggested that the judge should not seek to answer the second question beyond reiterating that the jury had to be sure of guilt before they could convict.

What the judge eventually said to the jury in response to that note was this at page 57 of the transcript: 'The first of your questions I read to remind you, and to read into the record is this: what constitutes reasonable doubt? My answer to the question is this: a reasonable doubt is the sort of doubt that might affect the mind of a person dealing with matters of importance in his own affairs. Your second question is this: how certain do you have to be? And my answer to that question is that you do not have to be certain. You have to be sure. Which is less than being certain. Thank you.'

No criticism is made on behalf of the appellant of the answer to the question about reasonable doubt and indeed that answer closely follows the formulation which the Privy Council regarded in Walters [1969] AC 26 as being unobjectionable. But the answer to the second question is the main basis of this appeal, being the ground, as we say, upon which leave was granted.

Mr Femi-Ola on behalf of the appellant submits that in normal usage one cannot distinguish between the words 'certain' and 'sure'. Consequently he contends the jury may well have been confused. It is argued that the judge should have said no more than saying to the jury 'You need to be satisfied so as to be sure'. Mr Femi-Ola argues that the direction given may have lowered the standard of proof which the jury should apply and he emphasises also the fact that the jury here returned their verdict only on a majority basis of 10 to 2. Emphasis is placed on behalf of the appellant on the importance of the standard of proof being got right by any judge when directing a jury.

For the Crown Mr Jackson has emphasised in his skeleton argument that the two answers given in response to the jury's note should be taken together and once that is done there can be no doubt that the jury had to be sure of guilt before they could convict and there is no possibility that they were confused in this case. It is clear to this court, having read the transcripts of the discussion between counsel and the judge, that the judge took his formulation of his answer to the jury's question from the passages in Archbold which appear in the 2002 Edition at paragraph 4–384. Reference is there made to authorities indicating that the prosecution does not have to make the jury feel certain of the accused's guilt but must satisfy them beyond reasonable doubt. The authorities cited are Miller v Minister of Pensions [1947] 2 All.E.R 372 and Bracewell, a decision of this court, reported at 68 Cr.App.R 44. After referring to the formulation by Lord Goddard CJ in Summers 36 Cr.App.R 14 at page 15, that the jury must be satisfied so that they are sure of guilt before they can convict, the learned authors of Archbold go on to say at sub-paragraph (d): 'Apart from this, it is well established that the standard of proof is less than certainty (see (a), ante). As in ordinary English "sure" and "certain" are virtually indistinguishable, it savours of what the late Sir Rupert Cross might have described as "gobbledegook" to tell the jury that while they must be "sure" they need not be "certain".'

That is a passage relied on by Mr Femi-Ola in his short but attractive submission to us. The Judicial Studies Board in its specimen direction on the standard of proof adopts Lord Goddard's formulation, that having been approved in a number of other cases including Walters. It is now, it seems to this court, very well established that the jury should be told that they have to be satisfied so that they are sure of guilt before they can convict.

The two authorities referred to in Archbold dealing with certainty are upon examination perhaps not as authoritative as might at first blush appear. The point which was being made by this court in Bracewell was that the jury is not required to be satisfied with scientific certainty, a degree of certainty such that an expert witness could exclude any other possibility at all. It was therefore a very limited point being made in that case and it is one which should not be used as the basis for drawing any general distinction between being certain and being sure. The other case cited, the well-known one of Miller v Minister of Pensions was a civil case where there are indeed dicta of Mr Justice Denning (as he then was) at first instance.

However, it does not seem to this court to be helpful to a jury to seek to draw distinctions between being certain of guilt and being sure of guilt and in our view judges should avoid doing so. Most people would find it difficult to discern any real difference between the two. That far we accept Mr Femi-Ola's argument. A trial judge faced with the questions put by the jury's note in this case would be better advised simply to remind the jury that they had to be sure of guilt before they could convict, indicating, if he felt it necessary, that that was the limit of the help which he could give them.

However, while the judge here would have been wiser to have adopted such a course, it does not follow that this appeal should be allowed. As was emphasised in the case of Walters to which we have referred: 'It is the effect of the summing-up as a whole that matters.' In the present case the judge repeatedly emphasised that the jury had to be sure of guilt before they could convict. He did so not only at the outset of his summing-up, as we have already indicated in the passage quoted earlier, but subsequently. It is unnecessary to repeat all his references to it, but they can be found in the transcript at pages 28H and again at 29B, again at page 39G and again at 47G. Moreover, he repeatedly indicated to them that if they concluded that the appellant might not have intended to cause really serious bodily harm then they should acquit. He did of course repeat again in the answer which is criticised that they had to be sure. But of some significance also to our minds is the fact that after giving the jury that answer in response to their note, he had to deal with another subsequent note from them. In so doing he again repeated the formula that they had to be sure of guilt before they could convict. Moreover, as the Crown now stresses, the jury had the benefit of the answer given as to what was meant by a reasonable doubt, an answer which is not criticised on behalf of the appellant. Nothing emerged from the jury by way of a note after they had been directed in the way now attacked to suggest that they were confused by the direction in the way which is suggested.

When all these matters are put together, while it might well have been wiser for the judge to have avoided drawing the distinction which he did, this court cannot see that this provides any basis for doubting the safety of the conviction. We have no doubts as to the safety of the conviction in this case and it must therefore follow that this appeal is dismissed.

Standard of Proof in Reverse Onus Burdens

As previously noted, some statutes place a legal burden on the accused in a criminal case to establish a defence, either expressly or by implication. However, where this is the case, they do not have to be established to the same standard as burdens placed on the prosecution; instead, the civil standard is used. Thus, in *R v Carr-Briant* [1943] 2 All ER 156 Humphreys J noted that: '…in any case where, either by statute or at common law, some matter is presumed against a person "unless the contrary is proved"…the burden may be discharged [by the defendant] by evidence satisfying the jury of the probability of that which the accused is called upon to establish.' This will also apply in those rare cases when insanity is advanced. As will be seen, when civil burdens are considered, and unlike the inherently intangible nature of 'beyond reasonable doubt', this is something for which a mathematical definition can be attempted (see below).

JSB Crown Court Bench Book: Specimen Directions, August 2005

2. C. If an issue arises on which the defence bears the burden of proof

If the prosecution has not made you sure that the defendant has (set out what the prosecution must prove), that is an end of the matter and you must find the defendant 'Not Guilty'. However, if and only if, you are sure of those matters, you must consider whether the defendant [e.g. had a reasonable excuse etc. for doing what he did]. The law is that that is a matter for him to prove on all the evidence; but whenever the law requires a defendant to prove something, he does not have to make you sure of it. He has to show that it is probable, which means it is more likely than not, that [e.g. he had reasonable excuse etc. for doing it]. If you decide that probably he did [e.g. have a reasonable excuse etc. for doing it], you must find him 'Not Guilty'. If you decide that he did not, then providing that the prosecution has made you sure of what it has to prove, you must find him 'Guilty'.

NOTE

Direction C is appropriate where the defence bears the 'legal' or 'persuasive' burden of proof, but not where the defence bears only an 'evidential' burden. For a recent example of the former see Lynch v DPP [2002] 1 Crim App R 420. For recent examples of the latter see R v Lambert [2001] 2 Crim App R 511 and R v Carass [2002] 2 Crim App R 77.

Standard of Proof in Civil Cases

The standard used in civil cases is the 'balance of probabilities.' This means, as Denning J noted in *Miller v Minister of Pensions* [1947] 2 All ER 372, 'more probable than not'. This normally presents few problems in theory as, unlike a standard of 'beyond reasonable doubt' or 'satisfied so that you are sure', it allows for a mathematical formula. Theoretically, a 51 per cent likelihood (or even 50.01 per cent), being more probable than not, will discharge it. In practice, such close cases will be extremely rare. However, if after the evidence has been heard the judge (as it will normally be in a civil case) is only persuaded 50/50 as to what occurred, he will find against whoever has the burden of proof on that issue.

Despite this, civil judges dislike having to decide a case on such a basis and are discouraged from doing so, rather than by finding specific issues in the trial to be proved or not proved on the evidence. Nevertheless, it is sometimes the only way to resolve a case. Thus, in *Verlander v Devon Waste Management* [2007] EWCA Civ 835, the claimant alleged that he had injured his back at work, after being required to lift a heavy freezer some considerable distance. This was denied by the defendants. The first instance judge in the County Court found the claimant an unimpressive witness, describing him as evasive and inconsistent in his testimony. However, he did not find the defendant's evidence very convincing either. Ultimately, the judge found against the claimant on the basis that the burden of proof was on him, and had not been discharged. This approach was subsequently approved by the Court of Appeal. However, that court also noted that a judge should only resort to such a disposal where he was genuinely unable to resolve an issue of fact, and after he had unsuccessfully attempted to do so by an examination and evaluation of the evidence (as was the situation in the instant case).

Nevertheless, it should also be noted that the balance of probabilities is judged in absolute terms: *Rhesa Shipping Co. SA v Edmunds* [1985] 1 WLR 948. It is not enough for a litigant to adduce more plausible evidence than his opponent, if this does not satisfy the tribunal of fact that his version is 'more probable' than the combined other possibilities. Thus, in a negligence action, if the judge decides that a claimant's version of events (ie an allegation of negligence) is 40 per cent likely, and the defendant's version only 30 per cent likely, other possibilities accounting for the remainder, the claimant will still fail, as having failed to reach the balance of probabilities.

Rhesa Shipping Co. SA v Edmunds [1985] 1 WLR 948, HL

Lord Brandon

...the judge is not bound always to make a finding one way or the other with regard to the facts averred by the parties. He has open to him the third alternative of saying that the party on whom the burden of proof lies in relation to any averment made by him has failed to discharge that burden. No judge likes to decide cases on burden of proof if he can legitimately avoid having to do so. There are cases, however, in which, owing to the unsatisfactory state of the evidence or otherwise, deciding on the burden of proof is the only just course for him to take...In my opinion Bingham J. adopted an erroneous approach to this case by regarding himself as compelled to choose between two theories, both of which he regarded as extremely improbable, or one of which he regarded as extremely improbable and the other of which he regarded as virtually impossible. He should have borne in mind, and considered carefully in his judgment, the third alternative which was open to him, namely, that the evidence left him in doubt as to the cause of the aperture in the ship's hull, and that, in these circumstances, the shipowners had failed to discharge the burden of proof which was on them.

Within civil cases, there is, ostensibly, normally only one standard of proof. Even allegations that would amount to criminal offences, such as assault, when heard in a civil court, need only be proved on the balance of probabilities. It is forum, not the nature of the allegation, which determines standard. Thus, the balance of probabilities was employed in *Hornal v Neuberger Products* [1957] 1 QB at 247, where the allegation was one of fraudulent misrepresentation. The reasoning in *Hornal* was followed in *Re Dellows's Will Trusts* [1964] 1 WLR 451 and other cases. These ended occasional earlier suggestions that such allegations must normally be established to the criminal standard.

Pause for reflection

Is it right that any court can find that someone has committed a crime on the balance of probabilities?

Despite this, it should also be noted that there are a few exceptions to this general position. In a very few, extremely serious disciplinary tribunals, where a defendant's livelihood has been at stake, or where the allegation almost amounts to a criminal offence, the criminal standard has sometimes been employed. Thus, in *Re a Solicitor* [1993] QB 69, where a solicitor was accused of serious professional misconduct, the tribunal decided that the case should be established beyond reasonable doubt. Subsequently, in the Privy Council case of *Campbell v Hamlet* [2005] 3 All ER 1116, Lord Brown reiterated that their Lordships had 'no doubt' that the correct standard for disciplinary proceedings involving the legal profession was that found in criminal cases. Where the allegation against a lawyer is of poor performance but not misconduct, a lower standard is likely to apply. Thus, in Scotland, the Scottish Solicitors' Discipline Tribunal expressly provides that allegations of professional misconduct must be proved beyond reasonable doubt by the complainer, but those of inadequate professional service need only be established to the balance of probabilities.

Re a Solicitor [1993] QB 69, DC

Lord Lane CJ

The tribunal do not state in so many words what standard of proof they applied in coming to their conclusion. In reciting the cases put forward by the applicant Law Society at the hearing, the tribunal at paragraph 20 of their findings said: 'There was much to be said for adopting the criminal standard of proof in disciplinary cases but there was no conclusive authority which bound the tribunal on that point.' There is no indication of what the view of the tribunal was upon that point. All that is stated in the following paragraph is: 'The tribunal wish however to state clearly that the tribunal's decision is not made on a finding of any criminal offence.... The tribunal has no criminal jurisdiction any more than the Barristers' Board of Western Australia.' Perhaps one could infer from those words that it was something less than the criminal standard of proof which the tribunal applied. The industry of counsel has brought to light no English authority directly in point. In Bhandari v. Advocates Committee [1956] 1 W.L.R. 1442, the Privy Council, on appeal from the Court of Appeal of East Africa in the case of a solicitor who had been found guilty of professional misconduct, concluded that the following exposition of the onus of proof in such cases was adequate, at p. 1452: 'in every allegation of professional misconduct involving an element of deceit or moral turpitude a high standard of proof is called for, and we cannot envisage any body of professional men sitting in judgment on a colleague who would be content to condemn on a mere balance of probabilities.' It seems to us, if we may respectfully say so, that it is not altogether helpful if the burden of proof is left somewhere undefined between the criminal and the civil standards. We conclude that at least in cases such as the present, where what is alleged is tantamount to a criminal offence, the tribunal should apply the criminal standard of proof, that is to say proof to the point where they feel sure that the charges are proved or, put in another way, proof beyond reasonable doubt. This would seem to accord with decisions in several of the Provinces of Canada.

Another undisputed exception to the general situation occurs with regard to allegations of contempt of court in a civil hearing, where the contempt must be proved to the criminal standard. The reasons for this are obvious; it 'partakes of the nature of a criminal charge', and can result in imprisonment: *Comet Products U.K. Ltd v Hawkex Plastic Ltd.* [1971] 1 All ER 1141. Thus, in *In the Matter of J-C (a Child)* [2007] EWCA Civ 896, the appellant had been the subject of a non-molestation order after he separated from his girlfriend on acrimonious terms. It was alleged that he had subsequently breached this order on eight occasions. A circuit judge, sitting in the County Court, decided that three of the eight allegations had been made out, after applying the criminal standard of proof to the evidence of breach. His direction to himself in this respect was subsequently approved by the Court of Appeal.

In the Matter of J-C (a Child) [2007] EWCA Civ 896, CA

Wall LJ

An important feature of it is that the judge in paragraph 3 gives himself what I regard, as a non-criminal lawyer, as an immaculate direction. He says this:

> 'The first thing I do is to remind myself and state in public that I am fully aware that the criminal standard applies, that is, I must be satisfied so that I am sure. Speculation of course is out of the question and it is not sufficient for me to be suspicious.' In my judgment that is the correct direction on the law and as I read the judgment, the judge faithfully throughout the judgment correctly applied the criminal standard of proof.

The presence of such rare exceptions explains why, where something is apparently on the boundary between a civil and criminal wrong, a statute might make clear that the civil standard applies. For example, when, under s. 240 of the Proceeds of Crime Act 2002, the Assets Recovery Agency applies to the High Court for a recovery order for 'property obtained through unlawful conduct', s. 241 of the Act provides that such conduct need only be established on the balance of probabilities.

Less clear-cut has been the situation with regard to what are, essentially, allegations of exceptionally serious crimes, such as murder or rape, being heard in civil forums. The great bulk of authority and principle indicates that, like any other criminal matter being determined in a civil forum, these should be decided on the balance of probabilities as occurred in the case of a felonious killing (a murder/suicide pact) in *Re Dellows's Will Trusts* [1964] 1 WLR 451. Nevertheless, it should also be noted that in the first instance decision of *Halford v Brookes* (1991) *The Times* 3 October, where the plaintiff brought a tortious action for assault and battery resulting in the death of her daughter (ie a murder) 13 years earlier, it was held by Rougier J that such an allegation had to be proved beyond reasonable doubt (which he decided it was in the instant case).

In an unprecedented ruling, the judge declared that the defendant was the dead woman's killer and ordered him to pay damages to her mother. (The judgment also paved the way for a successful criminal prosecution that the Crown Prosecution Service had earlier declined to pursue.)

Subsequently, however, judges trying similar cases appear to have followed the civil standard, and, as a matter of principle, this must be correct: *Francisco v Diedrick* (1998) *The Times* 3 April. Nevertheless, even if not formally subject to the criminal standard, such cases are classic situations in which the notion of 'standards within standards' will become relevant (see below).

Re Dellows's Will Trusts [1964] 1 WLR 451, HC

Ungoed-Thomas J

I have decided that, in accordance with the presumption raised by section 184 of the Law of Property Act, 1925, the husband, as the older of the two, died first. The result of that is that the husband's will in favour of the wife would take effect, unless she feloniously killed him. But if she did so kill him, then it is clear that neither she nor anybody claiming through her could claim his estate, and the gift to her in the husband's will would not take effect. A passage in Theobald on Wills (1963), 12th ed., para. 385, states that since the passing of the Forfeiture Act, 1870, the provisions of which I need not refer to, 'it has been held that it is against public policy for a person who is guilty of feloniously killing another to take any benefit in that other person's estate. And this principle applies to a case of manslaughter as well as one of murder. It applies to an intestacy as well as to a will. But it does not apply if the killer is insane. If there is no evidence as to the killer's state of mind, the killing is presumed to be felonious.'

In this case there is clearly no substantial evidence of insanity within the legal meaning of that term and no case is made out before me on that ground. Is it, then, established that the wife killed the husband? It is conceded that, in a case of this kind before me in the Chancery Division dealing with the devolution of property, the standard of proof required is not so severe as that required by the criminal law. The standard of proof was considered in Hornal v. Neuberger Products Ltd., [FN3] where Morris L.J. stated [FN4]: 'Though no court and no jury would give less careful attention to issues lacking gravity than to those marked by it, the very elements of gravity become a part of the whole range of circumstances which have to be weighed in the scale when deciding as to the balance of probabilities.'

---

7. 'Standards Within Standards'

Ostensibly, there are only two standards recognized by English law: beyond reasonable doubt/satisfied so that you are sure (on the Crown in criminal cases) and on the balance of probabilities (used in civil cases and placed on the defendant in criminal matters). However, it has 'long been recognised', in the words of Lord Brown in the Privy Council case of *Campbell v Hamlet* [2005] 3 All ER 1116 that there might be 'standards within standards'. That is, different degrees of cogency might be required to satisfy either of the two formally recognized standards of proof, depending on the gravity of any given case.

This can sound confusing, and it should be noted that the theoretical justification for such an approach has been questioned; nevertheless, it clearly operates in practice. The notion of 'standards within standards' is of most significance in civil cases, but has also reared its head in criminal matters. Thus, while it can be argued that a single standard in criminal cases may have been appropriate for felonies carrying a potential death sentence in the eighteenth century, this is no longer the case. Even in the 1760s, the judge and celebrated jurist, William Blackstone demanded especially clear proof in cases of rape and buggery, arguing that forensic evidence 'ought to be the more clear in proportion as the crime is the more detestable'.[12] Similarly, Denning LJ (as he then was), in *Bater v Bater* [1950] 2 All ER 458, made the (obiter) comment that: 'In criminal cases the charge must be proved beyond reasonable doubt, but there may be degrees of proof within that standard.' He approved earlier *dictum* made by Lord Best CJ that: 'in proportion as the crime is enormous, so ought the proof to be clear'. Arguably, the need for such an approach has been exacerbated by the many regulatory or 'quasi-offences', carrying relatively mild punishments and little social stigma, that exist in the modern era. Essentially, it means that, for example, although driving without due care and attention and murder are both criminal matters that must be proved 'beyond reasonable doubt' the former offence is much easier to establish than the latter.

In civil cases, there is a great deal of authority for such an approach. Thus, in the 1950s and 1960s, there was a raft of cases, many involving allegations of adultery, at a time when it was widely considered to be an exceptionally grave matter, which stressed that the gravity of the allegation went into the balance: *Bater v Bater* [1950] 2 All ER 458 and *Bastable v Bastable and Sanders* [1968] 1 WLR 1684.

Bastable v Bastable and Sanders [1968] 1 WLR 1684, CA

Willmer LJ

When Blyth v. Blyth and Pugh was before this court I ventured to say that I agreed with the view expressed by Denning L.J. in Bater v. Bater and adopted by this court in Hornal v. Neuberger Products Ltd. In that oft-quoted passage Denning L.J. said: 'The difference of opinion which has been evoked about the standard of proof in recent cases may well turn out to be more a matter of words than anything else. It is, of course, true that by our law a higher standard of proof is required in criminal cases than in civil cases. But this is subject to the qualification that there is no absolute standard in either case. In criminal cases the charge must be proved beyond reasonable doubt, but there may be degrees of proof within that standard. As Best C.J. and many other great judges have said: "in proportion as the crime is enormous, so ought the proof to be clear". So also in civil cases, the case may be proved by a preponderance of probability, but there may be degrees of probability within that standard. The degree depends on the subject-matter. A civil court, when considering a charge of fraud, will naturally require for itself a higher degree of probability than that which it would require when asking if negligence is established. It does not adopt so high a degree as a criminal court, even when it is considering a charge of a criminal nature; but still it does require a degree of probability which is commensurate with the occasion. Likewise, a divorce court should require a degree of probability which is proportionate to the subject-matter.' Until the matter has been further considered by the House of Lords, and further guidance has been received, I propose to direct myself in accordance with that statement of principle.

In the present case, what is charged is 'an offence'. True, it is not a criminal offence; it is a matrimonial offence. It is for the husband petitioner to satisfy the court that the offence has been committed. Whatever the popular view may be, it remains true to say that in the eyes of the law the commission of adultery is a serious matrimonial offence. It follows, in my view, that a high standard of proof is required in order to satisfy the court that the offence has been committed.

---

[12] W Blackstone, *Commentaries on the Laws of England* (1796, Clarendon Press) vol 4, at 214.

In more recent years, numerous cases have reiterated this general analysis for civil matters. Thus, in the wardship case of *Re G* [1987] 1 WLR 1461, Sheldon J concluded that a 'higher degree of probability' would be necessary to satisfy the court that a child's father had been guilty of sexual misconduct with her, than would be needed to decide that the child had been the victim of some such behaviour *whoever* may have been the perpetrator. In *R v Hants CC, ex p Ellerton* [1985] 1 WLR 749 it was held that the notion of a 'flexible' standard was particularly significant at disciplinary tribunals, where the civil standard is generally used. This has been expressly reflected in the 'Guidance on investigating complaints about poor performance and misconduct' by officers issued to police forces by the Secretary of State under ss. 83 and 87 of the Police Act 1996. This notes (at para. 3.70) that in deciding matters of fact the burden of proof lies with the presenting officer, and the tribunal must apply the standard of proof required in civil cases to such proceedings, that is, the balance of probabilities. It goes on to observe that the 'straightforward' legal definition of this is that the adjudicator is persuaded by the evidence that it is more likely or probable that something occurred than that it did not. However, it then notes that: 'Relevant case law makes it clear that the degree of proof required increases with the gravity of what is alleged and its potential consequences. It therefore follows that, where an allegation is likely to ruin an officer's reputation, deprive them of their livelihood or seriously damage their career prospects, a tribunal should be satisfied to a high degree of probability that what is alleged has been proved.'

In *Campbell v Hamlet* the Privy Council took the existence of such standards within standards as axiomatic. This approach is also supported by much recent domestic authority. Thus, in the Divisional Court case of *B v Chief Constable of Avon and Somerset Constabulary* [2001] 1 WLR, Lord Bingham CJ observed that, in a serious non-criminal case, such as the making of a sex offender order, the: '...difference between the two standards is, in truth, largely illusory. I have no doubt that...a Magistrates Court should apply a civil standard of proof which will for all practical purposes be indistinguishable from the criminal standard.'

The same analysis was followed by the Court of Appeal in *Gough v Chief Constable of the Derbyshire Constabulary* [2002] QB 1213, where Lord Phillips MR held that, because of the serious consequences of making a banning order under the Football Spectators Act 1989, magistrates should apply an: '...exacting standard of proof that will, in practice, be hard to distinguish from the criminal standard'. Such an approach has also received statutory support in Australia, under s. 140(2)(c) of that country's Evidence Act 1995, which requires a civil court to take into account the gravity of the matters alleged when deciding whether a matter has been proved on the balance of probabilities.

Campbell v Hamlet [2005] 3 All ER 1116, PC

Lord Brown

It has, of course, long been established that there is a flexibility in the civil standard of proof which allows it to be applied with greater or lesser strictness according to the seriousness of what has to be proved and the implications of proving those matters. . . . Most recently, in the House of Lords in R (McCann) v Crown Court at Manchester [2003] 1 AC 787, Lord Steyn agreed (para 37 at p 812) with what Lord Bingham had said in B about 'the heightened civil standard and the criminal standard [being] virtually indistinguishable' and concluded: 'In my view pragmatism dictates that the task of magistrates should be made more straightforward by ruling that they must in all cases under section 1 [of the Crime and Disorder Act 1998, providing for anti-social behaviour orders] apply the criminal standard'. Lord Hope of Craighead (para 83 at p 826) similarly recognised that in all these cases 'the civil standard of proof will for all practical purposes be indistinguishable from the criminal standard' and held that 'the standard of proof that ought to be applied in these cases to allegations about the defendant's conduct is the criminal standard'. Perhaps more directly in point, however, is the decision of the Divisional Court in In Re A Solicitor [1993] QB 69, concerning the standard of proof to be applied by the Disciplinary Tribunal of the Law Society. Lord Lane CJ, giving the judgment of the Court, referred to the Privy Council's opinion in Bhandari and continued at p 81: 'It seems to us, if we may respectfully say so, that it is not altogether helpful if the burden of proof is left somewhere undefined between the criminal and the civil standard. We conclude that at least in cases such as the present, where what is alleged is tantamount to a criminal offence, the tribunal should apply the criminal standard of proof, that is to say proof to the point where they feel sure that the charges are proved or, to put it another way, proof beyond reasonable doubt. This would seem to accord with decisions in several of the Provinces of Canada.' 21. A little later in the Court's judgment Lord Lane referred to the provision in the Bar's Code of Conduct requiring the tribunal to apply the criminal standard of proof and observed at p.82: 'it would be anomalous if the two branches of the profession were to apply different standards in their disciplinary proceedings'. This last observation, of course, clearly warranted the Law Society Disciplinary Committee thenceforth applying the criminal standard in all cases rather than merely in those, earlier referred to, 'where what is alleged is tantamount to a criminal offence'.

The Justification for 'Standards Within Standards'

To many, the notion of standards within standards is an inherently difficult one. Some commentators have questioned its theoretical basis. Does it mean, for example, that an allegation of dishonesty, such as one involved in a theft case, should be less easily proved than that of driving without due care and attention? There are three possible approaches to this issue: one is to say expressly that that is the case, as was done on occasion by Lord Denning.

Pause for reflection

Do you feel that the notion of 'standards within standards' of proof is a contradiction in terms?

The problem with this approach is that it can be argued that it is, effectively, a 'backdoor' way of introducing a third standard of proof (between the civil and criminal ones) into the English Law of Evidence. Such a standard already exists in some foreign common law jurisdictions. For example, in several American states it is termed 'clear and convincing evidence' and is used, inter alia, in civil cases involving the compulsory hospitalization of psychiatric patients. It is a standard that has been defined, in a case from Texas, as being that 'measure or degree of proof which will produce in the minds of the trier of fact a firm belief or conviction as to the truth of the allegations sought to be established.'[13]

However, although it might be a desirable introduction for certain types of regulatory offence (such as minor traffic cases) or very serious civil allegations, there is (at present) no such intermediate standard in English law. Indeed, in Re a Solicitor [1993] QB 69 the Divisional Court

[13] See BC Ingram, 'The Right of Silence, The Presumption of Innocence, The Burden of Proof And a Modest Proposal' (1996) Journal of Criminal Law and Criminology, vol 86, no 2, 559–595, at 573.

suggested that it was 'not altogether helpful' to have an undefined floating standard between the two normal ones. Nevertheless, there has been some academic support for its adoption, particularly where a finding against the defendant will have potentially drastic consequences (such as a loss of liberty). Despite this, as the following extract also suggests, criticisms of any addition of further layers of complexity to what is a very practical area of the law, can also easily be envisaged.

Mike Redmayne, 'Standards of Proof in Civil Litigation' (1999) The Modern Law Review, vol 62, no 2, 167–195, at 194

In this article, I have developed a conceptual framework for understanding standards of proof in civil litigation, and defended the 0.5 'more probable than not' standard as the default standard for civil cases. I have argued that the principles developed in the case law are confused and difficult to defend, and that the law would be improved by the adoption of a single third standard of proof. To pull the various strands of my argument together I used three examples to demonstrate when and how the application of the higher standard of proof might be justified. The arguments that I have presented are, of course, open to the criticism that they attempt to impose precision and clarity on an area where these are not virtues. It is certainly true that there is little uncontested understanding of just what it means to prove a case to a certain standard and that, while fact-finders may know when the cases they judge have been proved, they may well find it difficult to articulate precise reasons in every case. It is not surprising that the subject of the civil standard of proof moved Morris LJ to trot out a version of Holmes' well known aphorism: 'the life of the law is not logic but experience'. However, while I am very much aware of the shortcomings of attempts to explain proof in terms of decision theory and probability theory, I am not convinced that the project of providing a clear conceptual framework for understanding the civil standard of proof is misconceived.

Alternatively, the notion of 'standards within standards' can be rejected outright as being inherently illogical. According to this analysis, being 'sure' of a defendant's guilt, or satisfied 'on the balance of probabilities' of a claimant's case, must be the same whatever the allegation. Such a view appears to have attracted the sympathy of Lord Lloyd in the (grave) civil case of *Re H and others* [1996] 1 All ER 1. The distinguished judge declared: 'In my view the standard of proof... ought to be the simple balance of probability, however serious the allegations involved'. There has also been some academic criticism of the vagueness inherent in the position reached by the courts in this regard, as the following extract suggests.

Mike Redmayne, 'Standards of Proof in Civil Litigation' (1999) The Modern Law Review, vol 62, no 2, 167–195, at 167

Indeed, the civil standard of proof appears to be one of the simplest concepts in the law of evidence, requiring little explanation or illustration. But scratch the surface of this most basic of evidentiary notions and an altogether more complex picture is revealed: the case law provides a range of conflicting interpretations of what the civil standard proof requires in different contexts. When an area of the law is this confused, one starts to suspect that the problem lies in more than a failure by the appellate courts to resolve conflicting authorities and to lay down clear guidance (though this has certainly added to the difficulties in this area); one is drawn instead to the conclusion that the confusion lies at a deeper, conceptual level and that it is driven by the lack of a clear understanding of the basic building blocks of forensic proof.

Nevertheless, a possible way around this problem (at least in some situations) was suggested by the other members of the House of Lords involved in the same case. In *Re H and others* a child had made allegations of rape against her father. The child was fostered and the father then tried and acquitted of the offence. The local authority subsequently wished to take into care the three younger sisters of the complainant, fearing for their safety. The case turned on the standard of proof that had to be established by the authority under s. 31(2) of the Children Act 1989. The House of Lords held that the burden of showing that the children involved were likely to suffer significant harm lay on the applicant and that the standard of proof was the normal civil standard, ie the balance of probabilities (unsurprisingly, given precedent).

However, their Lordships also held that the very gravity of a matter was something that could go into the balance of likelihood. The more serious an allegation of abuse the less probable it was, and the more convincing was the evidence required to prove it. According to this analysis, it is much more common, and therefore likely, that a driver, at some point, will fall below the standard of the ordinary prudent road user than that the same individual will deliberately steal, this is something that can be considered when deciding whether an allegation has been made out.

8. The Tactical Burden

The tactical burden is also sometimes called the 'provisional' burden. It merely means that, once a clear prima facie case has been made out against a party to litigation, they will be well advised, even if they have no legal or evidential burden on any of the facts in issue, to call some evidence in rebuttal (if it is available to them). This is because doing so will make it very much harder for the opposing party to discharge their legal burden on the various issues in the trial than would otherwise be the case. Thus, once the prosecution in a criminal trial has called some cogent evidence to suggest that the defendant is a thief, simply reminding a jury or bench of magistrates that the legal burden in the case is on the Crown, and that the accused need do nothing to establish his innocence, though entirely true, will often not be enough to secure an acquittal. It will need to be backed up by some tangible defence evidence to the contrary (such as an alibi defence or evidence of ownership of the goods in question). Consequently, the tactical burden is nothing more than 'common sense' for lawyers. It is devoid of legal significance because it is impossible to tell when it has come into existence or when it has been discharged.[14] Nevertheless, in *Abrath v Northern Eastern Railway Co.* (1883) 11 QBD 440 (CA) Bowen LJ discussed the relationship between the legal and tactical burdens, albeit without formally annunciating the status of the latter.

Abrath v Northern Eastern Railway Co. (1883) 11 QBD 440, CA

Bowen LJ

Whenever litigation exists, somebody must go on with it; the plaintiff is the first to begin; if he does nothing, he fails; if he makes a prima facie case, and nothing is done to answer it, the defendant fails. The test, therefore, as to the burden of proof or onus of proof, whichever term is used,

---

[14] C Tapper, *Cross & Tapper on Evidence* (10th edn, 2004, LexisNexis) at 139.

is simply this: to ask oneself which party will be successful if no evidence is given, or if no more evidence is given than has been given at a particular point of the case, for it is obvious that as the controversy involved in the litigation travels on, the parties from moment to moment may reach points at which the onus of proof shifts, and at which the tribunal will have to say that if the case stops there, it must be decided in a particular manner. The test being such as I have stated, it is not a burden that goes on for ever resting on the shoulders of the person upon whom it is first cast. As soon as he brings evidence which, until it is answered, rebuts the evidence against which he is contending, then the balance descends on the other side, and the burden rolls over until again there is evidence which once more turns the scale. That being so, the question of onus of proof is only a rule for deciding on whom the obligation of going further, if he is to win, rests.

 ## Summary

- The legal burden is the risk of non-persuasion that falls on one of the parties to litigation with regard to any given issue, such that they will fail on that issue if they do not satisfy their burden by proving it to the appropriate standard.

- Generally speaking, in criminal matters, the legal burden on all issues is on the Crown. This is the 'golden thread' of English justice.

- There are three exceptions to the 'golden thread', in which a legal burden is placed on a defendant in a criminal case: insanity; express and implied statutory burdens.

- All reverse legal burdens in criminal cases, whether express or implied, must be compliant with the ECHR. If they are not, they will normally be 'read down' under s. 3 of the HRA 1998, so that they merely place an evidential burden on the defendant. Compliance is determined on a case-by-case basis, using the principle of 'proportionality' identified by the ECtHR and considering a range of policy and other factors.

- In civil cases, the rough equivalent of the golden thread is the maxim that 'he who asserts must prove'. As a result, the legal burden is usually on the claimant to establish the facts in issue. However, as with criminal cases, there are some situations in which the burden is placed on the defendant, as he is deemed to be 'asserting'.

- There are two main standards of proof. One is 'beyond reasonable doubt'/'satisfied so that you are sure', which is placed on the Crown in criminal cases (it is the effect, not the wording, of the standard that is vital). It is also used to determine civil contempt of court cases and, very rarely, disciplinary proceedings before certain tribunals. The other is the 'balance of probabilities', which is used in civil cases and in those situations in which a legal burden is placed on a defendant in a criminal case. This standard (unlike 'satisfied so that you are sure') can be reduced to a percentage of probability (anything over a 50 per cent likelihood).

- Within these two main standards there are often 'standards within standards'. In practice, very serious matters when determined in civil and (less commonly) criminal trials will require more cogent evidence to achieve the designated standard of proof than less serious cases, though some observers have questioned the theoretical basis for this difference.

- An evidential burden is the obligation placed on a party to make an issue 'live' by adducing some evidence on it, so that it is justified in going to the tribunal of fact. Evidential burdens do not have to be 'proved,' merely satisfied by the adduction of tangible evidence, from whatever source.

- All legal burdens carry an evidential burden. However, occasionally, an evidential burden will be placed on a party without him carrying a corresponding legal burden. For example, certain defences only need to be rebutted by the prosecution in a criminal case if they have already been raised on the evidence. However, if such defences are raised, wherever the evidence comes from (even if it is from the complainant), the judge is under an obligation to put the defence to the jury, even if it has not been mentioned by the defendant. This is the trial judge's 'invisible burden'. The prosecution then acquires a fresh legal burden, on top of the essential elements of the offence, namely, to rebut the defence raised.

- Although a party to litigation, whether criminal or civil, may not carry any burden in the case, whether legal or evidential, once the other party has adduced some evidence it will often be prudent for him to counter with some rebutting evidence of his own, if he wishes to prevent his opponent from proving his case. This is often termed the 'tactical burden'. It is, essentially, a practitioner's concept.

 ## Further reading

Andrew Ashworth and Meredith Blake, 'The Presumption of Innocence in English Criminal Law' [1996] Crim LR 309

Francis Bennion, 'Statutory Exceptions: A Third Knot in the Golden Thread' [1988] Crim LR 31

Ian Dennis, 'Reverse Onuses and the Presumption of Innocence: In Search of Principle' [2005] Crim LR 901–936

Gavin Dingwall, 'Statutory Exceptions, Burdens of Proof and the Human Rights Act 1998' (2002) Modern Law Review, vol 65, 450

Stephen Doran, 'Alternative Defences: The Invisible on the Trial Judge' [1992] Crim LR 878

Bruce P Smith, 'The Presumption of Innocence and the English Law of Theft: 1750–1850' (2005) Law and History Review, vol 23, no 1, 133–173

Paul Roberts, 'Taking the Burden of Proof Seriously' [1995] Crim LR 783

 ## Questions for Discussion

1. A new statute, the Protection of Rictoyds Act 2008, makes it a criminal offence to be found in possession of a Rictoyd (a recently discovered, small, fluffy, rare and threatened mammal): '...unless the individual concerned has a degree in veterinary science awarded by a British University'. Additionally, the Act makes it a defence for those in possession of the animals to 'prove that it is for the purposes of their religious devotions, the burden whereof shall be on the accused'. The maximum penalty is two years in prison. Fiona, George, Horace, Iqbal and John are accused of being in possession of several of the animals that were found in a flat that they share in Kingston. All of them, apart from John, plead 'not guilty'. Fiona does not deny that she was in possession of the Rictoyds, but says that she has a degree in veterinary science from Leeds University, though she is worried that she has lost her graduation certificate since leaving. George also admits being in possession of the Rictoyds, but says that it was for the purposes of a religious ceremony, as the animals are ascribed mystical qualities by New Agers like himself. Horace, too, admits to being in possession of the animals, but claims that it was only because a local criminal, Rasputin, threatened that he would kill him if he did not look after them. Iqbal, who has been away from the flat for long periods in recent months, proposes to say that he had no knowledge at all of the animals. Although John admits the crime, he claims that PC Sniff took £2,000 in cash from his desk when searching the house. When the CPS refuses to prosecute Sniff, John decides to sue the policeman for the return of the money in the local County Court.

Advise all of the parties as to the burden and standard of proof in the two cases.

For suggested approaches, please visit the Online Resource Centre

2. Alan, a haulier, contracts with Brenda to carry a consignment of highly flammable goods from Carlisle to London. The contract stipulates that Alan will not be responsible for any damage to the goods occasioned by fire, unless he was negligent in his anti-fire precautions. On the way south, Alan's lorry bursts into flames, and all the goods are destroyed. Brenda claims that the fire resulted from Alan carelessly discarding a cigarette butt into the back of his vehicle. Alternatively, she claims that Alan deliberately started the fire, with a view to claiming on the lorry's insurance policy.

Discuss any issues as to burden and standard of proof raised on the above facts.

3. Under s. 2(1) of the (fictitious) Bicycle Safety Act 2008 anyone found sitting on a stationary bicycle, without a helmet, is guilty of a summary offence, for which they can be fined a maximum of £200. However, under s. 2(2): 'It is a defence for a person charged with an offence under subsection (1) above to prove that at the time he is alleged to have committed the offence the circumstances were such that there was no likelihood of his riding the bicycle without a helmet.' Jim is seen sitting on a bicycle outside his house without a helmet, and prosecuted for the offence. He says that he had no intention of riding it, and was merely testing its suspension.

Advise Jim on the burden and standard of proof in the case.

4. Daniel is accused of murdering his girlfriend, Edwina. The two were well known to neighbours for having a stormy relationship and frequent domestic rows. Daniel denies any involvement in the killing and says that Edwina's injuries occurred when she fell off the roof of their house while he was in a betting shop. The Crown calls Fiona, a forensic pathologist, to say that the injuries to Edwina's body are consistent with a frenzied attack with a blunt instrument. Neighbours say that they heard raised voices coming from the house shortly before Edwina's death, though they were unable to discern any words. After Daniel is convicted of murder he asks to appeal on the basis that the trial judge should have directed the jury to consider a manslaughter verdict due to provocation.

Advise Daniel.

5. Consider the correctness of the following directions by a trial judge to a jury in the Crown Court:

'You must be positive of the defendant's guilt before you can convict.'

'The defendant has said that he killed the deceased man because he was in fear of his life. It is for him to prove this to you if you are to acquit.'

'The defendant claims that he should not be convicted of murder, but only manslaughter, as he was suffering from diminished responsibility. He must establish this, beyond reasonable doubt.'

4 PRESUMPTIONS

Definitions

Legal presumption Doctrine under which on the proof of fact A, fact B will be presumed, *unless* the opposing party does something to prevent the presumption taking effect.

Persuasive presumption A legal presumption that places a legal burden on the opposing party to prove that the presumed fact is not true.

Evidential presumption A legal presumption that places an evidential burden on the opposing party to suggest that the presumed fact is not true; ie, that requires him to adduce some tangible evidence that the presumption should not operate, before it will cease to do so (but does not require him to prove that it should not apply).

Presumption of fact A judicially identified form of circumstantial evidence in which, on the establishment of fact A, fact B *may* (but need not) follow.

Irrebuttable presumption of law A rule of substantive law couched in the language of presumptions.

---

1. Introduction

Legally, 'presumptions' are often closely linked in their effects to the operation of the legal and evidential burdens, and an understanding of these concepts (dealt with in chapter 2) is vital before this chapter will be readily comprehensible. However, the term is also employed, in a rather looser fashion, to refer to other situations where this is clearly not the case, so engendering a degree of confusion. Indeed, as far back as the case of *Chard v Chard* [1956] P 259, Sachs J was lamenting that the: '...demarcation lines between classes of presumption are, even when visible, not always regarded in the dicta of judges and textbook writers'. It also means that it is impossible to reduce the subject to one coherent doctrine or a comprehensive theory. In general, it can be said that the term 'presumptions' refers to four quite distinct situations. However, it is only really accurate to use the word in relation to two of these.

 Exam tip

Because 'true' presumptions are so closely linked in their operation to the legal and evidential burdens they are often combined with this topic in problem questions in examinations.

In the law of evidence, a 'true' legal presumption is found in those situations where, on the establishing of matter A by a party to litigation, conclusion B will inevitably follow, *unless* the other party does *something*. The actual terminology used varies, depending on the judge or academic commentator involved; thus, matter A is sometimes called the 'primary' or 'basic' fact, and B the 'presumed fact'. As will be seen, what precisely the 'something' that the other party must do will depend on which of the two types of 'true' presumption is involved. True presumptions constitute one of the rare situations in which evidence does not have to be called *directly* on an issue (in this case the presumed fact) for it to be deemed to have been established at trial.

Cross-reference Box

There are several other, very different, mechanisms by which this may also occur. For example, a judge might take 'judicial notice' of a fact. For more on this go to chapter 1 at pp. 20–24.

The bulk of this chapter will consider these two genuine types of presumption. Nevertheless, the terminology of presumptions is also frequently (and inaccurately) used in two other very different situations. These are so-called 'irrebuttable presumptions' of law and 'presumptions of fact,' which will be considered first. Further complicating matters, it must also be noted that there is a doubt, in some situations, as to precisely what type of presumption is created in any given situation, while some legal areas, such as marriage, attract several separate and different presumptions.

2. Irrebutable Presumptions of Law

Irrebutable presumptions of law (sometimes called 'conclusive' presumptions) are not really evidential rules at all. They are merely rules of substantive law, couched in the terminology of presumptions. Under them, if a certain fact is proved, the existence of the 'presumed' fact *must* be assumed, and no evidence can be heard in rebuttal. The burden or onus of proof is not contingent on the proof of a basic fact. For an example, can be considered the presumption, under s. 50 of the Children and Young Persons Act 1933, that a child below the age of 10 cannot commit a crime. Once it is shown that the child is, for example, nine, he cannot be found guilty of an offence. This is unlike the old, 'true', and consequently rebuttable, presumption that a child between the age of 10 and 14 was *doli incapax* (abolished by s. 34 of the Crime and Disorder Act 1998). The 1933 statute could equally have said, quite simply, that no child under 10 years of age can be guilty of an offence, without having recourse to the language of presumptions.

Similarly, it is sometimes said that everyone is 'presumed' to know the law, which is simply another way of saying that ignorance of the law is no defence. In like manner, in a defamation action, where the issue is whether a certain individual has committed a crime, if it is proved that he stands convicted of that offence, it is deemed to be 'conclusive evidence' for such proceedings that he committed the relevant crime, as a result of s. 13(2) of the Civil Evidence Act 1968. There are numerous other such 'irrebutable' presumptions to be found, in all areas of the law.

3. Presumptions of Fact

Introduction

So-called called 'presumptions of fact' are also not 'true' presumptions, being, in reality, nothing more than common-sense inferences drawn from what is usually circumstantial evidence. They are not true presumptions because there is no *requirement* that the tribunal of fact adopt the presumption and assume the presumed fact once the preliminary facts are established, any more than there is for any other type of telling circumstantial evidence. Their only effective significance, beyond such other forms of evidence, seems to be that a judge summing up to a jury (or magistrates directing themselves) can expressly refer to the presumption when doing so, ie it serves to direct the tribunal of fact to possible inferences that might be drawn from the evidence. In practice, this may give them some added or pre-ternatural significance.

Paul Roberts and Adrian Zuckerman,*Criminal Evidence* (2004, Oxford University Press), at 341

. . . presumptions of fact arise where, as a matter of common sense rather than by operation of law, the court may draw a particular factual inference from the existence of a certain set of facts. On a charge of handling stolen goods, for example, if the accused fails to provide a credible explanation for his possession of recently stolen goods, a presumption of guilty knowledge is said to arise. But notice that this so called 'presumption' merely restates the normal inferential process, articulating what the jury might, as a matter of ordinary logic and common sense, infer from the accused's possession of recently stolen goods. Presumptions of fact link circumstances which commonly occur in conjunction: where fact B may be inferred from fact A because A and B usually occur together; and the inference is even stronger where A seldom occurs without B. . . . such 'presumptions of fact' do not involve any formal distribution of risk of error. Indeed, since factual inferences remain to be drawn in the normal way, talk of presumptions in this context is strictly redundant.

Examples of Presumptions of Fact

Under the so-called 'doctrine of recent possession', alluded to above, if someone is found in possession of stolen goods very shortly after they have been stolen, and does not give any satisfactory explanation as to how he came by them, a number of conclusions can (but need not) be drawn about the person in whose possession they are found. In particular, it might be presumed that he knew or believed the goods were stolen when they came into his possession, and so have the requisite *mens rea* for, for example, an offence of handling: *R v Ball* [1983] 1 WLR 801.

R v Ball [1983] 1 WLR 801, CA

McCullough J

The so-called doctrine of recent possession is misnamed. It has nothing to do with goods recently possessed. It concerns possession of goods recently stolen. It is not even a doctrine. It is in fact no more than an inference which a jury may, or may not, think it right to draw about the state of mind of a defendant who is dealing in goods stolen not long beforehand. It is based on common sense. Stolen goods frequently pass quickly from hand to hand. Many of those who deal in them knowing or believing them to be stolen tell lies when they are asked to explain how the goods came into their possession. Others prefer to give no explanation. That has been the experience of the courts for generations. So when a defendant is found to have been in possession of goods recently stolen and either gives no explanation of how he came to acquire them innocently or gives an explanation which is patently untrue, it is the practice of judges to tell juries that they may, if they think it right, infer that he acquired them knowing or believing that they were stolen. The innocent man has nothing to fear from this. He has no need to lie. He will, as a rule, be only too willing to give his explanation. It is, in any event, an inference which a jury will only draw if they think it right to do so.

 Pause for reflection

Why should presumptions of fact be distinguished from other forms of circumstantial evidence?

Similarly, the 'presumption of continuance' suggests that, if a certain state of affairs has been shown to exist at a specified time, it can (but need not) be assumed that the same state of affairs is likely to have existed shortly before or after that time. For example, if, in a negligence case in which it is alleged that a pedestrian has been knocked down due to careless driving, it can be shown that, very shortly prior to the collision, a certain man was the driver of the vehicle involved, the court may infer from this that he was also the man driving it when he hit the pedestrian: *Beresford v Justices of St Albans* (1905) 22 TLR 1.

The 'presumption of continuance of life' is another, regularly encountered, presumption of fact, and, in many ways, analogous to other forms of the presumption of continuance. If it can be shown that a certain person was alive at a specified time, he may be presumed to be still alive a reasonable time afterwards. Because it is only a presumption of fact, there is no requirement that this be assumed and, as Sachs J observed in *Chard v Chard* [1956] P 259, this means that due weight can be given in each case to the differing circumstances of the individual concerned. For example, whether, when last seen, the relevant person was in: '...good or in bad health, and whether following a quiet or a dangerous occupation'. Thus, if a period of 25 years has elapsed since a 60-year-old man with prostate cancer, who was earning a living as a deep sea diver, was last seen, any inference drawn is likely to be very much weaker (if present at all) than that drawn where a 30-year-old secretary in perfect health was last seen five years earlier.

In like manner, there is a presumption of fact that people intend the natural consequences of their acts. For example, if you stab someone in the heart, that you intend to kill them. However, as s. 8 of the Criminal Justice Act 1967 makes clear, there is no *requirement* that jurors or magistrates in criminal trials draw this inference. This statutory restatement of what had previously been a common law doctrine was made necessary by the decision in *DPP v Smith* (1961) AC 290, which suggested that it was a presumption of law, rather than fact.

A number of other, more arcane, presumptions of fact have been identified by the courts. Amongst them is generally considered to be that of unseaworthiness. Under this presumption, if a vessel capsizes and sinks less than a day after leaving port, without having encountered a storm or other known cause sufficient to account for its loss, there is a presumption that it was unseaworthy when it sailed, one on which a court might (but need not) act, in the absence of evidence to the contrary. However, where evidence is given on the issue, for example, that the loss was due to bad handling of the vessel while she was at sea, the presumption obviously cannot be drawn: *Ajum Goolen Hossen & Co v Union Marine Insurance Company Ltd* [1901] AC 362. It should be noted that the precise status of this presumption is open to question. It has been argued by some observers that it is a true evidential presumption (see below), not merely one of fact, one which a tribunal must follow if no rebutting evidence is adduced.

4. Legal Presumptions

Introduction

Legal (ie 'true') presumptions are the creatures of both common law and statute. They are not necessarily the result of a process of logical reasoning. Instead they normally reflect a variety of policy considerations. Some, such as the various presumptions of marriage are aimed at preserving important social institutions. Others, such as the common law presumption of death, provide a mechanism whereby a contested issue with major implications and legal consequences (a missing individual's death) can be determined in a predictable and conclusive manner. For similar policy reasons, the statutory presumption contained in s. 184 of the Law of Property Act 1925, provides that where two (or more) people have died in circumstances rendering their precise order of death uncertain, for example a very serious car crash resulting in near instantaneous death, it is assumed that they died in order of their seniority, with the eldest expiring first and the youngest last.

There are two types; so called 'persuasive' and 'evidential' presumptions, though it should be noted that, occasionally, other terminology is used by both the courts and academic observers; for example, the former are sometimes termed 'compelling presumptions'. Where a persuasive presumption applies, once fact A has been proved, conclusion B will necessarily follow, *unless* the opposing party can prove, on the balance of probabilities, that it should not; ie he has a legal burden on that issue.

Where an evidential presumption applies, once fact A has been established, conclusion B will follow, unless the party against whom the presumption is being employed adduces *some* evidence to suggest that it should not do so; ie he has an evidential burden on that issue. However, although he must adduce some tangible evidence to avoid the presumption applying, there is no onus on him to prove anything, as he does not have a legal burden. Unfortunately, matters are occasionally complicated because, in some situations, there is a doubt as to whether a presumption is persuasive or evidential, with conflicting case law on the subject, as there is, for example, with regard to the presumption created by the doctrine *of res ipsa loquitur* (see below).

Cross-reference Box

Evidential burdens place an obligation on a party to adduce some evidence on an issue to make it 'live' and so warrant being considered by the tribunal of fact. There is no onus on that party to 'prove' anything, that is to persuade the tribunal of fact that it is so. For more information on evidential burdens, go to chapter 3 at p. 118.

5. Persuasive Presumptions

Introduction

Examples of these include the presumption of legitimacy, the presumptions relating to marriage and the statutory presumption under s. 11(1) of the Civil Evidence Act 1968 that a person convicted of an offence by a British court is guilty of that crime. These will be considered in detail; however, it should be noted that there are numerous others.

Legitimacy

The presumption of legitimacy provides that, once it is established that a woman was married at the time that her child was conceived or born, the child is presumed to be the offspring of her husband. In the modern era, when DNA testing can establish such matters to near certainty, this presumption is usually of little practical significance, though it might become important with regard to the beneficiaries of, for example, a trust or will that was drawn up many years ago and which was limited to the legitimate offspring of unions that occurred in the distant past.

However, where it operates, it creates a legal presumption, so that once it comes into operation, the opposing party will have to rebut the presumption on the balance of probabilities, by dint of s. 26 of the Family Law Reform Act 1969. This provision lowered (or formally recognized as being the same) the standard of proof to that found in all other civil matters, whereas previously it had often been argued that it was 'beyond reasonable doubt' at common law (an indication of the gravity of allegations of illegitimacy in earlier times). The presumption applies even though conception occurred prior to marriage, or birth takes place after a marriage has been terminated. Traditionally, it could be rebutted by matters as diverse as a husband's lack of access to his spouse or his impotence.

S v S [1972] AC 24, HL

Lord Morris

If there was no other evidence than that a child was born during wedlock then legitimacy would not be assailed. But in cases where paternity is repudiated by a husband there will be much evidence.

The spouses themselves may give evidence. Older rules by which they were restricted have been abrogated. On a weighing of all the evidence a court will have to decide. The presumption of legitimacy will merely have been at the starting point. Once that is left behind it is the effect and the weight of all the evidence that will count.

The Presumptions of Marriage

There are, effectively, three persuasive presumptions with regard to marriage. These mean, for example, that if a couple have been through a ceremony of marriage or, alternatively, cohabited together as man and wife, it is presumed that they are or were validly married and also had the legal capacity to marry when they did so. In an era of ever better records, they are only rarely encountered with regard to domestic (as opposed to overseas) marriages. The three presumptions must be considered separately.

Formal Validity

The presumption of 'formal validity' means that, if a marriage has been celebrated, there is a presumption that the essential legal formalities of the ceremony were complied with. For example, that banns were duly published and a licence issued in a Church of England marriage, or that a licence was duly issued in a civil wedding: *Piers v Piers* (1849) 2 HL Cases 331. The presumption is reinforced by post-marriage cohabitation, though this does not appear to be essential to its operation. This presumption applies to foreign as well as domestic marriages. Thus, in the Divisional Court case of *Mahadervan v Mahadervan* [1964] P 233, a woman had been through a ceremony of marriage in Ceylon and lived with the groom for a period in the same country. Her husband had then come to England and contracted a second marriage. Subsequently, the Ceylonese wife came to England, and made an allegation of adultery against her spouse. In response, her husband claimed that the marriage in Ceylon was invalid, because it had failed to comply with the necessary formalities as to location, and content, of the ceremony, required on the island. The Divisional Court rejected this argument, on the basis that once the marriage had been celebrated, the onus was on the husband to establish that the ceremony was fatally flawed (which he could not do).

Once the presumption has come into play, the party who seeks to persuade the tribunal of fact that a marriage is not valid will have a legal burden to establish that this was, in fact, so. In older cases, it was frequently suggested that this would have to be to the criminal standard of beyond reasonable doubt, even in civil trials such as *Mahadervan*. (Again, this was a reflection of the perceived gravity of the allegation.) However, in the modern era, the criminal standard of proof is normally eschewed in civil matters, and this is almost certainly the case with the presumption of marriage, albeit that this is also a classic situation in which the notion of 'standards within standards' is likely to come into operation, so that the courts seek particularly cogent evidence that the marriage was not valid.

> ### *Mahadervan v Mahadervan* [1964] P 233, DC
>
> **Sir Jocelyn Simon P**
>
> Where there is a ceremony followed by cohabitation as husband and wife, a strong presumption arises that the parties are lawfully married. The leading case as to this is Piers v. Piers. The validity of the marriage in question depended on the issue of a special licence; but there was no trace of its issue and the bishop of the diocese had no recollection of issuing it. Nevertheless the House of Lords affirmed the marriage.

> Cross-reference Box
>
> Although the appellate courts have stressed that there is only one standard in civil cases, that is 'on the balance of probabilities', they appear to accept that the more serious the allegation the harder it will be to discharge this burden. For more on this topic go to chapter 3 at p. 138.

Essential Validity

The presumption of 'essential validity' provides that, once it has been established that a formally valid marriage has been celebrated, it will be presumed that the parties were themselves of an age and status to be married. For example, that they were over 16 years of age and not already married at the time. This presumption appears to be persuasive, rather than evidential, despite comments by Pilcher J in *Tweney v Tweney* [1946] P 180, but can clearly be rebutted on the balance of probabilities: *Axon v Axon* (1937) 59 CLR 395. Thus, the adduction of a birth certificate, showing that someone was 15 when they wed would probably be more than sufficient. In *Tweney*, it was argued that a woman who had remarried some 11 years after her first husband had deserted her might not have been a widow when she contracted a second marriage, which would have made the subsequent marriage a nullity.

> ### *Tweney v Tweney* [1946] P 180, HC
>
> **Pilcher J**
>
> The only point which I have to decide is whether this was a good marriage. There is no question that the marriage between the petitioner and respondent was attended by all proper formalities. I think that this court ought to regard the petitioner, who comes before it and gives evidence of a validly contracted marriage, as a married woman, until some evidence is given which leads the court to doubt that fact.

Living as 'Man and Wife'

Finally, there is a persuasive presumption (in civil cases) that, if a couple have cohabited as 'man and wife', they did so as the result of a valid marriage: *Re Taylor* [1961] 1 WLR 9. In the modern era, when cohabitation before marriage is extremely common, simply sharing a residence will not be enough. However, if a man and woman have lived together, and publicly held themselves out as being married, perhaps using the same surname, bank accounts and also paying their bills jointly, the presumption will come into play.

> ### *Re Taylor* [1961] 1 WLR 9, CA
>
> **Lord Evershed MR**
>
> The question raised in the action is whether the intestate and Izender were ever, and were more particularly at the date of the birth of the plaintiff, lawfully married. No certificate of marriage has been found or produced: nor is there any evidence of a ceremony of marriage. But Danckwerts J. concluded, nonetheless, that the evidence of reputation and of admissible declarations were such that he could and should conclude that John Taylor and Izender were lawfully married or were at least lawfully married at all relevant dates for the purpose of this action and, therefore, that the plaintiff was entitled to claim as a lawful son and one of the next-of-kin of the intestate. I will say at once that upon such a matter I am not prepared to say that the judge's conclusion was wrong.

Section 11(1) of the Civil Evidence Act 1968

An important, statutory, persuasive presumption is that established by s. 11(1) of the Civil Evidence Act 1968, whereby, in any civil proceedings, the fact that a person has been convicted of an offence by a criminal court in the United Kingdom can be admitted into evidence to establish a persuasive presumption that he committed that offence. However, this presumption will not apply if the defendant can rebut it, on the balance of probabilities. This presumption is considered in more detail in chapter 1.

 Pause for reflection

In the modern era, when the state of marriage can be ascertained much more easily than may have been the case 200 years ago, is there any role for such presumptions, or should they be formally abolished?

6. Evidential Presumptions

Mechanical Instruments

Evidential presumptions include the presumption that mechanical instruments of a type that are usually in working order, such as speedometers, breath-testing machines and traffic lights, were in working order at the time they were used. To rebut the presumption, the opposing party must adduce *some* evidence to the contrary: *Nicholas v Penny* [1950] 2 KB 466. Thus, in *Fearnley v DPP* [2005] EWHC 1393, the Divisional Court noted that there would have to be positive evidence before the presumption that an intoximeter, challenged by a driver accused of drink-driving, was operating properly, would not apply.

Pause for reflection

How can you distinguish instruments that are normally in working order from those of a less dependable type?

For a recent example of this presumption in operation, consider *Carter v Director of Public Prosecutions* [2007] RTR 22. In this case, the defendant gave the police a specimen of blood (rather than breath) for analysis, after being stopped for drink driving and failing the ensuing breathalyser test. The accuracy of such a blood analysis was partly dependent on the presence of a certain preservative in a specimen phial in the appropriate testing kit. No positive evidence was adduced at trial by the expert who had analysed the defendant's blood sample to the effect that this preservative had been present in the phial. However, after conviction, the defendant's appeal was dismissed by the Divisional Court, which held that, unless there was something in the material before the court to suggest to the contrary, the magistrates were entitled to presume that the procedures laid down for the preparation of such blood kits and phials, including the addition of the relevant preservative, had been carried out correctly.

Carter v Director of Public Prosecutions [2007] RTR 22, DC

Latham LJ

Unless there is something in the material before the court to suggest to the contrary, I would accordingly conclude that the court is entitled to presume that the procedures laid down for the preparation of kits such as the ones we are concerned with here have been carried out correctly. In those circumstances the district judge was clearly entitled to come to the conclusion that she did, having heard the evidence of Sergeant Hardie that the procedures were properly carried out at the police station and the evidence of Dr Porter which did not suggest in any way that he concluded or considered that the sample might have been contaminated or otherwise affected by any failure to place in the phials the appropriate preservatives and other substances. I would accordingly reject Mr Ley's arguments on the basis that I have indicated. I should add, since Mr Ley has submitted that this raises an issue under Article 6 [of the European Convention on Human Rights] as to evidential presumptions, that the presumption that I considered appropriate in this case is one which is essentially based on common sense and, in my judgment, is entirely proportionate bearing in mind the opportunities, on the one hand, for the defendant to have his own sample analysed and, secondly, the opportunity, in any event, to raise any proper questions based upon material available to him which could undermine the presumption in any way. The moment there is such material clearly it will be for the prosecution to satisfy the court that any doubts have been entirely resolved before the court could properly convict.

Presumption of Regularity

A close cousin of the above evidential presumption is that of regularity, which is that public and official acts and duties have been properly performed and that public officers have been duly appointed. Once it has been established that someone acted in an official capacity, it will be presumed that they were properly appointed to that office, unless some evidence is adduced to the contrary. This presumption is sometimes summed up in the Latin maxim *omnia prae-sumuntur rite esse acta*. Thus, and for example, if there is evidence that a police constable acted as such, it will be presumed that he was a duly appointed police officer. Thus, in the following case, it became an issue on appeal as to whether the judge who had presided over the case at first instance had been properly appointed.

R v Roberts (1878) 14 Cox 101, CCR

Lord Coleridge CJ

I am of opinion that the conviction should be affirmed. One of the best recognized principles of law, *Omnia presumuntur esse rite et solemniter acta donec preobetur in contrarium,* is applicable to public officers acting in discharge of public duties. The mere acting in a public capacity is sufficient prima facie proof of the proper appointment; but it is only a prima facie presumption, and it is capable of being rebutted . . .

To prevent the presumption operating, the defence will have to adduce *some* tangible evidence suggesting, for example, that the official was not properly appointed, in which case the prosecution will then have to *prove* that the official was, in fact, duly appointed. The same principle will apply to, inter alia, a customs and excise officer, a postman and an inspector appointed by the Health and Safety Executive: *Campbell v Wallsend Slipway and Engineering Co. Ltd.* [1978] ICR 1015. Thus, and as a hypothetical illustration, if a defendant is accused of assaulting a police officer in the execution of his duty during a disturbance, the prosecution will not have to prove that the victim of the assault had this status (was a PC) unless, and for illustrative example, the defendant adduces some evidence that the 'officer' was, in reality, the police station cleaner who had been given a uniform to wear and was 'helping out' at a busy time. Thus, the prosecution might call one of her fellow cleaners to give oral evidence to this effect. The prosecution would then have to satisfy the court (beyond reasonable doubt) that she had been duly appointed; for example, by adducing her warrant in court.

Pause for reflection

For what practical reasons might such a presumption exist?

Presumption of Death

There is a presumption that if a person has not been heard of for seven years, by people who might be expected to have heard of them during that period, and all due enquiries have been made to ascertain whether he is still alive, the person will be presumed to have died at some point during that period. Thus, in *Chipchase v Chipchase* [1939] 3 All ER 895, it was held that it could not be argued that a woman who had been married in 1915, but had been deserted by her husband in January of the following year, without subsequently hearing from him, did not have any evidence that he was dead when she contracted a subsequent marriage in 1928.

Similarly, in *Re Newson-Smith's Settlement* [1962] 1 WLR 1478 a man who had last been seen on his way to the Great War (1914–1918), and last heard from by letter in the 1920s, could be presumed to be dead in 1960. However, as *Chard v Chard* [1956] P 259 makes clear, for the presumption to operate there must be people available who might have been expected to hear from the missing person during this period. In *Bullock v Bullock* [1960] 1 WLR 975, where the police had been unable to find a husband after he had disappeared, with a view to serving a committal order, it was held that his abandoned wife, who had not made her own enquiries, could still rely on the presumption to prevent a subsequent marriage, contracted many years later, being held to be void.

Bullock v Bullock [1960] 1 WLR 975, DC

Lord Merriman P

There is one other thing which I think may be stated to be settled, and that is that reliance on the presumption that a man who is completely unheard of for seven years may be presumed to be dead does depend to some extent on the question whether all due inquiries have been made having regard to the circumstances; and that the circumstances may vary between one case and another is plain from various authorities which have been cited to us, quite properly, in the course of the argument. In this case the importance of the failure to execute that warrant in the case of a man said to be living in or near Sheffield at the time when he left his wife, and certainly at the time of the celebration of the marriage and during the marriage, seems to me to be this, not merely that he could not be found then, but that he could not be found then in circumstances that he had the police, with all the resources that are open to them, after him; and if he could not be found by the police any woman might be fully justified in assuming that he could not be found by her, and it may be a very sensible and satisfactory explanation of the admitted fact that after that time, at any rate, she did not make any inquiries.

Although, in such circumstances, the subject of the presumption will have been presumed to have died during the course of the seven-year period, there is no presumption as to *when* this occurred, which will have to be proved by other evidence. Thus, in *Re Phene's Trusts* (1870) 5 Ch App 139, a sailor who had deserted a vessel in America, and not been heard of since, could not be presumed to have died in the first 24 months of the seven-year period.

The presumption is clearly one of law, not fact. Otherwise, as Sachs J observed in *Chard*, there would be no reason to have a definite seven-year period. It must also be an evidential presumption, because as soon as evidence is adduced that someone has heard from the subject it will necessarily cease to operate, as the absence of such evidence is a prerequisite for the presumption's operation. In this case a husband and his second wife sought decrees of nullity with regard to their marriage in 1933. The judge granted the decrees as the wife, who had been a normal healthy woman, would have been only 44 in 1933, and thus likely to still be alive, applying the presumption of continuance (a 'presumption of fact') and, although she had not been heard of since 1917, eight years after the original marriage, it was not possible to find someone who would naturally be expected to have heard from her in the intervening period after 1917 (and she had reasons not to wish to hear from the husband or his family). As a result, the husband was deemed to have been already married in 1933, when he contracted his second marriage.

Chard v Chard [1956] P 259, HC

Sachs J

By virtue of a long sequence of judicial statements, which either assert or assume such a rule, it appears accepted that there is a convenient presumption of law applicable to certain cases of seven years' absence where no statute applies. That presumption in its modern shape takes effect (without examining its terms too exactly) substantially as follows. Where as regards 'A.B.' there is no acceptable affirmative evidence that he was alive at some time during a continuous period of seven years or more, then if it can be proved first, that there are persons who would be likely to have heard of him over that period, secondly that those persons have not heard of him, and thirdly that all due inquiries have been made appropriate to the circumstances, 'A.B.' will be presumed to have died at some time within that period. (Such a presumption would, of course be one of law, and could not be one of fact, because there can hardly be a logical inference from any particular set of facts that a man had not died within 2,555 days but had died within 2,560.)

7. Disputed Presumptions

Res Ipsa Loquitur

Occasionally, as previously noted, there is some doubt as to whether a presumption is persuasive or evidential. For an example of this can be considered the doctrine of *res ipsa loquitur* (literally 'the thing speaks for itself') which traditionally assisted claimants in tortious actions who were attempting to prove negligence. Essentially, the preliminary facts for the doctrine to apply require that the claimant establish that a state of affairs was under the control of the defendant, and that it occasioned an accident that would not normally happen, in the ordinary course of events, in the absence of negligence on the part of the defendant. In these circumstances, the presence of negligence will be presumed. For example, in *Byrne v Boadle* (1863) 159 Eng. Rep 299, the plaintiff was injured by a barrel of flour falling from a second-storey window of the defendant's premises. As Baron Pollock noted, prima facie: 'A barrel could not roll out of a warehouse without some negligence, and to say that a plaintiff who is injured by it must call witnesses from the warehouse to prove negligence seems to me preposterous.' The doctrine was further clarified by the following case.

Scott v London and St Katherine Docks Co.
(1865) 3 H & C 596, Exchequer Chamber

Erle CJ

But where the thing is shown to be under the management of the defendant or his servants, and the accident is such an in the ordinary course of things does not happen if those who have the management use proper care, it affords reasonable evidence, in the absence of explanation by the defendants, that the accident arose from want of care.

In the modern era, these requirements have been interpreted quite strictly. For example, in a dissenting judgment in *Mahon v Osborne* [1939] 2 KB 14, Scott LJ was not even willing to accept that the doctrine applied so as to shift the burden to a defendant surgeon, accused of negligence, who was found to have carried out an operation in which a swab was left in a patient's body, as a result of which the patient subsequently died. Nevertheless, few judges would take such a strict approach to the doctrine.

 Pause for reflection

Can you think of any scenario in which this might have occurred without the surgeon demonstrating a degree of negligence?

Even more significantly, the continuing value and importance of the whole doctrine has been questioned in many common law jurisdictions, including England and Wales. Indeed, in some countries, it no longer operates at all, or has been relegated to being merely a 'presumption of fact'. In England, this process has been greatly assisted by the absence of the jury from civil cases, something that means that the doctrine is likely to be, at most, a footnote in a trial judge's judgment. In *Fryer v Pearson* (2000) WL 281274, several members of the Court of Appeal went further, and questioned its continuing use, leading some academic commentators to believe that the doctrine was moribund if not dead.

Christian Witting, 'Res Ipsa Loquitur: Some Last Words' (2001) Law Quarterly Review, vol 117, 392–397 (extract)

His Lordship's point, that the concept expresses 'no defined principle' is another way of saying that it has no coherent part to play in deciding cases. Although *Fryer v. Pearson* did not turn upon the issue whether it could be pleaded or not, so that any comments were strictly *obiter*, May L.J.'s opinion that it should no longer be applied renders it increasingly difficult to believe that *res ipsa loquitur* has any future role to play in the proof of negligence. In *Ratcliffe*, Hobhouse L.J. (as he then was) added his voice to a growing chorus of dissatisfaction with the concept, opining that "the expression *res ipsa loquitur* should be dropped from the litigator's vocabulary": [1998] Lloyd's Rep. Med. 162 at p. 177. Even if *Fryer* proves not to have dealt it the fatal blow, this is, perhaps, a taste of what is to come when the concept is next discussed in the House of Lords. Is it dead now? It may be hoped so.

Nevertheless, despite these publicly voiced doubts, the doctrine continues to make occasional appearances, in special circumstances, as can be seen from *Widdowson v Newgate Meat Corp* [1998] PIQR 138. In this case, the claimant, who suffered from serious mental illness, was struck by the defendant's van while walking on a dual carriageway. The seriously injured (and disturbed) pedestrian did not give evidence in his action, nor (crucially) did the defendant. The Court of Appeal held that, on the facts of the case, the plaintiff was entitled to establish liability using the maxim of *res ipsa loquitur*.

Widdowson v Newgate Meat Corp [1998] PIQR 138, CA

Brooke LJ

It appears to me that the suggestions put forward in this passage of cross-examination do not amount to a plausible explanation, consistent with an absence of negligence on the defendant's part, sufficient to rebut a prima facie inference of negligence by the defendant, and a plausible explanation is what the law requires if a defendant is to escape liability in such circumstances (see Moore v. R. Fox and Sons [1956] 1 Q.B. 596 per Evershed M.R. at 607 and Colvilles Ltd v. Devine [1969] 1 W.L.R. 475, per Lord Guest at 477. In Clerk & Lindsell on Torts (17th ed.) paragraph 7–180, the editor observes that the defendant cannot hope to redress the balance merely by putting up theoretical possibilities: 'his assertion must have some colour of probability about it'.

The situation might have been very different if Mr Scullion had given evidence. As Lord Griffiths pointed out in the Privy Council case of Ng Chun Pui v. Lee Chuen Tat [1988] R.T.R. 298 at 301, if a defendant does adduce evidence, that evidence must be evaluated to see if it is still reasonable to draw the inference of negligence from the mere fact of the accident. 'Loosely speaking this may be referred to as a burden on the defendant to show he was not negligent, but that only means that faced with a prima facie case of negligence the defendant will be found negligent unless he produces evidence that is capable of rebutting the prima facie case.' Mr Stewart showed us two reported cases, in both of which the defendant gave evidence, in support of his submission that his client should not be held liable on the facts of the present case, but those two cases were quite different.

Even allowing for its continued existence, there has been considerable debate, throughout the common law world, as to exactly what sort of presumption is created by the doctrine. In some countries, it appears to be nothing more than a presumption of fact, ie an inference of negligence that may (but need not) be inferred, once the prerequisites for the doctrine have been established.

In England, however, it has generally been treated as a true presumption, in that once its pre-conditions have been proved, the defendant's negligence will necessarily be presumed, unless he forestalls such a conclusion by doing 'something'. This then raises the obvious question, 'doing what?' Is it a persuasive or an evidential presumption? Does the defendant merely have to raise some evidence that he was not negligent for the presumption not to operate? Alternatively, does he have a legal burden to prove that he was not negligent? It is even possible that its effect will depend on the circumstances in which it is adduced, ie on some occasions it will be a persuasive presumption, in others an evidential one.

The case law differs on this issue, with some older decisions suggesting that the doctrine places a legal burden on the defendant, and so is a persuasive presumption, at least in some situations. Thus, in *Barkway v South Wales Transport Ltd.* [1949] I KB 54, Asquith LJ observed that: 'When a balance has been tilted one way, you cannot redress it by adding an equal weight to each scale. The depressed scale will remain down…the defendants must go further and prove…' Similarly, in *Ward v Tesco Stores* (1976) 1 WLR 810 the Court of Appeal suggested that it created a persuasive presumption.

However, insofar as it exists, the bulk of recent authority suggests that the doctrine merely creates an evidential presumption: *Ng Chun Pui v Lee Chuen Tat* (1988) RTR 298. In this case, it was held that it was misleading to talk of the burden of proof shifting to the defendant in a *res ipsa loquitur* situation, as the burden of proving negligence rested on the plaintiff (now termed the claimant) throughout the trial. However, in an appropriate case, once the plaintiff had established a prima facie case, by relying on the occurrence of an accident, if the defendant adduced no evidence to rebut it, the plaintiff would be taken to have established his case; the doctrine placed an evidential burden on the defendant.

In *Ng Chun Pui* a bus, driven by the defendant, had crashed through the central reservation of a busy main road into the path of another vehicle, resulting in death and personal injury. The plaintiffs were the injured passengers and representatives of those bereaved by the collision. At trial, they did not call oral evidence of their own, but relied on *res ipsa loquitur,* arguing that the fact of the accident alone was enough to prove negligence.

Nevertheless, in his defence, the defendant gave oral evidence that an untraced car had cut in on him, forcing him to swerve to avoid a collision, and so leading to the accident; thus, he satisfied an evidential burden by adducing some evidence that would suggest that the accident could have occurred without his negligence. At trial, the first instance judge felt that this evidence was not enough to disprove negligence (ie to satisfy a legal burden on the issue), and found for the plaintiffs. This decision was reversed on appeal, a conclusion that was subsequently upheld by the Privy Council, which held that there was no legal burden on the defendant to disprove negligence in the instant case, and that the doctrine had consequently ceased to operate once the defendant had adduced evidence on how the accident could have occurred without negligence. There was then no other evidence for the plaintiffs to establish their case.

Ng Chun Pui v Lee Chuen Tat (1988) RTR 298, PC

Lord Griffiths

So in an appropriate case the plaintiff establishes a prima facie case by relying upon the fact of the accident. If the defendant adduces no evidence there is nothing to rebut the inference of negligence and the plaintiff will have proved his case. But if the defendant does adduce evidence that evidence must be evaluated to see if it is still reasonable to draw the inference of negligence from the mere fact of the accident. Loosely speaking this may be referred to as a burden on the defendant to show he was not negligent, but that only means that faced with a prima facie case of negligence the defendant will be found negligent unless he produces evidence that is capable of rebutting the prima facie case. Resort to the burden of proof is a poor way to decide a case; it is the duty of the judge to examine all the evidence at the end of the case and decide whether on the facts he finds to have been proved and on the inferences he is prepared to draw he is satisfied that negligence has been established. In so far as resort is had to the burden of proof the burden remains at the end of the case as it was at the beginning upon the plaintiff to prove that his injury was caused by the negligence of the defendants.

---

8. When Presumptions Conflict

Occasionally, presumptions come into conflict. Often such conflicts will be more apparent than real. For example, a 'presumption of fact', such as the presumption of continuance of life, will always be 'trumped' by a legal presumption, such as the presumption of death, not least because the former is not a 'true' presumption. Very exceptionally, however, there will be a conflict between two legal presumptions of equal weight.

This is most commonly encountered with regard to marriage. For example, a party may be accused of having committed bigamy because his marriage to wife 1 was subsisting when he married wife 2. He may claim that he was not legally married in the first alleged ceremony and argue that the presumption of 'essential validity' should mean that it will be presumed that when he married wife 2 he was of a status to be married, ie he was single. Against this, it may be argued that the presumption of 'formal validity' means that, if a marriage to wife 1 has been celebrated, there is a presumption that the essential legal formalities of the ceremony were complied with (so that he can be presumed to have been married when he wed for a second time).

In these very rare, and complicated, situations, different approaches have been adopted by the judiciary and academic observers. Thus, in some (especially criminal) situations, it may be correct to follow Lord Coleridge's suggestion in *R v Willshire* (1881) 6 QBD, and work on the basis that the conflicting presumptions should cancel each other out, leaving the presumed facts to be decided on the rest of the evidence, in the case as a whole. In others, and especially in civil cases, it has been suggested that it would often be best to adopt a chronological approach. That is, to ask if the party who has the burden of proof on an issue has overcome any presumption that is against him, and which is earlier in time to a conflicting presumption on which he intends to rely, before he is allowed to rely on that conflicting presumption.[1]

 SUMMARY

- A true presumption, termed a legal presumption, describes a situation in which, once fact A has been proved, conclusion B must follow, unless the opposing side does 'something'.

- If this 'something' is limited to adducing some evidence to rebut the presumption (ie the opposing side has an evidential burden on that matter), it will be termed an evidential presumption. If it puts a burden of proof on the opposing side to show that the presumption is wrong, on the balance of probabilities, it will be termed a persuasive presumption. Occasionally, as with the doctrine of *res ipsa loquitur*, there is some doubt as to what type of presumption, evidential or persuasive, is involved.

- Such presumptions have been created both at common law and by statute. For a typical example of the former, consider the persuasive presumption that a child born within marriage is legitimate. Section 11(1) of the Civil Evidence Act 1968 provides an example of a presumption that has been created by statute; this provides that, in civil proceedings, a party is deemed to have committed the offence for which he was earlier convicted in a criminal court.

- However, the word 'presumption' is used, less precisely, in two other situations in the law of evidence; these are not really 'true' presumptions. They are the so-called 'presumptions of fact' and 'irrebuttable presumptions of law'.

- A presumption of fact is nothing more than a commonsensical inference that can (but need not) be drawn by the tribunal of fact once the preliminary fact is established. In theory, the only difference between these situations and any other examples of circumstantial evidence is that they have been specifically identified by case law. Examples of such a presumption are that a person intends the natural consequences of his acts, or has come by stolen goods improperly if they are found in his possession very shortly after a theft or burglary.

- An irrebutable presumption of law is really a substantive legal rule, couched in the terminology of presumptions. For an example, consider the presumption that a child under the age of 10 years cannot be guilty of a crime.

[1] P Murphy, *Murphy on Evidence* (9th edn, Oxford University Press) at 620–621.

Further reading

AT Denning, 'Presumptions and Burdens' (1945) Law Quarterly Review, vol 61, 379

M McInnes, 'The Death of Res Ipsa Loquitur in Canada' (1998) Law Quarterly Review, vol 114, 547–550

Daniel Mendonca, 'Presumptions' (1998) Ratio Juris, vol 11, no 4, 399–412

Christian Witting, 'Res Ipsa Loquitur: Some Last Words' (2001) Law Quarterly Review, vol 117, 392–397

GH Treitel, 'The Presumption of Death' (1954) Modern Law Review, vol 17, 530

Questions for Discussion

For suggested approaches, please visit the Online Resource Centre

1. Amanda lived with her partner Brian, an unsociable and elderly man, for several years. One day, he disappeared while on his way to a local tobacconist. Over the following year, Amanda asked his few friends and surviving family members whether they had seen him, but got no positive news. Eight years later, Amanda, who inherits all of Brian's property under his will, decides that she would like to have him declared dead, so that she can liquidate his stocks and shares and spend the resulting money.

Advise Amanda.

2. A High Street camera shop is burgled at 11.30 pm one night. At 1.30 am the following morning, Charles is arrested two miles away, in possession of three cameras that are subsequently found to have come from the shop. He claims that he found them in the street. There is no other evidence linking him to the burglary.

Advise the CPS as to how, if at all, they could establish that Charles has committed a crime.

3. Fiona and George lived together for five years, during which period they regularly referred to themselves as 'Mr and Mrs Smith' and jointly paid their bills under this title. George dies suddenly, without leaving a will. Fiona wishes to inherit his property as his wife and so, under intestacy rules, his closest relative. George's blood nephew, Harold, resists this on the basis that the couple were not married. Fiona is unable to adduce any formal documentation of her marriage to George, which she says took place in an Anglican Church in rural Norfolk, ministered to by a scatterbrained and long dead cleric.

Advise Fiona.

5 CHARACTER EVIDENCE

Definitions

Good character This normally signifies nothing more than that a defendant in a criminal case has no previous convictions.

Blemished defendant A defendant who does not meet all of the normal requirements of having a good character but, in some situations, may be treated as if he does.

Similar fact evidence Common law test for admitting evidence of previous bad character evidence to suggest misconduct in the present, at variance to the general common law exclusionary rule against adducing bad character evidence. Abolished in criminal cases by the Criminal Justice Act 2003, though a form of the test still survives in civil matters.

Credibility The likelihood that a witness is telling the truth.

Propensity The likelihood that a person who has behaved in a certain manner in the past will have done so again, and so 'acted in character' in the present.

---

1. Introduction

Human beings are, to some extent, creatures of habit. As a result, behaviour in the past, both good and bad, can provide an indication as to likely conduct in the present. A neat illustration of this phenomenon is, perhaps, provided by an old case from Worcester, in which it was recorded that a: '...fellow that stood in the pillory last Assizes, for attempting to commit a rape upon a girl, being suffer'd to go on an errand, attempted lately in like manner a young woman in the fields.'[1] Obviously, evidence of previous behaviour is never conclusive of that in the present and will, sometimes, be of relatively minor significance. Saints can turn sinner and thorough reprobates go 'straight'. Nevertheless, in many cases, and as the case from Worcester suggests, previous conduct is of some probative value at trial.

This can operate in two ways. Assuming that an individual has provided evidence in some form, whether orally or via a written statement, their personal history may have some bearing

---

[1] Mist's Weekly Journal, 23 July 1726.

on the weight that can be attributed to their testimony. To take an extreme example, it is likely that someone with numerous previous convictions for perjury will place little importance on the duty to speak the truth when under oath. This does not mean that in any given trial they will lie. It is, however, a factor that most tribunals would take into consideration when deciding how much importance should be placed on their evidence. Thus, their previous misconduct can be said to go to the issue of credibility, ie is what this individual has said worthy of belief?

Of course, the illustration given is an extreme one. Whether a previous conviction for an offence not involving dishonesty, or even a minor crime of dishonesty, should have a significant effect on the way in which an individual's evidence is considered is much more debatable, especially where they have no vested interest in the outcome of a case. In the latter situation, many behavioural psychologists in the modern era would question its significance.

Pause for reflection

Would you put less weight on the evidence of a man who was convicted of stealing a steak from a supermarket a year earlier?

Previous behaviour also has a second use; it can be a valuable indication as to likely conduct in any given situation, irrespective of whether the party gives evidence or not. Let us assume that in the case from Worcester the incident in the fields founded another prosecution for attempted rape, and the defendant denied that it had occurred. Would his very recent previous conviction for an identical offence, at the earlier assizes, be relevant to the case currently before the court? Employing Lord Simon's classic definition of relevance in *DPP v Kilbourne* [1973] AC 729, as meaning 'logically probative or disprobative' of the facts in issue, it would. It is now known that the defendant falls within the (hopefully) very small group of men who are willing to use force to gain sexual satisfaction. Consequently, it can be argued that he has acted in accordance with an established character trait. Such evidence can be said to go to the issue of propensity.

Cross-reference Box

Relevance is a key concept in the law of evidence and a prerequisite for the admissibility of all forms of evidence at trial, although some evidence that is relevant will not be admissible, because it is caught by an exclusionary rule. For a more detailed discussion of relevance see chapter 1, at pp. 30–33.

Of course, such earlier misconduct is certainly not conclusive of a defendant's guilt. That someone has misbehaved in a very serious manner in the past does not mean that they have done so in the present. However, there is often a danger that this will be assumed, for two reasons. First, a tribunal of fact, especially if made up of laymen, may give the evidence more significance than it properly deserves. This is sometimes referred to as 'reasoning prejudice'. Secondly, if they come to the conclusion that the accused is a 'bad man', they may decide not to give him the benefit of any doubt. This is sometimes referred to as 'moral prejudice'.

Unfortunately, it is often almost impossible to distinguish prejudice from legitimate reliance. Research with mock juries and magistrates hearing simulated cases suggests that lay tribunals that have been exposed to a defendant's bad character are, in some (but not all) situations more likely to convict. However, this may be because, despite the risk of prejudice, past misconduct has considerable, and proper, evidential weight.

S Lloyd Bostock, 'The effects on Lay Magistrates of Hearing that the Defendant is of "Good Character", Being Left to Speculate, or Hearing that he has a Previous Conviction' [2006] Crim LR 189

The results of the study confirm, not only the compelling nature of information about previous convictions, but also the complexity of its effects. Armchair speculation, or what decision-makers themselves believe about the likely effects of revealing or concealing previous convictions to magistrates or juries may well turn out to be wrong. Some significant results could not be predicted, though post hoc explanations have been suggested above, whilst other possible findings did not appear. As with the simulated jurors, it seems that very sparse information is sufficient to evoke a quite rich and potentially damaging stereotype. Significant effects were found even though only minimal information about the previous offence was provided (namely the offence charge), and there was only one conviction. The probative value of such information, without any details of the earlier offence and its circumstances, is arguably very limited. As in the Jury Study, the effects shown are not large, but they are significant and follow a consistent pattern. The results with bench verdicts indicate that they may make the difference between a guilty and a not-guilty verdict. Despite their difference experiences, the magistrates and simulated jurors seemed to have similar perceptions of typical patterns of criminality, except that magistrates seemed to view propensity as more fixed. For the magistrates, hearing about an old conviction could be as powerful as hearing about a recent one. Any previous conviction, recent or old, affected magistrates' assessments of the defendant's likely guilt and verdicts unfavourably, unless it was both recent and dissimilar to the current charge. On the other hand, absence of information, or information that the defendant is of good character, had a weaker impact than is sometimes assumed. It seems that it is specific, concrete information that does the damage. Despite the assumptions the magistrates said they made about prior record, 'no information' was significantly more favourable than information about a single previous conviction.

Obviously, evidence of propensity will be highly significant with regard to defendants in criminal trials. Even so, it is not confined to them. For an example of other situations, consider a trial for assault in which the accused man is advancing self-defence as the basis for a plea of 'not guilty'. He claims that the alleged victim and chief prosecution witness was, in fact, the aggressor in the incident. In such circumstances, the fact that the 'victim' has a long history of violence, resulting in numerous previous convictions for such offences, is likely to be highly relevant to the accused's defence.

Indeed, evidence of propensity is not even confined to criminal trials, though it is most commonly encountered there. It can also be relevant to civil matters. For example, in a copyright action it is alleged that the creator of a piece of music has, in reality, copied it from an earlier piece composed by another artist. In his defence, he argues that any similarities are coincidental. In this situation, the fact that the defendant has been successfully sued for breaches of copyright, in similar cases, on earlier occasions, may be highly relevant to the likelihood of his defence being accepted at trial.

Thus, previous conduct, good or bad, can go to issues of both credit and propensity, in civil and criminal trials, and involve defendants, witnesses and even third parties. Sometimes, it will be of enormous significance; at others, of little or no relevance. The use of good character is largely a creature of case law, as is that of bad character in civil matters. Bad character in criminal cases is now primarily regulated by the Criminal Justice Act 2003. This statute, the introduction of which followed a major Law Commission report, has transformed the bad character regime in criminal matters, making older authority largely (though not entirely) redundant in this area. For the sake of convenience of exposition, good and bad character, in criminal and civil cases, can be considered separately.

2. Defendant Good Character Evidence in Criminal Cases

A defendant can call evidence to establish his 'good' character. This may be given during examination-in-chief by the defendant in person, by one of his witnesses, or be elicited from a prosecution witness on his behalf during cross-examination. This can include a witness speaking 'positively' to an accused person's virtuous character. Strictly speaking, such evidence is limited to the *general* reputation of the accused, and can refer neither to a witness's own personal view of the defendant nor to specific creditable incidents involving them, since neither reveal general reputation: *R v Rowton* (1865) Le & Ca 520. Thus, in theory, a clergyman might be called to say that an accused has a very good character in his neighbourhood, but should not give details of his voluntary work with the disabled or his own personal assessment of the individual's character.

Even in the nineteenth century, a time of lower social mobility than the present, this proved to be a difficult rule to apply in practice; in the modern era, a time when 'reputation' as a commodity is so much harder to establish due to population mobility, it is frequently tacitly ignored in practice. As a result, a defendant who moves from bedsit to bedsit around the London area may never acquire a 'general' reputation, but private individuals, who are familiar with him, are often called to give character evidence and frequently touch on their personal views of his virtues or specific aspects of his previous good conduct.

It can also be noted that the position in *Rowton*, taken to its logical conclusion, would enable a character witness who personally believes an accused to be a complete rascal, and who knows of highly discreditable incidents in his life, but who is unique in such knowledge, to provide an excellent reference as to his general reputation, though Cockburn CJ wisely anticipated this by also asserting that it was essential that any character witness also have a personally good opinion of the defendant, otherwise they would be 'deceiving' the jury.

R v Rowton (1865) Le & Ca 520, CCR

Cockburn CJ

The only way of getting at it is by giving evidence of his general character founded on his general reputation in the neighbourhood in which he lives. That, in my opinion, is the sense in which 'character' is to be taken, when evidence of character is spoken of. The fact that a man has an unblemished reputation leads to the presumption that he is incapable of committing the crime for which he is being tried. We are not now considering whether it is desirable that the law of England should be altered—whether it is expedient to import the practice of other countries and go into the prisoner's antecedents for the purpose of showing that he is likely to commit the crime with which he is charged, or, stopping short of that, whether it would be wise to allow the prisoner to go into facts for the purpose of showing that he is incapable of committing the crime charged against him. It is quite clear that, as the law now stands, the prisoner cannot give evidence of particular facts, although one fact would weigh more than the opinion of all his friends and neighbours....It is, moreover, most essential that a witness who comes forward to give a man a good character should himself have a good opinion of him; for otherwise he would only be deceiving the jury; and so the strict rule is often exceeded. But, when we consider what, in the strict interpretation of the law, is the limit of such evidence, in my judgment it must be restricted to the man's general reputation, and must not extend to the individual opinion of the witness.

However, although the 'rule' in *Rowton* is frequently ignored in practice (as even Lord Cockburn noted in 1865), very occasionally, it asserts itself in some form. For example, in *R v Redgrave* (1981) 74 Cr App Rep 10, the defendant was accused of an offence of gross indecency in a public lavatory (ie a 'homosexual' offence). At his first trial he was allowed to adduce cards and letters from various girlfriends, to suggest that he was not homosexual and thus was not likely to have committed the offence of which he was accused. (For evidential purposes, if no other, these must be considered analogous to specific creditable incidents.) This trial produced a hung jury, and a retrial was ordered. The (different) judge presiding at the second trial did not allow evidence of the correspondence to be given and the defendant was convicted.

The defendant appealed on the basis that it was wrong for such evidence to have been excluded. Dismissing his appeal, the Court of Appeal upheld the decision in *Rowton* forbidding the adduction of evidence of specific incidents. However, the court also accepted that it was proper for a trial judge, as a special indulgence in such cases, to allow a defendant to assert that he was happily married or had a steady girlfriend. Whether such an approach, which penalizes promiscuous heterosexuals, would be followed today, is, perhaps, debatable.

R v Redgrave (1981) 74 Cr App Rep 10, CA

Lawton LJ

In our judgment the defendant is bound by the same rules as the prosecution. He can call evidence to show that he did not commit the acts which are alleged against him, but he is not allowed, by reference to particular facts, to call evidence that he is of a disposition which makes it unlikely that he would have committed the offence charged. That this is the common law of England is shown clearly by the decision in Rowton (1865) Le. & Ca. 520. In the course of his judgment in that case Cockburn C.J. said at p. 530: 'It is quite clear that, as the law now stands, the prisoner cannot give evidence of particular facts, although one fact would weigh more than the opinion of all his friends and neighbours.' That is what the appellant was trying to do in this case. He was trying, by his evidence about his relations with particular women and by the production of these letters and photographs, to show that he had had intimate heterosexual relationships with the writers of the letters and the girls in the photographs, and he was relying on those particular facts to show that he had not got a disposition to behave in the sort of way which the prosecution alleged. The problem in this case is whether there is any exception in law to the general proposition laid down by Cockburn C.J. nearly 120 years ago. The Court of Crown Cases Reserved in Rowton (supra), made up of no less than 12 judges came to the conclusion, with two dissensions, that when a defendant wishes

> to show he has not got a disposition to commit the kind of offence with which he is charged, he is limited in what he can say. In 1866 he could call evidence to show that his general reputation made it unlikely that he would commit the kind of offence with which he was charged. He could do that by calling people who knew him, but beyond that he could not go. It follows therefore, so it seems to us, that in this case, although disposition to commit the kind of offence charged was relevant, the law is as decided in Rowton (supra), viz. that the defendant could do no more than say, or call witnesses to prove, that he was not by general repute the kind of young man who would have behaved in the kind of way that the Crown alleged.

In practice, although it is always useful for a defendant to be able to call a character witness, when it comes to enjoying its *legal* consequences, having a 'good character' in an English criminal trial usually means no more than that the defendant does not have previous convictions, rather than that he is an upstanding and community minded member of society, given to doing good works and helping his neighbours, and for whom others will vouch. As a result, at least 75 per cent of men (though not of defendants) over the age of 30 years are entitled to the legal benefits that flow from a good character. Whether juries always understand that this is all that the phrase entails is open to question; nevertheless, the Judicial Studies Board model direction does suggest that, where there is positive evidence of an accused person's good qualities, a trial judge can point this out this in his direction on character.[2]

 Pause for reflection

Do you feel that it is helpful to have 'good character' so widely defined?

Uses of Defendant Good Character

In *R v Aziz* [1995] 3 WLR 52 the House of Lords referred to the 'sea-change' that had occurred in judicial thinking, with regard to the uses to which a defendant's good character can be put, over the previous decade. By then, there was a general recognition that the good character of a defendant was both 'logically relevant to his credibility and the likelihood that he would commit the offence in question'. Thus, just as bad character can go to both propensity and credibility, so can good character. If a defendant has no previous convictions, their lack of a propensity to offend is something that can always be considered when deciding whether they would have committed the crime with which they are currently charged. Of course, how much weight this carries will depend, in part, on the age of the defendant, becoming stronger as he gets older. It will be more surprising, and so improbable, if a man of 60 suddenly starts to offend than it would be if the individual were 18 years old.

Additionally, *if* a defendant elects to give evidence at trial, his lack of previous convictions is a factor that the tribunal of fact can consider when deciding how much weight, if any, to place on his testimony. Thus, if a woman of 50, of previous good character, is accused of shop-lifting a pork chop, and, in her defence, gives sworn evidence that she had forgotten that she had picked

---

[2] Crown Court Bench Book 1, Specimen Directions, fifth edition, para. 23. Defendant's Character—Good.

up the meat, the tribunal of fact might properly say to themselves 'this woman is of previous good character, that is something that can go into the balance when we consider whether she would suddenly start to offend in this manner; additionally, she has given evidence that she forgot she had picked up the steak, when deciding how much, if any, weight we can place on her account we are entitled to put more significance on her testimony than if she had previous convictions'. Obviously, both aspects of good character are conducive to acquittal (though certainly not conclusive), albeit that the second aspect will have this effect indirectly.

Judicial Directions on Defendant Good Character

In *R v Vye and others* [1993] 1 WLR 471, the Court of Appeal gave clear guidance on the relevant principles to be applied when directing juries in 'good character' cases, though this has not prevented the need for further cases elucidating various aspects of such directions. The aim in *Vye* was to clarify issues relating to such directions that had begun with the case of *R v Berrada* (1989) 91 Cr App Rep 131. In this case, the Court of Appeal took the view that where a defendant of good character has given evidence, the judge must direct the jury about the relevance of good character to his credibility; this is now known as the 'first limb' of a good character direction.

In *Vye*, Lord Taylor CJ confirmed the necessity for such a 'first limb' (or credibility) direction where an accused testifies. He also ruled that a non-testifying defendant is entitled to a 'first limb' direction when s/he has not given evidence at trial but relies on exculpatory statements made to the police or others, which have been admitted as part of a 'mixed' statement. In such a situation, the judge should direct the jury to have regard to the defendant's good character when considering the credibility of those statements. However, Lord Taylor added that a judge would be entitled to point out that such out of court statements were not made on oath, unlike in court testimony.

Cross-reference Box

The favourable (to a defendant) parts of 'mixed' statements, ie those that are a blend of inculpatory and exculpatory material, are deemed to be 'evidence', and so something on which a tribunal is entitled to act (unlike the favourable material contained in a purely exculpatory statement made to the police). As such, they can satisfy evidential burdens, just as oral testimony in court could. Mixed statements are discussed in greater detail at pp. 315–319 below. On evidential burdens see pp. 118–126 above.

Lord Taylor further ruled that where a defendant is of good character, whether he has testified or not, a trial judge should always give a 'second limb' direction on the effect of good character on the issue of propensity. The court accepted that the specific form of the direction is for the judge to determine and it should be tailored to the particular circumstances of the case. An appeal court would be 'slow to criticise any qualifying remarks he may make based on the facts of the individual case'. A defendant was still entitled to a full *Vye* direction even if he was being tried with a co-accused who was of bad character (and whose lack of such a direction might then appear conspicuous to a jury).

Cases since *Vye* have stressed that a failure to give both limbs of the good character direction where appropriate, or the second limb direction on its own if the accused does not testify, will generally lead to a conviction being quashed. In *R v Teeluck* [2005] Crim LR 728 the Privy Council noted that an improper failure to give even a necessarily tailored good character direction would rarely allow an appellate court to say that the giving of such a direction could not have affected the outcome of a trial. Additionally, it should be noted that in the case of *R v Napper* [1996] Crim LR 591, Lord Taylor held that the requirement to give a *Vye* direction was unaffected by any need to give an appropriate 'inference' direction on defendant silence under s. 35 of the Criminal Justice and Public Order Act 1994.[3]

R v Vye [1993] 1 WLR 471, CA

Lord Taylor CJ

(a) Defendant of good character not giving evidence…In our judgment, when the defendant has not given evidence at trial but relies on exculpatory statements made to the police or others, the judge should direct the jury to have regard to the defendant's good character when considering the credibility of those statements. He will, of course, be entitled to make observations about the way the jury should approach such exculpatory statements in contrast to evidence given on oath…Clearly, if a defendant of good character does not give evidence and has given no pre-trial answers or statements, no issue as to his credibility arises and a first limb direction is not required.

(b) The 'second limb' direction
   …It cannot be satisfactory for uncertainty to persist so that judges do not know whether this Court, proceeding on a case by case basis, will hold that a 'second limb' direction should or need not have been given. Our conclusion is that such a direction should be given where a defendant is of good character.…We can see no logical ground for distinguishing in regard to a 'second limb' direction between cases where the defendant has given evidence and cases where he has not. Having stated the general rule, however, we recognise it must be for the trial judge in each case to decide how he tailors his direction to the particular circumstances. He would probably wish to indicate, as is commonly done, that good character cannot amount to a defence.…Provided that the judge indicates to the jury the two respects in which good character may be relevant, *i.e.* credibility and propensity, this court will be slow to criticise any qualifying remarks he may make based on the facts of the individual case.

(c) Two or more defendants of good and bad character…In our judgment a defendant A of good character is entitled to have the judge direct the jury as to its relevance in his case even if he is jointly tried with a defendant B of bad character. This leaves the question as to what, if anything, the judge should say about the latter. In some cases the judge may think it best to grasp the nettle in his summing-up and tell the jury they must try the case on the evidence, there has been no evidence about B's character, they must not speculate and must not take the absence of information as to B's character as any evidence against B. In other cases the judge may, however, think it best to say nothing about the absence of evidence as to B's character.

As with so many other areas of the law of evidence these principles have been reduced to a succinct set of directions by the Judicial Studies Board; they are usually (but not invariably) followed by trial judges when summing up to juries.

---

[3] On such directions see p. 387.

JSB *Crown Court Bench Book 1, Specimen Directions*, fifth edition, para. 23. Defendant's Character—Good

You have heard that the defendant is a man/young man of good character [not just in the sense that he has no convictions recorded against him, but witnesses have spoken of his positive qualities]. Of course, good character cannot by itself provide a defence to a criminal charge, but it is evidence which you should take into account in his favour in the following way/s:

First limb

If a defendant does not give evidence and he has not made any statement to the police, or other authority or person which is admitted in evidence, ignore 1 below.

1. (*If a defendant has given evidence*) In the first place, the defendant has given evidence, and as with any man of good character it supports his credibility. This means it is a factor which you should take into account when deciding whether you believe his evidence.

(*If a defendant has not given evidence, but has e.g. made a statement to the police or has answered questions in interview, see Note 2, below*). In the first place, although the defendant has chosen not to give evidence before you, he did, as you know give [an explanation to the police]. In considering [that explanation] and what weight you should give it, you should bear in mind that it was made by a person of good character, and take that into account when deciding whether you can believe it.

Second limb

2. In the second place, the fact that he is of good character may mean that he is less likely than otherwise might be the case to commit this crime now. (*In cases where it is necessary to give the Delay direction, see direction 37, para 4.*)

I have said that these are matters to which you should have regard in the defendant's favour. It is for you to decide what weight you should give to them in this case. In doing this you are entitled to take into account everything you have heard about the defendant, including his age, [...] and [...]. (*Obviously the importance of good character will vary from case to case, and becomes stronger if the defendant is a person of unblemished character of mature years, or has a positively good character, and at this stage the benefit of this to a defendant whose good character justifies it may be pointed out to the jury, with words such as:*) Having regard to what you know about this defendant you may think that he is entitled to ask you to give [considerable] weight to his good character when deciding whether the prosecution has satisfied you of his guilt).

Pause for reflection

Do jurors really need to be directed about the potential uses of a defendant's good character?

Good Character and 'Blemished' Defendants

As already noted, although, in *Vye*, the Court of Appeal did not provide full guidance as to what constituted evidence of good character, in England (unlike, for example, New Zealand) a defendant without previous convictions normally qualifies for a good character direction.

However, there will be cases in which an accused person has very minor or long past convictions that are, perhaps, even 'spent' under the Rehabilitation of Offenders Act 1974, and who might be thought deserving of a *Vye* direction, despite their earlier transgressions. Additionally, both *Vye* and *Aziz* expressly recognized that there were some situations in which it would be wrong to give a good character direction to defendants, even if they were without a formal criminal record. This could occur, for example, where they admitted committing serious crimes in their own evidence or (sometimes) where, after being charged with two offences based on the same incident, they pleaded guilty to the lesser one and went to trial on the more serious matter.

Defendants in these classes are sometimes referred to as having 'blemished' characters: *R v Aziz* [1995] 3 WLR 52. In such situations, case law suggests it might, sometimes, be proper for a trial judge to give the good character direction in full, to tailor it significantly, or refuse it altogether, depending on the circumstances of the individual case.

For example, the first course was followed in *Shaw v The Queen* (Belize) [2001] 1 WLR 1519, in which the appellant was tried and convicted on two charges of murder. He claimed that he had acted in self-defence. Amongst his grounds of appeal was that as a man without any previous convictions the trial judge should have given the standard direction on good character and its bearing on credibility and propensity. This submission did not impress the Privy Council. The jury knew that the appellant had never been convicted before. However, they also knew, from his own admissions, that he had dealt in a substantial quantity of cocaine and had been a member of a violent armed posse. Had the judge given the jury a full direction it would have been so qualified as to do the appellant more harm than good, so that its absence was not improper.

However, in some cases, as the court in *Vye* also made clear, it was appropriate to treat an accused person with blemishes as being of good character and thus entitled to one or both limbs of the full good character direction (depending on whether they gave evidence). Indeed, one of the co-accused in *Vye* was so treated, despite having acquired a conviction as a youth. Although there is considerable judicial discretion in such cases, it also appears that if the judge does decide that a blemished defendant should receive a good character direction he is entitled to both limbs (assuming he gives evidence). The Court of Appeal has held that a trial judge should not limit himself to the credibility limb without also giving the propensity direction (or vice versa), though a failure to do this will not *necessarily* make any ensuing conviction unsafe: *R v Corry* [2005] WL 1185457.

In *R v Aziz* [1995] WLR 53 the House of Lords gave more detailed guidance on the appropriate directions to be given to a jury when faced with a defendant with no convictions, whose character was, in fact, blemished. The court also suggested that wherever there is any doubt as to whether both limbs of the character direction apply, or wherever it is thought that it may be necessary in the particular circumstances to modify such a character direction, it is desirable to canvass the proposed direction with counsel before closing speeches.

How such directions could be modified was further considered in *R v Durbin* [1995] 2 Cr App R 84, where the court laid down more specific guidelines. In particular, it stressed that a jury should not be directed to approach the case on a basis that was either 'artificial or untrue'. Thus, for example, a jury should not be told that a defendant has no previous convictions, when this is untrue, even if he is held to be entitled to a full good character direction. In such a situation, a trial judge might direct them that the accused has 'no relevant previous convictions and should be treated as a man of good character', before going on to give the appropriate direction.

Applying such guidance in practice can be difficult, as can be seen when considering some recent cases on blemished defendants. Nevertheless, it is also apparent from these cases that the courts have taken a comparatively liberal approach towards granting such defendants a full good character direction, only refusing it comparatively rarely.

Thus, in *R v Payton* [2006] Crim LR 997 it was held that a defendant accused of possession of cannabis with intent to supply, who admitted simple possession, was entitled to a (suitably modified) good character direction, despite having a previous conviction and caution for simple possession of the same drug (he had pleaded guilty to the former and, of course, admitted the latter). Possession with intent to supply was considered to be a radically different offence from simple possession. Similarly, in *Durbin* the defendant was held to have been entitled to a full *Vye* direction, when charged with importing drugs in his lorry, despite having two recently spent convictions for offences of dishonesty, admitting to having lied to customs officers when initially questioned by them, and having confessed in his evidence to smuggling computer parts across European borders.

In the case of *R v Challenger* [1994] Crim LR 202, it was held that a plea of guilty to a separate offence predating the trial, albeit set out in a count or charge contained in the same indictment, would be a conviction to be taken into account by the judge when deciding whether to give a *Vye* character direction, ie it might be a reason to withhold such a direction. Nevertheless, in the same case, it was also suggested that the situation *might* be different if the plea of guilty had been tendered to an alternative to the charge upon which the defendant was standing trial; for example, where there has been a plea to manslaughter to a charge of murder.

This conclusion was reached despite obiter comments by Lord Taylor CJ in *Vye* suggesting that a second limb direction on the defendant's lack of propensity to offend might be of little assistance to a jury where the accused raised the partial defence of provocation in a murder trial. This was because the argument that significance could be given to the fact that he had never before stooped to murder would be countered by the fact that he had never previously sunk to manslaughter either. However, Lord Taylor did not suggest that the second limb direction could *never* be of relevance to whether a defendant was provoked to lose his self-control.

Subsequently, in *Langton v Trinidad and Tobago* [2000] WL 544226, in which both limbs of *Vye* were denied to the accused, the Privy Council took a far more generous approach than Lord Taylor, and concluded that the jury should have been reminded that a man of previous good character, who advanced the partial defence of provocation to murder, might be less likely to indulge in very serious violence without first being severely provoked (as well as being directed that it might bolster his credibility).

Similarly, in *Paria v The Queen* [2003] WL 1822938 the defendant, who had no previous convictions, also claimed provocation in a triple murder case. Some positive evidence of his good character was provided by witnesses testifying to the effect that he was normally a man of equable temperament. However, the trial judge, mindful that the accused freely accepted that he had committed three exceptionally violent manslaughters, decided not to give a second limb propensity direction. On appeal, the Trinidad and Tobago Court of Appeal, following *Langton*, concluded that it had been a mistake not to give the full second limb of the *Vye* direction, but also decided that, given the inherent brutality of the crimes that he had admitted, the jury would still inevitably have convicted the appellant of murder.

 Pause for reflection

Do you think that the defendant in *Paria* was a man of good character?

By contrast, the Privy Council concluded that the defect was not so minor that it could be ignored, and substituted manslaughter verdicts for the murder convictions. Thus, it appears that cases where provocation is advanced as a partial defence to a murder charge are not usually amongst those in which a full *Vye* direction can properly be refused to someone without previous convictions, and that a failure to give such a direction will often be considered so serious that it will make any ensuing conviction for murder unsafe.

R v Aziz [1995] 3 WLR 52, HL

D) WHAT IS GOOD CHARACTER?

Lord Steyn

The certified question, although phrased in very general terms, was intended to raise the problem whether a defendant without any previous convictions may 'lose' his good character by reason of other criminal behaviour. . . . A good starting point is that a judge should never be compelled to give meaningless or absurd directions and cases occur from time to time where a defendant, who has no previous convictions, is shown beyond doubt to have been guilty of serious criminal behaviour similar to the offence charged in the indictment. A sensible criminal justice system should not compel a judge to go through the charade of giving directions in accordance with *Vye* in a case where the defendant's claim to good character is spurious. I would therefore hold that a trial judge has a residual discretion to decline to give any character directions in the case of a defendant without previous convictions if the judge considers it an insult to common sense to give directions in accordance with *Vye*. . . . That brings me to the nature of the discretion. Discretions range from the open-textured discretionary powers to narrowly circumscribed discretionary powers. The residual discretion of a trial judge to dispense with character directions in respect of a defendant of good character is of the more limited variety. Prima facie the directions must be given. and the judge will often be able to place a fair and balanced picture before the jury by giving directions in accordance with *Vye* [1993] 1 WLR 471 and then adding words of qualification concerning other proved or possible criminal conduct of the defendant which emerged during the trial. On the other hand, if it would make no sense to give character directions in accordance with *Vye*, the judge may in his discretion dispense with them. Subject to these views, I do not believe that it is desirable to generalise about this essentially practical subject which must be left to the good sense of trial judges.

The most complete and coherent guidance on good character directions is now set out in the Court of Appeal judgment in *R v Gray* [2004] 2 Cr App R 30. In this case, a trial judge was held to have improperly refused a full good character direction to the defendant in a murder case who had convictions for driving with excess alcohol, no insurance and without a licence.

R v Gray [2004] 2 Cr App R 30, CA

Rix LJ

(1) The primary rule is that a person of previous good character must be given a full direction covering both credibility and propensity. Where there are no further facts to complicate the position, such a direction is mandatory and should be unqualified...

(2) If a defendant has a previous conviction which, either because of its age or its nature, may entitle him to be treated as of effective good character, the trial judge has a discretion so to treat him, and if he does so the defendant is entitled to a *Vye* direction . . . but

(3) Where the previous conviction can only be regarded as irrelevant or of no significance in relation to the offence charged, that discretion ought to be exercised in favour of treating the defendant as of good character . . . In such a case the defendant is again entitled to a *Vye* direction. It would seem to be consistent with principle (4) below that, where there is room for uncertainty as to how a defendant of effective good character should be treated, a judge would be entitled to give an appropriately modified *Vye* direction.

(4) Where a defendant of previous good character, whether absolute or, we would suggest, effective, has been shown at trial, whether by admission or otherwise, to be guilty of criminal conduct, the prima facie rule of practice is to deal with this by qualifying a *Vye* direction rather than by withholding it . . . but

(5) In such a case, there remains a narrowly circumscribed residual discretion to withhold a good character direction in whole, or presumably in part, where it would make no sense, or would be meaningless or absurd or an insult to common sense, to do otherwise . . .

(6) Approved examples of the exercise of such a residual discretion are not common. . . . Lord Steyn in *Aziz* appears to have considered that a person of previous good character who is shown beyond doubt to have been guilty of serious criminal behaviour similar to the offence charged would forfeit his right to any direction (at 53B). On the other hand Lord Taylor C.J.'s manslaughter/murder example in *Vye* (which was cited again in *Durbin*) shows that even in the context of serious crime it may be crucial that a critical intent separates the admitted criminality from that charged.

(7) A direction should never be misleading. Where therefore a defendant has withheld something of his record so that otherwise a trial judge is not in a position to refer to it, the defendant may forfeit the more ample, if qualified, direction which the judge might have been able to give . . .

3. Defendant Bad Character Evidence in Criminal Cases

Introduction

Prior to the advent of the Criminal Justice Act 2003, the adduction of defendant bad character evidence in criminal cases was governed by a complicated mixture of common law principles and statute. Thus, evidence adduced to suggest guilt via propensity was largely ruled by the common law 'similar fact' doctrine. Evidence that was produced to undermine defendant credit was primarily regulated by s. 1(3) of the 1898 Evidence Act (supplemented by common law provisions). One of the main aims of the 2003 Act was to put all of the rules governing bad character in criminal cases, whether for defendants, witnesses or third parties, and whether going to credit or directly to the issue in a case, into a single statute. However, there were other concerns about the old regime, several of which were explored in the Law Commission report, *Evidence of Bad Character in Criminal Proceedings* which (in part) prompted the statutory reforms.

Evidence of Bad Character in Criminal Proceedings Law Commission Report No 273, October 2001, Paras 1.3–1.7

1.3 Presently, evidence of misconduct of the defendant on an occasion other than that leading to the charge may be introduced by the prosecution as evidence of 'similar fact' or by the prosecution or the co-defendant in the limited circumstances provided for by statute, principally under section 1 of the Criminal Evidence Act 1898. Evidence of a person's bad character may, however, also be introduced by a defendant in respect of witnesses who are not co-defendants or in respect of people who are not witnesses. The only limitation to this freedom is the requirement that the evidence be 'relevant'. We consider each of these instances of the introduction of evidence of bad character....

1.4 We are aware that some of those who are interested in this report may approach it by focusing on the question: 'Will this report, if carried into effect, result in a significant increase in the number of occasions when fact-finders will be told about a defendant's previous convictions?' If we had taken the approach of recommending that previous convictions should, as a rule, be presented to the fact-finders however marginally relevant they might be and regardless of how prejudicial they might be, or conversely, of recommending that they should never be adduced save where it would be an affront to common sense to exclude them, then we might have been able to answer such a question with confidence.

1.5 In our view we would have been mistaken to have taken either of these approaches. Their apparently attractive simplicity ignores the complexity and variety of factual situations to which they would have to apply. Each of them would run the risk of endangering the vital interests of the individuals involved: whether defendant, complainant, witness, or investigator. The former would run the risk of wrongful convictions based on prejudice rather than evidence which would be liable to being overturned on appeal with consequential damage to the reputation of the criminal justice system.

1.6 In our judgment, the question: 'Should the fact-finders hear or not hear about the previous convictions of a defendant or a witness?' is not, in practice, sensibly addressed as one of a priori principle. Questions of admissibility of bad character arise in criminal trials daily, case by case, affecting the vital interests of those involved. It is our view that those individuals deserve that these important questions be decided by the careful and consistent application to each case by the court of a structured process, which reflects the fact that often a person's misconduct will have significance for determining the matters in issue, but also recognises that fact-finders, whether lay or professional, are susceptible, however much they may try to avoid it, to having their good judgment either overborne or distorted by prejudice. Such a process requires that the court, performing the exercise of balancing countervailing considerations, should be given sufficient guidance to enable it to reach decisions which are consistent and, to an extent, predictable but which focus on the judgment of the individual decision-taker who is in the best position to make a sound judgment as to where the interests of justice lie.

1.7 The present law suffers from a number of defects which we identify in a late chapter of this report. In summary, however, they constitute a haphazard mixture of statute and common law rules which produce inconsistent and unpredictable results, in crucial respects distort the trial process, make tactical consideration paramount and inhibit the defence in presenting its true case to the fact-finder whilst often exposing witnesses to gratuitous and humiliating exposure of long forgotten misconduct.

Abolition of the Common Law Rules

As a result of the Law Commission's criticism (and that of other bodies), s. 99(1) of the Criminal Justice Act 2003 abolished all existing common law rules governing the adduction of defendant bad character evidence. Several statutes that were relevant to this area of the law, including s. 1(3) of the 1898 Act, were also repealed (under Sch. 37, part 5 of the 2003 Act). Additionally, the meaning of 'bad character' evidence is now the subject of statutory definition.

Definition of Bad Character

Under s. 98 of the 2003 Act, bad character is succinctly defined as 'evidence of, or of a disposition towards, misconduct on his [a defendant's] part'. Misconduct is further defined in s. 112 as the commission of an offence or 'other reprehensible behaviour'. The first part is simple enough with regard to previous convictions and cautions, the latter being adduced in *R v Weir and Others* [2006] 1 Cr App R 19. Unsurprisingly, s. 101(1) will also apply to foreign convictions in many, though not necessarily all, situations: *R v Kordasinski* [2007] 1 Cr App R 17. However, in appropriate circumstances, it also extends to evidence of offending where there has been no conviction or even no previous charge.

In the pre-2003 Act case of *R v Z* [2000] 3 All ER 385 the House of Lords held that, in *some* situations, if facts that amounted to a crime met the 'more probative than prejudicial' test for similar fact evidence, they could be adduced as probative of guilt even if, at an earlier trial, the defendant had been acquitted of an offence based on them. This fairly liberal approach has been followed under the new statute.

Thus, in *R v Edwards (Stewart) et al* [2006] 2 Cr App R 4, the Court of Appeal held that evidence of allegations made against a defendant, which would have supported counts in an indictment that had been stayed as an abuse of process, could be admitted as evidence of bad character under s. 101(1)(d) of the 2003 Act, as being capable of establishing a propensity to commit the type of offence currently charged against the accused. In this case, the defendant was accused of five counts of gross indecency with a child. Three further counts of rape, indecency with a child, and indecent assault on a female had been stayed prior to trial, because the police had written to the defendant several years earlier to say that no further action would be taken against him in respect of them. Subsequently, evidence of the stayed incidents was admitted at trial, and, on appeal, the defendant argued that such allegations, untested by a judicial or quasi-judicial hearing, could not be evidence of bad character under s. 101. He relied on the doubt expressed by Rose LJ in *R v Bovell* [2005] 2 Cr App R 401, as to whether the mere making of an allegation was capable of being such evidence under s. 100(1) (see below).

However, the Court of Appeal observed that in *Bovell* doubt had been expressed in the context of an allegation of wounding with intent made and then withdrawn by the victim against the complainant. Additionally, s. 100 dealt with non-defendant bad character, whereas s. 101 addressed that of a defendant; different factors applied. In particular, the relevance of defendant bad character depended on an assumption that it was true, the question as to whether it was or not ultimately being determined by the jury. As a result, the court was persuaded that the allegations in the instant case were capable of constituting evidence of bad character under s. 101(i)(d), particularly in the light of s. 109(1).

Nevertheless, it is certainly not the case that the courts will invariably allow criminal allegations that have not resulted in convictions to be adduced. Each case will turn on its own facts, and it is likely that judges will be mindful of the warning given by Rose LJ in *R v Hanson, Gilmore and Pickering* [2005] 1 WLR 3169 to the effect that: 'Where past events are disputed the judge must take care not to permit the trial unreasonably to be diverted into an investigation of matters not charged on the indictment.'

R v Edwards (Stewart) & others [2006] 2 Cr App R 4, CA

Scott Baker LJ

The relevant underlying principle seems to us to be this. Prima facie all evidence that is relevant to the question whether the accused is guilty or innocent of the offence charged is admissible. In R. v Z [2000] 2 Cr.App.R. 281 it was accepted by the defendant that the evidence of the three complainants in respect of whose complaints he had been acquitted was relevant to the question whether he was guilty of the offence of rape with which he had been charged. The issue was not whether the defendant was guilty of having raped the three other complainants; he was not being put on trial again for those offences. The only issue was whether he was guilty of the fresh allegation of rape. Lord Hope of Craighead said at p. 283 that the guiding principle was that prima facie all evidence which is relevant to the question whether the accused is guilty or innocent of the offence charged is admissible. . . . If evidence of previous allegations is in principle admissible notwithstanding that the accused was acquitted of charges based on those allegations in a previous trial, it is difficult to see why in principle evidence relating to allegations that have never been tried (i.e. because of a stay for abuse of process) should not be admissible. The defendant's protection comes through the judge's discretion under s. 101(3) or, in an appropriate case, through s. 78 of the Police and Criminal Act 1984.

It should also be noted that s. 108(2) provides that for defendants accused of offences committed when over the age of 21, convictions that they accrued while still under 14 years old are not admissible, unless both the offences are triable only on indictment (ie are very serious matters) and the court is satisfied that the 'interests of justice require the evidence to be admissible'. Thus, if a 22-year-old is accused of murder, a conviction for the same offence when he was 13 *might* be admitted if justified under one of the other provisions of the 2003 Act, provided the court felt that it was in the interests of justice to do so. By contrast, convictions for offences such as theft, accrued while under the age of 14, cannot be adduced under any circumstances once the accused is over 21.

'Reprehensible Behaviour'

The meaning of 'reprehensible behaviour' poses greater difficulties. The Law Commission suggested that the best test for this would be to ask whether a reasonable man would disapprove of the conduct in question (at clause 1(b) of its draft bill). To some extent, this reflects the view of Stephenson LJ, in *R v Bishop* [1975] QB 274, that imputations on character (under s. 1(3)(ii) of the now repealed 1898 Evidence Act) included allegations of 'faults or vices, whether reputed or real, which are not criminal offences'. He suggested that what constituted a vice would be governed by contemporary social mores, as reflected in the average juryman. In the 1970s, *Bishop* indicated that this could include an allegation of homosexuality, although, by then, this was legal behaviour.

Pause for reflection

Do you think that homosexuality would be considered reprehensible behaviour in the modern era?

It seems that a broadly similar approach to that suggested by the Law Commission is being followed under the 2003 Act. However, their definition did not form part of the statute as enacted, and there are a number of inherent problems in the new provision. For example, it has been observed that the word 'reprehensible' is redolent of another age, and not easy to interpret in a modern, multi-value, society. Does it extend to matters such as wife-swapping, recreational 'dogging', bondage sessions, excessive gambling, private drunkenness, possession of (adult) pornography, Satanism, etc?[4]

In these circumstances, it is, perhaps, worth remembering Lord Hailsham's observation (made in another context), that it is important that judges stay close to current social mores: *Boardman v DPP* [1975] AC 421. Nevertheless, Lord Hailsham still assumed that, although values might change in society, there would still be some kind of consensus of opinion as to what was considered abnormal (and so, perhaps, wrong). Some might question whether this is still always the case. Happily, decided cases now provide a modest degree of elucidation as to what is meant by 'reprehensible'.

In *R v Weir and Others* [2006] 1 Cr App R 19, the Court of Appeal upheld a decision to allow evidence to be adduced pursuant to s. 101(1)(d), along with other gateways, from two women alleging that they had been subjected to sexually charged approaches and manipulation, at a vulnerable time in their lives, by a priest at their Hindu Temple, even though these had not resulted in any crimes. In the instant case, the priest was charged with raping another of his congregation, following similar approaches.

By contrast, in another of the conjoined appeals in *Weir*, it was held that an earlier consensual sexual relationship with a 'normal' (rather than physically or emotionally immature) 16-year-old girl, on the part of a man of 34, did not amount to misconduct, or a propensity towards misconduct, where the defendant was accused of an indecent assault on a 13-year-old girl. Nevertheless, in this case, the Court of Appeal left open the possibility of his behaviour being viewed as 'reprehensible' if the accused man had 'groomed' her for such a relationship prior to her turning 16 or (perhaps less obviously) if he was aware that her parents strongly disapproved of the relationship. The court was clearly influenced in its decision by the fact that the couple could, in theory, quite legally have got married.

Pause for reflection

Do you feel that it is reprehensible for a 34-year-old man to date a 16-year-old?

Similarly, in *R v Edwards (Stewart) et al* [2006] 2 Cr App R 4, it was held that a first instance judge, presiding over a drugs case, had been wrong to allow a defendant to be cross-examined about his quite legal possession of an antique, but functional, Derringer firearm (for which no licence was required because of its age). Such legitimate possession could not amount to

---

[4] R Munday, 'What Constitutes "Other Reprehensible Behaviour" Under the Bad Character Provisions of the Criminal Justice Act 2003' [2005] Crim LR, 24–43.

evidence of misconduct. Against this, in *R v Saleem* [2007] EWCA Crim 1923, it was held that the appellant's possession of a considerable number of downloaded photographs of the victims of violent street assaults (he was accused of a similar crime of violence himself) were capable of being considered as 'reprehensible behaviour'.

 Pause for reflection

Is this different to a gangster being in possession of large amounts of very violent and interactive computer games?

As will be seen when s. 100 is considered, making demonstrably false allegations to have been the victim of a serious sexual crime might also be viewed as reprehensible behaviour. However, in *R v Osbourne* [2007] Crim LR 712, it was considered relevant when deciding that severe verbal abuse towards a former partner was not reprehensible behaviour that it was motivated by concern about the welfare of the child the defendant had had by her.

Although it is not easy to draw general principles from these decisions, it seems that if something is legal and would be approved of, or at least accepted, by a significant section (albeit a minority) of the population, such as an early middle-aged man having intimate relations with a 16-year-old female, the courts will be reluctant to view it as coming within the definition of 'reprehensible', even if some people might view the conduct as abhorrent. However, if behaviour is legal but very widely (if not universally) viewed as 'bad', such as a minister of religion abusing his position to make predatory sexual advances towards vulnerable members of his congregation, it might then be considered 'reprehensible'.

Disposition

The definition includes evidence of a 'disposition' towards misconduct; this will, presumably, extend to matters such as the possession of literature advocating paedophile behaviour or describing how to seduce children; additionally, of course, it would include pornographic literature of this type, as in *R v Lewis* [1982] 76 Cr App R 33 (though this would, in any event, constitute an offence). It would also include literature on how to create a bomb or perpetrate terrorist acts or other crimes.

It was not initially obvious how behaviour that is probative, but which, arguably, does not necessarily constitute 'misconduct', such as consensual sexual relations of an unusual type, as in *R v Butler* [1986] 84 Cr App R 12, would be treated after the 2003 Act came into force. Although these were governed by similar fact principles prior to the advent of that statute, they would not appear to fall within the parameters of s. 98.

It seems that they are now governed by general principles of relevance (it would be absurd to preserve a special similar fact doctrine in criminal cases that was confined to such matters). Such an analysis is supported by *Weir*, in which the Court of Appeal concluded that although evidence of previous sexual relations with a 16-year-old did not constitute 'reprehensible behaviour' on the part of the 34-year-old man, it was, nevertheless, still admissible under common law principles as relevant to demonstrating his sexual interest in young girls, and, in the circumstances of the case, the admission of such evidence would not be unfair under s. 78 of the Police and Criminal Evidence Act 1984.

Part of the Offence Itself

It should be noted that s. 98 expressly excludes from the ambit of bad character evidence material that 'has to do with the alleged facts of the offence with which the defendant is charged' and also evidence of 'misconduct in connection with the investigation or prosecution of that offence'. Thus, and unsurprisingly, evidence can be admitted about aspects of the case before the court, however reprehensible; for example, the gratuitous violence shown towards victims during a robbery. Additionally, it will cover matters such as attempts to intimidate witnesses during the investigation following the commission of a crime. In *R v Edwards (Stewart) and others* [2006] 2 Cr App R 4 Scott Baker LJ stressed that courts should always consider whether these provisions applied before deciding whether a statutory 'gateway' was necessary and available to allow the adduction of evidence of misconduct.

The issue was further considered in *R v Saleem* [2007] EWCA Crim 1923, where the Court of Appeal concluded that a defendant's rap lyrics, made some months before the incident which had resulted in his trial for a serious crime of violence, and suggesting that he may have been interested in carrying out such an attack, did not constitute part of the offence for the purposes of s. 98, as they were not sufficiently connected in time that they were 'to do with the alleged facts of the offence', given the date when they were written.

Similarly, in *R v Tirnaveanue* [2007] 2 Cr App R 23, a lack of a sufficient nexus in time between the evidence that the prosecution wished to adduce, and the offence with which the accused was charged, prevented the defendant's dealings with other would be immigrants from being adduced as part of the offence before the court. He was accused of posing as a solicitor in order to obtain money dishonestly from people seeking to enter the UK, and also with providing those people with forged entry documents (though the evidence of other incidents was held to be properly admissible bad character evidence under s. 101(1)(d) of the 2003 Act).

R v Tirnaveanue [2007] 2 Cr App R 23, CA

Thomas LJ

The contention of the prosecution was that the evidence was 'to do' with the offences with which the appellant was charged. The consequence of that argument was that, if the evidence was within the exclusion, then it was not for the purposes of the statutory provisions evidence of bad character and, as this court said in Edwards and Rowlands (at [1(i)]) (as qualified in R. v Watson [2006] EWCA Crim 2308 at [19]), the evidence 'may be admissible without more ado'.

There is very little authority on the extent of this exclusion. In R. v Machado [2006] EWCA Crim 837, the defendant charged with robbing a victim wished to use evidence that the victim had taken an ecstasy tablet shortly before the attack and immediately before the attack had offered to supply him drugs. This court held that the matters were in effect contemporaneous and so closely connected with the alleged facts of the offence, and so were 'to do' with the facts of the offence. In Edwards and Rowlands, this court observed at [23] that the term was widely drawn and wide enough to cover the finding of a pistol cartridge at the home of one of the defendants when it was searched in connection with the drugs offences with which the defendants were charged.

In R. v McKintosh [2006] EWCA Crim 193, this court held that a matter immediately following the commission of the offence was 'to do with the offence'. In Watson , an assault committed was held to do with the charge of rape committed upon the same person later in the day. Professor J.R. Spencer, Q.C. in his useful monograph, *Evidence of Bad Character* at para. 2.23 suggested that it clearly covered acts which the defendant committed at the same time and place as the main offence and presumably covered acts by way of preparation for the main offence and an earlier criminal act which was the reason for the main crime.

23 The basis on which it was contended before us by the prosecution that the evidence which they sought to adduce was 'to do' with the facts of the alleged offence was that it was evidence which was central to the case in that it related to proving that the appellant was the person who had committed the offences charged in the various counts. We do not accede to that submission. As counsel for the prosecution accepted, if his submission was right, then in any case, where the identity of the defendant was in issue (including, by way of example, cases of sexual misconduct), the prosecution would be able to rely on this exclusion to adduce evidence of misconduct on other occasions which helped to prove identity. It seems to us that the exclusion must be related to evidence where there is some nexus in time between the offence with which the defendant is charged and the evidence of misconduct which the prosecution seek to adduce. In the commentary in the Criminal Law Review to R. v T [2006] EWCA Crim 2006; [2007] 1 Cr. App. R. 4 (p.43); [2007] Crim. L.R. 165 , it was argued that the court in Machado and McKintosh had taken too narrow a view of s. 98 thereby permitting prejudicial evidence to be admitted on the threshold test of relevance alone with no gateway having to be satisfied. We do not agree—the application of s. 98 is a fact-specific exercise involving the interpretation of ordinary words.

24 We respectfully agree with Professor J.R. Spencer, Q.C. *Evidence of Bad Character* at para. 2.23, where he suggests that there is a potential overlap between evidence that has to do with the alleged facts of the offence and evidence that might be admitted through one of the gateways in s. 101(1).

The Seven Gateways for Bad Character Evidence

Outside the ambit of s. 98, defendant bad character can only be adduced if it falls within one of the seven 'gateways' set out in s. 101 of the 2003 Act, though, in appropriate cases, it may be admissible through several of them simultaneously. If bad character evidence is wrongly admitted through one gateway, but would have been admissible through another, it will not *necessarily* make an ensuing conviction unsafe. However, in *R v M* [2007] Crim LR 637, the Court of Appeal noted that this would not be the case where evidence had been improperly admitted under one limb of s. 101, such as s. 101(1)(d), but which could have been legitimately admitted under another, such as s. 101(1)(g), if the defence case might have been conducted differently, and the jury instructed in a very different manner as to how they should use the previous conviction, and why it had been adduced, had it been initially admitted under the correct limb at trial.

The s. 101 gateways came into force on 15 December 2004, being effective for all trials that began after that date: *R v Bradley* [2005] 1 Cr App R 24. Late amendments, an extremely brief set of 'Explanatory Notes' (which are not, of course, binding on the courts in any event), a relatively succinct statutory provision, and significant departures from the draft Bill suggested by the Law Commission (despite government claims that its legislation had been 'closely informed' by the Commission's 2001 Report), meant that initially there was considerable uncertainty as to how the new section would operate.[5] Fortunately, a considerable body of appellate cases interpreting the provision now provide flesh to the bare statutory bones of the section.

Section 101 of the Criminal Justice Act 2003, Defendant's bad character

(1) In criminal proceedings evidence of the defendant's bad character is admissible if, but only if—

    (a) all parties to the proceedings agree to the evidence being admissible,

    (b) the evidence is adduced by the defendant himself or is given in answer to a question asked by him in cross-examination and intended to elicit it,

    (c) it is important explanatory evidence,

    (d) it is relevant to an important matter in issue between the defendant and the prosecution,

    (e) it has substantial probative value in relation to an important matter in issue between the defendant and a co-defendant,

    (f) it is evidence to correct a false impression given by the defendant, or

    (g) the defendant has made an attack on another person's character.

(2) Sections 102 to 106 contain provision supplementing subsection (1).

(3) The court must not admit evidence under subsection (1)(d) or (g) if, on an application by the defendant to exclude it, it appears to the court that the admission of the evidence would have such an adverse effect on the fairness of the proceedings that the court ought not to admit it.

(4) On an application to exclude evidence under subsection (3) the court must have regard, in particular, to the length of time between the matters to which that evidence relates and the matters which form the subject of the offence charged.

Section 101(1)(a)–(b)

Some of the gateways contained in s. 101 are relatively uncontroversial, and can be dealt with swiftly. Thus, under s. 101(1)(a) defendant bad character evidence can be admitted with the agreement of 'all parties to the proceedings'. For practical purposes, in most situations, this will be contingent on the accused person wishing to adduce it, although, presumably, there might be exceptional circumstances in which a co-accused might object to its admission. Nevertheless, a defendant could then have recourse to s. 101(1)(b), which allows him to adduce such evidence in person or via an answer to a question 'asked by him in cross-examination and intended to elicit it'.

Section 101(1)(c)

Section 101(1)(c), in part, replicates a specialist provision that previously existed at common law. It allows the adduction of a defendant's previous misconduct if it is 'important explanatory

---

[5] Explanatory Notes to the Criminal Justice Act 2003, para. 46.

evidence'. Guidance on what is meant by this is given in s. 102, which provides that it can be admitted if, without it, the jury or court would find it 'impossible or difficult properly to understand other evidence in the case' and (rather superfluously) its value for understanding the case as a whole is 'substantial'. As a result, it is apparent that this provision will replace the common law rules established in cases such as *R v Fulcher* [1995] 2 Cr App R 251 and *R v Anthony Sawoniuk* [2000] 2 Cr App R 220. These held that where it is necessary to place evidence before the jury of a background or history that was relevant to an offence charged in the indictment, and without which the account would be incomplete or incomprehensible, the fact that it included evidence establishing the commission of an offence with which the accused was not currently charged was not, of itself, a ground for excluding the evidence.

Thus, in *Sawoniuk*, the appellant was accused of two counts of murdering Jews in the town of Domachevo in wartime Belarus; evidence of his criminal acts against other Jews as part of a German allied police unit was admitted, not as 'similar fact' evidence, but because it was relevant to prove that he was involved in other violent wartime search operations in which Jews were his targets, and so made sense of the incident that formed the basis of the indictment. Of course, there are dangers that this doctrine could be extended too far, to allow in prejudicial material that should properly be excluded. However, this is a risk that the Court of Appeal appears to be alert to: *R v Dolan* [2003] Crim LR 41.

R v Anthony Sawoniuk [2000] 2 Cr App R 220, CA

Bingham CJ

Mr Clegg now submits to us that this evidence, relating to criminal acts against Jews other than the victims in counts 1 and 3, should have been excluded. He suggests that the appellant's membership of a group participating in the search and kill operation was not disputed. This evidence was not probative of his identity as the killer in counts 1 and 3. There were no special features of the case to justify the admission of this evidence, and there was nothing in the circumstances of this case or the evidence to bring it within the special and circumscribed exception relating to evidence of similar facts. . . . For the Crown it is argued that this evidence was admissible but not as evidence of similar facts. It was relevant to prove that the appellant was a policeman involved in the search and kill operation. It was not the criminal nature of his conduct which made the evidence admissible, but the fact that it identified him as a member of the group to which the killer in counts 1 and 3 belonged. Thus the effect of the evidence was to identify the appellant as one of the possible killers. The evidence did not identify him, but it supported the identification of the eye witnesses. The evidence was called to prove not the appellant's propensity for misconduct but his participation in a police operation of which the counts of the indictment were a part.

We would accept Sir John's submissions. But we incline to the view that the admission of this evidence could be upheld on a broader basis. Criminal charges cannot be fairly judged in a factual vacuum. In order to make a rational assessment of evidence directly relating to a charge it may often be necessary for a jury to receive evidence describing, perhaps in some detail, the context and circumstances in which the offences are said to have been committed. This, as we understand, is the approach indicated by this Court in Pettman, May 2, 1985 (unreported), approved in Sidhu (1994) 98 Cr. App. R. 59 at 65 and Fulcher [1995] 2 Cr. App. R. 251 at 258: 'Where it is necessary to place before the jury evidence of part of a continual background of history relevant to the offence charged in the indictment and without the totality of which the account placed before the jury would be incomplete or incomprehensible, then the fact that the whole account involves including evidence establishing the commission of an offence with which the accused is not charged is not of itself a ground for excluding the evidence.' This approach seems to us of particular significance in an exceptional case such as the present, in which a London jury was asked to assess the significance of evidence relating to events in a country quite unlike our own, taking place a very long time ago in the extraordinary conditions prevailing in 1941 to 1942. It was necessary and appropriate for the Crown to prove that it was the policy of Nazi Germany first to oppress and then to exterminate the Jewish population of its conquered territories in Eastern Europe. This was done by expert evidence, which was very largely unchallenged. No objection was taken to this evidence. But it was not the subject of any formal admission. It was next necessary and appropriate for the Crown to establish that locally recruited police in areas which included Belorussia and Domachevo played a significant part in enforcing the Nazi policy against the Jewish population. This was proved, partly by expert evidence and partly by the oral evidence of eye witnesses. There was no objection to this evidence, but nor was there any formal admission, and when in due course the appellant gave evidence he contradicted this salient fact. It was next necessary and appropriate for the Crown to prove that the appellant was a member of the local police in Domachevo. By the date of trial this was admitted. But the appellant had earlier denied it in interview, and when he gave evidence the police force which he described was in important respects different from that described in the Crown evidence. It was necessary and appropriate for the Crown to prove that the appellant, as a locally recruited policeman, played a leading and notorious role in enforcing Nazi policies against the Jews in Domachevo. This was not admitted, and when in due course the appellant gave evidence he strongly denied it. It was necessary and appropriate for the Crown to prove that, following the massacre of September 20, 1942 (in which the appellant personally was not said to play any part), the locally recruited police in Domachevo, including the appellant, engaged in an operation to hunt down and execute any Jewish survivors of the massacre. This was strongly denied. The Crown had to satisfy the jury that the killings on which counts 1 and 3 were based took place: given the nature of his defence, the appellant did not admit that these events took place at all, but it was plainly incumbent on the Crown to satisfy the jury that they did. Lastly, of course, and crucially, the Crown had to satisfy the jury that the appellant committed the murders specified in counts 1 and 3, which formed part of the post-massacre operation carried out by local police. It seems to us that evidence relevant to all these matters was probative and admissible, even if it disclosed the commission of criminal offences, other than those charged, by the appellant and his colleagues. It has not been suggested that the jury should have been invited to reach a verdict on counts 1 and 3 having heard no more than the evidence of a single eye witness on each; had these gruesome events not been set in their factual context, the jury would have been understandably bewildered.

That s. 101(1)(c) puts the analysis in *Sawoniuk* into statutory form appears to have been tacitly supported by *R v Edwards (Stewart) and others* [2006] 2 Cr App R 4, in which the Court of Appeal concluded that a trial judge had rightly held that evidence of allegations of an earlier rape and acts of indecency committed against a child by the defendant, which were similar to the counts on an indictment, could not be admitted as important explanatory evidence under s. 101(1)(c), though properly admitted under s. 101(1)(d) (see below). Similarly, the same forum made clear in *R v Ifzal Iqbal* [2006] EWCA Crim 1302 that a defendant's previous convictions for drugs offences could not be adduced under s.101(1)(c) to explain why his DNA might have been found on packets containing drugs; this was again the province of s. 101(1)(d).

Nevertheless, it should be stressed that the operation of s. 101(1)(c) is certainly not confined to cases like *Sawoniuk*. It goes much further. For example, in *R v Edwards (Karl) and others* [2006] 1 Cr App R 3 it was held that an important identification witness who had recognized the accused as he ran past her in the street, while he was fleeing from a crime scene, because she had regularly purchased heroin from him on earlier occasions, should be allowed to reveal this aspect of the defendant's bad character pursuant to s. 101(1)(c). It was important explanatory evidence in relation to her identification, the strength of which was vital to the case.

> ### Cross-reference Box
>
> Identifications, especially those made in 'fleeting encounter' cases, are governed by the very strict rules set out by the Court of Appeal in the case of *R v Turnbull* [1977] QB 224. These were intro- duced following a series of miscarriages of justice occasioned by sincere, but mistaken, identifica- tions. It makes the 'quality' of an identification of prime importance, hence the concern in *Edwards* about how reliable that of the witness was; the fact that it was of someone with whom she had had extensive previous dealings was obviously of great importance in bolstering it. For more informa- tion on the Turnbull guidelines, see pp. 539–552.

Similarly, in an unreported Crown Court case, where a woman, who was very familiar with her abductor/rapist's bad record for calculated and severe criminal violence, had made no attempt to escape from her captor, in circumstances where it might otherwise have been expected, his previous convictions were adduced as important explanatory evidence under s. 101(1)(c). They would explain an otherwise strange piece of evidence (her failure to avail herself of possible escape opportunities).

By contrast, in *R v Osbourne* [2007] Crim LR 712, the defendant was accused of murdering a close friend, in the latter's flat. At trial, evidence was given by a former partner of the accused man to the effect that, when he failed to take the medicine that normally controlled his schizo- phrenia, he could suddenly snap and shower her with verbal abuse, though he was never physi- cally violent. The trial judge ruled that this was evidence of bad character, and so admissible under s. 101(1)(c) as important explanatory evidence. (The appellant had not been taking his medicine at the time of the murder.) However, the Court of Appeal held that, in the context of a brutal murder, the earlier verbal abuse did not amount to 'reprehensible behaviour', and, in any event, was not important explanatory evidence and so admissible under s.101(1)(c) (though the conviction was held to be safe on the evidence).

It should, perhaps, also be noted that in *R v Edwards (Stewart) and others* [2006] 2 Cr App R 4, Scott Baker LJ expressly observed that there might be situations in which it would be difficult to decide whether evidence of bad character was part of the offence itself under s. 98 (and so exempt from requiring a gateway), or whether it might not more properly be adduced under s. 101(1)(c).

R v Ifzal Iqbal   [2006] WL 163 4992, CA

Diehl H

Gateway (c): 'Important explanatory evidence'. This has to be considered in the light of section 102 of this Act also, which is in these terms: 'For the purposes of section 101(1)(c) evidence is import- ant explanatory evidence if—(a) without it, the court or jury would find it impossible or difficult properly to understand other evidence in the case, and (b) its value for understanding the case as a whole is substantial.' The respondent has argued before us that the previous convictions con- stituted important explanatory evidence of the manner in which the appellant's DNA came to be found on one of the knotted packages: that is to say, to show that he was in possession of the drugs and not, as was his case, that the DNA came to be there innocently. It is clear to us that gateway (c) did not apply to this situation but that the respondent's argument should really have been directed to gateway (d). The previous convictions were said to be relevant to an important matter in issue between the appellant and prosecution: that is to say whether the appellant was in possession of these drugs on 26th January. The learned judge did not rule that these two previous convictions were admissible through gateway (d). If he had been minded to do so then clearly exclusion under section 101(3) would have had to be considered.

Section 101(d)–(g): Introduction

The most problematic gateways will be the four established by sub-ss. 101(1)(d)–(g). Of these, the most significant for the prosecution are: s. 101(1)(d), where character evidence is relevant to an important matter in issue between the defendant and the prosecution; s. 101(1)(f), where the evidence is adduced to correct a false impression given by the defendant, and s. 101(1)(g), where the defendant has made an attack on the character of another person. The use of s. 101(1)(e) is limited to co-defendants.

Under the old (pre-2003 Act) regime on defendant bad character evidence it was possible to make a rough and ready division between those provisions that allowed bad character evidence to be adduced which went directly to the issue of defendant guilt (such as the old similar fact doctrine), and those in which it went primarily to the issue of credibility (such as s. 1(3)(ii) of the 1898 Evidence Act). As a result, generally speaking, a trial judge who allowed evidence of bad character to be adduced, because the defendant had, for example, cast 'imputations' on a prosecution witness, would have to instruct jurors, when summing up, that evidence of the defendant's bad character (usually his previous convictions) merely went to the issue of credit, it did not go directly to the issue of his guilt (ie it was not to be used as propensity evidence).

The 2003 Act did not expressly identify the purpose for which bad character evidence admitted under any one of the gateways in s. 101 could be adduced. It did not make clear, for example, whether evidence adduced after an accused had made an 'attack' on another person's character, pursuant to s. 101(1)(g), would also be treated as going purely to credit (though its explanatory notes suggested that this would not necessarily be the case). However, its advent followed criticism from Lord Auld (amongst others) of the artificiality of directing juries that, in some situations, convictions went only to credibility and not propensity, as occurred under the old regime. Perhaps as a result, in a significant departure from the old system, case law since the 2003 Act came into force indicates that the former approach will not necessarily be followed.

In *R v Highton and others* [2005] 1 WLR 3472, the Court of Appeal concluded that the use to which bad character evidence could be put depended on the matters to which it was relevant, *after* being adduced, rather than being entirely dependent on the gateway through which it had been admitted. Although, as the same forum also noted in *R v Edwards (Karl) and others* [2006] 1 Cr App R 3, relevance might be *influenced* by the gateway through which bad character evidence had reached the trial, it would not invariably be decisive of the issue, especially with regard to s. 101(1)(g). (It should, perhaps, also be observed that the traditional rationale behind adducing such evidence under the old s. 1(3)(ii) 'second limb' was never entirely clear, and had been questioned by the Law Commission.)

As a result, in *Highton*, although the defendant's previous convictions had been admitted under s. 101(1)(g), because he had made an attack on another person's character, the Court of Appeal upheld the trial judge's decision to give a propensity direction on the potential use of the accused man's previous convictions for violence and dishonesty, where he was currently accused of kidnapping, robbery and theft. Of course, much will turn on the circumstances of the individual case. For the purposes of exposition, the four provisions in s. 101(1)(d)–(g) will be dealt with, in detail, in turn.

R v Highton [2005] 1 WLR 3472, HL

Lord Woolf CJ

The argument before us was as follows: as subsection 101(1)(d) is the only gateway that is referred to in s. 103(1), the reference it contains to propensity makes it clear that it is only if the evidence is admitted under s. 101(d) that bad character evidence can be used to show a propensity on the part of the defendant to commit the offences of which he is charged or a propensity to be untruthful. In our view, however, the force of this argument is diminished for a number of reasons. First, s. 103(1) prefaces s. 103(1)(a) and (b) with the word 'include'. This indicates that the matters in issue may extend beyond the two areas mentioned in this sub-section. More importantly, while this argument can be advanced in relation to s. 101(1)(d), it can also be advanced in respect of the other parts of sub-section (1), in particular in relation to s. 101(1)(a) and (b). In addition, s. 101(1) itself states that it is dealing with the question of admissibility and makes no reference to the effect that admissible evidence as to bad character is to have. We also consider that the width of the definition in s. 98 of what is evidence as to bad character suggests that, wherever such evidence is admitted, it can be admitted for any purpose for which it is relevant in the case in which it is being admitted. We therefore conclude that a distinction must be drawn between the *admissibility* of evidence of bad character, which depends upon it getting through one of the gateways, and the *use* to which it may be put once it is admitted. The use to which it may be put depends upon the matters to which it is relevant rather than upon the gateway through which it was admitted. It is true that the reasoning that leads to the admission of evidence under gateway (d) may also determine the matters to which the evidence is relevant or primarily relevant once admitted. That is not true, however, of all the gateways. In the case of gateway (g), for example, admissibility depends on the defendant having made an attack on another person's character, but once the evidence is admitted, it may, depending on the particular facts, be relevant not only to credibility but also to propensity to commit offences of the kind with which the defendant is charged.

Section 101(1)(d)

At common law, evidence of a defendant's bad character was revealed to a tribunal of fact as being directly indicative of guilt in only strictly limited circumstances, some understanding of which is necessary to make sense of the new Act. This general restriction on the adduction of such evidence only went back to the late eighteenth century. Indeed, the exclusionary rule against adducing bad character evidence, to which the 'similar fact' doctrine eventually emerged as an exception, only fully developed after 1800, and was first hinted at as late as 1762 (by Sir Michael Foster, in his treatise on *Crown Law*). Prior to that time, for example in the 1720s, as the visiting Frenchman Cesar de Saussure noted of the Old Bailey, if a witness was called to give evidence that the accused was a person of: '…bad antecedents, and suspected of such and such a bad action, he will be listened to with attention'. This can also be seen by considering details from individual trials conducted at that court in the early modern period.

Old Bailey Sessions Papers, 24 February 1686, Trial of George Cliff

George Cliff, indicted for stealing from, and defrauding one Brewer of a Basket value 6 d. and half a Bushel of Apples, value 2 s. and 10 s. in Money, on the 7th of December, it was proved that Cliff coming to one Lovejoys house, demanded of the Maid Servant a Basket, which she delivered him he carryed away, which Cheat being at length found out, and he appearing to be an Old Offender saying little for himself was brought in Guilty.

As these cases suggest, it has always been accepted that most propensity evidence was excluded at common law, under the late eighteenth/early nineteenth century exclusionary rule, not because it was 'irrelevant' (though sometimes this might be the case) but because of its potential to produce both reasoning and moral prejudice against the accused.

By the nineteenth century, it was a basic principle of English law that simply because someone had been guilty of wrongdoing in the past, or had an unusual character trait, this should not normally be used to advance a prosecution case against them. Thus, in the leading case of *Makin v Attorney-General for New South Wales* [1894] AC 57 Lord Herschell LC noted that: 'It is undoubtedly not competent for the prosecution to adduce evidence tending to show that the accused has been guilty of criminal acts other than those covered by the indictment for the purpose of leading to the conclusion that he is a person likely, from his criminal conduct or character, to have committed the offence for which he is being tried.' Such an approach was later termed the 'forbidden line of reasoning' by Lord Hailsham in the case of *Boardman v DPP* [1975] AC 421.

Nevertheless, even as the general exclusionary rule hardened, an exception emerged whereby evidence of bad character could be admitted, in rare cases, in the form of the now abolished (in criminal matters), and misleadingly named, 'similar fact' doctrine. This allowed previous bad conduct to be adduced, provided, as Lord Salmon observed in *Boardman*, that the evidence was capable of persuading a reasonable jury of the defendant's guilt on some ground other than his general bad character and general disposition to commit the sort of crimes with which he was presently charged. This might be, for example, because it rebutted a specific defence being advanced by the accused man, showed a highly singular and unusual *modus operandi* or had major probative value for some other reason. Defining the stringent (and rare) circumstances in which the similar fact exception operated vexed the higher courts throughout the twentieth century. The leading case on criminal similar fact evidence, at the time of abolition, was *DPP v P* [1991] 2 AC 447.

DPP v P [1991] 2 AC 447, HL

Lord Mackay

From all that was said by the House in Reg. v. Boardman I would deduce the essential feature of evidence which is to be admitted is that its probative force in support of the allegation that an accused person committed a crime is sufficiently great to make it just to admit the evidence, notwithstanding that it is prejudicial to the accused in tending to show that he was guilty of another crime. Such probative force may be derived from striking similarities in the evidence about the manner in which the crime was committed and the authorities provide illustrations of that of which Reg. v. Straffen [1952] 2 Q.B. 911 and Rex v. Smith (1915) 11 Cr.App.R. 229, provide notable examples. But restricting the circumstances in which there is sufficient probative force to overcome prejudice of evidence relating to another crime to cases in which there is some striking similarity between them is to restrict the operation of the principle in a way which gives too much effect to a particular manner of stating it, and is not justified in principle.... In the present case the evidence of both girls describes a prolonged course of conduct in relation to each of them. In relation to each of them force was used. There was a general domination of the girls with threats against them unless they observed silence and a domination of the wife which inhibited her intervention. The defendant seemed to have an obsession for keeping the girls to himself, for himself. The younger took on the role of the elder daughter when the elder daughter left home. There was also evidence that the defendant was involved in regard to payment for the abortions in respect of both girls. In my view these circumstances taken together gave strong probative force to the evidence of each of the girls in relation to the incidents involving the other, and was certainly sufficient to make it just to admit that evidence, notwithstanding its prejudicial effect.

During the late twentieth century there was a widespread (though far from universal) feeling that the common law and statutory exceptions to the general exclusionary rule on bad character evidence were inadequate, and meant that the tribunal of fact was often denied highly cogent material about defendants' histories, potentially occasioning injustice. There were a number of *causes célèbres*, involving very serious crimes, such as paedophile murder, in which juries were denied access to what many would consider was vital information about a defendant's previous criminal history (such as previous attacks on children). Additionally, the law appeared to be illogical, judges directing juries that they should consider a defendant's good character as going towards his innocence (the *Vye* direction), but only rarely that his bad character went towards guilt.

Furthermore, there were a number of practical problems associated with the old regime. For example, juries, and even more so, magistrates, would rapidly guess that a failure to mention good character in a defendant probably indicated a bad one, encouraging them to speculate as to what this might be. As a result, it was argued by the Law Commission and other bodies that they should be replaced by a new statutory regime.

The replacement for the similar fact regime (inter alia) is found in s. 101(1)(d), which provides that evidence of misconduct can be adduced, by the prosecution alone (a limitation imposed by s. 103(6) of the Act), if relevant to an 'important matter in issue between the defendant and the prosecution'. This phrase is given clarification in s. 103(1)(a), which provides a non-exhaustive description of such 'matters'. Significantly, these include, inter alia, the question as to whether a defendant has a 'propensity to commit offences of the kind with which he is charged'.

Under s. 103(2) (non-exhaustive) guidance is also given on how a defendant's propensity under s. 103(1)(a) can be established; namely, by adducing evidence that he has been convicted of offences of the same 'description' or 'category' as those charged. The former encompasses crimes in which the terms of the indictment for the earlier offence are the same as that subsequently charged (for example, a murder conviction and a murder charge). The latter covers situations in which the earlier conviction is listed in the same designated category as that charged.

So far, just two such categories have been established, though others may follow. The Criminal Justice Act 2003 (Categories of Offences) Order (SI 2004/3346), banded together offences of 'theft' (Part 1) and 'sexual offences against persons under the age of 16' (Part 2). The former encompasses various types of instrumental crime, such as theft, burglary and robbery; the latter, a lengthy list of sexual offences committed against those below the age of consent, such as rape and indecent assault.

The working of s. 103(2) is, inevitably, 'without prejudice to any other way' of establishing propensity. This means, for example, that the provision does not prevent, where appropriate: the adduction of evidence of the commission of offences that have not resulted in convictions; that have resulted in convictions for offences of a different type to those with which the defendant is presently charged; that are in different categories; or evidence that shows a general propensity towards misconduct. Conversely, as will be seen, it is not necessarily enough for a previous conviction to fall within the same 'category' as that presently charged for it to be adduced.

As with the old similar fact regime, the bad character adduced under the CJA 2003 can constitute other counts on the same indictment, provided the allegations are not thought to be the result of collusion or mutual infection. Thus, in *R v Chopra* [2007] 1 Cr App R 16, the defendant was a dentist, accused of indecently assaulting three young girls while examining or working on their teeth. One of the allegations was 10 years old, another related to events a year earlier, and one was current. They made up three separate counts on an indictment, and the trial judge ruled that the three allegations were relevant to whether any of the incidents had occurred and so could be mutually supportive of each other in the absence of collusion (though he manifested an unfortunate willingness to rely on the old, by then abolished, common law rules on bad character when making his decision). The defendant was convicted of the current allegation and acquitted of the other two (older) alleged offences. The trial judge's decision was upheld by the Court of Appeal, which felt that the similar allegations could quite properly be admitted under s. 101(1)(d) in the instant case, even though two had resulted in acquittals.

R v Chopra [2007] 1 Cr App R 16, CA

Hughes LJ

For the purposes of the present case the relevant gateway is s. 101(1)(d). The evidence of the several complainants is cross-admissible if, but only if, it is relevant to an important matter in issue between the defendant and the prosecution. Mr Coker would have us define the important matter in issue as whether it would be an affront to common sense for the complainants independently to make similar false allegations. The important matter in issue in relation to each count is whether there was an offence committed by the defendant or no offence at all and s. 103 expressly provides that the matters in issue between the Crown and the defendant include whether the latter has a propensity to commit offences of the kind with which he is charged, except where his having such propensity makes it no more likely that he is guilty of the offence charged. It is that provision, together with the abolition by s.99 of the common law rules as to the admissibility of bad character evidence which effects the sea change to which we have previously referred. The present case is one in which quite clearly if the evidence did establish a propensity in the defendant occasionally to molest young female patients in the course of dental examination, that did make it more likely that he had committed the several offences charged. We do not understand Mr Coker to submit otherwise. Of course, where propensity is advanced by way of multiple complaints, none of which has yet been proved, and whether they are proved or not is the question which the jury must answer, that is a different case from the case where propensity is advanced through proof of a previous conviction which may be incapable of contradiction. However, the 2003 Act governs all evidence of bad character, not only conclusive or undisputable evidence.

It follows that in a case of this kind the critical question for the judge is now whether or not the evidence of one complainant is relevant as going, or being capable of going to establish propensity to commit offences of the kind charged. We wish to make it clear that not all evidence of other misbehaviour will by any means do so. There has to be sufficient connection between the facts of the several allegations for it properly to be capable of saying that they may establish propensity to offend in the manner charged. But the answer to the question whether the evidence does so is not necessarily the same as it would have been before the common law rules of admissibility were abolished by s. 99. The test now is the simple test of relevance—s. 101(1)(d).

Judicial Discretion to Exclude Bad Character Evidence

Section 101(3) makes it clear that bad character evidence will not automatically be admissible under s. 101(1)(d), even if potentially relevant as indicative of propensity. It can be excluded, on defence application, if admitting the evidence would have 'such an adverse effect on the fairness of the proceedings that the court ought not to admit it'. In one of the appeals heard in *R v Weir and Others* (2006) 1 Cr App R 19 the Court of Appeal suggested that, if necessary, a trial judge could expressly encourage the making of such an application by a defendant. The wording of this provision would seem to render defence applications under the similarly phrased general exclusionary discretion contained in s 78 of the Police and Criminal Evidence Act 1984 superfluous.

Indeed, in *R v Hanson, Gilmore and Pickering* [2005] 1 WLR 3169, the Court of Appeal, giving guidance on the section, noted that the wording of s. 101(3) is actually stronger than the comparable provision in s. 78, employing the word 'must' rather than 'may' as to the court's power to reject such evidence. Additionally, under s. 103(3) convictions should not be adduced if the court is satisfied 'by reason of the length of time since the conviction or for any other reason that it would be unjust' so providing what is, ostensibly, a separate exclusionary discretion. However, the court in *Hanson* observed that the decisions required of a trial judge under s. 101(3) and s. 103(3), though not identical, were closely related; a considerable overlap between the two must be expected.

In *Hanson*, it was also noted that when considering what is just under s. 103(3), and the fairness of the proceedings under s. 101(3), a trial judge might, among other factors, take into consideration the degree of similarity between any previous convictions and the offence charged, even if they were both within the same description or prescribed category of offences. For example, theft and assault embrace a wide spectrum of criminal conduct. Nevertheless, the court stressed that this does not mean that what used to be referred to as 'striking similarity' (under the old similar-fact rule) must be shown before such convictions become admissible.

Additionally, in reaching a decision, the trial judge might take into consideration the respective gravity of the past and present offences; for example, it might be unjust to a defendant with a murder conviction who is on trial for common assault to allow the former to be adduced in support of the latter. Furthermore, the court held that a trial judge should always consider the strength of the prosecution case. If there was very little other evidence against a defendant, it would be unlikely to be just to admit his previous convictions, whatever they were (and so, perhaps, risking a conviction based on prejudice).

It should be noted that, under s. 101(4), the court, when considering a s. 101(3) application, must have particular regard to the age of the misconduct that the Crown seeks to adduce. This is reiterated in a slightly different context in s. 103(3). Although many of the factors identified as significant in *Hanson* when assessing probative value and where the interests of justice lay, were anticipated by the Law Commission (in clause 5(2) of its draft bill), only the age of the misconduct was expressly referred to in the new Act, suggesting that it will often be of prime importance. It also seems from the case law that a lapse of time will be more significant if there has not been any ensuing criminality in the meantime. Although the Commission recommended that leave would have to be sought from the court to adduce misconduct evidence (and this would only be granted if it was in the 'interests of justice')[6] under s. 101(3) the onus is on the accused, and it is necessary for a defendant to make an application to exclude such evidence (albeit that a trial judge might invite him to do so in appropriate cases).

Although the more proximate in time that the commission of the offences that led to previous convictions are to the offence presently charged, the more relevant they are likely to be for the purposes of s. 101, it does not normally matter that they were committed *after* the offence(s) that are currently before the court. It is their relevance to the defendant's propensity at the time that he offended that is vital. Thus, in *R v Adenusi* [2006] Crim LR 929, the Court of Appeal upheld a trial judge's decision to admit a defendant's convictions for using a false instrument, under s. 101(1)(d), even though they arose from crimes that had been committed five days *after* the similar offence with which he was presently charged.

The 'interests of justice' have to be decided at the time that an application is made, and having regard to the gateway on which it is based, and so can change over the course of a trial. Thus, in *R v Edwards (Karl) and others* [2006] 1 Cr App R 3, the Court of Appeal upheld a trial judge's decision to refuse a prosecution application to adduce the defendant's previous convictions when it was made at the start of the trial, pursuant to s. 101(1)(d), largely because of the age of the previous offences, but, subsequently, to permit some of them to be adduced under s. 101(1)(g), after the accused man had made a very serious and sustained attack on prosecution witnesses during cross-examination.

The discretion will not be used to exclude evidence that is highly probative, even if it is damning to the defendant. In *R v Kordasinski* [2007] 1 Cr App R 17, the appellant was accused of rape and false imprisonment. He claimed that he should not have had several previous, and very similar, convictions that he had accrued in his native Poland, some six years earlier, adduced under s. 101(1)(d). He argued that the evidence should have been excluded under s. 101(3) of the 2003 Act, on the grounds that, if the convictions were put before a jury, he would inevitably be convicted. Thus, he claimed, adducing his previous convictions would necessarily have 'such an adverse effect on the proceedings that the court ought not admit it'. This argument was swiftly dismissed by the Court of Appeal, which noted that the adduction of the convictions clearly met the standards outlined in *Hanson*.

R v Kordasinski [2007] 1 Cr App R 17, CA

May LJ

Mr Aylett, for the appellant, virtually conceded before the judge that the Crown could pass the gateways in s. 101(1)(d) and (g) but he submitted that the court should not admit the evidence because s. 101(3) should apply. Under that subsection, the court must not admit the evidence in the face of a defence application to exclude it, if it appears to the court that the admission of the evidence would have such an adverse effect on the fairness of the proceedings that the court ought not to admit it.

46 It is submitted that the appellant would almost inevitably be convicted if the jury heard the details of the previous convictions in Poland. The jury could not be asked to keep that from their minds....

---

[6] Evidence of Bad Character in Criminal Proceedings, no 273, published 9 October 2001, at 103–110.

49 We see no force in these grounds. The judge's ruling in substance measured up to the standards outlined by this Court in R. v Hanson [2005] 2 Cr. App. R. 21 (p. 299); [2005] EWCA Crim 824, not least with regard to the question to which the circumstances of the Polish convictions were plainly material, assuming they were otherwise admissible and duly proved.

50 As to s. 101(3) and fairness, convictions in the present case would not, if the jury so decided, depend wholly or mainly on the evidence of the previous convictions, nor indeed on the unsupported evidence of the complainant alone. There was, of course, an issue of credibility between her and the appellant. But there was other evidence supporting the complainant's account.

Section 101(1)(d) in Practice

A key question prior to December 2004 was whether s. 101(1)(d) would liberalize the common law situation by making it easier to adduce a defendant's previous misconduct to directly suggest present guilt. The Law Commission's 2001 Report, which underpins much of the regime set out under the new statute, was adamant that any new Act should see a 'final break' with the old similar fact formulae. As a result, it was widely assumed that such a liberalization would occur under any new statutory provision. Indeed, in *R v Edwards and others* [2006] 2 Cr App R 4, Scott Baker LJ expressly observed that it was 'apparent' that Parliament had intended that under the new statute evidence of defendant bad conduct should be put before juries more frequently than had previously been the case.

Even so, the Law Commission did not envisage that such evidence would be lightly adduced. It favoured an enhanced relevance test or threshold for allowing in evidence to prove a 'tendency' to act or think in a certain way, and argued that such evidence should only be adduced if it was of 'substantial' probative value. Although this has been effected in the new Act with regard to matters in issue between defendants and co-defendants under s. 101(1)(e), it was not expressly extended to prosecution evidence under s. 101(1)(d). Section 103(1)(a) does state that evidence of misconduct cannot be adduced by the Crown if the propensity it establishes makes it 'no more likely' that a defendant is guilty of the offence charged. However, this provision might seem superfluous; in such a situation it would merely occasion prejudice and would be irrelevant.

Arguably, this part of the section is not entirely helpful as, theoretically, a small amount of probative value could be attributed to most convictions of a similar type to those charged. In practice, it probably means that cases of minimal cogency, such as, for example, a situation in which a murder defendant has previous convictions for minor offences of violence, can be ignored on a *de minimis* basis (without necessitating the exercise of judicial discretion under s. 101(3) and s. 103(3) of the Act).

The 2003 Act clearly *has* led to an abandonment of the historic approach to 'tendency' evidence set out in cases such as *Makin*. Thus, in the first case on the new provisions to be heard at appellate level, *R v Bradley* 1 Cr App R 24, the Court of Appeal expressly noted that it was now possible to view a general propensity to offend in the past as indicative of present guilt (the previously 'forbidden line of reasoning'). Similarly, in *R v Antony Weir & Others* [2006] 1 Cr App R 19, the Court of Appeal stressed that bad character evidence which satisfied the requirements of s. 101(1) of the Criminal Justice Act 2003 was admissible, even though it might not have satisfied the pre-existing test for similar-fact evidence.

Illustrative of this, in *R v White and Hanson (Damien)* (2005) *The Times* 23 November, a defendant's previous conviction for attempted murder and robbery were revealed to the jury at his trial for a murder committed in the course of a robbery. They indicated that he was an extremely violent youth as well as being a robber. As a result, prosecuting counsel could inform the jury that, in the light of the new statute 'the [other] evidence not only suggests he was the robber but his bad character indicates that fact as well'. As a consequence of these changes, and as Lord Phillips CJ expressly observed in *Campbell v R* [2007] EWCA Crim 1472, prior to the advent of the CJA 2003, it was: '...rare for a jury to be given details of a defendant's previous criminal record. Since that Act has come into force it has become much more common'.

Unfortunately, *Bradley* did not provide detailed guidance as to how the new provisions should be interpreted. However, this was partially remedied by the Court of Appeal in the conjoined appeals considered in *R v Hanson, Gilmore and Pickering* [2005] 1 WLR 3169 and has been further elaborated by more recent cases. In *Hanson* the court considered and rejected three applications for leave to appeal that had been referred to the full court. All three cases involved the adduction of previous convictions (rather than other forms of 'bad character' evidence). Although the Court of Appeal made it clear that its comments were not intended to be a comprehensive treatise on the operation of the new provisions, Rose LJ made a number of important observations about their operation.

R v Hanson, Gilmore and Pickering [2005] 1 WLR 3169, CA

Rose LJ

The starting point should be for judges and practitioners to bear in mind that Parliament's purpose in the legislation, as we divine it from the terms of the Act, was to assist in the evidence based conviction of the guilty, without putting those who are not guilty at risk of conviction by prejudice. It is accordingly to be hoped that prosecution applications to adduce such evidence will not be made routinely, simply because a defendant has previous convictions, but will be based on the particular circumstances of each case....Where propensity to commit the offence is relied upon there are thus essentially three questions to be considered. 1. Does the history of conviction(s) establish a propensity to commit offences of the kind charged? 2. Does that propensity make it more likely that the defendant committed the offence charged? 3. Is it unjust to rely on the conviction(s) of the same description or category; and, in any event, will the proceedings be unfair if they are admitted?...In referring to offences of the same description or category, section 103(2) is not exhaustive of the types of conviction which might be relied upon to show evidence of propensity to commit offences of the kind charged. Nor, however, is it necessarily sufficient, in order to show such propensity, that a conviction should be of the same description or category as that charged....There is no minimum number of events necessary to demonstrate such a propensity. The fewer the number of convictions the weaker is likely to be the evidence of propensity. A single previous conviction for an offence of the same description or category will often not show propensity. But it may do so where, for example, it shows a tendency to unusual behaviour or where its circumstances demonstrate probative force in relation to the offence charged....Child sexual abuse or fire setting are comparatively clear examples of such unusual behaviour but we attempt no exhaustive list. Circumstances demonstrating probative force are not confined to those sharing striking similarity. So, a single conviction for shoplifting, will not, without more, be admissible to show propensity to steal. But if the modus operandi has significant features shared by the offence charged it may show propensity...It is to be noted that the wording of section 101(3)—'must not admit'—is stronger than the comparable provision in section 78 of the Police and Criminal Evidence Act 1984—'may refuse to allow'. When considering what is just under section 103(3), and the fairness of the proceedings under section 101(3), the judge may, among other factors, take into consideration the degree of similarity between the previous conviction and the offence charged, albeit they are both within the same description or prescribed category. For example, theft and assault occasioning actual bodily harm may each embrace a wide spectrum of conduct. This does not however mean that what used to be referred to as striking similarity must be shown before convictions become admissible. The judge may also take into consideration the respective gravity of the past and present offences. He or she must always consider the strength of the prosecution case. If there is no or very little other evidence against a defendant, it is unlikely to be just to admit his previous convictions, whatever they are . . . Old convictions, with no special feature shared with the offence charged, are likely seriously to affect the fairness of proceedings adversely, unless, despite their age, it can properly be said that they show a continuing propensity. It will often be necessary, before determining admissibility and even when considering offences of the same description or category, to examine each individual conviction rather than merely to look at the name of the offence or at the defendant's record as a whole. . . . As to propensity to untruthfulness, this, as it seems to us, is not the same as propensity to dishonesty. It is to be assumed, bearing in mind the frequency with which the words honest and dishonest appear in the criminal law, that Parliament deliberately chose the word 'untruthful' to convey a different meaning, reflecting a defendant's account of his behaviour, or lies told when committing an offence. Previous convictions, whether for offences of dishonesty or otherwise, are therefore only likely to be capable of showing a propensity to be untruthful where, in the present case, truthfulness is an issue and, in the earlier case, either there was a plea of not guilty and the defendant gave an account, on arrest, in interview, or in evidence, which the jury must have disbelieved, or the way in which the offence was committed shows a propensity for untruthfulness, for example, by the making of false representations. The observations made above in para 9 as to the number of convictions apply equally here. . . . Our final general observation is that, in any case in which evidence of bad character is admitted to show propensity, whether to commit offences or to be untruthful, the judge in summing up should warn the jury clearly against placing undue reliance on previous convictions. Evidence of bad character cannot be used simply to bolster a weak case, or to prejudice the minds of a jury against a defendant.

As can be seen from this extract, in *Hanson,* the court was relatively conservative in its interpretation of s. 101, expressing a hope that applications to adduce bad character evidence would not be made as a matter of course. It is apparent that there is still a *de facto,* if not statutory, quality threshold on the admissibility of propensity evidence, albeit that it is set at a significantly lower level than was the situation at common law. It also seems that some of the principles established under the old similar fact regime, when suitably modified, continue to be of limited significance with regard to the new provisions. Thus, although there is no minimum number of previous incidents necessary to demonstrate a propensity to offend, the more there are, the greater will be the cogency ascribed to such evidence, and the more likely it is that it will be admitted.

In *Hanson* the court also concluded that a single previous conviction, even if of the same description or category as that presently charged, would often not show propensity, especially if it was for a 'common' type of crime. However, this might not be the case if it demonstrated a tendency to 'unusual' behaviour, or where its circumstances had particular probative force in relation to the offence charged, such as cases of child sexual abuse (there are echoes here of the old regime as seen in *DPP v P* [1991] 2 AC 447).

As a result, one previous conviction for shoplifting, committed without a highly singular *modus operandi*, would not normally be admissible to show a propensity to steal under the new statute. However, several recent findings of guilt for that offence might well be admissible, even if the offence of theft presently charged was of a very different type. Thus, in *Gilmore,* the first instance judge's decision to admit three convictions for shoplifting during the defendant's trial for an opportunistic theft from a garden shed was upheld. The accused man's defence had been that he found the stolen items abandoned in an alley and assumed they were rubbish and so *bona vacantia*. A selection of other cases provide further elucidation of the approach now adopted.

In *Hanson, Gilmore and Pickering*, Rose LJ stressed the significance of the age of previous misconduct when he suggested that old convictions, which shared no special features with the offence charged, were often likely to seriously affect the fairness of proceedings, and so should not normally be admitted. Logically, the court also observed that, in most cases, if there was a substantial gap between the dates of commission and conviction for the earlier offence, it was the former that was indicative of propensity and thus of most significance when assessing admissibility under s. 101(1)(d).

In *R v M* [2007] Crim LR 637, it was reiterated that single convictions that were also 'old' would have to be particularly exceptional to be adduced. In this case, the Court of Appeal allowed the appeal of a defendant who had been convicted of possession of a firearm with intent to cause fear of violence, contrary to s. 16A of the Firearms Act 1968. At his trial, a previous conviction for possession of a firearm without a licence, which was some 20 years old, was admitted to support identification. The Court of Appeal held that this offence was not sufficiently unusual to warrant being adduced. The court further noted that it would be very rare, though not impossible, for a single conviction of this age to be admissible under s. 101(1)(d).

However, in the case of *Pickering*, where the applicant was convicted of rape and indecent assault on one of his young daughters, a decade-old conviction for indecent assault on an 11-year-old girl was held to be admissible. This was an 'unusual' type of offence, and even a single, old, conviction for a similar matter was considered to be highly probative of the offence charged.

By further contrast, in *R v Long (Darrell)* [2006] WL 690630, the Court of Appeal quashed the conviction of a defendant accused of robbery from the person, after an interpersonal dispute, because the trial judge had allowed a single previous conviction for robbery to be adduced pursuant to s. 101(1)(d). No special but common features between the crime alleged, and that which had previously resulted in a conviction, had been revealed by the prosecution. Indeed, the two robberies were of markedly different types; the earlier conviction stemmed from a 'conventional' armed raid on retail premises in which the till contents had been snatched. Having regard to the comments made in *Hanson* about single previous convictions without special features, the Court of Appeal felt that the conviction was unsafe.

In like manner, in *R v Beverley* [2006] Crim LR 1065, the defendant was accused of participating in a conspiracy to import cocaine. He had two previous convictions. One of these, from more than five years earlier, was for possession of cannabis with intent to supply, and one was from two years previously, for simple possession of cannabis. These were adduced at trial under s. 101(1)(d), as showing a propensity to commit the type of offence with which he was charged. However, on appeal, the conviction was quashed, on the basis that one of the convictions was old, and one was of a different character (simple possession), that they involved a different type of drug, and related to offences of a vastly lesser degree of seriousness, both in size and complexity, to the large-scale conspiracy charged in the instant case.

Although, as these cases suggest, most situations where evidence is adduced under s. 101(1)(d) will require either an 'unusual' offence or one committed in an unusual manner, or, alternatively, several previous offences, in exceptional cases this will not be so. For example, in *R v Isichei* [2006] EWCA 1815, a defendant's single conviction for importing cocaine some six years earlier was admitted under s. 101(1)(d), as it was adduced not to suggest a propensity to commit such offences, but to support the identification of a complainant in an assault occasioning ABH and robbery indictment, who had heard the defendant demanding money for 'coke'.

The approach adopted in *Hanson* is certainly at variance to that originally anticipated (in October 2004) by David Blunkett, the then Home Secretary, who suggested that there would be a 'strong presumption' (albeit rebuttable) that previous convictions that were in the same category as that subsequently being tried should be admitted. However, this is clearly not the case, as in *Hanson* the Court of Appeal made it very apparent that it is not necessarily sufficient to establish propensity for a single previous conviction to be of the same description or category as that presently charged. Illustrative of this, in *Hanson*, the court felt that convictions for handling and aggravated vehicle taking, although technically within the 'theft' category of the relevant statutory instrument, did not show, without more pertinent information, a propensity to burgle or to steal.

The Court of Appeal in *Hanson, Gilmore and Pickering* also observed that even if previous offences were of the same description or category as that presently charged, it would often be necessary, before determining admissibility, to examine the particulars of each conviction individually (though any sentence passed would not normally be viewed as probative). The court suggested, in the same case, that where propensity to commit the type of offence charged was relied upon there are, essentially, three questions that have to be considered: 1. Does the history of conviction(s) establish a propensity to commit offences of the kind charged? 2. Does that propensity make it more likely that the defendant committed the offence charged? 3. Is it unjust to rely on the conviction(s) or will they make the proceedings unfair if admitted? Although fairly vague, this approach does, at least, provide a structure for considering such applications.

Finally, in *Hanson*, the Court of Appeal noted that, provided a trial judge had directed him/herself correctly, it would be 'very slow' to interfere with their ruling on the admissibility of bad character evidence. The court would not normally intervene unless the judge's decision as to the capacity of prior convictions to establish a propensity to offend was plainly wrong or the discretion had been exercised unreasonably in the *Wednesbury* sense.

Indicative of the range of the trial judge's discretion, in this regard, is the case of *R v Awaritefe* 2007 [EWCA] Crim 706, where the Court of Appeal concluded that the defendant's two previous convictions for middle ranking offences of violence, from a decade earlier, and a recent, but relatively minor (of its type), conviction for assaulting a policeman in the execution of his duty, were admissible under s. 101(1)(d) as showing a propensity to offend in a violent manner, where the defendant was accused of two serious offences of causing grievous bodily harm with intent. The court noted that, although some trial judges would not have acceded to the prosecution request, the decision was within the first instance judge's margin of discretion, and so would not be overturned. (This appears to have been considered to be a 'borderline' decision.)

Determining such matters, on appeal, will be facilitated by the requirement under s. 110 that reasons for such a decision be stated in open court when making a ruling under s. 101 (or, for that matter, s. 100). The importance of this provision was reiterated on several subsequent occasions by the Court of Appeal, as first instance judges were occasionally somewhat lax about complying with this requirement, at least in the early days of the statute's operation.

Propensity to Untruthfulness

Although s. 101(1)(d) deals with bad character evidence going directly to the issue of guilt, s. 103(1)(b) makes it clear that the sub-section does not operate *purely* in this manner. It also deals with a defendant's propensity to be untruthful, a completely novel departure from the position at common law. The Law Commission accepted that, in most trials, the truth of the defendant's version of events was itself an issue in the case. However, it concluded that *normally* it would not be fair to allow the prosecution to adduce evidence of a defendant's propensity to be untruthful. Nevertheless, the Commission did believe that the adduction of evidence of such a propensity should be permissible in strictly defined circumstances, where it was especially probative. For example, where the prosecution sought to argue that the defendant's explanation was strikingly similar to one advanced by him on a previous occasion, and thus unlikely to be true.

This would normally require the defence to be of an unusual or singular kind (there are only a limited number of general defences to many crimes). It might cover situations like that identified in *R v Reid* [1989] Crim LR 719, in which the defendant was accused of robbing a mini-cab driver at knife-point, but claimed that he had entered the cab only after the robbery had taken place. This was almost identical to the defence he had raised earlier to another, and very similar, robbery. As such, it was highly probative as to the truth (or lack of it) of his defence on the second occasion in which it was employed. Similarly, it was suggested that the use of an alibi that was identical to one used at an earlier trial might come within this provision.[7] Thus, it could encompass cases similar to *Jones v DPP* [1962] AC 635, in which the defendant adduced detailed and near identical alibis, in two separate trials, involving sexual attacks on girl guides.

These are extreme cases. In practice, it seems that the provision as enacted will be interpreted more widely than this. The only statutory limitation is that propensity to untruthfulness cannot be adduced where it is 'not suggested that the defendant's case is untruthful in any respect'. As a result, in theory, most defendants who gave evidence to support a 'not guilty' plea would come within its provisions, which *could* be limited to cases in which the accused's defence was based on a point of law or in which there was nothing more than a simple denial of the charges, putting the Crown to strict proof of its case.

However, even if it is being interpreted in a broader manner than the Commission may have envisaged, the Court of Appeal stressed in *Hanson* that a propensity to untruthfulness is *not* the same thing as a propensity to dishonesty. It reflected a defendant's post-arrest account of his behaviour, or lies told when committing the offence itself. Thus, a 'straightforward' thief, such as a pickpocket, who always pleaded guilty to his crimes, and freely made full admissions to the police when caught, would not necessarily be treated as 'untruthful' although clearly 'dishonest'. By contrast, an earlier conviction for an offence that did not involve dishonesty per se, such as violence or assault, *might* be admissible to show a propensity to be untruthful if, in the earlier case, the defendant gave an account, on arrest, in interview, or in evidence (following a not guilty plea) that the jury must have disbelieved. Despite this, some offences involving dishonesty, by their inherent nature, *are* likely to involve untruthfulness, such as obtaining property by deception or perjury.

Perhaps a little surprisingly, it also appears, in the light of some recent cases, that if a trial judge decides that previous convictions are not admissible on the issue of untruthfulness, but are for a reason such as propensity, he should not normally direct jurors to consider the previous offences as being relevant to the issue of the defendant's credibility. The courts are clearly discouraging the use of 'run of the mill' offences as an indicator of general credibility when adduced under s. 101(1)(d).

For example, in *Campbell v R* [2007] EWCA Crim 1472, the (then) specimen direction on character issued by the Judicial Studies Board, had been read to jurors at the trial of a defendant in an assault case, after the accused man's previous and recent convictions for similar offences of violence had been revealed to them under s. 101(1)(d). However, the judge's direction was subsequently criticized by the Court of Appeal for suggesting that jurors could have regard

---

[7] No 273, October 2001, *Evidence of Bad Character in Criminal Proceedings*, at paras. 11.32–11.34.

to the convictions when deciding: '…whether or not the defendant's evidence to you was truthful'.

However, the restrictive position reached in *Hanson* with regard to the meaning of a 'propensity towards untruthfulness' and the use of offences of dishonesty when considering credibility does not necessarily apply to other limbs of the section (ie apart from s. 101(1)(d)). Thus, offences of ordinary dishonesty, such as theft, that are adduced under s. 101(1)(g) can assist the jury in making an assessment about the defendant's character, for the purposes of deciding whether or not to believe his evidence rather than that of the prosecution witnesses: *R v Williams* [2007] EWCA Crim 1951.

Fabrication and Concoction of Alleged Previous Misconduct

There was a long-standing fear in 'similar fact' cases of collusion between complainants or the deliberate fabrication of evidence; this would then destroy the probative value that flowed from the inherent unlikelihood of co-incidence in such cases. However, in *R v H* [1995] 2 All ER 865 the House of Lords suggested that a court should normally admit similar fact evidence on the assumption that it was true and, if there was a suggestion of collusion or fabrication, warn the jury that they could only rely on it if they were first satisfied that this was not the case. It was only in exceptional circumstances, where evidence emerged that *clearly* indicated that no reasonable jury could come to this conclusion, that a court should exclude the evidence altogether.

The same issue has been specifically addressed in s. 109 of the Criminal Justice Act 2003, with regard to the truth of previous misconduct being adduced under s. 101, and especially s. 101(1)(d). Similar conclusions have been reached. Comments by Kennedy LJ in *Weir* would appear to suggest that the approach to the risk of collusion, and the directions that should be given on the issue to a jury, under the new Act, will be much the same as in *H*.

Essentially, s. 109(1) provides that a reference to the relevance or probative value of evidence is to be 'on the assumption that it is true'. However, under s. 109(2) a court need not assume this if it appears that 'no court or jury could reasonably find it to be true'. Thus, if compelling evidence is adduced to suggest that alleged previous misconduct is fabricated, a trial judge can refuse to let it go to a jury under s. 101(1)(d).

Section 107 establishes a further safeguard. It provides that if, *after* evidence of bad character has been adduced under (inter alia) s. 101(1)(d), the court is satisfied that it is 'contaminated', perhaps, for example, by apparent fabrication, in such a way that any ensuing conviction would be unsafe, the judge must either direct the jury to acquit the defendant of the offence or discharge the jury and so allow a retrial. This is one of those unusual situations in which a trial judge, rather than the jury, has to make an assessment of fact in a criminal case. Rather oddly, however, s. 107 only applies to trials on indictment; presumably, magistrates at a summary trial are deemed to be capable of putting the evidence of bad character from their minds.

However, if he does not reach this conclusion, but collusion, or innocent contamination, has been raised, or is a possibility on the facts of a case, a trial judge must still direct the jury, in appropriate terms, about the potential dangers of such evidence. In *R v Lamb* [2007] EWCA Crim 1766, the appellant was a 33-year-old school teacher, convicted of sexual activity with two 17-year-old female pupils whom he taught at his school. The counts arose out of apparently entirely separate allegations, which were held to be cross-admissible, to support each other, for the purposes of s. 101(1)(d) (assuming the jury were satisfied of their truth).

Nevertheless, in this case, although there was no suggestion of collusion, there was a clear possibility that the two complainants had been consciously or unconsciously influenced in their accounts by hearing of, and discussing, the other's allegation. Despite this, the first instance judge failed to warn the jury adequately to consider whether it was possible that the complainants had influenced each other in this manner, and, if so, how this affected the weight of their evidence. As a result, the ensuing convictions were quashed.

R v Lamb [2007] EWCA Crim 1766, CA

Rix LJ

In our judgment, therefore, the judge's failure to warn the jury about the danger of innocent contamination was a material misdirection, which went to the heart of this case. We do not suggest that the judge was wrong not to have stopped the case himself, something that was never suggested, but we do think that in the circumstances the jury's verdicts are as a result of the judge's misdirection themselves unsafe. In this connection, the manner in which the judge dealt with the question of similarities, although it would not in our view by itself have called the verdicts into question, did not assist. As *Hanson* and *Chopra* have emphasised, sufficient similarity raising the issue of the likelihood or unlikelihood of innocent coincidence is a relevant and sometimes critical test. It is therefore necessary for the judge, if he outlines the similarities to the jury, to give a balanced and accurate account of them, so far as they evidence a propensity which makes it more likely that a defendant has committed an offence.

Notice Procedures

Section 111(1) of the 2003 Act authorized the creation of such rules of court as were 'necessary or expedient' to govern the adduction of bad character evidence, albeit with a judicial discretion to override such provisions: s. 111(3). These are now contained in r. 35 of the Uniform Criminal Procedure Rules 2005, and providing such notice is mandatory. They are accompanied by appropriate forms for service on the defence, the most important of them being form BC1 (for non-defendants) and BC2 (for defendants). These provide details of the bad character evidence that it is intended to adduce or elicit by cross-examination and the justification for doing so. Such applications can, in turn, be challenged prior to trial by the defendant (using form BC3) under r. 35.6.

A timetable for compliance is also set out in r. 35.2–4, though a trial judge always has a discretion to permit departures from it: r. 35.8. Such a discretion is obviously necessary; sometimes, as when 'attacks' are made on third parties on the part of the defendant, it will be quite impossible to envisage the need to adduce the accused's bad character prior to trial. In other cases, however, there will be less excuse for a failure to comply with the notice procedure, this will be especially the case with regard to s. 101(1)(d).

In *Hanson,* the court noted that in a case where the Crown intends to adduce evidence of a defendant's convictions it needs to decide, at the time of giving notice of its application to adduce previous bad character, whether it proposes to rely simply upon the fact of conviction or also upon the facts on which the conviction was based. The former might be enough if the circumstances of the conviction are sufficiently apparent from its description to justify a finding that it can establish propensity, either to commit an offence of the kind charged or to be untruthful, and that the requirements of ss. 103(3) and 101(3) can, subject to any particular matter raised on behalf of the defendant, be satisfied. For example, a succession of convictions for dwelling-house burglary, where the same offence is presently charged, may well call for no further evidence than proof of the convictions.

But where, as will often be the case, the Crown needs, and proposes, to rely on the circumstances of the convictions, those circumstances and the manner in which they are to be proved must be set out in the application. Thus, if a defendant is accused of theft and has a single previous conviction for the crime, the prosecution will normally have to find some special details underlying its modus operandi before they can adduce the earlier matter; for example, in a shoplifting case, by showing that he has used the same false bottomed bag to conceal the stolen item. This detail will have to be contained in the relevant notice. However, there is a similar obligation of frankness upon the defendant, which will be reinforced by the general obligation contained in the CPR 1998 to give active assistance to the court in its case management (see r. 3.3). Routine applications by defendants for disclosure of the circumstances of previous convictions are likely to be met by a requirement that the request be justified.

The Court of Appeal suggested in *Hanson* that, in most cases, the relevant circumstances of previous convictions should be capable of agreement, and put before the jury by way of admission. The requirement in many propensity cases for information to be disclosed that goes beyond the basic facts of conviction may discourage some prosecution applications and will certainly require more pre-trial preparation by the Crown. In *R v Bovell and Dowds* [2005] 2 Cr App R 27, the Court of Appeal reiterated the importance of complying with the rules on providing notice. *Hanson* and *Bovell* also make it clear that a trial judge's initial decision on such matters as to any consequences imposed as a result of noncompliance will not be lightly overturned on appeal. As a result, similar applications may receive different disposals at trial without founding an appeal.

More detailed consideration as to the consequences of non-compliance with notice procedures was provided by the Divisional Court in *R (on the application of Robinson) v Sutton Coldfield Magistrates Court* [2006] 2 Cr App R 13. In this case, the defendant was accused of assault. At a pre-trial hearing for a summary trial of the matter, the prosecution indicated that they would seek to introduce his bad character. However, despite this warning, the prosecution did not formally serve notice of this until the eve of the trial (ie well out of time).

The defendant argued that the evidence of bad character ought not to have been admitted at trial, as the court should only exercise its discretion to extend time limits in exceptional circumstances, and this did not apply to the instant case. This approach was rejected by the Divisional Court, though the court again stressed the importance of compliance with the notice procedures and stressed that any application for an extension of time limits would be closely scrutinized. In particular, it held that reasons for any failure to comply with the notice provisions would have to be set out. Perhaps most importantly, the court held that it would have to be satisfied that there was no conceivable prejudice to the defendant in admitting the evidence when there had been a failure to meet deadlines. In the instant case, the defendant had been made aware early in the proceedings that such an application might be made and was well aware of his own convictions, so there was no prejudice.

Nevertheless, despite regularly stressing the importance of compliance, it seems that the higher courts have rarely allowed an appeal on the grounds of non-compliance. It is possible that, as the procedures become better known and understood by lawyers, they will take a slightly more robust, and less forgiving, approach. Additionally, it can be noted that first instance judges appear to be taking markedly different approaches to such lapses. Some seem to take a relatively severe view of any failure to comply with notice requirements, and quite readily refuse to admit bad character evidence because of non-compliance (for example, *R v O'Neil*, unreported, Preston Crown Court, 22 February 2005); others are more lenient.

R (on the application of Robinson) v Sutton Coldfield Magistrates Court
[2006] 2 Cr App R 13, DC

Owen J

The first point to be made is that time limits must be observed. The objective of the Criminal Procedure Rules 'to deal with all cases efficiently and expeditiously' depends upon adherence to the timetable set out in the rules. Secondly, Parliament has given the court a discretionary power to shorten a time limit or to extend it even after it has expired: r. 35(8). In the exercise of that discretion the court will take account of all the relevant considerations, including the furtherance of the overriding objective. I am not persuaded that the discretion should be fettered in the manner for which the claimant contends, namely that the time should only be extended in exceptional circumstances. 15 In this case there were two principal material considerations: first the reason for the failure to comply with the rules. As to that a party seeking an extension must plainly explain the reasons for its failure. Secondly, there was the question of whether the claimant's position was prejudiced by the failure. 16 The reason advanced for the failure was that the police had made every effort to discover the facts of the previous convictions, but were not able to do so until June 7. For my part, I have reservations as to the adequacy of that explanation. In my view a court would ordinarily wish to know when the relevant enquiries had been initiated, and in broad terms why they have not been completed within the time allowed. Any application for an extension will be closely scrutinised by the court. A party seeking an extension cannot expect the indulgence of the court unless it clearly sets out the reasons why it is seeking that indulgence. But importantly, I am entirely satisfied that there was no conceivable prejudice to the claimant, bearing in mind that he would have been well aware of the facts of his earlier convictions; secondly, that he was on notice on April 14 that there could be such an application; and thirdly, that there was no application for an adjournment on June 16 from which it is to be inferred that the claimant and his legal advisers did not consider their position to be prejudiced by the short notice. In those circumstances I am not persuaded that the justices erred in the exercise of their discretion to admit the evidence of bad character, notwithstanding the failure to comply with the rules. This was not a decision at which no reasonable bench of magistrates properly directed could have arrived.

Obligations on Trial Judges and Appeals

As Dame Heather Steel observed in *R v Eastlake* [2007] EWCA 603, there is a paradox inherent in admitting evidence of bad character that is similar to that presently charged. The more recent and similar such offences are to those before the court, the more powerfully they may indicate a relevant propensity: '...but those factors may [also] strengthen the argument that they should be excluded to avoid the risk of the trial becoming unbalanced by their admission into evidence'. In these situations, the judge noted, one 'safety valve' was the giving of proper jury directions as to the use (and dangers) of such bad character evidence.

In *R v Hanson, Gilmore and Pickering* [2005] 1 WLR 3169, the Court of Appeal observed that, where evidence of bad character is admitted to show a propensity to offend or to be untruthful, a trial judge, when summing up, should warn the jury clearly against placing undue reliance on the defendant's previous convictions. In particular, the jury should be directed that they should not conclude that the defendant is guilty or untruthful merely because he has such convictions and that their presence did not mean that he had committed the offence charged or been untruthful in the case before the court. A trial judge should also direct the jury that whether the previous convictions adduced demonstrated such a propensity was a matter for them to decide and that they should also take into account what the defendant had said about them. Additionally, although they were entitled, if they found such a propensity to be established, to take it into account when determining guilt, it was only one relevant factor and must be assessed in the light of all the other evidence in the case.

In *R v Edwards (Karl) and others* [2005] 1 Cr App R 3, Rose LJ approved the first instance judge's jury direction (which reflected the guidance given in *Hanson*) on the uses of bad character evidence as being close to a model of its kind, one that might provide assistance to other judges.

R v Edwards (Karl) and others [2006] 1 Cr App R 3, CA

Rose LJ

Before leaving the case of Chohan, it is, as we foreshadowed at the beginning of this judgment, perhaps helpful to refer to the summing-up of His Honour Judge Mort in Chohan's case: 'In this case you have heard evidence that Mr Chohan has a bad character, in the sense that he has got criminal convictions and you have heard, it is alleged, that he otherwise misconducted himself by supplying heroin to Donna Marsh. It is important that you understand why you have heard this evidence and how you can use it. As I will explain in more detail later, you must not convict Mr Chohan only because he has got a bad character. You have heard of this bad character because, first of all, in relation to the allegation that he was supplying drugs to Donna (and bear in mind it is her allegation that that is the position) it may help you to understand other evidence in the case, namely how is it that Donna Marsh was so confident that the man running past her on Lee Street, running away from Mr Marsh and from the two women, was the defendant. The reason being because she was seeing him several times a day when acquiring drugs from him. So it may help you to consider the accuracy and reliability of her identification and it may help you to understand the case as a whole. You have heard, in relation to the previous convictions, of his bad character and it may help you to resolve an issue that has arisen between the defence and the prosecution, namely the question whether he has a propensity or a tendency or an inclination to commit offences of the kind with which he is charged. If you think it is right, you may take the previous convictions into account, in deciding whether or not Mr Chohan committed the offences with which he is now charged. The prosecution rely on the robbers in 1992 because they show that he has a tendency to use weapons to threaten violence to steal and two instances have been given to you where a sheath knife was used, one in order to steal and one whereby theft actually took place and it is said, ten years on, now he is using a handgun. The prosecution rely on the burglaries in 2000 because they say that they show that the defendant has a tendency to use bogus explanations to trick his way into older people's homes in order to steal from them...So the prosecution's case there is that it is, on this occasion, a combination of pretending to be looking for people who have robbed his mother, asking for a pen and paper to write down the description of the alleged robberies and then using the pretext, coming back and saying: "We have found them" going in, producing the gun and stealing wallet. So the crown are saying here there is a tendency to commit robberies with a weapon and to target the elderly with bogus explanations and, therefore, they say it makes it more likely that he is guilty of the offence. The defence, on the other hand, say, first of all, these robberies were ten years ago, he described himself, "I was about 16 or 17 at the time, the burglaries were three years old, I always pleaded guilty to offences that I had been arrested for" and it is, in fairness to the defence, a matter which you can take into account, deciding what impact the convictions had on his truthfulness. Mr Samuels put it in a well known phrase from Casablanca of "rounding up the usual suspects" and that is what obviously you must be very careful about...If you do conclude that, at the time of these offences in May, 2003, Mr Chohan did have a propensity to commit offences of that type, namely robberies with weapons or targeting the elderly with bogus explanations to get entry into the property, then you can consider whether it makes it more likely that he committed the offences in May, 2003. You have to decide to what extent, if at all, his character helps you when you are considering whether or not he is guilty. You must not convict simply because of his convictions, nor mainly because of them. The propensity or tendency amounts to some additional evidence pointing to guilt, but please bear in mind, even if he did have such a tendency, it does not necessarily prove that he would commit further offences or that he has committed these offences. You are also entitled to consider the evidence of Mr Chohan's previous convictions in the following way. If you think it right, you may take into account, when deciding whether or not his evidence to you was truthful, because a person with convictions for dishonesty may be less likely to tell the truth, but it does not follow that he is not capable of telling the truth. Indeed, Mr Chohan says, "the fact that on the previous occasions I have been arrested and I have always held my hands up means that, when I plead not guilty, I am likely to be telling the truth" and you decide to what extent his character helps you when judging his evidence. So that is the extent to which the evidence of his previous convictions may be used for the particular purposes I have just indicated, if you find it helpful.' That approach...provides an [almost] impeccable summing-up which may well afford useful guidance in other cases where summing up the significance of previous convictions.

The requirement that a jury be warned in proper terms about the significance of past bad character is interpreted strictly. In *R v Ifzal Iqbal* [2006] EWCA Crim 1302 the Court of Appeal quashed a conviction in a drugs case after concluding that a (repeated) warning from a first instance judge that jurors 'should not convict purely on the basis of these [past drugs] convictions' was still inadequate in the light of *R v Edwards (Karl) and others* [2006] 1 Cr App R 3. Additionally, it should be noted that in *Hanson* the Court of Appeal observed that if, after a ruling that evidence of bad character was admissible, a defendant pleaded guilty, it was highly unlikely that it would entertain an appeal against conviction.

Section 101(1)(e)

A defendant's bad character can be adduced under s. 101(1)(e) if it has 'substantial probative value in relation to an important matter in issue between the defendant and a co-defendant'. In some respects, this replaces s. 1(3)(iii) of the (now repealed) Criminal Evidence Act 1898, though it also deals with matters that were outside the scope of that provision.

Guidance is given on what is meant by the new sub-section in s. 104 of the Act. This states that evidence is only admissible under s. 101(1)(e) by, or at the behest of, a co-defendant: s. 104(2). In practice, this was *almost* the situation under s. 1(3)(iii). However, there was nothing in that part of the 1898 Act expressly limiting it to co-defendants, and there were very rare examples of the prosecution cross-examining under it: *R v Seigley* (1911) 6 Cr App R 106. Under the 2003 Act, the prosecution cannot have recourse to s. 101(1)(e). As with the prosecution under other gateways, a co-defendant who intends to adduce such evidence is normally required to serve notice of such an intention on his co-accused under r. 35.5 of the CPR 2005.

Again, as with other limbs of s. 101, a previous conviction is not *necessarily* essential. In *Ibrahim Musone v The Crown* [2007] EWCA 1237, a defendant was allowed to adduce an allegation of murder under s. 101(1)(e) made against a co-accused, for which his fellow defendant had already been tried and acquitted, where the co-accused had subsequently admitted to him (the defendant) that he (the co-defendant) truly had committed the killing for which he had been found 'not guilty', and provided details of the crime which suggested that such a confession had genuinely been made. The trial judge's decision on this issue was subsequently approved by the Court of Appeal.

Additionally, and vitally, it should be noted that a quality threshold is expressly set out in the sub-section, one that is absent with regard to prosecution evidence of defendant bad character adduced under s. 101(1)(d) (although imposed in practice by judicial interpretation of the provision), and which was also absent under s. 1(3)(iii) of the 1898 Act. This requires that the evidence have 'substantial probative value' before it can be admitted. This means that evidence of only minor cogency to a co-defendant's case, though technically relevant, will not be admissible.

Furthermore, evidence adduced under s. 101(1)(e) must relate to an 'important matter' in the trial, ie, a matter of 'substantial importance in the context of the case as a whole': s. 112(1). It will not be admissible if the issue to which it relates is marginal to the case overall, though, it could be argued, this provision will, to a considerable extent, overlap with the requirement that the evidence have substantial probative value.

Against this, and unlike prosecution evidence of bad character under s. 101(1)(d), once this threshold is satisfied, there is *no* judicial discretion to exclude such evidence. Section 101(3) does not apply to s. 101(1)(e); nor, of course, does s. 78 of the PCEA 1984 (which is confined to prosecution evidence). This also accords with the old situation under s. 1(3)(iii) of the 1898 Act: *R v Ellis* [1961] 1 WLR 1064.

The rationale for this continuing distinction is that it is one thing to handicap the prosecution in the interests of fairness to a defendant, another to prevent an accused person properly exploring an avenue of defence that is open to them. Of course, there was (and still will be) a discretion to order separate trials where it is in the interests of justice, though, as there are also usually compelling reasons for holding joint trials, the courts have always exercised this power very circumspectly in the past: *R v Hoggins* [1967] 1 WLR 1223. It seems very likely that they will continue to do so in future.

There are several reasons as to why a defendant might wish to adduce evidence of a co-defendant's bad character. One classic example would be where he is running a 'cut throat' defence, blaming the other defendant for the offence with which he stands accused, and wishes to adduce the co-defendant's bad character to suggest that his propensity to misconduct makes it more likely that he was the sole perpetrator of the crime. For example, where a defendant, of previous good character, facing a count of murder, wishes to suggest that his co-defendant was entirely responsible for the killing, and to support such a claim by adducing the co-defendant's extensive criminal record for offences of serious violence (a distant record for minor assaults might not satisfy the quality threshold).

Thus, in *Ibrahim Musone v The Crown* [2007] EWCA 1237, it was held that where two prison inmates were accused of murdering a third prisoner in his cell with a knife, and were running 'cut-throat' defences (blaming each other for the crime), one of the defendants was allowed to adduce evidence of an earlier murder, allegedly perpetrated by his co-accused, to suggest that it was more likely that he (the co-accused) had inflicted the fatal wound. This was because the earlier killing was considered to have substantial probative value with regard to an important matter in issue between the two co-defendants (ie who was more likely to be violently homicidal), and so was admissible under s. 101(1)(e).

Ibrahim Musone v The Crown [2007] 2 Cr App R 29, CA

Moses LJ

Once evidence of a defendant's bad character is admissible under s. 101(1)(e) the section confers no express power on a court to exclude such evidence on grounds of unfairness, let alone imposing any obligation to do so. Nor is there any power under s. 78(1) of the Police and Criminal Evidence Act 1984 to exclude the evidence since it is not evidence on which the prosecution proposes to rely.

In this situation, as s. 78 of the PCEA 1984 would not apply, the only thing that an implicated co-defendant could do to avoid prejudice would be to rely on his right to a fair trial under Article 6 of the ECHR, and argue that allowing such evidence to be adduced would be contrary to his human rights. If accepted, this argument might allow the provision to be interpreted, under s. 3 of the Human Rights Act 1998, in a manner that was favourable to him. However, *Ibrahim Musone* suggests that the courts are highly unlikely to be sympathetic to such an argument, because of the initial, relatively restrictive prerequisites that must be satisfied before s. 101(1)(e) will apply.

Ibrahim Musone v The Crown [2007] 2 Cr App R 29, CA

Moses LJ

We do not think that it is possible to identify a power to exclude evidence which, ex hypothesi, has substantial probative value, in reliance on Art. 6. The question whether such a power exists only arises in circumstances where the court has already concluded that the evidence of the defendant's bad character does have substantial probative value in relation to a matter of substantial importance in the context of the case as a whole. Once substantial probative value has been established it is difficult to envisage circumstances where it would be unfair to admit evidence of that quality, subject to the procedural protection contained in the Rules. That is reflected in the structure of the section itself which excludes from the scope of s. 101(3) evidence of substantial probative value in relation to an important matter. In short, it is difficult to envisage room for invoking the right to a fair trial enshrined in Art. 6. Once the judge concluded that the evidence was of substantial probative value, he had no power, absent the application of the rules made under s. 111, to exclude the evidence on the basis that to admit it would be to infringe Chaudry's right to a fair trial under Art. 6. The only apparent control on the deployment of evidence by one defendant against another is that which is contained in s. 101(1)(e). Admissibility rests solely on the court's assessment of the probative quality of that evidence.

53 We conclude that the judge erred in purporting to exercise a power to exclude evidence which reached the standard imposed by s. 101(1)(e) for admissibility. Admissibility under that subsection depends solely on the quality of the evidence. The judge had no power under that section to exclude the evidence on the grounds of unfairness.

Similarly, in *Johnson v R* [2007] EWCA Crim 1651, it was held that, on a charge of importing cocaine, where two defendants were running cut-throat defences, each putting all the blame for the offence on the other, a single, recent, previous conviction for possession of the same drug could be adduced, on the grounds that it had substantial probative value in relation to an important matter in issue between the co-defendants (who was more likely to be dealing in cocaine) and so was admissible under s. 101(1)(e). There are, however, other possible situations in which an accused person might wish to adduce a co-defendant's previous bad character.

Most importantly, and returning to the cut-throat defence situation, a defendant blamed by their co-defendant for a crime might wish to adduce the co-defendant's record for offences of dishonesty to suggest that their allegations are not credible (ie he has fabricated his evidence). This produces a much closer parallel with s. 1(3)(iii) of the 1898 Act. Section 104 of the 2003 statute permits the admissibility of evidence of a defendant's bad character, under s. 101(1)(e), that merely shows that he has a propensity to be untruthful (ie is not credible as a witness): '…only if the nature or conduct of his defence is such as to undermine the co-defendant's defence'. Obviously, in such a situation, his credibility will become highly relevant to the issues in the case.

No guidance is given in the new statute as to the meaning of 'undermine'. It may be that, in these circumstances, the extensive body of case law that developed on whether a co-defendant had given evidence 'against' a defendant under the 1898 Act will continue to be of some (albeit limited) significance. Thus, in *Murdoch v Taylor* [1965] AC 574, the House of Lords defined it as evidence: '…which supports the prosecution's case in a material respect or which undermines the defence of the co-accused'. The court made it clear that the co-defendant's motive (the presence or absence of hostile intent) was irrelevant. Cases since this decision have explored the issue further. Some of these may still be relevant when interpreting the new statute, though it is likely that the courts will also be mindful of Lord Bingham's observation, in *R v Crawford* [1997] 1 WLR 1329, that: 'The words used in the [1898] statute are simple and readily intelligible. There is…a danger in over-complicating what we feel sure was intended to be an easily applicable test.' Future decisions are likely to turn on the facts of each case rather than implementing set formulae.

There will also be a question as to what is meant by 'relevant' to a 'propensity to be untruthful'. Strictly construed, this might be limited to convictions for perjury, offences of deception and situations in which a defendant has been convicted after pleading not guilty and testifying in his own defence. This is the approach taken to untruthfulness with regard to s. 101(1)(d), in cases such as *Hanson*. However, it seems that an application by the prosecution under s. 101(1)(d) is viewed differently to one made by a co-defendant under s. 101(1)(e), and different considerations will sometimes apply.

Thus, in one of the cases considered by the Court of Appeal in *R v Edwards (Stewart) and others* [2006] 2 Cr App R 4, the prosecution was refused permission at the start of the trial to adduce a defendant's previous convictions for violence, under s. 101(1)(d), when he was tried on a count of wounding with intent. However, the following day, the same judge acceded to a co-defendant's application to allow cross-examination on the same convictions under s. 101(1)(e) when he ran what was effectively (if not explicitly) a cut-throat defence. The decision was upheld on appeal. When it comes to untruthfulness under s. 101(1)(e), it seems that a broader range of offences of dishonesty may be adduced.

R v Edwards (Stewart) and others [2006] 2 Cr App R 4, CA
Scott Baker LJ

The judge correctly directed himself that he first had to decide whether there was an important matter in issue between the two defendants and secondly whether the bad character had a substantial probative value. He referred to R. v Price [2005] Crim.L.R. 304 as illustrating that the propensity to violence of D1 may be relevant as making it less likely that the offender was D2. It was important which of McLean or Saunders was more likely to have been O'Toole's assailant and the fact of McLean's s. 18 conviction was of substantial probative value: see R. v Weir and Others [2006] 1 Cr.App.R. 19 (p. 303), para. [120].

51 The judge concluded that although this was not perhaps a cut-throat defence in the classic sense, their separate versions of what had occurred created an important issue between them. This seems to us to be plainly correct. Each individual tells an entirely different story as to what went on. Mr Stanniland, for McLean, sought valiantly to distinguish between important issues and ancillary issues, his argument really coming to this: that although there was a series of ancillary issues between the defendants there was no important issue. We remind ourselves that 'important matter' is defined in s. 112 as a matter of substantial importance in the case as a whole and this, as Sir Igor Judge P. pointed out in R. v Renda and Others [2006] 1 Cr.App.R. 24 (p. 380) para. [3], is very much a matter for the 'feel' of the judge. The judge went on to consider whether the previous convictions of McLean had substantial probative value as to the issue between the defendants. He said it seemed to him that if each defendant was saying he was not involved in the violence, and one has previous convictions for violence, that must have substantial probative value on the issue between them. 52 Mr Stanniland argued that the judge's ruling against him was even more perverse when one took into account that s. 101(1)(e) provided a more stringent test than s. 101(1)(d) and yet he had admitted the evidence under the former but not the latter. We are not, however, persuaded by any of Mr Stanniland's grounds. The judge applied the correct test and, contrary to Mr Stanniland's third ground of appeal, the bad character evidence did, in our view, have substantial probative value. The appeal is accordingly dismissed. 53 Before leaving this case we make two further comments. It was not a case where the judge had any discretion to refuse to admit the evidence under s. 101(3) and, in fairness, it was never suggested that he had. Once the s. 101(1)(e) gateway was open the evidence was in. Nor did s. 104(1) apply because the issue was propensity to violence not a propensity to untruthfulness.

Balancing the rights of co-defendants is inherently difficult. One accused person's interests are often protected at the expense of another's. At least the old regime, under which the courts were not required to mediate between co-accused once one had undermined the other's defence, spared judges any risk of being accused of partiality.[8] The 2003 Act attempts to strike a balance by permitting the adduction of evidence of a co-defendant's earlier misconduct where it is of substantial probative value to do so. Inevitably, however, there will be appeals as to where this line is drawn, especially in finely balanced cases. Defendants who have been refused permission to adduce evidence of a co-accused's previous, relevant, convictions, on the ground that they are not of sufficient value, may seek to argue that their right to a fair trial, enshrined in Article 6 of the ECHR, has been breached.

Pause for reflection

Do you feel that trial judges should be required to choose between the interests of co-defendants? What are the realistic alternatives?

---

[8] R Munday, 'Cut-Throat Defences and the "Propensity to be Untruthful" under s. 104 of the Criminal Justice Act 2003' [2005] Crim LR 623–637, at 636.

Section 101(1)(f)

Under s. 101(1)(f) evidence of a defendant's bad character can be adduced to 'correct a false impression given by the defendant'. This has obvious parallels with the old statutory regime, and the Law Commission freely accepted that it covered 'similar ground' to that of the 'good character' exception under the 'first limb' of s. 1(3)(ii) of the 1898 Act, whereby a defendant would lose his 'shield' from cross-examination on his convictions if he: '... asked questions of the witnesses for the prosecution with a view to establish[ing] his own good character, or has given evidence of his good character'.

The new section also has parallels with the common law position, both before and after the 1898 Act, under which the Crown could rebut an unfounded claim to good character, even if the defendant failed to testify, as in *R v Rowton* (1865) 34 LJMC 57. The sub-section applies whether a defendant has given evidence or not, and thus replaces both existing provisions. In *Hanson* it was held that, given the similarities between s. 101(1)(f) and the 'first limb' of s. 1(3)(ii) of the 1898 Act, some of the old cases on the latter provision might be of continuing significance.

Guidance on the operation of the new provision is given in s. 105(1)(a), which provides that an accused person falls within its ambit if he is responsible for making an 'express or implied assertion which is apt to give the court or jury a false or misleading impression about the defendant'. The use of 'implied' indicates that the approach already taken under the 1898 Act will be followed under the new statute. Thus, and for example, in the old case of *R v Ferguson* [1909] 2 Cr App R 250 a claim that the accused regularly attended mass was held to be an implied assertion of good character.

If a 'false impression' is given under the new Act, the Crown can call evidence in rebuttal, though this must have 'probative value in correcting it' under s. 105(6). Consequently, and as the Commission intended, the common law rule on the indivisibility of character, set out in *R v Winfield* [1939] 4 All ER 164, has been abolished. Prior to the 2003 Act, a man accused of an indecent assault, who called evidence with regard to his good character *vis-à-vis* sexual morality, could be cross-examined about convictions for dishonesty as, in the words of Humphreys J, there was: '... no such thing known to our procedure as putting half your character is issue and leaving out the other half'. This ceases to be the case.

Thus, if a man who is accused of assault claims to be as 'gentle as a lamb' his previous convictions for offences of dishonesty will probably not be adduced. Additionally, evidence admissible under s. 101(1)(f) must go no further than is necessary to correct the false impression. This, too, allows for selective revelation. For example, it would seem that if the same assault defendant had a murder conviction and also several lesser convictions for offences of violence, it *might* be considered that adducing his assault convictions would be sufficient to correct the false impression, without resorting to the damning prejudice occasioned by establishing the murder conviction. Alternatively, an agreed (by prosecution and defence) formula of words, admitting previous offences of violence without going into details, could be employed.

This selectiveness about the adduction of past crimes can be seen in *R v Campbell* [2007] 2 Cr App R 28, where the defendant, accused of assaulting his girlfriend, had numerous previous convictions, for a variety of offences, including violence, dishonesty and criminal damage, reaching back over 20 years. However, at trial, only two previous and recent convictions for assaulting former or current girlfriends were admitted, pursuant to s. 101(1)(d), being adduced on the issue of the defendant's propensity to use violence towards women.

R v Campbell [2007] 2 Cr App R 28, CA

Lord Phillips CJ

The question of whether a defendant has a propensity for being untruthful will not normally be capable of being described as an important matter in issue between the defendant and the prosecution. A propensity for untruthfulness will not, of itself, go very far to establishing the committal of a criminal offence. To suggest that a propensity for untruthfulness makes it more likely that a defendant has lied to the jury is not likely to help them. If they apply common sense they will conclude that a defendant who has committed a criminal offence may well be prepared to lie about it, even if he has not shown a propensity for lying whereas a defendant who has not committed the offence charged will be likely to tell the truth, even if he has shown a propensity for telling lies. In short, whether or not a defendant is telling the truth to the jury is likely to depend simply on whether or not he committed the offence charged. The jury should focus on the latter question rather than on whether or not he has a propensity for telling lies.

For these reasons, the only circumstance in which there is likely to be an important issue as to whether a defendant has a propensity to tell lies is where telling lies is an element of the offence charged. Even then, the propensity to tell lies is only likely to be significant if the lying is in the context of committing criminal offences, in which case the evidence is likely to be admissible under s. 103(1)(a).

Section 105(2)(a) deals with the various situations in which a defendant is to be treated as being responsible for giving such a false impression. Unsurprisingly, this occurs when it is given in person during the proceedings (whether during examination in chief or cross-examination). However, it also includes situations in which it is made by the defendant in an out of court statement that is adduced into evidence. Theoretically, this could mean that, in some cases, what the accused actually does at trial will have no bearing on whether his bad character is revealed. Additionally, the defendant will be held responsible for an assertion that is made by another witness called by him, or by any other witness (ie even one called by the prosecution or a co-defendant) in response to a question asked by the defendant or his counsel that is 'intended to elicit it, or is likely to do so'.

Nevertheless, under s. 105(3) a defendant who would otherwise be treated as responsible for an assertion made by another witness will avoid adverse consequences if he withdraws it or disassociates himself from it. To some extent, this provision builds on the position at common law laid down in *R v Redd* (1923) 1 KB 104, which suggested that an attribution of good character by a witness, if made spontaneously and entirely unsolicited by the defendant, would not constitute a claim to good character within the terms of s. 1(3)(ii) of the 1898 Act.

However, under the 2003 Act, the defendant will also *actively* have to take steps to dissociate himself from the statement. Exactly how this will be done is still not entirely clear. Thus, if a defence witness blurts out, without any prompting, that the accused man is a 'saint', will the defendant have to state explicitly that he is not a saint? In *R v Renda and others* [2006] 1 WLR 2948, it was held that a concession extracted in cross-examination from a defendant, to the effect that he was not telling the truth in his examination in chief as to his claimed good character, would not normally amount to a withdrawal or disassociation from the original assertion for the purposes of s. 105(3).

Provision is also made in the new Act for non-verbal impressions, the position of which was uncertain at common law (the Law Commission concluded that they fell outside the old regime). Thus, under s. 105(4), where it appears to the court that a defendant: '... by means of his conduct (other than the giving of evidence) in the proceedings, is seeking to give the court or jury an impression about himself that is false or misleading, the court may if it appears just to do so treat the defendant as being responsible for the making of an assertion which is apt to give that impression'. Further guidance is given on what this means by s. 105(5), which provides that in s. 105(4) 'conduct' includes appearance or dress.

This section addresses the problems occasioned by a long line of cases, such as that involving a defendant's regimental blazer in *R v Hamilton* [1969] Crim LR 486. As a result, a witness who, while in court, engaged in exaggerated clutching or kissing of a Bible, Koran or religious emblem, the wearing of some form of clerical dress (especially if not in holy orders) or who ostentatiously resorted to prayer, might be treated as if he had made a claim to good character. Consequently, it seems that cases such as *R v Robinson* [2001] EWCA Crim 214, in which a defendant who had overtly brandished a Bible while giving testimony was held not to have made a claim to good character under the 1898 Act, are unlikely to be followed under the CJA 2003.

Although the exclusionary discretion contained in s. 101(3) only applies to grounds (d) and (g) of s. 101(1), in *Weir*, the Court of Appeal noted that s. 78 of the PCEA 1984 provides trial judges with a discretion to exclude evidence that is prima facie admissible under s. 101(1)(f), as it applies to all prosecution evidence. However, given that the decision to claim a false good character is often gratuitous, unlike 'attacks', which may be necessary to provide a defence, it may be that the discretion will be exercised fairly circumspectly in such cases.

Cross-reference box

Obviously, the exclusionary discretion contained in s. 78 will not apply to s. 101(1)(e), as only co-defendants may adduce bad character under this provision, and s. 78 is limited to prosecution evidence. It will be irrelevant with regard to s. 101(1)(a)–(b), as both grounds require the defendant's consent. However, it seems that it will cover ground (c) as well. For a more detailed discussion of s. 78 see chapter 2 at pp. 74–86.

R v Antony Weir & Others [2006] 1 Cr App R 19, CA

Kennedy LJ

We note that the provisions of section 101(3) do not apply to subsection (1)(f), and we see no reason to doubt that section 78 of the 1984 Act should be considered where section 101(1)(f) is relied upon (see the judgement of Lord Woolf CJ in *Highton and others* [2005] EWCA Crim 1895 at paragraph 13, and the views of Professor Spencer at paragraph 21 of the paper to which we have already referred). In this case for the reasons which we have already given when dealing with the application of section 101(3) to section 101(1)(d) we do not see any way in which, in relation to subsection (1)(f), section 78 would assist the appellant.

Nevertheless, and in the same way that s. 1(3)(ii) of the 1898 Act was interpreted in *Malindi v R* [1967] 1 AC 439, it seems that if the alleged claim to good character was made as an integral part of the allegation which has come to court, and is narrated to the court as an inherent part of that incident, it will not be viewed as opening the gateway in s. 101(1)(f). For example, if a defendant in an assault case, with previous convictions, were to testify that, when approached by the alleged victim of the crime and challenged to a fight, he initially replied, 'I am a God fearing man of peace' this would not necessarily be treated as a claim to good character at trial.

Thus, in *R v Ifzal Iqbal* [2006] EWCA Crim 1302, the Court of Appeal held that an explanation by the defendant as to why his DNA might have been found on a package containing heroin, and which had been interpreted at trial as an unwarranted claim to good character, was a fundamental defence contention and as such did not invoke s. 101(1)(f).

R v Ifzal Iqbal [2006] EWCA Crim 1302, CA

Diehl H

Gateway (f): 'evidence to correct a false impression given by the defendant.' The learned Judge seems have said that the two previous convictions were possibly admissible through this gateway. The short submission on behalf of the appellant is that, at the stage when the Judge made his ruling, the appellant had not given any false impression. We have reminded ourselves of the terms of section 105 of the Act, more particularly (1) and (2). The respondent argues that the appellant's defence statement provided pursuant to section 5 of the Criminal Procedure and Investigations Act 1996 contains or may contain an express or implied assertion giving the court or a jury a misleading impression about him. Reference was made to assertions contained in that document which gave the appellant's explanation for his DNA being deposited quite innocently on this knotted package which contained heroin. Even if what is contained in a defence case statement can amount to an assertion made by a defendant in the proceedings, the document in reality is setting out the contentions of the defence in relation to a fundamental issue in the case, the nature of his defence and the matters of fact upon which he takes issue. This, in the court's judgment, is not an impression about him, let alone a false or misleading one without begging the very question which the jury would have to determine.

Section 101(1)(g)

Section 101(1)(g) deals with those situations in which the defendant has made an 'attack on another person's character'. Once again, close parallels can be seen between this sub-section and the 'second limb' of s. 1(3)(ii) of the 1898 Act, which provided that the shield would be lost if the: '...nature or conduct of the defence is such as to involve imputations on the character of the prosecutor or the witnesses for the prosecution; or the deceased victim of the alleged crime'. However, there are also important differences. For example, at common law, imputations could usually be made quite safely against those who were *not* prosecution witnesses, as in *R v Lee* [1976] 1 WLR 71.

By contrast, the new provisions are not limited in this way. Thus, in theory, a man accused of theft from his employer, who blames the crime on a workmate who is not present at court, can still put his character in jeopardy. The section also ends the old common law position by which a defendant who attacked a prosecution witness through his advocate, but did not himself give evidence, was safe from the adduction of his previous bad character, as in *R v Butterwasser* [1948] 1 KB 4.

In practice, much will depend on the circumstances of the individual case. Section 101(1)(g) will not invariably be applied where there has, technically, been some kind of 'attack'. For a very crude and extreme example, judges would be likely to ignore a spontaneous outburst against the Queen by a defendant of Republican sympathies, or, alternatively, would automatically exercise the discretion under s. 101(1)(3) or s. 78 of the PCEA 1984 to prevent his bad character being adduced in such a situation, even though it would (arguably) fall within the provision.

Some additional clarity to this situation was provided in *R v Nelson* [2007] Crim LR 709. In this case, the defendant, while being questioned by the police on an affray charge, had stated that his neighbour was a liar and a user of class A drugs. As it transpired, the neighbour did not give evidence at the defendant's trial. However, the first instance judge held that there had been an attack on the character of another, which fell within the terms of s. 106(1)(g) of the Act. As a result, the accused man's previous drugs convictions were adduced.

In *Nelson* the Court of Appeal noted that the wording of the 2003 Act clearly covered the instant case, as there was no longer a need for the subject of the imputations to be a witness (unlike the situation under the 1898 Act). However, the court also noted that, in such situations, a trial judge still had a discretion (under s. 78 of the PCEA 1984) to prevent cross-examination on bad character where the accused had merely made imputations about the character of someone who was a non-witness and non-victim. Normally, though not invariably, the Court of Appeal concluded, it would be unusual to allow cross-examination in such a situation. However, in the instant case, where there was a suggestion that the neighbour had conspired with the alleged victim to fabricate evidence, and where this might have affected the way in which a juror viewed the victim's evidence, it would have been appropriate (had the evidence of the police interview properly been placed before the jury). The Court of Appeal also concluded that it would be wrong for the prosecution to adduce evidence of a largely irrelevant out of court interview, simply as a way of invoking s. 101(1)(g).

R v Nelson [2006] EWCA Crim 3412, CA

Keene LJ

We take the gateway aspect of the case first. There is no doubt that the wording of section 101(1)(g), 'an attack on another person's character', does not confine that gateway to the situation where a defendant, personally or through his advocate, attacks the character of a prosecution witness. It goes beyond the wording used in the earlier statutory provision which dealt with this area of law, namely section 1(3) of the Criminal Evidence Act 1898 , which by paragraph (ii) referred to 'imputations on the character of the prosecutor or the witnesses for the prosecution or the deceased victim of the alleged crime'. Apart from the case where there was a deceased victim, the earlier statutory provision effectively confined this basis for admitting evidence of a defendant's bad character to situations where there had been an attack during the trial on the character of a prosecution witness, including a person whose statement was read at trial. It did not extend to cases where the defendant attacked the character of a non-witness, save that of a deceased victim (see the decision in R v Lee (1976) 62 Cr App R 33).

15 That has been changed by the 2003 Act, which simply refers to 'an attack on another person's character', apparently irrespective of whether that person is a witness at trial. It must be taken, in our view, as Parliament's intention deliberately to widen the gateway in this fashion. Nonetheless, we would emphasise that the trial judge still has a discretion as to whether the jury should hear about a defendant's bad character when he has merely made imputations about the character of a non-witness. Not only does he have such a general discretion under section 78 of the Police and Criminal Evidence Act 1984 , but section 101(3) of the 2003 Act specifically provides that: 'the court must not admit evidence under subsection (1)(d) or (g) if on an application by the defendant to exclude it it appears to the court that the admission of the evidence would have such an adverse effect on the fairness of the proceedings that the court ought not to admit it'.

16 How the trial judge exercises that discretion is a matter for him or her, but it seems to this Court that it would be unusual for evidence of a defendant's bad character to be admitted when the only basis for so doing was an attack on the character of a non-witness who is also a non-victim. The fairness of the proceedings would normally be materially damaged by so doing.

The new Act defines 'attacking the other person's character' to mean suggesting that the other person has either committed an offence or behaved, or is disposed to behave, in a 'reprehensible way'. As a result, the same meaning will be given to the latter word as for defendants. Thus, in *R v Weir and Others* [2006] 1 Cr App R 19, a defendant who accused a rape complainant who was a member of his former congregation at a Hindu Temple of being 'not a witness of truth', and who claimed that her allegation was part of a conspiracy of fabrications, was held to have made an attack.

In *Bovell* the court also suggested that, as with the old regime, if a complainant's conviction had been adduced by a defendant, bringing it up would have amounted to an 'attack' for the purposes of s. 101(1)(g), one that would have justified the adduction of the accused man's own extensive list of convictions, in turn. Similarly, in *Dowds*, the defendant had claimed that a co-accused who had already pleaded guilty to a burglary for which he was standing trial had committed another burglary the previous day. This was deemed to be enough to put his character in issue under the provision. In like manner, in *R v Renda and others* [2006] 1 WLR 2948, it was held that comments that suggested that the victim of a crime would consent to sexual intercourse with anyone, and that any refusal on her part of consent could be disregarded as meaningless, constituted an attack on her character.

For the purposes of s. 101(1)(g), a defendant makes an attack on another's character if he adduces evidence that has that effect, asks questions in cross-examination that are intended or likely to elicit such evidence, or (as already noted) if evidence is adduced of an out of court imputation made by the defendant about that person. As a result, an attack can be made during a police interview, not just when giving evidence at trial (unlike the old situation under s. 1(3)(ii)). For example, in *Pickering*, the applicant was indicted on two counts of indecent assault and three counts of rape, the victim being his young daughter. At trial, the judge admitted the defendant's conviction for indecently assaulting an 11-year-old girl in 1993 under (inter alia) s. 101(1)(g) on the basis that at interview he had asserted that the girl's claim was a false allegation aimed at having him removed from the family home, so that she could return to it from foster care. This was held to amount to an attack on the complainant's character within s. 106(1)(c)(i) and s. 106(2)(b).

The Law Commission had intended that any new statutory regime should avoid the distortions to the trial process occasioned by the existing rules on imputations under the 1898 Act. For example, that a defendant alleged to have made extensive admissions to investigating police officers would necessarily *have* to suggest that they had fabricated them to have any real defence and thus, if he had previous convictions, would be obliged to lose his shield under the 1898 Act (subject to an exercise of the judicial discretion), as in *R v Britzman and Hall* [1983] 1 WLR 350. Similarly, in *R v Chinn* (1996) 160 JP 765, the appellant, who was accused of assaulting a publican occasioning actual bodily harm, lost his shield by claiming to have been acting in self-defence, although this was the only realistic option open to him.

This could have serious tactical consequences under the old law, as defendants running such defences might refrain from giving evidence altogether to avoid cross-examination on their criminal records. The Commission proposed to avoid such problems by making anything said within a 'central set of facts' immune from the new rules on imputations. This was reflected in their draft Criminal Evidence Bill, at clause 9(2)(a)(i–ii), which excluded from the ambit of 'imputations' any evidence to do with: '…the alleged facts of the offence with which the defendant is charged, or evidence of misconduct in connection with the investigation or prosecution of that offence'.

However, the 2003 Act did *not* contain such a provision, which meant that there was nothing to preclude the traditional approach from being followed. Despite this, some decisions under s. 1(3)(ii) of the 1898 Act during the last decade of its operation indicated an increased degree of judicial sympathy and realism towards defendants in this situation: *R v Wignall* [1993] Crim LR 62. Arguably, judges now have the power under the 2003 Act to take this process further by exercising the discretion contained in s. 101(3) to prevent such attacks leading to the adduction of a defendant's bad character, provided they are necessary to his case and go no further than is required to establish his defence. This might be especially likely if the misconduct is old, a factor that is expressly drawn to the court's attention under s. 101(4).

Even so, the facts of *Pickering* and other recent cases on this area of the law appear to suggest that a revolution in judicial practice is unlikely. Indeed, the court in *Pickering* concluded that some of the pre-2003 Act authorities on 'imputations' in the 'second limb' of s. 1(3)(ii) of the 1898 Criminal Evidence Act will continue to apply, when assessing whether an 'attack' has been made on another person's character under s. 101(1)(g), at least to the extent that they are compatible with s. 106 of the new statute.

As a result, it seems that judges will consider that the necessity for a defendant to make an attack, to have a defence at trial, is merely one factor to be considered amongst others when making a decision on the exercise of the discretion, just as it was under the 1898 statute, and certainly not conclusive of the issue. Indeed, a month after *Hanson*, the Court of Appeal, considering the case of *R v Dowds* [2005] 2 Cr App R 27, observed that when deciding whether there has been any 'adverse effect on the fairness of the proceedings' that would justify exercising the discretion under s. 101(3) not to admit bad character evidence, the defendant's motive or intention in making an attack (rather than its effect) was not a relevant factor that would warrant investigation by the trial judge.

Nevertheless, in *R v Singh (James Paul)* [2007] EWCA Crim 2140, Hughes LJ expressly noted that, when it came to exercising the discretion contained in s. 101(3), with regard to an 'attack' that had brought s. 101(1)(g) into play, and as with the old law, it was relevant (though certainly not conclusive) to consider whether 'an attack on the complainant is an entirely gratuitous one' (though, this was not relevant to the initial decision as to whether the gateway under s. 101(1)(g) had been opened).

In *Singh*, the defendant, accused of robbery, made an (undisputed) attack on the complainant by stating that he (the complainant) had been smoking crack and had, effectively, fabricated evidence. The accused man had previous convictions for disorder, harassment, assaulting a policeman, drink driving and criminal damage. When refusing to exercise the discretion contained in s. 101(3), to refuse to allow the defendant's convictions to be adduced, Hughes LJ, giving judgment in the Court of Appeal, made a number of other important points about this gateway.

R v Singh (James Paul) [2007] EWCA Crim 2140, CA

Hughes LJ

As to the first of those arguments it may be relevant to the exercise of discretion if an attack on the complainant is an entirely gratuitous one. Gateway G is, however, not limited to such cases and the question is not relevant to whether the gateway is passed. The purpose of gateway G is to enable the jury to know from what sort of source allegations against a witness (especially a complainant but not only a complainant) have come. This court has said on more than one occasion that the new rules for the admission of bad character evidence do not mirror the former law and argument from the former law is usually unhelpful. We have, however, no doubt whatever that gateway G was formulated with the former law under the Criminal Evidence Act 1898 in mind. It was well established then that the fact that an attack on a witness was necessarily involved in the case which the accused chose to make was no reason not to enable the jury to assess the reliability and the truthfulness of that case by seeing the full nature of the source from which the allegation comes. We are sure that the same approach is implicit in gateway G. That Mr Marklew was duty-bound to put the questions that he did to the complainant and that he did his duty once his instructions from the defendant were as they were is nothing to the point.

As to the second argument, gateway G does not depend upon propensity to offend as charged or upon propensity to be untruthful in the sense of having a track record for untruthfulness. The purpose that it has is the one which we have identified. Of course it is well established that if a defendant's bad character admitted because gateway G has been passed does also go to show propensity to offend as charged or to be untruthful it is open to the jury to use it for the relevant purpose. For that see R v Highton and Others [2005] EWCA Crim 1985; [2006] 1 Crim App R 7 That, however, is not this case and such has not been suggested. It does not, however, follow, that it is admissible only if it also shows one or other of those propensities. To say that would be tantamount to saying that evidence which is admissible through gateway G ought to be excluded as a matter of discretion unless it also passes gateway D. There is clearly no warrant in the statute for construing it in that way—just the reverse. The Act plainly demonstrates that the gateways are independent, although of course in some cases more than one of them may be passed. The argument which we are addressing would, if accepted, deprive gateway G of much of its application.

The second argument was effectively encapsulated in the proposition that the appellant's convictions were irrelevant to his credibility. We do not think that they were. They may not have been such as to demonstrate a track record for untruthfulness. They would not have been independently admissible under gateway D if there had not been the attack on the credibility of the complainant that there was. But the attack on the complaint had been made. The relevance of the attack was that if it was true it provided a reason why the complainant should be disbelieved. When the jury was assessing the evidence of the two main parties to this trial it was judging the complainant's credibility against that of the accused. The attack having been made, it was entitled to have regard to the source from which came the accusations which might affect the jury's judgment of the complainant. It would be wholly artificial to say that this information about the appellant went to whether he was to be believed in what he said about the complainant being a user of crack cocaine and not to whether he was believed in what he said about how the complainant came to be parted from his chain and his mobile phone. We think that it is perfectly plain that, once admitted under gateway G, bad character evidence does go to the credibility of the witness in question. That accords with common experience. It is, among other things, the obverse of the reason why a defendant is entitled to plead his own good character in support of his claim that he should be believed. The reason why he is entitled to do that is because ordinary human experience is that people of proven respectability and good character are, other things being equal, more worthy of belief than those who are not. Conversely, persons of bad character may of course tell the truth and often do, but it is ordinary human experience that their word may be worth less than that of those who have led exemplary lives. Once gateway G is passed the consequence of the defendant's bad character falls to be weighed with all the other evidence when the jury decides whether or not he has been proved to be guilty, and in doing so it may think him less worthy of belief because of his history. We ought to add that what is in issue here in relation to the exercise of discretion is of course whether this court should interfere with the judge's conclusion. This court

> will not interfere with the exercise of the judge's discretion under section 101(3) any more than it would under section 78 of the Police and Criminal Evidence Act or similar provisions unless the judge has either misdirected himself or had arrived at a conclusion which is outside the legitimate band of decisions available to him.

It seems that the principles laid down by the Court of Appeal in *R v McCleod* [1994] 3 All ER 254 as to the (very limited) scope of cross-examination on the underlying details of previous convictions of a defendant who had made imputations on the character of Crown witnesses for the purposes of s. 1(3)(ii) of the 1898 Evidence Act, will not automatically be followed under the 2003 Act. Under the old regime, it was generally thought that as such cross-examination went to credit, not propensity, under a 'tit for tat' principle, prolonged cross-examination as to the details of previous convictions was normally undesirable. It risked their being treated as 'back door' similar fact evidence. By contrast, where a propensity direction is likely to be given to bad character evidence admitted under s. 101(1)(g), as *Highton* makes clear can be done in appropriate circumstances, such detail may well be entirely justified.

Nevertheless, the amount of character evidence adduced under the provision can be restricted by a first instance judge, just as it can under s. 101(1)(f). Thus, in a recent case, involving an application to adduce bad character made under s. 101(1)(g), with regard to a defendant accused of assault, older convictions for serious offences of dishonesty were adduced, more recent convictions for offences of violence were not: *R v Edwards (Karl) and others* [2006] 1 Cr App R 3. Even so, and as *Weir* indicates, this will not invariably be the case.

R v Antony Weir & Others [2006] 1 Cr App R 19, CA

Kennedy LJ

We turn now to the final gateway provision relied upon, namely that the appellant at interview and thereafter made an attack on the complainant's character (section 101(1)(g)). Mr Kovalevsky accepts that he did so, but he submitted that the opening of that gateway should not be regarded as rendering all available evidence of bad character admissible. That is a somewhat difficult submission because in the first place it must be noted that section 105(6) has no application to section 101(1)(g), and, secondly, it is clear from the decision in *Highton* that once this gateway is open the evidence admitted may be used not only in relation to credibility but also in relation to propensity. In our judgment the attack on the character of the complainant clearly opens the door to all of the evidence on which the prosecution sought to rely, subject to the requirements of section 101(3), which we have already considered in relation to section 101(1)(d).

Other Statutes on Defendant Bad Character Evidence

A handful of older statutory provisions that permit the adduction of defendant bad character evidence have survived repeal in the 2003 Act. Thus, s. 1(2) of the Official Secrets Act 1911 allows a defendant's 'known character' to be adduced to suggest that he intended to act in a manner that was prejudicial to the interests of the state. However, the most important of these surviving specialist statutes is s. 27(3) of the Theft Act 1968. This historic provision (the statute had numerous precedents) allowed in evidence of a general propensity to commit offences of dishonesty to establish that a defendant knew that items in his possession were stolen. Under s. 27(3)(a) evidence of the accused handling other goods that were stolen not more than 12 months before the offence charged can be adduced on this issue, as can convictions accrued during the previous five years for offences of theft or handling, provided the defence is given seven days written notice: s. 27(3)(b).

Thus, in the House of Lords case of *R v Hacker* [1995] 1 All ER 45, the defendant was tried on indictment with handling stolen goods (the body shell of a motorcar) in August 1991. The trial judge allowed the prosecution to adduce in evidence, under s. 27(3)(b), a certificate establishing the defendant's conviction at a Magistrates' Court, in May of the same year, for receiving a stolen motorcar. Additionally, in *Hacker*, their Lordships concluded that when previous convictions are admissible under s. 27(3), s. 73(2) of the PCEA 1984 is also operative, so that the substance of the previous certificate of conviction will be admissible.

Traditionally, s. 27(3) was strictly controlled by a robust exercise of the judicial discretion: *R v Perry* [1984] Crim LR 680. Prosecution applications were often refused. However, given that s. 27(3), where it operated, effectively 'watered down' the strict common law similar fact doctrine on propensity evidence, and that this has now been liberalized generally by s. 101(1)(d) of the CJA 2003, the provision's future is uncertain. It may be that its use, already restricted, will often be considered unnecessary.

4. Bad Character Evidence of Non-party Witnesses and Non-testifying Third Parties

Criminal Cases

The CJA 2003 preserved the existing division between the character of witnesses who are defendants (now governed by s. 101) and those who are not, who are subject to s. 100 of the Act, as are third parties who do not appear at trial at all. At common law, and unlike the relatively protected position of an accused person giving evidence, there were few legal constraints against making allegations against third parties or on cross-examining non-party witnesses on aspects of their 'bad character', though, since 1976, complainants in sexual cases have had special statutory protection with regard to their sexual histories (now contained in s. 41 of the Youth Justice and Criminal Evidence Act 1999).

Cross-reference Box

There was a growing fear during the 1970s that rape trials were turning into trials of a complainant's lifestyle, with juries sometimes being tacitly invited to disregard the evidence of a woman who was deemed to be 'promiscuous'. This led to the introduction of restrictions on the extent to which a complainant could be cross-examined about her sexual history. For more information on how such cases are regulated, see below at pp. 448–465.

The normal common law position respecting cross-examination as to credit was summarized in the libel case of *Hobbs v Tinling* [1929] 2 KB 1, in which Scrutton LJ, sitting in the Court of Criminal Appeal, suggested (in *obiter* comments) that a witness could be asked any question about his character or previous conduct from which the court could infer that he was 'not worthy of belief, not a credible person'. This meant that s/he could be asked about previous convictions and any reprehensible associations or way of life. Of course, such matters were collateral and, subject to important exceptions, such as s. 6 of the Criminal Procedure Act 1865 (which deals with previous convictions and applies to both criminal and civil cases), the witness's answer could not be challenged by rebutting evidence, even if it was readily available.

 Cross-reference Box

The rule on the finality of answer to a question on a collateral matter (ie one that goes to a witness's credit) is a common law rule that prevents a party to litigation from adducing evidence to show that an answer (usually a denial) given to such a question is false, even if such rebutting evidence is readily available. There are a number of exceptions to the general rule. Parties can always call rebutting evidence if the question goes to an 'issue' in the case, though distinguishing between collateral matters and issues can pose problems. For a detailed discussion of this subject see pp. 436–440.

Subsequent judicial interpretation suggested that only relatively trivial questions about a witness's bad character were exempt from being raised in court for this purpose. For example, in the perjury case of *R v Sweet-Escott* [1971] 55 Cr App R 316, Lawton J, presiding at first instance, decided that the defendant's failure to own up to distant and minor convictions, committed just after completing national service over 20 years earlier, was not 'material' to a trial in which he had been a witness. He directed the jury to acquit and argued, again in *obiter* comments, that a trial judge or magistrates should allow a line of questioning if they concluded that the matter would not affect the witness's standing with a 'fair-minded' tribunal of fact after cross-examination. In this case, he felt that the magistrates before whom the defendant had originally given testimony would not have been influenced by such petty and distant transgressions.

Some additional protection was provided by a 1975 Practice Direction ('Crime: Spent Convictions' [1975] 1 WLR 1065), issued by Lord Widgery CJ, with the express encouragement of Parliament, and intended to give effect to the rehabilitative ethos behind the Rehabilitation of Offenders Act 1974 (the Act itself only expressly barred cross-examination on spent convictions in civil proceedings, exceptional circumstances apart). This Practice Direction provided that spent convictions should only be referred to in a criminal trial with leave of the presiding judge. This should only be necessary if the 'interests of justice so require'. Cases since then have identified several situations in which this might occur, whether because the conviction[s] affected the witness's credit to a marked degree or went directly to the issue in the case. For example, in *R v Evans* [1992] Crim LR 125, the Court of Appeal held that counsel should have been allowed to cross-examine the chief prosecution witness in an assault case (where self-defence was being advanced by the accused man) on her own spent convictions for violence, which might have suggested that she was the attacker.

In recent years, as Lord Auld noted in his report of 2001, the Codes of Conduct regulating both sides of the legal profession have also gone some way towards discouraging 'oppressive' questioning of witnesses.[9] Thus, the Code of Conduct for the Bar of England and Wales provides that counsel should not ask questions that are 'merely scandalous or calculated only to vilify, insult, or annoy' the witness.[10] The Law Society's Code for Advocacy contains a similar provision.

The common law latitude on cross-examination was (and is) also constrained by practical considerations. Counsel will often only know about a witness's previous convictions, not other areas of reprehensible conduct in their lives. Additionally, in a multi-value society there may be considerable public dispute as to what is meant by reprehensible or discreditable conduct. Cross-examining witnesses about 'transgressions' that some people might not perceive as such, has the potential to alienate the tribunal of fact, especially if it is a jury. For example, it is likely that, in some cases, the fact that an independent eye witness to a 'road rage' incident was working as a prostitute at the time in question would not have much influence on many jurors' assessment of her credibility, while questioning her about her lifestyle and occupation could appear to them to be a sign of desperation in opposing counsel.

However, despite these restrictions (both legal and practical), and the limited degree to which the issue has been explored judicially, the theoretical ambit of cross-examination at common law remained very broad. This was heavily criticized on moral, practical and policy grounds. The first line of argument tended to stress that it was not right that every indiscretion of a witness's lifetime, however old or minor, should necessarily be exposed to public view. The second, that although misconduct may affect general credibility this (unlike specific credibility) is often of very limited value in assessing a witness's testimony. The final argument is that gratuitously allowing distressing and humiliating cross-examination contributes to the current, and very marked, reluctance of witnesses to come forward or testify in criminal cases. This was a claim that the Law Commission itself expressly accepted in its report, which in turn heavily influenced the new legislation.[11]

As a result, the Commission concluded that before the bad character of non-defendants (whether they were witnesses or not) could be adduced, it should satisfy a test of 'enhanced relevance' and that this should cover not just bad character evidence that went to credibility but also that which went to the issue in the case (if only to avoid the often difficult task of distinguishing between the two). It hoped that this would balance the rights and interests of both the defendant and other witnesses.[12] The new provision is contained in s. 100 of the CJA 2003.

Section 100 of the Criminal Justice Act 2003, Non-defendant's bad character

(1) In criminal proceedings evidence of the bad character of a person other than the defendant is admissible if and only if—

    (a) it is important explanatory evidence,

    (b) it has substantial probative value in relation to a matter which—

        (i) is a matter in issue in the proceedings, and

        (ii) is of substantial importance in the context of the case as a whole, or

    (c) all parties to the proceedings agree to the evidence being admissible.

---

[9] Sir Robin Auld, Review of the Criminal Courts of England and Wales, 2001, 527.

[10] Code of Conduct of the Bar of England and Wales, 7th edn., in effect 31 July 2000, at para. 708(g).

[11] Evidence of Bad Character in Criminal Proceedings, no 273, published 9 October 2001, at para. 9.20.

[12] ibid. para 9.2.

(2) For the purposes of subsection (1)(a) evidence is important explanatory evidence if—

    (a) without it, the court or jury would find it impossible or difficult properly to understand other evidence in the case, and

    (b) its value for understanding the case as a whole is substantial.

(3) In assessing the probative value of evidence for the purposes of subsection (1)(b) the court must have regard to the following factors (and to any others it considers relevant)—

    (a) the nature and number of the events, or other things, to which the evidence relates;

    (b) when those events or things are alleged to have happened or existed;

    (c) where—

        (i) the evidence is evidence of a person's misconduct, and

        (ii) it is suggested that the evidence has probative value by reason of similarity between that misconduct and other alleged misconduct,

    the nature and extent of the similarities and the dissimilarities between each of the alleged instances of misconduct;

    (d) where—

        (i) the evidence is evidence of a person's misconduct,

        (ii) it is suggested that that person is also responsible for the misconduct charged, and

        (iii) the identity of the person responsible for the misconduct charged is disputed,

    (e) the extent to which the evidence shows or tends to show that the same person was responsible each time.

(4) Except where subsection (1)(c) applies, evidence of the bad character of a person other than the defendant must not be given without leave of the court.

Essentially, s. 100 allows non-defendants' bad character to be adduced in three separate situations. Uncontroversially, one of them, s. 100(1)(c), occurs where both parties agree to the evidence being adduced; this is in keeping with the Act's general trend towards agreed evidence. Both of the other two 'gateways' to adducing bad character evidence require the leave of the court: s. 100(4). Of these, the first, s. 100(1)(a), provides that bad character evidence can be admitted if it is 'important explanatory evidence'. Section 100(2) states that for the purposes of s. 100(1)(a) evidence is important explanatory evidence if, without it, the court or jury would find it impossible or difficult properly to understand other evidence in the case, and, additionally, its value for understanding the case as a whole is substantial.

Thus, s. 100(1)(a) covers, inter alia, situations in which the proposed evidence goes primarily to the credit of the witness: *R v Antony Weir & Ors* [2005] EWCA Crim 2866. For example, not knowing that an alibi witness has a very serious and recent history of offences of dishonesty might make it 'difficult properly to understand other evidence in the case'. Of course, some bad character evidence will go to both credit and issue; thus, can be considered the situation in which there is an alibi witness with a perjury conviction (something that also explains the Commission's reluctance to differentiate between the two when imposing an evidential threshold).

The second provision, contained in s. 100(1)(b), provides that such evidence can also be adduced if it has substantial probative value in relation to something which is both a 'matter in issue in the proceedings, and is of substantial importance in the context of the case as a whole'. The Commission envisaged that this would cover situations such as that in which third parties (not necessarily witnesses) were blamed for the offence for which the defendant stands trial. It will also cover those situations in which a witness's previous conduct is directly relevant to the issues in the trial. Again, for example, this would cover the assault 'victim' with recent and serious previous convictions for violence, where there is a dispute as to who initiated a fight. In the light of *R v S (Andrew)* [2006] 2 Cr App R 31, it also appears to extend to witness credibility.

Pause for reflection

Is it right that a co-defendant should have to meet such a qualitative threshold before he is allowed to adduce relevant evidence in his own defence?

In making the qualitative decision as to whether something was of 'substantial' importance, the Commission proposed that a number of factors should be considered by the courts. These are set out in s. 100(3), which provides, inter alia, that in assessing the probative value of evidence for the purposes of s. 100(1)(b), the court must have regard to the nature and number of the 'events or other things' to which the evidence relates (ie convictions or other instances of 'reprehensible behaviour'), when they occurred, and, where relevant, the similarity between that misconduct and other alleged misconduct.

Thus, under s. 100(3)(d), if a defendant were to suggest that a third party had been responsible for the crime with which he was charged, as occurred, for example, in respect of a child murder in *R v Blastland* [1986] AC 41, the court would have regard to the extent to which the evidence shows that 'the same person was responsible each time'. For example, in a murder case, if the killing that the defendant was accused of had the singular hallmarks of an absent third party's *modus operandi* such evidence might well be admitted; if very different, it might not. Thus, a defendant accused of murder where the victim was strangled with an electric cord might argue that the killing was the work of a Mr Brown who lived locally at the time and subsequently transpired to be a serial killer who always used such means to kill his victim. (This is obviously an extreme illustration.)

Although s. 100(3) is only directly linked to s. 100(1)(b), some of the factors identified will also be relevant when considering applications under s. 100(1)(a). However, these factors are also not exhaustive; others may be taken into account. In *R v Eccleston* [2001] EWCA Crim 1626, the Court of Appeal expressly noted (about the old regime for non-defendant witnesses) that although circumstances are infinitely variable, the prime question was to determine how relevant the information was to the defence of the accused.

In *Eccleston*, the court felt that it was highly significant to the question of admissibility that it was not put to a witness with minor previous convictions that she was lying. The Law Commission also suggested the importance of a direct allegation to that effect before such character evidence could be adduced. In the light of this, and although not expressly identified as a prerequisite, it is possible that before a court will find that bad character evidence going to credit is 'important' there will have to be a direct assertion that the witness concerned has lied or fabricated their testimony.

Because the two provisions are close to those envisaged by the Law Commission in its draft Criminal Evidence Bill, unlike several other aspects of the statute, some assistance as to its interpretation can be drawn from the Commission's earlier work. Obviously, and as already noted, the new provisions are broad enough to cover both bad character evidence that goes to credit and that which goes to issue. Additionally, and vitally, the words 'important' and 'substantial' make it apparent that the Commission's proposals for a test of 'enhanced relevance' have borne fruit.

The broad effect of the new provision is to tighten up the theoretical ambit of witness cross-examination on bad character. As a result, it seems that cross-examination on bad character evidence, whether to credit or issue, that, though technically 'relevant', is of minor cogency, will not be permitted in future. Thus, in the hypothetical case of the 'road rage' incident, it seems that cross-examining the eye witness as to her working as a prostitute would not *normally* be permitted under the new Act.

Pause for reflection

Do you feel that a witness's sensibilities should ever take precedence over a defendant's right to pursue his defence as vigorously as possible?

The Law Commission expressed the hope that its recommendations would not mean that the sensibilities of witnesses were protected at the expense of a defendant's rights, merely that questions that did not *substantially* advance the accused person's case would not be permitted. However, this requires a difficult judicial balancing act, and, in *R v Bovell* [2005] 2 Cr App R 27, the Court of Appeal took what might be considered to be a surprisingly 'robust' approach towards the new provisions.

In *Bovell*, the defendant had been convicted of wounding with intent, having advanced self-defence at trial as the basis for his not guilty plea. At first instance he had been refused permission to adduce the alleged victim and chief prosecution witness's previous convictions for handling stolen goods and robbery in 1993 (when the witness was 20), for the latter of which he (the witness) had received four years' imprisonment following a guilty plea. On appeal, the defendant argued that these convictions should have been put to the alleged victim, especially the one for robbery, as it subsequently transpired that this had involved the use of a knife, and so, it was claimed, showed a propensity for serious violence (potentially relevant in a situation in which self-defence was being claimed). Nevertheless, the Court of Appeal upheld the conviction, although accepting that had the presence of the knife been known, the trial judge might have reached a different decision with regard to the admissibility of the robbery conviction.

In *Bovell,* the court also doubted that a charge made against the complainant, several years earlier, for wounding with intent, but which had not been proceeded with, and as a result was a mere allegation, was capable of being evidence for the purposes of s. 100 (though it seems that in the right circumstances it might be for s. 101). Although the latter point might make sense (otherwise, there is a danger of trials becoming bogged down in satellite issues), the decision on the robbery at knife-point is more questionable.

Whether, in *Bovell,* it can really be said that the alleged victim's record of violence did not put a significantly different light on the accused's claim of self-defence is, perhaps, doubtful. An excessively strict approach to this issue might also lead defendants who have had their applications refused to argue that they have also had their Article 6 ECHR right to a fair trial denied. (In passing, it should also be noted that for defendants with previous convictions, adducing a third party's misconduct may well be deemed to be an 'attack' for the purposes of s. 101(1)(g), see above.)

R v Bovell [2005] 2 Cr App R 401, CA

Rose LJ

As it seems to us, it may be that the judge's decision with regard to the admissibility of the robbery offence, in 1993, might have been different had he known that the complainant had then been carrying a knife. It is to be noted, however in relation to that offence, that, notwithstanding he was only prosecuted for it some years later, when fingerprint evidence came to light, the complainant immediately admitted his guilt. This would have been relevant to the judge's decision. It seems to us to be unlikely in the extreme that the judge, had he known of the events in 2001, would have admitted the allegation of a s.18 offence made against the complainant. We say that, first, because we entertain considerable doubt as to whether the mere making of an allegation is capable of being evidence within s. 100(1). As the allegation was, in the circumstances which we have identified, withdrawn, our doubt on this aspect is increased. It is apparent from the circumstances, as we have summarised them, that if there was to be any question of the s.18 allegation being admitted before the jury, it would necessarily have given rise to investigation of the other subsequent matters, including the aspersions on the credibility of the victim, the want of independent confirmation of his account, and the fact that he had withdrawn the allegation. An excursion into those satellite matters is, as it seems to us, precisely the sort of excursion which, as was suggested in para. 12 of the judgment in Hanson, a trial judge should be discouraged from embarking upon. All of this adds to the unlikelihood of the judge permitting evidence of the 2001 events even if they had been known about at trial.

Pause for reflection

Do you feel that the alleged victim's previous criminal record in *Bovell* puts the case in a different light?

Less controversially, in one of the cases considered in *R v Antony Weir & Others* [2006] 1 Cr App R 19, the Court of Appeal concluded that a defence witness (the defendant's girlfriend) in an assault case should not have been cross-examined about a caution for possession of cocaine, on the ground that it had substantial probative value to her credibility, where it had been put to her that she was lying and there was a stark difference between prosecution and defence accounts of what had happened. Nevertheless, the court did accept that s. 100(1) covered matters of credibility and also upheld the conviction on the ground that, in the circumstances, it was not unsafe (the trial judge had subsequently directed the jury to disregard the caution).

R v Antony Weir & Others [2006] 1 Cr App R 19, CA

Kennedy LJ

The appellant's submissions are put on two bases: first, that the evidence did not relate to a matter in issue in the proceedings as the section does not encompass matters of credibility. Secondly, that even if credibility is encompassed by the section, the evidence did not pass the test of admissibility as it had no substantial probative value in relation to the question of credibility and was not of substantial importance in the context of the case as a whole. It was submitted that the evidence had very little value in relation to credibility and no relevance at all to the offence in question because a) the caution did not relate to an offence of dishonesty or show evidence of untruthfulness; b) it related to an incident after the events in issue; c) the witness by agreeing to be cautioned had accepted her guilt; d) the witness was frank about her caution in evidence; and e) there was no suggestion that she was under the influence of drugs during the incident itself. 69 The appellant also submits that the conviction is unsafe in the light of the majority verdicts on each count on the basis that the evidence could have adversely affected their view of the witness despite the judge's strong warning. 70 On behalf of the respondent, it is submitted that s. 100(1) must cover the issue of credibility, for were it not to do so, unfairness would ensue. It was submitted that the evidence of the caution was relevant to credibility, but it was conceded that it was difficult to suggest that the evidence had substantial probative value in relation to credibility in the light of the witnesses' answers. Their primary submission therefore is that the conviction was safe and that the strong warning given by the judge corrected any harm done by the introduction of the evidence.

Judgment

We now deal with the submissions and the questions arising therefrom. Does s. 100(1) cover issues of credibility? 73 Although couched in different terms from the provisions relating to the introduction of the defendant's bad character, in our view, s. 100(1) does cover matters of credibility. To find otherwise would mean that there was a significant lacuna in the legislation with the potential for unfairness. In any event, it is clear from para. [362] of the explanatory notes that the issue of credibility falls within the section. Did the judge err in coming to the conclusion that the evidence of the caution had substantial probative value in relation to the witness's credibility? 74 In our view he did err for a number of reasons, including those which were put forward by the judge himself when directing the jury to ignore the evidence of the caution. It follows, therefore, that we find that the evidence of the caution was inadmissible under s. 100.

Many of the cases on what constitutes 'other reprehensible behaviour' under s. 101 will be relevant to s. 100 (though this will not invariably be the case). Nevertheless, there have also been a number of decisions specific to s. 100. Thus, in *R v V* [2006] EWCA Crim 1901, the first instance judge in the trial of a man accused of sexually assaulting and raping his young daughter refused to grant permission, pursuant to s. 100, for the complainant to be cross-examined about several matters which, it was claimed, constituted evidence of 'other reprehensible behaviour'. On appeal, the Court of Appeal considered whether these matters came within such a definition and, if they did, whether leave should have been granted under the section.

In particular, the court in *V* concluded that the trial judge had been wrong not to allow the complainant to be cross-examined about an apparently false allegation that she had made, on an earlier occasion, about being sexually assaulted. In this instance, as there was an admission to a friend that she had fabricated the allegation, the Court of Appeal concluded that there was a sufficient evidential basis for asserting that the complaint was untrue; such behaviour was both 'reprehensible' and cogent in the instant case. However, the court concluded that another application under s. 100, to allow cross-examination on an incident in which the complainant had been overheard falsely telling other pupils at her school that a teacher had hit her, when at most there had been accidental contact, had been properly refused; schoolgirl exaggeration did not constitute reprehensible behaviour.

R v V [2006] EWCA Crim 1901, CA

Crane J

The teacher incident was the subject of an application under section 100 to Judge Brodrick and had no sexual aspect. On 21 November 2003 J had been overheard asserting to two other pupils at school that a teacher had hit her. The teacher who overheard this invited her to explain. She admitted that she had been misbehaving and been sent out of the room. She said that the teacher stopped her by putting his arm out, but then pushed her back with his arm. Later she conceded that there had been no push, merely contact with the teacher's arm.

We are inclined to doubt whether a piece of exaggeration to fellow pupils after some everyday classroom misbehaviour attains the level of 'reprehensible' behaviour envisaged in section 112(1), read with section 98, of the Criminal Justice Act 2003. If it was, we consider that the judge was justified in ruling, as he did, that it did not have 'substantial probative value' for the purposes of the test in section 100(1)(b). If it was not, leave was not required, but we do not think any cross-examination on these lines would have taken the Appellant's case any further.

Cross-reference Box

Interestingly, the trial judge in this case did not address his mind properly to s. 41 of the Youth Justice and Criminal Evidence Act 1999 (YJCE Act 1999), which now regulates the cross-examination of rape-complainants about their sexual histories. For more on this topic, see pp. 448–465.

In *R v S (Andrew)* [2006] 2 Cr App R 31 the complainant in a case of indecent assault, was working at the relevant time as a prostitute. The defendant alleged that he had been masturbated by her for £10, but that she had subsequently demanded more money, threatening to allege rape, and, when he refused, tried to grab his gold chain.

At trial, defence counsel sought to put to the complainant her previous convictions for burglary, theft and going equipped to steal. These had been accrued some four years before the incident in question. The trial judge refused to allow this, feeling that they did not have 'substantial probative value'. On appeal, the Court of Appeal accepted that under s. 100(1)(b)(i), 'matter in issue in the proceedings' must include the creditworthiness of a witness, ie evidence to show that they were unworthy of belief. As the court noted, otherwise, the provision might be open to challenge under Article 6 of the ECHR. The Court of Appeal further noted that credibility under s. 100 might well be wider than a 'propensity to be untruthful' in a defendant under s. 103(1)(b). As a result, it appears that a very bad and recent criminal record for dishonesty (but not 'untruthfulness') in a case where simple credibility on its own was in issue, *might* be admissible under s. 100.

Even so, on the facts of the case, the Court of Appeal felt the trial judge had been right to refuse the application on the basis of simple credibility. The complainant had always pleaded guilty to her crimes, none of which had involved false representations.

However, the court went on to conclude that the convictions should have been put to her on the basis that her propensity to act in the way that the defendant had asserted must be part of the 'matters in issue'. In this case, the defendant had claimed that the allegation of indecent assault arose out of a demand for money with menaces. In the court's conclusion, the previous convictions, although old, had substantial probative value with regard to her propensity to be dishonest, and should have been admitted, as it supported the defendant's version of events. Given that the verdict was by a bare majority, and after a long retirement, the conviction was held to be unsafe.

R v S (Andrew) [2006] 2 Cr App R 31, CA

Laws LJ

The complainant pleaded guilty to each of the previous offences sought to be relied on. None of them involved making false representations. In addition, as the judge was at pains to note, the offences are of some antiquity. The fact urged by counsel for the appellant that the jury knew about the appellant's good character cannot as a matter of logic increase the probative value of the complainant's previous offences in relation to her credibility. In our judgment the judge was quite right to refuse the application on the distinct basis upon which it was put to him.

13 However, that is not the end of the matter. By focusing on credibility counsel may have lost sight of a different basis on which it might be said that the complainant's convictions had substantial probative value in relation to a matter in issue. It will be recalled that the appellant's case on the facts was that the complainant demanded cash from him beyond the £10 which he said was agreed, threatened to cry rape, and tried to take his gold chain. Might not her previous offences support an argument that she was liable to behave in that way or possess a propensity to do so—in short, a propensity to act dishonestly?

14 In the case of a defendant whose bad character is sought to be put in, propensity to commit offences of the kind charged is, by s. 103(1)(a), included within matters in issue for the purposes of s. 101. Section 100 contains no analogue to s. 103(1)(a), but in our judgment it can hardly be doubted, and Miss Beattie for the Crown accepts, that a complainant's propensity to act in the way the defendant asserts he or she acted must likewise be part of 'the matters in issue'.

15 Here the appellant's case was to the effect that the complainant demanded money with menaces and tried to take his property. Her persistent criminal record of offences of dishonesty, notwithstanding their antiquity, might in our judgment very well be said to possess substantial probative value upon this issue: did she have a propensity to act dishonestly? The judge, as we have indicated, was not faced with an application put on that basis. Had he been, we consider that it would have been proper for him to accede to it. The evidence of propensity thus described would have been a matter of some importance for the jury's consideration. We consider the fact that the jury proceeded in ignorance of it renders the conviction unsafe.

There is still some doubt as to the impact of the provision on the existing collateral/issue distinction with regard to questions that go purely to credit (rather than issue, which by definition will not be collateral). Will 'adduce' mean merely that such questions can be asked, but that a denial that does not come within an existing exception to the finality of answer to a collateral question rule, cannot be rebutted unless they fall within an exception (as convictions do)?

Given that the ordinary dictionary meaning of 'adduce' includes 'cite as proof or instance',[13] and that the abolition of common law rules on evidence of bad character under s. 99 *might* be deemed to extend to the rule of finality on collateral issues, it is *possible* that if the court does allow a question to be put to a witness on their non-conviction bad character (even if it goes to credit), it will have at least the discretionary power to allow a denial to be rebutted by other evidence. Thus, in the perhaps unlikely event that post-Act a court allowed the hypothetical prostitute eye witness to be questioned about her work, it could permit one of her clients to be called to rebut any denial.

---

[13] *The Concise Oxford Dictionary* (6th edn, 1976, Oxford University Press).

Civil Cases

The position established at common law with regard to witnesses remains in force in civil matters (obviously unaffected by the 2003 Act). However, the impact of the Rehabilitation of Offenders Act 1974 limits the extent to which the previous convictions of witnesses can be referred to in civil proceedings (see below).

5. Defendant Good Character in Civil Cases

Generally speaking, the good character of a party to civil proceedings, whether defendant or claimant, is not admissible, unlike the normal situation with regard to defendants in criminal cases. As Baron Martin noted in *A-G v Radcliff* (1854) 10 Exch 84, in most cases, no presumption would arise: '…from the good character of the defendant, that he did not commit the breach of contract or of civil duty alleged against him'. Of course, if a party to litigation has his credibility attacked by unwarranted aspersions on his character, he can call evidence of his good character to rebut the allegation.

6. Defendant Bad Character in Civil Cases

Introduction

A defendant's character can be attacked in civil proceedings with a view to undermining his credit, just like that of any other witness. There is no special regime for defendants in civil trials, unlike the situation that governs the accused in criminal proceedings. Thus, for example, a defendant with previous convictions can have them put to him in cross-examination.

Nevertheless, it should be noted that convictions that are 'spent' cannot normally be referred to in civil cases (for any witnesses) as a result of s. 4(1) of the Rehabilitation of Offenders Act 1974, though, under s. 7(3), the court may allow their adduction if satisfied that 'justice cannot be done in the case' without referring to them. In *Thomas v Metropolitan Police Commissioner* [1997] QB 813 the Court of Appeal concluded that, in appropriate cases, s. 7(3) could be invoked to adduce spent convictions that were relevant to credit as well as those that went directly to an issue in the case.

Section 4 of the Rehabilitation of Offenders Act 1974, (Partial extract), Effect of rehabilitation

(1) Subject to sections 7 and 8 below, a person who has become a rehabilitated person for the purposes of this Act in respect of a conviction shall be treated for all purposes in law as a

person who has not committed or been charged with or prosecuted for or convicted of or sentenced for the offence or offences which were the subject of that conviction; and, notwithstanding the provisions of any other enactment or rule of law to the contrary, but subject as aforesaid—

(a) no evidence shall be admissible in any proceedings before a judicial authority exercising its jurisdiction or functions in Great Britain to prove that any such person has committed or been charged with or prosecuted for or convicted of or sentenced for any offence which was the subject of a spent conviction; and

(b) a person shall not, in any such proceedings, be asked, and, if asked, shall not be required to answer, any question relating to his past which cannot be answered without acknowledging or referring to a spent conviction or spent convictions or any circumstances ancillary thereto. . . .

When a conviction becomes 'spent' depends on the sentence originally imposed following the finding of guilt. Thus, under s. 5 of the 1974 Act, a conditional discharge is spent at the end of the period for which the defendant was discharged or a year after conviction (whichever is the greater); however, a fine takes five years, and a prison sentence of less than six months, seven years, to become spent. A sentence of more than 30 months' imprisonment never falls within the Act, and so can always be put, as of right, to a defendant in civil proceedings.

Civil Similar Fact Evidence

Perhaps more significantly, past misconduct can be indicative of present behaviour in civil as well as criminal matters and thus can be used to establish propensity under the common law 'similar fact' doctrine. The legal use of this type of evidence was neglected in civil cases, at least when compared to the extensive jurisprudence on its criminal counterpart. It was only rarely mentioned in judgments, and then often by reference to criminal case law on the topic. Ironically, however, given the abolition of the similar fact doctrine in criminal trials under s. 99(1) of the CJA 2003, it is only in civil cases that it will be encountered in future. A number of cases, stretching back over a century, are indicative of the doctrine at work. Thus, in *Hales v Kerr* [1908] 2 KB 201, evidence from a barber's customers that they, too, had become infected with ring-worm, after having been cut and bandaged by the defendant in the recent past, was admitted to support the plaintiff's claim to having been negligently infected in a similar fashion. It suggested that the defendant had an unhygienic system of work.

Hales v Kerr [1908] 2 KB 601, King's Bench Division

Channell J

. . . in the doctor's opinion antiseptics ought to be used for cleansing the razors in a barber's shop. Then if there is evidence that a practice prevails in the defendant's shop of cleansing his razors and appliances in a particular way, and a question arises whether that practice is a dangerous one, evidence to shew that a similar practice in other barbers' shops had led to the communication of disease, and was therefore dangerous, would be admissible. If so, evidence to shew that the practice had led to the communication of disease in the defendant's own establishment would be equally admissible... where the allegation is of a practice to do or omit to do a particular act, and the material issue is the existence or non-existence of the alleged practice, evidence that the act or omission has happened on several occasions is always admissible to shew that its happening on a particular occasion is not a mere accident or a mere isolated event.

The whole area of civil similar fact evidence was the subject of extensive and long overdue consideration by the House of Lords in *O'Brien v Chief Constable of the South Wales Police* [2005] 2 WLR 1038. In this case, the claimant alleged that two of the defendant's officers had been responsible for his malicious prosecution for murder (in 1987) and guilty of misfeasance in public office by, inter alia, putting him under improper pressure to make admissions, making up statements that had allegedly been made by him ('verballing') and pressuring a vulnerable co-defendant to implicate him. He wished to adduce evidence that the same officers had been involved in similar misconduct during major investigations and prosecutions in 1983 and 1990 (though this was denied by the defendant). This was permitted at a case management conference prior to trial, a decision that was, broadly, upheld by the Court of Appeal.

On further appeal to the House of Lords, counsel for the defendant cited a Victorian civil case, *Metropolitan Asylum District Managers v Hill* (1882) 47 LT 29, to suggest that such evidence should not be admitted if it was of limited cogency, but only if it had an 'enhanced probative value', ie if it was of special weight. This is, in some respects, the situation that criminal similar fact evidence had reached in *DPP v P* [1991] 2 AC 447, the leading case on the subject prior to abolition. However, their Lordships rejected this argument and dismissed the appeal, upholding the decision of the Court of Appeal. Lord Phillips openly suggested that it was 'not obvious' that the test in *DPP v P* was appropriate to civil cases.

Pause for reflection

Would it make sense to replace this common law doctrine with a statutory provision, as has occurred in criminal cases?

Obviously, the dynamics of most civil trials are fundamentally different to criminal ones, and this has significant consequences for similar fact evidence in such forums. In particular, civil cases are usually presided over by an experienced professional lawyer (rather than by jurors or lay magistrates) who should be well trained in the art of giving evidence its due weight, even if it is superficially prejudicial. Even more importantly, the defendant does not face the sanctions and stigma of a criminal conviction, while there is an obligation on the trial judge to be equally fair to both claimant and defendant, in a manner that does not apply to the Crown in criminal matters. Consequently, the courts have traditionally been more willing to allow such evidence in civil matters, as Lord Denning noted in *Mood Music Publishing Company v De Wolfe Ltd.* [1976] 1 All ER 763.

> ### Mood Music Publishing Company v De Wolfe Ltd. [1976] 1 All ER 763, CA
>
> **Denning MR**
>
> In civil cases the courts have followed a similar line [to criminal ones] but have not been so chary in admitting it. In civil cases the courts will admit evidence of similar facts if it is logically probative, that is, it is logically relevant in determining the matter which is in issue: provided that it is not oppressive or unfair to the other side and also that the other side has fair notice of it and is able to deal with it.

The Two-stage Test

In *Mood Music*, Lord Denning asserted that in civil cases the courts would admit evidence of similar facts if it was: '…logically relevant in determining the matter which is in issue: provided that it is not oppressive or unfair to the other side'. The notion of such a two-stage test was revisited in *O'Brien*, where the House of Lords approved the approach adopted in the same case by the Court of Appeal. First, it had to be asked whether the proposed evidence was 'admissible'. By this, the court, like Lord Denning, meant was it relevant to the facts in issue? If a positive answer to this question was reached, the second question had to be considered; namely, whether such evidence *should* be admissible. By this, their Lordships meant that a judge had to consider whether there were policy factors that militated against its reception. In *Mood Music*, Lord Denning had been particularly concerned that notice be provided to the opposing party of any intention to adduce civil similar fact evidence, so that they could deal with it effectively at trial. This is of limited significance in the modern era, where advance disclosure of evidence is normal in the civil litigation process.

However, in *O'Brien*, Lord Bingham expressly considered a number of other factors that were potentially relevant to such a decision, and which might be expected to recur on a fairly regular basis. Amongst them was the danger of distracting the tribunal's attention from the main issue in the case to something that was essentially collateral. Additionally, a judge might consider the potential of the evidence to cause 'unfair prejudice'. Unless its probative value was judged to outweigh such prejudice by a 'considerable margin' it was likely to be excluded. Finally, admitting such material might draw out trials to an excessive degree, perhaps by many weeks, driving up litigation costs in the process and taxing witnesses by requiring them to answer questions about matters that were distant in time and poorly recorded. Other factors might also be important but would occur less frequently, being more case specific.

The Test in Practice

The first part of the test is relatively straightforward. In many situations, a litigant's misconduct in the past will be relevant to the likelihood of something happening in the present. Thus, to take the facts of *Mood Music*, the plaintiff was allowed to adduce evidence in a copyright case that the defendant had previously reproduced other works that were also the subject of copyright, something that cast a different light on his defence of coincidence as to the marked similarities between his song and that of the plaintiff. As Lord Denning observed: 'Whereas it might be due to mere coincidences in one case, it is very unlikely that they would be coincidences in four cases.' It strongly suggested that the defendant was a habitual copier.

The second stage is somewhat more difficult. It seems that all of the factors identified by Lord Bingham are likely to be highly case sensitive. Thus, as Lord Phillips expressly observed in *O'Brien*, in those rare situations in which a jury is employed in a civil hearing, the risk of prejudice is likely to be far more acute than in the vast majority of cases where the matter is presided over by a professional judge, who is experienced in 'putting aside irrational prejudice'. This might be particularly important where the extrinsic evidence is of a scandalous nature; for example, the previous misconduct cited consists of allegations of what would amount to serious crimes if proved.

Additionally, the risk of excessively prolonging and distorting the litigation process will also vary enormously, and needs to be weighed up against the probative value of the evidence and any other case specific factors. However, as Lord Phillips noted, this is also a 'consideration of general application' to civil trials and not unique to the adduction of similar fact evidence. Indeed, under rr. 1(1) and 32(2) of the CPR 1998, the courts are expressly empowered to allot an appropriate amount of time to each case and to exclude evidence that 'would otherwise be admissible' in doing so. It is apparent that r. 32(2) was primarily aimed at 'case management' (whatever other uses it may now have), and was designed to prevent civil trials being drawn out indefinitely by the adduction of evidence that, though technically 'relevant', was of little weight.

For example, suppose that in *Hales v Kerr* there was only one other customer to support the plaintiff's claim against the barber, and it was alleged that he had been infected by the defendant more than 20 years earlier, when the latter individual had been a trainee hairdresser, a claim that was also vigorously disputed by the defendant. Although it might still have a minimal degree of cogency with regard to the present trial, its value would probably be greatly outweighed by the amount of time consumed, and distraction occasioned, in pursuing it, along with the inherent difficulty in establishing what precisely had occurred two decades earlier.

Cross-reference Box

Rule 32.2 has introduced an unprecedented judicial discretion to exclude relevant evidence in civil cases. This appears to include the power to exclude evidence that has been obtained in improper circumstances, albeit that the discretion is likely to be exercised only very rarely in such situations. For a more detailed discussion of this discretion to exclude evidence see p. 66 above.

Nevertheless, although important and likely to be encountered quite regularly in practice, these factors are not exhaustive. There might be others, special to an individual case, which would also be highly relevant. Thus, in *O'Brien*, the court noted that the claimant's allegations were exceptionally serious; the alleged misconduct by the defendant had had very grave consequences (he had been imprisoned for 11 years) and also went to the heart of the integrity of the criminal justice system. This might be something that would warrant exploration, even if it meant a considerable extension to the trial (almost a month, it was thought, in that case). Similarly, Lord Bingham suggested that vindication of reputation might also be among such factors, while the Court of Appeal noted that in cases like *O'Brien* the claimant was often put in special difficulties because such trials often 'boiled down' to one man's word being tendered against that of a number of police-officers; this was a problem that similar fact evidence might help overcome.

The Impact of *O'Brien*

In *Berger v Raymond Sun Ltd* [1984] 1 WLR 625, Dillon LJ observed that the test for admissibility of similar fact evidence was 'in general the same in civil and in criminal cases'. However, in the light of *O'Brien*, and taking *DPP v P* as the final position in criminal trials, this no longer seems to be the case. The test in civil cases appears to be both more liberal and yet stricter than that which went before. It is less demanding when considering the weight such evidence must attain before it can be considered for admission. As a result, some older views on the topic, such as those advanced by Neil LJ in *Thorpe v Chief Constable of Greater Manchester Police* [1989] 2 All ER 827, would now appear to be incorrect. The judge felt that even in civil cases: 'Such evidence is not admissible...merely to show that the party concerned has a disposition to commit the conduct alleged.'

However, as Brooke LJ observed, at the Court of Appeal level hearing of *O'Brien*, nowadays, if the evidence was probative of a party's normal conduct, and that was relevant to an issue in the case, the: '...similar facts do not have to be elevated to a system of conduct before they are admissible'. The liberalization seen in *O'Brien* is not surprising. It would be strange if, after the advent of the CJA 2003, it were easier to adduce evidence of previous misconduct by a defendant in a criminal trial than in a civil matter, and it would, perhaps, be mistaken to continue to define the doctrine by reference to criminal cases that are no longer operative in criminal forums. Against this, however, the modern test is, arguably, 'stricter' in civil matters by allowing judges to consider the potential impact of such evidence on other factors, such as trial length and complexity, and permitting them to exclude it on those grounds alone.

In practice, in civil cases, previous misconduct or misfeasance that is highly cogent, has nothing particularly 'scandalous' about it (especially if a jury is being employed), and can be adduced and presented to the court relatively quickly and conclusively, is likely to be admissible. Evidence that is of limited weight (albeit theoretically 'relevant'), which will take a long time to adduce, has special features likely to occasion 'prejudice' and which can only be established with a degree of uncertainty is likely to be excluded. Between these two extremes, and having regard to any other special factors, a trial judge must conduct a delicate balancing exercise when deciding where to draw the line.

In the light of *O'Brien*, it might be argued that, despite the term still being in use, there is, in reality, no longer a special doctrine of similar fact evidence in civil cases. Many of the conclusions reached in the case are explicable by other evidential principles, such as simple relevance or as a response to the Civil Procedure Rules. However, this would be an exaggeration, as there is still a residual discretion to reject such evidence simply because it might occasion reasoning or moral prejudice, rather than for any other reason; this is a hallmark of the similar fact doctrine at common law. Nevertheless, this is likely to be exercised only rarely, jury trials, perhaps, apart. In the light of Lord Bingham's observation in *O'Brien*, that similar fact evidence can be 'very important, even decisive' in civil cases other litigants may be encouraged to adduce such evidence in future. Against this, the case may also remind the courts that a general exclusionary rule means that evidence of extrinsic defendant misconduct should not be adduced informally (as often occurs in practice in civil cases).

O'Brien v Chief Constable of the South Wales Police

[2005] 2 WLR 1038, HL

Lord Bingham

That evidence of what happened on an earlier occasion may make the occurrence of what happened on the occasion in question more or less probable can scarcely be denied. If an accident investigator, an insurance assessor, a doctor or a consulting engineer were called in to ascertain the cause of a disputed recent event, any of them would, as a matter of course, inquire into the background history so far as it appeared to be relevant. And if those engaged in the recent event had in the past been involved in events of an apparently similar character, attention would be paid to those earlier events as perhaps throwing light on and helping to explain the event which is the subject of the current inquiry. To regard evidence of such earlier events as potentially probative is a process of thought which an entirely rational, objective and fair-minded person might, depending on the facts, follow. If such a person would, or might, attach importance to evidence such as this, it would require good reasons to deny a judicial decision-maker the opportunity to consider it. For while there is a need for some special rules to protect the integrity of judicial decision-making on matters of fact, such as the burden and standard of proof, it is on the whole undesirable that the process of judicial decision-making on issues of fact should diverge more than it need from the process followed by rational, objective and fair-minded people called upon to decide questions of fact in other contexts where reaching the right answer matters. Thus in a civil case such as this the question of admissibility turns, and turns only, on whether the evidence which it is sought to adduce, assuming it (provisionally) to be true, is in Lord Simon's sense probative. If so, the evidence is legally admissible. That is the first stage of the inquiry. The second stage of the inquiry requires the case management judge or the trial judge to make what will often be a very difficult and sometimes a finely balanced judgment: whether evidence or some of it (and if so which parts of it), which ex hypothesi is legally admissible, should be admitted. For the party seeking admission, the argument will always be that justice requires the evidence to be admitted; if it is excluded, a wrong result may be reached. In some cases, as in the present, the argument will be fortified by reference to wider considerations: the public interest in exposing official misfeasance and protecting the integrity of the criminal trial process; vindication of reputation; the public righting of public wrongs. These are important considerations to which weight must be given. But even without them, the importance of doing justice in the particular case is a factor the judge will always respect. The strength of the argument for admitting the evidence will always depend primarily on the judge's assessment of the potential significance of the evidence, assuming it to be true, in the context of the case as a whole.

While the argument against admitting evidence found to be legally admissible will necessarily depend on the particular case, some objections are likely to recur. First, it is likely to be said that admission of the evidence will distort the trial and distract the attention of the decision-maker by focusing attention on issues collateral to the issue to be decided. This is an argument which has long exercised the courts (see Metropolitan Asylum District Managers v Hill (1882) 47 LT 29, 31, per Lord O'Hagan) and it is often a potent argument, particularly where trial is by jury. Secondly, and again particularly when the trial is by jury, it will be necessary to weigh the potential probative value of the evidence against its potential for causing unfair prejudice: unless the former is judged to outweigh the latter by a considerable margin, the evidence is likely to be excluded. Thirdly, stress will be laid on the burden which admission would lay on the resisting party: the burden in time, cost and personnel resources, very considerable in a case such as this, of giving disclosure; the lengthening of the trial, with the increased cost and stress inevitably involved; the potential prejudice to witnesses called upon to recall matters long closed, or thought to be closed; the loss of documentation; the fading of recollections. It is, I think, recognition of these problems which has prompted courts in the past to resist the admission of such evidence, sometimes (as, perhaps, in R v Boardman [1975] AC 421) propounding somewhat unprincipled tests for its admission. But the present case vividly illustrates how real these burdens may be. In deciding whether evidence in a given case should be admitted the judge's overriding purpose will be to promote the ends of justice. But the judge must always bear in mind that justice requires not only that the right answer be given but also that it be achieved by a trial process which is fair to all parties.

Summary

- Previous behaviour, good and bad, can be an indicator as to present conduct.
- It can affect the way a witness's testimony is viewed, ie go to credit.
- It can be a predictor as to likely conduct in certain situations, ie go to issue via propensity.
- Excessive and undeserving significance can be placed on the significance of previous conduct; ie it can occasion 'prejudice'.
- Defendants in criminal cases without previous convictions are normally referred to as having 'good characters'.
- Defendants in criminal cases with good characters are always entitled to the 'second limb' of the *Vye* direction on propensity.
- Defendants in criminal cases with good characters who give evidence are also always entitled to a 'first limb' credibility direction.
- Occasionally, 'blemished' defendants without previous convictions who admit to offences, or those with previous convictions that are minor or distant, may be refused or granted good character directions, depending on the circumstances of the case.
- Defendant bad character in criminal cases is now almost entirely regulated by Part 11 of the Criminal Justice Act 2003, and s. 101 in particular.
- Bad character usually consists of convictions, but can extend to other areas of reprehensible conduct in an individual's life.
- Such bad character normally has to satisfy one or more of the seven gateways in s. 101(1) to be adduced.
- Whenever the prosecution (but not a co-defendant) attempts to adduce such evidence under s. 101(1) a trial judge has a discretion to refuse to admit it, whether from the Act itself or as a result of s. 78 of the Police and Criminal Evidence Act 1984, even if one of the gateways is, prima facie, satisfied.
- The uses to which such bad character can be put by the tribunal of fact, once admitted, will depend, in part, on the gateway through which it entered the trial, but also on its wider relevance to the instant case. Gateway is not decisive of its use.
- A few older statutes, regulating specific areas of bad character, have survived the introduction of the 2003 Act, though their significance will now usually be relatively minor.
- The similar fact doctrine developed at common law survives in civil cases, despite being abolished in criminal trials.
- Such evidence appears to require less probative force that was formerly the case in criminal hearings to be admitted in civil forums.
- However, the court can have regard to a wider range of policy factors than was the case in criminal trials when deciding whether to exclude such evidence.
- These include the efficient use of court time, the risk of distracting the tribunal of fact, litigation expense and the creation of prejudice.
- The case of *O'Brien* may encourage more litigants to attempt to adduce such evidence in future.

Further reading

HL Ho, 'Similar Facts in Civil Cases' (2006) Oxford Journal of Legal Studies 26(1), 131–152

J James, 'Good Character Directions and Blemished Defendants' [1996] 2 Web JCLI

Law Commission Report No 273, *Evidence of Bad Character in Criminal Proceedings* (2001, London: The Stationery Office)

R Munday, 'What Constitutes a Good Character?'[1997] Crim LR 247

R Munday, 'What Constitutes "Other Reprehensible Behaviour" under the Bad Character Provisions of the Criminal Justice Act 2003?' [2005] Crim LR 24

R Munday, 'Bad Character Rules and Riddles: "Explanatory Notes" and True Meanings of Section 103(1) of the Criminal Justice Act 2003' [2005] Crim LR 337

R Munday, 'Cut-Throat Defences and the "Propensity to be Untruthful" under Section 104 of the Criminal Justice Act 2003' [2005] Crim LR 624

M Redmayne, 'The Relevance of Bad Character' [2002] Cambridge Law Journal 684

J Spencer, *Evidence of Bad Character* (2006, Hart Publishing)

C Tapper, 'The Criminal Justice Act 2003: Evidence of Bad Character' [2004] Crim LR 533

Questions for Discussion

1. Abdul, who writes jingles for advertisements, is accused of raping Balita. It is alleged that he offered her a lift in his car on a rainy day, and then drove her to a remote wood. There, it is claimed that he sucked her toes before raping her. Abdul argues that although Balita picked him out on an ID parade she was mistaken. Shortly before the trial the prosecution receive several pieces of information. One of Abdul's former girlfriends, Charlotte, comes forward to say that she regularly had sexual intercourse with him in the same wood several years earlier and that he quite frequently sucked her toes in the process. Another woman, Delia, informs the Crown that on the day in question she was offered a lift by Abdul, but turned it down as he seemed a little 'strange'. The prosecution has also found that, several years earlier, Abdul was convicted of committing an indecent assault in a (different) wood, and has another conviction, from 20 years ago, for raping a woman in his car after she accepted a lift from him. All of these women had their hair in dreadlocks and were wearing very short skirts at the time the offences were committed, as was Balita. To compound his problems, Abdul finds that he is being sued for breach of copyright by Eleanor, who alleges that one of Abdul's recent advertisement jingles is very similar to one that she produced seven years earlier. Abdul claims that this is sheer coincidence. However, Eleanor has found out that he was successfully sued by another advertising agency, two years earlier, for a similar breach of copyright.

   (a) Will the Crown be allowed to adduce the evidence of Charlotte and Delia, as well as Abdul's previous convictions, to support their case on the rape of Balita?

   (b) Will Eleanor be able to adduce evidence from the previous action in which Abdul was successfully sued for breach of copyright to support her own action?

2. Albert, Ben, Clare and David are charged with the theft of a camera from a shop. It is alleged that they set off a fire-alarm and took the camera in the ensuing confusion. They were detained outside the store by two plain-clothes store detectives, Edward and Frank, who had allegedly witnessed them taking the item from a shelf.

For suggested approaches, please visit the Online Resource Centre

Albert has a previous conviction for shoplifting, apparently carried out after he set off a sprinkler system. Clare also has a conviction for theft from a department store, but in her case committed while she was working for the shop itself as a sales assistant. Ben has a previous conviction for criminal damage. David is of previous good character, and works voluntarily on Saturdays at a soup kitchen for tramps; the manager of the kitchen is eager to tell the court about his good work. All the defendants decide to give evidence in their defence. During the trial, Ben says that Edward and Frank are 'lying thugs' and have fabricated their evidence. Albert says that the two detectives smelt faintly of beer, treated him 'robustly', and appeared to be 'confused and disorientated', something that may have led them to make a 'mistake' as to what had occurred. Clare, while testifying, states that she is a 'thoroughly decent human being'.

Discuss any issues raised on the above facts.

3. Ahmed, Brian, Charles and Diana are accused of murdering Edwina in the course of a burglary. The prosecution case is that the four defendants burst into Edwina's flat one evening, hoping to steal items of value and, when confronted by Edwina, beat her to death. All four defendants plead not guilty and all but Diana give evidence at trial in their own defence. Ahmed has four recent convictions for theft. Brian has a conviction for attempted murder. He has also been charged and acquitted of burglary and was sacked from his previous job because he was suspected of stealing from his workmates. Charles has a conviction for indecent assault, another for rape and a third for perjury. Diana has one previous conviction for criminal damage but has also faced disciplinary action several times for fouls committed while playing hockey. At trial, Ahmed denies being involved in the crime, but admits meeting the other defendants later on the same night that the crime occurred. He says that he saw blood on Charles' hand, and noticed that all three of them looked 'nervous'. Subsequently, one of the witnesses called by Charles, to support an alibi defence that he is running, suddenly states, while giving his evidence and without any prompting, that Charles is 'the kindest, gentlest man on earth'. Additionally, while describing his movements on the evening in question, Charles gives evidence that he gave a sermon on the perils of violence at his local Church during the relevant time. While cross-examining Fred, a policeman who attended the crime scene, and who is giving evidence for the Crown, Charles' counsel also suggests to him that he is 'mistaken' in claiming that Charles made a lengthy admission to the crime, while being driven to a police-station for interview after arrest. Further, Charles' counsel suggests that the crime may actually have been committed by Edwina's married lover, Fergus, who is not in court, because Edwina was blackmailing him. Diana, who does not give evidence, says through her counsel that the investigating police-officers, including Fred, are 'pathological liars'.

Will counsel for the Crown, or any co-defendants, be allowed to cross-examine any of the accused about their previous convictions, charges or misbehaviour, or adduce evidence of those matters? If they are, what are the limitations on such cross-examination?

4. What use, if any, is a 'good character' to a defendant in a criminal trial?

5. Albert is accused of assault occasioning actual bodily harm. The alleged victim, Boris, claims that Albert attacked him in a public house, after he accidentally trod on his (Albert's) toes. His account is supported by Clare, who says that she was an eyewitness to the incident, and by David, the barman. Boris has a previous conviction for common assault, from 10 years earlier. Clare has a recent conviction for perjury. David has a 15-year-old conviction for shoplifting.

Will Albert be allowed to adduce the previous convictions of the three prosecution witnesses?

6 HEARSAY EVIDENCE

Definitions

Hearsay An out of court statement tendered at trial for the truth of its contents.

Original evidence An out of court statement tendered for some other purpose.

Multiple hearsay A hearsay statement that has passed through more than one link in a chain of communication before being tendered at trial.

Res gestae A family of preserved common law exceptions to the hearsay rule, which recognizes that some statements are inextricably bound up with the incidents to which they relate.

---

1. Introduction

As a general rule, hearsay evidence is inadmissible at common law. Indeed, this has been identified as one of the most characteristic features of any common law system of evidence. However, like many other exclusionary rules, it only became a rigid doctrine after the middle of the eighteenth century. Prior to this period, the evidential status of hearsay was uncertain, especially when it was tendered for the Crown. In some cases, judges were reluctant to receive it at all. For example, as early as the 1660s, while presiding over the trial of the notorious bigamist Mary Carleton at the Old Bailey, Judge Howel declared to a prosecution witness: 'Hearsays must condemn no man: what do you know of your own knowledge?'[1]

Despite this, in many other cases, the hearsay nature of evidence merely affected its weight until well into the 1700s. In practice, witnesses at trial frequently recited what they had learnt from 'a man' or 'somebody' without challenge. Statements by people who had subsequently died were routinely accepted without any of the indicia of reliability later required in 'dying declarations'. Only in a few cases, usually involving blatant hearsay, do the sources suggest that, prior to the early 1700s, judges showed major concern about its very admissibility.[2] By the early 1800s, however, the situation had been transformed, the rule reaching almost ridiculous degrees of technicality and rigidity in *Wright v Doe d Tatham* (1837) 7 A & E 313 (see below).

---

[1] F Kirkman, *The Case of Madam Mary Carleton* (1663, printed for Sam Speed) at 84.
[2] T Gallanis, 'The Rise of Modern Evidence Law' (1999) 84 Iowa L Rev 499–560, at 503.

Nevertheless, even in the 1800s, in both criminal and civil matters, the hearsay rule was significantly limited by a number of long-standing common law exceptions, such as the doctrine of *res gestae,* several of which have been expressly preserved by s. 118 of the Criminal Justice Act 2003 (CJA 2003) and s. 7 of the Civil Evidence Act 1995 (CEA 1995). Even so, the effects of subsequent statutory reform have been much more significant than these judicially created exceptions.

In civil cases, the advent of the 1995 Act abolished the rule altogether as one of exclusion, though it retains some significance with regard to weight and notice requirements. In criminal matters, the hearsay rule was eroded by a series of major, and progressively wider, statutory exceptions in the years after 1965. Exceptions to the hearsay rule in criminal cases are now largely contained in s. 114 of the CJA 2003, as interpreted in ss. 115, 116, 117 and 118 (amongst others) of the same statute. These include a novel judicial 'inclusionary' discretion for admitting hearsay evidence that is otherwise inadmissible, set out in s. 114(1)(d).

Despite such reforms, the rule still exists as one of general exclusion in criminal matters, where one of these exceptions does not apply. As a result, in *Maher v DPP* [2006] WL 1546690, the Court of Appeal expressly noted that, although the purpose behind the new provisions contained in the 2003 Act was 'undeniably to relax the previously strict rules against the admission of hearsay', it is still important to ensure that any route of admissibility for hearsay be correctly identified before such evidence can be adduced. However, it is, of course, only necessary to find such an exception to the common law rule (or to persuade the judge in a criminal trial to exercise his inclusionary discretion to admit the evidence) if a statement is first defined as hearsay, and this will be the subject of initial consideration.

2. Definition of Hearsay

Over the years, hearsay evidence has been given many definitions by Parliament and the courts. A useful starting point is that found in s. 1 of the CEA 1995, which, although it applies to hearsay in civil hearings, is based on common law cases that also formed the basis of hearsay definitions in criminal matters. It declares that hearsay evidence consists of: '…any statement made otherwise than by a person while giving oral evidence in the proceedings, which is tendered as evidence of the matters stated'. In criminal cases, there is no express statutory definition of the rule, though there is an oblique one in s. 114(1) of the CJA 2003, which sets out exceptions to the general rule with the preface that: 'In criminal proceedings a statement not made in oral evidence in the proceedings is admissible as evidence of any matter stated….'

At an academic level, Sir Rupert Cross also attempted to define the hearsay rule, noting that, under it, an: '…assertion other than one made by a person while giving oral evidence in the proceedings is inadmissible as evidence of any fact stated'. Sir Rupert's definition was later expressly approved by the House of Lords in *R v Sharp* [1988] 1 WLR 7.

As can readily be seen from this selection of definitions, the term has two parts or tests, *both* of which must be satisfied before evidence is defined as hearsay and, as such, caught by the exclusionary rule at common law. These will be considered separately. However, it can be noted immediately that it makes no difference to the status of hearsay evidence if the out of court statement was made on oath, nor even that the maker of the original statement is present to give evidence at trial. A sworn out of court statement made by a witness who testifies is still hearsay if tendered for its testimonial effect.

An Out of Court Statement

The first test is not difficult. The statement must be one made 'out of court.' Thus, anything witness A tells the court that witness B said, or anything that is contained in a document prepared out of court which contains what witness A said, will be caught by this part of the definition. Examples of written hearsay include *Patel v Comptroller of Customs* [1966] AC 356, in which the defendant was charged with making a false entry in a Customs form about the provenance of bags of coriander seed, by alleging, untruthfully, that they came from India. Some of the bags were marked as 'Produce of Morocco'; the prosecution sought to adduce the labels on the bags to show that their contents did not come from India but instead were from North Africa. It was held that this was written hearsay and so, prima facie, inadmissible; the label was being adduced for the truth of its contents (the court also held that the list of common law exceptions to the hearsay rule could not be extended judicially to include such things as labels or markings).

Patel v Comptroller of Customs [1966] AC 356, PC

Lord Hodson

The next question was whether there was any evidence upon which the appellant could be convicted of making a false declaration as charged. The only entry as to which the allegation of falsity is made is the word 'India' in the column headed 'country of origin', which is part of the import entry form signed by the appellant. The only evidence purporting to show that this entry was false is the legend 'produce of Morocco' written upon the bags. Their Lordships are asked by the respondent to say that the inference can be drawn that the goods contained in the bags were produced in Morocco. This they are unable to do. From an evidentiary point of view the words are hearsay and cannot assist the prosecution.

Indeed, the rule also covers statements made by gesture. An example of this occurred in the Privy Council case of *Chandrasekera v R* [1937] AC 220. In this case, the victim of an attack had been stabbed in the throat, so that she could not speak. However, before she died from her wound, she made signs that possibly indicated the identity of her attacker and, more pertinently, when given a name, nodded her head in assent. This was held to be hearsay (albeit admissible under a statutory exception contained in the Ceylon Evidence Ordinance of 1895).

Tendered for its Testimonial Effect

The problem is that, by itself, being made 'out of court' is not enough to make a statement hearsay. To achieve this status, it must also satisfy the second test; that of being tendered for its 'testimonial' effect, ie for the truth of its contents. Thus, in *Myers v DPP* [1965] AC 1001, the records of a motor manufacturer as to engine stampings, compiled by persons with no personal knowledge of the events that they recorded, prepared from cards drawn up by factory workers who did have such knowledge, and subsequently reduced to microfilm, were held to be hearsay, despite their freely acknowledged reliability. This was precisely because they were being adduced to establish the truth of their contents.

Myers v DPP [1965] AC 1001, HL

Lord Reid

At the trial counsel for the prosecution sought to support the existing practice of admitting such records, if produced by the persons in charge of them, by arguing that they were not adduced to prove the truth of the recorded particulars but only to prove that they were records kept in the normal course of business. Counsel for the accused then asked the very pertinent question—if they were not intended to prove the truth of the entries what were they intended to prove? I ask what the jury would infer from them: obviously that they were probably true records. If they were not capable of supporting an inference that they were probably true records, then I do not see what probative value they could have, and their admission was bound to mislead the jury.

However, if a reported statement is being tendered for any other reason, it is quite admissible for that purpose, although, as with all cases of 'limited admissibility', magistrates, judges and jurors will have to (attempt to) exclude it from their minds for any other evidential use. In these situations, it is referred to by lawyers, slightly unhelpfully, as 'original evidence'. It is this second aspect of the test that poses the greatest difficulties for students of the subject.

The problem of distinguishing between hearsay and original evidence emerged almost as soon as the rule against hearsay evidence started to be applied, on a fairly regular basis, in the early eighteenth century. Thus, in 1702, at the trial of the fraudulent 'witch-monger', Richard Hathaway, a lengthy debate took place between Sergeant Jenner (representing the defendant) and Lord Holt (the trial judge) over whether the emerging rule covered reported conversations that were adduced for a purpose other than their testimonial effect. By 1717, William Nelson accepted that in treason cases, at least, such statements could be admitted to 'shew the temper of the prisoner' rather than to establish the truth of their contents.[3]

Because this part of the two-fold test is much harder to grasp, there has, in the past, sometimes been a tendency, especially in the summary courts, for the first limb alone to be considered. Many lawyers have embarrassing memories, from early on in practice, of successfully objecting to a reported statement that, in retrospect, was quite clearly 'original' evidence. However, this tendency is exacerbated because it can, sometimes, be very difficult to ascertain whether a statement is being tendered for its testimonial effect or for some other purpose; the dividing line can be extremely narrow.

Additionally, there have been occasions in the past, a time when legitimate exceptions to the hearsay rule were much more limited than they are today, when describing a statement as 'original' evidence was, in reality, probably an illicit judicial evasion, rather than a legitimate avoidance, of the hearsay rule, used to justify admission. Now that hearsay can be admitted so much more freely, as a result of the Criminal Justice Act 2003, there will be less temptation to do this, and much of the heat has gone out of the hearsay/original evidence debate. Nevertheless, it still warrants detailed consideration.

Hearsay or Original Evidence?

A very simple illustration of the distinction between hearsay and original evidence might be seen in a case in which it is alleged, and disputed, that an individual is unable to speak.

---

[3] State Trials Vol X at 654, W Nelson *The Law of Evidence* (1717, R Gosling) at 232.

While a reported statement that he was heard to shout 'Smith has attacked me' could not be admitted as evidence that Smith had done any such thing, it might be admitted to show that the individual could speak clearly. Similarly, in a slander case, the claimant necessarily has to repeat the alleged slander as part of his case, albeit that it is being tendered precisely so that its truth can be denied, rather than as evidence of the truth of its contents: 'He announced to everyone in the club that I was a thief.' Although the making of the statement must be proved in court, the very purpose for bringing proceedings is because the claimant denies that it is true.

Unfortunately, real examples can become rather more complicated than these facile illustrations. These issues were explored by the Privy Council in the leading case on the hearsay/original evidence distinction, *Subramaniam v Public Prosecutor* [1956] 1 WLR 965. Subramaniam was accused of, and admitted, carrying prohibited ammunition in Malaya during the emergency there in the 1950s. His defence was duress. At his trial he was not allowed by the judge to repeat threats allegedly made to him by terrorists, with a view to establishing such a defence. However, as the Privy Council accepted, for the purpose of his defence, the truth of these statements, if made, was irrelevant. Even if the 'threats' had been nothing more than a practical joke by the terrorists, it was the making of them, and the fact that they operated on Subramaniam's mind, that was relevant.

Subramaniam v Public Prosecutor [1956] 1 WLR 965, PC

Mr L M D De Silva

Evidence of a statement made to a witness by a person who is not himself called as a witness may or may not be hearsay. It is hearsay and inadmissible when the object of the evidence is to establish the truth of what is contained in the statement. It is not hearsay, and is admissible when it is proposed to establish by the evidence, not the truth of the statement, but the fact that it was made. The fact that the statement was made, quite apart from its truth, is frequently relevant in considering the mental state and conduct thereafter of the witness or of some other person in whose presence the statement was made.

A number of other examples can be considered. Thus, in *R v Chapman* [1969] 2 QB 436, s. 2(2) of the Road Safety Act 1967 provided that a person could not be required to take a breath-test at a hospital unless the medical practitioner in charge of his case had been informed, and did not object to the provision of a specimen. In this case, the doctor did not object. It was held that evidence could be given that he had not done so, without violating the hearsay rule. This was because the absence of an objection was a procedural requirement to the taking of the breath-test. In like manner, advice from a solicitor to an arrested defendant will often be original evidence, and can thus be repeated by the defendant when seeking to argue that his failure to answer questions in an interview should not attract an adverse inference under s. 34 of the Criminal Justice and Public Order Act 1994: *R v Davis (Desmond)* [1998] Crim LR 659.

More controversially, in several cases, written statements were treated not as hearsay but as original and circumstantial evidence, and thus deemed to be admissible. These cases usually involved names on pieces of paper or tickets that were admitted to show the likely proximity of someone by the same name (normally the defendant) to the writing: *R v Lydon* [1986] 85 Cr App R 221.

In the Privy Council case of *Ratten v R* [1972] AC 378, the words, 'get me the police please,' spoken by a woman to a telephone operator, were not considered to be hearsay, because their purpose was to show, regardless of the words used, that a telephone call had been made and that the woman who made it was frightened. As Lord Wilberforce observed: 'Words spoken are facts just as much as any other action by a human being.' Similarly, in *Mawaz Khan v R* [1967] 1 AC 454, identical alibi statements that were demonstrably false were held not to be hearsay for the purpose of showing that there had been an attempt to fabricate a joint story. In like manner, in *AG v Good* (1825) M'Cle & Y 286, a wife's clearly false statement that her husband was away from home was not hearsay for the purpose of establishing that his intention was to defraud his creditors.

The case of *Woodhouse v Hall* [1981] 72 Cr App R 39 was even more difficult, and less obvious, than the above examples. Magistrates, hearing a case in which the defendant was charged with managing a brothel, refused to allow undercover officers to give evidence that they had been offered masturbation at a massage parlour. This was reversed on appeal to the Divisional court. According to Donaldson LJ, the magistrates had been misled by their interpretation of *Subramaniam* into thinking that they had to be satisfied as to the truth of what the ladies involved had said. However, it was the making of the statements, not their truth, that was relevant to the instant case.

Nevertheless, arguably, the quality of the words only becomes irrelevant if a very narrow interpretation is placed on the offence in this case, ie that brothels are places where sexual services are offered for money. If, at a dinner party, a guest jokingly announced that s/he would have sex with another diner for £100, would this make the house in which the offer was made a brothel? The intention behind the words is, perhaps, important; ie, to some extent, the reported statements were being tendered for the truth of their contents, a genuine intention to provide sexual services for money.

Woodhouse v Hall [1981] 72 Cr App R 39, DC

Donaldson LJ

I suspect that the justices were misled by Subramaniam's case (supra) and thought that this was a hearsay case, because they may have thought that they had to be satisfied as to the truth of what the ladies said or were alleged to have said in the sense they had to satisfy themselves that the words were not a joke but were meant seriously and something of that sort. But this is not a matter of truth or falsity. It is a matter of what was really said—the quality of the words, the message being transmitted. That arises in every case where the words themselves are a relevant fact. The quality of the words has to be assessed, but that is quite different from the situation where the words are evidence of some other matter. Then their truth and accuracy has to be assessed and they are hearsay. There is no question here of the hearsay rule arising at all. The relevant issue was did these ladies make these offers? The offers were oral and the police officers were entitled to give evidence of them. The evidence, in my judgment, was wrongly excluded and should have been admitted.

Another extremely complicated situation, in which the same fine distinction was drawn, can be found in *R v Gilfoyle* [1996] 1 Cr App R 306. In this case, the appellant had allegedly murdered his wife while making it appear as if she had killed herself. He had, apparently, earlier asked his wife to write out suicide notes, stating that she was going to kill herself; he did this by telling her that he needed these as props for a course on suicide counselling that he was attending at the hospital at which he worked. His wife had done this, but, not surprisingly, being worried by it, had mentioned this strange request to three of her friends. After she was found hanging in their home, along with a suicide note in what was clearly her own handwriting, the question arose as to whether the conversations with these friends could be admitted into evidence. At first sight this could only be to establish the truth of the reported contents of the conversation, namely, that the wife had written the notes at her husband's request, and they were excluded at trial as hearsay (they would now be admissible under s. 116(2)(a) of the CJA 2003). Despite this, the defendant was convicted.

On appeal, the Court of Appeal took the opportunity to consider the correctness of the trial judge's decision on the hearsay point. The court came to the conclusion that, at least for one purpose, the statement *was* admissible as original evidence. Relying on the decision in *Subramaniam,* it concluded that such evidence is not hearsay when the fact that the statement was made (quite apart from its truth), is relevant in considering the mental state of its maker, provided that the mental state of that person is directly in issue at the trial, as was clearly the case in *Gilfoyle*. Consequently, the court decided that the statements made by the deceased wife were not hearsay when tendered as to whether she was in a frame of mind to kill herself, as they indicated that the notes were not written in a state of suicidal depression or anxiety (though they would be hearsay if tendered to show that she wrote the letters at her husband's behest). Perhaps significantly, the court also found it prudent to identify a common law exception to the rule that would justify its admission, whether it was hearsay or not. Nevertheless, *Gilfoyle* is probably close to the 'borderline' in the original evidence/hearsay divide.

R v Gilfoyle [1996] 1 Cr App R 306, CA

Beldam LJ

The statements attributed to Paula by the three witnesses can be separated as follows: 1. That she had been asked to write the suicide note. 2. That this had worried or frightened her. 3. That Eddie had asked her to write the note. 4. That he had told her what to write. 5. That after she had written the notes, he had taken her into the garage to show her how to put up the rope. Paula's state of mind was one of the principal issues in the case. The defence contended that the notes evidenced a suicidal frame of mind. It was our preliminary view that the fact that the first three of these five statements were made was relevant to Paula's state of mind when she wrote the notes and thus admissible to refute the inference which might otherwise be drawn from them. Our view was founded on the decision of the Privy Council in Subramaniam v. Public Prosecutor [1956] 1 W.L.R. 965 (P.C.) . . . Strictly speaking, therefore, proof that the statements were made falls outside the category of hearsay evidence.

First Hand and 'Multiple' Hearsay

Hearsay evidence can be first hand or 'multiple' hearsay. The latter category encompasses second/third/fourth hand statements and more extreme illustrations. The distinction depends on whether the witness in court received the hearsay evidence directly from an eye witness, or whether it has passed through two or more intermediaries. Obviously, all other matters being equal, multiple hearsay is likely to be less reliable than first hand hearsay and, as a result, the CJA 2003 makes a distinction between the two (see below).

First Hand Hearsay

Second-Hand/Multiple Hearsay

 Pause for reflection

Why do you think that multiple hearsay is less likely to be reliable than first hand hearsay?

3. Implied Assertions and the Hearsay Rule

The extent of the hearsay rule raised particular difficulties with regard to so-called *implied* assertions, an area of the law that has now been transformed by the CJA 2003. In this (legal) context, it is important to note that, unlike common parlance, 'implied' does not mean a statement that, although not expressly communicated, is *meant* to be inferred from what is said (as in 'nudge, nudge, wink, wink'). It refers to a statement that, although not intended to assert a fact, appears to rest on an assumption that the maker of the statement believes to be true, and which is subsequently advanced at trial to suggest the existence of that assumption.

The notion that the hearsay rule extended to such evidence was first canvassed in *Wright v Doe d Tatham* (1837) 7 A & E, 313. This involved the will of John Marsden, a Lancashire gentleman of somewhat defective intellect, who was cared for by his aunt. A servant, George Wright, became the aunt's lover and steward of Marsden's estate, continuing in office after the aunt's death. When the unmarried Marsden also died, his will, which left the estate to the steward, was contested by the heir on intestacy, Admiral Tatham, who asked for it to be set aside because of the alleged mental incompetence of his cousin. As a result, Marsden's mental state went to the heart of the case.[4]

At trial, Wright attempted to prove Marsden's competency by adducing several fairly complicated letters, written to the testator, the detail and complexity of which suggested that the correspondents assumed the sanity of the recipient. Wright's case was that no one would have written in such terms to Marsden unless he was of sound mind, though the letters' authors had no intention of conveying such an impression. This then raised the issue as to whether an out of court statement, tendered to prove the truth of an implied assertion contained within it, was hearsay. It was held, inter alia (in what was not the clearest of judgments), that the rule did apply to implied assertions of fact made in oral or written statements, just as it did to express ones, and thus the letters were inadmissible. (Baron Parke's more extreme examples, suggesting that implied assertions extended to conduct as well, subsequently found little favour.)

Perhaps because the decision to exclude the letters was, in part, also influenced by the law on opinion evidence, the issue continued to be the subject of legal debate. However, in the modern era, case law firmly supported the notion that implied assertions were caught by the hearsay rule, despite frequent dissenting opinions by individual judges. Thus, the Court of Appeal gave support to the conclusions reached in *Wright v Doe d Tatham* in *R v Harry* [1987] 86 Cr App R 105. A few years later, a majority of the House of Lords also supported Parke's approach, in *R v Kearley* [1992] 2 WLR 656. In this case, the issue was whether, on a charge of possessing drugs with intent to supply, a prosecutor could rely on evidence by the police that, while at the home of the defendant, they had received telephone and personal calls from people (not called as witnesses) asking about drugs that they thought the defendant had for sale. Their Lordships concluded, by a bare majority, that even had these calls been relevant (something they doubted), they would have been hearsay, as the only reason that the prosecution could have to adduce such statements would be to rely on the implied assertion contained within the calls, namely that Kearley was a drug dealer. This was a controversial decision. As the dissenting minority argued, a strong case could be made for viewing such material as circumstantial evidence. Nevertheless, the decision was reiterated in the very similar case of *R v O'Connell* [2003] EWCA Crim 502.

⟶ Cross-reference Box

Generally speaking a witness's opinion is inadmissible in evidence, though there are exceptions for experts and for laymen whose 'opinion' is, in reality, simply a shorthand way of conveying facts. For more on this topic go to chapter 11 at pp. 469–525.

However, the Law Commission, in its 1997 Report, recommended introducing a statutory formulation of criminal hearsay that declared that a matter should be considered to have been 'stated' (and thus hearsay) *only* if it appeared to the court that the purpose, or one of the purposes, of the person making the statement was to cause another person to believe it. Thus, the rule would not preclude evidence of 'implied assertions' by those whose words or conduct were not intended to communicate any information at all.[5] The justification advanced for such a

---

[4] See on this generally, E Garnett, *John Marsden's Wil—The Hornby Castle Dispute, 1780-1840* (1998, Hambledon).

[5] Law Commission Report No 245, *Evidence In Criminal Proceedings: Hearsay and Related Topics*, published 19 June 1997, 'Summary of Principal Recommendations' at para. 1.5.

change was that the risk of deliberate fabrication of evidence was greatly reduced in these situations. The Commission's suggestions were enacted by s. 115(3) of the CJA 2003, which declares that: 'A matter stated is one to which this Chapter applies if (and only if) the purpose, or one of the purposes, of the person making the statement appears to the court to have been—(a) to cause another person to believe the matter, or (b) to cause another person to act or a machine to operate on the basis that the matter is as stated.'

Although there was, initially, some doubt as to whether the rule on implied assertions had been effectively abolished by s. 115(3), whatever the (undoubted) intention of the parliamentary draftsmen, this was resolved in *R v Singh* [2006] 1 WLR 1564, which made it clear that ss. 114 and 118 of the 2003 Act, taken together, had abolished the common law rule against the admissibility of hearsay and created a new rule against hearsay which did not extend to implied assertions. This means that cases like *Kearley* will be decided differently in the future, were they to recur, with such communications being treated as admissible circumstantial evidence.

R v Singh [2006] 1 WLR 1564, CA

Rose LJ

The interrelationship between sections 114 and 115 is deeply obscure. But, in our judgment, as Miss Blackwell for the prosecution contends, the answer to Mr Csoka's submission is provided by the editor of *Archbold, Criminal Pleading, Evidence & Practice* (2006), paras 11–14. Contrary to Professor Uglow's premise, the common law rule against the admissibility of hearsay is abolished by the clear express terms to that effect of section 118, to which Professor Uglow does not refer. When sections 114 and 118 are read together they, in our judgment, abolish the common law hearsay rules (save those which are expressly preserved) and create instead a new rule against hearsay which does not extend to implied assertions. What was said by the callers in R v Kearley [1992] 2 AC 228 would now be admissible as direct evidence of the fact that there was a ready market for the supply of drugs from the premises, from which could be inferred an intention by an occupier to supply drugs. The view of the majority in R v Kearley, in relation to hearsay, has been set aside by the Act. So, in the present case, the telephone entries are not a matter stated within section 115. They are implied assertions which are admissible because they are no longer hearsay. Furthermore they are also admissible under section 118(1) 7, as statements by an admitted co-conspirator against another party to the enterprise: see also *Cross & Tapper on Evidence,* 10th ed (2004), p 612 note 295, approved in R v Jones (Brian) [1997] 2 Cr App R 119, 129. A third possible route to admissibility is provided by section 114(2)(d). It follows that the judge was right to admit this evidence against the defendant and ground 2 fails.

As a result of this reform, it can be argued that a third 'limb' has been added to the test for hearsay in criminal matters. Namely, hearsay is an out of court statement, *intended to cause another person to believe the matter stated,* tendered for the truth of its contents. Inevitably, some novel problems are raised by the new provision. For example, the courts now have to investigate the dividing line between the 'purpose' of the person making a statement being to induce the recipient to believe something and it merely being an underlying assumption. This may not always be entirely clear. Suppose, for example, one of Marsden's correspondents had included in his letter a sentence declaring, 'you're a sane man Jack, so I know what your view on this sort of thing would be'? Additionally, the possibility that a party to a criminal investigation might fabricate such material, with a view to having it admitted at trial, cannot be entirely excluded. Nevertheless, this possibility applies to most evidence, without it resulting in special protection.

The Meaning of 'Statement' in Section 115

Despite reform, there are still difficulties with regard to the precise meaning of s. 115. In *R v Isichei (Marvin)* [2006] EWCA Crim 1815, the defendant in a robbery case was called Marvin. The alleged victims of his crime had earlier been with a man, who had telephoned another individual, whom he mentioned was also called Marvin. One of the issues at trial was whether this comment could be adduced to support the defendant's identification. (As its maker could not be identified, s. 116 of the 2003 Act was of no assistance to the prosecution; see below.) However, was the comment hearsay at all? If it was not, it did not, of course, need an exception to the general rule. The first instance judge concluded that it probably was not. The matter was governed by the definition of 'statement' set out in s. 115. The trial judge held that the word 'Marvin' was not a statement amounting to hearsay because it had not been said for the purpose of making anyone believe anything. Even so, he prudently added that if he was wrong about that he would still have held it to be admissible under the discretion contained in s. 114(1)(d) of the 2003 Act, as being in the interests of justice. On appeal, however, the trial judge's conclusion as to whether the comment constituted a statement, and so was hearsay, was doubted, though his decision on the exercise of the discretion was upheld.

By contrast, consider *R v K N* [2006] EWCA Crim 3309, in which a man was accused of having sexual intercourse with his 13-year-old niece. An entry in the girl's diary recording such an occurrence that had been exhibited to the jury, but which was written purely for personal use, rather than to convey information to others, was not held to be a statement for that very reason. The Court of Appeal concluded that, as a result, the entry was not hearsay for the purpose of the definition in s. 115. The court also concluded that this meant that the entry was admissible, as the statutory restrictions on the adduction of hearsay were not applicable, and thus it was simply evidence from which it could be inferred that intercourse had occurred, in exactly the same way that an inference might be drawn from seeing the man and his niece in a passionate kiss or sharing a hotel room. Consequently, the court concluded that: '...if the diary was intended to be read by anyone else, it fell within section 115 and was admissible under section 119 [as a previous inconsistent statement]. If it was not, it was outside the hearsay rule and was admissible providing it was relevant.'

R v Isichei (Marvin) [2006] EWCA Crim 1815, CA

Auld LJ

In our view, the judge may have been wrong in concluding that it was not a statement within section 115(3) and so governed by the Act. That would require a semantically correct and somewhat highly artificial application of the provision in this context in an analysis to what was essentially an inconsequential part of the story so far as the speaker on the telephone at the time was concerned. It is common sense that it is a possible inference that he spoke to Marvin, or someone whom he knew who was at the club, leading, as a result of the conversation, for them all to go there. But even if the man on the telephone had not, in the words of section 115(3)(a), had the purpose of causing the others in the cab to know that he was talking to Marvin, the evidence, if that were the case, would be, if anything, more probative than otherwise. Why should he care, if the story was true, what the others believed as to the truth of the person to whom he was talking or as to what was being said. Their only interest at the time was whether as a result of the telephone call they would be able to find another club to go to which was open. Whatever the position, it seems to us that the evidence about that was clearly admissible in the interests of justice under section 114(1)(d) as part of the story of a common sense series of events, the one leading from the other.

4. Justifications for the Hearsay Rule

Having defined hearsay evidence, it is worth considering why common law should have been so nervous about admitting it at trial. Traditionally, justifications for the general exclusionary rule against hearsay have tended to revolve around a number of themes. Some of these were identified by Byles J as far back as *R v Jenkins* (1869) LR 1 CCR 187, when he suggested that the rationale for the rule, at least in criminal cases, was that such statements were not made on oath (though this is not invariably the case, and their status does not alter where they have been sworn) or in the presence of the defendant, and were not made by witnesses who could be cross-examined on the truth and reliability of the statements, or who could be prosecuted for perjury.

Other traditional anxieties included a concern about the risk of distortion through repetition (the 'Chinese whispers' effect), deliberate concoction for forensic use, and the loss of nuance, subtlety and witness demeanour inherent in admitting such statements. Some observers have also expressed a fear that adducing hearsay could cause excessive delay in the trial and litigation process by allowing the adduction of evidence of marginal value, and voiced concern that people are sometimes willing to make statements behind someone's back they would not make to their face. Certainly, there is a widespread emotional attachment to the notion of making unpleasant claims in person.[6] Additionally, there is a long-standing anxiety that untested hearsay evidence, if admitted, might be treated as having a probative force which it does not properly deserve, especially by laymen. In Lord Devlin's words (taken from his Fifth Hamlyn Lecture of 1956), the: '…danger of hearsay is that the juryman, unused to sifting evidence, might treat it as first hand'.

 Pause for reflection

Which of these concerns do you find the most plausible?

Not all of these concerns explain the initial emergence of the hearsay rule. According to *Cross and Tapper on Evidence*, legal historians are divided between those who ascribe its development to distrust of the capacity of jurors to evaluate hearsay, and those who largely attribute it to the unfairness of depriving a party of the opportunity to cross-examine the witness.[7]

Whichever was initially most important, both of these two major arguments were periodically reiterated during the twentieth century by senior members of the judiciary. Thus, in

---

[6] R Friedman, 'Thoughts from Across the Water on Hearsay and Confrontation' [1998] Crim LR 697–709, at 707.

[7] 8th edn, 1995, at 565.

R v Blastland [1986] AC 41, Lord Bridge claimed that: 'The rationale of excluding [hearsay] as inadmissible, rooted as it is in the system of trial by jury, is a recognition of the great difficulty, even more acute for a juror than for a trained judicial mind, of assessing what, if any, weight can properly be given to a statement by a person whom the jury have not seen or heard and which has not been subject to any test of reliability in cross-examination.' Similarly, in *Teper v R* [1952] AC 480, Lord Normand observed that: 'The truthfulness and accuracy of the person whose words are spoken by another witness cannot be tested by cross-examination and the light which his demeanour would throw on his testimony is lost.'

In recent decades, some of these concerns have been recognized as valid, while others are now seen as greatly exaggerated. Thus, the Law Commission's report, *Evidence in Criminal Proceedings: Hearsay and Related Topics* (Law Com Report No 245 of 1997) concluded that oral evidence is preferable to hearsay primarily because it can be challenged in cross-examination, but was sceptical about many other justifications. Indeed, the Commission suggested (at para. 3.37 of its report) that this was the: '... main, if not the sole, reason why hearsay is inferior to non-hearsay'. However, it also felt that multiple (as opposed to first hand) hearsay raised legitimate anxieties about the risk of deliberately manufactured evidence and of errors being introduced by repetition. Additionally, the Commission was concerned that admitting hearsay evidence of very low probative value would excessively draw out cases and lead to a substantial waste of court time. By contrast, the Commission was much less impressed by arguments that hearsay evidence was fundamentally defective because it deprived the tribunal of fact of an opportunity to examine the demeanour of witnesses.

Evidence in Criminal Proceedings: Hearsay and Related Topics (Law Com Report No 245 of 1997)

SUMMARY OF PRINCIPAL RECOMMENDATIONS

1.29 Our basic philosophy is that oral evidence is preferable to hearsay, principally because in the former case the witness can be cross-examined. First hand hearsay is, in turn, preferable to multiple hearsay, because of the risk of manufacture and the errors that may be introduced by repetition. We are satisfied that the discretion provisions in the Criminal Justice Act 1988 have not worked satisfactorily: for example, many judges are consistently refusing to exercise their discretion to admit evidence under that Act. Uncertainty as to the admissibility of evidence means that the prosecution cannot confidently assess the prospects of a conviction in deciding whether to prosecute, and if so on what charges; and those acting for the defendant cannot confidently advise on the plea or on the conduct of the defence. Our concerns on this issue were confirmed on consultation.

1.30 We therefore recommend that there should continue to be an exclusionary hearsay rule, to which there would be specified exceptions, plus a discretion to admit hearsay evidence which would otherwise be inadmissible where this is in the interests of justice. (48)

1.31 Hearsay adduced by the prosecution would continue to be subject to the general power to exclude prosecution evidence, either at common law or under section 78 of the Police and Criminal Evidence Act 1984 ('PCEA'). (49) Evidence of no probative value would, as now, be excluded as irrelevant; but we have also been concerned about the possibility of a party seeking to adduce hearsay of very low probative value which would lead to a substantial waste of court time. (50) We believe that the court should have power to refuse to admit such evidence where it is satisfied that the probative value of the evidence is substantially outweighed by the danger that it would result in undue waste of time if admitted.

In 2001, the issue was further considered by Sir Robin Auld, as part of his *Review of the Criminal Courts of England and Wales*. This was even more radical in its proposals. Sir Robin would have liked the hearsay provenance of evidence to be limited to a factor affecting weight (as occurs in civil cases), rather than admissibility. Nevertheless, although the law on hearsay has been significantly liberalized, this course has not been followed in the 2003 Act, perhaps because of what is at stake in criminal proceedings. There is still a feeling, in many quarters, that in some situations at least, the rule against hearsay can operate to prevent the admissibility of evidence of doubtful reliability that might otherwise lead to an unjust conviction, especially in a jury trial. As a result, the evidence of absent witnesses *must* still satisfy one of the requirements set out in s. 114 of the 2003 Act to be allowed into evidence in a criminal trial.

Sir Robin Auld, Review of the Criminal Courts of England and Wales, 2001, paras 79 and 100

Para 79: A common justification for our system of orality of evidence, including the rule against hearsay, is that seeing the demeanour and hearing the evidence of a witness in the witness box is the best means of getting at the truth. But there is much judicial, academic and psychological scepticism about the weight that even seasoned observers of witnesses should attach to the impressions they form of them in the witness box. It may be a factor, depending on the witness and what he has to say and on the experience and good judgment of the fact finder. But it is only one factor and I respectfully agree with the Law Commission that it is not of such significance, on its own, as to justify the exclusion of hearsay. I would go further and join Lord Bingham and a growing band of other distinguished jurists who, on the whole, doubt the demeanour of a witness as a reliable pointer to his honesty.

Para 100: A number of contributors to the Review have suggested that those recommendations do not go far enough in their relaxation of the rule. And there is much distinguished academic support, past and present, for substituting for the present, exclusionary rule subject to exceptions, an inclusionary approach, leaving the fact finders to assess its weight—also the approach, as I have indicated, of the Runciman Royal Commission. Professor John Spencer, as a consultant to the Law Commission in preparing its consultation paper and to this Review, is among them. Praying in aid the views of such eminent writers in the common law world as Jeremy Bentham, JB Thayer, CT McCormick and Glanville Williams, he has argued that there should be a generally inclusionary system subject to a 'best available evidence' principle. That is, each side would be obliged to produce the original source of the information if the source is still available. He also suggested as part of that solution, the establishment of some regular means of deposing witnesses who, for one reason or another, it is thought might not be available to give evidence at trial. Professor John Jackson and the Standing Advisory Committee on Human Rights are of a similar view, arguing that the Law Commission 'should . . . have approached the subject on the basis that relevant hearsay should be admissible except where there is good reason for exclusion'.

Furthermore, although the Law Commission was fairly dismissive of some of the arguments traditionally advanced against hearsay evidence, they still feature in judicial warnings to juries about the inherent weaknesses and limitations of such evidence (where it has been admitted under an exception to the general rule). Thus, the Privy Council noted in the case of *Grant v Jamaica* [2006] Crim LR 836, that a jury should always be reminded that an admitted hearsay statement was not (normally) made on oath, had not been tested by cross-examination and did not afford them an opportunity to assess in person its maker. Similar warnings are mandatory in domestic courts where hearsay evidence is admitted, although it is the overall tenor of the summing up as to the limitations of such evidence, rather than any precise formula, that is important: *R v Denton* [2001] Crim LR 225.

In *R v McCoy* [2000] 6 Archbold News 2, Laws LJ suggested that where the evidence of a crucial witness is read a trial judge must, at the least: '...explain that it means that they may feel quite unable to attach anything like as much weight to the evidence in the statement, as they might were it tested in cross-examination; and where appropriate it would be necessary, certainly desirable, for the judge also to indicate to the jury by way of illustration the sort of matters that might well be put in cross-examination in the particular case'. However, subsequently, in *R v Hardwick* (2001) 3 Archbold News 2, the Court of Appeal concluded that *McCoy* should not be read as imposing any hard and fast rules. In practice, trial judges often follow the appropriate JSB specimen direction for such evidence (still to be updated to encompass the 2003 Criminal Justice Act).

JSB Specimen Direction 35, 'Hearsay' and/or other Evidence admitted under the Criminal Justice Act 1988

As you know, the general rule in the courts is that unless evidence is agreed it has to be given orally from the witness box. Then you have the opportunity to see the witness for yourselves and judge his evidence accordingly. However, there are certain circumstances where a witness is unavailable and the statement of that witness is read out. That has happened here in the case of the witness X. That statement is evidence in the case which you can consider, but as he did not come to court, his evidence has certain limitations which I must draw to your attention:

1. When someone's statement is read out you do not have the opportunity of seeing him/her in the witness box, and sometimes when you do see a witness you get a much clearer idea of whether that evidence is honest and accurate.

2. His evidence has not been tested under cross-examination, and therefore you have not had the opportunity of seeing how the evidence survived this form of challenge. You must therefore consider the evidence of X in the light of these limitations. You should only act upon it if, having taken these matters into account, you are nevertheless sure that it is reliable.

It should be noted that, despite Sir Robin Auld's observation about academic criticism of the hearsay rule, there has also been a considerable body of academic support for viewing hearsay as markedly inferior to oral evidence, as the following two extracts suggest.

Terence Anderson et al, *Analysis of Evidence* (2nd edn, 2005, Cambridge University Press) 306

The Hearsay problem.

A rule preferring live testimony rather than hearsay finds strong support in the logical principles of proof. In any case in which a statement made by a declarant, otherwise than while testifying, is offered to prove the truth of the matter asserted, the number of steps in the inferential chain increases and the sources of possible error multiply. Consider, for example, the testimony of William in a case in which Sam is accused of murdering John: 'I heard Donald say, "I saw Sam shoot John".' In determining whether Donald said, 'I saw Sam shoot John', the decision-maker must consider William's credibility and the factors that might affect his veracity, his objectivity, and his observational sensitivity. In doing so, they must answer four questions creating at least four possible sources of error. Did William believe he had heard Sam's statement at the time at which William testified? Did William have any expectations that might have caused him to misinterpret Donald's statement? (For example, Donald may have already suspected that it was Sam who murdered John and, for that reason, he may have thought he heard 'Sam' when in fact Donald actually said, 'I saw Pam shoot John'.) Given the lapse of time, did William accurately remember what he heard John say? Was William's hearing good and was he close enough to hear what John said?

A Zuckerman and P Roberts, *Criminal Evidence* (2nd edn, 2004, Oxford University Press) 597

Everyday experience teaches that information generally becomes less reliable the further one moves away from its original source, and it is a forensic commonplace that evidence is virtually always harder to test if it is provided to the court indirectly, at one or more removes from a witness who could vouch directly for the truth of the matter stated. It also seems unfair to the accused if he cannot effectively test the prosecution evidence against him, because the witness in court is a mere cipher relating what somebody else told him, whilst the originator of the evidence—the one who really knows the truth of the matter, if anybody does—is not available for further questioning. Even if cross-examination is not nearly as effective at winkling out the truth as lawyers have sometimes believed, depriving the accused of an opportunity to test evidence vigorously through cross-examination might still impact adversely on the fairness of proceedings, not least because people tend to trust in the efficacy of cross-examination, whatever behavioural science experts might think. It has been a constant refrain of this book that justice cannot fully be done unless justice is seen to be done, by the accused, by the witnesses, and by society at large. Seeing justice done might well entail a fair opportunity for cross-examination, at least for as long as this procedure is popularly embraced as a feature of procedural justice.

Reform in Criminal and Civil Cases

As the various reports cited above indicate, there have been numerous proposals over the years for reform of the hearsay rule, in both criminal and civil matters. For example, the Law Commission's 1997 Report concluded that the indiscriminate nature of the hearsay rule made it a 'blunt instrument' in criminal cases; of value in some situations, inappropriate in others; it felt that preserving the status quo was not acceptable. The same body had earlier (in 1993) reached even more dramatic conclusions with regard to hearsay in civil trials in *The Hearsay Rule in Civil Proceedings* (LC Report No 216). Both its reports included numerous recommendations for reform, and draft Bills to effect such changes. These saw fruition, with some amendments, in the CJA 2003 and Civil Evidence Act 1995, which will be dealt with in turn.

5. The Criminal Justice Act 2003

Hearsay evidence in criminal cases is now largely governed by the CJA 2003, and, in particular, s. 114 of that Act, which lays down four routes by which hearsay can be admitted at trial.

However, it should be noted that there are a variety of other, often rather arcane, statutes still in force, whereby hearsay evidence can sometimes be admitted. Amongst these is the Bankers' Books Evidence Act 1979, which, under s. 3, allows a copy of any entry in a banker's book to be received as prima facie evidence of the entry. The four routes set out in s. 114 of the CJA 2003 will be examined separately, though not in sequential order.

Section 114 of the Criminal Justice Act 2003 Admissibility of hearsay evidence (extract)

(1) In criminal proceedings a statement not made in oral evidence in the proceedings is admissible as evidence of any matter stated if, but only if—

    (a) any provision of this Chapter or any other statutory provision makes it admissible,

    (b) any rule of law preserved by section 118 makes it admissible,

    (c) all parties to the proceedings agree to it being admissible, or

    (d) the court is satisfied that it is in the interests of justice for it to be admissible....

Hearsay Admitted by Agreement

As with many of the other evidential provisions found in the 2003 Act, if the parties to a criminal trial agree to the adduction of hearsay evidence it is admissible: s. 114(1)(c). This already occurred, prior to the Act, with regard to non-controversial evidence admitted via an agreed statement under s. 9 of the Criminal Justice Act 1967.

Preserved Common Law Exceptions to the Rule

Even as the hearsay rule hardened into a rigid exclusionary rule in the late eighteenth and early nineteenth centuries, it was appreciated that it would exclude some vital types of evidence that were otherwise unobtainable from any other source or that were considered to be inherently very reliable. As a result, a number of common law exceptions to the general exclusionary rule developed, some of them drawing on much older roots. These developments were largely complete by 1850. In recent decades, the higher courts have been adamant that the era of new, judicially created, common law exceptions to the hearsay rule is over: *Sparks v R* [1964] AC 964. In *Myers v DPP* [1965] AC 1001, Lord Reid stressed again that any further relaxation of the hearsay rule could only come from Parliament. Over 20 years later, the same forum noted, in *R v Blastland* [1986] AC 41, that it was 'for the legislature, not the judiciary, to create new exceptions to the hearsay rule'.[8] This has occurred in successive, and progressively wider, statutory provisions, and, in particular, in the Criminal Evidence Act 1965, Police Civil Evidence Act 1984, Criminal Justice Act 1988 and, of course, the CJA 2003.

Prominent amongst the historic common law exceptions was the so-called 'dying declaration' whereby, if there had been a death, followed by a trial for murder, manslaughter or, arguably,

---

[8] However, it is at least arguable that such an exception was created by *R v Osbourne and Virtue* [1973] QB 678 in which two eye witnesses who had attended identification parades could not identify the accused at court and could not remember having picked out anyone at the parade. The defence objected to the evidence of the police inspector about what had happened at the parades, but it was still permitted.

causing death by reckless driving, pertaining to that death, a statement relating to the cause of death, made by the dead person in a settled hopeless expectation of death, was admissible. Thus, if a man was stabbed and before he died declared, 'I'm a gonner, it was Tommy who stabbed me', this could be admitted as evidence at Tommy's murder trial that he was the perpetrator of the killing. Its existence owed much to the belief that a person knowingly facing the awful prospect of imminent divine judgment would not dare to dissemble: *R v Woodcock* (1789) 1 Leach 500. However, all common law exceptions have been abolished in England and Wales by virtue of s. 118(2) of the CJA 2003, except insofar as they are preserved by s. 118(1). Thus, the dying declaration, which was not preserved, has finally expired, though such a statement will now usually be admissible under s. 116(1)(a) of the CJA 2003.

Pause for reflection

Do you think that people are less likely to lie when facing imminent death?

Nevertheless, s. 118(1) expressly retains most of the other long-standing common law exceptions, as the Law Commission felt that they occasioned few problems in practice. Given that s. 118 refers to the 'preservation' of the common law rules, it seems that the entire body of earlier case law governing these exceptions will continue to apply; the new section does not attempt to reduce them to a fresh set of statutory principles.

Res Gestae

Amongst the most important of the surviving common law exceptions is the *res gestae*, which is retained in all its four limbs, being preserved by subsections 118(1)(4) (a)–(c) of the CJA 2003. It should be noted that although grouped together under a single Latin tag (which literally means 'things done') they are, in many ways, separate common law exceptions, with *comparatively* little in common. As Lord Wilberforce observed in *R v Andrews* [1987] AC 281, the expression, like many Latin phrases, is often used to cover situations insufficiently analysed in clear English terms.

Section 118(1)(4)(a): 'Excited Utterances'

The first, and most significant, of the limbs, is the so-called 'excited utterance' rule (the phrase is not used in the statute). It deals with statements relating to a startling event, made while the declarant was under the stress of that event and emotionally overpowered by it, which were originally considered to be 'part' of the event rather than a report about it. A typical example might be a statement made by the victim of an attack, in the presence of another witness, just after the assault took place, indicating the identity of his attacker. In the event that the victim could not be called, because, for example, he was dead, this statement could be tendered by the witness to whom it was made to identify the dead man's assailant.

Although this would now, normally, automatically be admissible by dint of s. 116(2)(a) of the Act, in the (perhaps unlikely) event that the victim could not be identified, the statement would be inadmissible under this section, but could still be admitted under s. 118. However, and even more significantly, in theory, the statement can also be adduced, even if its maker does give evidence, or does not testify but is not otherwise 'unavailable'. Nevertheless, in *Andrews,* the House of Lords deprecated any attempt at using the *res gestae* doctrine as a way to avoid calling an available witness, and, were this to occur, such a statement might well be excluded under s. 78 of the PCEA 1984, if tendered by the prosecution. Their Lordships' analysis was supported by the Divisional Court in *Tobi v Nicholas* [1988] RTR 343.

Historically, the requirements for this exception were interpreted very strictly. Thus, in the Victorian case of *R v Bedingfield* (1879) 14 Cox CC 341, virtual contemporaneity with the incident to which a statement was related was held to be necessary before it could be adduced. In this case, a statement made by a woman who had had her throat cut (from which injury she died a few minutes later) saying, 'See what Harry [Bedingfield] has done', was not admitted under the doctrine as evidence against the defendant because she had walked out of the room in which it occurred before making it. However, in the modern era, the requirements for the adduction of such a statement have been considerably relaxed. The test is no longer the uncertain one as to whether the making of the statement was, in some sense, 'part' of the event or transaction. This change was first manifest in the decision of the Judicial Committee of the Privy Council in *Ratten v R* [1972] AC 378.

Ratten v R [1972] AC 378, PC

Lord Wilberforce

The possibility of concoction, or fabrication, where it exists, is on the other hand an entirely valid reason for exclusion, and is probably the real test which judges in fact apply. In their Lordships' opinion this should he recognised and applied directly as the relevant test: the test should be not the uncertain one whether the making of the statement was in some sense part of the event or transaction. This may often be difficult to establish: such external matters as the time which elapses between the events and the speaking of the words (or vice versa), and differences in location being relevant factors but not, taken by themselves, decisive criteria. As regards statements made after the event it must be for the judge, by preliminary ruling, to satisfy himself that the statement was so clearly made in circumstances of spontaneity or involvement in the event that the possibility of concoction can be disregarded. Conversely, if he considers that the statement was made by way of narrative of a detached prior event so that the speaker was so disengaged from it as to be able to construct or adapt his account, he should exclude it. and the same must in principle be true of statements made before the event. The test should be not the uncertain one, whether the making of the statement should be regarded as part of the event or transaction. This may often be difficult to show. But if the drama, leading up to the climax, has commenced and assumed such intensity and pressure that the utterance can safely be regarded as a true reflection of what was unrolling or actually happening, it ought to be received.

The approach adopted in *Ratten* was subsequently approved by the Court of Appeal and, in due course, by the House of Lords, in *R v Andrews* [1987] AC 281, which is still the leading case on the topic, and which laid down firm guidance as to how the question of admissibility should be determined. In *Andrews* it was held that the overriding question for the trial judge to decide is whether the statement was made at a time when the declarant was so emotionally overpowered by an event that the possibility of concoction, deliberate distortion, or fabrication by him can be ruled out. In answering this question a judge must consider all the circumstances in which the statement was made, assessing whether the statement was so direct, immediate and impulsive a reaction to events as to preclude any reasonable possibility that the declarant fabricated it. If, in his view, the reliability of the statement is tainted by factors other than the ordinary fallibility of any human observation, he should rule against its admission; otherwise, however, the reliability of the statement would be a matter for the jury. This would be the case, for example, if its maker may have been confused, forgetful or intoxicated. Thus, in *R v Turnbull* [1985] 80 Cr App R 104, the declarant had a strong Scottish accent and was fairly drunk when he made his statement, slurring some of his words. Nevertheless, his statement was still admitted.

Although the test may be difficult to apply in practice, a number of factors appear to be important; in particular, how 'dramatic' was the incident to which it relates, how involved was the maker of the statement in that incident, and how long a period of time elapsed between the incident and the making of the statement? Additionally, it must be asked whether the maker had any personal motivation to distort or fabricate the nature of the event? For example, if the very seriously wounded victim of an attempted murder identified his attacker as a man that he knew, but otherwise held no animosity for, some two minutes after the incident itself, the statement would be very likely to be admissible. At the other extreme, if a passer-by had been peripherally involved in a minor robbery, perhaps jumping out of the way of a getaway car, had not made a statement for two hours after the incident, and had then identified as the robber a man against whom he nurtured a profound grievance for running off with his wife, the statement would almost certainly not be admissible under the doctrine. In between, there is a grey area, where much will depend on the facts of a case and the interpretation placed on them by an individual trial judge.

With regard to the gravity of the incident, the decision in *Tobi v Nicholas* [1988] RTR 343 is significant. A statement in a damage only road accident was held not to be admissible, some 20 minutes after the incident, as it was a 'commonplace situation', unlikely to dominate the mind of a victim for any length of time. However, in grave cases, a significant amount of delay can be countenanced. Thus, in *R v Turnbull* [1985] 80 Cr App R 104, a statement made by the mortally wounded victim was received about half an hour after the crime. In perhaps the most extreme case, *R v Carnall* [1995] Crim LR 944, the victim of a fatal beating and stabbing, who had suffered terrible injuries and was in great pain, had crawled for over an hour from the scene of the attack before identifying his assailant. This appears to be about the maximum length of time that is normally permissible (though there is no set limit). More controversially, perhaps, in *R v Nye and Loan* [1977] 66 Cr App R 252, a period of some minutes had elapsed between an assault and the making of the statement. This decision might be viewed as slightly suspect. The incident, although extremely unpleasant, was not of the same magnitude as in *Turnbull* or *Carnall* and, given this, the delay was fairly significant, allowing an opportunity for reasoned reflection.

As to the maker's degree of involvement in the incident, most declarants are victims or complainants (usually the most intimately involved and so most likely to be 'dominated' by the event). However, more rarely, they can be other witnesses; very unusually, in *R v Glover* [1991] Crim LR 48, it was held that a statement made by the defendant during a criminal incident as to his own identity, 'I am David Glover', was subsequently admissible as an excited utterance, because he had been furiously angry at the time that he made it. Obviously, the court would have to be able to discount the considerable risk of concoction in such a situation.

R v Andrews [1987] AC 281, HL

Lord Ackner

My Lords, may I therefore summarise the position which confronts the trial judge when faced in a criminal case with an application under the res gestae doctrine to admit evidence of statements, with a view to establishing the truth of some fact thus narrated, such evidence being truly categorised as 'hearsay evidence?' The primary question which the judge must ask himself is—can the possibility of concoction or distortion be disregarded?

To answer that question the judge must first consider the circumstances in which the particular statement was made, in order to satisfy himself that the event was so unusual or startling or dramatic as to dominate the thoughts of the victim, so that his utterance was an instinctive reaction to that event, thus giving no real opportunity for reasoned reflection. In such a situation the judge would be entitled to conclude that the involvement or the pressure of the event would exclude the possibility of concoction or distortion, providing that the statement was made in conditions of approximate but not exact contemporaneity.

In order for the statement to be sufficiently 'spontaneous' it must be so closely associated with the event which has excited the statement, that it can be fairly stated that the mind of the declarant was still dominated by the event. Thus the judge must be satisfied that the event, which provided the trigger mechanism for the statement, was still operative. The fact that the statement was made in answer to a question is but one factor to consider under this heading.

Quite apart from the time factor, there may be special features in the case, which relate to the possibility of concoction or distortion. In the instant appeal the defence relied upon evidence to support the contention that the deceased had a motive of his own to fabricate or concoct, namely, a malice which resided in him against O'Neill and the appellant because, so he believed, O'Neill had attacked and damaged his house and was accompanied by the appellant, who ran away on a previous occasion. The judge must be satisfied that the circumstances were such that having regard to the special feature of malice, there was no possibility of any concoction or distortion to the advantage of the maker or the disadvantage of the accused. As to the possibility of error in the facts narrated in the statement, if only the ordinary fallibility of human recollection is relied upon, this goes to the weight to be attached to and not to the admissibility of the statement and is therefore a matter for the jury. However, here again there may be special features that may give rise to the possibility of error. In the instant case there was evidence that the deceased had drunk to excess, well over double the permitted limit for driving a motor car. Another example would be where the identification was made in circumstances of particular difficulty or where the declarant suffered from defective eyesight. In such circumstances the trial judge must consider whether he can exclude the possibility of error.

Pause for reflection

Do you think that a non-victim witness is ever so dominated by an event that they will meet the excited utterance criteria for admissibility set out in *Andrews*?

Section 118(1)(4)(b): Statements Accompanying an Act and Necessary to Evaluate it

A statement made by someone who carries out an act, referring to that act, may be the best evidence of the act's significance; indeed, it may be the only available evidence. This exception recognizes that it is often impossible to separate statement and deed. However, the prerequisites before this limb of the *res gestae* operates are quite strict. Thus, in *Howe v Malkin* (1878) 40 LT 196, Grove LJ noted that: 'The rule is that, though you cannot give in evidence a declaration per se, yet when there is an act accompanied by a statement which is so mixed up with it as to become part of the res gestae, evidence of such statements may be given.'

The statement must have been made by the person who carried out the act, relate to the act, and have been made contemporaneously with the act. Thus, in *R v Bliss* (1837) 7 Ad & El 50, a passing statement by a man when planting a tree, that it was being rooted on the boundary of his estate, could not, subsequently, be admitted as evidence of where the boundary lay, because his planting the tree was not a deliberate act of demarcation, and the making of the statement was coincidental. As Williams J noted in this case: 'The declaration here had no connection with the act done; and the doing of the act cannot make such a declaration evidence.' By contrast, had the planter said, as he rooted the tree, 'I am planting this tree to mark where the boundary of my estate lies', his statement *might* have been admissible. In *Peacock v Harris* (1836) 5 Ad & El 449, Lord Denman stressed the importance of contemporaneity for this exception to apply, noting that: '…an act done cannot be varied or qualified by insulated declarations made at a later time'.

Section 118(1)(4)(c): Contemporaneous Statements of Physical or Emotional Sensation

A contemporaneous statement of physical or emotional sensation may be admitted, as an exception to the hearsay rule, as evidence of that sensation. Thus, in *Aveson v Lord Kinnaird* (1805) 6 East 188 the statement of a woman to a friend, to the effect that she was ill, made at the same time that her husband took out an insurance policy on her life, was admissible to show that she was not in good health when insured (insurance contracts are contracts of the utmost good faith and so require the disclosure of anything that might affect the insurer's decision to issue a policy).

However, the exception is limited purely to the physical sensation, and does not cover any attribution as to its cause. As Charles J noted in *R v Gloster* (1888) 16 Cox CC 471, under this head of the *res gestae*: '…statements must be confined to contemporaneous symptoms, and nothing in the nature of a narrative is admissible as to who caused them, or how they were caused'. Similar views were expressed by Lord Pollock in *R v Nicholas* (1846) 2 Car & K 246. Consequently, if a child who had been a victim of domestic abuse told a friend that she had a pain in her stomach because her father had punched her there, the exception would allow her statement to be admitted as evidence of the pain, but not as to its cause.

The statement must be made 'contemporaneously' with the sensation, but this is not interpreted literally. A small degree of delay appears to be acceptable. For example, in *R v Black* [1922] 16 Cr App R 118, Salter J felt that the doctrine would extend to statements such as 'Yesterday I had a pain after meals'. Thus, a statement to a doctor by a patient to the effect that he (the patient) had had a headache the previous day might still be admissible under this limb of the *res gestae*.

Just as with statements of contemporary physical sensation so those of contemporary emotion are admissible as evidence of those emotions: *Thomas v Connell* (1838) 4 M & W 267. For example, if a witness was to say that they were very angry, this could be repeated as evidence that that was their emotion at the relevant time. In *R v Moghal* [1977] 65 Cr App R 56, it was held that a defendant in a murder trial, who claimed that the killing was entirely the work of a third party, should have been allowed to adduce evidence that the third party had said, shortly before the murder, that she intended to kill the dead man. As Scarman LJ (as he then was) noted, these statements were indicative of her state of mind, were made contemporaneously with that state of mind at the time and were relevant to the appellant's defence. In *Gilfoyle*, the existence of this exception allowed the Court of Appeal to conclude that, even if the statements made by the dead women were not original evidence (they decided that they were), they were still admissible hearsay by dint of this part of the *res gestae* as indicative that she was not suicidal.

R v Gilfoyle [1996] 1 Cr App R 306, CA

Beldam LJ

But, in any event, hearsay evidence to prove the declarant's 'state of mind' is an exception to the rule which has been accepted by the common law for many years. Where the intentions or state of mind of a person making the statement are relevant to a fact in issue, hearsay evidence is admissible. In R. v. Blastland (1985) 81 Cr.App.R. 266, [1986] A.C. 41 (H.L.), Lord Bridge said, at p. 271 and p. 54: 'It is, of course, elementary that statements made to a witness by a third party are not excluded by the hearsay rule when they are put in evidence solely to prove the state of mind either of the maker of the statement or of the person to whom it was made. What a person said or heard said may well be the best and most direct evidence of that person's state of mind. This principle can only apply, however, when the state of mind evidenced by the statement is either itself directly in issue at the trial or of direct and immediate relevance to an issue which arises at the trial. In the present case the statements made by Paula tended to prove that she was not depressed or worried to the point of suicide when she wrote the notes, but rather wrote them in the belief that to do so would be assisting the appellant in a course at work.' On this basis the statements were not admissible to prove the truth of the fact that the appellant had asked her to write them, or that he had told her what to write or what he had done after she had written the notes.

Additionally, it was noted that if the statements could be regarded as accompanying the writing of the notes in the sense of having been made sufficiently soon after they were written, it might be argued that the statement that the appellant had asked her to write them could be admitted to prove that he had in fact done so, under the exception now preserved by s. 118(1)(4)(b) (discussed above), though it would seem that the lack of contemporaneity would prevent this.

Other Preserved Common Law Exceptions

Under s. 118 several other common law exceptions to the hearsay rule are expressly preserved, though one of them, confession evidence, is, arguably, now a statutory exception by dint of the wording of s. 76 of the PCEA 1984; this vital exception to the hearsay rule is dealt with in detail in chapter 6. Another preserved common law exception is that which allows experts to base their opinions on research carried out by others, without violating the hearsay rule: s. 118(1)(8). This is dealt with fully in chapter 10. The other exceptions cover matters as diverse as family tradition, general evidence of reputation, as laid in *R v Rowton* (1865) 29 JP 149 (dealt with in chapter 4) and admissions made by agents.

Some of these exceptions are of considerable importance, others of lesser significance. Amongst the former is that by which public documents, such as public registers, can be admitted as evidence of the facts stated in them: s. 118(1)(b). Of course, in many of these situations, the document would also be admissible under s. 117 of the 2003 Act as a business record. A number of prerequisites apply to the operation of this doctrine. In particular, it seems that to be a public document, the document must have been made for public use, made without delay by someone who was under a duty to inquire into the matters recorded, and it must be open to public inspection. It was this last prerequisite that proved fatal to the adduction of regimental records as to a soldier's movements in *Lilley v Pettit* [1946] KB401. As Lord Goddard observed, such records were not kept for the information of the public, nor were they accessible by them; they were for the use of the Crown and executive. Perhaps the leading case on this area of the law is still *Sturla v Freccia* (1880) 5 Cap Ass 623.

Sturla v Freccia (1880) 5 Cap Ass 623, HL

Lord Blackburn

I do not think that 'public' there is to be taken in the sense of meaning the whole world. I think an entry in the books of a manor is public in the sense that it concerns all the people interested in the manor. And an entry probably in a corporation book concerning a corporate matter, or something in which all the corporation are concerned, would be 'public' within that sense. But it must be a public document, and it must be made by a public officer. I understand a public document there to mean a document that is made for the purpose of the public making use it, and being able to refer to it. It is meant to be where there is a judicial, or quasi-judicial, duty to inquire, as might be said to be the case with the bishop acting under the writs issued by the Crown. That may be said to be quasi-judicial. He is acting for the public when that is done; but I think the very object of it must be that it should be made for the purpose of being kept public, so that the persons concerned in it may have access to it afterwards . . . . Can the document in this case be said to come within that class of cases? I think it impossible to look at it in this way. There is not the slightest evidence, or the least circumstance, to lead me to the conclusion that it was ever intended that this private and confidential report should be seen by anyone interested in it. It was meant for private information, to guide the discretion of the Government. It was not, like the bishop's return of the first-fruits, for public information, to be kept in the office and to be seen by all in the diocese who might be concerned when there came to be any litigation.

6. Unavailable Witnesses

The 2003 Act greatly expanded the circumstances in which hearsay evidence could be admitted automatically. Most importantly, statements made by witnesses who are unable to testify at trial, or which are contained in business records, are often now admissible under ss.116 and 117 of the Act. It should be noted that it seems that if an appellate court concludes that a hearsay statement was mistakenly admitted under one provision, but should still have been admitted under another or, for that matter, by an exercise of the statute's inclusionary discretion contained in s. 114(1)(d), it will not uphold an appeal: *Maher v DPP* [2006] WL 1546690.

Section 116

Section 116 of the CJA 2003 allows earlier statements made by witnesses who are subsequently unavailable to testify at trial, for a variety of reasons, to be adduced in evidence. To a significant extent, the section is a reworking of s. 23 of the Criminal Justice Act 1988 (which is repealed by s. 136 of the 2003 Act). However, there are a number of major differences between the two statutes.

Section 116 of the Criminal Justice Act 2003 (Partial extract)

(1) In criminal proceedings a statement not made in oral evidence in the proceedings is admissible as evidence of any matter stated if—

    (a) oral evidence given in the proceedings by the person who made the statement would be admissible as evidence of that matter,

    (b) the person who made the statement (the relevant person) is identified to the court's satisfaction, and

    (c) any of the five conditions mentioned in subsection (2) is satisfied.

(2) The conditions are—

    (a) that the relevant person is dead;

    (b) that the relevant person is unfit to be a witness because of his bodily or mental condition;

    (c) that the relevant person is outside the United Kingdom and it is not reasonably practicable to secure his attendance;

    (d) that the relevant person cannot be found although such steps as it is reasonably practicable to take to find him have been taken;

    (e) that through fear the relevant person does not give (or does not continue to give) oral evidence in the proceedings, either at all or in connection with the subject matter of the statement, and the court gives leave for the statement to be given in evidence.

(3) For the purposes of subsection (2)(e) 'fear' is to be widely construed and (for example) includes fear of the death or injury of another person or of financial loss. . . .

Section 116 Extends to Oral Statements

Perhaps most importantly, a major limitation on s. 23, that only documentary (rather than oral) statements could be adduced under its provisions, does not apply to the new section; the Law Commission's suggestion that the exceptions should extend to spoken as well as written hearsay have been followed. Thus, the new statute provides that an admissible statement is a representation made by 'whatever means': s.115(2). This is not qualified elsewhere in the Act.[9] Consequently, if Alfred makes a verbal statement to Brenda, and is subsequently not available to give evidence for one of the designated reasons, she will be able to repeat it in court.

Additionally, s. 23(1) of the 1988 Act only allowed in earlier statements as evidence of any fact of which 'direct oral evidence by him [the witness] would be admissible'. As a result, it was limited to first hand hearsay, ie what the witness who made the statement would have said themselves if they had given evidence in court. This qualification is not contained in s. 116. Nevertheless, it should be noted that adduction 'as of right' under s. 116 is normally limited to first hand hearsay statements by dint of s. 121 of the Act (see below).

---

[9] *Evidence In Criminal Proceedings: Hearsay and Related Topics*, 1997, at para. 8.4.

Lack of an Integral Discretion within Section 116

Unlike the Criminal Justice Act 1988, admission of first hand hearsay under s. 116 is normally *automatic* if the section's prerequisites are satisfied. The new statute contains no equivalent of ss. 25 and 26 of the 1988 Act, which (effectively) gave the courts a discretion to refuse to admit such evidence, even if one of the grounds of unavailability had been established, where it was not deemed to be in the interests of justice to do so. (This also meant that the courts could be relatively liberal when interpreting the wording of s. 23.) The Law Commission was concerned that this discretion resulted in a lack of consistency in the way in which the unavailability provisions were applied. Some judges would regularly exercise their discretion to prevent such evidence being adduced; others were more liberal in admitting it. Additionally, the Commission felt that the criteria considered when exercising the discretion did not have sufficient regard to the interests of the prosecution (as opposed to those of defendants).[10] Unlike the 1988 Act, if one of the provisions set out in s.116(2)(a)–(d) of the 2003 statute is made out, the evidence is admissible. However, this is still subject, of course, to the court's power to exclude prosecution evidence generally under s. 78 of the PCEA 1984, and all hearsay evidence (from whatever source) under s. 126 of the 2003 Act. As will be seen later in this chapter, the courts are very willing to invoke these provisions to exclude hearsay evidence where they deem it to be necessary.

Grounds of Automatic Admissibility under Section 116

The grounds of automatic admissibility set out in s. 116(2)(a)–(d) are that the witness is: dead; unfit to be a witness because of his bodily or mental condition; outside the United Kingdom and it is not reasonably practicable to secure his attendance; or that he cannot be found, although such steps as are reasonably practicable have been taken to find him. The phraseology is very close to that used in s. 23(2)(a)–(c) of the Criminal Justice Act 1988, and the large number of cases that explored unavailability under the earlier statute will often still be relevant to the new one, though a body of 2003 Act specific decisions is now developing. Taken together, these cases provide fairly detailed guidance as to its likely interpretation in any given situation.

Thus, the grounds of unavailability will normally be established, in the absence of the jury, on the *voir dire* procedure, by calling otherwise admissible evidence; for example, by witnesses giving oral evidence or by the adduction of statements that are themselves admissible hearsay. As a result, death will continue to be proved (in most cases) by adducing a death certificate or tendering someone who can testify to the witness's demise.

When considering bodily and mental unfitness the courts will usually require a medical report setting out the relevant condition and explaining why it makes the witness unfit to give evidence. Cases such as *R v Sed* [2004] 1 WLR 3218 in which a video interview of the 81-year-old victim of an attempted rape was admitted under s. 23 of the 1988 Act, after expert evidence indicated that she was no longer fit to give evidence in court owing to the onset of dementia, will still be influential under the new statute. More recently, in *DPP v R* [2007] EWHC 1842, Hughes LJ stressed (unsurprisingly) that, for the purposes of s. 116(2)(b), fitness meant fitness to give evidence; not a physical ability to get to court. In another post-2003 Act case, that of *The Queen on the Application of Crown Prosecution Service v Uxbridge Magistrates* [2007] EWHC 205 the Divisional Court felt that magistrates should have acceded to a prosecution application to allow

---

[10] Paras 2.18, 4.29–4.30.

the complainant's statement in a domestic violence case to be adduced under s. 116 (on the proper adduction of a doctor's medical report) where she had been sectioned under the Mental Health Act, and where they had previously refused an application to adjourn the matter until she was in a better frame of mind and could attend personally. In this case, the complainant was the only prosecution witness, albeit that the defendant had made very limited admissions to the police, in which he had also raised self-defence as an issue.

The Queen on the Application of Crown Prosecution Service v Uxbridge Magistrates
[2007] EWHC 205, DC

Clarke J

Section 116 of the 2003 Act provides specifically for the admission of a written statement of a witness unavailable through ill-health. On such an application the court must consider the matters set out in section 116(4) and the interests of justice. The witness statement had been taken on 26th July, the same date on which photographs were taken. The defendant was able to challenge the contents of the statement by giving evidence, and his ability to do that was not hampered. This is not to say that adducing the written evidence would have been an ideal form of trial, but it would have been a good second best which would, in my judgment, have enabled the trial to proceed without unfairness to the defendant.

In like manner, pre-2003 Act cases on what steps are 'reasonably practicable' to find a missing witness or secure their attendance (if abroad) will continue to be of significance. Thus, it will still not mean 'physically possible' to find the individual or bring him to England; other factors must be put into the equation. For example, the degree of prejudice to the defendant in adducing the statement, the importance of the evidence to the case overall and the amount of expense involved in securing the witness's attendance will all need to be considered: *R v Castillo* [1996] 1 Cr App R 438. (To an extent, this will sometimes require a cost/benefit analysis.) This analysis is now supported by cases that are specifically on the 2003 Act. Thus, in *R v C* [2006] Crim LR 637, the Court of Appeal accepted that 'reasonably practicable' for the purposes of s. 116(2)(c) must be judged on the basis of the steps taken (or not taken) by the party seeking to adduce the relevant witness's evidence.

For example, in *R v Gyima* [2007] EWCA 429, the defendant was accused of a violent street robbery. The incident was witnessed by a 14-year-old boy, who was on holiday in London from America at the time. The boy was questioned by the police about what he had seen, which interview was also video recorded. Subsequently, the police tried to bring the boy over to London for the trial. However, problems occasioned by communications difficulties (numerous police telephone calls and emails being ignored), the boy's age and the illness of his mother, meant that they were unable to do this, despite considerable (and well evidenced) efforts. As a result, the prosecution gave notice to the defendant that they would seek to have the 13-minute video of his police interview admitted under s. 116(2)(c), on the basis the youth was outside the United Kingdom and that it was not reasonably practicable to secure his attendance at trial. The trial judge allowed this, and, on conviction, this decision was appealed.

The appeal was primarily founded on the failure by the prosecution to use a (very expensive) video-link at trial, so that the child could give evidence live from America, and also premised on an alleged violation of Article 6(3), occasioned by the inability of the defendant to cross-examine the boy on his evidence (see below). Both these grounds were rejected (the appeal was allowed on others). Similarly, under s. 116(1)(d), the party seeking to adduce the statement will have to give evidence as to what steps have been taken to find its maker, and that despite such measures he cannot be located.

R v Gyima [2007] EWCA 429, CA

Gage LJ

There can be, in our judgment, no doubt that the prosecution did make considerable effort to secure Kemar's attendance. As to the point taken on behalf of the appellants, that there was no evidence of the cost of making the arrangements for the video link, it is not possible for this court to know and assess whether it was too expensive to arrange. However, as Mr Carrasco points out, DC Quirk was available to give such evidence if required to do so. It has to be said, however, that the transcript shows that the judge rather brushed aside this aspect of the submissions. DC Quirk could, we are told, have given some evidence about the costs involved. Counsel did not ask for her to give such evidence. We know that it would have involved an officer going to New York to make arrangements and to be present when Kemar gave evidence. We think we are quite entitled to recognise that the expense would have been not inconsiderable. In our judgment, the judge would have been entitled to find that it was not reasonably practicable to secure Kemar's attendance by this means and we so find. In any event, it is clear that Kemar's parents would not co-operate with the Crown Prosecution Service which, since Kemar lived in the United States of America, presented a very considerable difficulty in communications with him and his mother and the ability of the police to persuade them to co-operate with any arrangement for a video interview or for him to come to this country. In the circumstances, we are of the opinion that, on the unchallenged evidence, the prosecution had proved that they had taken all reasonable steps to secure Kemar's attendance.

As with s. 23 of the 1988 Act, the existence of such a state of affairs (whichever limb is used) will have to be proved to an appropriate standard, depending on which party is the proponent of the evidence. Thus, the prosecution will have to establish one of the grounds set out under s. 116 beyond reasonable doubt; the defence only on the balance of possibilities: *R v Minors* [1989] 1 WLR 441. This was specifically reiterated with regard to s. 116(2)(b) of the CJA 2003 in *R (on the application of Meredith) v Harwich Magistrates Court* [2006] EWHC 3336.

Of course, under s. 116(1), and as with its immediate predecessor, a hearsay statement is only admissible if the same evidence given orally by the person who made the statement would also be admissible. For example, a witness could not have his statement admitted under the section if he was not competent to testify personally, because he did not satisfy the test set out in s. 53 of the Youth Justice and Criminal Evidence Act 1999. This might be because he was 'incapable of understanding questions put to him and of giving intelligible answers'. The provision also precludes (again for example) evidence of expert opinion being given by a layman via an out of court statement.

Identification of Witnesses

The Law Commission proposed that recourse should not be had to the unavailability exception unless the person who (allegedly) made the statement was identified to the court's satisfaction.

It feared that, otherwise, the opposing party would not be able to properly challenge the declarant's credibility and reliability. It gave, as a hypothetical illustration, the case of a defendant in a murder trial who called a witness to say that when he was on a train in a foreign city he overheard two men, whom he did not know, talking about how they had carried out the murder with which the defendant was charged.[11] Such scenarios have been a long-term concern for hearsay reformers, and also influenced the Criminal Law Revision Committee's 11th Report on Evidence of 1972. As Glanville Williams (a member of that committee) observed, professional criminals might arrange for anonymous 'witnesses', who had since conveniently disappeared, to call at the offices of 'bent' solicitors and admit to their crimes, raising enough doubt in the minds of a jury to secure an acquittal. (The committee suggested that no hearsay statement whose maker could not be called due to being abroad, unfindable or unidentifiable, should be admitted if made *after* an accused had been charged or warned that he might be prosecuted.)[12]

Pause for reflection

How real a risk do you consider this to be?

The Law Commission's proposals were followed in s. 116(1)(b) of the CJA 2003. This means that, to be admissible, hearsay statements made by unidentified witnesses, such as the female passer-by in the arson case of *Teper v R* [1952] AC 480 who was heard to say, 'Your place burning and you going away from the fire', will either have to be adduced under the discretionary power contained in s. 114(1)(d), or (in rare cases) under the *res gestae* principle preserved in s. 118(1)(4). However, 'identified to the court's satisfaction' is itself rather vague. Does it mean identified by a verifiable name that could be the subject of a criminal record investigation, a name that cannot be tested in this manner, a description, or even membership of a class? The Law Commission implicitly rejected the latter possibility, and it appears that it will not be sufficient.

Fear: Section 116(1)(e)

Although leave will no longer be necessary for most cases of unavailability, it was expressly preserved for statements admitted under s. 116(1)(e) because their maker was too frightened to testify at trial or, if they had started giving evidence, too afraid to continue doing so. The Law Commission fully accepted that the reluctance of witnesses to testify for this reason was a serious social problem, one that justified a special exception to the hearsay rule with regard to any earlier statements the frightened witness had made. These might include, for example, an account of a violent incident provided by an eye witness when first interviewed by the police. The Commission's conclusion was not, perhaps, very surprising, given the plethora of evidence, both anecdotal and statistical, about witness intimidation. For example, the most recent British Crime Survey found that 8% of witnesses that it questioned had been threatened in some way.

However, and in contrast to other forms of unavailability, the Commission did not think that *automatic* admissibility was appropriate in this situation. In particular, it was concerned that because fear was a state of mind, unlike physical conditions like death or illness, it was

---

[11] Paras. 8.5–8.6.

[12] G Williams, 'The Proposals for Hearsay Evidence' [1973] Crim LR 76–77.

harder to tell whether a witness was genuinely too frightened to testify or merely personally reluctant to give evidence. Additionally, it was concerned that if such evidence was admitted too readily it might enable dishonest witnesses to make a statement and then claim to be afraid, with a view to avoiding cross-examination on its contents at trial. As a result, the Commission recommended that the leave of the court should still be necessary before such a statement could be adduced (at paras 1.40 and 8.58 of their Report). This suggestion was followed in s. 116(1)(e), which provides that such leave will only be granted if the court is satisfied that it is 'in the interests of justice' to do so.

Pause for reflection

Do you feel that it is difficult to determine whether a witness is genuinely too afraid to afraid?

Furthermore, s. 116(4) provides a loose statutory structure for deciding whether or not this is the case. In particular, the court must consider a number of identified factors. These include the statement's contents; the risk of it occasioning unfairness to any party to the proceedings (i.e. prosecution, defence or any co-defendant); the possibility that a special measures direction issued pursuant to s. 16 or s. 17 of the Youth Justice and Criminal Evidence Act 1999 (such as the use of a live-link or strategically placed screens) could deal effectively with the witness's fear, and any other relevant circumstances. As with the factors identified with regard to an exercise of the discretion under s. 114(1)(d), it would appear that although he must consider them, a judge does not have to reach a firm conclusion on any of them.

Although fairly conservative in this respect, in others, the 2003 Act has liberalized and clarified the circumstances in which such material can be admitted. Thus, under s. 116(1)(e), there is no limitation on *who* the earlier statement was made to. By contrast, under the equivalent provision in s.23(3)(a) of the Criminal Justice Act 1988, it had to be made to a 'police officer or some other person charged with the duty of investigating offences or charging offenders'. The Law Commission felt that such a restriction was both unnecessary and potentially unfair to defendants (para. 8.67). Under the new statute, the earlier statement can be made to anyone, whether friend, neighbour, business associate or work colleague. Thus, if a defendant's solicitor takes a statement that provides an alibi for his client, from a witness who is subsequently threatened into not giving evidence (for example, by a co-defendant) the statement could be admitted at trial (with leave of the court).

Cross-reference Box

The array of special measures directions regulated or established by the YJCEA 1999 were designed to reduce the stress and fear occasioned to potentially vulnerable or intimidated witnesses by the traditional method of giving oral evidence in open court. For more on these, go to p. 414.

The Law Commission was keen that the wording of the new statute should encourage courts to be 'more sympathetic' to claims of fear. As a result, under s. 116(3) 'fear' is to be 'widely construed', and expressly includes fear of death or injury to another person, not just the maker of the statement (for example, his/her children or spouse) and also fear of financial loss (rather than simple physical violence), such as that produced by a threat to burn down a witness's house if s/he testifies. Tidying up flaws in the earlier statute, the Law Commission also felt that it was not obvious that witnesses who began to testify at trial but were afraid to continue doing so were still covered by s. 23 of the 1988 Act (though case law suggested that they usually were). The new statute makes it clear that the section will apply irrespective of the amount of evidence a witness has already given at trial.

However, even under the 2003 Act, establishing fear will probably remain fairly difficult. As with the 1988 statute, the courts will continue to view the use of the hearsay statement of a frightened witness, in lieu of their oral evidence, as a serious matter, one that is not to be undertaken lightly, and which requires the tribunal to be satisfied that the fear is genuinely held: *R v Waters* (1997) 161 JP 249. Additionally, the courts appear to be reluctant to reach such conclusions on a purely circumstantial basis. Where a key witness is subjected to subtle intimidation by a defendant, the decision will require a difficult balancing act to be performed between a subjective assessment of the witness's fear and an objective assessment of overall fairness in the case: *R v Doherty (Michael Patrick)* (2006) WL 3006848. It should also be noted that it is particularly important, when determining the question of fear on the *voir dire* procedure, that a trial jury remains ignorant of the application, because of the risk of serious prejudice to the defendant (obviously, it suggests that he is a potentially violent and dishonest man).

A good illustration of the operation of s. 116(1)(e) can be seen in *R (on the application of Robinson) v Sutton Coldfield Magistrates Court* [2006] 2 Cr App R 13, in which the Divisional Court approved the adduction of a police statement made by a complainant in an assault case. It had been followed, some six months later, by another statement in which she declared that she did not wish to give evidence in person because of her great fear of the defendant, and her concern that her appearance at court would furnish him with an opportunity to find her, when she had gone to great lengths to become untraceable by him (changing her appearance, etc.). By contrast, one reason (there were others) that the police video recording of a complainant in a rape case was deemed to be inadmissible in *CPS Durham v CE* [2006] EWCA Crim 1410, was that although the woman was in fear of the defendant, he had not deliberately done anything to induce such fear, with a view to preventing her from testifying.

Section 116(1)(e) does not provide a complete solution to the problems occasioned by witness fear. To operate, it requires that a witness has at least initially made a statement to someone before succumbing to anxiety. For example, it will not deal with the increasingly prevalent reluctance of many witnesses to serious crimes, especially in inner city areas, to identify themselves and so 'get involved'. Additionally, the new provision will occasion some novel problems. Although the requirement in s. 116(1)(b) that the person who (allegedly) made the statement be identified to the court's satisfaction will help prevent fabrication, the provision's extension to oral statements, and to those made to people other than police officers, might occasion difficulties. For a potential example, consider the case of an oral statement, made to a neighbour by an eye witness to a serious crime, committed by a notoriously violent man, which the witness subsequently refuses to reiterate to the police, let alone at trial. However, the provision will make a small contribution towards ameliorating the position of witnesses who are subsequently threatened into not testifying.

Self-induced Unavailability: Section 116(5)

It should be noted that s. 116(5) provides that if any of the reasons for unavailability set out in s. 116(2) are brought about by the proponent of the evidence, or someone acting on his behalf, the out of court statement will not be admissible. Thus, if a witness makes a favourable statement to the police on behalf of an accused person, and that individual, concerned about how this witness will fare under cross-examination, then threatens him into refusing to give evidence, he will not be able to invoke s. 116(1)(e) to have the earlier statement admitted. Similarly, if the same defendant were to murder the witness, he would not be able to adduce his statement under s. 116(1)(a). This provision is unsurprising, it would obviously be wrong if one of the parties to a trial could benefit from his own misconduct.

Section 121 and Multiple Hearsay

The Law Commission was acutely concerned that multiple hearsay was susceptible to being manufactured, did not allow a proper investigation into the circumstances in which the original statement was made, might lead to an undue waste of forensic time, and was frequently unreliable.[13] As a result, multiple hearsay (whether second, third or fourth hand, etc.), for example, a statement such as, 'Abdul said that Belinda said that Charles said that he saw…', is normally subject to judicial discretion by virtue of s. 121. This provides that a hearsay statement is not admissible to prove the fact that an earlier hearsay statement was made unless: either of the statements is admissible under ss. 117, 119 or 120; all the parties to the proceedings agree to its adduction; or (and most significantly) the court is satisfied that the value of the evidence in question: '…taking into account how reliable the statements appear to be, is so high that the interests of justice require the later statement to be admissible for that purpose'.

An example of the first situation occurred in *R v Xhabri* [2006] 1 Cr App R 26, where evidence of a recent complaint to two women was admissible under s. 120 of the 2003 Act. This was passed on to a police officer by the women, who could, as a result, repeat it, although it was, by then, double hearsay (victim to women to officers): s. 121(1)(a). In the second situation, it seems that when determining the interests of justice, much will depend on the number and reliability of the intermediaries through whom the original statement was transmitted to the witness who intends to repeat it in court, along with any other relevant circumstances. Thus, an important statement, originally made by someone of credit, relayed through a small number (ideally only one) of disinterested witnesses, who are themselves creditworthy people, would be much more likely to be admitted than a statement of marginal value, transmitted via numerous intermediaries who are themselves criminals who had a potential interest in the matter.

Arguably, this provision creates a mild (and rebuttable) presumption against the adduction of multiple hearsay. How strong this is can be elucidated by examining judicial decisions. Thus, in *Xhabri*, it was noted that even if the complaint to the two women passed on to the policeman had not been admissible under s. 121(1)(a), it would still have been admitted as being in the interests of justice under s. 121(1)(c), because it was very damaging to the defendant (ie cogent) and the absent intermediaries were merely passing on information provided to them by the complainant, who was herself available for examination at trial.

7. Section 117

Section 117 of the 2003 Act allows the adduction of 'business' records. It is the lineal descendant of (much narrower) provisions that were first introduced in the Criminal Evidence Act 1965,

---

[13] *Evidence in Criminal Proceedings: Hearsay and Related Topics* (1997) at paras. 8.16 and 8.17.

passed, in a hurry, after the decision in *Myers v DPP* [1965] AC 1001 appeared to render most business records inadmissible as hearsay. Section 117(1) provides that a statement contained in such a document is admissible as truth of its contents, assuming, of course, that oral evidence would otherwise be admissible on that matter; thus, and again for example, inadmissible opinion evidence, contained in a business document, would still not be admissible under the statute.

Section 117 of the Criminal Justice Act 2007 (Partial extract)

(1) In criminal proceedings a statement contained in a document is admissible as evidence of any matter stated if—

    (a) oral evidence given in the proceedings would be admissible as evidence of that matter,

    (b) the requirements of subsection (2) are satisfied, and

    (c) the requirements of subsection (5) are satisfied, in a case where subsection (4) requires them to be.

(2) The requirements of this subsection are satisfied if—

    (a) the document or the part containing the statement was created or received by a person in the course of a trade, business, profession or other occupation, or as the holder of a paid or unpaid office,

    (b) the person who supplied the information contained in the statement (the relevant person) had or may reasonably be supposed to have had personal knowledge of the matters dealt with, and

    (c) each person (if any) through whom the information was supplied from the relevant person to the person mentioned in paragraph (a) received the information in the course of a trade, business, profession or other occupation, or as the holder of a paid or unpaid office.

(3) The persons mentioned in paragraphs (a) and (b) of subsection (2) may be the same person....

Under s. 117(2)(a), the document containing the statement must have been created or received by a person in the course of a trade, business, profession or other occupation, or as the holder of a paid or unpaid office. This extensive list encompasses not just the records made by commercial enterprises but also those created by local and national government, clubs, schools, colleges, charities and societies, etc. For example, it would include a scoutmaster's list of the scouts who had attended a particular evening's training, which could subsequently be adduced at trial to suggest that a certain boy had been present at the scout hut on a set date.

Under s. 117(2)(b) the person who supplied the information contained in the statement must have had, or reasonably be supposed to have had, personal knowledge of the matters dealt with in it. For example, in *Myers* the vehicle engine block numbers were provided by workers on the car production line to clerks whose duty it was to record them. Under s. 117 this would not occasion any problems; the workers would have, or might reasonably be supposed to have had, personal knowledge of the relevant information, and the clerks would have a duty to record what the workers passed on to them. As a result, nowadays, the records would be admissible under the provision.

In the sexual assault case of *R v Humphris* [2005] EWCA Crim 2030 the requirement of personal knowledge under s. 117(2)(b) occasioned problems, when the prosecution sought to adduce bad character evidence of the defendant pursuant to s. 101(1)(d) of the same Act by admitting, under s. 117, a statement as to the defendant's earlier convictions for similar offences and their underlying details that had been prepared by police officers (the more normal method is to do so under ss.73 and 74 of the PCEA 1984). Although the officers who supplied the information in the document had personal knowledge of the conviction, they did not have personal knowledge of the facts on which it was based (unlike the complainant). As a result, it was held that this part of the statement should not have been admitted (although the safety of the ensuing conviction was upheld).

R v Humphris [2005] EWCA Crim 2030, CA

Lord Woolf CJ

Having looked at section 117, it is necessary to return to the document which was sought to be admitted in this case. That document contained partly details relating to the appellant's conviction. As to that there is no difficulty. The fact of the conviction can be admitted under section 117. Alternatively, the provisions of PCEA, to which we have already referred, could be relied upon. However, in regard to the entries dealing in the case of each previous conviction which described the method used, Mr Smith contended that the details of what the appellant is alleged to have done in order to commit the previous convictions was information dependent upon the complainant involved in those offences. The complainant was the relevant person under section 2(b) she did not apply the information; a police officer personally did so. That affair does not fall within subsection (2)(b). Accordingly, it is submitted, the right course to have adopted was that which was adopted prior to the Criminal Justice Act coming into force. A statement should have been obtained from the complainant. . . . In this case the Crown wanted to rely on the statement in the document as to the method used by the appellant in committing those previous convictions. . . . The necessary foundations for the admissibility of the method used by the appellant was not laid in this case.

It should be noted that the requirement under s. 116 that the unavailable maker of a statement must be 'identified' does not apply to business records admitted under s. 117. This is because of the inherent reliability ascribed to such records. Thus, although in the *Myers* scenario the maker of the record, or, indeed, the supplier of information, could not be personally identified, the record would still be admissible. It should also be observed that, under s. 117(3), the person who provides the information and the person who records it can also be the same individual. For example, if the scout master personally notes which scouts are present at a drill, and then, acting under a duty, enters their names in a register, he will fulfil both roles, and his register can, again, subsequently be admitted at trial to suggest (for example) that a particular boy was present at the scout hut on a certain night.

 Pause for reflection

Do you feel such records are inherently reliable, and if so, why?

Nevertheless, if the information is transmitted via one or more third parties, the resulting record will only be admissible if the intermediaries were themselves under a duty to pass it on (the individual with personal knowledge does not have to be under any duty to pass it on). Thus, returning to the *Myers* scenario, if one of the workers on the production line decided that he could not be bothered to walk over to the relevant clerk, but, instead, verbally gave the relevant number to a passing commercial traveller, who was visiting the plant to sell machinery, and asked him to repeat it to the recording clerk on his way out of the factory, the resulting entry would not be admissible, as the traveller would be under no duty to repeat it.

By contrast, if the factory employed a 'runner' whose job it was to carry the information from the workers to the recording clerks any resulting entry would be admissible. Indeed, if there were a series of runners under a duty to pass it on to each other, rather like a relay race, it would still be admissible. However, in *Maher v DPP* [2006] WL 1546690 the requirement under s. 117 that multiple hearsay be admitted through a chain of duty meant that a message that had, during its journey, been transmitted from an eye witness, via a victim, to the police, was not admissible, as the victim was not under any duty to pass it on to the police (though it was held to be admissible under the inclusionary discretion contained in s. 114(1)(d) of the Act).

Records Prepared for Criminal Proceedings

Statements taken by police officers from witnesses to a crime, or those taken by defence solicitors, are, prima facie 'records' for the purposes of the 2003 Act, just like any other business records. However, in these situations, the record was prepared for the purposes of criminal proceedings or investigation, and it is felt that as such should be subject to extra safeguards, as there is much less reason for the record to be viewed as inherently reliable. Consequently, one of the five requirements set out in s. 116(2) must also be satisfied for such records to be admissible under s. 117 (ie death, fear, physical incapacity, etc. on the part of the supplier of the information); alternatively, it must be concluded that the supplier of the information cannot reasonably be expected to have 'any' recollection of events. The latter provision is likely to be interpreted strictly; if they have any recollection, a witness could, instead, be allowed to refresh his memory from the statement and then testify orally. The provision might, for example, encompass a police statement that was taken several years earlier, in a 'cold case' crime that has been belatedly 'solved', long after it was committed.

However, it should be noted that under the section there is no need for either of these prerequisites to be established if the record, although prepared for the purposes of pending or contemplated criminal proceedings, was obtained pursuant to a request under s. 7 of the Crime (International Co-operation) Act 2003 or an order under para. 6 of Sch. 13 to the Criminal Justice Act 1988; these provisions relate to overseas evidence.

Previous (In)Consistent Statements

Previous consistent or inconsistent statements made by a testifying witness can be adduced at trial in a variety of circumstances, which are discussed in detail in chapter 8. At common law, such statements, when put to the witness or adduced by them, normally went only to credit, rather than being evidence of the truth of their contents (which would have violated the hearsay rule). However, by virtue of ss. 119 and 120 of the CJA 2003, all previous statements made by a witness, that are admitted at trial, whether inconsistent or consistent, are now evidence in their own right.

8. Section 114(1)(d) and the Inclusionary Discretion

Although the CJA 2003 greatly broadened the situations in which hearsay evidence could be adduced automatically, it did not abolish the rule altogether. Hearsay *must* still satisfy one of the requirements set out in sub-ss. 114(a)–(c) of the Act to be allowed into evidence 'as of right'. However, and very significantly, s. 114(1)(d) also provides that if the court is satisfied that it is 'in the interests of justice' for otherwise inadmissible hearsay to be admitted, it can now be received. Thus, an inclusionary judicial discretion to admit hearsay has been brought into existence.

The potential value of such a discretion has been discussed for several decades, as can be seen from the Privy Council case of *Sparks v The Queen* [1964] AC 964. In this case, which is often taken as a classic indication of the potential injustice occasioned by a rigid application of the hearsay rule, the defendant, a white American soldier, was convicted of assaulting an infant in Bermuda. The child, who did not give evidence at trial (being under four and so considered too young to do so) had told her mother, after the incident, that she had been assaulted by a 'coloured boy'. However, the jury did not hear of this, because of its hearsay provenance. On appeal, the Privy Council held that the evidence had been properly excluded and swiftly rejected counsel for the appellant's argument that there was, or should be, a discretion to admit cogent hearsay where it would be 'manifestly unjust' not to do so. Nevertheless, and perhaps significantly, the conviction was overturned on other grounds. The Law Commission expressly cited *Sparks* as justification for introducing an inclusionary discretion, as it was acutely conscious that whatever care was taken in drafting the categories of automatically admissible hearsay: '…some unforeseeable instances of very cogent hearsay will fall outside them'.[14]

The provision covers hearsay tendered by both prosecution and defence, some earlier proposals that it be limited to the accused having been rejected. It also covers multiple, written and oral hearsay. As a result, no evidence will now be irrevocably inadmissible simply because it is hearsay. However, much will turn on how liberally the sub-section is interpreted. The Law Commission clearly envisaged a fairly conservative approach to this issue. It called its original draft proposal a 'limited' discretion that would 'only be used exceptionally' (at para. 8.133 of their Report).

However, the provision as enacted is not in the form recommended by the Commission. Parliament appears to have been influenced by Lord Justice Auld's view, expressed in his *Review of the Criminal Courts of England and Wales*, that the Commission's recommendations did not go far enough and, after several amendments, accepted a slightly more robustly worded and prominent provision. This divergence from the original proposals, combined with the large degree of discretion accorded to courts in interpreting such an Act by virtue of s. 3 of the Human Rights Act 1998 (to ensure convention compliance), meant that making predictions about the likely use of s. 114(1)(d) was fairly difficult before it came into force.

The Law Commission's original recommendation was that the discretion should be exercised if the court was satisfied that, despite any difficulties there might be in challenging a hearsay statement, its 'probative value is such that the interests of justice require it to be admissible' (s. 9 of its draft evidence bill). This effectively introduced a qualitative test.[15] However, the phrase 'probative value is such' and the reference to difficulties in challenging the statement were omitted from s. 114(1)(d) as enacted. Thus, it was at least arguable that it should not be subject to a qualitative bar. Something could be of minimal relevance or cogency, yet its admission might

---

[14] Para. 1.39.   [15] At 8.141–8.142.

still be in the interests of justice. Taken to extremes, such an approach could render s. 114(a)–(c) almost superfluous.

Nevertheless, this interpretation always appeared unlikely, not least of all because the use of the new discretion was not entirely unguided. When deciding whether it is in the interests of justice that a statement be admitted under s. 114(1)(d), the court is required by s. 114(2) to have regard to a number of expressly identified factors (along with any others it considers relevant). As a result, it seemed probable that some kind of qualitative threshold would be seen as implicit in its employment. A relatively cautious approach to the use of discretion has been confirmed by recent case law on the provision. Thus, in *R v O'Hare* [2006] EWCA Crim 2512, the Court of Appeal stressed that: '…as a matter of generality, section 114[(1)(d) cannot and should not be applied so as to render section 116 nugatory'. (In this case, it was held that the statement of an absent witness could not be adduced under s. 116 of the 2003 Act, necessitating consideration of the discretion.)

Section 114 of the Criminal Justice Act 2003 Admissibility of hearsay evidence (extract)

(2) In deciding whether a statement not made in oral evidence should be admitted under subsection (1)(d), the court must have regard to the following factors (and to any others it considers relevant)—

(a) how much probative value the statement has (assuming it to be true) in relation to a matter in issue in the proceedings, or how valuable it is for the understanding of other evidence in the case;

(b) what other evidence has been, or can be, given on the matter or evidence mentioned in paragraph (a);

(c) how important the matter or evidence mentioned in paragraph (a) is in the context of the case as a whole;

(d) the circumstances in which the statement was made;

(e) how reliable the maker of the statement appears to be;

(f) how reliable the evidence of the making of the statement appears to be;

(g) whether oral evidence of the matter stated can be given and, if not, why it cannot;

(h) the amount of difficulty involved in challenging the statement;

(i) the extent to which that difficulty would be likely to prejudice the party facing it.

(3) Nothing in this Chapter affects the exclusion of evidence of a statement on grounds other than the fact that it is a statement not made in oral evidence in the proceedings.

Some of the factors identified in s. 114(2) have been considered in the context of other statutes and, in particular, the discretionary aspects of the now repealed Criminal Justice Act 1988 (especially ss. 25 and 26). Although the courts will not be bound by these earlier decisions when interpreting the 2003 statute, it is likely that they will often be followed. It should also be noted that several of the factors 'overlap' to some extent. Thus, the court must have regard to how much probative value the statement has ('assuming it to be true'). The more important the evidence, the more likely it is to be in the interests of justice that it be admitted. It must also consider what other evidence has been, or can be, given on the above evidence, and ask how important the matter or evidence is in the context of the case as a whole. If the tendered hearsay statement is the only evidence in a case it is less likely (though not impossible) that it will be admitted under the discretion contained in s. 114(1)(d).

DPP v R [2007] EWHC 1842, DC

Hughes LJ

Section 114 of the same Act separately provides for the admission of a hearsay statement, that is to say a statement not made in oral evidence in the proceedings, if (amongst other circumstances) according to section 1(d) the court is satisfied that it is in the interests of justice for it to be admissible. The difference between those two sections needs to be noted. If section 116(2)(b) applies then the evidence is automatically admissible, subject only to a possible submission under section 78 of the Police and Criminal Evidence Act. If section 114 alone is available as a possible route to admissibility, the court has a judgment to make and it must apply itself carefully to all the circumstances in the case, including the specific ones set out in section 114(2). Essentially the overall question is whether it is in the interests of justice for the hearsay statement to be admitted. Where it is the sole evidence, it will often, though not necessarily, not be safe to admit it.

Additionally, a court must consider the circumstances in which the statement was made: for example, if it was made several months after the event to which it relates, in a public house, by someone in their cups, it may have less value than one made immediately after the incident by a sober eye witness. Similarly, the court must consider how reliable the maker of the statement appears to be; a statement made by someone with no axe to grind in a case, and who is of a reputable background, will obviously carry more weight than one made by a party who is in some way 'interested' in the trial's outcome and is of generally bad character. Analogous to this, the court must ask how reliable the evidence of the making of the statement appears to be; ie, how reliable is the person who purportedly transmits the statement (rather than makes it)? Finally, the court must consider whether oral evidence of the matter stated could be given (and, if not, why not); how much difficulty is involved in challenging the statement, and to what extent that will prejudice the party facing it.

Although a trial judge should consider the factors identified in s. 114(2), there is no obligation on him to embark on an investigation, so that he reaches a definitive conclusion on each or any one of them: *R v Taylor* [2006] 2 Cr App R 14. In *Taylor*, the defendant was accused of causing grievous bodily harm, and the trial judge allowed the video-evidence statements of two prosecution witnesses to be admitted, in which they named the accused youth as the perpetrator. They had learned his identity from others. As this case also suggests, the discretion allows the adduction of multiple hearsay; however, in this situation, it would appear that s. 121(1)(c) might have to be considered. Nevertheless, there would be a major overlap here with the wording of s. 114(1)(d); if admitting the statement was deemed to be in the interests of justice under the latter provision it would necessarily be so under the former.

R v Taylor [2006] 2 Cr App R 14, CA

Rose LJ

As it seems to us, the first and crucial issue raised by this appeal is as to what is meant in s. 114(2) by the words 'the court must have regard to the following factors'. If Mr Sinclair is correct and those words denote an obligation on a trial judge to embark on an investigation, resulting in some cases in the hearing of evidence, in order that he may reach a conclusion established by reference to each of the nine factors, it is apparent that trials are likely to be considerably elongated. Proper investigation of each of those factors, if carried out in that way, may well be a very lengthy process. But do the words in the section require that course to be followed? In our judgment, they do not. They do not impose an obligation on the judge to reach a conclusion. What is required of him is the exercise of judgment, in the light of the factors identified in the subsection. What is required of him is to give consideration to those factors. There is nothing in the wording of the statute to require him to reach a specific conclusion in relation to each or any of them. He must give consideration to those identified factors and any others which he considers relevant (as expressed in s. 114(2) before the nine factors are listed). It is then his task to assess the significance of those factors, both in relation to each other and having regard to such weight as, in his judgment, they bear individually and in relation to each other. Having approached the matter in that way, he will be able, as it seems to us, in accordance with the words of the statute, to reach a proper conclusion as to whether or not the oral evidence should be admitted. That is a process which, as it seems to us, the trial judge followed in this case. He followed it in the exercise of his discretion, in a way which, in our judgment, cannot be effectively challenged. So far as the multiple hearsay point is concerned, it was, as it seems to us, entirely open to the judge, in the exercise of his discretion, to decline to revisit his earlier ruling bearing in mind the jury had already heard the evidence. There was, as we have already sought briefly to indicate, a considerable body of evidence against this applicant, quite apart from the naming of him by the two witnesses to whom we have referred.

The new discretion will certainly allow the courts to 'tidy up' any anomalies that emerge under the 2003 Act. For example, previous inconsistent statements proved against a hostile witness pursuant to s. 3 of the Criminal Procedure Act 1865 become evidence in their own right under s. 119(1)(b) of the Act. However, no mention is made in the statute to the (very rarely used) residual common law discretion to allow such statements to be put to a hostile witness, identified in *R v Thompson* [1976] 64 Crim App R 96. The discretion in s. 114(1)(d) could allow such statements to be treated in a manner that was consistent with those proved under s. 3 of the 1865 Act (ie as evidence of the truth of their contents). Arguably, when combined with the liberalization of automatically admissible hearsay under the statute, the discretion means that hearsay will cease to be a major exclusionary rule, even in criminal cases.

 Cross-reference Box

A 'hostile' witness is a witness who unexpectedly and maliciously fails to give favourable evidence on the part of the party calling him. This could be for a variety of reason, fear, bribery, etc. Such witnesses can normally be cross-examined on their earlier statements pursuant to s. 3 of the Criminal Procedure Act 1865. For further details on hostile witnesses go to pp. 409–413.

However, although the discretion will ensure that extreme cases like *Sparks* will not recur in future, it is not quite so obvious as to how more 'borderline' situations will be dealt with. In general terms, and having regard to the factors identified in s. 114(2), it seems likely that prosecution evidence will be treated slightly less sympathetically than that tendered for the defence. Additionally, there have now been a considerable number of cases specifically on the exercise of the discretion, which also provide significant guidance. Thus, in *Maher v DPP* [2006] WL 1546690, a statement that was inadmissible under s. 117, because of a technical breach in the chain of duty, was held to be admissible under s. 114(1)(d). In *R v Xhabri* [2006] 1 Cr App R 26, it was also noted that even if relevant evidence in that case was inadmissible under s. 120 of the 2003 Act, it 'plainly' fell within the judge's discretion under s. 114(1)(d).

R v Xhabri [2006] 1 Cr App R 26, HL

Lord Phillips

Even if s. 120 was not satisfied, the evidence in question plainly fell within the judge's discretion under s. 114(d), always provided that admission of the evidence was in the interests of justice. We can see no basis upon which it could be suggested that the admission of this evidence was not in the interests of justice. It was probably not clear at the time that the judge made his ruling whether the Defence case would be that L never made the alleged statements or whether it would be that, when making them, she was lying. If the former, then there was every reason why the jury should hear evidence from those to whom L made the statements. If the latter, the introduction of the evidence could not unfairly prejudice the Defendant. As we understand it the only argument raised by Mr Offenbach against the admission of this evidence was that it was unreliable. We see no merit in this argument. . . . The evidence was of substantial value and, according as it did with the evidence of Mrs L and the evidence of L, apparently reliable.

By contrast, in *R v Finch (David Barry)* (2007) WL 2843, the Court of Appeal upheld a trial judge's decision not to admit statements made, on arrest, by a co-defendant who had pleaded guilty (and, as a result, whose out of court statements were not admissible at the behest of his co-accused under s. 76A of PCEA 1984), under s. 114(1)(d). This was, in large part, because the witness had been produced from prison and so could have been called by the defendant to testify at his trial (he was unwilling to do this because the witness in question had earlier evinced a reluctance to give evidence, making the defendant nervous as to the testimony that he would give if called).

R v Finch (David Barry) (2007) WL 2843, CA

Hughes LJ

The judge worked through the relevant factors set out in section 114(2). He accepted that the evidence was, if true, of substantial probative value. He was plainly well aware that the assertion went to the heart of the defence of Finch and that there was otherwise only the evidence of Finch himself, so that the assertion was of considerable importance to the case as a whole. He concluded, however, that oral evidence of what Richer said about Finch was available to be given. He was unable to see how Richer could damage his own position by giving evidence that Finch was an innocent passenger. He also considered, in reference to sub-paragraph (e) of section 114(2), the potential unreliability of Richer if he was not prepared to support in the witness box what he had said to the police. He correctly addressed the difficulty for the Crown of controverting or challenging Richer's assertion if Richer were not in the witness box to make it. His conclusion was that the interests of justice did not call for the interviews to be admitted as hearsay. Plainly in reaching that conclusion the principal factor was the fact that Richer was available to give oral evidence if compelled to do so, together with the various consequences which that entailed. This was a situation calling for the exercise of the judgment of the trial judge. This court will interfere if, but only if, he has exercised it on wrong principles or reached a conclusion which was outside the band of legitimate decision available to him. We are unable to see that his decision can be criticised on either ground. We do accept that there are some difficulties for an appellant and his counsel in this situation when faced with a potential witness who is reluctant to give evidence. Richer would not of course have been called entirely blind. There may not have been a recent proof of evidence but there were the interviews with the police, properly recorded, available as an indication of what he could say. Had he in evidence not supported them it would have been open to Miss Radcliffe to seek to treat him as adverse and, had that been done and his previous inconsistent statements put to him, the latter would under the modern law have stood as evidence of any matter stated in them—see section 119 of the new Criminal Justice Act 2003. We understand, nevertheless, that an appellant might well decide, as this one did on advice, that calling such a witness was a risk that he was unprepared to take. It does not, however, follow that wherever that happens the interests of justice call for the admission in evidence of something which the reluctant witness has said out of court but is not prepared to support on oath. On the contrary, the reluctance only undermines the reliability of the evidence. We agree with the judge that in this case Richer's refusal to give evidence voluntarily plainly carried the suggestion that he was anxious that he would not be believed. . . . it will, as it seems to us, often not be in the interests of justice for evidence which the giver is not prepared to have tested to be put untested before the jury. It is not in short the law that every reluctant witness's evidence automatically can be put before the jury under section 114. We are satisfied that in this case the judge was right on both issues and this appeal must in consequence be dismissed.

In *Ibrahim Musone v The Crown* [2007] EWCA 1237, a prisoner had murdered a fellow inmate. Another inmate had made a statement to the police, shortly afterwards, in which he had implicated the accused man, both with regard to what he (the witness) had seen and with regard to what the dying man had told him. The latter was, of course, multiple hearsay, 'He said that the dead man told him. . .' Subsequently, however, the witness had refused to testify, and, when brought to court, refused to answer any of the prosecutor's questions. The question arose as to whether his post-incident statement to the police could be adduced pursuant to the inclusionary discretion contained in s. 114(1)(d) of the CJA 2003. The trial judge ruled that it could, and also that the statement satisfied s. 121(1)(c) insofar as it constituted multiple hearsay, as it was in the interests of justice to admit it.

On appeal, the first instance judge's decision on this issue was upheld, the court noting that it would not lightly interfere with such a decision as a trial judge was: '. . . best placed to make an accurate assessment of the fairness of admitting evidence in the context of the trial as a whole'. The judge had considered the relevant factors under s. 114(2) and, as both he and the Court of Appeal noted, a dying declaration implicating a murderer had traditionally been accorded considerable weight at common law (even though now abolished as a specific exception to the hearsay rule).

Capability and Credibility: Sections 123 and 124

By virtue of s. 123 of the 2003 Act, the maker of an admitted hearsay statement under ss. 116, 119 or 120 must themselves have the 'required capability' when they made the statement. Similarly, with regard to s. 117, if the supplier or receiver of information in a record did not have, or, if he cannot be identified, 'cannot reasonably be assumed to have had' the required capability at the relevant time, the record cannot be admitted. Under s. 123(3) 'required capability' means that the relevant person must be capable of understanding questions put to him about the matters stated, and giving answers that can be understood (this is the same as the requirements for any competent witness in a criminal case). In trials on indictment, such matters must be determined in the absence if the jury and the court may also receive expert evidence on the issue: s. 123(4)(a)–(b).

Interestingly, whichever party is seeking to admit the statement, whether prosecution or defence, only has to prove capability on the balance of probabilities by dint of s. 124(4)(c). (In some analogous situations in the law of evidence, the prosecution must prove the admissibility of their evidence beyond reasonable doubt.) Thus, and for example, if a statement was made by a severely retarded individual, it is possible that it could not be repeated as hearsay under s. 116. When determining this, the trial judge might hold a *voir dire*, and hear evidence about the witness's abilities from the person to whom the statement was made, and, perhaps, a psychiatrist.

Cross-reference Box

The *voir dire*, or 'trial within a trial', is most commonly used to determine the admissibility of confessions, though it is certainly not confined to such cases. It is held in the absence of the jury and allows the calling of evidence on a question of admissibility, with the trial judge sitting as both tribunal of fact and law on that issue. For more on this procedure go to chapter 7 at pp. 320–324.

Under s. 124(1), various credibility safeguards also apply where hearsay evidence is adduced and the maker of the statement does not give evidence in connection with its subject matter. This means, unsurprisingly, that s. 124 will not apply to those situations, such as with ss. 119 and 120 of the 2003 Act, in which the previous (in)consistent statements of a witness are adduced as evidence of the truth of their contents. Obviously, in such cases, the witness can be personally challenged about them, directly in court.

The provisions allow a defendant to adduce any evidence that is relevant to the absent witness's credibility, and also allow him to produce evidence of anything that could have been put in cross-examination, had the witness been called live, even if it was a collateral matter in which the witness's answer would normally be taken as final: s. 124(2)(a) and (b). This power is necessary, because, of course, the maker of the statement is not there to have the question put to him in the first place. The opposing party may also adduce any statement made by the witness that was inconsistent with the statement adduced at trial. However, the court can also allow evidence in rebuttal of such an allegation to be adduced by the calling party: s. 124(3). It should be noted that, where documentary hearsay is admitted under s. 117, s. 124(4) provides that these provisions also apply to any intermediaries through whom the statement was conveyed.

Cross-reference Box

A collateral matter is usually something that affects a witness's credit, rather than going directly to the issue in a case. The 'collateral-finality' rule means that such a question can usually be asked (assuming it is relevant) but, if its substance is denied, it cannot be rebutted by calling further evidence, even if it is available. There are a number of exceptions to the general rule (such as evidence of bias, etc.). For more information on this rule go to pp. 436–445.

As a result, and for example, if the maker of a hearsay statement, who has since died, had his statement admitted for the prosecution at trial under s. 116(2)(a) of the 2003 Act, evidence could be adduced that he was biased against the defendant, just as it could if it was put to him during the hearing as a 'live' witness, and he denied it: *R v Phillips* [1936] 26 Cr App R 17. Thus, if it transpired that the maker of the statement had had his girlfriend 'stolen' by the defendant some years earlier, this could be established. Similarly, if the witness's previous convictions would have been admissible pursuant to s. 100 of the CJA 2003, they can be adduced in his absence.

Cross-reference Box

Section 100 of the CJA 2003 regulates the circumstances in which the bad character of someone (usually a witness) other than the defendant can be adduced at trial. Previous convictions that are both minor and distant in time, especially if they are for an offence that does not involve dishonesty, will often be inadmissible under this provision. For more information on this section go to pp. 221–230.

Judicial Power to Exclude Admissible Hearsay

There are a number of grounds by which hearsay evidence that is potentially admissible under the 2003 Act can be excluded, and the integrity of the trial process guarded. Some of these overlap, further complicating matters. Thus, hearsay evidence being tendered by the prosecution, like all prosecution evidence, can be excluded under the ubiquitous s. 78 of the PCEA 1984 (something that is also expressly set out in s. 126(2)(a) of the 2003 Act). This is of particular importance because, for most of its gateway provisions (ie 'fear' apart), s. 116 of the Act allows hearsay evidence to be adduced automatically, without the exercise of a dedicated exclusionary discretion having to be considered (unlike the now repealed 1988 Criminal Justice Act). Consequently, the general exclusionary discretion may be vital in ensuring that a defendant receives a fair trial.

Even if the prerequisites for one of the statutory hearsay provisions are met, if the statement is being tendered by the Crown it can be excluded under s. 78 of the PCEA 1984. This will not be done lightly. Thus, the exercise of s. 78 was considered, but not applied, by the trial judge in *R v Taylor* [2006] 2 Cr App R 14. In *Ibrahim Musone v The Crown* [2007] EWCA 1237 (also discussed above), the defendant was accused of murdering a fellow prisoner. The dead man had made a statement to another inmate, implicating the accused, before expiring. This satisfied the prerequisites of s. 116(2)(a), because the maker of the statement was dead. However, on appeal, the defence argued that the evidence should have been excluded under s. 78, because the man to whom it was made was also a prisoner, had a bad criminal record, was a friend of the deceased, had been very reluctant to testify and had also initially delayed reporting what he had allegedly heard. Nevertheless, the Court of Appeal concluded that the trial judge had rightly declined to exclude the evidence.

Additionally, there is the discretion contained in s. 126 of the Act to be considered. This was initially thought to be primarily relevant to hearsay evidence that, although technically admissible under one of the provisions set out in s. 116, would unduly prolong a trial because it was of little cogency (in civil cases such evidence can be excluded under the judicial discretion contained in r. 32.2 of the CPR 1998). Certainly, this appears to have been the intention of both the Law Commission and Parliament. However, the wording of s. 126, although clearly aimed at such situations, does not confine the section's operation to them.

Cases since the 2003 Act came into force suggest that the section is also being pressed into service as a 'general' discretion to exclude what is considered to be 'unfair' hearsay evidence and, in particular, to prevent the automatic admissibility of statements under s. 116, in situations where it might occasion injustice. Unlike s. 78, it theoretically applies to *all* tendered hearsay evidence; not just that advanced by the prosecution, though this does appear to go against some of the Law Commission's aims. It was expressly noted in *R v Xhabri* [2006] 1 Cr App R 26 that a court might have a duty to exclude hearsay under s.126 if it was necessary to ensure compliance with the Human Rights Act 1998. As a result of these two provisions, even if a hearsay statement is prima facie admissible under s. 116, the court can still exercise its discretion to exclude it under s. 78 (if it is being tendered by the Crown) or under s. 126 (whichever party is seeking to adduce it).

With regard to s. 117, a business document being tendered by the prosecution can, in theory, also be excluded under s. 78 of the PCEA 1984. However, more generally, s. 117(6) and (7), taken together, also provide that a court may make a direction that a statement that is otherwise admissible under s. 117(1) should not be admitted, if satisfied that its reliability as evidence is doubtful, in view of: its contents, the source of the information contained in it, the circumstances in which the information was supplied or received, or the manner in which the document was created. Thus, s. 117(7) effectively provides a judicial discretion to exclude business records that appear unreliable (though not for any other reason). Without it, such defects in documentary evidence would normally go to weight rather than admissibility. For example, a record might be excluded under s. 117(7) if it transpires that the supplier of the information contained in it was, personally, acutely hostile to the defendant in a trial, and the record favours the prosecution (of course, in this situation, s. 78 of the PCEA 1984 could also be used to effect exclusion).

Additionally, s. 125(1) provides that, in a prosecution that is based wholly or partly on a hearsay statement (presumably, whether it is admitted under either s. 116 or 117), the court can direct an acquittal or discharge the jury if, at any time after the close of the prosecution case, it is satisfied that the evidence is: '…so unconvincing that, considering its importance to the case against the defendant, his conviction of the offence would be unsafe'. The provision is limited to trials on indictment conducted before a jury, rather than those heard summarily. In a case where hearsay evidence constitutes an important part of the Crown's case, it allows a trial judge who has belatedly developed serious reservations about that evidence, *after* admitting it, to withdraw the case from the jury. This avoids the risk that, despite the judge's likely direction as to its limitations when summing up, it will still be excessively influential on the jury's deliberations. This is something that s. 78 of the PCEA 1984 might not be able to effect, as the wording of the section is 'prospective', 'proposes to rely'. In summary trials, as the tribunal of fact and law are the same, there is, it seems, deemed to be no need for such a discretion.

9. The Impact of Article 6(3)(d) of the ECHR on Hearsay Evidence

Introduction

The hearsay provisions of the CJA 2003 allow an unprecedented degree of access to out of court statements made by an absent witness. However, a combination of the European Convention for the Protection of Human Rights and Fundamental Freedoms (ECHR) and the advent of the Human Rights Act 1998 (HRA 1998) have occasioned concern that the adduction of hearsay evidence, that cannot be tested by cross-examination, might be incompatible with Article 6(3)(d) which, as part of the general right to a 'fair trial' enshrined in Article 6(1), requires that an accused person should have the right to 'examine or have examined witnesses against him'.

When interpreting this provision, it can be noted that the European Court of Human Rights (ECtHR) appears to be primarily concerned with the risk posed to correctness of adjudication by an absence of cross-examination, rather than any wider jurisprudential considerations. This has been recognized by domestic courts. Thus, the House of Lords concluded that there was no infringement of Article 6 generally, and Article 6(3)(d) in particular, when a child gave evidence via a live link pursuant to s. 21(5) of the Youth Justice and Criminal Evidence Act 1999. In such circumstances, the defendant was present when the evidence was put before the tribunal, and had ample opportunity to challenge it, both by adversarial argument in court and by questioning; the only thing that was denied to him was face-to-face confrontation with the witness, and this was not guaranteed by the Convention: *R. (on the application of D) v Camberwell Green Youth Court* [2005] Crim LR 497.

However, and as with reverse onus clauses in the burden of proof, the issue of convention compliance and hearsay evidence does not allow for a simple 'yes' or 'no' answer. In some cases, where the untested statement of an absent witness has been adduced in a domestic court, the ECtHR has subsequently found that there has been a violation of the Convention; in many others, the Court has held that admitting a hearsay statement was convention compliant. This contextual approach has also been reflected in English domestic law. As Lord Phillips observed in *R v Xhabri* [2006] 1 Cr App R 26, Article 6(3)(d): '...does not give a defendant an absolute right to examine every witness whose testimony is adduced against him. The touchstone is whether fairness of the trial requires this'. As with reverse onus provisions, the difficulty lies in distinguishing statements that are convention compliant from those that are not.

The Definition of 'Witnesses'

It is obviously important in this context to identify exactly who is deemed to be a 'witness against' an accused person. In particular, does the definition extend to the makers of hearsay statements, where those statements are tendered against a defendant? However, the makers of hearsay statements can be further sub-divided into those who made them with a view to contemplated criminal litigation, whether in investigative interviews conducted by the police or some other form of pre-trial hearing, and the remainder. Cases emanating from the ECtHR make it clear that the former are 'witnesses' for the purposes of Article 6: *Trevedi v United Kingdom* (1997) 89 D & R 136.

The status of the latter is less clear. However, in 1997, the Law Commission noted that everyone who had been categorized as a 'witness' by the ECtHR at Strasbourg had consciously 'fed' information into the criminal justice system via depositions and police statements; ie they had made statements as part of an investigation. It did not, therefore, necessarily follow that a casual remark allegedly made by a third party would be classified as that of a witness and so trigger a defendant's right to cross-examine under Article 6(3)(d).[16]

---

[16] Law Commission Report No 245, at para. 5.7.

Case Law

The impact of Article 6(3)(d) on hearsay was considered in a reserved judgment by the Court of Appeal, with regard to ss. 23 and 26 of the (now replaced) Criminal Justice Act 1988, in *R v Sellick and another* [2005] 2 Cr App R 15. In this case, the defendants (two brothers) were accused of shooting dead a man in a dispute over drug deals. During the ensuing murder trial, the judge gave permission for the statements of four witnesses to be read out, on the basis that he was sure that two of them were being kept out of the way through fear, while he was persuaded to a high degree of probability that the other two were being kept out of the way for the same reason, and he was sure, in any event, that they could not be traced.

The defendants appealed on the grounds that the lack of a proper opportunity to challenge the statements constituted an infringement of their rights under Article 6(3)(d), especially as the statements constituted the sole or decisive evidence in a case. However, the appeal was dismissed and the trial judge's decision to admit the evidence upheld. On its facts, the court's decision is not surprising. It would be strange if a defendant could deliberately bring about the absence of a crucial witness from his hearing and then complain that his convention rights under Article 6(3)(d) had been violated, even if the witness's statement was the decisive evidence in the case against him. Even vehement supporters of a defendant's right to confront witnesses have accepted that if a witness's unavailability was brought about by the accused's wrongdoing he should be deemed to have forfeited his right to object to such testimony.[17]

However, many situations will be less clear-cut. In *Sellick*, the Court of Appeal firmly rejected prosecution suggestions that, provided the statutory requirements of the 1988 Act had been met, little assistance could be gained from the Strasbourg authorities. Section 2(1)(a) of the HRA 1998 expressly requires the courts to have regard to any judgments of the ECtHR. Additionally, a court must either interpret a provision that is apparently inconsistent with the Convention in a way which is compatible with it, under s. 3(1), or, alternatively, make a declaration of incompatibility under s. 4 of the HRA 1998.

Periodically, the ECtHR reiterates that, in most cases, rules of evidence are for national law to determine: *Miailhe v France No. 2* (1997) 23 HERR 491. Nevertheless, in practice, all this seems to mean is that the court will not lightly decide that domestic law violates convention rights and will not attempt to set out detailed guidance for convention states to follow. Instead, it prefers to deal with such matters on an ad hoc and case-by-case basis. This has prompted complaints that the decisions emanating from Strasbourg have 'little predictive value'. Certainly, many of the judgments show a reluctance to establish firm principles rather than vague generalizations.[18] This applies to a defendant's right to cross-examine witnesses as much as to any other evidential provision. Additionally, as the Court of Appeal noted in *Sellick*, questions as to whether Article 6 has been infringed are always 'very fact sensitive'. Nevertheless, a number of specific factors can be identified from ECtHR case law as being important when reaching a compliance decision.

Importance of the Evidence to the Overall Case

The more important the proposed evidence is to a case (taken as a whole), the less likely it is to be convention compliant; in *Kostovski v Netherlands* (1989) 12 EHRR 434, one reason that the

---

[17] R Friedman, 'Thoughts from Across the Water on Hearsay and Confrontation' [1998] Crim LR 697–709, at 707.

[18] A Choo, 'Crawford v Washington: A View from Across the Atlantic' [2004] International Commentary on Evidence, vol 2, no 1, Art. 4, at 9.

ECHR found that there had been a breach of Article 6 was that the convictions were based to a 'decisive extent' on read out statements. By contrast, one reason that the evidence tendered under s. 23 of the 1988 Act in *Trevedi v United Kingdom* (1997) 89 D & R 136 was deemed by the Commission to be compliant with Article 6 was that it was not the sole evidence of the facts in issue to which it related.

Nevertheless, *Sellick* firmly rejected any suggestion that simply because the tendered evidence was 'decisive', this, on its own, would conclusively indicate a violation of Article 6(3)(d). Subsequent cases have firmly reinforced this analysis, even if a hearsay statement is the only evidence in the case. In *R v Cole and Keet* [2007] 1 WLR 2716, there was held to be no breach of Article 6 where the evidence of a very elderly woman was admitted under s. 116 of the CJA 2003, and was the vital, if not only, evidence in the case. She had been the victim of bogus roofing contractors who had absconded before their trial, and disappeared for several years, before subsequently being tried for obtaining property by deception from her, by which time she was suffering from dementia. Indeed, the Court of Appeal endorsed the first instance judge's view that s. 116 provided an important weapon in the prosecution armoury in offences against elderly and vulnerable people of the type charged, where it was inevitable, in some cases at least, that a witness would be unable to attend trial.

In the conjoined appeal in *Cole and Keet* a conviction for assault occasioning actual bodily harm that was based on the statement of a dead woman about her boyfriend's conduct (she had committed suicide), combined with a post-death forensic examination of pre-mortem injuries to her body, was also upheld.

R v Cole and Keet [2007] 1 WLR 2716, CA

Lord Phillips CJ

Once one moves away, as both the Strasbourg and our domestic jurisprudence clearly have, from the proposition that there is an absolute rule that evidence of a statement cannot be adduced in evidence unless the defendant has an opportunity to examine the maker, it seems to us that there can be only one governing criterion. Is the admission of the evidence compatible with a fair trial? It is that question alone with which Article 6 is concerned.

There are many reasons why it may be impossible to call a witness. Where the defendant is himself responsible for that fact, he is in no position to complain that he has been denied a fair trial if a statement from that witness is admitted. Where the witness is dead, or cannot be called for some other reason, the question of whether the admission of a statement from that witness will impair the fairness of the trial will be depend on the facts of the particular case. Factors that will be likely to be of concern to the court are identified in section 114(2) of the 2003 Act.

Was it 'Tested' on an Earlier Occasion?

An obvious problem with the jurisprudence emanating from the ECtHR is that it is, predominantly, rooted in the civil law tradition, in which the parties' 'day in court' is often the culmination of a lengthy and judicially supervised investigative process that will have afforded the accused or his representative an opportunity to examine witnesses on an earlier occasion. The ECtHR has made it clear that, in the right circumstances, testing witnesses at such interlocutory hearings *can* satisfy the requirements of Article 6(3)(d).

The highly concentrated criminal trial that characterizes the common law tradition normally makes this impossible in England and Wales, something that has become even more marked since the abolition of oral evidence in 'old style' committal hearings. However, a failure to take advantage of any provision that could have allowed an accused person to test the evidence, for example under s. 3 of the Criminal Justice (International Co-operation) Act 1990, might preclude its adduction: *R v Radak* [1999] 1 Cr App R 187. Of course, if the maker of the hearsay statement that is admitted also gives evidence at trial, there will be no question of a violation of Article 6(3)(d): *R v Xhabri* [2006] 1 Cr App R 26.

 Cross-reference Box

For a discussion of the common law's emphasis on a 'day in court' trial process, rather than the judicially supervised system sometimes found in civil law systems, go to chapter 1, at pp. 10–17.

Policy Reasons for Admitting Hearsay Statements

There are a multitude of policy factors that might encourage admission, even where there has been no opportunity to cross-examine the maker of a statement. Some might be considered fairly arcane; for example, the requirement that an allegation of indecent assault by a doctor on his patient, made by a declarant who had since died, be confronted at trial: *R v Al-Khawaja* [2006] 1 WLR 1078. Others, such as the reality of elderly witnesses who have been victimized in their homes being able to give evidence after a lengthy delay are of more general significance: *R v Cole and Keet* [2007] EWCA 1924.

Presence of Other Safeguards

As the Court of Appeal noted in *Sellick*, the safeguards, or 'counterbalance', contained in s. 28 and Sch. 2 to the 1988 Act were important when considering whether a defendant's rights have been infringed under Article 6. These allowed a defendant to adduce evidence relevant to the (absent) witness's credibility. These have been replicated in s. 124 of the 2003 Act. Additionally, in *Sellick,* the court noted that the trial judge had carefully directed the jury as to the limitations inherent in receiving evidence in such a manner. For example, that the maker of the statement cannot be tested by cross-examination, etc. Such directions are now *de rigueur*.

The Criminal Justice Act 2003 and the Convention

As the Court of Appeal expressly noted in *Sellick,* questions of convention compatibility will be of even greater significance under the 2003 Act, which allows hearsay evidence to be admitted much more freely than its immediate predecessor. However, a trial judge always has the power to effect convention compliance. Thus, the judicial discretion to admit hearsay that is not otherwise admissible, under s. 114(1)(d), would necessarily have to be interpreted and applied by a trial judge so that it complied with Article 6(3)(d). Although ss. 116 and 117 of the Act might appear to pose more problems, because of the absence of an integral statutory discretion (unlike ss. 25–26 of the Criminal Justice Act 1988), this, too, can be circumvented. Section 78 of the PCEA 1984 *could* be used to exclude hearsay statements tendered for the prosecution, and so effect compliance with Article 6, on the basis that anything that would preclude a fair trial under the Convention would also necessarily have 'an adverse effect on the fairness of the proceedings' Even more significantly, the Court of Appeal in *Xhabri* noted that a judge might have a duty to exclude hearsay under s. 126 if it was necessary to ensure compliance with the HRA 1998. This would prevent the need for a declaration of incompatibility under s. 4 of that Act (always a last resort for the courts). Nevertheless, it is apparent that the courts are not lightly excluding hearsay evidence simply because of a potential breach of Article 6, as can be seen in *R v Al-Khawaja* [2006] 1 WLR 1078.

R v Al-Khawaja [2006] 1 WLR 1078, CA

Jack J

The important factors in the present case are the following. The witness, Miss Tampsett, could not be examined on behalf of the appellant because she had died. She was the only witness whose evidence went directly to the commission of an indecent assault on her by the appellant. If her statement had been excluded, the prosecution would have had to abandon the first count. The appellant was able to attack the accuracy of Miss Tampsett's statement by exploring the inconsistencies between it and the witnesses, Mr Fish and Mrs Hewlett, and through the expert evidence relating to 'altered perception' under hypnosis. The relevant sections of the 1988 Act contained provisions designed to protect defendants, which were properly considered by the judge, before the statement was admitted in evidence. Lastly, the tribunal of fact, here the jury, could and should take proper account of the difficulties which the admission of a statement might provide for the appellant, which should be provided by an appropriate direction to the jury.

Where a witness who is the sole witness of a crime has made a statement to be used in its prosecution and has since died, there may be a strong public interest in the admission of the statement in evidence so that the prosecution may proceed. That was the case here. That public interest must not be allowed to override the requirement that the defendant have a fair trial. Like the court in R v Sellick we do not consider that the case law of the European Court of Human Rights requires the conclusion that in such circumstances the trial will be unfair. The provision in Article 6(3)(d) that a person charged shall be able to have the witnesses against him examined is one specific aspect of a fair trial: but if the opportunity is not provided, the question is 'whether the proceedings as a whole, including the way in which evidence was taken, were fair': see Doorson v The Netherlands 22 EHRR 330, para 67. This was not a case where the witness had absented himself, whether through fear or otherwise, or had required anonymity, or had exercised a right to keep silent. The reason was death, which has a finality which brings in considerations of its own, as has been indicated at the start of this paragraph.

It was suggested by Mr Bennathan that one important consequence of the absence of Miss Tampsett, which made it unfair for her statement to be admitted, was that 'there were real areas that the defence would have sought to explore about the complainants' knowledge of each other's complaints'. This ignores the stance taken on behalf of the appellant both at the hearing before Judge Rennie when he ruled the statement admissible, and at the trial, not to explore the possibility of collusion between the witnesses: collusion was not suggested. Further, as we have stated, there was nothing to suggest that the women knew the details of each other's allegations.

> We have concluded that the rights of the appellant under Article 6 were not infringed by the admission of the statement. We consider that his rights were sufficiently protected in the circumstances of his case. His trial was not unfair. We refer to the matters we have set out in paras 25–27. That conclusion must be subject to the question whether the trial judge gave an appropriate direction to the jury as to the statement. It is well established that such a direction must be given.

By contrast, can be considered the situation in *CPS Durham v CE* [2006] EWCA Crim 1410, in which a rape complainant made a police video statement alleging rape. However, the video recording was not admitted under s. 116—although the trial judge was satisfied both that she was unfit to be a witness and that she would not give oral evidence through fear—in large part because it would have led to a violation of Article 6. This decision was made more likely because the video recording was itself not ideal. The defendant's condition had precluded the investigating officers from challenging and exploring some aspects of the complainant's video evidence while she made it, even though some obvious questions had been raised by it.

In contra-distinction, and perhaps because the complainant in the case was dead, in *R v Gilbert* (2006) *The Times,* 15 December, the defendant was tried for raping his daughter, the evidence against him being almost entirely in the form of police videos, in which the daughter had made her allegations, before subsequently committing suicide. (The defendant was acquitted by the trial jury.)

CPS Durham v CE [2006] EWCA Crim 1410, CA

May LJ

The sole or decisive evidence against the respondent was this hearsay, uncross-examined and untested video statement. The proposal was to adduce this as evidence without calling the complainant. She would not give evidence in part through fear, but not fear relevantly induced by the respondent. To admit this evidence would, we think, be a breach of Article 6.3 of the Convention, denying the respondent his minimum right and a breach by the court of section 6 of the Human Rights Act 1998. Subject to this, the judge had a discretion under section 116(4) of the 2003 Act, which was evaluative and fact sensitive. We are quite unpersuaded that his decision was unreasonable, let alone perverse. Indeed, we think that a conviction on the basis of this hearsay evidence, uncross-examined, was likely to result in a successful appeal against conviction, if conviction there were. The respondent would have been denied an important component of his minimum rights to a fair trial.

---

10. The Civil Evidence Act 1995

Major inroads were made into the hearsay rule in civil matters by the Civil Evidence Act 1968. However, this statute did not abolish the rule as one of admissibility, and had complicated procedural requirements. In 1988, the Civil Justice Review recommended a fresh inquiry into the rule's operation in civil cases. This was conducted by the Law Commission, which, in September 1993, published a report entitled *The Hearsay Rule in Civil Proceedings* (Law Commission

Report No 216). It recommended the abolition of the exclusionary rule against hearsay in civil cases, subject to certain procedural safeguards, such as a duty to give notice of hearsay evidence where it was reasonable and practicable to do so, and giving an opposing party the power to call a witness for cross-examination on his hearsay statement.

This development would, inter alia, reflect changes in the nature of civil litigation over the previous two decades (the exchange of witness statements, etc.). As the Commission observed in para. 1.5 of the Report: '….recent developments in the law and practice of civil litigation point to a new approach, where the main emphasis is upon ensuring that, so far as possible and subject to considerations of reliability and weight, all relevant evidence is capable of being adduced.' The Law Commission further recommended that a failure to give any (or adequate) notice should still not affect admissibility of a hearsay statement, but instead go to its weight and/or lead to costs sanctions being imposed.

The Civil Evidence Act 1995 was passed to implement these recommendations. It ended objections to the adduction of evidence in civil trials based purely on the ground that it is hearsay. Thus, s. 1(1) of the statute provides that: 'In civil proceedings evidence shall not be excluded on the ground that it is hearsay.' Additionally, there is no distinction between multiple and first hand hearsay when it comes to admissibility; by virtue of s. 1(2)(b) 'references to hearsay include hearsay of whatever degree'. As a result, statements such as 'Jim said that John said that Jerry said' are admissible.

Nevertheless, hearsay remains as an evidential 'class apart', even in civil cases. This reflects the traditional common law view that, in an ideal world, witnesses would usually be present to testify in person at trial, something that would allow them to be cross-examined, so that their credibility could be assessed; it would also reduce the danger of error inherent in the repetition of a statement, a risk that is compounded in the case of multiple hearsay. There was also a fear that trials might be unduly prolonged by admitting excessive amounts of hearsay, something that 'could lead to a proliferation of evidence of little probative value'. Unsurprisingly, many of these concerns are the same as those subsequently expressed about criminal hearsay, albeit that the exigencies of civil litigation allow a rather different response.[19]

Hearsay evidence still requires special treatment. In particular, a party should give notice to their opponent that they intend to rely on hearsay evidence. Additionally, there is a power to call for cross-examination of a person whose statement has been tendered as hearsay evidence, and there are statutory guidelines to assist the court in assessing the weight which should be attached to hearsay.

Notice Provisions

By s. 2(1) a party proposing to adduce hearsay evidence is required to give to the opposing party notice of that fact, and, if they are requested, such particulars of the evidence as is reasonable and practicable in the circumstances for the purpose of enabling him or them to deal with any matters arising from its being hearsay. No time was specified in the Act but s. 2(2) of the statute envisaged that rules of court would be made specifying when and how the notice was to be given, and any categories of evidence that would be exempt from such a requirement. These are now contained in rr. 33.2 and 33.3 of the CPR 1998.

[19] See on this also Law Commission Consultation Paper, *Hearsay in Civil Proceedings* Consultation Paper No 117 (1991) at paras. 33–39 and n. 1 at para. 4.41.

In its report, the Law Commission indicated that the notice provisions contained in the Act should operate in a manner that was complementary to the other means by which parties become aware of the strength of their opponents' case. It envisaged that notice would normally be given at the same time as witness statements were exchanged. This has been reflected in the CPR 1998. Thus, under r. 33.2(4)(a) the party seeking to rely on the hearsay evidence must serve notice of it no later than the latest date for serving witness statements during the litigation process.

Contents of a Hearsay Notice

A hearsay notice should identify the hearsay evidence that is to be given in evidence, the person who made it, and state why that person will (or may) not be called to give oral evidence. If the hearsay evidence is contained in a witness statement (as it often will be), it should refer to the part of the witness statement where it is set out. Additionally, s. 2(1) of the 1995 Act provides that the recipient of such a notice may request such further particulars of the hearsay evidence as is 'reasonable and practicable in the circumstances for the purpose of enabling him or them to deal with any matters arising from its being hearsay'.

Failure to Give Notice

Even if a party fails to give notice at the requisite time, or at all, or fails to give particulars of the hearsay evidence pursuant to a request from the recipient of a s. 2 notice, the consequences are relatively modest. The 1995 Act was fairly generous to defaulters as, under s. 2(4) the court has no power to exclude hearsay evidence simply for a failure to comply with the notice provisions, however glaring it might be. Instead, the sanctions for default range from adjournment of the trial pursuant to s. 2(4)(b), so allowing the other party time to consider the evidence concerned, via a penalty costs order under s. 2(4)(a), to regarding the default: '...as a matter adversely affecting the weight to be given to the evidence in accordance with the guidelines contained in s 4'. This last is likely to be the most significant consequence of such a failure, especially in a 'high value' action, where legal costs are small in comparison to the outcome of the case.

Power to Cross-examine

Section 3 of the Act envisaged that rules of court would be made to allow a party, with leave of the court, to call a witness whose evidence has been tendered as hearsay by another party, so that they could cross-examine that witness on their statement, treating it as their evidence in chief. Thus, the onus is on the recipient of a notice to apply for leave to cross-examine the maker of a hearsay statement. The application will have to be made prior to the trial in order for the court to determine whether it is reasonable or practicable for the witness to attend. In coming to this decision, the court will have regard to a number of criteria. The need to seek leave of the court to call and cross-examine a hearsay witness is not invoked as frequently as might be imagined, as, in the words of the Commission, normally: '...no party would willingly put forward hearsay evidence if better direct evidence were available'. Under r. 33.4 of the CPR 1998 such leave should be sought within 14 days of receiving notice of the intention to rely on the hearsay statement.

> **Cross-reference Box**
>
> This attitude also lies (in part) behind the abandonment of the historic 'best evidence' rule. For more on this go to chapter 1 at p. 60.

Interestingly, at the Court of Appeal stage of *Polanski v Conde Nast Publications Ltd* [2004] 1 WLR 387, Simon Brown LJ noted that the court could exercise its general exclusionary discretion under r. 32.1(2) of the CPR to refuse to admit evidence where the maker of a hearsay statement had failed to comply with an order that he attend for cross-examination at trial made under r. 33.4(1) of the CPR. In these circumstances, the judge felt, this would: '...in no way offend against section 1 of the 1995 Act: the evidence would not be excluded on the ground of being hearsay but rather because the witness refused to attend for cross-examination as required'. (Indeed, theoretically, there appears to be no reason as to why such an exclusionary discretion should not also be exercised where there has been a failure to comply with the notice requirements established by the 1995 Act.) However, it seems that this would be very unlikely to occur in practice, especially as Lord Nicholls, considering the same case in the House of Lords, concluded (in *obiter* comments) that it would not normally be appropriate.

Polanski v Conde Nast Publications Ltd [2005] 1 WLR 637, HL

Lord Nicholls

I agree with the Court of Appeal that the court's case management powers under CPR r 32.1 are wide enough to enable the court to make the orders indicated by the Court of Appeal in this passage. But I do question whether in the present case, had a VCF order been refused, the court would have been 'bound' to make an order excluding Mr Polanski's statements from evidence if he did not present himself in court for cross-examination. Such an exclusionary order should not be made automatically in respect of the non-attendance of a party or other witness for cross-examination. Such an order should be made only if, exceptionally, justice so requires. The overriding objective of the Civil Procedure Rules is to enable the court to deal with cases justly. The principle underlying the Civil Evidence Act 1995 is that in general the preferable course is to admit hearsay evidence, and let the court attach to the evidence whatever weight may be appropriate, rather than exclude it altogether.

Guidelines as to Weight

The Law Commission proposed the development of statutory guidelines as to how hearsay evidence should be assessed, if only to prevent abuse arising from the abolition of the rule as one of exclusion in civil cases. As a result, under s. 4 of the 1995 Act, a court, when estimating the weight to be given to hearsay evidence, should have particular regard to: whether it would have been reasonable and practicable to produce the maker of the original statement as a witness; the contemporaneity of the making of that statement; whether the evidence involves multiple or first hand hearsay; whether anyone involved in the making or transmission of the statement had any motive to conceal or misrepresent matters; whether the original statement was an edited account, or was made in collaboration with another or for a particular purpose; whether the circumstances in which the evidence is adduced as hearsay are such as to suggest an attempt to prevent proper evaluation of its weight, for example, failure to give notice or to reply to a request for further particulars of the hearsay evidence (see above).

Arguably, these factors are fairly obvious and little more than common sense, being matters that any experienced trial judge would automatically consider, though they may provide a useful structure for directing laymen in those few civil cases that still employ juries (such as defamation actions). In appropriate situations, it seems that hearsay evidence can be accorded so little weight that, effectively, it is almost excluded, as the following case makes clear.

Solon South West Housing Association Ltd v James [2005] HLR, CA

Mance LJ

On the face of s. 4, the availability of the maker of an original statement to be called is a matter going to weight not admissibility, but there is certainly power under the Civil Procedure Rules to exclude hearsay evidence. We were referred in that connection to the case of Grobbelaar v News Group Newspapers Ltd, August 12, 1999 in this court, although we were only shown this in The Times Law Reports for that date. To my mind, there is very little, if any, relevant difference between asking a judge to exclude evidence (which in this case does not appear to have happened) and asking him not to rely on it, since under s. 4 a judge could determine that evidence was not worthy of any particular weight even after it had been admitted. So in one sense it does not matter that there was no application to exclude the evidence. The question is whether the judge put weight on particular evidence and whether he was justified in doing so. When one reads the judge's account of the hearsay evidence which I have incorporated in this judgment, it seems to me that, far from endorsing generally the hearsay evidence in the bundle without discriminating between hearsay evidence coming from witnesses who were expressly unwilling by reason of fear to give evidence and other witnesses, the judge was careful in relation to the anonymous witnesses to confine himself to evidence where there was evidence of fear of identification or reprisals precluding the disclosure of their names or their calling. As I have said, in the other cases where the names were identified, the obvious position is that it would have been open to Mr Cottle to require them to attend for cross-examination under CPR 33.4, something which he never did at trial. ... Mr Cottle emphasised before us the importance of cross-examination and the prejudice, as he submitted, of inability to cross-examine in cases of admission of hearsay evidence. That inability is a natural consequence of the admission of hearsay evidence, where the maker of a statement is not identifiable or available to be called.

In *Welsh v Stokes* [2007] PIQR P27 two motorists were in the vicinity of a riding accident, in which a young woman was thrown from, and then crushed by, her riding school horse. She sued the defendant for negligence and liability under the Animals Act 1971. However, the complainant had no memory at all of what had occurred due to a head injury. Only one of the motorists had witnessed the accident, the details of which he reported to the other before disappearing without trace. At trial, the second motorist was allowed to give (hearsay) evidence as to what the first motorist had told him about how the accident occurred. This was the only real evidence in the case, and central to the first instance judge's decision to find for the claimant. The defendant appealed on the basis that the trial judge should not have given it significant weight, and that, as matter of law, the uncorroborated and untested hearsay evidence of the unknown motorist should have carried insufficient weight to allow a court to make specific findings of fact based on it. This argument was rejected by the Court of Appeal, which noted that the trial judge had directed himself properly with regard to all of the factors identified as relevant to weight in s. 4(2) of the Civil Evidence Act 1995.

Welsh v Stokes [2007] PIQR P27, CA

Dyson LJ

The judge was plainly alive to the difficulty of assessing the reliability of the account given by the unidentified witness. But he did have expert evidence to the effect that the account was 'credible'. I take 'credible' to mean 'plausible'. That was important evidence which the judge was entitled to take into account in deciding to give weight to the evidence. I accept that the defendants were unable to explore the reliability of the account or to raise issues of the kind that Miss Rodway would have wished to canvass in cross-examination. But there was no doubt that the claimant fell off Ivor and as a result sustained a head injury. In these circumstances, there was a limited number of plausible explanations for the accident. Miss Rodway suggested to Mr Mackie in cross-examination that the claimant might simply have lost an iron and tipped off herself. Another possibility was that the horse could have reared causing her to fall off as the judge found. No doubt there are other possibilities too, but Miss Rodway did not suggest any in the course of argument. In these circumstances, the expert evidence that the account attributed by Mr Wragg to the unidentified witness was 'credible' assumed particular significance. I do not accept that the opinion of Mr Mackie that the account given by the unknown motorist was credible was in any way dependent on the truth of that account. All that Mr Mackie was saying was that the account given by the motorist provided a plausible explanation of how the claimant came to be injured.

In my judgment, therefore, the judge was entitled to infer that the hearsay evidence was reliable and conclude that he should give it weight. He reached a conclusion that was reasonable and well within the ambit of conclusions that were reasonable for a court to reach. Even if the hearsay evidence were the only evidence on which the claim was based, I would not accept that this was necessarily a reason for giving it no weight. It would depend on all the circumstances. I accept that there will be cases where it is so unfair to hold a defendant liable solely on the basis of hearsay evidence that a court should place little or no weight on the evidence. Consideration of the factors stated in s. 4(2) will point the way, but will not necessarily be determinative. In some cases the defendant may be able to adduce evidence to contradict, or at least cast doubt on, the hearsay evidence. But there will also be cases, like the present, where the defendant is not in that position. Apart from the unidentified motorist and the claimant, there were no witnesses to the accident. In such a case, there may be said to be unfairness to the defendant in having to face hearsay evidence which he cannot directly challenge. On the other hand, there would be unfairness to the claimant to place no weight on the hearsay evidence, since without it her claim would inevitably fail.

The decision what weight (if any) to give to hearsay evidence involves an exercise of judgment. The court has to reach a conclusion as to its reliability as best it can on all the available material. Where a case depends entirely on hearsay evidence, the court will be particularly careful before concluding that it can be given any weight. But there is no rule of law which prohibits a court from giving weight to hearsay evidence merely because it is uncorroborated and cannot be tested or contradicted by the opposing party. I do not consider that the statements in the authorities relied on by Miss Rodway in her skeleton argument support such an extreme proposition. . . . For these reasons, I would dismiss the appeal in so far as it is based on the hearsay point.

Business and Computer Records

Under the simplified regime introduced by the Act, business records, whether or not generated by a computer, are admissible and subject to the same notice and weighing provisions as oral hearsay. In order to ensure that it is easier for such records to be admitted in evidence, they may be proved by the production of a certificate from an officer of the relevant business confirming that the document forms part of the records of the business. The form and contents of the certificate are a matter for rules of the court. The Commission recognized that in the case of computer records, in particular, there is widespread scope for abuse 'through the capacity to hack, corrupt or alter information'. However, the Commission was confident that the weighing provisions of s. 4 would offer a sufficient safeguard with 'parties being encouraged to provide information as to the security of their systems'.

Preserved Common Law Exceptions in Civil Cases

As with s. 118 of the CJA 2003, s. 7(2) of the CEA 1995 expressly preserved a number of common law exceptions. At first sight, this might appear strange; if the hearsay rule has ceased to operate as one of exclusion, what significance could there be in identifying hearsay evidence as admissible under one of the historic common law exceptions? One answer is that such provisions do not attract the procedural requirements for the admission of hearsay set out under s. 2 of the 1995 Act. Many of the preserved common law exceptions are the same as those found in s. 118 of the 2003 Act (see above). Amongst them are evidence of family tradition and reputation, admissions, public records and published works.

Credibility under the Civil Evidence Act 1995

As with the CJA 2003, the 1995 statute made provision for assessing the competence and credibility of the maker of a hearsay statement. Thus, s. 5 of the Act establishes that where hearsay evidence is adduced, and the person who made the original statement is not called as a witness, evidence is still admissible to attack or to support his credibility or to challenge his competence to testify. For example, under s. 5(2)(a) the fact that the maker of the statement has an 'unspent' conviction (under the Rehabilitation of Offenders Act 1974) might be adduced, as this could be put to him and proved under s. 6 of the misleadingly named Criminal Procedure Act 1865 if he testified in person. Additionally, under s. 5(2)(b) of the 1995 Act, the party against whom a hearsay statement is tendered can show that, at some point, he has made another statement that is inconsistent with it provided that he would be able to do so had the witness been called 'live' (ie it must not be collateral to it for the purposes of the Criminal Procedure Act 1865 as interpreted in *R v Funderburk* [1990] 1 WLR 587).

 Summary

- The exclusion of hearsay was one of the most important evidential rules developed in English law, and originally subject only to a number of common law exceptions.

- Some of these common law exceptions, such as the various limbs of the *res gestae*, still operate, having been expressly preserved by s. 118 of the CJA 2003 and s. 7 of the CEA 1995. The remainder, such as the 'dying declaration', have been abolished by statute.

- To constitute hearsay a statement must satisfy two tests, it must be an 'out of court statement' whether oral, written or made by gesture and, vitally, must be 'tendered for the truth of its contents'. An out of court statement tendered for any other purpose is not hearsay and is admissible as 'original' evidence. In criminal cases, the hearsay definition no longer extends to so called 'implied exceptions'.

- A number of rationales have been advanced for the emergence and survival of the rule. For example, that most hearsay evidence is not made on oath, cannot be subject to cross-examination, prevents the tribunal from making an assessment of witness demeanour, risks distortion by repetition, is vulnerable to being manufactured, etc. In the modern era, some of these, such as the absence of cross-examination, are still considered to be serious deficiencies; others are now viewed as exaggerated.

- Hearsay evidence is always admissible in civil cases, the hearsay rule having been abolished as one of exclusion by the CEA 1995. However, it retains significance with regard to weight and notice requirements.

- In criminal cases, the law on hearsay has been greatly liberalized by the CJA 2003. However, it remains as a prima facie rule of exclusion, albeit that it is much easier nowadays to find an exception through which it can be admitted.

- In criminal trials hearsay statements made by witnesses who are unable to testify at trial, because they are, for example, dead, too afraid to do so, etc., can be admitted under s. 116 of the CJA 2003, provided the maker of the statement can be identified. Documentary records are admissible under s. 117 of the same Act, provided that the technical prerequisites of the section are met.

- Section 114(1)(d) of the CJA 2003 has introduced a novel inclusionary discretion in criminal cases, whereby hearsay evidence that is otherwise inadmissible, whether tendered by the prosecution or defence, can be adduced, provided it is in 'the interests of justice'. However, it appears that such a discretion will not be exercised lightly.

- There are a number of provisions whereby hearsay evidence that appears, for some reason, to be unfair or unreliable can be excluded from a criminal trial, even though it is otherwise admissible. Any hearsay evidence tendered by the prosecution can, of course, be excluded under s. 78 of the PCEA 1984. Additionally, all hearsay evidence can be excluded under s. 126 of the CJA 2003. Despite its wording, this provision is being given a wide interpretation, and not confined to cases where admitting hearsay would occasion an undue waste of court time.

- These exclusionary discretions can also be used to ensure that a hearsay statement tendered by the prosecution in a criminal trial does not result in a violation of Article 6 of the ECHR, because of the inability of the opposing party to cross-examine its maker (though, in practice, it seems that this will only rarely be deemed to be the case).

 ## Further reading

A Ashworth and R Pattenden, 'Reliability, Hearsay Evidence and the English Criminal Trial' (1986) 102 LQR 292

D Birch, 'Hearsay: Same Old Story, Same Old Song?' [2004] Crim LR 556

P Carter, 'Hearsay: Whether and Whither?' (1993) 109 LQR 573

A Choo, *Hearsay and Confrontation in Criminal Trials* (1996, Oxford Univeristy Press)

Law Commission Report No 216, *The Hearsay Rule in Civil Proceedings* (1993, London: The Stationery Office)

Law Commission Report No 245, *Evidence in Criminal Proceedings: Hearsay and Related Topics* (1997, London: The Stationery Office)

R Friedman, 'Thoughts from Across the Water on Hearsay and Confrontation' [1998] Crim LR 697

J Jackson, 'Hearsay: the Sacred Cow that Won't be Slaughtered?' (1998) 2 E & P 166

P Murphy, 'Hearsay: The Road to Reform' (1997) 1 E & P 107

Questions for Discussion

For suggested approaches, please visit the Online Resource Centre

1. Adam is accused of possessing drugs with intent to supply. The Crown's case is that he is a large-scale dealer in cocaine. His house was raided by the police who discovered a cache of 500 grams of cocaine under his bed. Adam denies the charge, but admits simple possession, saying that he is a heavy drug user and that the cocaine was for his personal consumption. The police took possession of Adam's mobile phone after he was arrested, and answered the calls of a number of people, who typically asked, 'Is that Adam? Do you have any charley? Can I have some coke?' Adam is also accused of assault occasioning actual bodily harm. He allegedly approached Boris, whom he suspected of informing on him, accompanied by another man, and then punched Boris in the face. However, 10 minutes later, while they were still at the scene of the crime, a police officer, Clare, arrived and arrested both men. When she did so, Boris pointed Adam out and said, 'That's the one what hit me'. By an oversight, no subsequent identification of Adam was made, and, at trial, Boris cannot remember which of the two men struck him. Nevertheless, much later that day, an eye witness to the incident, Dana, aged six, tells her mother, Edwina, that that the punch was 'definitely' thrown not by Adam, but by his colleague, Fergus. Unfortunately, immediately after saying this, Dana develops acute post-traumatic stress disorder and is unable to make any further statement about the incident, or even to mention it again.

(a) Can the Crown adduce the evidence of the telephone calls to Adam to suggest that he was dealing in drugs?

(b) Can the Crown call Clare to give evidence of the statement made by Boris, at the scene of the assault, to suggest that it was Adam who struck him?

(c) Can Adam's defence counsel call Edwina to give evidence about what Dana told her about the identity of Boris's assailant?

2. Dick has been convicted of possessing heroin with intent to supply. He seeks to appeal against his conviction on the ground that the trial judge admitted evidence from police officers relating to several telephone calls, made to Dick's house after his arrest, and answered by those officers. Some of the callers, who could not be traced, enquired as to the price of heroin; others asked whether they could collect their 'usual supply'. They all hung up once they realized that Dick was not there.

Advise Dick as to whether the judge's ruling was incorrect.

3. Is it true to say that, since the advent of the Civil Evidence Act 1995, classifying evidence as hearsay is of no significance in civil cases?

4. Adam is accused of murdering his wife Brenda, who was found dying, in her bedroom, from arsenic poison, apparently administered over a period of time. The prosecution case is that Adam regularly put the poison in her night-time milk. Adam denies the charge, and says that his wife committed suicide, probably because she believed that she was terminally ill (the autopsy found a benign tumour in her colon). In his defence he relies upon the fact that by her body was found a brief note, in her handwriting, saying: 'I have decided to end it all. Brenda'. The prosecution wishes to adduce the following pieces of evidence in support of their case. Just before

she lost consciousness, she said to the housekeeper, who found her: 'I think Adam must have put something in my milk'. She died shortly afterwards. Additionally, they wish to adduce the evidence of Charlotte, a friend of Brenda, who will say that shortly before her death, Brenda had told her that Adam had asked her (Brenda) to write the note found by the body, saying that it was needed as a stage prop by his local amateur dramatics society. The prosecution also wishes to adduce a statement, made by Brenda, a week before her death, to another friend, Edwina, in which she said to her friend: 'My guts feel rotten; I think Adam is poisoning me'.

Advise as to any evidential issues raised on the above facts.

5. Richard is accused of committing murder during a botched burglary at Simon's house. The Crown's case is that Simon disturbed Richard while the latter was stealing his pictures, at which point Richard bludgeoned him. Richard admits that he went into the house, but says it was by mistake and that Simon accidentally fell down the stairs cracking his (Simon's) skull, after which he (Richard) ran away in a state of shock. The Crown says that after being hit on the head, Simon staggered from the house into his garden and collapsed. About 30 minutes later, his friend Patrick arrived and rushed over to him. Simon then groaned and muttered 'Murder! Murder! Dicky did it!' He then expired. A few hours before his death, Simon had told his doctor that he was experiencing dizziness and difficulty keeping his balance.

Will the Crown be able to adduce the statement to Patrick to support the count for murder at the criminal trial? Will Richard be able to adduce Simon's statement to the doctor to support his version of events?

6. How does hearsay evidence differ from original evidence? Give examples.

7. How does the Criminal Justice Act 2003 affect the definition of what is hearsay in criminal cases?

8. In *Jones v Metcalfe* [1967] 1 WLR 1286 Diplock LJ stated that hearsay was: '...a branch of the law that has little to do with common sense'. Is this still the case?

9. Monica is accused of murdering her neighbour, Nigella, with a knife. A postman says that he heard a scream from Nigella's living room while he was delivering a parcel to her house. He forced his way in, to investigate, after unavailingly trying to pick the lock of the front door for some 20 minutes. In the lounge, he found Nigella clutching her stomach. Nigella says to him, 'Monica cut me', before dying. Subsequently, defence solicitors receive a letter from another former neighbour of Nigella, Omar, which has a Marbella postmark. In the letter, Omar says that he saw Nigella deliberately fall on the knife, without Monica being present. Enquiries suggest that Omar cannot be found in Spain.

Consider ALL possible grounds for admitting the evidence of Nigella and Omar.

10. Poppy is charged with illegally importing endangered parakeets under the Protection of Rare Birds Act 2008 (fictitious). It is claimed that she smuggled young chicks into England via a secret compartment in a tin trunk, in order to sell them in her pet shop in Newcastle, once they had grown to adulthood. The prosecution wishes to put in evidence an airline ticket bearing Poppy's full name and the city from which the flight originated, which is also the capital of the small Central African country where the parakeets have their natural home.

Advise Poppy as to whether this is hearsay (IGNORE statutory and other exceptions to the hearsay rule).

7 CONFESSION EVIDENCE AND RELATED MATTERS

Definitions

Confession A statement in a criminal trial by a defendant that is adverse to his interests and which is adduced as an exception to the hearsay rule to indicate guilt.

Voir dire Procedure by which the admissibility of a confession is determined, in the absence of the jury, by a trial judge.

Oppression Statutory ground for excluding confessions obtained by this means.

Trial within a trial Alternative description of a *voir dire*.

Unreliability Statutory ground for excluding confessions obtained in circumstances where it would not be reliable.

---

1. Introduction

Status of Confession Evidence

At common law, confessions were received into evidence as an exception to the hearsay rule, being, of course, an out of court statement tendered in a criminal trial for the truth of its contents. Essentially, when it tenders a confession, the prosecution is seeking to advance its case by saying 'he said he did it so he must be guilty of it'. Arguably, it is now a statutory exception to the hearsay rule by dint of the wording of s. 76(1) of the Police and Criminal Evidence Act 1984 (PCEA 1984), which provides that in any proceedings a confession may be 'given in evidence against' an accused person, unless excluded by that section. However, and rather confusingly, it is also expressly preserved by s. 118(5) of the Criminal Justice Act 2003 (CJA 2003) as a common law exception to the hearsay rule.

A confession is sometimes referred to as a criminal form of 'informal admission', to contrast it with formal admissions made at trial by a defendant pursuant to s. 10(1) of the Criminal Justice Act 1967. Unlike a formal admission, the maker of a confession will not normally want it to be admitted into evidence, as it will damage his defence, and so will usually strongly challenge its truth, the circumstances in which it was obtained, or even whether it was made at all. By contrast, it is very difficult for a defendant to go back on a formal admission, which is usually taken as conclusive of the issue to which it relates, unless made by mistake or under a misunderstanding: *R v Kolton* [2000] Crim LR 761.

Cross-reference Box

For a further discussion of formal admissions, and the circumstances in which they might be made, see chapter 1, at pp. 18–19.

Rationale for Admitting Confession Evidence

The traditional rationale for receiving confessions was that such statements, unlike other forms of hearsay, were inherently reliable, because it was so unlikely that a suspect: '...would confess to any crime he had not committed that it was safe to rely upon the truth of what he said': *R v Sharp* [1988] 86 Cr App R 274. Indeed, a confession, even if unsupported by any other evidence, can found a conviction on its own, though this happens comparatively rarely in practice.

Pause for reflection

Do you feel that people never make untruthful statements that are against their own interests?

In this, England differs from some other jurisdictions, including Scotland, where there is a corroboration requirement for confessions, even if, as in Scotland, it is rather a loose one. In 1993, the Runciman Commission on Criminal Justice decided (by a majority) against recommending that such a rule be extended to England and Wales, though it was in favour of a mandatory judicial warning on the extra dangers of convicting on unsupported confessions (still not the law). Instead, over the last 250 years, the courts and Parliament have sought to ensure that confessions were obtained in circumstances that would preclude abuse or unreliability. As will be recalled from chapter 1, there has always been a general discretion at common law to exclude evidence of a confession that has been obtained by underhand means. However, in the modern era, the powers contained in the PCEA 1984 (especially ss. 76 and 78) are more important.

2. Confession Evidence Implicating Co-defendants

Introduction

A confession that implicates a co-accused is not evidence against that person. This is primarily because the rationale for such a statement being true does not apply in this situation, as many suspects would have a strong motive to lie and implicate others in a crime. As a result, it is viewed as ordinary hearsay evidence. Nevertheless, it is not normally considered appropriate to edit out parts of an adduced confession that implicate others, as this might give a misleading impression to the tribunal of fact, which would not know precisely how much personal involvement the confessor was admitting to.

In some situations, the identities of implicated co-defendants can be concealed by hiding their identity behind a letter or number, as occurred in *R v Silcott* [1987] Crim LR 765, reducing the degree of prejudice. This is obviously more practical where there is a multi-handed prosecution, rather than simply two co-defendants standing trial, when, even if the confession refers to a 'Mr. X', it may become obvious that the implicated man is also the defendant standing next to the maker of the confession, in the dock.

Nevertheless, although courts will not normally allow the name of an implicated co-defendant to be removed from a confession, a trial judge *must* direct the jury that the statement is only evidence against its maker: *R v Gunewardene* [1951] 2 KB 600. The current approved Judicial Studies Board specimen direction suggests that where the maker of the statement has not given evidence at trial to support it, a trial judge warns the jury that: 'The statement which B [or any other person] made [to the police] in A's absence implicating A is not and cannot be evidence against A.... You must therefore disregard it when you consider the case against A.'

Of course, a judge has the power to sever trials, under the 1915 Indictment Act and the 1971 Indictment Rules, if it is deemed to be in the interests of justice to do so, and this would avoid the problems attendant on such cases. However, joint criminal trials for co-defendants are strongly favoured in English law, as there are believed to be good policy reasons for co-offenders being tried together. As Lord Widgery noted, these include the need to avoid delay, cost and witness inconvenience. Most importantly, however, there is a perception that a just outcome is more likely to be established by a joint trial than in separate hearings: *R v Lake* [1976] 64 Cr App R 172. This view has been reaffirmed more recently by the Privy Council in *Lobban v The Queen* [1995] 1 WLR 877 and by the House of Lords in *R v Randall* [2004] 1 WLR 56. As a result, an application to sever an indictment on the ground that otherwise the jury would be exposed to hearing one of the defendants being implicated in a co-defendant's confession will usually be met by a refusal, and an assurance that the judge will give appropriate directions on the limited uses that the jury can make of the statement. However, because a confession that implicates a co-defendant is not evidence against that co-defendant, if it is the only 'evidence' against him, at trial, the case (against that defendant) will be thrown out on a submission of 'no case to answer', after the prosecution closes its case.

R v Gunewardene [1951] 2 KB 600, CCA

Lord Goddard CJ

As we have said, there is no doubt that the statement made by the prisoner Hanson incriminated the appellant in a high degree. This is a matter of very frequent occurrence where two or more prisoners are charged with complicity in the same offence. . . . If no separate trial is ordered it is the duty of the judge to impress on the jury that the statement of one prisoner not made on oath in the course of the trial is not evidence against the other and must be entirely disregarded, and that warning was emphatically given by Hilbery J., in the present case. But it would be impossible to lay down that where two prisoners are being tried together counsel for the prosecution is bound, in putting in the statement of one prisoner, to select certain passages and leave out others. As Alice Hanson had pleaded not guilty, counsel for the prosecution was bound to prove the case against her, and, so far as she was concerned, the evidence mainly consisted in the statement which she had made. The judge not only warned the jury that they must not regard her statement as evidence against the appellant but was at pains not to read, in his summing-up, the whole of the statement which she made, confining himself to those parts which bore on her guilt and not on that of the appellant, though he did read one passage which implicated the appellant, again warning the jury that it was not evidence against him. He went so far as to advise the jury not to ask for the woman's statement when they retired, so that they should not have before them matter prejudicial to the appellant. If we were to lay down that that statement of one prisoner could never be read in full because it might implicate, or did implicate, the other, it is obvious that very difficult and inconvenient situations might arise. It not infrequently happens that a prisoner, in making a statement, though admitting his or her guilt up to a certain extent, puts greater blame upon the co-prisoner, or is asserting that certain of his or her actions were really innocent and it was the conduct of the co-prisoner that gave them a sinister appearance or led to the belief that the prisoner making the statement was implicated in the crime. In such a case that prisoner would have a right to have the whole statement read and could, with good reason, complain if the prosecution picked out certain passages and left out others.

Refinement in *Hayter*

The principle laid down in cases such as *Gunewardene* has also been construed quite narrowly, as can be seen in the recent House of Lords case of *R v Hayter* [2005] 1 WLR 605. In *Hayter*, three defendants were charged with murder. According to the prosecution, the first defendant (Bristow) wanted to arrange a contract killing of her husband. There was strong evidence against her. The third defendant (Ryan) was alleged to be the 'hit man' who actually shot and killed her spouse. The evidence against Ryan was based purely on a confession that he had, allegedly, made to his girlfriend. The second defendant (Hayter) was alleged to have been the intermediary who engaged the killer. It was common ground that the evidence against the appellant was entirely circumstantial, and that the case against him depended upon the prosecution being able to prove that R was the killer and B the procurer. If the case against either R or B should fail, then the case against the appellant as go-between would also inevitably fail. The trial judge allowed the matter to go to the jury, and directed them that only if they found both the actual gunman, and the woman who arranged the killing, guilty of murder, would it be open to them (if they wished) to convict the middleman. The jury convicted all three defendants.

The principal argument on behalf of Hayter (the alleged middleman) was that the rule that an out of court confession by one defendant may not be used by the prosecution against a co-defendant had, effectively, if indirectly, been breached by the manner in which the judge directed the jury. At trial, it was submitted for the appellant that, since the jury could only convict Ryan on the basis of his confession, using any subsequent conviction against Hayter would also be (albeit indirectly) to convict Hayter on the basis of his co-defendant's confession. Additionally, it was argued that as the jury had to determine Ryan's guilt before using it to decide on that of Hayter, the case against Hayter should be thrown out on a submission of no case to answer at the end of the Crown's case. The submission was rejected, the judge finding that, where the prosecution was not using, and did not seek to use, the alleged confession of Ryan to confront any part of the appellant's defence, there was no erosion of the fundamental principle that the alleged confession of one defendant, in the absence of the other defendant, was not evidence against that other defendant. The appellant was convicted and appealed, ultimately to the House of Lords.

The majority of the House of Lords rejected the appeal and (Lord Rodger and Lord Carswell dissenting) concluded that, in a joint trial, the confession of one defendant was admissible against a co-defendant only in so far as the confessor's guilt helped to establish the co-defendant's guilt. Provided the jury were sufficiently sure of the truth of the confession to convict the confessor on that basis alone, the ensuing conviction could be used against a co-defendant. The jury must be directed that, when deciding the case against the co-defendant, they must disregard everything said out of court by the confessor that might otherwise be thought to incriminate the co-defendant. Thus, and in summary, if A says 'I killed B at the behest of C', in circumstances where C cannot be guilty without A also being guilty, if they are sure that A is guilty as a result of his confession, they can use his guilt as evidence against C, provided they are warned that it is the conviction that is evidence against C, not anything that he said in his confession implicating C.

Pause for reflection

Is this a valid distinction or merely intellectual games?

R v Hayter [2005] 1 WLR 605, HL

Lord Steyn

Counsel for Hayter relied on the general rule that a confession is only relevant and admissible against the maker of it. The existence of this rule, as well as the auxiliary rule that a trial judge in a joint trial must direct a jury not to rely on the confession of one defendant against other defendants, is not in doubt. The controversy is about the application of the rule in the present case. Counsel for Hayter said that his central submission was that the judge, by permitting the jury to use their finding that Ryan was guilty, in effect permitted the jury to rely on the words and content of the confession of Ryan as evidence against Hayter.

In my view counsel for Hayter has not established this proposition. In clear terms the judge directed the jury not to take into account the words or content of Ryan's confession in the case against Hayter. Subject to the jury being satisfied of the guilt of Ryan and Bristow, he directed the jury that they could take into account those findings, together with other evidence, in the case against Hayter. There is, therefore, no direct or indirect infringement of the rule. This becomes even clearer when one bears in mind that the mischief at which the rule is directed is to prevent the content or words of a confession to be used against anybody but the maker. The judge, of course, directed the jury that they could not use the content or words of any part the confession of Ryan against Hayter. And there is no reason to doubt that the jury would have understood and given effect to this direction.

This conclusion is reinforced if one postulates, contrary to the facts of the case, that Ryan made no out of court confession but that his guilt was established by an eye witness, a fingerprint or circumstantial evidence. In such circumstances counsel for Hayter rightly accepted that the judge would have been entitled to direct the jury that they may take into account their finding that Ryan was guilty of murder in considering the case against Hayter. What is the difference? Counsel for Hayter said that in the case of evidence by an eye witness, a fingerprint or circumstantial evidence, the evidence is 'evidence in the whole case'. This is analytically not an answer. It obscures the true position. It is necessary to consider the case against each defendant separately. That is part of the very alphabet of criminal practice.

Confessions Repeated in Court

It should be noted that where the maker of the statement has given evidence at trial, and repeated the allegation that he made against his co-defendant in his confession in his in court testimony, it becomes evidence for all purposes. A trial judge should point out to the jury that although the admitted confession cannot be evidence against the implicated man, the allegation has been repeated in court, in the co-accused's presence, and is therefore: '… evidence in the case generally, which you are entitled to consider'. Nevertheless, although it then becomes evidence in its own right, it should also be noted that the Judicial Studies Board's specimen direction number 26 suggests that, in such situations, a trial jury should also be warned that the evidence needs to be examined with particular care, because the witness: '… may have been more concerned about protecting himself than about speaking the truth'.

Cross-reference Box

It should also be remembered that if a co-defendant with a criminal record makes such an 'attack' on his fellow accused he risks having his bad character adduced under s. 101(1) (g) of the CJA 2003. For more information on this topic go to chapter 5, p. 215.

3. The History of Confession Evidence

Introduction

As far back as the eighteenth century, it was appreciated that the rationale for adducing confessions would only apply if they were made voluntarily, and that receiving involuntary confessions into evidence was potentially dangerous because they could be unreliable. In particular, it was feared that people could be deceived, bribed, tricked or threatened into making admissions. As a result, safeguards were gradually developed by the courts to prevent this occurring. Thus, by the mid-1700s, Chief Baron Gilbert could note that confessions 'must be voluntary and without compulsion' to be admitted, if only for the practical reason that 'extorted Confessions are not to be depended on'.[1]

By the late eighteenth century, a more precisely formulated rule forbidding the admission of involuntary confessions had emerged. For example, the confession of a defendant tried at the Kent Assizes in 1774 was only admitted after prosecution witnesses had been closely questioned as to whether it was made freely, read over to him before he signed it, and subject to any threats or promises. Confessions obtained in violation of such prerequisites were increasingly excluded.[2] The decision in *R v Warwickshall* (1783) 1 Leach 263 was important in crystallizing such an approach, though, in reality, it merely reiterated what had already become widespread and long established practice. In subsequent years a number of cases appeared in which confessions were excluded in criminal cases on the same basis as in *Warickshall*, ie that they were induced by a promise of advantage or by fear of a threat and an absence of such factors was adopted by various treatise writers as indicative of voluntariness.[3]

Thus, in *Ibrahim v R* [1914] AC 599 Lord Sumner noted that: 'It has long been established... that no statement by an accused is admissible in evidence against him unless it is shown by the prosecution to have been a voluntary statement, in the sense that it has not been obtained from him either by fear of prejudice or hope of advantage excited or held out by a person in authority.' In the twentieth century these two exclusionary grounds were extended to include confessions that were extracted by 'oppression' (a development that was itself influenced by the advent of the ECHR). At common law, this was defined as: '...something which tends to sap and has sapped, that free will which must exist before a confession is voluntary': *R v Isequilla* [1975] 1 WLR 716.

R v Warwickshall (1783) 1 Leach 263, KB

Nares J

Confessions are received in evidence, or rejected as inadmissible, under a consideration whether they are or are not intitled [sic] to credit. A free and voluntary confession is deserving of the highest credit, because it is presumed to flow from the strongest sense of guilt...but a confession forced from the mind by the flattery of hope, or by the torture of fear, comes in so questionable a shape...that no credit ought to be given to it; and therefore it is rejected. This principle respecting confessions has no application whatever as to the admission or rejection of facts, whether the knowledge of them be obtained in consequence of an extorted confession, or whether it arise from any other source.

---

[1] G Gilbert, *The Law of Evidence* (2nd edn., 1760, printed by Catherine Lintot) at 140.
[2] P King, *Crime, Justice, and Discretion in England 1740–1820* (2000, Oxford University Press) at 225–226.
[3] S Penney, 'Theories of Confession Admissibility: A Historical View' (1998) American Journal of Criminal Law, vol 25, 332–372, at 309.

Abolition of Common Law Rules of Exclusion

As a result of numerous cases over more than 200 years, the common law concept of voluntariness became highly technical in its interpretation. This attracted criticism from various bodies, such as the Criminal Law Revision Committee, and eventually led to their replacement by s. 76 of the PCEA 1984, which came into force in early 1986. All confessions in England and Wales are now governed by this statutory provision.

Justifications for Excluding Improperly Obtained Confessions

It should be noted that in *Warwickshall* the primary (if not the only) reason for excluding confessions obtained in dubious circumstances was a concern that they were inherently unreliable, rather than a fear that admitting them encouraged abusive policing or brought the criminal justice system into disrepute. Such views have occasionally been reiterated, in some form, in the modern era. Thus, in *R. v Mason* [1988] 86 Cr App R 349, Watkins LJ, commenting on a deceit practised by the police to obtain a confession, observed that it was not excluded simply because it was police misbehaviour of a particularly serious kind. He went on to say that the courts are: '… not the place to discipline the police. That has been made clear here [the Court of Appeal] on a number of previous occasions'.

However, other cases interpreting various aspects of the PCEA 1984, and the statute itself, cast serious doubt on the accuracy of this observation, and suggest that other factors, including a disciplinary function, are sometimes at work when confessions are excluded. Thus, in *R v Mushtaq* [2005] 1 WLR 1513 a majority of the House of Lords concluded that the rule against admitting involuntary confessions was not based solely upon their potential unreliability but also on the principle that a man cannot be compelled to incriminate himself and upon the importance attached in a civilized society to proper behaviour by the police towards those in their custody.

R v Mushtaq [2005] 1 WLR 1513, HL

Lord Hutton

It is clear that there are two principal reasons underlying the rule that a confession obtained by oppression should not be admitted in evidence. One reason, which has long been stated by the judges, is that where a confession is made as a result of oppression it may well be unreliable, because the confession may have been given, not with the intention of telling the truth, but from a desire to escape the oppression imposed on, or the harm threatened to, the suspect. A further reason, stated in more recent years, is that in a civilised society a person should not be compelled to incriminate himself, and a person in custody should not be subjected by the police to illtreatment or improper pressure in order to extract a confession.

Pause for reflection

Do you feel that factors other than reliability should be considered when determining the admissibility of a confession?

Of course, the potential unreliability of a confession that has been obtained in dubious circumstances remains an important justification for having a special regime for such evidence, as it is this that has contributed towards many of the most notorious miscarriages of justice in recent years. Amongst a fairly lengthy list of such cases might be considered the experiences of the 'Cardiff Three', the 'Guildford Four', Judith Ward, etc. In this area, however, society has also moved on in its understanding of the risk of untruthful confessions since the 1980s, let alone the 1700s. For example, the seminal work of psychologists such as Gisli Gudjonsson has made the courts much more aware than previously that false confessions can be obtained from suspects with psychological vulnerabilities, even where the interview is conducted in circumstances which are not overtly malign. This might be, for example, because the suspect is highly suggestible.[4]

Gisli H Gudjonsson, 'Unreliable confessions and miscarriages of justice in Britain' (2002) International Journal of Police Science & Management, vol 4, no 4, 332–343 (Extract)

Unprecedented scientific and legal advances have been made in Britain in recent years in relation to cases of disputed confessions. The attitude of High Court judges to expert psychological evidence in cases of disputed confessions, and their level of sophistication in evaluating it, have greatly improved since the late 1980s. The cases presented in this paper show that it is wrong to assume that only persons with learning disability or those who are mentally ill make unreliable or false confessions. The cases demonstrate the importance of personality factors in potentially rendering a confession unreliable, which is supported by recent empirical research into the nature of false confessions (Gudjonsson, 2003; Gudjonsson, Sigurdsson, Bragason, Einarsson, and Valdimarsdottir, submitted). The general thrust of the legal criteria developed over the past 10 years has broadened the admissibility of expert testimony to include abnormally marked personality traits (eg extreme suggestibility, compliance, anxiety proneness, poor self-esteem, impulsivity). Of course, these must be of the type to render a confession potentially unreliable (ie their relevance to the disputed confession must be demonstrated). Admissibility of expert testimony is no longer restricted to conditions of mental or psychiatric disorder, such as mental illness, learning disability, or personality disorder. Court of Appeal judgments are important in influencing the attitude and practice of the lower courts towards expert psychological and psychiatric testimony. Furthermore, the rulings in relation to both psychological vulnerability and police impropriety are also important in terms of influencing the behaviour of the police in the future. As McKenzie (2002) puts it: 'A 25-year police background, coupled with close to 40 years of observations and analysis of police behaviour, leads me to conclude that there is no more effective way for the courts to encourage police officers to toe the line than by throwing out cases in which they have breached procedures' (p. 447). The psychological understanding of unreliable and false confessions has progressed greatly since the Fisher Inquiry (1977) into the wrongful convictions of three youths who had made false confessions to the murder of Maxwell Confait. The recognition and acceptance by

---

[4]   See generally GH Gudjonsson, *The Psychology Of Interrogations And Confessions: A Handbook* (2002, John Wiley & Sons).

the judiciary that false confessions to serious crimes do occur on occasions, even in the absence of learning disability or mental illness, are fundamental to reducing the number of miscarriages of justice cases resulting from unreliable confessions.

The following extract shows the increased judicial awareness that has emerged in recent years from exposure to such research.

R v Blackburn [2005] 2 Cr App R 30, CA

Keene LJ

The essence of Dr Shepherd's evidence before us was that the key feature giving rise to a coerced compliant confession is fatigue, which, together with an inability to control what is happening, may induce the individual to experience a growing desire to give up resisting suggestions put to him. Eventually he can take no more and is overwhelmed by the need to achieve his immediate goal of bringing the interrogation to an end. That may not seem rational to an outsider, but it becomes rational if the individual finds the circumstances becoming intolerable. The age of such a person, said Dr Shepherd, is significant. Generally the younger he is, the less able he is to withstand sustained pressure. After more than three hours' interview without a break and references to new sexual allegations about the 1976 Irlam incident, one could well get a coerced compliant confession. Whether true or false, it is not reliable, said Dr Shepherd, because of such circumstances. He noted the appellant's evidence at trial that he had confessed because he wanted to get out of the interview and he 'felt sick of it'. Dr Shepherd also described the phenomenon of persons in such a position inventing details when under stress, something he termed 'confabulation' or conversational polyfilla. This can sometimes lead to a person describing things which could not have happened. Such details needed, said Dr Shepherd, to be checked out before they should be accepted.

    30 He distinguished these phenomena from the characteristic of suggestibility. The latter is related to personality, whereas the former are more the result of fatigue and vulnerability because of age or other factors. Consequently normal people, not suffering from any personality disorder or abnormal disorder, could be rendered compliant by prolonged interrogation. Dr Shepherd regarded Mr McVitie as having allowed the interviewing process to continue for too long and in that sense not to have acted properly.

Confessions after the PCEA 1984

The historic grounds for excluding confessions, dating back to the eighteenth century, were replaced by the grounds set out in the PCEA 1984 and, in particular, ss. 76 and 78 of that statute (the former being dedicated to confession evidence). It should be noted immediately that the 1984 Act is a codifying rather than a consolidating statute or one that is stipulated to be declaratory of the common law. As a result, earlier authority on, for example, the meaning of words, such as 'oppression' (one of the grounds of exclusion at common law after the 1950s), set out in cases like *R v Priestly* [1965] 51 Cr App R 1, are of little or no value in the modern era, and so largely ignored, even where they use identical terminology to that found in the 1984

Act: *R v Fulling* [1987] 2 WLR 923. Instead, as Lane CJ pointed out in *Fulling*, the principles of statutory construction for codifying Acts set out in *Bank of England v Vagliano Brothers* [1891] AC 107 apply.

4. Definition of a Confession under the PCEA 1984

Introduction

Since the PCEA 1984 came into force, confessions have been the subject of a statutory definition. Under s. 82(1) of the PCEA 1984 they 'include…any statement wholly or partly adverse to the person who made it, whether made to person in authority or not and made in words or otherwise'. This definition is important, as only a confession can be excluded under s. 76 of the statute. If a defendant's statement is tendered by the Crown, but does not amount to a confession, it may be possible to exclude it under the general judicial discretion contained in s. 78(1), but not under s. 76, the provision specifically dedicated to confessions.

A confession does not have to be made to a person 'in authority'. For example, confessions can be made to neighbours and work colleagues, or, as in *Hayter*, to a partner or spouse. Although a confession made to such individuals can be excluded under the same grounds as those made to the police, ie under ss. 76(2) and 78, their recipients are not, of course, subject to the extensive codes of practice and rules that regulate those who are professionally engaged in investigating crime. Thus, in *R v Elleray* [2003] 2 Cr App R 11, a youth confessed to a rape to probation officers preparing pre-sentence reports for an offence of indecent assault to which he had earlier pleaded guilty. The Court of Appeal upheld the trial judge's decision to admit the confession at a subsequent trial for rape, in which the admissions were the only evidence against the defendant, although they were not made under caution or with legal representation present (or offered), and without being contemporaneously recorded. These deficiencies would have been fatal to admissibility had police officers received confessions in such circumstances.

Pause for reflection

As (indirect) agents of the state, should probation officers have to meet the same safeguards as policemen when adducing confessions made to them in a professional capacity?

In recent years, 'cell confessions' have occasioned considerable problems for the courts in this regard. These are admissions made by a suspect, who has been held in custody, to another prisoner. The obvious difficulty is that, by their nature, such prison associates are likely to have criminal records and a potential interest in currying favour with the authorities. Nevertheless, they are admissible, although a trial judge will normally warn jurors about the need for caution when considering them: *R v Stone* [2005] Crim LR 569.

Cross-reference Box

This is one of comparatively few situations in the modern era where a judge will normally be obliged to warn a jury about the dangers of a certain type of witness evidence. For more on this go to pp. 535–539.

R v Elleray [2003] 2 Cr App R 11, CA

Lord Woolf CJ

Mr Priestly now advances to this Court the submissions which he made before the judge. He says that the judge came to the wrong decision in concluding that the evidence of the probation officers should be admitted before the jury.... A probation officer is under a duty to prepare a report which clearly and frankly sets out the probation officer's view, in particular in relation to sexual offenders, as to the degree of risk to the public that an offender constitutes. In order to do this in many cases they have to ask questions of an offender as to the precise circumstances in which the offender came to commit the offence to which he may have already pleaded guilty, or in relation to which there may be an agreed basis of facts between the prosecution and the defence. If in the course of that interview the offender volunteers an admission of committing the particular offence or some other offence which is relevant to the task of the probation officer in preparing their report for the court, they cannot ignore what they have been told. They are under a duty to provide a full and frank report which includes those details. Usually there will be little risk of any danger of action being taken in relation to an offender in consequence of anything said to the probation officers or anything said in a report. However, as this case illustrates, there can be a situation where that can arise.... The matter has to be considered, as was done by the trial judge in this case, by deciding whether there is a basis for excluding it under s. 78 of the Police and Criminal Evidence Act 1984. However, the fact that the evidence may be admissible in criminal proceedings does not mean that the fact that the admission was made in the course of an interview between an offender and a probation officer should be ignored. It is clearly important that there should be frankness in the exchanges between a probation officer and an offender as this furthers the role of the probation officer in the sentencing exercise. If it were to be the practice that the prosecution regularly rely upon what is said by an offender to a probation officer as evidence for further prosecutions then clearly this would have an adverse effect upon this need for frankness. Indeed a situation could soon arise where probation officers would be hampered in performing their important duty to assist the court in determining the correct sentence for offenders. So in the case of an admission the prosecution should first carefully consider whether it is right to rely upon evidence provided by a conversation between a probation officer and an offender and only rely upon it if they decide it is in the public interests so to do. If they do decide to rely upon that evidence, having taken into account the considerations of public interest to which we have made reference, then the court still has a discretion under s. 78 of the 1984 Act to ensure that no unfairness will occur because of the reliance on the admissions which an offender is alleged to have made. In deciding whether to exclude the evidence it is perfectly appropriate for the court to have in mind the contrast between the position that exists where an offender is interviewed by the police and that which exists when the offender is interviewed by a probation officer. The court should bear in mind the need for frankness between the offender and the probation officer; the fact that there may not be a reliable record of what was said; that the offender has not been cautioned; and that the offender has not had the benefit of legal representation. The protection which the court can provide under s. 78 in the majority of cases should be sufficient to ensure that no unfairness occurs to an offender.... Having said that, and returning to the facts of this case, we are conscious here that once the appellant had disclosed that he had committed rape on more than one occasion, in order to perform that responsibility of protecting the public the probation officers could not ignore what the appellant had said. They had to include the admissions in their report. It clearly was relevant to the degree of risk that the appellant constituted. 14 If the prosecution in this case had not adopted the course of charging the appellant with the offences of rape, then it would still have been necessary for the court to come to a conclusion as to the accuracy of the probation officers' record as to what the appellant said if he was challenging that record. 15 In the circumstances of this case we cannot say that it was wrong or unfair for the prosecution to have decided to prosecute the appellant for the offences of rape. We cannot criticise the judge for the conclusion to which he came as to the admissibility of the evidence of what was said to the probation officers.

'In Words or Otherwise'

Section 82(1) also makes it clear that a confession could, in the right circumstances, be made by a gesture such as a nod of the head, though establishing this to an appropriate standard might prove difficult for the police, if no one else, unless a videotape has been taken. This is what occurred in the Privy Council case of *Li Shu-Ling v R* [1988] 3 All ER 138 where a suspect's filmed re-enactment of a murder was held to be a confession. Doubtless, now that increasing use is being made of the video-recording of confessions (regulated by Code F) they may occur slightly more frequently in future.

Li Shu-Ling v R [1988] AC 270, PC

Lord Griffiths

It is conceded on behalf of the defendant that if a video recording had been made of his oral confession the video film would be admissible in evidence. If in the course of the video recording of the oral confession the accused had been asked to demonstrate how he placed his hands round the deceased's neck either using a dummy or a police officer it is conceded that this too would be admissible. This concession is rightly made for if an accused can say what he did there is no reason why he should not show what he did, indeed many illiterate people might find it easier to demonstrate an action rather than attempt to describe it in words. If it is permissible to allow the defendant to re-enact a part of the crime during interrogation there is no reason in principle why, if he is prepared to do so, he should not show how he committed the crime at the scene of the crime. The technique of video recording confessions in the form of a re-enactment of the crime is already established in Hong Kong although, as one would expect, it is confined to relatively few grave crimes. Such evidence has been held to be admissible in principle in Reg. v. Tam Wing-kwai [1976] H.K.L.R. 401 although, for reasons to which their Lordships will return later, it was held that it should have been excluded on the facts of that particular case. Video recordings of re-enactments of the crime by the accused and another participant have also been held to be admissible in Australia, Reg. v. Lowery and King (No. 1) [1972] V.R. 554, Collins v. The Queen (1980) 31 A.L.R. 257, in Canada Reg. v. Tookey and Stevenson (1981) 58 C.C.C. (2d) 421 and in the United States People v. Dabb (1948) 32 Cal. 2d 491 cited with approval in Hendricks v. Swenson (1972) 456 F. 2d 503. It should however be noted that some of these authorities warn of the caution that should be exercised when the judge considers whether he should exercise his discretion to exclude the video recording. It is self-evident that a re-enactment of the crime is likely to fall far short of a complete reconstruction of the actual event. Nevertheless in many crimes there should be little difficulty in re-enacting and demonstrating the essential features of the crime.

'Wholly or Partly Adverse'

A confession must be 'wholly or partly adverse' to its maker. The first part would encompass a statement such as 'Okay, you've got me bang to rights. I did it. It was premeditated. There's no excuse for what I did.' Such a statement is obviously damningly inculpatory. 'Partly adverse' is slightly more complicated, but would certainly extend to a statement that, while incriminatory with regard to some facts in issue, raises a partial or total defence: 'He lunged at me with a razor and I was terrified so I killed him.' Although admitting the *actus reus* of murder, this also raises self-defence. However, it seems that a statement that placed a suspect at a crime scene, or advanced the prosecution case in some other tangible manner, would also be viewed as partly adverse. In *R v De Silva* [2003] 2 Cr App R 5 the defendant was accused of importing cocaine from St Lucia. After being arrested at an airport with the drug in his possession he agreed to make telephone calls, under police supervision, to various contacts in England. It was held that the telephone calls, which contained incriminating material, constituted a confession.

R v De Silva [2003] 2 Cr App R 5, CA

Hughes J

These calls clearly did contain material which the jury might take to incriminate the appellant both in some of what he himself had said and in what had been said to him. They suggested that he had an arrangement to meet somebody to hand-over the suitcases containing the drugs. They suggested a reasonably close relationship with the people in the Caribbean, who clearly had an interest in the cases. They indicated that the appellant and Miss James had been in the company of such people before they left to come to England. The calls also revealed, through the mouth of one of the callers that there had at some stage been a third suitcase, which the appellant said on the telephone that he had left behind in the Caribbean. 16 There is no doubt that, quite apart from the relevance of these calls in the case of the co-accused Young, the Crown sought the admission of them as part of its case against this appellant. In due course, in deciding to admit the calls, the learned judge said this: 'It may well be that the jury can infer, and it would be a matter entirely for them, that certain passages here do show that the defendant was a party to a plan to bring in those suitcases.' 17 Then a little later: 'It will be for the jury to draw reasonable inferences from the contents of the telephone calls if they think it appropriate.' We are, accordingly, quite satisfied that these calls did contain evidence contrary to the interests of the appellant at the trial. It follows from that that, for the purposes of s. 76 of the 1984 Act, this was evidence which was within the extended definition of the expression 'confession', which is given by s. 82(1) of the Act; that is to say, a statement wholly or partly adverse to the person making it.

Exculpatory on its Face but Incriminating at Trial

What of a statement that, on its face, is wholly exculpatory or entirely neutral when made, but which turns out to be thoroughly inconvenient or damaging (and so 'adverse') to the defendant at trial? For example, suppose that, when interviewed, a murder suspect tells the police that he was 500 miles away on holiday at the time of the killing, which was nothing to do with him, and that he had a thoroughly harmonious relationship with the dead man. Subsequently, however, analysis of a security video reveals the accused man leaving the crime scene at the time of the killing and prompts him to change his defence from alibi to provocation or self-defence. The initial statement to the police, even if not defined as a confession, would normally be admitted as part of the prosecution's case, to show the defendant's reaction when taxed with incriminating facts (see below). Alternatively, it might be put to the defendant as a previous inconsistent statement under s. 4 of the Criminal Procedure Act 1865, were he to testify and to give evidence that was inconsistent with his earlier statement. Either way, if the defendant were to advance self-defence or provocation at trial, it is likely that his defence would be badly undermined by such an apparently evasive statement. However, were the statement to be defined as a confession under s. 82(1), it might be excluded under s. 76(2)(a) if, for example, there had been 'oppressive' questioning by the police. Of course, this would only be possible if 'adverse' extended to being adverse at trial, rather than meaning adverse on its face when made. Nevertheless, s. 82(1) does not make the time at which 'adverse' is to be considered clear.

In some common law jurisdictions the statement's consequences at trial are decisive. For example, this was the conclusion of the Supreme Court of Canada in *Piche v R* (1970) 11 DLR 700. However, in England, prior to the advent of PCEA 1984, Lord Widgery observed in *R v Pearce* [1979] 69 Cr App R 365 that: 'A denial does not become an admission because it is inconsistent with another denial.' After the PCEA 1984 came into force, the matter was examined in *obiter dicta* comments made by Lord Lane CJ in the Court of Appeal, in *R v Sat-Bhambra* [1989] 88 Cr App R 55. In this case, the judge adopted a purposive approach when considering ss. 82(1) and 76(2), assuming that the provisions were aimed at excluding statements that were obtained by words or deeds that were likely to be welcome to an interrogator; this could not be said about those that, on their face, were entirely exculpatory. As a result, he concluded that purely exculpatory statements did not fall within the meaning of s. 82(1). This approach was subsequently followed by the Court of Appeal in *R v Park* [1993] 99 Cr App R 270.

The matter arose again for consideration in *R v Hasan* [2005] 2 WLR 709. In this case, the defendant, accused of aggravated burglary, had had an 'off the record' interview with the police about a murder that had allegedly been committed by a third party. On its face, his comments in this interview were entirely exculpatory or neutral. However, his eventual defence to the burglary charge, at trial, was that he had acted under duress from this third party, something that was undermined by what he had said (or not said) about this person in the course of the earlier interview. The Court of Appeal, influenced by the advent of s. 3(1) of the Human Rights Act 1998 (HRA 1998), along with decisions emanating from the European Court of Human Rights (ECtHR) concluded that confessions extended to superficially exculpatory statements that had become disadvantageous at trial (reported as *R v Z* [2003] 1 WLR 1489). The court then certified for consideration by the House of Lords the question as to whether confessions included a statement 'intended by the maker to be exculpatory or neutral, and which appears to be so on its face, but which becomes damaging to him at the trial because, for example, its contents can then be shown to be evasive or false or inconsistent with the maker's evidence on oath'.

After reconsidering the matter, the House of Lords concluded that the Court of Appeal had misinterpreted cases from the ECtHR, and that there was nothing in the HRA 1998 that suggested that the interpretation given in *Sat-Bhambra* was incompatible with any Convention right. The House of Lords also rejected arguments that, as s. 82(1) employed the word 'includes', it was not intended to be exhaustive, and so confined confessions to statements that were, to some extent, adverse to their maker (unlike their conclusion with regard to s. 76(8)). As a result, it reversed the Court of Appeal's decision, restoring the approach that had originally been adopted in *Sat-Bhambra*.

R v Hasan [2005] 2 WLR 709, HL

Lord Steyn

That brings me to the reliance by the Court of Appeal on section 3(1) of the 1998 Act. Undoubtedly there is a strong obligation under section 3(1) to interpret legislation compatibly with Convention rights. There is a strong rebuttable presumption in favour of an interpretation consistent with Convention rights: Ghaidan v Godin-Mendoza [2004] 2 AC 557. Rix LJ held that the interpretation of section 76(1), read with section 82(1), which was suggested in R v Sat-Bhambra 88 Cr App R 55 would be incompatible with a Convention right. The House must, however, consider whether in truth any Convention right is engaged. While it is not spelt out in the judgment of the Court of Appeal, Rix LJ presumably had in mind that Article 6 is the particular Convention right in question. There is, however, nothing in the text of Article 6 or in the corpus of European jurisprudence which supports the view that sections 76(1) and 82(1) create any incompatibility with Article 6. Given the unrestricted capability of section 78 to avoid injustice by excluding any evidence obtained by unfairness (including wholly exculpatory or neutral statements obtained by oppression), sections 76(1) and 82(1) are in my view compatible with Article 6. The decision of the Court of Appeal to the contrary was wrong.

---

5. The Adduction of Exculpatory and 'Mixed' Interviews

Introduction

In *R v Garrod* [1997] Crim LR 445 the Court of Appeal noted that, although wholly exculpatory statements made in police interviews were not admissible as evidence, they were almost inevitably given at trial, usually as part of the prosecution case. This is because such statements are admitted not to show the truth of their contents (as they are not confessions, they would be hearsay if they were), but rather to show the defendant's reaction to being accused or taxed with incriminating matters: *R v Pearce* [1979] 69 Cr App R 365 and *R v Storey* [1968] 52 Cr App R 334. The trial judge is entitled to direct the jury accordingly.

Because they are not evidence, such statements cannot satisfy an evidential burden when one is placed on the defendant, unlike a partly adverse statement, which contains exculpatory as well as adverse material. Thus, in self-defence cases, it is possible that a police interview in which the suspect said: 'I stabbed him because he was threatening me with an axe' might turn out to be more advantageous to the accused at trial than declaring 'I had nothing to do with his stabbing at all'. The former would satisfy the evidential burden for self-defence, the latter would not. Because its material is not properly 'evidence' in the case, a purely exculpatory statement to the police that is adduced to show reaction does not require a *Vye* credibility limb direction, unlike a 'mixed' statement where the defendant does not give evidence but relies on the exculpatory parts, see *Aziz* 1995.

Cross-reference Box

Defences that go beyond a mere denial of the prosecution case, such as self-defence and provocation, place an evidential burden on a defendant to adduce some evidence on the issue before it has to be considered by the tribunal of fact. For a more detailed discussion of defence burdens see pp. 119–124.

R v Pearce [1979] 69 Cr App R 365, CA

Lord Widgery CJ

In our view the present case can be disposed of within the principles stated in Storey and Anwar (supra) and Donaldson (1977) 64 Cr App R 59. Those decisions will be found to contain all the guidance that is necessary in practice. We would ourselves summarise the principles as follows:

(1) A statement which contains an admission is always admissible as a declaration against interest and is evidence of the facts admitted. With this exception a statement made by an accused person is never evidence of the facts in the statement.

(2) (a) A statement that is not an admission is admissible to show the attitude of the accused at the time when he made it. This however is not to be limited to a statement made on the first encounter with the police. The reference in Storey to the reaction of the accused 'when first taxed' should not be read as circumscribing the limits of admissibility. The longer the time that has elapsed after the first encounter the less the weight which will be attached to the denial. The judge is able to direct the jury about the value of such statements. (b) A statement that is not in itself an admission is admissible if it is made in the same context as an admission, whether in the course of an interview, or in the form of a voluntary statement. It would be unfair to admit only the statements against interest while excluding part of the same interview or series of interviews. It is the duty of the prosecution to present the case fairly to the jury; to exclude answers which are favourable to the accused while admitting those unfavourable would be misleading. (c) The prosecution may wish to draw attention to inconsistent denials. A denial does not become an admission because it is inconsistent with another denial. There must be many cases however where convictions have resulted from such inconsistencies between two denials.

(3) Although in practice most statements are given in evidence even when they are largely self-serving, there may be a rare occasion when an accused produces a carefully prepared written statement to the police, with a view to it being made part of the prosecution evidence. The trial judge would plainly exclude such a statement as inadmissible.

Self-serving Exculpatory Defence Statements

Lord Widgery's third point presciently envisaged a situation that occurred the following year. Because it is tendered to show reaction, the trial judge has a discretion to prevent it being abused by a defendant using it to put a carefully crafted exculpatory statement before the tribunal of fact, which would have no value in showing their reaction to being taxed with allegations, but which might be designed to influence jurors: *R v Newsome* [1980] 71 Cr App R 325. In *Newsome* the defendant was accused of rape. At the first two interviews he was initially evasive, but eventually admitted intercourse had occurred. At his third police interview, with his solicitor present, he refused to answer any further questions, on legal advice. Later that same day, however, he made a detailed written statement to the police, again with his solicitor present, claiming that the alleged victim had, in fact, consented to intercourse. At trial, the first instance judge agreed with the prosecution decision not to adduce the statement. On appeal, the trial judge's decision was upheld, as it was clearly a self-serving statement, composed on legal advice, and in circumstances that revealed nothing relevant about the accused's attitude towards the allegations.

R v Newsome [1980] 71 Cr App R 325, CA

Ormord LJ

It is necessary, we think, to bear in mind exactly what was said there, and what was said was that a statement that is not an admission is admissible to show the attitude of the accused at the time when he made it, and for no other purpose. So whether it is relevant to know what the attitude of the accused was at the time of making the statement is clearly one of the matters which will have to be considered, but the broad indication of the second paragraph of this statement, we think, is that the prosecution should present the case fairly, not selecting bits of statements which favour the prosecution and shutting out bits which favour the defence. The prosecution should present the case fairly but, of course, in every case a line has to be drawn and the person to draw the line is, primarily, the learned judge. It is plain that the law of evidence does not, broadly speaking, permit accused persons to get in previous consistent statements merely because they are consistent with the evidence that they are proposing to give in the witness box. So the first rule, it seems to us, is that the prosecution should take the decision as to what statements to put before the jury. But it is the third paragraph of this statement of the law of evidence which is the important one in this case. That is purely a matter for the judge. He has got to decide whether a particular interview falls within (3) or within (2), and while recognising at once that that is not at all an easy task for any judge to perform—perhaps it is, regrettably, difficult for him to perform—we take the view that in this particular case the learned judge was fully entitled to exclude that written statement because it was clearly composed on legal advice with the solicitor present, and so could quite properly be regarded as a self-serving statement. The point about it is not so much that it is self-serving, but that a statement made in such circumstances reveals nothing relevant about the attitude of the accused, because it is clearly coloured by the circumstances in which it was made and the circumstances which immediately preceded its making. We think the learned judge was clearly entitled in this case to take the view that this was a paragraph (3) situation, that accordingly the prosecution was right not to put it in, and no one could compel them to put it in. That being so, the statement could only be got before the jury by counsel for the defence if he could show that it was admissible which, for the reasons we have given, we do not think he could possibly do. Consequently, the learned judge was right in his ruling, and on that part of his appeal, the appellant fails.

The Status of 'Mixed' Statements

As a matter of strict common law theory, 'mixed' statements, ie those which combine inculpatory and exculpatory parts, though confessions, should see a distinction being drawn between the evidential status of the two types of assertion, the former going to truth, the latter merely to reaction. However, this would require a difficult direction to jurors and, in *R v Sharp* [1988] 86 Cr App R 274, it was acknowledged that it would be an invitation to jury confusion. As a result, since *R v Duncan* [1981] 73 Cr App R 359, it has been accepted that the whole of a 'mixed' statement should be treated as evidence, if admitted. Thus, exculpatory portions, as well as inculpatory parts, will be go to the truth of their contents, albeit that the former might attract less weight.

This approach was approved by the House of Lords in *Sharp*, which observed that the: '...whole statement should be left to the jury as evidence of the facts but that attention should be drawn, when appropriate, to the different weight they might think it right to attach to the admission as opposed to the explanation or excuses'. In this case, two detectives investigating a burglary saw the defendant running away from the crime scene. They followed him but he escaped in a car. Three days later the defendant went to a police station and made a statement in which he admitted being in the vicinity of the burglary at the relevant time but gave an innocent explanation for his presence there. He was charged with burglary and, at his trial, did not give evidence. In his summing-up to the jury the judge treated the defendant's statement to the police as a 'mixed statement', ie partly admission and partly exculpatory. The jury were directed that they were entitled to regard that part of the account where he said he was in the area at the time of the burglary as an admission and therefore evidence of the fact he had been there, but that the other parts of the statement that explained his reason for being there were exculpatory and therefore not evidence of the facts related. This analysis was rejected by the court, which adopted the approach taken in *Duncan*.

As a result, in, for example, murder/provocation cases, where an accused person decides not to give evidence, it is possible that, in the right circumstances, stating at interview, 'I stabbed him because he called me a notorious child molester' would be more advantageous than saying, 'I had nothing to do with his stabbing at all'. The former might well satisfy the evidential burden for provocation. The latter, of course, would not.

Because the exculpatory parts of a mixed statement are evidence in their own right, if the accused was of previous good character he would also be entitled to the credibility limb of the *Vye* direction, even if he did not give evidence. Indeed, it was for this reason that, in *Garrod*, the Court of Appeal had to consider whether the (non-testifying) appellant's interviews were 'mixed' (and so requiring a *Vye* direction) or purely exculpatory. Although the court concluded that it was difficult to envisage a series of proper answers to questions (as opposed to simple denials) which did not involve some admission of relevant facts, a statement became mixed when it contained admissions which were significant to any issue in the case, that is, which were capable of adding some degree of weight to the prosecution case on a matter which was relevant to guilt.

 Cross-reference Box

A *Vye* direction is given to a defendant who is of previous good character (ie, without previous convictions). It directs the jury as to the uses that they can make of this information. Thus, if he has given evidence, more weight can sometimes be given to it than if he was not of previous good character. For more information on *Vye* directions see pp. 171–176.

R v Sharp [1988] 86 Cr App R 274, HL

Lord Havers

Evidence contained in a confession is however an exception to the hearsay rule and is admissible. . . . This exception became extended to include not only a full confession to the crime but also a partial confession in which the accused admitted some matter that required to be established if the crime alleged was to be proved against him and is now recognised in statutory form in the Police and Criminal Evidence Act 1984 in which confessions are defined by section 82(1) as including 'any statement wholly or partly adverse to the person who made it, whether made to a person in authority or not and whether made in words or otherwise . . . .' The difference in the authorities centres upon the status to be attached to those parts of a mixed statement that excuse or explain an admission and are intended to show that the admission does not bear the inference of guilt it might otherwise attract: for example, 'I admit that I stabbed him but he was about to shoot me', or, as in this appeal. 'I admit I was at the scene of the burglary but I was looking for something that had fallen off my car.' All the authorities agree that it would be unfair to admit the admission without admitting the explanation and the only question is how best to help the jury evaluate the accused's statement. The view expressed in Duncan (1981) 73 Cr App R 359 is that the whole statement should be left to the jury as evidence of the facts but that attention should be drawn, when appropriate, to the different weight they might think it right to attach to the admission as opposed to the explanation or excuses. The other view, which I might refer to as the 'purist' approach, is that, as an exculpatory statement is never evidence of the facts it relates, the jury should be directed that the excuse or explanation is only admitted to show the context in which the admission was made and they must not regard the excuse or explanation as evidence of its truth.

R v Garrod [1997] Crim LR 445 (Lexis Transcript by Smith Bernal), CA

Evans LJ

The fact that he volunteered a copy of the document and admitted having seen it at the time were certainly admissions of fact which might perhaps be sufficient to bring this statement within the 'mixed' category. But overall, even those passages read in their context show that the appellant essentially was making an exculpatory statement. This was because not only was the emphasis placed upon his lack of understanding of the document, but in fact the comment which he had made was precisely that. His manuscript note was 'I don't understand this', plus some further reference to the figures. It seems to us overall that what the appellant was saying in that interview, notwithstanding that he had volunteered the fact that he had seen the document, was that he did not understand the contents at the time any more than he did when these matters were put to him by the police. It seems to us that to regard that as anything other than an exculpatory statement, or as part of an overall denial, would not be correct. It seems also that little, if anything, was made of that particular answer and admission at the trial. We ask ourselves the question already posed: were these limited admissions 'significant' in relation to the central issue in the case against the appellant, or incriminating in the sense already described, the issue being did he have knowledge of the dishonest grant application scheme? It seems to us that it is only possible to classify this as an exculpatory statement, notwithstanding the presence of those limited admissions of fact. We therefore conclude that the summing-up cannot properly be criticised for failing to include the credibility aspect of the good character direction so far as the appellant was concerned.

6. Silence as a Confession

Generally speaking, remaining silent when accused of an offence could not amount to a confession at common law. However, there is some very limited authority suggesting that, in exceptional circumstances, a failure to answer allegations might be treated as a tacit acceptance of their veracity, and thus a confession. Thus, it has been suggested that, at common law, if an allegation is made orally to a person, by someone who is speaking to them on 'even terms', in circumstances in which they might be expected to deny the allegation or 'repel the charge', a failure to do so, will amount to an acceptance of the claim: per Cave J in *R v Mitchell* (1892) 17 Cox CC 503.

This principle was applied by the Privy Council in *Parkes v The Queen* (1977) 64 App R 25, when deciding that the defendant's failure to reply to two allegations that he had stabbed a woman's daughter (the mother found him near the bleeding and dying girl with a knife in his hands) was capable of amounting to an admission. The pre-requisite that the parties must be on equal terms is usually taken as precluding police interviews from the ambit of the principle (especially since the advent of the PCEA 1984), despite suggestions to the contrary in *R v Chandler* [1976] 63 Cr App R 1. However, this must now be seen in the light of s. 34 of the Criminal Justice and Public Order Act 1994, whereby an adverse inference might be drawn if a suspect refuses to answer questions when interviewed by the police (see below pp. 354–358).

7. The *Voir Dire*

Introduction

Whenever a confession is challenged by the defence or, under s. 76(3), by the judge on his own initiative (an important provision for protecting the rights of unrepresented or incompetently represented defendants), the prosecution is obliged to prove beyond reasonable doubt that it was not obtained in breach of s. 76(2). The determination of such challenges to the admissibility of confessions is made on a special procedure called the *voir dire* or, as it is colloquially known, a 'trial within a trial'. In *Ajodha v The State* [1982] AC 204 Lord Bridge set out the appropriate procedure for such hearings, noting that in the vast majority of trials where the admissibility of a confession statement is to be raised, prosecuting counsel will not mention the statement in his opening to the jury (having been warned by defence counsel that there is an issue as to admissibility), and at the appropriate time the judge will conduct a trial on the *voir dire* to decide whether the statement can be adduced. This will normally be done in the absence of the jury 'at the request or with the consent of the defence'.

However, as Lord Bridge also pointed out in *Ajodha*, in exceptional circumstances the defence may, for tactical reasons, prefer that the evidence bearing on that issue be heard before the jury, with a single cross-examination of the witnesses on both sides being conducted, even though this means that the jury hear the impugned statement whether it is deemed to be admissible or not. Indeed, in *R v Anderson* [1929] 21 Cr App R 178 it was held that there were very few circumstances in which a jury could be required to leave the court without the consent of the defence. Quite commonly, an application to exclude a confession by an exercise of discretion under s. 78 will be appended to one under s. 76, and argued at the same time.

To prove that the tendered confession was not obtained by oppression, or anything said or done that might make it unreliable, the prosecution will call witnesses who can testify as to the circumstances in which it was made. For example, the officers who conducted the interview that elicited the confession, the custody sergeant (with his custody record) and any others who saw the suspect during the relevant period, such as a police surgeon. These will be examined in chief by prosecuting counsel and cross-examined by defence counsel. The defence will then call their own evidence (if they wish), usually the defendant and occasionally other witnesses as well, and submissions will then be made to the judge by both sides as to the admissibility of the confession. The judge then makes a decision on the issue; if he is satisfied beyond reasonable doubt that there is no breach of s. 76(2), the confession will be admitted. If not, it is excluded.

Ajodha v The State [1982] AC 204, PC

Lord Bridge

It has to be remembered that the rule requiring the judge to be satisfied that an incriminating statement by the accused was given voluntarily before deciding that it is admissible in evidence is anomalous in that it puts the judge in a position where he must make his own findings of fact and thus creates an inevitable overlap between the fact-finding functions of judge and jury. In a simple case, where the sole issue is whether the statement, admittedly made by the accused, was voluntary or not, it is a commonplace that the judge first decides that issue himself, having heard evidence on the *voir dire*, normally in the absence of the jury. If he rules in favour of admissibility, the jury will then normally hear exactly the same evidence and decide essentially the same issue albeit not as a test of admissibility but as a criterion of the weight and value, if any, of the statement as evidence of the guilt of the accused. In the case presently under consideration, where the accused denies authorship of the statement but admits signing it under duress, the overlap of functions is more complex. Hearing evidence on the *voir dire*, the judge will of necessity examine all the circumstances and form his own view of how the statement came to be written and signed. In practice the issue as to authorship and that as to whether the signature was voluntary are likely to be inseparably linked.

Was a Confession Made?

Traditionally, if a defendant denied having made a confession at all, rather than claiming that he made one as a result of improper pressure or an inducement, a *voir dire* was not thought to be necessary. Whether the confession was made or not was simply a question of fact for the magistrates or jury to determine. Such allegations are much rarer nowadays, because of the use of tape-recording for interviews. However, the Privy Council case of *Thongjai v The Queen* [1998] AC 54 decided that, even if the actual making of a confession was disputed, if it was also argued that the circumstances that prevailed when it was supposed to have been made raised doubts about its voluntariness (had it been made) a trial judge should conduct a *voir dire* to determine the matter. If he decided that the confession was admissible, it was then for the jury to decide whether or not it had actually been made. In *Thongjai* the appellant had complained that he had been ill-treated immediately before or at the time of the alleged confession (the making of which he denied). This should have resulted in a *voir dire* hearing on admissibility.

Thongjai v The Queen [1998] AC 54, PC

Lord Hutton

The [Hong Kong] Court of Appeal was also in error in stating that a similar situation had arisen in Reg. v. Cheung Hon-yeung [1993] 1 H.K.C.L.R. 292 because, in that case, as their Lordships have already observed, there was no suggestion by the defendant that he had been ill-treated by the police before or at the time of the making of the alleged oral admission, and the Court of Appeal failed to distinguish between two situations. One situation is where the only allegation made by the defendant is that he had not made the alleged admission. The other situation is where the defendant alleges both that he had not made the admission and that he had been ill-treated before or at the time of the making of the alleged admission. In the latter situation the trial judge should hold a voire dire to decide whether (in case the jury find that the admission was made) the admission was made in circumstances which rendered it involuntary. Accordingly in the opinion of their Lordships in the trials of both defendants the trial judge should have made a ruling in the voire dire whether the Crown had proved that the alleged oral admission was voluntary, and in each case the judge wrongly held that he would not give such a ruling.

The Status of Evidence Given on the *Voir Dire*

Evidence given on the *voir dire* by defendants is without prejudice to their right not to testify in the substantive trial (though they will then be subject to the possibility of having an adverse inference drawn pursuant to s. 35 of the Criminal Justice and Public Order Act 1994). Additionally, allegations made on the *voir dire* did not constitute imputations for the purposes of s. 1(f)(ii) of the (now repealed) 1898 Criminal Evidence Act, because they were normally made in the absence of the jury, and the same approach will, presumably, be taken over 'attacks' made under s. 101(1)(g) of the CJA 2003.

 Cross-reference Box

As with s. 34 of the CJPoA (discussed at pp. 355–358) this provision replaced the common law rule whereby no adverse inference could be drawn from 'in court' silence. For more on this go to pp. 354–358.

If defendants give evidence in the main trial, what they said on the *voir dire* will not normally be admissible to the jury, *provided* it was relevant to the admissibility of the confession, even if it is highly incriminating to the defendant: *R v Brophy* [1982] AC 477. As a result, it can be said to be covered by a form of qualified privilege. In *Brophy*, this extended to an open admission to having been guilty of one of the counts in the indictment against him (membership of the IRA). The advent of the PCEA 1984, and in particular the wording of s. 76 of that Act, could have been interpreted as changing the law in this respect. However, this has not happened, although *Brophy* is a pre-PCEA case. It appears unlikely that *Brophy* would not be followed in future, even if it necessitated an exercise of the judicial discretion contained in s. 78 of the PCEA 1984 to do so. However, the privilege is not absolute. If a defendant goes beyond what is necessary or relevant to the issue of admissibility on the *voir dire*, for example, by openly boasting about his crimes, he might risk having his statement on the *voir dire* revealed to a jury.

R v Brophy [1982] AC 477, HL

Lord Fraser

I would rest my opinion of relevance also on a wider ground. Where, as in this case, evidence is given at the *voir dire* by an accused person in answer to questions by his counsel, and without objection by counsel for the Crown, his evidence ought in my opinion to be treated as relevant to the issue at the *voir dire*, unless it is clearly and obviously irrelevant. The accused should be given the benefit of any reasonable doubt. Of course if the accused, whether in answer to questions from his own counsel or not, goes out of his way to boast of having committed the crimes with which he is charged, or if he uses the witness box as a platform for a political speech, his evidence so far as it relates to these matters will almost certainly be irrelevant to the issue at the *voir dire*, and different considerations will apply to its admissibility at the substantive trial. But on any reasonable view of the respondent's evidence in this case, it cannot be said to be clearly and obviously irrelevant.... Once it has been held that the material part of the respondent's evidence was relevant to the issue at the *voir dire*, a necessary consequence is in my opinion, that it is not admissible in the substantive trial. Indeed counsel for the Crown did not argue to the contrary. If such evidence, being relevant, were admissible at the substantive trial, an accused person would not enjoy the complete freedom that he ought to have at the *voir dire* to contest the admissibility of his previous statements. It is of the first importance for the administration of justice that an accused person should feel completely free to give evidence at the *voir dire* of any improper methods by which a confession or admission has been extracted from him, for he can almost never make an effective challenge of its admissibility without giving evidence himself. He is thus virtually compelled to give evidence at the *voir dire*, and if his evidence were admissible at the substantive trial, the result might be a significant impairment of his so-called; 'right of silence' at the trial.... I do not overlook or minimise the risk that accused persons may make false allegations of ill-treatment by the police; some of them undoubtedly do. But the detection of dishonest witnesses on this, as on other matters, is part of the ordinary duty of the courts and it should be left to them. The possibility, indeed the practical certainty, that some accused will give dishonest evidence of ill-treatment does not justify inhibiting their freedom to testify at the *voir dire*. The importance of the principle was explained by Lord Hailsham of St. Marylebone L.C. in the recent Privy Council case of Wong Kam-Ming v. R. (1979) 69 Cr.App.R. 47, 55, [1980] A.C. 247, 261, where he said this: '...any civilised system of criminal jurisprudence must accord to the judiciary some means of excluding confessions or admissions obtained by improper methods. This is not only because of the potential unreliability of such statements, but also, and perhaps mainly, because in a civilised society it is vital that persons in custody or charged with offences should not be subjected to ill treatment or improper pressure in order to extract confessions. It is therefore of very great importance that the courts should continue to insist that before extra-judicial statements can be admitted in evidence the prosecution must be made to prove beyond reasonable doubt that the statement was not obtained in, a manner which should be reprobated and was therefore in the truest sense voluntary. For this reason it is necessary that the defendant should be able and feel free either by his own testimony or by other means to challenge the voluntary character of the tendered statement. If, as happened in the instant appeal, the prosecution were to be permitted to introduce into the trial the evidence of the defendant given in the course of the *voir dire* when the statement to which it relates has been excluded, whether in order to supplement the evidence otherwise available as part of the prosecution case, or by way of cross-examination of the defendant, the important principles of public policy to which I have referred would certainly become eroded, possibly even to vanishing point.'

Pause for reflection

Is it in the interests of justice for someone to be able to admit an offence with which they are currently charged, in court, without being convicted on such an admission?

Admissibility and Weight

The *voir dire* only determines the question of (legal) admissibility. If a confession is admitted, it does not prevent the defendant attacking it, and the circumstances in which it was made, and inviting the jury to ignore it altogether in the light of those circumstances. To that extent, at least, the defendant gets a second 'bite of the cherry'. Thus, the Court of Criminal Appeal quashed the conviction in *R v Murray* [1951] 1KB 391 after a trial judge, having ruled on a *voir dire* hearing that a confession was admissible, refused to allow defence counsel to cross-examine the police witnesses again, in the presence of the jury, as to the manner in which the confession had been obtained. Even worse, in his summing-up he told the jury that they must accept from him that the confession was a voluntary one obtained from the prisoner without duress, bribe or threat.

R v Murray [1951] 1 KB 391, CCA

Lord Goddard CJ

It was quite right for him [the trial judge] to hear evidence in the absence of the jury and to decide on the admissibility of the confession; and, since he could find nothing in the evidence to cause him to think that the confession had been improperly obtained, to admit it. But its weight and value were matters for the jury, and in considering such matters they were entitled to take into account the opinion which they had formed on the way in which it had been obtained. [Counsel for the defence] was perfectly entitled to cross-examine the police again in the presence of the jury as to the circumstances in which the confession was obtained, and to try again to show that it had been obtained by means of a promise or favour. If he could have persuaded the jury of that, he was entitled to say to them: 'You ought to disregard the confession because its weight is a matter for you'.

Indeed, in the case of *David Mitchell v The Queen* [1998] AC 695 the Privy Council concluded that a trial judge's decision on a *voir dire* to determine the admissibility of a confession should not be revealed to the jury, since to do so might cause unfair prejudice to the accused by conveying the impression that the judge had reached a firm view on the respective credibility of witnesses and of the defendant.

David Mitchell v The Queen [1998] AC 695, PC

Lord Steyn

In the present case the defendant insisted on a voire dire, one was held and it is common ground that it was right to do so. The right of a defendant in appropriate circumstances to require a voire dire to be held in the absence of the jury has been described as 'an important rule which exists to protect accused persons' and a 'very important safeguard': see MacPherson v. The Queen (1981) 147 C.L.R. 512, 522; Thongjai v. The Queen [1998] A.C. 54, 71, per Lord Hutton. A judge may not override this right by requiring a jury to stay if the defendant wants them to be excused: Blackstone's Criminal Practice, 7th ed. (1997), p. 1323. The reason why the voire dire must take place in the absence of the jury is that the jury should not be made aware of evidence which subsequently turns out to be inadmissible. But the question now arises whether a judge, who rules that a confession was voluntarily made, may properly inform the jury of his decision. Counsel for the defendant relied strongly on the analogy of the decision in Crosdale v. The Queen [1995] 1 W.L.R. 864. In that case the Privy Council held that a judge should invite the jury to withdraw while he heard submissions that a defendant has no case to answer and ruled on it. This holding was principally motivated by the need to protect the interests of the defendant. The Privy Council expressly dealt with the question whether the judge may inform the jury of his decision. The Privy Council held, at p. 873:

'That brings their Lordships to the third question, namely whether the jury should be present during the judgment on the application that the defendant has no case to answer or whether the jury should subsequently be informed of the judge's reasons for his decision. There is no reason why the jury should be privy to the judge's reasons for his decision. In order to avoid any risk of prejudice to the defendant the jury should not be present during the course of the judgment or be told what the judge's reasons were. If the judge rejects a submission of no case, the jury need know nothing about his decision. No explanation is required. If the judge rules in favour of such a submission on some charges but not on others, or rules in favour of it in respect of some defendants but not others, the jury inevitably will know about the decision. All the jury need then to be told by the judge is that he took his decision for legal reasons. Any further explanation will risk potential prejudice to a defendant or defendants.' (Emphasis supplied.) The principle that the judge must not inform the jury of his decision to reject such a submission is therefore squarely based on the need to avoid the risk of prejudice to a defendant. Counsel for the prosecution, who appeared before their Lordships, conceded that by analogy a judge, who conducted a voire dire as to the admissibility of a confession, ought not to inform the jury of his decision. Their Lordships accept that the analogy of Crosdale v. The Queen is helpful. An examination of the dynamics of a voire dire to determine the admissibility of a confession points in the same direction. The decision on the admissibility of a confession after a voire dire is the sole responsibility of the judge. There is no logical reason why the jury should know about the decision of the judge. It is irrelevant to the consideration by the jury of the issues whether the confession was made and, if so, whether it is true. There is also no practical reason why the jury need to be informed of the judge's decision. This is underlined by the fact that in modern English practice the judge's decision after a voire dire is never revealed to the jury. Moreover, if the judge reveals his decision to the jury, the risk of unfair prejudice to a defendant is created. That risk will often be greater than in the case of a no case submission. That is so because in the typical case, of which the present is a paradigm, the decision of the judge on the voluntariness of the confession may convey to the jury that the judge believed the police witnesses and disbelieved the defendant.... The reason why it is wrong for a judge to reveal his decision to a jury is not because it would amount to a withdrawal of an issue from the jury and it does not amount to a misdirection. The vice is that the knowledge by the jury that the judge has believed the police and disbelieved the defendant creates the potentiality of prejudice. A jury of laymen, or some of them, might be forgiven for saying: 'Well the judge did not believe the defendant, why should we believe him?' At the very least it creates the risk that the jury, or some of them, may be diverted from grappling properly and independently with a defendant's allegations of oppression so far as it is relevant to their decision. and such an avoidable risk of prejudice cannot be tolerated in regard to a procedure designed to protect a defendant.

However, traditionally, questions of admissibility relating to a confession were a judicial not a jury function. The latter body was concerned with the weight, if any, to be attributed to an admitted confession, not whether it should, legally, have been admitted. This was so even though many of the matters that they considered on the issue of truth were exactly the same as those considered by the trial judge on the question of admissibility. As a result, the jury was not normally directed by the trial judge that, if not themselves satisfied that the confession was made voluntarily, they should disregard it. Historically, the defendant did not have two bites of the cherry in relation to the issue of admissibility.

Eleventh Report of the Criminal Law Revision Committee (Cmnd 4991), 1972, at para. 67

The fact that the judge has decided at the trial within the trial that the confession is admissible will not prevent the defence from cross-examining the witnesses for the prosecution, or themselves giving evidence, at the trial proper about the way in which the confession was obtained with the object of convincing the jury that they should pay no attention to it. Even if the same evidence is given as that given at the trial within the trial, this will not prevent the jury from taking a different view from that which the judge took at the trial within the trial—even on the question, for example, whether there was any threat or inducement. This is in accordance with the present law. It would be wrong in our opinion to make any provision designed to require the jury to accept the judge's finding that a confession was not obtained in the ways mentioned, as this would be to usurp their function of deciding what weight to give to the confession. But the relevance of the issue for the jury will be only as to weight; and they will be under no obligation to disregard a confession, believed by them to be true, if it should so happen that (differing from the judge) they think that the test for admissibility was not satisfied. We have no doubt that the purpose for which the jury should consider the way in which a confession was obtained should be only that of deciding what weight to give to it. This is the present law and it will remain the law under [clause 2 of the Draft Criminal Evidence Bill annexed to the Report].

Nevertheless, this position has been slightly qualified by the House of Lords in *R v. Mushtaq* [2005] 1 WLR 1513 (Lord Hutton dissenting). In this case, a trial judge had directed a jury that they could rely on a confession that he deemed admissible, even if they concluded that it had been obtained by oppression, provided they concluded that it was also true (ie that they accorded it weight). Although this was, arguably, logical given the 'traditional' approach to such matters, a majority of the House of Lords felt that in the light of the ECHR, especially Article 6, this was a misdirection, and that the jury should have been directed that if they concluded that the confession was obtained by oppression or any other improper conduct they should disregard it (though, if they had concluded that the defendant was guilty, this might require 'mental gymnastics').

R v Mushtaq [2005] 1 WLR 1513, HL

Lord Rodger

The appellant submits, however, that the present practice is defective because the jury is limited to considering the circumstances for the purpose of deciding the weight and value to be attached to the confession. Rather, they should be directed that, if, having heard all the evidence, they find that the confession was, or may have been, obtained by oppression or any other improper means, they must disregard it…. In my view, therefore, the logic of section 76(2) of PCEA really requires that the jury should be directed that, if they consider that the confession was, or may have been, obtained by oppression or in consequence of anything said or done which was likely to render it unreliable, they should disregard it…. It follows, both on the basis of section 76(2) when viewed without regard to the Convention and on the basis of the appellant's Article 6(1) Convention right against self-incrimination, that the judge misdirected the jury when he said that, if they were sure that the confession was true, they might rely on it, even if it was, or might have been, made as a result of oppression or other improper circumstances.

It is only fitting to acknowledge that, in giving this direction, the judge was following the guidance from the Judicial Studies Board that was current at the time. That guidance was modified to reflect the comments of the Court of Appeal in this case. Clearly, neither version will afford appropriate guidance in the light of the decision by the House today. Having indicated the approach which should be applied in principle, I would not usurp the function of the Judicial Studies Board by attempting to draft model directions to give effect to that approach. I would only observe that there is often no dispute that, if what the defendant said happened did indeed happen, the confession should be excluded under one or other of the paragraphs in section 76(2) of PCEA. The only real dispute is as to whether the defendant's account as found in the evidence is true. In such a clear-cut case it may well be enough for the judge to indicate that, if the jury consider that the confession was, or may have been, obtained in the way described by the defendant, they must disregard it.

Mr McNulty submitted that, if the House reached the view that there had been a misdirection in relation to the confession, the appellant's conviction could not be regarded as safe and should accordingly be quashed. Like the Court of Appeal, I would reject that submission.

As I mentioned at the outset, this was a case where the appellant chose not to give evidence…. What it shows is that in this case there was no evidence whatever of oppression, or of any other improper means, for the prosecution to disprove or for the jury to consider. The direction to the jury as to what they might do if they found that the confession had been obtained by oppression or any other improper means was, accordingly, unnecessary and unduly favourable to the appellant. In those circumstances, the fact that the judge did not go further in his direction cannot possibly affect the fairness of the appellant's trial or the safety of his conviction.

Perhaps strangely, when determining the admissibility of confessions, it has been held that a *voir dire* should also be held in the summary courts: *R v Liverpool Juvenile court, ex parte R* [1988] QB 1. If the magistrates then decide that a confession is inadmissible they must put it out of their mind, though, if they decide to admit it, they do not need to have it adduced again in the substantive trial (which would be superfluous given that they themselves had only just heard it). Concern has periodically been voiced that much court time is spent by trial judges, sitting alone, hearing the witnesses in a *voir dire* so as to determine confession admissibility, only to have the same witnesses called again before the trial jury to consider the question of evidential weight (assuming the confession is admitted). An alternative approach to such issues would save court time and cost. Against this, it can be argued that the procedure provides an important protection for the rights of the accused. Helpfully, in the modern era, the admissibility of confession evidence can also often be raised in the course of a preparatory hearing in the Crown Court, held pursuant to s. 29 of the Criminal Procedure and Investigations Act 1996. This might be particularly useful where a confession is almost the only evidence against the defendant, so that, if it is ruled inadmissible, the prosecution will offer no evidence without the need to empanel a jury.

Pause for reflection

Do you feel that the benefits of the *voir dire* procedure warrant its expense? Are there any viable alternatives?

The Codes of Practice and Sections 56 and 58

As will be seen, there are a variety of grounds for excluding confessions; these are contained in ss. 76(2) and 78 of the PCEA 1984, and (although of much reduced significance in the modern era) in the common law power to exclude confessions obtained by trickery or because they are deemed to be more prejudicial than probative, preserved as a result of s. 82(3) of the same statute. However, many of these provisions exist in what might be loosely termed a cultural vacuum. Beating a man savagely to make him confess will clearly be oppressive, but what about depriving him of a meal or two? Custody standards that would be considered oppressive today might have been thought the height of luxury during the reign of Henry VIII. What standards should govern those who are held in detention for questioning, a major departure from which might be thought to render a confession unreliable?

These questions vexed the courts even in the nineteenth century. Thus, Baron Gurney was sure that although the police should not 'induce' confessions, it was not their business to caution: '. . . persons in their custody, and who are about to make statements, not to do so'. This would, he believed, be absurd and also help prevent the detection of criminals.[5] However, many other observers, including members of the judiciary, strongly disagreed. Confusion about this issue continued until 1906, when general cautioning of suspects was enjoined in a letter sent by the then Lord Chief Justice, Lord Alverstone, to the Chief Constable of Birmingham. It was subsequently reinforced by the Judges' Rules, which provided guidance on investigative 'good practice' and were first issued in 1912; they were updated on several occasions over ensuing decades (most recently in 1964). However, the legal status of these rules was uncertain, and their extent limited. As a result, the Royal Commission on Criminal Procedure (1981) concluded that this area of the law was too little regulated.

Consequently, s. 66 of the PCEA 1984 provided for Codes of Practice to be issued, governing in detail most areas of police activity and interaction with suspects, and setting out 'correct practice' in different situations. Section 67(9) provides that police officers and any other person charged with the duty of investigating offences, along with the courts, must take account of these codes. Thus, customs and excise officers come within their scope, as do a number of other bodies, in certain situations; precisely how far the duty to observe the codes extends is a question of fact in each case: *R v Seelig* [1992] 94 Cr App R. 17. Breaches of the Codes are themselves

[5] *R v Dickinson* 8 March & *R v Watts and others* 22 August 1844, reported Cox's Criminal cases, vol 1 1843–1846, (1846, J Crockford) at 27 and 75.

admissible in evidence, pursuant to s. 67(11), and, if deemed to be relevant, can be taken into account when determining any question before the court. Indeed, breaches of the Codes will often constitute much of the 'ammunition' used to establish one of the primary grounds for exclusion (whether under s. 76 or 78 of the PCEA 1984). The most important Codes for confessions are Code C, which regulates the detention, treatment and questioning of suspects in some detail; Code E, which controls the tape-recording of interviews; and, where carried out, Code F, which regulates the video-recording of confessions. A special Code, Code H, was added in the summer of 2006 to regulate questioning of suspects under s. 41 of the Terrorism Act 2000.

Under Code C, para. 1.3, detained suspects must be informed that they have a right to inspect the Codes of Practice, although the courts will not allow this process to be abused: *DPP v Billington* [1988] 3 All ER 435. Some protections afforded to suspects are so fundamental that, not only are they provided for as part of the Codes of Practice, they are also expressly set out in one of the substantive sections of the 1984 Act. Foremost amongst these are ss. 56 and 58, which provide, respectively, for suspects to be able to make a telephone call to inform someone of their whereabouts after arrest and for them to have access to legal advice.

Although too extensive to detail exhaustively in a work of this nature, amongst the various rights established under Code C, and indicative of their scope, are rules requiring the cautioning of suspects before they are questioned (para. 10.1), requiring that adequate breaks be provided during periods of questioning (subject to some exceptions, this should include a short refreshment break every two hours: para. 12.8), insisting that interviews be held in rooms that, 'as far as practicable', are properly lit, heated and ventilated (para. 12.4) and with the suspect being allowed to sit down during questioning (para. 12.6). Additionally, there is a requirement that detention cells and bedding be clean (para. 8.3) and that in any one 24-hour period the suspect should be allowed a continuous period of at least eight hours' rest, free from questioning, travel or any other interruption arising out of the investigation. In exceptional circumstances, the police are allowed to deviate from this rule if it is necessary in order to avoid harm to other persons or property, etc. Two light meals and one main meal should normally be provided to the suspect every 24 hours (para. 8.6).

To help ensure that the rights provided for under the Act and relevant Codes do not just exist in 'theory', the designated custody officer (a policeman of the rank of at least sergeant, who is independent of the investigation) is required to open a detailed custody record on each suspect, in which will be entered details of everything that happens to him while he is detained. Thus, the initial entries on the custody record usually document the cautioning of the suspect and that he has been read his rights regarding access to legal advice. If the right to see a legal adviser has been waived, this, too, will be recorded.

Nowadays, interviews with suspects are usually audio-taped, although this is only legally required if the offence in question is indictable or triable 'either-way' (rather than purely summarily). Some terrorist and Official Secrets Act offences are also exempt from tape recording. Additionally, the custody officer may authorize a non-tape recorded interview if the necessary equipment or facilities are broken or otherwise unavailable, in which case the traditional method of recording in longhand is used. Tape recording is governed by Code E, which lays down strict procedures to ensure that the whole of an interview is recorded and to minimize the possibility of the record being tampered with. The tape itself may be introduced into court as evidence, though, normally, the investigating officer will use it to prepare a written record of the interview which both he and the suspect will sign to certify its accuracy. Of course, such a tape, though a great advance on the old system of documenting a police interview, cannot record what happens outside the interview room, for example in cells or corridors (where inducements or threats might still be offered or made).

Section 56: Right to Inform of Arrest

Section 56 provides for a right for a person to be informed by a suspect of his arrest. This can be delayed under broadly similar (but not identical) circumstances to s. 58 (see below). Thus, such a delay must involve a serious arrestable offence and the maximum period of delay is 36 hours. The decision to delay notifying friends/family must be taken separately from the decision to delay access to a solicitor. This is because, in some circumstances, there might be very good reasons not to let friends or family know about an arrest, which reasons would not be remotely applicable to keeping the suspect from his legal representative.

Section 58: Access to Legal Advice

Section 58(1) of the PCEA 1984 provides that a person who has been arrested and is held in custody in a police station is entitled to consult a solicitor in private at any time. There should be prominent notices to this effect displayed in the charging area of the station. Additionally, the Custody Officer must advise the suspect of their right to legal advice and inform him/her that free legal advice is available via the Duty Solicitor Scheme. Once the suspect has requested legal advice, Code C provides that they must not be questioned further until it is received. Once the solicitor has seen his/her client any further interviews must be conducted with the solicitor present; *R v Samuel* (1988) 1 QB 615 makes it clear that a suspect's access to legal advice cannot be delayed merely because the police fear that the solicitor will advise the suspect not to answer questions. Code C says that s/he cannot be ejected from an interview unless they are making it impossible for the police to put questions to the suspect. Merely advising their client not to answer those questions is not a good reason for the police to eject the legal adviser. Nor can the police remove the solicitor because s/he questions the propriety of questions being asked or seeks a break in the interrogation for further private consultations with the suspect.

However, the suspect's right to legal advice is not entirely unqualified. Code C does provide that if the solicitor chosen by the suspect is not available, or will not attend the police station, and the suspect does not want to nominate another or be advised by the duty solicitor, interviewing can commence provided a senior officer has agreed. More significantly, under s. 58(8), an officer of the rank of superintendent or above may delay the suspect's access to their solicitor for up to a maximum of 36 hours (longer if an offence under the Prevention of Terrorism Acts is involved) if the possible charge involves a *serious arrestable offence* as defined in s. 116 of the PCEA 1984, and if the senior officer has reasonable grounds to fear that witnesses or property will be interfered with, accomplices will be enabled to escape, or stolen property will be more difficult to recover, as a result of the suspect's contact with his solicitor. However, the case law makes it clear that this provision will be very tightly construed indeed by the courts. As Hodgson J noted in *Samuel*, the right to legal advice, enshrined in s. 58 of the PCEA 1984, is of fundamental importance. Legitimate denial of such legal advice, under s. 58(8), normally requires that the police officer must believe (and have goods grounds for doing so) that a solicitor would, if allowed to consult the person in police detention, subsequently either commit a crime or, at the very least, be extremely foolish or stupid. Additionally, a solicitor's visit cannot be denied because relatives or friends sent the lawyer in question to the police station rather than the suspect having requested him in person. If, as often happens, the solicitor sends a representative, such as a legal executive, the police are obliged to give them the same access as they would the solicitor, *provided* they are capable of advising on the matter at hand.

R v Samuel (1988) 1 QB 615, CA

Hodgson J

The Court of Appeal is always reluctant to interfere with the exercise of a judge's discretion but the position is different where there was no discretion to exercise on the judge's ruling and all the court has is an indication of how the judge would have exercised it. This is particularly so in this case where, on the section 58(8) point, the judge failed properly to address his mind to the point in time which was most material and did not in terms give consideration to what his decision would have been had he ruled in favour of the defence on this more fundamental issue before him. In this case this appellant was denied improperly one of the most important and fundamental rights of a citizen. The trial judge fell into error in not so holding. If he had arrived at correct decisions on the two points argued before him he might well have concluded that the refusal of access and consequent unlawful interview compelled him to find that the admission of evidence as to the final interview would have 'such an adverse effect on the fairness of the proceedings' that he ought not to admit it. Such a decision would, of course, have very significantly weakened the prosecution case (the failure to charge earlier ineluctably shows this). In those circumstances this court feels that it has no alternative but to quash the appellant's conviction on count 1 in the indictment, the charge of robbery.

Use of the Codes at Trial

Because breaches of the codes are admissible under s. 67(11), counsel can use them (along with breaches of ss. 56 and 58) to support applications being made under both ss. 76 and 78. Thus, it might be argued that a confession is unreliable under s. 76(2)(b) because it was made after the suspect had been held for 24 hours without food, contrary to Code C, para. 8.6, prompting him to confess in the hope that this would allow him to seek nourishment. Similarly, it might be suggested that a confession should be excluded under s. 78 because of a failure to allow legal advice, contrary to both s. 58 of the Act and Code C, para. 6.1. Obviously, some violations of the Codes will be viewed more gravely than others. A failure to caution or allow access to legal advice will always be viewed with great seriousness; a short-term delay in allowing a light refreshment break during questioning will attract much less concern.

8. Grounds for Exclusion under the PCEA 1984

Introduction

The most common grounds under which improperly obtained confessions are excluded in the modern era are to be found in s. 76 of the PCEA 1984 (though s. 78 of the same Act is also very important).

Section 76 of the PCEA 1984. Confessions (Partial extract)

(1) In any proceedings a confession made by an accused person may be given in evidence against him in so far as it is relevant to any matter in issue in the proceedings and is not excluded by the court in pursuance of this section.

(2) If, in any proceedings where the prosecution proposes to give in evidence a confession made by an accused person, it is represented to the court that the confession was or may have been obtained—

(a) by oppression of the person who made it; or

(b) in consequence of anything said or done which was likely, in the circumstances existing at the time, to render unreliable any confession which might be made by him in consequence thereof

the court shall not allow the confession to be given in evidence against him except in so far as the prosecution proves to the court beyond reasonable doubt that the confession (notwithstanding that it may be true) was not obtained as aforesaid.

(3) In any proceedings where the prosecution proposes to give in evidence a confession made by an accused person, the court may of its own motion require the prosecution, as a condition of allowing it to do so, to prove that the confession was not obtained as mentioned in subsection (2) above. . . .

Section 76(2)(a): Oppression

Under s. 76(2)(a) of the PCEA 1984 a confession *must* be excluded if obtained by 'oppression'. It should be noted that, as the Court of Appeal observed in *R v Paris* [1993] 97 Cr App R 99, in such cases, the burden of proof is on the Crown to establish (beyond reasonable doubt) that it was not obtained in this manner, and the truth of the statement is irrelevant if it was obtained by oppression. Although 'oppression' had existed as a ground for exclusion at common law, the statutory provision is narrower than that which went before.

R v Paris [1993] 97 Cr App R 99, CA

Lord Taylor CJ

Three points on that section [s. 76(2)] require emphasis. First, the issue having been raised by the defence, the burden of proving beyond reasonable doubt that neither (2)(a) nor (2)(b) applied was on the Crown. Secondly, what matters is how the confession was obtained, not whether or not it may have been true. Thirdly, unless the prosecution discharged the burden of proof, the judge was bound as a matter of law to exclude the admissions. His decision was not discretionary.

Narrow Definition of 'Oppression'

The word 'oppression' for the purposes of s. 76 of the PCEA 1984 is defined under s. 76(8) as including: '…torture, inhuman or degrading treatment, and the use or threat of violence'. This definition reflects the wording of Article 3 of the ECHR. However, as the word 'includes' suggests, it is only a partial definition, not an exhaustive one. In practice, in the monitored and controlled environment found in modern police stations, relatively few confessions will be excluded under this narrow definition of oppression. Early on in the life of the PCEA 1984, the courts made clear that other behaviour could be oppressive, even though it did not fall within the wording of of s. 76(8).

Wider Definition of Oppression

In *R. v Fulling* [1987] 85 Cr App R 136 the defendant was charged with obtaining property by deception via a staged and bogus burglary that she claimed had occurred at her flat. She was interviewed at a police station for over two days, but said nothing. It was alleged that one of the police officers then informed her, rather spitefully, that her lover was having an affair with a woman who was being held in an adjacent cell. After hearing this, Ms Fulling confessed to the charge, subsequently claiming that she thought it was the only way she would be released quickly from custody, the circumstances of which had now become intolerable for her. At her trial, she unsuccessfully argued that the confession had been obtained by oppression and was thus inadmissible under s. 76(2)(a), although the trial judge also concluded that the prosecution had failed to satisfy him beyond reasonable doubt that the conversation with the police officer had not taken place.

Upholding this decision in the Court of Appeal, Lord Chief Justice Taylor made a number of observations about the prerequisites necessary for the provision to apply. In particular, he noted that 'oppression' should be given its ordinary dictionary meaning, ie the exercise of authority or power in a burdensome, harsh or wrongful manner, etc. He also observed that oppression would be likely to entail some form of deliberate impropriety on the part of the interrogator. However, this was a prerequisite that certainly did not apply to its sister provision in s. 76(2)(b). The court also noted that as the new statute was a codifying Act, it was not bound by earlier common law definitions of oppression, set out in cases such as *Prager*, which, the court concluded, were 'artificially wide'.

R v Ruth Fulling [1987] 85 Cr App R 136, CA

Lord Taylor CJ

This in turn leads us to believe that 'oppression' in section 76(2)(a) should be given its ordinary dictionary meaning. The Oxford English Dictionary as its third definition of the word runs as follows: 'exercise of authority or power in a burdensome, harsh, or wrongful manner; unjust or cruel treatment of subjects, inferiors, etc., or the imposition of unreasonable or unjust burdens.' One of the quotations given under that paragraph runs as follows: 'There is not a word in our language which expresses more detestable wickedness than oppression.' We find it hard to envisage any circumstances in which such oppression would not entail some impropriety on the part of the interrogator. We do not think that the judge was wrong in using that test. What however is abundantly clear is that a confession may be invalidated under section 76(2)(b) where there is no suspicion of impropriety. No reliance was placed on the words of section 76(2)(b) either before the judge at trial or before this Court. Even if there has been such reliance, we do not consider that the policeman's remark was likely to make unreliable any confession of the appellant's own criminal activities, and she expressly exonerated—or tried to exonerate—her unfaithful lover. In those circumstances, in the judgment of this Court, the learned judge was correct to reject the submission made to him under section 76 of the 1984 Act. The appeal is accordingly dismissed.

Intentional Misconduct and Oppression

Intentional misconduct was examined again in *R v Beales* [1991] Crim L R 118, where it was held that deliberately heavy-handed questioning and misleading suggestions amounted to oppression. It was the deliberateness of the police breaches that was significant in this context. By contrast, in *R v Hughes* [1988] Crim L R 545, where the police failed to put a suspect in contact with a solicitor after a request for legal advice and kept him in a cold cell, the Court of Appeal commended defence counsel for not making a case for excluding the defendant's confession on the grounds of oppression. This was because it was apparent that the police had acted on a misunderstanding. There was no intentional misconduct on their part. However, deliberate impropriety does not appear to be an absolute requirement, although, as Watkins LJ observed in *R v Seelig* [1992] 94 Cr App R 17, cases in which oppression would occur without it would be extremely rare.

No Need for Physical Mistreatment

Although oppression may require deliberate impropriety, it does not require the use or threat of physical mistreatment. In *R v Paris* [1993] 97 Cr App R 99 it was held that bullying, hectoring and shouted questioning by police officers, over a 13-hour period, with questions being repeated up to 300 times, was oppressive, the court noting that: 'Short of physical violence it is hard to conceive of a more hostile or intimidating approach by officers'. This remained the case even though the defendant had a (apparently incompetent) solicitor present throughout the interview.

R v Paris [1993] 97 Cr App R 99, CA

Lord Taylor CJ

We are bound to say that on hearing tape 7, each member of this Court was horrified. Miller was bullied and hectored. The officers, particularly Detective Constable Greenwood, were not questioning him so much as shouting at him what they wanted him to say. Short of physical violence, it is hard to conceive of a more hostile and intimidating approach by officers to a suspect. It is impossible to convey on the printed page the pace, force and menace of the officer's delivery . . . We have no doubt that this was oppression within the meaning of section 76(2). . . . Of course, it is perfectly legitimate for officers to pursue their interrogation of a suspect with a view to eliciting his account or gaining admissions. They are not required to give up after the first denial or even after a number of denials. But here . . . Having considered the tenor and length of these interviews taken as a whole we are of opinion that they would have been oppressive and confessions obtained in consequence of them would have been unreliable, even with a suspect of normal mental capacity. In fact, there was evidence on the *voir dire* from Dr. Gudjonsson, called on behalf of Miller, that he was on the borderline of mental handicap with an IQ of 75, a mental age of 11 and a reading age of eight. It is fair to the learned judge to say that, although he was invited to listen to part of tape 7, it was played only up to page 17 of the transcript. The bullying and shouting was from page 20 onwards. Why the most important part was not played to the learned judge has not been explained to us. Had he heard the rest of it, as we did, we do not believe he would have ruled as he did.

In the upshot, it is sufficient to say that in our judgment the Crown did not and could not discharge the burden upon them to prove beyond reasonable doubt that the confessions were not obtained by oppression or by interviews which were likely to render them unreliable. Accordingly, in our view these interviews ought not to have been admitted in evidence.

However, 'verbal oppression' is a matter of degree. Other cases make it clear that mere repetition and simple raised voices will not necessarily be enough. Indeed, in *Paris* it was accepted that it is: '...perfectly legitimate for officers to pursue their interrogation of a suspect with a view to eliciting his account or gaining admissions. They are not required to give up after the first denial or even after a number of denials.' Thus, in *R v Emmerson* [1991] 92 Cr App R 284, it was held that limited expressions of exasperation or bad language did not amount to oppression, unlike a deliberate course of 'hectoring and bullying'. The appellant had been interviewed by a police officer over allegations of minor embezzlement from his employer. At times the officer spoke in a raised voice and swore at the appellant. However, the Court of Appeal was unwilling to view this as oppression. Much will depend on the characteristics and experience of the interviewee; what could be oppressive for an old and frail person might be acceptable for a young man. Similarly, 'intelligent, sophisticated, self-confident and articulate' individuals will be in a different position to the 'weak, the inarticulate, the suggestible': *R v Seelig* [1992] 94 Cr App R 17.

R v Emmerson (1991) 92 Cr App R 284, CA

Lloyd LJ

The question which we have to ask ourselves is whether the confession may have been obtained by oppression. The interview was conducted by two officers. Most of it was very low-key. There was a short passage about three-quarters of the way through the interview when one of the officers raised his voice and used some bad language. He was saying in effect that it was plain that the appellant had committed the offences and why was he wasting their time. The impression given is one of impatience and irritation. The judge found it rude and discourteous. In deciding whether the police officer's conduct and the circumstances surrounding the interview as a whole amounted to oppression, we have to apply the ordinary meaning of that word: see Fulling (1987) 85 Cr App R 136. The appellant says that he was intimidated. We have all listened to the tape. We have each come to the conclusion independently that the conduct of the police officer was not in any sense oppressive. In ruling on the voire dire the judge said that to exclude this evidence would be to give oppression a completely false meaning. We agree with the judge. In our view the evidence was rightly admitted.

Unreliability: Section 76(2)(b)

The essence of the test for exclusion under s. 76(2)(b) is, first, whether the police or a third party have done or said something to prompt the making of a confession, and, secondly, whether the circumstances prevailing at the time were such as to make any ensuing confession likely to be unreliable. What is meant by 'unreliable'? In *R v Crampton* [1991] 88 Cr App R 338 the Court of Appeal concluded, in rather cautious terms, that it meant something that 'cannot be relied upon as being the truth'. However, it is important to note that a 'worm's eye view' of this issue is taken. As with oppression, the actual truth or otherwise of the confession is (at least in theory) entirely irrelevant, though this has sometimes posed difficulties for the courts.

In ordinary parlance, if something is true, it must be reliable. However, a confession that, in hindsight, is quite obviously 'reliable', because clearly true, must be excluded under s. 76(2)(b) if, at the point at which it was made, any hypothetical ensuing confession might be suspected of being unreliable. It is almost as if the situation is 'freeze-framed' just as the suspect opens his mouth to start his admissions.

Thus, in *R v Kenny* [1994] Crim LR 284 the conviction of the defendant was quashed by the Court of Appeal because, although the trial judge found there had been a breach of the Code of Practice when a mentally deficient suspect had been interviewed without an appropriate adult being present. The judge had gone on to rule that he was sure beyond reasonable doubt that the admissions were reliable and admitted them in evidence. The defendant had then changed his plea to guilty. Despite this, his appeal was allowed on the ground that the trial judge had not addressed his mind to the right question. He had first considered whether the particular confession was reliable and then gone on to exercise his discretion. What he should have done was to consider whether, in the circumstances, the confession, whether true or not, was obtained in consequence of anything done which was likely to render any confession unreliable, the burden being on the prosecution to prove beyond reasonable doubt that it was not so obtained. This approach was reiterated in *R v Blackburn* [2005] 2 Cr App R 30. Such an approach helps to preserve the separate functions of judge and jury.

R v Blackburn [2005] 2 Cr App R 30, [2005] EWCA Crim 1349, CA

Keene LJ

The argument advanced by the Crown, that the confession could still have gone before the jury because its reliability could be established by other evidence pointing to the appellant's guilt, is, in the view of this Court, wholly misconceived. It amounts to an argument that if other evidence tends to show the confession is true, that may overcome the sort of problem which existed here. Lord Carlile Q.C. seeks to say that such evidence is directed towards the reliability of the confession and consequently satisfies the terms of s. 76(2) of PCEA. In our judgment, the only relevance of such factors as he refers to, for example the evidence about the hair cuts, is to suggest that the confession may have been true. But the truth of the confession is not the test under s. 76(2). The wording of that statutory provision makes that entirely clear by the phrase '(notwithstanding that it may be true)', and several authorities have confirmed that obvious interpretation: see R. v Cox [1991] Crim.L.R. 276; R. v Kenny [1994] Crim.L.R. 284. One cannot overcome problems about the reliability of a confession by using extrinsic evidence to show that it is likely to be true. 63 Consequently the appellant's admissions made during the July 21 interview were wrongly admitted in evidence at trial. is therefore allowed and the convictions are quashed.

Circumstances

'Unreliable' confessions (unlike most of those obtained by oppression) may occur where there has been no deliberate impropriety in any form by the police or other investigating authorities. The circumstances to be considered by the trial judge, on a submission under s. 76(2)(b) of the PCEA 1984, include psychological evidence as to intelligence, even where the suspect's IQ is above 70 but still very low, as in *Raghip* (74 points), though the same evidence would not be admissible in the substantive trial on issues such as *mens rea*.[6] The Court of Appeal has also made it clear that any mental or personality abnormalities may be of relevance when deciding

---

[6] Expert evidence on intelligence and personality are discussed in chapter 11 at pp. 474–484.

the likely effect of things said or done upon a person being interviewed, even if they do not amount to a mental handicap. They form part of the relevant circumstances to which the court must have regard when considering a challenge to admissibility under s. 76. This is so even if the police were completely unaware of such circumstances: *R v Barry* [1992] 95 Cr App R 384. However, the court has also stressed that each case on reliability turns on its own facts, and is highly defendant specific as there are so many variables; it is inappropriate to attempt direct analogies with previously decided cases: *R v Wahab* [2003] 1 Cr App R 15.

Unlike 'oppression' the scope of 'unreliability' under s. 76(2)(b) of the PCEA 1984 is extremely broad. For example, it can extend to confessions obtained as the result of an inducement such as a promise of bail, the offer of better conditions of detention, an undertaking to have a 'word' with the sentencing judge or not to extend a criminal enquiry to another family member, etc. It can also encompass a threat that does not necessarily amount to oppression, a simple failure to record accurately what was said or accidentally leaving the suspect in harsh environmental conditions from which he feels compelled to escape.

Thus, in *R v Mathias* (1989) *The Times* 24 August, the police denied the defendant access to his solicitor for legitimate and exceptional reasons. An offer of immunity from prosecution was allegedly made and the defendant confessed. The confession was excluded as unreliable because the police had offered an inducement (the immunity) and the circumstances (denial of legal advice) made him especially vulnerable to such an offer. Similarly, in *R v Trussler* [1988] Crim LR 446 the suspect was a drug addict who was arrested at 9 a.m. and eventually made a statement at 2 a.m. the following morning. Although a doctor had been provided, and the suspect had spoken to his lawyer, there were long periods of questioning without adequate rest periods so that his confession was excluded as potentially unreliable under s. 76(2)(b).

R v Blackburn [2005] 2 Cr App R 30, CA

Keene LJ

Looked at by today's standards, this Court is in no doubt that this appellant, who was just past his fifteenth birthday at the time of the interview, should have been advised of his right to legal advice. That right today is provided for in Code C, paras 3.1 and 6.1 of the PCEA Codes, and while that is related to someone under arrest at a police station, it is to be remembered that under Code C a person under arrest must in most circumstances only be interviewed at a police station: see para.11(1). That is not a provision to be circumvented by delaying arrest and interviewing him elsewhere. The right to such advice is regarded by the courts as a fundamental one (see R. v Samuel (1988) 87 Cr.App.R. 232, [1988] Q.B. 615), breach of which may, depending on the circumstances, require a confession to be excluded.

56 We consider, therefore, those other circumstances. One of them is that no parent or guardian was present at this interview. Although the appellant was in the care of the local authority, it would have been his allocated social worker who performed the role of guardian on behalf of the local authority, not Mr McVitie. That social worker appointed by the local authority was Mr Smith, whose unchallenged evidence before us is that he was not told about the intended interview on July 21. It seems to us that the structure of para.4 of the Administrative Directions, as well as its wording, indicates that a parent or guardian of a young person should be present at interview, and that only if they are not available should some other adult be present instead. But irrespective of whether or not there was a technical breach in this respect, it seems to this Court that Mr McVitie was, in reality, doing little at the interview to safeguard the appellant's interests.

57 This is linked to the next circumstance, the duration of the interview. The appellant, just 15 years old at the time, had been questioned for three hours and ten minutes by these two senior police officers before he made any admission. There is no record of any break for refreshment during that period or indeed during the whole interview of four hours twenty minutes. We put it like that because if there had been such a break, the Administrative Directions in force at the time required it to be recorded. None is recorded. DI Marsh said at trial that cups of tea were brought in at one stage, but we find it difficult to rely on that statement, given his evidence about the way in which the confession statement was written, now shown to be untrue. Such a lengthy questioning of a 15-year-old boy without a parent or guardian present gives us real cause for concern.

58 Finally, there is the evidence about the use made by the interviewing officers of the new material which they had gathered about the 1976 incident at Irlam. At the *voir dire*, both officers gave evidence to the effect that the appellant, while he was told about the new material, was not told that there might be new charges in respect of the 1976 incident. Mr McVitie, however, testified that the officers did say that there was a possibility of a further charge, though he did not get the message that this was a threat. Given what we now know about the officers' credibility, it seems likely to this Court that the possibility of a further charge was raised. The trial judge placed emphasis on Mr McVitie's impression that this was not done as a threat, but it seems to us that one needs to ask how such references would have been perceived by the appellant. That was never considered. It is difficult to avoid the conclusion that, whatever the officers' intention, a boy of this age would have been likely to have regarded those references to the new evidence and the possibility of a further charge as a threat, to be made good if he did not co-operate.

59 When we put all these circumstances together—the duration of the interview, the age of the boy, the absence of a solicitor and of any indication that he was entitled to legal advice, the absence of a parent or guardian and the references to a possible further charge in respect of the Irlam incident—we are clear that none of the appellant's admissions should have gone before the jury. Certainly in the light of current standards they cannot be seen as reliable.

60 Lord Carlile Q.C. suggests that the appellant, despite his youth, could be seen as being sophisticated or at least familiar with police procedures because of his criminal record. We do not accept that the existence of previous convictions would have rendered this 15-year-old able to stand up to the conditions in which the interview took place.

'Anything Said or Done'

What is required is that the contested confession was obtained: '…in consequence of something said or done which was likely in the circumstances existing at the time, to render unreliable any confession'. There must be a causal connection between something 'said or done' and the making of the confession to lead to exclusion under s. 76(2)(b). In *R v Goldenberg* [1989] 88 Cr App R 285 it was suggested that this must be external to the defendant, a purely internal cause would not be enough to invoke the provision. In this case, a drug addict had sought an interview with the police after being arrested, hoping that if he made admissions it would lead to him getting bail swiftly and so securing a 'fix' to satisfy his craving. However, his confession was not excluded as there was nothing extrinsic to the defendant that was 'said or done' to justify this.

R v Goldenberg [1989] 88 Cr App R 285, CA

Neil LJ

In our judgment the words 'said or done' in section 76 (2)(b) of the 1984 act do not extend so as to include anything said or done by the person making the confession. It is clear from the wording of the section and the use of the word 'in consequence' that a causal link must be shown between what was said or done and the subsequent confession. In our view it necessarily follows that 'anything said or done' is limited to something external to the person making the confession and to something which is likely to have some influence on him.

Similarly, in *R v Crampton* [1991] 88 Cr App R 338, a confession was made by a withdrawing heroin addict. The appellant sought to distinguish *Goldenberg*, on the ground that in his case it was the police, not the suspect, who had sought the interview. The Court of Appeal was 'doubtful' if this made a difference to the situation, though it did not decide the point firmly. In general terms, it approved of the decision in *Goldenberg*. Nevertheless, some other, superficially similar, cases are fairly difficult to distinguish from the decisions in this case, although reaching different conclusions on their facts. Despite this, *Goldenberg* was reconsidered, and broadly approved, in *R v Wahab* [2003] 1 Cr App R 15. It appears that self generated hopes or motivations, even those with what might be considered a minimal external stimulus, will not trigger exclusion under s. 76(2)(b).

Although there must be a causal connection with something external to the defendant, this clearly does not have to come from the police or other investigating authorities. In *R v Harvey* [1988] Crim LR 241 the defendant was a mentally disturbed woman, with a psychopathic personality disorder and below normal intelligence. She heard her lesbian lover confess to a murder, and then confessed herself. It was held that the confession was unreliable. There was 'something done or said' (the confession of the lover) in circumstances which were likely to make Harvey's confession unreliable—the circumstances being her mental state, which was said to be such that she might confess merely to take the blame away from her lover and onto herself.

R v Wahab [2003] 1 Cr App R 15, CA

Judge LJ

The answers given by the appellant during the course of the fourth interview amounted to confessions. No one suggested that his answers resulted from oppression. The issue was reliability. Normally that question involves a decision whether the police, or investigating authorities, have 'said or done' anything likely to make the confession unreliable. However, significantly in view of the common law principles which formerly guided this issue, the statutory language is not confined to the actions (or omissions) or words of persons 'in authority'. Given her precarious mental state, we can quite understand why the defendant's confession in R. v Harvey [1988] Crim LR 241 was held to be inadmissible. Although the investigating police officers had said and done nothing relevant, the confession to murder made to the police in the defendant's presence by her lover, and the realistic possibility that in her confused mental state she might realistically have decided, 'childlike to protect her lover', made her subsequent confession unreliable. Our attention was drawn to R. v Barry (1992) 95 Cr App R 384. We agree that the reference in the judgment to things said and done 'by the police' was not intended to restrict the ambit of s. 76(2). Rather it reflected the fact that in Barry everything relevant said and done emanated from the police.

40 Mr Shepherd focused on the decision in Barry arguing by analogy, that Barry's anxiety to be granted bail, and the consequent exclusion of his confession in this court, should be equated with Wahab's anxiety that members of his family should be released. In our view it is inappropriate for the question of reliability under s. 76(2), when it arises, to be decided by reference, directly or by analogy, to circumstances which have arisen and been decided in different appeals. The question is always fact specific, and in particular, defendant specific: hence the express references in s. 76 to the 'accused person' and things said and done at the time which might make the confession 'by him' unreliable. The focus must be concentrated on the reliability of the confession made by the individual defendant, given the circumstances as they existed when the confession was made. Thus we doubt whether the decision in Harvey would have been the same if the defendant herself had not been of low intelligence and suffering from psychopathic disorder which may have served to produce her possible 'child-like' reaction to what she heard. Equally, if the members of the appellant's family and his girlfriend had been wrongly arrested in order to provide the police with a weapon to wield against Wahab, which was then deployed in the way he had alleged, we very much doubt whether the judge's decision in this case would have been the same.

41 We have considered R. v Goldenberg (1989) 88 Cr App R 285, which suggests that the phrase in s. 76(2), 'anything said or done' does not extend to things said and done by the defendant himself. Mr Shepherd suggested that this decision did not assist. We disagree. In Goldenberg one issue said to affect the reliability issue was the defendant's anxiety to obtain bail for himself, or to obtain credit for helping the police. It was held that s. 76(2) was concerned with something extraneous to the person making the confession. In the present case, when the appellant instructed his solicitor to see whether some convenient arrangement could be procured with the police, he was uninfluenced by anything said and done by anyone else. Everything thereafter originated from the appellant himself.

42 Advice properly given to the defendant by his solicitor does not normally provide a basis for excluding a subsequent confession under s. 76(2). One of the duties of a legal advisor, whether at a police station, or indeed at a pre-trial conference, or during the trial itself, is to give the client realistic advice. That emphatically does not mean that the advice must be directed to 'getting the client off', or simply making life difficult for the prosecution. The advice may, and sometimes ought to be robust, sensibly considering the advantages which the client may derive from evidence of remorse and a realistic acceptance of guilt, or the corresponding disadvantages of participating in a 'no comment' interview. The exercise of the professional judgment in circumstances like these is often very difficult, often dependent on less than precise instructions from the defendant. We do not, of course, rule out the possibility that a particularly vulnerable defendant (for example, Harvey) may make an unreliable confession after receiving advice from a solicitor, but such a conclusion would reflect the defendant's unfortunate mental weakness rather than any adverse comment on the solicitor's advice. The efforts of a solicitor acting for two clients to act in the best interests of one—seeking, for example, to persuade one client to make a confession to enable some advantage to be extracted for the other—or the advice of a solicitor at a police station, purporting to act in his client's best interests, but party to a corrupt understanding with the police to persuade the client to confess, would be tainted advice. For confessions made in such cases, s. 78 would provide an ample basis for exclusion, notwithstanding that the reliability of the confession was not in doubt....We have examined Mr Shepherd's submissions in the light of the facts found by the judge. We can see no reason to interfere with his decision. In summary, Wahab was an intelligent man, who instructed his solicitor to approach the police to see if any arrangement, consistent with his own wishes might be made. The police acted properly. The solicitor accurately conveyed the police response to Mr Wahab. Mr Wahab knew precisely what he was doing when he made his confession. Even if his mind was influenced by the possibility that a confession might lead to the release from police custody of members of his family, that was one

factor among several which served to explain his decision to confess. The judge held, and we agree, that none of these factors, taken individually or cumulatively, had any adverse effect on the reliability of his confession.

Section 78 of the PCEA 1984

The admissibility of confessions is primarily governed by s. 76, the provision that is dedicated to this form of evidence. However, early on in the life of the PCEA 1984 it was recognized that s. 76 did not provide the sole grounds for exclusion. In the right circumstances, s. 78 of that statute could be invoked as well (and frequently is in practice), because, of course, it applies to *all* prosecution evidence. This provision is dealt with in detail in chapter one, which discusses, inter alia, several cases where s. 78 was employed to exclude confession evidence, some of which can be further considered in this chapter.

Exam tip

When faced by a problem question on confession evidence it is always worth mentally considering all possible limbs under which it could be excluded: s. 76(2)(a); s. 76(2)(b); s. 78; and even the almost never used common law discretion preserved by s. 82(3) of the PCEA 1984.

In *R v Mason* [1988] 86 Cr App R 349, the appellant was charged with arson. It was alleged that he had set fire to the car of his former girlfriend's father, with whom he was on bad terms. Before his arrest the police had no significant evidence connecting him with the cause of the fire. One or more police officers decided to trick the appellant by telling him, untruthfully, that they had found one of his fingerprints on some fragments of a bottle used in starting the fire. This was subsequently confirmed to the appellant's solicitor, who then advised him to answer police questions and explain any involvement in the incident. The appellant then admitted that he had filled the bottles used in the attack with petrol and paint thinner. He claimed that a friend had then set the car alight for him, though he was not present at the time. The appellant did not give evidence at trial.

The prosecution sought to put the confession into evidence, and the judge overruled the defence objection to its admissibility. He appealed against conviction on the ground that the trial judge wrongly exercised his discretion in admitting the evidence of the confession. It was held that a trial judge has a discretion exclude a confession under s. 78, regardless of the power to exclude such evidence conferred by s. 76 of the same Act. The Court of Appeal concluded that the trial judge should have excluded the confession under this provision in the instant case because of the police conduct.

R v Mason [1988] 86 Cr App R 349, CA

Watkins LJ

The law is, as I have already said, that a trial judge has a discretion to be exercised of course upon right principles to reject admissible evidence in the interests of a defendant having a fair trial. The judge in the present case appreciated that, as the quotation from his ruling shows. So the only question to be answered by this Court is whether, having regard to the way the police behaved, the judge exercised that discretion correctly. In our judgment he did not. He omitted a vital factor from his consideration, namely the deceit practised upon the appellant's solicitor. If he had included that in his consideration of the matter we have not the slightest doubt that he would have been driven to an opposite conclusion, namely that the confession be ruled out and the jury not permitted therefore to hear of it. If that had been done, an acquittal would have followed for there was no other evidence in the possession of the prosecution. For those reasons we have no alternative but to quash this conviction. Before parting with this case, despite what I have said about the role of the court in relation to disciplining the police, we think we ought to say that we hope never again to hear of deceit such as this being practised upon an accused person, and more particularly possibly on a solicitor whose duty it is to advise him, unfettered by false information from the police.

Relationship Between Sections 76 and 78

Unfortunately, in some cases, it is not always easy to predict in advance whether the court will exclude a confession under s. 76 or under s. 78, both having been used for fairly similar situations in the past. It also seems that there is a considerable overlap between the two provisions. Thus, any confession that falls foul of s. 76(2)(a) would almost certainly be held to have been obtained in circumstances that would have an adverse effect on the fairness of the proceedings. Indeed, it seems likely that most confessions that might be excluded under s. 76(2) could also be excluded under s. 78 (just as most cases excluded under s. 76(2)(a) could be excluded under s. 76(2)(b)). However, the converse is clearly *not* the case. Further complicating matters, it is probable that, in some cases, judges have mistakenly used what is technically the 'wrong' section to exclude a confession. In practice, defence counsel will often adopt a 'belt and braces' approach to such applications, appending a s. 78 submission to a s. 76 application, if it is at all appropriate.

Section 78 will also cover situations where there is an irregularity which does *not* involve the situational specifics set out in the two limbs of s. 76(2). For example, because there is no deliberate misconduct by the police (usually required for oppression) or anything 'said or done' which would allow s. 76(2)(b) to be invoked. Thus s. 78 offers protection in situations which fall outside the boundaries of s. 76(2).

Nevertheless, there are some very important differences between the working of the two provisions. For example, in *Goldenberg,* it was suggested that it was not necessary to consider s. 78 on appeal if it had not been raised during the trial (unlike s. 76) and this has been alluded to by appellate courts on several other occasions. Additionally, unlike s. 76, where the exclusion of evidence is mandatory, s. 78 is discretionary (see chapter 1), though it is totally implausible to imagine that a court would fail to exclude a confession once satisfied that its reception would have such an adverse effect on the fairness of the proceedings that it ought not to admit it.

However, and more significantly, there is no burden on the prosecution to disprove unfairness beyond reasonable doubt under s. 78. Instead, there is a judicial duty to balance the interests of, and be fair to, both sides, including the prosecution: *R v Hughes* [1988] Crim LR 519. Such an analysis was supported by the Divisional Court in *Regina (Saifa) v Governor of Brixton Prison and another* [2001] 1 WLR 1134, which firmly rejected defence arguments that s. 78

placed an evidential burden on an accused person to raise the issue, which, once satisfied, then imposed a legal burden on the prosecution to rebut the section's operation beyond reasonable doubt (this case is discussed and excerpted in chapter 2). Because of this, it seems that appellate courts are even more reluctant to 'second guess' applications that were made under s. 78 than they are for those made under s. 76. In *R v Elleray* [2003] 2 Cr App R 11 the Court of Appeal observed that it would be slow to interfere with a trial judge's exercise of his discretion in this respect, as each case would ultimately turn heavily on its facts.

Cross-reference Box

Saifi case discussed other important aspects of the general exclusionary discretion under s. 78. For more on this, and an extract from the case itself, go to chapter 1, at pp. 75–76.

Factors that Might Lead to Exclusion under Section 78

A number of grounds will justify a challenge under s. 78 to the admissibility of a confession. These will include, for example, breaches of the ECHR and, perhaps most importantly, of the Codes of Practice issued pursuant to s. 66 of the PCEA 1984.[7] Of course, these only apply to confessions obtained by the police or other investigating authorities, such as officers from the Customs and Excise. In *R v Elleray* [2003] 2 Cr App R 11, a youth confessed to committing rape to probation officers preparing pre-sentence reports for another offence. The Court of Appeal upheld the trial judge's decision not to exclude the admissions under s. 78, despite the lack of protective procedures: they were not made under caution, were made in the absence of a solicitor and without being contemporaneously recorded. Although the court accepted that public policy factors were involved, for example, that it was necessary for defendants to speak freely to probation officers, such individuals were not charged with investigating crimes.

R v Elleray [2003] 2 Cr App R 11, CA

Lord Woolf CJ

Although that case referred to an offender being interviewed by a doctor, there are clear analogies as it seems to us between that situation and an interview by a probation officer for the purpose of preparing a pre-sentence report. A probation officer is under a duty to prepare a report which clearly and frankly sets out the probation officer's view, in particular in relation to sexual offenders, as to the degree of risk to the public that an offender constitutes. In order to do this in many cases they have to ask questions of an offender as to the precise circumstances in which the offender came to commit the offence to which he may have already pleaded guilty, or in relation to which there may be an agreed basis of facts between the prosecution and the defence. If in the course of that interview the offender volunteers an admission of committing the particular offence or some other offence which is relevant to the task of the probation officer in preparing their report for the court, they cannot ignore what they have been told. They are under a duty to provide a full and frank report which includes those details. Usually there will be little risk of any

---

[7] See chapter 2, pp. 76–77.

danger of action being taken in relation to an offender in consequence of anything said to the probation officers or anything said in a report. However, as this case illustrates, there can be a situation where that can arise.

11 We are grateful to Mr Greene for drawing our attention to the judgment of this Court in R. v Stokes (unreported, February 2, 2000), where on an application for leave a similar situation arose. As was indicated in the judgment of the Court in that case given by Sir Charles McCullough on the application for leave, there can be no question of the evidence being automatically excluded because it consisted of an admission made to a probation officer. The matter has to be considered, as was done by the trial judge in this case, by deciding whether there is a basis for excluding it under s. 78 of the Police and Criminal Evidence Act 1984. However, the fact that the evidence may be admissible in criminal proceedings does not mean that the fact that the admission was made in the course of an interview between an offender and a probation officer should be ignored. It is clearly important that there should be frankness in the exchanges between a probation officer and an offender as this furthers the role of the probation officer in the sentencing exercise. If it were to be the practice that the prosecution regularly rely upon what is said by an offender to a probation officer as evidence for further prosecutions then clearly this would have an adverse effect upon this need for frankness. Indeed a situation could soon arise where probation officers would be hampered in performing their important duty to assist the court in determining the correct sentence for offenders. So in the case of an admission the prosecution should first carefully consider whether it is right to rely upon evidence provided by a conversation between a probation officer and an offender and only rely upon it if they decide it is in the public interests so to do. If they do decide to rely upon that evidence, having taken into account the considerations of public interest to which we have made reference, then the court still has a discretion under s. 78 of the 1984 Act to ensure that no unfairness will occur because of the reliance on the admissions which an offender is alleged to have made. In deciding whether to exclude the evidence it is perfectly appropriate for the court to have in mind the contrast between the position that exists where an offender is interviewed by the police and that which exists when the offender is interviewed by a probation officer. The court should bear in mind the need for frankness between the offender and the probation officer; the fact that there may not be a reliable record of what was said; that the offender has not been cautioned; and that the offender has not had the benefit of legal representation. The protection which the court can provide under s. 78 in the majority of cases should be sufficient to ensure that no unfairness occurs to an offender.

12 Reference has already been made to the steps which were taken by the probation officers in this particular case. A course which in some cases may be appropriate if an offender starts making a confession is to stop him and ask him whether he would like to see his solicitor before he makes any further remarks. Probation officers should exercise judgment as to the appropriate course to adopt in the particular case. It is not possible for this Court to lay down guidance for probation officers as to what they should do, other than to indicate that if they fear that there is any risk of unfairness to an offender, they should take whatever appropriate action they think is necessary to protect the offender from any unfairness.

13 Having said that, and returning to the facts of this case, we are conscious here that once the appellant had disclosed that he had committed rape on more than one occasion, in order to perform that responsibility of protecting the public the probation officers could not ignore what the appellant had said. They had to include the admissions in their report. It clearly was relevant to the degree of risk that the appellant constituted.

14 If the prosecution in this case had not adopted the course of charging the appellant with the offences of rape, then it would still have been necessary for the court to come to a conclusion as to the accuracy of the probation officers' record as to what the appellant said if he was challenging that record.

15 In the circumstances of this case we cannot say that it was wrong or unfair for the prosecution to have decided to prosecute the appellant for the offences of rape. We cannot criticise the judge for the conclusion to which he came as to the admissibility of the evidence of what was said to the probation officers. As we have already indicated, the summing-up is one which cannot be criticised. The jury came to the conclusion that the rape offences which the appellant admitted were ones which he had committed. In those circumstances we have no alternative but to dismiss this appeal.

16 Like the judge in the court below, we are grateful to counsel for the clarity and conciseness with which the argument has been advanced. Appeal dismissed.

Exclusion under Section 78 for Breaches of the Codes of Practice

As was noted in chapter 1, three factors appear to be operative when it comes to excluding a confession under s. 78 for breach of the Codes of Practice: the gravity of the breach, whether or not it was deliberate (ie committed in 'bad faith'), and what its practical consequences were. However, perhaps the most important factor is the degree of gravity of the breach of the Codes of Practice and substantive sections of the PCEA 1984.

Violation of some provisions, such as the right to legal advice and the requirement that a suspect be cautioned are nearly always viewed as exceptionally serious and are usually fatal to the adduction of an ensuing confession, even if made inadvertently. Of course, in the latter case this assumes that the person being interviewed was a suspect and so required cautioning.

The duty to caution only arises under Code C when there are reasonable grounds to suspect that the defendant has committed an offence: *R v Shah* [1994] Crim LR 125. Thus, if a person is interviewed prior to such grounds arising, for example, as a potential witness, or to eliminate them from enquiries, and during that interview makes incriminating or unhelpful remarks that lead to them being interviewed under caution (as soon as there are reasonable grounds to suspect that the person has committed an offence) and charged, the incriminating remarks from the non-cautioned interview, or part of the interview, will still be admissible. Whether there are reasonable grounds to suspect the defendant is a question of fact. Courts will be particularly influenced by whether the officers involved acted in 'good faith' when deciding that there were, ostensibly, no reasonable grounds to suspect the accused when he was initially interviewed: *R v Shillibier* [2007] Crim LR 641.

Similarly, if a suspect makes an entirely spontaneous confession, without being questioned by the police, for example, he blurts out on his way to hospital in an ambulance, to an accompanying police officer, that he is guilty of the incident for which officers have attended a disturbance, without any questions being put to him, a failure to caution may not lead to exclusion under s. 78. However, where there has been an oral exchange between them, prior to the making of the admissions, the courts will not lightly decide this is the case, and that such a statement is unsolicited: *R v Noden* [2007] EWCA Crim 2050.

In *R v Walsh* [1990] 91 Cr App R 161 it was held that if there were 'significant and substantial' breaches of s. 58 of the 1984 Act (the right to legal advice) or the Codes of Practice the trial judge should consider whether the evidence ought to be excluded as it would, prima facie, be indicative of unfairness. Other breaches, such as a delay in minor refreshment breaks, are viewed less seriously.

R v Walsh [1990] 91 Cr App R 161, CA

Saville J

To our minds it follows that if there are significant and substantial breaches of section 58 or the provisions of the Code, then prima facie at least the standards of fairness set by Parliament have not been met. So far as a defendant is concerned, it seems to us also to follow that to admit evidence against him which has been obtained in circumstances where these standards have not been met, cannot but have an adverse effect on the fairness of the proceedings. This does not mean, or course, that in every case of a significant or substantial breach of section 58 or the Code of Practice the evidence concerned will automatically be excluded. Section 78 does not so provide. The task of the court is not merely to consider whether there would be an adverse effect on the fairness of the proceedings, but such an adverse effect that justice requires the evidence to be excluded. In the present case, we have no material which would lead us to suppose that the judge erred in concluding that the police officers were acting in good faith. However, although bad faith may make substantial or significant that which might not otherwise be so, the contrary does not follow. Breaches which are in themselves significant and substantial are not rendered otherwise by the good faith of the officers concerned.

Deliberation and the Consequences of a Breach of the Codes

Of secondary, but still significant, importance is whether the violation was deliberate. It is clear that bad faith, in terms of either conscious deceit (as in *Mason*), or an awareness of wrongdoing (such as a premeditated violation of the PCEA and its related Codes), is an important factor operating in favour of exclusion. An absence of bad faith will not normally 'cure' a major breach of the Codes, such as a wrongful denial of legal advice. However, its presence might make lesser breaches fatal to the adduction of a confession.

In exceptional circumstances, where there has been an absence of bad faith, the practical consequences of the violation might also be considered, and as a result, even potentially grave breaches may not lead to a confession being excluded. Thus, in the somewhat strange case of *R v Alladice* [1988] Crim LR 608, a confession to robbery was admitted at trial, despite the wrongful refusal of access to a solicitor, because there was evidence of bad faith by the police and, with almost foolish candour, the defendant, who had had many previous dealings with the police, freely admitted in court that he was well aware of his legal rights throughout the interview and that the absence of a solicitor had made no difference at all to his situation. (This case must be viewed as exceptional, and largely confined to its special facts.)

R v Alladice [1988] 87 Cr App R 380, CA

The Lord Chief Justice

What the appellant himself said in evidence was that he was well able to cope with the interviews; that he had been given the appropriate caution before each of them; that he had understood the caution and was aware of his rights. Indeed he asserted that he had said nothing at all after the first four (innocuous) questions, and what had been written down by the interviewing officer was nothing that he said but had been invented by the writer. His reason for wanting a solicitor was to have some sort of check on the conduct of the police during the interview. The judge rejected the allegations that the police had invented the admissions. He found as a fact that the interviews had been conducted properly. He concluded that the only difference the presence of a solicitor would have made would have been to provide additional advice as to the appellant's right to say nothing, a right which he knew and understood and indeed at times during the interview exercised. It may seldom happen that a defendant is so forthcoming about his attitude towards the presence of a legal adviser. That candour does however simplify the task of deciding whether the admission of the evidence 'would have such an adverse effect on the fairness of the proceedings' that it should not have been admitted. Had the solicitor been present, his advice would have added nothing to the knowledge of his rights which the appellant already had. The police, as the judge found, had acted with propriety at the interviews and therefore the solicitor's presence would not have improved the appellant's case in that respect. This is therefore a case where a clear breach of section 58 nevertheless does not require the Court to rule inadmissible subsequent statements made by the defendant. This appeal is accordingly dismissed.

Common Law Discretion to Exclude Confessions

Section 82(3) of the PCEA 1984 provides that: 'Nothing in this Part of this Act shall prejudice any power of a court to exclude evidence (whether by preventing questions being put or otherwise) at its discretion.' Thus, the general and very limited common law discretion to exclude evidence, identified in *R v Sang* [1980] AC 402, survives into the modern era. This allows (inter alia) a trial judge to exclude confessions obtained by, for example, trickery, or some other improper means, or because admitting them is more prejudicial than probative. This is likely to be of very limited significance in the modern era given that, in most cases, the discretion is clearly less extensive than that now contained in s. 78 of the PCEA 1984. Normally, if a confession cannot be excluded under s. 78, it will not be possible to exclude it under the common law discretion, while the corollary is clearly not the case.

Despite this, a continuing potential use for the discretion was identified in *R v Sat-Bhambra* [1989] 88 Cr App R 55. In this case, the Court of Appeal suggested that where a trial judge had initially ruled that a confession was admissible under ss. 76(2) and 78, he could not subsequently exclude it retrospectively under these same provisions, because they employed the phrases 'proposes to give in evidence and proposes to rely', suggesting that it has not already happened. Obviously, in such a situation, 'reliance' no longer lies in the future as the word 'proposes' clearly suggests it must. In this situation, of course, a trial judge would usually discharge the jury and abort the trial, with the agreement of the defence. However, there might be exceptional circumstances in which defence counsel will wish to continue with the trial. In such circumstances, the judge could direct the jury to disregard the confession, which was no longer deemed to be admissible, by employing his common law discretion.

R v Sat-Bhambra   [1989] 88 Cr App R 55, CA

The Lord Chief Justice

In Watson (1980) 70 Cr App R 273, [1980] 1 WLR 991, decided before the 1984 Act, it was held that a judge who has second thoughts about the voluntariness of a statement which he has earlier ruled admissible upon the voire dire may, where it is appropriate so to do, change his opinion as to its admissibility, and may take such steps as are necessary to put matters right, by, for example, directing the jury to disregard it or discharging the jury. The words of section 76 are crucial: 'proposes to give in evidence' and 'shall not allow the confession to be given' are not, in our judgment, appropriate to describe something which has happened in the past. They are directed solely to the situation before the statement goes before the jury. Once the judge has ruled that it should do so, section 76 (and section 78, for the same reasons) ceases to have effect. The judge, whatever his change of mind may be, is no longer acting under section 76 as the appellant contends. To that extent the decision in Watson does not survive the wording of the 1984 Act. That does not mean that the judge is powerless to act. He has the power, if only under section 82(3), to take such steps as are necessary, depending on the circumstances, to prevent injustice. He may, if he thinks that the matter is not capable of remedy by a direction, discharge the jury; he may direct the jury to disregard the statement; he may by way of direction point out to the jury matters which affect the weight of the confession and leave the matter in their hands. He is not, as is the submission here, obliged to discharge the jury and to order a new trial. If a defendant wishes under section 76 to exclude a confession, the time to make his submission to that effect is before the confession is put in evidence and not afterwards.

Confessions Tainted by Earlier Impropriety

What if a factor, which would preclude the adduction of an initial confession, is no longer present at a later interview when a fresh confession, in similar terms to the first, is made? For example, an improper inducement to make admissions has been expressly withdrawn, and an improper refusal to allow access to a solicitor has been reversed. At first sight, it might seem that the second confession will, as a result of being conducted in proper circumstances, be admissible, even though the earlier one will not. However, it can also be argued that the ensuing confession can no longer be seen independently of the factual nexus (the earlier admissions) in which it was made, and thus remains tainted.

If a suspect has made full admissions to a particular police officer, a few hours earlier, having been improperly denied legal advice, when interviewed again by the same policeman in the presence of his solicitor he is much more likely, it might be thought, to be too embarrassed to go back on what he said a short while before. As a result, it can be argued that the second confession will remain tainted by the first. This seems to have been the approach followed in *R v McGovern* [1991] 92 Cr App R 228. In this case, the defendant, suspected of murder, with an IQ of only 73 and at the same time heavily pregnant, was improperly denied access to a solicitor and at interview appears to have had some difficulty in understanding the terms of the caution. After initially prevaricating, she eventually confessed to having stabbed the victim. After this initial interview she was allowed access to a solicitor who, although aware of the content of the first interview, was unaware that she had been denied her request for a solicitor. He was present at a second interview when she again made a full confession. It was argued that, had the solicitor been told of the earlier refusal of legal advice, he would have realized that the first confession was suspect and, in all probability, would have advised against allowing the second interview to proceed. The Court of Appeal held that the first interview was inadmissible under s. 76(2) and, accepting the contention that the subsequent confession was a direct consequence of the first, they held that the very fact that admissions had been made at an earlier stage was likely to have such an adverse effect on the appellant thereafter that any repetition of them was likely to be unreliable.

Nevertheless, in *R v Glaves* (1993) WL 965633 the Court of Appeal rejected the view that 'there must inevitably be a continuing blight on any subsequent confessions'. For an ensuing confession to be admitted, it seems that the continuing influence of the initial one must be 'broken'. This might be done, for example, by the suspect receiving legal advice that the initial admissions had been obtained improperly, were unlikely to be received into evidence and that, as a result, he had a 'clean slate' for the (properly conducted) interview that was about to take place. However, the quashing of the manslaughter conviction in *Glaves* would suggest that the prosecution will not easily persuade the court that a later confession is untainted by an earlier, and improperly obtained, set of admissions.

R v McGovern [1991] 92 Cr App R 228, CA

Farquharson LJ

We are of the view that the earlier breaches of the Act and of the Code renders the contents of the second interview inadmissible also. One cannot refrain from emphasising that when an accused person has made a series of admissions as to his or her complicity in a crime at a first interview, the very fact that those admissions have been made are likely to have an effect upon her during the course of the second interview. If, accordingly, it be held, as it is held here, that the first interview was in breach of the rules and in breach of section 58, it seems to us that the subsequent interview must be similarly tainted.

Evidence Discovered as a Result of an Excluded Confession

At common law anything discovered as a result of an excluded confession was still admissible into evidence, albeit that no mention could be made as to how it came to be found: *R v Warwickshall* (1783) 1 Leach 263. The 'fruit of the poisoned tree' was not rendered inadmissible. This has been restated in s. 76(4)(a) of the PCEA 1984, whereby the fact that a confession has been excluded under s. 76(2) of 'any facts discovered as a result of the confession'. Thus, if a confession to a jewel robbery was obtained in circumstances that might render it unreliable, and, acting on the information contained in the confession, the police had occasion to dig under an old oak tree in a designated place, where they then discovered the stolen jewels, the finding of the gems would be admitted into evidence. No mention could be made as to why the police searched in that spot, the customary euphemism being to say that 'in the course of our enquiries we had occasion to search'. Obviously, how cogent the finding of the jewels would be would depend on other factors. If the oak tree was on land owned by the defendant, and his fingerprints were found on the jewels, it would be extremely important circumstantial evidence. If it was in a place with no connection to the accused and there was nothing else to connect him to the jewels it would be of minimal value.

Additionally, even if a confession is excluded under s. 76(2), part of it can be adduced to show, for example, that the defendant can speak in a certain manner: s. 76(4)(b). Thus, if it became an issue at trial as to whether the defendant could, or could not, speak with a strong Glaswegian accent, part of an otherwise excluded taped confession might be adduced to show that this was, or was not, the case. Obviously, in such situations, the part selected would normally be one that dealt with non-contested matters, rather than containing anything incriminating to its maker.

Handicapped Suspects

Section 77 of the PCEA 1984 establishes additional safeguards for those who suffer from a 'mental handicap', defined as applying to any person who is in a state of 'arrested or incomplete development of mind which includes significant impairment of intelligence and social functioning'. It provides that unless such people are interviewed in the presence of an 'appropriate adult', if a confession results, and the case depends 'wholly or substantially' on that confession, a trial judge is required to warn the trial jury that there is a 'special need for caution' before convicting in reliance on it. He must also explain why this is so, though he is not required to use a particular form of words when doing so.

In practice, the provision rarely operates, because of its rather restrictive ambit, and because it has largely been eclipsed by its neighbouring sections. Thus, a failure to arrange an appropriate adult before interviewing a handicapped suspect might well constitute 'something said or done' that would lead to exclusion under s. 76(2)(b) for unreliability, while it might also have such an adverse affect on the fairness of the proceedings that it should also result in exclusion under s. 78.

The discretion to exclude evidence is exercised relatively freely with regard to vulnerable defendants. Exclusion is certainly not contingent on malicious conduct by the police. Thus, in *R v Brine* (1992) WL 8936775 a confession was excluded under s. 78, on appeal, where the suspect had been interviewed for several hours with a lack of appropriate meals and breaks, and medical evidence subsequently established that he was suffering from a mild form of paranoid psychosis. However, where s. 77 is operative, *R v Bailey* [1995] 2 Cr App R 262 makes it clear that it is strictly applied. Nevertheless, a failure to give a specific and formal warning pursuant to s. 77(1) of the PCEA 1984, where it is deemed to be necessary, though serious, will not invariably be fatal to a conviction, *provided* that the trial judge has made clear to the jury, elsewhere in his summing-up, the importance of taking the defendant's mental condition into account: *R v Qayyum* [2007] Crim LR 160.

R v Bailey [1995] 2 Cr App R 262, CA

Roch LJ

What is required of a judge in a summing up in such cases, in our judgment, is a full and proper statement of the mentally handicapped defendant's case against the confessions being accepted by the jury as true and accurate. Because the defendant is significantly mentally handicapped, this duty will include a duty to see that points made on the defendant's behalf and other points which appear to the judge to be appropriate to his defence that the confessions are unreliable or untrue, are placed before the jury. That, in our view, is consistent with the general duty referred to at the start of section 77 of the court at a trial on indictment to direct the jury on any matter on which it appears to the court appropriate to do so and with the observations of Lord Ackner in R. v. Spencer and Smails (1986) 83 Cr.App.R. 277, 287, 288, [1987] A.C. 128, 141(A) to 142 (H). We would draw attention particularly to this observation by his Lordship at p. 288 and p. 142(H): 'The overriding rule is that he [the trial judge] must put the defence fairly and adequately.' What had to be included in the summing-up in this case for the defence to be put fairly and adequately before the jury? One matter was the fact that the experience of the courts has shown that persons with significant mental handicaps do make false confessions for a variety of reasons. The jury had to be reminded of the possible reasons for this appellant making false confessions in this case.

9. The Admissibility of a Co-defendant's Confession

Introduction

At common law, admissions made by a third party, not involved in the trial, were inadmissible because they constituted hearsay: *R v Turner* [1975] 60 Cr App R 80. (This must now be seen in the light of the discretion to admit hearsay evidence contained in s. 114(1)(d) of the CJA 2003.) What happens, however, if this third party is also a co-defendant, one who has made a confession that would be helpful to his fellow accused, but which is inadmissible for the prosecution against its maker? The traditional approach was that such confessions remained inadmissible: *R v Treacy* [1944] 2 All ER 229. This was qualified by the Court of Appeal in *R v Rowson* [1986] QB 174, which concluded that an otherwise inadmissible confession, which was at variance to its maker's testimony at trial, might be adduced by a co-defendant as a previous inconsistent statement under s. 4 of the Criminal Procedure Act 1865. However, this left several problems. In particular, as the inadmissible statement was being adduced as an inconsistent statement it went to credit and was not evidence in its own right (now changed by s. 119 of the CJA 2003). Additionally, to be applicable, it required that the co-defendant who had made the confession elected to give evidence.

Section 78 and Co-defendants' Confessions

Following a period of confusion in the early 1990s, some resolution to these problems, in limited circumstances, was reached by the House of Lords in *R v Myers* [1998] AC 124. In this case, two people were accused of murdering a taxi driver in the course of a bungled robbery. During a conversation with a police constable at the police station Melanie Myers was alleged to have said: 'I didn't do it, well I did do it. I did not mean to stab him. I had the knife and he kept coming forward at me.' She also made a number of other personally incriminating statements to this man and to three other officers while on the way to a Magistrates' Court. However, these were not admissible as part of the prosecution case because an absence of normal safeguards, such as a failure to caution Myers, meant they would have been excluded under s.78 (the prosecution did not even seek to adduce them for this reason).

At trial, each defendant blamed the other for the murder. Obviously, Myers' male co-defendant wished to adduce the statements made by her, as they were highly relevant to his defence. The first instance judge extended previous case law and decided that a co-defendant in a joint trial should be allowed to put voluntary statements made by the other defendant to those to whom the statements were made, where such statements were relevant to the co-defendant's defence, even if they incriminated their maker and were regarded as inadmissible for the prosecution as against that person. Myers was convicted of murder, while her co-defendant was found guilty of manslaughter. The court certified that a point of law of general public importance was involved in their decision, namely, whether in a joint trial: '... an out of court confession by A which exculpates B but which ... is conceded to be, inadmissible as evidence for the

Crown nevertheless admissible at the instigation of B in support of B's defence, or does such a confession in all circumstances offend the rule against hearsay?'

The House of Lords held that a defendant had a right to lead relevant evidence in his defence and the trial judge had no discretion to exclude such evidence. There was long-established authority showing that a defendant should be allowed to cross-examine a co-accused as to a previous inconsistent confession, so long as the material was relevant to the defendant's own defence. By extension, a defendant should also be allowed to put a co-defendant's confession to witnesses to whom the confession was made, provided it was relevant to the defendant's defence and it appeared that the confession was obtained *voluntarily*. This provision was important, as a co-accused might not give evidence at trial, making it impossible to put the confession directly to him. Additionally, and very importantly, their Lordships held that such a confession, if admitted, would be relevant both to credibility *and* to the facts in issue, ie in this case it was evidence that Myers was the actual killer and was not caught by the hearsay rule.

R v Myers [1998] AC 124, HL

Lord Hope

While it would appear not to be accurate to describe such a confession [obtained in breach of s. 76(2) of the PCEA 1984] as irrelevant, in a case where the defendant's case is that the offence was committed by the co-defendant, the circumstances in which it was obtained may be said to have been such as to render it worthless for all purposes, whoever it is who seeks to rely on it. On this view it would be a proper exercise of his discretion by the trial judge to exclude such evidence even although the other defendant wished it to be put in evidence. Section 78 of the Act of 1984, on the other hand, is a provision of a different character. This is the provision under which, as Mr. Harman for the Crown pointed out, the trial judge in this case would be likely to have held that the statements to the police ought not to be admitted in evidence if the prosecution had sought to lead that evidence. But once counsel for the co-defendant had made it clear that he wished to lead that evidence from the police officers, the trial judge was faced with a situation to which section 78 makes no reference. That section refers only to evidence on which the prosecution proposes to rely. It does not confer a discretion on the trial judge to exclude evidence of the kind which it describes on which a co-defendant wishes to rely.

Co-defendants' Confessions that are 'Involuntary'

The case of *Myers* involved a 'voluntary' confession that would have been excluded under s. 78, not because it was obtained in breach of s. 76(2) by oppression or something said or done that might make it unreliable. What would the situation have been if Myers had been induced by a promise or threatened with violence into making her admissions (in breach of s. 76(2) (b) and (a) respectively)? On this issue, their Lordships were less certain, and the majority suggested that any resulting confession would still be inadmissible, even for a co-defendant. Subsequently, the Law Commission suggested reform and clarification of this area, and this has been effected by s. 128 of the CJA 2003, which has added a new provision, s. 76A, to the PCEA 1984.

Section 76A

Under s. 76A(1) a confession may be given in evidence for a co-accused provided it is relevant to a matter in issue and is not excluded by the court under the new section. The rest of the provision goes on to mirror s. 76 with one important difference. Thus, s. 76A(2)(a) and (b) allow for the exclusion of an accused person's confession, on a co-defendant's application to adduce it, if it was obtained by oppression or in circumstances that might make it unreliable. Consequently, all of the existing case law on s. 76(2), such as *R v Fulling* [1987] QB 426, will be directly applicable. Similarly, as with s. 76, these issues can be raised by both the defendant and by a judge acting on his own initiative.

However, unlike s. 76, the absence of oppression and reliability need only be 'proved to the court on the balance of probabilities'. This is, of course, at variance to the standard placed on the Crown under s. 76(2), which is beyond reasonable doubt. This raises the possibility that, given the great difference between the two standards of proof, in the event that both prosecution and co-defendant sought to adduce a confession on the *voir dire*, a judge might only be persuaded to allow its adduction by the latter, not by the Crown.

In such a case, the co-defendant's counsel would, presumably, indicate before the *voir dire* that he, too, wished to rely on the confession and take his turn in questioning the officers who received it. More complicated would be the situation in which the Crown acknowledged in advance that they would not be able to meet the appropriate standard and did not attempt to adduce it. In which case, the trial within a trial would, presumably, have to be conducted by the co-defendant's counsel. Additionally, in any case where the confession was not admitted at the behest of the Crown, but was allowed on behalf of a co-defendant, the trial judge would have to direct the jury very carefully (albeit confusingly) that this was not evidence for the Crown but only for the co-accused.

In *Johnson v R* [2007] EWCA Crim 1651, the defendant had entered a guilty plea to importing cocaine with another person. He also tendered a signed basis of plea, claiming merely to have been a 'delivery man' in the importation. Subsequently, however, he claimed that he had not been in the 'right frame of mind' when he had pleaded guilty, and also claimed he had done so because he had not appreciated the law relating to such activity. He was allowed to change his plea to one of 'not guilty'. At trial, he and his fellow accused ran 'cut throat' defences, each blaming the other for the importation. The co-defendant sought to adduce the (now withdrawn) plea of guilty and the basis of plea statement as a confession, pursuant to s. 76A of the PCEA 1984 to support their own case. At trial, this was allowed, and the decision upheld on appeal. The Court of Appeal concluded that the basis of plea: '...clearly was a confession within the meaning of the Section [76A]'. As the judge had (quite reasonably) decided on the balance of probabilities that the plea had not been obtained by anything said or done that was likely to make it unreliable, it was admissible under s. 76A.

Johnson v R [2007] EWCA Crim 1651, CA

Pill LJ

We understand the frustration of a defendant who is permitted to vacate a guilty plea but not then permitted to enjoy the fruits of vacation by way of a trial unencumbered by the earlier plea. On the evidence, however, the issue at this trial was essentially between the two defendants and the decision in Myers and Section 76A of the 1984 Act, are designed to ensure a fair trial in that situation.

Arguably, the distinction in co-defendant situations between confessions that could be excluded for the prosecution under s. 76, and those excluded under s. 78, is not entirely helpful. Nevertheless, it seems that a co-defendant seeking to adduce a confession that is vital to his case will not normally have to concern himself with breaches of the codes of practice that might lead to a successful application to exclude the evidence for the prosecution under s. 78. However, any suggestion that the confession was obtained by oppression or in circumstances that might lead to unreliability will require the judge to be persuaded under s. 76A(2) that these factors did not apply, albeit to the civil standard.

10. Adverse Inference Directions

Introduction

Given that a police interview might result in a confession, it might be wondered what advantage a suspect has in co-operating with police questioning. One facet of what was traditionally referred to as the 'right to silence' was the entitlement not to have an adverse inference drawn from a refusal to answer such questions. This was the subject of fierce debate over several decades. Thus, the Criminal Law Revision Committee's 11th Report on Evidence (1972) concluded that it was wrong that it should not be permissible for a jury or magistrates: '...to draw whatever inferences are reasonable from the failure of the accused, when interrogated, to mention a defence which he puts forward at his trial. To forbid it seems to us to be contrary to common sense and, without helping the innocent, to give an unnecessary advantage to the guilty'.

Cross-reference Box

The other aspect of the common law 'right to silence', the right not to have an adverse inference drawn from a failure to give evidence at trial, has also been abolished, by s. 35 of the CJPOA 1994. For a detailed discussion of how this has operated in practice see below, p. 387.

Amongst the Committee's justifications for this recommendation was a belief that a failure to mention a defence relied on at trial was relevant to the case against the accused, and so ought to be admissible in evidence. Additionally, it was concerned that sophisticated professional criminals were refusing to answer questions put by the police, and then manufacturing false evidence for use at trial, which would then be 'sprung' on the prosecution leaving them little chance to investigate the defence adduced. (It should be noted that others questioned whether this was occurring in practice.)

After much debate, over several decades, and criticism from a variety of sources, including the Lord Chief Justice, s. 34(1)(a)–(b) of the Criminal Justice and Public Order Act 1994 Act permitted an adverse inference to be drawn by the court, following an accused's failure to mention facts during the investigative stage. This would apply where, at any time before he was charged with the offence, on being questioned under caution by a constable trying to discover whether or by whom the offence had been committed, he failed to mention any fact subsequently relied upon in his defence in those proceedings.

As s. 34(1)(b) indicates, an adverse inference can also be drawn if a defendant failed to mention such facts on being charged with an offence or officially informed that he might be prosecuted for it. This provision might be particularly important if the suspect has refused to be interviewed at all by the police after arrest (for example by refusing to come out of his cell).

Section 34 of the CJPOA 1994, Effect of accused's failure to mention facts when questioned or charged (partial extract)

(1)   Where, in any proceedings against a person for an offence, evidence is given that the accused—

(a) at any time before he was charged with the offence, on being questioned under caution by a constable trying to discover whether or by whom the offence had been committed, failed to mention any fact relied on in his defence in those proceedings; or

(b) on being charged with the offence or officially informed that he might be prosecuted for it, failed to mention any such fact,

being a fact which in the circumstances existing at the time the accused could reasonably have been expected to mention when so questioned, charged or informed, as the case may be, subsection (2) below applies.

(2)   Where this subsection applies—

(a) a magistrates' court inquiring into the offence as examining justices;

(b) a judge, in deciding whether to grant an application made by the accused under paragraph 2 of Schedule 3 to the Crime and Disorder Act 1998;

(c) the court, in determining whether there is a case to answer; and

(d) the court or jury, in determining whether the accused is guilty of the offence charged,

may draw such inferences from the failure as appear proper.

(2A) Where the accused was at an authorised place of detention at the time of the failure, subsections (1) and (2) above do not apply if he had not been allowed an opportunity to consult a solicitor prior to being questioned, charged or informed as mentioned in subsection (1) above.

(3)   Subject to any directions by the court, evidence tending to establish the failure may be given before or after evidence tending to establish the fact which the accused is alleged to have failed to mention.

(4)   This section applies in relation to questioning by persons (other than constables) charged with the duty of investigating offences or charging offenders as it applies in relation to questioning by constables; and in subsection (1) above 'officially informed' means informed by a constable or any such person. . . .

However, both provisions only apply if the fact in question is of a type which the accused 'could reasonably have been expected to mention' in the circumstances existing at the time. Section 58 of the Youth Justice and Criminal Evidence Act 1999 amended s. 34 of the 1994 Act by adding s. 34(2A) which provides that, if the accused has not been allowed an opportunity to consult a solicitor prior to being questioned, charged or informed, s. 34 will *not* apply. This amendment was made to ensure compliance with convention rights as interpreted by the ECtHR in *Murray v United Kingdom* (1996) 22 EHRR 29. It is for the trial judge to decide whether to give an adverse inference direction, the jury then decides whether drawing an adverse inference is appropriate on the facts of the case.

The wording of s. 34 has now been the subject of detailed judicial interpretation, and has generated a substantial body of case law. A number of points can be noted. If a defendant does not give evidence or adduce any other evidence at trial, and so does not rely on any 'facts', an adverse inference cannot be drawn against him: *R v Moshaid* [1998] Crim LR 420. It seems from this case that the provision is interpreted as being designed to prevent the prosecution being surprised at trial, rather than aimed at affording the police an opportunity to cross-examine a suspect about his explanation of events.

Thus, if a suspect mentions facts in a prepared statement that he gives to police at interview, and then refuses to answer any further questions, he has not 'failed to mention' those facts if he subsequently relies on them, and so no adverse inference can be drawn. For example, in *R v Knight* [2003] Crim LR 799, the defendant, accused of indecently assaulting a 10-year-old girl, had provided the police, at interview, with a prepared statement, which he read out in the presence of his solicitor. This gave his account, in narrative form, of what had (and had not) happened. He then refused to answer any further police questions. The narrative account was totally consistent with his evidence at trial. Nevertheless, the trial judge left to the jury the possibility of drawing adverse inferences from the defendant's failure to answer police questions (after finishing the statement).

On appeal, it was held that, on the facts of the case, this was wrong and the ensuing conviction was quashed. The Court of Appeal noted that the aim of s. 34(1)(a) of the 1994 Act was to secure disclosure of the defendant's account, not to allow cross-examination by the police on that account. However, the court noted that a read-out statement might still lead to an adverse inference if (unlike the instant case) it was not complete or was subsequently found to be inconsistent with the defendant's case at trial. Additionally, because s. 34 deals with 'facts,' hypothetical possibilities that *might* explain something, and which are first advanced at trial by a defendant, are not covered by the provision: *R v Nickolson* [1999] Crim LR 61.

The phrase 'could reasonably have been expected to mention' has been construed as being contingent on a large variety of circumstances, amongst them, the suspect's age, intelligence, sobriety, personal experience, character and legal advice. Thus, a failure to mention a fact might be deemed to be reasonable in one suspect but not in another, even though the factual nexus was almost identical: *R v Argent* [1997] 2 Cr App R 27. Obviously, the nature of the fact itself might be important. Failure to mention something that is personally embarrassing, such as an alibi based on a visit to a brothel by a married man, might be more 'reasonable' than a failure to bring up something that is mundane, but subsequently of vital importance to the accused's defence.

It should be noted that legal advice not to answer police questions, given by a solicitor to a suspect at a police station, will not constitute 'reasonable' grounds per se as to why an inference should not be drawn from a failure to mention facts. Otherwise, the 1994 Act would be readily circumvented: *R v Condron* [1997] 1 WLR 827. Thus, in *R v Howell* [2003] Crim LR 405 it was held that a suspect's silence at interview, on the advice of his solicitor, would only prevent an adverse inference being drawn under s. 34 if there were sound, objective reasons, for that silence.

'Reliance' has also been heavily defined by the case law. Obviously it will include a fact that is advanced as part of his defence by the accused in examination in chief. However, it seems that in some cases it will also apply to an assertion of a fact, put to a prosecution witness during cross-examination, even if that witness does not accept it. In this regard, the House of Lords has sought to distinguish between putting a specific case to a prosecution witness and asking questions that are simply intended to probe the Crown's version of events: *R v Webber* [2004] 1 WLR

404. By contrast, in *R v Betts* [2001] 2 Cr App R 257, the Court of Appeal concluded that a simple admission at trial by a defendant of a fact asserted by the prosecution during cross-examination could not, without more, amount to 'reliance' on that fact.

R v Condron [1997] 1 WLR 827, CA

Stuart-Smith LJ

It is common ground that, absent an acceptable explanation for not doing so, there were facts relied upon in the appellants' defences which they could reasonably be expected to have mentioned during interview. These included the purchase the previous day of the heroin in small wraps; the innocent explanation of the package and the cigarette packet; and the explanation for the matching wrap found in Curtis's flat. At one time Mr. Shaw was disposed to argue that in any case where the defendants' solicitor advised, for whatever reason, that his clients should not answer questions in interview, the judge should rule that a 'no comment', or refusal to answer, interview should be excluded, because it would be reasonable for the defendants in such circumstances not to answer. However, in the event, he resiled from this extreme position, recognising that if it was correct it would render section 34 wholly nugatory, at least in any case where the defendants had a competent solicitor, since this would be the advice that such a solicitor would be bound to give.

He sought, therefore, to distinguish between what he called tactical reasons for giving such advice and non-tactical reasons. Into the former category would fall these cases: (a) where the client's account to the solicitor suggests guilt, but the client refuses or is unwilling to accept guilt and confess; or (b) where the client refuses to give the solicitor any rational account of the matters in issue; or (c) where there is a risk that two or more defendants may give differing and conflicting accounts. In the latter category, he submitted, fall cases: (d) where the solicitor believes that the evidence is insufficient to charge, justify further detention or secure a conviction; (e) where he cannot personally advise because the police have not sufficiently disclosed their case; (f) where the solicitor forms the view that his client cannot give a fair account of his defence in interview because of some impairment of his mental or physical faculties.

He submitted that if the advice was given for non-tactical reasons, and the solicitor so stated, the judge should exclude the evidence of a 'no comment' interview on the basis that the jury could not, in such circumstances, be invited to draw adverse inferences.

But there are obvious difficulties in this submission: first, the advice may not be bona fide, though there is no suggestion in this case that that was so; secondly, there may be more than one reason for giving it, the other reasons being tactical; thirdly, it is not so much the advice given by the solicitor, as the reason why the defendant chose not to answer questions that is important, and this is a question of fact which may be very much in issue. To take this case as an example: both appellants knew that the force medical examiner certified that they were fit to be interviewed and therefore that medical opinion differed from that of their solicitor. Both were clearly advised by Mr. Delbourgo that, if they failed to mention material facts at the proposed interview, they could be criticised if the matter came to trial. That advice was understood. He also made it plain that this was entirely their choice. At the beginning of the interview both were given the caution in its current form, namely 'You do not have to say anything but it may harm your defence if you do not mention, when questioned, something which you later rely on in court. Anything you say may be given in evidence.' Both indicated that they understood that caution. Both were told that if they felt unwell during the interview they should let the interviewer know and it could be stopped. In these circumstances the fact-finding tribunal might well consider that if the appellants had an innocent explanation of the incriminating evidence, about which they were specifically questioned, they would have mentioned it. We use the expression fact-finding tribunal because, on an application to exclude evidence following a voire dire at which only the solicitor gave evidence, the judge is the fact-finding tribunal, and he is being asked to hold, in effect, that it would be perverse of a jury to draw an adverse inference in these circumstances. We have no doubt that the judge was right to reject this submission and conclude, subject to reviewing the matter at the conclusion of the evidence, that it was a matter for the jury.

Even if he gives an adverse inference direction, a trial judge must direct the jury carefully on its uses and limitations. In *R v Petkar* [2004] 1 Cr App R 22, Rix LJ observed that, in the light of the current JSB direction for such situations, and along with the requirements set out in earlier cases such as *Argent*, *Cowan* and *Condron*, it was desirable that other matters be put in a well-crafted judicial direction to the jury. For example, the facts that the accused failed to mention, but which are relied on in his defence, should be expressly identified and the jury warned that, even if they drawn an adverse inference, they should not convict 'wholly or mainly' on the strength of it.

 ## Summary

- Confessions are admitted as an exception to the hearsay rule, the rationale being that it is unlikely that anyone would make such a statement unless it was true.

- A confession is defined in s. 82(1) of the PCEA 1984. It includes statements that are only partly adverse to their maker (on their face when made); all elements of 'mixed' statements are evidence in their own right, including exculpatory parts.

- Purely exculpatory statements are frequently adduced by the prosecution at trial. However, they merely go to show a defendant's reaction to being taxed with incriminating facts; they are not normally evidence in their own right.

- Most, but not all, confessions are made in response to police questioning. A failure to reveal any facts during this questioning that are subsequently relied on at trial can result in an adverse inference direction being given to the jury. Police questioning of suspects is heavily regulated by Code C of the Codes of Practice issued pursuant to s. 66 of the PCEA 1984.

- Confessions can be excluded pursuant to the two grounds contained in s. 76(2), that is that they were obtained by oppression or in circumstances that might render them unreliable.

- For both of the grounds contained in s. 76(2) the truth (or otherwise) of the confession is irrelevant to the question of admissibility; it is the circumstances in which it was obtained that are decisive.

- To rely on a challenged confession the prosecution must prove beyond reasonable doubt that neither provision applies to the confession.

- Admissibility is determined, normally in the absence of the jury, on a special procedure known as the *voir dire*. The defendant's evidence on the *voir dire* attracts a qualified form of privilege at the substantive trial.

- Additionally, a confession, like any other form of evidence, can be excluded as a result of an exercise of the discretion contained in s. 78 of the PCEA 1984, if adducing it would have such an adverse effect on the fairness of the proceedings that the court ought not to admit it. There is considerable overlap between ss. 76 and 78.

- A confession is not evidence against a co-defendant implicated in it, unless repeated by the maker of the confession in court. However, a co-defendant may adduce a confession made by his fellow accused, if it advances his own case, provided that he can establish (on the balance of probabilities) that it was not obtained in breach of s. 76A of the PCEA 1984.

Further reading

Gisli H Gudjonsson, 'Unreliable confessions and miscarriages of justice in Britain' (2002) International Journal of Police Science & Management, vol 4, no 4, 332–343

John Hartshorne, 'Defensive Use of a Co-Accused's Confession and the Criminal Justice Act 2003' (2004) International Journal of Evidence and Proof, vol 8, 165

Peter Mirfield, 'Expert Evidence and Unreliable Confessions' (1992) Law Quarterly Review 528–534

Peter Mirfield, *Silence, Confessions and Improperly Obtained Evidence* (1998, Oxford University Press)

Rosemary Pattenden, 'Should Confessions be Corroborated' (1991) Law Quarterly Review 317

David Wolchover and Anthony Heaton-Armstron, *Confession Evidence* (1996, Sweet & Maxwell)

Questions for Discussion

1. Rachel, a cocaine addict, is arrested for taking part in an armed robbery in a bank. She is held in a very cold and unheated cell, in January, for 12 hours, before being interviewed by Shaun, a Detective Sergeant. Shaun, who is unaware of Rachel's addiction, observes to her that: '...being cooperative can influence bail decisions'. Rachel, who is desperate for a 'fix', makes full admissions to the crime, implicates Delia in the offence, and gives detailed information as to where the proceeds of the robbery (packets of money) can be discovered, buried under an old beech tree. The police search the location she has described, and discover the missing packets of money, which are found to have Rachel's fingerprints on them.

For suggested approaches, please visit the Online Resource Centre

   a) Advise as to the admissibility of Rachel's statement to the police.
   b) Assume it is *not* admissible, what would the evidential status be of the packets of money found buried under the tree?
   c) How will Rachel's statement affect Delia, if it is admitted into evidence?

2. Arthur and Barry are accused of murdering Cuthbert, a security guard, during an armed robbery at a bank. Both men are arrested shortly after the crime, and interviewed by Derek, a Detective Sergeant. Arthur, who is quite frail, is held in a filthy cell, for 10 hours, without food or drink before being questioned. Arthur refuses to have a solicitor present when interviewed but makes full admissions as to his role in the crime (though without mentioning Barry). Arthur says that he only made admissions because, before the interview, Derek threatened to arrest his mother as part of the investigation if he did not do so. Barry is also interviewed by Derek, though, in his case, shortly after arrest. He too makes full admissions to the crime. However, he says that he was not cautioned prior to the interview and that he only talked because Derek repeatedly raised his voice when questioning him, banged the desk and called him a 'horrible little man'. In his statement, as well as admitting his own role in the crime, Barry implicates Arthur in the robbery and killing.

   Advise as to any evidential issues raised on the above facts.

3. Richard is arrested on suspicion of murdering Sandra. At the police station he is told of his right to a solicitor, but says that he does not want one because he feels they are 'stuck-up prats'.

He is held in a cell for several hours, at the end of which he is interviewed by Detective Inspector Twining. After four hours of questioning, Twining produces a photograph of Samantha's badly decomposed body and says to Richard: 'Look what you did to her, you swine, will you cough now, or do I have to use my special interrogation methods to get the truth out of you?' Richard groans and says: 'OK, I killed her, but I didn't intend to do it. She kept taunting me about my love handles, I must have snapped.' The next day he is interviewed again by DI Twining, but this time he does have the duty solicitor present, and he is questioned in an entirely correct manner. He again admits to the killing.

Discuss any evidential issues that arise on the above facts.

4. Are the rights of an accused person being questioned by the police satisfactorily protected?

5. Fergus, George and Hussein are accused of murdering Iris, during a bungled burglary at her house. After their arrest, on the way to the police station, and without being cautioned, George is gently asked by DC Johnson about what happened in the house. He immediately says that he and Hussein killed Iris when she suddenly disturbed them, and that Fergus had nothing to do with the killing, which occurred while he was in another room. He says nothing more after consulting the duty solicitor. Hussein is interviewed at the police station and eventually confirms precisely what George said on the way to the police station. However, he subsequently claims that he only did this because Johnson threatened him (in his cell) with a 'good thrashing' if he did not do so. When interviewed, Fergus admits the burglary but denies any involvement in the killing.

Advise both the prosecution and Fergus as to the admissibility of the statements made by George and Hussein.

8 COMPETENCE AND COMPELLABILITY

> **Definitions**
>
> **Competence** The ability to give evidence at trial.
>
> **Compellability** The extent to which a witness can be forced to give evidence at trial, even if they do not wish to do so.
>
> **Affirmation** Secular equivalent of an oath, and with the same legal consequences, for those who do not wish to invoke a divine sanction when giving evidence.

1. Competence

Introduction

The law pertaining to competence governs the ability of a witness to give evidence at trial, ie it determines whether or not he can be 'heard' by the court. As will be seen, that regulating compellability governs whether the same witness can be forced to testify, even if he does not wish to do so, in the sense that he will be punished if he does not appear to give evidence when required. Historically, at common law, many groups of witnesses were deemed not to be competent to give evidence, and so could not testify, even if they could provide potentially important information. Among them were: atheists, convicted felons and 'interested' parties to both civil and criminal litigation (ie the litigants themselves). Additionally, spouses could not normally give evidence for or against each other. A variety of reasons lay behind this rather restrictive situation.

> **Exam tip**
>
> Competence and compellability are only rarely set as problem questions in their own right, unless, of course, a lecturer/exam setter has a particular interest in the subject. More commonly, they are appended to a question on other aspects of the law of evidence.

Atheists were barred from testifying as they would not be able to take an oath, or fear its religious sanction if they did. However, Jews were allowed to swear on the Old Testament,[1] while, by the

---

[1] GD, *Tryals Per Pais: or, the Law of England concerning Juries, By nisi prius, & c.* (3rd edn, 1695, printed by Edward Atkins) at 159.

eighteenth century, those of other non-Christian faiths were also often allowed to testify with appropriate oaths: *Omychund v Barker* (1745) 1 Atk 21. The rationale for the (perhaps surprising) incompetence of interested parties was based on a pervasive fear that, without it, litigants might be encouraged to manufacture evidence to support their cases. As Sir Geoffrey Gilbert noted, whether a party was the plaintiff or defendant in a civil matter, or a defendant in a criminal trial: '…the Law removes them from Testimony, to prevent their sliding into Perjury'. Because the victim of a crime did not stand to directly benefit from any fine (or other penalty) enforced on the defendant by the Crown, he was not considered a party to criminal proceedings and could give sworn evidence as a prosecution witness.[2] The law viewed married couples as being almost a single entity, the wife's legal identity being subsumed in that of her husband under the doctrine of *coverture*. Since a defendant was (at that time) incompetent to testify, it was logical that a wife could not testify if her husband was on trial, even as a defence witness, unless she was the victim of her husband's crime of violence (where, for practical reasons, an exception was made).

All of the witnesses listed above became competent to testify as a result of a series of Victorian statutes, the enactment of which were influenced by the earlier work of Jeremy Bentham and a growing recognition of the value of such evidentiary sources. Thus, convicts were made competent by the Evidence Act of 1843; the parties in a civil case by virtue of the Evidence Act 1851; atheists by the Evidence (Further Amendment) 1869; and all criminal defendants by the 1898 Criminal Evidence Act (there had been earlier statutes limited to specific offences allowing criminal defendants to give evidence). The Evidence (Further Amendment) Act of 1853 had made spouses competent in civil proceedings and the Criminal Evidence Act 1898 made them competent (and compellable) for the defendant in criminal matters. In the modern era, under s. 80 of the Police and Criminal Evidence Act 1984 (PCEA 1984), as amended by Sch. 4 to the Youth Justice and Criminal Evidence Act 1999 (YJCEA 1999), spouses are always competent to give evidence in criminal trials for both the prosecution and defence. As a result of these reforms, the vast majority of adult witnesses became competent to testify.

This 'inclusive' approach to competence was encouraged even further by the Home Office Report of 1998, *Speaking Up For Justice*. This suggested that only wholly unintelligible testimony should be withheld from a criminal tribunal, and influenced subsequent reform.

Speaking Up for Justice: Report of the Interdepartmental Working Group on the Treatment of Vulnerable or Intimidated Witnesses in the Criminal Justice System, Home Office, June 1998, paras. 11.25–11.26

11.25 If the basic principles of evidence are that relevant evidence is included and that it is for the tribunal of fact to weigh it, it could be argued that public policy should allow for its inclusion in all but he most exceptional of cases. This would involve reviewing both the present system of exclusions by category based on what we now consider to be outdated assumptions of human nature as well as the assumptions on the jury's ability to understand, weigh, and consider evidence where the manner of its expression may be difficult or unusual.

11.26 This approach would retain the right of the jury or tribunal of fact to test the credibility and weight of the evidence. It would also be right to allow the jury to hear expert evidence as to the ability of the witness to give reliable evidence based on the witness's faculties while not usurping the jury's function by testing the evidence. However, unless incoherency is such that it

[2] Sir Geoffrey Gilbert, *The Law of Evidence* (2nd edn, 1760, printed by Catherine Lintot) at 122 and 126.

renders the witness' evidence without appropriate aid wholly unintelligible, the option would be based on a presumption that in the case of all witnesses over the age of 14 years evidence will be called to be tested by the jury as best it can. The oath can be dispensed with in such cases but the need to tell the truth will be explained to the witness, who will be required to provide some form of acknowledgement.

Competence in Criminal Cases

This encouragement of general competence is reflected (in criminal matters), to a degree at least, in the presumption contained in s. 53(1) of the YJCEA 1999, which provides that: 'At every stage in criminal proceedings all persons are (whatever their age) competent to give evidence.' However, the Act itself allows for two exceptions to this general rule. One of them, a lack of mental or intellectual competence, whether occasioned by retardation, mental illness or infancy, has occasioned problems for centuries. Even in the 1700s, it was appreciated that some 'ideots, madmen, and children under the Age of common knowledge' were unable to give evidence because of their 'want of skill and discernment' or because they were 'incapable of any Sense of Truth'.[3] This remains the case today, at least in some situations. Additionally, defendants are not competent to give evidence for the prosecution.

Section 53 of the YJCEA 1999, Competence of witnesses to give evidence

(1) At every stage in criminal proceedings all persons are (whatever their age) competent to give evidence.

(2) Subsection (1) has effect subject to subsections (3) and (4).

(3) A person is not competent to give evidence in criminal proceedings if it appears to the court that he is not a person who is able to—

    (a) understand questions put to him as a witness, and

    (b) give answers to them which can be understood.

(4) A person charged in criminal proceedings is not competent to give evidence in the proceedings for the prosecution (whether he is the only person, or is one of two or more persons, charged in the proceedings).

(5) In subsection (4) the reference to a person charged in criminal proceedings does not include a person who is not, or is no longer, liable to be convicted of any offence in the proceedings (whether as a result of pleading guilty or for any other reason).

Determining Competence in Criminal Cases

By s. 54 of the YJCEA 1999, it is for the court to decide in a criminal case, whether on a motion by either party or of its own accord, if a tendered witness is competent to give evidence. However, it

---

[3] ibid at 147.

is for the party calling the witness to satisfy the court that s/he is competent, albeit only on the balance of probabilities, under s. 54(2) of the Act. It must do so in the absence of the jury, if the trial is on indictment, and expert evidence may be called on the issue. For example, this might include the evidence of a child psychiatrist called to testify that a tendered (infant) witness can give intelligible answers.

When making a decision as to competence, a court must also determine whether a special measures direction issued under s. 19 of the YJCEA 1999 would assist in making a prospective witness competent for the purposes of the Act, in a 'best case' scenario. Thus, when deciding whether a child would be able to give intelligible answers to questions, the court must decide whether he would be able to do so if, for example, he gave his evidence in chief via a video recording, and were cross-examined via a video-link, rather than testifying in open court.

Cross-reference Box

A range of special measures directions, most issued under the YJCEA 1999, have been introduced to reduce the trauma of testifying and with a view to enhancing the quality of such evidence. These provide alternatives to testifying in open court for certain witnesses, especially, for example, children and sexual complainants. For more information on special measures directions go to pp. 414–423.

The Test for Mental/Intellectual Competence

In the modern era, under s. 53(3) of the YJCEA 1999, a person is not competent to give evidence in criminal proceedings if it appears to the court that he cannot understand questions put to him as a witness, and cannot give answers to them which can be understood. This might be, for example, because of mental defect, insanity or infancy.

This two-part regime replaced the complicated mixture of common law and statutory rules that had previously governed this area of the law. As a result, the 1999 Act repealed, inter alia, s. 38 of the Children and Young Persons Act 1933 and s. 33A of the Criminal Justice Act 1988. Whether or not the test set out in s. 53(3) is satisfied appears to be a question of degree, as can be seen from the following case, which involved the ability of a woman, the victim in a rape case, who was 81 years old and suffering from the effects of Alzheimer's disease, to give evidence at trial.

R v Sed [2005] 1 Cr App Rep 55, CA

Auld LJ

Mr Carter-Stephenson's second point was that, unless the complainant understood all the material questions put to her and all her material answers were understandable, she could not qualify as competent within the terms of s. 53. It should be noted that s. 53 does not, in terms, provide for 100 per cent mutual comprehension of material exchanges giving rise to potential evidence. And, in our view, depending on the length and the nature of the questioning and the complexity of the matter the subject of it, it may not always require 100 per cent, or near 100 per cent, mutual understanding between questioner and questioned as a pre-condition of competence. The judge should also make allowance for the fact that the witness's performance and command of the detail may vary according to the importance to him or her of the subject matter of the question, how recent it was (in this case the interview took place within two days after the alleged attempted rape) and any strong feelings that it may have engendered. It is thus for the judge to determine the question of competence almost as a matter of feel, taking into account the effect of the potential witness's performance as a whole, whether there is a common and comprehensible thread in his or her responses to the questions, however patchy—bearing always in mind that, if, on critical matters, the witness can be seen and heard to be intelligible, it is for the jury and no-one else to determine matters of reliability and general cogency.

In *DPP v R* [2007] EWHC 1842, a 13-year-old girl, who was severely mentally handicapped, was the complainant in a sexual assault case. Her initial police interview about the incident was video-recorded and was considered to be coherent. This was tendered at trial as her examination in chief (under a 'special measures' direction). However, when it came to cross-examination, the girl was unable to recall anything about the incident at all. The question then arose as to whether this lack of independent recollection of the incident that had brought her to court rendered her incompetent. The Divisional Court concluded that it did not. The girl satisfied the test set out in s. 53 of the YJCEA 1999, in that she could understand and answer questions coherently, even if her answer was limited to saying that she did not remember anything.

DPP v R [2007] EWHC 1842, DC

Hughes LJ

This was not a case, on the Justices' findings, of incompetence. The girl may have had her learning difficulties. Her evidence may have needed treating with some care in consequence, but the problem at trial was not capacity to understand or to give intelligible answers, it was loss of memory. Recollection is quite different from competence. Of course, absence of recollection may, in some cases, co-exist with absence of competence, but they do not necessarily run together. Persons who have no recollection for an event may be perfectly competent. A simple example is the witness who is knocked out in the course of whatever happened which founds the charges, and has absolutely no recollection of what occurred, but is otherwise fully functioning.

22 This girl was not like the child in R v Powell. She could understand the questions and she could give intelligible answers. The problem was that her perfectly intelligible answer was, 'I cannot remember'. She was not incompetent. It may be that she could not, for lack of memory, give useful evidence by the time of trial, but that is a different question. The ruling that she was incompetent was erroneous. That does not, of course, mean that such evidence as she had given to the court by way of the video interview was necessarily reliable. The inability to test it by cross-examination either might or might not mean that it was unsafe to rely upon it. That, as I previously said, is an assessment which the trial court has to make individually in every case. An account originally given might, in some cases, be so obviously accurate that it would be wrong to discount it. In a good many more cases, no doubt, the inability to test it will mean that one simply cannot know whether what was said in the original account was accurate or not.

Pause for reflection

Did this decision afford the defendant a proper opportunity to test the complainant's evidence?

Competence and Children

The wording of s. 53(1) means that children of any age are, potentially, competent to testify in criminal trials, unless, under s. 53(3), they cannot understand questions or give comprehensible answers to them. However, until late in the twentieth century, the courts were reluctant to receive evidence from very young infants, especially those who were below the age of seven years. Thus, in comments made in the Court of Appeal in the case of *R v Wallwork* (1958) 42 Cr App R 153, Lord Goddard deprecated the calling of a five-year-old girl in an incest case and expressed the hope that it would not occur again.

Nevertheless, nowadays, and partly as a result of the new means whereby a witness (especially children) can testify pursuant to a 'special measures' direction (such as via a video-link or with the use of an intermediary), and partly because of psychological research that suggests that the evidence of infants is often of considerable value, and not necessarily inherently unreliable, younger children are sometimes allowed to testify.

It is increasingly recognized that small children can frequently give a coherent account of their experiences, while there is often a strong public interest in allowing them to testify, particularly in, for example, child abuse cases, where they may be the only witness available. For example, research into the information provided by 'Susie', a three-year-old girl who had been abducted in 1983, sexually assaulted and then abandoned for dead in a cesspit, and who gave an account of her experiences shortly after she was found, established that she had given a remarkably accurate narrative of what had occurred, though her recollection of what had happened subsequently deteriorated very much faster than with an older child.

D Jones, 'The Evidence of a Three-Year-Old Child' [1987] Crim LR 677 (Extract)

This case report illustrates that a child as young as three can provide a convincing account of a traumatic event which she had experienced. Additionally she could correctly identify her assailant. Part of the video taped assessment at day 14 consisted of assessments of her general reliability as well as the reliability of her ability to identify from photographs. In this case the information obtained from the child's account was able to be matched with the defendant's eventual confession. Susie's account and the defendant's show that this little child, at least, was a reliable informant. The 'account' itself consisted of demonstration with toys, her observed behavioural reactions as well as direct statements that she made. Part of the child's account was obtainable by the proper utilisation of techniques which have recently caused controversy, e.g. anatomically correct dolls. These techniques were only used in the later portions of the interview, where details of the assault were being probed for. The case therefore vindicates the claims of clinicians and researchers that cues and play material are necessary tools for the proper interviewing of young children, as opposed to being unreliable encumbrances.

As a result of a change in attitudes engendered by such research, in *R v C.A.Z.* [1990] 91 Cr App R 203, a six-year-old was allowed to give evidence against her father in a sexual abuse trial. Even more significantly, in this case, Lord Lane also observed that, although it might be very rare for a five-year-old child to be permitted to give evidence, it could happen, if the child's circumstances and abilities allowed it. More recently, in the unreported (and exceptional) case of *R v Dean* (2007) *The Times*, 13 January, this actually occurred, and a five-year-old girl gave evidence, using a video recording, to the effect that she had been raped by the defendant, who was also her babysitter, when she was only three. (Her cross-examination was conducted via a live link.)

Pause for reflection

In what circumstances would you be willing to convict on the evidence of a five-year-old?

Even so, there are, of course, still limits on the ages at which most infants can give evidence without falling foul of s. 53(3). In *R v Powell* [2006] Crim LR 781, a three-and-a-half year-old sexual complainant was initially treated as (just) competent to give evidence, in the light of her pre-recorded police video, which was both coherent and relevant. However, when it came to cross-examination, via a live link, it was apparent that she was a much less satisfactory witness than the video had suggested; she failed to articulate many answers and, at one point in the process, appeared to be accepting the defence case. It was held that what was relevant to the judge's decision on admissibility was competence at the time of trial, and, in the light of the complainant's cross-examination, it was apparent that she was not competent to testify. As a result, the trial judge should have reversed her initial decision and rejected all of the infant's evidence, including the video.

R v C.A.Z. [1990] 91 Cr App R 203, CA

Lord Lane CJ

So far as Wallwork is concerned, that decision, some considerable number of years ago, in 1958, has really been overtaken by events. First of all it will be seen from the words of Lord Goddard that part of the concern which he expressed was concern over the position of the child itself in court, when he mentions the fact the court was cleared so far as it was possible to have it cleared. That particular problem has now to a great extent been cured by the system of video links, which of course in Lord Goddard's days were not even imagined. But more recent developments are exemplified by the very fact which we have already emphasised that the proviso to the old section 38(1) has now been repealed by section 34(1) of the 1988 Act. It is to be observed also that so far as the decision in Wright and Ormerod (supra) is concerned, that decision, as we understand it, was before the coming into force of the material provision of (s. 34(1)) of the Criminal Justice Act 1988). It seems to us that Parliament, by repealing the proviso to section 38(1), was indicating a change of attitude by Parliament, reflecting in its turn a change of attitude by the public in general to the acceptability of the evidence of young children and of increasing belief that the testimony of young children, when all precautions have been taken, may be just as reliable as that of their elders.

In former years, the competence of a child (or any other witness) to give evidence (whether on oath or not) was normally determined in the presence of the jury, on the basis that this would also assist jurors when it came to weighing the child's testimony if they were (ultimately) permitted to give evidence. However, this is no longer the case, such questions normally being determined in the absence of the jury, being a matter for the judge alone. In *R v Deakin* [1995] 1 Cr App R 471 the victim and proposed prosecution witness was a woman with Down's Syndrome, who had been indecently assaulted by a care assistant. At the competency hearing, the judge heard from her in the presence of the jury and also took expert testimony from two psychologists, whose opinion was that the woman was capable of telling the truth, in the same circumstances. The defendant appealed on the basis that this evidence should not have been heard in front of the jury, who might have been influenced by the experts' acceptance of the complainant's story. The Court of Appeal agreed, at least insofar as the experts were concerned (although applying the proviso and dismissing the appeal). This applies equally to children and also now extends to the witness's own examination by the judge, as can be seen from the following extract.

R v Hampshire [1995] 2 Cr App R 319, CA

Auld LJ

It follows, in our judgment, that a judge who considers it necessary to investigate a child's competence to give evidence in addition to or without the benefit of an earlier view of a video-taped interview under section 32A of the 1988 Act, should do so in open court in the presence of the accused because it is part of the trial but need not do so in the presence of the jury. The jury's function is to assess the child's evidence, including its weight, from the evidence he or she gives on the facts of the case after the child has been found competent to give it. The exercise of determining competence is not a necessary aid to that function. Put another way, the Court's view in Reynolds of the ratio in Dunne cannot in itself be a basis for imposing, or for construing, the recent statutory change as continuing to impose, a duty upon the judge to conduct a preliminary investigation of the competence of a child witness in the presence of the jury.

Defendant Competence for the Prosecution

The previous and long-standing rule whereby a defendant was not competent to give evidence for the prosecution in his own trial, or in that of any co-defendant charged in the same proceedings, has also been preserved by dint of s. 53(4) of the YJCEA 1999. What this means is that (obviously) an accused person cannot give evidence for the Crown against himself, nor, when two or more defendants are being tried together, can he be called by the prosecution to give evidence against one of his co-defendants. However, under s. 53(5), the definition of a person who is 'charged in criminal proceedings' does not include someone who is no longer liable to be convicted (rather than sentenced). Most commonly, as the provision itself suggests, this state of affairs might be occasioned by the relevant individual pleading guilty. Having done so, he could then be called to give evidence for the prosecution against a former co-defendant.

However, such a situation could also be achieved by some other mechanism, or for 'any other reason' to quote the statute. This could be done, for example, by the Attorney General entering a *nolle prosequi* against the defendant, that is, a writ bringing the prosecution to an end. Converting a joint trial into separate trials of the individual co-defendants would also have this effect. However, cynical attempts to do this purely as a way of ensuring that co-accused become competent to give evidence against each other have usually been deprecated by the courts. In theory, an accused person may be called (though he cannot be compelled) to give evidence for the defence of a co-defendant, though, if he does so, he will, of course, be liable to be cross-examined about his own involvement in the alleged crime, making such a scenario highly unlikely.

Competence in Civil Cases

An adult witness will be competent to testify in a civil case if he can take the oath/affirm prior to doing so (see below). There is no power to allow an adult to give evidence except on oath (unlike the situation in criminal matters), so that competence and the ability to be sworn are synonymous. However, a child witness in civil matters who does not 'understand the nature of an oath' can testify without being sworn, provided he satisfies the test set out in s. 96(2) of the Children Act 1989, which is that he understands the duty to speak the truth and has sufficient understanding to justify his evidence being heard. The duty to speak the truth is, presumably, the duty to be truthful in 'normal' social intercourse (rather than the added duty imposed when on oath). For these purposes, s. 105 of the Children Act provides that 'children' are young people under the age of 18 years. The 1989 statute was the first to allow unsworn evidence from children in civil matters.

However, adults in civil cases who are, in some way, so mentally defective that they cannot meet the test for taking an oath, cannot give unsworn evidence, even if they meet the same standard of understanding as children testifying under s. 96(2) of the Children Act 1989 or, for that matter, unsworn adults giving evidence in criminal matters pursuant to s. 53(3) of the YJCEA 1999. This could, in theory, produce some strange results. Thus, a slightly mentally backward 17-year-old might be able to testify (unsworn) on one day, but could not do so a month later, after he had turned 18. Of course, not all forms of mental disturbance will preclude a witness from reaching the requisite level of understanding to take an oath. Thus, in *R v Hill* (1851) 2 Den 254, the inmate of an insane asylum, who believed that he was occasionally being spoken to by spirits, but who, despite this delusion, had a clear understanding of the duty imposed by an oath, was allowed to be sworn and testify on a manslaughter charge; the same principle would apply to a civil matter.

2. Testifying on Oath/Affirming

Introduction

When a party in a case calls a witness to give evidence, the witness will normally either take the oath or, alternatively, affirm, before testifying. Indeed, for adult witnesses in civil trials the test for competence and that required to take the oath/affirm are synonymous, though this is not the case for children in civil matters, or for adults and children in criminal trials. Affirmation will occur if the witness is not religious, is of a faith that cannot be readily accommodated by the court (perhaps because it lacks the requisite holy text) or because, like members of the Society of Friends (Quakers), they do not believe in swearing a religious oath. Nowadays, in most urban courts, all of the major religions found in modern England are catered for, with copies of the Bible (both Old and New Testament), Koran, Gita, etc., being available. However, if an arcane religious belief cannot be catered for, the witness can be asked to affirm.

The terms of the oath and affirmation are set out in s. 1(1) of the Oaths Act 1978 and have the same legal effect vis-à-vis subsequent prosecutions for perjury. The former is: 'I swear by Almighty God that the evidence I shall give shall be the truth, the whole truth and nothing but the truth.' The terms of the affirmation are: 'I do solemnly and sincerely and truly declare and affirm that the evidence I shall give shall be the truth, the whole truth and nothing but the truth.' In his 2001 report, Lord Justice Auld suggested that, although it was necessary to mark the beginning of a witness's evidence in some manner, a solemn promise to tell the truth would be superior to the current oath/affirmation regime, with its combination of 'archaic words' and (in the case of the oath) the invoking of God, which were, nevertheless, often uttered in a perfunctory manner. An inadvertent failure to administer the oath to a witness who ought to have been sworn is not a mere technicality, one that can usually be ignored on appeal, as such a witness may have given different evidence if they had testified on oath: *R v Sharman* [1998] 1 Cr App R 406.

R v Sharman [1998] 1 Cr App R 406, CA

Mantell LJ

It might be said that it is extremely unlikely that had P been sworn she would have deviated in a single instance from the answers which she returned to questions both in chief and cross-examination. But for the court to make that assumption would be to diminish the requirement that evidence be sworn or affirmed to the point where the procedure becomes virtually meaningless. As Evans L.J. said in Simmonds: 'The courts proceed on the basis that the oath imposes a sanction, temporal if not religious, and for those reasons the courts do not receive un-sworn evidence except where it is expressly permissible for them to do so.' So as Evans L.J. went on to say in that case: 'The evidence ostensibly given was not evidence at all.' That means and can only mean in the present case that the evidence received from P viva voce was inadmissible.

Oaths in Criminal Cases

In criminal matters, the criteria set out in s. 55 of the YJCEA 1999 now determine whether or not a witness is to be sworn. In particular, it should be noted that, under s. 55(2)(a) and (b), only a person aged 14 or more years can be sworn, and that, to do so, he must have a sufficient appreciation of the solemnity of the occasion and of the particular responsibility to tell the truth which is involved in taking the oath.

This means that the Act provides a statutory definition of competence to give sworn testimony, replacing that which previously existed at common law (though it is largely the same as the test that developed in the 1970s), and which still applies in civil cases. If the witness is able to give intelligible testimony, ie he can understand questions and answer them so as to be understood, he will be presumed to be able to give sworn evidence unless there is evidence (which may include expert evidence) to the contrary: s. 55(3). However, once such evidence is adduced, for example, by the opposing party demonstrating that the witness may not understand the responsibilities inherent in taking an oath, the calling party must persuade the court, on the balance of probabilities, that the witness is competent to be sworn, ie that they are over 14 and appreciate the requirements of the oath: s. 55(4) of the Act. This will usually be determined on the *voir dire* procedure (see chapter 1).

The question as to whether or not an oath has been lawfully administered does not appear to rest on the theological intricacies of the specific religion of the witness concerned. For example, in *R v Kemble* [1990] 1 WLR 1111, it was held that the fact that a Muslim witness took an oath using the New Testament did not constitute a material irregularity in the course of the trial, even though this was contrary to Islamic rules on oath taking.

R v Kemble [1990] 1 WLR 1111, CA

Lord Taylor CJ

We take the view that the question of whether the administration of an oath is lawful does not depend upon what may be the considerable intricacies of the particular religion which is adhered to by the witness. It concerns two matters and two matters only in our judgment. First of all, is the oath an oath which appears to the court to be binding on the conscience of the witness? And, if so, secondly, and most importantly, is it an oath which the witness himself considers to be binding upon his conscience?

So far as the present case is concerned, quite plainly the first of those matters is satisfied. The court did obviously consider the oath to be one which was binding upon the witness. It was the second matter which was the subject so to speak of dispute before this court. Not only did we have the evidence of the professor, the expert in the Muslim theology, but we also had the evidence of the witness himself. He having on this occasion been sworn upon a copy of the Koran in Arabic gave evidence before us that he did consider himself to be bound as to his conscience by the way in which he took the oath at the trial. Indeed he went further. He said, 'Whether I had taken the oath upon the Koran or upon the Bible or upon the Torah, I would have considered that to be binding on my conscience.' He was cross-examined by Mr. Banks in an endeavour to show that that was not the truth, but we have no doubt, having heard him give his evidence and seen him give his evidence, that that was the truth, and that he did consider all of those to be holy books, and that he did consider that his conscience was bound by the form of oath he took and the way in which he took it. In other words we accept his evidence.

Consequently, applying what we believe to be the principles which we have endeavoured to set out to those facts, we conclude that the witness was properly sworn. We conclude accordingly that there was no irregularity, material or otherwise.

Oaths in Civil Cases

As already noted, adult witnesses in civil cases must give evidence on oath, so the test for the oath and that for competence is the same. Children in civil cases can also give evidence on oath, provided they meet the requisite test to do so. Historically, at common law (which still governs civil cases), to have a sufficient understanding of the oath to justify being sworn required an appreciation of its divine sanction: *R v Brasier* (1779) 1 Leach 199. In the modern era, however, a time when religious belief is less prevalent, this has been replaced by the more secular test enunciated in the criminal case of *R v Hayes* [1977] 1 WLR 234, which still governs the situation in civil matters (the principle has been reduced to a similar statutory formula, in criminal cases, under s. 55 of the YJCEA 1999). This asks whether the witness has a sufficient appreciation of the solemnity of the occasion, and the added responsibility to tell the truth, which is involved in taking an oath.

Normally, *Hayes* suggests, infants below the age of eight will be too young to take an oath, while most children over 10 will be able to do so; the most keenly contested cases will fall in the two-year watershed between these ages. However, each case will turn on its own facts; an immature child of 11 might not be sworn, a very 'advanced' child of seven might be able to take an oath. The Court of Appeal will not lightly interfere with a judge's exercise of his discretion in this respect. Usually, an inquiry as to whether children are capable of taking an oath will only be carried out on those who are under the age of 14: *R v Khan* [1981] 73 Cr App R 190. (Although this was a criminal case, the principle survives in civil matters.)

R v Hayes [1977] 1 WLR 234, CA

Bridge LJ

It is unrealistic not to recognise that, in the present state of society, amongst the adult population the divine sanction of an oath is probably not generally recognised. The important consideration, we think, when a judge has to decide whether a child should properly be sworn, is whether the child has a sufficient appreciation of the solemnity of the occasion and the added responsibility to tell the truth, which is involved in taking an oath, over and above the duty to tell the truth which is an ordinary duty of normal social conduct.

Against the background of those general considerations of principle, we think it right also to approach the matter on the footing that this is very much a matter within the discretion of the trial judge and we think that this court, although having jurisdiction to interfere if clearly satisfied that the trial judge's discretion was wrongly exercised, should hesitate long before doing so. The judge sees and hears the boy or girl, which means very much more than the bare written word....

Unsworn Evidence

As will be appreciated from the above, competence in criminal matters, and an ability to give sworn evidence, are not synonymous. As a result, s. 56 of the YJCEA 1999 permits the reception of unsworn evidence that is given either by witnesses who are under the age of 14 or by older witnesses who do not appear to understand the solemnity of the proceedings required in taking an oath (perhaps because they have a mental handicap) but who can, nevertheless, still give intelligible testimony (ie they are competent under the Act).

In *R v Hampshire* [1995] 3 WLR 269, Auld LJ suggested that, where a young child gives unsworn evidence, a judge might find it appropriate to remind him/her, in the presence of the defendant and jury, of the importance of telling the truth. For example, he might say: 'Tell us all you can remember of what happened. Don't make anything up or leave anything out. This is very important.' Under s. 57 of the YJCEA 1999, it is an offence to give false unsworn evidence in circumstances that would constitute perjury, had the evidence been given on oath, though, for those under 14, the penalty is limited to a fine not exceeding £250. A deposition of unsworn evidence may also be taken, pursuant to s. 56(3). In civil matters, unsworn evidence can be given by children who satisfy the test set out in s. 116 of the Children Act 1989 (discussed above).

Section 56 of the YJCEA 1999, Reception of unsworn evidence (Partial extract)

(1) Subsections (2) and (3) apply to a person (of any age) who—

    (a) is competent to give evidence in criminal proceedings, but

(b) (by virtue of section 55(2)) is not permitted to be sworn for the purpose of giving evidence on oath in such proceedings.

(2) The evidence in criminal proceedings of a person to whom this subsection applies shall be given unsworn.

(3) A deposition of unsworn evidence given by a person to whom this subsection applies may be taken for the purposes of criminal proceedings as if that evidence had been given on oath.

(4) A court in criminal proceedings shall accordingly receive in evidence any evidence given unsworn in pursuance of subsection (2) or (3)....

3. Compellability

Introduction

Compellability determines whether or not a witness can be legally forced to testify, irrespective of his personal wishes. This can be done by a relevant party securing a subpoena, witness order or witness summons, requiring him to attend to give evidence, depending on the forum in which the witness is asked to testify. If the witness then fails to obey it, ie he does not attend court, refuses to enter the witness box when called or, having done so, is unwilling to answer specific questions, he risks being found to be in contempt of court and punished accordingly (which can include imprisonment) or, under s. 3 of the Criminal Procedure (Attendance of Witnesses) Act 1965, sentenced to a maximum of three months' imprisonment. Additionally, under s. 67 of the Criminal Procedure and Investigations Act 1996, judges have the power to issue arrest warrants for witnesses who fail to attend to give evidence at the Crown Court. The Court of Appeal has periodically stressed the importance of witnesses co-operating with the courts, warning that if a witness chooses to ignore a summons they can 'expect to be punished': *R v Yusuf* [2003] 2 Cr App R 32. Nevertheless, the sanction of contempt is very rarely used with regard to children under the age of 16 who refuse to testify.

Normally, any witness who is competent to give evidence is also compellable to do so, in both civil and criminal cases. However, there are a limited number of exceptions to this general rule, some of which are quite arcane. For example, the Queen and diplomatic ambassadors are competent but not compellable to testify. Additionally, no judge, of whatever level, including masters of the Supreme Court, can be compelled to give evidence in relation to their judicial functions (though they are competent to do so). For example, a District Judge cannot be compelled to give evidence as to the extent of a wife's undertaking in matrimonial proceedings conducted in the County Court: *Warren v Warren* [1997] QB 488. Much more important, in practice, is the position of spouses in criminal cases.

Spousal Compellability in Criminal Cases

A spouse, although always competent for the prosecution against their husband or wife in a criminal matter, cannot normally be compelled to give evidence against their partner. This is unlike the situation that prevails in civil proceedings, where spouses are usually treated like any other type of witness. The very limited number of situations in which a spouse can be compelled to give evidence against their husband or wife in a criminal trial are governed by s. 80 of the Police and Criminal Evidence Act 1984, as amended by Sch. 4 of the YJCEA 1999.

Section 80 of the Police and Criminal Evidence Act 1984, Competence and compellability of accused's spouse or civil partner

(2)   In any proceedings the spouse or civil partner of a person charged in the proceedings shall, subject to subsection (4) below, be compellable to give evidence on behalf of that person.

(2A)   In any proceedings the spouse or civil partner of a person charged in the proceedings shall, subject to subsection (4) below, be compellable—

(a) to give evidence on behalf of any other person charged in the proceedings but only in respect of any specified offence with which that other person is charged; or
(b) to give evidence for the prosecution but only in respect of any specified offence with which any person is charged in the proceedings.

(3)   In relation to the spouse or civil partner of a person charged in any proceedings, an offence is a specified offence for the purposes of subsection (2A) above if—

(a) it involves an assault on, or injury or a threat of injury to, the spouse or civil partner or a person who was at the material time under the age of 16;
(b) it is a sexual offence alleged to have been committed in respect of a person who was at the material time under that age; or
(c) it consists of attempting or conspiring to commit, or of aiding, abetting, counselling, procuring or inciting the commission of, an offence falling within paragraph (a) or (b) above.

(4)   No person who is charged in any proceedings shall be compellable by virtue of subsection (2) or (2A) above to give evidence in the proceedings.

(4A)   References in this section to a person charged in any proceedings do not include a person who is not, or is no longer, liable to be convicted of any offence in the proceedings (whether as a result of pleading guilty or for any other reason).

(5)   In any proceedings a person who has been but is no longer married to the accused shall be compellable to give evidence as if that person and the accused had never been married.

[(5A) In any proceedings a person who has been but is no longer the civil partner of the accused shall be compellable to give evidence as if that person and the accused had never been civil partners.]

(6)   Where in any proceedings the age of any person at any time is material for the purposes of subsection (3) above, his age at the material time shall for the purposes of that provision be deemed to be or to have been that which appears to the court to be or to have been his age at that time.

(7)   In subsection (3)(b) above 'sexual-offence' means an offence under the Protection of Children Act 1978 or Part 1 of the Sexual Offences Act 2003.

(9)   Section 1(d) of the Criminal Evidence Act 1898.

It should immediately be noted that a husband or wife is always compellable to testify on *behalf* of an accused spouse, by dint of s. 80(2). This is, of course, subject to the predictable exception, set out in s. 80(4), which provides that a spouse who is charged in the same proceedings as their husband or wife, is not compellable to testify for them. This is in conformity with the position with regard to any other co-defendant. Obviously, without such a provision, a spouse, if forced to give evidence, would have no choice as to whether to answer questions about their own involvement in any alleged crime.

Section 80(4A) of the 1984 Act provides that 'a person charged' does not include a person who is not, or is no longer, liable to be convicted of any offence in the proceedings. Thus, if the spouse of an accused person, who is also a defendant in the same proceedings, pleads guilty, s/he is outside the ambit of s. 80(4) and, consequently, is treated as an ordinary witness, and so subject to the traditional rule of compellability for the defence.

Over the years, a number of different rationales have been advanced for the spousal exemption from being compelled to give evidence for the prosecution. Several would no longer be treated seriously. Nevertheless, the preservation of marital harmony is still considered to be important. Thus, in the pre-PCEA 1984 case of *R v Hoskyn* [1979] AC 474, Lord Salmon ascribed the general exemption of a wife to: '... the supreme importance attached by the common law to the special status of marriage and to the unity supposed to exist between husband and wife'. The judge also referred to the 'natural repugnance' that the public would feel at seeing a wife give evidence against her husband in many situations.

One major criticism of such a justification is that the exemption only applies to those defendants who are legally married. As a result, parties who are merely cohabiting with each other, no matter for how long a period, are outside the scope of s. 80 and are, accordingly, treated as ordinary witnesses. An attempt in *R v Pearce* [2002] 1 Cr App R 39 to argue that respect for family life under Article 8 of the ECHR required that long-term cohabiting partners be treated in the same way as married spouses in this regard was swiftly rejected by the Court of Appeal, which saw benefits in restricting the number of potential witnesses who were not compellable to testify and also in limiting uncertainty in this area of the law; it would be difficult to determine what was a long-term relationship.

 Pause for reflection

In the modern era do you feel that this is a fair conclusion to reach on this issue?

R v Pearce [2002] 1 Cr App R 39, CA

Kennedy LJ

In any event we do not accept the proposition which underlies Mr Wood's submissions in relation to this aspect of the case, namely that proper respect for family life as envisaged by Article 8 requires that a co-habitee of a defendant, whether or not married to him, should not be required to give evidence or to answer questions about a statement which he has already made. This is plainly, as Ms Joseph submits, an area where the interests of the family must be weighed against those of the community at large, and it is precisely the sort of area in which the European Court defers to the judgment of States in relation to their domestic courts. There may be much to be said for the view that with very limited exceptions all witnesses who are competent should also be compellable, and certainly the material before us does not enable us to conclude that because a concession has been made to husbands and wives proper respect for family life requires that a similar concession be made to those in the position of a husband or a wife. As Ms Joseph points out, if the concession were to be widened it is not easy to see where, logically, the widening should end.

However, it should be noted that a civil partnership, between same sex couples, does have the same evidential effect as marriage, as a result of s. 84(1) of the Civil Partnership Act 2004. This provides that any enactment or rule of law: '...relating to the giving of evidence by a spouse applies in relation to a civil partner as it applies in relation to the spouse'. As a result, someone in a subsisting civil partnership cannot normally be compelled to give evidence against their partner. Additionally, it should be noted that, if a marriage has been celebrated abroad, it is essential that it is recognized as valid under English law for the spousal exemption to apply. Thus, in *R v Khan* [1987] 84 Cr App R 44, a 'second' Muslim marriage, made abroad, had no legal consequences for the purposes of giving evidence.

R v Khan [1987] 84 Cr App R 44, CA

Glidewell LJ

...what is the position of a lady who has gone through a ceremony of marriage which under the religious observances of a faith, and under the law of some other countries, is entirely valid, but which, because it is a second polygamous marriage, is of no effect in the law of this country? In our judgment the position so far as her ability and competence to give evidence is concerned is no different from that of a woman who has not been through a ceremony of marriage at all, or one who has been through a ceremony of marriage which is void because it is bigamous. Exactly the same principles in our view apply, and therefore we hold that the learned judge was entirely correct in his reasoning in deciding that Hasina Patel was a competent witness for the prosecution, both in respect of her husband and in respect of this appellant.

Provided that they are still legally married, it is irrelevant that the parties are separated from each other or are no longer living in amity. Perhaps more logically, once divorced, the previous status of the witness/defendant, ie that they were once married but are now no longer so, becomes irrelevant. They are treated as if they had never been married at all, by dint of s. 80(5). The material time for determining whether a witness is a legal spouse of the person charged is the point at which that person is called to testify. Some academic authorities have suggested that there is a measure of doubt as to whether the spousal exemption will apply to a marriage that has been entered purely and cynically for that purpose (ie to prevent compellability for the prosecution). However, it seems unlikely that it would not apply, both for theoretical and practical reasons (it would not be easy to prove motive).

R Munday, 'Sham marriages and spousal compellability' (2001) J Crim L, vol 65, no 4, 336–348 (Extracts)

Another point to be borne in mind is that English law is now governed by legislation which must be taken to have given proper consideration, both via PCEA and via the Youth Justice and Criminal

Evidence Act 1999 amendments, to the delicate task of balancing the maintenance of the institution of marriage against the public interest in the effective fight against crime. There is no history of English courts inquiring into the reality of parties' marriages, and there is no hint in the statute that the courts should begin to do so. In any case, one might infer from the fact that s. 80(5) of PCEA regulates the position of parties who are no longer married to one another (those who are divorced, whose marriages have been annulled, etc.), that had Parliament wished to insist that s. 80 only applies to marriages truly founded upon the understanding that the partners will observe those mutual obligations of care and support upon which Minton J insisted in Lutwak, it would have done so expressly.

Although this article has not explored the question, thorny, if not morally insoluble policy choices lie at the root of spousal compellability. Section 80 of PCEA offers a crude but workable accommodation between a desire to uphold the dignity of the married state and the need to promote the effective administration of criminal justice. As noted above, the drafting of s. 80(3)(a), in particular, offers the courts some leeway in determining the range of cases in which spouses may be compelled to testify against one another. It would undoubtedly be improper for the courts simply to employ this looseness of legislative language as a means of circumventing marriages that looked to be shams. However, should the courts elect to give a generous construction to the concept of an offence which 'involves an assault on, or injury or threat of injury to' the spouse, the issue of sham marriages would lose some of its force simply because such an interpretation would significantly diminish the potential pool of serious offences in which it would be likely to arise.

Indeed, it also appears that there is no power to prevent a prisoner from marrying, even where there is a suspicion that it is being done for the purpose of taking advantage of the spousal exemption, as the following case, involving a defendant who wished to marry a prosecution witness (also his partner) in a murder case, suggests.

R (On the Application of the Crown Prosecution Service) v Registrar General of Births, Marriages and Deaths

(2003) QB 1222, CA

Waller LJ

The right to marry has always been a right recognised by the laws of this country long before the Human Rights Act 1998 came into force. The right of course is also enshrined in article 12 of the European Convention for the Protection of Human Rights and Fundamental Freedoms. It has more recently been held that prisoners are not to be denied that right in the cases cited by the judge. The right, furthermore, must not be denied to Miss B who has indeed born a child to J. It seems to me that the right of marriage carries with it the incidences of marriage, including that the wife may not be compelled to give evidence against her husband or vice versa.

Changes in the general nature of society, in patterns of cohabitation, in the way in which marriage is widely viewed, and in perceptions of the social need to prosecute crime effectively have cast considerable doubt on whether it is appropriate to preserve a marital exemption from compellability in the modern era. However, alternative approaches, whether making exemption entirely a matter of judicial discretion, one that is purely dependant on a judge's perception of the nature of a relationship (and consequently uncertain as to its application), or, alternatively, abolishing it altogether, also pose serious problems.

Deirdre Dwyer, 'Can a Marriage be Delayed in the Public Interest So as to Maintain the Compellability of a Prosecution Witness?: R (On the Application of the Crown Prosecution Service) v Registrar General of Births, Marriages and Deaths' (2003) E & P, vol 7, no 3, 191–196 (Extract)

This case [*R (On the Application of the Crown Prosecution Service)*], along with Pearce, raises concerns about the circumstances in which the s. 80 privilege is provided. At the time of the Criminal Evidence Act 1898, marriage was the dominant form of long-term sexual relationship, and marriage was all but indissoluble. There were (at least in the eyes of Parliament) few unmarried families, and it was unlikely that two people would enter into marriage simply to invoke the privilege of incompetence and non-compellability. Following Pearce (which was not referred to in judgments in the instant case), B would have been a compellable prosecution witness against her partner of seven years. By marrying J, she ceased to be compellable. There is no reason why J and B could not divorce by mutual arrangement soon after J's trial, having made use of that privilege. Conversely, if J and B had been married but separated for seven years, B would have automatically been non-compellable (subject to the exceptions of specific offences). In this case, the Court of Appeal would appear to have sought to prioritise the right to marriage over the effective running of the criminal justice system. It has been submitted that to have done otherwise would have been to breach J and B's Convention rights.

One possible solution, suggested by Andrew Choo, is to follow the approach taken in Australia by the Evidence Act 1995. In all cases, except those concerning domestic violence and particular offences against children, s. 18 of that Act provides that the question of prosecution compellability for spouse, 'de facto spouse', parent and child is subject to the court's discretion. The court shall consider (s. 18(7)) the nature and gravity of the offence, the substance and weight of any evidence, whether other evidence is reasonably available, the relationship between defendant and witness, and whether a matter might have to be disclosed that was received in confidence. The merit of such an approach is that it avoids scenarios in which marriage is used to gain privilege, or where the accused and witness feel that marriage is forced upon them as a means to protect their relationship. The demerit is that it encroaches further on Article 8 rights, in that the police, the Crown Prosecution Service and the court will be required to investigate and scrutinise the private lives of the accused and of certain witnesses as part of the criminal justice process.

Pause for reflection

Do you feel that, in the modern era, it is appropriate that spouses or civil partners should ever be allowed not to testify for the prosecution against their partners?

Spousal Compellability for the Prosecution/Co-accused

The rules governing those rare situations in which a defendant's spouse is compellable for the prosecution or for a co-defendant are the same, and so may be considered together. Although the general rule is that a spouse is not compellable to testify for either of these parties, this is subject to the major statutory exceptions set out in s. 80(2A) and (3) of the PCEA 1984, as amended by Sch. 4 of the YJCEA 1999. This establishes a limited number of 'specified offences,' found in s. 80(3)(a)–(c), where a spouse is compellable to give evidence; they constitute an attempt by

Parliament to balance the perceived need for the institution of marriage to be respected, and marital harmony preserved, against the desirability that certain types of crime be prosecuted effectively.

The original legislation was heavily, if belatedly, influenced by the recommendations of the Criminal Law Revision Committee's 11th Report of 1972. It was particularly aimed at addressing domestic violence and sexual abuse. The specified offences comprise: those involving an assault on, or injury (including threats of injury) to the wife or husband of the accused person, or to a victim who was under the age of 16 years at the material time; a sexual offence, as defined in s. 80(7) of the Act, alleged to have been committed against a person under the age of 16 at the material time (such as rape or indecent assault); or being charged as an accessory, in any fashion, to the commission of the above offences.

It should be noted that the expression, 'offences involving an assault', although somewhat vague, appears to be wider than a simple charge of assault. For example, it would seem to extend to situations in which a drunken husband 'robbed' his wife of cash to fund a visit to a public house, as robbery necessarily entails the use or threat of violence. However, in this situation, in order to make the spouse compellable to testify for the co-accused or the prosecution, s/he must be a victim of the offence; for example, the victim in a case of domestic violence. By contrast, if a spouse witnesses a child under the age of 16 being the victim of an assault perpetrated by their husband or wife, it does not matter that s/he is not a child of the spouses' family or household. This is broader than the provision originally proposed by the Criminal Law Revision Committee. Thus, if a man were to assault the 14-year-old offspring of a neighbour, in the presence of his own wife, she would be compellable for the prosecution in any ensuing trial.

Of course, the dividing line inevitably produces certain anomalies. For example, if a man slapped his neighbour's 15-year-old daughter, his wife would be compellable to give evidence on the matter; if he raped her sixteen-year-old sister, she would not. It should also be noted that the limitation enacted in s. 80(4) is equally applicable in this context. Thus, if the spouse of the accused is also charged with an offence in the proceedings (for example, she aided and abetted the attack on the neighbour's child), she is not competent to testify for the prosecution, and not compellable to testify for the co-accused.

Waiving the Spousal Exemption

Although a spouse is not compellable to testify for the prosecution against their husband or wife (in most situations) or for a co-defendant, they may, of course, waive that right and elect to give evidence (as they are always competent to testify). This is an important step. Once they make this decision, they cannot later refuse to answer questions in the witness box, simply because they were not initially obliged to enter it. However, to waive their right not to testify they must also first be aware of it. In the past, this led to a rule of practice whereby a trial judge would warn a spouse, in the absence of the jury, that s/he was not required to testify: *R v Acaster* [1912] 7 Cr App R 187. In this case, Darling J observed that: 'In any case where the spouse of the accused comes to give evidence against her husband, the judge ought to ask her, "Do you know you may object to give evidence?"' In the case of *R v Pitt* [1983] QB 25, the Court of Appeal noted that this warning should be given *before* the individual takes the oath.

In *Pitt*, the defendant was charged, on two counts, with assault occasioning actual bodily harm to his baby daughter. His wife made a police statement implicating the defendant. At his trial, she was called to testify for the prosecution. However, the trial judge failed to inform her that she was not compellable to give evidence for the prosecution (as the law then stood; this is no longer the case, as a baby is obviously under the age of 16 years). She reluctantly testified, but during her evidence in chief she gave answers that were inconsistent with her earlier statement. The judge then granted the prosecution leave to treat her as a hostile witness and the prosecutor was allowed to cross-examine her. The defendant was convicted and appealed to the Court of Appeal on the basis that his wife had not appreciated that she did not have to testify. The Court of Appeal allowed the appeal because the trial judge had failed to inform the witness that she was not required to testify. Although decided before the advent of the Police and Criminal Evidence Act 1984, this decision still appears to be good law.

Cross-reference Box

A hostile witness is a witness who bears a hostile animus, for whatever reason, to the party calling him, and who, as a result, does not give the evidence expected of him. In such situations, the witness can be declared hostile by the judge, and some of the normal restrictions placed on a calling party during examination in chief, such as the rule against asking leading questions, are then relaxed. Hostile witnesses are discussed in greater detail at pp. 409–414.

R v Pitt [1983] QB 25, CA

Pain J

This case illustrates very powerfully why it is necessary for the trial judge to make certain that the wife understands her position before she takes the oath. Had that been done here, there would have been no difficulty. Up to a point where she goes into the witness box, W [the wife] has a choice: she may refuse to give evidence or waive her right of refusal. The waiver is effective only if made with full knowledge of her right to refuse. If she waives her right of refusal, she becomes an ordinary witness. Once W has started upon her evidence, she must complete it. It is not open to her to retreat behind the barrier of non-compellability if she is asked questions that she does not want to answer. This makes it particularly important that W should understand when she takes the oath that she is waiving her right to refuse to give evidence. It seems to us, desirable that where W is called as a witness for the prosecution of her husband, the judge should explain to her in the absence of the jury, that, before she takes the oath she has the right to refuse to give evidence but that if she chooses to give evidence she may be treated like any other witness.

Of course, if a wife is reluctant to give evidence because she is afraid to do so, it might be possible to admit an earlier statement, made to (for example) the police, under s. 116(2)(e) of the Criminal Justice Act 2003, as an exception to the hearsay rule.

Cross-reference Box

Any statement that has been made out of court, and which is tendered as evidence of the truth of its contents at trial, constitutes hearsay evidence. In criminal cases such statements can only be adduced if they come within a statutory or (preserved) common law exception to the rule, or alternatively, are admitted via an exercise of the judicial discretion under s.114(1)(d) of the Criminal Justice Act 2003. For more on this go to pp. 256–283.

Summary

- Competence governs the ability of a witness to testify, ie whether the witness can be 'heard' by the court.

- In the modern era, most witnesses are competent to give evidence in both civil and criminal matters. However, very small children, and those with limited intellectual functioning, may not meet the designated tests set out in the YJCEA 1999 in criminal cases. In civil matters, adults who do not understand the sanction of taking an oath, and children who do not satisfy the more modest test set out in s. 96 of the Children Act 1989, will also not be competent to testify.

- Compellability governs whether a potential witness can be forced to give evidence, even if they do not wish to do so. This is usually effected by an order of the court, disobedience to which can be punished as a contempt.

- The normal rule is that competent witnesses are also compellable. However, there are a few exceptions to this general position. Most importantly, the spouse of a defendant in a criminal matter can only be compelled to give evidence against their partner in the limited situations set out in s. 80(3) of the PCEA 1984. These attempt to balance the social need to prosecute crime with respecting the institution of marriage, and only force a spouse to give evidence where s/he is the victim of an assault or the offence involves a child under the age of 16.

- When it comes to compellability, a civil partner is treated in the same way as a spouse by dint of s. 84 of the Civil Partnership Act 2004. However, unmarried partners, no matter how long-standing their relationship, and those who, although previously married, are now divorced, are treated in exactly the same manner as any other type of witness for the purposes of compellability.

- Witnesses normally either swear an oath or affirm, before testifying. However, in criminal cases, children under 14, and those above this age (including adults) with intellectual handicaps or deficiencies who, as a result, do not reach the test set out in s. 55 of the YJCEA 1999 for taking an oath, but who are, nevertheless, capable of giving intelligible evidence, can testify unsworn. Similarly, children in civil cases who do not satisfy the common law test for taking an oath set out in *Hayes*, but can meet the test set out in s. 96 of the Children Act 1989, are allowed to give unsworn testimony. However, adults must give evidence on oath in civil matters.

- Affirmation has the same legal effects—for example, with regard to subsequent prosecutions for perjury—as taking the oath, but does not employ a religious sanction in its wording.

 Further reading

P Creighton, 'Spouse Competence and Compellability' [1990] Crim LR 34

D Dwyer, 'Can a Marriage be Delayed in the Public Interest so as to Maintain the Compellability of a Prosecution Witness?: R (On the Application of the Crown Prosecution Service) v Registrar General of Births, Marriages and Deaths' (2003) E & P, vol 7, no 3, 191–196

A Gillespie, 'Compellability of a child victim' (2000) J Crim L, vol 64, no 1, 98–105

D Jones, 'The Evidence of a Three-Year-Old Child' [1987] Crim LR 677

R Munday, 'Sham marriages and spousal compellability' (2001) J Crim L, vol 65, no 4, 336–348

JR Spencer and R Flin, *The Evidence of Children: The Law and the Psychology* (2nd edn, 2003, Blackstone Press)

Questions for Further Discussion

For suggested
approaches,
please visit the
Online Resource
Centre

1. Amanda tells the police that she has been raped by her husband, Bertie. However, shortly before trial, Amanda tells the police that she does not want to give evidence. The CPS wish to proceed with the case, and ask for advice as to whether she can be compelled to testify against Bertie.

Advise the CPS.

2. Fred is an intelligent four-year-old; he sees his mother being stabbed to death by a neighbour, George, with whom she was having a stormy affair.

Will Fred be allowed to testify against George?

3. Arthur is accused of assaulting Boris, the 12-year-old son of one of his neighbours, occasioning actual bodily harm, after he caught Boris 'scrumping' [stealing] apples in his orchard. Claudia, Arthur's wife, was with him when the incident occurred and made a statement to the police, incriminating her husband, shortly afterwards. However, she has since informed the CPS that she does not wish to testify against her spouse.

Advise the CPS.

4. Is it right that a married person should be exempt from being compelled to give evidence against their spouse, except in the most limited circumstances? Should these circumstances be expanded or reduced, and how should other social relationships be treated in this respect?

5. Percy is suing Quincy in his local County Court, accusing Quincy of knocking him (Percy) down with a mechanized lawnmower, inflicting moderately serious injuries in the process. Quincy denies that he was involved in any such collision. The incident was witnessed by Rachel, a seven-year-old girl, and Simon, a local simpleton who suffered a brain injury at birth (50 years earlier). Both of these people identified Quincy as the driver of the lawnmower.

Will Percy be allowed to call Rachel and Quincy to give evidence?

6. Maurice and Nick are civil partners. Nick is accused of assaulting Maurice during an argument over burnt toast, occasioning actual bodily harm in the process. Maurice is now very reluctant to testify for the prosecution against his partner, but the police and CPS are keen to proceed.

Advise Nick.

9

THE COURSE OF THE EVIDENCE: EXAMINATION IN CHIEF

Definitions

Aide memoire A document used to refresh memory when (or before) testifying.

Special measures Alternatives to the conventional means of giving evidence orally in open court.

Hostile witness A witness who deliberately changes his evidence to prejudice the party calling him.

Leading Question A question that suggests a particular answer or assumes the existence of disputed facts.

---

1. Introduction

The calling and questioning of witnesses follows the same general pattern in both civil and criminal cases. The prosecution in a criminal trial—or the claimant in a civil matter—calls its evidence first, formally closing its case when it has done so. Assuming that he does not make a successful submission of 'no case to answer' at this point in the process, the defendant then calls his own evidence (if any) in reply. The examination of each witness, called by any party to the litigation, normally goes through three stages. First, the party who called the witness engages in examination in chief. After he has finished this, the opposing side cross-examines the witness. The calling side then has the opportunity to re-examine the same witness, to clarify any issues raised in cross-examination. Thus, when calling police officers as part of its case, the prosecuting counsel in a criminal trial examines them in chief, while counsel for the defendant cross-examines them. When the defendant calls his own witnesses, including the defendant, the situation is reversed.

Cross-reference Box

Submissions of no case to answer in the criminal courts are normally governed by the principles enunciated in the case of *R v Galbraith* [1981] 1 WLR 1039. This case is considered in more detail at p. 10 in chapter 1 above.

Examination in chief

WITNESS BOX

Cross-examination

WITNESS BOX

Re-examination

WITNESS BOX

Calling party

Witness

WITNESS BOX

Opposing party

However, some of the rules regulating examination in chief and cross-examination are very different. This chapter will consider examination in chief, and, in particular, the use of memory refreshing documents, previous consistent statements, hostile witnesses and 'special measures' to assist witnesses when testifying, along with some other, less important, topics that will be dealt with more briefly. Nevertheless, it is difficult to hermetically seal the various stages of examination. As a result, some matters, such as non-traditional methods of conducting cross-examination (via a video-link, etc.) will, for convenience sake, also be examined in this chapter, together with alternative means of presenting evidence in chief.

Witness Familiarization

It has always been a cardinal rule in English litigation (both criminal and civil) that a party should not 'school' or coach his witness in advance of trial. Thus, he should not, in any way, suggest that a certain form of evidence is desirable, or that questions should be answered in a certain manner. This is still the case; however, there has been some relaxation in recent years with regard to general pre-trial preparation, or 'familiarization', of witnesses, aimed at making them aware of the layout of the court, the likely sequence of events, and the different responsibilities of the various participants in the trial process.

Additionally, it has been held that experts and similar types of witness can be trained in the technique of providing comprehensive evidence of a specialist type to a judge or jury, *provided* the training is not arranged in the context of a specific and forthcoming trial (ie it must be general in nature): *R v Momodou* [2005] 1 WLR 3442. In this case, the Court of Appeal also laid down guidance as to what procedural steps should be followed, and who informed, when such familiarization occurs in the criminal arena, for both defence and prosecution witnesses. This area of the law is fraught with potential dangers and, it is submitted, any further relaxation in this direction should be avoided.

R v Momodou [2005] 1 WLR 3442, CA

Judge LJ

There is a dramatic distinction between witness training or coaching, and witness familiarisation. Training or coaching for witnesses in criminal proceedings (whether for prosecution or defence) is not permitted. This is the logical consequence of the well-known principle that discussions between witnesses should not take place, and that the statements and proofs of one witness should not be disclosed to any other witness: see R v Richardson [1971] 2 QB 484, R v Arif The Times, 22 June 1993, R v Skinner (1993) 99 Cr App R 212 and R v Shaw [2002] EWCA Crim 3004. The witness should give his or her own evidence, so far as practicable uninfluenced by what anyone else has said, whether in formal discussions or informal conversations. The rule reduces, indeed hopefully avoids, any possibility that one witness may tailor his evidence in the light of what any-one else said, and equally, avoids any unfounded perception that he may have done so. These risks are inherent in witness training. Even if the training takes place one-to-one with someone completely remote from the facts of the case itself, the witness may come, even unconsciously, to appreciate which aspects of his evidence are perhaps not quite consistent with what others are saying, or indeed not quite what is required of him. An honest witness may alter the emphasis of his evidence to accommodate what he thinks may be a different, more accurate, or simply better remembered perception of events. . . .

   This principle does not preclude pre-trial arrangements to familiarise witnesses with the layout of the court, the likely sequence of events when the witness is giving evidence, and a balanced appraisal of the different responsibilities of the various participants. Indeed such arrangements, usually in the form of a pre-trial visit to the court, are generally to be welcomed. Witnesses should not be disadvantaged by ignorance of the process, nor when they come to give evidence, taken by surprise at the way it works. None of this however involves discussions about proposed or intended evidence. Sensible preparation for the experience of giving evidence, which assists the witness to give of his or her best at the forthcoming trial is permissible. Such experience can also be provided by out of court familiarisation techniques. The process may improve the man-ner in which the witness gives evidence by, for example, reducing the nervous tension arising from inexperience of the process. Nevertheless the evidence remains the witness's own uncon-taminated evidence. Equally, the principle does not prohibit training of expert and similar wit-nesses in, for example, the technique of giving comprehensive evidence of a specialist kind to a jury, both during evidence-in-chief and in cross-examination, and, another example, developing the ability to resist the inevitable pressure of going further in evidence than matters covered by the witnesses' specific expertise. The critical feature of training of this kind is that it should not be arranged in the context of nor related to any forthcoming trial, and it can therefore have no impact whatever on it.

Pause for reflection

What do you feel are the potential dangers in allowing witness preparation?

The Order of Witness Appearance

Not only do the parties usually select the witnesses that they want to call, but the actual order in which they give evidence is also normally a matter for the calling party (or, more commonly, their counsel). A natural structure often presents itself, assisting the tribunal of fact to make sense of what has occurred. For example, for the prosecution, in a criminal case such as a street robbery, it might mean first calling the victim to testify, then any eye witnesses to the crime, followed by the investigating police officers.

Cross-reference Box

As the Court of Appeal periodically points out, although parties in the common law system of litigation normally select their own witnesses, there is no 'property' in a witness: *Harmony Shipping v Saudi Europe Line* [1979] 1 WLR 1380. For more on party selection of witnesses and its critics see chapter 1 at pp. 10–17.

However, one exception to this general principle is that if a defendant elects to give evidence he must normally do so *before* other defence witnesses are called: s. 79 of the Police and Criminal Evidence Act 1984 (PCEA 1984). The rationale for this provision is obvious. Unlike other witnesses in criminal cases (apart from expert witnesses), the defendant is in court (in the dock) throughout the trial. Section 79 makes a small contribution towards reducing the opportunity that this gives to the accused person to tailor their evidence to fit that of the other defence witnesses in the case. (In civil cases witnesses can be present in court, unless specifically asked to withdraw on the application of one of the parties.)

Comment on a Failure to Testify

A failure to call a witness, who might reasonably have testified, can often be the subject of adverse comment by an opposing party or by a trial judge. Thus, in civil cases, opposing counsel (and, in those rare civil matters heard with a jury, a presiding judge) could certainly comment negatively on any failure by a party to give evidence in support of his claim, where appropriate. It would normally be strange if a claimant in a negligence action was reluctant to give evidence about the accident that occasioned his injury, but instead relied purely on the testimony of bystanders. In a criminal trial, the situation is broadly the same, but adverse comment by judge or counsel is more constrained in a number of specific situations. For example, a presiding judge can comment on a failure by the defendant to call a potential witness, who might reasonably have testified: *R v Robertson* [1987] 85 Crim App R 304. However, he must exercise a degree of caution when doing so, as there might be legitimate reasons for not calling such a witness: *R v Khan* [2001] Crim LR 673.

R v Robertson (1987) 85 Crim App R 304, CA

The Lord Chief Justice

The first [ground of appeal] is that the judge commented unfairly on the appellant's failure to call Poole or Long as witnesses. Having referred to the appellant's evidence of a conversation that he had with Poole prior to the final interview with the police, the judge continued: '...you should consider why the police allowed Robertson to see Poole, and why Poole suggested that Robertson should put his hands up—but, members of the jury, you should bear this in mind: that no one knows better than Poole and Long if Robertson was one of their number concerning the "Comet" burglaries. Both had been dealt with, neither would have anything to lose by giving evidence for Robertson. There is no obligation, of course, on Robertson to call either of them, but had he wished you to hear their evidence they could have been compelled to go into the witness box, and you may think it is surprising neither was called on his behalf if the admissions of Robertson are wicked inventions on the part of corrupt policemen.' That was a reference to the alleged fabrication of the last interview. Mr. Tansey was unhappy about it and, after the jury had retired, invited the judge to retract it. The judge declined. It is submitted that the comment was so unfair as to prejudice the appellant's case, particularly as it was linked to the controversial issue of the final interview. It was particularly unfair, it is said, because neither Poole nor Long could assist as to the genuineness of the record of that interview. If, which is doubtful, the judge was entitled to comment, it should have been done with more circumspection. In our view the judge was entitled to comment. There is no doubt that the comment was strong. The judge is entitled to make a comment which in appropriate circumstances may be strong. These were appropriate circumstances.

Furthermore, under s. 80A of the PCEA 1984, as inserted by Sch. 4 of the Youth Justice and Criminal Evidence Act 1999 (YJCEA 1999), the prosecution cannot comment on the failure of the spouse of a person charged in any proceedings to give evidence at trial. This prohibition does not extend to a judge or a co-accused. Nevertheless, a judge's comments are always constrained by the general need to ensure a fair trial and, as a result, he should again show a degree of circumspection in his remarks on such matters: *R v Naudeer* [1985] 80 Cr App R 9. There appear to be few restrictions as to the comments that can be made on this issue by a co-accused. In criminal cases, adversely commenting on the failure of a defendant to testify is closely regulated by statute and needs detailed consideration.

Comment on a Criminal Defendant Not Testifying

A defendant in a criminal trial cannot be compelled to give evidence, for example, by being punished for not doing so via the contempt of court procedure. To that extent, at least, the 'right to silence' still applies. Nevertheless, the position that had developed in England at common law prior to 1994 went much further than this. In criminal cases, the Crown, represented by the prosecutor, could make no mention of, nor invite the tribunal of fact to draw any adverse inferences from, a defendant's failure to give evidence at his own trial. Indeed, this was enshrined in the 1898 Criminal Evidence Act. Furthermore, trial judges could comment in only the most guarded terms about such a failure to testify, and not invite a jury to draw adverse inferences from it.

Despite this, throughout the twentieth century, a number of senior judges, lawyers, politicians and academics condemned the prohibition on drawing such inferences. For example, the radical 11th Report on Evidence, published in 1972, by the Criminal Law Revision Committee (a body made up of judges and lawyers concerned with improving substantive and procedural law in the criminal area), recommended drastic reform, suggesting that, once the prosecution had established a prima facie case at trial, the accused should formally be asked to go into the witness box and told that if he failed to do so, adverse inferences might be drawn. Sir Rupert Cross, a strong proponent of the report, claimed that abolition of the right not to have an adverse inference drawn from a failure to testify would prevent judges from talking 'illogical gibberish' to the jury.[1] Judicial hostility to the prohibition was most clearly seen in an observation made by the then Lord Chief Justice, Lord Lane, in the case of *R v Alladice* [1988] 87 Cr App R 380, who suggested that: '... the balance of fairness ... cannot be maintained unless proper comment is permitted on the defendant's silence in such circumstances'.

Pause for reflection

What inferences might you draw from a defendant's failure to testify?

Despite such criticism, other observers were strongly in favour of the existing situation, for a variety of reasons. Thus, it was claimed that the right not to have an adverse inference drawn from in court silence marked out the limits of state power, protected the dignity of the subject and was an assertion of democratic rights against the state. Others opined that, sometimes, a witness might wish to remain silent for reasons that had nothing to do with guilt; for example, to conceal an embarrassing alibi or to avoid incriminating a friend. Indeed, this was the one argument that Sir Rupert Cross saw as having merit, though he felt that such an analysis could be applied to every other type of incriminating circumstantial evidence, without anyone suggesting that it should result in special protection from adverse comment.[2]

Eventually, criticisms of the right not to have an adverse inference drawn from silence at trial prevailed, and reform was effected by s. 35 of the Criminal Justice and Public Order Act 1994. As a result of this provision, if a criminal defendant refuses to give evidence, or if, having elected to testify, he refuses to answer a question without good cause, the court or jury may draw 'such inferences as appear proper'. However, and, perhaps reflecting widespread reservations about the change, the operation of the provision is tightly constrained by both the Act itself and by subsequent judicial interpretation of the statute.

Section 35 of the Criminal Justice and Public Order Act 1994 (Partial extract)

(1) At the trial of any person who has attained the age of fourteen years for an offence, subsections (2) and (3) below apply unless—

(a) the accused's guilt is not in issue; or

(b) it appears to the court that the physical or mental condition of the accused makes it undesirable for him to give evidence;

---

[1] See generally, R Cross, 'A Very Wicked Animal Defends the 11th Report of the Criminal Law Revision Committee' [1973] Crim LR 329.

[2] R Cross, 'The Right to Silence and the Presumption of Innocence—Sacred Cows or Safeguards of Liberty?' (1970) 11 JSPTL 66.

but subsection (2) below does not apply if, at the conclusion of the evidence for the prosecution, his legal representative informs the court that the accused will give evidence or, where he is unrepresented, the court ascertains from him that he will give evidence.

(2) Where this subsection applies, the court shall, at the conclusion of the evidence for the prosecution, satisfy itself (in the case of proceedings on indictment, in the presence of the jury) that the accused is aware that the stage has been reached at which evidence can be given for the defence and that he can, if he wishes, give evidence and that, if he chooses not to give evidence, or having been sworn, without good cause refuses to answer any question, it will be permissible for the court or jury to draw such inferences as appear proper from his failure to give evidence or his refusal, without good cause, to answer any question.

(3) Where this subsection applies, the court or jury, in determining whether the accused is guilty of the offence charged, may draw such inferences as appear proper from the failure of the accused to give evidence or his refusal, without good cause, to answer any question.

For the section to operate, it is vital that the defendant is first warned in advance as to the consequences of not giving evidence, though a failure to do this will not be fatal to a conviction if no adverse inference direction is actually given to the jury or drawn by magistrates. Additionally, the section will not apply where the physical or mental condition of an accused person makes it undesirable for him to give evidence: s. 35(i)(b). This situation will, in practice, not occur very frequently, as it would require that the defendant be well enough physically and mentally to stand trial, but yet not well enough to testify. Possible situations in which this might occur were set out in *R v Friend* [1997] 2 All ER 1012, where the Court of Appeal suggested that they could cover, for example, a physical condition on the part of a defendant such that giving evidence might prompt an epileptic attack, or some type of latent schizophrenia where the experience of testifying might trigger a florid state. However, in *Friend*, a defendant of 15 with a mental age of nine was held not to come within s. 35(i)(b).

Section 35 has generated an enormous amount of case law, which needs detailed consideration. Perhaps the most important case is *R v Cowan and others* (1995) 3 WLR 818, in which the appellants had been charged before, but tried after, the new law came into effect. None of them had answered police questions when interviewed or subsequently given evidence at their trial. Because the Act was not in force when they were questioned, but had come into force when they were tried, the Court of Appeal was purely concerned with the interpretation of s. 35 of the statute (rather than s. 34 of the same Act, which is dealt with in chapter 6). The appellants were convicted and appealed on the ground that the trial judge had failed to give a correct direction as to the circumstances in which an inference could be drawn from a failure to testify, and what such inferences could properly be. In particular, it was argued that the discretion to draw inferences from silence should only apply in exceptional circumstances, not routine cases.

Cross-reference Box

Section 34 of the CJPOA 1994 abolishes the right, in some circumstances, not to have an adverse inference drawn from a failure to answer police questions prior to trial. This provision was even more controversial than s. 35, and its operation has been made subject to tight preconditions. For more on this topic, go to p. 354.

In firmly dismissing these arguments, the Court of Appeal observed that their acceptance would drive a 'coach and horses' through the statutory provisions, rendering them largely nugatory. The court also emphasized the significance of s. 38(3) of the Act, which prevents the tribunal of fact from convicting solely on an inference drawn from a defendant's silence. As a result, Lord Taylor CJ could still (albeit controversially) observe: 'It should be made clear that the right of silence remains. It is not abolished by the section.'

However, in *Cowan*, the Court of Appeal also stressed that a trial judge must direct a jury very carefully on what uses can be made of a defendant's failure to testify, and that a failure to do so would usually lead to any ensuing conviction being quashed. In particular, it was essential that a judge direct the jurors that: the burden of proof remained on the prosecution throughout the trial; that the defendant was entitled to remain silent; that an inference from a failure to give evidence cannot on its own prove guilt; that the jury must be satisfied that the prosecution have established a case to answer before drawing any inferences from an accused's silence; if, despite any evidence relied upon to explain his silence, or the lack of such an explanation, the jury conclude the silence can only sensibly be attributed to the defendant's having no real answer, or one that would stand up to cross-examination, they may then draw an adverse inference.

Of course, a defendant can call evidence as to why he might decide not to give evidence from the witness box, which, even if it does not persuade a trial judge not to give an adverse inference direction, might go to the jury and dissuade them from drawing any adverse inference from his failure to testify. However, in *Cowan* Lord Taylor also stressed that there had to be tangible evidence for such a decision before the issue needed to be considered. It was not proper for a defence advocate to give the jury reasons for his client's silence at trial in the absence of evidence to support them. As a result, a first instance judge should stop defence counsel from seeking to give reasons for the very first time in his closing speech.

R v Cowan [1996] 1 Cr App R 1, CA

Lord Taylor CJ

However, there are criticisms of the trial judge's directions to the jury which preceded the issue by the Judicial Studies Board of the specimen direction. Mr Mansfield alleged there were three defects. First, he claimed that the judge blurred the burden of proof by his directions to the jury as to the drawing of inferences from silence. This complaint in our view is unfounded. The judge gave the normal direction on burden and standard of proof. Nothing he said about drawing inferences from silence in our view qualified that direction. However, we do consider that there is merit in the other two complaints. The judge failed to tell the jury that they could not infer guilt solely from silence. Secondly, he did not warn the jury that the condition for holding a defendant's silence at trial against him was that the only sensible explanation for that silence was that he had no answer to the case against him or none that could have stood up to cross-examination. This was a case involving a clear conflict of evidence. Strong feelings had been aroused not only by the incident outside the public house but by the earlier fracas within it. We consider that without the omitted directions the jury may have attached undue importance or weight to the appellant's absence from the witness box. Accordingly, we are not sure that the verdict can be regarded as safe and satisfactory and the appeal must be allowed. We should add that we have sympathy with the judges in both the present case and the case of Gayle who had to cope with the new provisions shortly after their introduction and without guidance.

These requirements have been followed closely in subsequent decisions, as the following case makes clear.

R v El-Hannachi (Samir) and others [1998] 2 Cr App R 226, CA

May LJ

It is accepted on behalf of the prosecution that this direction fell short of that required in Cowan [1996] 1 Cr.App.R. 1, [1996] Q.B. 373. In that case at pages 7 and 380, the Court of Appeal in its judgment delivered by Lord Taylor of Gosforth C.J. considered the terms of a specimen direction suggested by the Judicial Studies Board and expressed the view that this was in general terms a sound guide. It may be necessary to adapt or add to it in the particular circumstances of an individual case. But the Court explained that there are certain essentials. The third and fourth essentials were expressed in these terms: '(3) An inference from failure to give evidence cannot on its own prove guilt. That is expressly stated in section 38(3) of the Act. (4) Therefore, the jury must be satisfied that the prosecution have established a case to answer before drawing any inferences from silence.' The judge's direction in this case expressed the third essential but did not express the fourth. This is accepted on behalf of the prosecution, who nevertheless submit that, notwithstanding this omission, Tanswell's conviction should be regarded as safe. In particular we understood Mr Dennison to submit that the safety of Tanswell's conviction could be supported by the safety of the convictions of the other three appellants.

We do not agree that in the circumstances of this case and in the light of the omission from the Cowan direction Tanswell's conviction was safe. The jury had to consider the case against each appellant separately. In his case, there was no supporting evidence for Eve Robertson's identification of him, as there was for Cooney (the blood on his shirt and his knuckle injury) and El-Hannachi (his hand injury). Without a proper direction on the subject, the jury were plainly likely to have considered that Tanswell's failure to give evidence was significant. They convicted him by a majority only. Some omissions from a summing up are more important than others.... The drawing of inferences from silence was a particularly sensitive area, not least in the light of Article 6(1) and 6(2) of the European Convention for the Protection of Human Rights and Fundamental Freedoms [1953] Cmd. 8969. Inescapable logic demanded that a jury should not start to consider whether to draw inferences from a defendant's failure to give oral evidence at his trial until they had concluded that the Crown's case against him was sufficiently compelling to call for an answer by him. What was called 'essential 4' in Cowan was correctly described as such. These observations apply directly to the present case. In our judgment, in the light of them and of the matters to which we have referred, Tanswell's conviction must be regarded as unsafe.

The principles established in these, and other, cases, as well as a relevant practice direction, have been reduced to an appropriate Judicial Studies Board (JSB) specimen jury direction, which is widely followed. However, where a trial judge decides that the prerequisites for an adverse inference to be drawn have not been met, he should direct a jury accordingly, something that is covered by the following JSB specimen direction.

JSB Specimen Directions. 44. Defendant's Right to Silence Where Judge Directs Jury that no Adverse Inference Should be Drawn

B. Failure to give evidence—The defendant has not given evidence in this case. That does, of course, mean there is no evidence from him to undermine, contradict or explain the prosecution case and that is a matter you may take into account. However, in this case, I direct you not to hold his failure to give evidence against him. This means that it cannot, by itself, provide any additional support for the prosecution case.

Absence of Leading Questions

The purpose of 'examination in chief' is to furnish the court with relevant and admissible evidence that supports the case of the party who calls the witness being questioned. However, such a witness cannot normally be asked 'leading' questions by the calling party. This provides a (modest) degree of protection for witness independence, as witnesses tend to be favourable to the parties who call them, and might otherwise agree with most suggestions put to them. Leading questions are those that suggest the answer required or which assume the existence of disputed facts. For an example of the former might be considered a question such as: 'Did you see a tall red headed man attacking Mr Green?' An example of the latter might include questions such as: 'What did you do when you saw Mr Green push Mr White over the cliff?' when no evidence has yet been adduced that Mr Green pushed Mr White over the cliff. In many respects, leading is a question of degree; even asking a witness 'what happened next' might be taken to suggest that something occurred, but would certainly be permissible. Borderline cases are matters of judgment and, usually, within the trial judge's discretion.

It should also be noted that openly leading questions are often allowed during examination in chief, by an opposing party, when they deal with facts that are not in contention; for example, formal or routine matters such as a witness's name and occupation. (His occupation is also normally the only detail that can be elicited about a witness's character; further questions, designed to bolster credibility, are not usually permitted.) Such 'leading' saves court time. Additionally, as will be seen, if a witness is declared 'hostile', the calling party may also ask leading questions. However, even where it is not allowed, information elicited improperly by a leading question is, strictly speaking, still admissible, though its weight will be considerably affected, perhaps, in some cases, to the point of being almost worthless: *Moor v Moor* [1954] 2 All ER 458.

Moor v Moor [1954] 2 All ER 458, CA

Evershed MR

From time to time, this court, and I think the President also, has drawn attention to the way in which, in cases of this character [an undefended divorce petition], evidence is given by a series of leading questions, which every experienced advocate knows to be quite irregular, and which have the effect of making the answers either not at all impressive or far less impressive than they otherwise would be. In spite of the attention which has been drawn to this matter, nobody, so far as I can see, has paid the slightest regard to what has been said, and I do not forget that the judges who try these cases might, I should have thought in all conscience, be expected to have stopped this irregularity.

2. Memory Refreshing and Aides Memoires

Introduction

As a general rule, witnesses are not allowed to give oral evidence by reading out written statements, prepared on an earlier occasion. However, if a witness's memory of an incident is poor, he may refresh his recollection from an appropriate document while testifying. Nevertheless, the item shown to the witness is not normally evidence in its own right; it is merely a stimulus to produce evidence in the form of oral testimony. In practice, aides memoires are frequently very important in the litigation process, as it can often take a long time for trials to be held, sometimes months, or even years, elapsing between the subject of the hearing and its adjudication. In some situations, perhaps because a criminal defendant is not apprehended until long after an investigation has been conducted, a decade or more might elapse. In these circumstances, it might be very helpful for a witness to refresh his memory from a document or note that he prepared or verified at an earlier date, while giving his evidence.

Preparation, of course, means that the witness personally wrote the note himself. However, a witness can also use a note to refresh his memory if it was prepared by another person, provided he 'verified' it, as being accurate, at an appropriate time. Thus, in *Burrough v Martin* (1809) 2 Camp 111 a witness was allowed to use the logbook of a ship's voyage to refresh his memory, even though he had not written it himself. He first gave evidence that he had regularly checked the entries, while the events they recorded were still fresh in his mind, and always found them to be accurate. As Lord Ellenborough noted, in such a situation, for the purposes of memory refreshing, the document was: '...as good as if he had written the whole with his own hand'.

As the above case suggests, verification is usually done by the witness personally reading the document through, and so checking that it is correct. Although, in such situations, the verifier will sometimes initial the aide memoire, to make it easier to prove that he has done this if it is ever questioned at trial, this is not essential. Of course, simply signing a document without verifying it, by (for example) reading it through, will not allow the document to be used as an aide memoire: *R v Eleftheriou* [1993] Crim LR 947.

However, even personally reading the document is not vital when it comes to verification. If it is merely read back to the verifier, and they acknowledge it as accurate, without reading it personally, it can still be used to refresh memory. Nevertheless, in this situation, the witness will first have to go through the laborious process laid down in *R v Kelsey* [1982] 74 Cr App R 213 before it can be used. Thus, the person to whom it was dictated, and who read it back to the witness, and who also noted that the witness had confirmed its accuracy, must first testify to that effect at trial, before the document can be passed on to the witness and used to refresh his memory.

R v Kelsey [1982] 74 Cr App R 213, CA

Taylor J

The question we have to decide is, therefore, whether witness A can verify a note he dictates to B only by reading it himself, or whether it is sufficient if the note is read back by B to A at the time for confirmation. In most cases we would expect the note to be read by A if it is made in his presence. But what of the instant case, or cases involving the blind or the illiterate? In our view there is no magic in verifying by seeing as opposed to verifying by hearing. Mills and Rose (supra), the tape recording case, illustrates this, and shows that Winn J.'s words were somewhat too restrictive. What must be shown is that witness A has verified in the sense of satisfying himself whilst the matters are fresh in his mind, (1) that a record has been made, and (2) that it is accurate.

It is generally accepted as (legally) quite proper for police officers to collaborate when writing up their notes of an incident, pooling their recollection of it, and even for them to produce a single document that can be used by more than one officer (each customarily initialling the document after they have done so), though a failure to admit that this has occurred might seriously affect the officers' credibility: *R v Bass* [1953] 1 All ER 1064. This appears to be an exception to the general position, whereby witnesses should not normally discuss the evidence that they will give: *R v Skinner* [1993] 99 Cr App R 212.

Pause for reflection

Why should such an indulgence be allowed to police officers when it is denied to other witnesses?

Time Limits for the Creation of Aides Memoires

At common law, which still governs the situation in civil matters, an aide memoire that could be used in court had to be made or verified 'contemporaneously' with the events that it recorded. However, as *R v Richardson* [1971] 2 QB 484 made clear, this was not to be interpreted literally, and, depending on the circumstances of the case (for example, how unusual or complex was the event recorded), it might allow for a day or two of delay. Nevertheless, aides memoires created a week or more after an event could not usually be employed in court by a witness while giving evidence, and it was normal for opposing counsel to question the use of any aide memoire that had not been made on the same day as the events it recorded.

Even in this situation, however, the note could be read by the witness *before* testifying, for example, while outside the court room; and it was (and is) common practice, and quite proper, for witnesses to be given copies of their police or solicitors' statements prior to giving evidence: *Owen v Edwards* [1983] 77 Cr App R 191. A judicially permitted relaxation of the strictness of the rules on aides memoires, during the 1990s, meant that such a statement could even be used during short adjournments from testifying when actually in the witness box, *provided* it was not used to refresh memory simultaneously with the giving of evidence: *R v South Ribble Magistrates Court, ex parte Cochrane* [1996] 2 Cr App R 544. However, the advent of s. 139 of the Criminal Justice Act 2003 (CJA 2003) has further transformed the situation in criminal cases.

Section 139 of the Criminal Justice Act 2003

In criminal matters, as a result of s. 139 of the CJA 2003, some of the common law pre-requisites that must be satisfied before an aide memoire can be used in court have been relaxed. A witness can now use a document to refresh his memory *while* giving oral evidence in criminal proceedings, provided: it was made or verified by the witness at an 'earlier time'; the witness testifies that the document records his recollection of the matter at that earlier time; and, under s. 139(1)(b), his recollection of the matter is likely to have been significantly better at that time than it is at trial. This provision effectively abolishes the requirement of 'contemporaneous' creation that previously existed at common law, even though it was not applied literally. This meant that statements that were made much closer to an event than the trial, but too late to be deemed contemporaneous, such as a police statement made a month after a criminal incident, could not be used to refresh memory *while* giving oral evidence. As a result of s. 139, such documents can now be used in the same way as 'contemporaneously' created aides memoires.

Section 139 of the CJA 2003, Use of documents to refresh memory (partial extract)

(1) A person giving oral evidence in criminal proceedings about any matter may, at any stage in the course of doing so, refresh his memory of it from a document made or verified by him at an earlier time if—

    (a) he states in his oral evidence that the document records his recollection of the matter at that earlier time, and

    (b) his recollection of the matter is likely to have been significantly better at that time than it is at the time of his oral evidence....

Nevertheless, the court must still be satisfied that the witness's recollection was 'significantly better' when they made their note; a written statement made shortly before trial would be unlikely to satisfy this requirement, even if it allowed the witness to focus their evidence. This was discussed by the Court of Appeal in *R v McAfee (John James)* [2006] EWCA Crim 2914, in which a police statement, made four and a half months after an incident, was used to refresh the memory of a witness in a murder trial held some 13 months further on again. The court approved the trial judge's decision and made it clear that it would not lightly interfere with a first instance judge's decision on such an issue. There is no equivalent to s. 139 for civil matters; however, in such cases, the court always has a discretion to allow a previous consistent statement to be adduced as evidence by virtue of s. 6(2)(a) of the Civil Evidence Act 1995, and this could apply to an aide memoire, such as a police notebook, just as it could to any other type of statement.

R v McAfee (John James)   (2006) WL 3880356

Tuckey LJ

We deal first with the judge's decision to allow Nicola Smith to refresh her memory. Section 139 of the Criminal Justice Act 2003 changed the law about this.... The statement to which the witness was allowed to refer was made on 11th September 2004, 4 1/2 months after the murder.... At trial when the witness said the old man had been killed, she added that she could not recall the exact words McAfee had used. She could not remember if he had said how the man had been killed. She was then reminded of the police interviews in September 2004 without being shown anything, and asked whether her recollection would have been clearer at that time, the time of the trial being 13 months later. She said it would have been. The prosecution therefore made their application under section 139 which was opposed by Mr Burbidge. He made similar submissions to the judge to those which he has made to us. It could not be shown that the witness's recollection was likely to have been significantly better in September 2004 than it was in October 2005.... This was not her original statement. She was a drug taker and had told many lies. There was no corroboration for her assertion that her recollection had been better the previous year. There was ample scope for mistake in the precise words which had been used because she had changed her story and Ellis had told her many different stories. The judge rejected Mr Burbidge's submission and allowed the witness to refresh her memory from the September 2004 statement. After referring to her statement, the witness said: 'My memory when I made the statement was better because I knew what they were asking me and what I was telling them. Things now seem muddled with times and dates.' Unfortunately we do not have a full transcript of what transpired, but there is no dispute about the account which we have just given. Mr Burbidge submits that the judge should not have allowed the prosecution's application and that this court should say that it was wrong. Even if the statutory conditions were fulfilled, he submits, the judge should have refused the application in her discretion. We disagree. The statutory conditions were met. It was for the judge to decide, having heard what the witness had to say, whether it was likely that her memory would have been significantly better or not. The statute contains no requirement of contemporaneity. This is just the sort of decision which a trial judge is in the best position to make, and just the sort of decision which this court is in no position to second-guess. Judges' decisions should be accepted unless they are obviously wrong, unreasonable or perverse. None of these things can be said of the judge's decision in this case. A judge must have a residual discretion to refuse a section 139 application even if the statutory conditions are met. But there were no good reasons for doing so in this case. The prosecution were entitled to present their best case to the jury. That is the object of many of the provisions in the 2003 Act.

Exhibiting Aides Memoires

Although the status of exhibited aides memoires has been altered by statute (see below), the common law rules, set out in cases such as *Senat v Senat* [1965] P 172 and *Owen v Edwards* [1983] 77 Cr App R 191 as to *when* such statements will be exhibited have not been affected, in either civil or criminal matters. Indeed, s. 6(4) of the Civil Evidence Act 1995 expressly states that the common law rules as to *when* an aide memoire is exhibited remain the same, and the wording of s. 120 of the CJA 2003 leads to the same conclusion.

Thus, such documents do not become exhibits merely because a witness refreshes his or her memory from them; cross-examining counsel may also *examine* them quite safely, and use any part of the document as a basis for questions during cross-examination. However, if questions are asked about entries other than those relied on by the witness to refresh his/her memory, the party that called the witness may apply to have the document entered as an exhibit and, if successful, it can be physically given to a judge, jury or magistrates for examination: *R v Sekhon* [1987] 85 Cr App R 19. These rules apply in both civil and criminal cases, and as much to defence aides memoires as to prosecution ones in criminal matters; for an example of this, can be considered the trade unionist defendant's note as to what had occurred in a strike-related disturbance in *R v Britton* [1987] 85 Cr App R 14.

Senat v Senat [1965] 2 WLR 981, HC

Sir Jocelyn Simon P

In my view the mere inspection of a document does not render it evidence which counsel inspecting it is bound to put in. I think that the true rules are as follows: Where a document is used to refresh a witness's memory, cross-examining counsel may inspect that document in order to check it, without making it evidence. Moreover he may cross-examine upon it without making it evidence provided that his cross-examination does not go further than the parts which are used for refreshing the memory of the witness.

R v Britton [1987] 85 Cr App R 14, CA

The Lord Chief Justice

Then it was Mr. Aylett's turn, on behalf of the prosecution, to cross-examine the appellant. Mr. Aylett did not confine his cross-examination, so far as the *aide memoire* was concerned, to those matters upon which the appellant had refreshed his memory in chief from the *aide memoire*. In other words he referred the witness to matters outside merely the arrest and the surrounding circumstances which were the only matters on which the appellant had in chief sought to refresh his memory from the document.... There appears to be a long standing rule of the common law regulating the admissibility of the *aide memoire* in these circumstances. That rule is as follows: cross-examining counsel is entitled to inspect the note in order to check its contents. He can do so without making the document evidence. Indeed he may go further and cross-examine upon it. If he does so and succeeds in confining his cross-examination to those parts of it which have already been used by the witness to refresh his memory, he does not make it evidence. If on the other hand he strays beyond that part of the note which has been so used, the party calling him—in this case the defendant represented by Mr. Buchan—may insist on it being treated as evidence in the case, which will thereupon become an exhibit.

It should also be noted that an aide memoire can become an exhibit in situations in which the state or nature of the document itself has become an issue at trial. This is usually done at the behest of the opposing party. Thus, in *R v Bass* [1953] 1 All ER 1064, the police officers denied at trial that they had collaborated over the making of their notes. It was held that the trial judge should have acceded to a defence application that both notebooks should have gone to the jury, who would then have had the opportunity to observe that their accounts were almost identical.

Status of Exhibited Aides Memoires

At common law, an exhibited aide memoire was not evidence in its own right, as to the truth of its contents; it went merely to consistency and credit: *R v Virgo* [1978] 67 Cr App R 323. In civil cases, however, by virtue of ss. 1 and 6(5) of the Civil Evidence Act 1995, an exhibited aide memoire is evidence of the truth of its contents. In criminal matters such exhibits are also now evidence in their own right, as a result of s. 120(3) of the CJA 2003, which provides that a statement made by a witness in a document, used by that witness to refresh his memory while giving evidence, on which he is then cross-examined, and which, as a consequence, is 'received in evidence' (ie exhibited) in the proceedings, becomes 'admissible as evidence of any matter stated of which oral evidence by him would be admissible'. Together, these statutory provisions mean that a judge, magistrates or jurors, in both civil and criminal matters, can act directly on information in an exhibited aide memoire, which have consequently also become exceptions to the hearsay rule.

Section 122 of the Criminal Justice Act 2003

Nevertheless, in criminal cases, although the theoretical value of an exhibited document is greatly enhanced by the 2003 Act, the statute also reflects the Law Commission's view that such documents, like any other written previous statement, might attract more value than oral evidence and be disproportionately influential if placed physically into the possession of the jury.[3]

As a result, their practical importance is limited by s. 122, which provides that a document that has been exhibited must not accompany the jury when they retire to consider their verdict unless the court considers it 'appropriate' or all the parties to the proceedings agree: s. 122(2). This provision does not just relate to exhibited aides memoires, but covers all documents or their copies that are exhibited under ss. 119 and 120; for example, a written inconsistent statement proved against a hostile witness under s. 3 of the 1865 Act. It should also be noted that the section is limited to trials conducted by a judge and jury: s. 122(1). Thus, it does not preclude magistrates from taking such material into their retiring room. Presumably, the experience of the latter is deemed to be enough to prevent them placing excessive reliance on such a document.

Section 122 of the CJA 2003, Documents produced as exhibits

(1) This section applies if on a trial before a judge and jury for an offence—

    (a) a statement made in a document is admitted in evidence under section 119 or 120, and

    (b) the document or a copy of it is produced as an exhibit.

(2) The exhibit must not accompany the jury when they retire to consider their verdict unless—

    (a) the court considers it appropriate, or

    (b) all the parties to the proceedings agree that it should accompany the jury.

This provision may well be prudent; unlike oral testimony, which is inherently transient, a written note can be highly (and disproportionately) influential on jurors, especially in a long trial. In civil matters, where written witness statements are commonplace, and matters normally determined by a professional judge, who will, presumably, be even more able to avoid placing undue importance on them than is a JP, an equivalent provision is (unsurprisingly) not deemed to be necessary. The courts will not lightly consider that it is appropriate for such a document to accompany the jury as the following case indicates.

R v Hulme [2007] 1 Cr App R 26, CA

Richards LJ

In our judgment the judge was wrong to allow the witness statement to accompany the jury when they retired to consider their verdict. The reason given by the judge that the document was needed in order to make sense of the case and for the evaluation of Miss Durao's evidence was in our view an insufficient reason to justify the course adopted. The jury would have been in a position to make sense of the case and to evaluate the evidence if the matter had been dealt with in the normal way by a reminder in the summing-up of the contents of the witness statement and of what Miss Durao had said about that document and the circumstances in which it was made. There was no special feature of the document that made it necessary for the jury to have the document

---

[3] Law Com No 245, para. 10.61.

itself before them. The jury could have been reminded orally of the one manuscript correction admittedly made before Miss Durao signed the document—a matter relied on by the Crown as showing that she had exercised some care before signing the document. The jury did not need the document itself for that purpose.

3. The Rule Against Previous Consistent Statements

Introduction

At common law, a witness was not allowed to adduce an out of court statement that was consistent with his/her evidence at trial with a view to bolstering their present testimony. This was referred to as the rule against previous consistent statements or, less commonly, as the rule against narrative. In the case of *White v R* [1999] 1 AC 210 the Privy Council adopted a passage from *Cross and Tapper on Evidence* (8th edn, 1995 at 294) as being a proper definition of the rule: 'The general rule at common law is that a witness may not be asked in-chief whether he has formerly made a statement consistent with his present testimony. He cannot narrate such statement if it was oral or refer to it if it was in writing (save for the purpose of refreshing his memory), and other witnesses may not be called to prove it.'

For example, and to take a very obvious illustration, in an assault case where self-defence is being asserted, it prevents the defendant saying: 'I am saying this today and have done so all along, as can be seen by the identical statement I made a day after the incident to Mr Jones in which I said that I was only protecting myself; this earlier identical statement makes it more likely that I am telling the truth now.' Of course, if the previous out of court statement were tendered not just to support the *credibility* of the in-court testimony, but also to establish the *truth* of the earlier statement's contents, it would also impinge on the distinct and separate exclusionary rule against hearsay.

Cross-reference Box

The hearsay rule prevents the adduction of an out of court statement as truth of its contents; if it is tendered for any other reason, it is not hearsay (for that purpose) and is admissible as 'original' evidence. For a more detailed discussion of this issue see chapter 6 at pp. 343–346.

A classic example of the rule in action involves the defendant in *R v Roberts* [1942] 1 All ER 187, who was accused of murdering his wife with a gun, and who was not allowed to adduce an earlier conversation with his father, held while he was awaiting trial in prison, in which he had said that the weapon had gone off accidentally. This was consistent with his eventual trial defence of accident.

R v Roberts [1942] 1 All ER 187, CCA

Humphreys J

The law upon the matter is well-settled. The rule relating to this is sometimes put in this way, that a party is not permitted to make evidence for himself. That law applies to civil cases as well as to criminal cases. For instance, if A and B enter into an oral contract, and some time afterwards there is a difference of opinion as to what were the actual terms agreed upon and there is litigation about it, one of those persons would not be permitted to call his partner to say: 'My partner a day or two after told me what his view of the contract was and that he had agreed to do' so and so. So, in a criminal case, an accused person is not permitted to call evidence to show that, after he was charged with a criminal offence, he told a number of persons what his defence was going to be, and the reason for the rule appears to us to be that such testimony has no evidential value. It is because it does not assist in the elucidation of the matters in dispute that the evidence is said to be inadmissible on the ground that it is irrelevant. It would not help the jury in this case in the least to be told that the appellant said to a number of persons, whom he saw while he was waiting his trial, or on bail if he was on bail; that his defence was this, that or the other. The evidence asked to be admitted was that the father had been told by his son that it was an accident. We think the evidence was properly refused.

Similarly (and perhaps less obviously), in the civil case of *Corke v Corke & Cook* [1958] P 93 the issue was whether a woman had committed adultery with her lodger. The husband found them in the lodger's bedroom and, having heard the bed creaking, challenged his wife with having had sexual intercourse, which she vehemently denied. She and the lodger were so incensed that, though it was then after midnight, she telephoned her doctor requesting him to come immediately and examine both her and the co-respondent with a view to establishing their innocence of misconduct. The doctor did not examine them, being of the opinion that any negative evidence which he might obtain would be valueless. However, evidence of the conversation between wife and doctor was admitted at trial, and the husband's petition was dismissed. He appealed, contending that the judge had been mistaken in admitting the contents of the telephone conversation. The Court of Appeal rejected this argument; Sellers LJ even went so far as to assert that the evidence of what the wife did and said was valueless and potentially misleading to the court. (Such a previous consistent statement in a civil case would now be admissible at the court's discretion by dint of s. 6(2)(a) of the Civil Evidence Act 1995.)

The rationale for excluding previous consistent statements was largely based on the long-standing common law fear of fabricated evidence and, in particular, concern that such statements could easily be manufactured in advance of trial by a witness, specifically for later forensic use. Thus, in *Corke v Corke & Cook* [1958] P 93 Sellers LJ claimed that without it a 'skilful witness might well embark on circumstantial matters to bolster up his or her story'. There was also concern about the delay that might be occasioned to the trial process by allowing such evidence to be admitted.

Pause for reflection

Do you feel that this is a real risk, and, if so, in what sort of trials would it be most likely to occur?

However, at common law there were a small number of well-established exceptions to the general exclusionary rule, whereby previous consistent statements could be adduced at trial. Amongst them was the situation in which a statement was being admitted to rebut an allegation of 'recent fabrication'; another was a recent complaint in a sexual case.

Status of Previous Consistent Statements

Where admitted at common law under an exception to the general rule, previous consistent statements normally only went to credit and not the truth of their contents. As a result, the judge, magistrates or jury would (theoretically) have to go through the complicated and, arguably, somewhat illogical, process of disregarding the statement except in so far as it affected the weight of oral testimony heard in court.

However, under s. 6(1) of the Civil Evidence Act 1995, and s. 120 of the CJA 2003, such statements, if admitted, have become evidence in their own right, abolishing the notion of previous statements being admitted purely for the purposes of credit. This is unsurprising, given that the Law Commission concluded that the main justification for the hearsay rule was the impossibility of cross-examining the maker of a statement. As this obviously does not apply to a witness's own earlier statements, it is logical that that body also concluded that the hearsay rule should not apply to admitted previous (in)consistent statements. Furthermore, the Commission accepted that the common law position (which applied until 2004 in criminal cases) required a conceptually difficult direction for jurors as to the limited uses to which a previous (in)consistent statement could be put.[4]

Hearsay and Related Topics Law Commission Report No 245 (Published 19 June 1997) 'Summary Of Principal Recommendations'

1.23 We now turn to the case where witnesses are present at court and can be cross-examined. This fact offers greater scope for the admission of a witness's previous statements, although they are technically hearsay, than where the maker of the hearsay statement is absent and cannot be cross-examined. We believe that a previous statement of a witness should be admitted either where it falls within one of the above exceptions to the hearsay rule (for example, res gestae) or (1) to rebut an allegation of recent invention; (2) as evidence of a previous identification or description of a person, object or place; or (3) as evidence of recent complaint. In each of these cases the statement would be evidence of the matters stated in it.

1.24 Such statements would frequently be in written form, and, if admissible, would therefore be exhibits. Normally this would mean that the jury would take the statements with them when they retire, and they might attach greater weight to these written statements than to the evidence given orally. We believe that this would be undesirable, because the emphasis on the oral evidence might be weakened. We therefore recommend that the written statements should not accompany the jury when they retire to consider their verdict, unless all the parties agree or the court considers it appropriate.

---

[4] Law Com Report No 245, *Evidence In Criminal Proceedings: Hearsay and Related Topics*, Cm. 3670 (1997), hereinafter Law Com No 245, at paras. 10.11 and 1.47.

Admissible Previous Consistent Statements in Civil Cases

Previous consistent statements can always be admitted in civil trials at the discretion of the court, by virtue of s. 6(2)(a) of the Civil Evidence Act 1995. However, the only circumstances in which a party in a civil case can adduce a previous consistent statement as of right, without the 'leave' of the court, applies where it is advanced 'for the purpose of rebutting a suggestion that his evidence has been fabricated': s. 6(2)(b) of the Civil Evidence Act 1995. As this latter situation is also an exception in criminal cases, it will be considered in detail below.

Admissible Previous Consistent Statements in Criminal Cases

In criminal cases, the 2003 Act expanded and, in some cases, altered, the situations in which previous consistent statements could be admitted at trial. Despite this, it should be noted that the general exclusionary rule still operates in criminal matters, where an exception does not apply. The Law Commission rejected suggestions dating back to the Criminal Law Revision Committee's 11th Report, of 1972, and reiterated more recently by Lord Justice Auld, that previous consistent statements *generally* should be admitted in criminal matters.

Although such statements might have been made when a witness's memory was at its freshest, the Commission felt that admitting them would often be superfluous, waste court time, raise a multitude of collateral issues as to the precise terms of the earlier statement and undermine the primacy of oral evidence.[5] The continuing existence of 'bright line' rules in this area will aid certainty, though some observers will regret Parliament's failure to at least provide trial judges with a general discretion to admit such material, where it can be justified on the facts of an individual case. Section 120 refers to five exceptions, some novel, others well established. These will be dealt with in turn.

Section 120 of the CJA 2003, Other previous statements of witnesses

(1) This section applies where a person (the witness) is called to give evidence in criminal proceedings.

(2) If a previous statement by the witness is admitted as evidence to rebut a suggestion that his oral evidence has been fabricated, that statement is admissible as evidence of any matter stated of which oral evidence by the witness would be admissible.

(3) A statement made by the witness in a document—

    (a) which is used by him to refresh his memory while giving evidence,

    (b) on which he is cross-examined, and

    (c) which as a consequence is received in evidence in the proceedings,

is admissible as evidence of any matter stated of which oral evidence by him would be admissible.

---

[5] Law Com No 245, at paras. 10.12–10.15.

(4) A previous statement by the witness is admissible as evidence of any matter stated of which oral evidence by him would be admissible, if—

(a) any of the following three conditions is satisfied, and

(b) while giving evidence the witness indicates that to the best of his belief he made the statement, and that to the best of his belief it states the truth.

(5) The first condition is that the statement identifies or describes a person, object or place.

(6) The second condition is that the statement was made by the witness when the matters stated were fresh in his memory but he does not remember them, and cannot reasonably be expected to remember them, well enough to give oral evidence of them in the proceedings.

(7) The third condition is that—

(a) the witness claims to be a person against whom an offence has been committed,

(b) the offence is one to which the proceedings relate,

(c) the statement consists of a complaint made by the witness (whether to a person in authority or not) about conduct which would, if proved, constitute the offence or part of the offence,

(d) the complaint was made as soon as could reasonably be expected after the alleged conduct,

(e) the complaint was not made as a result of a threat or a promise, and

(f) before the statement is adduced the witness gives oral evidence in connection with its subject matter.

(8) For the purposes of subsection (7) the fact that the complaint was elicited (for example, by a leading question) is irrelevant unless a threat or a promise was involved.

Rebutting an Allegation of 'Recent Fabrication'

Under s. 120(2), if a previous statement by a witness is admitted to rebut a suggestion that his oral evidence has been fabricated, the statement becomes evidence of any matter contained in it (assuming its maker could give oral evidence on it in court), rather than merely going to credit. However, unlike the situation with regard to 'recent complaints' (see below), and although the Law Commission criticized the limitation of the exception to allegations that the witness's oral evidence is a 'late' invention,[6] s. 120(2) does not appear to alter the common law requirements that must be met before such statements are *admitted*, merely the use to which they can be put once this has occurred. As a result, the considerable body of case law on this area, regulating admissibility, will continue to apply. (It should be noted that this exception also applies in civil cases, by virtue of s. 6(2)(b) of the Civil Evidence Act 1995.)

In particular, there must be a suggestion, express or implied, that the witness's statement has been *recently* fabricated, ie made up at a point that can be identified, chronologically, as being subsequent to the making of the statement that is consistent with it, as in *R v Oyesiku* [1971] 56 Cr App R 240. In this case, Karminski LJ observed that the statement must have been made 'sufficiently early to be inconsistent with the suggestion that his account is a late invention or reconstruction'. In *Oyesiku* the prosecution insinuated that the accused's wife had made up her testimony to support her husband's account, the latter individual being accused of

---

[6] Law Com No 245, at para. 10.16.

assaulting a policeman. She had, however, made a statement to her husband's solicitors *before* he was released from custody (the earliest time at which she would have become acquainted with his version of events), and, as a result, her statement tended to show that her evidence was independent.

Fox v General Medical Council [1960] 1 WLR 1017, PC

Lord Radcliffe

If in cross-examination a witness's account of some incident or set of facts is challenged as being a recent invention, thus presenting a clear issue as to whether at some previous time he said or thought what he has been saying at the trial, he may support himself by evidence of earlier statements by him to the same effect. Plainly the rule that sets up the exception cannot be formulated with any great precision, since its application will depend on the nature of the challenge offered by the course of cross-examination and the relative cogency of the evidence tendered to repel it.

The Irish case of *Flanagan v Flahy* [1918] 1 IR 361 can be considered as an example of an implied suggestion that a statement has been recently fabricated. In this case, it was put to a witness that he had invented his version of events because of hostility that existed between himself and the defendant. As a result, he was allowed to adduce evidence that he had made a statement that was consistent with his in court testimony prior to the time at which this hostility (which was the result of a specific incident) had occurred.

It should be stressed that merely impeaching a witness's credibility does not allow a previous consistent statement to be introduced. It is always safe to accuse a witness of lying, without risking the adduction of such a statement. It is the allegation of 'late' invention that brings the exception into play. Additionally, of course, if the previous consistent statement is made subsequently to the date contained in the allegation, it will not become admissible. For example, a question in cross-examination suggesting, 'You made this up a month ago' will not permit a consistent statement from two weeks earlier to be admitted. However, if cross-examining counsel were rash (or confident) enough to say to a witness, 'You're making this up as you go along' all earlier consistent statements would, in theory, become admissible. The strictness of these requirements (which still operate under the CJA 2003) explain why, as Lord Radcliffe observed in *Fox v General Medical Council* [1960] 1 WLR 1017, there are comparatively few reported instances of the rule being successfully invoked. This was also noted in the following Australian case.

The Nominal Defendant v Clements (1961) 104 CLR 476, Aus HC

Dixon CJ

...inasmuch as the rule forms a definite exception to the general principle excluding statements made out of court and admits a possibly self-serving statement made by the witness, great care is called for in applying it. The judge at the trial must determine for himself, upon the conduct of the trial before him, whether a case for applying the rule of evidence has arisen and...must exercise care in assuring himself not only that the account given by the witness in his testimony is attacked on the ground of recent invention or reconstruction or that a foundation for such an attack has been laid ... but also that the contents of the statement are in fact to the like effect as his account given in his evidence and that having regard to the time and circumstances in which it was made it rationally tends to answer the attack.

Section 120(4) of the Criminal Justice Act 2003

Section 120(4)(a) sets out three other exceptions under which a previous statement made by a 'live' witness can be adduced in criminal matters. However, before this can happen (for any one of them), s. 120(4)(b) provides that the witness must testify that he made the statement and that to the best of his belief it states the truth. One of the three is entirely novel, while two are based on existing common law exceptions, albeit considerably expanded. (As previously noted all of them become evidence in their own right.)

Section 120(5): Previous Identifications

At common law, an exception existed from 'time immemorial' whereby a previous identification of the accused, made by a witness out of court, could subsequently be adduced at trial. The rationale for this long-standing exception to both the hearsay rule and the rule against narrative was the desirability of excluding any suggestion that an identification of the prisoner in the dock was a mistake. More recently, the exception has been extended to cover situations in which the victim composed an out of court photofit of the accused as in *R v Cook* [1987] QB 417 or guided a police artist in sketching the accused's likeness: *R v Constantinou* [1990] 91 Cr App R 74. Both sketch and photofit could later be adduced at trial. Thus, in *Cook*, the victim of an indecent assault and robbery had directed the making of a photofit portrait of her attacker. At trial this was adduced both as evidence of the accused's appearance (potentially infringing the rule against hearsay) and to corroborate the victim's later identification of the defendant with her earlier description (infringing the rule against narrative). Watkins LJ circumvented these problems by arguing (neatly but implausibly) that photofits were analogous to real evidence such as photographs.

However, even when extended to sketches and photofits the exception only covered visual identifications of people, not verbal descriptions or, for example, descriptions of vehicles and their attendant number plates. Thus, in *Jones v Metcalfe* [1967] 1 WLR 1286 the prosecution sought to establish the registration number of a car involved in an incident. An eye witness related the number to a police officer, who had not personally seen it. It was deemed to be inadmissible hearsay for the latter individual to relate the vehicle's number at trial, for the purpose of identifying the car involved. The Law Commission felt that this discrepancy between visual identifications of people and objects, and between identifications/photofits and descriptions, was anomalous and a 'deficiency in the law'.[7]

As a result, under s. 120(5) of the new Act, an earlier statement can be admitted if it 'identifies or describes a person, object or place'. Thus, were *Jones v Metcalfe* to come before the court again, the witness's statement to the police officer could be adduced at trial to identify the car involved. There is, however, uncertainty as to how much 'surrounding' detail might

---

[7] Law Com No 245, at paras. 10.6 and 10.21.

be admitted under this provision. For example, if the description of an object was made in the body of a police statement, to what extent would it be ripped from its immediate context, even if this made it hard to evaluate at trial?

Section 120(6): Forgetfulness

Under s. 120(6) of the CJA 2003, a statement can be adduced if it was 'made by the witness when the matters stated were fresh in his memory but he does not remember them, and cannot reasonably be expected to remember them, well enough to give oral evidence of them in the proceedings'. This is an entirely novel provision, founded on the (incontrovertible) proposition that a witness's memory of an incident is likely to be most accurate shortly after it occurs rather than months (or even years) later. It will also obviate the need for witnesses to 'refresh' their memories from documents (whether made contemporaneously or not) when, in reality, they can have no real recollection at all of the matter to which it relates, and are, in truth, swearing to the accuracy of their note. Thus, a traffic policeman patrolling a busy road, and dealing with several incidents a day, would be allowed to adduce his note of, for example, a routine case of careless driving that occurred many months earlier, as evidence of its contents.

However, this provision raises complicated issues as to the degree of forgetfulness that must be present before the witness 'cannot reasonably be expected to remember'. In deciding this, the court is likely to consider the nature of the witness (is s/he elderly, etc.?), the incident (was it of a sort that would 'stick' in the mind?) and the time lapse prior to trial. Nevertheless, given the advantages of 'live' witnesses and the relaxation on the use of aides memoires, the degree of 'forgetfulness' required to invoke the provision might be considerable. Evidence tendered this way will also lose some of its cogency, as the 2003 Act's 'Explanatory Notes' expressly recognized.[8]

Section 120(7): 'Recent Complaints'

Under s. 120(7) of the CJA 2003, a statement in the form of a complaint by a witness who claims to have been the victim of an offence, which crime also forms the subject matter of the proceedings, which was made 'as soon as could reasonably be expected' after the conduct it relates to, and in a trial in which the witness has first given evidence, is admissible. This is clearly a development of the common law doctrine of 'recent complaint' in sexual cases. Prior to the Act, such complaints were a well-established exception to the general rule against previous consistent statements. However, when admitted, they only went to credit and consistency, and were not evidence of the truth of their contents, which would obviously have violated the hearsay rule: *R v Osborne* [1905] 1 KB 551. As a result, and as the Court of Appeal noted in *R v Islam* [1999] 1 Cr App R 22, it was necessary for trial judges to direct juries carefully on the 'very limited' evidential use that could be made of such complaints. This is no longer the case, since the advent of the CJA 2003, as, under s. 120(4) such complaints, if admitted, become evidence in their own right.

Nevertheless, the Act does not merely alter the status of admitted recent complaints it also changes the very circumstances in which they can be adduced. At common law, after c.1800, the adduction of such complaints was limited to sexual cases (rape or indecent assaults, whether

---

[8] Explanatory Notes at para. 415. These are issued by the Home Office, do not form part of the Act, are not approved by Parliament and, of course, are not binding on the courts.

committed against males or females). However, the Law Commission suggested that the doctrine be extended beyond sexual cases to cover all offences. This recommendation was followed in the 2003 Act.

Furthermore, the Commission also felt that the preconditions for adducing recent complaints that had been established in sexual cases were too strict and should be relaxed. Historically, case law required that a complaint in a sexual case be made 'voluntarily'. This was deemed to exclude statements made as the result of a suggestive or 'leading' question to the complainant: *R v Osborne* [1905] 1 KB 551.

However, under s. 120(8) of the 2003 Act such questions will not prevent complaints being adduced, being deemed 'irrelevant' to the issue of admissibility (though, presumably, still affecting weight). The only situation in which such a statement will be inadmissible is where it has been elicited by a threat or promise: s. 119(7)(e). This might, for example, cover the situation in which a complaint was made to his mother, by her obviously injured son, after she said to him: '... unless you got that cut lip defending yourself from an unprovoked attack by the boy down the road you will lose your pocket money for a year'.

It was, at first, less clear as to whether time limits on the making of complaints had also been altered by the statute, as some judges certainly hoped.[9] At common law, recent complaints had to be made at the first reasonable opportunity to be admissible. A key question was whether the prerequisite under s. 120(7)(d), that a complaint be made 'as soon as could reasonably be expected after the alleged conduct', extended the time available for complaints to be admitted or simply restated the common law position. The former may well have been the intention of the parliamentary draftsmen.

However, it should be noted that in the years after World War II, the courts had, on their own initiative, taken an increasingly understanding approach towards delays in complaints about sexual assaults, having greater regard to the distressing nature of the offence, the nature of the complainant and her relationship to potential confidantes: *R v Valentine* [1996] 2 Cr App R 213. Arguably, this reduced the scope for a relaxation in time constraints (at least for complaints in sexual offence cases).

Nevertheless, in *R v O* [2006] 2 Cr App R 27, the Court of Appeal rejected a defence argument that the Act merely codified the common law rules on admissibility. As a result, it seems, there has been some further relaxation, and increase in flexibility, in time limits for such a complaint to be admissible. Of course, much will depend on the nature of the offence. A significant delay in reporting a distressing crime, such as a rape or indecent assault, will usually be a lot more understandable than in a more 'routine' offence, such as the non-violent 'snatch' of a handbag in a restaurant.

The end of an exception purely limited to sexual complainants is unsurprising. The justification for its continued survival was regularly questioned in the modern era. Even judicial explanations for its special status, such as those advanced by Tudor Evans J in *R v Jarvis and another* [1991] Crim LR 374, had a rather strained quality. The judge felt that the reason for: '... singling out such offences is that more hinges on questions of the credibility of the participants than in most other areas, just because sexual activity tends to take place in private and is usually kept secret'. However, the same argument could be advanced for many other types of serious offence, such as allegations of domestic violence, where the normal exclusionary rule applied in full. Despite this, a total abolition of the exception, rather than its general extension to other offences, might have appeared a more likely outcome in the early 1990s. Nevertheless, the Law Commission preferred the latter option, feeling that early post-crime statements were

---

[9]   See, for example, Rix LJ in *R v Birks* [2003] 2 Cr App R 122.

more likely to be accurate accounts and that they also ran a smaller risk of being 'corrupted' by subsequent events.[10]

In the pre-Act case of *White v R* [1999] 1 AC 210, the Privy Council stated that it was necessary not only that the complainant testify to the making of the complaint but also that its terms should be proved by the person to whom it was made. If the recipients of the complaint did not give evidence, the complainant's own evidence that she made a complaint could not assist in proving her consistency or in negating consent. To do this, there needed to be independent confirmation of what the complainant said; the girl's own evidence in chief that she complained did not assist the jury when deciding whether she was worthy of belief. It is likely that this will continue to be the case under the new statute. It should also be noted that in the post-Act case of *R v O* [2006] 2 Cr App R 27, the Court of Appeal held that more than one complaint could be admitted under the provision.

R v O [2006] 2 Cr App R 27, CA

McCombe J

There was much debate in the written arguments before us as to whether technically the old rules as to recent complaint had been abolished by the 2003 Act. That seems to us, in spite of the erudition of those arguments to be largely an arid discussion. The application to admit the evidence was made under the new Act. The judge, in our view, correctly concentrated on deciding whether the test of admissibility provided by that Act had been satisfied. 19 In dealing with the complaints to L and to her mother the judge decided this and we quote from the transcript of his ruling as follows: 'This is no longer a question of considering whether a complaint is made at the first reasonable opportunity, although that may well be a consideration when one comes to consider subsection (d). It is now a question of determining whether the complaint was made as soon as could reasonably be expected after the alleged complaint, which is a different test. When one looks at a case such as this with a history, or alleged history, of abuse over a period of time affecting a child who started to experience problems at the age of 9 and left home at the age of 17, shortly after the last of those problems was experienced, it seems to me that it is relatively straightforward to reach the conclusion that it would be a complaint made at the time, or shortly after she left home, to the person to whom she had gone in circumstances where that person was seeking to persuade her to return home. I have no difficulty, therefore, in determining that...the complaint made to (L) [is admissible]...Indeed, in fairness, the defence did not really seek to argue otherwise.' Mr Bagley did not argue otherwise before us today. We set out that passage as being a preliminary to the learned judge's consideration of the second complaint about which this appeal is directly concerned. The judge then proceeded to consider the proposed evidence of the complaint to S, which, as he put it, posed greater difficulty. He considered the point as to whether this complaint was made, as the statute requires 'as soon as could reasonably be expected' after the alleged conduct. The judge's decision was as follows: 'As I indicated a moment ago, I need also to consider the context of this because when one looks at what is reasonably to be expected and when one considers whether a complaint is made as soon as could reasonably be expected after the alleged conduct, as indicated during the course of the argument, it seems to me that that very much depends upon the circumstances and the person to whom any complaint is made; whether something is reasonably to be expected depends upon the context in which it takes place and the person to whom the information is imparted. As I have indicated a moment ago, what happened in

---

[10] Law Com No 245, at paras. 10.53–10.55.

the early summer of 1996 was that there was a row between brother and sister arising out of family circumstances and, in particular, a card sent to the defendant, but it is fair to say that in explanation and during the course of that row things were said to the older brother (S). In my judgment, so far as these circumstances and the person to whom the information was imparted I consider that that was made as soon as could reasonably be expected after the alleged conduct.' The judge considered two further points made by the defence. The first was whether s. 120 of the 2003 Act allows the admission of more than one hearsay statement as to a complaint by the alleged victim of crime. He held it did. The contrary was argued in written argument but has not been pursued before us this morning. We can say quite shortly that we agree with the judge's conclusion on that point and there is no need to say any more about it. There is no such limitation in the Act and we see no reason to import such limitation.

The judge also considered the relevance of the second complaint and whether there was any evidential weight in a repeated complaint over and above the first that had been made. ... It has to be remembered that a statement admitted under the new statutory provisions is admissible to prove the truth of the matter stated and not merely to demonstrate consistency of the complainant's account as was the case under the old law. There is obviously a need in fairness to restrict evidence of 'complaint upon complaint' which may merely be self-serving. But broadly for the reasons given by Judge Swift we agree that the evidence in this case had a relevance over and above that of the complaint to L and her mother some months earlier. The appellant sought to argue that the new hearsay provision as to complaints merely codify the old law of recent complaint and should be regarded as importing the restrictions inherent in some regards to that law. Again we disagree. The statutory provisions are freestanding and provide their own criteria. In our view, the learned judge applied those criteria correctly for the reasons that he gave. In our view, in the context of this case, the timing of the second complaint was, in all the circumstances, made 'as soon as might reasonably could be expected' after the alleged conduct, in the words of para.(d) of s. 120(7). In the circumstances, we do not consider it is necessary to address the additional point made by Miss Whyte for the Crown that the statement, was inevitably going to be admitted under s. 120(2), namely as rebuttal of an allegation of recent fabrication [see above].

4. Hostile Witnesses

Introduction

Prosecution witnesses were effectively compellable from the sixteenth century onwards under the examining magistrates' recognizance provisions, though defence witnesses could not be forced to give evidence until slightly later. This immediately raised problems as to how to deal with reluctant witnesses who were called to testify against their wishes. For example, when James Dunne was sworn as a Crown witness in the elderly Alice Lisle's trial for treason, in 1685, prosecuting counsel informed the Court in advance that he was an 'unwilling witness, and desir'd he might be examin'd strictly'. On hearing this, Lord Chief Justice Jeffreys immediately warned Dunne about the 'danger of swearing falsely', and threatened that if he caught him prevaricating he would punish him severely.[11]

---

[11] T Salmon, *Tryals for High-Treason, and other Crimes* (vol 4, 1720, printed by D Brown) at 384–402.

Cross-reference Box

Any witness who is able to give evidence is said to be competent. Most (but not all) competent witnesses are also compellable, that is they can be made to testify even if they do not wish to do so. In the modern era, this is done by issuing witness orders or subpoenas, depending on forum, that require an individual to attend court to testify. Any failure to comply with them can be treated as a contempt of court and punished as such. For more information on competence and compellability go to chapter 8.

A rather more effective procedure for dealing with such 'hostile' witnesses was gradually developed at common law, before statute, in the form of s. 3 of the Criminal Procedure Act 1865, intervened (it applies to civil cases as well, as s. 1 of the statute states that ss. 3–8 apply to all courts authorized to hear evidence 'as well criminal as all others').

Section 3 of the Criminal Procedure Act 1865

A party producing a witness shall not be allowed to impeach his credit by general evidence of bad character; but he may, in case the witness shall in the opinion of the judge prove adverse, contradict him by other evidence, or, by leave of the judge, prove that he has made at other times a statement inconsistent with his present testimony; but before such last-mentioned proof can be given the circumstances of the supposed statement, sufficient to designate the particular occasion, must be mentioned to the witness, and he must be asked whether or no the has made such statement.

It should be noted that the word 'adverse' has been interpreted as meaning 'hostile' in this context: *Greenough v Eccles* (1859) 5 CBNS 786. A witness can be deemed to be hostile at any time during examination in chief, or even, theoretically, during re-examination. The meaning and consequences of hostility must be examined in detail.

The Distinction Between Unfavourable and Hostile Witnesses

Sometimes, a witness does not 'come up to proof', that is, he does not give the evidence that was expected of him, having regard to any pre-trial statement he may have made to a solicitor or the police, and depending on the nature of the case and party. There might be a legitimate reason for this; for example, the witness might have genuinely changed his mind about what he has seen, or his memory may have faded in the intervening time between incident and trial (though he will normally have been allowed to refresh his memory from any earlier statement before, and even while, giving evidence). Such witnesses are termed 'unfavourable'.

However, sometimes, the change in evidence is deliberate, and motivated by 'hostility' towards the party who has called the witness. There might be many reasons for this, ranging from overt bribery, via intimidation and fear of the physical consequences of giving evidence adverse to the other party, to the situation in a domestic violence case where the parties have 'patched up' their differences in the period since the incident occurred. Such witnesses are termed 'hostile'. Thus, a hostile witness is a witness who not only fails to give the evidence expected of him, but does so because he has no wish to tell the 'truth' at the behest of the party calling him, ie he bears a hostile animus towards that party. (This does, of course, assume that his original version was the truth.) Although, in many cases, hostility will come as a surprise to the calling party, this is not invariably the case, and a party (including the prosecution in a criminal matter) can call a witness even if they know in advance that he is likely to become hostile: *R v Dat* [1998] Crim LR 488. This might occur, for example, where he has evinced a conspicuous reluctance to testify prior to trial.

Decisions as to whether witnesses are hostile or merely unfavourable are a matter for the trial judge. Guidance on the procedures and criteria by which this determination should be made was provided in *R v Maw* [1994] Crim LR 841, which also suggested that, initially, when a witness failed to come up to proof, he should be invited to refresh his memory from an earlier statement before the question of hostility is considered. However, in *R v Pestano* [1981] Crim LR 397, it was suggested that an application to treat a witness as hostile should be made as soon as he manifested unmistakable signs of hostility. A manifest and inexplicable difference between the testimony given at trial and that in any earlier statement will always be very significant, although Lord Goddard was probably slightly overstating the case when he suggested that if the two were in flat contradiction it would always be conclusive of hostility: *R v Fraser and Warren* [1956] 40 Cr App R 160. Nevertheless, it was because of such a discrepancy that cross-examination was allowed in *R v Prefas and Pryce* [1987] 86 Cr App R 111.

In most cases, a decision as to the presence of hostile animus depends on a combination of the witness's present testimony compared to any previous statement they have made, along with the inherent nature of the case and witness, and their 'in court' demeanour and responsiveness. For example, a very elderly witness is more likely to be genuinely forgetful than is a youthful one. As a result, it is difficult to challenge a trial judge's decision on this issue on appeal, not least of all because he has seen the witness in the flesh: *R v Manning* [1968] Crim LR 675.

R v Prefas and Pryce [1988] 86 Cr App R 111, CA

The Lord Chief Justice

We have been referred helpfully to Stephen's Digest on the Law of Evidence, Article 147, in which the common law rules are set out. It may be helpful if I just read them: 'Unfavourable and Hostile Witnesses: If a witness called by a party to prove a particular fact in issue or relevant to the issue fails to prove such fact or proves an opposite fact the party calling him may contradict him by call-ing other evidence, and is not thereby precluded from relying on those parts of such witness's evidence as he does not contradict. If a witness appears to the judge to be hostile to the party calling him, that is to say, not desirous of telling the truth to the Court at the instance of the party calling him, the judge may in his discretion permit his examination by such party to be conducted in the manner of a cross-examination to the extent to which the judge considers necessary for the purpose of doing justice. Such a witness may by leave of the judge be cross-examined as to—(1) facts in issue or relevant or deemed to be relevant to the issue; (2) matters affecting his accuracy, veracity, or credibility in the particular circumstances of the case; and as to (3) whether he has made any former statement, oral or written, relative to the subject-matter of the proceeding and inconsistent with his present testimony...In the case of a witness who is treated as hostile, proof of former statement, oral or written, made by him inconsistent with his present testimony may by leave of the judge be given in accordance with Articles 144 and 145.' It is plain that the foundation for treating the witness as hostile was there, because all the ingredients in that Article of Stephen's Digest were present. The fact that the statement was oral rather than written, although making the task of the cross-examiner more difficult, does not seem to this Court to affect the principle. By saying he did not recognise Chris the witness showed himself to be sufficiently hostile to bring into operation the procedures mentioned.

There can be more than one application to treat a witness as hostile; for example, if the initial request is unsuccessful, but further material emerges to suggest hostility, even after the end of examination in chief, a fresh application can be made. This occurred in *R v Hulme* [2007] 1 Cr App R 26, where there were two applications by the Crown to treat a witness as hostile. The first occurred in the course of her evidence in chief, and was refused by the trial judge. The second, made at the end of cross-examination, was allowed.

The distinction between the two types of case, a genuine change of mind or forgetfulness in an unfavourable witness and animus in a hostile witness, is very important. In the first situation, unhelpful evidence that is not motivated by hostility, all the party calling the witness can do is to call another witness (presuming, of course, that such a person is available) to fill the lacuna that has been left in his case. He cannot impeach his own witness by cross-examining him about their earlier, and now inconsistent, statement. Often, having received no joy on the relevant issues from an unfavourable witness, he will cut his examination short, especially if under pressure from opposing counsel, who might be complaining: 'My learned friend has received an answer to this question/is seeking to lead the witness.' As Holroyd J observed in *Ewer v Ambrose* (1825) 3 B & C 746, normally if: 'A party calls a witness to prove a fact, he cannot, when he finds the witness proves the contrary, give general evidence to shew that that witness is not to be believed on his oath, but he may shew by other evidence that he is mistaken as to the fact which he is called to prove.'

However, if a witness is declared hostile, a very different result ensues from the situation in which he is merely deemed to be unfavourable. Although, generally, examining counsel may not ask leading questions during examination in chief (ie a question that suggests to the witness the answer desired by the questioner) such questions are allowed during the examination in chief of a hostile witness, ie the calling party can cross-examine his own witness. Additionally, a hostile witness's previous statements can be put to them. If they deny making them, examining counsel can call evidence to prove the making of the statement, pursuant to s. 3 of the Criminal Procedure Act 1865.

Nevertheless, if a witness *does* fully admit to making a previous inconsistent statement, when it is put to him under s. 3 of the 1865 Act, it seems that the calling party cannot normally adduce evidence to prove the circumstances in which the statement was made, even if they feel that the point would appear more impressive to the tribunal of fact if they were permitted to do so: *R v P (GR)* [1998] Crim LR 663. Although the previous statement, inconsistent with the in-court testimony, will usually be in writing (for example, a police statement) it can also be oral, as was the case in *R v Prefas and Pryce* [1988] 86 Cr App R 111. In the latter situation, as the Court of Appeal noted in *Prefas*, the principle is exactly the same as where the earlier statement was made in writing, albeit that it poses some extra practical problems for the examining party.

Although nearly all applications to treat a witness as hostile are now made under s. 3 of the Criminal Procedure Act 1865, it appears that the 1865 statute did not abolish the then existing common law power to treat a witness as hostile. This residual power was considered in

R v Thompson [1976] 64 Cr App R 96. In this case, the prosecution called a young girl to give evidence against her father in (inter alia) an incest case. However, once in the witness box she froze, refusing to give evidence, despite being warned that she risked being held in contempt of court. Eventually, the trial judge deemed her to be hostile and allowed her to be cross-examined about an earlier statement she had made to the police. As she had not actually said anything material in the witness box, it was argued, on appeal, that there was nothing for her evidence at trial to be inconsistent with, and therefore, given its wording, that the 1865 Act did not apply. Although Lord Widgery refused to give a firm view on this, it was held that s. 3 of the CPA 1865 had supplemented, but not replaced, the existing common law power to treat a witness as hostile, which power could still be invoked. In the instant case, there was no dispute that the child's silence was motivated by hostility, something that would certainly allow her to be cross-examined about the earlier statement at common law: *Clarke v Saffery* (1824) Ry & M 126.

R v Thompson [1976] 64 Cr App R 96, CA

Widgery CJ

Thus, one comes from there to Mr. Mylne's main point today, his best point as he described it, which is that the girl Anne ought never to have been treated as hostile. He concedes that she was a hostile witness and that the provisions of section 3 of the Criminal Procedure Act 1865 applied to her, but he says, for a reason which I will endeavour to explain in a moment, that that section did not apply to this case. . . . It is to be observed in the text of that section that the party producing a witness is permitted in certain circumstances to contradict, and that he may produce a statement inconsistent with present testimony. The argument of Mr. Mylne is that in order to get the benefit of section 3 it is not enough to show, as in this case, that the girl was hostile and stood mute of malice. It is essential, so the argument goes, that there should be a contradiction of a previous statement and an inconsistent current statement, and since in this case there was no such contradiction, the previous statement standing alone and the girl refusing to produce a second statement either consistent or otherwise, it is contended that the section has no application.

 We do not find it necessary to express any view upon the section as applied to cases where there is an inconsistent statement. We think this matter must be dealt with by the provisions of the common law in regard to recalcitrant witnesses. Quite apart from what is said in section 3, the common law did recognise that pressure could be brought to bear upon witnesses who refused to co-operate and perform their duties. . . . We are dealing here with a witness who shows himself decidedly adverse, and whereupon, as Best C.J. says, it is always in the discretion of the judge to allow cross-examination. After all, we are only talking about the asking of leading questions. If the hostile witness declines to say anything at all, that is as inconsistent with his or her duty as making a second and inconsistent statement about the facts. Best C.J. is recognising as a feature of the common law the right, in the discretion of the judge, always to allow cross-examination in those circumstances. . . . The short question after all is: was the judge right in allowing counsel to cross-examine in the sense of asking leading questions? On the authority of Clarke v. Saffrey (supra) and Bastin v. Carew (supra) it seems to us that he was right and there is no reason to suppose that the subsequent statutory intervention into this subject has in any way destroyed or removed the basic common law right of the judge in his discretion to allow cross-examination when a witness proves to be hostile.

It must also be stressed that, in some other respects, the position of a hostile witness with regard to the party calling him is not the same as that of an opposing party's witness. In particular, the calling party cannot impeach the hostile witness's testimony by questioning him about his 'general evidence of bad character' (if he has one) to quote the wording of s. 3 of the 1865 Act. Thus, he cannot ask questions, or adduce evidence, about the witness's previous convictions or other aspects of reprehensible behaviour. The rationale for this restriction is fairly obvious. If the witness is of such bad character as not to be worthy of belief, why was he called in the first place?

In the light of s. 119 of the CJA 2003, any previous statement by a hostile witness will not now merely go to credit, it will also be an exception to the hearsay rule and so evidence of the truth of its contents, even if its veracity (or its making) is rejected by the cross-examined witness.

5. Special Measures and Alternative Methods of Giving Evidence

Introduction

Traditionally, the paradigmatic manner for a witness to give evidence at common law has been to testify orally from the witness box, in open court, in full sight of any other party to the trial or, indeed, anyone else present in court. As has been seen, the relaxation of the hearsay evidence has altered this situation considerably. However, even where a witness does testify in person, a combination of modern technology and an increased sensitivity to the trauma inherent in giving evidence, mean that the traditional model is often no longer followed.

This sensitivity is not purely the result of an increase in general compassion for the (frequently) unenviable lot of a witness. There are thoroughly pragmatic reasons as well. As the Royal Commission on Criminal Justice expressly noted, as far back as 1993, without victims and other witnesses being willing to come forward to make statements to the police, and then to give evidence at trial, prosecutions will founder, and the guilty escape conviction. This has always been a problem in some (often urban) areas. However, it appears to be an expanding phenomenon in the modern era and has prompted comment from some senior members of the judiciary, as the following extract indicates.

R v Davis and Ellis [2006] 2 Cr App R 32, CA

Sir Igor Judge P

In the Davis appeal there is undisputed evidence from a detective officer who has specialised in murder investigations for the last seven years, and in particular, gun related violence. He said: 'Most people opt not to co-operate and do not get involved. Doors are not opened, arranged meetings result in a witness not turning up, telephone messages go unanswered and messages left at home addresses/work, although discreet are ignored. This is not a problem that exists on an occasional basis...it is a problem that exists in practically every investigation in one way or another. Such problems exist on a daily basis. I have spoken to witnesses about a reluctance to give evidence. The common factor between all of them is fear. They are in fear of their lives and that of their families and friends. There is a very real danger to such persons of death or serious injury, either to prevent them from giving evidence, or to punish them for giving evidence and to send a warning to those who may be thinking of assisting the police. This risk I know and the witnesses know, is not necessarily at the hands of the defendants themselves, but at the hands of the associates of the defendant. If the defendant is in custody, it is often the associates who are the physical threat. In many but not all cases, the witness knows of the defendant and their associates. They know they have easy access to firearms and the "ease" with which they are prepared to use them.' In summary, quite apart from the ghastly callousness involved in the use of firearms to kill, and the devastation suffered by the families of the deceased, it is not an exaggeration to point out that, whether they are aware of it or not, these gun carrying criminals are challenging the rule of law itself. One common feature of both these cases, and many others like them, is the absence of any or any significant attempt at concealment. People are gunned down in busy crowded areas. Although the offences are witnessed, those who use their guns expect to escape justice. They anticipate that the guns which have been used to kill will also serve to silence, blind and deafen witnesses. Without witnesses, justice cannot be done. Dealing with it generally, there are in principle, two ways to address these problems. The first is a witness protection programme. However in reality, and certainly for the individual of good character, with established roots, this kind of programme is unacceptable. It requires a complete change of identity, and home, and work, not only for the witness himself or herself, but for his family, and a likely permanent separation between them, and other members of their extended family, and a subsequent life which is dominated by the need for continued security, and constant supervision of that security by police officers. This process is grossly invasive of the right of the witness and his family to private and family life. It is likely to be appropriate when the identity of the witness is already known to the defendant, and may be suitable for the professional criminal who has decided, for reasons of his own, to give evidence against his former colleagues and who is treated as a 'supergrass'. The alternative to the witness protection programme is for appropriate steps to be taken to protect and reassure the witness about the process leading to and the giving of evidence. This includes voice modulation, and screening, and other special measures, and witness anonymity. It is this last feature of possible steps to protect witnesses, and their lives and the lives of their families, that is engaged in these appeals. The administration of protective arrangements of this kind is not unduly problematic in itself. The difficulty arises from the potential conflict between them and the over-arching principle of the common law, once memorably described by Lord Bingham of Cornhill C.J. as the 'birthright' of every British citizen, the right to a fair trial.

In 1989 the report of Judge Pigot's influential Advisory Committee on Video Evidence recommended that children be allowed to give not just their examination in chief by pre-recorded video (subsequently termed 'half Pigot'), but also that their cross-examination should be video recorded prior to trial ('full Pigot'). As new technologies became more widely available, and attitudes changed, a variety of statutes (such as the CJA 1991) and common law measures, instigated under the court's inherent discretion, effected considerable change to the process of giving evidence (though not 'full Pigot'). In June 1998, the report 'Speaking up for Justice' addressed the considerable stress that can be caused to witnesses by giving evidence, and identified a need to introduce further measures to support and protect vulnerable and intimidated witnesses ('viws') in particular. Its conclusions, which included 78 suggestions for change, were not entirely unsurprising, as the report was written by a working group that included representatives from victim support schemes. The following year, the Youth Justice and Criminal Evidence Act 1999 introduced a number of its recommendations. In particular, ss. 16 to 33 of the Act provided for an array of 'special measures directions' that courts can or must order in respect of various classes of 'vulnerable' witnesses in criminal cases, and which allow for a departure from the normal method of giving evidence in open court. These measures included the use of: video-recorded evidence, live CCTV links, screens and communications aids for adult and child witnesses likely to be intimidated and distressed by facing the defendant in court.

These provisions have replaced, supplemented, or put on a statutory basis, the more modest variety of older statutory and common law aids for such witnesses; for example, live link and video-recorded evidence in chief were already available by statute to child witnesses, prior to the 1999 Act. In turn, the advent of ss. 51 and 137 of the CJA 2003 has introduced the possibility of some special measures being extended to 'normal' witnesses (see below). In civil cases, r. 32 of the CPR now also allows for departures from the traditional approach to witnesses giving evidence.

Special Measures and Human Rights

It was initially a matter of considerable debate as to whether some of these provisions might not violate the accused person's right to a fair trial set out in Article 6 of the ECHR. This was especially the case as special measures did not extend to defendants. It was argued that, in appropriate situations, this might be deemed to have produced an 'inequality of arms' between prosecution and defence. For an example of this, consider the situation in which a child defendant had to give his evidence in open court, while a child witness for the prosecution was allowed to testify via video and live link. It could be argued, in these circumstances, that the accused child had been denied an opportunity to give his evidence under the most favourable circumstances, unlike the prosecution witness.

However, this argument was rejected by the House of Lords in *R v Camberwell Green Youth Court* [2005] 1 WLR 393. In this case, two under-17-year-old victims were allowed to give their evidence against two under-16-year-old defendants via a video-link. Their Lordships concluded that ss. 20(2) and 24(3) of the YJCEA 1999, which allow the discharge or variation of special measures directions if it is in the interests of justice to do so, gave the courts ample power to ensure a fair trial in such situations, while also noting that, in the instant case, the accused youths had not been prejudiced in conducting their defences. Indeed, in a prescient consideration of the new provisions, Laura Hoyano concluded as early as 2001 that none of them were likely to violate Article 6, her analysis being borne out by subsequent judicial interpretations.

L Hoyano, 'Striking a Balance Between the Rights of Defendants and Vulnerable Witnesses: Will Special Measures Directions Contravene Guarantees of a Fair Trial?' [2001] Crim LR 948

It is submitted that the special measures for child witnesses should be impregnable under the Convention. The principles upon which the special measures for child witnesses are predicated, that all children under 17 are deemed to be vulnerable, and that complainants of sexual and (to a lesser degree) of physical abuse are presumptively entitled to protective measures, will find substantial support in the existing jurisprudence from Strasbourg. I would venture to predict that the European Court will not require a specific finding of potential harm to a particular child witness, along the lines of the American 'harm hearings', as a prerequisite to an SMD, Redbridge Youth Court notwithstanding. That said, all of the Strasbourg cases thus far have dealt with ad hoc measures devised by the trial judge to deal with a particular problem with a witness, not with legislation permitting, and indeed requiring, such special measures. One provision vulnerable to an Article 6 challenge is section 27(4), if a trial judge were to admit a video interview when the defendant would be deprived of the opportunity of cross-examination. For vulnerable adult witnesses, the requirement that the court make an evidence-based finding that an SMD is likely to improve the quality of the witness's testimony, after considering whether the measure might inhibit the evidence being effectively tested by the opposite party, should also be sufficient to insulate an SMD from challenge under Article 6. To revert to the concerns of parliamentarians expressed at the beginning of this article: clearly the rights of witnesses cannot be coterminous with those of the defendant, because only the defendant is in jeopardy. However, affording witnesses some protection by mitigating the rigours of the orthodox adversarial trial does not necessarily mean that one is hollowing out the defendant's rights. The defendant's birthright under any rational criminal justice system is to a fair trial, that is, a public process whereby the probative value of all of the available admissible evidence can be fairly, thoroughly and effectively tested in the court's quest to ascertain the truth about past events. Enabling witnesses to give the best evidence of which they are capable not only does not collide with the defendant's rights, but, it is submitted, is entirely compatible with them. Extending the special measures to child defendants, and possibly also adult defendants with handicaps, could be the most effective means of refuting the critics of the new régime.

Special Measures under the YJCEA 1999

Most of the 1999 Act's special measures directions came into effect in July 2002. However, the use of video-recorded cross-examination (ie 'full Pigot') and the general employment of witness intermediaries remain to be implemented, partly for logistical reasons and partly because of difficulties posed by advance disclosure. In 2004, a Home Office Research Study on the effects of the new Act suggested that increasing numbers of witnesses had had recourse to the measures established in it, and that, in some cases, this had been decisive in their decision to give evidence.

'Are Special Measures Working? Evidence from Surveys of Vulnerable and Intimidated Witnesses' (Home Office Research Study 283, Published June 2004) at xiii

SPECIAL MEASURES AND OTHER MEASURES TO ASSIST VIWS

The phase 2 survey was conducted after the implementation of many of the special measures, while the phase 1 survey took place while only a limited number of such measures was in place, and these were only available for certain groups, in particular child witnesses. The results from the two surveys show an increase in the proportion of witnesses using certain measures, and the vast majority of witnesses using these measures in phase 2 found them helpful. The largest increases in use of special measures were found among: video-recorded evidence-in-chief (from 30% to 42% among child witnesses); live television link for giving evidence (doubling from 43% to 83% among child witnesses); and removal of wigs and gowns (from 8% to 15% among Crown Court witnesses giving evidence). Other forms of assistance including pagers, escorts and intermediaries 2 were used only rarely among VIWs at both stages (in the case of pagers, not at all). Witnesses using special measures in phase 2 rated them very highly; for example nine in ten witnesses using the live TV link found this helpful, and a similar proportion found using video-recorded evidence-in-chief useful. The importance of special measures is further vindicated by the finding that 33 per cent of witnesses using any special measure said that they would not have been willing and able to give evidence without this. . . . The value of special measures is further highlighted by the extensive level of demand for measures among witnesses who were not given access to them. Screens and/or live TV link were thought to be particularly useful, with around three-fifths of all VIWs who gave evidence and did not use these measures stating that they would have found them useful.

Who is Eligible for Assistance?

It should, perhaps, be noted straight away that the relevant provisions of the YJCEA 1999 are drafted in a particularly dense, obscure and unclear fashion, making comprehension quite difficult. Nevertheless, s. 18 enacts that assistance by means of a special measures direction may be provided to 'eligible' witnesses. The Act creates three classes of such witnesses (none of them extend to a defendant who gives evidence). Section 16 of the Act provides assistance to two categories of witness (ie it makes them eligible).

The first category consists of children or young people who are under the age of 17 at the time of the hearing. Under s. 16(3), the 'time of the hearing' means the time when the court makes a determination as to whether or not to make a special measures direction. The second category consists of witnesses the quality of whose evidence the court considers is likely to be diminished because they suffer from a mental disorder within the meaning of the Mental Health Act 1983, have a significant impairment of intelligence and social functioning, or because they have a physical disability or disorder: s. 16(2). By s. 16(5), the phrase 'quality of evidence' means its quality in terms of completeness, coherence and accuracy; 'coherence' is defined as meaning the witness's ability when giving evidence to provide answers which address the questions put to him and which can be understood both individually and collectively. No further guidance is provided by the section on this issue, so any decision as to whether or not a special measures direction is required will be very much a matter for the court's discretion.

Section 17 of the 1999 Act makes provision for assistance to be given to a third category of witness: those who are in fear or distress about testifying and the quality of whose evidence the court feels is likely to be diminished as a result. Before making the order, there are certain matters that the court must take into account under s. 17(2); in particular, it must consider: the nature and alleged circumstances of the offence; the age of the witness; the domestic and employment circumstances of the witness (where relevant), along with their religious or political beliefs; the behaviour towards the witness of the accused, members of the accused's family and associates, or anyone else likely to be a defendant or a witness in the proceedings. Any views expressed by the witness must also be considered. However, complainants in proceedings for sexual offences are automatically eligible for assistance under this ground, unless they inform the court that they do not wish to have recourse to such special measures: s. 17(4).

As a result of ss. 16 and 17 of the Act, the following (purely illustrative and non-exhaustive) selection of witnesses are likely to be (or will be) considered 'eligible': children, rape complainants, witnesses with acute agoraphobia, those who have been threatened on behalf of a defendant.

Under s. 19(2) of the 1999 Act, where a court, whether of its own motion or as a result of an application by a party to the proceedings, has decided that a witness comes within ss. 16 or 17 of the statute, and so is potentially eligible for assistance, it must then determine whether or not the quality of the witness's evidence would be improved by one or more of the special measures available. If it does come to such a conclusion, it should then give a 'special measures direction' to that effect. Under s. 20(5) of the Act, reasons for giving, refusing, varying or discharging such a direction must be given in open court. In the case of a Magistrates' Court, the reasons must also be entered in the register of its proceedings.

It should be noted that s. 19(6) specifically provides that the courts retain any existing powers to make an order in respect of a witness who is not eligible for assistance within the Act. Thus, and for example, the common law power to screen a witness giving evidence is preserved and could still be used for a witness who is not deemed to be eligible under the statute. The court may also make an order in respect of an eligible witness about a matter falling outside the ambit of ss. 16 or 17, for example, in relation to the provision of a foreign language interpreter.

In most cases, it is the party calling the witness who will be making the application for a special measures direction. However, the court can make a direction on its own motion, though, before doing this, it should consult the party calling the witness, the witness him/herself, and, in appropriate situations, the witness's parents, social workers and any other source of expert advice.

The Special Measures Directions Available

Under s. 23 of the 1999 Act, a vulnerable witness can be protected from seeing the accused by means of a strategically placed screen or some other arrangement. (As with the removal of wigs and gowns, courts relied on a common law power to do this prior to the enactment of this section.) The witness must be able to see, and be visible to, the judge and jury, or magistrates, the legal representatives in the proceedings, and any interpreter or person appointed to assist the witness by virtue of s. 23(2).

Section 24 allows the court to permit a vulnerable witness to give evidence via a 'live link' so that he does not have to be in the courtroom. This is defined by s. 24(8) as meaning a 'live television link or other arrangement whereby a witness, while absent from the courtroom, can see and hear and be seen and heard by persons in the courtroom'. Amongst such persons are the judge and jury or magistrates, legal representatives, interpreters, etc. If, in a Magistrates' Court, live link facilities are not available at that particular location (as is sometimes the case in the summary courts), the court may sit, for these purposes, at some other place where the facilities are available: s. 24(5).

Under s. 25, a special measures direction may exclude certain people, such as members of the public, from the court, while a vulnerable witness gives evidence. This section applies only to sexual offences, or cases in which the court believes that someone other than the accused has sought or will seek to intimidate the witness in connection with testifying in the proceedings. Certain people cannot be excluded under the provision. Amongst them are (unsurprisingly) the accused himself, as well as any legal representatives acting in the proceedings, interpreters, etc. Additionally, if reporters are to be excluded by such a special measures direction, one nominated media representative must be allowed to remain in court as a result of s. 25(3).

Under s. 26 of the 1999 Act, wigs and gowns may be removed if the court gives a special measures direction to that effect. In practice, common law had permitted this for many years prior to 1999, and it is, for example, now routine in those rare cases in which children are tried on indictment.

Section 27 of the 1999 Act, which replaces older provisions such as s. 32A of the Criminal Justice Act 1988, is particularly important. It allows for a special measures direction that permits vulnerable witnesses (not just children, unlike the 1988 statute) to give evidence in chief via a video recording made at an earlier time than the hearing. In practice, for prosecution witnesses, this will usually be made to the police early on in an investigation. In the case of children under 17 years of age, their evidence in chief will automatically be given on video unless the court determines otherwise, but in the case of other types of vulnerable witness the court may not admit such evidence if it is of the opinion that it would be against the interests of justice to do so. The court must consider whether any prejudice to the defendant that may arise from this procedure is likely to outweigh the desirability of showing the interview. Some of the factors that might be considered when exercising such a discretion were examined by the Court of Appeal in *R v C* (2001) WL 535694. In this case, a 17-year-old complainant in a rape case, where there was a similarly aged defendant, was allowed to give evidence in chief via a video and to be cross-examined via a live link, having been told some time earlier by the defence that this would be acceptable. The earlier assurance precluded any change of heart being deemed to be in the interests of justice.

If a special measures direction is made under this section, but the parties to the proceedings have not agreed that the witness will be available for cross-examination, or it appears that Rules of Court as to the manner in which the recording is to be made have not been complied with, the court may direct that the evidence is not to be admitted. A witness who gives evidence on video must be called by the party tendering the recording except where there is a special measures direction providing for the witness to be cross-examined otherwise than in court (via a video-link), or the parties to the proceedings have agreed that it is not necessary. Where a witness gives video-recorded evidence in chief s/he cannot give evidence by other means (for example, via live testimony), so long as the video-recorded evidence is, in the court's opinion, adequate.

Of course, evidence that is adduced pursuant to such a direction can raise some novel difficulties. For example, it appears that, where evidence has been heard via this mechanism, the trial judge has a discretion as to whether or not the video can be replayed to a jury, if they ask to hear it again. Alternatively, he may exercise his discretion to read from the transcript of the evidence. However, in this situation, there should be appropriate warnings to the jury about the dangers of any prejudice arising from hearing the same evidence twice: *R v Rawlings and Broadbent* [1995] 1 WLR 178. Although this decision was made under the old law, there is no reason to think that the result will be any different under the 1999 Act. Another potential difficulty would involve a child who has given evidence via a video recording and who then sought to retract the allegations made in it, prior to it being adduced at trial. It seems that, in such a situation, the court should not normally admit the recording as evidence.

It should be noted that the circumstances in which a video recording of a witness's evidence in chief can be taken by the police, with a view to later forensic use, are now guided by the extensive advice contained in a Home Office publication, *Achieving Best Evidence in Criminal Proceedings: Guidance for Vulnerable or Intimidated Witnesses, including Children*, which addresses, in some detail, the circumstances and manner in which such interviews should be conducted, as the following short extract indicates. However, the guidance is advisory, an indication of normal 'best practice', and does not constitute a legally enforceable code of conduct. Nevertheless, following it will, presumably, help to avoid the strong criticism that was expressed by the Court of Appeal in *R v Powell* [2006] Crim LR 781 about a delay of nine weeks that occurred in taking a video from an infant under four years of age in a sexual assault case.

Achieving Best Evidence in Criminal Proceedings: Guidance for Vulnerable or Intimidated Witnesses, including Children, vol 1, 2001, paras. 2.56–2.57

TIME AND LENGTH OF VIDEO RECORDED INTERVIEW

2.56 Professionals whose experience of interviewing has been mostly with adults may be tempted to adopt too fast a pace for the child, while those with only child care experience may adopt an overcautious approach and spend too long in the Rapport phase, when the child is ready to proceed with his/her account.

2.57 The investigating team should pay particular attention to when the interview takes place, as research has shown this to be one of the main concerns of child witnesses. Although the interview will normally take place as soon after an allegation or referral emerges as is practicable, rushing to conduct an interview, without properly considering the child's needs and consulting them as far as possible, and without proper planning, can undo any of the benefits of obtaining an early account from the child.

The 1999 Act also provided that a special measures direction might be given under s. 28 for the cross-examination and re-examination of a witness to be admitted by means of a video recording if his or her evidence in chief has been admitted by similar means under s. 27 (ie via video). However, this provision has not been brought into force, and in July 2004 the government announced that it had decided not to implement the provision in the form in which it had been enacted.

Section 29 of the 1999 Act permits the court to provide for the witness to be examined with the assistance of an 'intermediary' or other person approved by the court. Such an intermediary will be someone who may be trained in the necessary skills or who may have unique knowledge of the witness. The section does not alter existing arrangements for the provision in court of interpreters for the deaf who can choose either such an interpreter or an intermediary within s. 29. This provision has yet to be brought fully into force, being used in pilot trials in six areas of the country.

Section 30 authorizes the use of aids to overcome any physical difficulties on the part of the witness. Such aids might include, for example, signboards or other communication aids for the disabled (but not devices for disguising speech).

A combination of such special measures will often be used to deal with vulnerable witnesses. Thus, in *R v H* [2006] EWCA 853 three children between the ages of six (the victim) and 13 were witnesses in a case of rape by oral penetration. Their video-recorded police interviews constituted their evidence in chief (in the case of two of the witnesses there were two such interviews, both of which were played). They were then cross-examined by live link.

R v H [2006] EWCA 853, CA

Rix LJ

E, T and D gave evidence, as would be expected given their age, by having videos of their pre-recorded interviews played to the jury, and then they were asked further questions by way of further examination, cross-examination and re-examination over a video-link. Mr Jeary recognised that this was the proper procedure: it was in accordance with Youth Justice and Criminal Evidence

Act, 1999. He justifiably pointed out, however, the contrast between how the young witnesses were protected from the formidable atmosphere of the courtroom and the position of the appellant during the trial. The House of Lords has determined that it does not contravene article 6 of the Convention for young witnesses to give evidence in this way, even where the defendant is of a similar age: see R (D) v Camberwell Green Youth Court, [2005] 1 WLR 393. However, the difference in their treatment that Mr Jeary observed does underline that the court must adapt its procedures to ensure that a young defendant is not wrongly prejudiced by it and ensure that he has a fair trial in which he can effectively participate: see [2005] 1 WLR 393 at para 17 per Lord Rodger and para 57 per Baroness Hale.

The Future for Special Measures

Even the strongest supporters of special measures accept that their introduction/expansion under the 1999 Act has not been without problems. These have been engendered, in part, by logistical difficulties in the courts and partly by problems in the wording of the statute itself. Given that the changes effected by the YJCEA 1999 produced the most radical reforms to the traditional system of giving evidence yet seen in any common law country, such problems are not, perhaps, surprising. As a result, in December 2004 the government announced a review of special measures, the Review Group producing a consultation paper in June 2007, along with proposals for further reform. Some of these have been supported by academic observers, others received with less enthusiasm.

Laura Hoyano, 'The Child Witness Review: Much Ado about too Little' [2007] Crim LR 849–865 (Extract)

It was sensible for the Office for Criminal Justice Reform to pause for a rethink of SMs. It is indisputable that much progress has been made in their implementation, to the manifest benefit of many vulnerable witnesses. However, the government built several perilous traps for itself into the highly prescriptive YJCEA 1999: the rigidity of the primary rule which could thwart children's preferences as to how they will give evidence; the mandatory application of the primary rule to child witnesses called by the defence; and the denial of SMs to child defendants. The government should not be hesitant about approaching further legislative reform, and soon.

The *Child Witness Review CP* itself is disappointing in its failure to tackle difficult issues with detailed proposals. Rather, the Review Group expects the consultees to do the hard thinking, asking them to identify practical difficulties in implementation of the recommendations and to suggest solutions to them. This makes it doubly unfortunate that the government decided not to publish the review itself.

Judicial Warnings on Special Measures

By dint of s. 31 of the 1999 Act, all evidence given under a special measures direction will be treated as if given as direct oral testimony. However, where, on a trial on indictment, evidence is given in accordance with such a direction, the trial judge must give the jury whatever warning he considers necessary to ensure that the jury do not allow the presence of the special measures to prejudice them against the accused: s. 32. This is normally done when the witness gives evidence, and there is no requirement that it be repeated during the summing up: *R v Brown (Christian Thomas)* [2004] Crim LR 1034.

In *Brown*, two of three alleged victims in an aggravated burglary case, all of whom were prosecution witnesses, elected to give their evidence shielded by screens. The Court of Appeal approved the trial judge's direction to the jury, in which he informed them that the use of such screens was quite commonplace in serious cases (like the instant one) and warned them that they must not allow the use of screens to prejudice them against the defendants in any way. The court also noted that, in some cases, reiterating such a direction in the summing-up might give the procedure more emphasis in jurors' minds than was desirable. In the pre-Act case of *R v XYZ* [1990] 91 Cr App R 40, where screens had been used, the first instance judge directed the jury that their purpose was to prevent the child witnesses in the case from being intimidated by their surroundings, and that the jury should not let them occasion prejudice against the defendants.

Sections 51 and 137 of the Criminal Justice Act 2003

Section 24 of the YJCEA 1999, by which vulnerable witnesses could give evidence in chief via a live link, was considered a useful measure when applied to 'vi ws'. As a result, it was argued that the provision should be extended, in some situations, to cover 'ordinary' witnesses. This was effected by s. 51 of the CJA 2003. This provides that a witness (other than the defendant) can give their evidence via a live link if the court is satisfied that it is in the interests of the efficient or effective administration of justice and there are suitable court facilities for receiving such evidence in this manner: s. 51(4).

In deciding whether the test under s. 51 has been met, the court must consider all the circumstances of the case, including, 'in particular', the availability of the witness, the need for them to attend in person, their importance to the proceedings, their views, the suitability of facilities, whether giving evidence in this manner would inhibit another party from effectively testing the witness's evidence: s. 51(7). What this means is that, and for example, in appropriate circumstances, a witness located in Newcastle could testify at a trial being held in a Crown Court in Bristol.

Additionally, it was felt that the adduction of a video recording, made at an earlier time than the hearing, was a particular success under the 1999 Act, such evidence having the advantage of being recorded much closer to the incident to which it relates than in-court testimony (by which time witness memories have often deteriorated). As a result, s. 137 of the CJA 2003 gives the court a discretion to allow a video recording of a witness's evidence (other than that of the defendant) to be adduced as *part* of their examination in chief, provided that the account was given at a time when the events were fresh in the maker's memory, and provided that, in his oral testimony, the witness asserts the truth of the statements made by him in the video account.

The court will only allow such a recording to be adduced if the witness's recollection of events when the video was recorded is significantly better than it would be at trial and admitting such a recording is deemed to be in the interests of justice: s. 137(3). The exercise of the discretion to admit such a video recording is shaped by the factors set out in s. 137(4); these include the quality of the recording and the length of delay between the incident and the recording, as well as the views of the witness as to whether his evidence in chief should be given orally or via video recording.

Obviously, such evidence could be considered to be hearsay, ie it is an out of court statement being tendered for the truth of its contents. This problem was addressed by s. 137(2), which simply provides that such evidence will treated as if made by the witness in his own evidence at trial. As a result of s. 137, if an earlier video recording dealt fully with the witness's evidence, the witness will be sworn, the video played, the witness will vouch for the recordings truth, and will then be tendered for cross-examination. Of course, there will still be many attractions to calling a witness 'live', not least because many barristers feel that seeing a witness in the flesh has more influence on a tribunal of fact.

Pause for reflection

Why do you think that lawyers believe that 'live' witnesses normally have more influence on the tribunal of fact?

'Special Measures' in Civil Cases

The general rule, under r. 32.2(1)(a) of the CPR 1998 is that in civil trials a witness will give his evidence orally in public. However, under r. 32.2(2) of the CPR 1998, this is subject to any contrary provision in the CPR 1998 themselves or under statute and also any order of the court. As a result, the 'general rule' is very frequently departed from in practice. Obviously, this will happen with hearsay statements. Additionally, however, in civil litigation, witness statements, normally served prior to trial pursuant to r. 32.4 of the CPR 1998, are often taken as the witness's examination in chief by virtue of r. 32.5 of the CPR 1998. In these circumstances, although the witness will still attend court, and may amplify his statement with the court's permission (updating it, etc.), the statement itself will normally stand as the witness's evidence in chief. He will then be cross-examined on it in open court. Furthermore, even when it comes to 'live' witnesses, the court has enormous discretion as to how they give evidence by dint of r. 32.3 of the CPR 1998, which states that the court may allow a witness to give evidence through a video link or by other means.

Nevertheless, this provision can raise complicated policy issues. In *Polanski v Conde Nast Publications Ltd* [2005] 1 WLR 637, the claimant in a defamation action, a celebrated filmmaker, was resident in France. He was unwilling to give evidence in person in the High Court for fear that he would be arrested and extradited to the United States, where he was wanted for having underage sexual intercourse with a 13-year-old girl, and from where he had fled many years earlier after pleading guilty to the same offence. His action would probably fail if he were not allowed to give evidence from France via a video-conference link. This was permitted by a High Court judge, at a pre-trial hearing, and the judge's decision was then appealed to the Court of Appeal by the defendants. Their appeal was allowed by this forum, as it was held that the court's general policy should be to discourage litigants from escaping from the normal processes of the law, rather than facilitating it, especially in the circumstances found in the instant case. However, on further appeal to the House of Lords, the first instance judge's decision was restored, and the claimant permitted to give evidence via a video link.

The approach taken in *Polanski* was subsequently followed in *McGinn v Waltham Contractors Ltd.* [2006] WL 2794144, in which the claimant in a building dispute was allowed to give evidence from abroad, via video link, pursuant to r. 32.3 of the CPR, because, if he had attended the court in person, he might have become liable to UK capital gains tax of £50 million. Although the court found this an inherently unattractive basis for such an application, it also noted that there was a real risk of prejudice to the claimant (the tax) and that no significant prejudice would be occasioned to the defendant by having to conduct his cross-examination via video link, not least of all because the claimant's testimony was not of critical importance, much of the case turning on expert evidence.

Polanski v Conde Nast Publications Ltd [2005] 1 WLR 637, HL

Lord Nicholls

Despite his fugitive status, a fugitive from justice is entitled to invoke the assistance of the court and its procedures in protection of his civil rights. He can bring or defend proceedings even though he is, and remains, a fugitive. If the administration of justice is not brought into disrepute by a fugitive's ability to have recourse to the court to protect his civil rights even though he is and remains a fugitive, it is difficult to see why the administration of justice should be regarded as brought into disrepute by permitting the fugitive to have recourse to one of the court's current procedures which will enable him in a particular case to pursue his proceedings while remaining a fugitive. To regard the one as acceptable and the other as not smacks of inconsistency. If a fugitive is entitled to bring his proceedings in this country there can be little rhyme or reason in withholding from him a procedural facility flowing from a modern technological development which is now readily available to all litigants. For obvious reasons, it is not a facility claimants normally seek to use, but it is available to them. To withhold this facility from a fugitive would be to penalise him because of his status. That would lack coherence. It would be to give with one hand and take away with the other: a fugitive may bring proceedings here, but his position as a fugitive will tell against him when the court is exercising its discretionary powers. It would also be arbitrary in its practical effect today. A fugitive may bring proceedings here but not if it should chance that his own oral evidence is needed. Then, despite the current availability of VCF, he cannot use that facility and a civil wrong suffered by him will pass unremedied. For this reason I consider the judge was entitled and, indeed, right to exercise his discretion as he did. Rowland v Bock [2002] 4 All ER 370 was correctly decided. There Newman J made a VCF order in respect of a claimant who risked arrest and extradition to the USA on charges of fraud. No doubt special cases may arise. But the general rule should be that in respect of proceedings properly brought in this country, a claimant's unwillingness to come to this country because he is a fugitive from justice is a valid reason, and can be a sufficient reason, for making a VCF order. I respectfully consider the Court of Appeal fell into error by having insufficient regard to Mr Polanski's right to bring these proceedings in this country even though he is and will continue to be a fugitive from justice. I would allow this appeal and restore the judge's order. Mr Polanski was convicted of a serious crime. His reluctance to return to this country is grounded in a fear that he may be extradited and receive a custodial sentence in California. That does not take the case out of the general rule. However, at the trial the jury will be told these facts and will take them into account on all issues to which they are relevant.

 Summary

- Examination in chief is conducted by the party calling a witness, who also decides in which order his witnesses should be heard. However, a defendant who decides to testify must normally give his evidence before other defence witnesses are heard.

- Witnesses should not be 'coached' prior to testifying, but can be given training that will familiarize them with forensic procedure.

- A criminal defendant who fails to give evidence in his own case may be the subject of an adverse inference direction to the jury, though the prerequisites for giving such a direction are very strict. Such inferences can be routinely drawn in civil matters.

- Leading questions, that is questions that suggest a desired answer, cannot normally be asked by the calling party during examination in chief (unless a witness is declared to be 'hostile'). An exception is often made for purely formal matters.

- Witnesses may refresh their memory, while giving evidence, using an aide memoire. In criminal cases this must have been made or verified at an earlier time, when the witness's memory of events was significantly better than it is at trial, under s. 139 of the CJA 2003. In civil cases, it must have been made 'contemporaneously' with the events that it records, though this is not interpreted literally, and allows for a significant measure of delay. In certain circumstances, these aides memoires can be exhibited and given to the tribunal of fact. When this occurs, in both civil and criminal cases, they become evidence of their contents by dint of the CEA 1995 and the CJA 2003.

- If a witness shows 'animus' towards the party calling him, he may be treated as 'hostile' allowing that party to cross-examine him, and to adduce a previous inconsistent statement made by him, but not to impugn his general character. This is usually done pursuant to s. 3 of the Criminal Procedure Act 1865.

- Normally, a party cannot adduce a recent consistent statement during examination in chief. However, he may do so in certain specific circumstances, for example (and inter alia) if it constitutes a complaint about a crime made at the first reasonable opportunity or is adduced to rebut an allegation of recent fabrication. Under both the CJA 2003 and the CEA 1995 such statements, if admitted, are evidence of the truth of their contents, and no longer simply bolster witness credibility.

- Vulnerable witnesses, such as children or complainants in sexual cases, can be assisted when giving evidence by an array of 'special measures directions' under the YJCEA 1999; these are intended to reduce the stress of testifying. Amongst them are the use of screens, video-recorded examination in chief and video links, etc. More generally, provision is made in the CJA 2003 for ordinary witnesses to give evidence via live link and, in appropriate circumstances, to adduce an earlier video recording as part of their evidence in chief.

 Further reading

D Birch, 'A Better Deal for Vulnerable Witnesses' [2000] Crim LR 223–249

R Cross, 'A Very Wicked Animal Defends the 11th Report of the Criminal Law Revision Committee' [1973] Crim LR 329

L Hoyano, 'Variations on a Theme by Pigot: Special Measures Directions for Child Witnesses' [2000] Crim LR 250–273

L Hoyano, 'Striking a Balance Between the Rights of Defendants and Vulnerable Witnesses: Will Special Measures Directions Contravene Guarantees of a Fair Trial?' [2001] Crim LR 948

J McEwan, 'Evidence, Jury Trials And Witness Protection—The Auld Review Of The English Criminal Courts' (2002) International Journal of Evidence and Proof, vol 6, 163

R Munday, 'Calling a Hostile Witness' [1989] Crim LR 866

D Wolchover and A Heaton-Armstrong, *Witness Testimony: Psychological, Investigative and Evidential Perspectives* (2006, Oxford University Press)

Questions for Discussion

1. Edwina is called as a prosecution witness at the trial of Fred Kroy, a notorious and very violent gangster. She had earlier made a lengthy and detailed statement to the police about what she had observed when working as Fred's cleaner, which evidence was highly significant in implicating Fred in a variety of serious crimes. During her examination in chief, however, Edwina appears very nervous and hesitant; she eventually announces that she 'never saw a thing' while at work, other than the vacuum cleaner and Fred's rubbish.

Advise prosecuting counsel as to the conduct of his examination in chief.

2. Mohammed is accused of assaulting Nasreen, with a rolling pin, during an argument after they met while out fishing in the Thames. Nasreen did not get home until six hours after the incident, and when she did, her mother, seeing that she was bruised, asked her whether she had been 'attacked by a horrid man'. Nasreen then told her all about the incident. Mohammed, who is in custody, tells his brother, who visits him in prison before trial, that although the two of them had a disagreement, he did not intend to hit her with the rolling pin, but rather that he slipped with it in his hand, while showing Nasreen the size of a fish he had caught earlier that day. When he gives evidence to this effect at trial, prosecuting counsel tells him that he is making up his account 'as he goes along'.

(a) Will Nasreen be allowed to adduce the conversation with her mother, and if so, what will its evidential effect be?

(b) Will Mohammed be allowed to adduce the conversation with his brother while he was in custody, and if so, what will its evidential effect be?

3. How do the courts distinguish between a witness that is hostile and one who is merely adverse? What are the consequences of this distinction?

4. How does the Criminal Justice Act 2003 affect the use of aides memoires in court?

5. Miles claims that he was assaulted by Nobby (whom he knows), while walking past a public house late one evening. He sustains a black eye and cut lip, and runs home, where, early the following morning, he tells Oscar, a neighbour, about the incident. Some two weeks later he decides to report the matter to the police. Nobby is arrested shortly afterwards this, and charged with assault occasioning actual bodily harm.

Will the prosecution be allowed to adduce the evidence of the conversation between Miles and Oscar, and if so, to what effect?

6. Arnold is out walking and camping on Dartmoor, when he sees Brian stab Edwina to death (both of them being strangers to Brian). He then watches Brian get into a Ford Fiesta motorcar and drive off. He has no paper with him, but makes a mental note of the car's number. Unfortunately, because Arnold twists his ankle shortly afterwards, it takes him three days to get off the moor. As he arrives in a small village, he meets a police officer, Fiona, and tells her the registration number of the car, but little else that is precise about the incident. She makes a note of it, and reads it back to him, but forgets to let him read her note himself. A month later, by which time he has forgotten the registration number, he makes a full statement to the police, describing in detail the circumstances of the incident (but not the number of the car). Brian is arrested a week after the murder, and says little to the police when interviewed. However, he tells his aunt, when she visits him in prison, that he was sick in bed on the day of the alleged crime, and did not leave his house. The trial occurs 10 months later. During the course of cross-examination,

For suggested approaches, please visit the Online Resource Centre

prosecuting Counsel suggests to Brian that he has 'made up' his story about being sick at the time from 'start to finish'.

(a) Will Brian be allowed to adduce the conversation with his aunt to bolster his testimony in court?

(b) Will Arnold be allowed to use the police officer's note to refresh his memory in court?

(c) What use, if any, can Arnold make of the statement he made to the police a month after the incident?

(d) Can defence counsel ask to inspect, and cross-examine on, the contents of Fiona's note-book, or the statement, if it is used by Arnold? What, if any, risks will defence counsel need to be aware of if s/he is permitted to do so?

7. Arthur, a frail 16-year-old, claims that he has been indecently assaulted by a local man named Billy, a nightclub bouncer of 30. Arthur is terrified of Billy, and fears giving evidence in his presence. When he is under severe stress, Arthur tends to stutter uncontrollably.

Advise the prosecution as to how Arthur might give his evidence.

8. Paul is accused of robbery. He tells his solicitor that he is very reluctant to give evidence at trial because the stress of doing so might bring on a 'funny turn'. Additionally, he is concerned that, if he does so, he might say something that Quincy, a fellow suspect and notoriously violent criminal, might object to, producing lethal consequences for Paul when he leaves the court.

Will Paul be able to avoid an adverse inference direction?

10

THE COURSE OF THE EVIDENCE: CROSS-EXAMINATION AND RE-EXAMINATION

Definitions

Collateral question A question that (usually) goes to credit, rather than directly to the issues in the case.

Collateral-finality rule Evidential rule that normally prevents a party from rebutting the denial of a collateral question, posed in cross-examination, even if rebutting evidence is readily available.

Putting the case Confronting an opposing witness with a party's version of events, where the witness's own version is different, so that he (the witness) can deal directly with the party's account of what happened.

---

1. Introduction

As a general rule, all witnesses may be cross-examined by the opposing side to litigation, though there are a few minor exceptions, such as that of a witness who is called purely to formally produce a document. The object of cross-examination is to weaken the opponent's case or the standing of their witnesses, and to elicit facts favourable to that of the cross-examining party. A cross-examining party may ask about any matter, provided it is either relevant to the issues in the case or (with some major limitations) is relevant to the credit of a witness, even if it was not raised during examination in chief. For example, if a confession has been made in a criminal case and a tape of the relevant interview adduced by the prosecution, defence counsel can ask about earlier threats allegedly made to the defendant by officers in a corridor of the police station, outside the interrogation room, even though no mention was made of anything happening in the corridor by the officers concerned. A trial judge will only intervene to prevent cross-examination if the questions being asked are irrelevant or merely vexatious (or are subject to other, specific, statutory controls): *R v Kalia* [1974] 60 Cr App R 200.

The importance of such relatively unfettered cross-examination was stressed by the Court of Appeal in *R v Kepple (John)* [2007] EWCA Crim 1339. In this case, the defendant was accused of a very serious assault. He disappeared on the day of the trial, having given extensive instructions to his solicitor and having also held a conference with counsel at court. The prosecution successfully applied to proceed with the trial in the defendant's absence, which was apparently quite deliberate (this decision was upheld on appeal). Obviously, in this situation, defence counsel could not call evidence, but, nevertheless, sought to put the defendant's case, in some detail, to the prosecution witnesses. At trial, the first instance judge limited defence counsel to putting it in outline, on the basis that the defendant's instructions would not be supported by any formal evidence (given the defendant's absence). On appeal, however, the ensuing conviction was quashed. Although it was stressed that counsel could not give any indication, when cross-examining prosecution witnesses, as to what his absent client's evidence would or might have been, had he been present at trial, he was entitled to put as many relevant details, contained in his instructions, as he wished.

R v Kepple (John) [2007] EWCA Crim 1339, CA

Thomas LJ

In our judgment, counsel for the appellant was entitled to ask questions of witnesses for the prosecution in as much detail as he wished based on his instructions, but without indicating what the appellant's evidence might have been and in the knowledge that he would not be able to call evidence to contradict the answers given. He was entitled to conduct cross examination on this basis in the hope of either showing that his absent client's instructions were accepted by the witnesses or casting doubt upon the coherence or accuracy of their accounts. The ruling, however, had the potential effect of preventing counsel doing this. If it in fact did so, then it rendered counsel's presence at the trial largely nugatory and removed the valuable safeguard provided by that attendance to put the appellant's case based on his instructions. Although this was a case that in the circumstances could properly, as the judge had found, be tried in the absence of the appellant, the effect of the ruling could be thereby to deny the appellant the right to a fair trial which the common law afforded him and which was guaranteed by Article 6.

Putting the Case

Additionally, and very importantly, the cross-examining party must 'put their case', ie put to their opponent's witnesses every part of their own version of events about which those witnesses can speak, even if, as commonly occurs, it simply elicits a denial. For example, in an assault case, where a defendant is claiming self-defence as the basis for his 'not guilty' plea, his counsel must put it to the alleged victim (and chief prosecution witness) that he (for example) threw the first punch or ran at the accused man with a weapon in his hand.

Failure to do this amounts to a tacit acceptance of the evidence given by the opposing witness during their examination in chief, and prevents advocates from basing their case on a contradictory version of events, or from attacking the version given in examination in chief, in their closing speech: *R v Bircham* [1972] Crim LR 430. In *Bircham*, the Court of Appeal approved a trial judge's intervention when defence counsel, in a wounding case, suggested in his closing speech, and for the very first time, that the injury might have been inflicted by a co-defendant or a prosecution witness. Nevertheless, this rule is interpreted with some flexibility, especially in the summary courts or where a litigant is unrepresented. Thus, magistrates do not have to accept unchallenged evidence as true: *O'Connell v Adams* [1973] RTR 150.

The requirement of putting their case extends to defence counsel who intend to suggest that a co-defendant has not given truthful evidence. In such a situation counsel must make it plain in his cross-examination of the co-defendant that his evidence is not accepted and make clear in what respects this is so. In the absence of such cross-examination, it would be a trial judge's duty to comment to the jury on the fact that one defendant's case had not been put to the other, even though the two cases were diametrically opposed: *R v Fenlon* [1980] 71 Cr App R 307.

Quite commonly, counsel will initially ask 'non-confrontational' questions during their cross-examination, aimed at eliciting information that is favourable to their client, and which *may* be accepted by the witness, and then put their case to the witness in a more direct manner.

R v Fenlon [1980] 71 Cr App R 307, CA

The Lord Chief Justice

Now, my Lords, I cannot help saying that it seems to me to be absolutely essential to the proper conduct of a case, where it is intended to suggest that a witness is not speaking the truth on a particular point, to direct his attention to the fact by some questions put in cross-examination showing that that imputation is intended to be made, and not to take his evidence and pass it by as a matter altogether unchallenged, and then, when it is impossible for him to explain, as perhaps he might have been able to do if such questions had been put to him, the circumstances which it is suggested indicate that the story he tells ought not to be believed, to argue that he is a witness unworthy of credit. Mr. Goldberg submits that that is a rule which applies to counsel prosecuting on behalf of the Crown. It is his clear duty, he concedes, to put to witnesses the version of events for which he contends, so that they can answer it. But he further submits that it is not the duty of one defendant to put to another defendant his version of events where it differs from the version given by that other defendant. We can see no distinction in principle between the one situation and the other. The basis of the rule, as Lord Herschell pointed out, is to give a witness of whom it is going to be said or suggested that he was not telling the truth an opportunity of explaining and if necessary of advancing further facts in confirmation of the evidence which he has given. There seems to be no reason why there should be any different rule relating to defendants between themselves from that applying to the prosecution *vis-à-vis* the defendant or the defence *vis-à-vis* the prosecution. It is the duty of counsel who intends to suggest that a witness is not telling the truth to make it clear to the witness in cross-examination that he challenges his veracity and to give the witness an opportunity of replying. It need not be done in minute detail, but it is the duty of counsel to make it plain to the witness, albeit he may be a co-defendant, that his evidence is not accepted and in what respects it is not accepted.

Cross-examination as an Evidential Safeguard

Traditionally, common law has reposed considerable confidence in the ability of a properly conducted cross-examination to expose falsehood. This might be done using a variety of mechanisms; for example, asking about inconsistencies in the witness's testimony, exposing any lack of corroborating detail, prompting a nervous response or 'guilty' demeanour from a dishonest witness, etc. To some extent, the Law Commission has shared this faith, identifying the inability of a party to cross-examine an absent witness as the primary justification for the preservation of a hearsay rule in criminal cases. The American nineteenth-century evidence scholar, John Henry Wigmore was even more impressed with its worth, believing it to be 'beyond any doubt the greatest legal engine ever invented for the discovery of truth'. He felt that it was cross-examination rather than trial by jury that was the common law's greatest contribution to improved methods of criminal procedure. Even Jeremy Bentham, a generally iconoclastic jurisprudential philosopher, was confident that it was a 'grand security' against mendacious testimony. However, not everyone has had such faith in the process.

More recently, for example, Professor Langbein, although accepting that cross-examination was the only substantial safeguard against what he saw as the systematic bias inherent in party adduced testimony, also felt it was a 'frail and fitful palliative'. Additionally, because cross-examination allowed much latitude for bullying and other 'truth-defeating' stratagems, he feared that it was frequently the source of fresh distortion when brought to bear against truthful testimony.[1] Such concerns are certainly not new, having been in circulation for over 200 years.

Cross-examination, in its modern form, only fully developed in criminal cases in the last quarter of the eighteenth century. One of its early masters was the barrister William Garrow. Although generally well regarded, it was noted, even in the 1790s, that he sometimes blatantly played to the jury or spectators by indulging in witty repartee with witnesses or by openly ridiculing and disorientating them. One woman famously declared, in the middle of her cross-examination: 'Mr Garrow confuses me so, I do not know what to do.'[2] As a result, some judges of the era held Garrow and similar colleagues in considerable suspicion.

John Langbein, *The Origins of Adversary Criminal Trial* (2003, Oxford University Press) 246–247

The puzzle about the ready acceptance of cross-examination as the guarantor of truth is that contemporaries were well aware how easily cross-examination could be abused for partisan and truth-defeating ends. In 1787 Sir John Hawkins, the prominent London magistrate, expressed the concern that fear of abusive cross-examination had become a deterrent to prosecution. Potential prosecutors worried, said Hawkins, that 'they may be entangled or made to contradict themselves, or each other, in a cross examination, by prisoner's counsel...' In 1819 John Payne Collier spoke of the 'abuses of the Bar' in cross-examining witnesses, which cause truthful testimony to 'be defeated by those who have attained such skill in confusing what is clear, and involving [that is, making complex] what is simple'. Contemporaries knew that the purpose of cross-examination was to win, whether that entailed seeking or distorting the truth.

Other modern observers have been much more critical of the process, and, in particular, have strongly questioned the value of witness demeanour and reaction to questioning as an indication of testimonial veracity, especially when 'unusual' individuals or minority groups and communities are involved. Additionally, it seems that believing oneself to be a 'good judge of character' is a widespread human conceit. The normal results of stress in the courtroom, especially on a witness with a slightly nervous disposition, can easily appear to be, or be portrayed

---

[1] JH Langbein, 'The German Advantage In Civil Procedure' (1985) University of Chicago Law Review, vol 52, no 4, 823–866, at 834.

[2] JH Beattie, 'Garrow for the Defence' (1991) History Today, vol 41, issue 2, 49–53.

as, the symptoms of dishonesty, particularly as the tribunal of fact will have no familiarity with the witness's 'normal' behaviour. By contrast, one of the classic indicia of a psychopathic personality is the ability to lie, in any environment, without evincing signs of anxiety.

In the 1980s, Professor Paul Ekman, after conducting very extensive psychological research on the subject in the United States, concluded that there are almost no conclusive signs of deceit, and that although most people believe they can detect falsehoods, this is not the case in reality. Indeed, when tested in an experimental environment, some subjects' success rate at detecting untruthful testimony was less than what would be achieved by random selection.[3] This is partly because ordinary observers tend to rely on body language as a sign of mendacity, rather than more subconscious and less controllable aspects of communication, such as the pitch of a speaker's voice, which might be more revelatory (though again never conclusive). The following two extracts catch some of the 'flavour' of much recent work on witness psychology in this regard and, in particular, its significance for cross-examination.

Paul Roberts and Adrian Zuckerman, *Criminal Evidence* (2004, Oxford University Press) at 215 and 219

No barrister's memoirs would be complete without a good sprinkling of anecdotes recounting how through skilful cross-examination the heroic advocate was able to expose his opponent's main witness as a liar, or at least to reveal some crucial gap or inconsistency in the witness's evidence, thus winning the day for his client.... If cross-examination were truly such a magnificent asset to criminal adjudication, the law's reluctance to dispense with live oral testimony, at least for the phases of proceedings in which evidence is tested rather than merely conveyed, would be entirely understandable. But in recent times cross-examination has attracted a barrage of criticism, to the point where it is now widely regarded as an obstacle, rather than the royal road, to effective forensic fact-finding. These days Wigmore's peroration is more likely to be cited as evidence of the legal profession's collective self-delusion, than as a serious proposition about the best way to discover the truth about past events.... Behavioural science research confirms that potential jurors are frequently influenced by non-verbal cues of veracity. Indeed, many research subjects consider themselves quite accomplished in distinguishing truthfulness from falsehood on the basis of demeanour. Unfortunately, these same studies show that such confidence is largely misplaced.

Marcus Stone, 'Instant Lie Detection? Demeanour and Credibility in Criminal Trials' [1991] Crim LR 821–830 (Extract)

There is no sound basis for assessing credibility from demeanour. There is no known physiological connection between the brain processes of a lying person and any bodily or vocal signs. Also, psychological research confirms that there are no specific physical signs of lying, although there are physical expressions of emotions, including anxiety. Bodily or vocal emotional clues to sincerity in normal relationships tend to be neutralised in court. Witnesses are strangers. They are controlled, can only answer questions and give edited testimony. Witnesses tend to be inhibited and to lose their spontaneity. The demeanour of witnesses tends to be flattened and sterilised so that it has

---

[3] M Stone, 'Instant Lie Detection? Demeanour and Credibility in Criminal Trials' [1991] Crim LR 821–830 at 823–824.

minimal, if any, value for assessing credibility. Anxiety or relaxation, even if detected correctly, cannot be relied on to indicate veracity. Truthful witnesses may be anxious, and liars may be, or seem to be, relaxed. Evidence is evaluated holistically by integrating all of it from every angle. This includes assessing witnesses' personalities, characters and motives, as well as objective analysis of evidence, ie its consistency and probability. Any significance of demeanour for veracity, would, at best, be relatively minor in this context. Courts should refrain from practising 'instant lie detection' from the demeanour of a single witness. This should never be the basis of crucial decisions, particularly convictions.

Even strong supporters of the adversarial system occasionally express reservations about the merits of cross-examination, at least in certain situations, as the following extract from a newspaper editorial, published after the collapse of the criminal trial in a notorious child murder case, suggests.

'Truth and Justice', editorial in the *Daily Telegraph* on the Damilola Taylor case, 28 April 2002

...one of the strengths of the adversarial system of justice is that the prosecution's evidence is tested in as strong a way possible. If the jury is not convinced that the evidence passes those tests beyond reasonable doubt, then it is their duty to acquit. The jury was not convinced in this case, largely, it seems, because the 14-year-old girl given the pseudonym 'Bromley' performed so badly in the witness box. Bromley was the only person who claimed to have seen the killing of Damilola Taylor. In the course of an aggressive, six-day cross examination by defence barristers—who, as is their right under the adversarial system, gave her no quarter whatever—she was shown to have told lies. Those lies destroyed her credibility. When her credibility collapsed, so did the whole prosecution case.... It seems extraordinary that no one from the CPS made a serious effort before the trial to test Bromley's evidence, or at least to inquire about her ability to withstand what would inevitably be extremely intrusive and aggressive questioning.... The destruction of Bromley in the witness box by the accused boys' QCs has been widely thought to demonstrate that her whole testimony was fabricated. That conclusion, of course, is not warranted: that Bromley was lying about something in particular does not show that she was lying about everything. What is true is that her experience demonstrates that the adversarial system may not be the best way of getting at the truth in cases where child witnesses come from the same milieu as those they accuse. Witness Bromley was impoverished in every sense: intellectually, educationally, even morally. The problem is, it is almost impossible to find anyone who is part of the gang-culture that dominates the council estates of London who is not impoverished in that way. That presents a profound difficulty in the way of prosecuting the criminals such as those who ended the life of Damilola Taylor, and who are busy ruining the lives of thousands of other children. The gangs can intimidate most of those who have knowledge of their crimes into silence. Their barristers can destroy the credibility of those who decide to testify against them.

 Pause for reflection

Do you feel that you can normally tell when someone is being untruthful?

Cross-examination in Person

Generally speaking, a defendant always has the right to conduct his own defence in person, without the assistance of a lawyer, though this is very rare in practice (minor criminal matters, being tried summarily, apart). A major exception to this general rule occurs with regard to the cross-examination of complainants in sexual offence cases, certain 'protected' witnesses (mainly but not solely children in sexual cases) and, at the court's discretion, some other types of witness in a criminal trial.

Pause for reflection

Do you feel that a defendant should ever be forbidden to confront his accuser in person?

No person accused of a sexual offence may cross-examine a complainant either in connection with that offence, or any other offence, of whatever nature, with which the accused is charged at the same time, as a result of s. 34 of the Youth Justice and Criminal Evidence Act 1999 (YJCEA 1999). Thus, an alleged burglar who raped the occupant of a house and is then charged with both rape and burglary cannot cross-examine the complainant about the burglary. This provision was introduced after public concern that some defendants appeared to be conducting long, drawn out cross-examinations, with a view to humiliating or intimidating the complainants whose allegations had brought them to court, rather than to elicit information. In these situations, the defendant will be required to appoint counsel (whether a barrister or solicitor advocate) to conduct the cross-examination. If he fails to do so, under s. 38(4) of the same statute, the court may appoint a lawyer to cross-examine the complainant on his behalf. However, under s. 39 of the Act, if the defendant is prevented from cross-examining the complainant in person, the judge must give the jury a warning to ensure that the accused is not prejudiced by the procedure.

Additionally, s. 35 of the statute affords similar protection to so-called 'protected witnesses' with regard to certain types of (mainly sexual) offences.

Section 35 of the YJCEA 1999, Child complainants and other child witnesses (partial extract)

(1) No person charged with an offence to which this section applies may in any criminal proceedings cross-examine in person a protected witness, either—

    (a) in connection with that offence, or

    (b) in connection with any other offence (of whatever nature) with which that person is charged in the proceedings.

(2) For the purposes of subsection (1) a 'protected witness' is a witness who—

    (a) either is the complainant or is alleged to have been a witness to the commission of the offence to which this section applies, and

    (b) either is a child or falls to be cross-examined after giving evidence in chief (whether wholly or in part)—

        (i) by means of a video recording made (for the purposes of section 27) at a time when the witness was a child, or

        (ii) in any other way at any such time. . . .

It should also be noted that, under s. 36(2) of the YJCEA 1999, a defendant can be prevented from cross-examining a particular witness, in person, for any offence (not just a sexual crime), if the court concludes that it would improve the quality of the witness's evidence and is not contrary to the interests of justice. Thus, and for example, if a wife in a serious domestic violence case were to find that she was so intimidated by her husband that she could not testify properly if he questioned her in person, this could be prevented, and counsel appointed in his stead, even if the process of cross-examination had already started.

Leading Questions Permitted

During cross-examination, the opposing (ie cross-examining) party can ask leading questions of a witness, though they should not be in a form that is an invitation to comment or argument, as the aim of cross-examination is to elicit facts: *R v Baldwin* [1925] 18 Cr App R 173. Thus, and for example, in a domestic violence case in which it is claimed that a husband had beaten his wife, but where the accused is alleging self-defence, prosecution counsel, having suggested that the defendant struck his spouse, should not ask a question such as 'that was not a very manly thing to do was it?' However, evidence that is inadmissible as part of examination in chief, does not become admissible if put in cross-examination. Thus, if prosecution counsel has not been allowed to adduce a defendant's confession as part of the Crown's case he cannot normally ask questions about it when cross-examining the defendant: *R v Treacy* [1944] 2 All ER 229. Additionally, it should be noted that, in some situations, the cross-examining party cannot adduce evidence to rebut a denial of his questions by the witness, even if it is readily available, because of the 'collateral question' rule.

2. The Collateral-Finality Rule

Introduction

The right to call a witness, to contradict the evidence given by an earlier one, is limited by the rule on 'finality of answer to a collateral question'. By this common law rule, certain types of issue are deemed to be of such collateral interest to the case in hand that a witness will not be allowed to testify to them, if their sole purpose is to contradict another witness who has already given evidence on those matters. Such a rule exists to prevent excessive delay in the trial process and to avoid the confusion that would be engendered by raising a multiplicity of 'side' matters which are not directly relevant to the key issues in a case (and so, whether a defendant is guilty of an offence or a claimant's case has been made out). As Rolfe B observed in *Attorney-General v Hitchcock* (1847) 1 Exch 91, if humans lived for a thousand years, examining such collateral issues in detail might often be warranted, but 'in fact, mankind find[s] it to be impossible'. Where the rule does not apply, a party can rebut a denial by calling evidence, even if it has closed its case (for example, where the prosecution cross-examines a defence witness).

Questions going purely to credit are normally considered to be collateral. As a result, answers given in reply to such questions (usually denials of allegations put to the witness) are treated as final, even if rebutting evidence is readily available to the other party. This does not mean that the opposing party is deemed to accept the answer as true, merely that they cannot pursue the matter any further.

A simple illustration of this rule can be seen in *R v Burke* (1858) Cox CC 44. In this Irish case, it was put to a witness in cross-examination, who had earlier claimed through a translator that he could only speak Irish (very similar to Scottish Gaelic), that he could also speak English perfectly well. When he denied this, the cross-examining party was not allowed to call the evidence of a witness who had heard him speaking English to rebut his denial. Obviously, the trial in question was not about whether a particular witness could speak English or not; consequently, the matter was collateral.

However, the evidence excluded as collateral by the rule's operation can be much more significant than *Burke* might suggest. For an extreme (and borderline) example, consider the Australian negligence case of *Piddington v Bennett and Wood* (1940) 63 CLR 533. In this case, a supposed eye witness to a road accident, who gave important evidence for one of the parties, explained (with some hesitation) his presence at the scene of the incident by saying that he was on his way to a local bank, where he had later conducted some business. At trial, the opposing side was allowed to call a manager from the bank to say that, according to the bank's records, the witness had not conducted any business there that day. On appeal to the Australian High Court, the decision to allow the calling of the bank manager was criticized by a narrow majority of the court, and a retrial, without the bank manager's evidence, was ordered. Dixon J expressly observed that although the evidence going to the witness's credit was clearly important, that alone did not make it admissible. As this case suggests, one problem is that there is often not a neat dividing line between questions that go to credit and those that go to the issues in a trial. In many situations it would probably be more accurate to say that questions that go to *general* credit are normally deemed to be collateral.

Pause for reflection

Was the decision with regard to this evidence 'fair' to the opposing party?

The Test for Distinguishing Collateral Matters

Distinguishing a collateral question from one that goes to issue is not always easy. The traditional approach was set out in *Harris v Tippet* (1811) 2 Camp 637 and reiterated in the important case of *Attorney-General v Hitchcock* (1847) 1 Exch 91, where Pollock CB said that the test as to: '… whether the matter is collateral or not, is this: if the answer of a witness is a matter which you would be allowed on your own part to prove in evidence—if it had such a connection with the issue, that you would be allowed to give it in evidence—then it is a matter on which you may contradict him'. Nevertheless, in the modern era, this test has been described as 'circular'. Thus, in *R v Funderburk* [1990] 90 Cr App R 466, it was noted that: 'If a fact is not collateral then clearly you can call evidence to contradict it, but the so-called test is silent on how you decide whether that fact is collateral.'

In *Funderburk*, the court took a more pragmatic approach to the test, suggesting that the general rule was that rebutting evidence may not be called unless relevant to an issue in the case and that the decision as to whether this was so or not, was largely 'an instinctive one based on the prosecutor's and the Court's sense of fair play rather than any philosophic or analytic process'.

However, this case should not be taken to suggest that there is a total absence of analysis or a general laxity when deciding the question. Initially, when determining the matter, it seems that it is necessary to identify the issues in a case, after which, it appears, a mixture of logic and common sense come into play. Although evidence is relevant and not collateral if it is probative of an issue in the case, this is always a matter of degree. Additionally, it should be noted that, in practice, it seems that the limits are slightly less strict for the defendant in a criminal trial than they are for the prosecution.

Pause for reflection

Is it satisfactory that such an important test is couched in such vague and uncertain terms?

The defendant in *Funderburk* was accused of having sexual intercourse with the 13-year-old daughter of his girlfriend. He claimed that the allegation had been made maliciously. When testifying, the complainant's evidence strongly suggested that her intercourse with the defendant had been the occasion on which she lost her virginity (though she did not say this expressly), mentioning an effusion of blood and having experienced physical pain at the time that it happened. That such intercourse had actually occurred with the accused man would also explain why she was able to give a highly graphic and detailed account of the sexual act, despite her youth.

The defendant wished to put to the complainant that she had admitted, in a statement made to another woman, that she had had sexual intercourse with other boys, of her own age, and, if she denied this allegation, to call the woman to whom the statement had been made to prove it. This, of course, could then explain why she was able to give such a convincing account of intercourse with the accused man, even if it had not occurred; she could simply have been transposing her experiences with the youths to the allegation being made against the accused. At trial, the first instance judge refused to allow this, on the grounds that it was merely collateral. However, on appeal, the ensuing conviction was quashed, as the evidence was not deemed to go purely to credit.

R v Funderburk [1990] 90 Cr App R 466, CA

Henry J

When it came to the detail which she gave it seems clear to us that the transcript shows that the account she gave in her evidence-in-chief of the first of those incidents was a clear and pathetically moving account of the loss of virginity. If that account is true the tears, which we see from the transcript, accompanying the giving of that evidence were wholly unsurprising. Though the loss of virginity was never spelled out by any direct question from the Crown it would, in our judgment, have been superfluous to do so, not only because of the detail the child had gone into, but because the Crown's introductory questions which were cited by the learned judge in his summing-up in relation to the innocence of her previous experiences with her boyfriends. It seems to us very likely that this particular detailed account of that first incident would be the most vivid picture which the jury took with them into their retiring room. Even disregarding the tears and the pathos it was an account of something which only happens once in a lifetime. Accordingly we do not find it surprising that the defence submit that it was necessary for them to challenge that account in order properly to put their defence, namely, a denial that there had been any acts of intercourse between the parties. Unchallenged, the descriptive details could give the account the stamp of truth: detail often adds verisimilitude, and it seems to us that it certainly would have here. But if a detail of such significance is successfully challenged it can destroy both the account and the credit of the witness who gave it. Therefore, it is submitted that this is not a challenge which goes merely to credit but that the disputed questions go directly to the issue and not merely to a collateral fact or, alternatively at least, in the words of Denman's Act, that her account of having lost her virginity on a previous occasion were statements 'inconsistent with her present testimony' made by her 'relative to the subject matter of the indictment'.

Whatever the test's precise definition, in recent decades there have been signs of a slightly more liberal approach being adopted by the courts when deciding whether or not it has been satisfied, and a greater general willingness to allow rebutting evidence to be called, especially in criminal cases. Thus, in *R v Busby* [1985] 75 Cr App R 79, it was suggested that police witnesses for the prosecution were determined to convict the accused, had fabricated an oral confession to a handling charge allegedly made by him, and had also threatened a potential defence witness to prevent him from testifying. Both allegations were rejected by the officers. The defence sought to call the threatened witness to rebut their denial of having made such a threat. Counsel for the prosecution objected and the evidence was excluded by the trial judge on the ground that it went solely to the credit of the police officers, not to the issue in the case, under the collateral matter rule.

Nevertheless, the Court of Appeal quashed the ensuing conviction on the basis that the defence should have been allowed to rebut the police officers' denial. This was because it actually went to a fact in issue; if it was true that the officers concerned had threatened a defence witness against testifying it would have supported the defendant's case that they were also prepared to go to improper lengths to secure a conviction, so evidencing a willingness to invent evidence against the accused (such as fabricating a confession). It was, therefore, relevant to an issue that had to be tried. This seems at variance to some older decisions, and, in effect, to be substituting 'substantial relevance' as the test for allowing rebuttal. However, and problematically, *Busby* can also be explained as an example of 'bias' and so an exception to the collateral rule (see below). Further complicating matters, it has also been suggested that the case created a new exception, specifically with regard to police officers willing to go to improper lengths to secure a conviction, again limiting its impact on the general rule.

In *R v Marsh* [1986] 83 Cr App R 165, a (slightly) more obviously liberal approach was followed, one that cannot be quite so readily explained under an established exception. This case involved an assault where the defendant was claiming self-defence. During the course of cross-examination, it was put to the alleged victim and chief prosecution witness, a man named Armstrong, that he had, on previous occasions, uttered threats towards the appellant. This he denied doing. Subsequently, the defendant sought to call a witness to give evidence of the making of the threats that Armstrong had denied when they were put to him. After argument, the first instance judge ruled the evidence to be inadmissible on the ground that it went solely to the credit of Armstrong. On appeal, however, the conviction was quashed and the judge's decision criticized. It was held that the threats went to the root of the issue at trial, namely, the question as to who was the aggressor in the incident.

In *R v Nagrecha* [1997] 2 Cr App R 401, the defendant was accused of indecently assaulting one of the women who worked in the restaurant that he ran, on her first night in his employment. His defence was a simple denial that any such incident had occurred. The complainant had earlier made allegations of indecent behaviour against other men, including one of her managers in an earlier employment, which had subsequently not been pursued. When these allegations were put to her, she denied making them. The question then arose as to whether these denials could be rebutted by calling evidence from, for example, the manager who had been the subject of her earlier complaint. At trial, the defence application was refused, on the ground that the evidence went merely to credit and so was collateral. On appeal, it was held that it went to the issue in the case, which was whether the allegation been entirely fabricated, and so should have been allowed.

R v Nagrecha [1997] 2 Cr App R 401, CA

Rose LJ

In our judgment, the answer to this appeal is, in the light of the authorities to which we have referred, that the judge ought to have permitted the defence to lead evidence from Mr Lee in the light of the complainant's denial in cross-examination. Such evidence went not merely to credit, but to the heart of the case, in that it bore on the crucial issue as to whether or not there had been any indecent assault. As to that matter, only the complainant and the appellant were able to give evidence. In our judgment, that being so, the learned judge ought to have permitted the evidence to be called because it might well have led the jury to take a different view of the complainant's evidence.

More recently, in *R v Robinson (Paul Stephen)* [2004] EWCA Crim 2726, the defendant was accused of indecently assaulting the 13-year-old daughter of a friend after meeting her in the street near a bus stop on a certain day, while she was excluded from school. The defence case was that none of this had happened, and that, in reality, no such meeting took place. The complainant explained her presence at the bus stop by saying that she had gone there to talk to, and see off, a youth named Craig Burrows. It was put to her that at no point during the relevant week had she seen Burrows at the bus stop. When she denied this, an application was made to the trial judge to call Burrows to rebut her denial and to say that he had not seen the complainant at the bus stop during the relevant period. The defence took the view that this was an important issue because, if the complainant's evidence was wrong about seeing Burrows at the bus stop there was serious doubt as to whether the basis of her evidence with regard to seeing the defendant there was correct. The trial judge refused the application. The Court of Appeal, however, concluded that his decision was mistaken, as the presence or absence of Burrows at the bus stop went to an important issue in the case.

R v Robinson (Paul Stephen) [2004] EWCA Crim 2726, CA

Scott Baker LJ

The judge dealt very peremptorily with the matter. The Crown were not called on for any assistance. He simply said: 'It goes to credit, I am not allowing it, thank you.' It had, in our judgment, become clear, when the judge made this ruling, that it was a key issue in the case whether the complainant had been in Netherseal or Main Street at around 8.30 on the morning of Tuesday 7th May. She said that she went there specifically to talk, among others, to Craig Burrows and that he was there. His evidence, had he been allowed to give it, would, as we understand it, have been that he never saw KA at the bus stop at any time during that week.... The question is: does the evidence go to an issue in the case? It may be that in answering that question the judge has to exercise his judgment in forming a conclusion. But, once he has concluded that the evidence does go to an issue in the case, there is, as we understand it, no discretion, the matter has to be admitted. We would add, of course, a relevant issue in the case. In our judgment, the evidence of Craig Burrows in this case did plainly go to an issue in the case, namely, whether the complainant was or was not at the place where the offence is alleged to have occurred at the time that she alleged that it did occur.... In our judgment, the failure of the judge to allow this evidence in before the jury makes the conviction unsafe. In these circumstances, the appeal against conviction must be allowed on this ground and accordingly the conviction quashed.

3. Exceptions to the Collateral-Finality Rule

Introduction

Irrespective of the general rule, there are several well-recognized exceptions, both statutory and at common law, whereby answers to what are clearly collateral issues *can* be rebutted by the calling of further evidence. In *Funderburk,* the Court of Appeal suggested that these included situations in which a witness denied the presence of bias, previous convictions, a general reputation for untruthfulness or medical causes that would have affected his ability to give reliable testimony. At first sight, ss. 4 and 5 of the Criminal Procedure Act 1865, which deal with previous inconsistent statements, might also be thought to be statutory exceptions to the general rule. However, as will be seen, this is not the case.

Previous Convictions

In both civil and criminal cases, where a witness denies that s/he has a previous criminal conviction, proof of that conviction can be adduced as a result of s. 6 of the (misleadingly named) Criminal Procedure Act 1865. This provides that: 'A witness may be questioned as to whether he has been convicted of any felony or misdemeanour, and upon being so questioned, if he either denies or does not admit the fact, or refuses to answer, it shall be lawful for the cross examining party to prove such conviction.' Under the provision, this can be done by adducing a certificate of conviction from the relevant court.

However, it should be remembered that in civil cases such questions can normally only be put if the previous convictions are not 'spent' for the purposes of the Rehabilitation of Offenders Act 1974, as a result of s. 4 of that statute. In criminal matters, the court will now first have to be satisfied that such cross-examination is permissible under s. 100 of the CJA 2003 (see chapter 5). Prior to the advent of these provisions, the situation was rather different. Thus, in the civil case of *Clifford v Clifford* [1961] 3 All ER 231, Cairns J felt that it had 'never been doubted' that a conviction for any type of offence could be put to a witness by way of cross-examination to credit, even though it did not concern a crime of dishonesty. This is no longer invariably the case.

 Cross-reference Box

Traditionally, at common law, there were very few constraints as to the allegations of previous misconduct (including that of having earlier criminal convictions) that could be put to a non-defendant witness with a view to undermining their credit. Today, the situation is much more regulated, as a result of statutory intervention. For more on s. 100 of the CJA 2003, and s. 4 of the Rehabilitation of Offenders Act 1974, go to pp. 221–230.

Bias

If it is suggested that a witness is biased in favour of one of the parties to litigation, or in a relationship from which bias might be inferred (even if, in reality, it may not be present), and the witness denies that this is the case, the presence of bias may be shown by the use of extrinsic evidence. Normally, the examiner will ask the witness about the alleged bias, and, if he denies it, will be allowed to call the testimony of another person to rebut it. Such cases might typically include those in which a witness, after giving evidence favourable to one party, denies that they are a relative of, or romantically involved with, that person. For example, in *Thomas v David* (1836) 7 C & P 350, a witness's denial that she was the lover of the party calling her could be rebutted by extrinsic evidence.

However, bias is also interpreted rather more broadly than such an example might suggest. A willingness to go to improper lengths on the part of the witness, so as to secure a certain result in litigation, might also be deemed to be indicative of its presence. Thus, in *R v Phillips* [1936] 26 Cr App R 17, the defendant was accused of committing incest with his 12-year-old daughter. This child, and her young sister, gave evidence for the Crown. The defendant claimed that the girls were fabricating their allegations, having been schooled to do so by their mother. When it was put to the children that, with regard to an earlier (and similar) allegation, they had later told other people that they had merely repeated what their mother had told them to say, rather than what was true, their denials to the allegation were taken as final by the trial judge. On appeal, this was held to have been wrong; rebutting evidence should have been allowed as it showed bias.

Similarly, in *R v Mendy* [1977] 64 Cr App R 17, it was held that a witness's improper interest in the outcome of a case might also be proved as a form of bias. In this case, during the trial of a female defendant, a man was seen making a careful note of the prosecution evidence from the public gallery. He was later seen conferring with the defendant's husband, who was also a defence witness, and who had been waiting outside court to give evidence. When this was put to him in cross-examination, the husband denied it, and the prosecution was then allowed to call evidence (a court official who had witnessed the incident) to rebut his denial. His behaviour indicated a willingness to go to improper lengths to support the defendant's case. However, and unsurprisingly, evidence that someone has been offered a bribe, without accepting it, is not evidence of bias and does not allow for rebutting evidence: *Attorney-General v Hitchcock* (1847) 1 Exch 91. It is *accepting* a bribe that indicates bias.

R v Mendy [1977] 64 Cr App R 4, CA

Lane LJ

The truth of the matter is, as one would expect, that the rule is not all-embracing. It has always been permissible to call evidence to contradict a witness's denial of bias or partiality towards one of the parties and to show that he is prejudiced so far as the case being tried is concerned. Pollock C.B. in Attorney-General v. Hitchcock (1847) 1 Ex. 9 puts the matter thus at p. 101: 'It is no disparagement to a man that a bribe is offered to him; it may be a disparagement to the man who makes the offer. If therefore the witness is asked about the fact and denies it or if he is asked whether he said so and so and he denies it he cannot be contradicted as to what he has said. Lord Stafford's Case [(1680) 7 How.St.Tr. 1400] was totally different. There the witness himself had been implicated in offering a bribe to some other person. That immediately affected him as proving that he had acted the part of a suborner for the purpose of preventing the truth. In that case the evidence was to show that the witness was offered a bribe in a particular case, and the object was to show that he was so far affected towards the party accused as to be willing to adopt any corrupt course in order to carry out his purposes.' In Lord Stafford's Case, (*supra*) the evidence was admitted. Those words apply almost precisely to the facts in the present case. The witness was prepared to cheat in order to deceive the jury and help the defendant. The jury were entitled to be apprised of that fact.

Medical Causes which Affect the Reliability of Testimony

Medical (or other) evidence may be called to rebut the denial of a suggestion, put in cross-examination, that a witness's testimony is unreliable due to their suffering from an inherent physical or mental defect. As Lord Pearce noted in *Toohey v Metropolitan Police Commissioner* [1965] AC 595, human testimony shares the frailties of the witnesses who provide it; these will include the effects of prejudice, self-interest and imagination. However, these are matters for the jury to assess as best it can, aided by cross-examination and its own common sense. Nevertheless: '…when a witness through physical (in which I include mental) disease or abnormality is not capable of giving a true or reliable account to the jury, it must surely be allowable for medical science to reveal this hidden fact to them'. As this judgment makes clear, such conditions must affect a witness's *ability* to give reliable testimony, not their *willingness* to do so (the latter normally being a matter for the tribunal of fact to assess).

Cross-reference Box

The courts are traditionally reluctant to receive opinion evidence on the credibility of witnesses, feeling that judges, jurors and magistrates are as well placed as any expert to determine this, and that allowing expert opinion on such topics will undermine the role of the tribunal of fact. For a more detailed discussion of this general rule, and the limited exceptions to it, go to pp. 474–488.

Thus, it will include evidence of a witness's capacity to accurately observe events. For example, if it is put to an identification witness, who claims to have made out a defendant at some considerable distance, that he has such poor eyesight that he could not have seen clearly at that range, and the witness denies having such defective vision, evidence might be called to rebut his denial (perhaps from his optician or a friend). A similar situation would occur with a deaf witness who claimed to have overheard a whispered conversation.

However, this exception also extends to mental defects that affect the ability of a witness to give reliable testimony. The facts of *Toohey* itself provide an example of this. In this case, the alleged victim and chief prosecution witness in a street robbery had been examined by a police surgeon, shortly after the incident. This doctor had formed the impression that the complainant was in a state of acute hysteria; nevertheless, at trial, the defendant was not allowed to adduce evidence to suggest that the alleged victim's hysterical personality and condition might have led him to imagine that the defendants were attacking him, when, as they claimed, they were actually trying to assist him. On appeal, the first instance judge's decision was held to have been wrong; the evidence should have been admitted. Again, the mental factor must affect ability, not willingness, to give reliable testimony. That a witness is a pathological liar is normally a matter for the jury to determine unaided.

Toohey v Metropolitan Police Commissioner [1965] AC 595, HL

Lord Pearce

But when a witness through physical (in which I include mental) disease or abnormality is not capable of giving a true or reliable account to the jury, it must surely be allowable for medical science to reveal this vital hidden fact to them. If a witness purported to give evidence of something which he believed that he had seen at a distance of 50 yards, it must surely be possible to call the evidence of an oculist to the effect that the witness could not possibly see anything at a greater distance than 20 yards, or the evidence of a surgeon who had removed a cataract from which the witness was suffering at the material time and which would have prevented him from seeing what he thought he saw. So, too, must it be allowable to call medical evidence of mental illness which makes a witness incapable of giving reliable evidence, whether through the existence of delusions or otherwise.

A Reputation for Untruthfulness

A witness's evidence can also be rebutted where s/he has a 'reputation for untruthfulness' and denies it when this is put to him/her in cross-examination. This long-standing rule is rather obscure and very rarely applied in practice, but was referred to by Lord Pearce in *Toohey v Metropolitan Police Commissioner* [1965] AC 595, who also noted in that case that none of the judges or the counsel before them could recall personally seeing it invoked. Its ambit and limitations were also discussed by Edmund Davies LJ in the case of *R v Richardson and Longman* (1969) 1 QB 299. In the modern era it has been preserved as an admissible common law hearsay exception by virtue of s. 118(1) of the CJA 2003 (such evidence must necessarily be founded on hearsay). However, although an individual can give an opinion as to the general reputation for veracity of a witness, and also his own opinion on this subject (based on personal knowledge), he cannot refer to particular incidents of untruthfulness.

Whether the rule is worth preserving is debatable; someone might, in theory, acquire such a 'general reputation' undeservedly, and the fact that specific incidents cannot be adduced would make it difficult for the tribunal of fact to determine whether this was the case. Although not commonly encountered in practice, in *R v Bogie* [1992] Crim LR 302, several witnesses were allowed to testify to a rape complainant's general reputation for untruthfulness. They included a former employer, who was called to say that she was a liar and often behaved like a frustrated actress.

R v Richardson and Longman (1969) 1 QB 299, CA

Edmund Davies LJ

The legal position may be thus summarised: 1. A witness may be asked whether he has knowledge of the impugned witness's general reputation for veracity and whether (from such knowledge) he would believe the impugned witness's sworn testimony. 2. The witness called to impeach the credibility of a previous witness may also express his individual opinion (based upon his personal knowledge) as to whether the latter is to be believed upon his oath and is not confined to giving evidence merely of general reputation. 3. But whether his opinion as to the impugned witness's credibility be based simply upon the latter's general reputation for veracity or upon his personal knowledge, the witness cannot be permitted to indicate during his examination in chief the particular facts, circumstances or incidents which formed the basis of his opinion, although he may be cross-examined as to them. This method of attacking a witness's veracity, though ancient, is used with exceeding rarity. Nevertheless it was sought to be made use of in the present case by Mr. Lassman who appeared for Longman. He called a Dr. Hitchens, a geologist, who occupied with his wife a flat immediately above that of Mrs. Clemence, and the material part of the transcript reads in this way:

> 'Q. Are you aware, doctor, of her reputation for veracity?
> A. 'In a general way, yes.'
> Q. 'Would you believe that lady on her oath?'

4. Impeachment by Prior Inconsistent Statement

Introduction

A witness's credibility can be impeached by showing that he has made an earlier statement, whether written or oral, that is inconsistent with his present testimony. This is regulated by ss. 4 and 5 of the Criminal Procedure Act 1865 (which provisions also apply to civil matters). Section 4 provides that: 'If a witness, upon cross-examination as to a former statement made by him relative to the subject matter of the indictment or proceeding, and inconsistent with his present testimony, does not distinctly admit that he has made such statement, proof may be given that he did in fact make it; but before such proof can be given the circumstances of the supposed statement, sufficient to designate the particular occasion, must be mentioned to the witness, and he must be asked whether or not he has made such statement.'

The wording of s. 4, 'former statement', is broad enough to cover both written and oral statements, but, because the former have their own dedicated provision in s. 5, it is normally used to deal with oral statements. Section 5 provides that a witness may be cross-examined as to previous statements made by him: '...in writing, or reduced into writing, relative to the subject matter of the indictment or proceeding, without such writing being shown to him; but if it is intended to contradict such witness by the writing, his attention must, before such contradictory proof can be given, be called to those parts of the writing which are to be used for the purpose of so contradicting him'. The wording of s. 5, 'previous statements made by him in writing', means, of course, that it is limited to written statements.

Before a prior inconsistent statement can be adduced under s. 4, a foundation must be laid. In particular, the witness must be told the substance of the alleged statement, the time, the place, and the person to whom it was made. He must then be given a chance to deny having made the statement, or to explain away any apparent inconsistency. Only after all this has been done may the prior inconsistent statement be introduced into evidence (by calling the person to whom it was made). With regard to s. 5, before the statement can be formally proved, the witness's attention must be drawn to the parts of the written statement that will be used to contradict him. Thus, a witness can be asked whether he made a (written) statement to the police on a certain date and his attention drawn expressly to the relevant passages. Under s. 5, the trial judge can also, at any time, require the production of the written document for his own inspection.

As an example as to how s. 4 might operate in practice, consider the following hypothetical case. Albert is in a bank when a robber enters with a shotgun and forces a cashier to hand over £10,000 before fleeing. Subsequently, Albert purports to identify the robber as a well-known local man called Boris, making a statement to the police, in which he says that he got a good view of the robber and easily recognized him. A few days later, however, while drinking at the bar of the 'Bull and Bush', Albert tells the publican, Charles, that he was so frightened when the man came into the bank that he threw himself to the ground and 'didn't see a thing'. At trial, after Albert has testified to identifying Boris, and has been asked if he remembers making a statement to the landlord of the 'Bull and Bush' public-house and denied doing so, Charles can be called to give evidence of Albert's previous inconsistent statement.

In *R v Derby Magistrates' Court ex parte B* [1995] 3 WLR 681 it was held that ss. 4 and 5 of the Criminal Procedure Act 1865, presupposed that the statements were already available to the cross-examiner, so that if the witness denied making them or denied their inconsistency they could then be proved in evidence; as a result, where the cross-examiner did not have the previous statements to put to the witness they could not be admitted under the 1865 Act.

R v Derby Magistrates' Court ex parte B [1995] 3 WLR 681, HL

Lord Taylor CJ

It is therefore necessary to consider the statutory provisions governing the use which can be made of previous inconsistent statements. They are to be found in the Criminal Procedure Act 1865 ('Lord Denman's Act').... It was contended by Mr. Goldberg for the stepfather that section 4 applies only to oral statements and section 5 deals with written statements.... Although section 5 clearly refers only to written statements, we see no reason to confine section 4 to oral statements. Its wording does not so confine it and its content is apt to cover statements both oral and written.... Section 4 allows proof that a previous inconsistent statement was made if that is not distinctly admitted. Section 5 additionally permits (a) cross examination of a witness as to a previous inconsistent written statement without showing him or her the statement and (b) contradiction of the witness's testimony by putting the previous statement to him. If he denies making it, the statement can be proved: section 4. Even if he admits making the statement but adheres to evidence inconsistent with it, the statement, or such part of it as the judge thinks proper, may be put before the jury: section 5, and see Reg. v. Beattie (1989) 89 Cr. App. R. 302. . . . Lord Denman's Act contemplates cross-examining counsel having the inconsistent statement (e.g. a deposition) in his hand so that the procedure which may culminate in the document becoming admissible can be begun.

Not an Exception to the Collateral-Finality Rule

At first sight, it might appear that the adduction of an earlier statement under the 1865 Act could, in some circumstances, result in another, statutory, exception to the finality of answer to a collateral question rule. If a witness was asked a question on a collateral issue, and the opposing side was allowed to adduce a previous inconsistent statement under ss. 4 or 5 to rebut his answer, this would certainly be the case. However, in *Funderburk*, the Court of Appeal made it clear that the wording of these two sections and, in particular, their use of the phrase 'relative to the subject matter of the indictment or proceeding', meant that the sections only applied where the inconsistent statement itself related to a matter in issue; thus, extrinsic proof of a prior inconsistent statement is *not* allowed if the statement involves only a *collateral* matter.

To take the facts in *R v Burke* (1858) Cox CC 44 as an illustration, if the witness who declared that he could not speak English at trial had made an earlier, inconsistent, statement in which he said 'I can speak English perfectly', this would not be admissible, because, whether he spoke English or not was not a fact in issue, and so not 'relative to the subject matter' of the proceedings, unlike the hypothetical identification case considered above.

The Status of Previous Inconsistent Statements

At common law, if a previous inconsistent statement was put to a witness by opposing counsel under ss. 4 or 5 of the 1865 Act (and its making either admitted or proved), it went merely to their credibility, in the same way that a previous inconsistent statement put to a hostile witness under s. 3 of the same Act did, and was not evidence in its own right, *unless* the witness expressly accepted or adopted it as true. Judges, jurors and magistrates were not allowed to choose between the witness's present evidence and the differing version given in the earlier statement: *R v Golder* [1960] 1 WLR 1169. However, the common law position no longer applies in either civil or criminal matters.

In civil cases, under s. 6(1) of the Civil Evidence Act 1995, such statements are evidence of the truth of their contents, ie they are exceptions to the hearsay rule. Similarly, in criminal cases, by dint of s. 119 of the CJA 2003, previous inconsistent statements, the making (but not the truth) of which has either been admitted by a witness, or proved against a witness pursuant to the 1865 Act, become evidence of any matter stated in them of which oral evidence by the witness would also be admissible.

Cross-reference Box

Under the common law hearsay rule out of court statements could not be tendered for the truth of their contents. For more on this doctrine and its exceptions, go to chapter 6.

In *Johnson v R* [2007] EWCA Crim 1651, a defendant's account to a probation officer as to his involvement in an offence (he had pleaded guilty and then been allowed to change his plea), which was quite inconsistent with the account that he gave at trial, was held to be admissible under s. 119 of the 2003 Act (and, as the Court of Appeal went on to conclude, quite properly not excluded under s. 126 of the Act or on the grounds of fairness).

 Pause for reflection

Should information provided to probation officers be admissible in a criminal trial?

This change in criminal matters also extends to inconsistent statements made by absent witnesses whose evidence is tendered under one of the hearsay exceptions contained in the 2003 statute. Thus, if an out of court statement is given as evidence pursuant to s. 116 of the 2003 Act (because its maker is unavailable due to death, illness, etc.), its maker's credibility can be challenged by adducing any other statement that s/he has made that is inconsistent with the statement admitted: s. 124(2)(c). Obviously, this will show that s/he contradicted him/herself. However, under s. 119(2), the inconsistent statement will also be evidence of the truth of its contents.

For example, if a statement made by an eye witness, who has since died, to the effect that a murder was carried out by a man wearing a bright red jersey, is adduced pursuant to s. 116(2)(a), an inconsistent statement that he made to another party to the effect that the killer was wearing a dark green anorak can be adduced under s. 124(2)(c), and will then be evidence that the killer was so attired. However, and very significantly, s. 119 of the new Act does not alter in any way the initial circumstances in which such statements become admissible.

Despite this theoretical change in status, the courts have shown some caution about the use of previous inconsistent statements as evidence in its own right. Thus, in the rather unusual case of *R v Coates* [2007] Crim LR 887, the complainant in a rape case had given evidence at trial that may, technically, have allowed a previous statement that she had made as to what occurred on the night in question to be adduced under s. 119. At a Court Martial, the court used this version to convict the defendant, rather than the somewhat different account that she gave at the hearing itself. However, the Court of Appeal held that statement should not have been admitted in the context of overall fairness, given the complainant's in-court testimony, which was fundamentally different (ie it should have been excluded under s. 78 of the PCEA 1984), and quashed the ensuing conviction.

5. The Cross-examination of Sexual Offence Complainants

Introduction

In all trials, especially (but not solely) those conducted in an accusatorial and adversarial criminal justice system, there exists the potential for grave attacks to be made on the dignity of a witness. While 'putting their case' advocates must regularly make extremely unpleasant allegations. This is often done by suggesting that witnesses have fabricated their evidence and any earlier allegations that they may have made to the police. Given the inherent nature of the crime, this is likely to be especially unpleasant in rape and sexual assault cases, particularly where consent is the key issue to be decided at trial. The dynamics of such trials often lead to exceptionally personal questioning: 'Precisely how did he remove your knickers?'

However, in recent years, steps have been taken to ameliorate the unenviable situation in which the complainant in a sexual offence case finds her/himself (though the apparent level of reporting of such crimes, and the ensuing conviction rates, remain depressingly low). The most straightforward of these is a statutory restriction on defendants in such cases from cross-examining complainants in person (see above). More difficult, have been attempts at constraining cross-examination about complainants' sexual history.

Cross-examination on Complainant Sexual History

The last two centuries have seen acute tensions between two competing aims when it comes to sexual offence trials. On the one hand, there is a need to protect the dignity and feelings of the complainant, on the other, it is necessary to admit evidence and questioning that might help to establish a defendant's innocence. Such a conflict does not usually occur where the complainant has been attacked by a total stranger, who has jumped out from the shadows. Instead, it normally happens in situations where the forensic evidence is consistent with either consensual intercourse or rape, involves people who have some previous social knowledge of each other (if only transiently), and which requires the trial jury to make an assessment of the witnesses' likely veracity.

Prior to 1976, common law normally allowed questions relating to a complainant's sexual history with other men to be asked, on the basis that they went to her credit (ie a collateral question to the issues in the trial). However, the complainant's answer to these questions, even if it was not accepted as true by opposing counsel, was usually final (the rule as to finality of answer to a collateral question) and the question could not be pursued once an answer had been received, even if cogent rebutting evidence was readily available. Thus, if a complainant denied having had a boyfriend on a previous occasion, it was not normally permissible for the defence to call the boyfriend to give testimony proving the relationship. Otherwise, as Kelly CB remarked in *R v Holmes* (1871) LR 1 CCR 334, the whole history of the complainant's life might be gone into; this would: '...not only involve a multitude of collateral cases, but an enquiry into matters as to which the prosecutrix might be wholly unprepared, and so work injustice'.

Even at common law, however, the courts felt that some questions about third party sexual experience not only went to the witness's credit, but also went directly to the issue of the defendant's innocence or guilt. As such, they were not collateral and, as a result, the defendant could adduce rebutting evidence if such allegations were denied. These included being a prostitute, which was always deemed to be relevant to the issue of consent, and could always be proved on denial: *R v Bashir* [1969] 3 All ER 692. The list of such situations was never finally closed at common law, and as late as 1973 it was suggested that it might extend to a complainant with a history of serious sexual promiscuity alone: *R v Krausz* [1973] 5 Cr App R 466 (though this case was somewhat unusual in its facts). This common law situation ended in 1976.

During the 1960s and 1970s there was a growing level of awareness of the prevalence of rape in England (and many other countries), and an appreciation that it was, for so serious an offence, a very under-reported crime. There was also an increasing degree of concern (though this was certainly not a totally novel worry) that in many cases the trial of rape defendants, especially where consent (as opposed to identity) was in issue, often became, effectively, trials of the complainant and her lifestyle. This would usually be manifest in a humiliating cross-examination about her sexual history with other men. While such cross-examination was, theoretically, advanced as being relevant in some way to the accused man's defence or the complainant's credibility, it was sometimes of no real probative value, but rather motivated by a desire to unfairly prejudice the jury against the complainant. It was felt that a fear of undergoing such an experience, might also, in part, explain the low level of reporting in rape cases. This change in attitudes towards the crime was discussed by Lord Steyn in *R v A* [2002] 1 AC 45.

R v A [2002] 1 AC 45, HL

Lord Steyn

Following the Second World War the general principle of the equality of men and women in all spheres of life has gradually become established. In the aftermath of the sexual revolution of the sixties the autonomy and independence of women in sexual matters has become an accepted norm. It was this change in thinking about women and sex which made possible the decision of the House of Lords in R v R [1992] 1 AC 599 that the offence of rape may be committed by a husband upon his wife. It was a dramatic reversal of old fashioned beliefs. Discriminatory stereotypes which depict women as sexually available have been exposed as an affront to their fundamental rights. Nevertheless, it has to be acknowledged that in the criminal courts of our country, as in others, outmoded beliefs about women and sexual matters lingered on. In recent Canadian jurisprudence they have been described as the discredited twin myths, viz 'that unchaste women were more likely to consent to intercourse and in any event, were less worthy of belief': R v Seaboyer (1991) 83 DLR (4th) 193, 258, 278c, per McLachlin J. Such generalised, stereotyped and unfounded prejudices ought to have no place in our legal system. But even in the very recent past such defensive strategies were habitually employed. It resulted in an absurdly low conviction rate in rape cases. It also inflicted unacceptable humiliation on complainants in rape cases.

Although Parliament rejected the 1975 recommendation of the Heilbron Committee (set up to examine this issue) that questioning on third party sexual history be limited to cases of 'striking similarity' (effectively a 'similar fact' type evidential situation) between the behaviour of the complainant on a previous occasion, with another man, and that in the instant case, it accepted the need for reform. This need was ultimately met by the enactment of s. 2 of the Sexual Offences (Amendment) Act 1976, regulating such cross-examination and evidence. It gave enormous discretion to the trial judge by providing that such questions should not normally be allowed, unless it would be 'unfair' to exclude them. At about the same time, other common law countries introduced equivalent legislation (albeit using different mechanisms to control such evidence).

 Cross-reference Box

The doctrine of 'similar fact' evidence was the now abolished (in criminal matters) common law test for adducing defendant bad character. It only applied in exceptional circumstances. For more on this go to chapter 5 at pp. 190–192.

However, after a few years, some (but by no means all) commentators began to complain that the post-1976 situation was little better than that which had existed at common law, and that the 1976 Act had been 'emasculated' by subsequent judicial interpretation. Several individual decisions by trial judges allowing cross-examination on sexual history, or by the Court of Appeal quashing convictions where permission to conduct such cross-examination had been denied, were heavily criticized.[4] Defence counsel often proved adept at finding 'issues' in a case that would justify adducing sexual history evidence, so that about three-quarters of such applications were ultimately successful. For example, and as an extreme illustration, in *R v SMS* [1992] Crim LR 310 it was suggested that the complainant's sexual history was relevant to whether or not she would have consented to sexual intercourse with a much older man with a wooden leg (allegedly unlikely in a virgin, more probable in a sexually very experienced female).

A variety of alternative (to s. 2) solutions were proposed; these often involved more precise and rigid limitations on the situations in which a judge would be allowed to admit evidence or permit questioning on a complainant's sexual history (very broadly, the approach adopted by the Heilbron Committee). In June 1998, the influential report, 'Speaking up for Justice' also proposed greater restrictions. This resulted in new legislation in the form of ss. 41–43 of the YJCEA 1999, which replaced s. 2 of the 1976 Act. This imposed much more specific restrictions on the adduction of evidence about a complainant's sexual history.

Section 41 of the YJCEA 1999, Restriction on evidence or questions about complainant's sexual history (partial extract)

(1) If at a trial a person is charged with a sexual offence, then, except with the leave of the court—

    (a) no evidence may be adduced, and

    (b) no question may be asked in cross-examination,

    by or on behalf of any accused at the trial, about any sexual behaviour of the complainant.

(2) The court may give leave in relation to any evidence or question only on an application made by or on behalf of an accused, and may not give such leave unless it is satisfied—

    (a) that subsection (3) or (5) applies, and

    (b) that a refusal of leave might have the result of rendering unsafe a conclusion of the jury or (as the case may be) the court on any relevant issue in the case....

It should be noted immediately that there are some important differences between this statute and the 1976 Act. Thus, the 1999 Act relates to the trial of any 'sexual offence', including, for example, indecent assault, not just 'rape' offences (whether substantive or inchoate), unlike the earlier statute. Additionally, the 1976 Act did not cover previous consensual sexual behaviour between defendant and complainant (which could always be adduced as of right), unlike the newer statute. Under the 1999 Act, a man accused of raping a woman with whom he 'went out' and enjoyed sexual relations several months (or even days) earlier, will not be able to bring up their sexual history at trial as of right, but only if it can be admitted through one of the statute's gateways.

---

[4] An obvious example would be J Temkin, 'The Ravishment of Section 2' [1993] Crim LR 3.

Section 41 of the Youth Justice and Criminal Evidence Act 1999

Section 41(1) of the YJCEA 1999 provides that a defendant charged with a sexual offence cannot adduce evidence, or ask questions in cross examination, about 'any sexual behaviour of the complainant' without the court's permission, which will only be granted in certain situations. This obviously raises the questions as to exactly what is meant by 'sexual behaviour' and when such permission should be granted.

'Sexual Behaviour'

Under s. 42(1)(c) sexual behaviour is defined, rather briefly, as 'any sexual behaviour or other sexual experience', whether with the accused or a third party, *apart* from conduct that forms part of the offence charged. This definition has posed problems. Obviously, it includes sexual intercourse, or other behaviour that is clearly sexual in nature, but which falls short of full intercourse; for example, oral sex, mutual masturbation and 'heavy petting'. However, after this, the dividing line between 'sexual' and 'non-sexual' behaviour becomes progressively harder to determine. Does it extend to occasional (clothed) bottom pinching (almost certainly it does); statements that constitute overtly 'sexual' advances (again, yes); the possession of 'sex toys' (very probably); or extremely 'bawdy' conversations (less likely)?

However, it is clear that statements recounting previous sexual experience constitute evidence of 'sexual behaviour' as defined in s. 42(1)(c), and so fall within the reach of s. 41. This applies whether the defence seek to assert the truth of the statement or merely to assert that the statement was made. To reach any other conclusion would be to seriously weaken the level of protection provided by s. 41 to complainants in sexual cases: *R v TW* [2005] Crim. LR 965. For example, it would cover a witness who attempted to give evidence that a complainant had, at a dinner party, told other diners about her sexual encounters.

The term also covers experiences that might not have been defined as such by their participants, because of youth or mental incapacity. For example, in *R v E* [2005] Crim LR 227, it was claimed on appeal that what had happened to the infants in the case could not be described as sexual behaviour or experience on their parts, because they were too young to have the understanding of sexual matters that would lead them to appreciate the true nature of the experience. This argument was rejected by the Court of Appeal, which noted, inter alia, that to do otherwise would deny mentally handicapped complainants protection.

Inevitably, some situations will be 'borderline'. Thus, in *R v Mukadi* [2004] Crim LR 373, the complainant in a rape case had had an admitted degree of consensual sexual conduct with the defendant at his flat, immediately after meeting him at his place of employment (a supermarket), but claimed that she had refused consent to full intercourse. The accused man wished to cross-examine her to the effect that she had been seen, on the same evening, standing on a nearby pavement and then getting into a car driven by a much older man, with whom she subsequently exchanged telephone numbers. This line of questioning was not permitted by the trial judge, on the basis that it had no bearing on the issue of consent.

However, in *Mukadi*, the Court of Appeal, although not sure whether this conduct constituted sexual behaviour, thought that it 'probably' did, as the defendant wished to raise the matter to suggest that the complainant was close to acting as a prostitute at the relevant time, and must have anticipated sexual activity subsequently occurring at his flat. (The Court of Appeal also concluded that if it was sexual behaviour, it would have been admissible under s. 41(3)(b) of the 1999 Act as occurring 'at or about the same time' and, if it was not, it was admissible under general principles of relevance.)

False Complaints

In *R v T* [2002] 1 WLR 632, the Court of Appeal decided that, normally, questions or evidence about false statements made, in the past, by a complainant concerning non-existent sexual assaults were not 'about' any sexual behaviour of the complainant: 'They relate not to her sexual behaviour but to her statements in the past.' Such false utterances are simply evidence of untruthful conduct. As a result, they are not covered by s. 41, and questioning and evidence about the false complaint is not, prima facie, constrained by the provision.

However, the court was also aware that allowing such questioning on this basis could be open to abuse by defence counsel, who might allege that any previous allegation that did not result in a conviction should be deemed to be false, and so not covered by the Act. To guard against this, the Court of Appeal stated that where it had been unequivocally suggested that a previous statement or allegation made by a complainant in a sexual offence case was false, the trial judge was entitled to seek assurances from the defence that it had a proper evidential basis both for asserting that the statement was actually made and also that it was untrue. If these requirements were not met, the questions would be deemed not to be about lies but would be 'about the sexual behaviour of the complainant', within the meaning of s. 41(1), and so inadmissible. Inevitably, this raises the difficult question (for a trial judge) as to exactly when a proper evidential basis for such an accusation has been established.

This issue was further examined in *R v Garaxo (Shino)* [2005] EWCA Crim 1170, where the Court of Appeal concluded that a first instance judge should have permitted cross-examination as to the two previous allegations of sexual assault made by the complainant. Before trial, the prosecution had given the defence material that showed that, on two previous occasions, she had made allegations of sexual assault and common assault against men, which were recorded in CRIS (Crime Report Information System) reports. The first report stated that the complainant had asked for a crime reference number for the 'Social' and the second reported that the complainant had refused to co-operate with the police. The defence sought permission to cross-examine the complainant on the basis that those complaints had been false. The judge ruled that there was not sufficient evidence that the previous allegations made by the complainant were untruthful and, accordingly, he refused leave to cross-examine. However, as the Court of Appeal noted, the evidence was such that, depending upon the answers given by the complainant, a jury *could* have been satisfied that both previous allegations were untrue, and so the questions should have been allowed.

By contrast, in *R v E* [2005] Crim LR 227, the Court of Appeal concluded that counsel for a man accused of indecently assaulting his very young daughters had properly been refused permission to cross-examine the infants about complaints that they had made against a large number of other people (their mother, aunt, nephew, etc.) of sexual abuse, similar to that alleged against the appellant, some 15 months after the incident involving the defendant. No-one was interviewed, let alone charged, as a result of those allegations and, at trial, defence counsel's case was that, as it was wholly implausible that the children would have been abused by so many people, the later allegations were almost certainly a fabrication and, as a result, questioning the children about them would not relate to a 'sexual experience'. In turn, it was argued that this cast considerable doubt on the veracity of the allegations brought against the defendant. However, the Court of Appeal upheld the first instance judge's decision and concluded that, because there was no evidence of the falsity of the complaints, it was impossible for the court to know, or even to speculate, as to where any enquiry into the girls' allegations might lead. Such an enquiry would effectively require the girls to undergo an investigation, conducted on an unclear and unformulated basis, into other occasions of alleged abuse, in the speculative hope of establishing something that might add to the significant matters relating to their credibility that the judge had already permitted to be adduced. In general, courts would not embark upon such enquiries.

Pause for reflection

Do you feel that these later allegations cast a different light on the complainants' evidence?

It should also be noted that a claim that an alleged sexual offence victim has made a false complaint in the past will often amount to an allegation of 'reprehensible behaviour' on the part of a witness (or non-defendant). In these circumstances permission to question the complainant about the complaint will only be granted if the terms of s. 100 of the CJA 2003 are satisfied. However, case law suggests that this will be a rather less onerous hurdle to satisfy than s. 41. It is likely that permission to cross-examine on such matters will be granted in most cases where an evidential foundation for the falsity of the complaint is established.

Cross-reference Box

This statutory provision regulates, and limits, the circumstances in which the 'bad character' of a non-defendant can be adduced in a criminal trial. For more on the section go to pp. 221–230.

The Test for Admitting Complainant Sexual History

Under s. 41(2)(b) of the statute, permission can only be given if the court is satisfied that refusing it might render unsafe any conclusion drawn on a relevant issue in the case by the court or jury and, *additionally*, that one of the four gateways set out at s. 41(3)(a)–(c), or under s. 41(5), also applies. This means that it is a two-stage test. It is not enough that one of the gateways applies, if the court is not satisfied that refusing leave would render unsafe a conclusion on a relevant issue. Thus, in *R v Bahador* [2005] EWCA Crim 396, the Court of Appeal held that although in an indecent assault case the complainant's earlier public exposing of her breasts and simulation of oral sex in a night club was, technically, relevant to his defence of belief in consent under s. 41(3)(a), it was not sufficiently cogent, in the circumstances, that a refusal to allow cross-examination would render unsafe any relevant conclusion in the case. As a result, the evidence was quite properly excluded under s. 41.

The four 'gateways' are: that the issue at trial is not one of consent (subsection a); or, if it is an issue of consent, that the sexual behaviour of the complainant to which the evidence or question relates is alleged to have taken place at or about the same time as the event which is the subject matter of the charge against the accused (subsection b); or, the sexual behaviour of the complainant to which the evidence or question relates is so similar to the sexual behaviour of the complainant which took place as part of the alleged crime, or at or about the same time as that event, that the similarity cannot reasonably be explained as a coincidence (subsection c). Additionally, under s. 41(5), it is provided that permission can be granted if the evidence or question about the complainant's sexual behaviour goes no further than is necessary to allow the evidence adduced by the prosecution to be rebutted or explained.

Section 41(3)(a)

Section 41(3)(a) deals with those situations (inter alia) in which it is the defendant's belief in the complainant's consent that is in issue, rather than whether there was actual consent. This is, of course, a defence to most sexual offences, albeit that the defendant must now have a 'reasonable' belief, in the light of the Sexual Offences Act 2003. This defence has raised evidential problems for the courts for many years. Arguably, whenever there is an allegation of consent, there is also an implied allegation of belief in consent. Ostensibly, there is nothing to prevent a defendant, in most cases, from saying: 'Even if she wasn't, I genuinely believed she was consenting. In part, this was because she is notoriously free with her sexual favours in such situations.' He could then ask to put questions, or adduce evidence, about her sexual conduct with third parties to explain why he had this impression, so circumventing the shield established by s. 41. However, the courts have been alert to the risk that this defence could be abused, and do not lightly accept it.

In *R v Barton* [1986] 85 Cr App R 5, a decision under the 1976 Act, the defendant claimed that he had earlier seen the complainant behaving very promiscuously and willingly engaging in group sex, during which her behaviour, for example, kicking and screaming, was the same as that manifested by her during their own sexual encounter. He argued that these factors led him to genuinely believe she was consenting to intercourse with him, even if this was not the case. However, the trial judge refused leave to cross-examine on the earlier sexual behaviour, under s. 2 of the 1976 Act (then in force).

Upholding his decision, the Court of Appeal noted that whether such evidence should be adduced was a question for the judge to decide in the context of the facts before him, and, in the instant case, the prosecution case was very strong. Additionally, O'Connor LJ noted that there is a difference between believing that a woman is consenting to intercourse and believing that a woman will consent if advances are made to her. He also observed that: 'In the end it is the application of common sense to the facts of the individual case.' It seems that a similar approach will be followed, with at least the same degree of robustness, under s. 41 of the 1999 Act, and that defendants will not lightly be able to adduce evidence or ask questions to support such a defence. This does, of course, put trial judges in a slightly awkward position as they will be required to decide whether enough evidence of 'ambiguous' behaviour on the part of the complainant is before the court to justify it going to a jury. Essentially, this means that the defendant must satisfy an unusually high 'evidential burden' on the issue before a trial judge will let the defence be considered, though, as the following extract suggests, this is not necessarily unfair.

Jenny McEwan, '"I Thought She Consented": Defeat Of The Rape Shield Or The Defence That Shall Not Run' [2006] Crim LR 969–980 (Extract)

The obligation on the defence to adduce sufficient evidence of equivocality does not undermine the presumption of innocence. The evidential burden to raise accident fell upon the accused in Woolmington simply because the prosecution had already discharged its own evidential burden on mens rea by dint of the substantial inference of intention arising from the accused pointing a gun at his wife and firing it. Some credible evidence of lack of intention was clearly required. In rape and sexual assault cases, similarly unambiguous prosecution evidence would cast an evidential burden on the accused to suggest a belief in consent. Thus the presumptions under s. 75 of the Sexual Offences Act 2003, which in certain instances impose on the defence an obligation to adduce sufficient evidence to raise the issue of reasonable belief in consent, are necessary only when the prosecution evidence of mens rea is not strong enough on its own to impose an evidential burden upon the accused.

Nevertheless, s. 41(3)(a) is not necessarily confined to cases where a genuine but mistaken belief in the complainant's consent is in issue. In *R v Mokrecovas* [2002] 1 Cr App R 20, the issue at trial was consent. However, the defendant sought to cross-examine the complainant under s. 41(3)(a), to the effect that she had twice, within 12 hours of the disputed incident, had intercourse with his brother, at the flat where all three of them had stayed on the night in question. He argued that he did not wish to cross-examine her under this limb to suggest consent (which would clearly not be possible), but to explain why, shortly after returning home to her parents' house, she would make up a false allegation of rape. According to the defendant, her parents would be cross that she had been out and intoxicated during the night, and would suspect that sexual intercourse had taken place. Her allegation would, therefore, mitigate in their eyes what they already suspected had happened. On the facts of the case, the Court of Appeal rejected this submission, noting that the accused man's ability to cross-examine the complainant about the fact that she had voluntarily spent the night at the flat was quite enough to found his defence, without needing details of the alleged intercourse with the brother, and that coming to any other conclusion would severely undermine the statute. Again, the decision is indicative of a judicial reluctance to allow the effect of the 1999 Act to be circumvented.

R v Mokrecovas [2002] 1 Cr App R 20, CA

Lord Woolf CJ

He submits that it is not an issue of consent. We are prepared to accept his submissions this far. He contends that the issue goes to the motive which the complainant may have for lying to her father when she made the complaint of rape for the first time. In other words, it provides an explanation as to why she might have made up an allegation of rape against the defendant. Mr Owen submits that that is an issue which is distinct from the issue of consent. He says that on the facts of this case the position was, first, that the complainant had stayed away from home without the permission of her parents and when her parents would be likely to be upset; secondly, that she had drunk excessively; thirdly, that she had stayed in the flat of the two brothers and that her parents may well have thought that she had been guilty of sexual behaviour of which they would disapprove and that she had returned late the following morning in a condition where she immediately had to go to bed. In those circumstances she would want to persuade her parents that she should not be blamed and so she alleged that she had been the victim of a rape. That is why she made the allegation of rape against the defendant, albeit that consensual sexual intercourse had taken place. Having regard to the judge's ruling as to the permissible cross-examination, we ask ourselves to what extent, if at all, is the defendant inhibited in suggesting that there was a motive for the complainant to tell untruths to her parents? How would the ability of the defendant to argue that the complainant had a motive to lie be improved if she were to be allowed to be cross-examined to suggest that the brother had had sexual intercourse on two previous occasions? In our judgment, the position of the defendant would not be improved in any way. The refusal of leave to ask the specific questions that Mr Owen wishes to ask will not result in any lack of safety or unfairness in the proceedings or in any relevant issue not being explored.

Section 41(3)(b)

Section 41(3)(b) covers situations where consent is an issue, and provides that leave might be given to admit evidence or questioning about the complainant's sexual behaviour where the behaviour was alleged to have taken place 'at or about' the same time as the event that forms the subject matter of the charge. However, it was uncertain from the Act as to whether 'at or about' meant, for example, within an hour, a day, or a week. This has now been resolved to some degree, and appears to be limited to within 24 hours of the incident (see below).

It should be noted that the sexual behaviour that took place at or about the same time as the incident in question must still satisfy a test of relevance, such that it would risk making any ensuing verdict unsafe if it were not permitted. Thus, in *R v Stephenson* [2002] EWCA Crim 1231, the defendant was not allowed to question the complainant as to whether she had kissed a number of men on the same evening that the rape had allegedly taken place. This was not deemed to be relevant to whether the defendant would have consented to intercourse with the defendant.

Section 41(3)(c)

Section 41(3)(c) allows leave to be given where consent is in issue and the sexual behaviour of the complainant to which the evidence or question relates is alleged to have been, in any respect: '... so similar to any sexual behaviour of the complainant which (according to the evidence adduced or to be adduced on behalf of the accused) took place as part of the event which is the subject matter of the charge... [that] the similarity cannot reasonably be explained as a co-incidence'. Prima facie, this would cover situations like those envisaged by the Heilbron Committee, in which there is a striking similarity, manifest in unusual features, between the past sexual behaviour of the complainant and the subject matter of the indictment. For example, and to take an absurdly extreme illustration, a middle-aged nun who, during walks in a public park, regularly and aggressively solicits total strangers for ad hoc, al fresco sex in a shrubbery, where the defendant claims that this was also the background to an act of consensual intercourse between himself and the complainant, which is the subject of an allegation of rape. The allegation is so utterly bizarre and extraordinary that, without knowing about the other incidents, a jury might find it difficult to seriously entertain the accused man's account.

Impugning Complainant Credibility

Parliament was very keen not to perpetuate what was referred to in the Canadian case of *R v Seaboyer* (1991) 83 DLR (4th) 193 as the myth that unchaste women are less worthy of belief. As a result, under s. 41(4) of the 1999 Act it is also provided that, for the purposes of s. 41(3)—no express mention is made of s. 41(5)—no evidence or question shall be regarded as relating to a relevant issue in the case if it appears to the court to be: '…reasonable to assume that the purpose (or main purpose) for which it would be adduced or asked is to establish or elicit material for impugning the credibility of the complainant as a witness'. This does, of course, require the courts to make a fine distinction between a 'main' and a subsidiary purpose, something that is all the more difficult because of the blurring that inevitably occurs, in this area of the law, between matters that go to credit and those that go to issue; this is a problem that has vexed the courts since 1976: *R v Viola* [1982] 3 All ER 73. As long as impugning credit is a subsidiary purpose of cross-examination, the provision does not operate.

The distinction was examined by the Court of Appeal in the indecent assault case of *R v Martin* [2004] 2 Cr App R 22. In this case, the defendant alleged that the complainant had fabricated her allegation about a lack of consent to oral sex because he spurned her repeated request for full sexual intercourse. At trial, the judge had refused to allow cross-examination on her behaviour, on the basis that it went primarily to impugning credit. However, the Court of Appeal concluded that the judge had erred, as this was not the sole or main purpose behind the proposed cross-examination (though the court also held that the ensuing conviction was not rendered unsafe thereby).

R v Martin [2004] 2 Cr App R 22, CA

Crane J

We consider that one purpose of the proposed questions clearly was to impugn, in the ordinary sense of the word, the credibility of the complainant. However, it can also realistically be said that one purpose was to strengthen the defence case. The appellant wished to contend that the complainant was making a false allegation, because he had rejected her advances on the Monday night. Arguably that rejection could have been said to be more hurtful if she had gone on to perform an act of oral sex upon him and then been rejected. We also consider that one purpose of the questions was to add emphasis to the appellant's case that he on the Monday had not wanted a sexual relationship with the complainant. True he had allowed her, so he sought to say, to perform oral sex upon him, but it was she who was pestering him. We are impressed by the fact that, in this case, it was the prosecution who called evidence relating to the events of the Monday night, and rightly so. The situation might have been different if the prosecution had relied simply on the events of the Wednesday and therefore it was the defence who sought to canvass the events of the Monday. We have to consider whether, in these circumstances, the appellant has received a fair trial, if his version or part of his version of the events on the Monday was excluded from the jury's consideration. In our judgment, it was a significant part of the defence case that the complainant had not merely pestered him for sex but performed an act of oral sex upon him and then been rejected. He was alleging she had fabricated the Wednesday incident. He was alleging she had done so because he had rejected her advances. The jury might have interpreted a rejection after the performance of oral sex as more hurtful than rejection after verbal advances, at least if they had heard evidence of the performing of oral sex on the Monday. In any event, part of the relevance of the appellant's version of the Monday night events was to demonstrate that, far from pursuing a sexual relationship with the complainant, he had emphatically not wished to do so despite her willingness to provide sexual favours for him. In other words, it could be said that the proposed evidence went to his credibility rather than simply to hers. We conclude that, on ordinary principles of interpretation, it was one purpose but not 'the purpose' or 'the main purpose' of the questions to impugn the credibility of the complainant.

Section 41(5)

The remaining ground is set out under s. 41(5), whereby, if the prosecution itself adduces evidence about sexual behaviour on the part of the complainant, the defendant can adduce evidence to rebut it, provided it would go no further than is 'necessary' to explain such behaviour. The ambit of this section was considered in *R v F* [2005] 2 Cr App R 13. In this case, the prosecution and complainant freely conceded that the appellant, who was the complainant's stepfather, and who, it was claimed, had subjected the complainant to systematic sexual abuse and rape from the age of about seven until she was 16 years old, had subsequently lived together when she was a young adult (18–24) and shared a full and consensual sexual relationship when doing so. The Crown claimed that this apparently strange behaviour towards someone who had abused the complainant was consequential on her 'grooming' as a child, so that she was a passive participant in the process, and did what she was pressurized to do, just as she had done when she was much younger.

The appellant alleged that her complaints (about childhood sexual activity) were untrue, and motivated by a desire for revenge after he had brought their adult relationship to an end. The trial judge ruled that although the fact of the adult relationship could be adduced by the defendant, no evidence could be admitted or questions asked of the complainant about some photographs and two video-tapes in the accused man's possession. These showed the complainant stripping and posing for the appellant while describing in graphic and obscene terms what she would like to do to him sexually, and also appearing to be totally at ease with him. As such, it was argued that they (potentially) rebutted her suggestion that her adult sexual contact with the accused man was a result of pressure stemming from childhood abuse.

However, the Court of Appeal quashed the conviction and ordered a retrial. As evidence of the adult relationship evidence was given at trial by the prosecution/complainant, the case fell within s. 41(5), which entitled the appellant to rebut her account of it. To do this, he should have been allowed to support his case that the complainant was not submitting but fully participating in the activity by adducing the videos, as they cast light on the adult relationship and so were relevant to the jury's decision as to whether there had been an earlier abusive relationship. If such evidence was prima facie admissible, the court lacked any discretion either to prevent it from being adduced or to limit (relevant) parts from being heard. Without the video and photographic evidence the appellant's account was deprived of worthwhile support, which the complainant's demeanour in the films could well have provided. As a result, the jury might have concluded that the complainant had simply submitted to the appellant's demands as an adult and, therefore, that the relationship did represent the logical conclusion of childhood abuse, so that the motive for the false complaint attributed to her by the appellant was itself untrue.

R v F [2005] 2 Cr App R 13, CA

Judge LJ

She reiterated that until the age of 24 she was the victim of a sexual abuser, and that she was unhappy and was reluctant to engage in sexual activity with him. In the context of the adult relationship she was asked in terms whether the appellant was her lover or her abuser, and she replied, 'He was always my abuser.' She insisted that she did not want to have sex with him and only did so because she was scared. The appellant asserted that the complainant had initiated the sexual relationship between them when she was about 18 or 19 years old. Her complaints were false, motivated by a desire for revenge . . . The importance of this conflict of evidence is readily appreciated. If the complainant enjoyed a full and happy adult relationship with the appellant, neither being raped nor dutifully submitting to his dominant control, although not amounting to positive proof that she had not been abused as a child, the relationship would have called into question how she could ever have brought herself into enthusiastic participation for a number of years with her former abuser.

Convention Compliance and the 1999 Act

In essence, the YJCEA 1999 replaced judicial discretion to control the adduction of such evidence with a number of rigid categories of admissibility. The inherent problem with such an approach is, of course, that it is very difficult, if not impossible, for a parliamentary draftsman to envisage in advance every possible situation in which evidence of a complainant's sexual history might become highly relevant to an accused person's defence. Arguably, this problem should have been anticipated, given the problems occasioned in Canada by a similar (and now modified) statutory approach: *R v Seaboyer* [1991] SCR 577. In England, it manifested itself fairly quickly after the 1999 Act came into force.

 Pause for reflection

Why do you think this problem might not have been anticipated?

In *R v A* [2002] 1 AC 45, the defendant was accused of raping a woman, the girlfriend of his flat-mate, with whom he claimed to have had a discreet sexual relationship over the three weeks prior to the alleged rape. He claimed that the most recent sexual activity between them had taken place a week before the incident that formed the subject matter of the indictment. The alleged rape took place as the complainant and defendant walked along a riverbank on their way to visit the flat-mate/boyfriend, who was in hospital after a drinking binge. The accused man's defence was consent. The House of Lords concluded that, as in the instant case, a prior consensual sexual relationship between a complainant alleging a sexual offence and a defendant might, in some circumstances, be so relevant to the issue of consent that forbidding evidence relating to it would infringe the defendant's right to a fair trial, as enshrined in Article 6 of the ECHR. This would not invariably be so; everything would turn on the facts of the case. Nevertheless, as Lord Hutton observed, in some situations: '. . . evidence of such a relationship will show the complainant's specific mindset towards the defendant, namely her affection for him'. However, using conventional canons of statutory interpretation, it was extremely unlikely that any of the gateways in s. 41 would allow the adduction of such sexual history evidence.

Having reached this conclusion, their Lordships had a choice. They could either make a declaration of incompatibility under s. 4 of the Human Rights Act 1998, or they could find a s. 41 gateway through which to admit it, even if this required straining the section's normal statutory interpretation by having recourse to s. 3 of the 1998 Act. Ultimately, this latter course was pursued, the courts being generally reluctant to make declarations of incompatibility if they can be avoided. As Lord Steyn observed, it was realistic to proceed on the basis that the legislature would not have wished to: '...deny the right to an accused to put forward a full and complete defence by advancing truly probative material'. This then required the court to select a gateway that was susceptible to such interpretation.

Cross-reference Box

Section 3 of the Human Rights Act 1998 allows the courts to ensure compliance with the ECHR by interpreting a provision so that it is consistent with the requirements of the convention. It is an alternative to making a declaration of incompatibility under s. 4 of the 1998 Act. For more on this go to chapter 1, at pp. 51–54.

Attention initially fell on s. 41(3)(b) as having potential in this regard. Could not 'at or about' the same time be extended to cover a period of a week? However, after some consideration, the House of Lords concluded that the provision was too obviously aimed at behaviour that had occurred within 24 hours of the alleged incident for this to be possible. Instead, their Lordships settled on s. 41(3)(c), on the basis that sexual behaviour with the same man, even if it occurred some time earlier, could be interpreted (albeit rather artificially) as being 'so similar' to the incident in question that the similarity could not reasonably be explained as a coincidence, where it was also so relevant to the issue of consent that to exclude would threaten the fairness of the trial with regard to Article 6 of the ECHR. Such evidence was, of course, also relevant to the instant case.

R v A [2002] 1 AC 45, HL

Lord Steyn

Although not an issue before the House, my view is that the 1999 Act deals sensibly and fairly with questioning and evidence about the complainant's sexual experience with other men. Such matters are almost always irrelevant to the issue whether the complainant consented to sexual intercourse on the occasion alleged in the indictment or to her credibility. To that extent the scope of the reform of the law by the 1999 Act was justified. On the other hand, the blanket exclusion of prior sexual history between the complainant and an accused in section 41(1), subject to narrow categories of exception in the remainder of section 41, poses an acute problem of proportionality. As a matter of common sense, a prior sexual relationship between the complainant and the accused may, depending on the circumstances, be relevant to the issue of consent. It is a species of prospectant evidence which may throw light on the complainant's state of mind. It cannot, of course, prove that she consented on the occasion in question. Relevance and sufficiency of proof are different things. The fact that the accused a week before an alleged murder threatened to kill the deceased does not prove an intent to kill on the day in question. But it is logically relevant to that issue. After all, to be relevant the evidence need merely have some tendency in logic and common sense to advance the proposition in issue. It is true that each decision to engage in sexual activity is always made afresh. On the other hand, the mind does not usually blot out all memories. What one has been engaged on in the past may influence what choice one makes on a future occasion. Accordingly, a prior relationship between a complainant and an accused may sometimes be relevant to what decision was made on a particular occasion. In a balanced review of the voluminous critical literature in the United Kingdom between 1975 and 1999 Mr Kibble has shown that the principal focus throughout has been on the irrelevance and prejudicial impact of sexual experience of the complainant with other men. The target of the literature was the 1976 Act. When the issue of the relevance of sexual experience between a complainant and a defendant was raised there was broad agreement that such evidence is sometimes relevant (e g an ongoing relationship) and sometimes irrelevant (e g an isolated episode in the past). There was no case made out in the literature for the blanket exclusionary scheme incorporated in section 41 in respect of prior sexual experience between a complainant and accused. ... After all, good sense suggests that it may be relevant to an issue of consent whether the complainant and the accused were ongoing lovers or strangers. To exclude such material creates the risk of disembodying the case before the jury. It also increases the danger of miscarriages of justice. These considerations raise the spectre of the possible need for a declaration of incompatibility in respect of section 41 under section 4 of the Human Rights Act 1998. In my view ordinary methods of purposive construction of section 41(3)(c) cannot cure the problem of the excessive breadth of the section 41, read as a whole, so far as it relates to previous sexual experience between a complainant and the accused. Whilst the statute pursued desirable goals, the methods adopted amounted to legislative overkill. On the other hand, the interpretative obligation under section 3 of the 1998 Act is a strong one. It applies even if there is no ambiguity in the language in the sense of the language being capable of two different meanings.

It should be stressed that *A* did not drive a 'coach and horses' through s. 41 (albeit that it restored a judicial discretion that the Act had been intended to abolish). Indeed, Lord Steyn's *obiter* comment that the 1999 Act dealt 'sensibly and fairly' with previous sexual relationships between the complainant and third parties (ie someone other than the defendant himself) is significant. His view was, perhaps, most clearly supported by *R v White (Andre Barrington)* [2004] EWCA Crim 946, where the defendant to a rape charge, in which consent was alleged, was not allowed to cross-examine the complainant to the effect that she had previously been, for many years, a habitual prostitute in Coventry and, by her own admission, still worked occasionally in this capacity from home. Evidently, it will be very much harder, in many situations, to adduce evidence of a complainant's sexual history under the 1999 Act than was the case under its 1976 predecessor, let alone at common law.

R v White (Andre Barrington) [2004] EWCA Crim 946, CA

Laws LJ

In any case, however, there are in our view great difficulties in fitting the case within any of the provisions contained in section 41(3). Counsel's formulation of the issues which we have read shows that in truth the question here was whether or not the complainant was to be believed on the consent issue. It might be thought that the excluded material was sought to be introduced merely to impugn her credibility. As we have made clear, that would be prohibited by section 41(4). But let it be supposed, though we would not in fact accept it, that her acts as a prostitute were potentially objectively relevant as an explanation of why she might make up a false allegation of rape against a man who refused to pay her. It is important to see precisely what was the evidence she might have given about those activities. Apart from the long list of previous convictions, the material is contained in the first two paragraphs of her witness statement of 25th May 2000. It is effectively already summarised but we read if for convenience: 'I worked as a prostitute in Coventry from about the age of 21 till the age 30 and I was then working on the streets. I didn't like doing this any longer, it was dangerous, and so I eventually stopped and started just having clients coming to my house instead. I decided to move out of Coventry and I stopped with a friend in Handsworth and eventually I was given the flat I'm in now by Focus Housing, this was about four years ago. Since being in Handsworth I still have one regular client come to my flat who I've known for 14 years, and there are a couple of other regulars who also come to my house on an infrequent basis. I'm not working otherwise so this is the only reason that I carry on doing prostitution as I can't manage financially.' On the face of it, and even taking into account the list of convictions, this material is in too general terms for it to be asserted that any acts of the complainant's as a prostitute were in fact sufficiently contemporaneous with the alleged rape to engage section 41(3)(b), and there is nothing to show any significant similarity between those acts and the alleged rape for the purposes of 41(3)(c). Mr Muller submits that the necessary degree of similarity can be found between her taking money for sex in her trade as a prostitute and such details of the episode in question here as might have suggested to the appellant that she would be prepared to have sex for money. In our judgment, on the facts of this case, that submission is entirely insubstantial.

Nevertheless, the interpretation adopted in *A* has taken some of the 'sting' out of criticisms of s. 41, which was widely viewed as defective by both lawyers and members of the judiciary, as research by Neil Kibble indicates (in 2003, he interviewed 78 judges involved in criminal trials about the section's operation). More encouragingly, Kibble's work also suggests that trial judges currently manifest a substantial degree of consistency when determining questions of relevance and admissibility, and they adopt a far more thoughtful and considered approach to such questions than is sometimes popularly believed.

N Kibble, 'Judicial Discretion and the Admissibility of Prior Sexual History Evidence under Section 41 of the Youth Justice and Criminal Evidence Act 1999: Sometimes Sticking to Your Guns Means Shooting Yourself in the Foot: Part 2' [2005] Crim LR 263–274 (Extract)

There was a substantial consensus among the judges that s. 41 was not a workable provision prior to the decision of the House of Lords in R. v A (No.2), which restored a measure of judicial discretion in relation to the consent gateways and particularly s. 41(3)(c). A central theme of the judges' responses was the necessity of preserving judicial discretion. Judges drew attention to the difficulty of framing legislative rules to regulate decision-making in this area, and many judges warned of the injustice that would flow from s. 41 if they adhered to its provisions literally: 'It is very difficult to frame appropriate rules to apply to evidence which is infinitely variable. And it is the judge who has to decide that with regard to the facts in the case before him. I think it would be a terrible mistake for Parliament to lay down rules which we must inflexibly apply. I think it would be a recipe for filling the Court of Appeal even further. That is certainly a recipe for injustice, massive injustice.' 'There is nothing wrong in Parliament setting out criteria for admissibility but it is fundamentally wrong for Parliament to rob judges of discretion as to the admissibility of evidence, as it is to rob them of the discretion as to sentencing and other matters.'

Many judges spoke of their determination to avoid injustice and of how, faced with a section which threatened to result in injustice, they and practitioners had felt obliged to respond: 'I don't think it's a question of judges really bending the law. But I'd be prepared to bend one or two things, on timing whether it's contemporaneous, if it's a few days rather than 24 hours and that sort of thing. But it's a question of fairness at the end of the day. You've got to consider the complainant of course. Is it fair to the complainant and is it fair to the defendant? It's a balancing exercise. You do what you think is right.' 'I did think at the beginning of section 41 that it made life impossible. There were situations where one thought that it was deeply unjust or might be if a way wasn't found around it. I did find that the prosecution exercised their powers quite responsibly and actually said, "If the defence aren't going to cross-examine about this, I'm going to put it in."'

A recurrent theme of the vast majority of interviews was that, without the decision in R. v A, s. 41 was unworkable in relation to sexual history between the defendant and complainant: 'Were it not for R v A it would place all of us in insuperable difficulties, because of the requirement to exclude what would otherwise be manifestly admissible.' 'Obviously this Act was designed to cut back the judicial discretion that existed under the previous Act because judges were not trusted to ensure that improper questioning was not allowed . . . However, without the House of Lords decision in R v A I think undoubtedly that injustice would be done in some cases. Of course prosecutors are aware of that and of Article 6, which is why they often don't object to the application and that is why we allow sensible limited questioning. Without R v A we would have a straitjacket which at times would render unfairness.' Of course, it is hardly surprising that judges are critical of legislation that imposes rigid constraints upon their discretion. As one of the judges said during the interview, 'We would say that wouldn't we.' However, if we turn to other jurisdictions and examine both the operation of rape shield legislation and the debates over legislative reform, we will find powerful echoes of the judges' comments and a widespread rejection of the non-discretionary approach.

It is apparent that s. 41 has had a practical impact on the willingness of the courts to allow cross-examination on complainant sexual history, especially with regard to that with third parties, and that this has also accompanied a change in advocacy style in many such cases, though the extent to which the former has brought about the latter is, inevitably, open to question. Additionally, it should be noted that the 'attrition' rate in reported rape cases, that is the number that do not proceed to trial or which result in acquittals, remains alarmingly high, even after the advent of the provision.

Ian Dennis, 'Sexual History Evidence: Evaluating Section 41' [2006] Crim LR 869–870 (Extract)

Until recently the debate has lacked an empirical grounding; there was a gap in our knowledge as to how s. 41 is actually working in practice. A recent Home Office Online Report 20/06 by Liz Kelly, Jennifer Temkin and Sue Griffiths, Section 41: an evaluation of new legislation . . . provides much valuable data to fill this gap and inform future discussion.... The case-tracking exercise provided a sample of almost two-thirds of all rape trials heard in England and Wales during a three-month period in 2003. The analysis of the 236 cases in which the data were complete shows that s. 41 applications by the defence to use sexual history evidence were made in just under one quarter of the trials. Two thirds of the applications were allowed. One view is that these figures indicate some failure of the legislation, if the object of s. 41 is taken to be to restrict the use of sexual history evidence to exceptional cases. An alternative interpretation is that the section has in fact succeeded in reducing the numbers of applications from what they were under the old s. 2 of the Sexual Offences (Amendment) Act 1976, and that the majority of applications have some merit, as shown by their high success rate. In this connection it is worth noting that more applications are made where a prior relationship between the complainant and the defendant is alleged, and such applications are more frequently allowed. The influence of the House of Lords decision in R v A [2001] UKHL 25 has been considerable.... Defence lawyers do not generally come well out of this report; they are accused at various points of evading the legislation by not making necessary applications, or flouting the judge's rulings, or of using devious ploys to attack the complainant's credibility in contravention of s. 41(4). Such judgments will inevitably be contested. What cannot reasonably be contested are two other significant findings. One is that the former Crown Court Rules providing for written pre-trial applications under s. 41 were very largely ignored. The vast majority of s. 41 applications were made at trial, usually verbally, and often only when the complainant was actually giving evidence. Some of the judges and barristers interviewed were unaware of even the existence of the Rules. These Rules are now contained in Pt 36 of the Criminal Procedure Rules 2005. It will be a major test of the case management responsibilities of judges to see how they enforce the application procedure from now on and whether they do effect a change in the culture of defending rape cases. Secondly, the report points to convincing evidence of widespread ignorance and misunderstanding of s. 41. The legislation is undoubtedly complex and difficult, but that is no excuse for some judges and barristers to have only a vague or non-existent grasp of it.... It does appear that all-out attacks on complainants are now seen as poor advocacy. If s. 41 is responsible for at least this change then we should certainly be grateful. But there is clearly still scope for improvement, even if one does not support the authors' recommendations for further tightening of the section.

6. Re-examination

A witness can be re-examined by the party that originally called him/her following cross-examination by the opposing party. If there has been no cross-examination of a witness, there is no right to re-examine him. The purpose of re-examination is to allow the calling party to attempt to repair any damage done to the witness's story and credibility during cross-examination, and to clarify, explain or expand any matters that were raised during that process but which still appear unclear; this is a situation that can easily be produced by the asking of leading questions. For example, opposing counsel may have asked the witness to assent to, or deny a proposition 'yes or no' without allowing him to qualify his answer.

Re-examination follows the same rules as examination in chief, so that leading questions are not normally allowed on the part of the calling party. It must also be restricted to those matters arising out of the cross-examination and no new matters may be introduced without the court's permission, although this is often granted if a relevant matter was overlooked during examination in chief. The witness should not simply reiterate the evidence that he earlier gave in chief. A witness can be re-examined even if they have been declared hostile during examination in chief (though the circumstances for this to occur would have to be quite exceptional) and, in theory, can even be declared hostile at this late stage in the proceedings: *R v Wong* [1986] Crim LR 683 and *R v Norton and Driver* [1987] Crim LR 687.

Summary

- Leading questions are always permitted during cross-examination. They can be on any issue relevant to the facts in issue or (subject to statutory controls) the credit of an opposing witness, even if not raised during examination in chief.

- The cross-examining party must also 'put' his case to a witness, at the risk of being deemed to have accepted that witness's evidence if he does not do so, though this rule is not applied inflexibly.

- Although a question that goes to credit, rather than issue, can often be asked (subject, inter alia, to s. 100 of the CJA 2003), the 'finality of answer to a collateral question' rule means that a denial cannot normally be rebutted, even if the evidence to do so is readily available.

- Distinguishing between collateral questions, and those which go to issue, can be difficult; to an extent, it is as much an instinctive as an analytical process, and always a matter of degree.

- Even where a question is collateral, an answer can be rebutted with evidence if it falls within one of the exceptions to the general rule; for example, if it concerns bias, a reputation for untruthfulness, or a medical defect affecting the witness's ability to give valid testimony, etc.

- Complainants in sexual cases are given special protection from cross-examination about their previous sexual behaviour, by virtue of s. 41 of the YJCEA 1999. They can only be cross-examined, or have evidence adduced, about previous sexual behaviour, even with the defendant if a refusal to allow it might render unsafe any conclusion drawn on a relevant issue in the case and one of the gateways set out in the section is made out. These are, on their face, quite restrictive. However, the courts have evinced a willingness to interpret them constructively if that is necessary to ensure a fair trial for a defendant and avoid a violation of the ECHR.

- Complainants in sexual cases cannot be cross-examined in person by a defendant, contrary to the general position, as a result of s. 34 of the YJCEA 1999.

- Re-examination allows a party who has called a witness to clarify anything that has emerged in cross-examination. The same evidential rules governing examination in chief apply, but questions cannot be asked about an entirely new matter without permission of the court.

Further reading

A Dein, 'Police Misconduct Revisited' [2000] Crim LR 801

I Dennis, 'Sexual History Evidence: Evaluating Section 41' [2006] Crim LR 869–870

N Kibble, 'The Sexual History Provisions: Charting a Course Between Inflexible Legislative Rules and Wholly Untrammelled Judicial Discretion?' [2000] Crim LR 274

N Kibble, 'Judicial Discretion and the Admissibility of Prior Sexual History Evidence under Section 41 of the Youth Justice and Criminal Evidence Act 1999: Sometimes Sticking To Your Guns Means Shooting Yourself in the Foot: Part 2' [2005] Crim LR 263–274

J Langbein, 'The German Advantage in Civil Procedure' (1985) University of Chicago Law Review, vol 52, 823–866

J McEwan, '"I Thought She Consented": Defeat Of The Rape Shield Or The Defence That Shall Not Run' [2006] Crim LR 969–980

M Stone, 'Instant Lie Detection? Demeanour and Credibility in Criminal Trials' [1991] Crim LR 821–830

Questions for Discussion

1. Do the laws of evidence treat a complainant in a sexual case fairly? Discuss with special reference to evidential provisions that are specific to such cases.

2. Simon is a witness to a robbery, in which he claims that he heard one of the gang involved refer to their leader as 'Hudson', the surname of one of the defendants at a subsequent trial for the crime. Jim, counsel for Hudson, wishes to cross-examine Simon on the following points, and if this is allowed, to call evidence to rebut any denials that he might make: that Simon suffers from severe deafness (he has a statement from one of Simon's work colleagues to this effect); that Hudson had earlier had an affair with Simon's wife; that Simon has a spent conviction for theft (shop-lifting) from five years earlier; that Simon was overheard by Agatha, in the Rose and Crown Public House, saying that he 'didn't hear a thing' during the robbery, and that Simon has worked as a male prostitute in the past.
    Advise Jim.

3. Harold, a well known footballer, is charged with raping Joanna and committing an armed robbery at his local post-office. With regard to the rape, the prosecution case is that Harold raped Joanna in his hotel room late one night after meeting her at a night club. Harold admits that sexual intercourse occurred but states that it was entirely consensual. He says that Joanna is a premier league fan, who may have made up the allegation because he 'dumped' her quite bluntly the next morning. The prosecution wish to call the evidence of Joanna's mother, who will say that when she met her daughter, the following evening, Joanna was looking morose and, on being asked what was troubling her, was told, 'I've been raped by Harold'. Harold wishes to question Joanna about a conversation she had with Kyra, at the night club, shortly before they met, in which she is alleged to have said that she was determined 'to sleep with every player in the league'. Additionally, he wishes to call Lenny, another premier league player, to say that Joanna had 'picked him up' in a public house the previous week and had sexual intercourse with him in a nearby motel the same night.
    With regard to the robbery, the Crown propose to call Mavis, who was a customer in the post-office, and who positively identified Harold on an ID parade shortly afterwards. However, Harold has been approached by Nigel, a neighbour of Mavis, who says that Mavis told him that she was so frightened during the incident that she 'hadn't a clue' as to the robber's identity. Additionally, he says that he knows that Mavis has chronic astigmatism in her eyes and hates Harold because she fanatically supports a rival football team that Harold has regularly scored against. Harold wishes to cross-examine Mavis about these matters and, if necessary, call Nigel to give evidence about them.
    Advise all the parties as to any evidential issues raised on the above facts.

4. Karl is accused of raping Lola, the offence allegedly occurring at a New Year party. His defence is that she consented to sexual intercourse, asking him for a kiss and then leading him into a broom cupboard where she initiated the sexual activity. Karl wishes to question Lola about, and adduce evidence of, a previous incident of consensual intercourse that occurred between the two of them nine years earlier, when they lived in neighbouring rooms in a university hall of

For suggested approaches, please visit the Online Resource Centre

residence. He also wishes to question her about her behaviour at the party, and, in particular, about reports that she went around the room pinching the bottoms and rubbing the crotches of a number of men there. Karl also wishes to conduct his own defence and to carry out the cross-examination of Lola in person.

Advise Karl.

5. Do you share Lord Steyn's view that: '…the 1999 Act deals sensibly and fairly with questioning and evidence about the complainant's sexual experience with other [than the accused] men'?

6. Provide two examples of a 'leading question'.

11 OPINION EVIDENCE

Definitions

Expert A witness who is considered, by the court, to be 'peritus' or specially knowledgeable within a certain field.

Expert ad hoc A witness who is an expert in a very narrow field of knowledge by dint of his experience (the phrase is not normally used by English courts).

Expert Opinion The considered opinion of an expert on a matter relating to the facts in issue in a case that is within his area of expertise.

Lay Opinion A shorthand way of conveying facts observed by an ordinary (non-expert) witness.

Ultimate Issue The very issue that the tribunal has to decide; was the defendant negligent, insane, suffering from diminished responsibility, etc?

---

1. The Rule Against Opinion Evidence

Introduction

The general rule in both criminal and civil litigation is that witnesses speak to facts; their personal opinions, that is, any inferences they have drawn from facts that are before the court, are not normally admissible. This is a longstanding evidential rule. Even by the early 1700s, ordinary witnesses were being discouraged from providing the court with opinion, as opposed to evidence of facts. They were increasingly being told to state: '…not what they believe, for they are to swear nothing but what they have heard or seen'.[1]

---

[1] W Nelson, *The Law of Evidence* (1717, R Gosling) at 7.

Several rationales have been advanced for such a rule. One is that it is the role of the court to form any opinions necessary in a case, so that allowing witnesses to give their personal opinions would usurp the function of the tribunal of fact. Additionally, it is suggested that there is a risk that a court might be unduly influenced by the opinion of a witness who is either not impartial or who, because of his status, attracts more credence than would otherwise be justified; for example, a religious leader who has several acolytes on a jury or bench.

A number of other rationales, perhaps of lesser significance, have been mooted over the years, such as the difficulty of proving perjury on a matter of opinion. As Sir George Jessell MR noted in *Lord Abinger v Ashton* (1873) 17 LR Eq 358: '…although the evidence is given upon oath, in point of fact the person knows he cannot be indicted for perjury, because it is only evidence as to a matter of opinion'. Adopting another tack, Goddard LJ (as he then was) felt that opinion evidence from an ordinary witness was not sufficiently relevant to warrant being admitted at trial: *Hollington v Hewthorn & Co Ltd* [1943] KB 587.

However, whatever its justification, there are two important exceptions to the general rule: an expert witness may give opinion evidence on a matter that calls for expertise and which is within his specialist field, and a layperson can give opinion evidence as a shorthand way of conveying facts that they have personally perceived. These will be dealt with in turn.

Exam tip

Opinion evidence is a very important topic for those involved in the litigation process. However, academically, it has sometimes been neglected in England, at least when compared to the scrutiny the subject has received in the United States. Reflecting this, its importance in evidence courses and examinations varies. Sometimes, it is a major topic and is the subject of a dedicated question in its own right in an examination. At others, it is dealt with swiftly and is normally merely a facet of an exam question that is primarily about something else; for example, the examination of witnesses. Of the two aspects of opinion evidence, expert witnesses and lay opinion evidence, the former is much the most important. Because the subject is, in outline, relatively straightforward, students must have a detailed grasp of the more arcane aspects of the topic, such as the present status of the ultimate issue rule, as these are likely to be stressed in any problem question or essay title. Lay opinion evidence almost never forms a question in its own right, usually being an aspect of a wider question, whether on opinion evidence generally or some other evidential matter.

2. Expert Evidence

Introduction

If scientific, technical, or specialized knowledge will assist the tribunal of fact to understand other evidence adduced in a case, or help it to determine facts in issue, a witness who is deemed by the court to be qualified as an expert may provide evidence in the form of an opinion, provided it is within his field of competence. Even in the 1550s, English law recognized that expert opinion evidence might be received at trial where it was required. In *Buckley v Rice-Thomas* (1554) 1 Plowd 118 at 124, Judge Saunders observed that: 'If matters arise in our law which concern other sciences or faculties we commonly apply for aid of that science or faculty which it concerns.' A similar view was expressed by Lord Mansfield in *Folkes v Chadd* (1782) 3 Doug KB 157, the first important case on the topic in the 'modern' era, in which the opinion evidence of a Mr Smeaton, a celebrated engineer, was allowed on whether a certain bank, created for the purpose of preventing the sea overflowing adjacent meadows, had also contributed to the choking and decay of a nearby harbour.

Folkes v Chadd (1782) 3 Doug KB 157, KB

Lord Mansfield

It is objected that Mr Smeaton is going to speak, not as to facts, but as to opinion. That opinion, however, is deduced from facts which are not disputed—the situation of banks, the course of tides and of winds, and the shifting of sands. His opinion, deduced from all these facts, is, that, mathematically speaking, the bank may contribute to the mischief, but not sensibly. Mr. Smeaton understands the construction of harbours, the causes of their destruction, and how remedied. In matters of science no other witnesses can be called....On certain matters, such as those of science or art, upon which the court itself cannot form an opinion, special study, skill or experience being required for the purpose, 'expert' witnesses may give evidence of their opinion.

Although easy to state in outline, expert evidence presents a number of difficult challenges to the legal system. For example, how can the courts ensure that the scientific evidence they admit is reliable? On what aspects of human nature should experts be allowed to testify? How can the effect that adversarial tactics have on expert witnesses be limited? Nevertheless, despite such problems, the basic rules governing the admissibility of expert opinion evidence are, at least superficially, quite simple to state and can be summarized as providing the answers to several key questions. These are: does the tribunal of fact (whether judge, magistrates or jurors) need assistance on some matter? Can the proposed witness provide such assistance? On what did the proposed witness base their opinion? Is the tendered opinion within a forensically proper field for expert evidence? How is the witness constrained when giving evidence and what is his professional duty to the court? Additionally, it must be asked how a court should treat expert evidence when it is admitted and how a trial jury should be directed on its use. However, although easy to outline, these questions are sometimes harder to answer in practice.

3. When does the Tribunal of Fact Need Expert Assistance?

Introduction

English law reposes considerable faith in the experience, common sense and native abilities of judges, jurors and JPs. It does not lightly countenance the adduction of expert evidence where it may be unnecessary. In the leading criminal case of *R v Turner* [1975] 60 Cr App R 80 Lawton LJ observed in the Court of Appeal that: 'An expert's opinion is admissible to furnish the court with scientific information which is likely to be outside the experience and knowledge of a judge or jury. If on the proven facts a judge or jury can form their own conclusions without help, then the opinion of an expert is unnecessary.'

It was for this reason, amongst others, that the appeal in *R v Land* [1999] QB 65 failed. In this case, the defendant had been convicted of possessing indecent photographs of a child. At trial, there was no direct evidence as to the age of the youths in the pictures. The first instance judge directed the jury that they should use their own experience, judgment and critical faculties in deciding this issue. On appeal, it was argued that the prosecution should have called a paediatrician to give expert evidence as to their likely age, having regard to their physical development and appearance. However, this was rejected, the court pointing out that expert evidence on such a matter was inadmissible, as jurors were as 'well placed as an expert' to decide whether the prosecution had established that the children featured were under the age of 16. Similarly, in *R v Wahab* [2003] 1 Cr App R 15 it was held that neither court nor jury needed expert assistance from a solicitor on whether legal advice to a suspect (by another solicitor) being interviewed at a police station was mistaken, and might have rendered his ensuing confession unreliable.

Pause for reflection

Do you feel as well placed as a paediatrician to make such an assessment from physical appearance?

Nevertheless, the reality is that there are numerous specialist areas in which the tribunal of fact is recognized as needing such assistance when reaching their decisions. As a result, expert evidence has been received on a huge and ever growing number of subjects, running now into literally hundreds of fields, including, inter alia, matters as diverse as: insanity, road accident reconstructions, the working of a tachograph, DNA evidence, toxicology, real estate valuation, medical matters, pathology, aesthetic worth, commercial practise, child psychology, ballistics, etc.

Generally, it can be said that expert evidence is receivable on most specialist areas of study, knowledge or technology. Indeed, it has been observed that even a 'perfectly ordinary murder case' can be bristling with experts. Thus, a pathologist might be called to attribute cause of death, a doctor to describe cuts and bruises sustained by the defendant during the incident and their likely cause, while forensic scientists could give evidence on fibre traces, blood stains and DNA matches. A statistician might then address the court on the likelihood of such a match occurring by chance, and a psychiatrist could give evidence as to any mental abnormality on the part of the accused.[2]

It is easy in such cases to conclude that the expertise in question is outside the competence of the tribunal of fact; for example, most laymen have no idea about the range, trajectory and penetration of a specific type of bullet. However, some areas pose greater difficulties. Many of these do not relate to distinct fields of technical expertise, such as ballistics, but rather to evidence on the psychological or intellectual characteristics of people (often criminal defendants) involved in the trial process itself. These are frequently matters that might, for example, affect the ability of such individuals to form the appropriate *mens rea* for the offence with which they are charged, the probability of them telling the truth when giving testimony, or even the likelihood of a defendant having committed the offence charged at all.

---

[2] P Thornton, 'A New Look at eye witness testimony' (1995) New Law Journal, vol 145, 94–100, at 94.

Cross-reference Box

In *Toohey v Metropolitan Police Commissioner* [1965] AC 595 the House of Lords held that medical evidence might be adduced to demonstrate that a witness is incapable (rather than unwilling) of testifying accurately in the witness box due to some mental illness or condition, just as medical evidence would be admissible to demonstrate that a person was, for example, too short-sighted to have witnessed clearly at a distance what they claim to have seen of an incident as an eye-witness. Nevertheless, it is a subtle distinction. For a discussion of this and similar cases see pp. 443–444 below.

The approach manifested by the courts towards these areas has been to guard them jealously from falling into the province of the expert unless the matter in question is *clearly* outside a tribunal's normal experience, this being defined very widely. The 'classic' and still leading (albeit now somewhat modified) exposition of this approach was given by Lawton LJ in *R v Turner* [1975] QB 834, sometimes referred to as the 'rule in *Turner*', though most of the points made were extrapolated from earlier decisions, such as *R v Chard* [1972] 56 Cr App R 268.

R v Peter John Chard [1972] 56 Cr App R 268, CA

Roskill LJ

...one purpose of jury trials is to bring into the jury box a body of men and women who are able to judge ordinary day-to-day questions by their own standards, that is, the standards in the eyes of the law of theoretically ordinary reasonable men and women. That is something which they are well able by their ordinary experience to judge for themselves. Where the matters in issue go outside that experience and they are invited to deal with someone supposedly abnormal, for example, supposedly suffering from insanity or diminished responsibility, then plainly in such a case they are entitled to the benefit of expert evidence. But where, as in the present case, they are dealing with someone who by concession was on the medical evidence entirely normal, it seems to this Court abundantly plain, on first principles of the admissibility of expert evidence, that it is not permissible to call a witness, whatever his personal experience, merely to tell the jury how he thinks an accused man's mind—assumedly a normal mind—operated at the time of the alleged crime with reference to the crucial question of what that man's intention was. As I have already said, this applicant was by concession normal in the eyes of the law. Mr. Back suggested that if this evidence were of no value, it could have been demolished by counsel for the Crown or perhaps by the learned trial judge in the summing-up. That submission, with respect, is of no relevance on the question whether or not the evidence was admissible. That consideration, if relevant at all, would go to weight, and questions of weight are in general irrelevant on questions of admissibility. Dr. Mansbridge is a doctor, if I may be allowed to say so, very widely known in his own field, the field of mental illness and in particular mental illness in prisons, but neither he nor anyone else can claim to be an expert on the question of the intent of the ordinary man. The applicant at his trial stood before the jury as an ordinary man and his intent fell to be judged by them on the facts of the case in the light of what they thought the Crown proved his intent to have been. For those reasons, which I have endeavoured to give in deference to Mr. Back's argument, this Court thinks that the judge was abundantly right in the ruling he gave.

The 'Rule' in *Turner*

Turner was a murder case in which the defence wished to adduce the evidence of a psychiatrist in support of a partial defence of provocation under s. 3 of the Homicide Act 1957. The defendant had killed his girlfriend, allegedly after she had provoked him by her admissions to extensive infidelities and to carrying another man's child. The proposed evidence was to the effect that the defendant had a personality type that would probably have been severely provoked by such admissions and that also made him likely to be telling the truth about the incident. Very importantly, however, there was no suggestion that the defendant was suffering from any kind of psychiatric illness or form of insanity (something that would have been outside the normal province of the jury and within the remit of an expert, such as a psychiatrist).

Upholding the trial judge's decision that such evidence was not admissible, Lawton LJ opined that allowing it to be adduced would undermine the very function of, and rationale for, the tribunal of fact, so that 'trial by psychiatrists' would take the place of trial by jury and magistrates. Additionally, the judge expressed concern that although an expert witness's possession of impressive scientific qualifications do not, for that reason alone, make his opinion on matters of human nature and behaviour within the 'limits of normality' any more helpful than those of the jurors themselves, they might attribute excessive significance to it, especially if couched in scientific terminology. The judge also stressed that jurors did not need psychiatrists to tell them how 'ordinary folk who are not suffering from any mental illness' are likely to react to the stresses and strains of life, such as distressing news from intimates; nor did they need assistance when determining whether a normal witness is likely to be telling the truth.

Consequently, the rule precludes the use of expert psychological evidence on both a defendant's *mens rea* (where this is relevant) and his credibility. Such matters are normally deemed to be within the jurors' ordinary experience. Thus, they do not need to be told that a quick tempered man is more likely to be provoked by an 'unpleasing situation' than a placid one, and that a witness with a 'florid imagination' is likely to be less reliable than a precise and careful one.

Although many of the cases relate to defendants, it should be noted that, normally, expert evidence of credibility cannot be called to suggest that any other type of witness is worthy of belief. Such experts are sometimes termed 'oath helpers' after the procedure used in the ancient ecclesiastical courts (amongst other forums), where oath helpers were an intrinsic part of a hearing. Thus, in *R v Robinson* [1994] 97 Cr App R 260 the defendant was charged with indecently assaulting a 15-year-old with severe learning difficulties. At trial, the judge allowed the prosecution to call the evidence of an educational psychologist who gave evidence on whether the complainant was suggestible and likely to fantasize. The defendant was convicted and his subsequent appeal upheld. The Court of Appeal noted that the Crown could not 'call a witness of fact and then, without more, call a psychologist or psychiatrist to give reasons why the jury should regard that witness as reliable'.

R v Turner [1975] QB 834, CA

Lawton LJ

What, in plain English, was the psychiatrist in this case intending to say? First, that the defendant was not showing and never had shown any evidence of mental illness, as defined by the Mental Health Act 1959, and did not require any psychiatric treatment; secondly, that he had had a deep emotional relationship with the girl which was likely to have caused an explosive release of blind rage when she confessed her wantonness to him; thirdly, that after he had killed her he behaved like someone suffering from profound grief. The first part of his opinion was within his expert province and outside the experience of the jury but was of no relevance in the circumstances of this case. The second and third points dealt with matters which are well within ordinary human experience. We all know that both men and women who are deeply in love can, and sometimes do, have outbursts of blind rage when discovering unexpected wantonness on the part of their loved ones; the wife taken in adultery is the classical example of the application of the defence of 'provocation'; and when death or serious injury results, profound grief usually follows. Jurors do not need psychiatrists to tell them how ordinary folk who are not suffering from any mental illness are likely to react to the stresses and strains of life. It follows that the proposed evidence was not admissible to establish that the defendant was likely to have been provoked. The same reasoning applies to its suggested admissibility on the issue of credibility. The jury had to decide what reliance they could put upon the defendant's evidence. He had to be judged as someone who was not mentally disordered. This is what juries are empanelled to do. The law assumes they can perform their duties properly. The jury in this case did not need, and should not have been offered, the evidence of a psychiatrist to help them decide whether the defendant's evidence was truthful. Mr. Mildon submitted that such help should not have been rejected by the judge because in Lowery v. The Queen [1974] A.C. 85 the Privy Council had approved of the admission of the evidence of a psychologist on the issue of credibility. We had to consider that case carefully before we could decide whether it had in any way put a new interpretation upon what have long been thought to be the rules relating to the calling of evidence on the issue of credibility, viz. that in general evidence can be called to impugn the credibility of witnesses but not led in chief to bolster it up. In Lowery v. The Queen evidence of a psychologist on behalf of one of two accused was admitted to establish that his version of the facts was more probable than that put forward by the other. In every case what is relevant and admissible depends on the issues raised in that case. In Lowery v. The Queen the issues were unusual . . . We adjudge Lowery v. The Queen [1974] A.C. 85 to have been decided on its special facts. We do not consider that it is an authority for the proposition that in all cases psychologists and psychiatrists can be called to prove the probability of the accused's veracity. If any such rule was applied in our courts, trial by psychiatrists would be likely to take the place of trial by jury and magistrates. We do not find that prospect attractive and the law does not at present provide for it.

Turner in Practice

When it comes to psychological conditions, the key question is to ask whether the relevant mental state amounts to a serious and identifiable psychiatric disorder. Obviously, by its very nature, insanity or mental illness will be outside the province of the jury; it is not something that jurors will come across in their 'normal' lives and expert evidence is always received on this issue. The statutory partial defence of diminished responsibility under s. 2(1) of the Homicide Act 1957, requiring 'such abnormality of mind (whether arising from a condition of arrested or retarded development of mind or any inherent causes or induced by disease or injury)', is also a subject on which, by definition, expert opinion can always be heard. However, in areas like provocation, a separate defence under s. 3 of the 1957 Act, where there is no necessary suggestion of such abnormality, this type of evidence is normally excluded.

Similarly, in *R v Weightman* [1991] 92 Cr App R 291, the Court of Appeal upheld a trial judge's decision to exclude psychiatric evidence that a defendant in a murder trial, who had confessed to her husband, probation officer and the police that she had deliberately suffocated her two-year-old child, but who, it was freely admitted, was not suffering from mental illness or of below normal intelligence, had an impaired capacity to develop enduring relationships with other people, was emotionally superficial, attention seeking and also impulsive under stress, something that may have led her to make false admissions to the killing. Such a diagnosis probably applies to a significant proportion of 'normal' people. As a consequence of the general requirement that an identifiable psychiatric disorder be present before such evidence is received, the cases appear to limit the evidence of psychologists to a greater extent than they do that of medically trained psychiatrists; the former profession is often primarily concerned with 'normal', rather than pathological, mental conditions (though the limitations will also apply to psychiatrists giving evidence on 'normal' individuals).

R v Beverley Anne Weightman [1991] 92 Cr App R 291, CA

McCowan LJ

At the end of the day however it is very much a question of the facts in a particular case. It seems to us that the principle to be learnt from the cases, notably the case of Turner (supra), is that a psychiatrist's evidence is inadmissible where its purpose is in effect to tell a jury how a person who is not suffering from mental illness is likely to react to the stresses and strains in life. The point taken here is that the appellant has an abnormal personality, as was conceded by Mr. Hunt for the prosecution at the trial. What does that abnormal personality amount to however? It seems to us that it is not something which is beyond the experience of normal non-medical people. She is histrionic, theatrical and likely to say things to draw attention to herself. The jurors had already heard this without objection from the probation officer. They would know that there are people like that. They knew that the defence was that in accordance with her nature that was what she had done here. The jury had the advantage not merely of seeing her in the witness box, but also of hearing her on the tapes that had been made of the police interview. We must conclude that the jury did not believe that this was a case where she had falsely confessed in order to draw attention to herself. They concluded that her confession was true. In our judgment they would not have been helped by having a psychiatrist talking about 'emotional superficiality' and 'impaired capacity to develop and sustain deep or enduring relationships'. In fact as Lawton L.J. pointed out in the Turner case (1975) 60 Cr.App.R. 80, 83, [1975] Q.B. 834, 'dressed up in scientific jargon it may make judgment more difficult'. For these reasons our conclusion is that the learned judge was entirely right in the ruling that he made, and this appeal must be dismissed.

Intellectual Deficiencies

A similarly robust approach is taken by the courts to inherent intellectual (as opposed to personality) defects in defendants and witnesses. Although most jurors and, it is to be hoped, all magistrates and judges, are not themselves unintelligent, they have everyday experience of people who are. As a consequence, the present state of the law does not normally permit expert assistance in areas relating to intellect unless the level of intelligence in question is deemed to be 'pathological.' By this is meant something that falls outside the most generous range of 'normality' and amounts to an identifiable and severe disorder.

Establishing the parameters for this has resulted in extremely fine distinctions. Thus, and for example, current practice suggests that when the defendant slips below the point on the IQ scale that is considered to separate people who are deemed to be very unintelligent (but normal) from those who are considered to be mentally defective, ie below 70 IQ points, expert evidence on the special intellectual characteristics of such people can normally be adduced to assist the tribunal of fact. This might be over, and again for example, their ability to form the requisite *mens rea* for an offence.

However, if the figure is slightly to the 'right' side of this limit, as was the case in *R v Masih* [1986] Crim LR 395, such evidence is not normally admissible. In *Masih*, the defendant was accused of rape, and the question arose as to whether his lack of intelligence might have contributed to his being unaware that the complainant was not consenting to intercourse. He had no mental disorder, nor was he intellectually quite 'defective', having an assessed IQ of 72 (just within the supposed realm of normality, and a level present in only 3% of the population). Because of this, tendered expert evidence as to the defendant's likely understanding of the incident that led to his indictment was held to be inadmissible. A judge or juror is deemed to be able to make allowances for the understanding of a very unintelligent but 'normal' individual that he would not make for a NASA scientist, without receiving professional assistance on the point, as Lord Lane observed, where a defendant was: 'within the scale of normality, albeit, as this man was, at the lower end of that scale, expert evidence, in our judgment, is not as a rule, necessary and should be excluded'.

Of course there is a risk in such a situation, to quote Burt CJ in the Australian case of *Schultz v R* [1982] WAR 171, that the jury will not appreciate the defendant's limited intellect from 'merely seeing and hearing the [defendant] in the witness box'. This clearly places a heavy onus on counsel, when calling such an accused to 'set the scene' in his preliminary questions during examination in chief, by, for example, asking the defendant for details about his school and employment record, so that the jury or bench is given some opportunity to make an assessment of his mental faculties.

Long Established Departures From the Principle in *Turner*

It should be noted that one Privy Council case is at apparent variance to the general position reached in *Turner*. In the Australian murder case of *Lowery v The Queen* [1974] AC 85, evidence of a psychologist (Professor Cox) given on behalf of one of two co-accused (King), was admitted to establish that his version of the facts was more probable than that put forward by his co-defendant. In this case, a young girl had been sadistically killed in the outback by one or both of two (mentally 'normal') youths. The defendant (Lowery), to whose disadvantage the psychologist's evidence was given, had run a 'cut-throat' defence and had, in effect, said before it was called that he was not the sort of man who would commit such a crime so that it must have carried out by King. It was held that the evidence of Professor Cox, who had examined both youths, and which was to the effect that Lowery was the more aggressive and assertive of the two, King the more passive, was both relevant to, and admissible for, the co-defendant's case, as it involved negating what Lowery had put forward.

However, the following year, in *Turner* Lawton LJ concluded that *Lowery* was: '...decided on its special facts. We do not consider that it is an authority for the proposition that in all cases psychologists and psychiatrists can be called to prove the probability of the accused's veracity'. Nevertheless, although very rarely, if ever, encountered in practice, non-expert aspects of the decision in *Lowery* were (broadly) followed by the Court of Appeal in *R v Bracewell* [1979] 68 Cr App R 44. More pertinently, in *R v Randall* [2004] 1 Cr App R 26, another cut-throat defence, the House of Lords expressly declined an opportunity to comment on the correctness of expert evidence of propensity in such situations (and thus the decision in *Lowery*). It is possible that if the situation in *Lowery* were closely replicated in the future, the same approach would be followed.

Lowery v The Queen [1974] AC 85, PC

Lord Morris

In these circumstances it was most relevant for King to be able to show, if he could, that Lowery had a personality marked by aggressiveness whereas he, King, had a personality which suggested that he would be led and dominated by someone who was dominant and aggressive. In support of King's case the evidence of Professor Cox was relevant if it tended to show that the version of the facts put forward by King was more probable than that put forward by Lowery. Not only however was the evidence which King called relevant to this case: its admissibility was placed beyond doubt by the whole substance of Lowery's case. Not only did Lowery assert that the killing was done by King and not only did he say that he had been in fear of King but, as previously mentioned, he set himself up as one who had no motive whatsoever in killing the girl and as one who would not have been likely to wreck his good prospects and furthermore as one who would not have been interested in the sort of behavior manifested by the killer. While ascribing the sole responsibility to King he was also in effect saying that he himself was not the sort of man to have committed the offence. The only question now arising is whether in the special circumstances above referred to it was open to King in defending himself to call Professor Cox to give the evidence that he gave. The evidence was relevant to and necessary for his case which involved negativing what Lowery had said and put forward: in their Lordships' view in agreement with that of the Court of Criminal Appeal the evidence was admissible.

Another apparent exception to the general situation relates to young children. Although all adults have been children, and most adults either have them or know people who do, case law indicates that this is not invariably viewed as enough to make all matters of juvenile psychology involving 'normal range' children within their unassisted competence. Thus, Lord Parker CJ noted in *R v AB & C Chewing Gum* [1968] 1 QB 159 that: '...any jury and any justices need all the help they can get...as to the effect [of something] on different children'. In this case, the Divisional Court opined that expert evidence was admissible on whether graphic picture cards sold with bubble gum, depicting gruesome American Civil War battle scenes, might 'corrupt or deprave' the juveniles purchasing them. Nevertheless, it should be noted that this decision has since been questioned and is largely confined to its facts.

Similarly, and less controversially, although the form of non-insane automatism termed sleep-walking might not be categorized as a mental illness, Lane LJ (as he then was) noted in the Court of Appeal that it was clearly outside the ordinary juryman's experience and something on which they could receive assistance: *R v Smith* [1979] 1 WLR 1445.

R v Smith [1979] 1 WLR 1445, CA

Lane LJ

The next point he made is this: as a matter of discretion these reports should not be admitted. In effect, he says this: that in order to be admissible at all the reports must be relevant; that is to say, relevant to some issue which the jury have to determine. He submits that since there was no question of insanity or diminished responsibility, automatism or not was a matter which could and should be decided by the jury in the light or their own experience and they should not be assisted by medical or expert evidence as to the state of mind of the defendant. That being so, he suggests the doctors' evidence was irrelevant and, on that basis, should not have been admitted. Here, again, he cites a number of authorities....So, the question seems to be whether or not the applicant exhibited the type of abnormality in relation to automatism that would render it proper and, indeed, desirable for the jury to have expert help in reaching their conclusion. It seems to us without the benefit of authority that that is clearly the case. This type of automatism—sleepwalking—call it what you like, is not something, we think, which is within the realm of the ordinary juryman's experience. It is something on which, speaking for ourselves as judges, we should like help were we to have to decide it and we see not why a jury should be deprived of that type of help.

Any mental defect that renders a witness incapable (rather than unwilling) of testifying reliably can also be the subject of expert evidence as to credibility, though most such conditions will, necessarily, be defined as mental illness, and thus cannot be seen as departures from the principle in *Turner*. Nevertheless, there might be conditions, such as hysteria, that could not properly be so defined, and yet which can still be the subject of expert evidence.

Toohey v Metropolitan Police Commissioner [1965] AC 595, HL

Lord Pearce

Human evidence shares the frailties of those who give it. It is subject to many cross-currents such as partiality, prejudice, self-interest and, above all, imagination and inaccuracy. Those are matters with which the jury, helped by cross-examination and common sense, must do their best. But when a witness through physical (in which I include mental) disease or abnormality is not capable of giving a true or reliable account to the jury, it must surely be allowable for medical science to reveal this vital hidden fact to them. If a witness purported to give evidence of something which he believed that he had seen at a distance of 50 yards, it must surely be possible to call the evidence of an oculist to the effect that the witness could not possibly see anything at a greater distance than 20 yards, or the evidence of a surgeon who had removed a cataract from which the witness was suffering at the material time and which would have prevented him from seeing what he thought he saw. So, too, must it be allowable to call medical evidence of mental illness which makes a witness incapable of giving reliable evidence, whether through the existence of delusions or otherwise.

Criticisms of *Turner*

The general restrictiveness of the approach adopted in *Turner* to the admissibility of expert opinion evidence has not gone unchallenged. For example, it has been asserted that the courts have 'misled' the public into believing that there is a clear dividing line between 'normality' and 'abnormality' and that the testimony of experts (especially psychiatrists) cannot help jurors determine the criminal responsibility of 'normal' people or the weight that should be accorded to ordinary witnesses.[3]

This is, perhaps, a slightly harsh analysis. There has to be a dividing line somewhere in such cases, however imperfect, unless an evidential 'free for all' is to be permitted. This line cannot be chosen by the tribunal of fact (otherwise all such evidence would have to be admitted for its consideration) and whatever one is chosen will, to an extent, be arbitrary. Doubtless, Lawton LJ would have been the first to accept that there would be borderline cases and, even in *Turner*, he expressly accepted that such evidence was often potentially relevant, albeit excluded for sound policy reasons. For this reason, the decision in *Turner* has been influential, or independently replicated, in much of the common law world and continues to be the bedrock of the modern approach to such evidence.

For example, the same general approach has recently been taken in a case from the Northern Territory of Australia. In *The Queen v Joyce* [2005] NTSC 21 the appellant was convicted of an offence of indecency with a nine-year-old boy. The child was not suffering from any abnormal psychological condition. At trial, the defendant wished to adduce expert evidence from a psychologist to undermine the credit of videos recorded by the alleged victim giving his version as to what had occurred (for example, by discussing the possibility of the boy suffering from hyperamnesia and 'interviewer bias', etc.). The first instance judge's decision not to admit this evidence was robustly upheld on appeal, even though it related to a child. The court stressed that the assessment of a 'normal' witness's credibility was a function that juries had traditionally conducted without expert assistance, such expertise not being necessary to enable the fact-finder to reach a just conclusion.[4]

It should, perhaps, also be noted that even if the opinion of some types of expert may not be directly admissible as evidence, this does not preclude parties (or more accurately their lawyers) from making *any* use of them. There is nothing to prevent them, in suitable cases, from obtaining such reports from, for example, psychologists, employing them as 'advising experts' and then using them to spot potential weaknesses in an opponent's case, or avenues of defence in their own. They could also be used to shape the appropriate manner of questions for the examination of witnesses.[5]

Recent Modifications to the Strictness in *Turner*

Perhaps as a consequence of the criticisms that have been levelled at the judgment, the strictness of the limitations placed on expert evidence of mental characteristics enunciated in *Turner* have been subtly modified over the last 30 years. This is also in line with the situation in some other common law countries (if often more modest in extent). As a result, expert evidence is received on the *voir dire* as to the admissibility of confessions and to mental states that do not amount to full mental illness in circumstances where it would not have been 30 years ago.

---

[3] RD MacKay and AM Colman, 'Excluding Expert Evidence: a tale of ordinary folk and common experience' [1991] Crim LR at 801.

[4] Discussed in [2006] Crim LR at 276–277.

[5] See on this D Sheldon and M Macleod, 'From normative To Positive Data: expert psychological evidence re-examined' [1991] Crim LR 819.

Expert Evidence, Confessions and the *Voir Dire*

When it comes to evidence of intellect or personality, submissions on the admissibility of confessions, made on the voir dire, are now clearly a 'case apart'. This has produced a rather strange dichotomy whereby such evidence is inadmissible if tendered to establish *mens rea* (or the lack of it) in the substantive trial, when the rule in *Turner* will apply, and situations where it is being adduced on the *voir dire* to establish the potential unreliability of a confession under s. 76(2)(b) of the Police and Criminal Evidence Act 1984, when it normally will not.

> ### Cross-reference Box
>
> Confessions are admitted as an exception to the hearsay rule. However, to prevent abuse, s. 76(2)(b) of the Police and Criminal Evidence Act 1984 requires that a confession be excluded unless the prosecution can prove that it was not obtained by anything said or done that would be likely, in the circumstances, to make it unreliable. Such hearings are usually heard, in the absence of the jury, on a special procedure known as the voir dire. For more information on this and confessions generally, see pp. 320–350.

This is a result of the case of *R v Silcott, Braithwaite, Raghip* (1991) *The Times*, 9 December, which extended the earlier Court of Appeal decision in *R v Everett* [1988] Crim LR 826. In *Everett,* the defendant, a 42 year-old man with the mental functioning of a child of eight had an IQ of 61 (clearly severely sub-normal) and, unsurprisingly, evidence of this had been adduced on the *voir dire* as relevant to reliability on the ground that it was part of the 'circumstances of the case'. This became regular practice in such cases. In *Raghip*, however, the defendant had an IQ of 74 (like *Masih*, at the lower end of 'normality'). However, the House of Lords concluded that when it came to considering the application of s. 76(2)(b) it was undesirable to have an 'artificial' distinction between cases fractionally one side or the other of the line of 'normality'. The court felt that although Raghip's IQ was on the 'right side' of that borderline, as a 19 year-old man who, when interviewed, had the level of intellectual functioning of an average child of less than 10, he could not be said to be normal in any proper sense; as a result, the evidence was held to be admissible on the issue of reliability (and thus the admissibility of his confession).

Nevertheless, the court also made clear that this development was limited to the reliability of confessions being determined on the *voir dire*: '…nothing we say in this judgment is intended to reflect upon the admissibility of psychiatric or psychological evidence going to the issue of the defendant's *mens rea*'. Despite this observation, shortly after *Raghip* was decided, some observers suggested that it might undermine the approach taken to withholding such evidence from the tribunal of fact when it came to questions of mens rea.[6]

However, the distinction was reiterated in the case of *R v Coles* [1995] 1 Cr App R 157, where the defendant was accused of arson, being reckless as to whether life was endangered, and wished to adduced the evidence of a psychologist to the effect that he was in the 'low average range of intellectual functioning', something which may have provided a basis for the conclusion that

---

[6] P Mirfield, 'Expert Evidence and Unreliable Confessions' (1992) Law Quarterly Review, 528–534, at 534.

he lacked a capacity for foresight (ie which went to the issue of *mens rea*). Hobhouse LJ, in the Court of Appeal, reiterated the principle in *Turner*. He held that the judge had rightly excluded this evidence as it related to characteristics of the defendant that could be properly evaluated by a jury without the assistance of expert evidence. The principle in *Raghip* did not apply.

R v Coles [1995] 1 Cr App R 157, CA

Hobhouse LJ

The other ground of appeal advanced on behalf of the appellant related to the exclusion of the evidence of Mr Kirby Turner. The judge rightly refused to admit this evidence. It was not evidence of any abnormality of the mind of the defendant. It related to characteristics of the defendant which could be competently evaluated by a jury by reference to the facts of the actual case without the assistance of expert evidence. Adolescents of varying stages of maturity and brightness are all within the common experience of jurors. The appellant relied upon the case of Raghip, Silcott and Braithwaite, The Times, December 9, 1991, where the Court of Appeal held that expert evidence as to the mental characteristics of a defendant ought to have been admitted. But this was expressly in relation to the exercise of a judge's discretion whether or not he ought to admit a confession under section 76 of the Police & Criminal Evidence Act 1984. Such evidence had been admitted in the case of Everett [1988] Crim.L.R. 826, and the court was of the opinion that such evidence ought to have been admitted in the case of Raghip in order to assist the judge in deciding whether or not the defendant was particularly susceptible to suggestion and whether or not it was fair to him to admit in evidence what he had said in response to questions by the police. The Court of Appeal expressly drew a distinction between such evidence and evidence which was said to go to the defendant's mens rea: 'We emphasise that nothing we say in this judgment is intended to reflect upon the admissibility of psychiatric or psychological evidence going to the issue of the defendant's mens rea.' Unless some factor of the mental health or psychiatric state of the defendant is raised, such evidence is not admissible.

 Pause for reflection

Do you feel that it is right that an experienced trial judge can be assisted by expert evidence on the *voir dire* when this is not open to lay in the substantive trial?

This conclusion was reaffirmed more recently by the Court of Appeal in *R v Henry* [2006] 1 Cr App R 6. In this case, the defendant was accused of conspiracy to murder. His defence was that he had had no intention of harming the proposed victim and had merely played along with his manipulative co-conspirator in order to keep her quiet. He argued that his conviction should be quashed in the light of new evidence revealing that he had an IQ of about 75 and that his personality meant that he was an impulsive individual who was easily imposed upon, ie that went to his ability to form the requisite *mens rea*. However, the Court of Appeal concluded that expert evidence of neither his low intellect nor his personality would have been admissible at trial, and upheld his conviction.

R v Henry [2006] 1 Cr App R 6, CA

Kay LJ

In our judgment, the evidence of Dr Lowenstein and Prof. Gudjonsson is no more admissible on the issue of intention in the present case than the disputed evidence was in Masih and Coles. This is not a case of mental illness nor is it a case in which the IQ of the appellant is below that considered by the Lord Chief Justice to be the threshold for admissibility in Masih. Whilst it is true that persons with an IQ as low as that of the appellant form a small part of the population at large, sadly they form a somewhat larger part of those charged with criminal offences. An intention that someone should be killed is a visceral matter of no great complexity. In our judgment, it is not a matter which, on the authorities, lends itself to expert evidence in relation to a person such as this appellant. Moreover, it is not without significance that, in any event, the reports of Dr Lowenstein and Prof. Gudjonsson do not opine that the intellectual impairment of the appellant acted or may have acted as a contra-indication of the specific intention. Indeed, to the extent that they portray the appellant as easily led and ineffective in coping with stress and demands placed upon him by someone such as Donna Bailey, their views are entirely consistent with the prosecution case.

Severe Mental Abnormality

The borderline between outright mental illness and a 'normal' scale personality peculiarity can be even more vague than that between defective and low-normal intelligence (which is at least roughly 'testable'). In *R v Ward* [1993] 2 All ER 577, this ambiguity allowed the Court of Appeal to soften some of the strictness of the decision in *Turner* by concluding that the expert evidence of a psychiatrist or psychologist might be admitted if it was to the effect that a defendant was suffering from a condition which, though not properly definable as mental illness or insanity, amounted to a personality disorder 'so severe as properly to be categorised as mental disorder'. Although the court felt that this was likely to be particularly relevant when such evidence related to the validity of a confession, unlike evidence of intelligence, it was not *limited* to such situations. This slightly more liberal approach allowed the court to avoid some of the semantic problems occasioned by the debate as to what exactly constitutes a psychiatric 'illness'.

This flexibility has been reflected in a number of decisions in the ensuing years. Thus, in the case of *R v White* [1995] Crim LR 393, the Court of Appeal accepted that new psychiatric evidence to the effect that a nightclub doorman, convicted of a s. 18 assault under the Offences Against the Person Act 1861 (OAP Act 1861), was suffering from post-traumatic stress disorder, producing a dissociative state, as a result of an earlier violent incident, would have been admissible at trial. It was something that might have affected his ability to form the specific intent needed for a conviction under s. 18 of the OAP Act 1861 (ie which went to the issue of *mens rea*). An identical approach was adopted, to the same mental condition, in *R v Huckerby* [2004] All ER (D) 364. Such a disorder, though not extremely uncommon, is outside a normal juror's experience.

Similarly, in *R v Strudwick and Merry* [1994] 99 Cr App R 326, Farquharson LJ noted that there could be psychiatric conditions 'other than mental illness' in relation to which a jury might require expert assistance. In this case, expert psychological evidence of the effects of her own experience of child abuse on the mother of an abused child, such as an irrational belief that the child would survive and a personal 'emotional cut-off' from its situation was refused on the facts of the case. However, the judge indicated that, in other circumstances, it might have been permitted, even though it did not amount to mental illness. This position was reaffirmed, and further guidance provided, in *R v O'Brien, Hall and Sherwood* [2000] Crim LR 676, where it was noted that such evidence would show a substantial deviation from the norm and would normally be evidenced prior to trial. As a result of these decisions, the grey area between mental illness and a normal personality disorder has been redefined to emphasize the borderline between severe mental disorder (including but not limited to mental illness) and a 'normal' range personality defect, such as attention seeking and a histrionic nature.

R v Strudwick and Merry [1994] 99 Cr App R 326, CA

Farquharson LJ

It is not suggested here that the appellant is suffering from a mental illness, but that is not in itself conclusive against the admission of this evidence. The law is in a state of development in this area. There may well be other mental conditions about which a jury might require expert assistance in order to understand and evaluate their effect on the issues in a case. Miss Hallett submits that the psychological damage said to have been suffered by her client falls into that category. If the prosecution allegation had been that the signs of ill treatment on Sophie were not readily apparent, but nonetheless showed the sort of ill treatment which any normal mother would have recognised and acted upon, there would have been considerable force in that submission. But by the time the judge was asked to admit the evidence he and the jury had heard that this child was showing the signs of brutal ill treatment and had been for a long time, particularly during the days up to September 15, 1991, and that the second appellant had denied both in interview and in her evidence that there were any such signs. In these circumstances, while we are of the opinion that the judge could usefully have inquired further as to the weight of the opinions expressed in the experts' reports, we consider that he was correct in concluding that there was nothing in the case which a jury would be unable to deal with unaided by the experts. In coming to that conclusion he applied the correct test when he said that the experts were 'not likely to afford the jury the kind of help without which they would be unable to do justice to Mrs Merry's case'. Their evidence was, and is, highly relevant to understanding why the second appellant may have behaved in the way that she did, and is therefore of great importance when considering the appropriate sentence. Although we found Miss Hallett's argument attractive, we do not feel able to hold that the judge, as a matter of law, was in error.

The belated final appeal (on a CCRC referral) in *R v Pinfold and Mackenny* [2004] 2 Cr App R 32 (more than 20 years after the initial conviction) suggests that, even when it comes to questions of witness credibility, the courts are sometimes now willing to accept expert evidence on how this might be affected by serious personality disorders that do not prevent a witness from giving reliable testimony (a well established exception under the principle in *Toohey*), but which might affect the witness's willingness to do so; traditionally, under *Turner*, this was a matter purely for the jury to assess.

In this case, which involved a gruesome series of murders, the presiding judge's decision not to allow in expert evidence of a key prosecution witness's psychopathic personality, and its likely effect on his veracity, was upheld on appeal in 1981. Psychopaths are quite capable of giving reliable evidence if they wish to do so; they are merely prone to lying and often adept and adroit at doing so if they choose to adopt such a course of action. At the initial trial, and the first appeal, of the matter a 'traditional' approach had been followed.

R v Mackenney [1981] 72 Cr App R 78, CA

May J

If a witness is suffering from a mental disability, in a proper case, it may well be permissible to call psychiatric evidence to show that the witness is incapable of giving reliable evidence; but this, in my judgment, is very different from calling psychiatric evidence with a view to warning a jury about a witness who is capable of giving reliable evidence, but who may well not be doing so. If the witness is mentally capable of giving reliable evidence, it is for the jury, with all the warnings from counsel and the Court which the law requires, to decide whether or not that witness is giving reliable evidence.

However, when the matter was reconsidered by the Court of Appeal in 2004, a more liberal approach was taken. The court concluded that expert evidence could be given of the same witness's psychopathic personality, which meant that he could give apparently convincing evidence which was untrue, even though he retained the ability to give truthful evidence if he wished to do so.

Nevertheless, it should be noted that this relaxation does not abolish the general application of the rule in *Turner* with regard to credibility; it merely moderates it to allow evidence to be adduced of a very severe abnormality that affects a witness's willingness to give truthful evidence. Indeed, only a few years prior to this decision, in *R v Pendleton* [2002] 1 Cr App R 441, Lord Hobhouse had reiterated the decision in *Turner* in the House of Lords, noting that the courts: '... should be cautious about admitting evidence from psychologists, however, eminent, as to the credibility of witnesses. The assessment of the truth of verbal evidence is save in a very small number of exceptional circumstances a matter for the jury.' He went on to observe that the suggestibility of some witnesses was well within the experience of ordinary members of a jury, and that admitting evidence from psychologists on such a matter would be contrary to the established rules of evidence and the principle of trial by jury. As the contrast between these cases suggests, it is a matter of degree. Nevertheless, there remains a tension between the decision in *Toohey* and that in *R v Pinfold and Mackenny* [2004] 2 Cr App R 32.

R v Pinfold and Mackenny [2004] 2 Cr App R 32, CA

Lord Woolf CJ

Turning to the question of admissibility of expert medical evidence to assist the jury as to the weight, if any, to be attached to the evidence of a particular witness, it is important to appreciate that the approach of this court has over the years developed and is now more generous towards the admission of expert evidence than was once the case...The same approach [to evidence of credibility] applies whether the expert evidence that is being considered relates to a witness or a defendant. However, especially in the case of a witness it is necessary to take into account the importance of the evidence that the witness gives. If the evidence of the witness is of little significance to the issues at the trial, the admission of expert evidence is unlikely to be justified. This approach has to be contrasted with the more restricted approach adopted by May J. and the Court of Appeal in this case. (See R v Mackenney (1980) 72 Cr App R 78 and R v Pinfold (1983) 76 Cr App r 271). Miss Coen accepts that, since the date of the trial, there has been a greater willingness to accept medical expert evidence on the issue of the credibility of a witness than existed at the time of those decisions. However, in view of the decision in R v Fell [2001] EWCA Crim 696, she contends that the expert evidence has to be based on a physical examination of the witness whose credibility is being impugned before it can be admitted...The Court has to determine whether the evidence could be considered credible evidence by the jury as to an abnormality from which the witness suffered at the time of giving evidence and which might mean that the jury would not attach the weight it would otherwise do to the witness's evidence. The absence of an examination by the expert goes to the weight to be attached to the expert's opinion and not to the admissibility of that opinion. What a court must be on its guard against is any attempt to detract from the jury's task of finding for themselves what evidence to believe. The court should therefore not allow evidence to be placed before the jury which does not allege any medical abnormality as the basis for the evidence of a witness being approached with particular caution by the jury. Ultimately, it remains the jury's task to decide for themselves whether they believe a witness' testimony.

Additionally, in the light of recent cases, it seems that the effect of highly unusual circumstances on people with 'normal' personalities might be deemed to be outside the competence of a tribunal of fact, and so the subject of expert evidence. This might extend, for example, to the effects of an excessively prolonged interrogation: *R v Blackburn* [2005] 2 Cr App R 30.

R v Blackburn [2005] 2 Cr App R 30, CA

Keene LJ

The Crown resisted the appellant's application to call fresh evidence by Dr Eric Shepherd, a consultant forensic psychologist, who has extensive experience of interrogation methods and of their effects. Lord Carlile Q.C., on behalf of the Crown, did not question Dr Shepherd's expertise, but argued that his evidence was not admissible because it did not address matters outside the range of experience of a jury. Dr Shepherd, said Lord Carlile Q.C., would merely be giving general evidence about how 15-year-old boys might react to lengthy questioning. Moreover, there was no suggestion here of any abnormal disorder on the part of the appellant, who had not even been examined or interviewed by Dr Shepherd before the latter had written his report. The Crown placed some reliance on a passage from the case of R. v O'Brien, Hall and Sherwood [2000] Crim.L.R. 676, which suggested that, in cases where the expert evidence related to the existence of an abnormal disorder on the part of the accused, the disorder had to be of a kind which might render the confession unreliable.

28 We ruled during the hearing that Dr Shepherd's evidence was admissible and we received it under s. 23. His evidence concerns the phenomenon of false confessions and the circumstances in which research has shown that a vulnerable individual, after a prolonged period of questioning, may give what is termed a coerced compliant confession. It seemed to the Court that this was a topic which would generally fall outside the normal range of experience of a jury and that it was therefore one on which expert evidence was properly admissible. The case of O'Brien has little bearing on this issue. The passage there relied on by Lord Carlile Q.C. applies where there is some evidence about an abnormal disorder on the part of the accused. That is not this case. O'Brien was not intended to be a comprehensive statement as to the circumstances when expert evidence will be admissible on the reliability of a confession.

29 The essence of Dr Shepherd's evidence before us was that the key feature giving rise to a coerced compliant confession is fatigue, which, together with an inability to control what is happening, may induce the individual to experience a growing desire to give up resisting suggestions put to him. Eventually he can take no more and is overwhelmed by the need to achieve his

immediate goal of bringing the interrogation to an end. That may not seem rational to an outsider, but it becomes rational if the individual finds the circumstances becoming intolerable. The age of such a person, said Dr Shepherd, is significant. Generally the younger he is, the less able he is to withstand sustained pressure. After more than three hours' interview without a break and references to new sexual allegations about the 1976 Irlam incident, one could well get a coerced compliant confession. Whether true or false, it is not reliable, said Dr Shepherd, because of such circumstances. He noted the appellant's evidence at trial that he had confessed because he wanted to get out of the interview and he 'felt sick of it'. Dr Shepherd also described the phenomenon of persons in such a position inventing details when under stress, something he termed 'confabulation' or conversational polyfilla. This can sometimes lead to a person describing things which could not have happened. Such details needed, said Dr Shepherd, to be checked out before they should be accepted...He distinguished these phenomena from the characteristic of suggestibility. The latter is related to personality, whereas the former are more the result of fatigue and vulnerability because of age or other factors. Consequently normal people, not suffering from any personality disorder or abnormal disorder, could be rendered compliant by prolonged interrogation.

Future Developments

As these cases suggest, the whole area of expert opinion evidence is also in the process of continuing evolution. Further developments might be expected over the next few years. Thus, to help address the very low conviction levels found in rape cases, in 2006, a government consultation paper, *Convicting Rapists and Protecting Victims-Justice for Victims of Rape* proposed that another exception to the general pattern be allowed, whereby an appropriate expert, such as a psychologist, could give evidence (in general terms) on rape trauma syndrome and similar conditions to assist jurors with understanding why allegations of rape by complainants are often made some time after the incident to which they relate, etc. Such behaviour, if unexplained, might appear suspicious to jurors, mistakenly leading them to feel that an allegation must have been fabricated.

Convicting Rapists and Protecting Victims—Justice for Victims of Rape Office for Criminal Justice Reform (2006) 16–18 (Extract)

General expert evidence goes to the heart of this problem as it will explain to jurors and judges that such apparently problematic features of a person's evidence are common and should not necessarily lead to the conclusion that the victim/witness is lying or unreliable. The court will be informed of the acknowledged psychological reactions that occur after a prolonged relationship of abuse and/or after a deeply traumatic event. Such reactions can affect a victim's ability to give a coherent, consistent account of their experiences and cause behaviour which, to an onlooker, is puzzling as it does not match the expectation as to how 'genuine' victims act or react. For example, a court could be told that it is not unusual for a rape victim to delay reporting and an expert would provide alternative explanations that the jury could consider. Alternatively, general expert evidence could be used to counter the commonly held view that if a person has been raped by their partner, then the victim would leave. However, there are many practical reasons why people feel compelled to stay with violent partners—fear of poverty, social ostracism and child care. The inclusion of such evidence will also assist in challenging the erroneous assumptions and preconceptions that surround victims. These misperceptions and myths have been the subject of much research and academic debate. (Annex C contains a list of references on this area.) For example, in the recent Amnesty poll, a blame culture was identified against the victims of rape. This February, the British Psychological Society published research following a hypothetical study, which did not involve actual rape trials. This found that if a judge summarised a rape case to a jury and in so doing invited them to consider the evidence from a perspective of accepting stereotypes and myths, then a juror would be more likely to find the defendant not guilty of the rape. It is hard not to conclude that certain societal attitudes do amount to a substantial contributing factor to the low conviction rates in rape cases.

We propose that such general expert evidence should only be called in rape cases. This is because rape is a unique offence. The majority of rapes occur between acquaintances. Often, there is little outside evidence that supports the victim's account given that such offences usually occur in private. In the majority of non-stranger rape cases the identity of the attacker is not disputed and there will be no conclusive forensic or medical evidence. At the moment, the only evidence as to what allegedly occurred is being considered against a background of misperceptions and myths as to how 'proper' victims should behave which is going unchallenged.

4. Problems Pertaining to Expert Evidence

Introduction

When considering the criticisms levied at *Turner,* it must be remembered that there are major problems inherently involved in the admission of expert evidence. There is a genuine danger that unnecessary recourse to such evidence risks creating confusion rather than illumination. Thus, the late Dr Zakaria Erzinçioglu, former director of the Forensic Science Research Centre at Durham University, and himself a world renowned expert, and frequent expert witness, on the interpretation of insect presence (in, for example, dead bodies), claimed that incompetent and dishonest forensic scientists were undermining the criminal justice system. He argued that 'quack practitioners' were infesting the courts because of the unregulated manner in which their services were marketed.[7]

Although Dr Erzinçioglu's view may be an exaggeration, experts can often be found to support a wide range of sometimes diametrically opposed opinions. Even though the bulk of them might agree on general principles, it is rare for this to be unanimous across a field of expertise. When it comes to the application of such principles to the facts of individual cases, the divergence in opinion often becomes much more acute. For example, in the civil courts, experienced Personal Injury practitioners, litigating in the realm of back injuries (a medical condition that often produces little 'concrete' or conclusive medical evidence either way) are well aware that there are 'robust' consultants (often favoured by defendants) who, probably quite sincerely, attribute most of these conditions to 'functional overlay' (ie psychosomatic issues), and 'sympathetic' ones (favoured by claimants) who usually attribute them to genuine physical trauma.

---

[7] '"Quack" forensic scientists "pose threat to justice"' *Daily Telegraph,* 30 April 1998.

It has also been argued that forensic scientists are often presented with a 'line' that they are tacitly required to support, and that the forensic scientist's popularity rests on whether or not he has rendered good service to those who paid him. The Court of Appeal explicitly recognized this risk with regard to prosecution expert evidence in the criminal case of *Ward*. This is not entirely the experts' fault, as (especially in the past) lawyers have sometimes explicitly encouraged them to modify unhelpful parts of their opinions.[8] This situation is also not assisted by the ambiguous position of experts; at one moment, they are part of the litigation 'team' of the party calling them, at the next, ostensibly impartial experts helping the court. As a result, Auld LJ suggested that in criminal cases there should be reforms to: '...strengthen the quality and objectivity of expert evidence and improve the manner of its presentation both from the point of view of the court and experts'.[9]

R v Ward [1993] 96 Cr App R1, CA

Glidewell LJ

For the future it is important to consider why the scientists acted as they did. For lawyers, jurors and judges a forensic scientist conjures up the image of a man in a white coat working in a laboratory, approaching his task with could neutrality, and dedicated only to the pursuit of scientific truth. It is a sombre thought that the reality is sometimes different. Forensic scientists may become partisan. The very fact that the police seek their assistance may create a relationship between the police and the forensic scientists. And the adversarial character of the proceedings tend to promote this process. Forensic scientists employed by the government may come to see their function as helping the police. They may lose their objectivity. That is what must have happened in this case...we propose to limit our observations about the lessons that can be learnt to two matters which we regard as of crucial importance. First we have identified the cause of the injustice...on the scientific side...as stemming from the fact that the three forensic scientists at R.A.R.D.E. regarded their task as being to help the police. They became partisan. It is the clear duty of governmental forensic scientists to assist in a neutral and impartial way in criminal investigations. They must act in the cause of justice. That duty should be spelt out to all engaged or to be engaged in forensic services in the clearest terms. We trust that this judgment has assisted a little in that exercise. Secondly, we believe that the surest way of preventing the misuse of scientific evidence is by ensuring that there is a proper understanding of the nature and scope of the prosecution's duty of disclosure.

Civil Cases

Fears about partisan experts are certainly not confined to the criminal courts. Lord Woolf's recommendations for expert evidence in his report *Access to Justice*, the final version of which was published in July 1996, revealed an underlying anxiety that experts all too often act, effectively, as 'hired guns' for the party that calls them, rather than as truly independent specialists assisting the court. He was also concerned that the excessive use of expert witnesses had contributed to the enormous rise in litigation costs over recent years, as parties sought to 'out-gun' each other in the forensic arena. However, there is nothing new in such concerns; more than

---

[8] See, for example, letter by Dr L Field in *Counsel*, Jan/Feb 1995 at 6.
[9] Auld LJ, *A Review of the Criminal Courts of England and Wales* (2001) chapter 2, para. 18.

120 years earlier, Sir George Jessell MR complained that experts 'employed and paid in the cause of gain' were inevitably biased in favour of those who paid them and eager to do something helpful for their employer: *Lord Abinger v Ashton* (1873) 17 LR Eq 358. Similar worries were expressed by Sir Thomas Bingham MR in *Abbey National Mortgages plc v Key Surveyors Nationwide Ltd.* (1996) 3 All ER 184; the judge further noted that party appointed experts sometimes became even 'more partisan than the parties'.

Lord Woolf, *Access to Justice; Final Report* (1996) Chapter 13, paras. 25–30

25. There is wide agreement that the expert's role should be that of an independent adviser to the court, and that lack of objectivity can be a serious problem. This may sometimes arise because of improper pressure on experts from solicitors, as was found in a survey of clinical and educational psychologists, the results of which were reported in the May 1996 issue of The Psychologist.

26. The present system has the effect of exaggerating the adversarial role of experts, and this helps neither the court nor the parties. As the Court of Appeal has recently remarked:

'For whatever reason, and whether consciously or unconsciously, the fact is that expert witnesses instructed on behalf of parties to litigation often tend...to espouse the cause of those instructing them to a greater or lesser extent, on occasion becoming more partisan than the parties.' (Abbey National Mortgages plc v Key Surveyors Nationwide Ltd and others [1996] EGCS 23)

27. The clear implication of this is that a new approach is required which emphasises experts' impartiality. In cases where the option of a single expert is not pursued, it is particularly important that each opposing expert's overriding duty to the court is clearly understood. This is partly a matter of good practice on the part of instructing solicitors, who may themselves need guidance as to the appropriate form of instructions to experts. In my view, clarification in the rules of court is also needed.

28. Contributions to the Inquiry from experts themselves suggest that there is a degree of uncertainty among them as to their duties, and a perceived conflict between their professional responsibilities and the demands of the client who is paying their fee. Experts would welcome some formal recognition of their role as advisers to the court rather than advocates of the parties.

29. The rules will provide that when an expert is preparing evidence for potential use in court proceedings, or is giving evidence in court, his responsibility is to help the court impartially on the matters within his expertise. This responsibility will override any duty to the client. The rule will reaffirm the duty which the courts have laid down as a matter of law in a number of cases, notably Whitehouse v Jordan, [1981] 1 WLR 246, when Lord Wilberforce said:

'It is necessary that expert evidence presented to the court should be and should be seen to be the independent product of the expert uninfluenced as to form or content by the exigencies of litigation.' (Cited by Cresswell J in The 'Ikarian Reefer' [1993] 2 Lloyds Reports 68).

30. There was wide support for the proposal in my interim report that an expert's report intended for use as evidence in court proceedings should be addressed to the court. I now propose that there should be a requirement to this effect in the rules of court to apply whenever litigation is contemplated. This is a formal but important requirement. It does not imply that the expert is to be instructed by the court, but is intended to concentrate the expert's mind as he writes the report on his paramount duty to the court.

Court Appointed Experts

A fear of partisanship is so serious that some commentators, and several members of the judiciary, have proposed the establishment of a court appointed system of experts, in both criminal and civil cases, to avoid the problems inherent in a system in which a party to the proceedings can often 'shop around', discarding unhelpful reports until it finds one that is favourable (especially if a defendant in a criminal case or involved in civil litigation). Alternatively, they can call an 'expert,' who, although technically qualified, is 'cranky, senile, or generally ill thought of within the profession'.[10]

For example, in *Abbey National Mortgages plc v Key Surveyors Nationwide Ltd.* (1996) 3 All ER 184, Sir Thomas Bingham suggested that a court appointed expert 'with no axe to grind' was more likely to prove a valuable source of forensic information. It has been argued that the essential strength of the civil law tradition is that it accepts that credible expertise must be neutral. In most continental systems, the primary responsibility for selecting and informing experts is placed on the courts. Thus, German courts, if they need an architect's expertise, do not commission a pair of them to take what some might argue are preordained and opposing positions. As Lord Woolf observed, in continental jurisdictions there is an underlying assumption that party appointed experts: '... will tell the court only what the parties want the court to know'.[11] Instead, a German court selects and instructs the expert, whether on its own initiative or at the request of one of the parties. The German code of civil procedure allows the court to ask the parties for nominations, and requires it to use any expert upon whom they agree, but, normally, the court takes the initiative in nominating and selecting the expert from a previously approved list.[12]

Dr Erzinclioglu urged that such a system be adopted in England, with an expert being answerable to neither side in a case but, instead, employed and paid by the court. He felt that such an arrangement, would remove the temptation to please one side or the other. He went even further by proposing that a statutory body of forensic science be established, answerable solely to the judiciary, which could be consulted by either party in the adversarial process, but not under pressure to accommodate the wishes of either side for reasons of monetary gain or misplaced loyalty.[13]

John H Langbein, 'The German Advantage in Civil Procedure' (1985) University of Chicago Law Review, vol 52, 823–866 at 835–836

The European jurist who visits the United States and becomes acquainted with our civil procedure typically expresses amazement at our witness practice. His amazement turns to something bordering on disbelief when he discovers that we extend the sphere of partisan control to the selection and preparation of experts. In the Continental tradition experts are selected and commissioned by the court, although with great attention to safeguarding party interests. In the German system, experts are not even called witnesses. They are thought of as 'judges' aides'.

---

[10] JR Spencer, 'The Neutral Expert: an implausible bogey' (1991) Crim LR 107. For an opposing view see MN Howard, 'The Neutral Expert: a plausible threat to justice' (1991) Crim LR 99.

[11] Lord Woolf, *Access to Justice,* chapter 13, para. 9.

[12] JH Langbein, 'The German Advantage In Civil Procedure' (1985) University of Chicago Law Review, vol 52, no 4, 823–866, at 837–839.

[13] '"Quack" forensic scientists "pose threat to justice"' *Daily Telegraph,* 30 April 1998.

...At the American trial bar, those of us who serve as expert witnesses are known as 'saxophones'.' This is a revealing term, as slang often is. The idea is that the lawyer plays the tune, manipulating the expert as though the expert were a musical instrument on which the lawyer sounds the desired notes. I sometimes serve as an expert in trust and pension cases, and I have experienced the subtle pressures to join the team—to shade one's views, to conceal doubt, to overstate nuance, to downplay weak aspects of the case that one has been hired to bolster. Nobody likes to disappoint a patron; and beyond this psychological pressure is the financial inducement. Money changes hands upon the rendering of expertise, but the expert can run his meter only so long as his patron litigator likes the tune. Opposing counsel undertakes a similar exercise, hiring and schooling another expert to parrot the contrary position. The result is our familiar battle of opposing experts. The more measured and impartial an expert is, the less likely he is to be used by either side.

At trial, the battle of experts tends to baffle the trier, especially in jury courts. If the experts do not cancel each other out, the advantage is likely to be with the expert whose forensic skills are the more enticing. The system invites abusive cross-examination. Since each expert is party-selected and party-paid, he is vulnerable to attack on credibility regardless of the merits of his testimony. A defense lawyer recently bragged about his technique of cross-examining plaintiffs' experts in tort cases. Notice that nothing in his strategy varies with the truthfulness of the expert testimony he tries to discredit:

A mode of attack ripe with potential is to pursue a line of questions which, by their form and the jury's studied observation of the witness in response, will tend to cast the expert as a 'professional witness'.' By proceeding in this way, the cross-examiner will reap the benefit of a community attitude, certain to be present among several of the jurors, that bias can be purchased, almost like a commodity.

Thus, the systematic incentive in our procedure to distort expertise leads to a systematic distrust and devaluation of expertise. Short of forbidding the use of experts altogether, we probably could not have designed a procedure better suited to minimize the influence of expertise.

However, court appointed 'neutral' experts, although curing some problems, raise many others of their own, as the following extract suggests.

Deirdre Dwyer, 'The effective management of bias in civil expert evidence' (2007) Civil Justice Quarterly 57–78 (Extract)

Although there have been attempts to suggest that a party expert need not be biased, the analysis in this article suggests that bias (at least structural if not personal) on the part of a party expert is almost inevitable, and the CPR contains elements, such as the continuance of litigation privilege, that encourage the development of expert bias. If we remove the party's right to choose their own expert, on the other hand, then we not only limit the party's adversarial right to identify and lead the evidence that best supports their case, but also reduce the court's exposure to a range of possible genuine expert opinions. There is a real danger that the court will simply accept the single expert's opinion in a specialist field in which there might be a wide range of possible opinions.

In many fields, there is a broad consensus amongst most (but not all) experts on many (but not all) issues, such that an expert could be selected from what is deemed to be 'mainstream' opinion. Thus, in the area of spinal trauma, it seems that considerably over 90% of questioned experts in a recent survey thought that severe trauma would increase the rate of degenerative change to the vertebrae. Nevertheless, and very significantly, this still leaves a (sincere) minority who do not subscribe to such views.[14]

Who is equipped to say whether an expert whose opinion is currently deemed to be eccentric might not be propounding what will be tomorrow's orthodoxy? This has frequently occurred in science. Thus, the views of professors Marshall and Warren, recent joint Nobel prize winners, that many stomach ulcers were caused not by stress (received wisdom in 1980) but by a bacterium, and so could be treated by antibiotics, were considered heretical when first enunciated. Nevertheless, they were ultimately accepted by nearly all specialists in the field. Court appointed experts can still be mistaken, and party appointed ones correct. Additionally, the adversarial system does normally ensure that experts take care when preparing their reports, knowing that they will be rigorously challenged and tested by one of their peers. A lazy or incompetent court appointed expert might ultimately pose greater risks to the correctness of adjudication, being less likely to be exposed at trial.

Reflecting such concerns, inter alia, the establishment of court appointed experts in criminal matters was considered and expressly rejected by Auld LJ in his 2001 report, and Lord Woolf ultimately did not settle on it, except in the most limited circumstances, for civil cases.[15]

Auld LJ, *A Review of the Criminal Courts of England and Wales* (2001) at 577–578, paras. 140–141

140 Interestingly, the Runciman Royal Commission, despite its drive to introduce a more inquisitorial flavour to the pre-trial stage, showed little interest in court appointed experts in criminal proceedings, either to the exclusion of parties' experts or in addition to them. The overwhelming majority of the many contributors to this Review were against it. Where the court has directed that expert evidence is appropriate, I too cannot see any scope for introduction to criminal trials of a system of court appointed experts to the exclusion, even in the court's discretion, of the right of each party to call its own expert evidence. Even without Article 6, it seems to me that there are fundamental difficulties in denying a criminal defendant that entitlement, particularly where the issue is highly controversial and central to the case and—I would add with Lord Bingham—whatever the weight of the case. He would have to instruct an expert to obtain advice as to whether to accept the court expert's view and, if not, he would probably need his assistance for the purpose of cross-examination of the court expert. Yet he would be unable, unless permitted by the judge, to call him to justify the points put in cross-examination or to give his contrary view on which they were based. To leave it to the judge's discretion, as under the Civil Procedure Rules, would, I believe, result in most judges allowing the defendant, or the prosecution for that matter, to call their own expert witness—effectively making the provision a dead letter. Otherwise, the court appointed or selected expert would effectively decide the issue and, depending on its importance, possibly the case.

141 Nor do I believe that it would be helpful for the court to appoint its own expert in addition to any expert witnesses called by the parties, since, in jury cases, the very nature of his appointment might suggest to a jury a greater authority than one or other or both of the parties' experts. Accordingly, where there is an issue on a matter of importance on which expert evidence is required, I can see no justification for empowering the court to appoint or select an expert,

[14] TJD Byrnes and FP Nath, 'Spinal Trauma and Degenerative Disease: The Range of Expert Opinion' (2005) Journal of Personal Injury Law, vol 2, 159–171.

[15] See generally Lord Woolf, *Access to Justice: Final Report*, 1996, chapter 13.

whether or not it excludes either party from calling its own expert evidence. Of course, where there is no issue or one in which the parties are content that the matter should be resolved by a single expert, they should be encouraged to deal with it in that way, agreeing his report or a summary of it as part of the evidence in the case.

Pause for reflection

Would you have more or less confidence in a pair of court appointed experts than in two experts selected by the parties to litigation?

Experts' Responsibilities in Civil Cases

Instead of following the continental route, the response of English courts has been to delineate the role and function of the expert more clearly and to stress that experts have a duty to the court that goes beyond that owed to the party instructing them. Additionally, in civil cases, the use of a single jointly instructed expert has been actively promoted (though it is not usually mandatory). This generally 'exhortatory' approach to experts and their duties was clearly manifest in the Commercial Court case of *The Ikarian Reefer* [1993] 2 Lloyd's Rep 68, which involved allegations of the fraudulent destruction of a ship, and in which extensive, often unsatisfactory, and sometimes irrelevant, expert evidence was given. Cresswell J, the trial judge, issued important guidance on the responsibilities of experts. In particular, he emphasized that an expert witness should make it clear when a question fell outside his competence and should provide an objective independent and unbiased opinion in court, uninfluenced by the exigencies of litigation. Additionally, the judge stressed that such a witness should never assume the role of an advocate. An expert should also state the facts or assumptions upon which his opinion was based and not omit to consider material facts that could detract from his concluded opinion.

Subsequently, in *Autospin (Oil Seals) Ltd v Beehive Spinning (a firm)* [1995] RPC 683, the first instance judge reiterated that an expert witness carries a heavy responsibility because their evidence is afforded special respect and weight by the court. Experts must expect to be strongly censured if they do not take their role seriously. This necessarily involves researching the case thoroughly. These, and similar, judicial views were reflected in aspects of Part 35 of the CPR 1998 (in force from January 1999) and an associated Practice Direction. Thus, r. 35.3(2) expressly states that an expert's duty to assist the court 'overrides any obligation to the person from whom he has received instructions or by whom he is paid'. In *Stevens v Gullis* [2000] 1 All ER 527, an expert who did not appreciate the duty that was imposed on experts by (the then newly in force) r. 35 was debarred from giving evidence.

Pause for reflection

Do you feel that a 'professional' expert witness, that is one who makes much of his living from giving expert testimony, can ever be totally uninfluenced in his evidence by external factors?

The Ikarian Reefer (1993) FSR 563, HC

Cresswell J

Expert evidence presented to the court should be, and should be seen to be, the independent product of the expert uninfluenced as to form or content by the exigencies of litigation. An expert witness should provide independent assistance to the Court by way of objective, unbiased opinion in relation to matters within his expertise. An expert witness in the High Court should never assume the role of an advocate. An expert should state facts or assumptions upon which his opinion is based. He should not omit to consider material facts which could detract from his concluded opinion. An expert witness should make it clear when a particular question or issue falls outside his area of expertise. If an expert's opinion is not properly researched because he considers that insufficient data is available, then this must be stated with an indication that the opinion is no more than a provisional one. In cases where an expert witness, who has prepared a report, could not assert that the report contained the truth, the whole truth and nothing but the truth without some qualification, that qualification should be stated in the report. If, after exchange of reports, an expert witness changes his views on a material matter having read the other side's report or for any other reason, such change of view should be communicated (through legal representatives) to the other side without delay and when appropriate to the court.

Autospin (Oil Seals) Ltd v Beehive Spinning (a firm)
[1995] RPC 683, HC

Laddie J

In particular the plaintiff relied upon the evidence of their expert, Professor Davies who, after describing the system, said: 'As far as I am aware no other previous seal manufacturer has used such a coding system.' The clear message and purpose of this evidence was to support the plaintiff's claim that its system was unique. In the course of the trial it became apparent that not only was this coding system used by others in the trade but that the Professor did not know what coding systems were used by other companies and had made no effort to find out. Indeed during the course of preparing his report, the Professor had access and referred to the catalogue of another seal manufacturer, Pioneer Weston. Had he looked even at that catalogue he would have seen that the same coding system was used by that company. I can only assume that had the Professor taken the simplest steps to find out what systems were used by others in the trade he would have felt quite unable to lend the weight of his reputation to the plaintiff's assertions. The evidence of expert witnesses tends to be treated with great weight by courts. There is always a risk that the evidence of those directly involved in the litigation may be tailored to coincide with the witness' interest in the outcome of the dispute. On the other hand courts expect experts to approach the litigation more dispassionately. Their evidence is of particular value precisely because normally it is not the evidence of someone who has an interest in the outcome of the litigation. However the special respect and weight given to experts' evidence carries with it the responsibility to approach the task seriously. An expert and those who help him prepare his report should not be surprised if the court expresses strong disapproval if that is not done. In my view it is lamentable that the Professor should have lent his weight to this claim without taking the trouble to satisfy himself that it was appropriate to do so. The maintenance of such an unjustified claim by the plaintiff and the support given to it by the Professor reflects poorly on both.

Additionally, excessive use of experts in civil cases is discouraged. Thus, under r. 35.1 of the CPR 1998 parties are limited to calling no more expert evidence than is 'reasonably required to resolve the proceedings'. The court may also place a limit on the amount of expert costs that can be recovered by a successful litigant, ensuring that they are commensurate with the gravity of the case and the difficulty of the matter to be resolved. The parties must also have the permission of the court before any such evidence can be adduced. Where two opposing experts are appointed, the court can also require that they meet in conference for discussion. The unnecessary calling of experts for cross-examination, after they have submitted written reports that are substantially unchallenged, is also discouraged and a general culture of transparency has been promoted. Perhaps most pertinently, under r. 35.7 litigants are required to agree on a single joint expert witness where the court directs; if they cannot agree, the court may select the expert from a list prepared by the parties or in some other manner.

The use of a single joint expert (SJE) appeared to hold out great promise as a way of saving costs and avoiding some of the worst effects of adversarialism. Nevertheless, it has not operated quite as effectively as might have been anticipated (or at least hoped). Parties often fail to agree on appointing an SJE and seek out their own experts, even in situations that might appear eminently suitable for the former. Thus, in *Roadrunner Properties Ltd v Dean* [2003] EWCA CIV 1816, Sedley LJ noted that the case was a prime example of one in which expert testimony should have been confined to an SJE. However, the parties had been unable to reach agreement as to who this should be, and had eventually been permitted to appoint their own experts. (The judge also suggested that, in this situation, the court might have exercised its powers under r. 35.7 of the CPR to name its own expert.)

Even where the parties do appoint an SJE, if they are unhappy with the result they will usually be allowed to call their own expert: *Daniels v Walker* [2000] 1 WLR 1382. Other problems include the time-consuming formality with which SJEs must be approached by the litigants. For reasons of fairness, almost all communications have to be in writing and with the opposing side kept informed at all stages. Additionally, in serious cases, there is a tendency for parties to appoint 'shadow' experts to examine the issues, so that costs (even if not recoverable) remain high. In practice, although widely used, SJEs are still most frequently employed for non-controversial issues. For hotly contested issues, in serious cases, each party often appoints its own expert.

Criminal Matters

In criminal cases, similar conclusions have been reached as to an expert's general duties as were arrived at in *The Ikarian Reefer* and other civil cases, although, despite the express recommendation of Auld LJ in his *Review of the Criminal Courts of England and Wales*, there has been no criminal equivalent of r. 35.3 of the CPR 1998: *R v Harris (Lorraine)* [2005] 1 Cr App R 55. In *R v Bowman* [2006] EWCA Crim 417 the Court of Appeal reiterated, and added to, the guidelines set out in *Harris*. Perhaps significantly, the bench in this case included Cresswell J who had provided the guidance in *The Ikarian Reefer*.

The court gave particular guidance on the factors that should be included in an expert report. Amongst them were: details of the expert's academic record and professional qualifications; his range of experience and any limitations on his expertise; the substance of the instructions that he had received; the questions upon which his opinion was sought; the materials provided and considered, and the information that was material to the opinions expressed; information about who carried out any measurements and tests, the methodology employed, and whether they were supervised by the expert; where there was a range of opinion in the matters dealt with in the report, a summary of that range and the reasons for the specific opinion given; any material facts or matters that detracted from the expert's opinion; relevant extracts of literature or other material that might assist the court; a statement that the expert had complied with his duty to the court to provide independent assistance by way of objective unbiased opinion, and an acknowledgement that the expert would inform all parties if his opinion changed on any material issue. Perhaps most importantly, cases such as *Bowman* make it clear that in a criminal trial the expert's duty to the court overrode any obligation to the party instructing him.

R v Harris (Lorraine) [2005] 1 Cr App R 55, CA

Gale LJ

As to expert evidence generally, the evidential rules as to admissibility are clear (see for example R. v Bonython [1984] 38 S.A.S.R. 45 and R.v Clarke (RL) [1995] 2 Cr.App.R. 425 (facial mapping)). We see no reason for special rules where medical experts are involved. There is no single test which can provide a threshold for admissibility in all cases. As Clarke demonstrates developments in scientific thinking and techniques should not be kept from the Court. Further, in our judgment, developments in scientific thinking should not be kept from the Court, simply because they remain at the stage of a hypothesis. Obviously, it is of the first importance that the true status of the expert's evidence is frankly indicated to the court. It may be helpful for judges, practitioners and experts to be reminded of the obligations of an expert witness summarised by Cresswell J. in the National Justice Cia Naviera SA v Prudential Assurance Co Ltd (Ikarian Reefer) [1993] 2 Lloyds Rep. 68 at 81. Cresswell J. pointed out amongst other factors the following, which we summarise as follows:

(1) Expert evidence presented to the court should be and seen to be the independent product of the expert uninfluenced as to form or content by the exigencies of litigation.

(2) An expert witness should provide independent assistance to the court by way of objective unbiased opinion in relation to matters within his expertise. An expert witness in the High Court should never assume the role of advocate.

(3) An expert witness should state the facts or assumptions on which his opinion is based. He should not omit to consider material facts which detract from his concluded opinions.

(4) An expert should make it clear when a particular question or issue falls outside his expertise.

(5) If an expert's opinion is not properly researched because he considers that insufficient data is available then this must be stated with an indication that the opinion is no more than a provisional one.

(6) If after exchange of reports, an expert witness changes his view on material matters, such change of view should be communicated to the other side without delay and when appropriate to the court. Wall J., as he then was, sitting in the Family Division also gave helpful guidance for experts giving evidence involving children (see In re AB (Child Abuse: Expert Witnesses) [1995] 1 F.L.R. 181). Wall J. pointed out that there will be cases in which there is a genuine disagreement on a scientific or medical issue, or where it is necessary for a party to advance a particular hypothesis to explain a given set of facts. He added (see p.192): 'Where that occurs, the jury will have to resolve the issue which is raised. Two points must be made. In my view, the expert who advances such a hypothesis owes a very heavy duty to explain to the court that what he is advancing is a hypothesis, that it is controversial (if it is) and placed before the court all material which contradicts the hypothesis. Secondly, he must make all his material available to the

other experts in the case. It is the common experience of the courts that the better the experts the more limited their areas of disagreement, and in the forensic context of a contested case relating to children, the objective of the lawyers and the experts should always be to limit the ambit of disagreement on medical issues to the minimum.' We have substituted the word jury for judge in the above passage. In our judgment the guidance given by both Cresswell J. and Wall J. are very relevant to criminal proceedings and should be kept well in mind by both prosecution and defence. The new Criminal Procedure Rules provide wide powers of case management to the Court. Rule 24 and Para.15 of the Plea and Case Management form make provision for experts to consult together and, if possible, agree points of agreement or disagreement with a summary of reasons. In cases involving allegations of child abuse the judge should be prepared to give directions in respect of expert evidence taking into account the guidance to which we have just referred. If this guidance is borne in mind and the directions made are clear and adhered to, it ought to be possible to narrow the areas of dispute before trial and limit the volume of expert evidence which the jury will have to consider.

Bias in Experts

Normally, actual or potential bias in a witness goes to weight, rather than admissibility, though, if denied in cross-examination, its presence can be proved in rebuttal as an exception to the finality of answer to a collateral question rule: *R v Phillips* (1936) 26 Cr App R 17. However, expert witnesses are, it seems, to some extent *sui generis* in this respect, at least where the potential for bias is extreme. Thus, in the High Court case of *Liverpool Roman Catholic Archdiocesan Trust v Goldberg* [2001] 1 WLR 2337 Mr Justice Evans–Lombe concluded that a QC from the same chambers as the defendant, and a long-term friend, should not be allowed to give expert evidence on his behalf in a claim by the corporate trustee of the Roman Catholic Archdiocese of Liverpool against the defendant for professional negligence, relating to the advice that he gave with regard to the trustee's tax affairs.

 Cross-reference Box

The collateral issue rule usually prevents a party exploring a matter that goes purely to a witness's credit; for example, by calling evidence in rebuttal of a denial by that witness of an allegation that reflects badly on his trustworthiness. However, there are a number of important exceptions to this general rule, of which a relationship from which partiality or bias might be suspected is one. To read more about this rule and its exceptions, go to chapter 19.

Liverpool Roman Catholic Archdiocesan Trust v Goldberg
[2001] 1 WLR 2337, HC

Evans-Lombe J

The role of an expert witness is special owing, as he does, duties to the Court which he must discharge notwithstanding the interest of the party calling him see per Cresswell J in the *Ikarian*

Reefer. I accept that neither section 3 [Civil Evidence Act 1972] nor the authorities under it expressly exclude the expert evidence of a friend of one or the parties. However, in my judgment, where it is demonstrated that there exists a relationship between the proposed expert and the party calling him which a reasonable observer might think was capable of affecting the views of the expert so as to make them unduly favourable to that party, his evidence should not be admitted however unbiased the conclusions of the expert might probably be. The question is one of fact, namely, the extent and nature of the relationship between the proposed witness and the party. With great respect to the preliminary views expressed by Neuberger J, it seems to me that Mr Flesch's admission of the nature and the closeness of his relationship with the Defendant made him unsuitable, on grounds of public policy, to be called as an expert witness in support of the Defendant's case and his evidence, although it would otherwise have qualified within section 3, should not be admitted.

Pause for reflection

Would you feel able to give impartial expert evidence on behalf of a friend?

The extent to which this applies is obviously a matter of degree. It does not appear to preclude a party calling an expert who is also his/her employee or who is even personally, to some extent, acquainted with him: *Field v Leeds City Council* [2000] 17 EG 165. Nevertheless, the general principle is a valid one. It is widely recognized that intimacy and over familiarity, even through contact at court that is excessively prolonged, can make independence of thought difficult, while detachment discourages bias, as the following extract suggests.

Deirdre Dwyer, 'The causes and manifestations of bias in civil expert evidence' (2007) Civil Justice Quarterly at 425–446 (Extract)

The close association of the expert with a case may give rise to sympathy with the instructing party, which may in turn give rise to conscious or unconscious adaptation of the expert's opinion: 'Human nature being what it is, there is a tendency to want the side that hired you to win the contest.' This may be particularly true where the subject is an emotive one, such as the recovery of damages in personal injury or medical negligence litigation, or where the expert also has a role in the treatment of the patient. In such cases, the expert may be able to justify bias to him- or herself ethically, as success for the claimant will have considerable personal benefits to the claimant.

In *Vernon v Bosley (No.2)*, in which the two claimant's experts were shown to have acceded to a solicitors' request for reports to be adapted, two mitigating circumstances were identified by Thorpe L.J. First, they had an extensive relationship with their patient and had been 'sucked into' the personal injury litigation, with deleterious effects on their objectivity as experts. Similar concerns had been expressed by the trial judge, Sedley J., about the defendant's experts. Secondly, neither was fully aware of his duties as an expert in Children Act proceedings.

Pause for reflection

How do you feel that expert detachment could be encouraged?

5. Can the Proposed Witness Provide Expert Assistance?

Introduction

Even where expert evidence is called for, there is no point in calling a witness to assist the tribunal if that witness is no (or little) better equipped to give an opinion on the case than the jurors themselves, ie an expert must possess expertise! The basic test is that the proposed witness must be deemed to be *peritus*, that is specially knowledgeable about the subject on which he is to testify, to use an old (and now rather unfashionable), but helpfully succinct and judicially employed word. This is a question for the trial judge, and a matter of degree.

In most cases, expertise does not have to have been acquired by a formal course of learning; practical experience from work, as in *R v Oakley* (1980) 70 Cr App R 7, or even a keen amateur interest in the subject, as with the solicitor graphologist in *R v Silverlock* [1894] 2 QB 76, may be enough. More recently, a Dutch ear-printing expert in *R v Dallagher* [2003] 1 Cr App R 12, who had no formal qualifications, was deemed to be an expert because of his personal and extensive experience of making comparisons between ears and their prints.

In practice, however, although not essential, in many fields formal qualifications are readily available and extremely helpful in establishing expert status: *Said Ajami v Comptroller of Customs* [1954] 1 WLR 1405 (PC). Normally, the very first thing an expert does when he is called to give evidence or prepares a report to be tendered at trial is to list his qualifications and experience along with any publications in the relevant field that he may have authored, etc. In a 'Battle of Experts', all other things being equal (which of course they never are), the better qualified person will usually prevail.

Nevertheless, in *O'Toole v Knowsley MBC* (1999) Env LR 29, it was held that it was not necessary for environmental health officers to possess medical qualifications before venturing an opinion as to whether tenanted premises were 'prejudicial to health' under the Environmental Protection Act 1990. It seems that English courts take a relatively generous attitude towards granting expert status, when compared to some other common law jurisdictions, usually being willing to receive evidence from a witness if there is any significant basis for attributing expert status to him. Only a forensic pathologist is required by the law to have formal qualifications. In any other field, from toxicology to DNA fingerprinting, from ballistics to document examination, from blood analysis to glass fragment identification, anyone can practise if they satisfy the court as to their expertise.

Pause for reflection

Do you feel that expert status should so readily be granted by the courts?

R v Silverlock [1894] 2 QB 76, CCR

Lord Russell CJ

We now come to the second objection, as to the proof of the handwriting, which affords a good illustration of that class of evidence called evidence of opinion. It is true that the witness who is called upon to give evidence founded on a comparison of handwritings must be peritus; he must be skilled in doing so; but we cannot say that he must have become peritus in the way of his business or in any definite way. The question is, is he peritus? Is he skilled? Has he an adequate knowledge? Looking at the matter practically, if a witness is not skilled the judge will tell the jury to disregard his evidence. There is no decision which requires that the evidence of a man who is skilled in comparing handwriting, and who has formed a reliable opinion from past experience, should be excluded because his experience has not been gained in the way of his business. It is, however, really unnecessary to consider this point; for it seems from the statement in the present case that the witness was not only peritus, but was peritus in the way of his business. When once it is determined that the evidence is admissible, the rest is merely a question of its value or weight, and this is entirely a question for the jury, who will attach more or less weight to it according as they believe the witness to be peritus.

R v Trevor Alan Oakley (1980) 70 Cr App R 7, CA

The Lord Chief Justice

It is not without importance—indeed it is of great importance—to appreciate the calibre of the man who was making the investigation on behalf of the police authority and his experience as a reconstructor of motor accidents, if he can be so described. . . . He was asked: 'How long have you been in the traffic division?' He answered: 'I have been driving traffic cars for about 15 years, sir, and prior to that I drove area patrol cars for a little over five years.' He was asked if he had any experience in accident investigation, and he said: 'I attended an accident investigation course, sir, at the police headquarters, Chelmsford, I should think some three and a half to four years ago, sir.' He was asked: 'Are you a qualified investigator?' He answered: 'Yes, sir. I have passed the examination that is required of me.' He was asked: 'Can you estimate how many road accidents you have attended in the course of your service?' He answered: 'It would be impossible to put a figure on it, sir. I would have to say thousands. I certainly have attended well in excess of 400 fatal accidents. Not that I have dealt with them all.'

One need not read from the transcript further to realise that here one has a highly experienced police officer who has a very deep and conscious experience of the problems of reconstructing motor accidents. At the trial, having given his qualifications in that way, he then described what he had found at the scene of the collision. He produced the plan which he had prepared and, in addition to that, ventilated a number of theories of such scientific consequence that they are not altogether easy for the Court itself to follow. But the basic argument in favour of quashing this conviction is that it was wrong for the judge to allow Police Constable Robinson, to whom I have referred, to give evidence for the assistance of the jury which went beyond the plain evidence of fact and ventured on or over the boundary between fact and opinion.

. . . we would like to make it quite clear straight away that there is no question of a police officer being prevented from giving evidence as an expert if the subject in which he is giving evidence as an expert is a subject in which he has expert knowledge, and if it is restricted and directed to the issues in the case. Consequently, it was perfectly proper, in our judgment, for this officer to give the type of evidence he did.

'Ad Hoc' Experts

Indeed, the courts have shown a willingness to attribute expert status (if not necessarily the title) to what might be considered 'ordinary' witnesses, at least with regard to very discrete issues or areas of knowledge. This is a long-standing phenomenon. At the notorious trial of the barrister, Spencer Cowper, in 1699, the key issue was whether a young woman had been murdered by Cowper or, as he claimed, had committed suicide by drowning herself. Two Royal Navy sailors who had witnessed men both drowned at sea, and others killed out of the water and then thrown into it, and a woman who had seen both the deceased's body and that of a boy who had indisputably drowned some months earlier, were called.[16]

In the modern era, in *R v Chatwood* [1980] 1 WLR 874, an addict who was familiar with the effects of heroin was, effectively, allowed to give opinion evidence identifying a disputed white powder as the drug rather than flour. In *R v Clare and Peach* [1995] 2 Cr App R 333, this issue was considered in some detail. This case involved charges of violent disorder arising out of a confrontation between rival soccer fans outside a pub; these incidents had been captured on CCTV video, but the quality of the video was very poor, due to the numbers milling around in the scene, etc. The video was shown to the jury. However, on a single, or even several, viewings it would have been difficult for unaided jurors to identify individual defendants in the film. Nevertheless, before trial, a PC Fitzpatrick had studied the film closely and analytically, having earlier also filmed the fans at the stadium. He had seen the 'pub' video in slow motion and frame-by-frame (a total of 40 times), leading him to identify the violent acts outside the pubs and also who was perpetrating them. The prosecution successfully sought to adduce the officer's evidence to accompany the showing of the videos.

The appeal was largely founded on the argument that even if the jury could view the video themselves, Fitzpatrick's concurrent evidence as to what was happening was inadmissible opinion evidence. There was a dearth of domestic authority on this point. However, the Court of Appeal expressly approved the decision by the Court of Appeal of New Zealand in a similar case, *R v Howe* (1982) 1 NZLR 618. In this case, videos of a disturbance taken during a Springbok rugby tour were shown to the jury, while a detective who had watched them many times gave the jurors a commentary and identified the accused. The New Zealand Court rejected the defence argument that the detective was not an expert. It accepted that the question as to whether a person was an expert in a particular field could be difficult to define, but felt that there was no reason why the detective should not be regarded as sufficiently 'expert ad hoc' to give such evidence. The Court of Appeal in England, considering this case, felt that while the label 'expert ad hoc' might not be appropriate, PC Fitzpatrick had 'special knowledge' that justified the reception of his evidence. Consequently, it dismissed the appeal, and also observed that as technology developed evidential practice might need to be evolved to deal with the new situation.

R v Clare and Peach [1995] 2 Cr App R 333, CA

Lord Taylor CJ

In Howe (1982) 1 NZLR 618, the Court of Appeal of New Zealand had to consider a case arising from very similar circumstances to those of the instant case. During the Springbok Rugby Tour

---

[16] Anon, *The Tryal of Spencer Cowper, Esq. . . . upon an indictment for the murther of Mrs. Sarah Stout*, London, 1699, 13.

there was a demonstration which ended in violence. Various video tapes and photographs were taken. When the films were shown to the jury, a detective identified individual accused by giving a commentary from the witness box. The detective had not personally known any of the appellants save one before the day of the match and he was not present when any of the incidents were recorded on film. However, he had viewed the edited version of the tapes many times and (as in the present case) he was allowed both to describe what was being done at a particular time whilst the video was played and to identify who was doing it. At p. 627, the judgment of the Court reads as follows: 'Here, the evidence was needed to make the tapes and film and even the still photographs more readily understandable. The action was complicated and confused. Important details could easily be missed without prolonged viewing or guidance from someone closely familiar with the material. Having viewed the pictures ourselves, we are satisfied that the commentary by Detective Parsons was legitimately required as an aid to the jury. Economy, convenience and despatch would commend the admission of such a commentary and we see no fundamental principle in the law of evidence which would be infringed. The original tapes, films and photographs had been properly proved and the identification made from them by Detective Parsons was no more secondary evidence than was any oral identification made from a photograph. It was argued however, that Detective Parsons was not an expert. Whether a person is an expert in a particular field is not always easy to define. A witness need not embark on a course of scientific study to qualify as an expert; he may acquire his knowledge merely from experience; it is not necessary for him to acquire it professionally: Silverlock [1894] 2 Q.B. 766, 771; Menzies [1982] 1 N.Z.L.R. 40. There seems no reason in principle why a person who has seen tapes and the like as many times as Detective Parsons saw this material and has made a study of them and compared them with other still photographs with the purpose of reliably identifying individuals, should not be regarded as sufficiently expert ad hoc to give identification evidence.' The trial judge adopted and followed that passage. In our judgment he was right to do so. The phrase 'expert ad hoc' seeks to put witnesses like Detective Parsons and P.C. Fitzpatrick into the traditional category of those qualified to give opinion evidence. Whether or not the tag is appropriate, we are clearly of the view that P.C. Fitzpatrick had 'special knowledge that the Court did not possess', to quote the Canadian judgment cited above. P.C. Fitzpatrick had acquired the knowledge by lengthy and studious application to material which was itself admissible evidence. To afford the jury the time and facilities to conduct the same research would be utterly impracticable. Accordingly, it was in our judgment legitimate to allow the officer to assist the jury by pointing to what he asserted was happening in the crowded scenes on the film. He was open to cross-examination, and the jury, after proper direction and warnings, were free either to accept or reject his assertions.

Refusal of Expert Status

Nevertheless, the courts do make a qualitative judgment and periodically refuse expert status to tendered witnesses who are clearly not *peritus*, or whose methodology, although once respected, is no longer accorded value: *R v O'Doherty* [2003] 1 Cr App R 77. Thus, in *R v Inch* (1989) 91 Cr App R 51, a medical orderly, trained to treat cuts and wounds, who had treated the injured man in an assault case, was held not to be sufficiently expert to venture an opinion, based on its depth and shape, as to whether a cut to the victim's forehead had been caused by a martial arts instrument or a head butt. Similarly, in *R v Davies* [1962] 3 All ER 97 it was held that a soldier who had had substantial personal experience of driving was not able to give evidence on the issue as to whether the defendant had drunk so much alcohol that he was unfit to drive.

Lord Parker noted that such a lay witness 'merely because he is a driver himself, is [not] in the expert witness category so that it is proper to ask him his opinion as to fitness or unfitness to drive'. In like fashion, in *R v Edwards (Christopher)* [2001] EWCA Crim 2185, a drugs charity worker who had held extensive conversations with addicts was not deemed to be an expert on the effects of particular narcotics.

R v Inch [1990] 91 Cr App R 51, Courts-Martial Appeal Court

Watkins LJ

...responsibility for ensuring, especially with regard to expert evidence, that evidence which does not properly come within that definition does not go before the jury, does not lie only at the door of defence counsel. The court itself has a responsibility in that respect, and here the judge-advocate himself should have ruled that that evidence was not admissible. We do not doubt that it would have been ruled inadmissible in criminal proceedings in a civilian court. Lance Bombardier Whitemore was treated as an expert witness and should not have been. If the prosecution at the court-martial sought to, in endeavouring to establish the guilt of the appellant, rely upon expert evidence, then clearly it was free to call upon the services of skilled medical assistance from the resources of the British army in Germany. Doctors, dentists and specialists are there. There would surely have been a number of experts, properly so called, who could have come before the court and expressed an opinion as to how this fairly trivial injury to the head of Gatenby might have been caused. That course was regrettably not adopted. Instead, as I have indicated, what was resorted to was an attempt, successful as it happened, to put before the court evidence which the court should never have heard, that is to say expert evidence, so called, which did not come from an expert. That is, we think, sufficient to highlight what, in our view, went wrong in these proceedings. It may well be—we cannot tell—that the court was right to convict. It may be that Gatenby was truly the victim of an unprovoked assault by the appellant. It may equally be that the appellant's story was the right one, for he showed his own injuries to whoever was in charge of the guardroom the moment he arrived there. He, it was, who insisted that the military police should be called. The evidence on one side or the other, medical opinion apart, was pretty evenly balanced, which leads us to the conclusion that the medical evidence, the opinion that is, was probably the determining factor in the end. Seeing that the court, in our judgment, should not have heard it, leaves us very uneasy as to whether there may have been an injustice thereby caused.

---

6. Limitations on an Expert's Opinion

Introduction

Simply because a party is allowed to call an expert does not mean that he has carte blanche to venture an opinion on any matter that might be put to him. There are a number of limitations placed on him when testifying; most importantly, an expert should not give opinions outside his area of expertise. Additionally, in theory, he should be slightly chary about venturing an opinion on the 'ultimate issue' to be resolved by the tribunal of fact in criminal matters, though, as will be seen, this rule appears to have largely fallen into desuetude.

Veering Outside Area of Expert Competence

An expert is only able to provide opinion evidence within his sphere of expertise; if he strays outside this, his opinion evidence (on the issue outside his competence) is inadmissible. Experts venturing opinions outside their remit or competence appear to be a permanent problem for the courts. Lord Woolf accepted in his report that it was a widespread criticism of those called in civil cases, and it is at least as big a problem in criminal ones.

A classic illustration of this can be seen in the unreported Court of Appeal case of *R v Reatchlous* (heard on 20 July 1984, LEXIS Transcript by Marten Walsh Cherer), where it became an issue at trial as to whether a police officer who had been carried and dragged along a road by a car, had been holding on with one hand or both (the former would support his contention that he had banged on the vehicle to gain the driver's attention). An expert engineer was called to give evidence for the defence, and gave some relevant evidence (ie obviously within his expertise), as to the 'mechanics' of the incident such as the braking distances of the vehicles involved.

However, he was also asked to give evidence of some tests carried out under his supervision by a stunt man for the purpose of seeing whether it was possible for a man to retain his hold on a vehicle travelling at the speed of the car in question with only one hand. Although prosecuting counsel and the trial judge expressed misgivings and questioned the value of such evidence (an experiment carried out by a separate person on a different type of car and road) the defence were initially allowed to adduce the evidence, including the engineer's opinion that a man could not have been dragged along the road at speed while holding on to the vehicle with only one hand. However, when the engineer was asked to give an opinion as to how a man who had been dragged at speed might have held the car prosecuting counsel objected and the trial judge accepted that such opinion evidence was outside the province of expertise of an engineer. On appeal, this decision was upheld as clearly correct.

A broadly similar position was reached in *R v Barnes (Derek)* [2005] EWCA 1158, where the appellant sought to argue that evidence from an arboriculturalist that finger prints 'lifted' from a wooden door at a crime scene did not show a pattern of woodgrain that was consistent with that door (suggesting that they had actually come from somewhere else), would have been admissible had it been tendered at trial, so rendering the ensuing conviction unsafe (as admissible 'fresh' evidence). The Court of Appeal concluded that, although an expert in his field (identifying woodgrain generally), the expert had no specialist knowledge of woodgrain in fingerprint lifts, or the comparison of different lifts. This was because the 'striations' in the lift, although derived from woodgrain, also reflected other factors, such the quantity of powder used in the process, the pressure employed, and the extent of any grease lifted. The expert had no expertise in this field and so could not have given expert evidence had he been called at trial.

R v Barnes (Derek) [2005] EWCA 1158, CA

Mance LJ

In all these cases, the making of the relevant comparison was itself treated as a matter to be undertaken by an appropriately qualified and skilled expert. Here, we are satisfied that Mr Murat has no experience or expertise in the relevant comparison; and indeed, as we have observed, Mr Kamlish does not put him forward as having this. Mr Murat does have expertise in identifying woodgrain in wood, including veneer, and also in doing so despite or making allowances for the presence of varnish. But he has no expertise in the interpretation of lifts, or in the identification of wood-grain on lifts. He himself said that he was relying on a fingerprint expert for an assumption that the striations in lift 6 reflected wood-grain. However, we are prepared to accept and to proceed on the basis that the striations which can be seen on lift 6 do derive from wood-grain. But the completeness and precision of the reflection depends on factors such as the quantity of powder and pressure used and the extent of any grease or other contaminants lifted. Mr Murat has no experience or expertise to enable him to judge the extent to which the striations which show on the lift are complete or do or may completely or precisely reflect the wood-grain evident on the door; we have already indicated why it appears that the striations are not and do not....In those circumstances, we do not consider that any expert evidence that it is said that Mr Murat could give could afford any ground for regarding the jury's verdict as unsafe or therefore for allowing an appeal.

The Ultimate Issue Rule

This is a historic common law rule forbidding an expert to give his/her opinion on the very issue that the tribunal of fact has to decide, such as whether or not the defendant in a murder case was suffering from diminished responsibility, rather than exhibiting symptoms that were 'not inconsistent' with such a state. An illustration of the strict common law position on the ultimate issue is provided by the Court of Appeal case of *Haynes v Doman* [1899] 2 Ch 13, where it was held that expert witnesses giving opinion evidence in a case concerning the reasonableness of a restrictive covenant in a hardware manufacturer's servant's contract of employment could give evidence about what was normal in that particular trade, and what precautions were necessary to protect employers in such a line of business, but not whether they believed that the restrictive covenant was reasonable or not. This was a question for the court.

 Pause for reflection

Do you feel that an expert should be able to give an opinion on the ultimate issue in a case?

However, the rule has been expressly abolished in civil cases by s. 3(1) of the Civil Evidence Act 1972, which provides that: 'Where a person is called as a witness in any civil proceedings, his opinion on any relevant matter on which he is qualified to give expert evidence shall be admissible in evidence.' Nevertheless, despite its statutory abolition, it is arguable that comments in the Court of Appeal in the early 1990s, suggesting that experts giving evidence in child abuse and wardship cases should not be able to express a direct opinion as to whether the complainants alleging abuse were telling the truth, threatened to revive it. However, in *Re M and R* (minors) [1996] 4 All ER 239 the Court of Appeal held that the remarks in those cases about the ultimate issue rule were made *per incuriam*. However, Butler-Sloss LJ observed that although, in cases involving children, expert medical and psychiatric evidence from paediatricians was often indispensable, such a witness's evidence on the ultimate issue would often be inadmissible because the expert has no expertise as to whether there has been child abuse, *not* because it goes to the ultimate issue.

Although, as yet, there is no criminal equivalent to the 1972 Act, despite a recommendation that such a provision should be introduced by the Criminal Law Revision Committee in its 11th Report on Evidence of 1972, it appears that the rule is usually ignored in practice in criminal cases. As Lord Parker CJ noted in *Director of Public Prosecutions v A and BC Chewing Gum Ltd* [1968] 1 QB 159 at 164, many inroads have been made into the rule, and those who practised in the criminal courts regularly saw experts in diminished responsibility cases being asked, 'Do you think he was suffering from diminished responsibility?' although, technically, he felt that such questions were not admissible. Similarly, in insanity cases, it appears to be quite normal for counsel to ask an expert whether the defendant was, in his opinion, insane: *R v Holmes* [1953] 1 WLR 686.

More recently, Lord Parker's views were reiterated in even stronger terms by the Court of Appeal in *R v Stockwell* (1993) 97 Cr App R 260. Indeed, this case appeared to mark the end of the rule in criminal matters, and it has been argued that all modern cases that relied on the ultimate issue rule could also be explained on other grounds.[17] Evidence will normally be allowed on the ultimate issue, provided the trial judge makes it clear to the jury that it is not bound by such opinion.

Nevertheless, the rule has not been expressly abolished in criminal matters and periodically has cropped up in judgments, even if not formally enunciated as such. Thus, in *R v Jeffries* [1999] Crim LR 819 the Court of Appeal quashed a conviction in which a senior police officer had been allowed to give opinion evidence that lists seized from a defendant related to drug dealing. The court accepted that by dint of her policing experience she was an expert for the purposes of providing details as to the value and street prices of drugs and the paraphernalia that accompanied drug dealing. However, the conviction was deemed to be unsafe because she had ventured an opinion that the defendant was guilty of possessing drugs with intent to supply as charged. Arguably, this would only be improper if the ultimate issue rule was viewed as having some continuing significance. Nevertheless, despite such cases, it appears that the rule is almost defunct in criminal proceedings.

R v Stockwell [993] 97 Cr App R 260, CA

Lord Taylor CJ

Mr. Clegg's third and final argument is that even if Mr. Neave was rightly allowed to state his findings, he should not have been permitted to give his opinion on the very issue before the jury. He said: 'My conclusion on count 1 is that the photos strongly support the view that the suspect and the robber are the same man.' He went on: 'There is limited information, but I think the exhibits reveal that there is support for the view that the robber and the suspect are the same man on count 2, but it is not anything like as strong as the support on count 1.' Whether an expert can give his opinion on what has been called the ultimate issue, has long been a vexed question. There is a school of opinion supported by some authority doubting whether he can (see Wright (1821) Russ & Ry. 456, 458). On the other hand, if there is such a prohibition, it has long been more honoured in the breach than the observance (see the passage at page 164 in the judgment of Parker L.J. in Director of Public Prosecutions v. A and B.C. Chewing Gum Ltd. [1968] 1 Q.B. 159 and the cases cited at page 501 of Cross on Evidence (7th ed.). Professor Cross at page 500 of that work said: 'It is submitted that the better and simpler solution, largely implemented by English case law, and in civil cases recognised in explicit statutory provision, is to abandon any pretence of applying any such rule, and merely to accept opinion whenever it is helpful to the court to do so, irrespective of the status or nature of the issue to which it relates.' The same view is expressed by Tristram and

---

[17]   See generally J Jacksson, 'The Ultimate Issue Rule: One Rule Too Many' [1984] Crim LR 75–86, at 75.

Hodkinson in their work on Expert Evidence Law and Practice at pages 152 to 153, where, after referring to the case of Wright they say that in that case the expert witness could not express an opinion as to whether the particular facts before the court constituted an act of insanity. He could, however, state what types of behaviour demonstrated insanity in persons generally, from which the jury could draw inferences in the particular case. The learned authors went on as follows: 'There is little doubt however that such a distinction is not now rigorously observed, and given that expert evidence of this kind is to be put before a jury, it may be suspected that the often casuistic distinction between the general and the particular is either ignored by juries, or seen as a distinction of form rather than substance. It has been suggested too that some defences in criminal proceedings can in effect only be raised by adducing expert evidence, and that: "it would put an insuperable difficulty in the way of insanity" if such evidence were to be excluded by an ultimate issue or other analogous rule.' The rationale behind the supposed prohibition is that the expert should not usurp the functions of the jury. But since counsel can bring the witness so close to opining on the ultimate issue that the inference as to his view is obvious, the rule can only be, as the authors of the last work referred to say, a matter of form rather than substance. In our view an expert is called to give his opinion and he should be allowed to do so. It is, however, important that the judge should make clear to the jury that they are not bound by the expert's opinion, and that the issue is for them to decide.

7. On What did the Expert Base their Opinion?

Introduction

Experts cannot pluck their opinions from the air. The facts on which the expert gives his opinion must themselves be established by admissible evidence, ie they must be proven: *English Exporters (London) Ltd. v Eldonwall Ltd.* [1973] Ch 415. Thus, if a ballistics expert were to conclude that a bullet must have been fired from a high velocity weapon because it penetrated a brick wall, evidence that this had occurred would have to be adduced at trial. Such facts may be established by the expert himself; for example, a pathologist might describe wounds that he identified on a dead body during a physical examination that he personally conducted, before moving on to give an opinion as to their cause. Alternatively, another witness, for example, a nurse who carried out an intimate examination of the dead body, might give evidence on them, prior to the expert interpreting the nurse's findings and venturing an opinion as to how they arose.

Experts and Hearsay

In civil cases, the effective abolition of the hearsay rule as one of exclusion, under the Civil Evidence Act 1995, means that, technically, an expert witness can give an opinion on facts that have been reported to him and which he repeats in court, even though he has not conducted an examination himself (albeit that he should provide notice of this and it might affect the weight of his evidence). Alternatively, and more commonly, a statement could be served under the 1995 Act. In criminal cases, the Law Commission suggested that where a party had nothing to put to an expert's assistant that could not equally have been put to the expert, the existing rules providing for advance notice of an intention to adduce such evidence be extended to require notice of the names of those who had supplied the information on which the expert would rely, and the nature of that information in each case. It further recommended that where such notice had been given, a new hearsay exception be created to enable the expert witness to base his opinion on any information supplied by that person, without his being called, unless the court directed otherwise. The onus would be on the party seeking to cross-examine the assistant to persuade the court that his attendance was necessary.[18]

This proposal was met by s. 127 of the CJA 2003, which allows an expert to 'base an opinion' on a statement prepared by someone else, who had personal knowledge of the matters stated, and which was prepared for the purposes of criminal proceedings, *provided* that appropriate notice is given. In such circumstances, under s. 127(3), the statement 'is to be treated as evidence of what it states', ie it becomes an exception to the hearsay rule. However, this will not apply if, under s. 127(4), the court decides that it is not in the interests of justice for it to do so, in which case the maker of the statement will have to be called to give testimony as to his findings.

Nevertheless, in some respects, the evidence of an expert is not subject to the rule against hearsay in quite the same way as that of witnesses of fact. Provided the primary facts on which an opinion is based are established, the expert, when giving his opinion, can draw on, and cite, the *corpus* of available knowledge in the appropriate field to support it, even though he may not have personally established the information contained in this body of knowledge. To illustrate this point can be considered the facts of *R v Abadom* [1983] 1 WLR 126. In this case, a robbery had occurred during which an internal window had been broken in an office. The appellant when arrested had glass embedded in his shoes, which on forensic examination by an admitted expert had the same refractive properties as that from the broken window. These were the 'primary facts' and it was not disputed that the expert had established them.

However, that the window and the shoe glass had the same refractive quality was only of substantial value as circumstantial evidence if it could be established that this was not a common phenomenon (if *all* glass had the same properties in this area it would have been a valueless observation). The expert used Home Office statistics to show that only 4% of glass had the refractive index of the samples analysed (important evidence that it was from the same source). On appeal, after conviction, it was advanced that as the expert had not personally established the Home Office statistics by his own experiments, it was hearsay evidence, and he should not have been permitted to have recourse to them.

This argument was firmly rejected by the court; Kerr LJ stated that it was an 'essential part of his function as an expert to take account of this material'. Taking account of information stemming from the work of others in the same field was a vital part of expert evidence. The hearsay rule did not apply to this type of information. Such evidence could be either in a published form (as in a textbook) or unpublished materials (as with the tables of Home Office statistics), though the source of the information should be clearly identified, to allow the tribunal to make a proper

---

[18] Law Commission Report No 245, *Hearsay and Related Topics*, published 19 June 1997, at paras. 1.19 and 1.38.

assessment of its weight (obviously, a medical article in the *Lancet* will carry more weight than one in *Homes and Gardens*). This common law exception to the hearsay rule has been expressly preserved in criminal cases by s. 118(8) of the CJA 2003, which provides that an expert witness 'may draw on the body of expertise relevant to his field'.

R v Steven Abadom [1983] 76 Cr App R 48, CA

Kerr LJ

First, where an expert relies on the existence or non-existence of some fact which is basic to the question on which he is asked to express his opinion, that fact must be proved by admissible evidence...Thus, it would no doubt have been inadmissible if Mr. Cooke had said in the present case that he had been told by somebody else that the refractive index of the fragments of glass and of the control sample was identical, and any opinion expressed by him on this basis would then have been based on hearsay. If he had not himself determined the refractive index, it would have been necessary to call the person who had done so before Mr. Cooke could have expressed any opinion based on this determination. In this connection it is to be noted that Mr. Smalldon was rightly called to prove the chemical analysis made by him which Mr. Cooke was asked to take into account....

These, however, are in our judgment the limits of the hearsay rule in relation to evidence of opinion given by experts, both in principle and on the authorities. In other respects their evidence is not subject to the rule against hearsay in the same way as that of witnesses of fact...Once the primary facts on which their opinion is based have been proved by admissible evidence, they are entitled to draw on the work of others as part of the process of arriving at their conclusion. However, where they have done so, they should refer to this material in their evidence so that the cogency and probative value of their conclusion can be tested and evaluated by reference to it. Thus, if in the present case the statistical tables of analyses made by the Home Office forensic laboratories had appeared in a textbook or other publication, it could not be doubted that Mr. Cooke would have been entitled to rely upon them for the purposes of his evidence. Indeed, this was not challenged. But it does not seem to us, in relation to the reliability of opinion evidence given by experts, that they must necessarily limit themselves to drawing on material which has been published in some form. Part of their experience and expertise may well lie in their knowledge of unpublished material and in their evaluation of it. The only rule in this regard, as it seems to us, is that they should refer to such material in their evidence for the reasons stated above. We accordingly conclude that Mr. Cooke's reliance on the Home Office statistics did not infringe the rule against hearsay and dismiss the appeal against conviction.

Civil Cases

Exactly the same principle applies in civil cases: *English Exporters (London) Limited v Eldonwall Limited* [1973] Ch 415. The approach adopted in this case was subsequently approved by the Court of Appeal in *H v Schering Chemicals Ltd* [1983] 1 WLR 143. This provision is still of some significance, even though the hearsay rule has been abolished in civil matters as a rule of exclusion, as it means that an expert can give evidence citing such research without having to serve notice of it pursuant to s. 2 of the Civil Evidence Act 1995.

Cross-reference Box

Since 1995, the fact that something is hearsay, that is, constitutes an out of court statement adduced for the truth of its contents, has not precluded it being admitted in civil cases. However, it does affect the weight that can be accorded to the statement, and there is a notice scheme that should be complied with on pain of being penalized in costs and having the cogency attributed to the admitted statement further undermined. For more details on hearsay go to chapter 6.

English Exporters (London) Limited v Eldonwall Limited
[1973] Ch 415, HC

Megarry J

As an expert witness, the valuer is entitled to express his opinion about matters within his field of competence. In building up his opinions about values, he will no doubt have learned much from transactions in which he has himself been engaged, and of which he could give first-hand evidence. But he will also have learned much from many other sources, including much of which he could give no first-hand evidence. Textbooks, journals, reports of auctions and other dealings, and information obtained from his professional brethren and others, some related to particular transactions and some more general and indefinite, will all have contributed their share. Doubtless much, or most, of this will be accurate, though some will not; and even what is accurate so far as it goes may be incomplete, in that nothing may have been said of some special element which affects values. Nevertheless, the opinion that the expert expresses is none the worse because it is in part derived from the matters of which he could give no direct evidence. Even if some of the extraneous information which he acquires in this way is inaccurate or incomplete, the errors and omissions will often tend to cancel each other out; and the valuer, after all, is an expert in this field, so that the less reliable the knowledge that he has about the details of some reported transaction, the more his experience will tell him that he should be ready to make some discount from the weight that he gives it in contributing to his overall sense of values. Some aberrant transactions may stand so far out of line that he will give them little or no weight. No question of giving hearsay evidence arises in such cases, the witness states his opinion from his general experience. . . . Putting matters shortly, and leaving on one side the matters that I have mentioned, such as the Civil Evidence Act 1968 and anything made admissible by questions in cross-examination, in my judgment a valuer giving expert evidence in chief (or in re-examination): (a) may express the opinions that he has formed as to values even though substantial contributions to the formation of those opinions have been made by matters of which he has no first-hand knowledge; (b) may give evidence as to the details of any transactions within his personal knowledge, in order to establish them as matters of fact; and (c) may express his opinion as to the significance of any transactions which are or will be proved by admissible evidence (whether or not given by him) in relation to the valuation with which he is concerned; but (d) may not give hearsay evidence stating the details of any transactions not within his personal knowledge in order to establish them as matters of fact. To those propositions I would add that for counsel to put in a list of comparables ought to amount to a warranty by him of his intention to tender admissible evidence of all that is shown on the list. I have spent some little time in dealing with this matter of evidence as it appears to be the subject of no direct modern authority, and experience suggests that it is a matter upon which there is considerable misunderstanding. When a list of comparables is being prepared for the trial, as is usual and convenient, it is all too common to include in the list transactions upon which there will be no admissible evidence but only hearsay of a greater or lesser degree of reliability. If the parties exchange lists of comparables at an early date, often much time and money can be saved by the experts on each side agreeing such of the transactions in each list as, after any necessary inquiry, they feel they can accept as being reliably summarised; and in this way the additional expense of proving a favourable comparable not within an expert's own knowledge can be avoided. But if the other side will not accept the facts, then either the transaction must be proved by admissible evidence or it must be omitted as a comparable.

H v Schering Chemicals Ltd [1983] 1 WLR 143, CA

Bingham J

It is, as I have said, common ground that these articles can be referred to by experts as part of the general corpus of medical knowledge falling within the expertise of an expert in this field. That of course means that an expert who says (and I am looking at it from the plaintiffs' point of view for purposes of my example) 'I consider that there is a causal connection between the taking of the drug and the resulting deformity', can fortify his opinion by referring to learned articles, publications, letters as reinforcing the view to which he has come. In doing so, he can make reference to papers in which a contrary opinion may be expressed but in which figures are set out which he regards as supporting his contention, In such a situation one asks: Are the figures and statistics set out in such an article strictly proved? and I think the answer is no. I think that they are nonetheless of probative value when referred to and relied on by an expert in the manner in which I have indicated. If an expert refers to the results of research published by a reputable authority in a reputable journal the court would, I think, ordinarily regard those results as supporting inferences fairly to be drawn from them, unless or until a different approach was shown to be proper.

Laymen are not Covered by such a Privilege

However, it should also be noted that only an expert may avail himself of this privilege. A layman cannot cite professional research to support his version of events. Thus, in *R v Edwards (Christopher)* [2001] EWCA Crim 2185 the defendant was accused of possessing a large amount of ecstasy tablets (on his person in a night club) with intent to supply. While admitting possession, he sought to argue that they were for his own consumption and that he had no intention of selling them. He claimed that he needed so many tablets because, as a hardened addict with an unusual constitution, such a quantity was necessary to satisfy his own needs, rather than to supply others.

At trial, the judge decided not to allow the accused to call as an expert witness a man who had worked for some years in a drugs charity. This individual had no qualifications but had had many conversations with addicts. These led him to conclude that, in exceptional cases, extremely high amounts of ecstasy might be consumed by certain individuals. The Court of Appeal concluded that the first instance judge was correct in his view that extensive conversations with addicts was not a: '…safe basis on any footing whatsoever to accredit him with the expertise fit to exempt his opinion from the rule against hearsay'. He (the charity worker) was not an expert and so the conversations became hearsay (and not covered by the *Abadom* principle). Similarly, in a road traffic case from 1989, a defendant was forbidden to adduce a journal article to suggest that he was not careless in his driving.

 Pause for reflection

Is it fair that lay witnesses cannot adduce such material, unlike their expert counterparts?

This limitation is important, because, in the modern era, the use of such material to support expert opinion is a regular occurrence, and often very important to the outcome of a hearing. For example, in *Wardlaw v Farrar* [2003] 4 All ER 1358, the main issue at trial was whether delays in admitting the claimant's wife to hospital had increased her risk of death, and expert evidence was given on both sides. Much of this centred on the respective merits of an article published in *The Lancet*, relied on by one of the experts, and a passage in the *Oxford Textbook of Medicine,* adduced by the other.

8. The Weight Accorded to Expert Evidence

Introduction

The weight accorded to expert evidence is almost entirely a matter for the tribunal of fact. Generally, a judge, jury or magistrates can chose to accept or ignore such evidence, to choose between conflicting experts, or to disregard both of them. Even if expert evidence is unchallenged by that of another expert, but merely contested by 'ordinary' evidence, a tribunal of fact is usually free to ignore it (having duly considered it). Thus, in *Armstrong and anor v First York Ltd* [2005] 1 WLR 275, the Court of Appeal concluded that a trial judge was entitled to prefer the evidence of two convincing claimants of good character in a road traffic case, though they were unsupported by expert testimony, to that of a jointly instructed expert, with whose work and reasoning the first instance judge could find no fault, albeit also expressly noting that the area in which the expert practised, that of 'bio-mechanics' was, in the words of Brooke LJ, an 'unusual and developing field'. Similarly, at first instance in *Fuller v Strum* [2002] 1 WLR 1097, the trial judge preferred the evidence of ordinary witnesses as to whether a signature was forged to that of a single joint expert graphologist; his conclusion on this issue was not challenged by the Court of Appeal.

Armstrong and anor v First York Ltd [2005] 1 WLR 275, CA

Brooke LJ

In my judgment, in this very difficult case the judge directed himself correctly as a matter of law. He was entitled to consider the evidence he had been given by the claimant extremely carefully, directing himself about the dangers of witnesses who may seem to be very plausible but in fact are telling a pack of lies, and directing himself to consider very carefully the evidence given on behalf of the defendant. He formed the view that he could not be satisfied that these witnesses were telling a pack of lies. He was very impressed by their evidence, and he concluded, when he had to balance the evidence of each side, that there must be-although he accepted fully that he could not say what it was-something which was not accurate in Mr Childs's evidence in this particular case.

In my judgment there is no principle of law that an expert's evidence in an unusual field-doing his best, with his great experience, to reconstruct what happened to the parties based on the secondhand material he received in this case-must be dispositive of liability in such a case and that a judge must be compelled to find that, in his view, two palpably honest witnesses have come to court to deceive him in order to obtain damages, in this case a small amount of damages, for a case they know to be a false one.

In Liddell v Middleton [1996] PIQR P36 Stuart Smith LJ, who had immense experience of personal injury litigation, said, at p 43: 'We do not have trial by expert in this country; we have trial by judge.' In the last resort it is for the judge-or it may be the jury in a criminal trial as the triers of fact-to determine, on the balance of probability, on all the evidence they receive, where the probabilities lie. It may be that they are impelled to that conclusion when they are weighing two different types of evidence, one from extremely honest-appearing witnesses of fact and the other from an expert doing his best in his particular field of expertise. In my judgment, if we dismiss the appeal in this case we are not opening the door to a whole lot of dishonest claimants to recover just because there may be cases in which the honesty and force of a claimant's evidence impresses a trial judge in the way the evidence of these claimants did on this particular occasion. In very many cases the evidence of a witness like Mr Childs may very well be sufficient to tip the balance strongly in the defendant's favour.

For these reasons, in my judgment, there is no point of law of the type on which Mr Grant sought to rely in support of this appeal. This was very much a matter for the judge to determine on all the different types of evidence he received. There was evidence which pointed one way, which he was entitled to accept from the claimant if he thought fit. There was evidence that pointed the other way for the defendant. I can find no flaw in the judge's reasoning in this case.

Very exceptionally, however, it seems that a tribunal of fact is not free to choose between expert evidence, or decide against such evidence. Thus, the Court of Appeal has held that in certain very specific murder cases, involving the sudden unexplained deaths of infants, a matter should not be left to a jury (ie should be thrown out by a first instance judge), where there is a serious disagreement between reputable experts and no other cogent evidence in the case: *R v Cannings* [2004] 1 WLR 2607. Nevertheless, this decision has been interpreted quite restrictively, being largely confined to cases that depended on inferences based on coincidence, or the likelihood of two or more infant deaths in the same family, especially where such cases were entirely dependent on conflicting expert evidence and unsupported by other cogent evidence; unlike, for example, a case which includes a previously, and publicly, admitted urge to kill the relevant infant: *R v Kai-Whitewind (Chaha'oh Niyoi)* [2005] 2 Cr App R 31.

R v Cannings [2004] 1 WLR 2607, CA

Judge LJ

With unexplained infant deaths, however, as this judgment has demonstrated, in many important respects we are still at the frontiers of knowledge. Necessarily, further research is needed, and fortunately, thanks to the dedication of the medical profession, it is continuing. All this suggests that, for the time being, where a full investigation into two or more sudden unexplained infant deaths in the same family is followed by a serious disagreement between reputable experts about the cause of death, and a body of such expert opinion concludes that natural causes, whether explained or unexplained, cannot be excluded as a reasonable (and not a fanciful) possibility, the prosecution of a parent or parents for murder should not be started, or continued, unless there is additional cogent evidence, extraneous to the expert evidence, (such as we have exemplified in para 10) which tends to support the conclusion that the infant, or where there is more than one death, one of the infants, was deliberately harmed. In cases like the present, if the outcome of the trial depends exclusively or almost exclusively on a serious disagreement between distinguished and reputable experts, it will often be unwise, and therefore unsafe, to proceed.

It also seems that in some cases very strong expert evidence is binding on a trial judge, unless properly controverted, especially if he cannot provide good reasons for not accepting it. Thus, in *re B (A Minor)* [2000] 1 WLR 790 it was held that a county court judge had erred in care proceedings in failing to analyse or give reasons for rejecting expert evidence as to fractures provided by a pair of consultant radiologists. He had preferred the lay evidence of the child's grandmother, even though he could not fault the reasoning of the radiologists and there was no significant expert evidence in reply. Similarly, in *R v Matheson* [1958] 1 WLR 474, it was held that a jury were not entitled to return a verdict of guilty to murder, in a case where the defendant had called three doctors to give unanimous and unchallenged psychiatric evidence that he was suffering from diminished responsibility under s. 2(1) of the Homicide Act 1957.

Generally, appellate courts are reluctant to 'second guess' a judge's qualitative assessment of an expert's evidence. Thus, in *Wardlaw v Farrar* [2003] 4 All ER 1358 Brooke LJ observed that it was well established that the Court of Appeal would be: '...very slow to interfere with a trial judge's views on the quality of the evidence of expert witnesses whom he has had the advantage of seeing and hearing'. However, this is not an inflexible rule. Chadwick LJ noted in *Roadrunner Properties Ltd v Dean* [2003] EWCA CIV 1816 that appeal courts could examine the reasons provided by expert witnesses for their conclusions, particularly where they were seeking to construct what had occurred from evidence of other facts.

The claim in this case was for damage to floor tiles and a wall, allegedly caused by work carried out with a heavy-duty drill in an adjoining property. At trial, in the County Court, the claimant's expert suggested that use of the drill might well have caused the damage, but since he had not been able to carry out a more detailed examination he was unable to confirm this. By contrast, the defendant's expert argued that the damage to the floor and tiles had been caused by moisture absorbed from the atmosphere. He further suggested that the fact that the damage to the tiles, which had been unaffected by atmospheric conditions for 13 years, coincided with the work done in the adjoining property was merely coincidental. There was no other evidence as to whether atmospheric conditions at the time of the work were unusual. The trial judge preferred the evidence of the defendant's expert.

In the Court of Appeal, however, Chadwick LJ disagreed. He felt that the fact that the claimant's expert had been unable to pursue his investigation did not mean that the defendant's expert's theory was therefore more probable. It was also his view that the coincidence between the buckling of the tiles and the work being done was a proper factor to be taken into account, and that in such a situation, the court: '...should be slow to discard common sense in favour of expert hypothesis'.

In many situations, there is an inherent tension in calling conflicting expert evidence, which is that laymen are then being asked to reach a conclusion on matters about which specialists do not agree, as the following extract from Auld LJ's report makes clear.

Auld LJ, *A Review of the Criminal Courts of England and Wales* (2001) at 576, para. 137

MANNER OF PRESENTATION OF EXPERT EVIDENCE

137 At the heart of this question is the seeming absurdity in our present system of entrusting to a tribunal, whether judge, magistrates or jury, unversed in a particular discipline the task of determining which of two conflicting experts is right. However, to hand over the decision to a single expert or body of experts would remove that part, possibly the crucial part, of the decision-making from the court. Lord Justice May ruminated on this central dilemma in an address to last year's Annual Conference of the Expert Witness Institute, when citing the following passage from a seminal article of Judge Learned Hand in 1901:

> 'The trouble with all this is that it is setting the jury to decide, where doctors disagree. The whole object of the expert is to tell the jury, not facts, as we have seen, but general truths derived from his specialised experience. But how can the jury judge between two statements each founded upon an experience confessedly foreign in kind to their own? It is just because they are incompetent for such a task that the expert is necessary at all.... If you would get at the truth in such cases, it must be through someone competent to decide.'

Judicial Directions on Expert Opinion Evidence

Broadly speaking, a trial judge must neither direct the jury (or, in theory, himself) to ignore nor to accept expert evidence, and this remains the case even if there is no opposing expert evidence: *R v Lanfear* [1968] 2 QB 77. In *R v Stockwell* [1993] 97 Cr App R 260 the court emphasized the importance of a judge making clear to the jury that it was not bound by an expert's opinion and that the issue was always one for them to decide, especially if the evidence went to the ultimate issue in the case. However, in *R v Fitzpatrick* [1999] Crim LR 832, the Court of Appeal indicated that there was no requirement that a set formula of words be adopted when warning a jury to this effect, *provided* such a direction was given. Even so, a failure to give such a direction would often result in a successful appeal. The approved judicial studies board direction makes it appropriately clear that jurors are not bound by such evidence and is commonly used by trial judges, though, as *Fitzpatrick* suggests (and as with most other such directions), its adoption is not essential.

Judicial Studies Board Crown Court Bench Book: Specimen Directions, August 2005

No. 33, Expert Evidence

In this case you have heard the evidence of X, who has been called as an expert on behalf of the prosecution/defendant. Expert evidence is permitted in a criminal trial to provide you with scientific [or eg accountancy] information and opinion, which is within the witness' expertise, but which is likely to be outside your experience and knowledge. It is by no means unusual for evidence of this nature to be called; and it is important that you should see it in its proper perspective, which is that it is before you as part of the evidence as a whole to assist you with regard to one particular aspect of the evidence, namely [...].

A witness called as an expert is entitled to express an opinion in respect of [his findings or the matters which are put to him]; and you are entitled and would no doubt wish to have regard to this evidence and to the opinion/s expressed by the expert/s when coming to your own conclusions about this aspect of the case.

You should bear in mind that if, having given the matter careful consideration, you do not accept the evidence of the expert/s, you do not have to act upon it. [Indeed, you do not have to accept even the unchallenged evidence of an expert.] (In a case where two or more experts have given conflicting evidence:) It is for you to decide whose evidence, and whose opinions you accept, if any. You should remember that this evidence relates only to part of the case, and that whilst it may be of assistance to you in reaching a verdict, you must reach your verdict having considered all the evidence.

9. Evidence of Handwriting

Introduction

A frequently encountered, albeit specialist, provision governing expert evidence is found in s. 8 of the Criminal Procedure Act 1865. Despite its name, this part of the Act applies to both criminal and civil cases (see s. 1 of the statute), though in civil hearings the provision had a precedent in the Common Law Procedure Act 1854. Section 8 governs the comparison of disputed samples of handwriting. It allows their authors to be determined by comparing a disputed sample with any writing 'proved to the satisfaction of the judge to be genuine'. As this suggests, a crucial step is to obtain a satisfactory 'control' sample, for in-court comparison with the disputed sample. The judge then decides whether the authenticity of the control sample has been proved to his satisfaction. This has to be done to the standard appropriate to the proceedings in which the evidence is being adduced, that is on the balance of probabilities in civil cases, and beyond reasonable doubt in criminal ones: *R v Ewing* [1983] QB 1039.

Section 8 of the Criminal Procedure Act 1865

8. Comparison of disputed writing with writing proved to be genuine.

Comparison of a disputed writing with any writing proved to the satisfaction of the judge to be genuine shall be permitted to be made by witnesses; and such writings, and the evidence of witnesses respecting the same, may be submitted to the court and jury as evidence of the genuineness or otherwise of the writing in dispute.

However, jurors should not be unassisted, and left to their own devices, when making a comparison between the two samples of handwriting. Instead, they should always have the aid of either an expert graphologist or, alternatively, someone who is intimately acquainted with the handwriting in question, such as a personal secretary (deemed to be a de facto expert for these purposes): *R v Tilley* [1961] 1 WLR 1309 and *R v O'Sullivan* [1969] 1 WLR 497. Strictly speaking, the 'ultimate issue' as to whether the disputed handwriting is the same as the control sample is a matter for the jury, the expert pointing out unusual similarities between the two samples, for example 'both writers press hard on their capital letters'; in practice, as elsewhere, this rule seems to be frequently ignored.

Thus, and for example, if the defendant in a criminal case has, allegedly, filled in, signed and issued stolen cheques the prosecution will wish to establish that he is the author of the cheques. The writing on the cheques will be the disputed sample. During the search of the defendant's premises the police seize a letter written and signed by him addressed to his local cricket club. This will be the control sample. If the trial judge is persuaded, beyond reasonable doubt, that the defendant is the author of the letter to the cricket club, perhaps by the police giving evidence that it was found in his house, had his name on it, was covered in his finger prints and that he was a member of the club, it can go with the disputed sample to the jury for assisted (by a graphologist or someone intimately acquainted with the defendant's handwriting) comparison.

Judicial Studies Board Crown Court Bench Book: Specimen Directions, August 2005

No. 33 Expert Evidence (Extract)

[In a case where e.g. handwriting (See Note 1, below) is in issue or there might otherwise be a danger of the jury coming to its own 'scientific' conclusions, add: With regard to this particular aspect of the evidence you are not experts; and it would be quite wrong for you as jurors to attempt to [compare specimens of handwriting/perform any tests/experiments of your own] and to come to any conclusions on the basis of your own observations. However you are entitled to come to a conclusion based on the whole of the evidence which you have heard, and that of course includes the expert evidence.

Note 1: In relation to a matter such as handwriting, it is desirable to give the jury (in addition to any directions in the summing up) an early direction when the matter arises in evidence that they should not embark upon a comparison exercise on their own. They may, e.g. be told, if the issue is likely to be of importance, that they must decide it on the evidence only (which may legitimately take the form of agreed facts, the evidence of the maker or alleged maker of the document, the evidence of a person proved to be familiar with the maker's handwriting, expert evidence and circumstantial evidence); but they must not decide it on the basis of any comparison carried out privately by them.

---

10. Novel Fields of Expert Evidence

Introduction

At trial, as well as deciding if something is outside the competence of the tribunal of fact and whether a tendered expert is deemed to be peritus, a judge must also conclude that the proposed evidence is within a legitimate 'field' of expertise. This is so, even if it is obviously outside the tribunal's competence and the tendered witness is clearly a specialist in the subject. To take an extreme example, although the evidence of a qualified pathologist is heard without demur, the courts would not, as Bingham LJ pointed out in *R v Robb* [1991] 93 Cr App R 161, receive the evidence of an astrologer, even if he had spent decades mastering his discipline.

The problem lies in identifying where the qualitative dividing line between pathologist and astrologer lies. In practice, of course, it is comparatively rare for the courts to be invited to consider expertise that has not already been received on numerous occasions in earlier cases. However, in a world of continuous change and innovation, new fields of alleged expertise, whether scientific, artistic or commercial, continue to emerge on a regular basis. The courts, when faced with such evidence, must attempt to impose some form of quality control.

It is extremely difficult, if not impossible, to produce a succinct test that can be applied to *all* forms of novel expertise that are tendered in evidence, largely because of the extensive range of potential areas of expertise. As Bingham LJ pointed out in *Robb*, these are not confined to the old academically based sciences but extend to matters as diverse as accident reconstruction and the artistic merits of literary works that are alleged to be obscene. In recent years, domestic appellate authority in England has sometimes cited approvingly the second part (part b) of the test set out by King CJ in the Australian case of *R. v Bonython* (1984) 38 SASR 45; however, though succinct, its application is difficult in practice.

R v Bonython (1984) 38 SASR 45, SACA

King CJ

…[the question] may be divided into two parts: (a) whether the subject matter of the opinion is such that a person without instruction or experience in the area of knowledge or human experience would be able to form a sound judgment on the matter without the assistance of witnesses possessing special knowledge or experience in the area, and (b) whether the subject matter of the opinion forms part of a body of knowledge or experience which is sufficiently organised or recognised to be accepted as a reliable body of knowledge or experience, a special acquaintance with which by the witness would render his opinion of assistance to the court.

Sub-dividing expert evidence into its three main categories, each of which, in practice, appears to have its own criteria for determining admissibility, makes the process somewhat easier. These are: new scientific methods and techniques; novel areas of 'knowledge'; and newly identified 'skills'. Amongst the first category will be anything that is susceptible to what might, loosely, be termed the 'scientific method'. Amongst the second, will be evidence as to what is 'approved' practice in a new profession, industry or form of business endeavour. The final category includes matters as diverse as lip-reading and the assessment of artistic merit.

New Fields of Scientific Expertise

In the Canadian case of *R v Mohan* [1994] 2 SCR 9, which involved an expert giving evidence on the likely psychological profiles of putative perpetrators of sexual offences, the Canadian Supreme Court made the uncontroversial observation that expert evidence that advances a novel scientific theory or technique should be subjected to 'special scrutiny to determine whether it meets a basic threshold of reliability'. However, such 'special scrutiny' also needs some specific criteria to be effective.

Traditionally, in the United States, the test for accepting new scientific techniques was contained in *Frye v United States (1923)* 297 F 1013, a decision of the Court of Appeal of the District of Columbia, with regard to the admissibility of evidence of the (then new) polygraph test. Although this has since been qualified in many American jurisdictions, it is still important and the court's observations bear repetition: 'Just when a scientific principle or discovery crosses the line between the experimental and demonstrable stages is difficult to define.... [it] must be sufficiently established to have gained general acceptance in the particular field in which it belongs.'

Adopting such an approach means that the tribunal of fact is much less likely to be exposed to fields of expertise that ultimately prove to be of little worth. However, it was also criticized as being excessively cautious; the requirement that new techniques should have gained 'general acceptance' *before* they could be admitted would necessarily preclude most 'cutting-edge' methodologies from the forensic environment. As a result, in American federal, and some state, courts the *Frye* test appears to have been superseded by the slightly more flexible, if less succinct and clear-cut, approach established in *Daubert v Merrell Dow Pharmaceuticals, Inc.,* 509 US 579 (1993).

English courts have, historically, been more adventurous about allowing novel fields of scientific expertise than was the case in America after *Frye*. A traditional starting point in such matters is the Scottish case of *Davie v Edinburgh Magistrates* 1953 SC 34, in which Lord President Cooper concluded that to be admitted expert witnesses must furnish the court with the: '... necessary scientific criteria for testing the accuracy of their conclusions, so as to enable the judge or jury to form their own independent judgment by the application of these criteria to the facts proved in evidence'.

The approach adopted in *Davie v Edinburgh Magistrates* was approved by the Court of Appeal in *R v Gilfoyle* [1996] 1 Cr App R 302. In this case, the judge presiding over the trial of a man accused of murdering his wife, whose defence was that the dead woman had actually killed herself, refused to allow the adduction of what was termed a 'psychological autopsy' of the deceased. The tendered expert had based this on a scrutiny of a diary and other documents written by the dead woman, her life experiences and the reports of a doctor, as well as the views of the appellant. The conclusion of his 'autopsy' was that the dead woman had taken her own life.

The Court of Appeal, when upholding the trial judge's decision not to admit such evidence, accepted without reservation that the proposed witness was a specialist in the systematic analysis of human behaviour, and so was an 'expert' in his field. However, it concluded that it was not expert evidence of a kind that should be placed before a court for a number of reasons. Most importantly, although being completely novel, the expert's reports identified no criteria by reference to which the court could test the quality of his opinions; there was no data base comparing real and questionable suicides. Additionally, there was no substantial body of academic writing approving his methodology. The court went on to observe that: '...unstructured and speculative conclusions are not the stuff of which admissible expert evidence is made'.

However, and by contrast, in *R v Dallagher* [2003] 1 Cr App R 12, a differently constituted Court of Appeal, although prepared to order a retrial (subsequently abandoned), so that the reliability of 'ear-printing' could be challenged (in front of a jury) in the light of newly available evidence that questioned the method, was unwilling to say that the field was one on which evidence should not have been received at all at trial in 1998 (more than four years earlier).

Indeed, the court suggested that as long as the tendered field of expertise was sufficiently well established that it passed ordinary tests of relevance, no enhanced test was required for its admissibility.

How can these two cases be reconciled? Most importantly, it seems, to be admissible, novel scientific techniques require that the expert who advances them can explain to the tribunal how and why he reached his conclusion, so that they can follow his reasoning and could, in theory, replicate the process. In doing this, he must lay an empirical basis for his conclusions. This could be done with regard to the evidence in *Dallagher* even if, as transpired, it proved to be erroneous, in a manner that was simply not possible in *Gilfoyle*; ie the former case (unlike the latter) was susceptible to the scientific method. Thus, the expert in *Dallagher* (a Dutch policeman) could identify the points of comparison between the ear prints of the suspected perpetrator and defendant, and could compare them with the hundreds of other tests he had conducted over several years on the singularity of prints to the ears that made them. As Judge LJ observed in *R v Cannings* [2004] 1 All ER 725, in these situations, the courts appear to be willing to accept the risk that later research might undermine the accepted wisdom of today, so: 'That does not normally provide a basis for rejecting the expert evidence.'

R v Dallagher [2003] 1 Cr App R 12, CA

Kennedy, LJ

As we have indicated, Mr Clegg's first ground of appeal is that in English law the evidence of Mr Van Der Lugt and Professor Vanezis is and should be held to have been inadmissible. He submits that if Mr Hatton had been equipped with the fresh evidence now relied upon he could and would have made that submission to the trial judge, and that his submission should have been accepted.... As to the English approach we have found it necessary to refer not only to Strudwick and Merry but also to a number of other decisions, especially Clarke, from which, as it seems to us, the analogy with rule 702 is clear. As is said in the current ninth edition of *Cross and Tapper on Evidence* at 523 after a reference to Frye—'The better, and now more widely accepted, view is that so long as the field is sufficiently well-established to pass the ordinary tests of relevance and reliability, then no enhanced test of admissibility should be applied, but the weight of the evidence should be established by the same adversarial forensic techniques applicable elsewhere.' We are satisfied that if a submission had been made to the trial judge that the expert evidence upon which the Crown proposed to rely was inadmissible, and if that evidence had been deployed on a *voire dire*, whether with or without expert evidence called on behalf of the defence, the trial judge could not possibly have concluded that the Crown's expert evidence was irrelevant, or so unreliable that it should be excluded. Accordingly in our judgment the first ground of appeal fails.

 Pause for reflection

Do you feel that a more cautious approach to novel fields of expertise would be sensible in criminal cases, or would that merely deny the court access to innovative scientific techniques and new forms of knowledge?

Field, Methodology and Minority Schools of Thought

The dividing line between deciding that a tendered witness should not be accorded expert status (is not 'peritus'), and a decision that his proposed area is not an acceptable field for expertise, can be an extremely narrow one, as, to an extent, the field and the methodology are inextricably interlinked. This can be seen clearly in the borderline case of *R v Robb* [1991] 93 Cr App R 161, in which the Court of Appeal upheld, with some hesitation, a trial judge's decision to admit evidence of voice-identification based exclusively on auditory techniques, unaided by any quantitative analysis of speech patterns, although this approach was rejected by the 'great weight of informed opinion'.

Voice identification generally is a topic on which expert evidence is regularly received. However, in *Robb*, the tendered expert, a Dr Baldwin, had published no experiments or tests on the accuracy of his own conclusions and had produced no material which would allow his methods to be tested. Against this, there was a handful of other specialists in England who shared his approach to voice-identification and he was also able to give coherent reasons for his preference for the method in question. Additionally, he was able to give clear reasons for his preference for the method in question and was a lecturer in the phonetics in the University of London, with impressive academic qualifications.

Should Dr Baldwin's evidence be admitted in the same manner in which those who employed analysis of speech patterns, was his specific methodology a potentially unacceptable subdivision of the field of voice-identification, one on which it was not proper to receive evidence, or did his unusual approach to the subject simply render him non-peritus? In this case, the Court of Appeal decided that it was an appropriate field on which to receive expert evidence and that the witness's unusual methodology merely went to weight. However, other common law jurisdictions have reached different conclusions. Thus, the Northern Irish courts declined to follow *Robb* and concluded that, in the light of recent developments, the expert's technique was unacceptable today: *R v O'Doherty* [2003] 1 Cr App R 77. It may be that if the same matter were to come before an English court today, a similar conclusion would be reached.

R v O'Doherty [2003s] 1 Cr App R 77, CA (NI)

Nicholson LJ

Despite Mrs McClelland's expression of scepticism we are satisfied, having heard Dr Nolan and Dr French and read the report of Dr Kunzel, that in the present state of scientific knowledge no prosecution should be brought in Northern Ireland in which one of the planks is voice identification given by an expert which is solely confined to auditory analysis. There should also be expert evidence of acoustic analysis such as is used by Dr Nolan, Dr French and all but a small percentage of experts in the United Kingdom and by all experts in the rest of Europe, which includes formant analysis.

60 We make three exceptions to this general statement. Where the voices of a known group are being listened to and the issue is, 'which voice has spoken which words' or where there are rare characteristics which render a speaker identifiable—but this may beg the question—or the issue relates to the accent or dialect of the speaker (see R v Mullan [1983] N.I.J.B. 12) acoustic analysis is not necessary. We do not gain any assistance from the decision in R v Gilfoyle [2001] 2 Cr. App. R 757 to which counsel for the appellant drew our attention.

61 A second plank (out of four) was 'the comparisons that the jury themselves could be invited to make having heard the ambulance control tape and the voice of the appellant as he gave evidence in Court'.

62 In R v Bentum (1989) 153 J.P. 538 the Court of Appeal in England held that the jury should be allowed to hear any tape recordings for themselves, so that they may form their own judgment of the opinions on voice identification expressed by experts or others claiming to have recognised the voice.

63 In the present case the Court of Appeal held that the issue was whether the jury considered that the voice on the ambulance control tape was the voice of the appellant. Expert evidence is received when the subject is one upon which competency to form an opinion can only be acquired by a course of special study or experience and it has been accepted that expert evidence is receivable in cases of voice identification. Expert evidence is rarely, if ever, admitted in cases of visual identification. The tribunal of fact is considered to be in as good a position to assess CCTV footage or video tapes or photographs as witnesses: See R v Murphy and Maguire [1990] N.I. 306. It seems to us that if evidence of voice recognition is relied on by the prosecution, the jury should be allowed to listen to a tape-recording on which the recognition is based, assuming that the jury have heard the accused giving evidence. It also seems to us that the jury may listen to a tape-recording of the voice of the suspect in order to assist them in evaluating expert evidence and in making up their own minds as to whether the voice on the tapes is the voice of the defendant.

New Areas of 'Knowledge'

A specialist area of knowledge can be the subject of expert testimony, *provided* it is outside normal human experience and will assist the tribunal of fact. Such knowledge does not require a reasoning process, merely that the tendered witness can provide accurate information. Thus, those who are intimately familiar with a market can be called to establish the value of goods normally traded in that market: *Bond v Barrow Co.* [1902] 1 Ch. 353. Similarly, businessmen can be called to prove the meaning of customary trade terms. Nevertheless, expert witnesses, allegedly possessed of specialist knowledge, cannot venture on what, in reality, is 'mere speculation'.

In this context, the decision of Oliver J, in *Midland Bank Trust Company Limited and anr v Hett Stubbs & Kemp* 1979 1 Ch 384 (subsequently approved by the Court of Appeal) is significant. The case concerned the alleged negligence of a solicitor instructed in a conveyancing matter. The judge freely acknowledged that expert evidence could and should be received of some standard of conduct or widespread practice in a particular profession, whether sanctioned by a professional body or by common usage. However, he went on to stress that evidence that amounted to no more than an expression of personal opinion by a particular practitioner, as to what he thinks he would have done in a similar situation, was of little assistance. Thus, the key test in such cases was to see whether there was an 'accepted standard of conduct', even if it had only developed as a result of common practise, against which the litigant's behaviour could be compared.

This approach was followed in *Barings plc & anr v Coopers & Lybrand* [2001] EWCA 1163. The crucial issue here was whether a competent derivatives manager, examining the size and profitability of a 'rogue' trader's reported dealing, should have realized that there was something fundamentally wrong with the patterns of risk and reward being disclosed. The defendants wished to adduce experts' reports, dealing with banking management, to suggest that this was indeed the case. As one of these experts expressly noted, he had attempted to assess the events at Barings 'against good business practise in the industry'. He then went on to criticize the bank's operations in the light of such alleged good practise. The claimants sought to exclude large sections of the tendered reports as being outside the sphere of expert evidence.

However, at trial, Evans-Lombe J ruled that they could be adduced in full. He decided that such expert evidence was admissible where there was a: '…recognised expertise governed by recognised standards and rules of conduct capable of influencing the Court's decision on any of the issues which it has to decide'. In this case, the judge was satisfied that a body of approved practice, with recognized standards, in relation to the managers of investment banks who were engaged in derivatives trading, existed. He was heavily influenced by the fact that, even at the time of the trader's misfeasance, this area of commerce was already highly regulated. Its practitioners were required to be licensed and the regulator had prescribed standards of required competence. When derivatives trading first emerged in the 1980s, this may not have been the case and expert evidence may not then have been receivable on the subject.

New 'Skills'

The precise dividing line between a skill and a science can be difficult to identify. The latter category appears to require that the tribunal of fact is able go through the expert's reasoning process and understand how and why he came to his conclusions. If, however, the witness is saying that they have a personal gift (whether received by dint of training, experience or providence) that allows them to reach a valid conclusion on some matter, over and above the ability or 'ordinary' people, their expertise will partake more of a 'skill'. Here, the key test appears to be that of verifiable witness reliability such that it can be inferred that the conclusion reached by the witness is highly likely to be correct and the tribunal of fact can also be properly instructed in the risk that it is wrong (and so make due allowance for that risk).

Thus, in *R v Luttrell and others* [2004] 2 Cr App R 31 the Court of Appeal held that as lip-reading evidence was capable of passing ordinary tests of relevance and reliability it was potentially admissible in evidence, provided it was accompanied by appropriate warnings. The expert had testified as to what had been said at various meetings between the appellants, which had been recorded on CCTV. This evidence was held to be admissible after detailed consideration of its possible shortcomings, and evidence from the expert herself as to her skills, experience and working methods.

The Court of Appeal noted that, over and above the basic requirement that it be relevant, the test required that two conditions be satisfied: '…first, that study or experience will give a witness's opinion an authority which the opinion of one not so qualified will lack; and secondly the witness must be so qualified to express the opinion.' The court concluded that lip-reading evidence from a good quality video was capable of being both relevant and reliable and so admissible. However, this would not always be the case; for example, it would not be so where the video footage or the view of the speaker's face was poor. Furthermore, such evidence should always be accompanied by a warning from the judge as to its limitations and the concomitant risk of error. Such a warning could, amongst other things, spell out the risk of mistakes as to the words that the lip-reader believed were spoken, as well as the inherent strengths and weaknesses of the material being reviewed; for example, the lighting, distance and angle of the speaker being scrutinized, and the awareness of the lip reader of the context in which their work was being carried out (had she been told in advance that the incident related to drugs, a robbery, etc.).

R v Luttrell and others [2004] 2 Cr App R 31, CA

Rose LJ

As we have indicated, the appellants argued that evidence should not be admitted unless it passes a further test, that the evidence can be seen to be reliable because the methods used are sufficiently explained to be tested in cross-examination and so to be verifiable or falsifiable. Where, as here, the Crown is seeking to adduce the evidence in a criminal trial, this could properly be considered by the court when deciding whether to refuse to allow the evidence, under s.78 of the Police and Criminal Evidence Act 1984 or otherwise, in order to ensure a fair trial. We cannot accept that this is a requirement of admissibility. In established fields of science, the court may take the view that expert evidence would fall beyond the recognised limits of the field or that methods are too unconventional to be regarded as subject to the scientific discipline. But a skill or expertise can be recognised and respected, and thus satisfy the conditions for admissible expert evidence, although the discipline is not susceptible to this sort of scientific discipline. Thus, in In re Pinion decd., [1965] Ch 85 the court was willing, indeed felt obliged, to hear expert evidence on the question whether a collection of paintings and other objects had aesthetic worth so that their display would be of educational value and for the public benefit, notwithstanding, as Harman L.J. observed, 'de gustibus non est disputandum'.

11. Lay Opinion Evidence

Introduction

It is not always possible to make a neat distinction between facts and inferences. For an easy example, when a witness says that someone was 'drunk' he is actually conveying an opinion based on a number of observed facts: the smell of alcohol on the person's breath; the presence of slurred speech; a loss of co-ordination; an inability to talk coherently, etc. In other, more extreme situations, facts and inferences are often almost inseparable. In these situations, statements of opinion by a layman will generally be admissible, as a shorthand way of the conveying the facts that he observed, as long as a proper appraisal of the facts does not call for any special expertise.

In reality, much lay opinion evidence is given without even being identified as such, and usually appears to cause few problems. Arguably, there is an element of opinion in any statement of fact. Frequently encountered examples of statements of opinion from an ordinary witness that are normally admissible include those relating to the speed of a vehicle involved in an accident, and the identification of persons, animals, places or things (which are all technically opinion statements). Thus, and for example, when a witness says that a car was moving 'extremely fast' he is, effectively, saying that he watched it cover a significant distance in a very short time, that it left a slip stream, etc.

In civil cases, this situation is now governed by statute, in the form of s. 3(2) of the Civil Evidence Act 1972, which provides that: '...where a person is called as a witness in any civil proceedings, a statement of opinion by him on any relevant matter on which he is not qualified to give expert evidence, if made as a way of conveying relevant facts personally perceived by him, is admissible as evidence of what he perceived.' In the United States, this position is also neatly encapsulated by r. 701 of the American Federal Rules of Evidence, which states that if a witness is not testifying as an expert, he can provide opinions or inferences that are: '... (a) rationally based on the perception of the witness, and (b) helpful to a clear understanding of the witness' testimony or the determination of a fact in issue, and (c) not based on scientific, technical, or other specialized knowledge within the scope of Rule 702 [Testimony by Experts].'

In English criminal cases, the position is the same, though the situation is still governed by common law rather than statute. Thus, in *R v Davies* [1962] 1 WLR 1111, a case involving driving whilst unfit through drink, it was held to be quite proper for prosecution witnesses to give their opinion as to whether the defendant had been drinking. However, and perhaps because this case was approaching the borderline of acceptable lay opinion evidence, the court also held that the witness should also be able give the factual basis on which they formed that opinion (for example, that the defendant was uncoordinated and unsteady on his feet, etc.). Obviously, at least to some extent, this was a situation in which it was possible to distinguish opinion from the facts on which it was based. However, in *Davies* it was held not to be permissible for the same witness to say that the defendant was unfit to drive because of his level of intoxication. Such an opinion would require expert evidence.

Similarly, in *R v Johnson* [1993] Crim LR 689 a witness gave evidence that a complainant in a rape case came to her house in the early hours of the morning. The trial judge allowed her to testify that she initially thought the complainant was play-acting but ultimately concluded that she was genuine in her distress. The Court of Appeal upheld this decision; although the witness's statement was lay 'opinion' evidence, questions could be asked of her about its factual basis (that the complainant was sobbing heavily, etc.).

R v Davies [1962] 1 WLR 1111, Court-Martial Appeal Court

Lord Parker CJ

The defence had strongly taken the stand that the witness should be allowed to speak only as to facts he had seen, because it was for the court to say what was the appellant's condition. Apparently the judge advocate advised the court that the witness could state the impression he formed as to the appellant's condition at the time he saw him if he was a witness who know what was entailed in the driving of a car.

It is to be observed that the witness was allowed to speak about two matters which are quite distinct; one is what his impression was as to whether drink had been taken by the appellant, and the second was his opinion as to whether as the result of that drink he was fit or unfit to drive a car.

The court has come clearly to the conclusion that a witness can quite properly give his general impression as to whether a driver had taken drink. He must describe of course the facts upon which he relies, but it seems to this court that he is perfectly entitled to give his impression as to whether drink had been taken or not. On the other hand, as regards the second matter, it cannot be said, as it seems to this court, that a witness, merely because he is a driver himself, is in the expert witness category so that it is proper to ask him his opinion as to fitness or unfitness to drive. That is the very matter which the court itself has to determine. Accordingly, in so far as this witness and two subsequent witnesses, the lance-corporal and the regimental sergeant-major gave their opinion as to the appellant's ability or fitness to drive, the court was wrong in admitting that evidence.

Summary

- Witnesses are normally only allowed to speak to facts, not the opinions that they have drawn from those facts.
- A variety of justifications have been advanced for this long-standing common law rule, amongst them being a fear that allowing opinion will usurp the function of the tribunal of fact, be excessively influential, prolong and confuse trials or introduce irrelevant material.
- There are two exceptions to this general rule: experts giving opinion evidence within their specialist field and laymen giving what appears to be opinion as a shorthand way of conveying facts that they personally perceived.
- Expertise will only be received on matters outside the tribunal of fact's experience. Credibility and the effects of 'normal range' intellectual and personality traits are usually deemed to be matters for the tribunal of fact.
- Expert status does not normally require formal qualifications; it can usually be gained by personal experience.
- Experts must not veer outside their area of competence (or expertise). Historically, they were also not supposed to give opinion on the 'ultimate issue' to be decided by the tribunal of fact. This rule has been abolished in civil cases and is widely ignored in criminal ones.
- The primary facts upon which an expert bases his opinion must be proved. However, an expert is free to draw on published and unpublished research in his field when forming his opinions, without infringing the hearsay rule.
- Experts are normally party appointed, though in civil matters the parties can agree to instruct a single joint expert. All experts owe a duty to the court that overrides their responsibilities to the litigants instructing them.
- The weight accorded to expert evidence is usually entirely a matter for the tribunal of fact, which is not normally obliged to accept it, even if it is not opposed by other expert testimony.
- The use of expert evidence in handwriting comparison is governed by a specialist provision, s. 8 of the Criminal Procedure Act 1865, which allows comparison between samples of writing in both civil and criminal matters. Such a comparison should normally be assisted by an expert.
- Novel fields of expertise will have to be recognized by the courts as valid to be admissible. The courts appear to apply different tests when deciding this, depending on the nature of the expertise tendered.
- A lay (ie non-expert) witness can only give opinion evidence as a shorthand way of conveying what he has personally observed.

Further reading

L Blom-Cooper, 'Experts and Assessors: Past, Present and Future' (2002) Civil Justice Quarterly, 341–356

D Dwyer, 'The effective management of bias in civil expert evidence' (2007) Civil Justice Quarterly 57–78

D Dwyer, 'The causes and manifestations of bias in civil expert evidence' (2007) Civil Justice Quarterly 425–446

E Butler-Sloss and A Hall, 'Expert witnesses, courts and the law' (2002) Journal of the Royal Society of Medicine, vol 95, no 9, 431–434

MN Howard, 'The Neutral Expert: a plausible threat to justice' [1991] Crim LR 98–105, at 99

J Jackson, 'The Ultimate Issue Rule: One Rule Too Many' [1984] Crim LR 75–86, at 75

RD MacKay and AM Colman, 'Excluding Expert Evidence: a tale of ordinary folk and common experience' [1991] Crim LR, 800–810, at 801

R Munday, 'Excluding the Expert Witness' [1981] Crim LR 688

P Roberts, 'Towards the Principled Reception of Expert Evidence of Witness Credibility in Criminal Trials' (2004) International Journal of Evidence and Proof, vol 8, 215

JR Spencer, 'The Neutral Expert: an implausible bogey' [1991] Crim LR 106–110, at 107

Questions for Discussion

For suggested approaches, please visit the Online Resource Centre

1. Albert is accused of stabbing his wife, Bella, to death with a stiletto dagger. Some of the incident was caught by a security camera in a nearby house, albeit that the footage is extremely blurred. Albert has an IQ of 79. At the police station he declines the opportunity to have a solicitor present when interviewed and admits that he had carefully planned the killing for several months before carrying it out. He now says that he only made this confession because he was anxious that the police would beat him up if he did not do so, a belief that he says was induced by watching Hollywood films and the brusque tone of his interviewers. At trial, he intends to run the partial defences of diminished responsibility and provocation, in the alternative. He wishes to call Charlotte, a psychiatric nurse, who initially assessed him. She intends to argue that his low intelligence renders the police interview unreliable, and to argue that it also means that it was unlikely that he could have planned the killing in advance. She also proposes to say that Albert has a volatile and emotional personality that would make him easily provoked. Additionally, she will say that Albert was experiencing a serious mental disorder at the time, and, as a result, was 'definitely suffering from diminished responsibility'. Furthermore, Charlotte plans to say that, from the nature of the wounds on Bella's body, it is unlikely that a purpose made dagger was used in the killing. Instead, she will argue that her scrutiny of the forensic photographs has led her to conclude that an ordinary kitchen knife was used. She proposes to rely on the information contained in an article taken from the *British Journal of Pathology* to support her argument on this issue. The prosecution wish to call Detective Constable Hawk, who viewed the blurred footage of the incident 20 times, to assist the jury in understanding it.

Advise Albert, Charlotte and DC Hawk as to any issues relating to opinion evidence raised on the above facts.

2. Harold is charged with causing the death by dangerous driving of Iqbal, a pedestrian who was hit while crossing the road. It is alleged by the prosecution that he was driving erratically, at about 70 mph in a 30 mph zone, when he struck Iqbal. After the accident, Harold ran off, and was not arrested until two days later. However, Harold proposes to say in his defence that he was driving entirely correctly, when Iqbal suddenly darted out into the road, and that he (Harold) only fled after the incident because he panicked.

The prosecution wish to call an eye witness, John, to say that Harold was swerving wildly about the road, travelling at 'motorway speed', and appeared drunk at the time of the accident. In support of his case, Harold wishes to call Kate, a friend who is also an experienced car mechanic, to say that she subsequently had a look at the accident scene and that the skid marks on the road were consistent with those of a vehicle being driven at 'about 30 mph'. She also wishes to say that the injuries to Iqbal are 'consistent with a low speed' impact. After the accident, Harold suffered considerable stress and was seen by Larry, a psychologist. At trial,

Harold wishes to call Larry to say that he (Harold) is an 'honest man, likely to be telling the truth about the incident'.

Advise both prosecution and defence as to any issues relating to opinion evidence raised on the above facts.

3. Should the circumstances in which expert evidence can be adduced be liberalized or further tightened?

4. Did the ultimate issue rule serve any useful function? What is its present status?

5. What justification is there for excluding evidence of opinion?

12 CORROBORATION AND IDENTIFICATION EVIDENCE

Definitions

Corroboration Evidence that supports other evidence in a case, in certain specific legal respects.

Dock identification Identification of a defendant made for the first time when a witness sees him in the dock at trial.

Weak identification evidence Evidence of identification that is considered sufficiently weak or poor that it must be supported by other evidence before it can be left to a tribunal of fact.

Strong identification evidence Identification evidence that is considered to be sufficiently strong that it can go to a tribunal of fact without requiring supporting evidence.

---

1. Corroboration

Introduction

What is corroboration, and when is it needed? Historically, common law, unlike the civil law tradition, was concerned with the quality of the evidence that it received (supposedly ensured by the presence of exclusionary rules), rather than its quantity. As a result, and as a general rule, there was (and is) nothing to prevent a conviction from being based on the testimony of a single witness or one piece of evidence, such as a confession. By contrast, and for example, Dutch criminal law expressly states that the testimony of a single witness is not sufficient to found a conviction.[1] Of course, in practice, this is fairly unusual, even in England, as it is often very much harder to persuade tribunals of fact to the appropriate standard in such a situation, and it is rare that there is no circumstantial or other evidence to support a witness's testimony. Nevertheless, there is usually nothing to stop it happening in theory, unlike the situation found in many continental countries, and even, to an extent, in Scotland, albeit that the requirement for corroboration is often interpreted quite loosely in these jurisdictions.

---

[1] M Malsch, 'Swings and roundabouts: the role of judges and psychologists in the determination of criminal responsibility in the Netherlands' (1999) 3 E & P 87–100, at 90.

Cross-reference Box

Circumstantial evidence is contrasted with 'direct' evidence. It is evidence from which an inference must be made to give it probative weight. If I watch someone stab another person to death, my testimony is direct evidence that they murdered that individual. If the same individual is found a short distance from the murder scene wearing a bloody shirt and carrying a dagger, this is circumstantial evidence that he is the murderer. For more on circumstantial evidence go to pp. 56–57.

However, at common law, and also under several statutes, a number of specific exceptions to this general rule developed, in which some form of 'supporting' evidence, termed corroboration, was required. Perhaps even more significantly, at least with regard to frequency of occurrence, a number of other situations were identified from the late 1700s onwards, involving the evidence of sworn children, accomplices testifying for the Crown and sexual offence complainants, in which a trial judge was required to warn jurors in the clearest terms about the dangers of convicting on uncorroborated evidence (though still leaving them the opportunity to do so if they wished). Additionally, he had to identify any evidence in the case that was capable of being corroborative and, if there was none, point this out to the jury.

Exam tip

Prior to reform of the area in the late twentieth century, corroboration was a popular area for exam questions. There is now not normally enough for a question on the subject to warrant being set on its own, rather than being added to a question that is primarily about something else. However, identification evidence continues to be popular with examiners.

Such warnings were not only mandatory but also required the trial judge to employ certain stock phrases (or their equivalent in strength) when cautioning the jury. This commonly included a warning in the summing-up that it might be 'dangerous to convict' in the absence of corroboration. By the twentieth century, these warnings had become highly technical, as can be seen from the case of *Davies v DPP* [1954] AC 378, in which Lord Simonds held that a failure to give a warning where an accomplice testified for the Crown would normally lead to any ensuing conviction being quashed, even if there was ample corroboration available in the case.

Greatly complicating the situation, the very notion of corroboration also became very technical. It was not enough that it supported the other evidence in the case in some way; it had to meet a number of specific requirements with regard to its independence and its ability to implicate the accused in a material particular of the crime, before it could be viewed as corroborative. Aggravating such problems, it was settled law that one witness who required corroboration could not corroborate another in a similar situation (for example, two unsworn children), and so provide what was termed 'mutual' corroboration: *R v Baskerville* [1916] 2 KB 658.

Other 'Suspect' Witnesses

To make matters even more difficult, along with the judicially established categories attracting a mandatory and full corroboration warning, in the years after World War II there developed a further type of case that involved what has been referred to as 'suspect witnesses'. These were people who might be thought to be inherently unreliable for a variety of reasons but who did not come into the existing corroboration warning categories. For example, a witness who had a strong personal interest in the outcome of a case (albeit that he was not an accomplice) or an accomplice who, when testifying on his own behalf, implicated his co-accused, rather than doing so on behalf of the prosecution.

The pre-1945 common law rules did not require a full corroboration warning to be given to the trial jury in such cases. However, after 1945, a number of appellate-level decisions concluded that some type of warning, albeit not the full warning, had to be given in these situations. Thus, in *R v Beck* [1982] 1 WLR 461, three of the prosecution witnesses, whilst not accomplices in a legal sense, clearly had a motive to shift blame from themselves on to the accused. The trial judge advised the jury to pay 'particular care and attention' to the evidence of these witnesses but did not give the full corroboration warning for accomplices. This direction, and his decision, was upheld by the Court of Appeal; nevertheless, the court also suggested that there was a requirement that *some* form of warning be given in such situations (as had occurred in the instant case). Ackner LJ (as he then was) noted: 'While we in no way wish to detract from the *obligation* on a judge to advise a jury to proceed with caution when there is material to suggest that a witness's evidence may be tainted by improper motive, and the strength of that advice must vary according to the facts of the case, we cannot accept there is any obligation to give the [full] accomplice warning.'

Subsequently, *Beck* was approved by the House of Lords in *R v Spencer* [1987] AC 128. In *Spencer,* the evidence against the accused was provided by a mental patient at a secure psychiatric hospital. Their Lordships held that, where the evidence for the prosecution was provided by a witness who was not within one of the existing categories which attracted a mandatory corroboration warning, but who, by reason of his mental condition and criminal history, fulfilled analogous criteria, the judge should warn the jury of the dangers of convicting in the absence of corroborating evidence. However, in such cases, it was not necessarily vital to use the word 'dangerous' in warning the jury, so long as the words used by the trial judge made the jury fully aware of the risks of convicting on the witness's evidence alone. Thus, the view taken in *Beck* and *Spencer* seems to have been that although the format of the warning in 'suspect witness' cases was discretionary, a warning of some sort was obligatory, albeit not the full and very technical corroboration warning seen in accomplice and sexual complainant cases.

Reform

In the years after World War II, increasing doubts were expressed about the whole of the existing corroboration regime, culminating in the criticism set out in a Law Commission Report in 1991. As a result, a series of statutory reforms in the last quarter of the twentieth century, accompanied by a degree of judicial pragmatism, transformed the situation, abolishing both the need for actual corroboration in most of the situations where it was previously required, as well as the need for full corroboration warnings to be delivered, in set terms, in other circumstances.

However, there are still a few statutory situations where actual corroboration is needed, while in others a judge must caution a jury on the dangers of certain types of evidence as part of his general obligation to direct them properly on the evidence in a case, to put the defence case fairly, and draw attention to items of the prosecution evidence that are potentially unreliable; this will sometimes require some kind of warning.

Surviving Statutory Requirements for Corroboration

The advent of s. 34(2) of the Criminal Justice Act 1988, which abolished the need for the evidence of unsworn children to be corroborated, ended the last major requirement in English law for actual corroboration to be found (rather than for a warning to be given as to its desirability). However, it remains mandatory for a few very specific statutory offences. Amongst them is s. 13 of the Perjury Act 1911, under which a defendant cannot be convicted of perjury or subornation of perjury 'solely upon the evidence of one witness as to the falsity of any statement alleged to be false'. This is aimed at preventing prosecutions for perjury being instigated as a means of reconsidering earlier (and unsuccessful) litigation.

It should be noted that it is the falsity of the statement, not its making, that needs to be supported. It appears that the Act is interpreted quite broadly. For example, an out of court confession to perjury, supported by the evidence of another witness, will satisfy the statute's provisions: *R v Threlfall* [1914] 10 Cr App R 112. Similarly, in *R v Peach* [1990] 1 WLR 976, the defendant admitted on one occasion, but to two witnesses, that he had lied to a treasure trove inquest conducted in a Coroner's court, also satisfying the requirements of the statute. A trial judge will normally identify the evidence that is capable of being corroborative to the jury and then direct them that they must find corroboration to be present before convicting. As a result, as Mustill LJ noted in *R v Rider* [1986] 83 Cr App R 207, in such cases there is a: '... need for more than one witness to prove the untruth and a corresponding need for a direction on the subject, unless it can fairly be said no longer to have been in issue when the time came for the judge to direct the jury'. However, the judge also went on to observe that, although the absence of such a direction would amount to a material irregularity, any direction could be fairly brief.

R v Peach [1990] 1 WLR 976, CA

Lord Lane CJ

That leaves the second question, namely, is section 13 satisfied if two witnesses testify to having heard the defendant admit the falsity on the same occasion? One reads the section and asks whether in those circumstances the jury is being asked to convict of perjury solely upon the evidence of one witness as to the falsity of the statement alleged to be false. The answer on any view seems to us to be certainly not. The evidence is evidence of the falsity and there are two witnesses testifying to it. That interpretation does no violence to the reasons given by Byles J. in Reg. v. Hook, Dears. & B. 606, 616, to which reference has just been made, and is giving the words of the Act of 1911, so it seems to us, the only meaning which, in the view of this court, they can be said to bear. The plain words of the Act also have the advantage of resolving the not inconsiderable conflict between the various pre-1911 decisions to which reference has been made.

Similarly, s. 1 of the Treason Act 1795 requires at least two witnesses to prove certain treason offences. Rather more commonly, with regard to incidence of occurrence, s. 89(2) of the Road Traffic Regulation Act 1984 requires that a defendant shall not be convicted of speeding under the statute: '... on the evidence of one witness to the effect that, in the opinion of the witness the person prosecuted was driving the vehicle at a speed exceeding a specified limit'. The justification for such a provision is fairly apparent. Assessments of speed are highly subjective and, consequently, often unreliable. As a result, the evidence of two eye witnesses can found a conviction in such cases, but that of a single observer cannot.

Pause for reflection

Why do you think that treason offences attracted such a requirement?

However, the two witnesses must view the vehicle at the same time. In *Brighty v Pearson* [1938] 4 All ER 127, it was held that the immediate statutory predecessor to s. 189 did not allow two witnesses who had observed a moving vehicle at (very slightly) different times to provide mutual corroboration. Nevertheless, it appears that the courts are fairly willing to find that the requirements of the statute have been met via other mechanisms. For example, it seems that a police officer who witnessed a speeding vehicle could have his personal assessment supported by a speedometer reading or that taken from a speed camera.

Abolition of Mandatory Corroboration Warnings

A growing dissatisfaction among judges, practitioners and academic commentators at the complex and inflexible nature of corroboration warnings, and their frequent tendency to confuse rather than assist the jury in its deliberations, also resulted in reform in this area of the law. Section 34(2) of the Criminal Justice Act 1988 abolished the requirement that a trial judge issue a warning on the dangers of convicting on the uncorroborated but sworn evidence of a child (simply because s/he was a child). The surviving two classes of witness regarded as being inherently suspect, and thus calling for such warnings, were accomplices of the accused giving evidence on behalf of the prosecution, and complainants in sexual cases; for example, rape or indecent assault victims. The requirement that trial judges warn juries of the dangers of convicting on the uncorroborated evidence of such witnesses was abolished by s. 32(1) of the Criminal Justice and Public Order Act 1994 (CJPOA 1994).

Pause for reflection

Can you think of any merits to the old system of mandatory corroboration warnings?

However, statute did not *expressly* deal with the *Beck* and *Spencer* type situation, and it was, at first, a matter of some debate as to whether the body of case law dealing with such 'suspect witnesses', made against the backdrop of the mandatory corroboration warnings, had also been abrogated. As they had not been expressly abolished, it could be argued that they had survived the CJPoA 1994. If this was the case, though, it would be bizarre if no warning at all was given with regard to an accomplice testifying for the prosecution, but a *Beck* warning with regard to an accomplice testifying on his own behalf was still considered necessary, despite this being a situation that the courts had traditionally considered to be less dangerous. Alternatively, it might be argued that a *Beck*-type warning was now also necessary for accomplices giving evidence for the prosecution, only the full, and technical, corroboration warning that had previously been required for such witnesses having been abolished by s. 32. Indeed, it could even be argued that although there was no longer an invariable requirement that a full corroboration warning be given in such situations, in the right circumstances a trial judge should still provide one. Fortunately, case law since the CJPoA 1994 came into force has clarified this matter.

Jury Warnings After the 1994 Act

The Court of Appeal case of *R v Makanjuola* [1995] 1 WLR 1348, provided important guidance, not just on the effect of s. 32 of the CJPOA 1994, but also on how 'suspect' witnesses generally should be treated in future. In this case, the appellant was convicted of indecently assaulting the complainant by squeezing her breasts when they were alone together in a storeroom at their place of employment. Counsel for the defendant had suggested to the complainant during cross-examination that the allegation had been invented because she was angry with the appellant following a disagreement at work a few days earlier. It was argued that the trial judge had erred in failing to give any direction to the jury on corroboration. However, the Court of Appeal dismissed the appeal, concluding that there was no reason to give any sort of special warning in the instant case, which was referred to as 'perfectly straightforward'.

In *Makanjuola* the Court of Appeal also took the opportunity to provide clarification as to how trial judges might approach cases where it was suggested that some form of warning (albeit not the full corroboration warning) to the jury was still necessary. Lord Taylor CJ felt that it was a matter for the judge's discretion as to what, if any, warning, he considered to be appropriate in respect of such a witness, just as it was in respect of any other sort of witness, in whatever type of case: 'Whether he chooses to give a warning and in what terms will depend on the circumstances of the case, the issues raised and the content and quality of the witness's evidence.' In some situations, it would be appropriate for a trial judge to warn the jury to exercise caution before acting upon the unsupported evidence of a witness. However, as *Makanjuola* itself indicated, this would not be so merely because the witness was a complainant in a sexual offence or alleged to be an accomplice. Nor would such a direction necessarily be confined to such situations.

Additionally, the Court of Appeal observed that an evidential basis for suggesting that the evidence of a witness might be unreliable was necessary to warrant a warning; mere suggestions by cross-examining counsel would not usually be enough. Where a first instance judge did decide to give some form of warning, it would normally be appropriate for it to be issued as part of his general review of the evidence rather than as a set-piece legal direction. It would also be for the judge to decide the strength and terms of any warning, any attempts: '…re-impose the straitjacket of the old corroboration rules [we]re strongly to be deprecated'. Subsequently, in *R v Muncaster* [1999] Crim LR 409, the Court of Appeal reiterated that s. 32 of the CJPOA 1994 had not only abolished the requirement that a corroboration warning be given in certain situations, but also that cases such as *Beck* and *Spencer* now had to be seen in the light of the new Act, even though they were not, theoretically, overturned by it. As a result, there was also no longer an automatic requirement that a warning be given in such situations.

The tenor of much of the guidance in *Makanjuola* and *Muncaster* suggested that such matters are entirely within a trial judge's discretion. However, at one point in his judgment in *Makanjuola*, Lord Taylor did suggest that there might be situations 'where some warning is required' with regard to a suspect witness. Clearly, this would only occur on rare occasions; Lord Taylor himself suggested in *Makanjuola* that a trial judge's decision on such an issue, that is a failure to give a direction, or giving an inadequate direction, would normally only be challenged if it constituted *Wednesbury* unreasonableness.

R v Makanjuola [1995] 1 WLR 1348, CA

Lord Taylor CJ

Given that the requirement of a corroboration direction is abrogated in the terms of section 32(1), we have been invited to give guidance as to the circumstances in which, as a matter of discretion, a judge ought in summing up to a jury to urge caution in regard to a particular witness and the terms in which that should be done. The circumstances and evidence in criminal cases are infinitely variable and it is impossible to categorise how a judge should deal with them. But it is clear that to carry on giving 'discretionary' warnings generally and in the same terms as were previously obligatory would be contrary to the policy and purpose of the Act. Whether, as a matter of discretion, a judge should give any warning and if so its strength and terms must depend upon the content and manner of the witness's evidence, the circumstances of the case and the issues raised. The judge will often consider that no special warning is required at all. Where, however the witness has been shown to be unreliable, he or she may consider it necessary to urge caution. In a more extreme case, if the witness is shown to have lied, to have made previous false complaints, or to bear the defendant some grudge, a stronger warning may be thought appropriate and the judge may suggest it would be wise to look for some supporting material before acting on the impugned witness's evidence. We stress that these observations are merely illustrative of some, not all, of the factors which judges may take into account in measuring where a witness stands in the scale of reliability and what response they should make at that level in their directions to the jury. We also stress that judges are not required to conform to any formula and this court would be slow to interfere with the exercise of discretion by a trial judge who has the advantage of assessing the manner of a witness's evidence as well as its content. To summarise. (1) Section 32(1) abrogated the requirement to give a corroboration direction in respect of an alleged accomplice or a complainant of a sexual offence, simply because a witness falls into one of those categories. (2) It is a matter for the judge's discretion what, if any warning, he considers appropriate in respect of such a witness as indeed in respect of any other witness in whatever type of case. Whether he chooses to give a warning and in what terms will depend on the circumstances of the case, the issues raised and the content and quality of the witness's evidence. (3) In some cases, it may be appropriate for the judge to warn the jury to exercise caution before acting upon the unsupported evidence of a witness. This will not be so simply because the witness is a complainant of a sexual offence nor will it necessarily be so because a witness is alleged to be an accomplice. There will need to be an evidential basis for suggesting that the evidence of the witness may be unreliable. An evidential basis does not include mere suggestion by cross-examining counsel. (4) If any question arises as to whether the judge should give a special warning in respect of a witness, it is desirable that the question be resolved by discussion with counsel in the absence of the jury before final speeches. (5) Where the judge does decide to give some warning in respect of a witness, it will be appropriate to do so as part of the judge's review of the evidence and his comments as to how the jury should evaluate it rather than as a set-piece legal direction. (6) Where some warning is required, it will be for the judge to decide the strength and terms of the warning. It does not have to be invested with the whole florid regime of the old corroboration rules. (7) It follows that we emphatically disagree with the tentative submission made by the editors of Archbold, Criminal Pleading, Evidence & Practice, vol. 1 in the passage at paragraph 16.36 quoted above. Attempts to re-impose the straitjacket of the old corroboration rules are strongly to be deprecated. (8) Finally, this court will be disinclined to interfere with a trial judge's exercise of his discretion save in a case where that exercise is unreasonable in the Wednesbury sense: see Associated Provincial Picture Houses Ltd. v. Wednesbury Corporation [1948] 1 K.B. 223.

The approach adopted in *Makanjuola* has been reiterated by subsequent cases. Thus, in *R v Gilbert* [2002] 2 AC 531, the Privy Council allowed an appeal by the prosecution from the decision of the Eastern Caribbean Court of Appeal (Grenada), quashing a conviction for attempted rape, because of a lack of sufficient warning, noting that: 'It will only be in clear and exceptional cases that an appellate court will feel justified in interfering with the trial judge's exercise of his discretion. Their Lordships do not believe that this case comes into that category.'

Nevertheless, it does appear that, in rare situations, and as part of his summing up of the evidence, a first instance judge must give some form of warning about potentially dangerous types of evidence, albeit not couched in technical terms, if he is to be deemed to have put the case 'fairly' to the jury. This is as part of his general judicial duty, rather than as a rule of law. In exceptional circumstances, a failure to give some form of warning *might* be a successful ground of appeal. Unfortunately, *Makanjuola* did not provide clear guidance as to the types of case where this could occur. However, subsequent case law does help identify some situations where a warning should normally be given, though it is vital to stress that every case will ultimately turn on its own facts, rather than being considered as a member of a more general class that invariably requires such a warning.

Amongst these situations, and for example, are so-called 'cell confessions', that is, informal admissions to a crime made by defendants to their fellow prisoners, prior to trial. It appears that in such cases, a warning, of some sort, is usually necessary, for obvious reasons. In *Benedetto and Labrador v The Queen* [2003] 1 WLR 1545, a Privy Council case from the British Virgin Isles, evidence of a cell confession to murder was provided by a fellow remand prisoner of the defendant. This man (the fellow prisoner) had an appalling criminal record and was still awaiting trial on the matter for which he was being held when the alleged confession was made to him. The prosecution case was largely founded on his evidence. The Privy Council noted that, in such cases, the prisoner testifying to the confession will normally have a strong motive to ingratiate himself with the authorities, while the normal safeguards for recording a confession when it is made to the police will, invariably, be absent. Consequently, a warning as to its inherent dangers is usually required.

Benedetto and Labrador v The Queen [2003] 1 WLR 1545, PC

Lord Hope

Their Lordships are conscious of the fact that it is undesirable to restrict the circumstances in which a judge may, as a matter of discretion, urge caution in regard to a particular witness when summing up to a jury, and the terms in which any warning should be given if the judge thinks that this is appropriate, by laying down rules as to when warnings of that kind must be given. But evidence of the kind on which the Crown relies in this case, where an untried prisoner claims that a fellow untried prisoner confessed to him that he was guilty of the crime for which he was then being held in custody, raises an acute problem which will always call for special attention in view of the danger that it may lead to a miscarriage of justice. . . . In the case of a cell confession it [the danger] is that the evidence of a prison informer is inherently unreliable, in view of the personal advantage which such witnesses think they may obtain by providing information to the authorities. Witnesses who fall into this category tend to have no interest whatsoever in the proper course of justice. They are men who, as Simon Brown LJ put in R v Bailey [1993] 3 All ER 513, 523J, tend not to have shrunk from trickery and a good deal worse. And they will almost always have strong reasons of self-interest for seeking to ingratiate themselves with those who may be in a position to reward them for volunteering confession evidence. The prisoner against whom that evidence is given is always at a disadvantage. He is afforded none of the usual protections against the inaccurate recording or invention of words used by him when interviewed by the police. And it may be difficult for him to obtain all the information that is needed to expose fully the informer's bad character.... It should be noted that there are two steps which the judge must follow when undertaking this exercise [warning a jury], and that they are both equally important. The first is to draw the jury's attention to the indications that may justify the inference that the prisoner's evidence is tainted. The second is to advise the jury to be cautious before accepting his evidence. Some of the indications that the evidence may be tainted may have been referred to by counsel, but it is the responsibility of the judge to examine the evidence for himself so that he can instruct the jury fully as to where these indications are to be found and as to their significance. Counsel may well have suggested to the jury that the evidence is unreliable, but it is the responsibility of the judge to add his own authority to these submissions by explaining to the jury that they must be cautious before accepting and acting upon that evidence.... The judge told the jury at the outset of his summing up that they would have to have careful regard to Plante's evidence. Later in his summing up he reminded the jury of its content, including the various admissions which Plante had made both in chief and in cross-examination as to matters bearing on his credibility. As he put it to the jury more than once, they had to have regard to whether Plante could be believed. But nowhere in his summing up did he draw the jury's attention to the various factors which would justify the inference that Plante's evidence was tainted by self interest and to their significance. It was not enough for him simply to mention them while he was going through the evidence which he had written down in his notebook. What he omitted from his summing up was the drawing together of these factors so that the inferences and conclusions that might be drawn from them were made plain for the jury's consideration when they were assessing their significance. Nor did he advise the jury to be cautious before accepting Plante's evidence.

However, such a warning does not have to be to a set formula. Thus, in *R v Causley* [1999] Crim LR 572, a man who was awaiting trial for murdering his wife allegedly made confessions to several fellow prisoners, which were subsequently admitted into evidence. The trial judge provided a warning to the jury as to the need for caution in relying on such evidence. Nevertheless, after conviction, the appellant argued that the judge's directions were not sufficiently robust in the light of *Spencer*. The Court of Appeal rejected this argument, feeling the summing-up, and the warning given, had been appropriate to the case. Clearly, the court was reluctant to go back to decisions like *Beck* and *Spencer* that had been made against the backdrop of the common law mandatory warnings.

Another situation that will usually require a warning, of some sort, to be given, was discussed in *R v Jones* [2004] 1 Cr App R 60. In this case, the Court of Appeal noted that, where co-defendants ran 'cut-throat' defences, including 'mirror-image' ones (that is, blaming each other for the offence) a trial judge's summing-up should normally include a direction to the jury to bear in mind that any co-defendant testifying in this situation might have an axe to grind and, as a result, that his evidence should be considered with care. Thus, in *Jones*, a murder conviction was quashed because the trial judge had failed to warn the jury that a co-defendant running a cut-throat defence might have an interest to serve in giving evidence. The importance of such a warning, where co-defendants ran cut-throat defences, was reiterated in *R v Petkar* [2004] 1 Cr App R 22.

R v Jones [2004] 1 Cr App R 5, CA

Auld LJ

We see no reason to depart from the approach of this Court in R. v Knowlden & Knowlden (1983) 77 Cr.App.R. 94, and confirmed by it in Cheema, that a judge, in exercising his discretion as to what to say to the jury should at least warn them, where one defendant has given evidence adverse to another, to examine the evidence of each with care because each has or may have an interest of his own to serve. Cheema was, as Mr Aubrey has observed, a cut-throat defence. There was also, as Mr Aubrey commented in argument, a particular need for some such warning in this case, where Jenkins, unlike Jones, had refused to answer questions in interview and was therefore able, if he wished, to tailor his defence to the facts in evidence. In our view, the failure to give such a warning was a serious omission and unfairly prejudicial to Jones' defence, and also, though possibly to a lesser extent, to that of Jenkins. Accordingly, we do not consider that the general directions as to evidence of the judge to which Mr Harrington referred us were sufficient for the purpose.

 Pause for reflection

Do jurors really need to be reminded that two people who are accused of a serious crime, and who are blaming each other for it, might have a personal axe to grind when testifying in such cases?

2. Identification Evidence

Introduction

Mistaken identification has been a major cause of wrongful convictions throughout history and, as a result, has occasioned concern for centuries. For example, the notorious case of Alfred Beck, who was wrongly picked out on several late Victorian identification parades, by at least eight women, as the man who had defrauded them of their jewellery, and who served more than five years in prison as a consequence, resulted in the establishment of the Court of Criminal Appeal in 1908. However, in the years after World War II there was a growing judicial recognition of the inherent unreliability of identification evidence, in many common law jurisdictions. Thus, in *The People (Attorney General) v Dominic Casey* [1963] (No 2) IR 33, the Supreme Court of the Irish Republic decided that it was desirable in all cases where the verdict depended substantially on the correctness of a visual identification to draw the attention of a trial jury to the inherent possibilities of mistake.

Subsequently, in its *Eleventh Report on Evidence* of 1972, the Criminal Law Revision Committee also expressed acute concern about the danger of wrongful findings of guilt that were based on mistaken identifications of the accused. It regarded this as 'by far the greatest cause of actual or possible wrong convictions'. In particular, the Committee highlighted the problem that was occasioned by identifying witnesses who were mistaken, but whose evidence, because they were obviously sincere and 'honest', might appear highly convincing. The majority of the Committee were in favour of a statutory requirement that a first instance judge warn a jury of the special need for caution before convicting in reliance on the correctness of one or more identifications of the accused, where a case depended wholly or substantially on such evidence.

Shortly afterwards, and partly influenced by the case of Luke Dougherty, who was incorrectly identified and imprisoned as a shoplifter in 1972, when he had what proved to be a cast-iron alibi, the then Home Secretary appointed a Committee under the chairmanship of Lord Devlin to consider identification evidence in criminal cases. The Devlin Report of 1976 produced a recommendation that was even stronger than that proposed by the Criminal Law Revision Committee four years earlier. It concluded that a general and imprecise warning about the dangers of identification evidence would not be good enough as: 'The extent to which a man may deceive himself is well known to psychologists and to experienced criminal lawyers, but it is not yet universally realised … [jurors] do not appreciate the extent to which an apparently convincing witness may be mistaken.' As a result, the Committee recommended that, where the evidence for the prosecution consisted wholly or mainly of visual identification evidence, the jury should be informed that it was unsafe to convict unless the circumstances of the identification were exceptional or the identification was supported by substantial evidence of another sort. More recent research has echoed the Committee's concerns and identified numerous factors that can affect both initial identification and subsequent recall, as the following extract suggests.

P Roberts, 'The Problem of Mistaken Identification: Some observations on process' (2004) 8 E & P 100 (Extract)

The range of factors that might affect the accuracy of any identification attempted by an eyewitness is substantial. Numerous commentators have formulated taxonomies which include characteristics inherent in the witness, such as age, respective ethnicity of witness and suspect, and degree of physiological arousal (as might occur when a violent event is witnessed). Environmental factors also have the potential to affect accuracy, for example, lighting conditions when the culprit is observed, the length of time that the witness has the culprit in view, whether the offence involved the use of a weapon. In providing structure to what would otherwise be a mere catalogue of factors, Wells' categorisation of factors as either system variables or estimator variables is of considerable importance for the evaluation and development of criminal procedure. Estimator variables describe those factors capable of affecting identification accuracy that have an existence independent of anything that might be done by those responsible for criminal justice system policy, and of the practices pursued by those working in the system. Environmental circumstances, and the physiological characteristics of witness and suspect, fall into this category. In contrast, the term 'system variable' describes a phenomenon believed to affect identification accuracy adversely which arises as a consequence of some conduct engaged in by agents (essentially police officers) in the pre-trial process. These include various forms of suggestive conduct engaged in by the agent while following the prescriptions of formal rules or exercising discretion conferred for the purposes of investigation. In the context of estimator variables, so named because they are not controllable and their influence can only be 'estimated', mitigating the risk of miscarriages of justice requires an awareness of their potentially adverse effect on identification accuracy. To employ a medical analogy; if we perceive mistaken identification as a disease, which in the criminal justice system we want to eradicate, there are two strains. We are powerless to prevent the 'estimator strain', the sources of which are the physical circumstances in which a culprit was observed committing an offence or the physiological characteristics of the actors involved. The most that the criminal justice system can do is to remain vigilant as to its various symptoms and implement an effective screening programme in an attempt to detect possible outbreaks of the disease. The 'system strain' of the disease is a rather different matter. While the disease remains difficult to diagnose outbreaks are caused by the practices and procedures followed in the criminal process. It is, therefore, possible to take preventative measures by adopting and adhering to appropriate regimens concerning the treatment of eyewitness identification. Wherever there is interaction between a number of witnesses, or police officers and witnesses, there is a danger that a witness's memory and recollection of relevant events will be distorted. There is a consensus among psychologists that the mind does not operate like a video recording, whereby once events are stored in the memory they can be recollected by accessing the discrete 'part' of the memory in which they are stored. Memory processes appear much more complex than this. Researchers have proposed models which differentiate different kinds of memory involving the processing of information between the various modes. One manifestation of malfunctioning in this process is the apparent malleability of memory. One study, in which participants observed a stranger whom they were later asked to describe, provides a vivid illustration of the danger of semantic suggestion on witness recall. In the study, one group of witnesses were told by the interviewer that the man was a truck driver while another group were told that he was a dancer. Those who were told he was the former estimated his weight to be significantly greater than those who were told he was the latter. Similarly, where interviewers described the stranger as a 'man' estimates of his age were significantly higher than when he was referred to as a 'young man'. As Kohnken has explained, the interviewee who experiences an event is unlikely to be able to perceive and encode all available information. Any additional information acquired from an interviewer might lead the witness to use general knowledge and fall back on social expectations to fill 'gaps' in his recollection of events.

However, shortly after the publication of the Devlin Committee's Report, the Court of Appeal pre-empted parliamentary intervention when, in the case of *R v Turnbull and Others* [1977] 1 QB 224, it laid down mandatory guidelines for the conduct of such cases. In particular, it set out in definitive terms the procedures, warnings and directions that must be given in almost every case involving a significant element of contested identification evidence. These are still applied in England and some Commonwealth countries.

Of course, such strict rules, though preventing false convictions, may also mean that, sometimes, the guilty will walk free. Thus, the decision by the CPS not to prosecute, and the failure of the subsequent private prosecution to survive a submission of no case to answer, in the *cause célèbre* involving the murder of Stephen Lawrence was entirely unsurprising to most lawyers. The identifying eye witness evidence of the murder was replete with phrases such as. 'It happened very quickly', 'I didn't have a chance to look at their faces', 'It was dark' and 'it was really, really quick. I was surprised.' As Lord Justice Macpherson subsequently observed, in his report on the incident: 'Any lawyer knows of the difficulty involved as to identification during such a fast happening in the dark. The shadow of *R v Turnbull* [1977] QB 224 was already upon the case.'[2] After the victim's companion, was cross-examined by defence counsel, further inconsistencies and problems with the identification were exposed, leading to the case being dismissed without going to a jury.

 Pause for reflection

Are such situations (certainly not unique to this case) an acceptable price to pay to avoid the conviction of the innocent through mistaken identification?

---

[2] Lord Macpherson of Cluny, 'The Stephen Lawrence Inquiry' (1999, The Stationery Office) para. 41.12.

The *Turnbull* guidelines have themselves been the subject of detailed judicial consideration, further elucidating the situations in which (and how) they will apply. These will require thorough examination. However, it should immediately be noted that, where the rules do apply, they are applicable to all identifications, including those made by police witnesses: *R v Reid and others* [1990] 90 Cr App R 121. It has also been held that the general guidelines on submissions of no case to answer subsequently set out in *R v Galbraith* [1981] 73 Cr App R 124, were not intended to affect in any way the operation of the *Turnbull* guidelines as to when a case that was dependent upon poor identifying evidence should be withdrawn from a jury: *Daley v The Queen* [1994] 1 AC 117. Thus, an identification case can be withdrawn, and an acquittal directed, even though the submission does not otherwise meet the test in *R v Galbraith* [1981] 1 WLR 1039. Additionally, it should be observed that, although it is defence counsel who will normally make a *Turnbull* submission, asking that a case be withdrawn from a jury (in the right circumstances), a trial judge is under a duty, in its absence, to invite such a submission if he is of the view that the identification evidence is poor and unsupported: *R v Fergus* [1994] 98 Cr App R 313.

 Cross-reference Box

Galbraith established the normal test for a submission of no case to answer in the Crown Court, setting out when a trial judge should prevent a case continuing after the end of the prosecution case, because the evidence, taken at its highest, could not found a conviction. For more on this go to chapter 1, at p. 9.

R v Turnbull [1977] QB 224, CA

Lord Widgery CJ

Each of these appeals raises problems relating to evidence of visual identification in criminal cases. Such evidence can bring about miscarriages of justice and has done so in a few cases in recent years. The number of such cases, although small compared with the number in which evidence of visual identification is known to be satisfactory, necessitates steps being taken by the courts, including this court, to reduce that number as far as is possible. In our judgment the danger of miscarriages of justice occurring can be much reduced if trial judges sum up to juries in the way indicated in this judgment. First, whenever the case against an accused depends wholly or substantially on the correctness of one or more identifications of the accused which the defence alleges to be mistaken, the judge should warn the jury of the special need for caution before convicting the accused in reliance on the correctness of the identification or identifications. In addition he should instruct them as to the reason for the need for such a warning and should make some reference to the possibility that a mistaken witness can be a convincing one and that a number of such witnesses can all be mistaken. Provided this is done in clear terms the judge need not use any particular form of words. Secondly, the judge should direct the jury to examine closely the circumstances in which the identification by each witness came to be made. How long did the witness have the accused under observation? At what distance? In what light? Was the observation impeded in any way, as for example by passing traffic or a press of people? Had the witness ever seen the accused before? How often? If only occasionally, had he any special reason for remembering the accused? How long elapsed between the original observation and the subsequent identification to the police? Was there any material discrepancy between the description of the accused given to the police by the witness when first seen by them and his actual appearance? If in any case, whether it is being dealt with summarily or on indictment, the prosecution have reason to believe that there is such a material discrepancy they should supply the accused or his legal advisers with particulars of the description the police were first given. In all cases if the accused asks to be given particulars of such descriptions, the prosecution should supply them. Finally, he should remind the jury of any specific weaknesses which had appeared in the identification evidence. Recognition may be more reliable than identification of a stranger; but even when the witness is purporting to recognise someone whom he knows, the jury should be reminded that mistakes in recognition of close relatives and friends are sometimes made. All these matters go to the quality of the identification evidence. If the quality is good and remains good at the close of the accused's case, the danger of a mistaken identification is lessened, but the poorer the quality, the greater the danger. In our judgment when the quality is good, as for example when the identification is made after a long period of observation, or in satisfactory conditions by a relative, a neighbour, a close friend, a workmate and the like, the jury can safely be left to assess the value of the identifying evidence even though there is no other evidence to support it: provided always, however, that an adequate warning has been given about the special need for caution. Were the courts to adjudge otherwise, affronts to justice would frequently occur.... When, in the judgment of the trial judge, the quality of the identifying evidence is poor, as for example when it depends solely on a fleeting glance or on a longer observation made in difficult conditions, the situation is very different. The judge should then withdraw the case from the jury and direct an acquittal unless there is other evidence which goes to support the correctness of the identification. This may be corroboration in the sense lawyers use that word; but it need not be so if its effect is to make the jury sure that there has been no mistaken identification: for example, X sees the accused snatch a woman's handbag; he gets only a fleeting glance of the thief's face as he runs off but he does see him entering a nearby house. Later he picks out the accused on an identity parade. If there was no more evidence than this, the poor quality of the identification would require the judge to withdraw the case from the jury; but this would not be so if there was evidence that the house into which the accused was alleged by X to have run was his father's.... The trial judge should identify to the jury the evidence which he adjudges is capable of supporting the evidence of identification. If there is any evidence or circumstances which the jury might think was supporting when it did not have this quality, the judge should say so.... A failure to follow these guidelines is likely to result in a conviction being quashed and will do so if in the judgment of this court on all the evidence the verdict is either unsatisfactory or unsafe.

When the police interview potential identification witnesses they are trained to question them specifically about the relevant *Turnbull* factors, and, in particular: the amount of time the suspect was under observation: the distance at which this occurred; the visibility at the relevant time (was it night or day, in street lighting, etc.); any potential obstructions to their view; did they already know the suspect or had they seen him before; was there something specific that made the suspect more memorable; how long has elapsed since the witness saw the suspect; are there any material discrepancies between descriptions provided by the eye witness in their first and subsequent accounts?

When do the *Turnbull* Guidelines Apply?

The rules set out in *Turnbull* come into operation whenever the case against a defendant depends 'wholly or substantially' on the correctness of identifications of the accused which the defence claims are mistaken. As this suggests, they do not operate in every case where some element of identification is involved. For example, they do not apply if the identification is not challenged. More controversially, according to Lord Widgery, *Turnbull* was 'intended primarily to deal with the ghastly risk run in cases of fleeting encounters': *R v Oakwell* [1978] 66 Cr App R 174. Nevertheless, although the distinguished judge was the primary author of the guidelines, his rather narrow interpretation as to when they will apply is not necessarily followed in practice, though it has been reiterated on occasion: *R v Curry* [1983] Crim LR 737.

There is clearly no need to give the *Turnbull* directions if the eyewitness merely provides a general description of a suspect, one which is subsequently advanced as circumstantial evidence at his trial, without there being any suggestion that there has been a positive identification or recognition of the accused person. Thus, in *R v Gayle* [1999] 2 Cr App R 130, a caretaker at a school where the theft of a handbag had occurred described seeing a man on the premises who was stocky, black and wearing a black bomber jacket with a distinctive logo. Subsequently, a man matching this description was discovered acting suspiciously and in close proximity to the stolen item, which was recovered.

R v Gayle [1999] 2 Cr App R 130, CA

Henry LJ

This was not an identification case because the witness was not purporting to have identified any individual person. All she was doing was giving evidence of her observation of an unknown man wearing certain distinctive clothes. It was thus in truth a circumstantial case raising the question: 'Was it remotely likely that there would be two identically dressed men in the vicinity of the commission of the crime?' The fallacy of Mr Lynch's submission is demonstrated by the qualitative difference between identification evidence and what the judge called 'evidence of description'. The special need for caution before conviction on identification evidence is because, as experience has often shown, it is possible for an honest witness to make a mistaken identification. But the danger of an honest witness being mistaken as to distinctive clothing, or the general description of the person he saw (short or tall, black or white etc., or the direction in which he was going) are minimal. So the jury can concentrate on the honesty of the witness, in the ordinary way.

Additionally, where a case revolves purely round the truthfulness or accuracy of a witness, rather than the correctness of his identification, a *Turnbull* warning may not always be necessary. For example, in *R v Courtnell* [1990] Crim LR 11, the prosecution case depended entirely on the identification of a publican who allegedly saw the incident. The defendant claimed that this witness was 'stitching me up', and denied being present at the crime scene at the relevant time. As the only issue was the publican's veracity, and there was no suggestion by the defence that he was simply mistaken, there was no need for a *Turnbull* direction. Similarly, in *R v Clements* [2004] EWCA Crim 3077, a witness claimed to have seen the defendant kicking and punching the victim of an assault, and subsequently picked her out during a video identification procedure (see below). The defendant admitted being at the scene of the crime, but denied any involvement in acts of violence. The Court of Appeal upheld the first instance judge's decision not to give the jury a *Turnbull* direction, as the only issue at trial was whether the prosecution witness was telling the truth.

R v Clements [2004] EWCA Crim 3077, CA

Hooper LJ

Mr Bowers gave evidence that he thought that the appellant, Clements, had delivered six to 12 blows, mostly as kicks and that she had been very aggressive. He gave evidence that the woman who had done what he was describing had been called 'Kelly' by others. Later, as we say, Bowers picked her out on the video identification procedure. 12. In cross-examination he confirmed his evidence. He at no stage saw Clements on the ground. 13. There was no dispute that Mr Bowers had correctly identified the appellant as being 'involved' in this second incident. Mr Bowers was not challenged as to the identity of the appellant but as to the alleged kicking and stamping. It follows, as was conceded during the course of argument by Mr Orton, that the Turnbull direction was not appropriate in so far as Mr Bowers was concerned. The issue was not identity. This issue was what the person (whom he correctly identified as the appellant) was doing. 14. Alan Christopher Priday gave evidence that he was in the public house with his girlfriend, Julie Clarke. He had heard a commotion outside. He had seen someone with a bloodstained hand apparently trying to come in. Walters had then stormed out saying: 'Right, that's it, I've had enough'. Priday then looked outside and could see Walters had knocked a man to the floor and was kneeling on his chest and punching him. The man was doing his best to defend himself. He saw five or six blows to the man's head. Another man then rushed past him and he also struck five or six blows. He then saw a girl with short black hair stamp on the complainant's head at least twice. He subsequently saw injuries. He accepted that he had not been asked to attend an identification parade and the dispute between him and the defence was not whether a woman answering that description had been there, but what that woman was doing.

However, and despite *Clements*, it should be noted that a simple admission to being at a crime scene, combined with a denial of involvement in an offence, will not *invariably* absolve the court from the need for giving a *Turnbull* direction. In *R v Thornton* [1995] 1 Cr App R 578, the Court of Appeal quashed the conviction of a defendant who admitted being present at a wedding reception, where an assault had occurred, but claimed that he was merely involved in assisting the victim to his feet, despite being identified by a witness. In the circumstances of the reception, where there were a number of other men attired in a very similar manner to the defendant, there was a clear possibility of mistaken identification, and a full *Turnbull* warning should have been given. Everything will turn on the facts of the case, and the possibility that a witness may have mistaken one person for another: *R v Slater* [1995] Crim LR 244.

Additionally, it can be argued that the two defences, falsity and genuine mistake, are not necessarily mutually exclusive. Whenever there is a defence based on a witness's alleged lack of truthfulness, the defendant is, perhaps, impliedly also suggesting that the witness, if not lying, must be mistaken. In *R v Giga* [2007] Crim LR 571, where the defence case was that the identified suspect was being falsely and deliberately implicated by two eye witnesses, the Court of Appeal, suggested that it would have been better if a 'qualified' *Turnbull* warning had been given along with directions on the credibility of the eye witnesses. Even so, the court refused to quash the ensuing conviction, and also stated that giving a full *Turnbull* warning would have led to confusion.

Can the Identification go to the Jury?

In *Turnbull*, the Court of Appeal held that some identification cases should be dismissed without even going to a jury, because no amount of warnings as to their inherent dangers could prevent the risk of a wrongful conviction. In particular, the court concluded that a judge should intervene, at the close of the prosecution case, to stop a trial proceeding further, if he concluded that the quality of the identification evidence was 'weak' and there was no other evidence capable of supporting the correctness of the identification.

In summary, strong but unsupported identification evidence could go to a jury, with appropriate warnings about the inherent dangers of such evidence; weak but 'supported' evidence could also go to the jury, again with appropriate warnings; however, weak and unsupported evidence, could not do so (or, in theory, survive a submission of no case to answer in a summary trial). This in turn raises a number of key issues. In particular, what is 'strong' identification evidence, and what is deemed to be 'weak'? What constitutes 'supporting' evidence? What should an identification warning consist of, and in what terms should it be couched?

What is Weak Identification Evidence?

There might be a number of reasons for identification evidence being deemed to be 'weak'. Thus, it might be a classic 'fleeting encounter' case, of the type identified in *Turnbull,* in which the witness has only a brief view of the perpetrator of a crime. This was also the case with regard to one of the appeals in the Privy Council case of *Reid and others v The Queen* [1990] 90 Cr App R 121, in which a police officer had a brief glance at a suspect in difficult circumstances. As the prosecution case was entirely dependent on this evidence, it was held that it should have been withdrawn from the jury.

Reid and others v The Queen [1990] 90 Cr App R 121, PC

Lord Ackner

At the trial Corporal Chambers estimated that the length of time during which he had been able to observe the men whom he identified as Reece and Taylor had been seven seconds and four seconds respectively. Throughout his observation of both men he had been lying flat on his chest on top of the embankment, some two yards above the road. As the facts set out above clearly demonstrate, the quality of the identifying evidence was indeed poor. In each case it depended solely on a fleeting glance made in difficult circumstances. The witness was lying flat on his front frightened for his life and trying to hide from the very men he subsequently purported to identify. Reece and Taylor formed part of a large group of seven men in all and there was no special reason to concentrate on them, since neither was armed whereas others were. Both men ran past the witness, and all seven men in the group were complete strangers to Corporal Chambers. In their Lordship's view this was a classic case where the uncorroborated identifying evidence was so poor, depending solely on fleeting glances and further made in difficult conditions, that the judge should have withdrawn the case from the jury at the end of the prosecution evidence and directed an acquittal.

As *Reid* also suggests, a weak identification might be one made in difficult circumstances, even if made over a longer period of time; for example, at a distance or by someone with poor eyesight, with an obstructed view, in bad light, or who was personally terrified by the incident. Thus, in *R v Fergus (Ivan)* [1994] 98 Cr App R 313, the defendant was accused of assault with intent to rob. It was alleged that he had followed his victim for about 10 minutes, prior to the assault, threatening him and demanding money. He subsequently attacked him. The Court of Appeal quashed the defendant's conviction because, in the circumstances, it deemed the identification to be weak, despite the duration of the incident, and there was no dispute that it was unsupported by other evidence.

Similarly, in *Daley v The Queen* [1994] 1 AC 117 a husband had purported to identify one of the men who had broken into his house and murdered his wife. His evidence was unsupported. The trial judge allowed the case to go to the jury, despite concluding (perhaps), in the light of the dark conditions prevailing at the time, and the presence of acute fear on the part of the (concealed) observer, that 'the identification has not been a very good one'. The Privy Council quashed the resulting conviction. Case law also indicates that identification evidence can be deemed to be poor, even though made by a number of witnesses. For example, they may all have had only the opportunity of a fleeting glance or a longer observation made in difficult conditions: *R v Weeder* [1980] 71 Cr App R 228.

By contrast, strong identification evidence might include situations in which there had been an extensive period of observation; for example, by a person who had been kidnapped and held by a defendant for a prolonged period before escaping or being released. Alternatively, it might be an observation made in satisfactory conditions by someone who is very well acquainted with the defendant, such as a workmate, family member or friend. However, in *R v Etienne* (1990) *The Times,* 16 February, the court was not at all sure that previous sightings of the suspect could render the identification more reliable if it still amounted to no more than a fleeting glimpse recognition.

Supporting Evidence

As Lord Widgery noted in his judgment in *Turnbull*, even when, in the opinion of the trial judge, the quality of identifying evidence was poor, as, for example, when it depended on a fleeting glance or on a longer observation made in difficult conditions, the judge would not have to withdraw the case from the jury and direct an acquittal if there was 'other evidence which goes to support the correctness of the identification'. In such cases, a judge should identify to the jury the evidence he considers capable of supporting the identification. However, he must then make it clear that it was for them to decide whether the evidence actually did support the identification: *R v Akaidere* [1990] Crim LR 808.

Nevertheless, in such situations, a trial judge is under no obligation to warn jurors that if they do not find the potential supporting evidence identified to them to be satisfactory they should acquit. By the time the jury retire, they will have heard other evidence in the case, from, for example, the defendant and any co-accused, or will have been able to draw an adverse inference under s. 35 of the CJPOA 1994,[3] all of which might affect the way in which they view the prosecution case, even if they are not satisfied by the potential supporting evidence initially referred to by the trial judge: *R v Ley* [2007] 1 Cr App R 25.

R v Ley [2007] 1 Cr App R 25, CA

Scott Baker LJ

The point of law to which the argument was mainly directed was this: the judge having decided that the identification was of such poor quality that he would not have left the case to the

---

[3] See on this, chapter 9, at p. 387.

jury in the absence of supporting evidence, must the jury be directed that they should not convict on the evidence of identification alone in the absence of supporting evidence? In the first place we are not satisfied the judge would have stopped the case in the absence of supporting evidence. But assuming that were so, we do not think the judge was required to give such a direction. Identification cases always require a careful direction from the judge drawing attention to the dangers of honest but mistaken identification along the lines of Turnbull. But the jury has to consider its verdict in the light of the whole of the evidence, it being a matter for them what evidence they accept and what evidence they reject. When a defendant gives or calls evidence, and especially so when there is more than one defendant, the picture may look very different at the conclusion of the whole of the evidence from how it looked at the end of the prosecution case.

 Cross-reference Box

Until the CJPOA 1994, a tribunal could draw, or not draw, any adverse inference from a defendant's failure to answer police questions when interviewed under caution or to give evidence at trial in their own defence. Since the advent of the 1994 Act, this is no longer necessarily the case. For more information on this topic go to pp. 354 and 387.

Perhaps fortunately, the notion of 'supporting evidence' has escaped the technicality that bedevilled corroboration during the twentieth century. Even so, the evidence must identify the defendant as the offender, rather than merely indicating that an offence has been committed. In *Turnbull* itself, Lord Widgery provided several illustrations of what might constitute such supporting evidence. For example, it would include a suspect who was seen (albeit fleetingly) to run into a particular house, was subsequently identified, and who, it transpires, is also the son of the owner of that house. The judge also approvingly cited the earlier case of *R v Long* [1973] 57 Cr App R 871, as an example of supporting evidence. In this case, the defendant, who had been identified by eye witnesses, had behaved in a bizarre fashion after the incident, claiming to know who had committed the crime and offering to help others find its perpetrators. Thus, strange coincidences can, in appropriate circumstances, constitute supporting evidence.

Obviously, a defendant's confession, if admitted, will support a disputed identification, as will circumstantial evidence that is considered to be sufficiently strong. For example, in *R v Sadler* [2002] EWCA Crim 1722, the shirt of the accused man was badly stained with the victim's blood. Unsurprisingly, this was deemed to be supporting evidence that his identification as the victim's attacker was correct. Separate eye witnesses can also support each other's identification, provided that their evidence is not considered to be weak: *R v Weeder* [1980] 71 Cr App R 228. In the right circumstances, it seems that convictions for previous and similar offences, adduced under s. 101(1)(d) of the CJA 2003, can also constitute supporting evidence. This was the case in *R v Eastlake (Nicky)* [2007] EWCA Crim 603, where youths with a previous record for offences involving street violence had their convictions adduced to support fresh and similar allegations of inflicting grievous bodily harm and assault occasioning actual bodily harm. A selection of other examples provides less obvious illustrations of supporting evidence.

Cross-reference Box

As a general rule, a defendant's previous convictions, like his other previous misconduct, cannot be adduced in evidence at trial. However, in certain circumstances, set out in s. 101(1)(d) of the CJA 2003, such a rule does not apply, and the convictions can be adduced to demonstrate, inter alia, a propensity to commit such crimes. For more information on this topic go to p. 190.

In *R v Baba (Omn)* (2000) WL 544197, the defendant was accused of burgling a flat, after forcing its front door open. A neighbour of the victim testified that, on the relevant day, she met a man running down the stairs from the flat. He stopped and spoke to her small child for about 8 to 10 seconds. The witness had a clear view of him and thought that she had seen him before. The victim subsequently found the defendant's wallet containing his photograph dropped in her flat. The owner showed it to the neighbour who immediately identified him as the man on the stairs. An identification parade held later produced the same result. The defendant testified that, on the relevant day, he was in a park when he realized that his wallet was missing. However, if the defendant did not personally drop his wallet in the victim's flat, it would have been necessary for the item to have been stolen, or lost and found, by the true burglar, and left in the flat within a period of 75 minutes. This was inherently unlikely, and, as a result, the Court of Appeal concluded that the finding of the wallet was 'undoubtedly' capable of supporting the identification.

In *R v Penny* [1992] Crim LR 184, the identified suspect owned one of four cars in the area that were similar to that used in a robbery. The defendant's vehicle was the only one that was unaccounted for at the relevant time. This was held to be capable of being supporting evidence. In *R v Walters* [2001] EWCA Crim 1261, a murder case, the Court of Appeal concluded that the fact that the man identified by the identifying witness turned out to be someone who had had telephonic communication with a person who lived at the address where the murder took place, some 50 minutes before the killing occurred, was also strong supporting evidence. In *The Queen on the Application of Pierre Wellington v The DPP* [2007] EWHC 1061, the fact that a suspect, when stopped by the police, had, before fleeing, given the same name as an alibi previously used by the defendant was held to be capable of being supporting evidence.

Defendant Lies as Supporting Evidence

A defendant's use of a false alibi was, in appropriate circumstances, capable of being corroboration at common law: *R v Lucas* [1981] QB 720. From the aspect of corroboration, this is no longer usually significant, because of the changes outlined above (the abolition of mandatory corroboration warnings and the ending of the requirement for actual corroboration in most situations). Nevertheless, such evidence can still advance the prosecution case in general and, where it does, it still requires a *Lucas* direction. In such situations, however, there should be independent evidence establishing that the statement is a lie. It is not enough that the jury simply disbelieves it. Additionally, as was noted in *Turnbull*, defendant lies can also constitute supporting evidence for a visual identification, at least in some circumstances.

However, as Lord Widgery observed in *Turnbull*, great care must be taken when directing a jury about the support that can be derived from their rejection of a defence alibi. This is because false alibis can be put forward for many reasons, not all of them indicative of guilt. For example, a defendant who is telling the truth about his lack of involvement in a crime might, foolishly, fabricate an alibi, perhaps to bolster what he is concerned may otherwise be viewed as a weak (if truthful) case or to hide something else about which he is ashamed (for example, that he spent an evening with a mistress), or because he made a genuine mistake about dates and places. As a result, a jury should be reminded that proving that the accused has told lies about where he was at a material time does not, in itself, prove that he was where the identifying witness places him. Only if satisfied that the defendant lied, and did not lie for an innocent reason but rather to deceive them, may the jury find support in a false alibi for otherwise poor identification evidence. These guidelines were developed further in *Lucas*.

R v Lucas [1981] QB 720, CA

Lord Lane CJ

In our judgment the position is as follows. Statements made out of court, for example, statements to the police, which are proved or admitted to be false may in certain circumstances amount to corroboration. . . . To be capable of amounting to corroboration the lie told out of court must first of all be deliberate. Secondly it must relate to a material issue. Thirdly the motive for the lie must be a realisation of guilt and a fear of the truth. The jury should in appropriate cases be reminded that people sometimes lie, for example, in an attempt to bolster up a just cause, or out of shame or out of a wish to conceal disgraceful behaviour from their family. Fourthly the statement must be clearly shown to be a lie by evidence other than that of the accomplice who is to be corroborated, that is to say by admission or by evidence from an independent witness.

The *Turnbull* Warning

If the identification evidence is strong or, alternatively, if it is weak but supported by other evidence in the case, it can be left to the determination of the jury. Nevertheless, the Court of Appeal made clear in *Turnbull* that, in either of these situations, a judge must still warn jurors of the special need for caution before convicting the accused in reliance on the correctness of the identification. Furthermore, this cannot be in vague or general terms. Case law has emphasized that a mere statement that a jury must treat visual identification evidence with extreme caution is not sufficient.

A judge should identify the inherent weaknesses and dangers of such evidence, both generally and in the particular circumstances of the case before the court. Thus, he should instruct the jury as to why there was a need for such a warning and should make some reference to the possibility that a mistaken witness can be a convincing one and that a number of such witnesses (where there is more than one) can all be mistaken. However, provided this is done in clear terms, it is not necessary for a judge to use a particular form of words or expressions when doing so. A first instance judge should also make it clear that the need for caution is rooted in the courts' actual experiences of miscarriages of justice.

Secondly, the judge should direct the jury to examine closely the circumstances in which the identification by each witness came to be made in the instant case. How long did the witness have the accused under observation? At what distance and in what light was the identification made? Was the observation impeded in any way, for example by buildings, passing cars or people? Had the witness ever seen the accused person before and, if so, how often? If he had only met him occasionally, did he have any special reason for remembering the defendant? How long had elapsed between the original observation and the subsequent identification to the police? Finally, the judge should remind the jury of any specific weaknesses which had appeared in the identification evidence. For example, any discrepancy between a witness's initial description of a suspect to the police and the defendants' actual appearance (the details of which the prosecution are under an obligation to supply to the defendant): *R v Nash (Paul)* [2005] Crim LR 232.

R v Fergus (Ivan) [1994] 98 Cr App R 313, CA

Steyn LJ

The submission that the judge should have withdrawn the case from the jury must now be examined. It was a case which depended solely on the visual identification of Ivan by the victim. There was no evidence which supported the identification. Andrew Maloney displayed and, it is plain, genuinely felt an invincible conviction in the correctness of his identification. That is a common feature in identification cases. The problem is to identify any specific weaknesses in the identification so that an informed judgment can be made whether unsupported visual identification evidence is too poor in quality to be left to the jury. In our judgment the following weaknesses in the identification evidence ought to have been obvious: (1) While it is true that the episode on March 28 between the assailant and his victim lasted altogether some 20 minutes, one had to set against that the fact that Andrew Maloney said that during the earlier part of the episode 'it was starting to get dark' and that in oral evidence he described himself as having 'not very good eyesight'. At the trial he said his identification was based on his recollection of the face of the assailant. But he said 'I did not take too much notice of his face'. (2) In his initial description he said that the assailant was about 16–18 years of age. In oral evidence he said that his assailant was at least 16. At the time when the offence was committed Ivan was 13. (3) In his original description to the police, and in his subsequent witness statement, Andrew Maloney described the height of his assailant as 5 feet 11 inches. Ivan was 5 feet 7 inches. (4) In his pre-trial statements, Andrew Maloney consistently said that his assailant had some stubble on his face. Ivan had not yet started to shave, and had no stubble on his face. (5) In his original statement to the police, and in his witness statement, he described his assailant as 'light-skinned'. By contrast Ivan is of a relatively dark Afro-Caribbean complexion. (6) In his original description, Andrew Maloney said that his assailant had a distinctive zigzag pattern in his hair. There was, however, nothing distinctive about it. It was a popular style among young people. It is true that when he was arrested Ivan had a zigzag pattern on the sides of his head and a stick-man motif at the back. But he explained in interview that he had acquired this style some two weeks earlier, i.e. sometime after the offence was committed. He said his uncle had given him the new haircut. The address of the uncle was given to the police. (7) Andrew Maloney was throughout confident that his assailant wore a brown jacket, jeans and trainers. In interview Ivan was asked about the brown jacket but he denied that he owned a brown jacket. A search of his home did not reveal any such articles. (8) The identification on the day before Ivan's arrest raised questions. On any view it was no more than a fleeting glance identification. Moreover, Andrew Maloney said that the person he identified had a blazer with a badge on. But in the interview Ivan and his mother explained that he was not wearing his blazer on that day because he had spilt something on it. More importantly, they explained that he had outgrown his old blazer with a badge on it. There was nothing to gainsay these easily verifiable statements. In these circumstances the following questions had to be posed: Did Andrew Maloney on April 24 correctly identify his assailant? If not, what faith can one have in his identification on the next day? If his identification on April 24 was correct, did he identify the same person on the next day? (9) Finally, Andrew Maloney said that on the day of the arrest there was a face-to-face confrontation between himself and the person he identified. The two police officers had no recollection of such a confrontation. Ivan denied that such a confrontation had taken place. This state of the evidence raised not only a general question mark over the reliability of Andrew Maloney's evidence, but it cast a shadow over his identification immediately before the arrest. These are the specific weaknesses which ought to have been considered at the end of the prosecution case. And it was necessary to consider the cumulative effect of these matters on the quality of the identification evidence. If the specific weaknesses had been properly analysed the judge would have been bound to withdraw the case from the jury.

In practice, most trial judges have recourse to a suitably tailored version of the Judicial Studies Board recommended direction for identification cases.

JSB Specimen Direction, No 30, Identification, Approach to Evidence of

This is a trial where the case against the defendant depends wholly or to a large extent on the correctness of one or more identifications of him which the defence alleges to be mistaken. I must therefore warn you of the special need for caution before convicting the defendant in reliance on the evidence of identification. That is because it is possible for an honest witness to make a mistaken identification. There have been wrongful convictions in the past as a result of such mistakes. An apparently convincing witness can be mistaken. So can a number of apparently convincing witnesses. You should therefore examine carefully the circumstances in which the identification by each witness was made. How long did he have the person he says was the defendant under observation? At what distance? In what light? Did anything interfere with the observation? Had the witness ever seen the person he observed before? If so, how often? If only occasionally, had he any special reason for remembering him? How long was it between the original observation and the identification to the police? Is there any marked difference between the description given by the witness to the police when he was first seen by them and the appearance of the defendant? (Where appropriate:) I must remind you of the following specific weaknesses which appeared in the identification evidence...

Consequences of a Failure to Give a Warning

Obviously, a failure to withdraw what is deemed to be weak and unsupported identification evidence from a jury will result in any ensuing conviction being quashed. However, as Lord Widgery also noted, even where this is not the case, a failure to give a *Turnbull* direction to a jury in an identification case where it is required will also normally lead to a conviction being overturned. In the Privy Council case of *Scott and Others v The Queen* [1989] 2 WLR 924, Lord Griffiths felt that it would only be in: '... the most exceptional circumstances that a conviction based on uncorroborated identification evidence should be sustained in the absence of such a warning'. However, as this suggests, in exceptional cases, where the identification is considered to be extremely strong, or (perhaps) very well supported by other evidence, it seems that this will not invariably be so. Thus, in another Privy Council case, *Shand v R* [1996] 1 WLR 67, the defendant was recognized at very close range in bright moonlight for up to two minutes and had also responded to his name being shouted out. The Privy Council concluded that the identification was 'exceptionally good' and upheld the conviction, despite the absence of a *Turnbull* direction. Nevertheless, such cases will be rare.

3. Identification Procedures

Introduction

Where an eye witness has identified, or might be able to identify, someone who has been arrested on suspicion of involvement in an offence, para. 3.12 of Code D, issued pursuant to s. 66 of the Police and Criminal Evidence Act 1984, requires that the police hold an 'identification procedure' prior to trial, if the suspect disputes the identification, unless it is not practicable, or would serve no useful purpose, to do so.

Paragraph 3.12 of Code D

Whenever: (i) a witness has identified a suspect or purported to have identified them prior to any identification procedure set out in paragraphs 3.5 to 3.10 having been held; or (ii) there is a witness available, who expresses an ability to identify the suspect, or where there is a reasonable chance of the witness being able to do so, and they have not been given an opportunity to identify the suspect in any of the procedures set out in paragraphs 3.5 to 3.10, and the suspect disputes being the person the witness claims to have seen, an identification procedure shall be held unless it is not practicable or it would serve no useful purpose in proving or disproving whether the suspect was involved in committing the offence. For example, when it is not disputed that the suspect is already well known to the witness who claims to have seen them commit the crime.

Normally, an identification made for the very first time at trial, a so-called 'dock identification', will not be allowed, on the basis that its prejudicial effect outweighs its value. This is because, inevitably, there will be a temptation for a witness simply to identify the defendant standing in the dock: *R v Johnson* [2001] 1 Cr App R 26. However, somewhat illogically, and largely for practical reasons, the rules on dock identifications appear to be applied slightly less strictly in the Magistrates' Courts than they are in the Crown Court, especially where summary only offences are being considered and where the defendant has not indicated in advance that identification is in issue: *Barnes v Chief Constable of Durham* [1997] 2 Cr App R 505. Interestingly, in Scotland there is, historically, less antipathy to dock identifications.

R v Johnson [2001] 1 Cr App R 26, CA

Lord Woolf CJ

The fact that Mrs Pintus over a period of time was more positive in her identification, particularly both at the magistrates' court and at the trial, is not a matter of surprise. It is common experience that a witness who is perfectly honest can become more positive in their identification as time passes, when it is well-known that identification becomes more difficult after a lapse of time. In particular, if someone is seen in the dock of a court and is identified, or if the person is identified on an identification parade, it is very easy subsequently not to be identifying the person originally observed at the scene of the crime, but the person seen in the circumstances just described. For that reason the practice of identification at court is now frowned upon. Dock identifications are not normally to be permitted in the course of proceedings.

The conduct of all identification procedures is regulated in great detail by Code D of the Police and Criminal Evidence Act 1984, and its attendant annexes. Traditionally, the main form of identification procedure was the identification (ID) parade, in which a suspect appeared in a line-up with eight different, but physically similar, individuals (12 if there were two suspects), while the witness attempted to identify them, either directly or from behind a screen. However, although still used (and regulated by Annex B to Code D), in recent years this has been supplemented and, to a large extent, replaced by the other procedures detailed in Code D. By far the most important of these is the video identification, which is normally the first choice of procedure under para. 3.14 of Code D, unless it is not practicable to hold one, or an identification parade is considered more suitable for some other reason. The vast majority of identifications are now conducted using this procedure. One reason for this is that a video identification can usually be arranged very much faster than an identification parade.

A third method of pre-trial identification, the so called 'group identification,' in which the witness sees the suspect in an informal group of people, for example, in a shopping mall, is generally considered to be less satisfactory than an ID parade or video identification, but may be resorted to if circumstances make it necessary. The weakest form of identification procedure, direct confrontation between a witness and suspect prior to trial, will only be accepted in exceptional circumstances. A defendant's failure or refusal to participate in any identification procedure might be given in evidence: *R v Doyle* [2001] EWCA Crim 2883.

Video Identifications

Video identifications are regulated by Annex A to Code D. They must be supervised by an identification officer, who must have no direct involvement in the investigation of the case. Under this procedure, a video is made by the police of a suspect, which is then matched by eight other individuals, usually taken from a pool held on a central databank (situated in Yorkshire), who must, as far as possible, resemble the suspect in 'age, general appearance and position in life' (under para. 2 of the Annex). Additionally, para. 3 requires that the nine people must be shown in the same positions or carrying out the same movements. The suspect and his solicitor must be allowed to see the selection of images used prior to the identification procedure, and the suspect's lawyer (but not the suspect) is allowed to be present when the viewing occurs. If no legal representative is present, the process itself must be recorded on video (under para. 9 of Annex A).

As with the old identification parade, and despite the very large number of video images held on the central database, the requirement that the eight other individuals be similar to the suspect in age can still occasion problems, especially where s/he is of an unusual appearance. For example, in *R v Ruel Marcus* [2004] EWCA Crim 3387, the defendant was accused of robbery.

He was a middle-aged black male of singular appearance. Most importantly, he was bearded and greying. The police were unable to find similar men in their (then) 19,000-image databank, particularly men with the same facial hair.

To circumvent this problem, they initially showed the victims photographs of nine men with their hair electronically masked (allowed under para. 2A(a) of the Annex). However, this did not produce any positive identifications. The police then showed the witnesses the same nine men with the masking devices removed, an obvious breach of Code D, producing several positive results. On appeal, the ensuing conviction was quashed: 'The course taken by the police here was a deliberate device to evade the provisions of the Code. That falls to be condemned by this court. In these circumstances, the judge should have excluded the evidence.' As the Court of Appeal noted, developing technologies may reduce the incidence of such cases in future, as it will soon be possible to generate features, such as facial hair, electronically.

Group Identifications and Confrontations

Group identifications are regulated by Annex C to Code D and may be used if the officer in charge of the investigation feels that it would be appropriate or more suitable in the circumstances. It might be conducted with the suspect's consent, or, if this is not forthcoming, might even be done covertly. This might be carried out, for example, by having the suspect pass in front of the witness as part of a group of people on a moving escalator or, alternatively, being stationary in a group of people, such as the clientele of a bar. When selecting the location for such an identification, the police must consider the appearance and number of people likely to be present. Obviously, a quiet country pub, just after opening time on a weekday, might not be appropriate if there was only one elderly man and his dog in it.

For an example of its operation in practice can be considered the case of *R v Stott* [2004] EWCA Crim 615, in which the defendant's solicitor had been unhappy with some of the images that the police proposed to use in a video ID. As a result, the police resorted to a group identification conducted in a bar in Newcastle International Airport, the witness being asked to walk through it, and look at everyone drinking there, to see if she could identify the person who had earlier attempted to burgle her house. During this process she asked that the suspect stand up, to confirm her initial suspicions. He was then positively identified by her. On appeal, it was argued that the group identification procedure (rather than an ID parade) should not have been used, and, in any event, the suspect should not have been asked to rise. Both arguments were rejected by the Court of Appeal. Once the video procedure was deemed not to be practical, there was no requirement that a parade (instead of a group identification) be held, especially as the defendant's solicitor had not objected to a group identification at the time. With regard to the second point, the suspect had only been asked to stand after an initial identification, ie to confirm the witness's view.

R v Stott [2004] EWCA Crim 615, CA

Brown J

In our view, none of these grounds, taken singly or together, result in this conviction being in any way unsafe. The logical starting point is the propriety of holding a group identification, and in our view the Crown's submissions are clearly right. The unchallenged evidence was that it was not practicable to compile another video. There is nothing in the code which compels the officer in charge to go first to an identification parade after a video parade is ruled out. He could have chosen a group identification in the first place. There was here no breach of the code, and nothing in the way in which the exercise was carried out to indicate any unsafe procedure. The initial viewing by Miss Griffiths was of a group of people seated in an area of the bar, either holding drinks or having drinks in front of them. It is clear from her evidence that she was very nearly sure she had made the correct identification but wanted to see the suspect standing because that is how she had seen the burglar. No complaint can be made that all the persons in the bar were not asked to stand as she had virtually picked out the man in the checked shirt and it was his height that she would have considered the second time she saw him. Such criticisms as could be made of this procedure were doubtless canvassed in cross-examination and were well within the jury's province after the proper directions as to identification which they received. The judge was not, in our view, in error in deciding that there was no breach of the code in this regard. There was no breach in holding a group identification and no deficiency in the way it was carried out. We agree with the Crown that the code does not prevent at a group identification, any more than it does at an identification parade, the officer in charge asking those taking part to adopt particular stances or clothing.

Confrontation, regulated by Annex D, is by far the least satisfactory pre-trial identification procedure as, like the dock identification, there is a strong suggestion that the suspect confronted is the perpetrator of the relevant crime. It will usually take place at a police station and normally only be used in exceptional circumstances, when none of the other forms of identification procedure are practicable: *Williams (Noel) v The Queen* [1997] 1 WLR 548. These conditions were satisfied in *R v Kelly* [2003] EWCA 596. In this case, the identifying witness had been held at knifepoint during a robbery. Subsequently, the suspect refused (in writing) to take part in a video ID, an identification parade and a group identification procedure. In these circumstances, the Court of Appeal concluded that holding a confrontation procedure at a police station, with the appropriate safeguards (insofar as such a procedure allows them), was acceptable. There was also no requirement in such situations for the police to arrange, for example, a 'covert' video procedure, as suggested by defence counsel.

Breaches of Code D

If there is a breach of Code D in carrying out one of the procedures, any resulting identification of a suspect *might* be rendered inadmissible. Whether it is actually admitted at trial will depend on an exercise of the judge's exclusionary discretion under s. 78 of the PCEA 1984, which will, in turn, be closely linked to the gravity of the breach and the quality of the identification. However, even if an application to exclude such evidence is refused for such a breach, the trial judge should still direct the jury on the circumstances and possible consequences of the breach of the code: *R v Forbes* [2001] 1 AC 473.

In *Forbes* (which involved an earlier version of Code D than that now in force), the House of Lords dismissed an appeal by the defendant from a decision of the Court of Appeal upholding his conviction for attempted robbery. The accused man had attempted to rob another man at a cash-point, who had escaped from him, called the police, and then been driven around the area until he spotted and positively identified his assailant. After his arrest, the defendant had asked for an identification parade, but this had been refused by the police. At trial, the judge concluded that as the prior street identification of the defendant had been 'full and complete', the parade requested by him was unnecessary. As a result, she decided that there had been no breach of Code D, and admitted the evidence without exercising her exclusionary discretion under s. 78. Accordingly, she also did not direct the jury as to any breach of the Code.

However, Lord Bingham, giving the judgment of the House of Lords, noted that a parade should be held, if the suspect consented and unless the specified exceptions applied (which they did not in the instant case) whenever a suspect disputed an identification. Nevertheless, despite the absence of an exercise of discretion under s. 78 of the PCEA 1984, their Lordships felt that the identification evidence in the case was compelling and had been rightly admitted. Whether the defendant's absolute right to a fair trial under Article 6 of the ECHR had been infringed would depend on an assessment of the whole history of the proceedings, though where that right had been infringed, any ensuing conviction would be held to be unsafe. Even if the evidence was admitted (and not excluded under s. 78), where a breach of Code D had occurred a direction should still be given to the jury explaining what had happened and its potential consequences. Nevertheless, in *Forbes*, and on its facts, the absence of such a direction had still not rendered the defendant's trial unfair or his conviction unsafe.

R v Forbes [2001] 1 AC 473, HL

Lord Bingham

We cannot accept that the mandatory obligation to hold an identification parade under paragraph 2.3 does not apply if there has previously been a 'fully satisfactory' or 'actual and complete' or 'unequivocal' identification of the suspect by the relevant witness. Such an approach in our opinion subverts the clear intention of the code. First, it replaces an apparently hard-edged mandatory obligation by an obviously difficult judgmental decision. Such decisions are bound to lead to challenges in the courts and resulting appeals. Second, it entrusts that decision to a police officer whose primary concern will (perfectly properly) be to promote the investigation and prosecution of crime rather than to protect the interests of the suspect. An identification parade, if held, may of course strengthen the prosecution, but it may also protect the suspect against the risk of mistaken identification, and a suspect should not save in circumstances which are specified or exceptional be denied his prima facie right to such protection on the decision of a police officer. Third, this approach overlooks the important fact that grave miscarriages of justice have in the past resulted from identifications which were 'fully satisfactory', 'actual and complete' and 'unequivocal' but proved to be wholly wrong. It is against such identifications, as well as against uncertain and equivocal identifications, that paragraph 2.3 is intended to offer protection to the suspect.

A similar conclusion was reached in *R v Lewis* [2006] EWCA Crim 2895, where there had been several breaches of Code D, including a failure to note the initial description provided by the identifying witnesses, who had also travelled together to the scene of the identification in breach of Code D, para 3.2(c). However, in this case, the first instance judge had described the breaches in detail to the jury, and stressed the need to consider the identification evidence with the greatest care in the light of them. Again, the ensuing convictions were upheld by the Court of Appeal.

In like manner, in *The Queen on the Application of Pierre Wellington v The DPP* [2007] EWHC 1061, the defendant was stopped, while driving a car, by police officers. As the officers were making enquiries about the defendant, he fled the scene. Although the officers made a note of the incident, they did not make a note of the driver's appearance. About two weeks later, one of the officers recognized the defendant's picture during a briefing at their police station. Two months further on again, he spotted the defendant at the police station and identified him as the driver who had been stopped 10 weeks earlier. The man was interviewed and charged with driving while disqualified (the time when he had initially been stopped). However, no identification parade was held. The defendant was convicted at a summary trial, one of the officers giving evidence about the incident and his subsequent identification of the defendant at the police station.

The defendant appealed to the High Court by way of case stated on the grounds that the failure to note his initial appearance was a breach of para. 3.1 of Code D, and the failure to hold an identification procedure was a breach of para. 3.12 of Code D. The Queen's Bench Divisional Court accepted that both of these constituted breaches of the Code, the former being more serious than the failure to hold an identification procedure as, given that the identifying officer had seen a slide of the defendant and then identified him at the police station it was almost inevitable that he would have identified him if a parade or some other procedure had been held. Nevertheless, despite these breaches, the court upheld the magistrates' conviction.

The Queen on the Application of Pierre Wellington v The DPP
[2007] EWHC 1061, HC

Jackson J

Two breaches of Code D occurred. Both breaches must weigh in the balance against the prosecution. The existence of those breaches called into question the admissibility of the identification evidence given by PC Leanne. The justices duly considered that question. They noted the breaches of Code D: see paragraphs 4 and 5 of the case stated. They expressly applied the test set out in section 78 of PCEA: see paragraph 7.1 of the case stated. In the exercise of their discretion under section 78 of PACE, the justices decided to admit the identification evidence given by PC Leanne. In my judgment, this was an exercise of discretion which was open to the justices. They reached a decision which was permissible on the facts before the court.

 Summary

- As a general rule, under English common law (and unlike the situation in some civil law countries), evidence does not need to be supported to found a conviction or to prove a civil claim.

- However, at common law, a small number of situations developed in which actual corroboration was necessary in criminal matters, while in others, there was a mandatory requirement that a jury be warned about the dangers of convicting in its absence. The notion of corroboration also became highly technical in its legal requirements.

- In the modern era, both of these two general categories have been abolished. There is no longer a need to give a corroboration warning, nor is there any requirement at common law for corroboration. Nevertheless, there remain a few, fairly arcane, statutory situations in which actual corroboration is required; for example, under s. 13 of the Perjury Act 1911.

- A trial judge retains a discretion to give a warning to jurors about evidence that appears potentially dangerous for some reason. Very occasionally, when directing a jury, the general requirement that the evidence in a case is presented fairly during a judge's summing up, will require that such a warning be given, and its absence might found an appeal, though every case will turn on its facts.

- Cases that turn wholly or substantially on identification evidence are regulated by the principles established by the Court of Appeal in the case of *R v Turnbull* [1977] 1 QB 224. These were introduced after a series of miscarriages of justice, in cases that were based on identification evidence, indicated that such evidence could be extremely unreliable, even when given sincerely.

- The guidelines set out in *R v Turnbull* [1977] 1 QB 224 require that weak identification evidence, which is not supported by other evidence in the case, should not survive a submission of no case to answer. In appropriate cases, this should be invited by the trial judge, if not made spontaneously by defence counsel.

- However, weak identification that is supported by other evidence, and strong identification evidence, even if it is unsupported, can be considered by jurors and magistrates. Nevertheless, in these situations, the trial judge must warn jurors (and magistrates remind themselves), in detail, about the potential dangers of identification evidence generally, and about the quality of the identification in the instant case in particular. A failure to do this will normally result in any ensuing conviction being quashed.

- If an identification is disputed by the suspect, an 'identification procedure' must normally be held by the police prior to trial. A 'dock identification', that is, one made for the first time at trial, will not normally be permitted. By far the most important of these procedures is the video identification, regulated by Code D, Annex A to the PCEA 1984. This has largely (though not totally) replaced the traditional identification parade (now regulated by Annex B). Group identifications can be held if appropriate in the circumstances (Annex C). In quite exceptional circumstances, a pre-trial confrontation between witness and suspect, usually at a police station, may be admissible; for example, where the suspect has refused to participate in any other procedure.

- The circumstances in which such identification procedures must be held are highly detailed and closely regulated by Code D. Any breach of these regulations may lead to the identification being excluded at trial under s. 78 of the PCEA 1984. Much will turn on the gravity of the breach and its likely effects on the identification in question. Even if they do not lead to its exclusion, a trial judge must direct the jury as to the existence and consequences of such a breach.

 ## Further reading

D Birch, 'Corroboration: Goodbye to All That?' [1995] Crim LR 524

A Dein, 'Non Tape Recorded Cell Confession Evidence' [2002] Crim LR 630

P Mirfield, 'An Alternative Future for Corroboration Warnings' (1991) 107 LQR 450

P Mirfield, 'Corroboration After the 1994 Act' [1995] Crim LR 448

P Roberts, 'The Problem of Mistaken Identification' (2004) 8 E & P 100

G Williams, 'Evidence of Identification: The Devlin Report' [1976] Crim LR 407

 ## Questions for Further Discussion

1. Simon is accused of raping Tina, his colleague, in a storeroom at the factory where they both work. He claims that nothing happened between them, and states that he thinks that Tina made up the allegation because she had an unrequited 'crush' on him. There is no other forensic evidence to support her claim. However, while Simon is held in custody, pending trial, Ulysses, a fellow remand prisoner awaiting trial for robbery, informs the police that Simon admitted to him, while they were in the showers, that he had raped Tina. Ulysses testifies to this effect for

For suggested approaches, please visit the Online Resource Centre

the prosecution. The trial judge gives no warning about the status of either Tina's or Ulysses' evidence in his summing-up. Simon is convicted and wishes to know if this might provide the basis for an appeal.

Advise Simon.

2. Should the surviving statutory requirements for corroboration be abolished?

3. Ali is accused of robbery. It is alleged that he crept up behind Brenda, the victim, and snatched her handbag, pulling it until she released her grip on the bag. Brenda had been out selling sprigs of 'lucky heather' for 50p each and, as a result, her bag was full of the multi-sided coins. The incident took place at dusk, in an area without natural lighting, and Brenda says that she was so shocked, that she only got a brief glimpse at her attacker before he ran off. She gave a description of him to the police, in which she mentioned that he had a visible scar on his left cheek. Ali was arrested and put on an identification parade (it not being deemed to be practical to hold a video identification), where Brenda subsequently pointed him out as her attacker, though no scar was found on his face. Additionally, although Ali is over six feet tall, three of the men on the parade were only five feet in stature. When he was arrested, Ali was also found to be in possession of a very large number of 50p pieces and a tiny sprig of heather.

Advise as to any evidential issues raised by Brenda's identification.

4. Do the *Turnbull* guidelines go far enough in preventing miscarriages of justice due to mistaken identifications?

5. Provide some examples of 'supporting' evidence in identification cases.

6. What is meant by a 'weak' identification?

PUBLIC INTEREST IMMUNITY

Definitions

Public Interest This refers to the interests of the state and the wider society.

Immunity This refers to immunity from being compelled to produce evidence at trial.

Crown Privilege This is an old term for Public Interest Immunity.

Informer Person who uses criminal contacts to provide the police with secret intelligence about the commission of offences.

---

1. Introduction

In general, all evidence that is relevant to the issues raised in legal proceedings should be admitted, as this is conducive to rectitude in decision-making. As has been noted in other chapters, the rules of evidence sometimes restrict this general principle, on certain occasions, for a variety of reasons, by deeming relevant evidence to be 'inadmissible'. Additionally, the law relating to privilege sometimes allows relevant and otherwise admissible evidence to be withheld by one of the parties (see chapter 12).

However, exceptionally, the adduction of evidence is also restricted in circumstances where admitting it, whether it be a document or oral evidence, might damage the state or be injurious in some other significant way to the national or public interest. In these situations, the personal interests of a litigant yield to those of the wider society. As Lord Morris observed in *Conway* v *Rimmer* [1968] AC 910, in some circumstances: 'If…national security would or might be imperiled by the production and consequent disclosure of certain documents, then the interest of a litigant must give way.'

Pause for reflection

Is it ever right to risk a mistaken decision at trial in order to protect other interests? If so, what interests would you feel were worthy of protection?

This area of the law has seen very considerable development over the past 70 years. It used to be termed 'Crown Privilege', but in the modern era Public Interest Immunity (PII) is preferred, because Crown Privilege suggests that the doctrine is solely concerned with great issues of state, whereas the reality is that it will usually involve much more mundane matters, such as the identity of a police informer or the efficient operation of a public service. Additionally, a privilege can be waived, whereas if the court concludes that PII is operative, it is conclusive of the matter. This is because a litigant who asserts that documents or other evidence is immune from production or disclosure on the grounds of public interest is 'not . . . claiming a right but observing a duty', in the words of Bingham LJ (as he then was) in *Makanjuola v Commissioner of Police of the Metropolis* [1992] 3 All ER 617.

Although a government minister might often be the most appropriate person to raise the public interest, it is open to anybody to bring up the issue. Indeed, in *D v NSPCC* [1978] AC 171, Lord Scarman noted that, in some cases, a court might be duty-bound to raise the issue of PII on its own initiative, even if neither of the parties to litigation or a government minister has first raised the matter. This important distinction between PII and privilege is neatly encapsulated in r. 31.3 of the CPR 1998, which notes that a party to whom a document has been disclosed—ie its existence has been revealed as part of discovery—has a right to inspect it, unless the disclosing party 'has a right or duty to withhold inspection of it'. In this context, 'right' refers to privilege (see chapter 12), 'duty' to PII.

There are other important differences between the doctrines of privilege and public interest immunity. For example, if a party wishes to claim privilege with regard to a document, he may object to its 'inspection', but he cannot normally refuse to disclose its existence during 'discovery'. This is the stage in proceedings when the existence of all documents that are, or have been, in a party's possession and that are relevant to the litigation in question, whether they are helpful or not to the case of the party in possession, are revealed to the opposing side: r. 31.6 of the CPR 1998.

By contrast, where PII is concerned, in civil cases, under r. 31.19(1), a person can apply to the court, without notice to the opposing side, for an order permitting him to withhold even the disclosure of a document, on the ground that 'disclosure would damage the public interest', thus, the application is, effectively, made *ex parte*. Of course, such an extreme step will often not be necessary. A party might feel able to disclose the identity of a document via discovery, without risking the public interest, but simply object to its inspection on the grounds of PII. In this situation, he must state in writing that he has such a duty, and set out the relevant grounds for doing so: r. 31.19(3) of the CPR 1998. In reply, the party to whom its existence has been revealed can challenge these grounds under r. 31.19(5) of the CPR 1998. In quite exceptional cases, *ex parte* PII applications can also be made in criminal cases.

Additionally, where PII does apply, secondary evidence of a relevant document, for example the oral testimony of a witness who has seen it, can never be adduced, under any circumstances. This is in contrast to the situation with regard to privilege, where secondary evidence of a privileged document will sometimes be received: *Calcraft v Guest* [1898] 1 QB 759.

 Cross-reference Box

Thus, in *Calcraft v Guest* the Court of Appeal held that where the appellant had obtained copies of privileged documents he was entitled to prove their contents by secondary evidence. However, this will not invariably be the case, as can be seen in *Ashburton (Lord) v Pape* [1913] 2 Ch 469. For more on this topic go to p. 613.

2. In What Situations does PII Operate?

When will PII apply? It should be noted that the classes of PII, that is, the types of evidence that it can cover, are never closed, and new situations emerge periodically. Most cases involve civil matters, but the doctrine also applies to criminal cases (see below), albeit that the inherent nature of criminal proceedings very significantly alters whether, and how, it operates: *R v Governor of Briston Prison ex parte Osman* [1992] 1 All ER 108.

In *Duncan v Cammell Laird* [1942] AC 642, Viscount Simon suggested that PII would normally be raised in three situations; namely, those where disclosure would be: '...injurious to national defence, or to good diplomatic relations, or where the practice of keeping a class of documents secret is necessary for the proper functioning of the public service'. The first of these situations would cover matters such as those that occurred in *Duncan v Cammell Laird* itself. This related to the accidental loss of the new British submarine 'Thetis' during diving trials in 1939, and was determined against the backdrop of World War II, which broke out only months after the submarine sank. In this case, the plaintiff was a dependant of one of the 99 men lost in the sinking and sued the defendant for negligence. The plaintiff sought the production of various documents relating to the construction of the submarine and the fatal test dive. However, the First Lord of the Admiralty issued certificates stating that it would be injurious to the public interest for any of these to be disclosed, and this claim was upheld by the court.

On its facts, the decision in *Duncan v Cammell Laird* is unsurprising. This was a time when the country could not afford to risk any information about the construction of its naval vessels being obtained by the enemy. Similarly, and perhaps equally unsurprisingly, in *Asiatic Petroleum Co Ltd v Anglo Persian Co Ltd* [1916] 1 KB 822, a case involving an alleged breach of contract to supply oil, the disclosure of a letter from the defendants to their agents in Persia, containing information about a campaign in the (then ongoing) Great War, was also refused, on the instructions of the Secretary of the Admiralty, because it was of potential value to the enemy and so held to be covered by privilege.

The second category would include situations such as that which arose in *Buttes Gas and Oil v Hammer (No 3)* [1981] 1 QB 223. In this case, a dispute as to drilling concessions between two oil companies turned on what was, essentially, a dispute between two neighbouring middle-eastern Emirates as to the extent of their respective territorial waters. The Court of Appeal recognized the public interest in preserving the United Kingdom's good diplomatic relations with other sovereign states, when it refused to order disclosure of government-held documents addressed to, or emanating from, the rulers of such states, and that were concerned with politically sensitive international disputes over territorial boundaries. (This case also made clear that foreign states could not advance their own national or public interest as a reason per se for withholding evidence in English courts.)

The third, and, statistically, by far the most common situation in which the doctrine is advanced, occurs where adduction of the evidence would have a negative impact on the 'public service'. As Lord Morris observed in *Conway v Rimmer*: '...if the production of a State Paper would be injurious to the public service, the general public interest must be considered paramount to the individual interest of a suitor in a court of justice'. This limb covers a very diverse range of matters, extending from the need to protect police informers from having their identities revealed in public to the need to preserve the effective operation of bodies such as the NSPCC or the Gaming Board.

Thus, and by way of example, in *D v NSPCC* [1978] AC 171, the NSPCC, although a charity rather than a governmental organization, was authorized under Act of Parliament to bring legal proceedings for the welfare of children. It received a complaint about the treatment of a 14-month-old baby girl, and one of its inspectors called at the child's home to investigate. The allegation proved to be unfounded, and the infant's mother sued the Society, which had guaranteed its informant (as they did all their informants) confidentiality in his allegation. The Society was successful in arguing before the House of Lords that it should not have to disclose any documents that might reveal the identity of this person. Without confidentiality, information about the ill-treatment of children might dry up, as people would fear exposure, and this would be contrary to the public interest in seeing children protected.

D v NSPCC [1978] AC 171, HL

Lord Diplock

...confidence, however, is not of itself a sufficient ground for protecting from disclosure in a court of law the nature of the information or the identity of the informant if either of these matters would assist the court to ascertain facts which are relevant to an issue upon which it is adjudicating: Alfred Crompton Amusement Machines Ltd. v. Customs and Excise Commissioners (No. 2) [1974] A.C. 405, 433–434. The private promise of confidentiality must yield to the general public interest that in the administration of justice truth will out, unless by reason of the character of the information or the relationship of the recipient of the information to the informant a more important public interest is served by protecting the information or the identity of the informant from disclosure in a court of law. The public interest which the N.S.P.C.C. relies upon as obliging it to withhold from the plaintiff and from the court itself material that could disclose the identity of the society's informant is analogous to the public interest that is protected by the well established rule of law that the identity of police informers may not be disclosed in a civil action, whether by the process of discovery or by oral evidence at the trial: Marks v. Beyfus (1890) 25 Q.B.D. 494. The rationale of the rule as it applies to police informers is plain. If their identity were liable to be disclosed in a court of law, these sources of information would dry up and the police would be hindered in their duty of preventing and detecting crime....I see no reason and I know of no authority for confining public interest as a ground for non-disclosure of documents or information to the effective functioning of departments or organs of central government. In Conway v. Rimmer [1968] A.C. 910 the public interest to be protected was the effective functioning of a county police force; in In re D. (Infants) [1970] 1 W.L.R. 599 the interest to be protected was the effective functioning of a local authority in relation to the welfare of boarded-out children. In the instant case the public interest to be protected is the effective functioning of an organisation authorised under an Act of Parliament to bring legal proceedings for the welfare of children. I agree with Croom-Johnson J. that this is a public interest which the court is entitled to take into consideration in deciding whether the identity of the N.S.P.C.C.'s informants ought to be disclosed. I also agree that the balance of public interest falls on the side of non-disclosure.

Similarly, in *Rogers v Home Secretary* [1973] AC 388, the plaintiff sought discovery of a letter sent to the Gaming Board by an Assistant Chief Constable (based on information he had received), with regard to his suitability to hold a gaming licence, with a view to bringing proceedings for criminal libel. The House of Lords concluded that the public interest required such communications to be immune from disclosure, so that the Board might obtain the fullest possible information without its informants fearing repercussions. Otherwise, it would be difficult, if not impossible, to make effective enquiries about someone's suitability to be involved in the gambling industry.

Rogers v Home Secretary [1973] AC 388, HL

Lord Reid

The ground put forward has been said to be Crown privilege. I think that that expression is wrong and may be misleading. There is no question of any privilege in the ordinary sense of the word. The real question is whether the public interest requires that the letter shall not be produced and whether that public interest is so strong as to override the ordinary right and interest of a litigant that he shall be able to lay before a court of justice all relevant evidence. A Minister of the Crown is always an appropriate and often the most appropriate person to assert this public interest, and the evidence or advice which he gives to the court is always valuable and may sometimes be indispensable. But, in my view, it must always be open to any person interested to raise the question and there may be cases where the trial judge should himself raise the question if no one else has done so. In the present case the question of public interest was raised by both the Attorney-General and the Gaming Board. In my judgment both were entitled to raise the matter. Indeed I think that in the circumstances it was the duty of the board to do as they have done. The claim in the present case is not based on the nature of the contents of this particular letter. It is based on the fact that the board cannot adequately perform their statutory duty unless they can preserve the confidentiality of all communications to them regarding the character, reputation or antecedents of applicants for their consent.... There are very unusual features about this case. The board require the fullest information they can get in order to identify and exclude persons of dubious character and reputation from the privilege of obtaining a licence to conduct a gaming establishment. There is no obligation on anyone to give any information to the board. No doubt many law-abiding citizens would tell what they know even if there was some risk of their identity becoming known, although many perfectly honourable people do not want to be thought to be mixed up in such affairs. But it is obvious that the best source of information about dubious characters must often be persons of dubious character themselves. It has long been recognised that the identity of police informers must in the public interest be kept secret and the same considerations must apply to those who volunteer information to the board. Indeed, it is in evidence that many refuse to speak unless assured of absolute secrecy.... So it appears to me that, if there is not to be very serious danger of the board being deprived of information essential for the proper performance of their difficult task, there must be a general rule that they are not bound to produce any document which gives information to them about an applicant. We must then balance that fact against the public interest that the course of justice should not be impeded by the withholding of evidence.... In the present case the board told the appellant nothing about the contents of this letter because they say that they had sufficient grounds for refusing his application without any need to rely on anything in the letter. Their good faith in this matter is not subject to any substantial challenge. If the appellant had not by someone's wrongful act obtained a copy of the letter there was no reason why he should ever have known anything about it. In my judgment on balance the public interest clearly requires that documents of this kind should not be disclosed...

Class and Contents

As several of the cases already cited suggest, in some of these situations the argument for PII is (or was) not necessarily based on the specific 'contents' of an individual document, but rather on the 'class' to which it belongs. To go back to the situation in *D v NSPCC*, even if the society's informer in that case was entirely happy for their identity to be revealed, doing so might still undermine the confidence that the public had as to the anonymity of such complaints, discouraging people from passing on information in future. In these situations, it might still be deemed necessary to resist disclosure on the grounds of PII.

Duncan v Cammell Laird [1942] AC 642, HL

Viscount Simon

The principle to be applied in every case is that documents otherwise relevant and liable to production must not be produced if the public interest requires that they should be withheld. This test may be found to be satisfied either (a) by having regard to the contents of the particular document, or (b) by the fact that the document belongs to a class which, on grounds of public interest, must as a class be withheld from production.

Similarly, in *Conway v Rimmer*, Lord Reid accepted that there were: '... certain classes of documents which ought not to be disclosed whatever their content may be'. He gave, as an example, cabinet minutes. A variety of justifications might be advanced for this, such as the need to promote candour amongst ministers when discussing affairs of state. However, even then, the House of Lords made it clear that there was a heavy burden of proof on those seeking to argue that a whole class of documents should be privileged.

In the modern era, the courts are very much more reluctant than previously to accept that entire classes of material should be covered by PII, without any reference to the specific contents of the document in question. This is particularly the case in criminal trials. Indeed, it seems now to be the situation that PII cannot be countenanced in such cases. In the 1990s, Sir Richard Scott observed, as part of his inquiry into the *Matrix Churchill* case (involving potential arms shipments to Iraq), that there had almost never previously been such class claims to immunity in criminal matters, there was no judicial authority for making a class claim in such proceedings, and that class claims should not be made again, in the future, in criminal cases.

Even in civil matters, it was suggested by the House of Lords in *Burmah Oil Co Ltd v Bank of England* [1980] AC 1090 that there were no class of documents that were totally immune from production, whatever the circumstances. Additionally, in 1996, the then Lord Chancellor suggested that the former division between 'class' and 'contents' applications would no longer normally apply to central government bodies. However, in practice, it appears that certain very limited and exceptional types of document, such as foreign office dispatches, are still likely to attract privilege, irrespective of their specific contents. Nevertheless, as the following civil case, where it was held that there was no justification for imposing a class based PII on all documents generated by an investigation into a complaint against the police, suggests they will be very rare (though note Lord Lloyd's caveat).

R v Chief Constable of West Midlands Police, Ex parte Wiley
[1995] 1 AC 274, HL

Lord Templeman

If public interest immunity is approached by every litigant on the basis that a relevant and material document must be disclosed unless the disclosure will cause substantial harm to the public interest, the distinction between a class claim and a contents claim loses much of its significance. As a general rule the harm to the public interest of the disclosure of the whole or part of a document dealing with defence or national security or diplomatic secrets will be self-evident and will preclude disclosure. On the other hand it is difficult to see how the disclosure of documents generated by the activities of the Police Complaints authority can cause any harm.

Lord Woolf

The recognition of a new class-based public interest immunity requires clear and compelling evidence that it is necessary. Yet as the present case has demonstrated, the existence of this class tends to defeat the very object it was designed to achieve. The applicants only launched their proceedings for judicial review to avoid the existence of a situation where their position would be prejudiced as a result of their not being given access to material to which the police had access.

Lord Lloyd

I would want to guard against inferring that the distinction between a class claim for public interest immunity and contents claim is now liable to lose much of its significance; and I would leave open the question whether there may not be a more limited class claim covering, for example, the report of the investigating officer.

Pause for reflection

Do you feel that there are certain types of document that should never be exposed, as a matter of principle?

Who Determines Whether PII Applies?

In *Duncan v Cammell Laird*, the House of Lords held that it was not open to the court to go behind a minister's certificate or affidavit declaring that production of the documents in question would cause damage to the public interest. As Lord Simon observed, the approved practice in both England and Scotland was to: '... treat a ministerial objection taken in proper form as conclusive'. Any weighing up of the benefits and disadvantages of disclosure was, effectively, the responsibility of the minister, whose decision on the issue was final.

Pause for reflection

What are the dangers of allowing a minister's view to be conclusive of such matters?

However, on this point, the House of Lords subsequently changed its collective mind in the important case of *Conway v Rimmer* [1968] AC 910. In this case, the appellant was a probationary police constable who sued the respondent, his Superintendent, for malicious prosecution, after being tried and acquitted of stealing a fellow officer's torch, and then being discharged from the police force. At trial, the appellant had sought disclosure of a number of reports, including several 'probationary' reports on his service, and others relating to his prosecution. The then Home Secretary objected to their production on the ground of Crown Privilege (now PII).

On appeal, their Lordships held that it was open to a judge to require the documents in question to be produced for the court's inspection, and then it was for the court to decide whether or not PII applied; the minister's view was no longer to be considered conclusive of the issue. Thus, in the modern era, the test for admissibility is always determined by the trial judge, not by a minister.

Conway v Rimmer [1968] AC 910, HL

Lord Reid

In my judgment, in considering what it is 'proper' for a court to do we must have regard to the need, shown by 25 years' experience since Duncan's case, that the courts should balance the public interest in the proper administration of justice against the public interest in withholding any evidence which a Minister considers ought to be withheld. I would therefore propose that the House ought now to decide that courts have and are entitled to exercise a power and duty to hold a balance between the public interest, as expressed by a Minister, to withhold certain documents or other evidence, and the public interest in ensuring the proper administration of justice.

 Pause for reflection

Is a trial judge always equipped to make a decision as to PII, in a way that, for example, a government minister might be?

The Test for PII

Although leaving the ultimate decision to a minister, in *Duncan v Cammell Laird* [1942] AC 642, Lord Simon made clear that a certificate asking for PII should not be issued lightly, but only in situations where the public interest would otherwise be 'damnified'. For example, it should not be issued simply because exposure might lead to embarrassment for a government agency, public criticism or litigation.

However, once the courts took responsibility for determining whether PII applied, in *Conway v Rimmer* [1968] AC 910, a formal test had to be annunciated. In *Conway v Rimmer*, the House of Lords concluded that if the requirements of justice in the instant case overrode the particular public interest invoked by the government minister claiming immunity, disclosure should be ordered. This decision established the so-called 'balancing act' that is the essence of any modern exercise of PII. This requires that a judge weigh up the competing benefits and disadvantages of disclosure, that is, that he balance the public interest in withholding evidence with the interests of justice (and so also of the public) in disclosing it, and then decides the case by considering whether one outweighs the other. As Lord Simon subsequently observed in *D v NSPCC* [1978] AC 171, excluding relevant evidence on an issue is a serious step, as it is in the public interest that the search for truth should, normally, be unfettered: 'Accordingly, any hindrance to its seeker needs to be justified by a convincing demonstration that an even higher public interest requires that only part of the truth should be told.'

Conway v Rimmer [1968] AC 910, HL

Lord Reid

I would therefore propose that the House ought now to decide that courts have and are entitled to exercise a power and duty to hold a balance between the public interest, as expressed by a Minister, to withhold certain documents or other evidence, and the public interest in ensuring the proper administration of justice. That does not mean that a court would reject a Minister's view: full weight must be given to it in every case, and if the Minister's reasons are of a character which judicial experience is not competent to weigh, then the Minister's view must prevail. But experience has shown that reasons given for withholding whole classes of documents are often not of that character. For example a court is perfectly well able to assess the likelihood that, if the writer of a certain class of document knew that there was a chance that his report might be produced in legal proceedings, he would make a less full and candid report than he would otherwise have done.

A variety of factors might be considered by the court when reaching such a decision. For example, they will include the potential evidential value of the material to the party who desires its disclosure. The more probative the evidence, the greater will have to be the potential harm to the public interest in disclosure, to counterbalance the desirability of it being adduced. Similarly, the more serious the allegation, the more important the public interest against disclosure will have to be. An initial judicial decision to accede to a PII application, and to refuse disclosure, is not conclusive of the issue. Having made such a decision, a trial judge must also keep the situation under review, during the course of the trial, to see if the 'balance' changes, so that ordering disclosure then becomes necessary: *R v Davis* [1993] 1 WLR 613 (although a criminal case the principle also applies in civil matters).

R v Davis [1993] 1 WLR 613, CA

Lord Taylor CJ

We should add that where the court, on application by the Crown, rules in favour of non-disclosure before the hearing of a case begins, that ruling is not necessarily final. In the course of the hearing, the situation may change. Issues may emerge so that the public interest in non-disclosure may be eclipsed by the need to disclose in the interests of securing fairness to the defendant. If that were to occur, the court would have to indicate to the Crown its change of view. The Crown would then have to decide whether to disclose or offer no further evidence. It will therefore be necessary for the court to continue to monitor the issue. For that reason, it is desirable that the same judge or constitution of the court which decides the [pre-trial] application should conduct the hearing.

In civil matters, a two-stage approach is normally adopted by the courts when a case involves adducing documents, with the person challenging the claim of immunity being required to demonstrate their potential relevance, before judicial inspection of the documents will be undertaken: *Air Canada* v *Secretary of State for Trade and Industry (No 2)* [1983] 2 AC 394. For example, if the courts decide that a litigant is seeking disclosure of a particular document as part of a 'fishing expedition' for evidence, rather than because they genuinely and reasonably suspect that it contains potentially valuable material to their case, the court will not proceed to inspect the relevant document. In recent years this has resulted in what is sometimes termed a 'threshold' test, whereby the party seeking disclosure must show that it may be necessary for the fair disposal of a case, and the possibility that the documents sought may contain something useful to his case must be real and not merely fanciful: *Goodridge v Chief Constable of Hampshire* [1999] 1 WLR 1558. If a judge does feel that inspection of a document is warranted, the claim may then be upheld, or a full or partial disclosure of the document's contents ordered, depending on the balancing process.

Case law suggests that the onus is on the claimant to persuade the court that discovery should be ordered, rather than on the defendant to satisfy the tribunal that it should not. Thus, in *Air Canada,* Lord Wilberforce observed that it was for the party seeking discovery to: '...establish clearly that the scale falls decisively in favour of [the public interest in the administration of justice] if he is to succeed in his quest. If he fails, even material clearly necessary...for disposing fairly of the case or matter must be withheld.'

Public Interest Immunity can be abrogated by statute, though very few Parliamentary Acts have this effect. Nevertheless, and for example, s. 42(3) of the Children Act 1989 provides that a guardian ad litem has the right to have access to, and to examine, local authority records relating to a child: '...regardless of any enactment or rule of law which would otherwise prevent the record in question being admissible in evidence'. In *A Metropolitan Borough Council v JJ S (a child by his Guardian)* [2003] EWHC 976, Wall J criticized a local authority for denying the guardian ad litem of a baby, in the authority's care, access to information in their files relating to that baby, on the grounds of PII. It was held that the wording of s. 42(3) prevented a PII defence being advanced in such a situation.

In A Metropolitan Borough Council v JJ S (a child by his Guardian)
[2003] EWHC 976, HC

Wall J

I need, however, to deal with the question that PII somehow trumps section 42. The answer to that seems to me very simple. If the document the guardian wishes to examine and take copies of falls within CA 1989 section 42, PII simply does not arise so far as the guardian's inspection is concerned. In this respect, it seems to me that the argument put forward by the guardian which I have summarised at paragraph 44 and 45 of this judgment is exactly in point, and I accept it....It must be remembered that CA 1989 section 42(3) gives the guardian the right to inspect 'regardless of any enactment or rule of law which would otherwise prevent the record in question being admissible in evidence' (my emphasis). That phrase manifestly embraces PII. In my judgment, therefore, the cases cited to me by counsel dealing with PII and identified at paragraph 43 of this judgment are irrelevant. The documents with which I am concerned all fall within CA 1989 section 42. The local authority's reliance on PII is misconceived.

3. PII in Criminal Cases

Introduction

The major cases on PII have involved civil rather than criminal matters. However, claims of PII have been made in criminal matters for well over a century. Thus, in *Marks v Beyfus* (1890) 25 QBD 494, Lord Esher observed that it was 'clearly established' that a witness would not normally be required to disclose the identity of a police informant. This was because of the public interest in protecting and encouraging such people to provide information and a fear that such sources would 'dry up' if protection was not provided. Indeed, such a rule can be noticed as far back as the eighteenth century.[1] Not only can a witness not be asked a question that would disclose a third party informer's identity, he cannot be asked whether he himself is an informer.

Nevertheless, when it comes to PII, the dynamics of civil and criminal cases are fundamentally different. In criminal trials, the adverse consequences of its exercise on correctness of adjudication, with the possible result that an innocent man is convicted and, perhaps, imprisoned for a lengthy period of time, are very much greater than they are for most civil matters, where the consequences are normally limited to financial loss (grave though this may be). In *R v Horseferry Road Magistrates' Court, Ex p Bennett* [1994] 1 AC 42, the House of Lords declared that it was axiomatic that if a person charged with a crime: '...cannot be tried fairly for that offence, he should not be tried at all'. As a result, even if it is accepted that a balancing process should occur in criminal cases, as it does in civil ones, the results would necessarily often be very different.

Police Informers

A manifestation of this is that where disclosure of an informant's identity is essential to prove a defendant's innocence, it has always been accepted that disclosure will be ordered, as Lord Esher expressly observed in *Marks v Beyfus* (1890) 25 QBD 494. This can be contrasted with the situation that currently prevails with regard to legal professional privilege in such situations, as established by *R v Derby Magistrates' Court, ex p B* [1996] 1 AC 487.

 Pause for reflection

Why should the law pertaining to PII and legal professional privilege have reached different conclusions on this issue?

Even in the eighteenth century, in the case of *R v Hardy* (1794) 24 St Tr 199, Lord Eyre CJ could observe that: '...if it can be made to observe that really and truly it is necessary to the investigation of the truth of the case that the name of the person [the informer] should be

---

[1] See, for example, Old Bailey Sessions Papers, 10 December 1783, Trial of James Roberts.

disclosed, I should be very unwilling to stop it'. Essentially, in such situations, the courts work on the presumption that the public interest is never best served by an innocent man risking conviction.

Marks v Beyfus (1890) LR 25 QBD 494, CA

Lord Esher MR

Now, this rule as to public prosecutions was founded on grounds of public policy, and if this prosecution was a public prosecution the rule attaches; I think it was a public prosecution, and that the rule applies. I do not say it is a rule which can never be departed from; if upon the trial of a prisoner the judge should be of opinion that the disclosure of the name of the informant is necessary or right in order to shew the prisoner's innocence, then one public policy is in conflict with another public policy, and that which says that an innocent man is not to be condemned when his innocence can be proved is the policy that must prevail. But except in that case, this rule of public policy is not a matter of discretion; it is a rule of law, and as such should be applied by the judge at the trial, who should not treat it as a matter of discretion whether he should tell the witness to answer or not. The learned judge was, therefore, perfectly right in the present case in applying the law, and in declining to let the witness answer the questions. The result of his so deciding was, of course, that the plaintiff's cause of action, which was founded on the alleged instigation of the Director of Public Prosecutions by the defendants, failed, for there was no evidence of any such instigation. I may add that the rule as to non-disclosure of informers applies, in my opinion, not only to the trial of the prisoner, but also to a subsequent civil action between the parties on the ground that the criminal prosecution was maliciously instituted or brought about.

Arguably, in such cases, no 'balancing' process is possible. Once the court concludes that disclosure is necessary to help the accused person establish his innocence, the issue is decided and disclosure must be ordered. Thus, in *R v Agar* [1990] 2 All ER 442, the defendant wanted to know what an informer had told the police. This would have revealed his identity, and was refused by the trial judge. However, on appeal, the ensuing conviction was quashed as the information was deemed to have been necessary to allow the defendant to establish that the police and the informer were acting in concert. In practice, in these (and similar) situations, the prosecution will usually decide not to offer evidence (so that a formal acquittal is returned), rather than compromise the identity of their informant.

For other, relatively recent, illustrations of this fundamental principle in operation can be considered the cases of *R v Hennessey* [1979] 68 Cr App R 419 and *R v Keane* [1994] 1 WLR 746. In the latter, the appellant was charged with having custody or control of counterfeit notes and counterfeiting materials, which were found in a car that he was driving. At his trial he applied for disclosure of the identity of the sources of information leading to his arrest, observation logs and other documents. The judge refused to order disclosure and ruled that it was for the police to decide whether or not to answer questions put in cross-examination. The appellant did not give evidence and was convicted. The Court of Appeal held that, in the circumstances of the case, since there was a public interest in not disclosing the material withheld and it would have been of no assistance to the defence if disclosed, the balance was clearly in favour of non-disclosure and of the restriction on cross-examination that had been imposed. Accordingly, the verdict was neither unsafe nor unsatisfactory.

R v Keane [1994] 1 WLR 746, CA

Lord Taylor CJ

If the disputed material may prove the defendant's innocence or avoid a miscarriage of justice, then the balance comes down resoundingly in favour of disclosing it. But how is it to be determined whether and to what extent the material which the Crown wish to withhold may be of assistance to the defence? First, it is for the prosecution to put before the court only those documents which it regards as material but wishes to withhold. As to what documents are 'material' we would adopt the test suggested by Jowitt J. in Reg. v. Melvin (unreported), 20 December 1993. The judge said: 'I would judge to be material in the realm of disclosure that which can be seen on a sensible appraisal by the prosecution: (1) to be relevant or possibly relevant to an issue in the case; (2) to raise or possibly raise a new issue whose existence is not apparent from the evidence the prosecution proposes to use; (3) to hold out a real (as opposed to fanciful) prospect of providing a lead on evidence which goes to (1) or (2).' As was pointed out later in that judgment, it is open to the defence to indicate to the prosecution a defence or an issue they propose to raise as to which material in the possession of the prosecution may be of assistance, and if that is done the prosecution may need to reconsider what should be disclosed. We also wish, in passing, to endorse the observations of the judge in that case as to the scope of the Crown's duty. It would be an abdication of that duty for the prosecution, out of an over-abundance of caution, simply to dump all its unused material into the court's lap and leave it to the judge to sort through it all regardless of its materiality to the issues present or potential. The prosecution must identify the documents and information which are material, according to the criteria set out above. Having identified what is material, the prosecution should disclose it unless they wish to maintain that public interest immunity or other sensitivity justifies withholding some or all of it. . . . Secondly, when the court is seized of the material, the judge has to perform the balancing exercise by having regard on the one hand to the weight of the public interest in non-disclosure. On the other hand, he must consider the importance of the documents to the issues of interest to the defence, present and potential, so far as they have been disclosed to him or he can foresee them. Accordingly, the more full and specific the indication the defendant's lawyers give of the defence or issues they are likely to raise, the more accurately both prosecution and judge will be able to discuss the value to the defence of the material. In the present case, the appellant had suggested in his interviews the nature of his case especially as to his own movements on the day of the arrest. Counsel, in making his application to the trial judge, was very forthcoming as to the issues he hoped that prosecution disclosure might have addressed. Having examined the material which the Crown put before us, we are wholly satisfied of two matters. First, there was undoubtedly a public interest in not disclosing the material withheld by the Crown. Secondly, that material, had it been disclosed, would not have assisted the defence at all. On the contrary, it would have assisted the prosecution. We have no doubt that if the judge had been shown the material, he would have decided that the balance was clearly in favour of non-disclosure. We are satisfied that no injustice was done to this appellant by his not having access to the documents we have seen.

Of course, this still requires a trial judge to make a difficult assessment as to whether disclosure actually is necessary to help the defendant establish his innocence (though, once he has decided that this is so, it must be ordered). It is a matter of degree, but the threshold appears to be relatively low. In *R v Hallett* [1986] Crim LR 462, the Court of Appeal suggested that a defendant must not be: '. . . deprived of the opportunity of casting doubt on the case against him'. It seems from this that there must be a real, not a fanciful, possibility that the documents or information will be of benefit to the defence.

Even this will not always be obvious, as can be seen from the facts of *R v Turner* [1995] 2 Cr App R 94. In this case, the defendant was accused of robbery and various firearm offences. His defence was alibi, and he sought disclosure of the identity of an informer who had given the police the location of a weapon used in the robbery, which was found concealed together with some of the defendant's clothes. The defendant argued that he was being 'set up' by someone who was probably personally involved in the crime. The trial judge refused disclosure, a decision that led the Court of Appeal to quash the conviction. On its facts, the nature of the evidence and the defence being run made disclosure necessary, though the court noted that the number of such defences had increased in the modern era, and that similar applications should always be scrutinized carefully to see that disclosure was warranted.

R v Turner [1995] 2 Cr App R 94, CA

Lord Taylor CJ

They will need to be astute to see that assertions of a need to know such details, because they are essential to the running of the defence, are justified. If they are not so justified, then the judge will need to adopt a robust approach in declining to order disclosure. Clearly, there is a distinction between cases in which the circumstances raise no reasonable possibility that information about the informant will bear upon the issues and cases where it will. Again, there will be cases where the informant is an informant and no more; other cases where he may have participated in the events constituting, surrounding, or following the crime. Even when the informant has participated, the judge will need to consider whether his role so impinges on an issue of interest to the defence, present or potential, as to make disclosure necessary.... Clearly, it would be impossible for this Court to describe in detail the factual material put before the learned judge. To do so would be to make public the very material which it was sought to maintain undisclosed. It is sufficient for us to say that in this case we are satisfied that the information concerning the informant showed a participation in the events concerning this crime which, coupled with the way in which the defence was raised from the very first moment by the defendant when he said that he was being set up, gave rise to the need for the defence to be aware of the identity of the informant and his role in this matter. We, therefore, conclude that if one applies the principle which has been quoted from Keane to the facts of the present case, there could only be one answer to the question as to whether the details concerning this informer were so important to the issues of interest to the defence, present and potential, that the balance which the learned judge had to strike came down firmly in favour of disclosure. That being so, whilst we appreciate the difficulty of this type of issue which faces judges, we have come to the conclusion that the learned judge's exercise of his discretion in the present case cannot be justified.... It is sufficient to say that on the first ground which has already been described, we feel bound to allow this appeal against conviction.

However, and irrespective of the wishes of the prosecution, a police informer can always voluntarily forgo his anonymity, without the risk of this being prevented by a PII application: *Savage v Chief Constable of Hampshire* (1997) WLR 1061. In this case, the informer revealed his own identity by bringing civil proceedings. At first sight, this is, to an extent, indirectly contrary to the general principle that PII cannot normally be waived. The rationale for the decision in *Savage* is that, as the purpose of the rule is to protect the informer's safety, he is free to expose himself to risk. Nevertheless, it seems that even in non-criminal cases, the attitude of a person, whose identity is being protected by a PII claim, towards public disclosure of their name, might sometimes be a relevant *factor* for the courts to consider when deciding whether or not to uphold such a claim.

Savage v Chief Constable of Hampshire (1997) 1 WLR 1061, CA

Judge LJ

It is well understood that on occasion the public interest requires that evidence which would otherwise be relevant and admissible in litigation should nevertheless not be disclosed or adduced in court. The need to conceal the identity of informers is justified, 'not only for their own safety but to ensure that the supply of information about criminal activities does not dry up:' per Lawton L.J. in Reg. v. Hennessey (Timothy) (1978) 68 Cr.App.R. 419, 426; see also D. v. National Society for the Prevention of Cruelty to Children [1978] A.C. 171. These are not the only considerations. In a limited number of cases, the claim for concealment is justified on the basis that the police service could not otherwise function properly and perform their public duty. . . . In Marks v. Beyfus (1890) 25 Q.B.D. 494 the plaintiff issued civil proceedings for damages for malicious prosecution. He called the Director of Public Prosecutions as a witness. He refused to identify the name of the person who had given him the information on which he had acted against the plaintiff. The Court of Appeal upheld the judge's decision that he should not do so. Lord Esher M.R. explained, at p. 498: 'this rule as to public prosecutions was founded on grounds of public policy, and if this prosecution was a public prosecution the rule attaches; . . . I do not say it is a rule which can never be departed from; if upon the trial of a prisoner the judge should be of opinion that the disclosure of the name of the informant is necessary or right in order to show the prisoner's innocence, then one public policy is in conflict with another public policy, and that which says that an innocent man is not to be condemned when his innocence can be proved is the policy that must prevail. But except in that case, this rule of public policy is not a matter of discretion; it is a rule of law, and as such should be applied by the judge at the trial, who should not treat it as a matter of discretion . . .'. At the end of his judgment, at p. 499, he added that the rule applied: 'not only to the trial of the prisoner, but also to a subsequent civil action between the parties on the ground that the criminal prosecution was maliciously instituted or brought about.' The principle firmly established and constantly repeated thereafter was that immunity from disclosure was not a privilege to be waived by one or other party to the proceedings. . . . Secondly, non-disclosure was not limited to criminal prosecutions but extended in some circumstances to civil proceedings as well. . . . Although there are numerous authorities which deal with the application and indeed the continuing development of the essential principles, one question not yet decided is whether the public interest requires that the principle should be applied when the informer himself positively wishes his activities to be identified. In such circumstances, and assuming that the informer is adult and of reasonable intelligence, it is difficult to see why the court should prevent disclosure of his activities on the basis that his personal safety would be in danger. Disclosure at his insistence could not serve to undermine one of the essential features of arrangements between the police and their informers that the informers and their identity will normally be protected from disclosure. . . . in my judgment, the wish of an informer that his identity should be disclosed could not without more be ignored on the basis of the immunity principle, certainly in relation to civil proceedings taken by him after the conclusion of any relevant criminal prosecutions. . . . if a police informer wishes personally to sacrifice his own anonymity, he is not precluded from doing so by the automatic application of the principle of public interest immunity at the behest of the relevant police authority. This follows, not from waiver of privilege attaching personally to the informer, but from the disappearance of the primary justification for the claim for public interest immunity. That, of course, is not an end of the matter. It is possible that, notwithstanding the wishes of the informer, there remains a significant public interest, extraneous to him and his safety and not already in the public domain, which would be damaged if he were allowed to disclose his role. However, I am unable to understand why the court should infer, for example, that disclosure might assist others involved in criminal activities, or reveal police methods of investigation or hamper their operations, or indicate the state of their inquiries into any particular crime, or even that the police are in possession of information which suggests extreme and urgent danger to the informer if he were to proceed. Considerations such as these might, in an appropriate case, ultimately tip the balance in favour of preserving the informer's anonymity against his wishes in the public interest. There is no evidence that any such consideration applies to the present case.

Police Observation Positions

The same aspect of PII that normally protects the disclosure of an informer's identity, and the exceptions to such protection, has been extended to the disclosure of premises from which police or other law enforcement officers (such as members of the customs and excise) have carried out observation or surveillance on a suspect. In these situations, many of the occupiers of such premises will be extremely frightened at the prospect of having their properties identified, for fear of being identified themselves and so suffering personal reprisals, especially in less salubrious areas. As a result, if the prosecution do disclose the location from which officers observed the defendant, others may well refuse to allow their property to be used for a similar purpose in the future, with very negative consequences for law enforcement in the wider society.

Against this, however, sometimes disclosure may be essential if a defendant is to properly test police evidence. He may argue, for example, that he is very doubtful as to whether the police officers concerned could possibly have seen what was going on from wherever their vantage point was located, as they claim, and insist that it is vital that its position be revealed in court, so that the question can be further explored.

This problem was considered in *R v Rankine* [1986] 83 Cr App R 18, in which the activities of an alleged drug dealer in Brixton had been watched by police officers hidden in private premises some 65 metres away. The Court of Appeal concluded that such cases were 'indistinguishable' from those involving police informers, so that it was quite proper to withhold the location of the observation point, provided that withholding such evidence was not likely to result in a miscarriage of justice.

R v Rankine [1986] 83 Cr App R 18, CA

Mann J

In our judgment the reasons which give rise to the rule that an informer is not to be identified apply with equal force to the identification of the owner or occupier of premises used for surveillance and to the identification of the premises themselves. The cases are indistinguishable, and the same rule must apply to each. That being so the only question could be as to whether the learned judge in the instant case was correct in not exercising the duty exceptionally to admit in order to avoid a miscarriage of justice. Mr. Offenbach for the appellant accepted that if the rule in regard to informers applied, the performance of the duty could not be criticised. We agree. For those reasons this appeal is dismissed.

The matter was further examined by the Court of Appeal in *R v Johnson (Kenneth)* [1988] 1 WLR 1377. In this case, the appellant was accused of drug dealing in the street, important evidence coming from officers who were stationed inside nearby buildings. The prosecution resisted disclosure of the precise whereabouts of these premises after police officers visited the occupiers (who had also been in residence at the material time) and were told that they did not want their names and addresses to be disclosed because they feared for their personal safety. The appellant argued that the layout of the street, which had trees and other objects in it that might have impeded the officers' vision, meant that disclosure was essential to prevent him from being disadvantaged when testing the police evidence.

However, the trial judge refused disclosure, on the basis that a miscarriage of justice was unlikely to occur as a result of such a ruling in the instant case, though he also carefully directed the jury on the limitations on the prosecution evidence that ensued from such a decision. This decision was upheld by the Court of Appeal, which concluded that evidence of location could be excluded if an application was made on a proper evidential basis, and provided the decision did not lead to injustice. Although, in the instant case, the appellant's questioning was to some extent affected by the restraints occasioned by non-disclosure, this was not deemed to be sufficient to risk injustice.

In *Johnson* the Court of Appeal also laid down the necessary basis for the prosecution to make an application to withhold the location of an observation point. In particular, it was first necessary for an officer of the rank of at least sergeant to testify that he had visited the premises and ascertained the attitudes of the occupants to the possible disclosure of the identity of the premises used and the occupier, and for an officer of at least the rank of chief inspector to testify that immediately before trial he had visited the premises to identify whether the occupiers were still the same (as previously) and, in any event, their attitude towards the disclosure of the use made of the premises and the identification of the premises and the occupants.

R v Johnson (Kenneth) [1988] 1 WLR 1377, CA

Watkins LJ

...he [the judge] had knowledge from previous trials conducted by him of the difficulties police encounter in obtaining help from the public in the area where the appellant's offence was found to be committed. He was, we think, in a sound enough position to balance the competing interests between the principle of full disclosure of material facts on the one hand and the need in the interests of justice to in some degree conduct a trial without conforming with it. It is risking condescension to say of him that he knew well the legal principles involved. Moreover, we cannot agree that his rulings went too far to meet the needs of the protection sought. We cannot accept that there was unfairness in this trial, nor that the verdict was either unsafe or unsatisfactory.... The paramount consideration here is whether the appellant had an unfair trial which led to a verdict which is either unsafe or unsatisfactory. Although the conduct of the defence was to some extent affected by the restraints placed upon it by the judge's rulings, which were in our view properly made, we are not persuaded that this led to any injustice. The Jury were well aware of those restraints and most carefully directed about the very special care they had to give to any disadvantage they may have brought to the defence. It was a summing up which was as a whole we think favourable to the defence and which contained safeguarding directions which could have left the Jury in no doubt of the nature of their task. The judge was not of course acquainted with the guidance we are about to give and did not receive evidence which conformed to it before making the rulings complained of. But he heard some evidence going part of the way to meet that guidance and he had knowledge

> from previous trials conducted by him of the difficulties police encounter in obtaining help from the public in the area where the appellant's offence was found to be committed. He was, we think, in a sound enough position to balance the competing interests between the principle of full disclosure of material facts on the one hand and the need in the interests of justice to in some degree conduct a trial without conforming with it. It is risking condescension to say of him that he knew well the legal principles involved. Moreover, we cannot agree that his rulings went too far to meet the needs of the protection sought. We cannot accept that there was unfairness in this trial, nor that the verdict was either unsafe or unsatisfactory.

Of course, and as with the disclosure of informers, such decisions require a qualitative judgment by trial judges as to when a failure to disclose the location of an observation point risks occasioning a miscarriage of justice. This will not always be easy to make. Additionally, and as with the identity of informants, if the police are required to disclose their observation point, they may often prefer to offer no evidence, rather than compromise their source.

However, it is not necessary that the owners/occupiers of premises from which the police observation was made fear 'serious' violence before protection is offered to them. In *Blake v DPP* [1993] 97 Cr App R 169, the graveyard of a London Church had become the regular scene of nocturnal sexual activity between men, two of whom were observed by officers keeping watch, prosecuted and convicted of a summary offence under s. 2 of the Ecclesiastical Courts Jurisdiction Act 1860 (for which they were fined). The Divisional Court concluded that a fear of, and protection from, 'harassment' (rather than simply violence) could be a reason for not disclosing the identity of the domestic premises used by the police officers to carry out their observation of the churchyard.

Article 6 of the European Convention on Human Rights and Criminal PII

Obviously, withholding information from a criminal defendant could, potentially, affect his ability to receive a fair trial under Article 6(1) of the ECHR. However, as Lord Hope observed in *Montgomery v HM Advocate* [2003] 1 AC 641, it is not the purpose of Article 6 to make it impractical to bring people accused of serious crimes to justice. In England, the fact that, if a defendant cannot have a fair trial in the absence of disclosure, disclosure must be ordered, usually ensures that such a decision will be convention compliant, provided (very importantly) appropriate procedures were also adopted when reaching a decision in those cases where it is concluded that this is not the case.

The ECtHR itself has expressly observed that permitting the prosecution to withhold material from the defence on the basis of PII does not *necessarily* violate Article 6(1), provided it is strictly necessary and any difficulties occasioned to the defence are sufficiently counterbalanced by the procedures followed at trial. This decision must always be made by a judge, not by the prosecution itself: *Rowe and Davis v United Kingdom* (2000) 30 EHRR 1. In this case, three defendants had been accused of a murder and a number of robberies. As a result of information received from informers, the police searched certain premises belonging to the accused and discovered property that had been taken during the robberies. The informers were not called to give evidence at trial and, on appeal after conviction, the defendants sought disclosure of their identities. Their convictions were initially upheld by the Court of Appeal. However, the matter subsequently went to the ECtHR in Strasbourg, which concluded that the applicants' rights had been violated because the procedures used when reaching the decision on disclosure had been unsatisfactory. As a result, when the matter went back before the Court of Appeal, their convictions were quashed.

Rowe and Davis v United Kingdom (2000) 30 EHRR 1, ECtHR

Judgement

However, as the applicants recognised, the entitlement to disclosure of relevant evidence is not an absolute right. In any criminal proceedings there may be competing interests, such as national security or the need to protect witnesses at risk of reprisals or keep secret police methods of investigation of crime, which must be weighed against the rights of the accused. In some cases it may be necessary to withhold certain evidence from the defence so as to preserve the fundamental rights of another individual or to safeguard an important public interest. However, only such measures restricting the rights of the defence which are strictly necessary are permissible under Article 6(1). Moreover, in order to ensure that the accused receives a fair trial, any difficulties caused to the defence by a limitation on its rights must be sufficiently counterbalanced by the procedures followed by the judicial authorities.

In the conjoined appeals in *R v H, R v C* (2004) 2 AC 134, the House of Lords approved a 'structure,' in the form of a series of questions, for judges to adopt in criminal cases where they have to consider PII applications to derogate from the normal 'golden rule' of full disclosure.

R v H, R v C (2004) 2 AC 134, HL

Lord Bingham

When any issue of derogation from the golden rule of full disclosure comes before it, the court must address a series of questions.

(1) What is the material which the prosecution seek to withhold? This must be considered by the court in detail.

(2) Is the material such as may weaken the prosecution case or strengthen that of the defence? If No, disclosure should not be ordered. If Yes, full disclosure should (subject to (3), (4) and (5) below) be ordered.

(3) Is there a real risk of serious prejudice to an important public interest (and, if so, what) if full disclosure of the material is ordered? If No, full disclosure should be ordered.

(4) If the answer to (2) and (3) is Yes, can the defendant's interest be protected without disclosure or disclosure be ordered to an extent or in a way which will give adequate protection to the public interest in question and also afford adequate protection to the interests of the defence?
This question requires the court to consider, with specific reference to the material which the prosecution seek to withhold and the facts of the case and the defence as disclosed, whether

the prosecution should formally admit what the defence seek to establish or whether disclosure short of full disclosure may be ordered. This may be done in appropriate cases by the preparation of summaries or extracts of evidence, or the provision of documents in an edited or anonymised form, provided the documents supplied are in each instance approved by the judge. In appropriate cases the appointment of special counsel may be a necessary step to ensure that the contentions of the prosecution are tested and the interests of the defendant protected (see para 22 above). In cases of exceptional difficulty the court may require the appointment of special counsel to ensure a correct answer to questions (2) and (3) as well as (4).

(5) Do the measures proposed in answer to (4) represent the minimum derogation necessary to protect the public interest in question? If No, the court should order such greater disclosure as will represent the minimum derogation from the golden rule of full disclosure.

(6) If limited disclosure is ordered pursuant to (4) or (5), may the effect be to render the trial process, viewed as a whole, unfair to the defendant? If Yes, then fuller disclosure should be ordered even if this leads or may lead *156 the prosecution to discontinue the proceedings so as to avoid having to make disclosure.

(7) If the answer to (6) when first given is No, does that remain the correct answer as the trial unfolds, evidence is adduced and the defence advanced?
It is important that the answer to (6) should not be treated as a final, once-and-for-all, answer but as a provisional answer which the court must keep under review.

Summary

- Very occasionally, potentially relevant and admissible information is withheld from the courts, not because it is caught by an exclusionary rule or is otherwise privileged, but because of the wider interest of society that it should not be exposed by forensic use. In the modern era, the doctrine under which this occurs is termed Public Interest Immunity (PII).

- Such evidence might be withheld for a variety of reasons, ranging from the need to protect great matters of state, such as defence secrets, to the effective operation of a public service.

- PII differs from privilege in several important respects. In particular, if it applies, it cannot be waived. If a document is covered by PII, secondary evidence of it will never be admissible. Even if the issue of PII is not raised by one of the parties (or a third party such as a government minister), the court may have a duty to raise it on its own initiative.

- In the modern era, it is for the courts to determine whether PII applies, not a government minister, though the latter will still usually issue a certificate or affidavit asking that disclosure be refused on the grounds of public interest. The courts decide this issue by adopting a 'balancing act', weighing up the public interest in the proper administration of justice against the public interest that certain potentially damaging material does not get into the public domain.

- PII applies to criminal, as well as civil, matters. However, the dynamics of criminal cases are fundamentally different, limiting its effect in such cases. Most importantly, it is felt that the public interest in not seeing innocent people convicted and punished will always outweigh other considerations, and so the courts will require disclosure of evidence if there is a realistic chance that it might lead to an acquittal. In these situations, the prosecution will often decide not to offer evidence, rather than reveal, for example, the identity of a police informer or the location of a police observation post.

- In appropriate, and limited, circumstances it is possible to withhold information from disclosure without violating a criminal defendant's right to a fair trial under Article 6 of the ECHR.

Further reading

Sir R Scott, 'The Use of Public Interest Immunity Claims in Criminal Cases' [1996] 2 Web JCLI

Sir R Scott, 'The Acceptable and Unacceptable Use of Public Interest Immunity' [1996] PL 427

C Taylor, 'What next for public interest immunity?' (2005) J Crim L, vol 69, no 1, 75–83

C Taylor, 'The courts and applications for public interest immunity: R v H and C' (2004) E & P 2004, vol 8, no 3, 179–185

AAS Zuckerman, 'Public Interest Immunity: A Matter of Prime Judicial Responsibility' MLR, vol. 57, no 5, 703–725

Questions for Discussion

1. Adam is a commercial fisherman, who operates a small one-man trawler. One day, while out fishing, his vessel is struck by a missile that, he believes, can only have come from a naval frigate. The trawler is badly damaged and Adam decides to sue the Ministry of Defence for negligence. He asks for details of the positions of all warships that were within a 40-mile radius of his boat at the relevant time. The MOD has a chart documenting this, but refuses to disclose it on the ground that to do so would endanger national security.

   Will the MOD be able to withhold the chart from evidence?

2. Pritash owns a small apartment, on the third floor of a purpose-built block of flats, which overlooks a scrap metal yard owned by Quincy. The police suspect that Quincy is the mastermind behind a notorious gang that steals silver and gold jewellery and tableware, and then melts it down in the yard. The police ask Pritash to allow them to place an observation unit on the balcony of his flat, which he permits. Subsequently, the officers involved propose to give evidence at Quincy's trial as to the various comings and goings at the yard. However, defence counsel argues that they could not possibly have had a clear view of the entrance to the yard, and so must be fabricating their evidence; he asks that the location of the observation post be revealed so that this can be tested. Pritash is terrified that he will be killed by associates of the defendant if this occurs.

   Additionally, a pair of gloves, containing Quincy's DNA, is found next to a quantity of stolen silver rowing trophies, which are discovered hidden under an oak tree near the yard. The police say that they searched there after receiving advice from an informer, whose identity they refuse to disclose. Quincy says that he suspects that this man is one of his former employees, who has a grudge against him (he has a reputation for very regularly sacking his workers), who planted the items under the tree to get revenge. He says that it is vital that the informer's identity be revealed in court to test this hypothesis.

   Will the prosecution be required to disclose the location of their observation post and the identity of their informer?

3. Should the courts be able to question and overrule a government minister's opinion as to whether PII should apply?

4. Why should the rules on PII in criminal cases differ from those found in civil matters?

For suggested approaches, please visit the Online Resource Centre

14 PRIVILEGE

Definitions

Privilege A privilege is the right accruing to a party in certain circumstances not to be forced to give or provide evidence that is otherwise both relevant and admissible.

'Waiving' a privilege Parties do not have to invoke their right to a privilege. They can disregard the right, in which case the privilege is 'waived', ie lost, and cannot be relied on again.

Without prejudice A communication made 'without prejudice' is made without the risk of its contents being adduced at trial on the issue of liability, even if it contains admissions.

---

1. Introduction

In general, a witness must answer any questions put to him at trial, albeit that some of them may require the express permission of the court before they can be asked (as with allegations of previous 'reprehensible behaviour' under s. 100 of the Criminal Justice Act 2003 (CJA 2003), or questions about a rape complainant's previous sexual history under s. 41 of the Youth Justice and Criminal Evidence Act 1999 (YJCEA 1999)). This remains the case, even if the answers might be highly damaging to the witness's own case (if they are a litigant), or otherwise extremely personal or embarrassing (whether they are a litigant or not). Additionally, a witness must normally produce any documents for the opposing side's inspection that are in their possession, if they are relevant to the issues in the case and requested, irrespective of their contents.

Cross-reference Box

In the modern era, a feeling that intrusive and distressing cross-examination about sexual history helped to explain why so few rape complainants came forward led to statutory controls on such questioning being imposed throughout most of the common law world. For more information on this topic, go to pp. 448–465.

Any failure to answer a question at trial, or to produce a relevant document, is likely to be treated as a contempt of court and punished accordingly. There are sound policy reasons for this. The need for correctness of adjudication requires that all relevant and available information should normally be placed before the tribunal of fact. As Lord Edmund-Davies observed in *Waugh v British Railways Board* (1980) AC 521, it is necessary to start from the assumption that the public interest is, on balance: '...best served by rigidly confining within narrow limits the cases where material relevant to litigation may be lawfully withheld. Justice is better served by candour than by suppression'. In the same case, he approved dicta in *Grant v Downs* (1976) 135 CLR 674 to the effect that the exercise of privilege normally detracts from the fairness of a trial, if it denies a party access to relevant evidence.

However, and despite this strong policy consideration, there are a small number of exceptions to the general position, whereby a person or body can legitimately refuse to answer relevant questions or to produce relevant documents, not because the evidence contained in them is 'inadmissible' under the law of evidence, but on the basis that the information is subject to 'privilege'. The most important aspects of privilege are those against self-incrimination, legal professional privilege, and the privilege attaching to communications made in 'without prejudice' negotiations.

It should be noted that an individual who is entitled to claim privilege is not obliged to do so; they may 'waive' their right to it in either of the first two cases, and allow the evidence to be adduced. With regard to 'without prejudice' negotiations, both parties to the correspondence must agree to the relevant documents being adduced before the privilege can be waived. As this suggests, privileged evidence is very different to inadmissible evidence. In this chapter, the three main types of privilege will be dealt with in detail, in turn. The chapter will finish by examining s. 10 of the Contempt of Court Act 1981, a specialist, and qualified, statutory privilege, which allows journalists to protect the identity of their sources, unless there are pressing reasons for such information to be disclosed.

2. The Privilege Against Self-incrimination

Introduction

This aspect of the law of privilege can be claimed by any witness (including a litigant) called upon to answer questions during a civil or criminal trial, or to disclose documents via (for example) pre-trial discovery, who feels that doing so might 'incriminate' them in the commission of an offence and so expose them to the risk of a criminal charge, penalty or (in criminal matters) a forfeiture under domestic law. Where this is held to be the case by the court, the witness may legitimately refuse to answer the relevant question or to produce the appropriate document. Although such a privilege is also recognized by the ECtHR at Strasbourg, it is not unqualified under European jurisprudence: *O'Halloran and Francis v United Kingdom* [2007] Crim LR 897.

The common law privilege is generally thought to originate in popular hostility to the processes of the early modern Court of Star Chamber, in which witnesses could be interrogated on oath, and so forced to inculpate themselves, even though not accused of an offence when initially questioned. It is also sometimes claimed that it helps to preserve the autonomy and dignity of the individual within the wider justice system.

It should be noted immediately that there are (unsurprisingly) special rules with regard to defendants in a criminal trial, who cannot refuse to answer questions that might incriminate them in the offence with which they are presently charged, if they elect to give evidence. The advent of the Criminal Evidence Act 1898, the first statute to allow all criminal defendants to give sworn evidence, necessarily required a modification to the general privilege; this is contained in s. 1(2) of the statute (as amended). Otherwise, it would have been pointless for the prosecution to cross-examine an accused person about the offence for which they were on trial, as they could simply rely on the privilege to refuse to answer awkward questions, while simultaneously enjoying all the benefits of giving their own version of events to the court during their examination in chief.

Section 1(2) of the Criminal Evidence Act 1898

Subject to section 101 of the Criminal Justice Act 2003 (admissibility of evidence of defendant's bad character), a person charged in criminal proceedings who is called as a witness in the proceedings may be asked any question in cross-examination notwithstanding that it would tend to criminate him as to the offence charged in the proceedings.

Cross-reference Box

Section 101 of the Criminal Justice Act 2003, determines whether the prosecution (or a co-defendant) can adduce evidence of a defendant's previous bad character; for example, previous convictions or other forms of reprehensible behaviour. For more information on this topic, go to pp. 184–220.

It should also be noted that the presence of the privilege does not preclude a question from being asked; it merely entitles the witness not to answer it. (In practice, a highly visible refusal to respond to such a question at trial may be damaging, whatever the legal theory.) The party calling the witness will often identify such a question, when it is put to their witness in cross-examination, and intervene. However, the opposing party might also anticipate the potential risk inherent in a question that they propose to ask, before posing it, and suggest that the witness does not answer until the judge or, in a summary court, the magistrates or their clerk have explained the existence of the privilege. Alternatively, the possibility that a reply might incriminate a witness will be spotted by the trial judge, who will personally intervene to advise the witness about their rights, before allowing them to decide whether or not to answer the question.

For a relatively trivial, but common, example of its operation in practice, consider the situation in a summary trial in which the defendant is accused of driving his car whilst disqualified, and, as often occurs, calls a friend to say that it was he (the friend) who had been behind the wheel at the relevant time. This witness might then be warned about the existence of the privilege before deciding to answer a prosecution question as to whether or not he was insured to drive the vehicle at that time.

It is, unsurprisingly, purely for the court to determine whether a claim to the privilege is well founded: *BSC v Granada TV* [1982] AC 1906. However, the onus is on the party who claims the privilege to persuade the tribunal that it should apply. It should also be noted that, at common law, the privilege applies only to the incrimination of the claimant, though it seems that, despite some dicta to the contrary in older cases, these can include artificial legal personalities, such as limited companies.

Nevertheless, it is a privilege against 'self' incrimination; there is, obviously, nothing to prevent an opposing party from adducing other evidence to incriminate a witness in having committed an offence, where it is relevant to his case to do so (subject, of course, to permission being granted under s. 100 of the CJA 2003, etc.). Additionally, because it is confined to self-incrimination, it will not cover a limited company (ie an artificial legal person) being questioned about its employees (or vice versa), even though the answers might incriminate the employees, and even if they are major shareholders in the relevant company. There is no privilege against incrimination by a third party; it seems that this remains the case even if it is closely linked to the person who claims privilege.

Cross-reference Box

Section 100 of the CJA 2003 regulates the situations in which the bad character of a non-defendant witness (or other party) can be adduced in criminal cases. For example, that a prosecution witness has previous convictions for theft. For more information on this topic, go to p. 223.

Tate Access Floors Inc v Boswell [1991] Ch 512, HC

Sir Nicholas Browne-Wilkinson

In order for a person to show that he has any privilege at all, the burden must be on him to show that he is being asked to incriminate himself: he has no privilege against incrimination by a third party and must prove that the company is his creature. Even if, contrary to my view, the individual defendants are entitled to put forward the claim to privilege on the basis that the defendant companies are their creatures, in my judgment they are still not entitled to object to the discovery against the company defendants. The privilege can only be claimed by the person who is likely to be incriminated: see In re Westinghouse Electric Corporation Uranium Contract Litigation M.D.L. Docket No. 235 (No. 2) [1978] A.C. 547, 637 per Lord Diplock. If people choose to conduct their affairs through the medium of corporations, they are taking advantage of the fact that in law those corporations are separate legal entities, whose property and actions are in law not the property or actions of their incorporators or controlling shareholders. In my judgment controlling shareholders cannot, for all purposes beneficial to them, insist on the separate identity of such corporations but then be heard to say the contrary when discovery is sought against such corporations.

Nevertheless, in civil matters, s. 14(1)(b) of the Civil Evidence Act 1968 has extended the privilege to questions tending to incriminate a claimant's spouse or civil partner. Thus, and for example, if a man is sued in the High Court for negligently injuring another person while driving his car, but denies being behind the wheel at the relevant time, he can refuse to answer a question as to who was driving the vehicle, if this was his wife, and, at the relevant time, she was disqualified from driving (ie she was committing a criminal offence).

Section 14(1)(a) and (b) of the Civil Evidence Act 1968

(1) The right of a person in any legal proceedings other than criminal proceedings to refuse to answer any question or produce any document or thing if to do so would tend to expose that person to proceedings for an offence or for the recovery of a penalty—

   (a) shall apply only as regards criminal offences under the law of any part of the United Kingdom and penalties provided for by such law; and

   (b) shall include a like right to refuse to answer any question or produce any document or thing if to do so would tend to expose the [spouse or civil partner] of that person to proceedings for any such criminal offence or for the recovery of any such penalty.

The privilege against self-incrimination has prompted mixed feelings in the modern era. To some, it is a bulwark against oppressive state power. To others, it is a potential source of injustice, one that sometimes denies the courts vital information. Thus, in *A.T. & T. Istel Ltd. v Tully* [1993] AC 45, Lord Griffiths asserted that the privilege was 'in need of radical reappraisal'. In the same case, Lord Templeman stated that he viewed the continued existence of the privilege in civil cases as an 'archaic and unjustifiable survival from the past'. Depending on where their sympathies lie, individual judges interpreting the privilege have adopted slightly different degrees of strictness when applying it, something that also makes its exact parameters somewhat uncertain.

Pause for reflection

Is it right that, even in a court of law, a witness can legitimately refuse to answer a potentially vital question on the basis that telling the truth might expose him to the consequences of his own actions? Would it be practical to make a distinction between civil and criminal cases in such matters?

3. The Scope of the Privilege

Introduction

The scope of the privilege against self-incrimination was considered in the important case of *Blunt v Park Lane Hotel* [1942] 2 KB 253, where Lord Goddard described it as being that: '…no one is bound to answer any question if the answer would, in the judge's opinion, have a tendency to expose the [witness] to any criminal charge or penalty, which the judge regards as reasonably likely to be preferred'. In this case, the plaintiff in a slander case objected to answering interrogatories on the ground that to do so might expose her to the risk of ecclesiastical penalties for her incontinent sexual behaviour. The Court of Appeal rejected this claim, on the basis that, in the modern era, such a jurisdiction has long been obsolete, at least so far as the laity was concerned, and that it was 'fantastic' to suppose that there was any real likelihood of ecclesiastical penalties being imposed on the claimant.

However, Lord Goddard's definition still raises the obvious questions as to: what is meant by a 'criminal charge or penalty' in more realistic scenarios, that is the threat to which the claimant is exposed; what is entailed in a 'tendency to expose', ie how incriminating must the answer to the question potentially be; and what is meant by 'reasonably likely to be preferred', that is what must be the degree of risk that such charges will be brought? Obviously, in the right circumstances, many answers, to even apparently innocuous questions, could have this effect. (To some extent the last two identified factors are interlinked.) These different questions must be addressed separately.

The Threat

Clearly, the privilege covers the risk of prosecution in the Magistrates' or Crown Courts. However, it is now apparent that the criminal charge must relate to a prosecution in the jurisdiction in which the privilege is being claimed, not a foreign country. In civil cases, this is by dint of s. 14(1)(a) of the Civil Evidence Act 1968 (see extract above); in criminal matters, it is as a result of the Privy Council decision in *Brannigan v Davison* [1997] AC 238. Thus, a witness could not refuse to answer a question in the Crown Court on the basis that his answer might incriminate him with regard, for example, to an offence and proceedings in Papua New Guinea.

Brannigan v Davison [1997] AC 238, PC

Lord Nicholls

Different countries have their own interests to pursue. At times national interests conflict. In its simple, absolute, unqualified form the privilege, established in a domestic law setting, cannot be extended to include foreign law without encroaching unacceptably upon the domestic country's legitimate interest in the conduct of its own judicial proceedings. Their Lordships respectfully agree with the views to this effect expressed in the Court of Appeal by Cooke P., Henry and Thomas JJ. Their Lordships' conclusion is that the common law privilege does not run where the criminal or penal sanctions arise under a foreign law.

Cases involving a threat of 'penalties', sufficient to bring the privilege into effect, are much rarer in the modern era than those involving the threat of a criminal prosecution. However, in *Cobra Golf Inc. and Another v Rata and Others* [1998] Ch 109, it was held that for a party to expose himself to the risk of proceedings for civil contempt (technically, not truly a crime, albeit punishable by a fine or imprisonment), was to expose himself to the risk of a penalty and brought the privilege into play.

Cobra Golf Inc and Another v Rata and Others [1998] Ch 109, HC

Rimer J

Accordingly, I propose to follow Knox J.'s decision in Bhimji v. Chatwani (No. 2) that proceedings for civil contempt are proceedings for the 'recovery of a penalty' in respect of which there is a privilege against self-incrimination. In view of Lord Oliver's dictum I do so with some diffidence;

but I find it a compensating comfort that I have arrived at a result in harmony with any assumption, suggestion or assertion in cases such as Comet Products U.K. Ltd. v. Hawkex Plastics Ltd. [1971] 2 Q.B. 67, A.J. Bekhor & Co. Ltd. v. Bilton [1981] Q.B. 923, Crest Homes Plc. v. Marks [1987] A.C. 829 (including by Lord Oliver) and the Exagym cases [1994] 2 Qd.R. 6; [1994] 2 Qd.R. 129 that there is a privilege against self-incrimination for civil contempt.

The Degree of Risk

In *Blunt v Park Lane Hotel* Lord Goddard spoke about a charge or penalty that was 'reasonably likely' to be brought. This was itself an apparent (albeit modest) relaxation of older *dicta*, set out in *R v Boyes* (1861) 121 ER 730, which suggested that the danger to be apprehended must be 'real and imaginable, with reference to the ordinary operation of the law'. It would not encompass threats that were 'unsubstantial', 'barely possible' or: '…so improbable that no reasonable man would suffer it to influence his conduct'. Incrimination is clearly still a matter of degree, and does not cover very remote or purely fanciful possibilities, as the following extract also suggests.

BSC v Granada TV [1981] AC 1096, HL

Sir Robert Megarry

It appears to me to be one thing to say 'To answer this question would tend to incriminate me', and another to say 'To answer this question might lead to a train of inquiry which, if pursued, might lead to some evidence which, if adduced, might tend to criminate me'. If the privilege extended that far, a witness who was guilty of a gang affray which had nothing to do with the case in which he is testifying could refuse to say who any of his friends were, since to identify them might lead to those who could give evidence against him, if he were charged with making an affray. However that may be, in this case I cannot see any reality in the fear of a charge of conspiracy. There is not the slightest evidence of any conspiracy. Indeed, Granada's explicit evidence is that the documents were volunteered, and reached them without any prior agreement or solicitation by them. If a question is put to a witness which itself indicates some jeopardy to him if he answers it one way, then that will normally support the privilege. But if there is nothing in the question or anything else to indicate anything save an innocent question, the court must be satisfied from some other source of the tendency to criminate: see In Re Genese, Ex parte Gilbert (1886) 3 Morr. 223, 226, 227, per Lord Esher M.R. He can claim the privilege if he 'states circumstances, consistent on the face of them with the existence of the peril alleged, and which also render it extremely probable': see Short v. Mercier (1851) 3 Mac. & G. 205, 217, per Lord Truro L.C. The words 'extremely probable' relate to the existence of the risk, and not to whether a prosecution will in fact be brought; for the latter, all that is required is an appreciable chance: see In Re Westinghouse Electric Corporation Uranium Contract Litigation M.D.L. Docket No. 235 (No. 2) [1978] A.C. 547, 581, per Shaw L.J.; and see at p. 574 per Lord Denning M.R., approved at p. 627, per Viscount Dilhorne. What is there in this case to show that there is any real risk of Granada being liable to be prosecuted for any offence save under the Theft Act 1968, which for this purpose Mr. Irvine accepted was of no avail to Granada? Mr. Irvine was reduced to contending that if the identity of the person who delivered the documents was disclosed, that person might falsely allege against Granada that there had been a prior conspiracy. In this world, I suppose, almost anything might happen: but it seems quite impossible to regard such a wild and speculative surmise as being a fear or apprehension with any substance in it.

In *Blunt v Park Lane Hotel* Lord Goddard spoke about 'tending' to show. It is apparent that the rule is not confined to answers that would *directly* incriminate the witness, as in 'I stole the car', but extends to those that might merely advance the prosecution case against him, such as: 'I admit that I was the man seen driving the [stolen] car.' As Lord Tenterden observed in *R v Slaney* (1832) 5 C & P 213: 'You cannot only not compel a witness to answer that which will criminate him, but that which tends to criminate him.' Otherwise, as Lord Tenterden also noted, a witness could go from question to question, which, although not individually enough to incriminate their maker, when taken together could, by a causal chain of reasoning, have this very effect. Inevitably, this, too, will be a question of degree.

Of course, if criminal matters have been concluded, or if the witness has been formally pardoned, as in *Boyes*, he will no longer necessarily be in jeopardy of further prosecution, and, if that is truly the case, the privilege will not apply. However, that the witness has already made incriminating statements outside court, for example, to the police, will not preclude him from arguing that repeating them, especially on oath, will further incriminate him. In *Den Norske Bank ASA v Antonatos* [1999] QB 271, the defendant was alleged to have taken bribes and engaged in fraudulent behaviour with regard to the claimant bank. He was ordered to disclose various assets and sought to argue that some of these were covered by the privilege against self-incrimination. In response, it was argued for the claimants that, as he had already provided a statement on such matters, he would not expose himself to further jeopardy by giving sworn evidence on the same subject. This argument was firmly rejected by the Court of Appeal.

Den Norske Bank ASA v Antonatos [1999] QB 271, CA

Waller LJ

It is one thing for someone to make a statement to the police or anyone else which he might afterwards try to retract. It is quite another for him some time later to be made to repeat any admission on oath in court in the presence of a judge and his own lawyers. It makes the potentially retractable impossible to retract. If there is a risk of self-incrimination and if there is no bad faith a 'no increase in risk' must be almost impossible to establish. It is of interest that it failed in the Tate Access case [1991] Ch. 512, 529 and the IBM case [1994] 1 W.L.R. 719, 732.

Waiving the Privilege

As with legal professional privilege (see below), there is nothing to prevent a witness answering an incriminating question if he wishes to do so, and so waiving the privilege, as the following extract also makes clear.

In Re L (a minor) [1997] AC 16, HL

Lord Jauncey

It was only when the report became available that its possible incriminating effect became known and it was at that stage when the mother was first in a position to advance her claim to privilege by seeking a variation of that part of the order which required the report to be filed. In the event she filed the report without taking any steps to assert a claim for privilege. Thus the mother voluntarily initiated the process, did not appeal the order when it was made and obtempered it without seeking a variation, notwithstanding that the unfavourable nature of the report had by then become apparent. In these circumstances she must be taken to have waived any claim which she may have had to privilege against self-incrimination consequent upon the order of the district judge.

Exceptions to the Privilege

The general statutory exception to the privilege for criminal defendants, under s. 1(2) of the Criminal Evidence 1898 Act, has already been noted (see above). However, there are also a few, more specific, statutory exceptions, covering distinct offences, where the privilege does not exist. For example, under s. 434 of the Companies Act 1985, if inspectors appointed to investigate the affairs of a company consider that an officer or agent of the company is in possession of information relating to a matter relevant to the investigation, they may require him to produce all documents relating to the company, attend before the inspectors when required to do so, and give the inspectors all assistance in connection with the investigation which they can. This remains the case even if the answers or documents might incriminate the company officer. Despite this, some of these statutes expressly provided for an alternative safeguard, by stating that, although the privilege is absent, any incriminating answer to what would otherwise be a privileged question cannot subsequently be adduced in evidence at trial. Foremost amongst these is s. 31(1) of the Theft Act 1968.

Section 31(1) of the Theft Act 1968

A person shall not be excused, by reason that to do so may incriminate that person or the wife or husband of that person of an offence under this Act—(a) from answering any question put to that person in proceedings for the recovery or administration of any property, for the execution of any trust or for an account of any property or dealings with property; or (b) from complying with any order made in any such proceedings; but no statement or admission made by a person in answering a question put or complying with an order made as aforesaid shall, in proceedings for an offence under this Act, be admissible in evidence against that person or (unless they married after the making of the statement or admission) against the wife or husband of that person.

Arguably, those statutes that did not provide such protection could be challenged on the basis that they were incompatible with Article 6 of the ECHR. This was raised in the case of *Saunders v UK* [1996] 23 EHRR 313, in which the ECtHR concluded that information obtained in violation of the privilege against self-incrimination might not be convention compliant. As a result, and in response, Parliament enacted s. 59 of the YJCEA 1999, which amended enactments providing for the use of answers and statements given under compulsion, so as to restrict their use in criminal proceedings against those who made them. The amended statutes are set out in Sch. 3 to the 1999 Act.

Nevertheless, it is also apparent that the privilege against self-incrimination is not absolute. Not every derogation from it will violate Article 6. Thus, in the Privy Council case of *Brown v Stott* [2003] 1 AC 681 (a devolution case from Scotland), it was held that the provision under s. 171(2)(a) of the Road Traffic Act 1988, by which an apparently intoxicated woman who had been arrested in a superstore was required to say who had been driving her vehicle at the time when she would have travelled in it to the shop (she admitted that it was her), did not violate Article 6, provided that it was necessary to achieve a legitimate aim in the public interest (as was the case with preventing drink driving) and was proportionate (as in the instant case, given that it was limited to the issue of who had been driving the vehicle and that a failure to answer the question was subject to a relatively modest penalty).

The courts have also been careful to restrict the boundaries of the privilege. Thus, in *C plc and another v P (Attorney General Intervening)* [2007] 3 WLR 437 the claimants in an action for copyright infringement obtained a search order (see chapter 1) against the defendants, allowing them to take possession of his computers and identify and copy any of their material found on them. On arrival at the defendant's premises, the latter's solicitor stated to the claimant's lawyer (supervising the search), in very general terms, that he (the defendant) would rely on the privilege against self-incrimination with regard to any material found on the computers.

A subsequent examination of the computers by an expert revealed (unexpectedly) that one of them contained obscene pictures of small children, possession of which was, of course, a serious criminal offence (the defendant denied having anything to do with them). The judge who had authorized the search order made a further order requiring this obscene material to be passed on to the police, with a view to possible criminal proceedings, on the basis that the common law privilege against self-incrimination did not apply to 'freestanding' evidence that was not produced under compulsion. Subsequently, a majority of the Court of Appeal upheld the decision after concluding that the privilege did not extend to documents or things that had an existence that was independent of the 'will' of the person relying on the privilege. Such evidence was considered by the court to be analogous to incriminating evidence found by dint of an otherwise inadmissible confession; this had always been deemed to be admissible at common law, independent of the (excluded) confession that led to it: *R v Warwickshall* (1783) 1 Leach 263. As a result, the situation was deemed to be on a par with that which would have arisen had an illegal firearm been discovered hidden inside the body of the computer.

C plc and another v P (Attorney General Intervening)
[2007] 3 WLR 437, CA

Longmore LJ

It is necessary to emphasise that the only issue before the judge and on this appeal is whether W should have the leave of the court to disclose the offending material to the police. It is in this context that I would hold that no privilege exists in the material itself which is itself 'real' and independent evidence and is not itself 'compelled testimony' from P.

Cross-reference Box

The common law principle with regard to confessions has been replicated in s. 76 of PCEA 1984. Thus if a defendant is threatened into admitting his guilt with regard to a burglary and, in the process also reveals that the proceeds of the crime are hidden in his loft, although the jury will not hear about the confession they can be informed about the discovery of the stolen items which will, of course, be important circumstantial evidence against the accused. For more on this go to p. 349.

4. Legal Professional Privilege

Introduction

In general, there is no privilege with regard to confidential statements made between a professional person and his client. Historically, this absence of privilege extends to statements made within highly confidential, but non-legal, relationships. Thus, in the *Duchess of Kingston's Case* (1796) 20 State Trials 572, it was held that a physician or surgeon was compellable to give evidence on matters which might have come to his knowledge in the course of his professional relationship to a litigant. Similarly, in *Wheeler v Le Marchant* (1881) 50 LJ Ch 793, Lord Jessel concluded that privilege does not extend to communications made to a priest in the confessional by a penitent, even on matters considered by him to be more important than his life or fortune.

In the modern era, this analysis has been reiterated by Lord Denning, who, in *Attorney General v Mulholland* [1963] 2 WLR 658, observed: 'Take the clergyman, the banker or the medical man. None of these is entitled to refuse to answer when directed to by a judge.' In this, England differs from some Roman law countries. Thus, and for example, accountants, although having limited statutory privilege when providing tax advice, are not generally exempt from giving evidence about matters that came to their notice in their professional capacity. However, it should be noted that another statutory exception to the general rule can be found in s. 280 of the Copyright, Designs and Patents Act 1988, whereby communications between client and patent agent on any matter relating to the protection of an invention, design or technical information are: '. . . privileged from disclosure in legal proceedings . . . in the same way as a communication between a person and his solicitor'.

Pause for reflection

Why should communications with patent agents be accorded greater protection than those with priests, bankers and doctors?

Nevertheless, although most professional/client communications are not privileged, they are not entirely unprotected. In some situations, at least, a trial judge does have a *discretion* as to whether such a witness should be compelled to testify about them. However, this is founded on public policy considerations, and can be viewed as an aspect of Public Interest Immunity (dealt with in chapter 13), rather than one of legal privilege. As Lord Scott expressly observed in *Three Rivers District Council v Bank of England* [2005] 1 AC 610, the protection afforded by the court to such witnesses not to answer questions will give way to more important policy factors. This is unlike legal professional privilege, which is normally absolute; it is currently viewed as rather more than an evidential rule, being seen, as Lord Taylor observed in *R v Derby Magistrates' Court, ex p B* [1996] 1 AC 487, as a fundamental condition on which the administration of justice as a whole rests.

Three Rivers District Council v Bank of England [2005] 1 AC 610, HL

Lord Scott

In relation to all other confidential communications, whether between doctor and patient, account-ant and client, husband and wife, parent and child, priest and penitent, the common law recognises the confidentiality of the communication, will protect the confidentiality up to a point, but declines to allow the communication the absolute protection allowed to communications between lawyer and client giving or seeking legal advice. In relation to all these other confidential communications the law requires the public interest in the preservation of confidences and the private interest of the parties in maintaining the confidentiality of their communications to be balanced against the administration of justice reasons for requiring disclosure of the confidential material. There is a strong public interest that in criminal cases the innocent should be acquitted and the guilty con-victed, that in civil cases the claimant should succeed if he is entitled to do so and should fail if he is not, that every trial should be a fair trial and that to provide the best chance of these desiderata being achieved all relevant material should be available to be taken into account. These are the administration of justice reasons to be placed in the balance. They will usually prevail.

The importance of legal professional privilege, and the need for it to remain inviolate, has been reiterated on several occasions in recent years by the Court of Appeal. For example, in *R v Grant* [2006] QB 60, the defendant was accused of conspiracy to murder his wife's lover. It was claimed that, while he was held in custody, the police deliberately eavesdropped on, and recorded, privi-leged conversations between the defendant and his solicitor, held in the exercise yard of a police station, with a view to obtaining useful information. At trial, the first instance judge concluded that the interceptions had not given rise to any evidence subsequently relied upon by the Crown and, as a result, that the defendant had suffered no prejudice. In consequence, he refused to accede to an application that the prosecution be stopped as an abuse of process. On appeal, however, the ensuing conviction was quashed, on the basis that deliberate interference with such an important right undermined the rule of law. Such a conscious violation of a suspected person's right to legal professional privilege was so great an affront to the integrity of the justice system that the associated prosecution ought to be stayed as an abuse of process by the court.

R v Grant [2006] QB 60, CA

Laws LJ

We are quite clear that the deliberate interference with a detained suspect's right to the con-fidence of privileged communications with his solicitor, such as we have found was done here, seriously undermines the rule of law and justifies a stay on grounds of abuse of process, notwith-standing the absence of prejudice consisting in evidence gathered by the Crown as the fruit of police officers' unlawful conduct. Newman J took the same view in Wheel. He had well in mind the gravity of the crime of which the defendant was suspected: 'A young man has been executed by a brutal shooting.' So of course do we, in this present case. As for prejudice, it is a particular vice of the police conduct in such circumstances as these (as, again, Newman J recognised in Wheel) that the court cannot know whether the police misconduct has in fact yielded fruit in the form of evidence, whether directly or indirectly, without enquiry as to what the covert surveil-lance revealed; but that would further violate the suspect's right of legal professional privilege. As Newman J said: 'The defendants having an absolute right not to waive the privilege, it cannot be right that the court can force them to do so in order to prove the case for a stay, for to do so would be to effectively take away the very fundamental right which the law has conferred.' In all these circumstances, we conclude that there was abuse of the process here and Astill J should have stayed the proceedings in consequence. We understand it to be accepted that if the court reaches this conclusion, the conviction falls to be treated as unsafe. In those circumstances the appeal will be allowed.

Scope of the Privilege

In practical terms, legal professional privilege, where it applies, allows a lawyer's client to refuse to reveal the contents of a privileged communication or document and also to insist that his lawyer or, in the case of its 'litigation privilege' aspect, third parties, do the same. For this rea-son, the phrase 'legal professional privilege' is somewhat misleading, as the privilege always belongs to the client, not the lawyer, who must assert it at all times unless the client instructs him to the contrary.

Nor does the privilege belong to any third party. Thus, in *Schneider v Lee* [1955] 2 QB 195, an expert witness who had been instructed by a solicitor to produce a report for litigation was not able to rely on privilege when he was sued for defamation by someone mentioned in his report. The client whose solicitor had commissioned the report could have insisted on its non-disclosure (it was his privilege), the expert could not, on his own initiative. Additionally, it should be stressed that the court will not be able to draw an adverse inference from any exercise of the privilege by the client.

The scope of legal professional privilege has been established by case law, but s. 10(1) of the Police and Criminal Evidence Act 1984, setting out the limits on police powers to search for and seize evidence, has been described as a statutory reflection of the common law position: *R v Central Criminal Court ex parte Francis and Francis* [1989] AC 346. As this section makes clear, there are two aspects to the privilege.

Section 10(1) of the PCEA 1984

(1) Subject to subsection (2) below, in this Act 'items subject to legal privilege' means—

  (a) communications between a professional legal adviser and his client or any person repre-senting his client made in connection with the giving of legal advice to the client;

(b) communications between a professional legal adviser and his client or any person repre-
senting his client or between such an adviser or his client or any such representative and any
other person made in connection with or in contemplation of legal proceedings and for the
purposes of such proceedings; and
(c) items enclosed with or referred to in such communications and made—
    (i) in connection with the giving of legal advice;
or
    (ii) in connection with or in contemplation of legal proceedings and for the purposes
    of such proceedings,
when they are in the possession of a person who is entitled to possession of them.

Although subsumed under the general title 'legal professional privilege', often overlapping and,
sometimes, as in *Re L (a minor)* [1997] AC 16, described as two facets of the same privilege, they
are somewhat different in their operation. The first category, identified in s. 10(1)(a) is termed
'legal advice privilege'. The second category, identified in s. 10(1)(b) is usually referred to as
'litigation privilege'. The prerequisites, and some of the justifications, for the two aspects of the
privilege are not always the same, and must be considered separately.

5. Legal Advice Privilege

Introduction

Legal advice privilege covers confidential communications between a legal adviser and his client
that were made for the purpose of giving or receiving legal advice. The privilege arises whether
the advice relates to contemplated litigation or to entirely non-contentious matters, such as the
drawing up of a will. However, it only operates with regard to *legal* advice. It would not, to take
an extreme example, cover a solicitor's recommendation to his client as to a likely winner in the
Grand National! More realistically, a record of the times of an appointment between solicitor
and client, and how long the appointment lasted for (rather than details of anything that passed
between them during that meeting), even if it involved a communication between lawyer and
client (which itself might not necessarily be the case), would not be covered if, for example, the
prosecution sought to adduce it to establish a defendant's whereabouts at a certain time. This
because the communication was not for the purposes of giving legal advice: *R v Manchester
Crown Court, ex parte Rogers* [1999] 1 WLR 832. Thus, if a defendant ran a defence of alibi with
regard to a robbery committed in London on 1 July, claiming to have been in Edinburgh at that
time, his attendance at the offices of 'Sue, Grabbit and Run' in Harley Street, London, on the
relevant day could be established using the record.

    In *Minter v Priest* [1930] AC 588, Lord Atkin made the important observation that it was the
nature of the comments, rather than the meeting in which they were made, that would decide
whether they were privileged. For example, even if a meeting is specifically held to provide legal
advice to a client, if the terms of discussion drift outside that of legal advice the privilege will
cease to apply.

R v Manchester Crown Court, ex parte Rogers [1999] 1 WLR 832, QBD

Lord Bingham CJ

It is in my judgment important to remind oneself of the well established purpose of legal professional privilege, which is to enable a client to make full disclosure to his legal adviser for the purposes of seeking legal advice without apprehension that anything said by him in seeking advice or to him in giving it may thereafter be subject to disclosure against his will. It is certainly true that in cases such as Balabel v. Air India [1988] Ch. 317, the court has discountenanced a narrow or nit-picking approach to documents and has ruled out an approach which takes a record of a communication sentence by sentence and extends the cloak of privilege to one and withholds it from another. It is none the less true that legal professional privilege applies, and applies only, to communications made for the purpose of seeking and receiving legal advice.

In this case we must consider the function and nature of the documents with which we are concerned. The record of time on an attendance note, on a time sheet or fee record is not in my judgment in any sense a communication. It records nothing which passes between the solicitor and the client and it has nothing to do with obtaining legal advice. It is the same sort of record as might arise if a call were made on a dentist or a bank manager. A record of an appointment made does involve a communication between the client and the solicitor's office but is not in my judgment, without more, to be regarded as made in connection with legal advice. So to hold would extend the scope of legal privilege far beyond its proper sphere, in my view. It is submitted on behalf of the applicant that the doctrine is to be applied on an all or nothing basis, that either a document is wholly entitled to legal professional privilege or none of it. That in my judgment is not so. The proposition is not in my view made good by Great Atlantic Insurance Co. v. Home Insurance Co. [1981] 1 W.L.R. 529. That case concerned a continuous memorandum. It was held that a party could not waive privilege in relation to one part of it without waiving privilege in relation to the whole. The good sense of that ruling is, I think, obvious since to permit such a course would raise an obvious risk of misleading the reader. It therefore was held, and properly held in my view, that a party cannot pick and choose. But that is not the position here. Production is sought of nothing relating to legal advice or the subject matter of legal advice. Any such reference in, for example, an attendance note can be covered up, blacked out or obliterated. The Crown have made it as clear as can be from the outset that they have no wish to go behind the veil which protects the exchanges between the applicant and his professional adviser with regard to his personal affairs. That is something to which the Crown are not entitled and it is something which they do not seek. In my judgment, subject to any necessary obliteration, blacking out or covering up, there is nothing in the documents to which the Crown seek access to which legal professional privilege can apply.

A key question is to decide how 'legal' advice differs from other forms of advice or communication, which are not covered by the privilege. Unfortunately, this is an uncertain area, in which the law is (perhaps necessarily) not always entirely clear. The distinction is particularly important, as lawyers, especially solicitors, often act in non-legal capacities for their clients, sometimes serving, effectively, as their 'man of business'. For example, in the modern era, many solicitors provide financial and investment advice.

To be seen as legal advice, and so to attract privilege, the advice must be given or requested in a 'legal context', according to *Three Rivers District Council v Bank of England* [2005] 1 AC 610. This clearly goes very much further than advice relating to even the most remotely possible litigation or the drawing up of non-contentious but formal legal documents or arrangements. Thus, in the *Three Rivers* case, privilege was held to attach to advice relating to whether the Bank of England had properly carried out the public law duties imposed on it by the Banking Acts of

1979 and 1987, for the purposes of the Bingham Inquiry into the collapse of the Bank of Credit and Commerce International (BCCI). This was despite the fact that the inquiry was inquisitorial (not adversarial) in its operation.

Three Rivers District Council v Bank of England [2005] 1 AC 610, HL

Lord Scott

If a solicitor becomes the client's 'man of business', and some solicitors do, responsible for advising the client on all matters of business, including investment policy, finance policy and other business matters, the advice may lack a relevant legal context. There is, in my opinion, no way of avoiding difficulty in deciding in marginal cases whether the seeking of advice from or the giving of advice by lawyers does or does not take place in a relevant legal context so as to attract legal advice privilege. In cases of doubt the judge called upon to make the decision should ask whether the advice relates to the rights, liabilities, obligations or remedies of the client either under private law or under public law. If it does not, then, in my opinion, legal advice privilege would not apply.

As this suggests, and as Taylor LJ also expressly observed many years earlier in *Balabel v Air India* [1988] Ch 317, the notion of legal advice is interpreted very broadly. The courts will not lightly decide that communications between a lawyer and his client were not made for the purposes of receiving legal advice, as the following comment by Lord Buckmaster also indicates.

Minter v Priest [1930] AC 588, HL

Lord Buckmaster

The relationship of solicitor and client being once established, it is not a necessary conclusion that whatever conversation ensued was protected from disclosure. The conversation to secure this privilege must be such as, within a very wide and generous ambit of interpretation, must be fairly referable to the relationship, but outside that boundary the mere fact that a person speaking is a solicitor, and the person to whom he speaks is his client affords no protection.

More recently, his analysis has been reiterated by Baroness Hale in the *Three Rivers* case.

Three Rivers District Council v Bank of England [2005] 1 AC 610, HL

Baroness Hale

There will always be borderline cases in which it is difficult to decide whether there is or is not a 'legal' context. But much will depend upon whether it is one in which it is reasonable for the client to consult the special professional knowledge and skills of a lawyer, so that the lawyer will be able to give the client sound advice as to what he should do, and just as importantly what he should not do, and how to do it. We want people to obey the law, enter into valid and effective transactions, settle their affairs responsibly when they separate or divorce, make wills which will withstand the challenge of the disappointed, and present their best case before all kinds of court, tribunal and inquiry in an honest and responsible manner.

Nevertheless, as these cases also make clear, there are still limits as to what will be considered as an appropriate legal context. Communications that are clearly outside such limits will not be protected.

Justification for Legal Advice Privilege

Legal professional privilege, especially its legal advice aspect, stretches back at least four centuries. It does not exist because the law attributes special status to lawyers or the confidentiality of their relationships per se. It is traditionally premised on an acceptance of the need for legal assistance in the administration of justice, something that would, it is feared, be threatened without the existence of such a privilege: *Greenough v Gaskell* (1833) 1 Mylne & Keen 103. As Sir George Jessel MR noted in *Anderson v Bank of British Columbia* (1876) 2 CH D 644, the complexity of litigation means that it can often only be properly conducted by professional lawyers and, as a result, it is essential that a layman, in order to pursue his rights, or to defend himself from an improper claim by others, whether criminal or civil, should have recourse to their assistance. This being so, it is equally necessary that he should be able to 'make a clean breast' of matters to his lawyer, so that the latter can do an effective job. More recently, this analysis has been broadly reiterated by the House of Lords in the *Three Rivers* case.

Three Rivers District Council v Bank of England
[2005] 1 AC 610, HL

Lord Scott

But the dicta to which I have referred all have in common the idea that it is necessary in our society, a society in which the restraining and controlling framework is built upon a belief in the rule of law, that communications between clients and lawyers, whereby the clients are hoping for the assistance of the lawyers' legal skills in the management of their (the clients') affairs, should be secure against the possibility of any scrutiny from others, whether the police, the executive, business competitors, inquisitive busybodies or anyone else (see also paras 15.8 to 15.10 of *Zuckerman's Civil Procedure* (2003) where the author refers to the rationale underlying legal advice privilege as 'the rule of law rationale'). I, for my part, subscribe to this idea. It justifies, in my opinion, the retention of legal advice privilege in our law, notwithstanding that as a result cases may sometimes have to be decided in ignorance of relevant probative material.

As will be seen, these traditional justifications are often more relevant to legal advice privilege, rather than litigation privilege, which appears to be justified by other factors as well (see below). Additionally, it might be argued that such justifications are more appropriate to legal advice tendered with regard to possible or actual litigation; for example, in regard to a criminal defendant's defence, or a possible cause of action in negligence, rather than non-contentious business like the drawing up of a will, although such matters are still clearly covered by the privilege. Nevertheless, Lord Rodger has firmly rejected such arguments.

Three Rivers District Council v Bank of England [2005] 1 AC 610, HL

Lord Rodger

Despite its long pedigree the Court of Appeal in this case appear to have been less than enthusias-tic about the very notion of legal advice privilege. In particular, they thought that it was not clear why it should attach to matters such as the conveyance of real property or the drawing up of a will: see [2004] QB 916, 935, para 39, per Lord Phillips of Worth Matravers MR. I do not share these doubts. A client's financial or tax position, or the financial or tax position of members of his family, may well be relevant to the way in which he asks his solicitor to structure a property transaction. Or else, for example, the client may have private worries about his son's ability to fend for himself which explain why he conveys a more valuable property to his son than to his more able daughter. People have a legitimate interest in keeping such matters private. The case for confidentiality is, if anything, even more obvious when it comes to the preparation of a will. Rightly or wrongly, the provisions are often shaped by past relationships, indiscretions, experiences, impressions and mistakes, as well as by jealousies, slights, animosities and affections, which the testator would not wish to have revealed but which he must nevertheless explain if the solicitor is to carry out his wishes. Divulging the provisions during the testator's lifetime or disclosing the reasons for them after the testator's death could often cause incalculable harm and misery. The public interest lies in minimising the risk of that happening.

Criticism of the Privilege

However, in recent years there has been an increase in criticism from legal academics, and even some lawyers, about the scope of the privilege, and the justifications that have traditionally been advanced for its existence. There have been suggestions that it is sometimes abused for nefarious purposes. These critics have frequently called for a radical reappraisal of the whole area, as the next extract shows.

CFH Tapper, 'Privilege, Policy and Principle' (2005) Law Quarterly Review, 181–185

These justifications [for the privilege] are, it is submitted, somewhat unconvincing in modern conditions, both in general and on the particular facts of this case. There is little empirical evi-dence that the availability of legal advice privilege does cause those who would not otherwise have consulted lawyers to do so. Increasing use of accountants for advice about tax avoidance fortifies doubt. It could however well be the case that lawyers believe that it may do so, and this no doubt explains the intervention in the argument by the legal professional bodies in this case. Such attitudes also surface in turf wars between different professions over such matters as statutory exemption on the basis of privilege from obligations to disclose information in relation to money laundering and taxation avoidance schemes. On the facts it seems highly unlikely that the Bank would have abstained from retaining lawyers to assist with the preparation of evidence for sub-mission to the Bingham inquiry were it not for the availability of legal advice privilege. The policy of preservation of privacy in respect of communications with a lawyer as set out by Knight Bruce L.J. in Pearse v Pearse (1846) 1 De G. & Sm. 12 at 28 in a famous passage approved by the House, has a somewhat archaic ring when a large public body consults a large firm of solicitors about a matter where the greatest concern is to reveal as transparently as possible what the conduct and motivation of the public body was in the relevant respect. It hardly accords with current espousal of the principle of freedom of information. It needs also to be remembered that there remains a quite separate obligation upon the lawyer to preserve his client's confidence unless and until required to disclose such information in the public interest in the administration of justice. It is not over cynical to suppose that the privilege is often invoked more to keep secret information about the substance of the case which will assist the other party, and to which he is entitled, than to preserve confidence in the advice which has been requested or received.

 Pause for reflection

Is it right that someone facing serious criminal charges can 'pick the brains' of a lawyer, when considering their defence, without any risk of this being exposed, even if the lawyer becomes so 'professionally embarrassed' by what he has heard that he can no longer act for the client?

Who is Covered by the Privilege?

Historically, the rule applied to all qualified lawyers whether attorneys (a now vanished legal profession), barristers, or solicitors.[1] In some situations, it will also cover their trainees and representatives, such as legal executives; for example, a trainee who attends a police station to advise a suspect. Legal professional privilege can still apply, even if the legal adviser is an employee of the client, such as an 'in house' lawyer working for a corporation, government department or a local authority. This is, of course, provided that the lawyer is engaged in giving legal advice to his employer at the relevant time. It will not apply to communications made in a non-legal capacity, for those legally qualified employees who (as is often the case) have a dual function, and, for example, do work of an executive as well as a legal nature. As Lord Denning noted, if there is a dispute as to which category a communication from an employed lawyer falls into, a trial judge can inspect it to assist him in making a determination: *Alfred Crompton Amusement Machines Ltd. v Commissioners of Customs and Excise* [1972] 2 QB 102. (His views were subsequently upheld by the House of Lords.) Similarly, in *Blackpool Corporation v Locker* [1948] 1 All ER 85, it was held that correspondence with the Minister of Health from a town clerk, who was also a solicitor, was not privileged as it was written when he was acting in his executive rather than legal role.

Alfred Crompton Amusement Machines Ltd v Commissioners of Customs and Excise
[1972] 2 QB 102, CA

Lord Denning MR

They [employed lawyers] are regarded by the law as in every respect in the same position as those who practise on their own account. The only difference is that they act for one client only, and not

---

[1] Lord Chief Baron Gilbert, *The Law of Evidence* (2nd edn, 1760, printed by Catherine Lintot) at 138.

for several clients. They must uphold the same standards of honour and of etiquette. They are subject to the same duties to their client and to the court. They must respect the same confidences. They and their clients have the same privileges. I have myself in my early days settled scores of affidavits of documents for the employers of such legal advisers. I have always proceeded on the footing that the communications between the legal advisers and their employer (who is their client) are the subject of legal professional privilege: and I have never known it questioned. There are many cases in the books of actions against railway companies where privilege has been claimed in this way. The validity of it has never been doubted.

Pause for reflection

In such situations, will it always be easy to distinguish between executive and legal functions?

Once Privileged Always Privileged

Once legal advice privilege attaches to a document it is permanent, even if it was made over a century before, as occurred in *Calcraft v Guest* [1898] 1 QB 759. In this case, the original copies of privileged documents relating to proceedings 110 years earlier, by one of the party's predecessors in title to a fishery, were held to still be covered by privilege when they came into the possession of their opponents (though this did not necessarily apply to copies of the relevant document, as will be seen). Lord Hindley observed that, as a general rule, it could be said that: '…once privileged always privileged. I do not mean to say that privilege cannot be waived, but the mere fact that documents used in previous litigation are held and have not been destroyed does not amount to a waiver of the privilege'.

6. Litigation Privilege

Introduction

The second aspect of legal professional privilege, 'litigation privilege', arises only when litigation is in prospect or pending. This is, of course, unlike 'legal advice privilege', which applies to any advice tendered on a legal matter, whether contentious or not. However, from the moment litigation is contemplated, any communications between the client and his solicitor or (and vitally) between one of them (client or solicitor) and a third party, such as a potential witness, will be privileged, if they come into existence for the sole or dominant purpose of either giving or receiving advice in regard to the pending litigation, or collecting evidence for use in that litigation. This is also unlike legal advice privilege, which does not extend to third parties.

Thus, litigation privilege covers information sought for the purpose of knowing whether the client ought to bring or defend an action, or evidence for the purpose of such an action.

In these circumstances, the client or solicitor cannot be asked what the information that he obtained was. This is the basis for claiming privilege for correspondence with witnesses of fact. For example, correspondence between either a solicitor *or* his client and an eye witness to a traffic collision about how the accident occurred, does not have to be produced, because it is the subject of litigation privilege.

Of course, this merely relates to the correspondence. The general principle that no party has property in a witness obviously still applies. Thus, and for example, if the solicitor of a defendant in a negligence action takes a statement from an eye witness to a road accident, the contents of which are unfavourable to his client, although the statement is privileged, there is nothing to prevent the claimant's solicitor from interviewing the same witness about what they observed, and adducing that witness's evidence at trial.

This principle extends to expert witnesses, such as forensic engineers. The reports generated by these witnesses might be privileged, but the expert is not. Were it otherwise, it might be possible, in a field that had only a small number of specialists, for one party to instruct all the leading experts in the subject, so precluding their availability to an opponent. However, this then raises obvious problems with regard to experts who have initially been consulted by one party to litigation, which party then decides not to call them, but who are then instructed by their opponent.

During the earlier consultation, a variety of communications, chattels, documents and information are likely to have passed between litigant and expert, much of it subject to legal professional privilege. In these situations, as Dunn LJ observed in *Harmony Shipping v Saudi Europe Line* [1979] 1 WLR 1380, the rule is that legal professional privilege attaches to confidential communications between the solicitor and the expert, but it does not attach to the chattels or documents upon which the expert based his opinion, nor to the independent opinion of the expert himself. Again, it is the document, not the facts that it contains, that are privileged.

Unfortunately, this can sometimes present problems, as it is not always easy to distinguish between communications and facts. For example, if a doctor carries out a physical examination of a litigant who has consulted him, what he personally saw and drew expert conclusions from (such as bruises on the litigant's body) is not privileged; but anything that he was told by the client, or the client's solicitors, in privileged circumstances, about the client (for example, that he suffered severe headaches), would attract privilege.

Thus, in *Harmony Shipping*, a handwriting expert had inadvertently given an opinion on whether certain documents were genuine or forgeries to both plaintiffs and defendants. He was professionally embarrassed and the question was whether he was obliged to give evidence under subpoena for the defendants and to produce an allegedly forged document that had been supplied to him for examination by the opposing side.

The Court of Appeal upheld the trial judge's decision that he was. The essence of the decision was that his opinion as to the documents did not depend on information provided to him in privileged circumstances. It was expressed by reference to facts that the expert had personally observed while examining the disputed documents provided to him by solicitors; because these documents were, effectively chattels, rather than confidential communications from or via the solicitor, they could not be the subject of privilege and so withheld. The principle is the same in criminal matters: *R v King* [1983] 77 Cr App R 1. Otherwise, as was noted in *King*, a forger, facing a potential police investigation, could quite legally ensure that none of his (forged) documents could ever be examined, by the simple expedient of sending all of them to his solicitors, so that they could be examined by an expert.

Harmony Shipping v Saudi Europe Line [1979] 1 WLR 1380, CA

Lord Denning MR

The question in this case is whether or not the principle [that there is no property in a witness] applies to expert witnesses. They may have been told the substance of a party's case. They may have been given a great deal of confidential information on it. They may have given advice to the party. Does the rule apply to such a case? Many of the communications between the solicitor and the expert witness will be privileged. They are protected by legal professional privilege. They cannot be communicated to the court except with the consent of the party concerned. That means that a great deal of the communications between the expert witness and the lawyer cannot be given in evidence to the court. If questions are asked about it, then it would be the duty of the judge to protect the witness (and he would) by disallowing any questions which infringed the rule about legal professional privilege … it seems to me that an expert witness falls into the same position as a witness of fact. The court is entitled, in order to ascertain the truth, to have the actual facts which he has observed adduced before it and to have his independent opinion on those facts. … In this particular case the court is entitled to have the independent opinion of the expert witness on those documents and on those facts—excluding, as I have said, any of the other communications which passed when the expert witness was being instructed or employed by the other side.

However, cases such as *Harmony Shipping* and *King* do not support the proposition that a court is also entitled to receive the opinion of an expert, called by an opposing party, that is largely based on material that is itself privileged, or which was provided to the expert in privileged circumstances by that party. Thus, in *R v Davies* [2002] EWCA Crim 85, the appellant's primary defence to a charge of murdering his brother during a drink-fuelled domestic quarrel was diminished responsibility. At trial, the first instance judge ruled that the opinion of a consultant psychiatrist, Dr Cope, who had been instructed by the appellant's solicitors to examine him, should be disclosed to the prosecution, as it was obtained in a doctor/patient rather than a legally privileged relationship. Having seen its conclusions, which were unfavourable to the accused, the prosecution then called Dr Cope to testify for the Crown. She opined that, although the appellant did suffer from an abnormality of mind at the time of the killing, it did not substantially diminish his responsibility for the crime.

The Court of Appeal quickly accepted that the primary purpose of her visit to the defendant was not as part of a doctor/patient relationship, but was instead for litigation purposes. As a result, they concluded that her report should not have been disclosed to the prosecution. However, on its own, this did not resolve the matter, because even if the report had been privileged, it would not have precluded the prosecution from calling her 'blind' and then asking her to give an expert opinion as to the defendant's mental state.

Nevertheless, the appellant argued that he was entitled to object to the doctor giving any evidence at all, because her opinion was partly based on a privileged proof of evidence, prepared by the defendant's lawyers on his instructions, and on what he personally had told her when she visited him in prison, which information was also privileged. As a result, because her opinion was based on such privileged material, it was itself privileged. This argument was accepted by the Court of Appeal, which concluded that, even if Dr Cope's opinion was, in part, based on her personal observation of the defendant, it was also inextricably dependent on the privileged material with which she had been supplied, and so should not have been admitted.

R v Davies [2002] EWCA Crim 85, CA

May LJ

Thus, in both Harmony Shipping and King, the handwriting expert's opinion was expressed by reference to material which was not itself privileged, that is by reference to facts which he himself had observed from documents provided to him by solicitors, for which the solicitor's client could not claim privilege. The court is entitled to have the independent opinion of the expert on such documents and on the actual facts which he has observed in circumstances which were not privileged. But these authorities do not, in our judgment, support the proposition that the court is additionally entitled to have the opinion of an expert which is based on material which is privileged and which is provided to the expert in privileged circumstances.

Rationale for Litigation Privilege

Many of the justifications advanced for the existence of legal advice privilege (see above) overlap with those for litigation privilege, especially where it relates to a lawyer. For example, if a client consults his solicitor with regard to pending litigation, any communications will be covered by both aspects of the privilege. However, as has been seen, this will not invariably be the case, as the privilege can extend to third parties. Litigation privilege is largely a creature of the adversarial system. Its rationale, insofar as it differs from that for legal advice privilege, appears to rest on a belief that, in such proceedings, the right not to reveal some types of communication forms part of the wider concept of a fair trial. It allows lawyers a 'protected' area within which they can safely investigate and prepare a matter for trial. Arguably, the adversarial system could not function properly if litigants and their lawyers knew their investigations and preparations might well be disclosed to the opposing side. For this reason, it is well established that litigation privilege does not survive past the end of the case to which it relates (unlike legal advice privilege).

Three Rivers District Council v Bank of England [2005] 1 AC 610, HL

Lord Rodger

Litigation privilege relates to communications at the stage when litigation is pending or in contemplation. It is based on the idea that legal proceedings take the form of a contest in which each of the opposing parties assembles his own body of evidence and uses it to try to defeat the other, with the judge or jury determining the winner. In such a system each party should be free to prepare his case as fully as possible without the risk that his opponent will be able to recover the material generated by his preparations. In the words of Justice Jackson in Hickman v Taylor (1947) 329 US 495, 516, 'Discovery was hardly intended to enable a learned profession to perform its functions either without wits or on wits borrowed from the adversary.'

Absence in Non-adversarial Proceedings

Because litigation privilege is rooted in the adversarial system, the House of Lords concluded (by a majority), in the case of *In Re L (a minor)* [1997] AC 16, that it did not apply to inquisitorial proceedings. In this case, a baby was admitted to hospital, after ingesting a quantity of metha-done, prescribed to her heroin addicted parents. In the ensuing care proceedings, pursuant to s. 31 of the Children Act 1989, the mother was given leave to disclose the court papers to an expert chemical pathologist. The expert made a number of observations in his report that were distinctly unhelpful for the infant's parents. The police became aware of the report's existence and sought disclosure, with a view to determining if a criminal offence had been committed by either or both of the parents. This was opposed on the grounds that the report was privileged. However, it was held that, as proceedings under Part IV of the 1989 Act were not adversarial, there was no privilege. It was also for this reason that litigation privilege (as opposed to legal advice privilege) did not arise in the *Three Rivers* case; the Bingham Inquiry into the collapse of BCCI, around which the case revolved, took the form of an inquisitorial proceeding, rather than an adversarial one.

In Re L (a minor) [1997] AC 16, HL

Lord Jauncey

I agree with Sir Stephen Brown P. that care proceedings are essentially non-adversarial. Having reached that conclusion, and also that litigation privilege is essentially a creature of adversarial proceedings, it follows that the matter is at large for this House to determine what if any role it has to play in care proceedings. . . . However, in these proceedings, which are primarily non-adversarial and investigative as opposed to adversarial, the notion of a fair trial between opposing parties assumes far less importance. In the latter case the judge must decide the case in favour of one or other party upon such evidence as they choose to adduce, however much he might wish for further evidence on any point. In the former case the judge is concerned to make a decision which is in the best interest of the child in question and may make orders which are sought by no party to the proceedings: sections 10(1)(b), 31(5), 34(5) of the Act. Furthermore, the court has wide powers under rule 4.11(9)(10) of the Rules to require the guardian ad litem to obtain expert reports and other assistance. Thus the court is seeking to reach a decision which will be in the best interests of someone who is not a direct party and is granted investigative powers to achieve that end. In these circumstances I consider that care proceedings under Part IV of the Act are so far removed from normal actions that litigation privilege has no place in relation to reports obtained by a party thereto which could not have been prepared without the leave of the court to disclose documents already filed or to examine the child.

Pending Litigation

If litigation has not already been initiated, how likely must it be to attract litigation privilege? This was explored in *USA v Philip Morris Inc (British American Tobacco (Investments) Ltd intervening)* [2004] 1 CLC 811, in which the court concluded that the mere possibility of litigation occurring at some point in the future did not suffice, nor was a belief that there was a 'distinct possibility' that 'sooner or later' someone would make some kind of legal claim against the defendant, or even a general apprehension about future actions being brought. Litigation must have reasonably been in prospect. Again, this will involve trial judges in making difficult assessments of fact and degree.

USA v Philip Morris Inc (British American Tobacco (Investments) Ltd intervening)
[2004] 1 CLC 811, CA

Moore-Bick J

It has been recognised on many occasions that there is a conflict between the need to enable clients to communicate freely with their legal advisers in relation to litigation and the need to ensure that all relevant material is before the court: see, for example, Lord Wilberforce in Waugh v British Railways Board at pages 531–532 and Lord Simon at pages 535–537. The point at which litigation should be regarded as sufficiently likely for confidential communications between client and his lawyer to attract privilege on this ground therefore involves striking an appropriate balance between these two factors. The requirement that litigation be 'reasonably in prospect' is not in my view satisfied unless the party seeking to claim privilege can show that he was aware of circumstances which rendered litigation between himself and a particular person or class of persons a real likelihood rather than a mere possibility. I am unable to accept that litigation against BATCo itself was reasonably in prospect in 1985 and 1986 when Lovells were first instructed. I quite accept that at that time Mr Cannar thought it a distinct possibility that sooner or later someone might make a claim against BATCo for smoking-related illness, if only because the burgeoning litigation in the US could be expected to provide an example to claimants in other countries, but at that stage no claim had been made or even threatened. The fact that Mr Cannar considered it desirable for BATCo to put its house in order because of a general apprehension of future litigation is not in my view sufficient to entitle it to claim litigation privilege in respect of communications made for that purpose. As time went on, of course, the position changed, but it is sufficient for present purposes to say that I am not persuaded that all communications which Mr Foyle might be asked to disclose in the course of the proposed examination are inevitably privileged on this ground.

It has been argued by some academics that litigation privilege, where it currently exists between expert and client, is inconsistent with the role of an expert as set out in r. 35.3 of the CPR 1998, and should be treated as having been waived once the report of an expert is disclosed. This is on the basis that r. 35.3 of the CPR 1998 invites the court to treat the expert as an independent source of information.[2] However, such an approach has yet to be followed by the courts or Parliament.

 Cross-reference Box

Rule 35.3 provides that an expert has an overriding duty to the court, above and beyond that to the client who has instructed him. It is one aspect of a general attempt in recent years to reduce partisanship in expert witnesses, and a public perception that they are often 'hired guns', willing to sell favourable opinions to whoever is employing them. For more information on this, and on the role of experts generally, go to pp. 494–496.

---

[2] A Edis, 'Privilege and Immunity: Problems of Expert Evidence' (2007) Civil Justice Quarterly, 40–56, at 53.

Documents with Multiple Uses

Many documents are not prepared solely with a view to potential litigation, but have multiple uses. In these situations, the document will only be privileged if the 'dominant purpose' for which it was brought into existence was to be used for the purpose of obtaining legal advice or being employed by lawyers in possible or probable litigation: *Waugh Appellant v British Railways Board Respondents* [1979] 3 WLR 150.

In this case, the plaintiff's husband, a train driver and employee of the defendants, had been killed by a collision between two locomotives. Very shortly afterwards, an accident report, termed an internal inquiry report, had been prepared by two of the Board's officers. It contained a number of statements, made by several witnesses to the incident, shortly after it occurred and was potentially extremely important (probably the best) evidence in the plaintiff's negligence action. However, the BRB claimed it was a privileged document. On examination, it appeared that such reports had two purposes; they were prepared, in part, to facilitate obtaining legal advice about any liability. Nevertheless, they were also commissioned so that railway safety might be improved and lessons learnt from any incidents.

The House of Lords concluded that, in this case, the dominant purpose of the document was the investigation of the accident that had occurred, and the making of recommendations by which similar accidents could be prevented in the future. Its legal function was subsidiary to this purpose, or, at the least, only of equal importance. Consequently, it was not deemed to privileged; the situation would have been different if its dominant purpose had been to advise the Railways Board about liability in any potential legal action for negligence. Ultimately, such a matter will be a question of fact for the trial judge to determine. For this reason, it is unlikely that, in finely balanced cases, the Court of Appeal will substitute its own judgment for that made at first instance.

Waugh v British Railways Board Respondents
[1979] 3 WLR 150, HL

Lord Wilberforce

The whole question came to be considered by the High Court of Australia in 1976: Grant v. Downs, 135 C.L.R. 674. This case involved reports which had ' as one of the material purposes for their preparation' submission to legal advisers in the event of litigation. It was held that privilege could not be claimed. In the joint judgment of Stephen, Mason and Murphy JJ., in which the English cases I have mentioned were discussed and analysed, it was held that ' legal professional privilege' must be confined to documents brought into existence for the sole purpose of submission to legal advisers for advice or use in legal proceedings. Jacobs J. put the test in the form of a question, at p. 692: '...does the purpose'—in the sense of intention, the intended use—'of supplying the material to the legal adviser account for the existence of the material?' Barwick C.J. stated it in terms of 'dominant' purpose. This is closely in line with the opinion of Lord Denning M.R. in the present case that the privilege extends only to material prepared 'wholly or mainly for the purpose of preparing [the defendant's] case.' The High Court of Australia and Lord Denning M.R. agree in refusing to follow Birmingham and Midland Motor Omnibus Co. Ltd. v. London and North Western Railway Co. [1913] 3 K.B. 850 and Ogden v. London Electric Railway Co., 49 T.L.R. 542, as generally understood. My Lords, for the reasons I have given, when discussing the case in principle, I too would refuse to follow those cases. It appears to me that unless the purpose of submission to the legal adviser in view of litigation is at least the dominant purpose for which the relevant document was prepared, the reasons which require privilege to be extended to it cannot apply. On the other hand to hold that the purpose, as above, must be the sole purpose would, apart from difficulties of proof, in my opinion, be too strict a requirement, and would confine the privilege too narrowly: as to this I agree with Barwick C.J. in Grant v. Downs, 135 C.L.R. 674, and in substance with Lord Denning M.R. While fully respecting the necessity for the Lords Justices to follow previous decisions of their court, I find myself in the result in agreement with Lord Denning's judgment.

Where Legal Professional Privilege will not Apply

Even where the prerequisites for legal professional privilege have been established, the privilege is not quite untrammelled. In particular, communications between a lawyer and his client will not be privileged if the advice was sought with a view to facilitating the commission of a crime. This applies whether or not the lawyer was a party to the crime, or knew for what purpose the advice was being sought. Thus, in the historic case of *R v Cox and Railton* (1884) 15 Cox CC 611, a client consulted his solicitor with a view to drawing up a fraudulent bill of sale. There was held to be no privilege to prevent the Crown calling the solicitor to testify that the defendant had consulted to give evidence of the relevant transaction. Similarly, s. 10(2) of PCEA 1984 notes that items held with the intention of furthering a criminal purpose are not subject to legal privilege.

R v Cox and Railton (1884–5) LR 14 QBD 153, CCR

Grove J

We must take it, after the verdict of the jury, that so far as the two defendants, Railton and Cox, were concerned, their communication with Mr. Goodman was a step preparatory to the commission of a criminal offence, namely, a conspiracy to defraud. The conduct of Mr. Goodman, the solicitor, appears to have been unobjectionable. He was consulted in the common course of business, and gave a proper opinion in good faith. The question, therefore is, whether, if a client applies to a legal adviser for advice intended to facilitate or to guide the client in the commission of a crime or fraud, the legal adviser being ignorant of the purpose for which his advice is wanted, the communication between the two is privileged? We expressed our opinion at the end of the argument that no such privilege existed. If it did, the result would be that a man intending to commit treason or murder might safely take legal advice for the purpose of enabling himself to do so with impunity, and that the solicitor to whom the application was made would not be at liberty to give information against his client for the purpose of frustrating his criminal purpose. Consequences so monstrous reduce to an absurdity any principle or rule in which they are involved.

Nevertheless, the courts will not lightly set aside privilege on this ground. As Stephen J observed in the same case, it ought to be exercised with the greatest care, so that defendants are not hampered when making their defences. For example, if a lawyer merely warns his client that certain conduct, if pursued, might result in prosecution, this will not lead to the privilege being lost: *Butler v Board of Trade* [1971] Ch 680. Similarly, it is not enough if the legal advice was sought by a party with a view to knowing what their legal liabilities might be were they to commit a civil wrong (rather than a crime), such as a tort or breach of contract, as was unavailingly suggested by the plaintiffs in the following case, and firmly rejected by Goff J.

Crescent Farm (Sidcup) Sports Ltd v Sterling Offices Ltd
[1972] Ch 553, HC

Goff J

I do not consider the principle requires any extension. On the contrary, I think the wide submission of the plaintiffs would endanger the whole basis of legal professional privilege. It is clear that parties must be at liberty to take advice as to the ambit of their contractual obligations and liabilities in tort and what liability they will incur whether in contract or tort by a proposed course of action without thereby in every case losing professional privilege. I agree that fraud in this connection is not limited to the tort of deceit and includes all forms of fraud and dishonesty such as fraudulent breach of trust, fraudulent conspiracy, trickery and sham contrivances, but I cannot feel that the tort of inducing a breach of contract or the narrow form of conspiracy pleaded in this case come within that ambit.

However, and by contrast, it should be noted that in *Barclays Bank PLC v Eustice* [1995] 1 WLR 1238, the privilege was held not to apply to legal advice given with regard to an assignment of real estate, designed to defeat a creditor, and described by the Court of Appeal as 'iniquitous', when the creditor sought, pursuant to s. 423 of the Insolvency Act 1986, that the transactions be declared void and unenforceable.

The fraud/crime exception applies to both aspects of legal professional privilege (that is, legal advice and litigation privilege), and can operate even if litigation has already begun: *Kuwait Airways Corporation v Iraqi Airways Co (No 6)* [2005] 1 WLR 2734. In this case, the defendant had, allegedly, communicated with their legal advisers with a view to committing systematic perjury, so as to deceive the court into resolving issues of state immunity and liability for wrongful interference in its favour, in earlier actions arising out of the Gulf War of 1991. The Court of Appeal upheld the trial judge's decision to apply the fraud exception to the communications and to order their production for inspection.

Kuwait Airways Corporation v Iraqi Airways Co (No 6)
[2005] 1 WLR 2734, CA

Longmore LJ

These two cases (together with the Hallinan case [2005] 1 WLR 766) show that the fraud exception can in principle apply even when litigation has begun with the result that privilege will not attach to documents which further the fraud or the criminal purpose. They also show that courts will be cautious about ordering disclosure or inspection of such documents. That caution has two aspects: (1) it may be unfair to a defendant to make such an order if all that is shown on the evidence is a prima facie case which may turn out on full investigation to be incorrect and (2) it may be unfair in what Glidewell LJ in the Snaresbrook case [1988] QB 532, 538 called the ordinary run of cases (such as cross-allegations of assault or drivers falsely saying they were driving on the correct side of the road) to order disclosure and inspection merely because communications with a party's solicitors are 'untrue and would, if acted upon, lead to the commission of the crime of perjury'—per Lord Goff of Chieveley in R v Central Criminal Court, Ex p Francis & Francis [1989] AC 346, 397. These two reasons for caution are, of course, somewhat interdependent. If all one has is disputed versions of events, it will be difficult to say that there is even a prima facie case of fraud. This will be particularly so if the disputed version of events is the very same issue that is to be tried in the proceedings. If, however, the evidence of crime or fraud is freestanding and independent and particularly if its evaluation 'does not require any judgment to be reached in relation to the issues to be tried' (per Rose LJ in the Hallinan case [2005] 1 WLR 766, 771), it may be perfectly possible, even on a prima facie case basis, to decide whether the fraud exception applies. It is significant that in Chandler v Church 137 NLJ 451 where there was only prima facie evidence of fraud and the fraud was alleged in relation to the issues that had to be tried, Hoffmann J refused to order disclosure. By contrast, in Dubai Aluminium Co Ltd v Al-Alawi [1999] 1 WLR 1964, 1968, where the alleged fraud did relate to issues to be tried on the application to discharge the search and seizure order and the freezing injunction, Rix J (following Barclays Bank plc v Eustice [1995] 1 WLR 1238, 1249) thought that before disclosure was ordered there should be a strong prima facie case of criminal or fraudulent conduct; he held that, on the facts, there was. He therefore ordered disclosure.

At one time, it was thought that the privilege would always yield to the need to prove the innocence of an accused man. Thus, in *R v Barton* [1972] 2 All ER 1192, Caulfield J observed that he could not: '. . . conceive that our law would permit a solicitor or other person to screen from a jury information which, if disclosed. . . would perhaps enable a man either to establish his innocence or to resist an allegation made by the crown'. This analysis was repeated in *R v Ataou* [1988] 2 All ER 321.

However, in the light of *R v Derby Magistrates' Court, ex p B* [1996] 1 AC 487, this principle no longer applies, the privilege being absolute, even in such circumstances. In this case, a defendant confessed to a murder, but subsequently retracted his confession at trial, and blamed his stepfather for the killing. He was acquitted, and the stepfather was later charged with the same murder. At committal proceedings, the stepson gave evidence for the prosecution, but refused to divulge the contents of the instructions he had given to the solicitors who had represented him at his own trial for murder. The magistrates decided that the defendant's need to make his defence, and establish his innocence, outweighed the stepson's legal advice privilege, and ordered that the instructions be produced by means of a witness summons. However, the House of Lords quashed the magistrates' decision to compel production. Lord Taylor observed that *Barton* and *Ataou* should be viewed as overruled and that: '. . . no exception should be allowed to the absolute nature of legal professional privilege'.

Arguably, this analysis might be challenged at a future date, at least in some circumstances, as being incompatible with a defendant's rights under Article 6 of the ECHR. If vital evidence was withheld from a tribunal by dint of such a privilege, it might be said that the accused person had not received a fair trial. It can also be noted that, although absolute under English common law, some other jurisdictions, such as Canada, have adopted a different approach to dealing with such situations, allowing a 'balancing' of the arguments for and against disclosure by a trial judge (as occurs with PII claims in England). *Derby Magistrates' Court* also establishes a clear distinction between privilege and PII, the latter (effectively) always yielding to the need to establish a criminal defendant's innocence, unlike the former.

R v Derby Magistrates' Court, ex p B [1996] AC 487, HL

Lord Taylor CJ

The client must be sure that what he tells his lawyer in confidence will never be revealed without his consent. Legal professional privilege is thus much more than an ordinary rule of evidence, limited in its application to the facts of a particular case. It is a fundamental condition on which the administration of justice as a whole rests.

Legal professional privilege can, of course, be qualified by parliamentary statute. However, for this to occur, in the post-Human Rights Act 1998 era, the statute must override the privilege by express words or 'necessary implication', not simply because it might be deemed to be more reasonable or sensible for it to do so: *R (Morgan Grenfell & Co Ltd) v Special Commissioners of Income Tax* [2003] 1 AC 563. Thus, and for example, the Solicitors Act 1974 allows the Law Society to investigate the conduct of a solicitor by accessing privileged documents in his client's files, even if the client objects, as does the Taxes Management Act of 1970.

R (Morgan Grenfell & Co Ltd) v Special Commissioners of Income Tax [2003] 1 AC 563, HL

Buxton LJ

We are therefore driven to conclude that the provisions of the 1970 [Taxes Management] Act taken as a whole do demonstrate a premise that the rule of LPP is excluded from them save where it is expressly incorporated. Applying then the approach in B's case [2000] 2 AC 428 referred to in paragraph 16 above, it is a necessary implication from that premise that arguments based on LPP cannot be used to resist an application for disclosure under section 20(1) of the 1970 Act.

Waiving the Privilege

As Lord Hindley's comment in *Calcraft v Guest* suggests, and as with the privilege against self-incrimination, the client (but only the client) can waive their right to claim legal professional privilege. However, once the privilege has been waived it is lost, and cannot be reasserted at a subsequent point by the client: *Lillicrap v Nalder & Sons* [1993] 1 All ER 724. As this case also noted, waiver can, in some very exceptional situations, be implied. By far the most (if not the only) important situation in this regard, occurs where a client sues his solicitor; in these circumstances, he impliedly waives his claim to privilege in relation to all matters that were relevant to any issue in the proceedings between them.

It is not normally possible to waive privilege selectively, for example, with regard to part of a privileged document (or communication), unless 'severance' of the document is possible, in those cases where it deals with several entirely different matters. In these situations, and as with partially privileged documents, those parts that preserve privilege can be removed, covered up or blacked out: *R v Manchester Crown Court, ex parte Rogers* [1999] 1 WLR 832. Normally, if a litigant wishes to use a privileged document (or communication), he must accept that the entire document will cease to be protected by privilege. Thus, if he employs an expert who produces a 'mixed' report (from his perspective), he cannot cite the report selectively during negotiations for a settlement of the action, simply referring to the favourable parts and holding back the unhelpful sections when the other party asks to see them.

Similarly, once a defendant in a criminal matter adduces evidence as to why his solicitor advised him not to answer police questions when interviewed prior to being charged, with a view to avoiding a negative inference being drawn from his silence during questioning under s. 34 of the Criminal Justice and Public Order Act 1994, the privilege with regard to that conversation is lost. This is significant, as, although it seems that a defendant can state that he remained silent on legal advice without waiving privilege, this alone is not usually enough to prevent an adverse inference from being drawn. The accused person will usually have to go into the particulars of the advice he was given if this is to occur, something that *will* normally result in the privilege being waived. This remains the case even if the advice is elicited in the course of a voir dire, but is not repeated in the substantive trial: *R v Bowden* (1999) 1 WLR 823. As Lord Bingham CJ observed in this case: 'The defendant cannot at any stage have his cake and eat it.'

 Cross-reference Box

At common law, no negative inferences could be drawn from a defendant's failure to answer police questions when interviewed at a police station. This changed as a result of the 1994 Act. However, an inference can only be drawn if an accused person failed to answer questions without reasonable cause. For more details on this topic go to p. 354.

More recently, the approach adopted in *Bowden* has been reiterated by the Court of Appeal in *R v Loizou (Lisa Joy)* [2006] EWCA Crim 1719. (There is still some doubt as to whether the prosecution, in such cases, can look at all of the defence solicitor's notes from the time of the interview.) This is particularly important because it appears that the courts are reluctant to accept non-defendant evidence as being sufficient to prevent an adverse inference from being drawn. Thus, in *R v Ullah* [2007] EWCA Crim 798, the Court of Appeal concluded that post-conviction psychiatric evidence that a defendant failed to give evidence in court because he suffered from a severe social phobia, unsupported by his own testimony, would not have been enough to prevent an adverse inference from being drawn.

R v Bowden (1999) 1 WLR 823, CA

Lord Bingham CJ

If, at trial, the defendant or his solicitor gives evidence not merely of the defendant's refusal to answer pre-trial questions on legal advice but also of the grounds on which such advice was given, or if (as here) the defence elicit evidence at trial of a statement made by a defendant or his solicitor pre-trial of the grounds on which legal advice had been given to answer no questions, the defendant voluntarily withdraws the veil of privilege which would otherwise protect confidential communications between his legal adviser and himself, and having done so he cannot resist questioning directed to the nature of that advice and the factual premises on which it had been based.

Privileged Material Obtained by an Opponent

The privilege protecting communications between lawyer and client relates to the production of the relevant document, not to its admissibility in evidence per se, let alone to secondary evidence of its contents. As a result, if a party comes into possession of an opponent's privileged documents, or obtains secondary evidence of them or of other privileged conversations, such evidence, assuming that it is relevant, will not *automatically* be rendered inadmissible at trial simply because it was privileged, though it might be excluded for another reason: *Calcraft v Guest* [1898] 1 QB 759. In this, privilege differs from public interest immunity (PII), where secondary evidence of a document that qualifies for PII will never be allowed.

In practice, much will depend on the circumstances in which the documents were obtained; in particular, was it improper in any way? For example, in *R v Tompkins* [1978] 67 Cr App R 181, it became an issue at trial as to whether a stolen stereo had a loose control button (as its loser stated). The appellant passed a note to his counsel, while in court, admitting that he had glued the button firmly back on to the stereo. This was subsequently dropped on the floor of the court, where it was recovered by a clerk working for the prosecution, and handed to prosecuting counsel, who then showed it to the defendant and asked in cross-examination whether he had tried to glue the button back on to the stereo. The defendant admitted that he had, and was convicted.

On appeal it was argued that the use of information obtained in breach of legal professional privilege was contrary to natural justice and should not have been allowed. However, this was rejected by the Court of Appeal, which observed that: 'The note, though clearly privileged from production, was admissible in evidence once it was in the possession of the prosecution.' Of course, had someone working for the prosecution deliberately gone through defence counsel's bundle, looking for such material, the trial judge would almost certainly have excluded the evidence. Today, as *R v Cottrill* [1997] Crim LR 56 suggests, this would normally be under s. 78 of the PCEA 1984, the provision by which the eavesdropped conversation in *R v Grant* [2006] QB 60 was also excluded.

In civil cases, if a party comes into possession of privileged documents improperly, or through inadvertence, they are also prima facie admissible under the principle in *Calcraft v Guest*. However, if he acts promptly, the opposing side can, traditionally, seek an injunction from the court ordering the return of any originals and preventing the use of any copies of them in litigation, where they have been obtained in an improper manner, under the principle set out in *Ashburton v Pape* [1913] 2 Ch 469. In this case, the defendant had obtained letters from the plaintiff to his (the plaintiff's) solicitor, which were covered by legal professional privilege, via nefarious means. Given that there is now a general, albeit rarely exercised, discretion to exclude improperly obtained evidence under r. 32.2 of the CPR 1998, as elucidated by *Jones v University of Warwick* [2003] 1 WLR 954, use of such documents could, presumably, also now be excluded at trial, even if there had been no application in advance.

Ashburton v Pape [1913] 2 Ch 469, CA

Swinfern Eady LJ

Then objection was raised in the present case by reason of the fact that it is said that Pape, who now has copies of the letters, might wish to give them in evidence in certain bankruptcy proceedings, and although the original letters are privileged from production he has possession of the copies and could give them as secondary evidence of the contents of the letters, and, therefore, ought not to be ordered either to give them up or to be restrained from divulging their contents. There is here a confusion between the right to restrain a person from divulging confidential information and the right to give secondary evidence of documents where the originals are privileged from production, if the party has such secondary evidence in his possession. The cases are entirely separate and distinct. If a person were to steal a deed, nevertheless in any dispute to which it was relevant the original deed might be given in evidence by him at the trial. It would be no objection to the admissibility of the deed in evidence to say you ought not to have possession of it. His unlawful possession would not affect the admissibility of the deed in evidence if otherwise admissible. So again with regard to any copy he had. If he was unable to obtain or compel production of the original because it was privileged, if he had a copy in his possession it would be admissible as secondary evidence. The fact, however, that a document, whether original or copy, is admissible in evidence is no answer to the demand of the lawful owner for the delivery up of the document, and no answer to an application by the lawful owner of confidential information to restrain it from being published or copied.

Cross-reference Box

Until the advent of the CPR 1998 it was generally felt that there was no judicial discretion in a civil case to exclude evidence that was relevant and admissible, no matter how it had been obtained. This is no longer the case, albeit that it seems that the courts will not exercise their r. 32.2 power other than in exceptional circumstances. For more on this topic go to pp. 66–69.

In the modern era, where a 'cards on the table' approach to civil litigation means that there is an enhanced risk that privileged documents will accidentally be disclosed to an opposing party, without any impropriety on their part, some protection is also provided by r. 31.20 of the CPR 1998.

Rule 31.20 of the CPR 1998

Where a party inadvertently allows a privileged document to be inspected, the party who has inspected the document may use it or its contents only with the permission of the court.

7. Without Prejudice Correspondence

Introduction

When a civil dispute arises, attempts are often made by the parties to settle matters before it comes to trial. Frequently, this will involve correspondence between the litigants (or potential litigants). The existence of the 'without prejudice' privilege means that such negotiations, provided that they entail a genuine attempt at producing a settlement, are privileged from subsequently being produced in court as evidence. Thus, if the parties involved in the negotiations fail to reach an acceptable resolution to their dispute, any concessions or proposals they may have made during negotiations cannot be disclosed at trial as evidence of the strength or weakness of their respective cases: *Cutts v Head* [1984] 1 All ER 597.

For example, the defendant in a road accident case, who is disputing liability, can make an offer to the claimant without being prevented from denying liability at trial or worrying that the claimant will adduce the letter in which he made the offer as indicative that he had accepted responsibility for what occurred. It is not necessary for litigation to have commenced for the privilege to attach to communications aimed at resolving such a dispute, it also applies to negotiations prior to the service of a writ: *Rabin v Mendoza* [1954] 1 WLR 271. Although such negotiations are nearly always expressly headed as being 'without prejudice' in the relevant documentation, it is not necessary to use the label for the privilege to attach, *provided* that the communication was a genuine attempt at producing a settlement.

Rush & Tompkins Ltd v GLC (1989) AC 1280, HL

Lord Griffiths

The rule applies to exclude all negotiations genuinely aimed at settlement whether oral or in writing from being given in evidence. A competent solicitor will always head any negotiating correspondence 'without prejudice' to make clear beyond doubt that in the even of the negotiations being unsuccessful they are not to be referred to at the subsequent trial. However, the application of the rule is not dependent upon the use of the phrase 'without prejudice' and if it is clear from the surrounding circumstances that the parties were seeking to compromise the action, evidence of the content of those negotiations will, as a general rule, not be admissible at the trial and cannot be used to establish an admission or partial admission.

 Pause for reflection

Is it right that a party to litigation should be able to deny any liability at trial having impliedly admitted responsibility in a 'without prejudice' communication?

Conversely, however, simply adding the label 'without prejudice' to a document will not necessarily be conclusive as to whether it is privileged on this ground; the courts can still examine the document to see if it was a genuine attempt at reaching a negotiated settlement, and so a true without prejudice communication: *Cheddar Valley Engineering Ltd v Chaddlewood Homes Ltd* [1992] 1 WLR 820. For example, this will be the case if there is no existing dispute at the time the document was written, and any admissions were made prior to the start of bona fide negotiations by the parties. To take an extreme example: if, many years after a debtor had failed to repay money, recovery of which was long statute-barred under the Limitation Act 1980 and had been written off by the lender, he chose to write in mocking terms, 'out of the blue,' to his creditor, acknowledging the debt, in a letter headed 'without prejudice', the creditor would not be precluded from adducing the document as evidence of the debt (something that would preclude a Limitation Act defence).[3]

Indeed, in *Bradford & Bingley plc v Rashid* [2006] 1 WLR 2006, the facts were only slightly less extreme. The defendant had disappeared for a decade owing more than £15,000 to the claimants, after the forced resale of a mortgaged property during a property slump. He subsequently contacted them via an advice centre, offering to pay a small part of the debt in full and final settlement of the whole. The correspondence was not labelled 'without prejudice', though, as has already been noted, this would not necessarily have precluded a claim to privilege. The question arose as to whether it constituted an acknowledgement of the debt for the purposes of the Limitation Act 1980 (without which the debt would be time barred and irrecoverable). It was held that the correspondence could be adduced as the without prejudice privilege did not apply to apparently open communications designed to discuss the repayment of an admitted liability, rather than to negotiate and compromise a disputed liability.

Bradford & Bingley plc v Rashid [2006] 1 WLR 2066, HL

Lord Brown

In my opinion the without prejudice rule has no application to apparently open communications, such as those here, designed only to discuss the repayment of an admitted liability rather than to negotiate and compromise a disputed liability. I find it impossible to regard the correspondence here as constituting 'negotiations genuinely aimed at settlement' (Lord Griffiths in Rush & Tompkins Ltd v Greater London Council [1989] AC 1280, 1299) or 'an attempt to compromise actual or impending litigation' (Sir Robert Megarry V-C in Chocoladefabriken Lindt & Sprungli AG v Nestlé Co Ltd [1978] RPC 287). Nor does the underlying public policy justification for the rule appear to have any application in circumstances such as these. That justification, as Oliver LJ observed in Cutts v Head [1984] Ch 290, 306 (see para 62 above) 'essentially rests on the desirability of preventing statements or offers made in the course of negotiations for settlement being brought before the court of trial as admissions on the question of liability'. No 'statements or offers' were made here with a view to settling a dispute. Since the debt was admitted, there was no dispute. As Mr Fenwick aptly put it in argument, Mr Rashid was simply asking for a concession; he was not giving one.

Justification for the Privilege

The primary justification for the existence of such a privilege is founded in the public interest that litigation be brought to an early and mutually acceptable solution, without the disruption, delay, expense and vexation occasioned by a matter going for trial. To this end, the privilege allows parties to negotiate freely, without fear of subsequent prejudice. However, it has also been argued that, in some situations at least, a secondary justification of the privilege is that the parties have impliedly agreed between themselves that such communications should be protected from exposure.

---

[3] See generally, S Magintharan, 'Lack of Dispute and its Effect on Without Prejudice Privilege in Common Law and s.23 of the Evidence Acts of Singapore and Malaysia' [2006] Civil Justice Quarterly, 367–379.

Cutts v Head [1984] Ch 290, CA

Oliver LJ

That the rule rests, at least in part, upon public policy is clear from many authorities, and the convenient starting point of the inquiry is the nature of the underlying policy. It is that parties should be encouraged so far as possible to settle their disputes without resort to litigation and should not be discouraged by the knowledge that anything that is said in the course of such negotiations (and that includes, of course, as much the failure to reply to an offer as an actual reply) may be used to their prejudice in the course of the proceedings. They should, as it was expressed by Clauson J. in Scott Paper Co. v. Drayton Paper Works Ltd. (1927) 44 R.P.C. 151, 156, be encouraged fully and frankly to put their cards on the table... The public policy justification, in truth, essentially rests on the desirability of preventing statements or offers made in the course of negotiations for settlement being brought before the court of trial as an admission on the question of liability.

Exceptions to the Privilege

However, and very importantly, the privilege, even where it applies, is not absolute; there are several situations where 'without prejudice' communications can be adduced in court. These include a disclosure to show that a concluded agreement has been reached: *Walker v Wilsher* [1889] 23 QBD 335. Additionally, where the documentation is headed 'without prejudice save as to costs', it can, subsequently, be adduced on the issue of litigation costs (rather than liability). For example, if an offer made to a claimant in correspondence, or under Part 36 of the CPR 1998, is rejected, and the matter goes for trial, and the sum awarded at trial to the claimant does not exceed that offered earlier, the communication can be adduced by the defendant to argue that the legal costs incurred since that time should be borne by the claimant, even though he has won on the issue of liability. It appears that it may well be necessary for the label on the documentation to have the words 'save as to costs' (or their equivalent) for this to occur. An offer made in a normal 'without prejudice' communication cannot be adduced for this purpose: *Reed Executive PLC v Reed Business Information Ltd* [2004] EWCA Civ 887. The justification for this requirement may be questioned.

Nevertheless, the courts do not lightly decide that the privilege should not apply. In *Unilever v Proctor & Gamble* [1999] 2 All ER 691, Laddie J reviewed the operation of the 'without prejudice' rule in some detail. He rejected the suggestion that an allegation of infringement of a patent made by Proctor & Gamble at a 'without prejudice' meeting could subsequently be relied upon by Unilever to found a claim for a declaration that Unilever was not breaching the patent. The essence of his decision was that the rule should be interpreted broadly to cover such situations.

Unilever v Proctor & Gamble [1999] 2 All ER 691, HC

Laddie J

...the spread of the without prejudice umbrella should be wide enough to cover all statements made bona fide without prejudice by each party touching on the strengths or weaknesses of its own and its opponent's case and any valuation, for whatever reason, it places on its or its opponent's rights...the without prejudice rule covers not only admissions but assertions also.

Section 10 of the Contempt of Court Act 1981

Traditionally, journalists have been very reluctant to disclose the identity of their sources, for fear of landing such individuals in trouble, something that, in the long run, is also likely to result in their sources 'drying up', as people, fearing disclosure, become nervous about passing on information. Furthermore, it has frequently been argued that, in a democratic society, a free press is vital to keep the public informed, and, in turn, that this requires that information can be provided with a reasonable assurance of confidentiality from the journalist receiving it. As Lord Wolf observed in *Ashworth Hospital Authority v MGN Ltd.* [2002] 1 WLR 2033, forcing journalists to disclose their sources has a 'chilling effect' on the freedom of the press.

At common law, the journalist's relationship with his sources was not covered by privilege, and there was no absolute right allowing him to withhold the identity of an informant. He was not in the same position as a lawyer who receives information from a client while providing legal advice, nor was he in a superior position to the doctor who receives confidential information from a patient or the priest who hears a confession. However, in many situations, and as with information passing between a priest and penitent in the confessional, a journalist could argue that the public interest should allow him to withhold the identity of his informant, so relying on principles of public interest immunity to persuade the court not to require him to disclose the relevant information. This was a claim to which the courts were generally sympathetic. As Lord Wilberforce observed in *BSC v Granada Television Ltd* [1981] 1 All ER 417, the courts should not compel disclosure of sources unless it was necessary in the interests of justice; he also noted that the public interest in the free flow of information would vary from case to case. Normally, a relatively strong justification would be required before disclosure was ordered.

Nevertheless, there remained some uncertainty about how far this doctrine would apply in any given case. As a result, Parliament intervened by providing for a qualified statutory privilege in s. 10 of the Contempt of Court Act 1981. As this is a qualified privilege, it could, almost as properly, have been addressed with Public Interest Immunity (see chapter 12).

Section 10 of the Contempt of Court Act 1981

No court may require a person to disclose, nor is any person guilty of contempt of court for refusing to disclose, the source of information contained in a publication for which he is responsible, unless it be established to the satisfaction of the court that disclosure is necessary in the interests of justice or national security or for the prevention of disorder or crime.

 Pause for reflection

Given that the current trend with regard to privilege is to treat it as prima facie absolute, might it be argued that a qualified privilege is an oxymoron and that s. 10 of the 1981 Act is really just a statutory rendering of PII principles, or would this be an exaggeration?

Under s. 10, the onus is on the party seeking disclosure to persuade the court that it is necessary: *Secretary of State for Defence v Guardian Newspapers Ltd.* [1984] 3 WLR 986. This inevitably involves a balancing act, with competing factors having to be weighed up by the court, as can be seen from the facts of *Ashworth Hospital Authority v MGN Ltd.* [2002] 1 WLR 2033. In this case, the defendant's newspaper, the 'Daily Mirror', published an article quoting verbatim extracts from the records of a notorious convicted murderer (the moors murderer, Ian Brady) being held in the claimant's secure psychiatric hospital. It was apparent that the records must have been extracted from the hospital's computer by an employee, who would, of course, be in breach of his duty of confidentiality in doing so, and thus also have committed a civil wrong. However, an internal inquiry conducted by the hospital failed to identify the relevant employee.

A High Court judge ordered that the identity of the informant be disclosed. This decision was appealed by the defendant, but upheld by the Court of Appeal. The matter went for further appeal to the House of Lords, which again upheld the first instance judge's decision. The hospital's need to protect the integrity of its records, something that had a major potential impact on both security and staff/patient morale, and so to be able to identify and punish the informant (via dismissal), made disclosure a necessary and proportionate response on the facts of the case.

Ashworth Hospital Authority v MGN Ltd [2002] 1 WLR 2033, HL

Lord Woolf CJ

The fact that journalists' sources can be reasonably confident that their identity will not be disclosed makes a significant contribution to the ability of the press to perform their role in society of making information available to the public. It is for this reason that it is well established now that the courts will normally protect journalists' sources from identification. However, the protection is not unqualified. Both section 10 and Article 10 recognise this. This leads to the difficult issue at the heart of this appeal, namely whether the disclosure ordered was necessary and not disproportionate.... The care of patients at Ashworth is fraught with difficulty and danger. The disclosure of the patient's records increases that difficulty and danger and to deter the same or similar wrongdoing in the future it was essential that the source should be identified and punished. This was what made the orders to disclose necessary and proportionate and justified. The fact that Ian Brady had himself disclosed his medical history did not detract from the need to prevent staff from revealing medical records of patients. Ian Brady's conduct did not damage the integrity of Ashworth's patient's records. The source's disclosure was wholly inconsistent with the security of the records and the disclosure was made worse because it was purchased by a cash payment.

However, this is yet another evidential area where it could be argued that the combined impact of the ECHR and the Human Rights Act 1998 might have an impact on the law. Article 10 of the ECHR, in particular, provides, that everyone has the right to freedom of expression and to receive and impart information.

Article 10 of the ECHR

1. Everyone has the right to freedom of expression. This right shall include freedom to hold opinions and to receive and impart information and ideas without interference by public authority and regardless of frontiers. This article shall not prevent States from requiring the licensing of broadcasting, television or cinema enterprises.

2. The exercise of these freedoms, since it carries with it duties and responsibilities, may be subject to such formalities, conditions, restrictions or penalties as are prescribed by law and are necessary in a democratic society, in the interests of national security, territorial integrity or public safety, for the prevention of disorder or crime, for the protection of health or morals, for the protection of the reputation or rights of others, for preventing the disclosure of information received in confidence, or for maintaining the authority and impartiality of the judiciary.

In theory, there is nothing to prevent a journalist claiming that his Article 10(1) rights have been violated if he is ordered to disclose a source, on the basis that it interferes with his right to receive information. However, and as with so many areas of the Convention, the European Court of Human Rights (ECtHR) does not take an all or nothing approach to such matters, especially as Article 10(2) expressly provides a number of caveats to the general principles set out in Article 10(1). As a result, the ECtHR allows for qualified and 'proportionate' exceptions to the general situation set out in Article 10(1): *Goodwin v UK* [1996] 22 EHRR 123. This means that ordering disclosure will not, per se, constitute a violation of Article 10. Additionally, in *Ashworth Hospital Authority v MGN Ltd.*, Lord Woolf was satisfied that, with regard to s. 10 and Article 10: 'The requirements of necessity and proportionality are here separate concepts which substantially cover the same area.' Thus, it appears that, in the present day, and ignoring the actual decision in *Goodwin v UK*, a proper interpretation of s. 10 will *normally* produce a result that is also consistent with the application of Article 10.

Cross-reference Box

The reluctance of the ECtHR to commit itself to 'bright line' rules on evidential admissibility, rather than to saying 'sometimes this is permissible, sometimes not, it all depends on whether it is proportionate' will already be well apparent to readers. For a similar analysis by the same court with regard to reverse burdens of proof and absent witnesses go to pp. 103–114 and 284–290.

Goodwin v UK [1996] 22 EHRR 123, ECtHR

As a matter of general principle, the 'necessity' for any restriction on freedom of expression must be convincingly established. Admittedly, it is in the first place for the national authorities to assess whether there is a 'pressing social need' for the restriction and, in making their assessment, they enjoy a certain margin of appreciation. In the present context, however, the national margin of appreciation is circumscribed by the interest of democratic society in ensuring and maintaining a free press. Similarly, that interest will weigh heavily in the balance in determining as must be done under Article 10 (2), whether the restriction was proportionate to the legitimate aim pursued. In sum, limitations on the confidentiality of Journalistic sources call for the most careful scrutiny by the Court.

Summary

- Generally speaking, all evidence must be admitted if relevant and not caught by an exclusionary rule, however damaging, personal or embarrassing it is to a party or witness.

- In exceptional circumstances, however, a witness or party can refuse to divulge information on the basis that it is privileged, without suffering any adverse consequences for doing so.

- The three most important situations where this occurs in the law of evidence are: the privilege against self-incrimination; legal professional privilege; and that pertaining to 'without prejudice negotiations'.

- The privilege against self-incrimination allows a witness to refuse to answer any question that will expose him to prosecution (or forfeiture) for a criminal offence, unless he is a defendant in a criminal matter and the question relates to the charge before the court, or the question is covered by some other specific statutory exception, such as s. 31(1) of the Theft Act 1968.

- A witness is not required to refuse to answer such a question. He may 'waive' the privilege and reply.

- Legal professional privilege comes in two forms. So called 'legal advice privilege', which covers communications between lawyer and client that are tendered for the purposes of giving/receiving advice in a legal context, and 'litigation privilege', which covers communications between client and solicitor (which will also normally be caught by legal advice privilege) and between lawyer or client and third parties (which will not) for the 'dominant' purpose of contemplated litigation.

- Where the legal advice has been obtained for the purpose of facilitating a crime or fraud, the privilege does not apply, and the lawyer can be questioned about what passed between him and his client.

- Legal professional privilege can be waived, but only by the client to whom it pertains, not by the relevant lawyer.

- The privilege pertaining to 'without prejudice' negotiations, means that admissions made in genuine attempts at resolving a civil dispute, the documentation in which is usually, but not invariably or necessarily, headed as 'without prejudice', cannot subsequently be adduced at trial on the issue of liability.

- There are a few exceptional situations where 'without prejudice' correspondence can be adduced without the assent of both parties to litigation. For example, to establish that an agreement was reached or, in some situations, on the issue of costs.

- Section 10 of the Contempt of Court Act 1981 provides a special, limited and qualified privilege to journalists, allowing them to refuse to divulge the identity of their sources of information. However, this will not apply if the opposing party can persuade the court that disclosure is in the interests of justice, national security or the prevention of crime. The correct application of s. 10 will normally (but not invariably) also prevent Article 10 of the ECHR from being breached.

 ## Further reading

Andrew Edis, 'Privilege and Immunity: Problems of Expert Evidence' (2007) Civil Justice Quarterly, vol 26, 40–56

Charles Hollander, 'Privilege, The Law Society and Mr Simms' (2006) Civil Justice Quarterly, vol 25, 433–438

Joan Loughrey, 'Legal advice privilege and the corporate client' (2005) International Journal of Evidence and Proof, vol 9, no 3, 183

S Magintharan, 'Lack of Dispute and its Effect on Without Prejudice Privilege in Common Law and s. 23 of the Evidence Acts of Singapore and Malaysia' (2006) Civil Justice Quarterly, 367–379

Colin Passmore, 'The Future of Legal Professional Privilege' (1999) 2 E & P, 71–86

Michael Stockdale and Rebecca Mitchell, 'Who is the client? An exploration of legal professional privilege in the corporate context' (2006) Company Lawyer, vol 27, no 4, 110–118

CFH Tapper, 'Privilege, Policy and Principle' (2005) Law Quarterly Review, 181–185

Constantine Theophilopoulos, 'The Anglo-American Privilege Against Self-Incrimination and the Fear of Foreign Prosecution' [2003] Sydney Law Review 14, 305–324

Questions for Discussion

For suggested approaches, please visit the Online Resource Centre

1. Adam occasionally plays golf with Brian, the solicitor who normally handles the conveyancing on his extensive range of commercial properties. One day, while putting on one of their club's greens, he (Adam) suddenly boasts to Brian that he has recently murdered an unpopular neighbour whose body had just been discovered buried in a field.

Will legal professional privilege preclude Brian from giving evidence of the conversation at trial? Suppose that, instead of suddenly boasting about the killing, Adam had first said, 'Brian, I need some professional help with a serious mess that I'm in', before quietly telling him about the murder. Would the situation be any different?

2. Charles runs an amusement arcade. Unfortunately, Delia is slightly injured (a modest bruise on her knee) on a 'little dipper'. Charles is very concerned that such an accident might happen again, in a more serious form, but is also aware that, at least in theory, Delia could sue him for negligently operating the machine. He prepares an 'Incident Report' describing what occurred, using evidence from his company operatives and eye witnesses as to what happened. Delia, who is a highly litigious individual, decides to sue Charles. Charles wishes to know whether the report will be privileged from being produced.

Advise Charles.

3. Fergus is accused of VAT fraud. He had earlier had a meeting with Gerald, a very knowledgeable but rather unworldly solicitor, during which he had asked about the mechanics by which 'carousel fraud' could be effected, 'just as a matter of interest', when discussing his own business affairs and legal problems. Fergus had then used the information provided by Gerald to carry out such a fraud.

Can the prosecution call Gerald to give evidence of his conversation with Fergus?

4. Lionel is accused of robbing Mavis of £10,000 worth of diamonds. He instructs a solicitor, Nobby, and explains to him exactly what happened, in considerable detail. However, at trial, a series of police and CPS errors leads to crucial evidence being lost and Lionel is acquitted without even having to give evidence. Some 10 years later, new information and evidence result in the case being reopened by the police, who arrest Oscar for the crime. Oscar has heard it rumoured that Lionel originally planned to plead guilty at his trial, until the evidential defects in the Crown's case became apparent. He suspects that Lionel made full admissions to his solicitor (Nobby), the adduction of which would greatly boost his own (Oscar's) case at trial.

Will the conversations between Lionel and Nobby be admissible at Oscar's trial?

5. Karla is accused of murdering a college acquaintance, at 11 pm one evening. She wishes to establish an alibi defence, claiming that she was smoking drugs in a well-known opium den, far from the crime-scene, at the time the killing occurred. She calls Julius to support her alibi, as she says that he was sharing her opium pipe with him before, during, and after the relevant time.

Can Julius be required to answer questions about where he was, and what he was doing, at that time?

6. Leroy purchases 500 widgets from Mitra, at a price of £10,000. However, after delivery, he argues that they are not of satisfactory quality under s. 14(2) of the Sale of Goods Act 1979, and seeks to reject the widgets and recover his money. Mitra responds by saying that there is nothing wrong with them and refusing to return the £10,000. Subsequently, there is an exchange of letters, the first of which came from Mitra, and was marked 'without prejudice'. In a much later (unmarked) letter, Mitra says, 'OK some of the widgets may have been a bit grotty, what do you say to me returning £3,000 to you in full and final settlement of our dispute?'. Leroy is not happy with this, and the matter proceeds to the local County Court for trial. Leroy asks you if he can adduce the letter as evidence that some of the widgets were sub-standard.

Advise Leroy.

7. Should privilege extend to non-legal but confidential relationships, such as that between a doctor and patient or a priest and penitent?

8. Mabel is a television celebrity and also a close personal friend of her solicitor, Nora. One day, Mabel writes to Nora, telling her that she has acquired syphilis after a brief liaison with a Venetian gondolier.

Will this letter be covered by legal professional privilege?

9. What arguments are advanced for the existence of legal professional privilege? Are they justified?

10. Larry is accused of bank robbery. He was arrested some months after the crime. A cashier at the bank gives evidence that, as Larry fled the crime scene, he (the cashier) struck him on the forehead with a ledger, occasioning a significant wound. Later that same day, Larry visited his solicitor, Mona. During their interview, Mona noticed a marked cut on Larry's forehead. The prosecution propose to call Mona to ask if she noticed anything strange about his face that day.

Advise Mona as to whether she can refuse to answer this question on the basis that it is covered by legal professional privilege.

11. Fiona is a reporter for a local paper, the 'Daily News'. George works for a large, privately owned, chemist's shop in the same town. George has become aware that the manager and owner of the shop occasionally sells drugs that are past their 'sell by' date. He arranges a meeting with Fiona, but, before passing on this information, asks whether she can guarantee that his identity will never be revealed, as he cannot afford to lose his job.

Advise Fiona.

INDEX